GEORGE R. TOLLES

LATIN
AMERICA

SECOND EDITION

LATIN AMERICA

The Development of Its Civilization

HELEN MILLER BAILEY

Chairman, Department of Social Sciences
East Los Angeles College

ABRAHAM P. NASATIR

Professor of History
San Diego State College

Prentice-Hall, Inc., *Englewood Cliffs, New Jersey*

Library of Congress Catalog Card No.: 67-12678

PRINTED IN THE UNITED STATES OF AMERICA

Current printing (last digit):

10   9   8   7   6   5   4   3   2   1

Prentice-Hall International, Inc., *London*
Prentice-Hall of Australia, Pty. Ltd., *Sydney*
Prentice-Hall of Canada, Ltd., *Toronto*
Prentice-Hall of India Private Ltd., *New Delhi*
Prentice-Hall of Japan, Inc., *Tokyo*

Preface

—To the First Edition:

The United States is being forced to make an "agonizing reappraisal" of its Latin American policies. Now, as never before, we must make friends with our neighbors to the south. It is important that we have an understanding of the cultural and social factors in Latin America as well as of political factors, and an awareness of the continuing influence of the Indian and colonial backgrounds. Without an appreciation of the forces at work among the Latin American nations, a new generation will find it increasingly difficult to hold them within our circle of friends.

Granted that there were many similarities of Indian heritage and colonial background in the independent Latin American nations as they developed in the nineteenth and twentieth centuries, today each country has its own pride of nationality and patriotism. Hence it seemed desirable to give each of the larger and more influential states—Mexico, Brazil, Argentina, and Chile—separate treatment, both in the nineteenth and again in the twentieth centuries. The other countries have been arranged in regional groupings, and treated similarly. If one prefers to study the entire history of a particular nation from independence to the present, the chapters in Parts Five and Six which deal with that nation can be isolated and read consecutively.

A bibliography of books in English is included at the end of each chapter, and a special bibliographical note appears at the end of the book.

In the spelling of Spanish and Portuguese names and terms, we have tried to be as consistent as possible by adopting the style used on modern maps of those countries; accordingly, we have used the newer spelling of the Portuguese names in Brazil, as adopted there in 1940. Spanish surnames are often very confusing to the reader when the father's and mother's family names are both combined in the name by which an historical character is known. Bowing to Spanish custom, we have given the entire name when the character is first mentioned. When he is again referred to, only the father's surname is used.

A number of scholars in the Latin American field aided us in preparing this book and read parts of our manuscript. We would be remiss if we did not single out two young professors, Dr. Ramon Ruíz of Smith College and Dr. Mark Van Aken of San Diego State College, who helped us immeasurably. Dr. Philip Powell of the University of California at Santa Barbara gave us ideas for division and chapter titles. Dr. Lionel U. Rideout of San Diego State College and María Grijalva spent many hours in improving the manuscript. Pauline Thurman of the Pan American Union assisted in procuring illustrative materials, and H. Morle Bailey advised us in technical matters concerning geography, exploration, and navigation. We are both indebted to our students, who often helped with research and with preparation of the manuscript, and who served as "guinea pigs" for lecture materials included in the book.

—To the Second Edition:

We, the authors, have been pleasantly surprised by the very favorable reception accorded *Latin America: The Development of Its Civilization,* since the first edition appeared in 1960. We have watched the reaction of students to its organization and to its treatment of social and economic subjects as well as political matters. Where our students, our friends, our general readers, and our critics have found errors of fact or interpretation, we have attempted to correct them. We are grateful to the many authorities in the field of Latin America who responded to our request and to the publisher for suggesting improvements in the revision, of which we have incorporated many.

We have endeavored in this revision to bring the narrative up to date in all aspects, from the new archeological discoveries to the latest material on the Alliance for Progress. We have rewritten many sections and portions of chapters and have completely rewritten Chapters 40 and 41. We have expanded our chapter reading lists and our "Aids to Further Study." We have emphasized the new interest in the Negro's contribution to Latin America, the "revolution of expectations" and the economic upsurge sweeping Latin America today. Since we both have been able to continue traveling and studying in Latin America, we are pleased to include new photographs of our own. Many critics deplored the inadequacy of maps in the first edition, and we hope this deficiency has been corrected. Finally, we have added a glossary of Spanish and Portuguese terms used.

H.M.B.

A.P.N.

Contents

Part V

MAJOR LATIN AMERICAN NATIONS LOOM LARGE IN TODAY'S WORLD   457

28

Mexico from Civil War to Modern Democracy   *461*

29

Indianism to Industrialization in Present Day Mexico   *484*

30

Modern Brazilian Politics: Regionalism Versus Unity   *506*

31

Brazilian Economic and Social Development in the Twentieth Century   *526*

Illustrations

Maps

LATIN
AMERICA

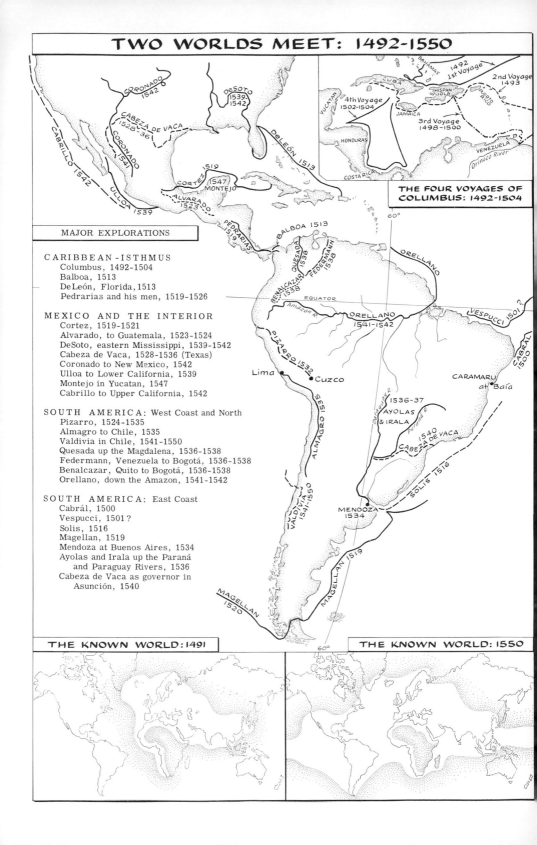

TWO WORLDS MEET: 1492-1550

THE FOUR VOYAGES OF COLUMBUS: 1492-1504

MAJOR EXPLORATIONS

CARIBBEAN-ISTHMUS
Columbus, 1492-1504
Balboa, 1513
DeLeón, Florida, 1513
Pedrarias and his men, 1519-1526

MEXICO AND THE INTERIOR
Cortez, 1519-1521
Alvarado, to Guatemala, 1523-1524
DeSoto, eastern Mississippi, 1539-1542
Cabeza de Vaca, 1528-1536 (Texas)
Coronado to New Mexico, 1542
Ulloa to Lower California, 1539
Montejo in Yucatan, 1547
Cabrillo to Upper California, 1542

SOUTH AMERICA: West Coast and North
Pizarro, 1524-1535
Almagro to Chile, 1535
Valdivia in Chile, 1541-1550
Quesada up the Magdalena, 1536-1538
Federmann, Venezuela to Bogotá, 1536-1538
Benalcazar, Quito to Bogotá, 1536-1538
Orellano, down the Amazon, 1541-1542

SOUTH AMERICA: East Coast
Cabrál, 1500
Vespucci, 1501?
Solis, 1516
Magellan, 1519
Mendoza at Buenos Aires, 1534
Ayolas and Irala up the Paraná
and Paraguay Rivers, 1536
Cabeza de Vaca as governor in
Asunción, 1540

THE KNOWN WORLD: 1491

THE KNOWN WORLD: 1550

Part I

TWO WORLDS MEET

THURSDAY, OCTOBER 11, 1492, at sunset! There had been several days of murmuring and mutinous talk among the hands on all three ships, the *Niña*, the *Pinta*, and the *Santa María*. Two days before, Christopher Columbus, the Admiral, had conferred with his captains, telling them, says the chronicle written from his logs, "that it was useless to complain, since he had come to go to the Indies, and so had to continue until he found them, with the help of Our Lord." Then he agreed with the captains to continue westward for three more days. Now on this second day, the eleventh, there came "floating by the vessel a green rush." The men of the *Pinta* picked up "a reed and a stick," and "those of the caravel *Niña* saw a branch of wild roses." Throughout the day the wind had blown a gale; there was a high sea, and the fleet made a record run of seventy-eight miles.

At sunset all hands were summoned; evening prayers were said in unison. On the *Santa María*, the Admiral stood on the sterncastle and gave the men a little talk, speaking of the "fair winds and clear course" throughout the voyage, and of the "comfort of signs of better things to come." Then, because of the

1

"great desire of all to see land," he ordered the ships to carry on at full sail at night despite the unusually high wind.

At 2:00 A.M. October 12, with the moon just past the full, the lookout on the *Pinta*, a seaman named Rodrigo de Triana, saw a "white sand cliff" gleaming in the moonlight, and a dark line of land beyond. As he shouted "Tierra!" his captain, Martín Alonzo Pinzón, set off a small cannon as a signal to the other two ships. The land was then about six miles distant. Since Columbus rightly feared reefs and breakers, he ordered the ships to lower sails and lay off shore till dawn. In the morning they came to a passage through the western reefs of a tiny island in the Bahamas and "found sheltered anchor in five fathoms of water." Here on the sandy beach, says the chronicle, "presently they saw naked people, and the Admiral went ashore in the armed ship's boat with the royal standard displayed."

Thus Old World and New had officially met—the old Latin Europe and the new America had come together to make Latin America. It was a moment for which Europe had been preparing for centuries. The nations had emerged from medievalism and the people were ready for new things. Their thoughts turned to geographic writings; their tastes yearned for Far Eastern luxuries; their skills developed better ships for exploration and trade. Christopher Columbus himself was a product of these thoughts and skills.

When Columbus came searching for a sponsor, it was the Spanish rulers who accepted his challenge. Why? For the answer to that question, the student must understand the backgrounds of Spanish history. Spain was, in fact, not only ready to back Columbus, but ready to follow him. Spanish America was to become a transplanted Spain in language and religion and family tradition, just as Portugal, the nation whose Atlantic exploration antedates that of Columbus, gave her lifeblood to Brazil.

Columbus was the first to see the lands of the Americas, and other Spaniards came after him, beating their way up and down the hemisphere. Thus, the reader must follow their footsteps to see the geography of this vast new world, to understand the environment in which Latin America was born. Columbus was also the first to see the Indians, the New World's inhabitants. Latin American people are today, in many areas, Indians with a European veneer. It is impossible to understand them without a knowledge of the pre-Columbian inhabitants, both north and south of Panama.

With such understanding, the reader returns to Columbus, for his life is the line which brought two streams of people into first contact. With Columbus as a colonizer, the Spanish empire began in the Caribbean, and spread into North and South America. Thus Columbus' voyage touched off the forces that shaped the New World in its first century.

Chapter 1

The Age of Discovery

A EUROPE AWAITING COLUMBUS

THE CHANCE SPOT WHERE Rodrigo de Triana first sighted land—probably the small island in the Bahamas called San Salvador—was a matter of accident. The discovery of America itself was no accident, however, but the culmination of a long period of European growth in geographic knowledge, in scientific and philosophic ideas, and in economic development. Medieval Europeans, largely preoccupied with the petty wars and the restricted commerce of feudal times, had centered their interest in the Mediterranean, forgetting the geographic knowledge of the ancient Greeks.

Not until the Crusades of the eleventh century did the narrow Europeans look outward. Cities on the Mediterranean prospered; better ships were built to carry the passenger traffic of the Crusades; kings, noblemen, squires, and monks took ships and went to the Near East. The individual Crusader became a traveler. He discovered that the Mohammedan infidels, against whom the Holy War was directed, had a civilization superior to his own, that they lived in greater luxury, and that they had desirable products to trade. He heard about other lands lying beyond the Near East, lands which produced silk and spices, camphor and musk, pearls and ivory. From the returning Crusaders, the other Europeans of the later medieval period acquired these same new tastes and interests. The subsequent growth of the trading cities and the distribution of routes throughout Europe produced a new mental stimulus; the outside world was coming inland. Meanwhile the creation of surplus wealth in young towns and cities permitted leisure and the cultivation of the arts and learning. A new learning produced more accurate geographic knowledge and more intelligent interest in the world beyond.

Meanwhile some faint contacts had been made beyond the Near Eastern lands of the Crusades. As early as 1160 Rabbi Benjamin of Tudela, a Jew from Spain, had been in Baghdad and written about possibilities of a route from that city to China. By 1245 a Franciscan monk, Giovanni de Plano Carpini, had been to the Great Khan's headquarters in Karakorum. His travel story, *The Book of Tartars*, described the empire of the Great Mogul and mentioned a mysterious Christian kingdom near India ruled by "Prester John." About eleven years later two Venetian brothers named Polo reached the court of the Chinese ruler and remained there for fourteen years before returning to Venice. On setting out a second time to trade in the empire of the Great Khan they took their young nephew Marco Polo with them. Marco grew up to serve the Khan as emissary to other Far Eastern nations. When he dictated a travel story long after his return to Europe, his readers would not believe his fabulous adventures. He described Chinese ports on an ocean facing east and told of the ships that came to these ports full of the spices and peppers for which Europeans were so hungry. He also wrote of the Island of Cipangu, or Japan, where the people roofed their houses with gold, and the ruler was so rich and powerful that Marco's employer, the Great Khan, could not conquer the island. According to Marco, it was only one of many rich islands that lay far off to sea along the coast of China. Only the land masses of Africa, Arabia, and Asia Minor lay between Europe and the direct sea route to these fabulous places, he implied.

Marco Polo made known to Europe the riches of the Far East. Other travelers, including some traders and some ecclesiastics, made their way to India and China during the next century. Meanwhile Castile expanded into the Atlantic by occupying the Canary Islands in 1405. Prince Henry the Navigator, son of the Portuguese king, set up a scientific headquarters for navigation at the southwesterly tip of Portugal, gathering maps and information about the west coast of Africa, in the hopes of reaching the mythical Christian king Prester John. His seamen sent colonists to the Madeiras and the Azores, and by the time of Henry's death in 1460 they had reached the coast of Guinea. From Henry's old headquarters, Bartolomeu Dias reached the Cape of Good Hope in 1487–1488.

While practical travelers and seamen pushed farther into the unknown, the medieval universities had begun to produce Renaissance thinkers who were studying the ancient Greek scholars—Greek mathematicians who had proved by figures that the world was round, mapmakers who had drawn the world as a sphere, a geographer of Alexandria who had implied, in A.D. 25, that circumnavigation of the globe could have been tried "except for want of resolution and the scarcity of provision." These Greek writers were forgotten for centuries, but were being reread in the Europe of 1450.

Mapmaking improved also with the rereading of classics. Geography, along with other Renaissance studies, became a scientific pursuit, and most learned men accepted a spherical earth. A writer named Pierre d'Ailly in his book *Imago Mundi* made a compendium of the geographical notions of his time, describing the continent of Asia as a land mass reaching far into the Pacific—with, of course, no Western Hemisphere continents in between—and implying that an ocean voyage to the west would be shorter than the ancients figured. "For, according to the philosophers and Pliny, the ocean which stretches between the extremity of further Spain and the eastern edge of India is of no great width. For it is evident that this sea is navigable in a very few days if the wind be fair." This book, first written in 1410, was printed and widely circulated when Columbus was a young man. So also was the *Historia Rerum Ubique Gestarum*, the *History of All Things*, by the learned Aeneas Sylvius, who afterward became Pope. In this book the ideas of the ancients on the shape and size of the world were given contemporary wording and credence, and the medieval superstitions of a flat world, the old theories about the impossibility of sailing round Africa, were shown to be outgrown. It is interesting to note that Columbus' own personal library, the books read in his youth, contained copies of Marco Polo's *Travels*, the *Imago Mundi*, and the *Historia Rerum*, all marked and commented on in Columbus' own handwriting. Thus all the learned world was ready for such a voyage as that of Columbus, for the books of all the travelers of the previous three centuries now were being printed by the spectacular invention of movable type, and were being read in a new light in the Europe of 1490.

An awakened Europe with new ideas of luxury hoped to enhance the trade in Far Eastern goods. However, the direct connection which travelers and traders had begun to establish between East and West was almost cut off by the time of Columbus' birth. In 1368 the descendants of Kublai Khan were driven from Peking, and personal contact with the Celestial Empire by inquiring travelers was ended. Even indirect trade via the ports of the Near East became a mere trickle when the Turks captured Constantinople in 1453. After that date, all trade came through Turkish hands. Though the Turks tried to stimulate trade, prices rose sky-high because of their excessive taxes. The Italian cities of Venice and Genoa were the only European centers in touch with this Turkish monopoly and they squeezed Western European traders out. If any nation could find a new route around the Turkish territory, it could corner the entire wholesale market on the Eastern luxury wares, silks and spices. What an opportunity for countries with windows on the Atlantic, countries which were becoming powerful and ambitious! In England, Portugal, Spain, and France, strong kings had the money, the need for trade, and the interest in expansion. The Black Death had depopulated their countrysides, had made many villagers footloose, had broken many of the still-existing feudal ties. The kings of such restless countries might be sold on the desire to send expeditions to find new sea routes. A single ship, following such an all-water route, could bring back more cargo than several caravans, and at much lower cost.

The seafaring world was now building ships that could weather such a trip. Venice and Genoa had forsaken the small, medieval, oared galley, carrying a single sail and guided by a standing oarsman. The ships of the early 1400s were "caravels" steered by a rudder. By the twelfth century some sailors had made use of the magnetic needle as a compass and no longer had to depend upon the position of the sun or the North Star when out of sight of land in the Mediterranean. The astrolabe, a very primitive type of sextant, gave a ship's position north or south of the Equator—what we call latitude. Though longitude was still a matter of guesswork till the 1700s, the clever mariner of the 1400s knew the direction in which he was going and his approximate distance from home. Knowledge of direction and latitude thus made possible the *portolani*, or sailing charts, of the Mediterranean and the western coast of Europe. The preparation of *portolani* for use by commercial seamen, quite apart from the abstract study of ancient maps of the world taking place in the universities, became a trade or career in itself, and enhanced seamanship in the Italian cities, in Spain, and in Portugal. In fact, Columbus and his brother were making their living drawing such maps in the Lisbon of the 1470s.

With more accurate charts to guide their courses, shipowners built bigger and better ships. Vessels built in Venice in 1450 had large holds for cargo, and also bore a forecastle and a sterncastle, those high platforms at each end for boarding enemy ships in case of war. By Columbus' time the sterncastle had become the poop deck with space for the captain's cabin. Later the forecastle became a covered quarters forward for the crew. Such ships could carry stores of provisions and drinking water and could be away from land for more than a month. The lateen-sailed galley of the Italian ports was giving way to the square-rigger, whose large sails could be held taut in a high wind. Ships equipped with such sails could always catch enough breeze to be independent of galley slaves and their banks of oars. Thus, shipbuilders, like scholars, kings, and traders, were ready to search for the all-water route to India.

The invention of gunpowder gave the ships, and the soldiers aboard them, greater striking power. This "improvement in war" also strengthened kings at home. Armed with the new weapons, they had allied themselves with the towns to bring the nobles under subjection and to produce strong monarchical states. Equally "explosive" in breaking up the old feudalism and strengthening the monarchies was the invention of printing, which disseminated ideas and made control of a wider realm an easier task for an enlightened king. Such a king would naturally encourage the shipbuilding industry and all sorts of commercial enterprises to be carried on by sea. From the standpoint of geography and commerce, the monarchs of Spain and Portugal were favorably situated at the western end of the Mediterranean with frontage on the Atlantic. They were prepared to undertake such enterprises as the search for the new routes; they had the desire, the power, and the surplus wealth.

Christopher Columbus' voyage was therefore no accident, no isolated event. He and Vasco da Gama were the culmination of the "best" of

Europe. They represented the finest ideas of the contemporary world. Had not Columbus found the New World in 1492, or had not Vasco da Gama found the all-water route to India in 1497, it would have been done by others within a very few years.

COLUMBUS, THE PRODUCT OF A NEW AGE

Columbus was not the first citizen of the Old World to see the New. His was the first *effective* discovery; he advertised the New World and made its occupation permanent and continuous. Surely, in remote times, Chinese or Japanese navigators touched on the Pacific Coast. Breton fishermen had known of the Grand Banks off Newfoundland for years before Columbus, and they may have wintered on Labrador or laid over on Nova Scotia to dry and salt their codfish. Leif Ericson the Viking sailed to North America from the Norse colony on Greenland about the year 1000; his discovery was kept alive in the Norse sagas which were still being told as true history in Iceland and Norway in the late 1400s. Sailors from Bristol, England, knew these stories, knew also of the fishing banks visited by the Bretons, and of Irish tales of missionaries who, centuries before, had visited on Saint Brendan's Island somewhere in the Atlantic to the west. Bristol sailors had contacted Portuguese sailors, perhaps the very ones who had been involved in Prince Henry the Navigator's attempts to have the African coast thoroughly explored, and had given ear to all kinds of stories of western islands. It was now the second half of the fifteenth century and discovery was in the air. By the time Bartolomeu Dias came home from the tip of Africa, Christopher Columbus, promoter, man of vision, and superbly skillful navigator, had already approached the Portuguese king with his more daring scheme to reach India by way of the western islands.

As the fortunate planner, the one who successfully advertised his discovery, Columbus typified the new age. He was born in 1451, at or near Genoa, the son of a wool weaver. Like other Genoese boys, he went to sea early, aboard small cargo ships in the Mediterranean. At some time in those early years he went to Bristol, and possibly to Iceland, where he himself heard the tales of islands. In 1476, French war vessels had attacked and wrecked a Genoese merchantship trading with England; the young Columbus was aboard her in charge of cargo. With other survivors, he swam ashore on the Portuguese coast, and made his way on foot and penniless to find help among Genoese seamen and traders who lived in Lisbon. At this time Portugal was the center of interest in the new navigation, the headquarters of exploration, the home of geographic discovery. Now Columbus was among the Portuguese, who knew how to handle ocean-going vessels well, how to load them for long trips, how to deal with primitive peoples (such as those among whom Portuguese captains traded and slave-raided on the West African coasts), and what kind of trade goods such savages liked.

We know he spent his late twenties and early thirties in Lisbon, that he and his brother Bartholomew went into the chart and mapmaking business, and that he became well known in the Genoese colony. He took trips with Portuguese captains to the Guinea Coast. Soon he was sufficiently acceptable to Portuguese society to arrange a marriage with Doña Felipa Perestrello, daughter of the governor of Madeira, a fortunate marriage for his and the world's future, since he doubtlessly heard talk of Portuguese explorations from his wife's family. Records show he lived in the Azores in 1479. In 1482 he was writing to and receiving letters from a famous Florentine scholar named Paolo Toscanelli, letters in which Toscanelli assured Columbus of the safety of a course "due west of Lisbon which will take you 5000 nautical miles to the Chinese Province of Mangi," and complimented him on "thy great and noble ambition to pass over to where the spices grow." Thus, though Columbus knew the world was a sphere, he greatly underestimated its size, since between Lisbon and the China coast stretch nearly 12,000 nautical miles. He also assumed that there were no lands to be discovered in between and that thus one only had to cross the Atlantic by as direct a route as possible.

No one knows just when Columbus decided on this "noble ambition." In the court of Portugal in 1484 he made his first request for a group of ships to sail west to Cipangu (probably Japan). The maritime commission which considered the proposal turned it down, but the Portuguese king remained interested; in fact, he went so far as to permit a private exploration westward in 1487, but it came to naught. Disappointed in two attempts to involve the Portuguese monarch, Columbus, now a widower, went to Spain in the middle of 1485 with his young son Diego. Here he soon contacted some important people close to the Queen. Isabella appointed a commission of learned men to study his plan while Columbus cooled his heels on a royal pension, busied himself gathering evidence for his contention that the voyage was possible, and supported a young mistress who bore his famous biographer son Fernando.

When the learned commission rejected the western voyage plan on the proper grounds that the ocean was too wide and that its proponent asked for too many personal rewards in return for the discoveries he might make, Columbus looked to France or England for help. Spain was busy expelling the Moslems and unifying the interior provinces; Columbus had already waited five years for Spanish action. But when his brother had started for England and he himself was on the road toward France, a royal messenger was sent after him with news that Queen Isabella had personally decided to back the project. Her treasurer and some others in the court had expressed willingness to invest money in the venture, and she had been attracted by Columbus' personality from the first.

We know little of his personality. He was probably a commanding figure, in the prime of life as he stood before the Queen. His contemporaries described him as "tall and well built, with a ruddy and freckled complexion, hawk-nosed and long of visage, blue-eyed and with high cheek bones." In character he was courageous, persistent, strong-willed, and deeply devout, but undoubtedly conceited and overbearing to the point of being irritable.

Thus, Christopher Columbus was called back to the Queen, and a basic agreement was made, the first in a long series of contracts between the Spanish crown and the men who went forth to conquer and colonize a whole New World. Under the contract, Columbus was to be "Admiral over all islands and mainlands he discovered not already under Christian kings," a title which was to go to his heirs in perpetuity. He was also to be the governor over all such lands, with power to nominate officials; he was to receive "one-tenth of all gold, silver, pearls, gems, spices, and other things produced or obtained by barter and mining within these new lands." He was to be addressed as "Admiral of the Ocean Sea, Viceroy, and Governor." Had all his rights and titles been continued, Columbus would have been ruler of all the Western Hemisphere! His heirs were to carry on lawsuits about these rights for a generation after his death. In addition to

Columbus: A portrait painted on the return from his second voyage. *Courtesy Pan American Union.*

the foregoing promises, the queen undertook to supply ships, sailors, and provisions for the voyage. The total cost of outfitting the expedition was about 2,000,000 *maravedis* (perhaps $30,000), with Columbus himself investing some funds in the enterprise. And, contrary to legend, Queen

Isabella did not have to pawn any of her jewels for the great venture. To the Queen, the voyage was a fresh adventure of expanding dominions and crusading zeal, as well as a lucrative enterprise.

The ships were prepared in the little southwestern port of Palos, partly because this Spanish town had had experience in the African trade and in the handling of caravels, and partly because Palos owed the Queen some ships as back taxes. The 'Pinzón brothers of Palos, Martín Alonzo and Vicente Yáñez, undertook the job of provisioning the ships and recruiting the crew. In later years the Pinzón family brought suit against Columbus' heirs, claiming greater credit on the voyage than they had received. It is true that the brothers captained two of the ships, and that their influence in Palos and their tales to the townsfolk of riches to be gained and fabulous lands to be explored, persuaded many men of that seafaring town to undertake the questionable voyage. In all, ninety men were recruited; again contrary to legend, none were convicts.

It took ten weeks to get the expedition ready, a fortunate delay which kept Columbus from the West Indies until after the hurricane season. The ships given Columbus were, as he himself said "very well suited for such an enterprise." They were small but fast. Though they would seem leaky little cockleshells to the modern sailor, for Columbus' purpose they were the best type of ships known at that time. In short, his little fleet— *Niña,* the best; *Santa María,* the biggest and the worst; and *Pinta*—was unusually well organized. Furthermore, commander Columbus himself was a skilled navigator, a man of determination who had faith in his own plans, as his subsequent achievements well proved. He was the Renaissance figure who put *theory* to the test.

Leaving Palos on August 3, 1492, the ships sailed southwest to the first stop in the Canary Islands off the African coast. The maps of Columbus' time indicated that the Canaries were on the same parallel as Cipangu, and Columbus proposed to sail straight west from them to the Far East. On the Islands, supplies, especially fresh food, were taken aboard and some repairs and adjustments made.

Throughout the first voyage, he himself worked hard and ably as navigator. He used the system called "dead reckoning." With a mariner's compass as his main instrument, he laid out his course and estimated distances on a chart, an art at which he was extremely accurate. From the standpoint of sailing, this 1492 trip was one of the easiest Columbus ever made. Once he had the men, the ships, and the monarchs' permission, his greatest problems were solved. The weather was fine, the season the best of the year. His principal difficulty was in handling the men, a skill in which he never excelled. His experienced seamen were not afraid of sea monsters, or of dropping off the end of a flat world; their main trouble was close confinement for such a long time on the small ships, and their fear of foundering so far from home.

By the first week of October, two months from home and twenty days from land in the Azores, they had exceeded all previously known records for ocean navigation beyond the sight of land. The crisis with the men came October 8 and 9. Then there were those conferences with the Pinzón brothers, captains of the *Niña* and the *Pinta,* the agreement to continue three more days, the glorious sunset October 11, and Rodrigo de Triana's cry of "Tierra!" in the early hours of the twelfth.

Stepping from the armed ship's-boat on the beach at San Salvador, Christopher Columbus stepped from the role of sea captain to the exalted title of Admiral of the Ocean Sea, and to immortality as *The* discoverer. Now came the strange, new things that Columbus and his men were to see, as they explored excitedly among the islands in search of supposedly near-by Cipangu. They were fascinated by the sight of human beings, naked and

Primitive Caribbean Indians still offer trade goods to the ships of strangers. San Blas Indians off the coast of Panama. *Photo by Helen Miller Bailey.*

of a color and type the Spaniards had never known. They saw the native *hamacas*, hammocks—a discovery that would soon enable sailors to sleep more comfortably on their ships. They obtained a small quantity of gold —at least enough to make their expedition even more important to those back home. They found the natives smoking cigars through their noses, the first European view of the tobacco habit. Busy looking for the mainland of Asia beyond the Bahamas, Columbus sailed on into the Caribbean waters.

He had not planned to begin colonization on this voyage. However, the *Santa María* was wrecked and had to be abandoned off Hispaniola, as he called the first large island he found, home of today's two republics of Haiti and Santo Domingo. The Admiral could not take all his men back to Spain on the two small remaining ships, and was forced to leave some of the men on Hispaniola in a makeshift fort he called Navidad. Thus began the first, though temporary, colony in the New World. Then, after much sailing among the islands, and touching on Cuba—which Columbus thought might be the China coast—the *Niña* and the *Pinta* started home. Returning to Europe from the Caribbean, Columbus hit upon the best route east, the one that would be used by Europeans to the end of the days of sail. The trade winds had pushed him over; now he went north far enough to pick up the prevailing westerlies which would take him rapidly back to Spain, where he was to become a famous personage overnight. Thus Columbus, in his first voyage, laid out the best westward and eastward routes across the Atlantic.

SIGNIFICANCE OF THE DISCOVERY

Columbus' discovery marked the inception of Latin America. The result of the impact of Europe on the life of the New World is the whole story of the rest of this book. European people were to begin an immigration which is still going on. Spanish and Portuguese languages, customs, food, religion, wheeled vehicles, and domestic animals were to change the life of the aboriginal inhabitants beyond measure. Spanish and Portuguese government was to rule the New World for three centuries, both politically and economically.

Columbus' voyage had great significance for the people of Europe as well. Once he had returned to Europe, the news of his discovery spread rapidly among learned circles in Italy, France, and England. A letter from Columbus to a friend at court, which was printed in Latin and circulated in the spring and summer of 1493, ran to nine editions. One item new for Europeans was that Columbus had found naked natives living in a state of nature. The Indians' apparent lack of religion aroused some general European curiosity, as did the stories that they seemed generous, rather timid, and in total ignorance of important weapons of war. All this sounded like something approximating the lost Garden of Eden! Old World excitement was also stirred by Columbus' glowing description of rivers yielding gold, since European markets were short of such metal for commercial exchange. As far as his discovery itself is concerned, Columbus' claim to have reached East India was generally believed, but there were skeptics from the start. The idea that these lands were really a "new" world was growing rapidly by the time Columbus died in 1506, though the Discoverer himself long held firmly to the conviction that he had reached Asia.

Because the Columbian discovery was the culmination of the Commercial Revolution then going on, the economic results for Europe came rapidly. With the discovery and colonization of the New World, the center of trade and finance began to shift from the Mediterranean to the Atlantic. The gold that was to pour through Spain into the rest of Europe from Mexico and Peru produced a price revolution, brought changes in banking and finance, and helped produce a new class of businessmen in Western Europe. There were now new sources of raw materials. The plantation system, producing sugar and, later, cotton, led to new wholesale methods in Europe, and eventually to machine production. Shipping processes developed rapidly as larger and larger vessels had to be built and provisioned to handle the flow of passengers and cargo. In the field of politics, the changes were to be as great. Spain's metallic wealth gave her an illusion of prosperity and forced her into a more vigorous foreign policy. She and her enemies enlarged their navies for both trade and war. New types of warfare, fought in both hemispheres, resulted in new balances of power and changes in the methods of diplomacy. Meanwhile the colonies overseas were a challenge to Spain and Portugal. Conquered peoples, completely different from any ever before ruled by Europeans, had to be controlled from the mother country. European concepts of government had to be modified for the colonies. New institutions grew up to handle these problems.

In religion and culture the changes were as great. Here was a whole pagan world for the devout to convert, with money pouring in by the millions to be spent on such conversions. Literature was vitalized by the impact of adventure. The map itself was to change most, as well as the method of drawing it accurately. Even in daily diet, Europeans changed, eating corn, potatoes, and chocolate for the first time, and smoking tobacco as a luxury. All in all, the New World was one of the most revolutionary things that ever happened to the Old.

For Spain in 1492 there was a need for haste if she was to prevent Portuguese encroachment on her discoveries. Thus the Spanish rulers opened the pages of diplomatic history in the Americas by appealing to the only international authority then in existence, one recognized by both Spain and Portugal, the Papacy. Portuguese authorities had been quick to claim that the new Spanish discoveries were in territory already guaranteed to Portugal by papal order and by Spanish treaty of 1481 in connection with discoveries on the coast of Africa. Now there was a new papal order. By two new Bulls or papal pronouncements, on May 2 and 4, 1493, the Pope drew a line between the respective areas of Spain and Portugal, in return for promises that those nations would evangelize the savages and colonize the new lands with Christians. This Line of Demarcation was indefinitely placed at one hundred leagues west and south of any "one of the islands commonly known as Azores and Cape Verdes." Disputes over the exact location led to a meeting of Spanish and Portuguese envoys at Tordesillas the next fall and settlement on a line at 370 leagues west of the Cape Verdes. Spain's apparent generosity in accepting this far western line was based on the erroneous assumption that the other half of the line would cut through the East Indies and allow Spain part of that rich trade. After Magellan's voyage, the line's extension did give Spain the Philippines. On the other hand, the demarcation line in the Atlantic gave Portugal her legal toe hold on Brazil, though uncertainty as to the exact measuring point in the Azores made Spain challenge the extent of Portuguese expansion inland in South America. Modern South American countries inherited boundary disputes which had their origin in the Line of Demarcation.

Thus Columbus' landfall in the morning of October 12, 1492, a result of centuries of build-up in Europe, brought changes to every phase of life in the Old World and the New, and even led to border disputes in the Far East and on the courses of the Amazon.

Readings

Abbott, W. C., *Expansion of Europe* (2 vols., 1924)

Baker, J. N. L., *History of Geographical Discovery and Exploration* (1937)

Beazley, C. R., *Dawn of Modern Geography* (3 vols., 1949)

Cheyney, E. P., *The Dawn of a New Era* (1936)

Diffie, B. W., *Prelude to Empire: Portugal Overseas before Henry the Navigator* (1961)

Hart, H. H., *Sea Road to the Indies* (1950)

————, *Venetian Adventurer, the Life and Times of Marco Polo* (1943)

Hechscher, E., *Mercantilism* (2 vols., 1935)

Helps, A., *Spanish Conquest of America* (4 vols., 1900–1904)

Lybyer, A. H., "Influence of the Rise of the Ottoman Turks upon the Routes of Oriental Trade," in *American Historical Association, Annual Report—1914*, Vol I, 127–33

————, "Ottoman Turks and the Routes of Oriental Trade," in *English Historical Review*, XXX (1915), 577–88

Marco Polo, *The Book of Sir Marco Polo the Venetian* (Yule ed.) (2 vols., 1903)

Morison, S. E., *Admiral of the Ocean Sea* (2 vols., 1942)

————, *The Caribbean as Columbus Saw It* (1964)

————, *Portuguese Voyages to America in the Fifteenth Century* (1940)

Newton, A. P., ed., *Travel and Travellers in the Middle Ages* (1930)

Nowell, C. E., *The Great Discoveries and the First Colonial Empires* (1954)

Nunn, G. E., *Geographical Conceptions of Columbus* (1924)

O'Gorman, E., *Invention of America* (1961)

Olson, J. E., and E. G. Bourne, eds., *The Northmen, Columbus and Cabot* (1906)

Penrose, Boies, *Travel and Discovery in the Renaissance, 1420–1670* (1952)
Prestage, E., *The Portuguese Pioneers* (1933)
Richman, I. B., *The Spanish Conquerors* (1919)
Sauer, C. O., *The Early Spanish Main* (1966)
Skelton, R. A., *et al., Vinland Map and the Tartar Relation* (1965)
Sykes, P., *The Quest for Cathay* (1937)
Thatcher, J. B., *Christopher Columbus* (3 vols., 1903–1904)

Chapter **2**

The Rich Heritage
of Spain and Portugal

THE SPAIN TO WHICH COLUMBUS RETURNED

Columbus, aboard the Niña, returned home to Palos on March 15, 1493. By the 31st, Palm Sunday, he was in Seville, jewel city of the Castilian province of Andalusia. He stayed on through Holy Week, watching the religious processions, worshiping in the churches, visiting with the archbishop, and chatting with young knights who begged for a chance to be with him on a second voyage, while he waited for word from Isabella's court. The city itself hummed with the activity of Holy Week and the fair. Seville was then a city of more than a quarter of a million people, one of the most pleasant places to live in Europe. In the crowds jostling at the market place were tradesmen from all southern Spain. Here were the fine horses of Andalusia, the bulls for the *corridas* or bull fights to be held Easter Sunday afternoon, the fat tawny oxen from Spain's uplands, as well as many sheep and goats and donkeys for sale—all those domestic animals which Spaniards were to carry to America. Here also were the handmade products of Spaniards and Moors from all the regions of Spain, products which deft Indian fingers were to copy in the New World: silks, embroideries, pottery, leather work. Seville merchants could not foresee that this Holy Week Fair was to be rivaled in its turn by the two great yearly fairs Seville's traders were to set up in the New World during the next two centuries.

Columbus himself was gone from Seville before the fair was over. A summons from the Queen had arrived on that Monday, an order to come overland quickly to the court being held at Barcelona, the width of Spain away. The new Admiral had purchased clothing of fine white linen and red velvet suitable to his new rank; he journeyed with his officers and servants in a long mule train. The mules in the rear bore six Bahama Island Indians; donkeys carried Caribbean parrots in wicker cages. After two weeks of cross-country travel the caravan reached Barcelona, seat of Ferdinand's power in Catalonia. "'All the court and the city came out to meet the Admiral," wrote Columbus' biographer son. He was received by Ferdinand and Isabella in a hall full of nobles and courtiers. The sovereigns stood up to greet him, and Columbus sat to tell of his adventures while the nobility remained standing. The members of the court were to find out within a decade that this royal guest had given a claim to a whole new continent to Spain, the Spain of the colorful cities, the great fairs, the gala processions, the deep religious devotion. The next century was to bring exploratory and colonizing activities in which much of the life of Spain that Columbus had seen in passing was to be transferred to the New World.

Spain's history gave her a drive for land and trade. The wars against the Moslems produced a spirit of national unity and expansion and created a fervent patriotism which expressed itself in terms of a fanatical religion. There was, by 1492, a strong military caste seeking an outlet for its energies, and a militant church, seeking souls to convert and new sources of funds. Columbus' discovery was an answer to all this seeking.

EARLY IBERIAN HISTORY
AS THE BACKGROUND FOR IBERIAN AMERICA

In the decade before 1493 Columbus had occasion to see many of the geographic features of the Iberian lands which had influenced the early Iberian peoples and which prepared them for life in the New World. With a land mass about two-thirds the size of the single modern Latin American nation of Venezuela, separated from the rest of Europe by the Pyrenees mountains, dominated by a high and dry central plateau, the Iberian nations of Spain and Portugal had been conditioned by their own difficult terrain and climate. The broken highlands, the rugged river valleys, the extremes of heat and cold, the great variations between dry and rainy seasons, between low altitudes at river mouths and high altitudes up steep escarpments away from the sea—the Iberian people knew all these handicaps of climate and geography at home and could cope with them when they encountered them in the New World.

As the Spaniards were to invade areas of the New World across many difficult geographic barriers, so their ancestors had been either conquerors or conquered through many epochs of history. Spain's people represent a blending of many races and cultures. The inhabitants of the Iberian peninsula were, by 1492, the most mixed peoples in Europe; not even the proudest Spanish knight could call himself a "pure-blood."

Perhaps a race known as Iberian had developed in Spain by the time history was being recorded in Egypt. Via the Pyrenean passes came Celts; via the Mediterranean and the Straits of Gibraltar came Phoenicians and Greeks and Carthaginians to mix into the Iberian bloodstream. When Carthage was embroiled with the Romans, the great General Hannibal used Spain as his base; another century saw Spain a thriving Roman colony. Out of Roman rule came governmental and cultural patterns that remained as foundations of Spanish civilization. The political administration was unified, the language standardized as a dialect of Roman Latin. The Romans superimposed their own system of law, indelibly stamping Roman law upon the Hispanic peoples and their descendants in America. Roman roads, public buildings, schools, and libraries showed the power of Rome in Spain. Spanish town and countryside used Roman ways of commerce and agriculture. Almost every form of scientific, literary, and artistic accomplishment that characterized Rome in her days of greatest glory was copied in Spain. Roman town and city government was later to form the basis for town strength in imperial Spain and in the Spanish American empire.

Even more important was the introduction of Christianity. The Spaniards in the Americas were to be famous for their religious devotion and the intolerance they felt toward other religions. Christianity had started as a religion in the Roman Empire, spreading from Palestine to Greece, to Rome, to North Africa, to Southern France, to Spain. Modern Spanish Christians believe that Saint James, brother of Saint John, traveled the length of Spain preaching, and that his bones are buried in a church in Galicia on the Bay of Biscay. Midway through the third century there were Christian communities all over Spain; and in 313 the Emperor Constantine made Christianity a legal religion throughout the Roman Empire. The church in Spain proceeded to hold its own conferences, to enjoy exemption from taxation, to perform all marriage ceremonies, and to take advantage of special legal rights such as maintaining separate courts for church leaders accused of crime—rights later famous as the *fueros*. The Spanish clergy developed a very high culture, traditional in Spanish American life to the present time.

Following the pattern of Mediterranean history, Spain fell to barbaric hordes at the time of the Germanic invasions. With the coming of the barbarians into Italy, Roman soldiers were called home; contacts between Rome and Spain diminished. Now Spain was open to conquest by a Christianized Germanic people called the Visigoths, who established a Christianized kingdom with its capital at Toledo. For three centuries the Visigothic kings ruled most of the Iberian peninsula, administering the country under an efficient code of laws, part Roman and part Germanic. The Visigothic pride in and respect for this code of laws created the strong Spanish pride in juridical practice which would later be transferred to America. The Visigoths also contributed a basic trait of the nobility—

the preference for living in the country rather than in the towns, the establishment of a landed aristocracy whose serfs tilled the land, as opposed to the city-dwelling ruling class of Roman times. Thus the Visigothic nobles may be distant progenitors of the modern Latin American *hacendados* or *estancieros,* the owners of large estates living in splendid rural isolation with their many servants and laborers. Toledo remained a cosmopolitan center, however, welcoming cultured Jews from the Near East, hiring Byzantine mercenaries from the Eastern Empire at Constantinople, and generating an atmosphere of tolerance and prosperity that was to be found in few other cities of the moribund Roman Empire.

In 711 Moslems from North Africa crossed the Straits of Gibraltar into Spain in a wave of expansionism for that new Arabian faith which was to surge across the Pyrenees until it was stopped by Charles Martel at Tours. This brought Spain into the orbit of the Mohammedan world. The invaders, called in Spanish history the Moors, settled throughout the Iberian peninsula, save for a few regions in the Pyrenean foothills. Gone was the Visigothic rule over the Ibero-Carthaginian-Roman-Byzantine peoples. The continuous presence of this new intrusive culture and its political rule until the final defeat at Granada in 1492 were the dominant factors in Spain during the Middle Ages. The Moorish influence was especially strong in Andalusia, the province around Seville which was to become the headquarters of New World trade and government.

The first two centuries of Moslem domination brought little stability to the peninsula, for when Moslems were not fighting Christians they were fighting each other, along tribal or regional lines. Finally by 950 Moslem rule was consolidated under the Caliphate of Cordova. The Caliphs formed the strongest navy in the Mediterranean and gained for Spain the reputation of being the greatest state and the seat of the highest culture in western Europe. This "golden age" of the Moslems lasted from about 900 to 1300.

The Moorish cities grew and prospered; and the twelfth century brought luxury in living and advances in culture to both Seville and Cordova. It is said that Arab mathematicians introduced into Europe by way of Spain the Arabic numerals, the use of the zero in arithmetic, and the study of algebra and geometry. The Moslem sages knew elementary physics and chemistry. Not only the wise men, but a great majority of the common people could read and write Arabic, and many of them the Latin of the European Christians as well. In these languages Caliphs and hermits, wise men and gay young blades wrote poetry—poetry of love, of spring, of the abstract values of life. This love of verse writing persists in Latin America, for young and old. In Toledo lived many learned Jews; astronomical tables and computations worked out by a group of Jewish astronomers in Toledo in 1065 became the foundation of the work that made latitude and longitude calculations possible, and thus helped chart the New World. From the Giralda tower in Seville—to be used as a cathedral tower when Christians retook the town—learned astronomers surveyed the stars. The city had seventy public libraries, that of the Caliph containing 600,000 volumes. Many of these volumes were history books; with their fondness for historical writing, the Arabs helped build a tradition that would live on in Spain and in Latin America.

Seville was filled with the tile-roofed houses of Moorish architecture, built square around a patio. Beyond lay the wide green acres of the valley of Andalusia. The people prospered from wise use of the land. Trees and vines were grafted to improve the fruit. Sugar cane, rice, and cotton were introduced from the Near East as products to be grown under irrigation. A textile industry developed from the cotton as well as from silkworms grown in Cordova. It is interesting to know that the conflict among farmers who used the land to graze sheep, those who raised cattle, and those who planted crops was present in Moorish Spain. The quarrel broke out again in the history of the Spanish-speaking frontier of the United States—the sheep men, the cattle men, the "nesters."

Society under the Moors consisted of the landed aristocrats, the freemen, the peasants, the merchants, the soldiers, and the slaves. Naturally, the nobility was made up chiefly of the Moslems, while the merchants were Jews and descendants of Christians who had adopted Mohammedanism. Still the culture was Moorish, and Moors comprised the chief racial element, an element so important in shaping Andalusian character and thus indelibly stamping the character of Spanish America.

THE INFLUENCE OF THE REVIVING CHRISTIAN NATIONS AND THEIR INSTITUTIONS ON THE NEW WORLD

Politically the Spain that was to administer the New World colonies grew from the persistence of Christianity during the Middle Ages in the north near the Pyrenees, and from the long "reconquest" as these northerners moved southward into the Moorish regions of the center and the south. Many Christians, fleeing from the Mohammedans, had hidden in the mountains in the northwest. Groups of them remained in the north as in Visigothic times, in areas that gradually became the independent kingdoms of Asturias, Navarre, Aragon, and Catalonia. Gradually two stronger kingdoms emerged in the northwest, León and Castile, which were destined to supplant Asturias and become a single nation under the ancestors of Isabella. By the eleventh century Castilians began the long process of reconquering Moslem Spain.

The influence of the church and the monastic orders gave vigor to this movement. The small northern kingdoms had become fanatically religious. The Christians had always remembered Saint James, whose bones were supposed to be in Spain. "Miraculously" discovered in Galicia, the bones were placed in a shrine called Saint James of Compostela. Saint James—San Diego or Santiago—became the patron saint of the reconquest; soldiers went into battle crying "Santiago!" Many are the towns in the New World today called Santiago.

In 1236 Cordova fell to a Castilian king known to history as San Fernando. Asked by the king of France to join in a Crusade against the

Holy Week parade in San José, Costa Rica—a direct heritage from Spain. *Courtesy United Fruit Company.*

Mohammedans in the Holy Land, this King Fernando had answered, "There is no lack of Mohammedans in my own land." In 1248 he came triumphantly into Seville as a conqueror. Meanwhile kings of Aragon, uniting with Catalonia, had advanced their own kingdom southward to include Valencia. By the time of Columbus' birth, the combined kingdom of Castile and León dominated most of central and northern Spain, flanked by Portugal on the west and tiny Navarre and powerful Aragon on the north and east, with the Moors on the defensive in Granada alone.

Although Christian Spain was not territorially united until after 1469, the Moors had been on the defensive since the middle of the thirteenth century. During the two centuries of the "reconquest," the powerful Christian kingdoms of Castile and Aragon were developing institutions that were to dominate the Spain of Renaissance times and to provide the pattern for government and social life in Spanish America. There was great pride in noble birth. Castilian nobility was made up of *ricos hombres*, or grandees. The "sons of somebody," *hijos de algo* (as opposed to "sons of nobody," *hijos de nadie*) came to be called *hidalgos;* they formed the bulk of the aristocracy. Below them were the *caballeros*, the men who fought as cavalry and could afford horse and equipment, and thus enjoyed privileges. *Hidalgos* and *caballeros* figured strongly in the development of Latin America throughout its conquest and settlement. In both Castile and Aragon these privileged classes were strongly individualistic and separatistic.

The nonprivileged class was composed of peasants and people of the towns. The Castilian town was not only a center of commerce but an agency for holding and consolidating lands in the reconquest of Spain from the Moors. The towns thus gained special rights, *fueros*, or charters granting privileges outside the royal authority and immunities from the law. They administered their own affairs rather democratically, through a *cabildo,* or council made up of elected members called *regidores.* They maintained their own police system separate from the king's—police groups called brotherhoods, or *hermandades.* The towns furnished revenue to the king in return for self-government, and were answerable only to royal inspectors, called *visitadores.*

During the reconquest, the kings gained increasing power over the feudalistic nobles. Now the subjugated nobles served in the capacity of royal officials or frontier military governors and were called *adelantados.* In the king's castle a court officialdom was developed. In some cases feudal positions were held by church dignitaries who recognized the king's nominal power over them. As the king grew in power, he formed a royal tribunal, which brought justice under royal rather than local control. Then the *audiencia,* or court, in which the king held an audience to hear complaints and administer justice, became a fixed institution. The church was also a centralizing authority; church agencies received large land grants in return for cooperation with the royal government, and became wealthy and powerful.

The king often made special fiscal grants to noble or military officials. This grant was called an *encomienda,* a term destined for a fateful history in the New World. In medieval Spain the grant consisted of the right to collect taxes in a given region in return for responsibility over the welfare of the inhabitants. Similar *encomienda* grants were to form the basis of distributing Indian laborers and their village lands in the New World. Sheep and cattle raisers formed their own guilds in Christian Spain as they had in Moorish Spain, and received certain chartered privileges. Their guilds were called *mestas;* their disputes were carried over to the colonies.

Special liaison officers between king and town were called *corregidores;* as the centuries passed, these royal agents served to strengthen the royal authority at the expense of self-government in the towns. Town government, chartered rights, provincial control, and strengthened royal authority in Castile were setting a pattern for the New World. The terms *cabildo, adelantado, audiencia, fueros, corregidor, visitador* all were to appear again and again in Spanish American colonial history. The system of royal taxation—a royal share on the output of the mines, ships to be contributed for royal use, such as those which the town of Palos had to give Isabella for Columbus, a tax on commercial transactions called *alcabala,* royal monopolies on certain products, customs duties on every shipment in and out of a Spanish port—this was a system to be used to tax the towns, the mines, and the trade of the colonies. All these functionaries together with the codes of legal jurisdiction, the code of the Visigothic kings, and the laws of Castilian rulers helped create respect for written law and bureaucratic procedure. The endless copies of detailed reports on all the taxes complying with all the laws were to fill the colonial archives of Seville during the three centuries after Columbus.

The treatment of minorities was to be reflected also in the colonial epoch in the New World. Special taxes were laid on Jews and Moors; they were confined to ghettos, forced to wear badges or distinctive types of clothing, kept from practicing certain trades. In fact, no occupations save those of merchant and moneylender were open to Jews. Many Moslems were also in the commercial class, but thousands of them worked as artisans and agriculturists. The quiet discrimination against such people turned at times to bitter persecution and forcible baptism. Meanwhile royal authority, and with it religious persecution, were to receive a new impetus in the second half of the fifteenth century.

THE STRONG UNIFIED SPAIN
OF COLUMBUS' TIME

In 1469 an eighteen-year-old girl named Isabella, heiress to the throne of Castile, married a seventeen-year-old boy named Ferdinand of Aragon. Within ten years' time, each of these young people had inherited his own throne; Castile, León, Aragon, and Catalonia and all their Moorish conquests were now ruled by one family. The marriage has been hailed as a love match; though that is not completely true, it was more so than most royal marriages. Isabella, auburn-haired, clear-skinned, fair of face, had a strong religious will and was determined to stamp out heretics, infidels, and Jews in her realm; the church became rich and powerful under her. Ferdinand, on the other hand, though perhaps not so sincerely religious, was a wily and successful diplomat. He made alliances with other great powers and the new Spain became a leading nation in Europe. After 1480 the young rulers, though still technically reigning separately, set about to complete the unification of all Spain within the borders it has today.

Territorially, they had first to rid the peninsula of Moslems, a goal for Isabella's religious zeal and Ferdinand's political ambition. Isabella and Ferdinand visited the holy shrine of Santiago at Compostela for inspiration in the war against Granada, the last Moorish stronghold. Then they received the support of the nobility and the blessings of the Pope, who gave them the title of The Catholic Monarchs. With their soldiers crying "Santiago!" the monarchs laid siege to Granada, and followed the campaign into the field with their entire family. Isabella was at her camp outside the city when she received Columbus. She had little interest in explorations until Boabdil, the last Moorish sultan, evacuated the Alhambra in the spring of 1492 and fled to North Africa. Now Spain was united territorially. The entire nation was still celebrating the victory when the successful Columbus went to the court at Barcelona in 1493.

Territorial unification itself is not sufficient to make a strong nation. Administratively, feudalism had to be made to bend to royal power. This The Catholic Monarchs proceeded to do. They gave special powers to the *Santa Hermandad,* the royal brotherhood which became the centralized police force. The chivalric military-religious organizations were taken over by Ferdinand, who became their "grand master" and thereby assured for himself a strong central army and a larger income. Chartered towns were restricted and *corregidores* and *visitadores* superseded *cabildos* or town councils in power. *Residencias,* reviews of an official's administration at the end of his term of office, were instituted to insure the honesty and efficiency of the *corregidores* and became an established institution a century later in the New World. The monarchs obtained income from many types of taxation and had no reason to summon a *cortes* or parliament to lay taxes, as the earlier Christian kings in northern Spain had done. Royal councils, as opposed to the *cortes,* grew in power and became the principal instrument of government for both Spain and the colonies. There were councils of state, of finance, of justice, of religious affairs as government became more complex and Spain's power expanded. Finally the Council of the Indies, which was to wield power in the New World for three centuries, was established.

Thus Ferdinand ruled Aragon and Isabella ruled Castile, though the Queen's idea was "all for Spain," not "all for Castile." As their power grew, they raised a son and three daughters for this new Spain. Ferdinand arranged marriages for his children into several of the courts of Europe, outlived the strait-laced Isabella by twelve years and his only son by a generation. Of his daughters, the youngest was Catherine of Aragon, ill-starred first wife of Henry VIII, whose only heir was the English queen "Bloody" Mary. His eldest daughter died as the young queen of Portugal. His mentally unbalanced second daughter, Juana, had the most brilliant match, marrying Philip, the heir to Austria, Belgium, and Holland, as well as to the title of Holy Roman Emperor, and with that title heir to the leadership of the federation of German states.

Juana became insane before she came to the throne of Castile, but her young son Charles inherited all these vast possessions. He was actually the first monarch of both Castile and Aragon, and Granada as well, and he called all these Iberian possessions Spain. Through his father he had vast possessions in Europe. During his reign as Charles V of the Holy Roman Empire and Charles I of Spain, while he was yet a boy, Magellan sailed around the world, Cortés conquered the Aztecs, and Martin Luther challenged the power of the Roman Catholic Church in his German possessions with the first successful "heresy." Charles was the king of Spain when many of the major grants for exploration were made. Harried and exhausted by religious disputes in Germany and wars in other parts of his realm, he could still put Castile's institutions to the test in an all-out attempt to transfer the Spanish royal will to the New World. His son enhanced the prestige and increased the power; he was that Philip II of Spain's Golden Age who "tangled" with Queen Elizabeth and lost the Armada in 1588, the first strong colonial ruler to be defeated by the British navy.

Ferdinand and Isabella and their heirs also brought about unification and strong central power in the field of religion. Before Isabella's time the Castilian clergy had been, by modern standards, scandalously lazy, immoral, and ignorant. During Isabella's reign the church and the religious orders were reformed and infused with piety and industry. The monarchs secured control of church appointments in Spain; bishops and archbishops were chosen, not by the Pope but by the Crown, a royal privilege called the *real patronato.* As "Divine-Right" monarchs, with more control over the church than had other rulers of Europe, The Catholic Monarchs transferred their religious authority to the New World. Indeed, the Latin American republics of modern times were to inherit disputes based on the same question—was the government or the Pope to choose religious leaders? In the Americas, as in the Spain of 1492, the church became a large landowner, possessing many peasant Indian villages and thousands of square miles of land, again creating an economic problem for modern times.

Once Granada had been taken, conformity in religion became synonymous with patriotism in the mind of the pious Isabella. Unity of the nation meant unity in faith, complete acceptance of Catholicism. Moors and Jews must be converted or exiled. To make sure that newly converted Christians did not backslide or secretly practice old ways, a Royal Council of the Inquisition was established to root out heresy, to make Spain orthodox from the mountains to the sea. The institution of the Inquisition was carried into the New World and used against heretics who turned up from Spain or elsewhere. It was not abolished in Latin America until the nineteenth century.

Religious unity was achieved when Jews and Moors were driven out, but economic activities were temporarily blighted in Spain as a result, and the effects were felt socially in the New World for centuries. The clever artisans, the skilled metal workers, the richest merchants, the ablest financiers were gone from Spain. Because darker-skinned "heretics" had carried on the handicrafts and commerce, "pure-blooded" Spanish *hidalgos* scorned such pursuits. In the New World the gallant young Spaniards would not undertake any such occupations; until recent times the Latin American republics were retarded because educated young men would not go into commerce, engineering, or the skilled trades.

For the future colonial empire the rule of Ferdinand and Isabella had great commercial and financial importance. Government administration was efficient; commerce and trade were rehabilitated after the years of the Moorish wars. A merchant marine was developed; the sheep raising industry was strengthened and agriculture prospered with hired labor. By 1500 The Catholic Monarchs were ruling over a people who could well afford the effort of colonizing the Caribbean islands. The centralization of political and economic power, combined with the riches brought from the further discoveries in Mexico and Peru, stamped the sixteenth century as one of Spanish dominance in Europe and the world, even though these riches soon produced an imbalance in Spain's' home economy. When Charles V served as ruler of both Spain and the Holy Roman Empire and controlled realms in Europe and the Americas of a size and strength unknown since the fall of Rome, a new imperialism developed, challenging the rest of Europe to expand in opposition. Spanish metallic wealth from the New World, Spanish unity under one crown and one religion— in contrast to northern Europe's quarrels over Protestantism—combined to give Spain unprecedented prestige. American gold helped Charles in his wars in Europe against the French. As accepted champion of Catholicism he fought Protestants in Germany and Turks in Eastern Europe. Charles' son Philip II inherited the prestige of Spain, though not all the Hapsburg possessions, and brought Spanish glory to its height just before the loss of the Armada in 1588. Even Portugal was to be ruled by Spain for sixty years after 1580. In the period from 1520 to 1588 two new civilizations were conquered, and Spain's empire was expanded the length of both American continents. It was the largest empire the world has ever known. The reign of Philip II was indeed Spain's "Day in the Sun," although shadows were already being cast at midday.

GOLDEN AGE OF SPANISH CULTURE

The serious-minded Isabella was interested in other things besides the "purification" of religion. She believed in "Culture" with a capital "C." She surrounded herself with scientific minds, some of whom eventually listened to Columbus. She sent for one of the famous figures of the Italian Renaissance, Peter Martyr, to be tutor to her children. He stayed on at her court to write the best-known contemporary account of the days of exploration. Printing had been introduced into Spain from North Europe while Isabella was still a girl, and German and Italian workmen were imported to run the presses. New universities were founded in the now united Christianized Spain to replace the great Moorish centers of learning. At Valencia, Valladolid, Barcelona, Seville, Salamanca, and Alcalá the university centers prospered. Italian teachers were brought in to tell of the new interests in ancient classics and modern science. Isabella encouraged religious painting and architecture. Spaniards in the united Spain wrote more love poetry and history-telling ballads than ever. Intellectual life was stimulated, although by modern standards it seems severely hampered by censorship and by the stress placed on theological education. The monarchs' own officials came from an educated class of lawyers, a closed administrative group which became a bureaucracy and which brought bureaucratic methods into colonial government.

During the reigns of Charles V and Philip II, the European Renaissance flowered contemporaneously with the religious conflicts over Protestantism; Spanish literature and art reflected these trends by the mid-1600s. The period from about 1550 to about 1650 has been called the Golden Age of Spanish literature. The scholars at Salamanca were concerned with eclipses and calendar reform; Luis Vives contributed to European philosophy on a level with Erasmus; Father Vitoria wrote of international law before Grotius. Lope de Vega and Calderón de la Barca wrote plays still read today; Cervantes produced Don Quixote, the greatest Spanish novel ever written. Velásquez, El Greco, and Murillo set patterns for portraiture and religious painting for the New World to copy. The religious revival of the Counter Reformation produced the militant order of Jesuits founded by Ignatius Loyola. Some of this Spanish Renaissance of the sixteenth century was due to the inspiration and zest brought to the peninsular peoples by the discovery and conquest of America. In its turn the influence of the Spanish Renaissance was reflected in many ways in the New World.

The language of Lope de Vega and of Cervantes was the language of old Castile, the language of Isabella's court. The history of Castilian, which became the official language of the new unified nation and survives as the present-day Spanish of Madrid, is the history of Spain, for it contains Iberian words as well as words from the "vulgar Latin" of the Roman soldiers and from the Arabic of the Moorish invasion. The old Latin of the soldiers, spoken differently in each province, had developed different pronunciations in Portugal, Castile, Aragon, and Catalonia. Students of Latin America should remember that the first "proud Castilians" who came to the New World were from Cadiz and Seville rather than Castile; they spoke the language of Andalusia with its "ss" sound rather than "th" for *c* and *z*, as in the language of the central plateau. Today in Latin America one says "*grassias,*" not "*grathias,*" so as not to be taken for a visitor from Madrid.

In this language, with the Andalusian pronunciation, Spanish words, Spanish place names, Spanish family names came to America. A glance at lists of the nobility, government officials, and church leaders in the Spain of 1250 to 1500 reveals many names familiar in the Americas. The names of viceroys, poets, explorers, and large landowners of the New World were the famous noble family names of Spain. But more important were the ordinary families named Chávez and Pérez, Domínguez and González, López and Morales and Fernández, who gave their names to the New World, for they are today the Smiths and the Joneses, the Browns and the Greens, the Millers and the Carpenters of Latin America. They brought their love of music and poetry, their almost Moorish seclusion of women, their pottery and weaving, their market squares, their styles of houses. Especially they brought their devotion to religion—the colorful pageants on holy days, the patron saints for each town, the religious place names. And those who came as farmers brought their domesticated animals, especially their patient burros and their draft oxen, their methods of caring for orchard and vineyard and their Old World grains. In fact, the Chávez and Pérez and López families brought their whole pattern of life.

Spaniards also stamped the New World with their own personal characteristics. The bigotry and intolerance born of the long crusade against the Moors, the excessive pride and arrogance of the *hidalgos* who laid siege to Granada came to New Spain in the next generation. Contempt for peasant workers and for heretic tradesmen and artisans caused the well-born young Spanish soldiers in America to prefer fighting on the frontier to manual labor. On the other hand, the knightly pride was accompanied by reckless irresponsibility and an almost Arab individualism which was to run rampant in America.

The many regions of Spain each contributed special characteristics. To the New World came self-reliant commerce-minded Basques, hard-working Gallegos from Galicia, cultured Castilians, peasants from Estremadura, and traders from Aragon. Especially is the carefree, emotional spirit of Andalusia found in the Americas—the joy of living, the gay colorful dances, the lighthearted poetry and song and speech. All these elements combined to form the psychological make-up of the sixteenth-century Spanish immigrants to America, dominated by honor, passion, and individualism, which are the best-known reflections of Spain in the development of Spanish America.

PORTUGAL AT THE TIME OF EUROPE'S RENAISSANCE

Little has been said of Portugal, that other Christian kingdom which remained outside the union of Castile and Aragon, which kept its own language separate from the Castilian tongue, and which was the first European nation to embark on a colonial career. The Lusitanians were a tribe of Iberians on the Atlantic coast. Their city in the valley of the Tagus River came to be called Olisipo when it was under Roman dominance, a name re-pronounced Lisboa or Lisbon when the Roman Latin was no longer spoken. The Moors were in Lisbon by 720 and stayed there 400 years. Moorish influence is evident in Portugal in place names, architecture, literature, and folklore.

Meanwhile, the Valley of the Douro, with its old Roman town of Portus Cali, or Portucale—today's Oporto—was conquered by the expanding kingdom of León. As the county of Portugal, this area was given as a dowry by the king of León to his daughter when she married a young count from Burgundy. Her son proclaimed independence from León and pushed southward, winning the Tagus Valley from the Moors in 1147. Nine successors of his direct line, called the House of Burgundy, drove the Moors out of the rest of present-day Portugal. By placing the kingdom under the protection of the papacy as a papal fief, and by fending off all attempts of León and Castile to conquer it by force, Portugal was able to develop itself into a unified new state under a strong monarch, with a national language and literature. Many of the factors involved in the early history and struggles of Spain were present in the story of Portugal. By the time of John I—King John the Great (1385–1433)—Portugal was a strong unified nation, completely separate from the expanding Castilian kingdom.

King John's rule resembled that of Isabella a half century later. He consolidated the royal power and allowed his *cortes* to put but slight restraint upon him. The towns looked to the monarch for their privileges, and the nobles were loyal to the king. Owing to the piety of the people, the church remained a powerful influence. Royal courts encroached upon ecclesiastical courts and the king acquired the right of approving Papal Bulls. Yet clergymen filled most of the positions of influence and power. The King, as Ferdinand was to do later in Spain, assumed mastership of the military orders, the command of a royal army and of the newly created royal navy. Meanwhile there developed a new middle class capable of handling an increase in commerce. This class supported the king and obtained concessions, while the military were rewarded with land grants. Peace, strength, and economic and social advances made Portugal ready to act on the inviting possibilities presented her by her geographic situation.

Portugal is located in the southwest corner of Europe facing the Atlantic Ocean, and has several good ports. The Italian states had gained prosperity from their Mediterranean ports; the Portuguese could circumvent the Italian monopoly and do the same on the Atlantic. The people, physically strong, brave, sober, accustomed to hot climates, and imbued with religious zeal and the spirit of medieval chivalry, were ready to embark on any adventure. Tales of distant lands, of Christian kingdoms like that of the mythical Prester John, egged on the Portuguese. King John began the expansion in 1415 with the capture of Ceuta, a rich port on the African side of Gilbraltar, terminal of caravan routes into the heart of Africa, and a stronghold of Moslem corsairs. In this conquest the nineteen-year-old Prince Henry, born in 1394 as the third son of John I, was in naval command and was given a governorship in the corner of North Africa. This campaign started his career of discoveries down the African Coast, discoveries so important in the story told in Chapter 1.

The religious Prince Henry hoped to find the land of the Christian Prester John; for profit to Portugal he sought gold, slaves, and ivory. He himself spent most of his years at home as administrator of the voyages of exploration. At his headquarters at Sagres on the southwest tip of Europe he established an "Institute," and here he surrounded himself with a group of scholars, cosmographers, cartographers, mathematicians, astronomers, and physicians. Here he built an observatory, made maps and charts, built ships, trained pilots, and received reports from his captains who were year by year working farther down the shoulder of Africa. The Madeiras were discovered by 1420 and colonized in 1425; a little later the Azores, known to antiquity, were rediscovered and explored. From Cape Blanco, Negro captives were brought back to Portugal. By the time of Henry's death in 1460, his mariners had gone within 6 degrees of the equator and had landed at Sierra Leone. His ships had started the trade in Negro slaves, gold dust, ivory, cotton, and pepper. Before the death of Henry, papal grants had confirmed the Portuguese claims along the African coast.

Far from ceasing when Henry died, the voyages down the African coast increased after the fall of Constantinople in 1453; the desire to circumvent the Turkish monopoly of the eastern trade routes created a new incentive for discovery of an all-water route to India. The eastern bend of Africa was discovered in 1462, and a settlement made on the Guinea coast. The Congo region was reached in 1484. Finally the work was climaxed by Bartolomeu Dias, who in 1488 doubled around the Cape of Good Hope; only a mutiny of his sailors prevented his achieving the goal reached ten years later by Vasco da Gama, who arrived successfully in India and returned with products of the Far East. Following up Vasco da Gama's voyage, Pedro Alvares Cabral, with a large trading fleet, touched at Brazil and then went on around Africa to lay the foundations for the Portuguese trade empire. There followed a rapid succession of Portuguese trading stations and colonies in the Far East—in India, Java, Sumatra, the Spice Islands, China, and even in Japan. Portugal, by thus finding an all-water route to India, wrested the lion's share of the India trade from the Italian city-states and became the great entrepôt of this lucrative business. The Portuguese ships, not the *Niña* and the *Pinta*, had actually reached Cathay. Thus Portugal had laid the groundwork for both trade and colonization.

Portugal now had her own century of glory. Her university at Coimbra was famous in Europe; the missionary St. Francis Xavier, though Spanish-born, took Christianity to India at the request of the Portuguese king and became a patron saint for all missionaries; the Portuguese poet Camões sang the glories of the age of East Indian exploration. Portugal's captains founded sugar-growing settlements in Brazil which she claimed under the Line of Demarcation agreement. Her merchants founded stations along the coast of Africa and became rich as slave traders for Europe and America, starting that tragic traffic in Negroes that was to be a black shadow on the New World.

But her decline as a world power came even before the defeat of Philip II's Armada at the hands of Elizabeth. For that same Philip, through his mother's line, had made himself King of Portugal when the male line died out, and thus what all early Portugal had dreaded—union with Castile —happened unexpectedly. Sixty years later, when Spain's own kings were weak, a Portuguese patriot, the Duke of Braganza, revolted and made Portugal an independent nation once again. The House of Braganza survived to see gold and diamonds discovered in Brazil. So, in the long run, Portugal had no reason for lasting regrets that she had turned Columbus down.

Spain and Portugal, by the evidence shown in this brief review of their earlier histories, were uniquely prepared for the task of colonizing the Americas which had been set for them by the voyages of Columbus.

Readings

Abbott, W. C., *Expansion of Europe* (2 vols., 1924)

Altamira y Crevea, R., *A History of Spain*, trans. Muna Lee (1949)

Atkinson, W. C., *History of Spain and Portugal* (1960)

Bertran, L., and Charles Petrie, *History of Spain* (1934)

Boxer, C. R., *Four Centuries of Portuguese Expansion 1415–1825* (1961)

Chapman, C. E., *History of Spain* (1918)

Cheyney, E. P., *European Background of American History* (1904)

———, *Dawn of a New Era* (1936)

Davies, R. Trevor, *The Golden Century of Spain 1501–1621* (1965)

Descola, J., *A History of Spain* (1963)

Diffie, B. W., *Prelude to Empire: Portugal Overseas before Henry the Navigator* (1961)

Foster, G. M., *Culture and Conquest: America's Spanish Heritage* (1960)

Haring, C. H., *Trade and Navigation Between Spain and the Indies in the Time of the Hapsburgs* (1918)

Keen, B., trans. and ed., *Life of Admiral Columbus by his Son Ferdinand* (1959)

Klein, J., *The Mesta: A Study in Spanish Economy, 1273–1836* (1920)

Lane-Poole, S., *The Moors in Spain* (1886)

Lea, H. C., *History of the Inquisition in Spain* (4 vols., 1906–1907)

Mariéjol, J. H., *Spain of Ferdinand and Isabella* (1961)

Merriman, R. B., *Rise of the Spanish Empire in the Old World and in the New* (4 vols., 1918–1934)
Nowell, C. E., *A History of Portugal* (1952)
Prescott, W. H., *Ferdinand and Isabella* (2 vols., 3rd ed., 1839)
Sanceau, E., *Henry the Navigator* (1947)
Stanislawski, D., *The Individuality of Portugal* (1959)
Stephens, H. M., *Portugal* (1893)
Ticknor, G., *History of Spanish Literature* (3 vols., 1965)

Chapter 3

The Land and Climate
of the New World

THE SURPRISING NEW LAND MASS

"AN AGE WILL COME after many years, when the Ocean will loose the chains of things, and a huge land lie revealed," the Roman-Iberian Seneca had written. Christopher Columbus had read such early prophecies and had written comments on them in the margins of his personal books. And he had also promised Queen Isabella that he "had the intention to make a new chart of navigation, upon which I shall place the whole sea and lands of the Ocean Sea in their proper position under their bearings." But Columbus never made such a chart personally; he evolved no conception of the two continents, "the huge land" revealed when the ocean "loosed the chains of things." Between him and his goal of the true Indies lay half the "space" of the world.

And what "space"! Toscanelli and Behaim, the great geographers of the 1490s, thought the coast of China would be 5,000 miles westward from Europe; by actual airline it proved to be 11,766. Nearly 7,000 miles of this distance was partly occupied by the new hemisphere—from the hump of Brazil on the east to San Francisco on the west—and Iberian peoples were to put settlements somewhere along the entire 7,000-mile stretch. Spain and Portugal, with an area of only 225,000 square miles, were to dominate 8,600,000 square miles, an area almost forty times as great. For 200 years after the discovery, mapmakers tried to draw the contours and positions of the new continents, adding lands and islands in the wrong places, hoping to plot the strait that would show the way through to the Far East. The royal courts of Spain and Portugal regularly employed expert pilots and mapmakers to keep up with the newest information about coastlines and river mouths brought in by ship captains, but accurate knowledge was acquired only slowly, for the project was so vast. While scholars, cloistered in Europe, drew maps from secondhand information, explorers, soldiers, friars, and homebuilders tackled the lands themselves. In a thousand ways they found the new areas to be fantastically beyond previous experience. Although Spain itself was a land of severe contrasts, Spaniards entering the New World were unprepared for the great extremes of size, wealth, climate, hardships, and sheer beauty that they found in the American continents. Nothing as exciting would happen to mankind again until the exploration of space beyond the earth's atmosphere.

It is impossible to understand the history of Latin America without knowing something of its geography and the influence of that geography on the people who came to live there. For history is the story of the lives of people, and people live when and where they can earn a living, with their living depending on the geography of their living places. This is especially true of the great land mass the Spaniards had just discovered; each region of Latin America has a distinctive situation of water, weather, or mountain that has affected the lives of people there.

Latin American history is more involved with geography than is the history of most places. Latin America's geography produced her isolation from the rest of the world and her slow changes in culture; the great distances separating Latin America from Europe, and separating her various regions from each other, produced fierce local feelings for independence.

That the culture of Mexico is different from that of Brazil or of Argentina today is to some extent a matter of geography. For convenience the term Latin America is applied geographically to the twenty different regions of Spanish, Portuguese, and French colonization that make up today's twenty republics. The Latin-Europeans explored the Western Hemisphere from Nootka Sound and the Chesapeake Bay to Tierra del Fuego, an area entirely surrounded by water, unconnected with any other continent. Most of South America lies east of the United States and much closer to Europe than does North America. By far the greater portion of the new continents lies within the Torrid Zone, a factor destined to make difficulties for the settlers, despite modification by some high plateaus.

Into this area, intervening between Europe and the eagerly sought-for lands of Asia, the Spaniards came—into an area unknown, uncharted, inhabited by strange red men who themselves had no concept of the extent of the land mass. The reader can follow the astounded Andalusians as they arrived in the Western Hemisphere via the Caribbean area and spread out

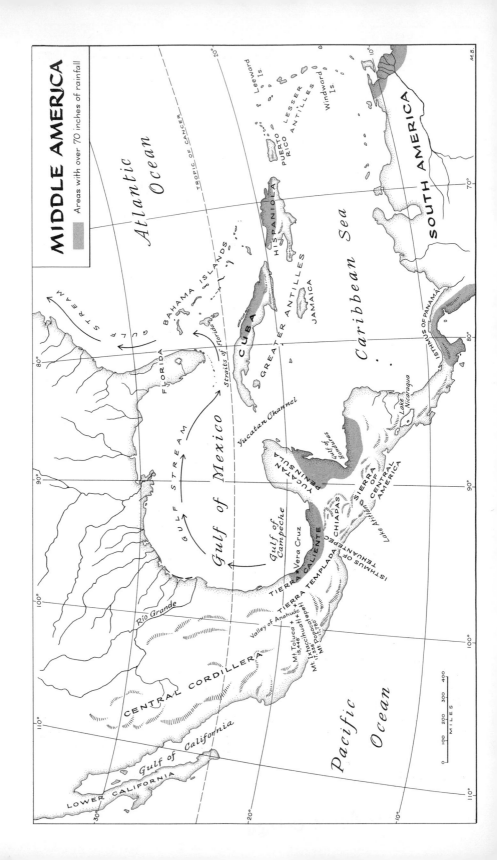

MIDDLE AMERICA

Areas with over 70 inches of rainfall

Atlantic Ocean

GULF STREAM

BAHAMA ISLANDS

TROPIC OF CANCER

Leeward Is.

PUERTO RICO

LESSER ANTILLES

Windward Is.

SOUTH AMERICA

HISPANIOLA

CUBA

Straits of Florida

FLORIDA

GREATER ANTILLES

JAMAICA

Caribbean Sea

Yucatan Channel

Gulf of Mexico

GULF STREAM

Lake Nicaragua

ISTHMUS OF PANAMÁ

Gulf of Campeche

YUCATAN PENINSULA

Gulf of Honduras

SIERRA OF CENTRAL AMERICA

Vera Cruz

TIERRA CALIENTE

Lake Atitlán

ISTHMUS OF TEHUANTEPEC

CHIAPAS

Rio Grande

TIERRA TEMPLADA

Valley of Anahuác

Mt. Toluca 15,448

Mt. Ixtacchuatl 17,338

Mt. Popocatepetl 17,760

CENTRAL CORDILLERA

Pacific Ocean

Gulf of California

LOWER CALIFORNIA

MILES
0 100 200 300 400

M.8.

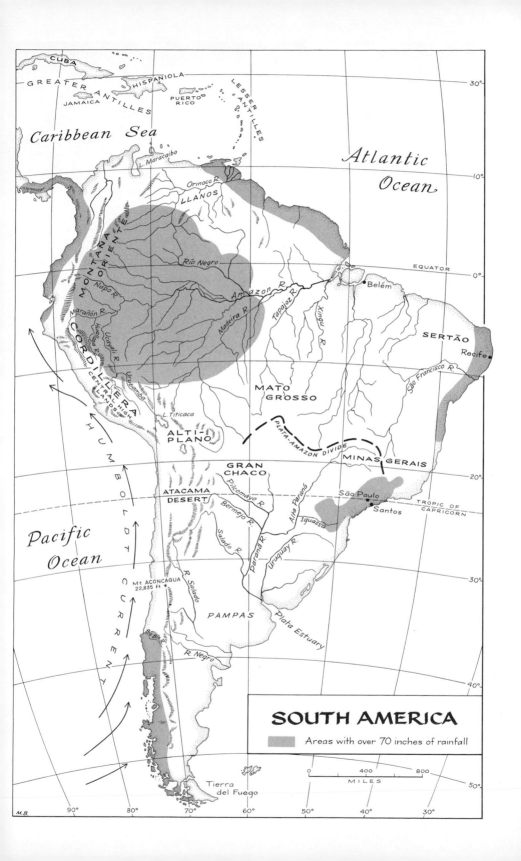

CUBA

GREATER ANTILLES

JAMAICA   HISPANIOLA

PUERTO
RICO

LESSER ANTILLES

Caribbean Sea

L. Maracaibo

Orinoco R.

LLANOS

*Atlantic
Ocean*

EQUATOR

Belém

MONTAÑA ORIENTE

Río Negro

Napo R.

Marañón R.

Amazon R.

Tapajoz R.

Xingu R.

0°

Huallaga R.

Madeira R.

SERTÃO

CORDILLERA

Ucayali R.

Urubamba

CENTRAL HIGHLANDS

Recife

São Francisco R.

HUMBOLDT

L. Titicaca

ALTI-
PLANO

MATO
GROSSO

PLATA-AMAZON DIVIDE

GRAN
CHACO

MINAS GERAIS

20°

ATACAMA
DESERT

Pilcomayo R.

São Paulo

TROPIC OF
CAPRICORN

Bermejo R.

Alto Paraná

Santos

*Pacific
Ocean*

Salado R.

Iquassú

Paraná R.

Uruguay R.

CURRENT

Mt ACONCAGUA
22,835 ft ★

R. Salado

30°

PAMPAS

Plata Estuary

Bío Bío

R. Negro

40°

SOUTH AMERICA

Areas with over 70 inches of rainfall

0   400   800
MILES

*Tierra
del Fuego*

50°

M.B.   90°   80°   70°   60°   50°   40°   30°

The falls of the Iguassú on the Argentine-Paraguay-Brazil border—one of the fantastic surprises the New World held for the Spaniards. *Courtesy Moore McCormack Lines.*

into North and South America. In general, the Europeans were delighted at first with what they saw. Columbus thought his new-found lands were "like April in Andalusia." The European invasion of the American hemisphere began with the jewel-like islands of the Caribbean.

THE CARIBBEAN AS SPANIARDS FIRST SAW IT

The Caribbean area is a great curve of islands of various sizes and elevations which extends from near the peninsula of Florida to Venezuela; these islands enclose the Caribbean Sea and the Gulf of Mexico, and protect the narrow isthmus connecting North and South America. Within this enclosure lie the Greater Antilles—Cuba, Puerto Rico, Jamaica, and Hispaniola—and the the Lesser Antilles, the long curve of small Windward and Leeward Islands, some volcanic in structure, some coral. These West Indies, consisting of dozens of islands of various sizes and elevations—islands which are the highest parts of a submerged mountain chain—contain an area of better than a million square miles.

Elevation and prevailing winds have always played a large part in the economy of the Caribbean. Some islands are relatively dry, lack sufficient level places for agriculture, and have failed to develop adequate food supplies. Others rise to a height of 5,000 feet—and in one case, the peak of Mt. Tina, almost to 10,000 feet—receive a great deal of precipitation during the season of the trade winds and hurricanes, and have a warm, moist climate.

Both the Greater and Lesser Antilles loom large in the first century of colonization. The Spaniards first introduced themselves as colonists in the former, and then introduced their animals and plants, especially sugar; here they first tried out their institutions. The Greater Antilles were the strategic steppingstones to North, Central, and South America, and the nearness to the mainland gave the region a continuing and enduring importance. The trade winds blew the first European ships directly to these islands; the important commercial routes from Europe led to the Caribbean as long as shipping depended on sails and wind directions.

Columbus came to Cuba two weeks after he first sighted land in the Bahamas. "I sailed along its coast some distance toward the west," he wrote of this Pearl of the Antilles, "and found it to be so large, without any apparent end, that I believe it was not an island but a continent, a province of Cathay." Actually, this large island stretches from east to west some 760 miles, though it averages only sixty miles in width. At all points Cuba is near the sea, and it has many good harbors and anchorages which invited Spanish explorers from the first. Sixty per cent of Cuban land is flat or gently rolling. Spaniards began to clear forests along the coast and raise sugar cane before Cortés went from there to the conquest of Mexico in 1519, and most of Cuba's subsequent history, to the present, was to revolve around the production of sugar. With rainfall averaging about fifty inches and temperatures averaging between seventy and eighty degrees, only an occasional hurricane disturbs this planter's idyll.

The first Spanish homes were built on the Caribbean's second largest island, Hispaniola, which now contains the two republics of Haiti and the Dominican Republic. Much more mountainous than Cuba, it has much less agricultural land. Though this island was the "mother of America," Spanish planters, miners, explorers, and administrators struck out for other islands of the Antilles or for the mainland within a decade of its settlement. However, Spanish settlers and traders continued to make fortunes from sugar and slaves in Cuba and Santo Domingo throughout the colonial period.

Puerto Rico, fourth of the Caribbean islands in size, is a continuation of the mountain range running from Cuba through Hispaniola. The island of Jamaica, third largest in the Antilles, lies directly south of Cuba. It long served Spaniards as a great producer of livestock; from here came many of the horses and cattle utilized in the settlement of mainland Mexico, Peru, and elsewhere. Then, for a century after it fell into the hands of the English, Jamaica was a thorn in the flesh of the Spanish American empire, serving as a base for naval attacks upon Spanish Caribbean cities.

The long line of the Lesser Antilles, exotic little islands with such pretty names as Dominica, Antigua, Martinique, Guadeloupe, and Marie Galante, was largely by-passed by the Spaniards after their first entry into the Caribbean. This chain of islands became, during the seventeenth and eighteenth centuries, hideouts for English and French freebooters, as well as important bases for the English and French when they began colonial development in the Americas.

HEIGHTS AND LOWLANDS OF MEXICO
AND CENTRAL AMERICA

Across the Gulf from Cuba lies the eastern coastal plain of Mexico, an area stretching from the Rio Grande to Yucatan and comprising sandy beaches, swampy lagoons, mosquito-infested rivermouths. Vera Cruz, to be founded from Cuba as a base for conquest of the Aztecs, lies in the middle of the curve. At the end of the arc, like a thumb, lies the peninsula of Yucatan, a flat limestone tableland resembling that other dangling finger into the Caribbean, Florida. Since its porous limestone surface absorbs the runoff, there are no rivers in Yucatan; the tropical rains run quickly underground, forming a below-surface water table used as a source of year-round deep wells by the Maya Indians. It was here that the Spaniards first saw such civilized peoples, and gained the desire to explore deeper into Mexico.

The base of Yucatan's peninsula leads into the plains of Mexico's tropical eastern lowlands in the states of Tabasco and Chiapas. Here is Mexico's narrowest point, but even here the traveler soon meets the main geographic feature of the Mexican nation, the *cordillera*, or mountain range, which forms Central America and runs on up into central Mexico where it serves as the sheltering walls for many highland valleys. The real Mexico is the highland plateau between its ridges. Between the two branches of the *cordillera*, above the coastal plain on the east and sweeping down into the Pacific on the west, lies an area 500 miles wide at its broadest, an area filled with valleys and basins. The altitude—4,000 feet for Oaxaca, 9,000 feet for Toluca, with many other valleys at elevations in between—produces a temperate climate conducive to European settlement.

Most important of these basins is the central valley of Anáhuac, site of the Aztec culture and home of today's Mexico City. Here is a cup 160 miles in circumference at an altitude of about 7800 feet. There are twenty-three inches of rainfall a year, distributed throughout the growing season to produce adequate crops, while temperatures stay near seventy degrees. The fertile and productive valley is rimmed by two snow-covered peaks, Popocatépetl and Ixtaccíhuatl. From the pine-covered mountains melting snows and rain pour down into the valley, and there is no outlet. In prehistoric times these streams formed a series of marshes and lakes. The Aztecs built their city on islands in the marsh known as Lake Texcoco; as it grew, they could not drain it in flood season. For the Spanish colonial city, as for the modern Mexican capital, there has been no natural drainage from the central sink of the Valley of Anáhuac, creating a problem for its rulers since 1400. Yet the valley itself has housed the population center of Mexico and is in many ways an ideal place to live.

North from the central valley lies a series of basins, some of them inhabitable areas where Indians had started agricultural settlements made possible by sufficient rainfall. On the edge of the rainfall line, just south of the Tropic of Cancer, quantities of mineral wealth lay hidden in the ranges in the silver-producing areas of Zacatecas and San Luis Potosí. One-third of the modern state of Mexico lies north of this region, outside the area of sufficient rainfall. It is an area of brush and cactus. Beyond it lie the Rio Grande, the plains of Texas, the mountains of Arizona and New Mexico, the barren peninsula of Baja California, and the Mediterranean-climate area of Alta California. All were to know the rule of Spain.

To the south of the central valley the highland country continues, beyond the mountain rim of the plateau of Anáhuac and at increasingly lower elevation. Two hundred thirty miles south from Mexico City the mountains open out to form the long, narrow, and rich valley of Oaxaca, with an average elevation of some 5,000 feet, where lived other civilized Indian tribes. Beyond this last valley the mainland of Mexico narrows down to 130 miles; here the two ridges form one in the low hills of the Isthmus of Tehuantepec, again a low hot country. Where Tehuantepec begins to widen out again, the mountains jut up steeply into the cooler valleys, deep slashing *barrancas*, or ravines, and active volcanoes standing guard over sapphire lakes of Guatemala—a land with a large Indian population that made the Spaniards fight hard for conquest. The Indian strain is still strong in Guatemala today, and the whole land is very nearly as colorful as the Spaniards found it.

Columbus himself had been the first to sail along the Central American coast, the deeps or *hondos* of Honduras, the "rich coast" of Costa Rica. The Central American area was to be colonized both from Panama northward and Mexico southward. Its 213,000 square miles of area comprise merely a narrowing and an extension of Mexico southward, running across the compass from northwest to southeast, containing many volcanic peaks and two high continuing ridges which unite at various points. The mountains tend to come closer to the Pacific Ocean side, dividing the smaller republics into tropical and unhealthy lowlands on the east and pleasanter highlands on the west. Most of the Spanish settlement in Central America took place in the valleys where an average altitude of some 3,000 feet lessens the heat of the tropics. The Negro slave population brought in by the Spaniards remained largely confined to the Caribbean coastal lowlands. Today's Central American population is white, Indian, and *mestizo*, or mixed bloods, in the thickly populated highlands on the west, and Negro in the small ports and banana plantations on the Caribbean coast.

Thus the *cordillera* of Mexico and Central America was to be a constant hindrance to conquest and settlement. But the greatest frustration this mountain chain was to offer the Europeans was at the place where it narrowed to its lowest strip in the dense jungle called the Isthmus of Panama. Only forty miles of land here separated the Caribbean from the Pacific, or South Sea—just enough land to shatter the hopes of easily reaching Marco Polo's China by water. This low mountain range of Panama is the connecting link between the Andean *cordillera* of South America and the great chain of *sierras* heading northward through Central America and Mexico. Half the voyages of exploration for a quarter century after Columbus were made in search of a way around or through this strip. The Isthmian link flattens out into swampy lands along the Caribbean coast—swamps which were to bring fever and death and to make the Isthmus famous as the pesthole of colonial trade and travel.

Pesthole the Isthmus was, but its very narrowness was to be a blessing for the Spanish empire. Its small width made it the shortest route to the riches of Peru, and it was naturally situated as the base of supply for Pizarro's Peruvian conquest. Throughout the whole colonial period Panama, with its terminal trading centers on either coast, handled the richest traffic in all the New World, the flow of silver and mechandise from Peru, Chile, and Ecuador to Mother Spain.

THE SOUTH AMERICAN CONTINENT

"We reached a land which we deemed a continent, which is distant westwardly from the Isles of Canary about a thousand leagues beyond the inhabited regions and within the torrid zone." Perhaps this was the first description of South America on the "hump" of Brazil, written by Amerigo Vespucci a few years after Columbus' first voyage. Here Iberians were to find and develop agricultural and mineral wealth untold, but the geography of the continent was so difficult, its whole area so much to the south of the main east-west trade routes as to make South America even today an isolated and underdeveloped region. It has been handicapped by its long, smooth coastline where good harbors lie so far apart, by the tropical climate of two-thirds of its land mass, by its rugged and lofty mountains unmatched save in the Himalayas. It was hard for Europeans to maintain contact and to interchange ideas across this difficult terrain; Spanish and Portuguese towns remained isolated, and in the mid-twentieth century whole regions are still only sparsely occupied by wild Indians.

Again, it is the contrast between mountains and lowlands that has set up the most difficult geographic barrier. In past geologic ages South America was made up of two great land masses, the Andes mass on the west, and the plateau known as the Brazilian Highlands on the east.

The Amazon and the Plata River basins make up the eastern side of the continent, and the Andes *cordillera* stands high as the backbone, dividing the continent into two unequal parts. Its ridges hug the Pacific shores, leaving only a narrow coastal strip as a shelf or stepping stone up into the highlands. The ridges and valleys that make up the Andes extend the length of the western coast from Panama to Tierra del Fuego. In southern Chile the *cordillera* is one single range forty miles wide, a region of forests, fogs, and fjords; in Bolivia the Andes area is a vast plateau of from ten to fifteen thousand feet elevation with the city of La Paz lying in a ravine. With the inhabited plateaus at lower elevations in Peru and Ecuador, the mountains continue into Colombia, where they divide into three narrow fertile valleys with rivers flowing down each. One of these chains sidetracks to form the ridges and valleys of Venezuela. Individual peaks in the Andes rival the famous mountains of the Himalayas. Illimani, at 22,000 feet, towers above Bolivia's windswept central tablelands. Osorno, a perfect cone like Fujiyama, stands snow-covered the year round in Chile's southern range, while Mount Aconcagua is the highest peak in the Western Hemisphere at 22,863 feet. Cotopaxi and Chimborazo are on the Equator in

Ecuador, but both are constantly snow-covered at the top because they reach upward of 20,000 feet.

Most prosperous of the long Andean valleys today is perhaps the Central Valley of Chile, a fertile area forty miles wide and 600 miles long, whose counterpart Spaniards were to find two centuries later in Alta California. The Inca Indians had built their capital at Cuzco in the Andean Valley to the north in Peru; Quito, capital of Ecuador, is similarly situated. The capital of the Colombian region was to be at Bogotá. The city itself is not in the river valley, but in a *savanna* or grassy plain, at 8,700 feet elevation in the Andes, 600 miles up the Magdalena River from the coast and 150 miles into the mountains beyond, extremely difficult of access until the air age. Despite their height, with few exceptions, the Andes have not formed the political boundaries of today's republics.

The geography of the Andes approaches never made transportation easy; routes to Bogotá, Quito, La Paz, and Cuzco were so precipitous as to slow down the development of those Spanish cities in the interior. The peaks of the *cordillera* raise their beautiful heads as the greatest handicap to development of five nations on the west coast, nations which are still trying to get across their mountains and develop their areas in the valleys of the Amazon's tributaries, nations whose isolated towns put sectionalism ahead of national pride. About one-sixteenth of this large area of South America has an elevation of 10,000 feet or more, a height at which Europeans have found life difficult. Along the *cordillera* from Central America to Chile runs an earthquake belt where active volcanoes have spewed out lava and destroyed farmland even in recent years. The Brazilian Highlands consist of a plateau broken by mountains along the coast, making passage north and south difficult. In the far north are the Guiana Highlands which even today are little explored.

As important as the mountains in the social and economic development of South America are the vast plains, which comprise about three-fifths of the land area of the continent, making eastern South America one of the largest lowland areas of the world. Inland from the coastal plains are three great areas of low-lying fertile lands. In the north are the *savannas* or tropical grass lands of the Orinoco, the *llanos* of Venezuela. Beyond the Guiana and Brazilian Highlands lie the tropical *selvas* or hot, wet forests of Brazil, merging in the south into the rolling, grassy, treeless pampas, the meat and wheat belt for South America. The pampas start in today's modern Brazilian state of Rio Grande do Sul, and run through Uruguay, a grassland nation two-thirds the size of Spain. So devoid of mountains is this land that when a Portuguese sailor, so the story is told in Uruguay, saw a hill 700 feet high, he called, *"Monte vejo!"*—"I see a mountain!"—and Montevideo itself is there today.

Below the Plata River are the pampas of Argentina, one of the greatest pasture areas on earth. On their east lie a thousand miles of open Atlantic, on the north the Plata-Paraná River system, on the west the Andes. At the widest point the pampas are 980 miles across, area enough to make thirty Hispaniolas. Spanish-speaking peoples, coming to it reluctantly at first as to a poor land of starvation and wild Indians, were to make of it four centuries later one of the world's richest agricultural regions, producing beef, mutton, wheat, corn, cotton, and flax for the city people of Europe. Its climate is right for this type of agriculture: warm for the crops in the heat of the Southern Hemisphere's January summer, chilly in July and August, but rarely below freezing. The flat pampas rise gradually into the Andes in the west. A mule-train-oxcart round trip from Buenos Aires to the Andes foothills behind Chile took four months as late as 1800. Geography south of the pampas stopped the Spaniards short, for here was windswept Patagonia. In mid-twentieth century there are still whole sections of it that have never been surveyed.

Equally difficult for colonization was another grassy plain of South America, the *llanos* of Venezuela, flood plain of the Orinoco, never actually settled, save by a few cattle ranchers. Lowlands on the western coastal strip, the bleak Atacama Desert of southern Peru and northern Chile, also proved uninviting for Spanish colonists. Nitrate and guano developments there, however, made the region a bloody battleground in the nineteenth century. Thus lowlands and highlands, in stark contrast with each other, both created a poor welcome to the Iberians as they wrestled with the land mass of South America.

THE INFLUENCE OF RIVER SYSTEMS

The Iberian peoples, accustomed to the Tagus and the Guadalquivir, would want to use the rivers of America as approaches to the hinterland. Mexico's geography offered them little in this regard. Indeed, in all of Mexico there are no large rivers. Even the famous Rio Grande is important today only for irrigation. In Central America, the Chagres forms part of the Panama Canal, and the San Juan River-Lake Nicaragua waterway has historic importance in colonial commerce and in diplomatic controversy over canal routes. Harbors are good in Mexico and Central America, but they are not necessarily on river mouths. Rivers in the Caribbean show as names on the map, but are not navigable, though the good harbors on the islands have been of great use since the days of discovery.

South America is as blessed with rivers as Mexico is lacking. It was at one such river that Columbus first saw South America; his third voyage touched on the mainland beyond the island of Trinidad. There he approached one of the mouths in the delta of the Orinoco, a river 1700 miles long, draining the *llanos*. Spaniards had not seen such a quantity of water issuing from so green a country. Columbus himself thought that as "neither the Ganges nor the Euphrates nor the Nile carried so much fresh water," it could not flow from a mere island, but from "a terrestrial paradise." Thus, because of the river, Columbus sensed that he had reached a continent. The Orinoco has proved of little economic use, however, though navigable for a thousand miles. There is little trade because of the floods during the rainy season. Not so the Magdalena, which, with its tributary the Cauca, served as the highway into Colombia's interior until the air age. Navigable for 600 miles, the Magdalena carried the nation's freight three-fourths of the way to Bogotá from the harbors of Barranquilla and Cartagena at its mouth until highways were completed in the late 1950s.

In southern South America the Plata estuary, a great body of fresh water a hundred miles wide at the sea, invited explorers to come in looking for a strait to the Far East. In itself, the Plata is not a hundred miles long, for it is actually a joint mouth for the Uruguay and the Paraná rivers. The latter, one of the great rivers of the Western Hemisphere, has its headwaters in little rivulets in Brazil's Goiás plateau, where drops of water running side by side cannot make up their minds to go either north to the Amazon or south to the Plata. One of the tributaries, near its junction with the Paraná a thousand miles upstream from the Plata estuary, rushes madly along a plateau and plunges 210 feet on a two-mile width in the second largest falls of the world, the Falls of Iguassú.

The Paraná has a sister river, the Paraguay, navigable to Spanish "brigantines" 500 miles above its confluence with the Paraná. Waters reaching it from Bolivian Andes, near Lake Titicaca down the Pilcomayo, and from the Mato Grosso plateau divide its sources from those of the Amazon. How could the Spaniard, accustomed to the short reaches of the Guadalquivir, comprehend the great river systems of South America? Pilcomayo, Paraguay, Iguassú, Bermejo, Paraná, Uruguay—draining over a million square miles of territory and providing as much navigation for his little barks as if he had crossed the Atlantic, these rivers spread out like a fan before him as he stood at the Plata estuary. Entering the estuary he was to find paths overland from it to reach his brother Spaniards in the Inca lands beyond the Andes. Today four modern republics are dependent on the Plata system for part of their life stream. The first European settlement was to be Asunción, where the Pilcomayo meets the Paraguay in the interior. To the north lay the jungles of the Mato Grosso. To the west lay the Gran Chaco, a region of swamps in the wet season, desert in the dry, through which comparatively few Spaniards passed safely in three centuries.

Largest river in the world is the Amazon, flowing majestically over 4,000 miles, draining a basin of 2,750,000 square miles, which contains 40,000 miles of navigable river. Spaniards first saw the mighty river as they worked down from the Andes at the river's sources. The first Spanish witness described the headwaters of the Amazon as a region "full of foul places, of rough forests, and rivers great and small," a region later to be called the *Montaña,* comprising the eastern sections of the modern republics of Peru, Ecuador, Colombia, and Bolivia. In fact, until very recent times the Amazon was the only means of penetrating large portions of South America, and it gives several Pacific South American republics a future hope and look toward the Atlantic. Here the rushing streams of the Andes, starting at some places less than a hundred miles from the Pacific, come leaping out of the easternmost canyons of the *cordillera,* through the humid forest belt of the foothills to form great rivers—the Napo, the Huallaga, the Urubamba, the Negro, and the Marañón. Forbidding access to the first Europeans, many Amazon tributaries are even yet unexplored; their tentacles stretch out into every South American country save three. Three thousand miles from the Atlantic the tributaries begin to meet, first one and then the other, to make the Amazon eight miles wide before it has flowed one-fourth of its journey. Many of its head streams almost touch fingers with headwaters of the Plata-Paraná system on the south, or the Orinoco system on the north.

Flood waters which start in eastern Peru in February, the rainiest season, reach the Atlantic down the Amazon four months later in June. The banks of this river that crosses a continent are so low and the tributaries are so many that the waters move sluggishly, overflowing and filling swamps as the water comes down, receding just in time for another flood. It reaches the sea in a stream fifty miles wide, goes around large islands at the mouth, and makes the ocean itself a muddy brown many miles out. The tributaries flowing from the south split the wilderness of Mato Grosso and Goiás. These rivers, the Tapajós, the Xingú, the Tocantins, are themselves half a continent long; the territory they cross is only now being opened to colonization by the air age.

There are other bodies of water in South America. Though west coast rivers are few, the Maule and the Bío Bío have been important in Chilean history, and the Guayas in Ecuador makes a harbor at Guayaquil. Lakes in the south of Chile form a vacation area today. Lake Titicaca, home of a very early Andean civilization, is one of the highest lakes in the world, while Lake Maracaibo, actually an arm of the sea on the Venezuelan coast, is one of the world's most important sources of petroleum, black gold far more valuable than the yellow gold the Spaniards sought.

The east coast does not lack harbors, from Belém on the mouth of the Amazon, to Recife with its protecting reefs, to the beautiful Bay of Salvador known as Baía where the Portuguese first settled in Brazil, to Santos Bay, port for the São Paulo interior. Rio de Janeiro itself remains one of the most spectacular harbors of the world. That these good ports did not help develop Brazil more rapidly was due to the facts that they were too far apart down the long coast and that their backlands were not inviting. Inland from Recife lies a highland region with only twenty inches of rainfall, the *Sertão* or pastoral country; few immigrants direct from Portugal were ever to go there. Inland from Baía runs the São Francisco River, south to north and then into the sea, but so full of rapids as to be unusable for navigation, and hence little assistance to penetration beyond. Inland 300 miles to the northwest of Rio, but still only an eighth part of the distance across the continent, vast mineral treasures awaited the Portuguese in Minas Gerais. Inland from Santos harbor lay the rich uplands of São Paulo, destined to produce wealth in coffee berries undreamed of by any gold-prospecting settler. However, much of this development was to come late in Brazilian history.

The natural beauties, the breathtaking scenery of mountain, lake, and river in Latin America make today's tourists gasp as did the first explorers. The Falls of the Iguassú, part of the Plata system, are wider and higher than Niagara; the *barrancas* of Mexico are almost as amazing as the Grand Canyon; Lake Atitlán in Guatemala is bluer than Crater Lake; a newly discovered cataract in the Guiana Highlands dims the wonders of Yosemite Valley. Spanish chronicles and letters are full of descriptions of the many such wonders Europeans saw for the first time in the New World.

TEMPERATURE, RAINFALL, AND SETTLEMENT

Climate has surely been an important influence on humanity and history in Latin America. It is impossible to do more than make a few generalities about climate conditions; a mere glance at the map does not tell the story. Spanish and Portuguese America stretches from 35 degrees north latitude to a few degrees from the Antarctic Circle, through temperate, torrid, and again temperate zones into the edge of the frigid zone, but there are greater variations in climate than that. The Tropic of Cancer crosses Mexico near Mazatlán a few hundred miles south of the United States border; the Tropic of Capricorn runs near Rio de Janeiro on the east, near the Bolivian-Peruvian border on the west. The areas north of Mazatlán have a cool season in December and January; south of Rio and Asunción Christmas comes in the summer, and June and July bring cold and rain to Buenos Aires and Santiago. Still, the areas within these zones vary in climate because of the presence of vast mountains and many different elevations. Winds, fog, rains, and ocean currents also enter the picture.

Thus there are many exceptions to any statements that can be made about climate in Latin America. A mere glance at a relief map does not reveal the climatic differences between Quito and Guayaquil, Mexico City and Vera Cruz, Lima and Baía. In Mexico and in the Andes nations the temperature is based not on north and south but on elevation. Mexicans refer to the coastal lowlands of Vera Cruz, Tabasco, and Yucatan as *Tierra Caliente,* the hot, humid lands, the home of the mosquito as well as of the banana. The *Tierra Templada,* or temperate country, lies at 2,000 to 8,000 feet above sea level. It is a land of perpetual spring, exemplified by Mexico City at 7,800 feet, with its year-round pleasant days but chilly nights. *Tierra Fría* lies above 8,000 feet where nights are cold and one wears a coat every evening, and where there can even be severe frost to hurt the crops. Thus in crossing from east to west, from Vera Cruz to Acapulco, one goes from hot to temperate to cold to temperate and back to hot, all on the same parallel of latitude. The plateaus north of Mexico City are *templada,* in varying degrees, depending on their altitude, while on the low west coast north of Acapulco, one finds the *Tierra Caliente* as far north as the Tropic of Cancer at Mazatlán and beyond. South of Mexico City the land slopes down to *Tierra Caliente* again at Tehuantepec, then up suddenly to the cool *Tierra Templada* in the highlands of Chiapas and Guatemala. Rainfall also varies; there is heavy precipitation on the Atlantic coastal plain, especially in the south, and hardly any rain at all in the barren west and northwest Pacific coastal area.

Central America presents the same spectacle of varying climate, for it is hot and humid on the Atlantic coastal plain, but cool, healthy, and in spots delightful in the highland areas near the Pacific where most of the city population lives. There is a difference in rainfall from fifty inches a year on the west coast to more than 200 in some points on the Caribbean side. In general the rainy season is in summer, May to October, but the winter seasons are by no means dry. The Caribbean climate is that of the torrid zone, though the altitude and insular position on each island temper the heat. For example, Puerto Rico's climate, dry on one side, moist on the other, is conditioned by the trade winds, the same breezes that blew Columbus to the islands in the first place. On each island, rainfall varies greatly from coast to coast, but it is always humidly warm.

In South America great variations take place, again explained by altitude, by winds, and by ocean currents. About two-thirds of South America is in the torrid zone, and the remainder in the south temperate zone. In general the lowlands of the Amazon are damp and hot, while the places of great altitude are cool and salubrious even at the equator. In the Andean regions of the torrid zone the majority of the population lives at an altitude of from six to twelve thousand feet. On the plain of the west coast the heat is not as excessive, owing to the cooling effects of the Humboldt Current, a cold ocean current that sweeps northward from the Antarctic, as the earth turns, along the coast of Chile and Peru. It is, however, turned away from South America by the shoulder south of the Guayas and runs northwest across the Pacific to become the Japanese Black Current in Asiatic waters. Coming from the frigid zone into the tropics, the air above this current holds little moisture, and cannot release it in the form of rain as would a warm current; it brings chilliness and fog to the coast of Peru, but hardly ever rain. The high Andes reach close to the shore and have already combed out the moisture from the trade winds blowing across the Amazon Valley, and have collected it on their peaks in the form of snow. None of this moisture reaches the west coast below the Guayas, except as it flows down in the form of melted snow in swift rivers through the desert coast. Thus the Andes on the west side in Peru, Bolivia, and northern Chile get no moisture and the coast is a rainless desert. The Inca capital was in an irrigated valley 11,000 feet in altitude and 200 miles inland from the coast. These Indians developed irrigation because although the Central Highlands in Peru are well watered from the melted snow, the streams that rise there find their way eventually into tributaries of the Amazon which flow in the *Montaña* area of Peru, Ecuador, and Bolivia, where there is heavy rainfall anyway.

North of the bulge at Guayaquil the coast of Ecuador and Colombia lies in one of the rainiest areas of the world. The steaming west coast part of Colombia has 200 inches of rainfall a year. To the south of Chile's northern coastal desert the Central Valley of Chile—the California of the Southern Hemisphere—needs irrigation on both sides of Santiago. Rain falls more heavily to the south, and the wooded hills beyond the Bío Bío are one vast area of lakes, rains, and chill fogs.

Southern Argentina, where the pampas begins along the Andean Piedmont, sees little rain, but from there to the Atlantic Coast rainfall increases to keep the pastures green. In Brazil the precipitation is heaviest in the Amazon Valley and fairly heavy along the coast from March to August. Here the trade winds also blow and help take the discomfort out of the heat. They come across the Atlantic from northeast and southeast toward the equator, bearing heavy loads of moisture, most of which has been dropped in the form of rain by the time they reach the *cordillera*. Hence, the tropical interior of South America on the whole gets excessive rain, a geographic factor that has made colonization difficult.

Rain, its excess or its lack, has been one of the most significant factors in Latin American history, determining as it does the character and distribution of the lakes and rivers, and making the ultimate decision as to location of settlements and methods of agriculture. Moisture also influenced the type of game settlers would catch, fruits they would pick, and their own state of health, good or bad. Most tropical climates bring the constant menace of insect pests and diseases which we have only recently learned to combat. Dysentery, hookworm, and bubonic plague are carried by bacteria, parasites, and fleas in the tropics. Malaria, to which natives and Negro slaves were more apt to be immune, slowed down the white European everywhere he tried to live in the tropics. So he built his most successful cities at higher altitudes—Mexico City, São Paulo, Bogotá, Puebla, Arequipa—or on drier irrigated plains such as the coast of Lima. Only the ports in the tropics flourished—ports which had to be placed there as steppingstones to something else. Mankind wants water for his civilization but not too much and not too often. Thus from this whole pattern of moisture versus dryness, a history of settlement, of successful agriculture, of the growth of cities, could be written.

THE WILD LIFE OF THE NEW WORLD

The Iberians were to see many strange animals: tapirs, iguanas, bison, jaguars, turkeys, emus, capybaras, guanacos. They noted immediately the lack of horses, cows, mules, sheep, goats, or donkeys. "So innumerable are the animals that they could not be counted," wrote an early explorer, "but all are savage, and of none of them do the natives make use for their service." When Pizarro came to Peru, he found the llama domesticated as a beast of burden, the alpaca and the vicuña raised as a source of wool; all of these animals were to be pressed into service for the Spaniards. Other New World animals were of less use to him, though deer, bison, and rabbits were often to serve him as meat, and beavers were to inspire a Spanish fur trade up into the Mississippi country in rivalry to the French. The fish of the New World—over two thousand varieties in the Amazon area alone—provided the colonist with a source of food, and led to a thriving industry into modern times, as did the pearl-bearing oysters which first brought the Spaniards to the islands off Venezuela and the Bay of La Paz in Lower California.

Tropical and subtropical fruits and many vegetables were usable for the Europeans in the New World. The Europeans were to learn to eat Indian corn, or maize, to use the beans, the squash, the tomatoes, the chiles, and the yams the Indians cultivated. The New World gave them cacao for chocolate, tobacco for smoking, quinine to cure malaria. Cortés wrote his king about a game played with a ball, which "when thrown to the ground rebounded to the player." The ball was made of rubber, one of Latin America's greatest gifts to Europe. Mexico alone produced eighty-seven kinds of fruits, fifty-two species of vegetables and cereals, 113 types of medicinal herbs and plants. South America provided the white potato, basic food of the Inca Indians, and soon to spread from Spain to Ireland and Germany to become a staple of Europe's peasantry.

Other plants produced fibers, the agave and henequén of Mexico. For building materials there were fifty-six species of lumber-producing woods, and twenty-one kinds of cabinet woods, including the mahogany of Central America and the Amazon. Quebracho trees of the upper Paraná were to produce a chemical valuable for the tanning of leather, and become one of the principal exports of Paraguay. In the soil lay mineral wealth—gold, silver, iron, tin, copper, nitrates, and finally oil. For the earliest civilized inhabitants there was stone for building materials and clay for pottery.

So the explorers and settlers were to know the islands and the Spanish Main, the Isthmus, and the *cordillera* of Mexico, with its *Tierra Caliente* at the foot and its *Tierra Templada* in the center. They were to meet and conquer the Andes, over Indian trails, or through new passes they themselves worked out. Deserts in Chile and Peru, in Sonora and Arizona and Baja California, were to be crossed by them. The Colorado and the Yaqui, the San Juan and the Chagres, the Orinoco and the Magdalena and the Bío Bío would be used for floating ships or for watering men or beasts or crops. The Amazon and the Plata drainage systems were to provide access to new regions and to become the sources of boundary disputes through centuries to come.

The settlements themselves were completely bound by geography. Where climate was temperate and soil fertile, native peoples had learned agriculture, had developed irrigation systems where they were needed, had built villages and then cities. Where mineral deposits were close to such peoples, they had begun to work them. To such areas, rich in agriculture, in mineral wealth, in labor supply, Europeans came in large numbers. Where high ranges separated these areas, even the European communities remained isolated. Where rivers helped them in and out, they kept in touch with one another. Where good harbors combined with river systems and easy passes through the mountains, they kept in touch with the world. Tropical diseases and heat drove them into the highlands; cold and barren ridges kept them in the temperate valleys. Sufficient rainfall brought them independence as to food supply and gave them products to export; excess rainfall flooded them out and made city-building impossible. Thus some areas were settled and some neglected; in some places one crop was raised and in some another; in some places natives were exploited to do the labor, in some Negro slaves were imported, and in some farmers from Spain did the work themselves—all depending on the geographic conditions. The New World offered a wide variety of such conditions.

Concerning most of this New World, later comers would agree with Amerigo Vespucci: "The land is full of immense rivers. The soil is very pleasant and fruitful; there are immense woods and forests, and it is always green, for the foliage never drops off. The fruits are so many that they are numberless."

The fruits were indeed to be many—from the pleasant soil, the immense woods, the riches under the earth, the toil of the settlers and of the natives. Truly had Columbus written to Ferdinand and Isabella that "great will be the benefit derived hence. It is certain, Lord Princes, that where there are such lands there should be profitable things without number."

Readings

Bain, H. F., and T. T. Read, *Ores and Industry in South America* (1934)

Bates, M., *Where Winter Never Comes: A Study of Man and Nature in the Tropics* (1952)

Bowman, I., *The Andes of Southern Peru* (1916)

———, *Desert Trails of Atacama* (1924)

Butland, G. J., *Latin America: A Regional Geography* (1960)

Carlson, F. A., *Geography of Latin America* (3rd ed., 1952)

Hargreaves, D. and B., *Tropical Trees in the Caribbean, South America, Central America and Mexico* (1965)

James, P. E., *Latin America* (rev. ed., 1959)

Jones, C. F., *South America* (1930)

Monge, C., *Acclimatization in the Andes*, trans. D. F. Brown (1948)

Platt, R. S., *Latin America: Countrysides and United Regions* (1942)

Price, A. G., *White Settlers in the Tropics* (1939)

Reid, W. A., *Ports and Harbors of South America* (1934)

Rich, J. L., *The Face of South America: An Aerial Traverse* (1942)

Russell, R. J., and F. B. Kniffin, *Cultural Worlds* (1951)

Shanahan, E. W., *South America: An Economic and Regional Geography with an Historical Chapter* (11th ed., 1963)

Smith, J. R., *North America* (1925)

Suman, A. L., *Geography of Middle America* (1937)

Verrill, A. H., *Foods America Gave the World* (1938)

Whitbeck, R. H., *et al., Economic Geography of South America* (3rd ed., 1940)

Wilgus, A. C., ed., *Colonial Hispanic America* (1936)

———, *Latin America in Maps* (1943)

Chapter 4

Pre-Columbian Americans
North of Panama

THE ORIGIN OF ABORIGINAL LIFE
IN THE NEW WORLD

On October 13, 1492, Columbus wrote that "at daybreak there came to the beach many of these men, all young men as I have said, and all of good stature, very handsome people." Their black hair "is not kinky but loose and coarse like horsehair." On each the "whole forehead and head is very broad, more so than any other race that I have seen, and the eyes very handsome and not small." These people were "of the tanned color of the Canary Islanders, neither black nor white." As for their figures, "their legs are very straight, all in a line; and no belly, but very well built." Columbus assumed these people were East Indians, and they looked about as he expected Hindus or Malayans to look. So he called them Indians.

Everywhere the Iberians were to go they found people of the same general appearance—copper-hued, with straight black hair—though the numbers, varieties, and differing degrees of culture among them proved constant sources of wonder. They had in common only physical appearance, the cultivation of cotton, maize, beans or mandioca, and the use of stone weapons. It seemed that the awe-inspiring geographical variety of the New World was matched by an equally variegated population.

The origin of these peoples is still a matter of controversy among anthropologists. Some say that the New World natives came to this hemisphere in remote prehistoric times over a land bridge from some common home of humanity in Central Asia. Others claim that migrations of partially civilized peoples from Siberia across the Bering Straits brought all the ancestors of the Indians here within the last 10,000 years. If the Siberian "visitors" came as nomadic hunters, unable to spin, weave, or make pottery, and unaccustomed to agriculture and village life, they certainly needed more than 5,000 years to learn to do all these things after arriving in the Western Hemisphere. In the last two decades paleontologists have found American Indian skeletons in geologic strata laid down in the Mississippi area by the first melting of Ice Age glaciers during the Pleistocene period. This would imply human existence in North America before 30,000 B.C. Arrow points, spearheads, and other human remains have been discovered imbedded in the bones of prehistoric bison, and human campfires have been found in caverns under layers of excrement left by long-extinct giant sloths.

If the Indians were all originally immigrants to the New World, perhaps the migration began at a time when the Bering area was solid land with a warmer climate than it has today. The growth of the polar ice cap may have driven the migrants from Asia southward after an era of warm climate, leaving only one group, the Eskimos, to adapt themselves to the increasing cold. The others roamed, ahead of the cold, along the coast of British Columbia, into the Mississippi Valley, finally to the Isthmus and into South America, some of them as far as Tierra del Fuego. Undoubtedly such a migration would have embraced thousands of years, and perhaps have represented many fairly distinct Asiatic origins. The wide variety of languages spoken by the Indians was quickly noted by the explorers and was to prove a problem to missionaries and governors.

Granted that the first Asiatics coming to this hemisphere knew nothing of agriculture, when and where was the planting of crops developed in the New World? Many migrant hunters, such as the Siboney of Cuba and the wandering tribes of northern Mexico and California, ate wild seeds and fruits when game was scarce; but it is a long historic step between this practice and the systematic planting of seeds to reap harvests months later. The basic seed plant which Spaniards found in most parts of the hemisphere was maize. How did the first Indian grower of corn happen to plant it? No one knows, but there is thorough agreement that the development of corn was one of the greatest of man's achievements.

"Corn-on-the-cob" grew nowhere in the Old World and was entirely unknown to Europe when the explorers found it in America. Barley, wheat, and rice were developed in the Old World from wild grains which still grow there, but there is nothing resembling a wild corn in the Western Hemisphere, no plant that grows large grains on a cob. The only native plant of the same botanical type as corn is a grass of the Mexican and Guatemalan plateaus, called *teozintle*. This plant does not produce a tempting food grain. It would require highly intelligent agriculturalists to take the tiny seeds from the *teozintle* cob, pick the largest ones, watch their growth, and in turn plant the best seeds from the new cobs. Some botanists claim that a type of "pod corn" which once grew in South America was the now-extinct ancestor of corn. In any case, from some plant a cob of corn was developed, but this took many, many years of careful planting and seed saving. By 1492 the Indians had developed a food grain more highly specialized than any wheat or rice known in the Old World.

Many of the descendants of the migrants from Asia had learned to settle in one place and to give up their nomadic hunters' life, to plant crops, and to group their huts and families into villages. From the maize they learned to make *tortillas* and mush; they roasted the whole ear; they fried, chilled, and stored it; they made intoxicating drinks by fermenting it. Other staple food plants brought into production were the white potato in Peru, the batata or sweet potato, the manioc root or mandioca in Brazil and the Caribbean, the yam, the peanut, tomato, and pumpkin, and several varieties of squash, lima beans, kidney beans, and peppers. For fruit the Indians had pineapples, persimmons, guavas, and strawberries. They found use for rubber, copal, Peruvian balsam, chicle, quinine, yerba maté, cascara, and indigo. The making of paper from the bark of the wild fig tree was perfected in Central America and Mexico long before the Spaniards came. Strangely enough the only domesticated animals were the dog, the llama, the alpaca, vicuña, guinea pig, and turkey. Sisal, cotton, and other fibrous plants were grown and used to make rope and clothes.

With all these products came increased skill in making utensils and in developing crafts which used clay and stone, gold and silver. Where agriculture was intensive and food supply constant, people had the leisure to work at these arts, to make figurines and small metal objects, to weave elaborate textiles. In the more advanced centers the people lived in substantial towns of stone houses and temples, built with engineering skill. They had time to think and reason also, and developed some knowledge of astronomy, mathematics, medical science, and hieroglyphic writing. In the main areas of such civilization, Guatemala, Mexico and the Andes nations, Indian blood is predominant today, for the Europeans employed the sedentary populations. Indians had learned to exploit the available gold, copper, and silver sources and had many objects made of these metals for the Spaniards to envy. Thus the stores of ready-made wealth exerted a tremendous influence on the direction of the Spanish conquest.

The great centers of the semicivilized peoples developed in the plateaus and mountain country of the Americas. Even the Maya cities on the lowland coast of Honduras and the flat peninsula of Yucatan were built by peoples who probably first became civilized in the mountain valleys of Guatemala and Honduras. Agriculture was not always so easy in these plateaus and valleys. The conflict between Indian groups for fertile lands and means of subsistence led them to develop the most efficient methods of agriculture, sometimes even under irrigation. There were four groups of civilized peoples: the Chibcha of the Isthmus and the Colombian highlands; the Maya of Guatemala, Honduras, and the flat peninsula of Yucatan; the Aztec and their predecessors in the central valley of Mexico; and the Inca and other west-coast people in Peru, Bolivia, and Ecuador. The Pueblos of New Mexico, the Guaraní of Paraguay were also settled agricultural peoples and played an important part in the story of Latin America. All around the periphery of the Spanish colonial empire were wild nomadic tribes

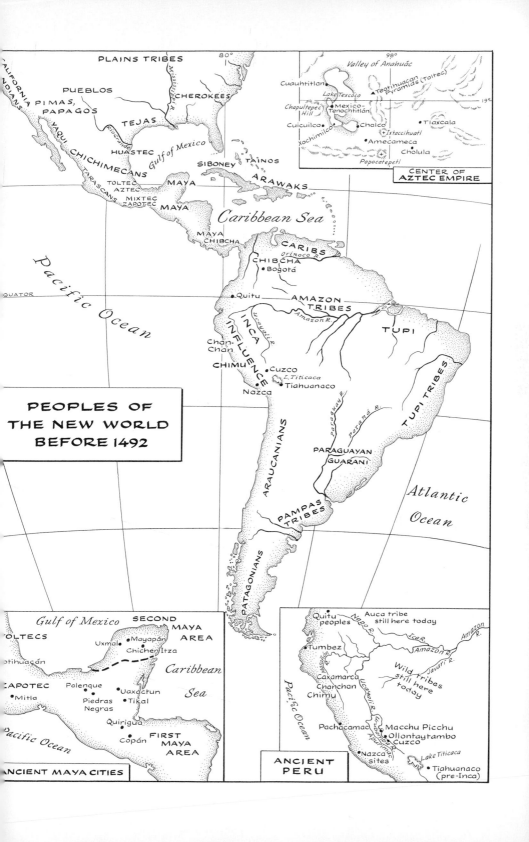

PEOPLES OF
THE NEW WORLD
BEFORE 1492

Main map labels:

CALIFORNIA INDIANS
PLAINS TRIBES
PUEBLOS
PIMAS, PAPAGOS
CHEROKEES
TEJAS
YAQUI
CHICHIMECANS
HUASTEC
Gulf of Mexico
TARASCANS
TOLTEC AZTEC
MIXTEC ZAPOTEC
MAYA
MAYA
SIBONEY
TAINOS
ARAWAKS
Caribbean Sea
MAYA CHIBCHA
CARIBS
CHIBCHA
• Bogotá
Orinoco R.
• Quitu
AMAZON TRIBES
Amazon R.
TUPI
INCA INFLUENCE
Chan-Chan
CHIMUENCE
• Cuzco
L. Titicaca
• Tiahuanaco
Nazca
Ucayali R.
TUPI TRIBES
ARAUCANIANS
Paraguay R.
Paraná R.
PARAGUAYAN GUARANI
PAMPAS TRIBES
PATAGONIANS
Pacific Ocean
Atlantic Ocean
EQUATOR

Inset (top right): CENTER OF AZTEC EMPIRE

Valley of Anahuác
Cuauhtitlan
Lake Texcoco
Teotihuacan Pyramids (Toltec)
Chapultepec Hill
Mexico-Tenochtitlán
Cuicuilco
Chalco
Ixtaccihuatl
Tlaxcala
Xochimilco
Amecameca
Cholula
Popocatepetl
80°
98°
19°

Inset (bottom left): ANCIENT MAYA CITIES

Gulf of Mexico
SECOND MAYA AREA
TOLTECS
Uxmal
• Mayapán
Chichen Itza
Teotihuacán
Caribbean Sea
ZAPOTEC
• Mitla
Palenque
Uaxactun
Piedras Negras
• Tikal
Quirigua
Copán
FIRST MAYA AREA
Pacific Ocean

Inset (bottom right): ANCIENT PERU

Quitu peoples
Auca tribe still here today
Napo R.
Tigre R.
Amazon R.
• Tumbez
Amazon R.
Javari R.
Wild tribes still here today
Caxamarca
Chanchan
Chimu
Ucayali R.
Pachacamac
Macchu Picchu
Ollontaytambo
Cuzco
Apurimac R.
Nazca sites
Lake Titicaca
Tiahuanaco (pre-Inca)
Pacific Ocean

whose people harried the Spaniards for years, but whose blood helped make the modern nations. In considering all these pre-Columbian peoples, let us approach them as did the first Spaniards, by way of the Caribbean.

THE ARAWAKS OF THE CARIBBEAN

The aborigines Columbus first encountered in the outer islands of the Caribbean were Tainos, a group of the general culture called Arawak. Columbus described them as a "gentle peaceful people of great simplicity." They came out to meet him "quite naked as their mothers bore them," but he spoke of their trading him "cotton threads in skeins." They had small spears, or darts, "a kind of rod without iron. . . . I showed them swords and they grasped them by the blade and cut themselves through ignorance; they have no iron." But they had tools of stone to build dugout canoes, "which are fashioned like a longboat from the bole of a tree and all in one piece and wonderfully made, and so big that in some came forty or forty-five men."

On Hispaniola and on Cuba Columbus found more of the related Arawak tribes, village dwellers who had driven hunting tribes away from the coasts. Their villages sometimes had three or four thousand inhabitants, and consisted of a "great house," made of reeds and thatch for the chief, and many "long houses" in which the lesser families lived. They had no "nation," but each village followed its own chief and its own medicine man, and worshiped its own crudely shaped idols in a primitive religion. At such worship Spaniards first saw the use of tobacco in smoking and as snuff.

The Arawaks were clever with their hands. They could carve wood, weave baskets, make pottery decorated in two and three colors, work their small amounts of gold into objects by hammering, and weave wild cotton into hammocks and netted bags. They planted and harvested various crops—corn, cassava, or mandioca roots for bread, yams, beans and peanuts.

The Carib tribes, enemies of the Arawaks, came from scattered islands throughout the Lesser Antilles and from the Venezuelan coast. Attacking the Arawak villages, the Caribs forced these weaker Indians into slavery or fattened them for cannibalistic feasts. Carib culture seems to have been no more advanced than that of the Arawaks; the way of life was generally similar throughout the Caribbean area. The Caribs survived in part among wild tribes in Venezuela, but the gentle Arawaks were eliminated by the diseases and the forced labor of the conquerors. Unprofitable as slaves, the first natives were as disappointing to Spain as was the treasure store of the islands. Disappearing early from the cultural scene, these Indians made no marked contribution to the race and culture of modern Latin America.

MAYA HISTORY AND CULTURE

Columbus was most nearly convinced that he had found China when, on his fourth voyage in 1502, he saw a large canopied canoe close to the coast of Central America. It was rowed by Indian slaves, and under the canopy sat a merchant, richly clad in white cotton embroidered with colors. He was taking his trading goods, bright bales of woven cotton, down the coast from Yucatan to trade in Honduras. It was evident that he represented a people far superior to the naked Arawaks Columbus had so far seen.

The ancestors of this merchant were the ancient Maya. Theirs was the first extensive civilization developed by the natives in Spanish North America, occupying southern Mexico from the Isthmus of Tehuantepec and extending to the northern regions of Nicaragua. Their greatest centers were in Honduras, Guatemala, Chiapas, and the Yucatan peninsula. They have been called the Greeks of the New World, for they passed their civilization on to the Aztecs and other Mexican peoples as the Greeks passed European civilization on to the Romans.

There is a good deal known of Maya history. Students of this culture have divided it into two periods, the Old Maya Era and the New Maya Era. During the Old Era to about A.D. 800, the Maya centers were on the eastern coast of Guatemala and Honduras and their influence spread north and south in Central America. During the New Era, from the ninth century to the period of Maya decline before the coming of the Spaniards, Maya government and culture centered in Yucatan, and Maya culture influenced other cities in Mexico. The story of the rise and decline of these eras can be pieced together.

On the wet Caribbean coast of Guatemala, thousands of years before Columbus, Taino-like naked nomads had settled. It is probable that migrants from the drier plateaus and highland valleys, who had already learned to harvest crops, make pottery, spin and weave with cotton, and build homes of stone, came down into this more luxuriant country and conquered the more primitive people. In these wet lands they were able to grow food for much larger numbers of people, with less labor, and the workers devoted their days to constructing roads and temples. As time went on, a leisure class evolved—a class with opportunity to study the heavens, design temples, and work out a complex religion and a sense of the passing of the years.

Modern authorities on the Maya peoples think the latter began to keep accurate track of time in their first cities on the Caribbean coast of Guatemala and Honduras. Perhaps one man, the god and culture hero, Itzamna, invented the calendar and numbering system. We have no way of knowing what event marked their "year one," nor what date it corresponds to in the Christian calendar. On many Maya monuments, however, can be read the dates in their carved inscriptions, telling the number of years since their "year one." The best approximations indicate that the great cities of Palenque in southern Mexico, Tikal in Guatemala, and Copán in Honduras were flourishing just before the time of Christ and for several hundred years thereafter. In these cities the priests and scholars perfected their knowledge of astronomy, and artists carved human figures in bas-relief on stone. By A.D. 300 the cities of the Guatemalan coastal lands were entering what archeologists call the "Great Period."

With natural expansion, colonists were sent to build cities in Yucatan, the Guatemalan highlands, and the Isthmus of Tehuantepec. At Copán, at

Faces of three Mayan priests carved in life-size relief, Palenque, Mexico. *Photo by Helen Miller Bailey.*

Piedras Negras, at Uaxactún, at Quiriguá, cities of perhaps 100,000 population prospered as centers of religion, government, and trade. Around them thousands of acres cleared for crop cultivation were inhabited by agricultural peasants. In this period all the great cities contained dated temple markers and "cornerstones" showing building activity up to one specific date, which is perhaps about A.D. 700 or 800. Then there are no more date carvings. This culture seemed to disintegrate and building to cease, all within a very short time.

The Maya people did not die out; they went to their more distant provincial cities and towns. From their founding to perhaps A.D. 1100, the cities of Yucatan grew and prospered as the centers of a Second Maya Era. Why did the Maya suddenly move from Guatemala toward Yucatan? Did a great epidemic force them to leave the mosquito-infested lowland? Possibly. Drought may have ruined their agriculture. A plant disease may have destroyed several successive crops. Quite probably the system of burning off and clearing forests just wore out the land, and food could not keep pace with population. Perhaps they even moved for some reason connected with their religion.

After the migration, Chichén-Itzá, formerly a small provincial city, became the center of Maya culture. Yucatan had less rainfall than did the area of the older cities, the forest was less luxuriant, and water was not found in running streams but in deep wells in the porous limestone. Two such natural wells, or pools, each more than eighty feet in diameter, were at the site of Chichén-Itzá, and thus it could support a large population.

The name of the city meant "the mouth of the wells where lives the Itzá tribe." A hundred miles from it grew a sister city named Uxmal, and between them a third, called Mayapán, near the site of the modern city of Mérida. These three cities, with some lesser ones, joined into a loose federation called the League of Mayapán, sometimes likened to the Greek federation of city-states in ancient Europe. Until after A.D. 1100 this league was peaceful enough, bothered occasionally by family squabbles but not molested by outside enemies. The league cities even had organized teams to play a sort of basketball game with each other in great courts adjoining the temples.

About 1100 or 1200, a bearded conqueror named Kukulcán came to this league of cities. He was said to be from the Land of the Feathered Serpent, probably one of the Toltec people of highland Mexico who handed down to the Aztecs a similar legend. Kukulcán brought many Toltec ideas to the Maya. He is said to have beautified Chichén-Itzá with newer and finer temples, but he also introduced religious rituals which called for human sacrifices. An old Spanish report of this story goes on to say that "This Kukulcán lived with the lords in the city (Chichén-Itzá) for several years, and, leaving them in great peace and friendship, he returned by the same way to Mexico." The Maya had heard that "after his return he was regarded in Mexico as one of their gods and called Quetzalcoatl."

At least as early as Kukulcán's time the cities of Yucatan carried on trade with the people of Mexico. They also began to wage war against one another; during the thirteenth century Uxmal fought against Chichén-Itzá and both cities against Mayapán. Other cities joined in. After a decade or so the ablest of the young men were killed off and fighting subsided. With the next generation, brought to manhood and trained to perpetuate the fighting, war began again. Through the fourteenth and fifteenth centuries the Maya men were so often at war that they had little time for building. The last date-carving on any monument so far found in the Mayapán region is the mid-1400s, according to the most accepted modern reading of the calendar. When Spanish conquerors arrived a century later, they found the Maya living in grass-hut villages near the old city sites. Priests lived in the temples of the stone cities and conducted religious ceremonies, but grass was growing through the paving. Many of the Maya writings were found, but few knew how to read them. Records indicate several years of epidemics and destructive hurricanes between wars. Not much doubt as to why the Spaniards found the cities of Yucatan in decadence! One of their chroniclers wrote down, in Spanish, this unhappy little Maya poem:

> Eat, eat while there is bread;
> Drink, drink while there is water.
> A day comes when a blight shall wither the land . . .
> When ruin shall fall upon all things . . .
> When eyes shall be closed in death . . .
> Father, son, and grandson hanging dead on the same tree,
> When ruin shall fall upon all things
> And the people be scattered abroad in the forest.[1]

[1] From *Columbus Came Late* by Gregory Mason. Copyright, 1931, Century Company. Reprinted by permission of the publishers, Appleton-Century-Crofts, Inc.

Thus there were two distinct periods in Maya history: the early epoch during which the southern area was at the height of its glory, and the later Maya Renaissance during which the rich culture flourished in the north. Not much is known of the institutions of the southern or early Maya, for most of our descriptive material is of the northern cities.

Whatever else may be said, the Maya were the great creators of the New World. They developed a calendar which was more exact than the Roman calendar of the time, and they became great astronomers and mathematicians. They discovered the secret of the mathematical zero and established a system of numbering far earlier than the introduction of Arabic symbols into Europe. Their writing consisted of paintings in pictograph with water colors on fiber paper which was bound within covers. In such ideographs priests seem to have kept scientific and historical records as well as civil and ecclesiastical accounts; they computed years, months, days, and the times for festivals and ceremonies. Most of their pictographs were burned by Christian zealots, though a few specimens are still extant. A literature in prose and poetry was passed down through the generations, perhaps orally. Some of their legends were later recorded through Christianized Maya, and at least a few have been translated into English, such as the books of *Chilam Balam* of Yucatan and *Popol Vuh* of Guatemala.

The Maya artistic and intellectual achievements were largely by-products of the religion that was their predominant interest. The art and architecture of their elaborately carved religious buildings excelled the work of all other Indian peoples. Their principal temples, astronomical observatories, homes for chiefs and priests, and their pyramids are as large and often as impressive as similar remains in the Old World. In their more massive structures, the temples and pyramids, they heaped up earth and rubble to make a central core, then faced this with carved stones. Since they did not know how to make a vaulted arch, they never constructed any imposing domed roof. The rooms of their important buildings, when roofed with stone, were very small; larger rooms were roofed with timber, which eventually rotted away. Recent excavations at Tikal in Guatemala have exposed many inner cores, layer on layer, inside the larger temples. The method of construction seems to prove that the temples were rebuilt at the end of a long time cycle, perhaps a two-hundred- or a four-hundred-year period, with the previous structure serving as the foundation, and a larger surface built up around the outside. Dated carvings and life-like bas-reliefs in the earlier period were covered over completely in the new buildings.

Much of Maya carving and stucco decoration is in geometric and elaborate formal designs. In every city there are some carvings of people, birds, and animals—sometimes conventionalized, often very realistic. In the cities of Yucatan the feathered serpent appears often on carvings. The "basketball courts" have carved friezes of the players, dressed in padded uniforms. The same elaborate, realistic picture art is found on Maya pottery. Small objects of gold and silver, worked in fine detail, are also to be found in the ruins of Yucatan, as are copper plates and knives. These may have come through trade from Mexico, for there are no ore deposits in Yucatan. Jade was much used for making small carvings. Seashells

Façade of a section of the House of the Nuns, Chichén-Itzá, Yucatan. *Photo by Helen Miller Bailey.*

from the Caribbean were evidently traded to the north to get turquoise, which was highly prized by the Maya for decorative purposes. The decorated dress of both men and women in the Maya paintings implies great skill in the textile arts.

Religion was dominant in their lives as well as in their art. In the Maya pantheon of gods there were about a dozen major deities and a host of lesser gods, some to secure prosperity and happiness, some to ward off evil. At the head was a creator, god of the sun, who was aided by lesser gods of the sky, of the north star, of thunder and lightning, and of rain. The rain god in particular was very important to Yucatan with its long dry season. There are many carvings of a maize god, who is a handsome young man with a headdress of corn tassels. The Maya firmly believed in immortality and ancestor worship. For all this religious devotion a large clergy was needed with orders of monks and nuns. Priests served in the temples, burned incense at the corners of fields to insure good crops, and presided over religious festivals. There had evidently been little human sacrifice among the Maya prior to the coming of Kukulcán; such sacrifices seem to have been the result of Mexican influence. Prisoners taken in the civil wars after 1100 were sacrificed at Chichén on a large platform decorated with carved skulls.

When the Maya were not taking part in religious ceremonies, they lived much as people live in Yucatan today. Farmers kept their land cleared of weeds, planted corn, beans, squash, and cotton, harvested the crops in big cooperative festivals, tended their fruit trees, and cared for their flower gardens. According to their mural paintings, their round huts with peaked roofs and their corn-grinding stones, or *metates,* are exactly the same as those used by Indian villagers in Yucatan today. The women of present-day villages wear the "Yucateca" costume, a long white gown with a square neck and bands of wide bright embroidery around the neck, sleeve, and skirt. The ancient paintings in the temples show women dressed this way.

The men were somewhat dandified, wearing plugs and ornaments in their lips and nostrils to show the social rank of the individual, and having headdresses of quetzal feathers and embroidered shawls and loincloths of bright cotton.

City dwellers also owned land and went out into the country to till it, or perhaps worked as stone carvers, jewelers, or potters, or as servants and orderlies in the temples. It took thousands of workers to build the temples, to make the roads—high, wide, paved causeways—which led to all the important religious shrines and which can still be seen in many places. It is not known whether these "public works" were done by farmers during slack seasons as a way of paying taxes, by hired laborers, by war captives, or by every adult male as a service to please the gods. On these roads a heavy roller was used, but the next step, the wheel, was never developed, so no carts traveled the roads. If the road workers were paid, they probably received cacao beans, feathers, cotton cloth, or small bells of copper, all of which were used as money in the markets and in inter-regional trade. In the ancient days, as today, men and women brought their rural produce and the results of their handwork into the markets and sold them to city dwellers. In these markets, products from many other parts of Indian America were offered for barter sale. Emeralds came from Colombia and turquoise from North Mexico, indicating that wandering traders on foot and in sea-going canoes covered great distances.

The markets were full of food products because the Maya were the great agriculturists of North America. The principal crop and the mainstay of their diet was corn, eaten in the form of *tortillas* and gruel. Maya farmers also harvested beans, tomatoes, red peppers, and yams, and cared for the great maguey cactus plants from which they made *pulque*.

Family life seems to have been serene enough. Marriages were arranged by the family, with divorce easily achieved by the husbands. Personal cleanliness was practiced by high and low, as it still is in Yucatan. For beautifying purposes, mothers tied their children's heads to boards until the head was conical and misshapen, filed their front teeth, and suspended beads in front of their eyes to make them permanently cross-eyed. How such cross-eyed babies grew up to be ball players is indeed something of a mystery, but a game of ball requiring great skill was one of the important Maya recreations. That this game had also some religious significance may be indicated by the presence of the ball courts in the center of their religious temples.

Very little is known of the government and society of the Mayas. Perhaps the only stable political unit was the individual city with its outlying district. Each of these cities was a theocratic despotism, the rulers being civil princes and high priests. The kings appointed the *caciques* or chieftains of outlying villages and the local magistrates for sections of the larger cities. The chieftains and their councils of elders were supported by locally paid taxes. The cities were organized into loose federations or leagues of city-states; hence the oft-made comparison between Maya and Greek city-states. In the Old Era there seem to have been four such leagues, the Petén area of Guatemala, the cities in the Usumacinta Valley of the Mexican state of Chiapas, the Honduran region with its capital at Copán, and the southwestern highlands. Yucatan had three such leagues, Chichén-Itzá, Uxmal, and Mayapán. These federations had no nationalism, no sturdy patriotism to hold them together, except during a war against another federation.

The people were socially stratified with an hereditary ruling class at the top. Government was distinctly oligarchic, since the families of the nobles provided magistrates, military leaders, and priests. The vast majority of people, such as artisans, serfs, and slaves, did not participate in the government. But below the privileged classes all commoners were equal, whether they tilled the fields, quarried stones, or worked as artisans in the cities. The only difference in social standing seems to have been measured by the distance a family lived from the center of the city. In the chieftains' houses, in the temples, and in the army there were also many slaves, who had been either captured in war, condemned to slavery because of crime, or sold into slavery because of debt. Children of slaves were usually free, so that a large permanent slave class did not develop. The feudal nobility and the hierarchy of priests on top, then the warriors, then the freemen tillers of the soil and the workers, then the slaves at the bottom—so ran the classes among the Maya.

Thus the Maya built twenty-five or more large cities, organized a religious society, developed a high level of handicraft culture, and transmitted their culture and institutions to the central Mexicans. The Spaniards who conquered Yucatan did not realize the full extent of the Maya area at its height, for ancient cities on the coast of Guatemala and Honduras have only been revealed in the last century. In their search for Maya cities and their painstaking efforts to reconstruct them, highly trained archeologists are joined by engineers, artists, anthropologists, and experts on textiles, ceramics, and sculpture. Their work has aroused so much interest that Chichén-Itzá, Uxmal, Palenque, Copán, and Quiriguá have been made accessible to tourists by plane and car, so that the readers of this book can see much more of the Maya empire than could the Spanish conquerors.

THE EMPIRES OF THE TOLTECS AND AZTECS

Cortés, the first Spaniard to see the Anáhuac valley of central Mexico, found there the Aztecs, inheritors of many Maya traditions. They were not the first city-builders there. From the far northwest, centuries before, Toltec peoples had come as waves of nomads who overran Mexico and settled in the valley of Anáhuac. Like the Maya, they built upon a foundation laid by previous archaic agricultural people. Conquering the sedentary peoples, the Toltecs continued to superimpose their culture on other groups that arrived from the north. They drew from the Maya civilization to the south, and became the master builders of Tula, Cholula, and Teotihuacán, where the great pyramids surpass those of Egypt in size. They were also skilled craftsmen, clever astrologers, and notable builders, and they invented a form of writing. Arts and institutions of the Maya adopted by the Toltecs

Head of a feathered serpent—the word *Quetzalcoatl* **means "feathered serpent"—on the steps of a Toltec temple, Teotihuacán Mexico.** *Photo by Helen Miller Bailey*

were transmitted to all central Mexico by means of conquest. By perhaps the eleventh century their warriors were fighting northward as far as the Tropic of Cancer and southward to the Isthmus of Tehuantepec. Their war canoes landed in Yucatan and brought Toltec influences to Chichén-Itzá. Their empire was a military state based on predatory warfare and coercion, but much of the cultural progress of the Toltecs was due to the semilegendary Quetzalcoatl who introduced the best fruits of Maya thought, mathematics, astronomy, and agriculture.

The Aztecs remembered this hero-god and they sang a hymn about him for the Spaniards, telling of his pyramid-building:

> There in grandeur reared his temple,
> Reared aloft its mighty ramparts.
> Reaching upwards toward the heavens;
> Wondrous stout and tall the walls were,
> High the skyward climbing stairway,
> With its steps so long and narrow . . .
> That there scarce was room for stepping.

And of Quetzalcoatl's teaching of his people:

> As master workmen worked they,
> Fashioned they the sacred emeralds,
> Smelted they both gold and silver,
> Other trades and arts they mastered . . .
> And in Quetzalcoatl all these
> Arts and crafts had their beginning;
> He the master workman taught them
> All their trades and artifices.[2]

[2] Quoted by permission from John H. Cornyn, *The Song of Quetzalcoatl*, Antioch College Press, 1930.

Quetzalcoatl may have been an idealized combination of several different leaders. But the Aztecs believed that he traveled away again to visit in Yucatan as Kukulcán, leaving word that he would return by sea. Montezuma was still waiting for the return of Quetzalcoatl, the "Fair God," five hundred years later, and thought at first that Cortés might be he.

The Toltecs, like the later Maya, fought among themselves. Their empire began to crumble about the middle of the thirteenth century when "feudalism" broke the empire into small principalities. Some of the Toltec cities in the valley of Mexico were abandoned, and others were conquered by military invaders from the north. Little is known of their institutions, except that they copied them from the Maya, and undoubtedly passed them on to the Aztecs. They must have had a strong central government with a warrior king, and a workable system of governing a vast empire. The size of their mighty pyramids—undoubtedly bases of temples—implies a deep religious devotion and a strong power of priestly class over working class. They must have been skilled agriculturists to have grown food enough to support cities as large as Teotihuacán and its neighbor Azcapotzalco. We are not even sure in what century Teotihuacán was abandoned, only that it was a complete ghost city during at least the two generations before the Spaniards came to the nearby Aztec cities in 1519.

Meanwhile Chichimecan peoples, wilder tribes from the north, had set up states among the marshy lakes of the valley floor. They gained the upper hand over the declining Toltecs, though at first inferior in culture, and in turn were superseded by another, more primitive migrant people from the north, the Aztecs, who absorbed the Maya-Toltec-Chichimeca culture. In the early years of the fourteenth century a group of nomadic tribesmen had wandered from the north into the Valley of Anáhuac, looking for a sign, so their priests told them—an eagle with a snake in its mouth perched on a cactus, the symbol which is today the national emblem of Mexico. These wanderers, led by their chief, Tenoch, found their augury, so the story goes, on the shores of marshy Lake Texcoco, and here they decided to establish their home. At this time of "founding" their city of Tenoch-titlán, traditionally in the year A.D. 1325, they were actually building mud and reed huts on islands in the shallow water. But in the next two hundred years they learned much from their more advanced neighbors, and finally they became the dominant politico-military power of the valley and even beyond. They enlarged the original islands, filled in land to make others, and connected their dwellings to the mainland with four giant causeways and numerous bridges.

Since the Aztecs were at the height of their military power and general culture when the Spanish invasion occurred, we have good descriptions of this city as the Europeans saw it. To them Tenochtitlán seemed fair and shining, with its buildings of white stucco and brightly colored ornamentation. There were wide streets and open paved plazas which served as market squares and as centers for religious pageantry. Around the inhabited islands smaller islands were built for flower and vegetable gardens. Some of these were originally "rafts" on which flowers were grown in a layer of mud; as the roots grew, these "floating gardens" became anchored. The floating

The plaza of Mexico Tenochtitlán, capital of the Aztec empire, as it might have looked when the Europeans first saw it. *Courtesy American Museum of Natural History.*

gardens of Aztec days are now the flower-raising group of islands and canals called Xochimilco.

From these islands and from the mainland shore, boatloads of produce, borne to the edge by long lines of carriers from the surrounding country-side, came across to the city markets. As in modern Mexican markets, one section on the city plaza was exclusively for vegetables and another one for the charcoal that is still used as cooking fuel in many Mexican homes. Cloth and clothing were sold in one section, sleeeping mats and basket work in another. Implements made of copper, knives of obsidian, stone-drilling tools, spinning whorls made of clay or deer horn were for sale in the "tools" section. Fresh fish from the Gulf could be bought, carried by runner in twenty-four hours from the coast, to grace the table of Montezuma and the nobles. The sale of bird feathers was profitable, for the highest ranking warriors and priests clothed themselves almost entirely in feather-embroidery. Jewelers offered objects made of jade, pink seashells, tortoise shells, and turquoise, as well as ornamental figurines cast from gold, copper, and silver. Trade was either by direct barter or with cacao beans as money, for chocolate was a favorite Aztec drink and the cacao tree did not grow in the central plateau. Medicine women had trays of herbs to sell, and barbers set up stands to shave men, using razors of volcanic glass. Women were in their element in the Aztec market life; Cortés' chronicler commented on their luxuriant raven tresses and on their faces which "although of a cinnamon hue were not unfrequently pleasing."

Because so much was written describing the Aztecs, one is apt to gain the impression that their culture was the most important attainment of Indian America. In reality, they were inheritors rather than originators and added little to what the Toltecs and the Maya had already achieved. The Aztecs themselves had kept an account of their rulers in a kind of picture record which some of the Spaniards learned to decipher. They could count back the years, coordinating their calendar to that of the Spaniards, and they set down the year 1376 as the date of accession of their first chieftain in Tenochtitlán. By the 1480s the Aztecs had begun to expand, joining with their neighbors in the city states of Texcoco and Tlacopán in a three-way confederacy in which each unit kept its own government but followed the Aztec emperor as a military leader in wartime. Soon the Aztec Confederacy, developing an intensively military phychology and aggressive warfare, extended its conquest from Tehuantepec to Mazatlán, from the Pacific to the Gulf. The civilized and highly artistic Tarascan Indians to the west in Michoacán, the Mixtecs and the Zapotecs of earlier advanced civilizations in Oaxaca were all forced to pay tribute. Here and there remained a few "independent" groups, such as the Tlaxcalans halfway down toward the Gulf, who were willing to help Cortés fight the hated Aztec Confederacy.

This Aztec Confederacy was, strictly speaking, not an empire, though its vassals paid the Aztec ruler heavy taxes. In fact, there were many revolts within the empire, and although they were suppressed, the conquered parts were independent enough to govern themselves locally without any garrisons stationed among them. Officials were merely sent to supervise the collection of tribute and perhaps to look out for signs of rebellion.

At the center was the city-state of Tenochtitlán, governed not so much by the emperor or war chief as by a council of elders representing the twenty clans in the various wards or neighborhoods of the city. Each clan in turn had its own council of elders. The over-all city council elected two chief officials, the *tlachautin*, who led the warriors in war and were responsible for the maintenance of order, and the *calpullec*, or principal civil officer who collected taxes, distributed land, and kept records. Montezuma II, the much-touted emperor, was at first simply the war chief whose family had been elected to this position for two generations. He was also a priest, and his power had some theocratic overtones; furthermore, Montezuma served as the highest court of appeal, above the neighborhood courts, and the punishments he meted out for crimes were extremely severe. The government seems to have been in a state of evolution at the time of the arrival of the Spaniards, for it was changing from a kinship-territorial form ruled by the council of elders to a one-man despotism.

As the Aztecs changed from a nomadic people to the rulers of a vast federation, they developed strict social classes. The great feudal lords and the high army officials soon formed the nobility. The priests were especially privileged; being in charge of education and religion, they held the future in the palms of their hands. The free citizens formed an element in society but all were organized in clans and tribes. At the close of the Aztec regime they were losing their freedom, being deprived of political privileges, and reduced to serfdom. Slaves—no one was ever *born* into slavery—consisted chiefly of prisoners of war, criminals, and others who sold themselves or were sold by their parents. It was not a harsh type of slavery, though every village had its slave market. The merchants were an important element in society, especially the leading tradesmen who were respected and influential. The rank and file of the nation were the free peasants and artisans. The most important occupation was that of warrior, for war was of greater worth than agriculture. Fanatical wars were carried on for spoils, for tribute, and for prisoners to be sold as slaves or used as sacrifices. The armies were well organized and well disciplined, and the military education of youth was stressed. Education of all youth was seriously attended to, the priests serving as teachers of music, arithmetic, reading of the hieroglyphic writing, and religion.

Family life was elaborately regulated. A child was given a name and a feast held in its honor within a few days of its birth; it is easy to see how Mexican people took so easily to the Catholic idea of baptism and still today hold such large parties in honor of a newly baptized child. Children were usually treated well and given serious advice on manners, some of which has come down to us in writing. At fifteen, boys took military or religious training in an organized "house of youth." Marriages were arranged by the parents with the young people's consent, for boys at twenty, for girls at sixteen. Descriptions of the three-day marriage feasts, at which much *pulque* and *tequila* flowed, at which endless speeches were made and many gifts exchanged, sound very familiar to anyone who has been a guest at a wedding in a Mexican rural community today.

From the tribal council the clans received the lands used for agriculture, divided them into lots, and distributed the lots among the heads of families. Thus the clans, not the individuals, actually owned the land. At the death of a land holder the tenancy passed to his son; if no son survived, or if the land had not been cultivated for two seasons, it reverted to the clan for redistribution. Large areas of land were reserved for the maintenance of religious and government officials and for the financing of wars. These public lands were evidently worked by slave labor or by "contributed time" on the part of nearby tenants. The pressure on land use was great; the Aztecs reclaimed much land in their swampy areas and were constantly adding new corn lands by conquest. The arrangements made by the Aztecs concerning irrigation systems and water rights worked so well that kings of Spain later ordered that they remain unchanged in rural areas.

More extensively than the Maya or Toltecs, the Aztecs engaged in long-distance commerce. Trade and commerce were highly respected occupations and received government protection. Away from the great market centers each village had its special product—mats or baskets or pottery—as do Mexican villages today. It seems hard to imagine a wandering Mexican peddler without the mules which the Spanish taught him to use, but Aztec travelers covered the length and breadth of Mexico and Middle America on foot, their packs on their backs. Parrot feathers from the tropics have been found in Indian ruins of the southwest United States, and much New Mexico and Arizona turquoise was used by the Aztecs. Aztec cotton cloth could be found in Panama. No one trader covered this distance; objects passed through many hands from tribe to tribe, but the contacts were made from the great center of Tenochtitlán.

For trade, for agriculture, and for religion, the Aztecs kept track of time. Their carefully divided solar years ran in cycles of fifty-two, but these half-century cycles were not themselves numbered or named in any order. Every 104 years, or at the end of two cycles, a great celebration was held. The Aztecs themselves had no record of two such 104-year celebrations, so their history becomes legendary a century into the past before Cortés' arrival. The Aztec calendar stone, kept in Mexico City's National Museum, has carvings to represent days, twenty-day months, and seasons.

The Spaniards considered the religion of the Aztecs the work of the Devil, and it is easy to see why. Many of the explorers and would-be conquerors were to be sacrificed to the pagan deities of Mexico. In the center of Tenochtitlán was a giant pyramid similar to that in Toltec and Maya cities. The priests, trained in ritual since childhood, led war captives and slaves up the narrow steps to the top on every public feast day, held them over an elaborately carved altar, and tore out their hearts with a sharp obsidian knife. Thousands of captives died this way every year. Wars were fought simply to capture more prisoners for sacrifice. On special occasions members of distinguished families were chosen for sacrifice, which may have been something of an honor; the victim was pampered by the populace for weeks beforehand. The pageantry, processions, and incense-burning which accompanied the sacrifices, especially those to their supreme deity and god of war, Huitzilopochtli, made religion very dramatic to the people as they watched the ceremonies. It was a brutal religion. The clergy were numerous, for the temple at Tenochtitlán had over 5,000 priests, each with his specialty of saying prayers and chants, leading processions and dances, keeping track of the calendar, educating the young, or preparing sacrifices. The people believed the human sacrifices appeased the gods and, in the same spirit, they fasted and went to confession. Like the Maya, they believed in life after death, with various purgatories on the way to paradise.

There seem to have been some more advanced abstract concepts in the Aztec religion, and many poems and songs were sung on the puzzle of life itself. The most famous poet was a king of Texcoco called Nezahualcoyotl, whose name means "hungry coyote."

"The goods of this life," he sang, "its glories and its riches, are but lent to us, its substance is but an illusory shadow, and the things of today shall change on the coming of the morrow. Then gather the fairest flowers from thy gardens to bind round thy brow, and seize the joys of the present ere they perish." In another song handed down by memory through the generations, Nezahualcoyotl said of the present, "The fleeting pomp of the world is like a green willow, . . . but at the end a sharp axe destroys it, a north wind fells it." [3]

The north wind that felled the Aztec culture was the Spanish army led by Cortés. Tenochtitlán was destroyed and Mexico City built on the lake site. But the imprint of the Aztecs remained strong in colonial Mexico. Art craft, home life, food, house construction, and marketing methods were still pure Aztec in the rural villages and among the poor of the new

[3] Frances Gillmor, *Flute of the Smoking Mirror, a Portrait of Nezahualcoyotl* (Albuquerque: University of New Mexico Press, 1949).

Mosaic designs made by thousands of small stones. Zapotec ruin at Mitla, Oaxaca, Mexico. *Photo by Helen Miller Bailey.*

Spanish cities. People continued to eat *tortillas* and beans as the main staples of diet, to use the *agave* or maguey plant for liquor and for fiber. The Aztec language, Nahuatl, was spoken commonly in Mexico as late as 1750. The mixed-blood descendants of the Maya and the Aztecs form the great majority of the population of modern Mexico.

Exploring and conquering through the passes south of Mexico City and into the Valley of Oaxaca, Spaniards found the remains of the Zapotecan empire. Two hundred fifty thousand Indians in southern Mexico were still speaking the Zapotec language in the middle of the twentieth century. Halfway between the Maya and the Toltecs, on what is still today a through trade route, Zapotecs built up a city civilization long before the Aztecs settled on Lake Texcoco. Their neighbors the Mixtecs, who seem to have been related to the Toltecs, built a "religious civic center" of pyramids and platforms, called today Monte Albán. Excavated in 1927, tombs there produced the greatest quantities of the finest gold work, both beaten and cast, ever found in the Western Hemisphere. Across the Valley of Oaxaca is the ruin of the Zapotec city of Mitla, elaborately decorated with an unusual geometric mosaic.

Southeast of the Aztec empire lived an early people called the Olmecs. Recent discoveries at a site called La Venta show them to have been a very early people, perhaps pre-Maya, who carved enormous, child-like heads, in the round, without bodies. Much is yet to be learned about all these people.

North of the Aztec empire were many seminomadic tribes who lived on the edges of the desert country of northern Mexico. Many of them are often lumped together under such names as the Chichimecs, who put up fierce resistance to the Spaniards; the Huastecas, who lived on the Gulf Coast; and the Tarahumaras, who roamed the northern ranges of the central plateau. Of all the peoples within the area of modern Mexico, the Yaqui fought the Spanish domination the longest, and remained unconquered into the first years of the twentieth century. North of the Yaqui were the Indians of Sonora, related to the Pima, the Papago, and the Yuma of Arizona, among whom Spanish Jesuit missions were founded late in the colonial period. Beyond them were the very primitive Indians of California, who lived on acorns and wore clothing made of animal skins, and who were brought into missions by the Spanish Franciscans as a last frontier effort of Spain in America. Spaniards also contacted the uncivilized Tejas Indians north of the Rio Grande. East of that area and across the Mississippi lived the Creeks, Cherokees, and Appalachian tribes. The nomads who hunted buffalo on the Great Plains—the Sioux, the Comanches, the Kiowa—though never conquered by Spanish soldiers, adopted abandoned Spanish horses and became the fast mounted terrorizers of wagon trains in a later century. The Pueblo of today's New Mexico, an advanced, sedentary people with a maize basis of civilization, became wards of Spain in the early seventeenth century.

Readings

Anderson, A. J. O. and C. Dibble, eds. and trans., *Florentine Codex* (Sahagun's, *General History of Things of New Spain* (12 vols., 1950 to date)

Astrov, M., *The Winged Serpent; An Anthology of American Indian Prose and Poetry* (1946)

Bandelier, A. F., and E. L. Hewitt, *Indians of the Rio Grande Valley* (1937)

Blom, F., *The Indian Background of the Conquest of Yucatan* (1936)

——, et al., *Studies in Middle America* (1934)

Borah, W., and S. Cook, *The Aboriginal Population of Central Mexico on the Eve of the Spanish Conquest* (1963)

——, *Indian Population of Central Mexico, 1531–1610* (1960)

Caso, A., *The Aztecs, People of the Sun* (1958)

Chevalier, F., *Land and Society in Colonial Mexico* (1963)

Clark, J. C., ed., *Codex Mendoza* (3 vols., 1938)

Cook, S. and W. Borah, *Population of Central Mexico, 1548* (1960)

Cornyn, J. H., *The Song of Quetzalcoatl* (1930)

Covarrubias, M., *The Eagle, the Jaguar and the Serpent: Indian Art of the Americas* (1954)

Díaz del Castillo, B., *True History of the Conquest of New Spain* (many editions)

Dockstader, F. J., *Indian Art in Middle America* (1964)

Driver, H. E., *The Americas on the Eve of Discovery* (1964)

——, *Indians of North America* (1961)

Duran, D., *The Aztecs: History of the Indians of New Spain* (1964)

Effler, L. R., *The Ruins of Chichén-Itzá* (1936)

Embree, E. R., *Indians of the Americas* (1939)

Emmerich, A., *Art Before Columbus* (1963)

Gann, T., and J. C. Thompson, *History of the Mayas* (1931)

Gann, T. W. F., *Glories of the Maya* (1939)

——, *Maya Cities* (1927)

Gates, W., *A Grammar of Maya* (1938)

Gibson, C., *Aztecs under Spanish Rule* (1964)

Gillmor, F., *The King Danced in the Market Place* (1964)

Goetz, D., S. G. Morley, and A. Ricinas, *Popol Vuh: The Sacred Book of the Ancient Quiche-Maya* (1950)

Griffin, C. C., ed., *Concerning Latin American Culture* (1941)

Hanke, L., *Aristotle and the American Indian* (1959)

Harrington, M. R., *Cuba Before Columbus* (2 vols., 1921)

Hewitt, E. L., *Ancient Life in the American Southwest* (1930)

———, *Ancient Life in Mexico and Central America* (1936)

Jenness, D., ed., *American Aborigines* (1933)

Jennings, J. D., and E. Norbeck, eds., *Prehistoric Man in the New World* (1963)

Joyce, T. A., *Central American and West Indian Archaeology* (1916)

———, *Maya and Mexican Art* (1927)

———, *Mexican Archaeology* (1914)

Keleman, P'al, *Medieval Ancient Art* (one vol. ed., 1956)

Kidder, A., and C. S. Chinchilla, eds., *Art of the Ancient Mayas* (rev. ed., 1959)

Kingsborough, V., *Antiquities of Mexico* (9 vols., 1830–1848)

Koebel, W. H., *Central America* (1917)

Kubler, G., *The Art and Architecture of Ancient America* (1962)

Landa, Diego de, *Yucatan Before and After the Conquest*, ed. Gates (1937); edition by A. M. Tozzer is better (1941)

Leon-Portilla, M., *Aztec Thought and Culture* (1963)

———, *Broken Spears: Aztec Account of the Conquest of Mexico* (1961)

Linne, S., *Archaeological Researches at Teotihuacan* (1924)

Lothrop, S. K., *Treasures of Ancient America* (1964)

Lumholtz, K. S., *Unknown Mexico* (2 vols., 1902)

MacGowan, K., *Early Man in the New World* (1950)

Martin, P. S., G. I. Quimby, and D. Collier, *Indians Before Columbus* (1947)

Mason, G., *Columbus Came Late* (1931)

Mayas and Their Neighbors: Studies Presented to A. M. Tozzer (1940)

Mitchell, J. L., *Conquest of the Maya* (1935)

Morley, S. G., *Ancient Mayas* (3rd ed., 1956)

Motolinía, T., *History of the Indians of New Spain* (1950)

Paddock, J., *Tomorrow in Ancient Mesoamerica* (1965)

Prescott, W. H., *History of the Conquest of Mexico* (many editions)

Proskouriakoff, T., *An Album of Maya Architecture* (1963)

Radin, P., *The Story of the American Indian* (1944)

Robertson, O., *Mexican Codices* (1959)

Rouse, I., *The Pre-History of Haiti* (1939)

Sauer, C. O., *Distribution of Aboriginal Tribes and Languages in Northwestern Mexico* (1934)

———, *The Early Spanish Main* (1966)

———, and D. Brand, *Aztatlan: Prehistoric Mexican Frontier of the Pacific Coast* (1932)

Sejourne, L., *Burning Water: Thought and Religion in Ancient Mexico* (1957)

Sellards, E. H., *Early Man in America* (1952)

Soustelle, J., *Daily Life of the Aztecs on the Eve of the Spanish Conquest* (1962)

Spence, L., *Civilization of Ancient Mexico* (1912)

———, *Gods of Mexico* (1923)

Spicer, E. H., *Cycles of Conquest: The Impact of Spain, Mexico and the United States on the Indians of the Southwest 1533–1960* (1965)

Spinden, H. J., *Ancient Civilizations of Mexico and Central America* (3rd rev. ed., 1928)

————, *Maya Art and Civilization* (1957)
Stacy-Judd, R. B., *Ancient Mayas* (1934)
Tax, S., ed., *Civilization of Ancient America* (1951)
Thompson, J. E., *Mexico Before Cortez* (1933)
————, *Rise and Fall of the Maya Civilization* (1954)
Tulane University, *Middle American Papers*
Unesco, *Mexican Wall Paintings of the Maya and Aztec Period* (1963)
Vaillant, G. C., *Indian Arts in North America* (1939)
————, *The Aztecs of Mexico* (1950)
Von Hagen, V. W., *The Aztec: Man and Tribe* (1958)
————, *The World of the Maya* (1960)
Wauchope, R., ed., *Handbook of Middle American Indians*, Vol. I (1964)
————, *They Found the Buried Cities* (1965)
Weatheraux, P., *Indian Corn in Old America* (1954)
Wissler, C., *The American Indian* (3rd ed., 1938)
Wolf, E. R., *Sons of the Shaking Earth* (1959)
Wormington, H. M., *Origins* (1953)

Chapter 5

Pre-Columbian Americans
from the Isthmus South

PRE-INCA PEOPLES ON THE COAST
AND MOUNTAINS OF WESTERN SOUTH AMERICA

OH, PACHACAMAC,
Thou, who hast existed from the beginning,
Thou, who shalt exist until the end,
  powerful but merciful,
Who didst create man by saying,
  "Let man be,"
Who defendest us from evil,
And preservest our life and our health,
Art Thou in the sky or upon the earth?
In the clouds or in the deeps?
Hear the voice of him who implores thee,
  and grant him his petitions.
Give us life everlasting,
  preserve us, and accept this, our sacrifice.[1]

[1] Translation given in Philip Ainsworth Means, *Ancient Civilizations of the Andes* (New York: Charles Scribner's Sons, 1931), p. 439. Reproduced by permission of the publishers.

When the Spaniards came to the coast of Peru in the 1500s they heard the Indian subjects of the Incas singing this hymn, a song which appeals to the universal religious sentiments of all mankind. Pachacamac, sometimes called Viracocha, was a god of the pre-Inca, a people who had lived on the coast centuries before the Incas swept down on them from the Andean highlands. Twenty-five miles from Lima there still stands a great stone ruin called today Pachacamac; it was once the religious center for several different groups of ancient Peruvians, whose abstract ideas of worship and whose songs of devotion were adapted to daily use by the later sun-worshiping Incas.

Portrait jugs made by Pre-Inca peoples on the Peruvian coast. *Courtesy Pan American Union.*

The Chimus, the most numerous of these coastal people, lived along the desert coasts north of Lima, occupying and irrigating the valleys around the present-day Peruvian towns of Trujillo and Chimbote. They had a unified kingdom and a large population, dominating the coast until conquered by the Incas about 1475. When Europeans first saw their city of Chan Chan it was a great roofless mass of adobe buildings, square streets, and elaborately decorated stucco walls in bright colors, little changed since the Incas had resettled its people almost a century before. Though an unprecedented rainstorm on this rainless coast in 1925 reduced Chan Chan to piles of mud, a recent aerial survey proved the city to have covered twelve square miles, with a thousand square miles of irrigated corn lands and truck gardens around it. A "Great Wall" had been built from the coast to the high Andes ridge as a defense against the Incas and other mountain tribes, for the Chimu people depended on their river; they had to keep invaders from stealing their water rights.

Equal to their irrigation projects in skill was the pottery of the Chimu. It is known that Chan Chan was inhabited over a long period of time, and that the pottery of the early period is much more interesting than that being made when the Incas conquered the city. Jugs made as portraits, perhaps of the person in whose grave they are found, have realistic man-sized faces, moulded in the round, in the rich terra cotta color so like an Indian's skin—faces which smile or frown or even wink at the visitor from the walls of museum shelves. The plates and vases of the Chimu made for daily use are decorated with scenes of home life, commerce, or religious ceremony. Some of their colored plates imply that they built large sail-bearing rafts and traded extensively on the coast.

South of the temple at Pachacamac other peoples had lived perhaps several centuries before the Chimu. Tribes known as Paracas had perhaps come first, followed by the Nazca people who had learned to irrigate the coastal valley. The Nazca were the best weavers of ancient America; their bright patterns are found in graves as mummy coverings, left by the rainless desert in as perfect condition as when they were first buried.

Perhaps both Nazca and Chimu peoples learned pottery-making and weaving from a very early mountain civilization on the shores of Lake Titicaca on the high Bolivian *altiplano*. There the ancestors of today's Aymará Indians built a stone city, for which archeologists have not yet set a date. Evidently the later Incas knew nothing of the history of this empty city, with its wide paved floor, its carved gates, and its representations of the human figure. The Incas themselves did not make carved decorations, so the Tiahuanaco builders are definitely non-Inca. It can be taken for granted that there was a city or religious center at Tiahuanaco when the Incas were a tribe of llama herders in some poor mountain village.

THE EMPIRE OF THE INCAS

When Europe discovered America, first and foremost among the semi-civilized Indians of South America were the Inca "Children of the Sun," whose civilization and imperial territory extended from the northern border of Ecuador a third of the way down Chile, and eastward through Bolivia into upper Argentina. Speaking the Quechua language, they were mistakenly called Incas by the Spaniards, who used the title of their ruler as a general name for all the civilized Andean peoples. These so-called Incas kept their empire together by a remarkable system of roads and communications. They emphasized the general welfare of the people as a basis for their state, and planned the development of the resources of the country in order that the surplus should be used for the state and the aristocracy after the needs of the workers themselves had been satisfied.

Of the Inca kings and their subjects we know a mass of detailed history, more than we know about the Aztecs and infinitely more than about the Maya. In Peru there was perhaps not as great a slaughter of nobility by the European conquerors as elsewhere; many upper-class Incas held their positions and married their daughters to Spaniards. The detailed memorized stories of Inca greatness were passed down in these families. Spanish priests and scholars seemed more interested in writing down facts about the Incas than about the Aztecs.

These memorized Inca legends say that the Sun created a man and his wife on an island in Lake Titicaca and made them "prince and princess." He then sent them to the high fertile Andes valley of Cuzco. "The prince and princess went throughout the valley calling the people together in the name of their Father, the Sun." With the "multitude thus assembled" they built the city of Cuzco. Their descendants conquered the surrounding territory and told their history to their children in turn.

By 1450 the Inca realm was as large as modern Peru. The Inca at that time, Pachacutec, required three years to make a complete tour of inspection of his realm—his empire had been so widely extended by combining guile and diplomacy with military aggression. It had become set policy of the Inca ruler to conquer peoples by arms and then to reconcile them by kindness. It was Pachacutec who absorbed the Nazca country, took over the shrine, and perhaps the religion, of Pachacamac, and advanced to the great wall of Chan Chan. It was his son, the crown prince Tupac Yupanqui, who subdued the Chimu.

In the next generation under Huayna Capac, the empire reached to the present Colombia-Ecuador line, and far down into the fertile valleys of central Chile as well as the sloping eastern *montaña* of Bolivia, an expanse 1500 miles long and 300 miles wide, all ruled by the Child of the Sun from Cuzco. With the death of the ruler about 1527 a quarrel ensued between two of his sons for whom he had divided the empire. Was it Huascar, born of his chief wife, a Cuzco princess, who should be the true heir, or was it Atahualpa, his favorite son, whose mother was a much-loved concubine, a princess from the recently conquered province of Quito? After a few years of armed truce, these two half-brothers fought openly over the Inca throne for three years; when Pizarro came, the Spanish conquerors were to profit from the disorganization caused by this quarrel.

Inca statesmanship was remarkable as the empire was extended. The new conquests were made integral parts of the highly centralized kingdom. Whenever lands were conquered, the subjected people were allowed to retain approximately a third of their territory; the Inca peoples were given a second third for their own expansion, while the Inca ruler kept a last third for his own use. The new area would be dominated by Inca-built roads and fortresses; its people would be won over by a policy of assimilation and Inca-acculturation. Transferred colonists from older parts of the empire came into the villages and farms to work side by side with the newly subjected inhabitants. These were always people who spoke Quechua, the language of the Incas. From them the subject people were forced to learn this official tongue. There were once more than eighty tribal groups and languages in the habitable west coast area. By the time the Spaniards came, some people in every village spoke Quechua; in fact, it was more widely spoken in the region than Spanish is today. This language helped unify the empire. No interpreters were needed, for the conquered peoples learned Quechua more quickly than the new officials could learn the speech of the conquered. The Quechuan word for the empire, *Tahuantinsuyo*, actually means *unity*. Thus were the vast Inca holdings solidified.

The actual government of the whole territory from the top was by means of a theocratic despotism. At the head of the empire of eight or ten million inhabitants stood the hereditary Inca or Sapa-Inca, descendant of the Sun. Tradition and precedent required that he rule wisely and justly. As the source of all laws, administrative decrees, and religious proclamations, he was surrounded by an aura of divinity and wore special and distinctive garb. His capital was at Cuzco, city of 100,000 inhabitants at 11,000 feet elevation; a secondary capital and court were maintained at

Ruins of the Inca city of Machu Picchu, perhaps an early capital, were discovered in 1911. *Photo by Helen Miller Bailey.*

Quito by the time of the arrival of the Spaniards. Four viceroys helped him in the actual rule of the empire and served as an advisory council. He also had an elaborate system of messengers and itinerant officers who kept him closely in touch with every part of his vast realm.

The absolute power of the Inca, the uniform level of knowledge and culture, the generally well-fed condition of the subjects, and the lack of any strong outside enemies made the empire a paternalistic and socialistic state. Such a state called for a bureaucracy of many officials. Below the four viceroys and the provincial governors, called *camayas,* were the tribes and villages, the *hunas,* each theoretically comprising a hundred households. At the bottom of the pyramid were the headmen, the *chuncas,* in charge of ten families each. These headmen reported on the physical needs of their people, and served as justices of the peace, though their decisions could be appealed all the way up to the Inca, the supreme judge. Justice was firm and prompt; capital punishment was the penalty for theft, adultery, murder, and blasphemy against the Sun God, with justice especially severe for violations committed by public officials.

The government was supported by income from lands belonging to the Inca, from monopolies of precious stones and metals, and from tribute in the form of forced labor. Work from each household was supposed to be equal; the whole governmental system emphasized equality of opportunity based solely on ability and age. But such a system called for rigid regimentation. Though no one was overworked, labor was highly specialized. Each age group was assigned a certain type of labor according to strength. Once an artisan of particular skill, always such an artisan. Young people below twenty-five and old people above fifty were exempted from tribute labor on the roads, on water supply systems, and on other public projects, and were assigned only light tasks. Transfers of population were sometimes made for the purpose of maintaining loyalty. If a region threatened rebellion, it was soon re-colonized with many loyal families—a system of *mitimaes.* Thus there was "social security" without individual liberty. Life was safe and pleasant enough, and the government efficient and respected.

This organization of all levels of life developed a rigid class system. The royalty included the legitimate descendants of the royal family who formed the highest nobility; from them were selected the principal military and civil officials and the chief priests. There was an upper class in the remote provinces also, consisting of the *curacas,* hereditary chiefs of the conquered governments whose children were educated at the court of Cuzco.

Below the official class, there was no inequality but that of physical strength, numbers of able-bodied sons and daughters in a family, or skill of craftsmanship and farming "know-how." There was also a class of slave-workers, who were confined to the lands of the Inca and of the temples, and who were kept in that position from generation to generation. In the families of the laboring class of people even marriage was arranged by the state; all the girls and boys of marriageable age in any one unit of a hundred households were married at one time in a gala public ceremony to provide a big fiesta, prevent private family parties, and to save time for the harvesting of crops and the building of roads.

Under such a system there was no individual ownership of land. Fields belonged either to the priests for the support of the sun-worship, to the Inca for support of the royal family and the government, or to the tribes (*hunas*) and villages (*chuncas*) for distribution to the families. From the village reserves enough land was given to each family for its own maintenance, according to the number of members, their assigned occupations, and their ability to work. No land was ever bought from and sold to individuals, and adjustments of holdings were made to fit family numbers in each new generation. Food from the land went into public storehouses; craftsmen received it in return for their manufactured goods, laborers in return for their work on roads, on public works, or in mines.

The lands produced well, for the Inca people were among the best farmers in the Americas. They terraced the mountainside, fertilized the soil with *guano* or seagull dung from the coast, and used well-planned systems of reservoirs, canals, and aqueducts for irrigation of the drier valleys and the coastal shelf. In their intensively cultivated plots they raised potatoes, corn, manioc or tapioca, peppers, tomatoes, beans, and squash. They had vast herds of llamas to be used as beasts of burden and alpacas to be sheared for wool.

Roads, used to maintain touch with all the empire and for military purposes, connected all sections, some of them on the flatland paved with stones, others made of chiseled stairsteps up mountain passes. On such trails the suspension bridges across deep chasms were better than many of those used on pack trails in the Andes today. Post runners, or chasquis, ran regular routes with messages on these trails, and storehouses and inns were maintained for such runners, for the Inca's packtrain leaders, traveling officials, and tradesmen. Signal fires helped the runners relay commands swiftly from post to post. The thousand-mile trip from Cuzco to Quito was covered by such messengers in eight days. Balsa boats on Lake Titicaca took the Inca's messages over into what is now Bolivia.

Religion naturally ruled the people's lives in a country where the absolute ruler was also a Child of God. The Inca himself, usually son of the previous Inca by his own sister to keep the blood line pure, was also the highest archpriest. For the cult of unquestioning devotion to Sun-worship there was an elaborate priesthood headed by the Villac Umu, a brother or close relative of the ruler, under whom there were hundreds of lesser priests, keepers of the temples, nuns or "Virgins of the Sun." Sacrifices of food and flowers, or articles of precious metals were made. For formal ceremonies on set occasions llamas were sacrificed, and, very rarely, a human life.

Among the more sophisticated Cuzco people, there was a belief in a life after death. Those who were good went to live with the Sun. Sinners— and disobeying the emperor or carelessness in worship was a sin equal to murder—went to the center of the earth, where they were constantly hungry and had no food but stones. Sins had to be confessed, and bad luck, illness, and accidents came to those who failed to do so. Priests in the temples received these confessions, much as the Catholic priests among the Quechua might do today, and made assignments of fasting and prayer for penitence. The temple in Cuzco was the finest building erected by the Inca; one of its spacious rooms was 296 feet long. A curved sanctuary at

Street in pre-conquest town of Pissac, Peru. Indian women here continue to dress in Inca costume. The terraced fields rising high above the town are planted with varieties of corn and po tatoes derived from plants developed by the early Incas. *Photo by Helen Miller Bailey.*

the end of it, made of beautifully smooth stones, still stands in Cuzco today in the foundation of a convent. Here the people prayed, "Oh, Sun! Thou art in peace and safety, shine upon us, keep us from sickness, and preserve us in health and safety." It was easy enough for these people to transfer their faith to a Christian God in the Cuzco cathedral.

Through their Sun-worship the Incas seem to have developed an abstract culture perhaps superior to that of the Maya. Though there was no system of writing, much religious poetry was recited orally and was written down by the Spaniards. The Inca sages also composed love songs and philosophical verses. Pachacutec, Inca in the 1480s, is best remembered for his wise proverbs, many of which were still being widely quoted when Spaniards wrote them down a half century later:

> Envy is a worm that gnaws and consumes the entrails of the envious.
>
> He that kills another without authority or just cause condemns himself to death.
>
> Judges who secretly receive gifts from suitors ought to be looked upon as thieves and punished with death as such.[2]

[2] Selections from Means, *Ancient Civilizations of the Andes*, p. 262. Reproduced by permission of the publishers.

Such poems and proverbs were part of the "college education" given to the sons of the upper class. In a four-year course in the temples they learned astronomy and mathematics as well as the history and legends of the Inca peoples. The classes for the noblemen's sons were taught by *amautas,* learned men of the priestly class who gave specialized training in law, priesthood, and principles of government. The noble youngsters, being trained themselves for a life of service to the empire as priests, tax collectors, and governors, were also taught the elements of science, bridge building, and road construction. Since they had no alphabet or picture writing, all this learning had to be by rote in oral recitation. The sons of officials were also taught the use of the *quipu,* an elaborate and ingenious method of keeping accounts by means of knotted cords of various sizes and colors, red for accounts concerning war, white for those of peace. With these cords officials recorded populations, taxes, road-building plans, increase of herds, and every item necessary for a vast realm. The children of commoners had no such fine training—in fact, no formal education of any kind.

With an efficient ruling class and an accurate system of accounts, the Incas developed an advanced culture in things practical, as is evidenced by their bridges and irrigation canals, their terraced fields on steep mountainsides. In such activities they surpassed all other Western Hemisphere peoples. Even in their art forms they developed along practical lines. The Inca conquerors could not improve on the pottery work of the Chimu nor on the textiles of the Nazca. But they could improve their "technical excellence" in the speed of manufacture, and could treble the quantity produced by the sheer force of the demand. For common use jars and dishes were so standard in form and decoration, so uniform in texture as to seem almost machine-made.

This functional design—well made, carefully finished, but simple in decoration for ordinary things—is evident also in architecture. Inca stone masons did not carve serpent heads on temple walls, nor decorate columns with mosaic patterns. Since as much time was spent by the builders erecting houses for workers as houses for Sun-worship, all building was of simple blocks of stone. Builders showed reverence only in the public buildings for the use of the Inca, priests, and Sun Virgins; in these structures they used larger stones, fitted them more closely, polished their surfaces more highly. The enormous size of the stones, brought by human labor from distant quarries and set together neatly without mortar, is a source of amazement to anyone who visits Inca ruins. To do such building, and to plan their other public works, the Incas required a knowledge of engineering techniques. They were almost as familiar with the movement of the stars as were the Maya, had an accurate calendar based on the solar year, and could foretell the equinoxes. They were as fine metallurgists as any people of the Western Hemisphere, working copper, bronze, and lead, as well as casting ornamental objects of the most intricate type in gold and silver. Though in conquering Inca civilization the Spaniards destroyed its higher aspects, they found much to adopt in modified form after the conquest. Andean civilization is a combination of native and Spanish culture, and many mountain villages in Ecuador, Peru, and Bolivia are still pure Indian today, retaining their language, dress, and agricultural customs.

TRIBES ELSEWHERE IN SOUTH AMERICA

Lying to the north of the powerful Inca empire were the less highly organized Chibcha peoples. Perhaps there were a million Chibcha altogether, organized into five federations of villages. They knew the names of only one generation of kings and had no long story of their history. Each of the rulers of the five federations was absolute in military and political affairs and lived in great pomp, collecting tribute or taxes in cloth and objects of gold. One such ruler, who controlled federated tribes in the Colombian highlands, was a chieftain named Bogotá, who gave his name to the later Spanish capital there. The Chibcha were an agricultural people growing a variety of crops including cotton, which they wove into fine cotton cloth and sold at their trade fairs. They had a well-developed language, a calendar system of enumeration, and a rudimentary coinage.

Stories of the fine Chibcha gold work, equal to any craft product of the New World, brought Spaniards on exploring trips up to the Colombian highlands and over into the *montaña* for generations in search of *El Dorado*, the Gilded Man. The chieftain of Guatavitá, a town in Colombia near a mountain lake in a region which today still is rich in gold and emeralds, was said to rub his greased body with gold dust just once a year,

Details of Inca stonework showing exact fittings made without mortar. *Photo by Helen Miller Bailey.*

exhort his people to throw golden objects into the lake as a sacrifice, and then plunge into the lake in religious ecstasy. This story, combined with the golden figurines the Spaniards found among the coastal peoples, gave rise to the *El Dorado* legend. In pre-Columbian times Chibcha influence spread to the Chiriquí and Darien Indians in Panama. Nicaragua, powerful chieftain of Central America in Balboa's day, was of Chibcha strain.

In 1967 an expedition from Lima discovered a complex of village, city, and fortress ruins at 10,000 feet elevation overlooking the Peruvian and Ecuadorian drainage area leading down into the Amazon Basin. The site was said to be of the Chachapoyas culture, pre-Chibcha and pre-Inca. It extended over an area of 100 square miles and has been named the Monte Peruvian ruins. This discovery has set up a new puzzle to be solved by archeologists working on the remote past of the Andes peoples.

South of the Incas in Chile lived the Araucanians, a name which perhaps comes from the word "auco" meaning "free." They were the best fighters in South America, and were never subdued by firearms or by missionaries. Their hero, a fiery youth named Lautaro, became synonymous with freedom, and the word Lautaro was used as a password during the wars for independence from Spain. They planted crops and wove with llama wool—witness their blankets, the first true poncho, that protection of today's Chilean cowboy, with a slit for the head in the center.

In governmental institutions the Araucanians were undeveloped beyond the patriarchal family and the small tribe. Only during a war did tribal groups ally themselves together, but these alliances broke up as soon as war was over. The tribal chieftains seem to have constituted the small upper class, as all families in the village settlements owned land, and there were no cities. The settlements consisted of groups of adobe and reed huts which were far below the level of building achieved in Inca villages to the north. Most knowledge of the Araucanians depends on a study of their tribal groups on the Chilean government reservations, where anthropologists can still observe their weaving, their religious cults, their love of oratory in public meeting, or their games of hockey, for they have proudly preserved their culture and independence to the present day.

Argentine history has been influenced by the fact that there were no large "civilized" Indian cities to be conquered on the Plata estuary; Brazilian history was partially to be made by the childlike Indian peoples who welcomed the Portuguese along South America's east coast.

The nomadic peoples of the Argentine plains, the pampa tribes, were like the North American Plains Indians; they were wandering huntsmen till the Spaniards abandoned horses among them; once mounted, they became the terror of the early settlers. On foot they had hunted the wild llama of Argentina, the *guanaco*, and caught it with *bolas*, weapons made of stones tied in a small bag of hide. Several bags were connected together with long thongs, and the whole was swung at the running animal, entangling his legs. The people used skins for clothing or went naked, made a poor grade of pottery, lived in temporary shelters similar to tepees, and used shells as ornaments. When the Spaniards first came the pampa Indians roasted and ate some of them, a fate as bad as being scalped by the Sioux. The first colonizers of Buenos Aires abandoned horses and cattle on the plains; the animals multiplied on the lush pastures, and the Indians learned to capture and ride them. The danger presented by these wild nomads, the impossibility of using them as peasants to till the land or as artisans in cities, made the whole pampa region unattractive to Spaniards for two centuries. Europeans would not settle there in any number till the wild savages were gone. They were still a problem when Argentina became an independent nation.

A stronger influence on present-day history has been the Guaraní Indians of Paraguay. Their language persists in Paraguay even among the city people, and modern Paraguayans are proud to claim Guaraní blood. The original Guaraní lived along the Paraná and in today's Chaco region. Closer to the civilizing influence of the Inca peoples, they were friendlier to the white man when he came than were the wilder tribes at the Plata mouth. They cultivated squash and maize and lived in permanent thatched houses. They also used silver ornaments which they had obtained from the Inca subjects in silver-producing Bolivia. Such silver ornaments found their way to the coast, reached the hands of the first Spanish explorers, and started the story of a rich country of silver—*argentum* in Latinized form, *plata* in Spanish.

There were many different tribal groups among the Guaraní, and their range was wide. The Portuguese found them as they explored Southern Brazil; they are related to many tribes along the southernmost tributaries of the Amazon. Cousins of the Guaraní, the Tupi-Guaraní, lived all along the tropical coast of Brazil and waded out to meet Portuguese explorers when they came. Real children of nature, these people of the warm climate and the lush jungle had no need for clothing, for irrigated fields, for stone shelters. They slept in hammocks, lived off fish, game, and fruit, and bothered to cultivate only the manioc root to make their flat bread. With the arrival of the Portuguese they were made slaves or retreated inland up the inaccessible tributaries of the Amazon. In the Mato Grosso of Brazil and the jungle area of the west coast countries they still live today as their ancestors did before them. The Jívaro of Ecuador's Amazon area make the shrunken heads which today horrify museum visitors. The Tupi people who once lived at the mouth of the Amazon and along the coast just to the north mingled with Arawaks and Caribs along the regions now known as the Guianas, and near the mouth of the Orinoco. These latter were the same peoples whom Columbus met on the islands of the West Indies.

Thus lived the Indian peoples of the New World when the conquerors and settlers came, peoples in cities and peoples in the jungles, waiting to become the allies, the servants, the mates of the Europeans, to join with them in producing the new Latin American strain.

Readings

Baudin, L., *A Socialist Empire: Incas of Peru* (1961)
———, *Daily Life in Peru under the Last Incas* (1962)
Beals, C., *Nomads and Empire Builders* (1961)
Bennett, W. C., and J. B. Bird, *Andean Cultural History* (1949)

————, *Ancient Arts of the Andes* (1954)

Bingham, H., *Lost City of the Incas, The Story of Machu Picchu and Its Builders* (1948)

Bram, J., *An Analysis of Inca Militarism* (1941)

Brundage, B. C., *Empire of the Incas* (1963)

Bushnell, G. H. S., *Ancient Arts of the Americas* (1965)

Church, G. E., *Indians of South America* (1912)

Embree, E. R., *Indians of the Americas* (1939)

Faron, L. C., *Mapuche Social Structure, Institutional Reintegration in a Patrilineal Society of Central Chile* (1961)

————, *Hawks of the Sea: Mapuche Morality and Its Ritual Attributes* (1964)

Garcilaso de la Vega, *Comentarios Reales de los Incas*, H. H. Lirteaga, ed. (5 vols., 1918–1920; shorter version in English, 1961)

Hammel, E. A., *Wealth, Authority and Prestige in the Inca Valley, Peru* (1962)

d'Harcourt, R., *Textiles of Ancient Peru and their Techniques* (1962)

Hewitt, E. L., *Ancient Andean Life* (1939)

Hrdlicha, A., *Early Man in South America* (1912)

Huber, S., *The Realm of the Incas* (1959)

Jenness, D., ed., *American Aborigines* (1933)

Joyce, T. A., *South American Archaeology* (1912)

Karsten, R., *The Civilization of the South American Indians* (1926)

Kosok, P., *Life, Land and Water in Ancient Peru* (1965)

Lothrop, S. K., *Treasures of Ancient America* (1964)

MacGowan, K., *Early Man in the New World* (1950)

Markham, C. R., *Incas of Peru* (1910)

Mason, J. A., *The Ancient Civilization of Peru* (1957)

Means, P. A., *Ancient Civilizations of the Andes* (1931)

Moore, S. F., *Power and Property in Inca Peru* (1958)

Osborne, H., *Indians of the Andes, Aymaras and Quechuas* (1952)

Otfinel von Haustein, *World of the Incas* (1925)

Poindexter, M., *The Ayar-Incas* (1930)

————, *Peruvian Pharaohs* (1938)

Posnansky, A., *Tihuanacu: The Cradle of Ancient Man* (2 vols., 1945)

Prescott, W. H., *History of the Conquest of Peru* (many editions)

Radin, P., *Indians of South America* (1942)

Restrepo, V., *Los Chibchas ante de la Conquista Española* (1895)

Sarmiento de Gamboa, P., *History of the Incas* (1907)

Sauer, C. O., *The Early Spanish Main* (1966)

Stewart, J. H., ed., *Handbook of South American Indians* (6 vols., 1946–1950)

————, and L. C. Faron, *Native Peoples of South America* (1959)

Tax, S., ed., *Civilization of Ancient America* (1951)

Thompson, J. E., *Archaeology of South America* (1936)

Von Hagen, V. W., *Incas, People of the Sun* (1961)

————, *Realm of the Incas* (1957)

Wissler, C., *American Indian* (3rd ed., 1938)

Chapter 6

Spain in the New World:
the First Quarter Century

THE CONTINUED SEARCH
FOR A ROUTE FROM WEST TO EAST

WE LEFT COLUMBUS at Barcelona, in April of 1493, being received in state by the whole court. In royal lodgings provided for him Columbus stayed six weeks, while baptismal services were held for the six Bahama Island Indians he had brought back, for whom the queen herself acted as godmother. Meanwhile plans for a second voyage were immediately under way. Columbus was declared "Admiral of the said Ocean Sea and Governor of the said islands and mainlands that you have found and discovered," a title to remain in his family as an hereditary right. He was to help make plans for the colonizing of Haiti, the land of Hispaniola on which he had left the men from the shipwrecked *Santa María,* and the court was busied preparing a large fleet which was to take settlers and their equipment to the New World.

Columbus, however, was interested in making further discoveries now that the Papal Bull on the Line of Demarcation gave Spain a free hand to search farther west for the route to India. As commander of the coloniz-ing fleet, he reached Hispaniola in November of 1493, after sighting the Virgin Islands and Puerto Rico. He found his year-old fort destroyed and no trace of the men from the *Santa María.* When he had finally succeeded in establishing the town of Isabella, the first real settlement, he set out in the summer of 1494 in his same little *Niña* to make further explorations along the coasts of Cuba and Jamaica. Never finding the tip of Cuba turning north, he was sure he had skirted a continent; he then returned to his colony at Hispaniola. His mistakes in governing the settlement are part of another story. Suffice it to say here that chaos and economic failure in the colony forced him home to explain his difficulties three years after he had brought the large fleet to the Indies.

Still in good favor with Isabella, Columbus talked the Queen into maintaining him as governor and outfitting another exploratory expedition. On this third voyage, in 1498, he sailed south of Hispaniola, found the island of Trinidad and saw the Venezuela coast. It was in the waters on the south side of Trinidad that he first sensed the might of the Orinoco, the great body of fresh water so far out to sea, a river which could not arise in a small island, but must come from a continent. "I believe that this is a very great continent, which until today has been unknown"—his first mention of a mainland other than the Asia he was looking for. "Your Highnesses have here another world!" On his return to Hispaniola from this exploration, with nothing but the story of a new continent and a handful of pearls from Margarita Island to bring the Queen, he found himself in deeper difficulties as governor, and in 1500 he was sent home under arrest.

Still honoring him as the Discoverer, Isabella freed him; however, she was tired of the chaos in his colony and his own bickering over titles and prestige, and never again allowed him to govern. Irritable and persistent, he persuaded the aging queen in 1502 to send him on one last expedition. The purpose of this fourth voyage was to find a strait to India through the Caribbean and Central America and "to discover lands rich in gold." With four ships and 150 men, including his brother Bartholomew, the mapmaker, and Ferdinand, the fourteen-year-old son who was to be his biographer, he cruised along the shore of the *hondos,* the deep waters he named Honduras, and the Rich Coast, Costa Rica. There he saw the trading raft of the civilized Maya, and assumed he was close to China. Disappointed in the search for a strait, however, he may have changed his mind. A map made by his brother on this expedition calls the South American mainland *Mondo Novo,* the New World. In Christopher's own writings in 1502 he spoke of the islands as the "West Indies Unknown to all the World." On this last voyage he was shipwrecked on Jamaica and marooned there a whole year, while the quarrelsome colony at Hispaniola 120 miles away, to which he had sent a messenger by canoe, did not even consider him important enough to rescue. Friends finally sent a caravel to take him home to Spain, where he died practically forgotten in 1506. But the stories of his findings were important factors in the rapid exploration, conquest, and settlement of the Americas.

Other European nations had not been content to let Spain alone capitalize on Columbus' discoveries. By 1525, a series of voyages had examined the shoreline of the entire Western Hemisphere from Labrador to the Straits of Magellan, with captains representing Portugal, France, and England as well as Spain taking part. The voyage of John Cabot, another Genoese mariner who had visited Bristol and who had been hired to sail for England, established the English claim to the Atlantic coast of North America in 1497. His son Sebastian unsuccessfully sought the northwest passage or strait for England, though he did receive fame later in exploring South America for Spain. France, too, hired an Italian seaman, Verrazano, a Florentine, who looked for the strait to Asia by way of Maine and New-foundland, and thus laid a claim to the northern area for the French kings in 1524. Portugal's mariners, the Corte Real brothers, had also looked for the elusive strait along the North Atlantic coast.

The Portuguese Vasco da Gama meanwhile had found the sea route to the Indies. On his return to Portugal in 1499 a fleet of thirteen ships was fitted out under Pedro Alvares Cabral, designed to make permanent trading contacts in India by the round-Africa route. Perhaps Cabral's instructions directed him to take a route straight west of the Cape Verde Islands and touch at the new southern "island" to the west before he turned south around Africa at all. At any rate, Cabral found land on the shoulder of Brazil, within the Portuguese area of Demarcation, in Easter Week of 1500. Twenty-five leagues of coastline were explored, according to Cabral's report, "flat, and full of great trees, and very beautiful inland." The natives were naked, "'painted black and red on the bodies and legs and looked very well." A ship was sent home to the king with the news of this land so close to the Cape Verdes, while Cabral continued his route around Africa. Another Portuguese expedition was immediately sent out, and by 1502 the land was opened to Portuguese commercial companies.

As no strait had yet been found, the desperate search for a northwest passage through or around the newly discovered lands, undertaken specifi-cally on Columbus' fourth voyage, was continued by Spanish ships. Despite Columbus' insistence that all exploring rights had been granted to him personally, other captains were sent out by Spain. A young man named Alonzo de Ojeda, who had gone with Columbus on the second trip to Hispaniola and who was a personal friend of Isabella's colonial adviser, Bishop Fonseca, was commissioned to explore the whole length of the northern coast of South America from Guiana to the Magdalena. It was Ojeda who first saw "lake-dwellers' huts" on stilts in the Gulf of Maracaibo, and called the region "Little Venice" or Venezuela. He was also successful in finding pearls and thus made a profit out of what was actually a piratical venture. Four or five other captains and navigators who had served under Columbus undertook similar exploring and pearl-hunting expeditions within the next few years with varying success. Thus in a little more than a decade four Columbian voyages and five trips by former companions of his had revealed the coastline from Honduras to Pernambuco and even beyond. Every larger island in the West Indies was known except Barbados. Though of great importance to the future, these voyages were disappointing to the captains themselves, for they had found only wild land without either eastern cities or a route through to them.

On several of these early explorations there may have been a spy for Italian commercial companies, a Florentine named Amerigo Vespucci. His trips are so uncertain that it seems a quirk of fortune that the continent is named for him. A commercial trader who was at one time an agent for the rich Italian house of de Medici, later a mapmaker, he claims to have made several trans-Atlantic voyages, and some of his adventures have been authenticated. At any rate, he was a profuse and interesting letter writer, describing the coast of South America in personal and readable letters sent back to Italian employers and friends. In all of them he considered the continent he had seen a "'New World," at a time when Columbus was still claiming that Cuba and Haiti were in the Far East. Some of his letters to the de Medicis were published in Florence under the title "The New World," and were widely read before any of Columbus' accounts of his later voyages were printed. Martin Waldseemüller, young geography professor in a college in Lorraine, published a textbook in 1507 to which he added Amerigo's "The New World Letters" as an appendix. In his text he enumerated the four parts of the world, ending "and the fourth part of the globe, which, since Amerigo discovered it may be called Amerigo's land." Copied by other geographers, this name was eventually applied to the whole Western Hemisphere.

Meanwhile the search for the strait was responsible for more voyages north and south which filled in the coastlines for the mapmakers. Cuba was circumnavigated by Sebastian de Ocampo; Florida was discovered by the Spaniard Juan Ponce de León; the Gulf coast was mapped by three different voyages out from Cuba and Jamaica between 1517 and 1519. Slave raiders from Santo Domingo worked up and down the Carolina coast. By 1525 the whole eastern coastline from Nova Scotia to the Straits of Magellan had been mapped.

Finally Europeans were convinced that the strait to India through the New World did not lie between the coast of northern South America and Nova Scotia. Europe thus lost interest in the all-water route through the Caribbean to the Indies. Isabella died in 1504; Ferdinand concentrated on Aragon, while Juana the Mad inherited Castile. The colony of Hispaniola languished and only occasional voyages were made to the northern South American coast for pearls and Indian slaves.

The only through passage, the Straits of Magellan, was eventually found after a series of explorations farther and farther south down the coast of South America. The Amazon mouth had been sighted by Pinzón in 1500; he and Juan Díaz de Solís were sent on an official expedition in 1508 to explore every salt-water inlet between Trinidad and the Amazon mouth in the search for the strait. When news of Balboa's discovery of a great sea to the south and west of the Isthmus reached Spain in 1514, Ferdinand sent Solís, co-pilot on the 1508 expedition, out again, ordering him to explore the coast of South America. In 1515 and 1516, Solís passed the shores of Uruguay, and entered with delight that sea of fresh water he called the Mar Dulce. This was no strait, but the Plata estuary, 100 miles wide at the mouth. When he left his caravel and went exploring in a small boat, he and the rest of a landing party were killed by Indians; Solís was roasted and eaten within sight of his crew anchored out in mid-stream. One of Solís' vessels was shipwrecked on the homeward voyage and eighteen survivors lived among the Brazilian Indians for eight years, where they heard stories of silver from Inca land to the west.

All this information combined to tell Europeans that America was an obstacle blocking the way to the Orient. Some route must be found through or around it. In 1519, a Portuguese nobleman named Ferdinand Magellan offered his services to the King of Spain—now Charles V, son of Juana— showing the interested young king a "well-painted globe in which the world is depicted," indicating on it a proposed route for circumnavigation. His expedition of five ships and 270 men, provisioned for a two-year voyage, reached the Plata estuary by January of 1520. Leaving no bay or river-mouth unexplored, Magellan spent the Southern Hemisphere winter on the bleak coast of Patagonia. He had lost two of his boats by the time he found the strait that bears his name. This was in October of his second year out. His ships had entered a harbor, driven ahead by a thirty-six-hour hurricane. The mariners of the lead ship "perceiving that this channel was not closed, threaded it, and found ourselves in another"—and thus eventually the remaining ships arrived safely through the straits. So Magellan came into the open Pacific, which his ships traversed, without fresh food or water, for three months and twenty days.

Magellan eventually stopped at Guam, landed in the Philippines, and claimed them for Spain as being inside the Demarcation Line in its extension round the globe. In the Philippines the natives understood the speech of his East Indian slave and interpreter; Magellan then knew he had reached the waters near Asia. Though he himself was killed fighting natives in the Philippines, one of his ships, captained by Juan Sebastian del Cano and loaded with spices enough to pay the expenses of the whole trip, "limped" into Spain around Africa after three years. The survivors aboard it were the first to fulfill Columbus' dream of obtaining riches from spices by sailing west. The voyage had brought a group of eastern islands into the Spanish empire, had shown the distance across the Pacific and the unexpectedly great size of the earth. Though the search for a better strait continued for another two centuries, Europeans now knew that the Indies were half a world away from the Caribbean and that a great land mass lay across the path. By this time, Spaniards and Portuguese had turned to the exploration of the New World for its own sake, for conquest and settlement rather than for routes through to Asia.

Under what conditions did these old Spaniards and Portuguese cross the Atlantic, explore a new continent, and search for straits? In every contemporaneous account we read of the difficult life on shipboard—the foul drinking water, the short rations of salt pork or pickled sardines, the prevalence of scurvy owing to lack of fresh supplies. There was constant work setting the sails, hauling them in, drying and repairing them, pumping out the bilges, scrubbing the deck, and splicing rope. Seamen had no quarters but slept on the open deck or in crannies in the cargo among the fleas, the rats, and the cockroaches. Passengers on board had to bring their own food and cook it themselves. To add to the confusion, the horses of the explorers and cattle for the colonists were carried on deck. On the larger galleons of a later day there were stalls below decks for livestock, private cabins for officers and government officials, and rooms with bunks for the passengers. Many later explorers built ships in the New World called brigantines, which had no decks or private quarters, and which were lucky to hold together.

The captains got them to land, however, with what would seem to a modern mariner impossibly crude instruments of navigation. They had the astrolabe with which they could measure the position of the sun at noon and thus know their approximate distance from the equator; but there were no maps showing longitude and latitude and no standardized ways of measuring them; the site of the Royal Naval Observatory in Greenwich, England, was not accepted as zero degree of longitude until 1675. Time was measured by hour glasses and water clocks. Captains did not have the education in mathematics to make use of the new science of the Renaissance and apply it to navigation. Slopping about in narrow channels between islands, taking a large ship into a shallow river estuary, seeking a strait in every cove, all were often more dangerous than the preliminary crossing on the trade-winds route pioneered by Columbus. By such coastwise risks the Spanish and Portuguese mariners of the thirty years from 1492 to 1522 plotted out the shores of almost a whole hemisphere.

HISPANIOLA: LABORATORY
OF COLONIAL ADMINISTRATION

In November of 1493 the actual colonization of Hispaniola had begun, that transfer of Spanish people and institutions which was to spread throughout Latin America and to set a colonial policy by the experimental method. Fifteen hundred settlers embarked with Columbus on his second voyage; his large fleet was loaded with equipment, seeds, and livestock for the colonists. Since La Navidad, the fort built for the *Santa María* crew, had been destroyed, Columbus established the newcomers at the new site of Isabella. Here he laid out streets and a plaza, and erected huts of thatch as temporary quarters. The Spaniards had not come to do heavy work in the tropics; they fell sick and made poor colonists. In 1498 the town of Isabella was abandoned as too unhealthy a site and too poor a harbor, and, after some gold had been discovered in the southern part of the colony, Santo Domingo, the oldest permanent European city in the New World, was founded (1496). Here the emaciated colonists—those who had not died or run off to the hills—were ready to mutiny against Columbus' own neglectful administration. During his third visit there, in October 1498, he sent a ship back to Spain with a report on "the abominable knaves and villains" he had in his colony; they in turn sent a message by the same ship calling Columbus and his brother "unjust, mean, cruel enemies and shedders of Spanish blood."

Shocked by the reports from Santo Domingo, Isabella appointed a judge and inspector of the island over Columbu' head. The man chosen was Francisco de Bobadilla, royal commissioner to investigate and adjust grievances. He reached Santo Domingo in the summer of 1500. The first

The first Spanish towns founded in the Caribbean area were similar to this Venezuelan coastal village. Only the burros and the plaster walls changed the appearance of the Indian villages. *Courtesy Standard Oil Company of New Jersey.*

sight that met Bobadilla's eyes in the new town was seven Spaniards hanging on the gallows. Already prejudiced against Columbus, the new governor put both the Admiral and his brother in chains and sent them back to Spain. That the monarchs had Columbus released as soon as they heard of his arrival and allowed him to make a fourth exploratory voyage does not lessen his failure as a colonial administrator. In the brief time that Columbus was in charge, however, a pattern for future rule had been set. Towns had been founded and fortresses had been built. Bobadilla, feeling that he had brought peace to the colony, embarked in his fleet to go home from Santo Domingo, only to lose the whole fleet and his own life in a West Indian hurricane.

Thus Columbus lost his monopoly and a royal governor was appointed in his place; Nicolás de Ovando set sail from Cádiz in February of 1502 with thirty ships. With him were 2,500 new colonists, including seventy-three married couples with families and twelve friars. Church policy was begun by these clerics, for soon two bishoprics were established. Agriculture prospered under Ovando; he brought hogs as well as cattle to the island and thus began a livestock industry. Ovando, the actual founder of Spain's empire in America, was efficient, firm, and fair. Though the royal policy toward the Indians was still wavering, Ovando himself was mainly interested in pacifying the island and putting down Indian rebellions so that the colony of Europeans could survive and prosper. The capital city of Santo Domingo, founded in 1496, now began to grow into a sizable village. Ovando tried to keep the interests of Spain at heart—the search for wealth, the spread of religion, the development of agriculture. By 1513 gold was

91

being mined in the interior, cotton and sugar were planted, roads had been built, and thirteen chartered towns had been founded. Though Spanish interest was soon transferred to Cuba and the mainland, Hispaniola remained a successful colony.

Meanwhile Diego Columbus, Christopher's elder son, had grown to manhood in the Spanish court and Ferdinand decided to make him governor, a position Don Diego claimed as his inherited right; Ferdinand considered the appointment merely a matter of the sovereign will to be rescinded after a short term. Disagreements between the rulers and the Columbus family over these points continued until 1536, when Don Diego's descendants received a dukedom and a pension and gave up all further claim to hereditary rights in America.

Don Diego's colony of Hispaniola has been called the "mother of Spanish America," for so many Spanish colonial institutions were experimented with and developed there—the councils and boards to handle colonial matters in New Spain, the titles and powers of administrators in the New World, the relationship between church and state, a humanitarian attitude toward the natives in the abstract, combined with a realistic "on the spot" economic exploitation of them in the "concrete." The encouragement and selection of immigrants, the granting of land and the Indians living on it to private owners, the economic policy in developing mines, the trade with the mother country via official fleets, the improvement of agriculture, the doubling and trebling of red tape and regulation as the empire grew, all these were to become set attitudes for more than two centuries, and they evolved from the first experimentation on Hispaniola. For Spain had no exact model to follow, no real precedent in the world's history of colonizing nations. Spain had to draw on her own historical experiences, and adapt them to the new situation. The West Indies from the first were meant to be more than just way stations on the route to the East Indies; they were permanent European communities to shine as a credit to Spain and Catholicism. Only approved Christian Spaniards were allowed to emigrate to the islands, and plans were made from the beginning to convert all the natives to Christianity.

Because of the complaints against his administration, Columbus' rule was canceled less than a decade after his discovery. Bobadilla in 1499, Ovando in 1502, and Diego Columbus in 1509 all were called "governor" and given orders for almost all-inclusive powers. They were the highest court of appeal, the collectors of taxes, the source of decisions concerning land grants. Such a governor was not called "viceroy" until later (see Chapter 9).

The governor's power as chief justice was soon curtailed by the transference of that Spanish judicial institution, the *audiencia*. As the city of Santo Domingo grew, complaints were made against the arbitrary justice of Diego Columbus; these complaints led to the establishment of a superior court there to which appeals from the governor-general could be carried. Such *audiencias,* formally decreed by a law of 1524, followed Spanish government to the other principal colonies. The *cabildo* or municipal council, locally elected, had already lost its autonomous powers in Spain under the unification policies of the Catholic monarchs and was curtailed in its authority soon after being established in the New World; in 1500 Santo Domingo had a *cabildo* which was appointed, not elected. The *cabildo* was to become a major institution of government in the New World, though its membership in many places was to become hereditary.

As the conquest branched out from Hispaniola into virgin territory, private individuals, such as Ponce de León in Florida, were given the joint rights of founder and governor, and called *adelantados*. The *adelantado* bore the expense of his venture in a new colony but could keep most of the profit from it, including what lands he chose to hold personally. Many grants of *adelantado* were to be made in the 1500s, similar to the old rights of Castilian noblemen to maintain feudal holdings along the Moorish frontier.

Such were the representatives of the crown in the New World in the earliest stages of their evolution. The colonies were considered a direct concern of the crown of Castile, unimportant though the pitiful little settlements seemed to the court at first. It was immediately foreseen that some special official or council must head up the colonial plans in Spain itself. When Columbus returned in the spring of 1493 and plans were made for his second voyage, Juan de Fonseca, Isabella's chaplain, was put in charge of collecting the supplies, interviewing the colonists, and chartering the ships. For a decade he acted as a sort of colonial minister, opposing Columbus' monopolies and concentrating colonial plans in his own hands for the benefit of his sovereigns. Columbus himself had suggested that all ships for the West Indies depart via Cádiz. Fonseca was able to have this port monopoly transferred to Seville, thus starting two centuries of feud between the towns and making Seville the headquarters of all colonial activity. In Fonseca's time a Board of Trade, called the *Casa de Contratación*, was set up to assist him in economic matters, and it became the clearing house for all trade, navigation, and immigration to the Spanish colonies. By the time Mexico had been added to the empire a Council of the Indies had been created to head up colonial affairs (described in Chapter 9).

Columbus had seen the need of encouraging agriculture if his lands were to be permanent homes for Europeans. On his second voyage he had taken brood mares, rams and ewes, donkeys, bulls and cows, as well as chickens and many types of seeds. Hard as it was to make either Indians or Spaniards till the soil, his new arrivals planted and harvested the first crops—wheat, barley, melons, and cucumbers. They set out grape cuttings for vineyards and planted sugar cane roots. He also sent prospectors to look for gold, which he found in some quantity at Cibao in the interior. There he built a fort and set miners to panning the streams.

Though the rumors of gold on the Caribbean Islands served to urge the Spaniards on to greater conquests, actually little gold was ever found there. The prosperity of the West Indies had to depend on agriculture. Between 1502 and 1508 Ovando increased the herds of domestic animals —cattle, pigs, horses, mules—and greatly encouraged the planting of grapes, olives, oranges, lemons, figs, and bananas. Sugar cane and cattle were to become the first two major sources of wealth in the islands. This kind of energetic and profitable colonization not only meant prosperity for those engaged in it, but also provided important supplies for the later conquests on the mainland. Without having to obtain their horses, mules, cattle, and grain across the broad Atlantic, the Spanish mainland explorers and conquerors could supply themselves over the relatively short distances from the Caribbean Islands. Ovando's success is strongly indicated by the arrival of many new settlers from Spain; by 1507 there were 12,000 Spaniards in the islands, many of them settled down in homes in the city of Santo Domingo or in the other thirteen towns of Hispaniola.

Already there were town councilmen, royal judges, treasury officials, friars, parish priests, artisans, merchants, planters, and small farmers. There were wives from Spain and Indian wives from the native population. By 1510 there were many Spanish children born in the New World, as well as half-breed children, called *mestizos*, already nearing adulthood. In the total population, those who worked at gold mining in the interior of Hispaniola made up a relatively small percentage, a fact which was prophetic of the future, for in the total story of Spanish conquest in America, gold and silver seekers were always a minor portion of the population. The work of agriculture, commerce, political administration, and religious direction was far more important and engaged many more people. Only good Catholics were to go to Hispaniola; they were to be kept "good" after they arrived by the constant presence of their own religious institutions. Thus, wherever Spain went, there also went the Catholic faith which Spain had agreed to support and to spread, as will be described in Chapter 11 below.

The greatest problem met by Spain in the Indies was that posed by the natives. How should they be handled—selfishly, for the use of the settlers and thus for the "good" of the colony; or humanely, for the good of the natives themselves? Queen Isabella had considered their protection and conversion one of the Spaniards' chief duties—to bring them to a life of industry and usefulness and to teach them to till their own lands or work for pay within the Christian fold. Columbus had written of the Arawaks, "I knew that they were a people who could better be freed and converted to our Holy Faith by love than by force." But he himself felt that the cannibalistic Caribs were fair game for slavery; when he found so little gold on his second trip, he broadened his rule allowing the enslaving of cannibals, and said it would include any "resentful" native.

Legally the Indians were wards of the crown as proclaimed in Spain, but that freedom availed them little in the far-off Indies where work had to be performed, for, true to their long tradition, many Spaniards disdained work. Because precious metals are useless if left in the ground, and no food will issue forth from the soil without some human labor, in the long run the Indians were forced into a system hardly distinguishable from slavery. As a result of an Indian uprising in 1495, Columbus had condemned the natives to pay tribute in gold or personal sacrifice; later demands for tribute to the Spanish government led to more forced work. From the beginning the economic motive clashed with the humanitarian.

How should Indian workers be managed, fed, and paid? Which Spaniards should have the rights to their services? Under Columbus, a system of apportioning Indians to the colonists had been started, in which groups of Indians were assigned to a colonist for a private job, or put to labor on a public project for a single set task. This was a temporary allotment of labor which was called a *repartimiento;* the policy of making such allotments was expanded under Bobadilla. Ovando, who had been instructed to consider the Indians legally free and to treat them with "kindness," was also faced with the necessity of finding cheap labor. He was allowed to enslave in the mines and on public works any cannibalistic Indians, or natives who "resisted Catholicism or the King," and was to hold all Indian villages responsible for tribute and tithes. These deviations from the "kindness" instruction served as the entering wedge for many abuses. Word of the abuses came to Isabella, and she ordered what seemed to her a greater protection to the Indians. They were to be congregated in villages, each one to be put under the permanent control of a "protector," or *encomendero,* to use an old Spanish word implying the feudal protection a lord owed his serfs. *Repartimientos* were "chain gangs" of Indians temporarily working for a colonist, separate from their land or their village; *encomiendas* were grants of Indian workers on their own settled land, in their own villages, villages in which the Indians worked permanently for the one lord, while the lord "converted, civilized and educated" them. As will be seen in a later discussion of conditions of labor in the colonies (Chapter 10), *repartimientos* and *encomiendas* were to figure large in Latin American history.

By 1514 there were 715 *repartimientos* in existence in Hispaniola, with perhaps 20,000 Indians bound to service. When the local Indians ran away into the interior, collapsed under the unaccustomed labor, or died in the epidemics of measles and smallpox, European diseases new to them, slave raiders brought Indians from other islands—hostile Caribs at first, but later thousands of peaceful Arawaks. The forced labor, the slave raids, and the diseases started a sharp decline in the number of the island's Indians during Columbus' own rule. Later on, when Spaniards invaded the principal Indian cultures of the mainlands, Spanish officialdom, both civil and religious, was much better prepared to prevent such a decimation of the Indian population.

Church officials in the New World became concerned for the Indians as early as 1511, when a Dominican friar who had returned from Santo Domingo persuaded Ferdinand to summon a group of theologians and learned men to suggest a remedy for the Indian problem. Out of their discussions emanated the so-called Laws of Burgos, a detailed paper consisting of a preamble and thirty-five decrees. In the preamble, the Indians were declared by nature idle and given to vice; the detailed decrees went on to provide for the congregating of Indians into villages on or near *encomiendas.* The *encomenderos* were to build churches, teach the rudiments of Catholicism, maintain priests, and feed the natives. The Indians in return were to work in the fields or mines. They could not take part in commerce and could keep only one wife. Any one *encomendero* could have no less than forty nor more than 150 Indians on his estate. Though Indians were not to be overworked and beaten, and inspectors were to be assigned to insist on good treatment in every village, distance and lax inspection made it impossible to enforce the humane provisions. *Encomenderos* themselves were appointed inspectors for their own villages; greed and economic necessity automatically carried out the exploitation features of the code, almost to the exclusion of the other sections.

Although one Dominican failed in his effort to ameliorate the laws governing the Indians, another famous Dominican preacher, Bartolomé de las Casas, called the "Apostle of the Indians," was to arouse the conscience of Spain. As a layman he had followed the conquerors to Cuba where he was granted an *encomienda*, and exploited his Indians just as did his fellow Spaniards. But he took holy orders in 1510, offered his services to the Dominican reformers, renounced his *encomienda* publicly and preached from the pulpit persuading other Spanish landholders to let the Indians go in peace. Five years more in the Indies made him determined to lay the matter before the authorities in Spain. Granted an audience with the young King Charles V, he made an impassioned plea for more consideration of the Indians. "These people, my most powerful lord, with whom the New World is crowded, are quite capable of practising the Christian faith, and likewise all the virtues and good customs," a people "by nature free, having their natural lords to govern them." As a result of Las Casas' pleas a commission was sent to enforce more liberal laws, to set at liberty "all capable Indians under their own chiefs." Las Casas himself returned to America with the title Protector of the Indians.

He spent the rest of his life trying experiments to solve the great problem of getting the work of the Indies done without enslaving the Indians. He continued to fight the landlords who held *encomiendas*, to plead for the enforcement of the old laws and the promulgation of better ones. He wrote a book in defense of the Indians, *Very Brief History of the Destruction of the Indies*, in which he described in gruesome detail much of the torture and persecution he had seen. This book, read widely in England, gave rise to an exaggerated idea of Spanish cruelty in dealing with the natives, an idea called by historians today "The Black Legend." Afterward, Las Casas attempted to found a Utopian colony on the mainland of South America, but through unfortunate circumstances it failed. Further experiments in converting the Indians in Guatemala were very successful, and the state in which he worked there is still called "The True Peace," Vera Paz.

As for the Indians themselves, they were always to be the minor, the weaker part of society, and hence perhaps inevitably exploited. It was not that Spain was soulless in the matter; the deep moral nature of Isabella held over into the new generations. The whole problem was to vex the Spaniards sorely, to bring many missionaries to the Indies, and to cause crown and church to spend vast sums. Spanish scholars were to study Indian languages, write grammars, prepare Indian chronicles and histories in an attempt to do them justice. Actually the Spaniards were probably no more cruel to the natives than any other Europeans might have been at the time. After all, if settlements are to be maintained, life in them must be attractive and profitable to the colonists from home; hence, the natives were exploited in mines and field. Church and crown meant well and set up careful laws, but there was always the conflict between humanitarian feelings on the one hand and vested interests on the other.

Las Casas' pleas had one bad social effect on the New World. Accustomed in Spain to the Portuguese slave trade in Negroes, and considering Negro slavery a lesser evil than the exploitation of natives which he had seen with his own eyes, he suggested that Negroes be introduced into the West Indies to do the work assigned the unfortunate Indians, as the Africans were better adapted to plantation life in the tropics. Later Las Casas repented his words and advocated abolition, but it was then too late. Ovando had brought a few Negroes to work in the mines, and they soon ran away to the hills. A consignment of 200 had been sent from Seville in 1510, but the Cardinal of Spain had stopped further trade. Now with the increased planting of sugar which called for human labor by hands accustomed to the tropics, Negroes were imported in large numbers. More than 8,000 slaves were sold in Santo Domingo from 1520 to 1530. After the middle of the sixteenth century, territorial expansion on the mainland and the official ban against the enslavement of Indians still further augmented the traffic, either directly from Africa or by way of the slave mart in Lisbon. Cuban plantations prospered on Negro slave labor from their beginning. Today in the West Indies it is the descendants of African Negroes, not of Arawaks and Caribs, who make up the great mass of the population. Thus the political problems of running the government, the economic problems of mining and agriculture, and the social problems created by the presence of Indians and Negro slaves all began for the Spanish empire on Hispaniola within the first quarter of a century.

EXPANSION TO OTHER AREAS
AROUND THE CARIBBEAN

Under Don Diego's governorship began that second phase of Spanish empire, the spread of conquest and colonization from Hispaniola as a base, with each conquest preceded and followed by exploration. The largest and most important island colony in the Caribbean was Cuba, which was to remain for the next two centuries a much greater source of wealth and bigger center of population than Hispaniola.

In 1508 Cuba had been circumnavigated by Sebastian de Ocampo; now in 1511 Don Diego Columbus sent Diego Velásquez, a wealthy and longtime resident of Hispaniola, to Cuba in command of settlement. Cuba provided so much better land that many *hidalgos* from Santo Domingo were glad to follow Velásquez. Though he had a difficult time subjugating the island, his first town, a tiny settlement called Baracoa, soon gave place as capital of Cuba to the city of Santiago, founded in 1514. Important for its fine harbor and its easy access from Santo Domingo, Santiago was soon the center of prosperous sugar plantations. Velásquez also founded Havana at the western end of the island in 1515: within a decade there were settlements along the coast between. Inland some mines were opened, and grants of Indian workers were given out.

Puerto Rico and Jamaica, third and fourth largest islands in the Greater Antilles, had been brought under Spanish sway a few years before this successful settlement of Cuba, though they were never destined to be as important. Juan Ponce de León, a picturesque and honorable *caballero* who had come out to Hispaniola in 1493 and had become a protégé of Ovando's, was given permission in 1508 to "trade with the Indians" on the nearby island of Puerto Rico. De León soon "pacified" the island, was made its governor, and organized a permanent settlement there in 1511. This was the town called San Juan, which was to be the seat of the third bishopric in the New World. De León left to discover Florida, but his island of Puerto Rico prospered without him. Meanwhile Jamaica, on which Columbus had been so long marooned, was conquered in 1509 by another *adelantado,* Juan de Esquivel, a "prudent man," who chased the Indians into the interior and ruled peacefully enough until his death three years later. Destined in a later century to be the base for English pirates and the home of English planters and traders, Jamaica in these early years was a thriving Spanish colony with a yard for shipbuilding.

From the islands, colonizing Spaniards spread to the mainland. The same Ojeda who had first seen Venezuela had returned again for pearls. Licenses to make permanent settlements on the Isthmus and the Colombian coast were granted in 1509 to him and to a rich Hispaniola planter named Diego de Nicuesa. Both *adelantados* attempted colonies and headed large expeditions to the pearl coast which came to grief and met starvation, and both leaders died. With one had sailed an illiterate adventurer named Francisco Pizarro, with the other a stowaway named Vasco Núñez de Balboa, who had escaped from his debts as a gentleman farmer on Hispaniola and hidden in an empty provision cask.

Then a man of thirty-five, Balboa may have failed in Santo Domingo, but on the Isthmus he was a successful commander of men and administrator of colonies. He was elected leader by the starving survivors of the disastrous Ojeda-Nicuesa expeditions, and helped them find a healthy site for a town at Darién. There he made friends with the Indians, who willingly brought in food. One of the chieftains told Balboa of a great body of water a few days' journey inland, and passed on to him the rumors of a highly civilized people with a "silver king" far to the south along that water. Though he had no legal status in the eyes of the government, Balboa decided to search for the western ocean, the so-called "South Sea." He set forth across the Isthmus on foot with a small force of the men he had, including the soldier Pizarro.

On September 25, 1513, Balboa stood on a hilltop from which he could see the Pacific, and four days later he waded out into the water and facing South took possession of all lands washed by the South Sea, in the name of the King of Spain. Before Balboa returned to the now thriving colony at Darién some sixty miles back on the other side of the Isthmus, Ferdinand in Spain had appointed a legal governor for the area, a seventy-four-year-old dynamo named Pedrarias de Ávila. When Pedrarias first arrived in Panama with many dapper gentlemen of the court dressed in silks and brocades, he allowed Balboa to continue his plans for exploring the South Sea. New orders from Spain made Balboa *adelantado* of the South Sea. With the help of his Indian allies Balboa built four brigantines at new docks he constructed on the Pacific side, and organized supplies to start down the coast. Now Pedrarias and his friends from court began to fear Balboa's ambition. The jealous and wily old governor sent for Balboa on a ruse, tried him for treason, and had him executed—some say that the executioner's sword was wielded by Pizarro, his companion in arms, who took over his private dream to find Peru. Balboa's ships were used in the exploration of the Pacific coast of Central America; his boat works were merged with Pedrarias' new town of Panama City. His name has been remembered for the view he had from a mountain top rather than for his natural leadership of men, his long-range plan, his town-building, or his Indian policy.

Pedrarias soon shifted the Isthmus capital from Darién on the Caribbean to Panama City on the Pacific, and a trail was begun to connect the two sides of the Isthmus. From these two bases the "Men of Pedrarias," as his followers were called, explored Costa Rica and Nicaragua, and established Spanish rule there. The Lake Nicaragua, so named from an Indian chief powerful in the region, had been discovered by an independent adventurer, Gil González Dávila, who had rebelled against Pedrarias, escaped to Santo Domingo, and there received a separate charter to exploit the Central American area. In the early 1520s, after Cortés had already conquered Mexico, the men of Gil González were involved in open warfare with the lieutenants of Pedrarias for control of the Nicaraguan area. The Indians were the ones to suffer most, being subject to every outrage, and were murdered and enslaved by the thousands at Pedrarias' order. One of Pedrarias' lieutenants, defeated by the adventurers in the squabble, was the handsome young Hernando de Soto, destined to play an important part in later history of the hemisphere, to help in the conquest of the Incas, and to die eventually on the shores of the Mississippi. As they advanced north into Honduras, all these warring Spaniards in the Nicaraguan and Costa Rican area were defeated in their turn by the agents and forces of Hernando Cortés.

The whole story of the conquest of Nicaragua, Costa Rica, and Panama is one of cruelty and jealous self-seeking. Pedrarias was removed from the governorship of Panama by royal order when news of his personal cruelty to Spaniard and Indian alike reached the young Charles V. He proceeded to rule as governor on the new frontier of Nicaragua, till he died of old age in his ninety-first year. Guatemala and Salvador were conquered by the "Men of Cortés" and the whole area was eventually ruled by Cortés' lieutenant from Guatemala City. With the Greater Antilles colonized, a pattern for administration worked out there, and the

Isthmus a part of the Spanish empire, attention turned to the invasion of the mainland of North America via Mexico.

Readings

Anderson, C. B. G., *Life and Letters of Vasco Núñez de Balboa* (1941)
d'Anghiera, Peter Martyr, *De Orbo Novo*, trans. F. A. MacNutt (2 vols., 1912)
Bancroft, H. H., *History of Central America* (3 vols., 1883–1887)
Benson, E. F., *Ferdinand Magellan* (1930)
Bolton, H. E., and T. M. Marshall, *Colonization of North America* (1921)
Bourne, E. G., *Spain in America* (1904; new ed., 1962)
Brebner, J. B., *Explorers of North America, 1492–1806* (1933; new ed., 1955)
Chamberlain, R. S., *Conquest and Colonization of Honduras, 1502–1550* (1948)
Fiske, J., *Discovery of America* (2 vols., 1896)
Gonzalo, Fernández de, *Natural History of the West Indies* (1959)
Guillemand, F. H. H., *Life of Magellan* (1890)
Hanke, L., *First Social Experiments in America* (1935)
———, *Spanish Struggle for Justice in the Conquest of America* (1949)
———, *Bartolomé de Las Casas* (1952)
———, *Aristotle and the American Indian* (1959)
Haring, C. H., *Spanish Empire in America* (1952)
Helps, A., *Life of Las Casas, the Apostle of the Indies* (1896)
———, *Spanish Conquest of America* (4 vols., 1900–1904)
Jane, C., *Select Documents Illustrating the Four Voyages of Columbus* (2 vols., 1930–1932)
Keen, B., ed., *Life of Admiral Christopher Columbus by his Son Ferdinand* (1959)
Kirkpatrick, F. A., *The Spanish Conquistadores* (1934)
MacNutt, F. A., *Bartholomew de Las Casas* (1909)
Means, P. A., *The Spanish Main: Focus of Envy 1492–1700* (1935)
Merriman, R. B., *Rise of the Spanish Empire in the Old World and the New* (Vols. II–IV, 1918–1934)
Morison, S. E., *Admiral of the Ocean Sea* (1942)
———, *Journals and Other Documents on the Life and Voyages of Christopher Columbus* (1964)
Moses, B., *Establishment of Spanish Rule in America* (1898)
Neasham, A., "Spain's Emigrants to the New World," *Hispanic American Historical Review*, XIX, 147–60
Newton, A. P., *European Nations in the West Indies (1493–1688)* (1933)
Nowell, C. E., ed., *Magellan's Voyage Around the World* (1962)
———, trans. and ed., *A Letter to Ferdinand and Isabella, 1503* (1965)
O'Gorman, E., *Invention of America* (1961)
Olson, J. E., and E. G. Bourne, eds., *The Northmen, Columbus and Cabot* (1906)
Parr, C. M., *So Noble a Captain—Life and Times of Ferdinand Magellan* (1953; 2nd ed. under title of *Ferdinand Magellan*, 1964)

Pohl, F. J., *Amerigo Vespucci—Pilot Major* (1944)
Richman, I. B., *The Spanish Conquerors* (1919)
Romoli, K., *Balboa of Darién, Discoverer of the Pacific* (1953)
Sauer, C. O., *The Early Spanish Main* (1966)
Simpson, L. B., *The Encomienda in New Spain* (1950)
———, *Laws of Burgos of 1512–1513* (1960)
Stevens, H., and F. W. Lucas, ed. and trans., *The New Laws of the Indies* (1892)
Vigneras, L. A., *Journal of Christopher Columbus* (1960)
Wright, I. A., *Early History of Cuba* (1916)
Zavala, S., *New Viewpoints on the Spanish Colonization of America* (1943)
———, *Political Philosophy of the Conquest of America* (1953)

Chapter 7

The Spanish Conquest
of North America to 1600

THE APPROACH TO MEXICO

BY 1519 THE ISTHMUS had been crossed and had yielded no great riches; the coasts of North and South America were being mapped, and neither golden kingdoms nor routes through to the riches of the Far East had been found. The Caribbean itself was now an old story. The killing and dying off of the natives led Spaniards on the search for slaves farther and farther away from their island bases and toward the east coast of the United States. There was a double movement in this advance during the next thirty years; one branch went directly west to the mainland of Mexico, one went northwest toward what is now the United States.

It seems ironical that in these movements away from the islands toward the mainland the Spaniards were so long in hearing of the Maya and the Aztecs. In 1512 a ship returning from Darién to Hispaniola had been wrecked on the coast of Yucatan and eighteen survivors had reached a Maya town. Perhaps the Maya had heard more about the Spaniards than the whites had heard about them; at any rate, all eighteen Spaniards were immediately seized when they came in to shore, and only two of them were saved from sacrifice on the local pyramid. One of them, Gerónimo de Aguilar, a priest, spent the next eight years fretting over his fate, serving cruel taskmasters who forced him to do women's work in the houseyards, and yearning for a Spanish ship which would free him from bondage. It was to Cortés' ship, anchored off Cozumel in 1519, that he finally escaped, and his knowledge of the local languages made him of great value to Cortés' expedition. The other survivor, a seaman named Guerrero, using his skills with rope and carpentry to win the respect of the Indians, became a petty chieftain among the decadent Maya, and helped the towns of Yucatan fight off the Spanish conquest as late as 1540.

Other men from the colony of Darién, men whose voyages were more successful than that of the marooned priest, reported the existence of stone cities on the peninsula of Yucatan. A group of veterans of Pedrarias' first campaigns on the Isthmus had returned to Cuba and were soon hired on slave-raiding expeditions back to the coasts they had heard rumors about. Their captain was Francisco Hernández de Córdova, whose venture was partially backed by Velásquez, governor of Cuba. In 1517 Córdova's men landed at several points on the Yucatan peninsula. They were attacked by the expert bowmen of the Maya, but not before they had traded for enough vessels and utensils of gold to whet the appetite of the Cuban governor. They were able to "limp" home to Cuba, having lost half of the men from the Darién colony. Their captain Córdova died shortly after his arrival in Cuba.

Governor Velásquez immediately dispatched another captain, his cousin

Hernando (or Fernando) Cortés.
Courtesy Pan American Union.

Juan de Grijalva, with orders to reconnoiter for information. Grijalva's well-armed expedition made forays along the Yucatan and Tabasco coasts, entered the river now named for the commander, and, cautious according to instructions, continued to skirt the coast as far north as the Pánuco River. When Grijalva returned without making any further landing, his cousin the governor chafed at his hesitancy and planned a bigger and better-equipped expedition under a more daring and able leader. The leader he chose was Hernando Cortés.

Just at the time that Cortés was to begin his great adventure in Mexico, the Gulf of Mexico coast was being mapped in greater detail. Francisco de Garay, governor of Jamaica, a rival of Velásquez, had sent Alonzo de Pineda out as his agent to explore the continental line of the Gulf in search of a strait. Pineda's work overlapped Grijalva's from the other direction; he had seen the mouth of a large river which was surely the Mississippi, and had then sailed counterclockwise around to overlap Grijalva's northward exploration, thus mapping the Gulf of Mexico coast from Florida to Vera Cruz. Pineda's master Garay then applied for and obtained permission to colonize Amichel, as the Texas-Tampico coast was first called; his grant and his efforts here were to run afoul of Cortés later on. In the story of the advance to Mexico, Córdova was the discoverer, Grijalva and Pineda the coastline explorers, but Hernando Cortés was the conqueror, the man who founded a really *New* Spain.

The story of Cortés and of his conquest of many millions of people with a few handfuls of soldiers is a romance for the ages, and has as its hero a natural leader of men. Born in Medellín, Estremadura in 1485, Cortés had been excited early by stories of the New World. He had left his student life as a young gentleman at the University of Salamanca and had gone to Santo Domingo in 1504. Here he soon made his mark in "gallantry about town," but found no quick fortune. Unwilling to farm in Hispaniola—"I did not come to till the soil like a peasant!"—he joined an expedition for the conquest of Cuba. There he attracted the attention of Velásquez by his potentialities as an organizer. He was then thirty-three, a vigorous, resourceful man, well set up and clean-cut, by nature a born gambler ready to stake his all on a single chance, but persistent and brave, fair in his treatment of the men who served under him, and capable of long-range planning.

He enthusiastically accepted the role of Grijalva's successor and was able to pay for the equipment he organized—in all, eleven vessels, 508 soldiers, and 109 seamen, as well as Cuban Indians, two Maya Indians previously captured by Córdova, sixteen horses, and several small cannon. We get to know his soldiers well, thanks to the description written afterwards by the famous chronicler and companion of Cortés, Bernal Díaz, who probably was also one of the original hundred men from Darién who had sailed with Córdova. Díaz, writing fifty years later, could still see the Men of Cortés "before his eyes," these future *conquistadores* destined for so many individual adventures in the next two decades. Díaz particularly remembered the sixteen horses which came on the first ships—"a light bay with three white feet";—"a gray mare who was a pacer but not fast";—

"a piebald horse inclining to black in the markings, with white forefeet, he turned out worthless";—"for Captain Cortés a vicious dark chestnut horse which died." How they wished there had been more horses, but they were so hard to come by in Cuba! The horses and the few small cannon were to be of great help in frightening the Indians who were unaccustomed to mounted soldiers or firearms.

Velásquez soon became suspicious and jealous of Cortés, who was so successful in acquiring all this retinue. When he revoked Cortés command, the dramatic Cortés upped anchor and sailed out of Santiago in defiance while the frustrated governor bellowed with rage. This was on November 18, 1518. Continuing secretly to enlist men in the smaller port towns along the coast of Cuba, Cortés was able to sail from the western point of the island in February, 1519. Men and equipment all organized, and himself in illegal command, he left for the mainland of Mexico and his destiny.

The expedition proceeded directly to the island of Cozumel off the coast of Yucatan. Here Cortés picked up that first Spaniard enslaved by the Maya, the priest Aguilar who was to act as interpreter among the Maya and other coastal tribes. With Aguilar aboard, Cortés' fleet landed on the Tabasco coast, where he had a first minor skirmish with the natives, terrorizing them with his seven cannon and his sixteen horses. After being defeated by these prancing mounted "gods," the Tabascans brought Cortés presents, among them twenty girl slaves. One of these, the beautiful girl Cortés was to name Marina, then about eighteen years old, was a chieftain's daughter from the Aztec highlands who had been a slave among these Maya-speaking Tabasco people. It was soon discovered that she spoke both the Aztec and Maya dialects; Aguilar, the marooned Spaniard, spoke Maya and Spanish. Thus Cortés, through two interpreters, spoke directly to all tribal leaders in the Aztec confederacy, and later to Montezuma. Doña Marina he took as his own mistress, kept her with him to Tenochtitlán, took her on an excursion to Honduras, and in later life granted her land and a position of respect and legitimized her son. Through her wise counsel the expedition was saved from disaster on many occasions.

From the Tabasco coast Cortés proceeded to the harbor of San Juan de Ulúa, familiar to several men on his expedition who had accompanied Grijalva a short time before. Here Cortés founded and laid out la Villa Rica de la Vera Cruz, first city of New Spain, on Good Friday, 1519. Immediately a *cabildo* or town council was elected; to it Cortés resigned the command bestowed upon him by Velásquez. Then the *cabildo* in turn appointed him *alcalde* and captain-general, thereby erasing the stigma of rebel, at least in his own conscience, and conferring legitimacy on the expedition in consonance with medieval Spanish practice. Thus Cortés could now consider himself independent of Velásquez and dependent directly on the crown. He persuaded his men to surrender their booty and shipped it off to Spain with a long explanatory letter in support of his position. Next he secretly scuttled his ships, thus preventing desertion and giving his men the alternative of fighting to win or dying in the attempt. On the Vera Cruz coast Cortés heard of the discontent rampant among the many tribes subject to the Aztec Confederacy—for example, the Totonacs of Cempoalla, axious to free themselves from Aztec control and willing to welcome an army with which they might make common cause.

THE FALL OF THE AZTEC EMPIRE

Montezuma, then "war chief" and emperor of the Aztec Federation, had heard of Córdova's and Grijalva's expeditions and he knew of Cortés' coming from afar; he feared that the Quetzalcoatl of song and story had returned in the white castles on the sea to claim his people. To placate this awe-inspiring rival Montezuma sent messengers bearing many beautiful gifts—masks and plates of gold, silver and turquoise, cotton cloth, feather mantles—giving Cortés greeting and asking him to leave peaceably. The golden objects whetted the Spanish appetite; news of disloyalty and disaffection in the empire encouraged the Spanish boldness. Cortés instructed the gift bearers to take back to Montezuma a picture story of the Spaniards' greeting and of their determination to visit the capital at Tenochtitlán.

Cortés had now spent several months at Vera Cruz; fortifications were built; a church had even been constructed and natives in the region converted. But men were dying of fever on the coast. The Cempoallans offered warriors and burden bearers by the hundreds. Leaving 150 men under Gonzalo de Sandoval to guard the Vera Cruz fort, in August, 1519, Cortés wound his way up through the luxuriant vegetation of the *tierra caliente* and climbed to the pine-clad slopes of the Sierra Madre, with snow-capped Orizaba gleaming on the left. Beyond Orizaba, Cortés' men fought a pitched battle with the independent nation of Tlaxcala. The natives were subdued after hard fighting and joined Cortés in an alliance against Montezuma. At Cholula, a religious capital and site of a sacred pyramid, the natives planned to murder Cortés. Dramatically, Marina, the faithful mistress, warned Cortés in time for him to turn the tables, massacre the nobles of Cholula, destroy the temple on the pyramid, and found a church in its place. Montezuma meanwhile had sent fresh envoys with more gifts and more requests to leave, but on hearing of Cortés' quick action against the Cholula conspiracy he felt that Quetzalcoatl's return was inevitable. A last brace of envoys arrived with their thousands of Indian allies and porters to guide Cortés' men to Tenochtitlán.

Now the Spaniards went in official convoy, having been proclaimed as gods. From the pass below Popocatépetl the whole valley of Anáhuac with its lakes and cities lay spread out before them. Pine forests gave way to corn fields, to villages with orchards and gardens—then to the large lake-shore towns of Xochimilco, Ixtapalapán, and Texcoco. The four causeways led across the lakes to the fair island city of Tenochtitlán. Chieftains from the four points of the compass around the lake came to greet the Spaniards ceremoniously at they advanced down out of the pass; crowds of common folk milled around in canoes to see the white gods and their supernatural animals. At last Montezuma came in a sedan chair. At this dramatic meeting between the Old World and the New, November 8, 1519, Cortés and Montezuma, both handsome leaders in their middle thirties, treated each other as equals. Their retinues joined in a single parade and went together into the city. Montezuma made the Spaniards his guests, and turned over a part of his own castle to them.

Here the Spaniards were sumptuously entertained for a week. They felt danger all around, however, for their Indian allies were outside beyond the causeways. Cortés decided on a bold move to strengthen his position. He brought Montezuma to the Spanish quarters by forceful "persuasion" and attempted to run the government through him. Montezuma lived thus as a hostage for several months, giving all the Spanish soldiers gold and other presents, providing them with both men and women slaves, and teaching them to play the Aztec equivalent of chess. They and he both seemed, on the surface at least, to live a gracious life of ease.

This domination of millions by a handful was rudely interrupted. Governor Velásquez back in Cuba, furious at Cortés, had sent a large expedition under Pánfilo de Narváez to arrest him. In May of 1520 Cortés was forced to make a quick journey to the coast to win over this force of over 1,000 Spaniards. The wily Cortés sent men ahead with gifts of gold to tempt the men from Cuba to join him, and easily won a brief battle with them. Most of the newcomers followed Cortés back up to Tenochtitlán. When he approached the causeways, however, Cortés' luck seemed to have deserted him and his former Indian friends avoided him.

Small wonder! Inside the city, Pedro de Alvarado, the impetuous lieutenant whom Cortés had left in charge, had become alarmed at the tension he sensed at an Aztec festival and had broken up the fiesta by force. Cortés and his new followers came back to the old quarters, but the air was hostile. Cortés blamed Alvarado, but the mischief was done. Montezuma sulked in the Spaniards' headquarters; Aztecs in the city brought Cortés and his band no food. Outside the palace, an Aztec prince aroused the citizens. Montezuma himself died from wounds received from stones thrown by his own people when he appeared on the palace roof to calm them.

There followed the sad night, *La Noche Triste*, of Mexican history, June 30, 1520. The Spaniards, deciding to sneak out of the city on the shortest causeway, secretly built a portable bridge to be carried out of the palace and through the streets. Drums on the pyramid aroused the populace; the Aztecs swarmed over the retreating Spaniards. The bridge helped them over the first gap in the causeway, but it stuck and could not be moved as other bridges ahead were hewn down by the Aztecs. The greedy Spanish soldiers who had loaded up with gold, especially the newcomers from Cuba, fell heavily into the water with their treasure. Their bodies became a bridge for others to pass over. Legend has it that Alvarado himself made a spectacular leap, using his lance as a vaulting pole, and cleared the gap. For every Indian the Spaniard killed, three took his place.

In the morning Cortés sat down beyond the lake shore to weep. A cypress tree under which he is reputed to have rested that night still stands today, marked by a plaque. His most trusted lieutenants, his two interpreters, a clever ship carpenter, and many Tlaxcalans had been saved, along with twenty-three cavalrymen. As for Spanish foot soldiers, of whom he had about 1300 the day before, no accurate count was kept of losses, but a third of the force must have perished.

Fighting other Aztec armies on the way, the little Spanish band returned to Tlaxcala. However, their Indian allies now determined to reorganize and destroy the Aztecs. Here Cortés showed himself to be a master strategist. Plans for the new campaign consumed a year of his time. More Spaniards and supplies intended for Narváez' men reached him from Cuba; munitions and reinforcements also came to him direct from royal officials at Hispaniola. His rescued ship carpenter and other craftsmen made the parts for thirteen brigantines which were carried over the pass below Popocatépetl and put together on Lake Texcoco. New-comers from Cuba had brought the smallpox to Mexico, a disease to which the Indians had no immunity and which acted as an ally to Cortés, killing the natives by the thousands. With the brigantines, the Spaniards had command of the lake and laid siege to the city, beginning April 28, 1521. For three months the brave Aztecs in Tenochtitlán, their fresh-water supply cut off, slowly starved, while the young son of Montezuma's brother, Cuauhtémoc, Mexico's national Indian hero, urged them on to a spirit of resistance. The Spaniards landed from the brigantines onto the causeways and destroyed the city block by block. It is said that Cortés grieved for the destruction of the city, hoping to have saved its beauty intact under the peaceful rule he had accomplished after seizing Montezuma. At last Cuauhtémoc surrendered when the city was five-sixths destroyed. All the survivors were allowed to go to villages in the country, and the corpse-ridden and disease-infested ruin was burned. So ended the Aztec Tenochtitlán. This was August, 1521. Martin Luther was defying papal authority for the first time in Germany, and Magellan's ships were sailing round the world.

EXPANSION FROM TENOCHTITLÁN
IN ALL DIRECTIONS

The fall of Mexico-Tenochtitlán was but the prelude to an extensive and far-flung series of conquests. The Spanish occupation spread in all directions and was carried on by the "Men of Cortés." He sent his lieutenants out north and south to pacify the country, while he himself gave the next three years to rebuilding the city. Indians were put to work laying out blocks on the plan of a Spanish city, with churches, monasteries, and government buildings, some of which are still standing today. The Spanish municipality of Mexico City was legally organized and city officials chosen. Paganism was uprooted, missionary fathers arrived to preach Christianity, and the Indians were given out in *encomiendas* to individual Spaniards. Cortés was made captain-general by order of the king in 1522.

While Cortés thus busied himself at constructive works, his lieutenants Sandoval and Orozco conquered the southern part of Vera Cruz, set up municipalities in the Valley of Puebla, and defeated the semicivilized

Dance of the Conquistadores, Sololá, Guatemala. Indians masked and dressed as Spanish conquerors still hold mock battles at yearly fiestas. *Courtesy Pan American Union.*

Zapotecs in the Valley of Oaxaca. North and west of Tenochtitlán, bands of Cortés' men, chiefly under Cristobal de Olid, conquered Michoacán and Jalisco. Thus, much of the most thickly settled area of modern Mexico was subdued by Spaniards while Cortés was still rebuilding the capital city. A shipyard was even constructed at Zacatula to prepare vessels for northward and southward expansion on the Pacific coast and to search for the elusive strait from the west side. Cortés himself left the capital again for the Gulf coast to crush a second group of Spanish rivals under Garay, who claimed the mouth of the Pánuco river. Here Cortés proceeded to subdue the Huasteca tribes and establish the town of Pánuco (modern Tampico), a settlement which was to remain the northeast outpost of Mexico for a number of years.

Meanwhile, Pedro de Alvarado had regained Cortés' confidence during the long months of the siege of Tenochtitlán and had served as the first *alcalde* or mayor in Mexico City. A handsome, swashbuckling captain with red, curly hair, he was called "Sunlight" by the Aztecs. When the Men of Cortés had gone out to the north and to the south, Cortés had sent the ambitious "Sunlight" off to far-distant Guatemala, from whence rumors of the highland Maya towns had reached Cortés in Mexico. Marching through the Isthmus of Tehuantepec, Alvarado and "a goodly company of cavalry and foot soldiers" reached the highlands of Guatemala in 1524. On the site of the modern Quetzaltenango he destroyed a well fortified city. Alvarado then successfully turned one highland tribe against another so that the towns fell easily, towns which are today sleepy Indian villages where weaving and spinning in the Maya pattern still go on. A Spanish capital, first established near the present site of Antigua, was destroyed by flood and earthquake within a decade and later moved twice to safer ground. Restless and always ambitious, Alvarado went on to conquer El Salvador, made a spectacular sea voyage down the west coast to Peru, returned to fight in northern Mexico, and met death there in a horseback accident.

More important rivals to Cortés and his lieutenants were the Men of Pedrarias, who were busy destroying Indian settlements in Central America. The lieutenant Cristobal de Olid was sent by sea to spread Cortés influence against Pedrarias and Gil González Dávila in the south. Going via Cuba, Olid arrived on the Honduras coast and proceeded to declare himself a separate adelantado free from Cortés' supervision. Cortés himself angrily set off for Honduras by land, leading a large expedition of soldiers, servants, and camp-followers over a route which is almost impassable even today. Cuauhtémoc, the heir to Montezuma, who had been in his turn the uneasy house guest of Cortés through these years, was dragged along, so that there might be no Indian revolt during Cortés' absence. On the forced march through the jungle terrain Cortés, himself physically ill, suspected a conspiracy among his Indian followers, and had Cuauhtémoc executed, an act which modern Mexicans consider the most infamous of all Cortés' deeds.

This expedition itself was unnecessary, for Olid had been killed in a mutiny of his own men by the time the exhausted Cortés found his camp in Honduras. When other loyal forces sent by Alvarado arrived from Guatemala to preserve Cortés' claims in northern Central America against the men from Panama, Cortés returned to Mexico by sea. Disappointed that the king had meanwhile stripped him of political authority and set up an appointed *audiencia* in Mexico, Cortés went to Spain in 1528, accompanied by forty Indian nobles and armed with rich presents for the king. Charles V was already carrying out plans for a vice-regal system to govern New Spain, plans which did not include the ambitious Cortés. He was merely given large land grants in Mexico, made a marquis, and allowed to return to devote himself to shipbuilding at Acapulco and to sea exploration on the Pacific for the next decade. Vainly he hoped to rebuild his prestige by discovering new islands and perhaps the elusive strait itself.

In 1532 Hurtado de Mendoza, sailing for Cortés, explored the Gulf of California. The following year two more ships were sent up the coast, and California and the pearl fisheries at La Paz were discovered. Cortés himself attempted to colonize La Paz, but the king's new governor in Mexico City blocked him at every turn. In 1539 Cortés' last fleet, under Francisco de Ulloa, returned from Lower California with the news that California was a peninsula, that its gulf dead-ended with the mouth of the Colorado. Cortés, faced with failure on the Pacific, returned to Spain to quarrel over the powers of the new viceroy in Mexico; he died near Seville practically unnoticed in 1547.

Yucatan, center of Maya culture, remained unconquered for two decades after the arrival of the Men of Cortés. This was partially due to the efforts of that marooned Spanish sailor, Guerrero, who enjoyed great prestige among the Maya and taught them how to drive every Spanish expedition away. Two Francisco Montejos, a father and then a son, spent their fortunes in fighting the Yucatan Maya, who blocked their trails, destroyed the sources of drinking water, and scorched their own earth to keep out the conquerors. Only when the Indians eventually quarreled among themselves, perhaps after the death of Guerrero, did the younger Montejo subdue the Maya tribes. The city of Mérida was founded on the site of Mayapán.

The rapid conquest of a goodly portion of Mexico by the Men of Cortés within a relatively few years was a remarkable feat. Indian unrest against the Aztec tyranny, the weakness and fatalism of Montezuma, the leadership qualities of Cortés and his able lieutenants, firearms, and horses, all had combined to make this possible. These men were not to be allowed to rule Mexico, however. The king sent officials to Mexico to assume Cortés' powers. A first *audiencia* was headed by the bitter enemy of Cortés, the Captain Nuño de Guzmán. When this court proved corrupt and inefficient, Charles sent a second group of judges, and finally appointed a viceroy. His first choice for this important post was Antonio de Mendoza who came to Mexico in 1535 with a large retinue and almost royal power. He ruled successfully and well until 1550, bringing peace and prosperity, sending out explorations north and south by land and sea, and governing the vast area from Guatemala to Guadalajara and beyond. After his term eight different viceroys served out the second half of the sixteenth century, while the wealth and area of New Spain expanded rapidly.

THE NORTHERN MYSTERY

The Spanish explorers of the first half-century after Columbus had not been satisfied merely to found Spanish settlements in the area from the Tropic of Cancer to the Isthmus of Panama. Beckoned by rumors of wealth in the north, stories of Gran Quivira and the Seven Cities of Cíbola, urged on by the quest for the Fountain of Youth and the hopes for the elusive strait, they unfolded the geography of a large part of North America. Certain fables remained to be exploded and the Spanish did so, following these fables in three directions, via Florida, New Mexico, and the California coast. Though not today part of Latin America, these regions still bear the stamp of Spain on their history, and the Spanish urge to see them had implications for the more rapid development of northern Mexico.

Florida, at first considered one of the large Caribbean islands, had been granted to Ponce de León, governor of Puerto Rico, as *adelantado* after he discovered the area in 1513. He was fatally wounded by Indians when he first attempted to colonize it and explore inland in 1521. A justice of the *audiencia* of Santo Domingo, Lucas Vásquez de Ayllón made an attempt to colonize in the area of South Carolina in 1526, and died of disease in his turn. A third unsuccessful try at colonizing Florida, by that time recognized as a peninsula, was made by that same Narváez whose troops had deserted to Cortés just before *La Noche Triste*. Narváez took 600 colonists, including the officer Álvar Núñez Cabeza de Vaca who was to figure in the future of both North and South America. Arriving at Tampa Bay in 1528, Narváez went ashore with half his men, leaving the other half to cruise along the coast to meet him later. Lured by stories of a golden land called Appalachee, Narváez traveled to an agricultural village of fifty clay huts near the present Talahassee. When he returned to the sea and found that his ships had deserted, he and his lieutenant, Cabeza de Vaca, went on to incredible adventures without them.

As far as Florida was concerned, that land waited for a fourth unsuccessful party under Hernando de Soto in 1539. This famous explorer of the southeastern area of today's United States had been one of the Men of Pedrarias who had helped conquer Nicaragua, had gone on to Peru with Pizarro, had amassed a fortune there for himself, and had returned famous to Spain as a charming and graceful young grandee. But the New World called him back; he received a grant from the king to explore and colonize Florida and persuaded 600 men from Spain to follow him. For two disappointing years in the interior of Alabama, northern Florida, and the southeastern Mississippi Valley, he tracked down every rumor of golden treasure and civilized cities. In May of 1541 he reached the Mississippi River just below Chickasaw Bluffs, Tennessee. Fever and disappointment killed de Soto on May 21, 1542; his survivors set his body adrift in the river, built a brigantine—which always seems to have been so easy for these Spanish explorers to do on the spot—and sailed down the Mississippi to the Gulf, to reach Pánuco four years after they had left Cuba.

Their description of the primitive state of the North American Indians and the lack of rich cities was born out by the adventures of the survivors of Narváez' expedition. Fourteen years before de Soto's death Narváez and his men, deserted by their ships on the coast of Florida, had killed their horses on the beach, and from the horsehides had constructed five small ships. In this "horsehide fleet" they hoped to cruise along the Gulf coast and reach Pánuco. By the time they had arrived at Galveston Island all the boats were wrecked and there were only 80 survivors, including the one officer, de Vaca. After a miserable winter on a diet of shellfish, only fifteen remained alive to become the slaves of the wild Tejas tribes. De Vaca tried to keep in touch with all the others, each held captive by a separate Indian group. For six years of degrading captivity the Spaniards refused to make a break for freedom by starting overland to find Pánuco. When only four remained alive, de Vaca persuaded them to follow him as wandering "medicine men," winning the Indians by giving simple remedies. Eventually they crossed the Rio Grande and worked south and west, by now revered as witch doctors and followed by many natives. In 1536 they came upon white men near the Spanish frontier town of Culiacán, after having been among the Indians eight years. They had crossed from Atlantic to Pacific, the first transcontinental hike in North America. The account de Vaca wrote of his adventures makes one of the most interesting stories of the period of exploration. From Mexico City de Vaca went to Spain and later obtained a governorship in the Plata region of South America.

The governor of the region around Culiacán, then called New Galicia, listened with excitement to the stories of the Pueblo Indians which de Vaca had heard while in Texas and New Mexico. One of the survivors of Narváez' horsehide fleet who had come all the way with de Vaca, a Negro slave named Estevánico, was glad to return across the Rio Grande as a guide for the missionary Friar Marcos de Niza, sent by the viceroy to scout the country of New Mexico and test de Vaca's stories. Estevánico was killed by Indians as he advanced on the first Pueblo Indian towns of the upper Rio Grande. The friar, walking several miles behind him, climbed a hill and saw a large town of two- and three-story houses; he returned to the northern Spanish outposts to report it as a "Silver City," one of those "Seven Cities" which had long been rumored among Spanish adventurers.

The friar's account spurred the governor himself, Francisco Vásquez de Coronado, to set out for the Pueblo country with 300 men and many horses. A sea expedition under Hernando de Alarcón paralleled their path and sailed up the Colorado River beyond the Gila. On a side trip, Lieutenant Cárdenas discovered the Grand Canyon of the Colorado. In the Zuñi country, Coronado soon found out that his Silver Cities were adobe pueblos. Ácoma and other villages in the Zuñi area of New Mexico, as well as the Rio Grande pueblos, are still on the same sites in New Mexico today. Coronado ravaged the crops, burned 200 Indians at the stake, and left hostility everywhere. The Indians finally persuaded him to leave by telling him of golden cities of Quivira out on the Great Plains. The misguided Spaniards crossed the Pecos into Texas to find only roving Apaches hunting buffalo.

With an advance guard Coronado went searching for Gran Quivira through the trackless grassland to the area near Wichita, Kansas. Some of the horses from his expedition ran loose and became the ancestors of the wild ponies of the plains, providing mounts for the Plains Indians. Coronado turned back to Mexico in 1542, two years after he had started, having found no city and no treasure. His journey had served only to disprove the existence of the legendary Quivira and Cíbola, and his report served to discourage further exploration in that area. Later advances were to be more gradual and solid, accompanied by town settlers, frontiersmen, and *encomenderos*—less romantic than Coronado, but more fundamental.

Further advance out into the Pacific was begun under Viceroy Mendoza during this first half-century. One expedition under Juan Rodríguez Cabrillo went in search of a strait along the coast of California. It was this expedition which discovered San Diego Bay in 1542. Cabrillo died en route but his ships, under Ferrelo, reached the present California-Oregon border. Another fleet under Ruy López d Villalobos sailed to the Philippines and made an unsuccessful attempt to oust the Portuguese from those islands legally claimed by Spain. By their very failure, these expeditions of Coronado, de Soto, Cabrillo, and Villalobos led the Spanish government to renew activity in areas closer to Mexico City and to concentrate on the economic development of agriculture and mining there.

THE MINES OF NORTHERN MEXICO

The second half of the sixteenth century (1542–1609) was to witness the occupation of parts of northern Mexico, Florida, New Mexico, and the Philippine Islands, and the further exploration of the Pacific coast. But the pace, the methods, and the reasons for this new half-century of conquest were different from those of the dashingly romantic first half. After 1550, the Spaniards, their first bloom of excitement over, were interested in developing silver mines, in raising cattle and planting crops to feed the new cities they had already founded, and in doing missionary work among primitive tribes. They also began to worry about foreign competition from other Europeans—the French and the English; they had to protect the treasure fleets and to push their farthest outposts against encroachments. Thus the expansion of this new period was less aggressive, and a little more defensive.

Since almost every advance was begun with the idea of permanent towns and settled agricultural or mineral development, the conquests were undertaken as an investment by men of means, great captains or *adelantados*. They came from settled New World communities where many docile Indians were already at work, and they used these Indians, the Tarascans or the Tlaxcalans, as settlers, farmers and miners, to countercolonize, and to guard the frontier against the wilder tribes of the north.

The first such *adelantado* was an arch enemy of Cortés, Nuño de Guzmán, "a natural gangster," who had governed in Pánuco, and who headed the first *audiencia* or "court" staff to discipline and control the Men of Cortés. He soon needed much more control himself. As governor along the Pánuco River he had amassed a fortune by shipping slaves to the Caribbean islands. *Persona non grata* in Mexico City because of these activities, he was nevertheless a friend of Velásquez and of the slave buyers in Cuba and, perhaps through them, was not punished for his Pánuco activities. Instead, he was soon carving out a private empire for himself in a region he was to call New Galicia. Cortés' lieutenants had conquered the Tarascans in Michoacán; much of the land south of the Río Santiago in the present states of Jalisco and Nayarit had already been granted as *encomiendas*. Now in 1529 came Guzmán, with a royal sanction as governor, to spend the next seven years exploring Nayarit and Sinaloa, granting *encomiendas* to himself and his friends, selling Indians into slavery, and destroying their villages. But he brought in the Spanish tradition of correctly founded Spanish towns, and set up Compostela and Culiacán on the two edges, north and south, of his "empire." Here were *cabildos*, the municipal councils which gave the faint color of legality to Guzmán's action. For lack of docile Indian labor and a ready market for their products, the *encomenderos* of New Galicia made no profits. Soon Guzmán was called before the reform government in Mexico City, there to be imprisoned by the new viceroy, Antonio de Mendoza. Francisco de Coronado was made governor in his place to establish firmer royal control over the frontier province, before taking off himself for Gran Quivira.

While Coronado was gone to the north an uprising occurred in New Galicia which is called the Mixton War. The natives, long abused and terrified by the Guzmán regime, took advantage of the new governor's absence in 1540 and carefully planned a full-scale war. Alvarado met his death ignominiously when a horse fell on him as he fled from an Indian ambush. Finally, the viceroy himself arrived in the midst of the Mixton carnage and crushed the revolt by force of numbers and the weapons of the fresh royal troops. By 1548 the area was organized as the province of New Galicia, with an *audiencia*, a bishop, and a cathedral at Guadalajara in 1550. It was subdivided into districts under governors, and the Indians organized under local *alcaldes* subject to *encomenderos*. The smallpox, which had helped Cortés devastate the area around Mexico City two decades earlier, came with the troops to New Galicia during the Mixton War; the Indians who survived it were forced into the heavy work in field and mine which brought a new prosperity to the region.

This was the prosperity of a "silver rush." In 1542 silver had been discovered in Michoacán, but that discovery was soon eclipsed in 1546 by the great silver strike made near today's Zacatecas by Juan de Tolosa, a captain sent out to subdue pockets of rebellious Indians left unconquered from the Mixton War. Setting the Indians to mining for him, Tolosa had several mule loads of ore on the way to Mexico City in a few weeks. Soon he was joined by three other veteran commanders of the Mixton War, Cristobal de Oñate, Diego de Ibarra, and Baltazar Termiño de Bañuelos, men who had money enough behind them from previous adventures to exploit the mines, establish mining camps, contract for laborers, hire muleteers for transporting the ore, and support all these people until the silver profits began to flow back. The four of them became the richest men in Mexico; their fabulous fortunes were to be used in making explorations and opening mines farther to the north, in establishing packroutes back to the larger towns, and in building up the frontier provinces. Guadalajara, and the *encomiendas* in Jalisco which had failed under Guzmán, now had a new reason for existence. The region lay on the silver route; Guadalajara was the new distributing center for goods for the silver rush, a market for food, a center of farming and cattle raising. The cattle prospered on the fields of Jalisco, but the Indians did not. Cattle trampled the corn fields and destroyed the native agriculture. The Indians lost land to the stockmen and were driven as slaves to the mines.

Under the new viceroy, Luis de Velasco, systematic exploration beyond the frontiers took place in the 1560s with the idea of establishing permanent Spanish and Indian towns for defense against the still unsubdued Chichimecas who were raiding the last line of settlement. Especially important here was the work of Francisco de Ibarra, nephew of one of the four developers of the silver boom. From New Galicia and Zacatecas he went farther north and, using his uncle's fortune to fit out mule drivers, soldiers, and Indian colonists, he worked for two decades carving out a future province called New Vizcaya, chiefly in the present states of Zacatecas,

Durango, and Sinaloa. A provincial government was organized on the same plan as all Spanish government in the new territories. Francisco de Ibarra himself was named governor in 1562; the town of Durango was founded in the next year and remained for many years the military capital of all the northern country, including the settlements in southern Chihuahua.

Mines were found in this new area, but native Indians were few. Who was to be forced to work in the mines? The frontier community of Santa Barbara, where silver deposits were found in 1563, was on the River Conchos, which drained into the Rio Grande. Down the canyons and valleys of the Conchos and across the Rio Grande went the slave raiders to capture the primitive Tejas Indians among whom de Vaca had served as a slave. Thus did the Spanish frontier reach into Texas in the time of the *adelantado* Ibarra. Interested in looking for new river valleys and harbors as well as for villages to be enslaved, Ibarra explored Sinaloa, ascended the Pacific slope from Culiacán up the river valleys and across into Chihuahua. When Ibarra died in 1570 he had over twenty years of exploring, mining, colonizing, and efficient administration to his credit. Cattle were brought into his Durango region, and they remain today the chief source of wealth there. San Luis Potosí, today one of the world's most productive silver mines, had been developed in 1576, and Tlaxcalan colonists were brought in to hold the frontier. By then the mines were being extended northeast of New Vizcaya and Durango by a father-and-son team, both named Francisco de Urdiñola.

On the Gulf coast, in today's state of Tamaulipas,[1] another province called New León was created in 1579, the area north and west from Pánuco and delimiting New Galicia and New Vizcaya. Its founder was Luis de Carabajal whose money-making slave raids to supply labor to the mines were stopped by the Inquisition, which condemned him as a heretic. In 1596 the lieutenant governor of New León, Montemayor, founded the city of Monterrey, which after 1600 became the center of Franciscan missionary activity. Today it is one of Mexico's chief industrial centers. Thus by the end of the century the frontier of settlement of Mexico was roughly a line drawn some hundred miles below the mouth of the Rio Grande on the Gulf of Mexico, and just north of Monterrey across Mexico to a point high up in Sinaloa on the Gulf of California. However firm that line might have been, during the same half-century several areas beyond it had been explored and occupied. Northern Mexico, with its mines, its forts, its cattle ranches, and its missions, was to be a base for Spanish expansion north of the Rio Grande.

SPANISH EXPLORATION AND OCCUPATION
IN THE PRESENT UNITED STATES

In the American Southwest—Texas, New Mexico, Arizona, and California—and to a lesser extent in Florida, Spanish colonial history is an important part of the regional heritage. Of little importance in the develop-

1 See map showing states of modern Mexico, p. 465.

ment of modern Latin America, these regions deserve some attention as points of the farthest Spanish frontier, and as areas where Spain was forced on the defensive against the encroachments of other powers. Rumors that Francis Drake had found the Northwest Passage in 1579 stimulated a renewed interest in the regions to the north, which had been called "the very worst country that is warmed by the sun," in Coronado's own reports. Indians caught on slave raids north of the Rio Grande reported again on the towns of the Pueblos. Working on the idea that these people should be Christianized and a frontier set for Spain farther north nearer the "strait," explorations were made into the area in 1580–1582 and in the early 1590s. Meanwhile, rich ores had been reported on a foray into Arizona. Don Juan de Oñate, wealthy relative of two of the Big Four, was made *adelantado* for the northern region in 1595, and in 1598 went at his own expense on an extensive exploration to the Arkansas River on the east and the Gulf of California on the west. Oñate, who had with him 130 soldiers and their families and 7,000 cattle and horses, made a temporary settlement. He fought and subdued the pueblo of Ácoma, but could make no money from the investment, so gave up his governorship and returned to the Zacatecas mines and from there to Spain.

The Crown then assumed control of the colony, considering the risk worth the time and effort. Under direct royal authority Governor Pedro de Peralta founded the city of Santa Fe in 1609, a town which still remains one of the symbols of Spanish influence in the Southwest. Its establishment a hundred years after Ojeda and Nicuesa received a grant to search for pearls on the Isthmus marks the end of a colorful century of discovery, conquest, and occupation in North America.

There had also been a renewal of activity on the Atlantic coast. Spanish attempts to colonize Florida had not ended with de Soto. That fourth effort at Florida settlement had been followed by a fifth in 1549 under Fray Luís Cancer, and a sixth in 1559–1561 under Tristán de Luna and Villafañe. This last failure was enough for King Philip II, who no longer considered Florida worthwhile.

The need for bases remained, however. The fleets of Spanish treasure ships had to have refuge from hurricanes and pirates. So, when French Protestants under Jean Ribault and René de Laudonnière successfully settled 300 colonists on the northern Florida coast in 1562–1564, Philip changed his mind. He sent an able organizer, Pedro Menéndez de Avilés, to found St. Augustine, first permanent settlement in today's United States, within a hundred miles of the French fort. His men massacred the French settlers; a French captain in turn massacred a Spanish coastal garrison, but Menéndez de Avilés held firm in his hold on the coast for Spain. From his successful colony further exploration was carried on inland to the interior of Georgia and along the coast up to Chesapeake Bay. Jesuits and Franciscans founded missions, and the little settlement became a buffer against both English and French in the Bahama Channel shipping lanes when Spain began to lose her monopoly on the Atlantic coast after 1600.

On the Pacific slope and in the Far West, Spain was also forced to action by the activities of other European nations. Portuguese merchants were making good in the Orient via their round-Africa route, and the Spaniards had no choice at first but to leave it to them, for though they had worked out a route from Acapulco across the Pacific, they could not find a way to return with the wind. The only way home led round Africa, Portugal's own private route. Finally in 1564, Miguel López de Legazpi was sent to lay an effective claim to the Philippines, first seen by Magellan, and to work out a route back. His chief navigator, Fray Andrés de Urdañeta, found such a route via the northern Pacific. Now the Philippines were within reach going and coming by an all-Spanish route; Manila was founded and Spanish rule established in the islands. An *audiencia* was established at Manila in 1583 and attached to the viceroyalty of New Spain. A single yearly ship, the famous Manila Galleon of the colonial trade fairs, went every year to the islands and came back loaded with the luxuries of the China and Philippine trade.

Because of the northern return route of the Manila Galleon, the California coast came again into importance in Spanish eyes. Sailors needed fresh supplies to ward off scurvy; pearl fisheries might be found; foreign intruders could be scared away if Spain developed California. Hence captains of the Galleon were instructed to search for suitable harbors as way stations along the coast. When none were found, it was decided to send explorers directly from Mexico. In 1596 a special expedition under Sebastián Vizcaíno established the colony of La Paz in lower California. Vizcaíno was also commissioned by the king to explore the upper coast, which he did in 1602, naming various points and recommending Monterey Bay as an important site for a colony. With the death of Philip II in 1598 an era ended, the project was forgotten, and nothing was done for another century and a half about the stopping points for ships on the return trip to Mexico from the Far East.

This exploration of the California coast marked the farthest northward advance of Spanish rule in the sixteenth century. Thus passed the heroic age of Spanish colonization in North America, an age of fantastic accomplishment.

Readings

Aiton, A. S., *Antonio de Mendoza: First Viceroy of New Spain* (1927)
Bannon, J. F., *The Spanish Conquistadores* (1960)
Bennett, C. E., *Laudonnière and Fort Caroline: History and Documents* (1964)
Bishop, M., *The Odyssey of Cabeza de Vaca* (1933)
Bolton, H. E., *Coronado on the Turquoise Trail: Knight of Pueblos and Plains* (1949)
———, *Spanish Borderlands* (1921)
———, *Spanish Explorations in the Southwest, 1542–1706* (1916)
Borah, W., *Early Colonial Trade and Navigation Between Mexico and Peru* (1954)
———, *Silk Industry* (1943)
———, *New Spain's Century of Depression* (1951)

Bourne, E. G., *Spain in America*, ed. B. Keen (1962)

Braden, C. S., *Religious Aspects of the Conquest of Mexico* (1930)

Brebner, J. B., *Explorers of North America, 1492–1806* (1933)

Cerwin, H., *Bernal Diaz: Historian of the Conquest* (1963)

Chamberlain, R. S., *Conquest and Colonization of Honduras, 1502–1550* (1953)

———, *Conquest and Colonization of Yucatan, 1517–1550* (1948)

Clissold, S., *Seven Cities of Cíbola* (1962)

Collis, M., *Cortés and Montezuma* (1955)

Connor, J. T., *Pedro Menéndez de Avilés* (1923)

Day, A. G., *Coronado's Quest* (1940)

Descola, J., *The Conquistadors* (1957)

Diaz del Castillo, B., *True History of the Conquest of New Spain* (many editions)

Fuentes, P. de, *The Conquistadors: First Person Accounts of the Conquest of Mexico* (1963)

Garcilaso de la Vega, *The Florida of the Inca*, ed. and trans. J. G. and J. J. Varner (1951)

Gardner, C. H., *The Constant Captain: Gonzalo de Sandoval* (1961)

———, *Naval Power in the Conquest of Mexico* (1956)

Gibson, C., *Tlaxcala in the 16th Century* (1952)

Guardia, R. F., *History of the Discovery and Conquest of Costa Rica*, trans. H. W. Van Dyke (1913)

Hallenbeck, C., *Alvar Nuñez Cabeza de Vaca: The Journey and Route of the First Europeans to Cross the Continent of North America, 1534–1536* (1934)

Hammond, G. P., and A. Rey, eds., *Narratives of the Coronado Expedition, 1540–1542* (2 vols., 1940)

———, *Oñate: Colonizer of New Mexico* (2 vols., 1953)

Hanke, L., *Bartolomé de Las Casas* (1952)

Hodge, F. W., and T. H. Lewis, *Spanish Explorers in the Southern United States, 1528–1543* (1907)

Horgan, P., *Conquistadors in North American History* (1963)

Kelly, J. E., *Pedro de Alvarado, Conquistador* (1932)

Kinigan, A., trans., *Barcías Chronological History of the Continent of Florida* (1951)

Leon-Portilla, M., ed., *Broken Spears: The Aztec Account of the Conquest of Mexico* (1961)

López de Gómara, F., *Cortés; The Life of the Conqueror by His Secretary*, trans. and ed. L. B. Simpson (1964)

Lowery, W., *Spanish Settlements Within Present Limits of the United States* (2 vols., 1911)

MacNutt, F. A., *Fernando Cortes and the Conquest of Mexico* (1908)

———, *Letters of Cortes to Charles V* (2 vols., 1908)

Madariaga, S., *Hernan Cortés* (1941)

Maynard, T., *De Soto and the Conquistadores* (1930)

Mecham, J. L., *Francisco de Ibarra and Nueva Vizcaya* (1927)

Menucy, A., *Florida's Menéndez, Captain General of the Ocean Sea* (1965)

Merriman, R. B., *Rise of Spanish Empire*, Vols. III and IV (1934)

Parry, J. H., *The Audiencia of New Galicia in the Sixteenth Century* (1948)

Powell, P. W., *Soldiers, Indians and Silver: The Northward Advance of New Spain, 1550–1600* (1952)

Prescott, W. H., *History of the Conquest of Mexico* (many editions)

Priestley, H. I., *Coming of the White Man; 1492–1848* (1929)

————, *Tristán de Luna* (2 vols., 1936)

Ribaut, J., *The Whole and True Discouerye of Terra Florida, 1563*, ed. D. L. Dowd (1964)

Richman, I. B., *Spanish Conquerors* (1919)

Sauer, C. O., *Colima of New Spain in the Sixteenth Century* (1948)

————, *The Early Spanish Main* (1966)

————, *Road to Cibola* (1932)

Simpson, L. B., *Exploitation of Land in Central Mexico in the Sixteenth Century* (1952)

Taylor, M., *Impetuous Alvarado* (1936)

Verrill, A. H., *Conquerors of South and Central America* (1943)

Wagner, H. R., ed., *Discovery of New Spain in 1518 by Juan de Grijalva* (1942)

————, *Rise of Fernando Cortés* (1944)

————, *Spanish Voyages to the Northwest Coast of America in the Sixteenth Century* (1929)

West, R. C., *Mining Community of North New Spain: The Parral Mining District* (1949)

Chapter 8

The Spanish Conquest
of South America to 1600

THE PIZARROS IN INCALAND

AN INDIAN CHIEFTAIN, watching Balboa in 1511 as the Spanish captain weighed golden objects taken from his Panamanian Chibcha tribe, is supposed to have struck the scales and cried, "If this is what you prize so much that you are willing to leave your distant homes, and risk even life itself for it, I can tell you of a land where they eat and drink out of golden vessels, and gold is as cheap as iron is with you." Balboa heard other stories of Birú, or Peru, lands to the south where the fabulous Incas lived. On the Pacific coast another Indian is said to have stooped on the beach and modeled for Balboa in the wet sand a representation of a llama, as he tried to tell Balboa's men of the glamorous lands where such animals were as tame as their own horses. With Balboa at his first sight of the Pacific in 1513 was a soldier named Francisco Pizarro who was eventually to find such lands and see such animals. Stories of the riches of the Incas had already reached the Europeans from various other directions when Pascual de Andagoya sailed south along the west coast of Colombia in 1522 and reached a region called Birú. He brought back alluring stories of riches to the south, riches which he himself could not reach owing to an incapacitating illness. Pizarro was still on the Isthmus restlessly looking for some way to travel south.

Francisco Pizarro, poor, proud, cruel, and adventurous, was actually an illiterate swineherd of Estremadura. Illegitimate son of a minor aristocrat, he spent his youth in the poorest peasant surroundings. When, through the influence of his father, he was able to sail to America, he had nothing save his "cloak and sword." He had come to Darién with Ojeda in 1509, a bold, resourceful, persistent man of unusual physical strength, already nearing forty. In Panama, granted an *encomienda* for his loyalty to Pedrarias, he had amassed some wealth, so life in the New World had not passed him by. But he was obsessed with Balboa's old dream of conquering Incaland, and so formed a three-way partnership with two other Men of Pedrarias. Diego de Almagro, second of the partnership, was, like Pizarro, a soldier of fortune of questionable birth. He had been a servant at the court of Spain, and, coming under a cloud when he stabbed a man, had left quickly for America; but he was more generous and frank than Pizarro.

The third partner was the vicar of Panama, a priest named Hernando de Luque; their business partnership was so formal and official that even Pedrarias owned a share. In 1524 each of the active partners, Pizarro and Almagro, took a ship south along the Colombian coast, returning with gold enough to interest their backers in a more elaborate expedition of 160 men. On this second trip one of their pilots made a contact with Túmbez, a prosperous port town in northern Peru, and both partners landed in rich villages of the Ecuadorean coast. Here they had such brisk opposition from the Indians—which cost Almagro an eye—that the partners decided they needed a larger force. Almagro returned to Panama for help, while Pizarro and a few loyal men stayed on tiny Gallo Island off the Ecuadorean coast till his partner should return. The next ship they saw was a vessel from Panama sent by the new legal governor there to force them to give up the whole plan. Dramatically, Pizarro appealed to his men to stay with him —"As for me, I go south!" Thirteen men stayed, half-starving on the island, till another ship came months later. This time, Pizarro and his men went as far as Túmbez, received gold vessels and vicuña wool in trade, and took a young Indian, Felipillo, to be trained as interpreter. They knew, however, that the governor was now hostile to them; any further help must come directly from Spain. Pizarro himself set out for the homeland.

It was the summer of 1529 when Pizarro appeared in the Spanish court. On July 26, Charles V gave Pizarro his written instructions for a larger expedition. In this document, both Almagro and Pizarro were given titles as legitimate gentlemen; even the thirteen who had stuck with Pizarro on Gallo Island were all made knights. Almagro was to be commander of Túmbez; their partner the vicar was to go there as bishop. Pizarro himself, being the only one on the spot at court, was granted 200 leagues of territory south of the Gulf of Guayaquil, and was made governor, captain-general, and *adelantado* for life. He had to recruit his own forces, however—a difficult task since everyone was more interested in going to Mexico. So Pizarro went to his old home in Estremadura, enlisted his two full brothers, Gonzalo and Juan, his father's one legitimate son, Hernando Pizarro, and Martín de Alcántara, a half-brother on his mother's side. These infamous and avaricious brothers were to bring destruction to the Incas and internecine strife to the Spaniards in Peru. Though they all survived many battles, each died by violence or imprisonment. With them also went a young nephew, Pedro Pizarro, as page; he alone was to leave a good record, and became a famous chronicler of the conquest.

Back in Panama, Pizarro picked up more recruits, including Hernando de Soto, who brought two ships down from Nicaragua. In January, 1531, with 180 men and twenty-seven horses, Pizarro set sail from Panama—with Almagro to follow as usual—and came again to Túmbez. After destroying that town, and founding another Spanish municipality named San Miguel on the coast, he decided not to wait for Almagro and reinforcements but to march directly east over the Andes into the central valleys at Caxamarca, where the Inca ruler was holding court.

Like Cortés, Pizarro came to his new kingdom at an opportune time. The old Inca ruler Huayna Capac had died about 1527, leaving a quarrel between his successors—Huáscar, the legal heir, and Atahualpa, son of a Quito-born concubine. When the Spaniards arrived, Atahualpa had just won this civil war and was consolidating his empire by setting up a capital at Caxamarca halfway between Cuzco and Quito. De Soto, now with the Pizarro brothers, had been in touch with the envoys of Atahualpa and reported this situation to Pizarro. To Caxamarca, then, came Pizarro, in November, 1532, after a difficult climb of forty-five days, with 102 infantrymen and sixty-two horses. Unlike Montezuma, Atahualpa heard with scorn of the coming of these interlopers, these destroyers of Túmbez; the llama-using Incas lacked the Aztecs' superstitious fear of the horses. When Pizarro arrived in Caxamarca, Atahualpa, who had an army of 40,000 near at hand, came in from a bathing spa at the hot springs outside his city leading a large retinue, and deigned to meet the Spaniards in the square. Pizarro's chaplain, Fray Vicente de Valverde, made a long speech through Felipillo the interpreter, telling Atahualpa that Charles V was the only true king, and the Christian God the only true God. When Atahualpa asked by what authority the Christian God stood over his god, the Sun, he was shown a testament. It was a book with clasps; Atahualpa struggled to open it, looked at the strange black lines on the white paper, and scornfully cast it down. The Spaniards needed only this excuse of sacrilege to rush in, fire their cannons into the Indian crowd, and take Atahualpa captive in the midst of a general slaughter of his followers.

Atahualpa, handsome, grave of countenance, with fierce flashing eyes, was in the prime of life, perhaps about thirty-five years of age. Held in captivity while the Spaniards lived in Caxamarca, he was treated much as the hostage Montezuma had been treated by Cortés. His servants and his wives waited on him; he learned to play chess with de Soto; and he was exposed to the doctrine of Christianity, expounded to him by Valverde. But Atahualpa was of a more determined character than Montezuma. He offered the treasure-hungry Spaniards gold enough to cover the floor of his quarters. When the Spaniards seemed scornful, he offered to fill the room up to a nine-foot height as a price for his release—a "king's ransom." Two smaller rooms were to be filled with silver. Pizarro hypocritically agreed, if it were to be done in two months.

Immediately runners went out with *quipu* messages to all points of the empire. Soon the treasure began to pour in; porters carried loads of vases and temple vessels, and even thrones. It has been estimated that the ransom amounted to about 13,265 pounds of gold and 26,000 pounds of silver. Spaniards who went out to get more were carried on Indian litters all the way to Cuzco, where they were hospitably received as emissaries of Atahualpa's new masters. Hernando Pizarro went to the ancient city of Pachacamac and there received the same treatment; the mass of the Incas were willing to accept the new rulers without a murmur. At this juncture Almagro and his men arrived from Panama.

It was not in the scheme of things to release Atahualpa, however. The Spaniards had to find some excuse to get rid of him. The half-brother Huáscar, held prisoner by Atahualpa, had offered the Spaniards even higher ransom money for his own release, but Atahualpa had secretly ordered him murdered in prison. Now the Spaniards could accuse Atahualpa of murder, ransom or no. He was condemned to be burnt at the stake for this crime. When he was told that if he accepted Christianity he would only be strangled, not burned, he became "converted." He submitted stoically to being garroted in the plaza of Caxamarca and was given a Christian burial on August 29, 1533.

The Pizarros now planned to march on Cuzco, take over the whole empire, and found a large Spanish capital on some good harbor to the south. The ransom gold was melted down and divided, one-fifth being sent to the king via that gentlemanly and only educated Pizarro brother, Hernando. The rest of the loot was given out to the soldiers under the eagle eye of "fair-play" de Soto. Here commenced the greatest difficulty Pizarro was to have in Peru—not battle with the Indians, but quarrels among the Spaniards. Almagro's men received a much smaller share than Pizarro's men, because they had reached Caxamarca three months after the seizure of Atahualpa, and Pizarro's men could claim to have had the greater peril and hardship. As soon as the treasure was distributed, gambling began for large stakes, fortunes were won and lost, and discipline broke down. Pizarro saw that action was necessary, and set out on a long march to Cuzco. Beautiful Cuzco, city of the children of the Sun, offered no resistance and was systematically looted. Then the ever legal-minded Spaniards set up a Spanish municipality there in March, 1534; two *alcaldes* and a town council of eight members were appointed from among themselves. Soldiers received houses in town and large tracts of agricultural land with many Indians in *encomienda*. A younger brother of Huáscar, Manco Capac, was set up as a puppet to maintain the pretence of Inca authority.

Now two years had passed since the subjection of Túmbez. Almagro, temporarily pacified by gold looted at Cuzco, set off to Quito, a city already conquered by a lieutenant named Benalcázar and organized into a Spanish municipality. Both of these Spaniards were hurrying to ward off the rumored coming of Alvarado, the conqueror of Guatemala, who was cruising with his fleet down the coast. Gonzalo and Juan Pizarro ruled Cuzco; Francisco went to seek a site for a new capital on the coast. The valley of Rimac near the harbor of Callao seemed the ideal place; there the capital was founded in 1535. The Indian word Rimac was corrupted to Lima, and Pizarro began the construction of a fine Spanish city. Here Pizarro was for a time an efficient administrator; colonists came and other cities were founded soon thereafter at Guayaquil and Trujillo. Alvarado himself, "welcomed" at Quito, was bought off for 100,000 pesos of gold, and after a pleasant visit with Pizarro, went happily back to Guatemala and his death in northern Mexico, though hundreds of men who came with him stayed in Peru.

PERU—THROUGH CHAOS TO RICH COLONY

Although the conquest of Peru now seemed over except for consolidation, it was to degenerate into civil war between factions of Spaniards. As knowledge of the new riches spread like wildfire and adventurers of all descriptions came to Peru, they soon divided into two factions owing to the Almagro-Pizarro jealousy. Hernando Pizarro had taken the king's share of Atahualpa's ransom to Spain, and had returned with a royal order for the division of the new territory. Territories, "in the north for an extent of 270 leagues," were granted to Pizarro; lands 200 leagues to the south of Pizarro's grant were given to Almagro. The bishop of Panama was to come to Peru and set the dividing line, a trip which he never found time to make. Naturally, a dispute arose as to who should own the former Inca capital of Cuzco. The inevitable bloodshed was temporarily averted when the Men of Pizarro were able to persuade Almagro that more riches lay in the unexplored south. Hernando Pizarro assumed control of Cuzco; Francisco went down to the coast to develop his new capital at Lima.

The *Almagristas*, the Men of Almagro, now spent all their gold in preparing for a journey to the unknown Chile. Spaniards to the number of 550, thousands of Indian porters, and flocks of llamas set out over the Bolivian highlands and through the mountainous deserts of northern Chile. When Almagro finally entered the fertile valley of central Chile, he found only poverty-stricken, hostile Indians living in adobe villages. The bankrupt *Almagristas* returned to Peru more embittered at the Pizarros than ever and determined to take Cuzco for their own.

While Almagro was gone and Francisco Pizarro was busy in Lima, the Inca puppet Manco Capac revolted and led a great army of Inca villagers in a siege of the Spaniards inside Cuzco. Other Indians harassed the new coastal cities till the return of the Men of Almagro ended the many months of rebellion. Manco Capac, hopeful that the two groups of Spaniards would kill each other off, withdrew his remaining forces and went into retirement in an Inca stronghold hidden away in the mountains, where he held court and harassed the Spaniards by forays until his death. His descendants considered themselves ruling Incas, albeit only over a few poor villages.

Manco's hope that the Spaniards would quarrel to the death among themselves almost came true. Almagro had returned from Chile and taken over Cuzco after defeating Pizarro's troops. This meant open civil war, for

Francisco Pizarro was not one to give in easily. The inevitable decisive battle took place at Las Salinas, a salt plain outside Cuzco, April 6, 1538. Six hundred *Almagristas* fought eight hundred *Pizarristas*, while bemused Indians looked on from the hills. Two hundred Spaniards were killed and Almagro himself was taken to prison, where Hernando Pizarro decided to execute him. Almagro, now a decrepit seventy-five-year-old man with no fortune to show for his years of campaigning, pleaded with Hernando, "I was the first ladder by which you and your brother mounted up." Hernando was deaf to these pleas and had him strangled in prison.

The Pizarro brothers were now in complete control. Juan had been killed in Manco's rebellion, but the other three fared well. Gonzalo went beyond Lake Titicaca to found the colony of Charcas, mother of today's Bolivia, where, at Potosí, a silver strike far richer than that of northern Mexico was to be made before the century was out. Gonzalo granted himself a rich *encomienda* among the Aymarás, and arranged for the founding of Chuquisaca, today's Sucre, in 1539. Francisco went on to found Arequipa and to organize his own *encomienda* with 100,000 Indians northeast of Lima. Pedro de Valdivia, a faithful Pizarro supporter, was sent to Chile to make a permanent settlement. Gonzalo was appointed governor of Quito, where he had further fantastic adventures. Hernando meanwhile had gone to Spain, but the king, who had already heard stories of the death of Almagro, threw him into prison. For twenty-two years he lay in jail, to be released eventually, in time to succumb to old age in his hundredth year, the only Pizarro to die a natural death.

Both Francisco and Gonzalo died by violence in the continued quarrels in Peru. A young *mestizo* son of Almagro, an eighteen-year-old called Almagro the Lad, rallied the remaining *Almagristas* and assassinated both Francisco and his half-brother Martín de Alcántara in their own house on June 25, 1541. When news of this continued feud reached the king he sent an experienced lawyer, Vaca de Castro, to restore order in Peru. His first problem was to destroy the forces of Almagro the Lad in a pitched battle in September, 1542, and to have this last of the *Almagristas* executed. This left Gonzalo, now backed by a large private army. To deal with him, Vaca de Castro, was replaced by an official viceroy, the aristocrat Blasco Núñez Vela, who with a group of judges to comprise an *audiencia* was ordered to end the rule of the Pizarro faction and to bring legal Spanish government to the chaotic new colony.

In the same year, 1542, the government in Spain had become increasingly concerned with the conditions of the Indians in all the New World colonies, and had promulgated a list of regulations to end hereditary *encomiendas* and to limit many abuses of forced labor among the Indians. These were known as the New Laws, and Núñez Vela came ready to enforce them in tumultuous Peru. But the *conquistadores*, who had gambled away most of the Inca gold, now owned thousands of acres of fertile lands worked by hundreds of thousands of Indian serfs. They bitterly opposed the New Laws and rallied behind Gonzalo to defy the viceroy.

Gonzalo Pizarro, popular man of the hour to all factions except those newcomers on the viceroy's side, took Cuzco, imprisoned the viceroy, and then made himself dictator of Lima. A few loyal Spaniards came to the viceroy's aid, helping him to escape and to collect a small army near Quito, where he was met and defeated by Gonzalo. Acting with kingly power, Gonzalo had the viceroy beheaded. This last of the Pizarros was now definitely an outlaw who had committed treason, though the whole colony including the settlements in Panama lived for two years under his unchallenged power. This time the king sent a scholarly priest, Pedro de la Gasca,

Inca towns in the Peruvian Andes. The Spaniards built the buildings but changed the Indians little.
Photo by Helen Miller Bailey.

to bring Gonzalo to heel. Under his blandishments Gonzalo's henchmen in the Isthmus "deserted" back to the king, as did the captains and sailors on the private "fleet" Gonzalo had been using to patrol the coast. By the time La Gasca landed at Túmbez with a large loyal force in June of 1547, Gonzalo realized the game was up. Retreating in a cat-and-mouse play with this new royal agent, Gonzalo was finally forced to surrender near Cuzco on April 9, 1548, while his men deserted to La Gasca by the hundreds.

Gonzalo himself was unceremoniously beheaded. Thus came the final doom of the Pizarro brothers, sixteen years after the death of Atahualpa. The "Age of the *Conquistadores*" in Peru was ended.

Pedro de la Gasca now turned his strong hand to reform in the face of seething discontent, working busily at balancing finances and founding new towns, including La Paz in Bolivia. He was clever in rewarding those of Gonzalo's friends who had switched to his side and was purposely lax in enforcing the New Laws against hereditary *encomiendas*. When La Gasca returned to Spain in 1550, the king replaced him with Antonio de Mendoza, who had been the successful first viceroy of Mexico for fifteen years; however, Mendoza was old and ill when he came to Peru in 1551, and died after ten months there. Subsequent viceroys, good and bad, came and went, accompanied by large retinues of servants, courtiers, and relations. Meanwhile settlers came in great numbers to Peru to take out grants of land worked by Indians, to operate mines in the Andes, to work as shopkeepers and artisans in the new Spanish cities.

Most famous and successful viceroy of Peru in the second half of the sixteenth century was Francisco de Toledo, who in his years in Peru from 1569 to 1581, really established the Spanish colonial system on South America's west coast. Philip II had given him a long list of detailed instructions. He toured the provinces personally, increased the output of the new silver mines in Bolivia, established a mint, sent silver home to Spain in fleet after fleet, planned the founding of a university in Lima, and encouraged the recording of Inca history. Though he ended the shadowy rule of the last Incas in their mountain fastnesses by the execution of Tupac Amaru, Manco Capac's youngest son, he improved conditions for the Indians at work in field and mine. He stiffened the morale of the clergy, introduced the Inquisition, built roads, aqueducts, and canals, and founded hospitals.

By 1600 Peru was Spain's most valuable colony, pouring silver down from the Bolivian Andes, supporting a cultured aristocracy in Lima, working its highland Indians in agriculture and handcrafts. Two sociological processes characteristic of all Spanish colonies were being developed— Spanish towns and cities had been founded, and Spanish blood had been injected into the population, often through legal intermarriage, for few women came from Spain in the early years, and Spanish law allowed marriage with Christianized Indian women. The rich silver veins of Potosí had been found by 1545, and in 1563 the Spaniards had stumbled on the remarkable mercury deposit at Huancavelica; silver refining by the mercury process became the basis of Peru's prosperity. All this was not easy for the Spanish rulers, however. A series of weak successors to Toledo faced problems of foreign rivalry in the Pacific beginning with Drake; earthquakes, internal disorders, and smallpox epidemics disturbed the population. The methods of government developed in Peru and in Mexico, the economic system, the interplay of the new social classes, the activities of missionaries and church officials, and the development of a scholarly culture in Lima all are topics that will be treated in Part III of this volume.

EXPLORATIONS AND SETTLEMENT
IN NORTHERN SOUTH AMERICA

The story of northern South America, including the area called "the mainland," the "Spanish Main," or *Tierra Firme*, is the history of present-day Venezuela, Colombia, and parts of Ecuador and of the Amazon Basin. Movements pushed into this area from all directions—from the Antilles, from Panama, and from Peru. It began with Columbus' first sight of the Orinoco beyond Trinidad. As it unfolded, the story was to include sagas of pearl fishing and slave hunting among the Caribs on the coast, the attempts of a German banking house over two decades to settle Venezuela, the explorations of the interior by way of the Orinoco and its tributaries on the one hand and from eastern Peru down the Amazon on the other, the advance north from Ecuador up into the southern valleys of Colombia, the search for *El Dorado*, the Gilded Man, and the final meeting of three such searching parties in the *savanna* or valley of Bogotá. It is a confusing story, with many swashbuckling heroes.

Ojeda, ill-fated commander of the expedition on which Balboa sailed, had named the Venezuela coast. Although the area had been put under control of the *audiencia* in Hispaniola, settlement was slow owing to the fierceness of the Indians and the exploitation of the coast by slave raiders. Actual permanent occupation began with the founding of Coro in 1527 by Juan de Ampués. Diego de Ordaz, who had been with Cortés in Mexico, was made *adelantado* of the Orinoco country and was the first to go inland in search of mythical kingdoms. All subsequent adventures in the same direction failed to bring about any permanent settlement. Caracas, today's capital of Venezuela, was not established until 1567. The whole Venezuelan coast waited for development until Negro slaves were imported to work in place of the untamed Caribs.

The Amazon Valley meanwhile was explored by accident from Incaland. Before he began his quarrels with the viceroy, Gonzalo Pizarro, as governor of Quito, had set out from Quito on Christmas Day, 1539, in search of a mythical Land of Cinnamon, the land of the Omaguas and the country of *El Dorado* in the *montaña* to the east. The expedition started with 210 Spaniards, driving 4,000 chained Indian bearers, 5,000 live hogs for food, and large flocks of llamas. After weeks of hardship they came down into a land where progress was difficult "without blows of the hatchet," so dense was the jungle. On an upper tributary of the Amazon, the versatile Spaniards built two boats. Many of the highland Indians they brought with them had died in the low altitudes; the herd of swine had all been eaten. A Captain Francisco de Orellana set out downriver in the boats with sixty men to find help and food; Gonzalo Pizarro never saw him again and always considered that he had deserted. Gonzalo and the survivors found their tortuous way back to Quito a year later (1542), half-starved, having eaten their 100 horses. Meanwhile, Orellana had gone rapidly on down the current until it was impossible to return. Eventually he reached the Amazon, which he named after the women of the Greek myth, saying that he had passed villages in which only the women came out with spears. Halfway down the river he built a brigantine, even "forging two thousand very good nails" over a charcoal fire from the weapons and armor the Spaniards carried. When the crew of this brigantine reached the river mouth eight months after they had left Gonzalo Pizarro, they were able to sail out into the Atlantic and reach Spanish settlements in the Caribbean. One passage from the Amazon across to and out down the Orinoco was made in 1559 under a group of illegal outlaws from Peru led by the infamous Lope de Aguirre.

At this time the Venezuelan interior was in non-Spanish hands. Charles V, with his German background, had borrowed money from a German banking house named Welser. He had given the Welsers a proprietary grant to the Venezuela area in 1528, from which they hoped to retrieve their loans to the king by slaves, pearls, and gold. Their agents made sporadic explorations along the coast from the Magdalena to the Orinoco, urged on by stories of Meta, Omagua, and *El Dorado*, the Gilded Man, far inland. One of these agents was Nikolaus Federmann, the wisest and most daring of the German leaders, who with 400 men started out up the Orinoco-Meta system in 1536, hoping to find a back-door route to *El Dorado*. By the time they came to the upper reaches of the Meta, he and less than half his men had survived the snow of the Andes passes to emerge from the mountains, emaciated, in skins, their beards long and matted. They were in the high Chibcha plateau of Bogotá, but Spaniards from the Colombian coast had come there ahead of them up the Magdalena. Meanwhile, other German agents of the Welsers on the coast had ravaged the Indians and plundered the country. They lost the company's investment, and their grant was canceled by the Council of the Indies in 1546. Venezuela itself was neglected by the Spanish kings for many years until pirates raided the coast and forced attention to its defense.

The story of the search for *El Dorado* must now shift to the Colombian coast. Facing the Caribbean and the Pacific, lying adjacent to Peru and Panama, Colombia was entered from all directions. The real beginning of permanent settlement was the founding of Santa Marta by Rodrigo de Bastidas in 1525 and of Cartagena by Pedro de Heredia in 1533. Explorers from these bases had explored the lower Magdalena, where they naturally heard many stories of the Chibcha kingdoms in the highlands. The final successful expedition which reached the highland valley was led by the chief justice of Santa Marta, Gonzalo Jiménez de Quesada, an earnest and honest servant of the king who took with him about 800 men. They left that colony on April 6, 1536, and, after suffering months of hardship in the lowlands of the Magdalena, 166 survivors found the upper reaches of the river and discovered an Indian trail up a steep escarpment into the Andes. Their fifty-nine remaining horses were lifted over cliffs in baskets; men and supplies were pulled up by ropes. A year after leaving Santa Marta, Quesada emerged upon the *savanna* of Bogotá, where he found the cultivated fields of the Chibchas, who decorated their wooden huts with gold discs and their persons with emeralds. By playing one tribe against the other, Quesada's soldiers easily conquered the Chibchas and then lived happily in the valley, counting their gold and jewels and talking idly of returning to report to Spain. Quesada named this new land New Granada; Santa Fé de Bogotá was founded as his Spanish capital on August 6, 1538.

It was upon this peaceful scene that two other parties arrived in search of *El Dorado*. In February of 1539 Federmann and his emaciated men came down from the east into the valley. Since they were only 160 and Quesada's well-fed, well-entrenched men were 166, there was at first no challenge, only succor and sympathy. Now, close on Federmann's heels, came word of still a third expedition, "Spaniards well clothed and supplied with arms, riding fine horses and driving 300 head of swine for food." This second group of interlopers, coming from the south through the highlands of Ecuador, were led by Sebastián de Benalcázar, whose single lifetime included half the story of the Spanish conquest of the Americas. He had sailed as a boy with Columbus, settled in Santo Domingo, served in Darién under Balboa, in Nicaragua under Pedrarias, and had followed Pizarro to Peru, where he soon became governor of Quito. Bored as soon as the conquest of Quito was over, he had struck north on his own to find *El Dorado*. He had come up through the rich valleys of the upper Cauca in 1536, founding Cali and Popayán on the way.

Thus, parties in the name of King Charles V had approached Bogotá from three directions to meet amicably in the year 1539. If the two new arrivals had combined, they could have replaced the first comers, but Quesada gave the Germans a gift of 4,000 gold pesos, and they stayed by him. After three months of guarded pleasantries, all three leaders went back down the precipitous trail to the Magdalena, to Santa Marta together, and so to Spain. Federmann asked for royal favor in vain, as the German grant was already in dispute. Quesada spent months traveling in Europe, spending the emeralds he had brought before he finally pleaded his case at court; then he was created "Marshal of Bogotá," a title of dignity but little power. He returned to live peacefully in his new city, to lead one more unsuccessful expedition looking for *El Dorado*, and to serve as town councilman until after his eightieth birthday. As for Benalcázar, he was made governor of the towns he founded in southwestern Colombia. When he returned from Spain to this royal grant, he made his rule there effective, setting up the town of Pasto and establishing successful agricultural and mining colonies.

New Granada, including the coast towns, Benalcázar's territory, and Bogotá, was made the seat of an *audiencia* in 1550; a bishopric was established there and missions started. The history of the area till 1600 is a confusion of disputes over grants of *encomienda*, the work of the Indians, and the power of the governors over the archbishops. The coast towns on the Spanish Main particularly suffered from the raids of Drake and other English privateers, ill omen of the destruction to be wreaked by pirates on that coast in the next century.

THE SETTLEMENT OF CHILE

From Peru the conquest had spread, moving north with Benalcázar from Ecuador to Colombia, east with Orellana down the Amazon, and south into Chile, a land only partially infiltrated by Inca civilization, and occupied by the fierce Araucanian Indians beyond the River Maule. The embittered men of Almagro had told all Spaniards in Peru that it was an inhospitable and unfruitful land. Four years after Almagro's failure there, however, one of the Men of Pizarro, Pedro de Valdivia, a persevering Estremaduran and a gentleman born, forty years old at the time of the invasion of Incaland, had asked Pizarro for the Almagrist grant in Chile. Pizarro, considering this territory unclaimed after the defeat and death of Almagro, had gladly given it to Valdivia, helping him raise an expedition of 150 Spaniards and 1,000 Inca farmers, with mares and swine for breeding and seed, grain, and tools for cultivation. Valdivia even took his own mistress, a Spanish woman named Inez Suárez, known in history as "the Conqueror's Lady."

The party left Cuzco in January of 1540. When Valdivia reached the central Chilean valley, he found that the local Indians remembered Almagro's mistreatment, and resisted the Spaniards' effort to force them to work. With the help of the colonists he had brought, however, Valdivia founded the city of Santiago—today one of South America's great capitals —just a year after he had left Cuzco. He laid out Santiago as the typical rectangular Spanish city, with central plaza, church, *cabildo*, and prison. He called the settlers into an open town meeting, and had them "elect" him "captain-general and governor." The first mayor was one of his lieutenants, who built an aqueduct to bring water into the town, made peace with the Indians, and set the men to planting crops and washing gold in the nearby river. Valdivia, like Cortés, was interested in expanding his colony and built ships for further exploration.

The good fortune did not last. Six months later the Indians rose up and destroyed Santiago; the crops were burned and the Spaniards had to live on roots while they sent to Peru for aid. They needed gold to persuade Pizarro to send reinforcements, and they had found very little in Chile, but they worked up all they had into golden stirrups to cajole the Peruvians. With this show of wealth their envoy was successful in getting more men to come to save Chile. Santiago was rebuilt, more colonists arrived, and Valparaiso was founded for sea communication with Peru in 1544. Meanwhile, the dashing Valdivia had himself been censured for mismanagement and debt and ordered either to marry or get rid of his mistress. Valdivia married her off to another Spaniard and returned to Peru to clear his name and get more help against the wild Araucanians. When he returned to Santiago in 1549 he had with him his own legal wife who had been left behind in Spain the first time; he also had clear title to the governorship granted him by the new viceroy.

Back in Chile, Valdivia, now in his fifties, was anxious to make more of a name for himself in conquests of wilder country. The town of La

Serena in the Valley of Coquimbo to the north had been founded to protect communications with Peru; now some settlements must be set up to the south to protect the central valley from the Araucanians. In 1550 Valdivia himself went beyond the Bío Bío River and founded the cities of Concepción, Imperial, Valdivia, and Villarica. Below these towns the Araucanians continued to inspire dissatisfaction and revolt among the Indians on the established *encomiendas* of the central valley, and to harass Valdivia's new towns to the south.

The leader of many guerilla raids made by the Araucanians into the valley was a young Indian named Lautaro, today one of the heroes of South America, a symbol of the struggle for freedom. As a fifteen-year-old boy, Lautaro had been captured by Valdivia, and had served for four years as head groom in charge of Valdivia's horses. But he burned with a zeal for the independence of all Indian peoples in Chile and secretly organized the guerillas, finally running away from Valdivia's service to lead them himself. Lautaro's insurrections gave Valdivia the excuse for a raid south of the Bío Bío with 200 men, but he was surrounded by Lautaro's men, captured, and put to death at the Indian town of Tucapel on New Year's Day in 1554.

To avenge the death of the Chilean leader another Spanish force went into Araucanian territory and fought Lautaro for three more years. Finally in 1557, while still in his early twenties, Lautaro was defeated and killed in battle, and the untamed Indians retreated south of the Bío Bío forever. The Araucanians never bowed to Spanish rule over their tribe, however, and remained a problem for the independent nation of Chile till the second half of the nineteenth century. The Spaniards had such respect for the independent spirit of these natives that Lautaro was made the hero of a long poem written by one of Valdivia's own men. Chile remained a "fighting frontier," and the war against the Araucanians continued as a great expense to the Crown.

After Valdivia's death his lieutenants quarreled over the succession till the king had to intervene, as he had done in Peru, by sending an official governor, young Hurtado de Mendoza, son of the viceroy. Under this governor, rival claimants to Valdivia's power were expelled, town founding went ahead, and explorations toward the Straits of Magellan and Patagonia were made by sea.

From Chile's central valley and from Peru, Spaniards crossed the Andes and founded towns in today's Argentina—Santiago del Estero in 1553, and Mendoza in the province of Cuyo just across the Andes from Santiago in 1561. All these, like Chile itself, were colonies that were planned from the first to live by agriculture. In spite of flood, earthquake, epidemic, and drought, Chile slowly improved by 1600. Cattle, horses, sheep, and pigs brought prosperity to the settlers, though insufficient revenue to please the king. The irrigated lands of the valley were planted to vineyards and orchards, to wheat, maize, and hemp. These things were raised by Indian laborers on the large estates, the feudal holdings of a white aristocracy around Santiago. The same types of crops were also raised on smaller holdings in the outpost regions. Thus Chile remained a fighting frontier, an agricultural colony, a pleasant enough place to live, in periods between wars. But it had to be subsidized from Peru and was never a source of pride and wealth for Spain.

THE PLATA RIVER, AN ENTRY
INTO THE FAR SOUTH

The Plata valley was an area long neglected by the agencies of the mother country, though today it is Spanish South America's most cosmopolitan and prosperous area. There was no treasure there, and only the wildest, most "unusable" Indians. When settlers finally came in any number —from Peru, from Chile, and from the Atlantic coast—they came for agriculture and livestock grazing, or to keep other nations out.

At first the Plata estuary had been the stopping place on the route round the new continents in search of the Orient. One such searcher, Juan Díaz de Solís, had been killed there and had left a group of survivors, some of whom were stranded on the coast of Brazil. As the story goes, one of his survivors, Aleixo García, crossed from the Atlantic coast and ascended the Pilcomayo, one of the tributaries nearest the Andes; after reaching Incaland, he returned to tell the remaining survivors among the Guaraní the fabulous stories of a "White King," a "Sierra de la Plata." Though García was himself killed later by the Guaraní, some of his fellow men were eventually found by other Spaniards, and the second-hand account they had of Inca silver soon brought Sebastian Cabot to the region on a disappointing search for silver in 1526. Then interest in the estuary died when Panama was accepted as a closer route to Inca silver.

Portuguese encroachments on the south Brazilian coast eventually frightened the Spanish king, and, though he was unwilling to spend royal money on this distant shore, he did grant the region to a very rich and famous man, Don Pedro de Mendoza, who would pay all expenses of colonization. Mendoza hoped to find an easy route overland to the rumored silver kingdom and planned for a big return on his investment. He came to South America with eleven vessels and over 2,000 settlers, including some of the most illustrious men of Spain, together with equipment for a large colony and many cattle and horses. Mendoza himself was old and ill; his men quarreled during a stop on the Brazilian coast for fresh water, and the expedition arrived disgruntled. In early February or March, 1536, Mendoza founded the town of Nuestra Señora de Buen Aire.

At first the primitive Indians brought in guanaco meat and fish, but it took a great deal of food to feed 2,000 Spaniards, who "did not come to till the soil but to find silver kings." When the Spaniards demanded more food, they had a bloody battle on their hands. From that time on the Indians were their enemies, while the Spaniards starved inside the stockade. Too sick to continue in the colony, Mendoza sailed for Spain and died on the way, his investment lost. An eyewitness account tells how the survivors at Buenos Aires ate the corpses of the dead.

Meanwhile, before Mendoza left he had sent a party of explorers up the Paraná to search for a better place for a colony and also, if possible, to find a route up into the Andes to Peru. It was commanded by Juan de Ayolas, the most trustworthy and devoted of those with Mendoza. His party established a fort at Corpus Christi; they went up the Paraguay River and found friendly Guaraní Indians living in villages, cultivating fields, and raising corn and manioc. How different from the guanaco-hunting pampas Indians who were howling around the stockade back at Buenos Aires! Here where the Pilcomayo runs into the Paraguay, a camp was set up named in honor of the Assumption of the Virgin, Asunción. A lieutenant named Domingo Martínez de Irala was left to found forts along the Paraguay while Ayolas set out across the Chaco following rumors of the silver in Bolivia. Historians think Ayolas reached Inca outposts but was murdered on the way back.

Irala meanwhile built a fort at Asunción in 1537, gathered supplies from the Guaraní Indians, and did some exploring on his own. When he knew Ayolas was dead, he assumed leadership. The starving colonists at Buenos Aires and on the Paraná ascended to Asunción, where Irala built a large town. It was the first permanent settlement in the area, and Irala was elected its first governor. Only a third of Mendoza's colonists had survived to reach Asunción. On the pampas were left a few horses of the expedition—perhaps seven mares and two stallions—which could not be captured and put on the "brigantines" for Asunción; from them sprang the wild horses of Argentina, numbering in the thousands before the century was out. Some cattle were perhaps "marooned" there also, as later comers found great droves of wild cattle.

Now there was no royally appointed governor in the colony; there was only Irala, who had been chosen by the settlers and had taken things into his own hands. He put the peaceful agricultural Guaraní to work, and settled down himself, marrying all seven daughters of a Guaraní chief. He and his associates were not to be left undisturbed by the home government in their happy seclusion of the forests of Paraguay, however. Charles V determined to help Mendoza's survivors, and to send them an official governor. Cabeza de Vaca, that famous pedestrian, had become bored with the life of retirement in Spain. He asked for a governorship in the New World, was sent with 400 men to the Plata as *adelantado* and governor in 1540. De Vaca landed four months later at Santa Catarina Island on the southern coast of Brazil. Being an experienced hiker, he sent his ships on down the coast and up to Asunción by the long river route, and walked himself, with 250 men and twenty-six horses, a thousand miles straight west to Asunción. He probably was the first white man to see the Iguassú Falls (unless it be that man of mystery, Aleixo García), and he described the lush land on his route as "a garden" compared to that which he had walked through in Texas and New Mexico.

When he arrived in March, 1542, the new governor received a very cold welcome in Irala's colony. He had been ordered to refound a city at the mouth of the Plata, but the Asunción settlers, remembering the miseries suffered there, refused to return downriver. He tried to set up a regal court in the wilds of Paraguay, and there was hostility between his men and the older settlers. Out of a sense of gratitude to the many Indians who had befriended him on his transcontinental hike in North America, Cabeza de Vaca meant to stop the abuse of Indian laborers and to check the polygamy practiced by the white men among the Indian women. While de Vaca busied himself with expeditions up the Pilcomayo, the settlers, determined to keep their many Indian wives and their easy way of life, rose up in rebellion against him. On his return from the futile trip into the Gran Chaco they put him in a dark little adobe prison in Asunción for eight months while they built a "caravel," not just a mere brigantine. When it was finished they shipped him back to Spain. The king seems to have sided with the rebels, for Cabeza de Vaca was in disgrace at home during many years of litigation. Eventually he was given a judicial office in Seville, where he lived to a very old age.

When the "caravel" was two days downstream with Cabeza de Vaca aboard her, Irala, who had returned from a search for the headwaters of the Paraguay River on which de Vaca had sent him, was re-elected governor. By this time the royal court had again lost interest in the Plata, so Irala's election was confirmed. He lived on as a successful governor for twelve more years, continually sending out exploring parties. On December 7, 1548, a messenger from one of his expeditions which had crossed the Bolivian Chaco reached the viceroy at Lima, having traveled all the way on foot. Sheep and goats were introduced over this mountain trail from Peru, and cows were later brought in from Brazil. Though Argentine historians deride Irala as a bad administrator and blame him for abandoning the first Buenos Aires and for sending Cabeza de Vaca home, Paraguayan historians praise him as a true leader of men, a friend to the Guaraní, and a national hero. By proclamation of the town council of Asunción in 1602, "they weep even today in this land for Domingo Martínez de Irala"—and who wept that long afterward for Pizarro or Cortés? Before his death in 1556, 1,500 Spaniards and who knows how many half-breeds and Guaraní were living in Asunción; the city covered three square miles, had three churches, two schools, and even a weaving establishment, while three less important Paraguayan frontier towns had been founded to hold the line against the Portuguese in Brazil. But the mouth of the Plata was still a "no man's land."

During the years that followed Irala's death there was a succession of governors, some chosen by the colonists, some royal appointees. Under one of these, Ortiz de Zárate, the project of refounding Buenos Aires was taken under serious consideration. As leader for this venture he chose his own nephew, Juan de Garay, a true pioneer spirit of the New World who had come to Peru when only fourteen. As a partisan of Asunción, Garay wanted to keep the Spaniards of Peru from advancing into the Plata. He also knew that a town at the Plata mouth would keep out the Portuguese and establish direct communication from the sea into the interior—a port for Paraguay. In 1573, as a first step in his new project, he had taken eighty-four settlers from Asunción to found the town of Santa Fé, halfway downriver to the Plata mouth. Various other pioneer projects involved Garay until 1580. In March of that year he set out downriver with sixty-three men, only ten of them from Spain, for he wanted young men born in Asunción and used to frontier life. He also took farm implements and munitions, perhaps 1,000 horses, 500 cows, and "other equipment for founding a city" at the Plata mouth.

Having arrived at the old site, these second settlers easily fought off the pampas Indians, now all mounted bareback on those wild horses descended from Mendoza's few. Three miles from Mendoza's old fort, Garay proclaimed Buenos Aires a city on June 11, 1580, and laid out 144 square blocks. An *alcalde* or mayor was elected, and he and Garay proceeded to divide the land for farming, with a parcel for each family to work by its own labor. Then he set the new colonists to killing the wild cattle and drying the hides. When a locally built ship carried his official report of all this activity back to Spain, it took a load to hides with it, a symbol of the source of the future wealth of Argentina. Buenos Aires was now permanently established; by 1600 it had a population of 3,000. Garay spent the rest of his life maintaining authority between Asunción, Santa Fé, and Buenos Aires and traveling to and from these places. On such a journey he was ambushed by hostile Indians and killed in 1583, though he had always been a friend of the Indians and a leader of communities composed almost entirely of settlers of half-Indian blood.

But what is now the area of Argentina was not settled from Asunción alone. A thin stream of colonists crossed the Andes from Chile in 1561, to settle at Mendoza and other places in the province of Cuyo; this area was governed from Santiago until 1776. A larger trickle of colonists —Peruvians, whom the Paraguayans hated—came down from Bolivia into the northwest. They founded Tucumán in 1565, Córdova in 1573, Salta in 1582, and Jujuy in 1591. This area was incorporated into a governmental unit under the *audiencia* of Upper Peru or Charcas. Agricultural crops were developed here which found ready markets in the mining areas of Potosí and in Lima. In spite of their Peruvian origin, Mendoza, Tucumán, and Córdova are all cities of Argentina today, built by second-generation sons of the New World, sons who loved freedom, chose their own leaders, and often did their own work. No gold was discovered, no docile Indians served as slaves. Democratic town councils often did the governing, as Peruvian influence faded after 1600. Thus the Argentines of this area pride themselves on their democratic origins. The Plata towns, involved in constant clashes with the Portuguese on the Brazilian border, remained a frontier for two centuries. The interior towns, Córdova, Tucumán, Santa Fé, and Salta for centuries were in large part dependent on overland trade between Buenos Aires and Peru, and were to resent Buenos Aires domination into modern times. By 1617, Asunción itself had been separated from Buenos Aires as a separate governmental unit.

Thus, by the end of the sixteenth century a great part of South America had been definitely colonized by Spain. The semicircle of settlement stretched from the Isthmus, down along the Andes through Bogotá, Quito, Peru, and Chile, eastward over the Andes to Mendoza, across the pampas to the Plata, and northward upriver beyond Asunción. This line enclosed an interior frontier over 7,000 miles long, everywhere bordered by savagery. Although such a frontier could not remain unchanged, yet by 1600 armed conquest had paused, and peace, if such it can be called, was to characterize the life of the colonists in the next century. Almost from the moment of the founding of all these new towns, as in Mexico, political, economic, social, and cultural institutions began to develop out of the new mixture of two races—institutions worth as serious consideration as has been given the exciting stories of exploration and conquest.

Readings

Arciniegas, G., *Germans in the Conquest of America* (1943)

——, *Knight of El Dorado* (fictionalized, 1942)

Bandelier, A. F., *The Gilded Man* (1893)

Bannon, J. F., *The Spanish Conquistadores* (1960)

Beals, C., *Nomads and Empire Builders* (1961)

Birney, H., *Brothers of Doom: The Story of the Pizarros in Peru* (1942)

Dawson, T. C., *South American Republics* (2 vols., 1903–1904)

Galdames, L., *History of Chile*, trans. I. J. Cox (1941)

Gibson, C., *Inca Concept of Sovereignty and the Spanish Administration in Peru* (1948)

Graham, R. B. C., *Conquest of New Granada, Being a Life of Gonzalo Jimenez de Quesada* (1922)

——, *Conquest of the River Plate* (1924)

——, *In Quest of El Dorado* (1923)

——, *Pedro de Valdivia, Conqueror of Chile* (1926)

Heaton, H. C., ed., *Discovery of the Amazon* (1934)

Henao, J. M., and G. Arrubla, *History of Colombia*, trans. J. F. Rippy (1938)

Kirkpatrick, F. A., *Spanish Conquistadores* (1934)

Lee, B. T., and A. C. Heaton, *Discovery of the Amazon According to the Account of Friar Gaspar de Caravajal* (1934)

Levene, R., *History of Argentina*, trans. W. S. Robertson (1937)

Lowry, W., *Lope Aguirre, the Wanderer* (1952)

Markham, C. R., *Conquest of New Granada* (1912)

——, *A History of Peru* (1892)

May, S. B., *The Conqueror's Lady, Inez Suárez* (1930)

Means, P. A., *Fall of the Inca Empire and Spanish Rule in Peru, 1530–1780* (1932)

Merriman, R. B., *Rise of the Spanish Empire*, Vols. III and IV (1934)

Moses, B., *Establishment of Spanish Rule in America* (1898)

——, *Spanish Dependencies in South America* (2 vols., 1914)

Muller, R., *Orellana's Discovery of the Amazon River* (1927)

Ober, F. A., *Pizarro and the Conquest of Peru* (1906)

Penrose, B., *Travel and Discovery in the Renaissance, 1420–1620* (1952)

Pizarro, P., *Relation of the Discovey and Conquest of the Kingdom of Peru*, ed. P. A. Means (2 vols., 1921)

Polmentary, H. C., *The River of the Amazons—Its Discovery and Early Exploration, 1500–1743* (1965)

Prescott, W. H., *History of the Conquest of Peru* (many editions)

Richman, I. B., *The Spanish Conquerors* (1919)

Sancho de la Hoz, P., *An Account of the Conquest of Peru* (1917)

Service, E. R., *Spanish-Guaraní Relations in Early Colonial Paraguay* (1954)

Vernon, I. W., *Pedro de Valdivia, Conquistador of Chile* (1946)

Verrill, A. H., *Great Conquerors of South and Central America* (1943)

Warren, H. G., *Paraguay. An Informal History* (1949)

Zahm, J. A., *Quest of El Dorado* (1917)

Zárate, A. de, *A History of the Discovery and Conquest of Peru*, ed. D. B. Thomas (1933)

Zimmerman, A. F., *Francisco de Toledo, the Fifth Viceroy of Peru, 1569–1581* (1938)

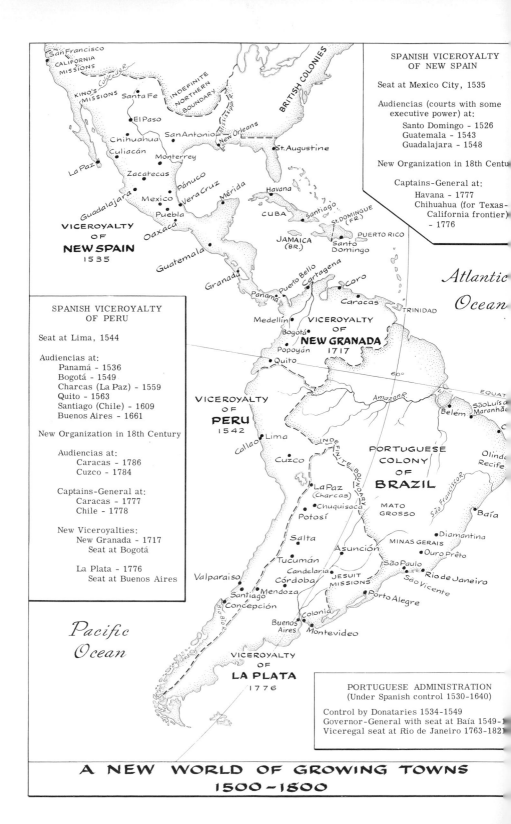

A NEW WORLD OF GROWING TOWNS 1500–1800

Part II

OLD WORLD AND NEW
CREATE A RICH NEW TAPESTRY

A Peruvian named Garcilaso de la Vega el Inca, whose interesting writings in the Spanish language give us the best pictures of Inca history, was born in Cuzco in 1539, one of the first generation of half-breeds or *mestizos* in Peru. His father was a soldier of a famous Spanish family, descendant of a well known poet; his mother, who had been baptized a Christian under the Spanish name of Doña Isabel, was an Inca princess, granddaughter of Tupac Yupanqui. Garcilaso's father had accepted her as the mistress of his household. With Doña Isabel at the head of his table, he daily fed 150 to 200 comrades in arms, many poor relations from Spain, and Inca dignitaries of Doña Isabel's family. Cuzco was still Inca in dress and tradition, but things were changing rapidly; for example, Garcilaso saw teams of oxen given away in his father's ceremonial hall as gifts to his Inca vassals. In return, the Indians brought gifts to Garcilaso''s mother on the Christian festivals of Saint John's

Day and Christmas. His father hired a Spanish tutor for his half-breed son, had him carefully trained in Christian doctrine, and took him on trips as a companion. His mother's relatives taught him to figure with a *quipu* and had him memorize the long stories of Inca history. Thus Garcilaso seemed to be a perfect blending of the best in Indian and Spanish life, a famous example of the *mestizo* society of the whole New World. But when his father was fifty, he took a young Spanish bride. Though Garcilaso was "beloved and cherished" in his father's new house, though he went to Spain as the son of a Spanish officer and served as a captain in the army of Philip II, his legal younger half-sisters inherited the estates.

Thus Indian and Spaniard combined to make a new race in a New World. In such combination the culture and the characteristics of both bloodstreams were present. However, as happened to Garcilaso, the *mestizo* or mixed-blood usually suffered economically as well as politically and socially. In much of Latin America he is only now coming into his own. During three centuries of colonial rule, the *mestizo* class multiplied, did the work, fought in the army, obeyed the Spanish administrators, and were dominated by the aristocrats born in Spain and the pure whites or creoles born in the New World. These two higher classes quarreled among themselves for prestige in the Spanish empire.

That the empire was successfully administered from Spain is attested by its long hold on the vast Spanish New World. To understand this success, and the attendant failures also, the reader must analyze the methods of administration in both central and local government, in control of trade, and in church authority. To understand the people of the New World one must make some analysis of their lives at all social and racial levels, as well as of their religious faith and its influence on their lives. Cities grew up as pleasant and prosperous as Seville or Barcelona, while at the same time missions and presidios held the frontier.

When riches poured from the mines and fleets sailed the oceans, other European nations became jealous of Spain. Thus the seventeenth and eighteenth centuries were full of intercolonial wars and frontier clashes, in which Spain held her own. In culture, always a reflection of European trends, the colonies also developed an interest in the "Enlightenment" which was to bring revolutionary changes to Europe in the eighteenth century. By the end of the century, all peoples were seeking more freedom from dictatorial governments. That the Spanish Americans should do so indicates that the Spanish colonial empire cannot be considered a three-century failure.

Parallel to the Spanish colonial empire in South America there grew up a Portuguese colonial empire in Brazil. Some analysis must also be made of Portuguese administrative methods, of the new mixed races from which modern Brazilians are descended, and of their culture in a tropical environment quite different from that of Lima or Mexico City. Thus we bring both Portuguese and Spanish colonial America up to 1800 in the following group of chapters.

Chapter 9

Political Administration
of the Spanish New World

A LONG DEVELOPMENT
FROM THE FIRST GOVERNOR AT SANTO DOMINGO

DIEGO COLUMBUS, eldest son of the discoverer, took as his bride María de Toledo, a cousin of King Ferdinand—a brilliant match for the young son of a wandering foreigner. With this extra influence he received the governorship the Crown had promised his father—full power as the king's representative, supposedly governor of the entire New World. On July 11, 1509, the newlyweds landed in the midsummer heat of Santo Domingo, that first frontier town in the Americas, but dignified by the term "Capital of the Island of Hispaniola and the Spanish Empire." With Don Diego came an escort of relatives, ladies in waiting, knights, plumed horses, and a crested gilt coach. All members of the party were dressed in velvet and brocade, sweltering as they walked up the beach into the soggy little town. There was no place for this pompous array of lords and ladies to stay in the tropical huts of Santo Domingo only a decade and a half after Columbus had first seen Hispaniola. But Don Diego's bride was determined to hold court in the manner of her royal cousins. For her Don Diego built a viceregal house, with arched colonnades front and back, and a fine view of the river and harbor from the

The palace built by Diego Columbus in Santo Domingo as repaired by the present Dominican government and furnished with authentic articles, including a portrait of Don Diego and his famous father. *Courtesy* Americás *Magazine.*

terrace. Doña María covered the walls with tapestries, paved the floor with majolica tiles, and planted lush gardens. While she tried to make raw Santo Domingo into a true royal capital, her husband quarreled with the kings of Spain over the titles and moneys due him on his father's death, and over his powers of appointment and inspection.

Don Diego's quarrelsome rule, the expansion of settlement into other islands and on the Isthmus, and the need of strong centralized agencies at home in Spain led the rulers to establish a permanent pattern for government in the New World. It grew into the full-fledged colonial political system for a vast empire which was to last three hundred years. For such an empire settlers and administrators were more important than the explorers and adventurers whose story has been told in Chapters 7 and 8.

Compared to the spectacular story of transplanting European government and culture to the Americas, the tales of the gold-hungry conquerors pale. Before Jamestown and the *Mayflower,* Spain had completed most of her full cycle of discovery, exploration, and settlement, and had transplanted her civilization, one of the richest cultures in Europe at the time. By 1574, over 160,000 Spaniards had followed Don Diego's courtiers on the route to America, Spaniards drawn from all walks of life. Santo Domingo was but the beginning; in 1600 there were over 200 chartered towns, many more mining centers and frontier garrisons. Don Diego's city of Santo Domingo declined in his lifetime, but the empire grew by leaps and bounds. So, too, the governmental institutions outgrew the pattern set up in the agreements with his father. To further the evolution of this colonial system, agencies of royal control were set up both in Spain and in the New World.

COLONIAL ADMINISTRATION
FROM THE MOTHER COUNTRY

The pattern for the rule in the colonies was largely established under the Hapsburg kings of the sixteenth century. In theory the colonies belonged to the Crown of Castile, and thus held as his personal property by Isabella's grandson, the young King Charles, called Charles I of Spain but Charles V in his Austrian holdings. He and his son Philip II did their best throughout the sixteenth century, trying to solve the explosive problems of a very New World for whose rule no kings could have been prepared. The age of discovery ended in their time and in that of their immediate successors. By the 1600s the New World was an old story to the Hapsburg descendants; the colonies no longer produced glamorous adventure stories but silver and hides and sugar for Spain. As the Hapsburg line weakened, its rulers in the late 1600s being misled by favorites, with the last of them, Charles II, even feeble-minded, neither colonies nor mother country were run well by them. After 1713 French-blooded kings of the Bourbon line were to rule Spain in an era of so many changes as to deserve a separate chapter.

The Spanish monarch was absolute at home and the royal monarchs intended to maintain the same exclusive control over the people in the new possessions, natives and Europeans alike. The new institutions, though modified to fit local conditions in the New World, were modeled on those of Castile. The power and control emanated from the monarch, and exercise of personal rights on the part of subjects often depended on the favor and will of whoever happened to be on the throne. When, as in the cases of Columbus, Cortés, and Pizarro, the reigning sovereigns had granted sweeping powers to the explorers and conquerors, royal jealousy and prerogative soon revoked the power and centralized the authority again in the hands of the king in Spain. This authority was from the first economic and religious as well as political.

It will be remembered from Chapter 6 that in 1493 Ferdinand and Isabella had appointed Bishop Fonseca to supervise the preparations for Columbus' second voyage. He was to serve until his death in 1524 as a counselor of the crown for American affairs. His appointment gave the position great prestige, for he was archdeacon of the cathedral of Seville and chaplain to Isabella. After a decade of control by Fonseca, the economic administration of the affairs of Hispaniola grew too large for him to handle, and the *Casa de Contratación,* or House of Trade, was created, perhaps at his suggestion. As described in Chapter 6, the *Casa* was a clearing house for commerce and immigration. As the empire expanded from the islands to the mainland, commercial regulations naturally became more complicated and the work of the *Casa* increased. Officials, secretaries, port collectors, a postmaster, a chaplain, a prison staff, and scores of lawyers were added to its force. Originally housed in Seville, it had to act as arbiter for over a century in the fierce struggle between the ports of Cádiz and Seville for a monopoly of the trade of the Indies.

Fonseca's troubles in the field of politics magnified also. He had to sign all decrees and orders from the king concerning colonies, and to act as colonial minister. On Fonseca's death in 1524, Charles set up the Council of the Indies to take over all Fonseca's political duties and all his employees and offices. It was to become Spain's chief agency for governing the New World, and was not abolished until after the Spanish American republics were declared·independent. It was the supreme legislative, administrative, judicial, and ecclesiastic body for colonial affairs, responsible only to the king.

The membership of the Council was always made up of high-born men, nobles from Spain's richest families, lawyers from the University of Salamanca, returned officials from the colonies serving emeritus. It had its own attorneys, reporters, clerks of accounts, treasurers, solicitors, a chaplain, a bailiff, a historian, a cosmographer, and a professor of mathematics. Distinguished mapmakers and historians served it. The actual membership of the board varied from nine to nineteen at different epochs of the colonial period. During the weak reigns of the last Hapsburgs, the top-heavy Council had three times as many officials and employees as it had had at its peak of success in 1600, though the salaries for all these extra dignitaries were in arrears and the state was bankrupt.

What were the duties of the Council in its heyday? Actually, it was the mouthpiece of the king in colonial affairs; it resided at court; its deliberations were secret. It proposed for the king's approval the names of appointees to fill all political positions in the New World except those few filled by the choice of the settlers themselves. The Council prepared all the laws and decrees, wording them, copying them, readying them for the king's signature, and distributing them to the officials concerned. It heard cases on appeals from the various courts in America, held powers of censorship of all books and papers going into the colonies, spied on all its own appointees as they worked in the colonies to carry out its orders, tried to preach good treatment of the Indians, and endeavored to maintain harmony among all the subjects of the king in the dependencies. It was responsible for all accounts and reports on every colonial subdivision—and there were more and more subdivisions as the colonies expanded from the Rio Grande to Tierra del Fuego.

Its members worked hard, from three to five hours every day in general council alone, as the meetings dragged on interminably. Then each member served many hours daily on small committees—committees that heard complaints from the colonies, committees that interviewed applicants for positions, committees that read books for censoring before shipment, committees that prepared the special reports for the king, committees that handled military affairs. Only of this last job were the committeemen relieved by the creation of a special committee for warfare, or *junta de guerra de Indias,* after 1600.

So many detailed records were kept of all these doings that historians know more about life in Spanish colonial times than they do about conditions fifty or a hundred years ago in many of the smaller Latin American republics. In general the records prove that the home government was trying to do a good job, and that it fell down where the frontiers were too distant, the differences in colony and homeland too great, the red tape needlessly complicated, the moneys too great a temptation to the very human administrators who handled them, or the laws themselves too involved to be successfully carried out.

The legislation for the colonies was voluminous and touched on every aspect of the duties and rights of both colonists and officials. The code of Castilian law, complicated enough of itself, had to be adjusted so that the legal spirit of the homeland was applicable to the peculiar conditions in the New World. Then there had to be elaborate new legislation with a distinct character of its own, including special laws for the Indians and even some judicial customs of Incas and Aztecs. As conditions changed, and parts of the New World became busy, settled, Europeanized places, many of these laws became obsolete but were still on the books. A codification of all the laws, decrees, ordinances, and regulations of the Council of the Indies was compiled eventually in the *Recopilación de Leyes de los Reynos de las Indias*, a notable monument of colonial legislation and a comprehensive and humane code for government. In its final form in 1681 the code contained 6,377 laws, arranged in nine books, classified by subject under 218 headings. With the law itself so confusing, small wonder that there was so much disregard of it, disregard often stemming from ignorance as well as corruption.

Two other institutions for the government of the colonies existed at home in Spain and controlled affairs from the home base. While the *Casa* or House of Trade existed to see that the Crown made money from the colonies, the merchants of Seville wanted their share of colonial profits also. When in 1543 the Crown made the regulation that all vessels trading with the New World sail in fleets officially sponsored and protected by the royal navy, the merchants in control of American commerce banded together in a merchant guild or *Consulado* to arrange these fleets to their own best advantage. The guild proceeded to lighten the burdens of the *Casa* with respect to the outfitting and dispatching of the fleets. It was almost official and served to settle disputes among its own members, the rival merchants, so that the Crown had little reason to interfere.

Though headquarters for the fleets were in Seville, the difficulty of the Guadalquivir entrance and the dangers of sandbars at its mouth forced many ships to load and unload at Cádiz. Thus an agency called the *Juzgado de Indias* was established at Cádiz; it handled the inspection and loading of ships, the embarkation and clearance of passengers to and from the Indies whenever tidal and river conditions made ascent to the port of Seville impossible. The fleets which left semiannually from one port or the other carried all paperwork, all officials, all cargo to the colonies; they were the link between the home government in Spain and the units of government scattered throughout the empire.

VICEROYS AS THE KING'S REPRESENTATIVES

As colonial organization in the homeland evolved slowly from the time of Columbus and Don Diego to 1800, so also did the agencies of control that had their offices in America. Thus the development of colonial institutions in the Americas was a gradual process; however, in order to provide an over-all picture of colonial administration, it is best to discuss it at the height of its power.

With Columbus in the settlement of Hispaniola there had been two treasury officials to regulate finances and to guard the king's rights. Thus central authority was present from the beginning. Only in municipal organization did any vestige of ancient Castilian democracy permanently survive, and even there local self-government was overshadowed by royal authority. Though the first settlements were often made by adventurers who put up their own capital and thus had some governmental power, this period of *adelantados* did not last long. Most of the *conquistadores* only held the powers of *adelantado* for a few years. Sooner or later a governor was chosen whose appointment was revocable at the pleasure of the Crown, and the colony was administered as a royal rather than as a proprietary colony. Colonization was thus conceived primarily as a function of the state. This called for an elaborate bureaucracy, for viceroys, judges, local governments, and financial officials. The age of Charles V and of Philip II was a period of great experimentation in government; centralization, uniformity, and routine were its keynote. Many of its experiments hardened into complex, inflexible institutions which remained unaltered until the eighteenth century.

The territorial organization, the viceroyalties, the captaincies-general and the *audiencias* all fit into this complex scheme. So large an area of settlement, from Rio Grande to Río Bío Bío, must have many subunits of central control. As time and the Spanish pioneers advanced, the lines of control became thinner, and the vast distance between the various New World cities became of itself a problem of administration and a cause of the weakening of the empire. The administrative subdivisions—viceroyalties, captaincies-general, and seats of *audiencias*—became the independent nations of today. The feelings of independence that Quito's judges had against Peru's viceroy, that Guatemala City inhabitants felt against Mexico City, are partially responsible for the existence of Ecuador and Guatemala as separate from Peru and Mexico in the twentieth century. The subdivisions had been created for administrative and geographic convenience. They were ruled by the judges of the regional *audiencias* through the person of their chairman or president, and by a captain-general, in whose office military and civil authority were combined on the frontier. The seat or subcapital of each such factotum, although regarded as part of the viceroyalty of Mexico or Lima, was for all intents and purposes independent of viceregal intervention.

The first permanent viceroyalty erected in America was on the mainland in New Spain. Antonio de Mendoza, the experienced diplomat, popular nobleman, decisive administrator, and devoted public servant who brought peace and prosperity to Mexico after the days of Nuño de Guzmán and the Mixton War, reigned there in the king's stead for fifteen years (1535–1550) and held much greater powers over a much vaster and more populous area than ever were held by Don Diego Columbus. This viceroyalty included the former Aztec empire, as well as New Galicia,

Central America, the Antilles, and, after Mendoza's time, even the Philippine Islands. Within this domain there were seats *of audiencias* at Mexico City, at Guadalajara for New Galicia, and at Guatemala City for Central America, which was later created a captaincy-general. As the frontier advanced in the next two centuries, New Spain's viceroyalty also included many military governments on the frontier in the silver-mining areas and as far north as California by 1769. The earliest governors, striving to bring order out of chaos in frontier Hispaniola in the first decade of the 1500s, could not have foreseen the extensive kingdom of New Spain as it existed in the 1700s.

The viceroyalty of Peru was even more far-reaching, including as it did by 1600 all of South America that was to be settled by Spain. The viceroy himself had more prestige in Lima than had his counterpart in Mexico City, and received a higher salary. Under him was the *audiencia* of Lima, 1544, the *audiencia* of Panama attached to Lima after 1567, the *audiencia* of Charcas, 1559, the *audiencia* of Bogotá, created in 1561, of Quito in 1563, of Chile in 1565, of Buenos Aires, at least temporarily in 1661, as well as others in the eighteenth century. Many of these capitals were so far from Lima that one by one most of them were made into small captaincies-general, or *presidencias,* with little subserviency to Lima. Bogotá, seat of government for New Granada, became a captaincy-general as early as 1563. Chuquisaca, today's Sucre, Bolivia, had a governor of its own by the seventeenth century, as did Santiago, Chile. Buenos Aires and Asunción, the Plata frontier, were considered so remote and unimportant for two hundred years that they were simply ruled from Charcas, high in the Bolivian Andes, till the 1660s. Further changes were made in the eighteenth century, as will be discussed in Chapter 15.

As for viceroys themselves, those alter egos of the king, they had broad powers and heavy responsibilities. The king needed a royal representative with fullest authority who would not declare independence in his own right. Thus the king had to choose his viceroys wisely. The royal officials, living so far from home supervision in both time and distance, must have an intense devotion to the royal power. It was hard to find men with these qualifications. In many cases the noblemen of the highest Spanish blood whom the king sent for these jobs were hampered by the pride and arrogance of the higher clergy, by the jealousy of the royal judges, and by the distrust of the governing councils in Spain in everything they did. Antonio de Mendoza, fifteen years in Mexico and a term afterward in Lima, pleased the king by his lack of independent initiative. "The secret of good ruling," he told his successor, "is to do little and to do that slowly," since most matters lent themselves to that kind of treatment. After the first viceroys, the normal term for this position was fixed at three years, then later raised to five. The viceregal salary, difficult to translate into modern dollars, provided a sumptuous living from the royal treasury, and the viceroy usually had a private fortune as well.

Throughout the three centuries many decrees were passed regulating the powers and activities of the viceroy. Politically and administratively he made appointments, distributed land and titles, issued instructions to subordinates, promoted colonization, founded new towns, took the periodic census, superintended public works, maintained public health rules, protected the Indians, and enforced all royal laws. On the economic side, he collected taxes, enforced commercial restrictions, and promoted industry where it did not come into competition with that of the homeland. Ecclesiastically, the viceroy was the representative of the king in America; he founded churches, set the boundaries of bishoprics, supervised the instruction of natives in religion, acted as vice-patron to all religious endeavor, and collected tithes to support the church. Thus he was the chief agency in promoting the advancement of the faith in the New World. As an ex-officio member of the judicial body, the viceroy sat with the *audiencia* judges, though he had no vote. That body acted as the highest court of appeal this side of Spain, and decided the competency of questions of jurisdiction between civil officials and church officials. The viceroy also acted in a military capacity, serving as commander in chief of all forces within his viceroyalty, and being held responsible for the "preservation of the peace." The viceroys thus became practically kings in the New World. At first they could do here in America almost everything that the king could do in Spain, but this great power of the earliest viceroys was afterward regulated by law from Spain, as the king became increasingly fearful of New World autonomy.

How well a viceroy did all these things depended on the character of the man himself. The viceroys of the sixteenth century were good administrators, carefully chosen by Charles V and Philip II. In the seventeenth century, military men were preferred; those of the period after 1650 were often weaklings to whom the Crown owed some favor. There were viceroys who worked for their own interests and for those of their families, viceroys who worked only for the king and for Spain, viceroys really interested in furthering the New World for its own sake. Of 103 different men who served as viceroys in the three centuries of Spanish rule in Mexico and Peru, only four were born in any part of the Americas, so determined were the kings to choose only men of noble Spanish families whose loyalty would be unquestioned. Forty-one of the viceroys served in Peru, sixty-two of them in Mexico; the portraits of all those in Mexico hang in a museum room of the Castle of Chapultepec. The subjects for these portraits were thin men and fat, old men mostly, but here and there a young one. Before 1700, they wore their own hair in curls or showed bald spots; after 1700, they wore the elaborate white wigs popularized by the kings of France. A few were church leaders in ecclesiastical robes; one or two seem to have been gallant horsemen.

We can read, in the records of their rule, the accounts of the elaborate celebrations given at the time of their arrival and departure. Two centuries after Mendoza served his term in Peru the Spaniards there had established the custom of processions of welcome stretching out over a hundred miles and lasting several weeks. The incoming viceroy, so an old account relates, is to land at a small port two hundred leagues north of Lima, so he can be entertained at every town en route. Each local governor along the coast "then provides litters, mules, and everything necessary for the viceroy and his retinue as far as the next jurisdiction," and also, at his own expense, "orders booths to be built for the entertainment of the viceroy in the halting places of the desert." In Lima the new arrival is the guest of the local town council; a parade "of all officials and all religious orders," which lasts the entire day, welcomes him as a mere civilian guest on the day of his arrival. The first evening he must attend a play "to which the ladies are admitted." Next day he goes at the head of a long line of open coaches to meet the retiring viceroy, who is delayed at the port of Callao while his record is being "inspected" by the other royal officials. The militia, the college students, the judges, and all the lesser officials of the court march in honor of the new viceroy. There are three days of such processions, with dinner parties in the homes of the elite every evening. Then follow five days of "Bull Fiestas" for the general public. For the next two weeks, the new viceroy must spend some days at ceremonies at the university, and others at every house of a religious order. There is a final celebration in which Lima "breaks loose" because all these formalities are finished. Don Diego Columbus had brought the pomp and splendor of Spain with him to a thatch-and-mud town; these later viceroys to Lima and to Mexico City found the pomp waiting for them in the rich new cities. Throughout the era, the first year of a viceregal term was given over to functions chiefly social.

The use of time and money in such welcomes was matched only by the account of a funeral of a viceroy who died in Mexico City. Parades, booths on the plaza, four hundred special readings of the mass, elaborate new mourning clothes for all well-to-do families were the order of the day. Some viceroys are famous for other things besides arriving and dying. The Count of Chinchon, a religious fanatic who would not allow ships in Lima to receive passengers who had not gone to confession the night before, and who tried to stop ladies from wearing seductive veils with one eye peeking out, is remembered because of his wife's severe case of malaria, cured by quinine bark, an Inca remedy still called *cinchona* in Peru. He introduced the malaria cure in Europe, while in Lima the defiant ladies used his anti-veil ordinance for curl papers. Another Peruvian viceroy is famous for the mistress he kept, La Pericholi, whose career as an actress and arbiter of social customs is still well known in Lima.

Few viceroys were actually corrupt, and real challenge to the royal authority was unthinkable, but furtive disobedience mixed with an outward show of respect for the king's wishes became a widespread fact. Yet for the viceroy there were many controls on his power both in theory and in actuality. He was furnished with detailed instructions when appointed, instructions which he must endeavor to carry out in every respect, and royal decrees were sent which, at least legally, had to be respected.

The kings and the Council of the Indies had a sure check on every viceroy at the end of his term of office. He was required to remain at the seat of his viceroyalty after his successor had been appointed and to submit to an inspection and auditing of his accounts which was called a *residencia*, or term of mere residence without authority. During this *residencia* a judicial review was made of the viceroy's administration. Notice was given in advance, and anyone among his subjects could bring any complaint against him, to be heard before officials appointed by the Crown. This formidable institution of royal control was probably more effectively enforced against lesser officials in the provinces than against the viceroys in Lima or Mexico City. If any official was involved in an unusually big scandal during the middle of his term, he was inspected by a special *visita* sent out by the Council of the Indies; or a general investigation could be made of a viceroyalty by a *visitador general*, and recommendations made to Spain which were reviewed by the Council of the Indies. In such investigations the *visitador general* had powers superior to the viceroy and could carry out his recommendations on the spot. His visits were usually followed by a period of marked honesty and efficiency. It was not that the Crown lacked machinery to maintain loyal, honest, efficient government, but that the long distance from Spain, the slowness of communication, the human weakness of the governors, and the lax conditions of the court life in Spain itself in the later period made real honesty in government a rarity, though flagrant dishonesty was the exception rather than the general rule. It was said of the Spanish empire the "government was never vigorously good, never intolerably bad."

In the remote capitals where a captain-general was the king's executive representative, he lived like a small-scale viceroy, kept as elaborate a court as he could afford in a frontier community, collected taxes, supervised the church, dealt with the Indians, maintained forts and garrisons, founded new towns according to royal specifications, and was a "big frog in a little puddle." He also was subject to a short inspection by a *residencia*. Captains-general reported directly to the Council of the Indies and were removable by the Council of the king, just as was a viceroy.

In all government the judicial branch is as important as the executive. Though viceroys and captains-general had some judicial function, the real center of judicial power was the *audiencia*, the court of appeal, the highest interpreter of the law. The first *audiencia* sent to Mexico had only four member judges, called *oidores*, or "hearers." By the seventeenth century the two large *audiencias* attached to the viceregal courts in Mexico City and Lima had twelve judges, some to hear criminal cases and some to hear civil cases. They listened to appeals from decisions made by various types of local governments and lower courts. *Audiencias* were required to "protect the Indians," and two days were set aside each week for the judges to hear cases involving Indians. In the two viceregal capitals, appeals of cases concerning Indians were so numerous that special branches of the *audiencias*, called *juzgado general de Indios*, had to be set up before 1600 to check abuses against the natives.

The *audiencia* judges corresponded directly with the king and acted as the king's advisors to the viceroy. They executed royal orders, administered royal property, reviewed credentials, and filled in for the viceroy. In Quito, Charcas, and other capitals where the *audiencia* was the chief agency of the Crown, the president of the court acted as governor of the province, and the area was often called a presidency. In the viceregal capital it was the president of the *audiencia* who served as viceroy during the many periods when the former viceroy had died or had served out his term and the new one was long in arriving. Since the terms of the judges were not limited, the *audiencia* was a more permanent and continuous body than any one viceroy, and thus was actually the center and core of the government of the Spanish Indies, often acting as a curb on viceregal power. Its judges were kept "Spanish" and, together with the viceroy, were not allowed to marry in the colony, to own real estate, to carry on business, or even to attend weddings or funerals in American-born families. The term *audiencia* was also often used for the territory of the *audiencia's* jurisdiction and some of these territories became modern republics in the present day.

There were many courts below the level of the *audiencia*. Some were administrative courts that acted in an executive capacity. Routine civil and criminal cases were heard by *alcaldes*, or justices of the peace. There were also special civil courts, courts of the *consulados* or merchant guilds, courts of the silver-mining interests, courts of the *mesta* or livestock ranchers' guild, a tribunal of accounts connected with the exchequer and a *proto-medicato* to regulate the medical profession. The church and the army maintained separate courts for those of their own personnel who might be in difficulties, for Spanish custom granted them *fueros*, privileges which set them apart from the jurisdiction of the civil courts.

PROVINCIAL AND LOCAL GOVERNMENT

Captaincies-general were areas as large as the modern republics of Latin America; naturally, they had to be divided into smaller units to facilitate administration. These provincial divisions differed greatly in size and importance, and were governed variously by officials called *gobernadores* if in large sparsely settled areas on the frontier, or *corregidores* if in areas of many Indian villages, or *alcaldes mayores* if in areas of Europeanized settlement. All three of these types of governors had approximately equal salaries and powers, and all had political and judicial as well as military authority.

Each governor usually served only a three-year term in any one district, and was often asked to give an inventory of his personal wealth before assuming office. He could not conduct a private business or marry within the district. Occasionally landowners or merchants already resident in the New World received these appointments. Such appointees in most cases had to serve in districts apart from their residences. As with the viceroy, the multiplicity of decrees and regulations often made honesty and integrity hard to maintain, and some governors became petty tyrants. Their salaries were so low compared to those of the captains-general that they were constantly tempted by the many opportunities for graft and corruption. In general they were closely associated with the town council and could intervene, either in the public interest or in the interest of the Crown, in all affairs conducted by local council meetings.

Corregidores especially had responsibility concerning Indians, and in this connection they were often guilty of petty graft. A *corregidor*, under the guise of being their chief protector, could force the Indians to render him or his friends personal services, to sell products to him below the market price for his own resale at pleasure, and to pay excessive tributes of any kind that pleased him. So widespread were these abuses that the relationship between the *corregidor* and the Indians became the notorious weak link in the Spanish colonial administrative system.

Viceroys, *audiencias*, and *corregidores* were not the government in town and village; the governor of New York State does not tell people how to light the streets of Poughkeepsie. In every empire there must be some local government. At home in Spain, the local unit of government was called an *ayuntamiento* or a *cabildo*. This body was transferred with little change to the New World. The urban tradition was as strong in Spanish America as it was in Spain. The *cabildo* was the first institution set up everywhere the Spaniards went. Cortés established a *cabildo* to legalize his acts in Vera Cruz before he ever met Montezuma; Balboa strove to legalize his position on the Isthmus by founding a *cabildo* in Darién. Later municipalities might have grown out of an earlier Indian mission or a mining settlement or even a garrison or *presidio* on the frontier, but each municipality was created consciously with a predetermined plan.

The *cabildo* is usually considered a democratic institution, for it was the only area of government open to creoles, the American-born sons and grandsons of the European immigrant. In the first *cabildos* the councilmen, the *regidores*, usually from five to twelve in number, were chosen by the settlers themselves. As soon as the frontier character of the town was lost the royal power moved in and *regidores* were usually no longer elected. By 1660 most *cabildo* members were chosen by the provincial governors, often from lists drawn up by retiring *regidores*. Some seats even became hereditary or were sold to the highest bidder. Thus the democracy of the *cabildo* did not last long. Municipal offices also became private property. By the beginning of the seventeenth century most local offices had become both proprietary and hereditary and municipal administration had passed into the control of a narrow circle of wealthy and influential families.

Cabildos exercised the normal routine functions of city councils today, distributing land, collecting local taxes, regulating the local militia and police force, issuing building permits, proclaiming public holidays, setting up rules for parades, supervising public markets, building bridges, controlling floods, distributing grain during famine. Because the revenues were limited, the budgets, and hence the public works and services, were small. There was nothing to create any community spirit; only in matters of grave importance—such as defense problems, floods, Indian raids, special gifts to be collected for the king to support new European wars or to honor the birth of an heir to the throne—was the main body of the citizenry called into consultation. Such a meeting was called *cabildo abierto*, or open council, even if it included only the most notable citizens, the landowners, the bishop and clergy, and the principal merchants. Though seldom held in the colonial period, open councils became of great importance during the Wars of Independence.

A number of lesser town officials were chosen by the *cabildo* members. The chief magistrate, sort of a combined mayor, city commissioner, and justice of the peace, was the *alcalde* elected by the *regidores*. He was also head of the local court system. Lesser officials, such as a constable, a public trustee of funds, an inspector of weights and measures, a collector of fines set by the court, a city attorney, a custodian of public property, all did the duties these dignitaries would perform in a modern town. There were also police magistrates for local districts, tax collectors, and officials of the exchequer. This in general is the type of town organization in the more Hispanized regions where European-type towns prospered.

Things were different on the frontier. Here the principal institutions were mission settlements in which the religious leaders formed the government, and *presidios* or garrisons in which the military officers commanded the soldiers. Such garrisons were necessary along the periphery of the empire to secure routes of travel, to protect commerce between the cities and the rich mines of northern Mexico or of Bolivia, and to check invasions of hostile Indians. Such a *presidio* consisted of a fort and a number of soldiers and their families who lived there and developed farms around the military post. Frequently, important towns grew up around the *presidio*. San Francisco, for instance, was once such a frontier garrison and mission.

A majority of the pure-blooded Indians still lived in their own *pueblos*. The Spanish government was interested in attempting to get the scattered Indians throughout the country to abandon their nomadic way of life and to settle down in concentrated villages of their own. Each such Indian village was to be provided with a church and priest of its own, in order to bring the Indians under Spanish tutelage, though the expenses of the church were to be borne by the Indians. There were to be from one to four Indian aldermen or *regidores* and an *alcalde* or magistrate, chosen with the consent of the *corregidor*. These *alcaldes* shared jurisdiction jointly with the old time *caciques* or hereditary tribal chieftains, though Spanish policy was to substitute the Spanish form of local government and the Spanish titles of officeholder wherever the idea of tribal chieftains could be forgotten in the new *pueblos*. Even sites of Indian *pueblos* had to be carefully selected and had to be provided with a common public land for pasturing cattle. *Caciques* and *alcaldes* could punish their fellow Indians for drunkenness, for failure to attend mass, and for minor infractions of tribal rule, but more serious offenses were taken to the *corregidor* who was always of Spanish blood and seldom interested in the social well-being of the Indians. In addition to paying into the royal coffers and the *corregidor's* own expense fund, Indian villagers maintained their community funds to defray expenses for local improvements and celebrations, as would any Indian town in Latin America today.

In conclusion, it must be admitted that in spite of the abuses of the *corregidor* system, the heavy tributes on the Indians, the scandals involving occasional viceroys, the disregard of Spanish laws in the colonies and of colonial well-being in Spain, the Spanish colonial empire was as well governed as any empire in history up to that time. The paternalistic administrative system actually worked remarkably well for three centuries over a vaster territory than that ever controlled by the empires of antiquity. Eventually, red tape and restrictions led officials to think up ways to get around them, obedience to royal and viceregal orders grew lax, and corruption increased. In the course of time the complications of administrative function and the multitudinous instructions from Spain inevitably sapped the vigor of the colonial regime.

Since government jobs brought such honor and prestige and were closed to so many classes of society born in the New World, job "mania" and nepotism became the order of the day. A job with the government meant the open door to quick wealth and social standing. As the centuries advanced, there was an excessive number of officials in Spanish America and jobs were created for relatives of relatives of those in power. "Get me a relative, I have an extra government job," was supposed to be a byword. However, Spain winked at a little graft in order to save the empire from larger graft, accepted a little lawbreaking and disobedience to prevent open rebellion and to make its system work. When, by the eighteenth century, the whole empire was decaying and the system cried out for reform both at home and in America, the Bourbon kings instituted the methodical changes that are described in Chapter 15.

Readings

Aiton, A. S., *Antonio de Mendoza, First Viceroy of New Spain* (1927)

Blackmar, F. W., *Spanish Institutions of the Southwest* (1891)

Bobb, B. E., *The Viceregency of Antonio María Bucareli in New Spain, 1771–1778* (1962)

Castañeda, C. E., "The Corregidor in Spanish Colonial Administration," *Hispanic American Historical Review*, IX, 446–70

Cunningham, C. H., *The Audiencia in the Spanish Colonies as Illustrated in the Audiencia of Manila, 1583–1800* (1919)

———, "The Residencia in the Spanish Colonies," *Southwestern Historical Quarterly*, XXI, 253–78

Diffie, B. W., *Latin American Civilization: Colonial Period* (1945)

Fisher, L. E., *Viceregal Administration in the Spanish American Colonies* (1926)

Haring, C. H., *Spanish Empire in America* (1952)

———, *Trade and Navigation Between Spain and the Indies in the Time of the Hapsburgs* (1918)

Hill, R. R., "Office of Adelantado," *Political Science Quarterly*, XXVIII, 646–68

Holmes, J. D. L., *Gayoso: The Life of a Spanish Governor in the Mississippi Valley, 1789–1799* (1965)

Jones, O. G., "Local Government in the Spanish Colonies as Provided by the Recopilacion," *Southwestern Historical Quarterly*, XIX, 65–90

Lynch, J., *Spanish Colonial Administration, 1782–1810: The Intendant System in the Viceroyalty of the Rio de La Plata* (1958)

Madariaga, S. de, *Rise of the Spanish American Empire* (1947)

Mecham, J. L., *Francisco de Ibarra and Nueva Vizcaya* (1927)

———, "The Real de Minas as a Political Institution," *Hispanic American Historical Review*, VII, 45–83

Merriman, R. B., *Rise of the Spanish Empire*, Vols. II, III, IV (1918–1934)

Moore, J. P., *Cabildo in Peru Under the Hapsburgs* (1954)

Moses, B., *Spanish Dependencies in South America* (2 vols., 1918)

Parry, J. H., *The Audiencia of Nueva Galicia in the Sixteenth Century* (1948)

———, *Spanish Theory of Empire in the Sixteenth Century* (1940)

Pierson, W. W., "Some Reflections on the Cabildo as an Institution," *Hispanic American Historical Review*, V, 573–96

Priestley, H. I., *Coming of the White Man, 1492–1848* (1929)

———, *José de Gálvez Visitor General of New Spain* (1916)

———, "Spanish Colonial Municipalities," *Louisiana Historical Quarterly*, V, No. 2, 125–43; see also *California Law Review*, 1919

Roscher, W., *Spanish Colonial System*, trans. E. G. Bourne (1914)

Schurz, W. L., *Latin America* (rev. ed., 1964)

Smith, D. E., *The Viceroy of New Spain* (1913)

Te Paske, J. J., *The Governorship of Spanish Florida, 1700–1763* (1964)

Wilgus, A. C., ed., *Colonial Hispanic America* (1936)

Zavala, S., *New Viewpoints on the Spanish Colonization of America* (1943)

Zimmerman, A. F., *Francisco de Toledo, Fifth Viceroy of Peru, 1569–1581* (1938)

Chapter 10

Economic Trends in the
New World and the Old

SPAIN'S MONEY-MAKING IDEAS FOR HER EMPIRE

DIGGING FOR GOLD and silver, breeding and grazing horses and cattle, planting and harvesting the agricultural products of Europe and the Americas, setting up small hand manufactories for weaving and ceramics, trading directly with Spain and with Spain only—by these means were the Spanish colonials to make profits for the mother country and, incidentally, to live well enough themselves. European countries of the sixteenth, seventeenth, and eighteenth centuries believed in mercantilism—the colonies existed for the benefit of the mother country. Only Spanish merchants in the towns of Spain and Spanish-born traders in the New World should benefit from commerce with the colonies; foreigners should be excluded positively from the bonanza of the colonial trade, and creoles or *mestizos* born in the Americas were to share in the wealth only when the citizens of the mother country were abundantly prosperous. Since bullion— silver and gold in pure metallic form—was considered by economists at the time as the only true wealth, and the American colonies were one of the greatest sources of bullion of all time, that wealth was intended for Spain only, to increase her own prosperity at home and abroad. In order that all the gold and silver should reach Spain, the colonists were to sell to Spain only, and to purchase processed goods from Spain with the metals whenever possible, rather than to process the goods in the Americas. Prices on both sides of such trade were to be set and qualities standardized by the Spanish government or by the trade guilds Spain approved at home.

Spain was the first European nation to face the problem of colonizing the New World; but she was also a country with little experience in colonization or in overseas trade of any kind. Furthermore, more than any other trading country, Spain was busy with the spread of religion and the waging of wars against the native population. There were other handicaps: the colonies with which this heretofore nontrading nation now carried on this vast commerce were thousands of miles away; the Spanish ruling class was a landed aristocracy, not a commercial class; upper-class Spaniards considered trade as manual labor and did not wish to dirty their hands. Most of the first colonial trading centers were in the tropics, with different needs and agricultural methods from those the colonists were used to. The work force was primitive and unwilling. The semicivilized Indian centers had been accustomed to subsistence economy and usually to barter trade. Neither the Old World colonizers nor the New World subjects had traditions of seafaring or large-scale commercial enterprises.

In spite of these handicaps, Spain transplanted herself to America in matters economic. That she succeeded is due to the great wealth of the New World in field and mine. The minor failures sprang from the position of Spain in Europe's economy. The flood of bullion into Spain produced inflation. Such enormous mineral wealth and the ease of its acquisition discouraged Spanish home enterprise and Spanish trade efforts in Europe. Big money meant big power and big power meant wars and big wars meant big debt. By 1700 Spain's military might was defeated on land and sea; her people were hungry and unemployed; her agriculture and industry had deteriorated. Her monopoly failed in the Americas when her businesses were failing at home, and foreign smugglers began to edge in on the colonial trade, supplying the articles the mother country no longer provided cheaply to the colonists. When the empire ceased to be self-contained by the beginning of the eighteenth century and most of the colonial silver was passing into foreign hands, then the new Bourbon kings tried to institute reforms.

AGRICULTURE AS THE BASIS FOR COLONIAL LIFE

The Spanish American colonies reflected both New World and Old World influences in their economic life. Side by side with the subsistence and tribute-paying economy of the Indians there arose a Spanish commercial agriculture, producing foods and fibers for home use, for sale in local markets, and for transport to Europe. Geographic differences and variations in native economies determined the trend of agriculture in the various regions of Latin America. Subsistence agriculture continued to support the sedentary Indians; grazing industries were introduced on the grassy plains regions, and plantation life developed in the Caribbean and along the coasts. Over vast areas the land was fine, fertile, and unused when the Spaniards came. Farms could be laid out as big as the holdings of several

Old World villages combined. Into the Indian culture producing maize, lima and kidney beans, manioc, potatoes, maguey, tobacco, cacao, pineapple, and peanuts there was transplanted the Spanish culture of wheat, barley, olives, grapes, and sugar. The pattern of land ownership varied with the type of planting, the level of Indian civilization, and the military history of each region. No matter who owned the land, its product meant wealth for Spain.

For despite the emphasis on metals, the cash value of agrarian products of the New World usually exceeded that of the metal shipped from the mines. Only in the Mexican colonies was the silver exported worth more than the various agricultural products shipped home to Spain. Even in that rich region the total value of all foodstuffs consumed on the *haciendas*, at the mines, in the cities, and in the Indian villages must have been far greater than the value of the silver ingots. The Indians had grown food to support themselves; now they and their Negro slave counterparts in the more tropical colonies produced sugar and tobacco, cacao and indigo on plantations for export, and added to their pre-Columbian products the cattle, swine, horses, and poultry introduced along with Spanish farming methods. Thus, for export and for home consumption, the geographic area of Spanish America was growing perhaps double the tonnage and the value that it had before the Spanish rule began. Indians tilled the land of their ancestors, but in most larger settlements they learned to use European animals to harvest both the old and the new crops. Nomadic Indians became herdsmen or forest gatherers for the new masters. In the Spain of 1492, the great mass of people labored in the fields; so also in the Spanish New World of 1592 or 1692, or even 1892, more Spanish-speaking and Indian peoples lived by agriculture than by any other means. Agriculture remains the basis of wealth in most of Latin America today.

At home, Spaniards lived on wheat bread and beef, on mutton cooked in olive oil, on the rich red wine of the Alicante and Malaga grapes, on the oranges of Valencia. All these things had to be grown in the New World if Spaniards were to live there happily. Though wheat was planted wherever possible for the Spanish settlers, maize remained the staple cereal crop of Latin America. In the irrigated coastal valleys of Peru the olive tree was introduced in 1560 and olive oil was exported from Lima to other colonies. Grapes did well on Mexico's plateau, in the Central Valley of Chile, and in the Argentine foothill province of Mendoza, and colonial wines competed briskly with wines imported from Spain.

The silk industry based on the mulberry-leaf-consuming worms was brought to New Spain, where many Spanish landowners encouraged the Indians to work with silk. Martín Cortés, son of Cortés and Marina, was one of those who prospered on the Indian manufacture of silk cloth; when Chinese silks began to come in cheaply on the Manila Galleon, the silk industry, and with it the mulberry trees, were allowed to die out. Hemp and flax, grown at first in abundance, also competed with the cordage and the linen of Spain, and their planting was discouraged after 1600.

Tobacco and cacao were developed as plantation crops in the New World for the European market—the gorgeous court ladies at Versailles had to have their cup of chocolate on retiring, and the gentlemen took up the use of snuff. Some of the fortunes of the Caribbean Islands were made on the private estates where these crops were grown. The largest single source of wealth from a planted crop, however, was the sugar grown to make rum; Negro slaves were imported to handle the crops.

The livestock industry was important from the first. Columbus brought cattle to Hispaniola and Cortés came with horses to Mexico. After a century, Indian farmers still did the work in Mexico and Peru, but their ways of farming were changed. A cow and a few pigs and a flock of chickens lived near the little farmhouses of corn and bean growers, just as they do today near the *casitas* of Mexican villagers. The Indian corn planters had oxen to pull a plow similar to that used in Spain, a step up from the primitive cornplanting stick of the Aztecs. Sheep provided wool for weaving and created a new industry. Pigs had come with the first colonists to Hispaniola, for the Spaniards wanted their pork, hams, and bacon wherever they settled. Today it is impossible for us to imagine the pampas without cattle, Uruguay without sheep, Mexico without horses and burros, any Latin American mountain community without goats. All these descended from the stock brought by the Spaniards.

The Crown had paid attention to stock raising from the early settlement of Hispaniola; in each new town there were to be "woods and grasslands for the common use of all colonists." Various decrees of the Council of the Indies attempted to regulate the size of lands to be distributed to those who were to make their living grazing cattle. An area one league in diameter was to accommodate no less than 2,000 head of cattle and to have built on it at least one permanent stone building. More than three square leagues could not be granted to one individual without a special royal license. The great cattle ranches that developed in Argentina, in northern Mexico, and on the plains of the Orinoco would indicate that it was either simple to get such a license, or else that this law to guarantee a just distribution of land was, like so many others, conveniently overlooked by the authorities in the New World. It may have been overlooked because the stockraisers' guild so powerful in medieval Spain, the *mesta*, was transferred to the colonies. Formally organized in Mexico in 1542, the *mesta* regulated branding, settled quarrels over land ownership, maintained a separate court for disputes concerning cattle, and represented the cattlemen before the authorities.

Equally important in many parts of the New World was the raising of mules and horses for transport. In the archives of Asunción there is a bill of sale, telling how Domingo Martínez de Irala, in the year 1551, bought "a black horse with the near forefoot white and some white about its face, from Alonso Parejo for 4,000 gold pesos." Fourteen years before, far down the Plata, Mendoza had abandoned seven mares and two stallions; when Irala's descendants came to refound Mendoza's colony, there were "wild horses in plenty," no need for gold pesos, nor even for bills of sale. The Crown had said that all such wild herds were royal property, but the settlers went to court in Asunción and won a case against the king in 1596. Then anyone could have the horses who cared to catch them—there were

Pack train in a muleteers' inn in the mountains above Toluca, Mexico—thus was carried most of the freight of the Spanish colonies. *Photo by Helen Miller Bailey.*

more than enough for all. In 1744, an English traveler in the Plata region reported that a young colt was not worth half a peso. He saw "great plenty of tame horses and a prodigious number of wild ones." The wild horses "wander in great troops about those vast plains."

There was more money to be made in Venezuela, Peru, or Colombia in raising mules, which were used by the hundreds on the Andes or the Isthmus crossing and which died in equal numbers from overwork, accidents on the precipitous trails, and poor fodder. On flat lands, burdens were carried by carts, the large-wheeled *carretas* pulled by oxen, but there was little profit in raising oxen for transport. Cattle produced meat for local consumption solely, as it could only be preserved by drying and salting. Profits from the grazing business lay in hides which were shipped across the pampas and up into the Andes to Lima for transport to Spain, or sent down to Vera Cruz from the interior. The Texas longhorn and the Indian pony of the Great Plains "grew" in the same way as did the stock of Argentina, probably from animals abandoned or lost by early expeditions. Thus, on the frontier of Spanish settlement both north and south, a cowboy-pony, bronco-busting, hide-and-jerked-beef industry developed unlike anything ever known in the Old World. So, too, developed the culture of those who worked with the cattle, the mixture of Indian and white which produced the life of the *vaqueros* near the Rio Grande, of the *gauchos* near the Plata, and the *llaneros* on the Orinoco.

If the Crown was to question private ownership of wild cattle and horses, and worry over the size of grazing acreage, how much more of a problem was the ownership of agricultural land—all those millions of acres of the new continents. Of the various factors that contributed to maintain an aristocracy in the Spanish American colonies—differences of race and religion, discriminatory economic legislation—the problem of land tenure was the most important. Land was the basis for political rights, the principal source of riches and prestige in a society which disdained trade and industrial pursuits. The value of the land was created, not by the landlord, but by the Indians and Negroes who worked it. The idea of a manor, a large area cultivated by an ignorant and depressed peasantry, was so common in Europe as to be easily transferred to the New World. Successful mine operators invested their gold and silver fortunes in land; creoles, the sons of Spanish families born in the New World but shut off from important government jobs, became wealthy through the inheritance of land.

How was land to be distributed in the first place? Most Indian communities had little conception of individual ownership; land had been owned by a tribe or village as a whole. As new lands were conquered by the Spaniards, they belonged automatically to the Crown, which granted out the tillable surface parcel by parcel and preserved the subsoil or mineral rights for royal ownership. Throughout the colonial epoch the Spanish rulers awarded deeds or charters to individual *adelantados*, town councils, or plantation developers. Of course, the lands were not surveyed, boundaries were indefinite, and many abuses were practiced. Squatters took over large areas; a decree of the late 1500s required squatters of ten years' standing to clear with the Crown. Many Indian villages theoretically kept their land, though they were often defrauded of it.

Favorites of the king or of the viceroys received great tracts of unsurveyed, new lands—estates called *haciendas* in New Spain and *latifundios* in South America. Indians on such lands were theoretically held in trust and protection by the new landowner. In actuality, of course, the Indians became the peasant workers of the feudal system. Smaller holdings—that is, free grants to a head of a family or to a common foot soldier, a *peón*, in lieu of wages—were called *peonías*, and comprised enough land for subsistence planting and pasturage for a small herd. The word *peón* came to be applied to the poor Indian who worked the lands of the rich landowner, but the *peonía* holding was the basis for an independent small-farmer class, the *rancheros*, who still farm these smaller holdings today. The church became a large owner of land, as described in Chapter 11. On the whole, land in the New World belonged to the wealthy, and was tilled by servile labor under primitive methods.

MINING, INDUSTRY, AND HANDCRAFTS

It was the lure of gold and silver that had brought many Spaniards to the New World in the first place. Mining remained one of the great industries of Latin America. Kings were interested in mining efforts, and issued early decrees that the subsoil rights on all agricultural land belonged to the king. Mines were worked on a sort of grant or lease from the royal court, with a fifth of all metals ordinarily going to the king, but there was large private profit in mining anyway. In fact, in the mines lay the origins of many of the private fortunes in America and the principal source of crown revenues. When the prosperity of the mines increased as the frontier advanced, there was more money in circulation, a greater demand for goods, and a sharp rise in the value of land, since mine operators invested their profits in agricultural land. Mine fortunes also brought a spur to the construction of churches and public buildings.

Gold soon gave out save in a few gold-bearing regions. The first silver mines were discovered in Michoacán, Mexico, in 1531. By 1550, Zacatecas, San Luis Potosí, Guanajuato, and later Taxco became silver-mining towns of fantastic wealth. Potosí in Bolivia became one of the most dramatic "boom" towns in all mining history; the hill of Potosí was thought to be the greatest "glory hole" on earth.

The mines produced so richly and easily that there was no need for efficiency. To bring the ore to the surface, small pits were dug with no connecting galleries; the ore was carried up ladders by Indian bearers who worked on a forced-labor basis. When the pits were flooded, they were drained by leather bags and the water handed up the same way, from Indian to Indian up the ladders. Once on the surface, the ore was crushed in an open "patio" by a revolving stone drag drawn round and round by a blindfolded mule. The ancient Indians had known how to smelt the silver out of the ore by fire. In 1554, after the ores from Zacatecas had been worked in this primitive way for six years, a German in Europe discovered a method of running mercury or quicksilver over the crushed ore and dissolving out the silver. The mercury could then be easily distilled off, leaving the pure silver. A Spanish miner, Bartolomé de Medina, heard of the method and brought it to Pachuca in 1556, and it was soon in use in both Mexico and Peru. Though at first all mercury was brought from Europe, a mercury deposit was soon found in Peru at Huancavelica, and its product was monopolized by the Crown. By the end of the seventeenth century even this method was no longer the best modern procedure, and the mining industry began to decline as a result of the lack of machinery, bad transportation, and underground flooding. Under the Bourbon kings at the close of the colonial period an attempt was made to bring technological improvements into the mines.

Silver was not the only mineral resource of the New World. Gold was still worked in some places in the late seventeenth century and was the source of boom conditions in the province of Chocó and in the Cauca Valley of Colombia and the mountains of Honduras. Diving for pearls was a major industry on Margarita Island near the Venezuelan coast and at La Paz in Lower California; a rich consignment of emeralds was sent to Spain from Colombia every three months for 150 years.

Since American treasure preserved Spain's balance of trade and financed her foreign wars, Spain endeavored to keep these valuable sources of wealth within the home country. Gold and silver were to be cast into ingots stamped with the royal stamp. At the time of stamping, the king's agents were to take his fifth. Naturally much gold and silver was never reported to the agents but was hidden away unstamped and traded to foreign smugglers for valuable French, English, or Dutch commodities. All the stamped bricks were contracted out to a half dozen private coin-making firms who minted up the pesos according to a standard set by royal decree. That is, they did so when strictly supervised; records indicate a loss to the Crown of 10,000,000 pesos in one twenty-year period because the minters made the coins "defective in weight or fineness."

This loss was small compared to all the wealth gained from Spain's New World minerals. In 1803 Alexander von Humboldt, a visiting scientist, figured the New World had sent the Old World, from 1492 to the year of his visit, a greater amount of precious metal than the entire known world had seen since the days of Solomon. In the final analysis, however, the mines proved a liability to Spain, as the great mass of metallic wealth meant inflation at home, and left Spain with an impoverished working class and a declining home industry. Only a small group of Spanish merchants actually benefited.

Naturally, manufacturing industries had no extensive development in the colonies, partly because the Spanish government discouraged or directly forbade any industry's competing with the manufacturing and trade of the mother country. The colonies existed to send raw materials to the mother country and to buy her manufactured goods. But the townspeople in the New World needed more than beef and hides, corn and wheat, or sugar and tobacco. They needed clothing in greater quantity and at lower prices than could be imported by the long slow journey from Spain. The manufacturing most widely developed in America was textile manufacturing. Factories called *obrajes,* hiring great numbers of skilled Indian hand weavers, appeared within the first decade of conquest. The Incas had always been expert textile weavers with llama wools; their descendants took easily to the use of sheep's wool. All types of fine cotton goods were produced; dyes for them were made from the cochineal insect, bright red parasite on the cactus plant, and from indigo. The weaving of velvet, taffeta, and other fine silk goods, at first from the silk produced in the new mulberry-tree industry and later from raw skeins brought over on the Manila Galleon, became a local industry, even though considered competitive to the mother country. The upper classes in the growing cities objected that "fine materials brought from Spain rotted and faded on the long sea journey."

Obrajes producing the cheap cotton and woolen goods for general consumption were found from Guadalajara to Tucumán. The exploitation of Indian labor in them was notorious, both by the Indian chieftains who abused their fellow Indians to make a profit and by the Spanish entrepreneurs. Efforts to control this exploitation were made from time to time by social-minded governors and viceroys, and by direct decree from the Council of the Indies, but to no lasting avail. Negro slaves and at one time even Chinese weavers were brought in to end the abuse of the Indians, and the number of *obrajes* was restricted by law.

Metal work, from ornamental iron bars for the windows of pretty girls' bedrooms to horseshoes, had to be made by smiths in the New World. Skilled metal craftsmen could cast anything from a cannon to a church bell, even the fine needles for the ladies' embroidery work. Equally skilled were leather workers who brought their trade from Spain; they turned out shoes for the wife of the viceroy and sandals for the Indian herdsmen, saddles and suits of leather clothing for the horsemen, hand-tooled scabbards for the swords brought out from Spain. Potters continued in their ancient crafts and had an importance in the economic life of every town and market place. The wines of Chile's central valley were stored in large earthern jars made in Santiago and, which are still to be seen in some old vineyards. Refined sugar, soap, gunpowder, tanned shoe leather, basketry, glass, hardware of all sorts, carved wood cabinets, and intricate jewelry, all were made in the New World for the New World consumption. The colonists could not wait for the fleets from Spain to bring them these products, and could not pay the high prices asked when they arrived.

The new towns needed skilled builders also. The records of Asunción, Paraguay, for instance, have preserved the names of the carpenters, ship-builders, and bricklayers, as well as of the adventurous captains who founded the town. Skilled wood-workers built ships for the Pacific coast of Mexico at San Blas and Acapulco, for the west coast of South America at Guayaquil and Valparaiso.

Many of these craftsmen, who created an in-between social class in the cities, were organized into *gremios* or guilds on the medieval pattern. The silversmiths of Mexico City were the first to organize such a guild, patterning it after the powerful one in Spain. By 1685, seventy-one silversmiths were listed in Mexico City; at the same time there were eighty organized silver workers' shops in Lima. The guild members were in evidence as leaders in public celebrations and religious processions. Only pure-blooded Spaniards could join; the years as apprentice and as journeyman were as long and arduous as in any craft guild of Europe. After two centuries of Spanish rule, Mexico had 100 other guild groups—gold beaters, harness and saddle makers, potters, weavers, hatters, candle makers. These organizations regulated apprenticeship, set standards for the quality of goods, kept up prices, and licensed journeymen, masters, and inspectors. They were also social, religious, and philanthropic organizations, the center of life and activity for their members and families.

To sample the economy of a smaller community, the people who lived in Panama City were checked by a royal "informer" as to how they made their living. "A few wealthy citizens have grain and livestock plantations for the local market; other wealthy ones own the brigantines which seek the oyster beds where the pearls are found, or are the owners of pack trains of mules which make the portage from the fleets of one sea to those of the other." There were also boat owners who "bring the wares from the fleets from Spain down the Chagres to the customs houses at Cruces and from there by mule train to Panama." There were "wealthy owners of saw mills where they make the planks used for houses and flat-bottomed boats." Some others superintended the cutting of logs in the forest, ran the slaughter houses, and owned fishing and shrimp-collecting boats. The Indians and Negro slaves, who were not even listed in the report, cut the logs and manned the boats, dived for the oysters, tilled the fields, and drove the mules.

COLONIAL LABOR SUPPLY

In every step of the conquest, the conquerors expected the conquered Indians to do the heavy work. In countries in which there is a preponderance of Indian blood the Indians still today remain the toilers, the hewers of wood and the drawers of water. How to allocate Indian workers and get them to work was the problem in Hispaniola at the beginning. Groups of Indians were distributed to a private party to do an assigned task— an institution called *repartimiento*. Theoretically they were to be paid wages for this work, but as they also owed tribute to the Crown, the work was soon considered the tribute. This granting of the use of Indian laborers as separate from the land became an abuse in Peru under a system called the *mita*. Chiefs were required to send a certain percentage of the men of free villages long distances from their homes to work in the mines. They were kept there for months on a pittance of wages, as a method of collecting "tribute" from the chiefs. Thousands of them died in the mines and never saw their native villages again.

A different institution for the use of Indian labor was the *encomienda*, also first used on the Caribbean islands. This was not intended to be a grant of land, for land grants had no legal connection with the work of the Indians who happened to be living on the land. The landowner was to "protect" the Indians, and could collect from them in work the tribute they were supposed to owe the Crown. If the Indians did not work the land to the capacity the landlord decreed, they had "failed to pay the royal tribute" and were considered in debt. Thus they were soon tied to the land in the manner of feudal peasants in Europe, working as serfs on estates. In Mexico the serfs were called *peones,* in Peru *yanacones,* in Chile *inquilinos.* If the Indians could prove themselves to be out of debt, they could go to work as paid laborers. Thus there was a gradual evolution away from the forced labor of *repartimiento, mita,* and *encomienda* to the use of free labor paid in wages.

Complicating the picture of the Indians' gradual rise to free labor status were the Negro slaves, supplanting the Indians on the plantations. The slave trade prospered, with Cartagena as its center. Once in the New World, the Negroes were well adapted to heavy work in the tropics, but did not multiply rapidly and often ran away to the hills to become *cimarrones,* or renegade slaves living as outlaws. Though there was always a demand for more Negro slaves freshly captured in Africa, actually Negro labor cost more than forced Indian labor.

White laborers entered the colonial picture to a smalled extent. The Crown encouraged farmers, artisans, and laborers from Spain to go to the New World, and granted free transportation for chosen emigrants, giving them tools, seed, and farm animals. But the restriction on emigration counterbalanced these inducements, and, save for the craftsmen who were members of the guilds and a few technicians from foreign countries, the laboring classes were not of pure European extraction. The social problems of labor and its exploitation will be discussed again in Chapter 12.

TRADE AND COMMERCE
AS CONTROLLED BY SPAIN

It should be apparent to the student of American history that Spain tried to control the trade of Latin America much as England did that of her colonies. Under the theory of mercantilism, the accepted theory in those days of new overseas empires, colonies existed to help the mother country, to provide the raw material for the manufacturers at home, and to buy back the manufactured articles. None of this colonial trade must be allowed to profit a rival foreign power. Spain's efforts to maintain such a policy forced her to spend large sums on army and navy to fight off foreign competitors, and on a large bureaucracy to restrict and control trade and keep foreigners from sharing it.

Control of trade in the Indies was handled through the *Casa de Contra-tación*, whose founding was described in Chapter 6. It remained a gigantic agency, licensing and supervising all ships and merchants, passengers and goods, crews and equipment passing to and from the New World. It handled all gold and silver, collected all customs taxes, and even maintained a whole staff devoted to improving the science of navigation. It was assisted by the *consulado* or merchant guild in Seville and by parallel merchant guilds in the chief trading centers of the Americas. *Consulados* were local "chambers of commerce" for the American cities, performing public services, improving roads, arranging parades, handling bankruptcies and breach of contract cases. Their members were the wealthiest and most important merchants in the colonies.

The system of sending goods to the Indies narrowed the monopoly, kept up the prices, and made trade slow and difficult. Only Cádiz and Seville could be used as ports of departure, only Vera Cruz and Porto Bello as ports of arrival. Not only must goods be sent on Spanish ships, but the ships must all sail together. To control the trade and to protect the ships against pirates, all cargoes were sent on yearly fleets of from forty to seventy ships. All the ships which were licensed to visit the colonies in any one year met at Seville or, in the years of shallow water, at Cádiz, and traveled with six or eight armed ships. Two groups sailed, a fleet in the spring called the *flota* which went to Vera Cruz with cargo for Central America, Mexico, and the islands, and a fleet in August called the galleons, *los galeones,* with cargo destined for Panama and transshipment across the Isthmus. The *flota* returned laden with hides, sugar, and Mexican silver, the *galeones* with Peruvian silver, Colombian emeralds, Venezuelan pearls, drugs, spices, cacao, and dyestuffs.

The Vera Cruz *flota*, often delayed in Spain until late summer, might be caught in the hurricane season of the Caribbean, or, if not caught by the hurricanes, might fall as booty to English pirates. When the *flota* arrived at fever-ridden Vera Cruz, the produce was transshipped to muleback and taken up into the *cordillera* to the pleasant town of Jalapa for a great yearly fair. Thousands of people came to Jalapa; profits for middlemen were enormous as goods were purchased to be transshipped to towns from Guatemala to Texas.

To the fair at Jalapa also came goods brought by the one ship which sailed alone without convoy, the Manila Galleon, the single ship a year which came from Spain's one colony in the Orient. All Spanish trade with the Philippines had to go via Mexico's west coast. If the ship survived its difficult passage, it came into Acapulco loaded with silk, both raw and woven, and all kinds of embroidery, porcelains, lacquers, carved ivories, and damascene ware. When the Oriental wares arrived in Acapulco they were transported by mule to Mexico City, and thence to other parts of the empire and to Spain via the Jalapa fair.

The fair to sell goods from the *galeones* was held at Porto Bello, the "Emporium of South America" on the Caribbean side of the Isthmus; in fact, the towns on the Isthmus existed for this fair. Here for the forty days of the fair came the wholesale merchants from Peru to exchange mule-train loads of silver and vicuña wool and Plata River hides for European-made things. To the fair through the rich Seville middlemen had come laces, tapestries, and silks from France, linens from Holland, crystalline glass from Venice, hand-tooled leather from Florence, wool hats from England, rugs and shawls from the Near East, beautiful things to find their way eventually into the colonial mansions in Lima or Quito, or even the frontier houses in Buenos Aires. In addition there were staples from Spain—cheeses, ink, shoes, hardware, Spanish pottery, wheat flour, and even beeswax.

At Porto Bello these things had already doubled in price. To sell them, booths were built of jungle logs around the plaza nearest the wharf and covered with sailcloth to "hold the vast stacks of merchandise." A special force of 5,000 soldiers patroled the town and the trails to Panama City across the Isthmus and protected the mule trains of silver out of Bolivia's "glory hole" from the thieves and hangers-on who followed the fairs. There was no place to sleep for the thousands who came, so they slept in the open, in the mosquito-ridden night, and died by the hundreds from yellow fever. Two thousand mules for the trans-Isthmian service were kept in near-by corrals, though they could not be carefully enough guarded, there on the edge of the jungle, from jaguars making their nightly kill. The European goods purchased by the wholesalers were taken, on the mules who survived the jaguars, to meet the "Armada of the Southern Seas" in Panama Bay, a fleet of ships mostly built in Guayaquil. At Callao and Lima smaller fairs were held; the goods were sold to other middlemen who would ship them to Valparaiso, send them by pack train up to Cuzco or to the fast-living silver towns of Bolivia, or pack them through the Andes to meet the caravans of oxcarts on the edge of the pampas at Salta to go the long trip to Buenos Aires. As far as the *Casa* and the Council of the Indies officially knew, no European goods ever reached Valparaiso or Buenos Aires except via the fair and the galleons at Porto Bello. Any bride in Córdoba or Santiago or Buenos Aires who wanted a wedding dress from Spain would wait two years from the time she ordered it until she got it, and then would pay ten times its original price.

And the bride, waiting for her wedding dress in Buenos Aires—could her father not get a better price for his hides and a lower price on the dress by dealing with a trader directly at the Plata harbor? This dependence of Buenos Aires on Lima and Porto Bello was an absurd situation creating high costs and retarding the growth of the Plata colony, but one which was perpetuated because the merchants of Lima and Panama were influential with the *Casa* and wanted to keep their cut of the Plata trade. What a temptation for smugglers, and how the settlers in these isolated ports welcomed them! English and Dutch ships often lay in Buenos Aires harbor, taking untold thousands of hides back to shoemakers in London or Amsterdam—and who in Seville was to know? Other centers of contraband trade were in the Antilles, especially at Jamaica and Curaçao, islands controlled by England and Holland in the eighteenth century.

Negro slaves were part of the contraband trade coming into the Caribbean. Spanish merchants had seldom handled slaves, since they had no access to the coast of Africa and had been forced to grant the Portuguese *asientos,* or rights to send slave ships into the island markets and to the mainland at Cartagena. As time went on these ships carried on much contraband trade as well, and England was able to cut into this profitable cargo. Spanish officials helped in the cheating, secretly opening ports as "haven for ships in distress," ships which had no greater distress than the anxiety to unload their rich cargoes.

Trade from one colony to another was less restricted by law than by poor roads, lack of bridges, difficult geography, and great distances. Every region was isolated from every other. The regions had little use for each other's products; a long trek by river boat was necessary even to start the climb to the Bogotá highland valley; the trek by oxcart across the pampas from Buenos Aires to Salta, only halfway to the hide markets at Lima, took several weeks; even the improved trail between Vera Cruz and Mexico City called for ten days on a good horse. On the Isthmus, that shortest route across the continent, the Cruces Trail was actually a primitive, overgrown mule path paved with irregular blocks of stone and seldom repaired, so muddy and so difficult that even though it was only sixty miles long a week's travel was necessary for a loaded mule. Meanwhile, in all parts of the New World, transportation of village food products to town markets was carried on by the same methods as in 1492, on the heads and backs of Indians. Tropical colonies needed to import cereals from temperate climate areas; tobacco, sugar, and cacao from the tropics went to Mexico City and to Lima. Commission men made fortunes supplying food and pack animals from the agricultural areas to the silver-mining regions of northern Mexico and Bolivia. From such trading a new middle class began to develop slowly by the 1700s.

MONEYS INTO THE ROYAL EXCHEQUER

More important than the trade and commerce of the New World— more important to the Crown and the Council of the Indies—was the wealth of funds that came from direct income on royal land, from Crown monopolies, and (mainly) from taxes. The revenues varied up and down through the decades; the total royal income from the New World had multiplied sixfold between 1550 and 1750. Though many of the smaller colonies and frontier communities never paid their own expenses, Peru and Mexico continually brought in a substantial revenue for the crown. Spain maintained a wide frontier, fought expensive wars in Europe, and championed the Catholic faith in Europe and America, so taxes could never be light. The royal exchequer hired a comptroller, a treasurer, inspectors, tax collectors, auditors, judges for special tax appeal courts, and hundreds of bookkeepers, all of whose records have been carefully preserved. The money came from more than forty different types of taxation.

A major source of income was the indirect tax on trade between Old World and New. Though such taxes brought income for the Crown, they actually hampered commerce and kept prices high. Merchants who sent goods on the fleet paid a special assessment to pay for and arm the fleet. A standard import and export duty, the *almojarifazgo*, ranging between 7 and 10 per cent, was charged on all articles coming through Seville, and another almost equal percentage was collected as a sales tax, the hated *alcabala*, on the same articles when they arrived in the colonies. At home in the colonies, individuals paid tithes to the Church, excise taxes on wines and liquors, luxury taxes on cockfights and tobacco, and many types of stamp taxes on legal documents. The Indians at the bottom paid a capitation or poll tax, as well as tribute to local authorities.

In addition to such taxes, the Spanish crown gained a personal profit from the New World. The *quinto* or fifth of all precious metal mined went to the king. He held vast tracts of agricultural land as direct proprietor and owned all cattle and crops on it. Mercury, gunpowder, playing cards, lotteries, salt, pepper, snow, and ice brought down from the mountains for cooling drinks in Mexico City and Lima—all were royal monopolies. In addition the king made private revenue from the sale of public offices, titles and honors, "forced loans," and from "kickbacks" into the treasury required of many seekers after lucrative political and ecclesiastic appointments.

To provide money to carry on all this financing, the Crown set up royal mints in Mexico City and in Lima. Here were minted the small coins called *reales* and the standard silver *peso* pieces of eight *reales* value, the "pieces of eight" of pirate days. The colonies always suffered from scarcity of small coins and had to resort to barter on the village-market level. There was never any paper currency, there were no banks, and thus there was little flexibility of credit.

Tax collecting was often farmed out to subcontractors, a system which always invites dishonesty. The heavy taxes on trade produced a chronic undersupply of manufactured goods, and all goods were sold at exorbitant prices. In return for the large tax revenue Spain gave the colonies an organized governmental system, roads, albeit poor ones, communications with the mother country, defense against Indians, the comforts of religion, and the luxury of a Spanish-born aristocracy. But there was much legitimate trade in spite of taxes, business was thriving, and wealth was being produced, no matter how badly distributed. The colonists accepted the conditions and learned to live with them, sometimes complying with the many restrictions and levies, sometimes getting around the system by bribery or smuggling.

Some historians of the Spanish colonial empire claim that the responsibility of the colonies bankrupted Spain. It is true that by 1700 the colonial cities were more prosperous than Seville or Madrid, and that the power of Spain in Europe was ended. But this was partially due to the wasteful line of weak kings, to the many wars they fought against England and France, to their quarrels with their dependencies in Holland, Italy, and the German states, and to their own corrupt tax collectors. Fifty per cent of all the fabulous wealth pouring into the royal treasury must have been used to defray these expenses, for the records seem to indicate that the costs of governing the New World—maintaining the viceroys and their courts, the customs houses and their employees, the fleets and their crews, the frontier forts and their soldiers—came to only 50 per cent of the total tax revenue. The lack of adequate law enforcement, the opportunities for smuggling and tax evasion, combined with the great natural wealth and vitality of the New World itself led to the ultimate downfall of Spain's commercial system, the end of mercantilism as a colonial policy.

Readings

Agricola, G., *De re Mettallica*, trans. H. C. and L. H. Hoover (1950)

Bannon, J. F., *Indian Labor in the Spanish Indies* (1966)

Barber, R. K., *Indian Labor in the Spanish Colonies* (1932)

Borah, W., *Early Colonial Trade and Navigation Between Mexico and Peru* (1954)

———, *New Spain's Century of Depression* (1951)

———, *Silk Raising in Colonial Mexico* (1943)

Chevalier, F., *Land and Society in Colonial Mexico* (1963)

Cobb, G. B., "Supply and Transportation from the Potosí Mines, 1545–1560," *Hispanic American Historical Review*, XXIX, 25–45

Diffie, B. W., *Latin American Civilization: Colonial Period* (1945)

Dusenberry, W. M., *The Mexican Mesta: The Administration of Ranching in Colonial Mexico* (1963)

Hamilton, E. J., *American Treasure and the Price Revolution in Spain, 1501–1650* (1934)

———, *War and Prices in Spain, 1651–1800* (1947)

Hanke, L., *Bartolomé Arzans de Orsura y Vela's History of Potosí* (1965)

———, *The Imperial City of Potosí* (1956)

Haring, C. H., *Spanish Empire in America* (1952)

———, *Trade and Navigation Between Spain and the Indies in the Time of the Hapsburgs* (1918)

Howe, W., *The Mining Guild of New Spain and Its Tribunal Guild* (1949)

Klein, J., *The Mesta* (1920)

Loosely, A. C., "The Puerto Bello Fairs," *Hispanic American Historical Review*, XIII, 314–335

McBride, G., *Land Systems of Chile* (1936)

———, *Land Systems of Mexico* (1923)

Merriman, R. B., *Rise of the Spanish Empire*, Vols. II, III, IV (1918–1934)

Motten, C. G., *Mexican Silver and the Enlightenment* (1950)

Nesmith, R. I., *The Coinage of the First Mint of the Americas at Mexico City, 1536–1572* (1955)

Parry, J. H., *Sale of Public Office in the Spanish Indies Under the Hapsburgs* (1953)

Powell, P. W., *Soldiers, Indians and Silver* (1952)

Priestley, H. I., *Coming of the White Man* (1929)

Schurz, W. L., *Latin America* (rev. ed., 1964)

———, *Manila Galleon* (1939)

Service, E. R., "The Encomienda in Paraguay," *Hispanic American Historical Review*, XXXI, 230–50

———, *Spanish-Guaraní Relations in Early Colonial Paraguay* (1954)

Simpson, L. B., *Encomienda in New Spain* (1950; rev. ed., 1966)

———, *Exploitation of Land in Central Mexico in the Sixteenth Century* (1952)

———, *Many Mexicos* (3rd ed., 1952)

———, *Repartimiento System of Forced Native Labor in New Spain and Guatemala* (1938)

Smith, R. S., *The Spanish Guild Merchant* (1940)

West, R. C., *Colonial Placer Mining in Colombia* (1952)

———, *Mining Community in Northern New Spain: Parral Mining District* (1949)

Whitaker, A. P., *The Huancavelica Mine* (1941)

———, "Spanish Contributions to American Agriculture," *Agriculture History*, III, 1–14

Wilgus, A. C., ed., *Colonial Hispanic America* (1936)

Zurita, Alonzo de, *Life and Labor in Ancient Mexico*, trans. B. Keen (1963)

Chapter 11

Church and Faith
in the Spanish Colonies

SECULAR AND REGULAR CHURCH
ORGANIZATION UNDER THE CROWN OF SPAIN

"**O**UR REDEEMER GAVE this victory to our illustrious King and Queen . . . whence all Christendom should rejoice for the winning of so many peoples to our Holy Faith," wrote Columbus to Isabella as he returned from the first voyage in the spring of 1493. When he discovered the mainland at the mouth of the Orinoco in 1498, his message was, "Your Highnesses have here another world where our Holy Faith may be spread." For the next fifty years explorers named their new finds after the Spanish equivalents of the Holy Trinity, the Name of God, Saint James, Saint Dominic, Flowery Easter, Thanks to God, the Body of Christ, the Assumption of the Virgin. Cortés' first meeting with Indians at Tabasco was blessed by the setting up of an altar to the Virgin. Whenever he won a victory on the march to Mexico, Cortés said, "Above all, the great mercy of God gave us strength."

This missionary spirit, this deep devotion, went with every Spaniard to the New World, no matter how personally ambitious or greedy he might have been, no matter how hard he was in his treatment of individual Indians. As each colony was founded, identical steps were taken to spread the faith—a chaplain with the conquerors, missionary brothers to convert the heathen, bishoprics created and churches built as soon as towns were founded, priests and friars trying to protect the Indians from exploitation.

Catholic Christianity was thus one of the strongest forces in colonial Spain. Great praise is due the devout church workers for their missionary spirit, their bravery, their persistence, their part in transplanting European culture and civilization to America over enormous distances to rugged frontiers. True, the Church in America had its faults; members of its personnel often failed to live up to the high standards incumbent upon them; the church organizations became rich and politically powerful; religious institutions controlled education sometimes to the extent of keeping out new ideas, and always with an intolerance of other faiths. Most of these conditions reflected the times in Europe. The faults of the Church peculiar to the New World were due to human frailties rather than to institutional evils. In almost every task the Church undertook it was the only agency in existence to attempt such work.

It is hard for the cynical modern to comprehend the intense religious feeling of the sixteenth century, that century which was to be remembered for its bitter wars between Catholic and Protestant, its fanatical punishment of heresies on either side, its missionary zeal, its close connection between church and state. Because of their championship of the cause of Catholic Christianity, Ferdinand and Isabella had been granted special powers by the Pope over the clergy in Spain, and were known as The Catholic Monarchs. The unity they had established for all Spain involved conformity to Catholicism, and their absolutism gave them the power to root out all nonconformists as heretics. Wherever Spain went in the New World, the Roman Catholic Church went also, upholding the sanctity of kings and transmitting Spanish institutions and culture.

A papal bull had set the Line of Demarcation in the first place to give Spain her legal claim to the new lands. In the next two decades other papal bulls were to give the Spanish kings direct control of the Church in America. The Crown made appointments under the *real patronato*, the right of the king in Spain to make appointments to positions usually filled in other countries by the Pope alone. The Crown was to control the church buildings and handle the taxes collected for the Church. In return for these unusual powers the Spanish Crown was obligated to back all church activity financially and, above all, to "instruct and convert the natives."

After the first few years on the islands the Church organization for the New World was completely separate from, though parallel to, the Church hierarchy of Seville or Madrid. Royal control over it was as thoroughly consolidated as Crown control of the courts or of the customs collection. Only in the *fuero*, the special privilege of church personnel to be tried only in church courts, did the clergy act independently of the Crown. No churchman could go to the New World for any reason without royal license. Appointments of bishops, creation of new dioceses, even communications between abbots and bishops in the New World and their counterparts in Seville, or between an archbishop in Mexico and the Pope in Rome were carried on by the Council of the Indies. Even papal bulls applying to the colonies had to be approved by the Council before they could be published in the Indies.

The Church returned the interest and devotion of the monarchs by serving as a bulwark of monarchy. The clerics were beholden to the king for finances and favors, and they in turn served the monarchs faithfully, instilling in the minds of their ignorant flocks an almost universal devotion to the royal person. Church organization both at home and in the colonies consisted of two branches, the "regulars" or members of holy orders of monks and nuns, and the "seculars," the clergy who directly served the public as parish priests and the archbishops and bishops above them. The head of the secular clergy for the colonies was called the Patriarch of the Indies, a position of great importance throughout the colonial period, as the Patriarch resided at court and served *ex officio* on the Council of the Indies.

Under the Patriarch were the archbishops and bishops in America. At first the Archbishop of Seville was the chief prelate for the island colonies, but as Spain's power stretched north and south, bishoprics were created in provincial capitals. Then, in the 1540s, archbishops were sent to the capitals of the new viceroyalties, Mexico City and Lima, with only nominal subservience to the archbishop at Seville. By the end of the colonial era there were ten archbishops in Spanish America and thirty-eight bishops' dioceses. These church divisions did not always coincide with the political divisions, a situation which was to lead to some confusion during the early days of independence. The men who were appointed bishops and archbishops were almost always Spaniards born in Spain, usually men of noble birth, of high ability, and the best education. Ten of them became viceroys of Mexico during their New World sojourn. American-born Spaniards, the pure whites called creoles, seldom received such eminence in the church, and had to be satisfied with positions as curates, priests, and missionaries. The archbishop of Mexico received 130,000 pesos in salary, and a parish priest about 125 yearly.

Under the bishop were the dignitaries of the cathedral chapters, for every diocese had a cathedral with its many canons and prelates. At the lower levels were the thousands of parish priests, who preached in the town and village churches scattered all over the Spanish colonies. The parish priests were responsible for the church buildings erected by law in every town, Spanish or Indian, and for such schools and hospitals as it was possible to maintain. Close to the common people as these priests were, many of them were to side with the colonists during the wars for independence, while the bishops were almost always royalists.

Since the Spanish Crown had taken the Christianizing and civilizing of the natives as its most serious obligations to the Pope and the Church, the missionary churchmen, members of the "regular" orders, were naturally the most numerous in the colonies. The conquest was considered a "crusade" against the heathen and virtually every fleet from the time of Columbus' second voyage bore a contingent of friars, Franciscans, Dominicans, or Augustinians, to carry on such a campaign of conversion. Once the Spanish power was spread to the mainland of Mexico, fifteen different organizations of regulars eventually appeared there, ready to convert millions of Indians over a vast terrain. After the founding of the Society of Jesus by Ignatius Loyola, a militant Spaniard, the Jesuits became very important in the fields of education and missionary work. The first Jesuits arrived in New Spain in 1572. Each order was a worldwide organization, of course, and had its own elaborate hierarchy, with its general resident in Rome, a commissary-general in Madrid, and various ranking officials in America.

The members of the orders in America were divided into two classes: there were those who worked in the actual frontier missions—that work for which the *padres* are best and most warmly remembered—and those who lived in or near the Europeanized cities in monasteries or convents, devoted themselves to social services and to educating the children of the Spanish town dwellers, or gave their lives to meditation.

SHRINES, SAINTS, AND RELIGIOUS CELEBRATIONS

Hispanized communities, with their culture imported entirely from Spain, centered their life around the Church and its parish priest as did their Spanish prototypes.

In every colonial village or town the church is the finest building, set on the central plaza, its interior richer, more colorful, and more magnificent than anything else the colonial children of the town had ever had a chance to see in their narrow little lives. Some of the larger colonial churches are famous examples of the architecture of the time. Mexico City had a church building for every three or four blocks of residences. Puebla, a hundred miles to the southeast, is said to have the most churches per population of any city in the New World: Romanesque churches with round domes, Italian Renaissance Churches, roofs of brilliant blue and yellow glazed tile, façades of ornate carving or of Majolica tiles in picture patterns.

Not only was the church building the center of the town, but its priest was the town's social arbiter and community leader, and church procedure was the center of social life. Family life was built around its traditions, just as most Latin American family life is today. A child's birth was registered in the parish register; he received a baptismal certificate rather than a civil birth certificate. Godparents who sponsored him at baptism promised to help him all his life, and the relationship was very close and personal. Probably a boy's elementary education, and certainly his secondary education, was in church schools. Marriage was a religious sacrament blessed by the priest and never to be broken by divorce. As a grown man, the town dweller belonged to a religious brotherhood, an *hermandad* or men's lodge which conducted social affairs and looked after charity cases. For every venture a man prayed to his own saint, promising penance and gifts if his requests were granted, and often offering to bear the whole expense of the next fiesta as a "major domo." If life became hard for him or he lost his family, he could go into a monastery and be cared for for life. At death he was given a church funeral and was buried in holy ground. A woman's life even more than a man's was bound by religious restrictions. Going into a convent was her only possible career other than marriage within the church fold. This pattern of life has remained unchanged for many families in Latin America since colonial times.

The public social events in a town or city were largely connected with religious celebrations. Pageants and parades for Carnival, Palm Sunday, and Easter, *posadas* for Christmas, miracle plays from medieval Europe, and especially the celebration of the birthday of a town's own patron saint—these were the high points of the year. A patron saint's birthday is even today a week-long festival for any town in rural Latin America; the processions and pageantry given in his honor may be identical to those of the 1670s or the 1770s.

Latin America has produced its own saints and beatified persons, all of them religious leaders remembered for their service to the unfortunate. Colombia has a beloved friar named San Pedro Claver, who worked for forty years among the slaves who built the fortifications of Cartagena, and kept a mission down in the slave pens where they were forced to live. Fray Pedro Gante, Peter of Ghent, came to Mexico City after Cortés and founded schools among the Aztec children. Don Vasco de Quiroga christianized the Tarascan Indians in Mexico's Lake Pátzcuaro region and helped them develop colorful handicrafts with lacquer which their descendants still sell to tourists today. Paraguay had its patron and first American saint in the missionary father San Francisco Solano, who died working in the inhospitable Gran Chaco. Two religious leaders of Lima were canonized by the Pope, the first an archbishop named Toribio who learned to speak Quechua and made a tour on foot and muleback to every community he could reach in Peru, the other a sanctified young girl who was canonized as Saint Rose of Lima.

Special shrines in the New World became as famous as spots for pilgrimages as any in Spain or Italy. In the church of Guadalupe, four miles from the center of Mexico City, is kept a miraculous painting of a dark-haired, brown-skinned girl, the Indian Virgin of Guadalupe, patron saint of all Indian people in Mexico. This painting is believed to have appeared on the *sarape* or blanket of Juan Diego, a poor Christianized Aztec Indian, on December 9, 1531. He had been visited by a vision of the Virgin when picking cactus apples on the Guadalupe Hill; she requested him to ask the bishop that a church be built there. As proof she caused roses to grow among the cactus; when he picked the roses and carried them to the bishop in his *sarape*, the picture appeared on the blanket. The shrine subsequently built by the bishop is today visited by thousands of devout Mexicans, many of whom climb the hill on their knees on December 9. The appearance of a brown-skinned Virgin was an enormous influence in helping the Spanish priests convert the Indians.

During colonial days, other statues and shrines became competitors of the Virgin of Guadalupe. Colonists of pure Spanish blood paid little attention to her, but worshiped at the shrine of Our Lady of Los Remedios. South Americans had their shrines also. The chapel of the Virgin of Copacabana on Lake Titicaca is still the goal of pilgrimages today. In a revered little town near Buenos Aires there is the statue of the Virgin of Luján;

when it was being carried inland by oxcart in 1630, the cart halted at Luján, and the oxen would go no further. Argentines consider that the Virgin wished to stay near Buenos Aires; all good Catholics of Argentina try to go to see this statue. Thus colonial life at all levels and in all regions was deeply influenced by the Church, and that influence is still a vital part of Latin America today.

THE INFLUENCE OF THE CATHOLIC FAITH ON THE INDIANS

Such a social life centered around the church was no new thing for the immigrant from Spain; he brought it with him as part of his heritage. But to the Indians the ideas and rituals and celebrations of Christianity were a whole new life. The conversion of the Indians was Isabella's fondest dream concerning the new islands of the Indies, and the speed with which the Indian religions were replaced by Christianity is one of the remarkable facts of the Western Hemisphere. Some criticism can be made as to the way in which vast numbers were "converted" at first; often a "requisition" was merely read aloud to them in Spanish, which of course they did not understand, giving a theological explanation of the history of Christianity. After hearing such reading, and watching the celebration of mass, Indians were content to be baptized in great numbers. The historian Motolinía tells us that over four million were baptized during the first fifteen years of the conquest of Mexico. Between 1524 and 1531 the Franciscan fathers there claimed more than a million conversions. One famous missionary, Fray Pedro de Gante, wrote to his king that 14,000 Aztecs had been baptized on a single June day in 1529; "many of us have baptized more than 100,000 each during our sojourn here." In order to "eliminate heathen practices," some of this conversion was by physical force, temples were torn down, idols destroyed, and severe punishments inflicted by the Spanish military on those who resisted. "Save their souls first, then teach and train them afterward," was the motto.

Teach and train them the missionaries proceeded to do, as more and more friars came, and as a new generation of Indians accustomed to Spanish ways grew up. Friars in coarse habits, pledged to poverty and simplicity, presented a different picture than did the inhabitants of the rich monasteries in Mexico City and Lima. Assigned to Indian agricultural villages or frontier missions, they devoted themselves to the well-being of their charges and became famous in the annals of their orders. They were sent out at royal expense and their early months of mission expenses were paid by the Crown. As the secular clergy were too few in number on the wide frontier, the papacy issued special dispensations giving the regulars the right to perform the duties of ordained priests. This caused much of the jealousy between seculars and regulars, and was ended in 1757 when secularization of well-established missions was ordered.

In most frontier missions the religion was a thin veneer on the old barbarism. The primitive natives had difficulty in comprehending the involved spiritual doctrines of the Church; Christianity for them was simply a new mixture of superstition and formalism. With the veneer of Christian faith, they also received a thin coating of European culture. They lost the old tribal ethical standards which they had understood, but they did not grasp the ethics of the new. That such great numbers of natives were involved in the first century of expansion indicates that the clergy worked for numbers rather than for high ideals. The *conquistadores* did not help in inspiring the Indians to follow Christian ethical principles and often by their example undid what the friars accomplished. From a governmental point of view, the missionaries did a splendid job, pacifying many tribes without arms, defending the frontier, and Hispanizing entire areas.

The greatest energy and zeal was exhibited on the barbarous frontier at the farthest limits of empire in both North and South America. The missionaries bravely contacted the tribes, studied the languages and customs of each region, endured hardships, hunger, disease, and martyrdom. The Indians were "reduced" into missions and were taught the elements of civil and religious life. Veneer or no, the culture they acquired included agricultural and craft training, arts, music, and letters, for the missions were really schools. Trained for their tasks at their own missionary colleges such as the Franciscan College at Querétaro, the friars were explorers, diarists, historians, architects, geographers, and linguists, as well as teachers of agriculture and agents of the Crown. They often acted as anthropologists,

Guatemalan Indians combining ancient Mayan rites with Christian worship in the Church of Santo Tomás Chichicastenango. *Courtesy Pan American Union.*

making studies of tribal life that are of value in analyzing primitive groups today. On the most remote frontiers—Upper California, Texas, Florida, the Guiana border of Venezuela, the Araucanian territory of southern Chile, the Guaraní country of Paraguay and Iguassú—the missions were the outposts of empire, and were often fortified by *presidios* or garrisons of soldiers.

The most famous missions are those in California and those in Paraguay. The Jesuits worked for two centuries in Durango, Sinaloa, and Sonora in northern Mexico, moving northward as their missions became villages taken over by the seculars. Finally their "farthest-north worker," Father Eusebio Kino, who had spent twenty-four years in the Nogales-Tucson-Yuma triangle of Arizona teaching the Pima Indians, extended his work to Lower California through his support of Father Salvatierra. His mission at Dolores on the mainland was so rich that he could send thousands of cattle to help start the farms for the mission on the inhospitable desert land of Lower California.

The Franciscans were later given the task of extending the mission chain into Alta California. The twenty-one missions in California, from San Diego north through Santa Barbara, Monterey, and San Francisco, are familiar landmarks to all Californians. Though life in them has been over-romanticized, it was typical of such settlements wherever the monastic orders went among uncivilized peoples throughout the length of Latin America. Father Junípero Serra, a sort of patron saint to California school children today, founded many of the missions in the chain, starting with San Diego in 1769. From the first reed huts, the mission buildings were transformed by skilled Indians in the second generation into large adobe-brick chapels, many of which, restored, still stand today. At the height of their power, the missions were surrounded by homes for the priest-teachers, barracks for a guard of Spanish soldiers, dormitories for unmarried Indians, huts for families, and long lines of blacksmith shops, olive and wine presses, smoke houses, leather-tooling shops, brick-making yards, pottery kilns, and tanneries. Do not think the Indians who lived there were always happy. If they longed for their former free life, where diet was sparse but heavy work and strict discipline unknown, they could not run away without Spanish soldiers chasing them; the mission fathers sometimes had them flogged when caught. Probably the young people of the second generation who were born into the mission life profited more from the mission experience than did their parents.

In South America missionaries were so much a part of local history that the Argentine province on the Paraguay is called Misiones, and Argentine tourists take cruises up into the semitropics to see the abandoned Jesuit missions in the jungle. The Jesuits arrived from Peru in 1605, having been ordered by the Crown to stop the encroachments by the Portuguese slave raiders from Brazil in the area to the northeast of Asunción. They founded missions on the upper Paraná and upper Paraguay. Though their early missions in Paraguay were destroyed by the slave raiders and perhaps 60,000 mission Indians carried into slavery in Brazil, the devoted Jesuits were able to retreat with 12,000 neophytes and settle south of the Falls of the Iguassú. Here they eventually had thirty successful mission *pueblos* with perhaps 100,000 neophytes. They were provided with arms and were able to keep the Brazilian slave raiders at bay as a frontier force, while they developed an almost independent community of their own called "The Jesuit Republic."

In Candelaria, the largest of these Paraguayan settlements, the pattern was set up for a happy and prosperous, though strictly regimented life. The fathers ruled in every detail, acted as judges and used corporal punishment. Their agricultural empire was enormous, producing oranges, olives, and grapes as well as wheat and livestock. The Jesuit fathers learned the Guaraní language, wrote books in that language, and had them printed on their own printing presses in their extensive workshops. Thanks to this literary effort the Guaraní, of all Indian languages in the Americas, remains a written language today, and is widely spoken in modern Paraguay. But the influence of the mission fathers was not permanent. They had kept their charges under constant tutelage and completely isolated from other Spaniards, had themselves managed all the funds and carried on all the outside trade, maintaining a theocratic quasi-communism under which the Indians never learned self-reliance. When the Jesuits were expelled in 1767 the mission buildings fell into decay and the Indians relapsed into barbarism.

Because Indians in most areas did not understand the Christian doctrine as it was taught in Rome, they developed variations of their own. This was particularly true of Indian villages that had always been settled and where there had never been missions. If such communities had a local deity, a protector whose stone statue stood in the temple and was guarded by the medicine man, it was easy for church teachers to persuade the people to adopt a patron saint instead. In Peru, for instance, the persistence of the Inca religion among the Quechuas was reported in 1620 as a great problem for the Spanish government. There was confusion, so the report went, between the help the saints gave in time of stress and the help the Quechuas hoped to enlist from the mummies of their ancestors, the spirit of their "luck pieces," the sacrifice of guinea pigs, and the "incantations" of sorcerers. In the mid-twentieth century, the same rituals are regular observances in Andean life where Quechua is still spoken, though the villagers attend mass regularly and observe the outward forms of the Christian ritual. This is also true of the highland Indians of Guatemala and of many remote parts of Mexico.

ACTIVITIES, POWERS, AND ABUSES
OF CHURCH OFFICIALS

The mission fathers had their activities cut out for them on the frontier, their days full. So also with the parish priest, who became the "little father" of his town and without whose influence no Spanish family could be well ordered, no Spanish community could function. Friars and nuns in larger towns led busy lives as social workers and as teachers, for all the social service in the colonies, the schools, the hospitals, the asylums, the personal relief, the family charity was done by religious orders. When fortunes were left to the Church, it was that the gifts might be spent in charity. Bequests to the Church cared for foundlings, educated the children of the poor, provided poorhouses for the destitute and hospitals for the periodic epidemics of the time. As a wealthy industrialist of today might set up a foundation for a cancer clinic or for a boys' club, so in the sixteenth to eighteenth centuries, with no other social agencies in existence to do such things, a social-minded person gave money to the Church and commissioned some church group to spend it for him.

A wealthy Spaniard in Mexico City in the mid-1500s, for example, gave liberally to missions on the savage frontier, endowed a chair of theology in the new University of Mexico, and left 140,000 additional pesos to Jesuit charities. The members of the religious orders were also in charge of education, from the primary schools for Indian children to the Jesuit universities described in Chapter 13. Thus charity work and education kept thousands of the clergy occupied during endless hours of self-sacrifice. Doubtless there was more actual social service work done in the New World by Catholic personnel than done during the same period in the Old World by Protestant and Catholic workers combined, so challenging were the demands on a true missionary spirit.

However, in many areas there were more members of the regular and secular branches than the new colonies needed for religious instruction and personal sacraments. The various branches of the Church, combining all properties owned, held more than half of the productive land in some parts of the New World. Land was acquired by bequest by gift, by mortgage, and by tithes collected in cattle or acreage. From this wealth the archbishops received salaries comparable to those of the viceroys, while a poor parish priest worked on a pittance. Bishops and archbishops lived like royalty in palaces with ornate furnishings, and ruled vast estates like feudal lords. The Indians who lived on these estates were just as subject to abuse, overwork, heavy tribute, and *mita* service in the mines—some of the mines were Church-owned—as were Indians working for any private person, and often had less redress in the courts. Monasteries were exceedingly numerous, and are said to have owned a fourth of all the buildings in the cities of Mexico and Lima by 1750. In the face of such wealth, the monks in luxurious monasteries sometimes forgot their vows, relaxed in their discipline, and lived lives of licentiousness, idleness, and political intrigue, in contrast to the self-sacrifice and zeal of the frontier missionaries.

The wealth and influence of the Church in politics was one of the most troublesome problems to be carried over from the colonial era to the new republics, and in some parts of Latin America it is still a cause of conflict. Many church leaders were given to misuse of funds for personal political advantage, and to undignified quarrels over jurisdiction with civil authorities and between regulars and seculars. Since the tradition in Spain and in Rome had been special church courts to try cases involving priests or monks, or concerning disputes over church lands or church fees, so in the New World special courts grew up to keep such cases out of the civil courts. This produced a condition of privilege or *fuero* for churchmen which helped cause a revolution later in Mexico, and was a sore point to the other citizens even in colonial days. Priests, friars, and nuns, supposed to live exemplary lives, were often no better than run-of-the-mill towns-people, and sometimes worse—in an age when hypocrisy and immorality were the rule in Spain under the later Hapsburgs and early Bourbons. Colonists born in the New World were always jealous of the powerful churchmen who were Spanish-born and were sent out to head some rich parish or diocese with no knowledge of colonial conditions, holding positions which colonial-born Spaniards could never hope to reach.

Only a small minority of the clergy was involved in this bad aspect of the Church in America, a reflection in many way of conditions in Spain, but many reports sent to the king on the affairs of the Church in the New World mentioned conditions with horror. A "plainclothes" inspector in the eighteenth century, Antonio de Ulloa, reported to the king a long list of church abuses and concluded that "in Peru the life of the clergy was scandalous to an unbelievable degree." Their luxurious daily existence was in sharp contrast to that of the heroic mission fathers martyred on the frontier.

That the king sent such inspectors indicates some conflict between Church and state. Viceroys were jealous of archbishops, captains-general of bishops. The clergy threatened to have the Pope excommunicate political administrators; administrators retaliated by cutting off funds to the Church. There were interminable litigations over jurisdictions and funds in the courts, with appeals to the king and court hearings dragging on for decades.

The Church received money to run its organizations and activities from tithes, amounting to a tenth or *diezmo* of income on all agricultural and industrial products of the New World. From these funds and from the income from the Church's own farmlands and herds, cathedrals and city and parish churches were supported, as well as the missions, parochial schools, hospitals, and orphanages. Secular churchmen also received large amounts of produce and cash for religious services, such as sacraments, weddings, baptisms, funerals. Sometimes such services became a cause for dispute with political authority when *audiencias* and *cabildos* tried to set standard prices and individual churchmen often continued to charge "whatever the traffic would bear."

One of the Church's activities was to exercise "thought control" over the citizens. Books were censored, school curricula supervised, any deviation from accepted belief punished. Students of Spanish history are familiar with the Inquisition, that board of judgment and censorship which tried to regiment Spanish religious thought, and was famous for having sent heretics to the stake in Spain. To protect the orthodoxy of the Church against heretical contamination in the New World, Inquisitorial agents were sent from Spain as early as 1522. By 1570 Phillip II had decreed that a separate Inquisition be established in the New World, and three different courts were subsequently set up, one at Lima in 1570, one at Mexico City in 1571, and one at Cartagena in 1610.

The declared purpose of these colonial Inquisitorial tribunals was to punish blasphemy and immorality among the clergy, adultery and witch-craft among laymen, to censor morals in the colonies and, above all, to "maintain the purity of the faith" and to protect it against heresy. Throughout the colonial period there were very few trials for heresy, as nonconformists seldom were able to obtain legal passage to the colonies. Penalties for minor offenses, like blasphemy and immorality, included fines, penance, and flogging, work in the galleys and exile for bigamists, and burning for "proven heresy and witchcraft." In the three centuries of colonial rule only thirty heretics were burned in Lima, only forty-one in Mexico City. Some of these victims were Protestant "heretics" (the *Luteranos*, as even the irreligious English pirates were called in Spanish) who were captured while raiding along the Spanish Main. On the rare occasions when heretics were burned or "flogged through the streets of the city," the crowds in Mexico City or Lima or Bogotá looked on as at a carnival, returned to their purely orthodox Catholic communities, and felt little of the religious upheaval and intolerance which wracked Europe in the wars of the time. Thus the Inquisition was never as fearsome in America as it was in Spain.

The Inquisition served religious and moral purposes, and so it had to "prevent" as well as punish disbelief. To do so it maintained the Index, that list prepared by the Inquisitorial courts in Rome and in Spain of books that were not to be sold, printed, nor read in the colonies, and naturally not shipped there from Europe. The forbidden list contained all works by Jews, Mohammedans, and Protestants. Any book containing the idea of popular sovereignty was considered heretical. The bishops and priests helped the Inquisition by closely supervising the reading of the parishioners. Church agents could enter private homes, question crews about cargo, and keep a watchful eye out for all smuggled books and papers, and check the wares of bookshops in the New World cities. Many hundreds of books listed by the Index got through this "thought-control screen" anyway, and some were even read by the members of the clergy themselves.

Thus the Inquisition attempted to keep out foreign ideas that were considered dangerous to Church and Crown, and thereby hindered intellectual progress and freedom of opinion; at the same time it suppressed heresy and punished public and private scandals, and served the empire by keeping people loyal and orthodox.

Contrary to popular modern belief, Indians were never subject to the Inquisition; because of their "ignorance and weak minds" they were excused from its regulation. It was not Inquisitorial judges, but a few misguided missionaries who destroyed Indian religious objects and punished recalcitrant pagans among the newly baptized. There is only one case on record of a converted Indian being put to death by a religious court for "backsliding to heathen practices."

Leaders in education in the colonies were the members of the Jesuit order. Their novices strictly trained, their leaders highly educated, and their monasteries among the richest in the New World, they were the most efficient and successful missionaries and university teachers. They were also extremely wealthy, and owned vast areas of fertile land. Defying lay authority, they often pursued profit for their order; they controlled the Peruvian market in wheat, brandy, sugar, and hides, for example, in spite of royal rules against clerics' participating in commerce. With such power and funds they could challenge the viceroy himself.

Then in 1750 came open defiance of royal authority from the very unworldly and unselfish Jesuit missionaries on the Paraguayan frontier. By treaty with Portugal, territory on the upper Paraná, which included the populous mission settlement of Candelaria, had been ceded to Brazil; the mission fathers refused to obey both the order and the Portuguese authorities from São Paulo who came to take over the missions. An open war against the transfer ensued, the Indians fighting in armies led by the Jesuits. At home in Europe, in Spain and in other Catholic countries as well, the rich and powerful Jesuit order had produced jealousy by its interference in politics. Suddenly, by royal order, the 2,260 Jesuits in America were expelled, their property confiscated by the government, and the clerics themselves sent to Italy. This unexpected action caused near rebellion in some parts of America, such as the riots in the streets in Guanajuato and San Luis Potosí in Mexico where the Jesuits were leaders in community social projects. The Jesuits who went to Italy remained fanatically opposed to the Spanish Crown, and were instrumental in circulating propaganda for independence thirty years later.

In favor of the church officials in the New World, it must be granted that no other religious organization in history has done a more complete job than the Spanish Catholic Church in the new continent. Charges can be made against this institution as it affected Latin American history, however. It sought to monopolize moral and educational leadership in every community, dabbled in politics, and failed to live up to its own high standard. This situation created problems with which Latin American republics are still wrestling.

Readings

Baird, J. A., Jr., *The Churches of Mexico, 1530–1810* (1962)

Barth, P. J., *Franciscan Education and the Social Order in Spanish North America, 1502–1821* (1945)

Bolton, H. E., *Rim of Christendom* (1936)

——, *Wider Horizons of American History* (esp. essay on the "Mission as a Frontier Institution") (1939)

Braden, C. S., *Religious Aspects of the Conquest of Mexico* (1930)

Cleven, N. A. N., *Readings in Hispanic American History* (1927)

Conway, G. R. G., *An Englishman and the Mexican Inquisition, 1556–1560* (1927)

Demarest, D., and C. Taylor, *The Dark Virgin: The Book of Our Lady of Guadalupe* (1959)

Diffie, B. W., *Latin American Civilization: Colonial Period* (1945)

Dunne, P. M., *Pioneer Black Robes on the West Coast* (1940; and other works by author)

Gannon, M. V., *The Cross in the Sand: The Early Catholic Church in Florida, 1513–1820* (1966)

Graham, R. B. C., *A Vanished Arcadia* (1924)

Greenleaf, R. E., *Zumárraga and the Mexican Inquisition* (1961)

Hanke, L., *The Spanish Struggle for Justice in the Conquest of America* (1959)

Haring, C. H., *Spanish Empire in America* (1952)

Harney, M. P., *The Jesuits in History* (1941)

Houtart, F., and E. Pin, *The Church and the Latin American Revolution* (1965)

Jacobsen, J. V., *Education Foundations of the Jesuits in Sixteenth Century New Spain* (1938)

Keyes, F. P., *The Rose and the Lily: The Lives and Times of Two South American Saints* (1961)

Lea, H. C., *Inquisition in the Spanish Dependencies* (1908)

Leonard, I. A., *Baroque Times in Old Mexico* (1959)

McClaskey, J. Y., *Inquisition Papers of Mexico* (1947)

Mecham, J. L., *Church and State in Latin America* (rev. ed., 1966)

Moore, J. P., *The Cabildo of Peru Under the Hapsburgs, 1530–1700* (1954)

Mörner, M., *Expulsion of Jesuits from Latin America* (1965)

———, *Political and Economic Activities of the Jesuits in the La Plata Region: The Hapsburg Era* (1953)

Moses, B., *Spanish Dependencies in South America* (2 vols., 1914)

O'Neill, G., *Golden Years on the Paraguay: History of Jesuit Missions* (1934)

Parry, J. H., *Audiencia of New Galicia in the Sixteenth Century* (1948)

Phelan, J. L., *The Millenial Kingdom of the Franciscans in the New World* (1956)

Pike, F. B., *Conflict of Church and State in Latin America* (1964)

Priestley, H. I., *Coming of the White Man* (1929)

Rippy, J. F., and J. Nelson, *Crusaders of the Jungle* (1936)

Scholes, F. V., *Church and State in New Mexico, 1610–1670* (2 vols., 1937–1945)

Shiels, W. E., *King and Church: The Rise and Fall of the Patronato Real* (1961)

Studies Presented at the Conference on the History of Religion in the New World During Colonial Times (Washington, D.C., 1958)

Tibesar, A., *Franciscan Beginnings in Colonial Peru* (1953)

Warren, F. B., *Vasco de Quiroga and His Pueblo Hospitals of Santa Fe* (1963)

Wilgus, A. C., ed., *Colonial Hispanic America* (1936)

Chapter 12

People and Society
in the Spanish Colonies

CASTES AND CLASSES: THE DOMINANT WHITES

As is shown by the story of Garcilaso de la Vega, el Inca, the people of Latin America, after a mere half-century, had begun to be a new race, a mixed people who combined elements and characteristics of three continents—America, Europe, and (with the introduction of the Negro culture) Africa. In this "melting pot" the amalgam did not all become a blending like Garcilaso, but the new metal formed in layers, determined by blood and color content, dictated by nature and by official document as well. Naturally there were three basic colors—white, red, and black. Within each there were variations, and the mixtures gradually outnumbered the "pure," for the small number of Spaniards who conquered America did not conquer an unpopulated expanse of territory, but a hemisphere already full of people. In those areas where the Indians were barbarous, they were annihilated and the population is today mostly white, as in Uruguay and Argentina. In the areas of sedentary Indians, of town and city civilization, the Indians remained as the work force; few white women came at first, and intermarriage and miscegenation ran rampant, to create modern nations of many mixed bloods. In both cases, however, the whites always kept the upper hand socially, politically, and economically, and remained the highest caste in which no one of color gained membership.

Spain, not always legally, but by actual consistent practice, evolved a very highly fixed differentiation of castes. The apex of this social pyramid was not just the white man, but the white man born in Spain. The mercantilist colonial theory said that colonies existed for the good of the mother country; by the same theory, the cream of jobs and profits in the colonies should go to the Spaniards born in the mother country. It was only by exceptional means that other whites of the same content of blood and color —pure white Spaniards of noble lineage, but unfortunate enough to have been born in the colonies—were able to "break into" the top social classes and to gain their special advantages and privileges. Such "breaks" were usually by way of purchased certificates which proclaimed the bearer to be of Spanish birth, or by way of licenses available only to colonials of great wealth.

The more the Spanish royal family at home declined physically and mentally, the more the Crown distrusted anyone not born close to the royal court. Thus, many jobs were given to impoverished Spaniards, parasites and relatives of the court, while the American-born were discriminated against. Spanish tradition disdained the commercial trades, the professions, or the crafts, and only government jobs were socially acceptable. These lush jobs were received in Spain before the office-seeker left, for Spain was the source of all patronage in the colonies.

Thus economic class lines also separated the creoles, the American-born, from the Spanish-born. The Crown did encourage farmers and artisans to come from Spain, but comparatively few did, and they went to such "democratic" frontiers as Argentina, Chile, or Costa Rica. The colonials called the Spanish-born variously *chapetones*, the tenderfeet, or *gachupines*, the "spurred ones" who overrode all others, and sometimes *peninsulares*, or else *Godos* or Goths, referring to the Visigothic barbarians who had conquered Spain so long before. The colonials hated them all, though they fawned on the Spanish aristocrats, aped their ways, and hoped to pass as Spanish-born themselves.

To stimulate industry, Madrid at times authorized the emigration to America of non-Spanish Europeans who were skilled artisans, engineers, or metallurgists. There were also often legally approved Italian, Flemish, or German missionaries. So it is not surprising to note the number of foreigners who showed up in the New World, despite the general Spanish restrictions on emigration. Many deserted from ships in New World ports; many entered clandestinely. Travelers and learned men came to visit and remained. Lima had Frenchmen, Italians, Germans, Flemings, Greeks, Irishmen, Englishmen, Moors from North Africa, and even East Indians and Chinese busy in various trades by 1700. Of the five wealthiest people in Guatemala, one was a Genoese and two were Portuguese. These foreigners were almost entirely occupied in trade and shipping—money-making pursuits scorned by the true *gachupines*. By 1600 there were 200,000 whites in Spanish America, settled in more than 200 towns and controlling more than 4,000,000 Indians and mixed-bloods.

The second class of whites, the American-born, were called creoles, in Spanish, *criollos*, a term misused today, but originally meaning anyone of pure European extraction but native to the New World. Though the emigration of single women from Spain was never favored, married men were required to take their families with them when they went as settlers rather than as soldiers, and to such families children were born. With these native-born Americans was born a pride of blood, a sense of aristocracy, a scorn of manual labor. They inherited the lands granted their fathers, and all the rights to control Indian workers, but they had less prestige and privilege, and were considered inferior by the aristocrats who came out from Spain. Of all the viceroys in Mexico up to 1813, only four were creoles; of 602 captains-general and governors, only fourteen.

The very philosophy about their inferiority worked against the creoles; they were born in an atmosphere where the work was done by servile races; they knew that they would inherit the vast lands and riches but that the opportunities at the top were closed to them. Thus the young creole men often did become worthless and indolent; vanity and pride kept them from working in commerce and industry. If related to distinguished families in Spain, they could occasionally buy their way into military offices, positions in the higher clergy, or, rarely, political jobs.

The colonial aristocracy remained a group of the utmost wealth held in land, a group which called themselves the *gente decente*, wore clothes of silk, and lived better than the aristocrats born in Spain from among whom the *gachupín* officials came. Spaniards wrote home that the creoles were "prone to gambling and love affairs, and attendance at bullfights and cock-fights" for lack of anything better to do, and expressed surprise when they found elegant manners and "gentle and discreet speech" at creole society gatherings. Young sons of such society were educated in the Jesuit universities in the colonies, or sometimes sent to universities in Europe for their last years of schooling. Then they became lawyers, doctors, professors, priests, and nursed their discontent. Such a wealthy creole was Simón Bolívar, richest young man in Venezuela, who had the breeding, the polish, the education both at home and abroad, to surpass most young Spaniards, but who by the very discrimination against his class was embittered enough to devote his life to freeing that class from Spain forever.

If the creole disliked the aristocratic peninsular, the *gachupín* who received all the lucrative and honorable positions, he bitterly hated the humbler classes of Spain, the *chapetones* or tenderfeet, who came in as farmers and artisans. With little education and no social standing in the homeland, they nevertheless rated in importance above any proud creole of no matter what education and inherited wealth. These humbler Spaniards, usually Basques or Catalans from Northern Spain, often gained an entrance into exclusive circles after they made a fortune from trade. They had the prestige of Spanish birth, were not too proud to start as peddlers, and lacked the inferiority complex of the bitter young creole. They often married wealthy creole women and created hostilities even within families. The antagonism generated between these two classes carried over into hostility even in church leadership, for a poor uneducated Spaniard could have a promotion in church or monastery over the most distinguished creole.

THE INDIANS AND THE MESTIZOS

The Western Hemisphere was the red men's continent. What, in general, do militant colonizing peoples do with native populations? Those natives who are leaders perhaps adopt the civilization of the colonizing power. Those who have done the work for the native leaders stay and work for the new masters. Those who lived off the beaten track of the colonizers remain unchanged. To a large extent this pattern held true in Latin America. Historians for centuries painted the Spanish treatment of the Indians in the blackest colors, told and retold many tales of torture or exploitation. Anglo-Saxons, too, have forgotten tales just as black in the treatment of natives within their own empire. Modern historians think that early reformers such as Las Casas exaggerated the cruelties, that the Black Legend of Spanish mistreatment of the natives was widely circulated in Europe by Spain's Protestant enemies, that captains and adventurers of the sixteenth century from any European nation would have reacted to the peoples of the New World in the same way. Spanish kings for a hundred years tried to enforce laws to protect the Indians, and friars served as their champions when the laws were broken. Spanish policy was to reduce the Indians to village life, separated from the Europeans but converted to the European religion, to "eradicate odious practices among them" and train them in essential trades.

However, the pure-blooded Indians remained near the bottom of the social scale, widely distributed and differing greatly from tribe to tribe, and often preserving their own language and customs. Their fundamental role in society was that of food-producer. Their living standards were low; they were wretchedly housed, undernourished, and addicted to alcohol in which they found solace. Held by law to be minors, considered in a

Young teacher-training students in an historical pageant in Oaxaca, Mexico, carry in their faces the evidence of the three classes of colonial times. The tall girl is of pure Spanish Blood, the girl to her left is *mestizo*, and the girl with the flowers is pure Indian, of the Zapotecan tribe, as are most of the girls in the background. *Photo by Helen Miller Bailey.*

"perpetual state of tutelage," and protected by a vast legislation against exploitation by their "betters," most of the Indians were serfs. They were subject to "unlimited exactions in labor and product" by *corregidores, caciques,* and priests. From the first they constituted a ready labor supply in a land where Spanish *hidalgos* avoided work. Governors and slave raiders broke Isabella's rules for good treatment from the first. Viceroys in Mexico and Peru were forced to soften the New Laws of 1542 which had been passed to stop the exploitation of Indian labor. Though the viceroy remained the Indians' legal protector, and they had their own special court of appeal, the *Juzgado de Indios* in Mexico, few Indians received real redress of grievances.

After three centuries, two general types of Indian labor persisted; peonage on agricultural lands and forced drafts in mines and on public works. When the *encomienda* system was abolished by law, landlords worked out other ways to hold the Indians in bondage. Advance payments for seeds and equipment for baptismal or funeral expenses for the Indian's family were granted as loans. Then the overseer saw to it that the Indian never got out of debt, and thus his family could never leave the land. This system persisted in Mexico till 1910, and was partially responsible for a violent Mexican civil war which began in that year.

In Peru and Bolivia the Indians suffered particularly under the *mita* system that sent them to labor in the mines and on public works. Almost every traveler to the mining country was distressed by the conditions there, and many are the reports in the archives which tell of slave labor conditions, limited rations, and high death rates among the miners. Some of these reports resulted in improved conditions; where royal laws as to the protection of Indians were enforced, conditions for gold or silver miners in Latin America were better in 1700 than for coal miners in England in 1800. Laws forbade Indians from free villages doing forced labor as textile weavers in *obrajes* or as pearl divers, but in years of weak rule in Spain these humane laws were violated in the colonies. Throughout the colonial period there were many Indian revolts, all repressed severely. The Indians were always looked on as children, though "subjects of the Crown" with souls.

Apart from the workers forced by the Spaniards to labor in mine and field, there lived the tribal Indians. Some Indian groups—the Tarascans north of Mexico City, the Zapotecans on the Isthmus of Tehuantepec, the Aymará in Bolivia, the Maya in Yucatan, the Cachiqueles of Guatemala— all of them semicivilized peoples in 1492—remained unchanged for generations, and many of their villages still speak their own languages and follow their ancient customs today. In every place that semicivilized agricultural communities had existed, hundreds of them continued to exist, unchanged by Spanish ways—except perhaps by the introduction of burros and oxen—and ruled still by their own *caciques* or chieftains. Under law, such *caciques* were allowed to retain oppressive powers over their tribesmen.

In Mexico, northern Central America, Peru, Ecuador, Bolivia, and Paraguay, Indian people are the basis of today's population. The villages remained intact where they were remote from colonial centers, or where there was no gold or silver to be mined and little flat land for plantation-type crops; in those cases the Spaniards never came in as actual occupants, but merely collected tribute. On the remote frontiers the Indians kept up the battle against the white man just as did the Sioux and the Pawnee in the Mississippi Valley. Popé, a medicine man, led the Pueblos in a revolt that caused temporary abandonment of the colony of New Mexico in the 1680s. The Araucanians in Chile staged one three-century-long revolt; they have sometimes been called the "Apaches of South America."

The Indians who came in and out of Mexico City to bring produce to market impressed Alexander von Humboldt, the scientific German observer who visited the New World in 1803, as being ignorant and lazy, "due to circumstances under which they have to live." They "built huts of wood, clay, and uncut stone; they did not eat beef, mutton, or wheaten bread, nor drink wine nor wear silk." Their dress was "that of a slave, linen breeches to the calves of the legs, a cotton shirt like a sack with three openings for head and arms, and, in winter, a blanket with a hole in the center," the present-day *sarape*. But von Humboldt did not find Mexico's Indians living as "'meanly as peasants of North Europe" lived in 1800, and he concluded that "not only has the number of natives increased for a century, but that also the whole vast region we describe as New Spain is more inhabited today [1803] than before the arrival of the Europeans."

In between the "pure" white on top and the "pure" red at the bottom, stand the great mass of Latin Americans, the mixed-bloods. Mixtures among the three races formed a kaleidoscope of color with great variations of shades and complexions and social castes. The laws of the Indies recognized differences between mulattoes, the mixture of black and white, *mestizos,* the mixture between red and white, and *zambos,* the mixture between red and black. These were rudimentary combinations, however; Spanish records noted differentiations down to the nineteenth degree of blood mixture and as many as eighty different castes, with legal Spanish terms for every variation, terms which often appear in documents of the time.

It was the *mestizo* who really made Latin America. The lack of white women and the presence of many beautiful and semicultured Indian women led to many legal unions in the first generation after the conquest. *Mestizos* were always legally *gente de razón,* people with the ability to reason, as opposed to the pure Indians, and were admitted to minor offices in church and state, and to the militia. In a sense, they constituted a lower middle class—farmers, stewards, shopkeepers, and artisans—and formed the majority of the population in large cities and towns. Their upper levels often became merged with the creoles, their lower level with the Indians. However, there was always a stigma attached to their birth, and by the end of the first century of colonial rule the terms illegitimate and *mestizo* were synonymously used. The frontier had an appeal for such disinherited people, and they became cattle herders on the plains, the typical *llaneros* of Venezuela and *vaqueros* of northern Mexico, the poor gauchos herding wild horses on the Argentine *pampas.* Since they were generally raised by Indian mothers, especially those who were the illegitimate sons of the casual white men, they had little choice but to stay near the bottom of the social ladder.

Naturally, after 300 years, there was much more mixture than most families would admit. Who was to prove that any creole family was pure white all the way back? Few were the families whose every member had the fair white skin and the wavy light brown hair of the Castilian strain. Thus, by 1800 there were some young men of "color" serving as officers in the militia, studying in the colonial universities, and becoming priests. As a class *mestizos* were ready to join with the creoles in winning independence from Spain. On the eve of the wars of independence, the scientific observer von Humboldt figured that the population of Spanish American numbered about 17,000,000 of which 44.5 per cent (7,530,000) were Indians, 31.5 per cent (5,328,000) were mixed-bloods, 19.4 per cent (3,276,000) were pure whites, and 4.6 per cent (776,000) were Negroes.

In this large hybrid population there was a class stratification parallel to the color-caste line. The upper strata, the aristocratic members of society, were entirely white. The European-born were the ruling class, the humbler *peninsulares* the commercial element, the wealthy creoles the leisure class, the university students, the members of professions, the scholars, and the lower clergy. *Mestizos* were to be found in trade and industry and military service, or as free laborers on the frontier, while Indians worked at agricultural pursuits and did the heavy work in the mines. Negroes were plantation workers or domestic servants. This class structure, an economic as well as a social stratification, is the basis of society today in those parts of Latin America where there is still a small middle class.

THE NEGRO SLAVES IN COLONIAL LATIN AMERICA

There was a group in Latin America who did live "more meanly than the peasants of North Europe," the Negro slaves whom the idealist Las Casas had once suggested as a means of getting the work done in the West Indies. With the opening up of Africa by the Portuguese, slaves had been sold in considerable numbers into Spain, and came with their masters as body servants on the earliest ships to the New World. With the settlements on Hispaniola the Spaniards were eager to gain wealth, but disdained work; the Indians were unwilling or unable to perform efficiently the various tasks so cruelly imposed upon them. Thus, even without Las Casas to make the suggestion, Negroes would have soon been imported to the Caribbean islands; they were the ideal source of labor on sugar and tobacco plantations. Because it was the Portuguese who had access to the Gold and Guinea Coasts and the Congo Basin, they also had a monopoly on the slave trade. Spanish kings granted *asientos,* or rights to bring in slaving ships to the Caribbean ports, to Portuguese captains and to certain French and English middlemen. A Flemish count in the court of Charles I received one of the first "middlemen" monopolies to trade with the

Portuguese and bring in 4,000 slaves a year. He in turn sold his right to a Genoese merchant for 25,000 ducats. Thus the king, the count, the Genoese, the Portuguese ship captain, and probably an Arab slave raider and a Gold Coast chieftain all made their "percentage" on this inhuman traffic. As far as crowded, unsanitary conditions, rations, and death rate are concerned, the slave ships of the 1600s made the Yankee slavers of the 1800s seem like pleasure cruisers.

Once the slaves were on Spanish soil evidence seems to show that they were better treated than slaves in the English and French West Indies, or in Carolina and Virginia. The same Crown that meant to protect the Indians passed "humane laws" for Negro slaves. By 1800 a Spanish colonial slave could seek a kinder owner of his own volition if a magistrate certified that he was abused, could marry as he pleased, and could buy his own freedom and that of his wife and children "at the lowest market price." Courts were to hear complaints of slaves and punish cruel masters, though von Humboldt sadly said, "Doubtless these laws are often eluded."

There must have been much cruelty, for the blacks ran away by the thousands, establishing communities of runaway Negroes, who were called *cimarrones*, in British Honduras, northern Panama, and the central parts of the larger islands. English and French pirates used them as allies; Havana was once sacked by a few French pirates cooperating with a band of *cimarrones* from the interior of Cuba. *Cimarrones* were so numerous in Panama that any travel away from the main trail was considered dangerous. There were several slave rebellions in the settled areas during colonial times. Creoles exaggerated the dangers of such revolts and rounded up freed Negroes on the slightest provocation, often considering them dangerous wildmen.

However, Negroes did not come to the New World as savages, as primitive children of nature from the jungle. They had a culture behind them from the Senegal, Guinea, and Gabon Coasts. Negroes from the Western Sudan had been cattle grazers on the grasslands or skilled craftsmen from the towns. Men from Dahomey knew how to work in bronze and copper. Their well organized villages had a complex tribal government which collected taxes and organized markets at which wood carvings, woven cloth, pottery, and even iron work were sold. Their tribal life had been enriched with an oral folklore which was almost literature. They had music and rhythmic forms far more advanced than those of most Indian peoples of the Americas.

Thus most of the strong young Negroes who survived the slave trade were already accustomed to hard work in yam or kaffir corn fields and were familiar with cattle raising. Slaves with this background were valuable property. There were never enough to meet the demand, for the Spaniard needed the Negro to turn the tropical lowlands into a permanent source of wealth. A *pieza de Indias* was "a prime slave, sound in wind and limb, usually between the ages of eighteen and thirty, and seven Spanish *palmos* high." Such a slave was worth 300 pesos. He was easier to teach than a nonagricultural Indian; also, he was stronger and healthier than an

Indian of similar age and height, and he was more docile, perhaps because he knew he could never return home. He was completely and forever lost from his own village culture and thus had no alternative except to become a *cimarrón*. So he assumed a cheerfulness and chanted in rhythm with his fellow slaves as he staggered under the heavy burdens on the broken cobbles of the Cruces Trail across the Isthmus, or sang as he cut cane on a Cuban plantation. Even when freed he had few rights. If he worked in the army or the mines as a freed wage-earner, his status was little above that of a slave. A *zambo,* the red-black half-breed, was spurned by all three color groups and considered a potential enemy of society.

Never so important in Spanish America as in Brazil, Negroes thrived and multiplied on the Caribbean coast of Venezuela and Colombia, in communities on the eastern side of Central America, on both sides of the Isthmus, in Cuba, Hispaniola, and Puerto Rico. By 1560 a report to the king listed 500 Spaniards and 15,000 Negroes in Puerto Rico, 2,000 Spaniards and 30,000 Negroes in Hispaniola. In all these regions the descendants of the slaves are still there in great number, many of them mulattoes, many of them Indian Negro mixed-bloods, and many of them as blue-black as their ancestors on the slave ships. In the twentieth century they comprise a third or more of the population in Brazil, Cuba, and the Dominican Republic, half the population of Panama, and at least a fifth of Venezuela, Colombia, and Ecuador. They are considered true Latin Americans.

SOCIAL LIFE IN THE COLONIES

High society in Mexico City and Lima, dominated by the wealthy, lived much as did the well-to-do in Madrid, Seville, Barcelona, or even Paris. Creole ladies who could afford it dressed with the best of Europe, buying their imported silks and satins from the annual fairs or the Manila Galleon. Silk stockings, kid slippers, lace sleeves, pearl-embroidered garters, and jeweled rosaries on long gold chains decorated these ladies. Unfortunately, the ladies usually covered all this with a long black shawl and left only one eye peeping out. The beautiful *mulata* and *mestiza* mistresses of the Spanish aristocrats displayed themselves in "bodices laced with gold and silver,...full white sleeves of Holland linen," and "petticoats of China colored silk." Men not only spent money on clothes for women, but for themselves as well—crimson velvet suits, lace cuffs, floral embroidered vests, gold knee buckles. Many letters, diaries, and travel accounts of the time tell of fancy masked balls and endless dinner parties with a rich variety of foods and wines.

The homes of the wealthy creoles, many of which can still be visited by the tourist, were almost like palaces. Carved balconies, tile floors, hand-wrought grillwork were the rule. Such homes had three patios, the first approached from the street by a main door wide enough for a carriage to enter. Around this patio, filled with plants, fountains, and birds in cages, were the living rooms of the family. An opening led to a second patio surrounded by kitchens and rooms for domestics. In a

Folk dancers of Mexico still wear the ranchero costumes similar to those worn in Spanish colonial times.
Photo courtesy Los Angeles County Board of Supervisors.

third patio were stables and carriage houses, and, in the great establishments, private blacksmiths, carriage makers, and craftsmen who served the one establishment only.

With the carriages thus provided, the aristocratic creole families paraded up and down the *alameda,* the one main, paved, tree-lined street in these colonial cities. Six thousand mule-drawn decorated carriages threaded the streets of Lima, where they met with mule pack trains from the Bolivian mines, and countless thousands of Indian burden bearers on foot. Wealthy grandees from the country estates often kept town houses and traveled back and forth twice a year by carriage or mule litter. The houses in the country resembled those in the city (though they often had to be fortified against bandits) and entertaining in them was on the same lavish scale. Huts of the Indian workers surrounded them as slave cabins did a plantation.

The city folks had other recreation besides parading in carriages. Gentlemen bet at cards, held lotteries, played at *pelota* or handball, raised gamecocks to fight at high wagers, took part in the constant religious processions and saint's-day fiestas, and watched the bullfights. For their friends they gave masquerade parties, held parlor games, and conducted *tertulias* or literary society meetings.

Thus the leisure class had a great deal of time and enjoyed it. Though self-indulgent, the colonials were an amiable, courteous people, hospitable in their entertainment. The creole landowners and their city counterparts had little else to occupy their time, though the youth took a classical education at the universities, and the occasional creole with advanced education worked as a lawyer or doctor or stayed in the university as a teacher. The artisan classes had their social contacts through their craft guilds. The total proportion of the population that was gainfully employed was small. Records of Mexico City describe large numbers of homeless beggars of all kinds and colors who swarmed in rags around the churches and plazas. There were many criminals, gamblers, and hold-up men in the cities and bandits in the country, frequenters of *pulquerías*, the poor-man's bars. A police force called the *Santa Hermandad*, holy brotherhood, was organized to stop them. Among these disinherited lower classes, with their color mixtures and the caste lines against them, there was a great deal of misery and ignorance.

Family life at all levels was patriarchal. The father or, if living, the grandfather, was the unquestioned arbiter on the comings and goings of all members of the family, even the married sons. Families were such close-knit units as to include cousins of several degrees removed, and co-godfathers and co-godmothers who sponsored children at baptism. In such a father-controlled society, woman's place was one of meek obedience. This type of family tie is seen today in many of the more provincial parts of Latin America, where fathers still order the lives of grown sons and where mothers and wives have only the indirect influence on family affairs that they can exert through the force of their own personalities.

Life for the well-to-do creole women was simple. Indian servants were to be had for their keep; even a skilled craftsmen's wife had to do hardly any actual housework, so the ladies had even more leisure than the men. They engaged in gossip, learned little besides embroidery, music, and religious devotions, and remained untouched by the outside world. They were usually devoted wives, raised large, well-mannered families, and kept the family unit, with its center in religious observance, as the central core of social life. There were a few outstanding women in the colonial period, remembered for literature, art, or charity organization, but most of the feminine members of society remain unsung.

Ladies helped the church workers in charity among foundlings and orphans and in hospitals. From the beginning there were never enough doctors and hospitals, and the spread of disease seems to have been worse than in Europe, owing to the Indians' lack of immunity to European diseases. Three times in the century after Cortés smallpox struck in Mexico, bringing waves of death for hundreds of thousands; there was also another mysterious epidemic which might have been influenza. The friars who tried to nurse the thousands of cases died themselves from this latter lung and throat infection. They blamed it on a comet one time, on volcanic eruption the next. The colonial hospitals not only took care of acute cases, but also served as refuge for destitute aged people, the blind, and the orphaned—in other words, they were actually poorhouses. The Indians themselves had known of many native medicinal plants, including quinine in Peru, which they taught the friars and nuns to use; such Indian remedies were often ahead of current European practices. But the mass of the people still followed quacks and sorcerers, and there was a strong belief in witchcraft.

THE TOWNS AND COUNTRYSIDE OF THE SPANISH-SPEAKING NEW WORLD

Mexico City, largest city in the Western Hemisphere, viceregal capital and social center, the equal of many European capitals, had 20,000 white inhabitants before there was an English town in North America. Today's narrow streets near the Zócalo, or main square in Mexico City, were laid off in the days of Cortés and Mendoza, and the great cathedral was begun on the old Aztec plaza of Tenochtitlán. The Aztec lake remained a main problem for the city builders; at one time the plaza was only three feet above the level of the marshes, and five great floods occurred in the city during the colonial period. Vera Cruz, chief port of New Spain, was always in a disadvantageous location. A high sea wall had been built to defend the town from pirates, but it could not protect it from yellow fever, for the wall kept the sea breezes out, the sewage in, and thus encouraged mosquitoes. Wrecked by hurricanes, attacked by pirates, and scourged by yellow fever, few cities had such a tragic history. Important during visits of fleets and viceroys, the town was almost depopulated the rest of the year.

Guatemala City had no quarrel with pirates; its enemy throughout history was the quaking earth itself. Alvarado's capital had been destroyed by earthquake and flood in 1543; on a new site there grew up Santiago de los Caballeros de Guatemala, "third in magnificence among Spanish colonial capitals," according to its own historians. Here, in a handsome city of Spanish Renaissance architecture, there was a great concentration of wealth, especially in church organizations. By 1773, when Boston was still a town of wooden buildings and muddy streets, Guatemala's luxurious capital was already 200 years old. But that year saw its death; it was a year of terror, with earth tremors week after week, people camping in the fields, and "some nobles spending the night in coaches." Disorganization and pestilence took the town. By the king's order the city was officially moved sixty miles away to the site of the present Guatemala City, while the old site, taken over by the Indians, slumbered on its uncleared debris as a provincial seat known as Antigua. Nicaragua, a region of two rival cities, Granada and León, was described by the English visitor Thomas Gage in 1637 as the "Paradise of America, so fertile, so abundant in the fruits of the earth," a place of gardens and thriving trade. He thought of Costa Rica, that settlement of middle-class farmers of European stock, as a country of "good valleys, planted with corn and prosperous farms."

Panama pleased no traveler or writer of the colonial period. "In the hot steamy town, men sickened and died; what with much eating of fruit and drinking of water, hundreds of merchants, soldiers and mariners died of the flux," wrote Gage of Panama. The town then consisted of 8,000 "souls who confessed," living in 750 houses along four streets. The harbor was inadequate and the town "could be moved to a better site, but for the great price of houses." Alligators "floated like large logs in the water" out behind the slaughter house. The people were forced to move from this unpleasant site when the English pirate, Sir Henry Morgan, sacked the town. Its ruins stand in a park ten miles from the present-day Panama City.

Across the Isthmus on the Atlantic side lay the harbor of Porto Bello. The first Spanish town in that general region had been called Nombre de Dios, a poor harbor and an unhealthy little settlement. In 1597 a wise governor surveyed the area for a new port and founded Porto Bello, "a fine harbor protected by three strong fortresses, the strongest bastion on the Spanish Main." Its long sea wall is lined with "cannon of the largest calibre ever cast up to the time." Some of them still lie there today in the picturesque ruin.

The finest fortification was to be seen at Cartagena on the Colombia shore of the Spanish Main. Bogotá prided itself on isolation, purity of Spanish speech and blood, and intellectual pursuits; it was so far inland from Cartagena that a Spanish viceroy sent to govern it stayed three years on the coast waiting for auspicious water level on the Magdalena to make the trip, and returned without ever having visited Bogotá at all. Medellín, in the valley of the Cauca, had been founded in 1675; at the end of the colonial period, this prosperous, agricultural city had 9,000 inhabitants, more people than had Vera Cruz or Panama City.

These Colombian towns were not connected with Caracas by overland trail of any kind. There an independent-spirited city, destined to be the mother of the revolution, grew up twenty-three miles from the sea and its sleepy little port of La Guaira. The twenty-three-mile trail was one of the most precipitous approaches to a city in Latin America, and took two days of "stair-step climbing" among the rocks on sure-footed mules. It was difficult to travel any place else from Caracas, but Bogotá was in mule-trail touch with Quito, by way of Popayán and Pasto, two fiercely loyal colonial towns founded by Benalcázar. Quito itself, important as the seat of an *audiencia*, was a center of art and science, though the "decent folk" were only one-sixth of the population, according to one of the king's plainclothes investigators. Guayaquil, not Quito, was considered the "jewel of the *audiencia's* crown." Large ships were built on its banks; mule trains came down from Quito with textiles, dyestuffs, and liquor; sugar cane, bananas, and rice from the coast went back up. Cervantes, the famous Spanish author of *Don Quixote,* asked in 1590 that he be sent to the Indies as "beneficiary of one of the royal offices," and specially mentioned Quito or Guayaquil as a choice spot for a government post.

In 1620, when Plymouth was founded, Lima "counted 4,000 houses, only 260 of which were of Indians." In the next decade a viceroy built arches around the square, brought clear spring water by aqueduct into the city, built local fountains "in all the quarters." As the streets "are ordered in squares and the water goes in pipes along the streets, it is easy to install it in the houses," said a report; thus houses in Lima had running water before New England had houses. Lima remained the literary, cultural, and social center of Spanish South America till 1800; by then it had upwards of 70,000 inhabitants. Arequipa, today the second city of Peru, was a sleepy, monotonous convent town, while Cuzco remained an Indian center, a provincial capital with a thin veneer of Spanish society.

The earthquake belt of the Andes extended to Santiago, Chile, which was destroyed on May 13, 1647, and rebuilt gradually over a period of years till it was all new "from the cathedral to the jail." To this calamity were added the floods of the Río Mapocho, so frequent that "every year the residents of this capital were liable to see their houses destroyed." Society in Santiago moved at a much slower pace than in Lima. There were no coaches, and the wealthiest families boasted only mule-drawn carriages with two wheels.

Down the mule trail from Bolivia, with its silver-mining cities and "wide-open" social life, into the valleys at Tucumán and Salta, onto the pampas below the aristocratic city of Córdova, a thin colonizing stream dribbled through the centuries into Buenos Aires. Asunción on the Paraguay was farther away from this current of traffic than St. Louis is from New Orleans. Travelers from Asunción went downriver to meet the wagon trails to Tucumán, then up the mule trails to Cuzco and over to Lima, if they wanted to go home to Spain. In Guaraní-speaking Asunción there was even less society than in Santiago; it was said that the ladies spent their time "in sewing, weaving, gardening, and taking care of babies and ducks." Few visitors to Asunción bothered to go back downriver to Buenos Aires, a town on the Plata estuary which was described in the 1650s as having "only four saloons paying the annual license tax" and "only sixteen horse-drawn coaches." A visitor called it "a dirty, unattractive town." Montevideo, across the estuary, was not even founded till 1726.

Out beyond Buenos Aires on the grassy pampas lived a still different type of society, the cattle herders later to be called *gauchos*. Descended from the colonists brought by Mendoza and Irala, or from Spaniards who came into the pampas from Peru or Chile, they took as wives Guaraní women or girls from among the wild pampas Indians. Their houses were mud huts thatched with pampa grass, set out on the treeless plain, their front door a steer hide, their furniture piles of hides for beds and steer skulls for stools, their hearth an open fire of cow dung, their diet beef and *yerba maté*. A trip for weeks on horseback brought them to Buenos Aires, Mendoza, or Córdova, which must have seemed metropolises to these children of the sun and wind.

The Spanish Indies by 1700 was a good place to live, full of color, excitement, and opportunity. In all these communities life was probably as pleasant as in most towns in Spain, and was certainly cleaner and more open to air and sun than was town life in seventeenth-century England. Here in these New World settlements was emerging the culture of today's

Latin America, where life is still open to air and sun, and where the progress of the combined red, black, and white races is one of the most significant things of the New World.

Readings

Bancroft, H. H., *History of Mexico* (6 vols., 1883–1887)

Bannon, J. F., *Indian Labor in the Spanish Indies* (1966)

Bourne, E. G., *Spain in America* (1904)

Chevalier, F., *Land and Society in Colonial Mexico* (1963)

Cooper, D. B., *Epidemic Disease in Mexico City, 1761–1813* (1965)

Diffie, B. W., *Latin American Civilization: Colonial Period* (1945)

Espinosa, A. V. de, *Compendium and Description of West Indies,* trans. G. U. Clark (1942)

Gage, T., *A New Survey of the West Indies, 1648,* ed. A. P. Newton (1929); ed. J. E. Thompson (1958)

González Obregón, L., *Streets of Mexico*, trans. B. C. Wagner (1937)

Hanke, L., *The First Social Experiments in America* (1935)

———, *The Imperial City of Potosí* (1956)

Haring, C. H., *Spanish Empire in America* (1952)

Kubler, G., *Indian Caste of Peru, 1795–1940* (1952)

Leonard, I. A., *Baroque Times in Old Mexico* (1959)

Lucero-White, A., *Folk-Dances of the Spanish Colonials in New Mexico* (1937)

Marshall, C. E., "Birth of the Mestizo in New Spain," *Hispanic American Historical Review*, XIX, 161–87

Moses, B., *Spain Overseas* (1929)

———, *Spanish Dependencies in South America* (2 vols., 1914)

Priestley, H. I., *Coming of the White Man* (1929)

Rodriques, J. H., *Brazil and Africa* (1965)

Schurz, W. L., *This New World* (1954)

Simpson, L. B., *Encomienda in New Spain* (1950)

Tannenbaum, F., *Slave or Citizen: The Negro in the Americas* (1947)

von Humboldt, A., *A Political Essay on New Spain* (4 vols., 1811)

Wilgus, A. C., ed., *Colonial Hispanic America* (1936)

Zavala, S., *New Viewpoints on the Spanish Colonization of America* (1943)

Chapter 13

Intellectual Life in the Colonies

SCHOOLS AND COLLEGES

IN 1663 THERE WAS BORN in Lima a creole named Pedro de Peralta Barnuevo who grew up to be as outstanding an intellectual as any university professor in Madrid or Paris in his lifetime. He lived successfully in Lima for eighty years, and apparently never left the city or the port of Callao even to go up to Cuzco. He was "mathematician, chief cosmographer and engineer of the viceroyalty" and a doctor of Roman and canon law, a professor of mathematics at Lima's University of San Marcos for thirty-four years, and its historian and rector. As a lawyer he pleaded cases before the Lima *audiencia* and acted as an official of that body. As an engineer he built the breakwater at Callao and worked out improved methods of assaying and extracting silver from ore. He did research in the fields of botany and medicine; as a geographer he accurately figured the latitude of Lima; as an astronomer he prepared almanacs giving the days of the phases of the moon. He also found time to write poetry—not merely in Spanish, but in Latin, Greek, French, and Italian—to write plays, and to produce a history of Spain. He was most highly praised by his contemporaries for a 10,000-line epic poem, *The Founding of Lima*. With such a learned man as an example, colonial Spanish Americans could not be too far behind the times. Education may not have been as widely spread in the New World as in the Old, but one should not think of the colonies as a raw, unlettered frontier.

As in Europe at the time, education was a class-conscious affair in the Spanish colonies. It reflected the society to which it administered, and provided a formal, classical education which was available only to the pure whites and the upper-level *mestizos*. The church maintained most of the teachers and the buildings; the Inquisition guaranteed the "purity" of the teaching. While many of the young creoles at the top went through the university, the lower classes remained in the most complete ignorance; thus illiteracy must have amounted to more than 90 per cent by 1800. Though all municipalities were theoretically supposed to support primary schools, they were usually too poor to do so, and in practice education was a church responsibility. Each parish church tried to maintain an elementary school for the children of its parishioners, often taught by the priest. Most well-to-do creole children were educated by private tutors when religious schools were distant or inadequate. Secondary schools or *colegios* maintained under church auspices may have been very good, but they were attended by only a very small fraction of the eligible boys in town. Dominicans and Jesuits, the two principal teaching orders, worked against difficult odds to keep their schools going, though they sometimes received financial aid directly from the Crown or from the bequests of private benefactors. In general, it was university education, rather than primary and secondary, for which these orders deserve credit in the New World, and which the Spanish colonials themselves were most interested in fostering.

At first primary education in America was provided for Indian children. During Cortés' lifetime, schools for the children of Aztec chieftains and nobility were set up to teach religion. The famous Brother Peter of Ghent (Fray Pedro de Gante) directed such an Indian school for over forty years. His graduates became Europeanized, and they worked as artisans and skilled craftsmen in the decoration and care of churches. Father Sahagún, also an early arrival, gathered together likely young Aztecs who taught him their tongue as they learned his, while they all worked together on a monumental history of the Aztecs.

As a second generation grew up, *mestizo* children cared for by *mestizo* or Indian mothers were raised without benefit of any education. Church authorities made an attempt to set up schools for them, though there were never enough. Schools for foundling boys and girls were erected in Mexico City and Lima and other large towns. Especially famous was the foundling school of San Juan de Letrán, founded by the Franciscans in Mexico City, which provided a vocational education for many orphan children of Indian blood for 250 years. By 1534 there were eight schools for Indian girls in New Spain, in which cooking, sewing, and homemaking were taught. The Council of the Indies had decreed that there be a school to teach Spanish in every Indian *pueblo,* but the decree was often ignored. Still today, in numerous villages with a preponderance of Indian blood only the village leaders can read and speak Spanish.

The second generation of creoles in Mexico and Lima saw the coming of full-fledged universities. The Royal and Pontifical University of Mexico predated Harvard by nearly a hundred years. Founded by royal order in 1551 and opened with pomp and ceremony in 1553, it was endowed with the status and privileges of the University of Salamanca, its mother institution in Spain. A permanent site was found for it on the same location as Montezuma's old palace, and the cornerstone was laid there in an elaborate ceremony by the archbishop. The building, a square two-story stone structure around a flowered patio, was the meeting place of classes till the 1700s and has been used in recent times as the National Conservatory of Music. In its first grant the university received a yearly sum from the Crown to pay the cost of its teachers—professors of Latin, rhetoric, philosophy, civil and canon law, and theology. Two of the first professors were judges of the *audiencia,* and the rest were churchmen. By the time the school was a half-century old there were twenty-four chairs, two of them in medicine and two of them specializing in ancient Indian languages, Nahuatl and Otomí, at that time still considered scholarly and important subjects.

Another royal decree of 1551 called for the establishment of the Royal and Pontifical University of San Marcos in Lima. For 25 years it consisted merely of classes housed in a Dominican convent and taught by monks there, but the Viceroy Toledo made it a separate institution similar to that in Mexico, and gave it buildings of its own in 1578. In addition to the usual classical subjects San Marcos offered courses in medicine and in the Quechua language. The universities of Lima and Mexico were models for other high-ranking colonial colleges, run by the Jesuits and Dominicans, of which there were ten major and fifteen lesser in the provincial capitals by 1625. These universities all gave the aristocratic young creoles a formal and impractical schooling to brighten the luster of their family standing. On a more practical level, the law schools trained men to conduct the government's business and to protect the legal interests of the landowners and clergy; the courses in medicine were as practical as those offered in Spain at the time, and the theology schools supplied the New World with priests.

University organization was patterned after that of Salamanca; college affairs were governed by a cloister and a rector who exercised police jurisdiction over the students and hired and paid the professors. Professors took the oath to "defend the doctrine of the Immaculate Conception, to observe modest conduct, and not to attend theaters and dances." They got their jobs after competition before an examining board, but received very low salaries; they all did something else for a living or were churchmen whose living was provided. It was a great honor to teach classes, but not a means of support. Occasionally a wealthy patron would endow a chair in some subject, and such a professorship paid better than the regular classes. The universities of the New World, like those in Europe, were made up of a group of professional schools, as they still are today in many parts of Latin America. The school of theology would be in a different part of town than was the school of law; the school of medicine would be someplace else, with none of them really grouped on a campus in the modern North American sense.

Student life was similar to that at Oxford or any other European university in the seventeenth century. Students wore cassocks, long cloaks, and brimless hats to class, a style inherited from the same medieval student's garb as gave rise to our present-day academic caps and gowns. They lived a strict life under the control of the rector, chosen from among all professors who had doctorates, and under the "masters," who corresponded to our graduate students and teaching fellows. The classes were taught by rote; the students memorized lectures which the professor had himself memorized.

Scholasticism, Aristotelian logic, was the central idea, and there was no experimental science until late in the era, though mathematics, "including the geometry of Euclid," was taught to all who tried for the bachelor's degree. Classes were conducted in Latin, and there was little or no discussion. Cost of classes in yearly tuition was small, but matriculation fees were high, and fees charged at the time of granting a degree seem exorbitant. Once a student earned a doctor's degree and was passed by a strict "committee of judges" he could teach classes, of itself a great honor. There was criticism of San Marcos, however, because most of its teachers through the centuries were its own graduates, thereby generating a great deal of "inbreeding" in scholarship. Indians and freed mulattoes were supposed to be eligible for university work, but the records indicate few degrees granted to them after 1600. By 1700 a "certificate of legitimacy and purity of race" and of "freedom from the taint of heresy" was being required for matriculation.

In spite of the restrictions and the methods, the colonial universities did produce some very distinguished scholars and students, such as Dr. Peralta Barnuevo. All in all, the University of Mexico in its 268 years of existence before independence granted 37,732 bachelor's degrees, several thousand master's degrees, and 1,655 law degrees and doctorates. As in every phase of colonial life, there were many changes in the later eighteenth century.

SCHOLARLY RESEARCH AND SCIENTIFIC PURSUITS

University graduates and professors made contributions to scholarship in the New World that received recognition in Europe. But even these results of colonial education were achieved under some restrictions from Spain. The mother country, at the peak of her golden age in the sixteenth and seventeenth centuries, did not want the colonies to outshine her but was anxious that they be a credit to her. American scholars were encouraged to interest themselves in specialties in which the Spanish scholars were making no contribution; thus American researchers studied the pre-Columbian Indians, their history, customs, and language. They were interested in the geography, botany, zoology, and metallurgy of the New World, and in the astronomical phenomena visible along the equator and from the Southern Hemisphere which could be studied only in the South American colonies. In all these fields contributions were made during the colonial period.

The descriptions of Indian civilizations and their conquest, written by Garcilaso de la Vega, Bishop Landa of Yucatan, and especially Friar Bernardino de Sahagún, are the best modern sources of information on the ancient cultures. There was a great interest in such materials during the colonial days even though the poor Indian peasants themselves were the objects of scorn. Indian stories, songs, and epic poems were recited by the Indians from their rich tribal memories during the first and second generations of the conquest, and the friars who had studied the Indian tongues in their own mission schools heard the recitations, translated them into Spanish, and wrote them down. As late as 1700 the learned Dominican Francisco Jiménez, living among the Maya-Quiché in Chichicastenango, Guatemala, discovered the records of Mayan history and mythology known as the *Popul Vuh;* it is from his Spanish translation of these legends that modern students of the Maya have gleaned so much information.

Colonial Spaniards were even more interested in histories of the conquest, told as exciting personal-experience stories. Foremost historian of the early days in the New World was Gonzalo Fernández de Oviedo (1478–1557), who came to Panama with Pedrarias in 1514 and later, as an authorized chronicler, crossed the Atlantic at least twelve times. He found time to write down in the greatest detail everything that he himself had seen and all the roistering history he had heard from those who came and went through Panama. The most scientific historian of these early days was the Jesuit professor, Father José de Acosta, who read all the accounts written by eye-witnesses, wrote down many Indian stories, and then tried to write a unified history of the New World from pre-Columbian times. Published in 1571 under the title *Natural and Moral History of the Indies,* it was one of the best sellers of its day. The story of the conquest of Peru was well told by Pedro Pizarro, the nephew, as well as by other soldiers and friars such as Pedro Cieza de León and Friar Montesinos, who came to Peru early in the conquest. Bernal Díaz, with his story of Cortés' adventures, and Cabeza de Vaca, with his account of the long walk in the southwest, both contributed popular books to the history of the conquest. Other more formal historians such as Juan Matienzo, Juan de Solórzano Pereira, and Bernabé Cobo (1582–1657), with his *History of Lima,* added detailed studies of the law and government, as well as of civil and judicial procedures of the new *audiencias.* All these learned men contributed to scholarship and are sources of authentic information for today's historians of colonial Latin American.

The years from 1550 to 1700 brought to Europe a new interest in science; though Salamanca and its sister universities in Spain may have lagged, the New World was not asleep. Philip II sent careful instructions out to Peru to have an eclipse of the moon observed there and to see the lunar body from the Western half of the world and just below the equator. Scientists at the University of Mexico figured the longitude of their capital more accurately than it was being figured out in Europe. Since their calculations were not published outside Mexico, geographers of the Old World kept making maps with the incorrect longitude on them for another century. In the year 1680 a comet was studied in an unusually scientific spirit in the University of Mexico by a famous teacher, writer, and scientist, Carlos de Sigüenza y Góngora (1645–1700), who quarreled with church authorities as to its causes. "Comets, contrary to popular belief, have nothing to do with the wrath of Providence," he courageously wrote at the time.

Practical applications of science were made in the colonies. In 1608 Enrico Martínez, an engineer, worked out a fairly modern plan to drain the swamps of Mexico City, temporarily solving Mexico's age-old drainage problem. Serious scientific commissions studied the possibilities of a canal through the Isthmus of Panama, and no less than twenty plans were formulated and filed away in the archieves. The Nicaragua Lake route was also studied by a scientific committee. Kings and viceroys maintained royal cosmographers at their courts to keep government ships posted on new exploration and improvements in navigation, though Spanish sea captains themselves were sometimes way behind the times.

Medical science lagged behind the other sciences in America as it did in Europe before the eighteenth century. Medical practice was limited to medieval usages and Indian herb-doctoring. *Protomédicos* were appointed by royal order to examine and license physicians and druggists and to collect information on medicinal plants. As early as 1535 there were royal orders against "quackery and dishonesty" in medical practice in the New World. The first *protomédico* sent out to enforce these decrees in Mexico was appointed by Philip II in 1571 to improve standards and to collect botanical specimens. When he returned in 1577 he brought fifteen or more volumes of studies of natural history and Indian lore.

By the eighteenth century, as in Europe, medical science was making great strides. Attention was being paid to clinical surgery, to obstetrics, pharmacy, and scientific anatomy based on observation and dissection. In 1723, however, a debate was held in Lima on the possibility of the circulation of the blood, with learned professors taking the negative on a subject that had been proved by William Harvey in England almost a century before. Eighty years later von Humboldt mentioned the use of vaccination against smallpox in an epidemic in Mexico.

Not only in medical advance was the eighteenth century a new age. French thought and letters were penetrating into the colonies in the Age of Enlightenment. The influence of this spirit on education in general and on politics in particular will be discussed in Chapter 15. Reforming kings introduced classes in chemistry, mineralogy, botany, astronomy, engineering, and navigation into the universities, and had founded schools of mines. More and more lay teachers of a new scientific bent were teaching in the classical old universities. Spanish-Americans traveled to Europe and other parts of the colonies; famous European scientists visited America, and whole new fields of thought opened up.

In the latter half of the eighteenth century botany had become a new science, and where could be found a better field for plant collecting and classification than the lush American tropics? Botanical gardens to house specimens were set up in Bogotá and Mexico City, and a Museum of Natural History was founded in Guatemala. To the Bogotá gardens came a friend of Linnaeus, the father of botany, a Spaniard from Cádiz named Dr. José Celestino Mutis. A doctor by training, he had come to Colombia as physician to one of the first viceroys Charles III sent there; he stayed on twenty-five years, fascinated by the wealth of plant life. The king granted him 10,000 pesos a year to hire fifteen engravers and water colorists to make exact reproductions of each species. More than 3,000 miniature drawings of plants were left by him to be sent to Madrid. He had time and interest of found an astronomical observatory in Bogotá in 1802, as well as to collect plants. A creole pupil of Mutis, Francisco José de Caldas, carried on his botanical work.

To visit Mutis in Bogotá came the era's most distinguished natural scientist and geographer, Alexander von Humboldt, who has already been mentioned as an explorer and observer. Bogotá was so "science-conscious" that the city declared a public holiday on his arrival. During a five-year period, 1799 to 1804, von Humboldt and a French scientist named Aimé Bonpland journeyed through Mexico and northern South America, and afterward published a monumental work in French called *Voyage to the Equinoctial Regions of the New Continent*. From von Humboldt we know a great deal about cultural improvements in Spanish America resulting from the intellectual interests of the eighteenth-century kings and the general new enthusiasm for learning reflected from Europe. He found in Mexico "youth gifted with a rare facility for understanding the principles of the sciences," and he thought the students in the School of Mines were "animated with the finest zeal, and capable of using instruments which could be placed in their hands." He concluded, "No city of the new continent, not excepting any of the United States, can show scientific institutions as big and solid as those of the capital of Mexico."

BOOKS WRITTEN AND BOOKS READ

There was a certain book publisher in the city of Seville so fortunate as to handle the sale of all books sent for pleasure and profit to the New World. Every year at fleet-sailing time long mule trains carried boxes of books to the storage sheds for the fleet alongside the Guadalquivir River. The boxes were opened by customs officials, those forbidden to good churchgoers were removed, and the boxes "resealed with the stamp of the Holy Inquisition." In the 1601 shipment this single Seville dealer sent 10,000 books—eighty boxes each for Puerto Rico, Santo Domingo, and Cuba, the rest for Mexico and Panama, an order that would surely delight any modern publishing house. More than 75 per cent of the order consisted of heavy religious tomes, law books, and school books, but there was a surprising amount of popular fiction. Laws of the day indicate that "romances of chivalry" were prohibited in the colonies, but the shipping lists show that hundreds of Horatio-Alger-type light novels got by the censors. The first edition of *Don Quixote* was not only boxed in great quantity in a ship's hold on the way to the colonies, but was also being read by passengers in the cabin. Books on history, mathematics, and medicine were sent, together with much of the poetry of which Spaniards were so fond. And all this sale of books took place in spite of the strict censorship carried on jointly by the House of Trade and the church courts. The House of Trade itself kept lists of every title in every box of printed materials shipped to the colonies. Many bills of lading used subterfuges, however, and many "illegal" books reached the colonies. A study of such lists reveals a surprising amount of reading going on in the New World.

What the Spanish colonial liked to read varied with the century. Books of the sixteenth century were chronicles, translations of native Indian books, *relaciones* on the conquest. The century of expansion and mission work called for religious books, the lives of saints, catechisms, books of sermons and missionary chronicles as well as primers and grammars in Indian languages. The romances, the picaresque novels, the dramas and comedies of famous Spanish playwrights, as well as more histories and travel books began to appear in the seventeenth century. The eighteenth century saw the new popularity of secular philosophy, science, and even books in French and English, frowned upon as they were.

Though printing presses spread very slowly in the colonies, not all books came from Spain. The Bishop of Mexico had petitioned in 1533: "It would be a very useful and convenient thing to have here a printing press and paper mill...surely there are persons of these skills who would like to come over if Your Majesty would favor them with means of support." In answer, the monopolistic Seville publishing house sent an Italian craftsman who brought plates for engraving, and soon was able to produce, at the king's expense, a "Brief Christian Doctrine" for use with the Indians. Within twenty years thirty-four other such books were produced on this press, a total of 174 different works before 1600. Craftsmen were sent from Mexico to Lima and another generation saw similar work being done in Peru by the 1580s. Even by 1800, at the end of the colonial period, the reading public was so small and the price of books was so prohibitive that only twenty-five presses existed in the whole of Spanish America, of which ten were in New Spain.

Presses had no occasion to print newspapers till the eighteenth century. Spanish-Americans had no learned journals, magazines, or newssheets describing the life of their own times, except the *Hojas Volantes,* newssheets distributed on the arrival of the fleet. Intellectual circles in Mexico City and Lima also had occasional copies of the special court news letters from Spain. One such document from the year 1671, called the *Gazeta,* was issued to tell about the "adjustment of the peace between the crowns of Spain and Great Britain in America" and to describe the "repression of raids and robberies on the high seas." The same *Gazeta* carried stories of fights against the Turks in the Mediterranean and an account of a "bull-running in Mexico on the anniversary of our monarch

Charles II." Actual periodicals printed in America including both literary efforts and news did not appear until the first monthly *Gazeta de Mexico* in 1722, which lasted only six issues. The rapid increase of such periodicals and their part in the "Enlightenment" and the movement for independence are a part of Chapter 15.

In actual literary effort colonial Spain, as has been described, excelled in meaty research materials and produced little in the way of *belles-lettres.* The Spanish writer Luis de Góngora (1561–1627) influenced all literary efforts in Spanish America for decades after his death. The artificial, bombastic style, heavy with mythological allusions, known as "Gongorism" in Spanish literature, was so reflected in American circles in the seventeenth century that little Latin American writing of that era is even remembered today, other than the historical chronicles. From this same historical material came the few masterpieces, such as the long epic poem of the conquest of Chile, *La Araucana,* written by Alonzo de Ercilla y Zúñiga (1533–1594), a soldier in Valdivia's company of pioneers. This history in verse in praise of Lautaro, first published in 1569, lives on today as the national epic of Chile. Ercilla made the Spaniards seem "full of swollen importance," their "souls made of so much wind and glory." This poem was counterbalanced by Pedro de Oña's (1570–1643) epic, *Arauco Domado,* which gave high praise to the Spaniards.

An Inca drama telling the love story of an Inca prince was translated into Spanish as a long metrical poem called *Ollantay.* Revived as a colonial Spanish masterpiece, it has been an inspiration for a modern musical drama. The longest poem in Spanish literature is a history called *Elegies of the Illustrious Men of the Indies* and was written in praise of Spain in the New World by Juan de Castellanos (1522–1606), a priest who had grown up in the Caribbean islands. Its 150,000 lines are of interest today as a key to usages of the Spanish language in the Caribbean area in the 1580s. Garcilaso de la Vega's (1539–1643) masterpiece, the *Royal Commentaries,* glorified Inca civilization and is a great chronicle of distinguished literary merit. Apart from the religious works, the historical epics, and the scientific studies, there were occasional essays on contemporary life, but little other prose of a purely literary type and no important novel was produced, though the presses of the New World were busy turning out short poetry and dramas.

POETRY, MUSIC, AND ART

Poetry was to all Spaniards the preferred form of literary expression. By the middle of the seventeenth century Spanish colonial poetry was classical in form and written in a stilted spirit. But formal or not, everyone in the colonies who could write wrote poetry. Scientists, drainage engineers, theology professors, judges, and even governors wrote lyrical verses. Priests encouraged their flocks to write sonnets to the Virgin and the saints. There were many poetic contests in the universities. Of all these gentlemen poets,

Bernardo de Balbuena (1568–1627) stands out. Born in Spain in the 1560s, he was educated in Mexico and was appointed Bishop of Puerto Rico after his poetry made him famous. He seemed to have loved Mexico City most, and wrote a poem, *La Grandeza Mexicana*, in praise of the colonial metropolis. He praised the "skillful artifice" which "contributes interest and pleasure to this noble city." Here, in contrast to European cities, he could "live a life of plenty, peace and happiness." The best sacred epic in the

Façade of San Francisco Acatepec Church, Puebla, Mexico, showing ornate Spanish tile used in decoration. *Photo by Helen Miller Bailey.*

Spanish language, *La Cristiada*, was produced in a Lima monastery by Diego de Hojedo (1570[?]–1615).

But the most famous poet of colonial Latin America was a woman, a beautiful little nun who lived in Mexico City a century after Balbuena. Born Juana Inés de la Cruz in 1651 near Mount Popo, she learned to read at the age of three; at fourteen she begged to go to the university like a man; instead she was allowed to live in her grandfather's city house, where there was a fine library and where many socially prominent people gathered. Her wit and beauty brought her to the attention of the viceroy's wife, who made her a lady-in-waiting. In the lax society of the age she was soon disillusioned and decided at sixteen that she could best devote herself to writing and peaceful study if she became a nun. As Sor Juana she busied herself writing plays, sonnets, and critical essays. Her work was in many metrical forms, and she used several foreign languages. Words she coined

Sor Juana Inés de la Cruz, Mexican poetess, 1651-1695. *Courtesy Pan American Union.*

became popular expressions; her ideas on art, science, and education were the intellectual fashion of the day. Cultured men of the time came to her convent for the privilege of talking to her. At forty she became a nun in spirit also, sold her 4,000-book library for charity, and went out to nurse cases of the plague during the great epidemic of 1695, in which she herself died. Ahead of her time even in science, she had worked out a theory of the mathematics of harmony in music.

But Sor Juana, a nun of a scientific and charitable spirit, will live always as a poetess of love. She urged her readers, if not herself, to live the full life. "If my displeasure from my pleasure comes, Heaven give me pleasure even at the cost of my displeasure," she wrote, in favor of burning the candle at both ends. She approved of the life of a rose. "Happy it is to die while young and fair and not to endure the insults of old age." In rhymed couplets, she blamed men for the frustrated loves of womankind. "You blame women alike whether they favor or scorn you, complaining of them if they treat you ill, making mock of them if they love you dearly." Sor Juana pleaded for freedom of the mind and the soul; her philosophic as well as her love poems became famous in Spain, and her works are read today for their sheer artistry.

Dramatists in Spain and the New World wrote often in verse form. The most famous dramatist, whose works were actually produced on stage but are still read as poetry by devotees of Spanish literature, was Juan Ruiz de Alarcón y Mendoza (1581[?]–1639), who was born in the Mexican town of Taxco. As a young lawyer he pleaded cases before the *audiencia* but wrote sad poems about a "somewhat grey world." He had reason to be sad, for he was a short and ugly hunchback. No one paid attention to his poems in Mexico, so when he received a legacy he went to Spain and began to write plays in verse for the Madrid theater. His contemporaries spurned him; though his plays were popular, even Spain's most famous dramatist, Lope de Vega, tried to break up his audiences and called him the "poet with a trunk on his back." Alarcón then wrote a play called *The Walls Have Ears*, in which one of his leading characters addressed the audience and said, "Thou shalt not look for beauty and gentility in man's physique. His beauty lies in nobility of soul, his gentility in wisdom." Alarcón wrote thirty-five plays altogether, many of them with scenes laid in Mexico. He is best remembered for his play *La Verdad Sospechosa (The Liar)*. Mexico gladly claimed him as a native son and credited his ability to his colonial boyhood; he finally received a post with the Council of the Indies and retired from the theater, still in a "somewhat grey world."

In Mexico City before 1600 there was a permanent public theater to which all classes of society came, and which had its own buildings and acting companies with a repertoire of plays and a paying audience—this when the Shakespearean theater was young in London. Traveling companies from Spain played the dramas of Lope de Vega and some products of local talent as well, such as the more than fifty light comedies by the Mexican Eusebio Vela. Lima claimed to have an even more sophisticated theater in its *Casa de Comedias* of the 1590s and its Coliseum Theater of the early 1600s. There were private theaters—sometimes in convents and universities, one at the court of the viceroy—though the clergy denounced them. The Indians in the villages never saw these sophisticated dramas, but they had pageantry of their own in the festivals and religious plays on saints' days.

Churches throughout Spanish America are filled with art done in the colonial epoch—sugary paintings of saints and Virgins, dark pictures of martyrdom, poor copies of Spanish and Italian subjects, crude tempera drawings by mission Indians. All formal art was church art, save for the occasional portrait of some dignitary.

Spaniards of the upper classes were interested in religious arts, with which they filled their houses and churches in the colonial period; Spanish artisans and Indian craftsmen produced a new art in the beautiful handiwork they learned from each other. As to formal art, the New World learned the type the Old World taught, especially the school of the Seville painters. A school of painting had existed in Quito and some noteworthy canvasses were done there, but all subjects were pious, with church decoration as the motive. Benalcázar, that adventurous *conquistador* who saw so much of South America, had a half-breed son who devoted his life to being "painter and gilder of the churches of Quito." Art lovers who visit Quito today can see many of his religious canvasses. Mexico had its counterpart in Miguel Cabrera, a pure-blooded Zapotec, who decorated several churches, although in the ornate Churrigueresque style and not in any Zapotec tradition. Francisco Eduardo Tresguerras (1745–1833), a sculptor, architect, and painter of Guanajuato, is remembered for the fine decoration of the church of Carmen at Celaya. He lived to see the people of Guanajuato join the revolt against Spain, and is called "the last figure of importance in Mexican art until 1920." Painting reached its apogee in the seventeenth century and declined in the eighteenth.

The true Latin American art was in crafts, combining Indian skills with European methods. Puebla was famous for its tile-making in the Majolica style; much of the product can be seen in the churches and homes of Puebla today. To Guadalajara came glass blowers in the Venice tradition, who founded a "blue glass" industry. Talavera-type pottery was made in polychrome—blue with yellow, red, or black—with an amazing variety of effect. To Indian pottery methods were added all the tricks from Spain, from the use of a potter's wheel to bright Spanish glazes. Indian craftsmen learned to copy Chinese pieces that came on the Manila Galleon. Chinese methods of painting on ivory were reproduced for the delicate fans of delicate creole ladies; some creole miniature artists copied French methods and learned to make portrait brooches on imported ivory. Indian designs in textiles were used with new dyes; the blankets of Chile had Araucanian motifs in geometric patterns of red and blue, conventional plant and flower designs in pink and green, stripes in harmonizing colors. Saddlebags of plush and velvet, as well as rugs or tapestries for women to kneel on in the Santiago churches, show the ingenious flower designs of the Araucanians. The mosaic patterns on the ruins of Mitla crept into the new sheep's-wool blankets of Oaxaca. The old Indian artistry of fine gold casting was kept alive by the Spanish taste for gold jewelry and silver table service, saddle decorations, spurs, and sword hilts.

In both formal religious painting and informal craft work there was no classical art education offered in New Spain until the cultural renaissance brought by the late Bourbon kings, which is a part of the story of the eighteenth century. Then a School of Fine Arts was founded in Mexico

City in 1773 and a famous Spanish architect and sculptor, Manuel Tolsa (1767–1825), was imported to teach in it. Sculpture was religious in nature; marble and wood carvings were done as church decorations.

Architecture in the New World was essentially of European origin, with a few Indian contributions. Churches reflected the periods of Spanish art—the Moorish styles, the Italian Renaissance, the ornate façades of the declining Spanish Renaissance with its baroque styles and "gingerbread" ornamentation. Private dwellings continued to be built in Moorish style, with rooms and balconies around an interior patio, adobe walls on the outside, and much tile decoration within.

Latin America is famous for its music today, in the homes, in the streets, on the concert stage. The true Latin American music evolved from the melancholy strains of the Indians, the rhythmic genius of the Negro, and the technical influences of Europe. Unfortunately, little record remains of music in colonial times. Every convent had its chorus, every church its singing choir boys, many big cities their own public bands. Indian villages still had their drummers, their harpists, and their pipers. In the Caribbean, Negro rhythms were transplanted into Spanish melodies during slave times. Gauchos in the Plata Colony produced a dance form in the rural area and on the waterfront that was condemned by the Bishop of Buenos Aires in 1743. No good churchgoer could dance the *malambo*, a "nervous, jumpy, contagious form" of the staid old Spanish *fandango*. Only after 1780, when it was given sweep and grace and became the *tango*, did it come into the drawing rooms, such as there were, in Buenos Aires. Everywhere that Indian and *mestizo*, Negro and mulatto danced, for religion or pleasure, new dances and songs developed, but only in very recent times have their tunes and steps been recorded. Meanwhile, staid creole society members sat in their stuffy city parlors and listened to their marriageable daughters play European classics on the harpsichord, while their suitors out in the street sang to a guitar the current popular songs of Spain.

What then were the intellectual tendencies of the Spanish colonials? To the dominant creoles and *gachupines*, it was European culture that mattered; few were interested in what the New World produced that was new. Different intellectual epochs in Europe were reflected in the colonies: the Golden Age of the Spanish Renaissance, the days of El Greco, Velásquez, Lope de Vega, and Cervantes, saw a paler "golden age" of culture come to Spanish America. By this time Mexico City was the intellectual center of the New World, with Lima and Bogotá as secondary centers. By the eighteenth century, scientific thought was turning the leisure and wealth of the creoles into new channels. Throughout the colonial period the underlying culture of the Spanish New World was the *mestizo*, the combination of the thin European veneer, reflecting Old World moods and tendencies, with the Indian cultures at the base.

Readings

Adams, E. B., and F. V. Scholes, "Books in New Mexico," *New Mexico Historical Review*, XVII, 226-255

Anderson, L., *The Art of the Silversmiths in Mexico, 1519–1936* (2 vols., 1941)

Appleton, L. H., *Indian Art of the Americas* (1950)

Barth, P. J., *Franciscan Education and the Social Order in Spanish North America, 1502–1821* (1945)

Caso, A., *et al., Twenty Centuries of Mexican Art* (1940)

Charlot, J., *Mexican Art and the Academy of San Carlos, 1785–1915* (1962)

Coester, A., *Literary History of Spanish America* (rev. ed., 1928)

Conway, G. R. G., ed., *Friar Francisco Naranjo and the Old University of Mexico* (1939)

Diffie, B. W., *Latin American Civilization: Colonial Period* (1945)

Englekirk, J. E., *et al., Outline History of Spanish American Literature* (3rd ed., 1965)

Friedrich, C. J., *Age of the Baroque, 1610–1660* (1952)

Gonzalez-Pena, C., *History of Mexican Literature* (rev. ed., 1943)

Griffin, C. C., ed., *Concerning Latin American Culture* (1940)

Hague, E., *Latin American Music, Past and Present* (1934)

Haring, C. H., *Spanish Empire in America* (1952)

Henriquez-Ureña, P., *Brief History of Hispanic American Culture* (1964)

———, *Literary Currents in Hispanic America* (1945)

Jacobsen, J. V., *Educational Foundations of the Jesuits in Sixteenth Century New Spain* (1938)

Kelemen, P., *Baroque and Rococo in Latin America* (1951)

Kubler, G., *Mexican Architecture in the Sixteenth Century* (2 vols., 1948)

———, and M. Soria, *Art and Architecture in Spain and Portugal and their American Dominions, 1500–1800* (1959)

Lanning, J. T., *Academic Culture in the Spanish Colonies* (1940)

———, *Eighteenth-Century Enlightenment in the University of San Carlos de Guatemala* (1956)

———, *University in the Kingdom of Guatemala* (1955)

Leonard, I. A., "Best Sellers in the Lima Book Trade," *Hispanic American Historical Review*, XXII, 5–33

———, *Baroque Times in Old Mexico* (1959)

———, *Books of the Brave* (1949)

———, *Don Carlos de Siguenza y Gongora: A Mexican Savant of the 17th Century* (1929)

———, *Romances of Chivalry in the Spanish Indies* (1933)

Mandel, O., *The Theatre of Don Juan: A Collection of Plays and Views, 1630–1963* (1963)

Moses, B., *Spanish Colonial Literature in South America* (1922)

Nettl, B., *Folk and Traditional Music of the Western Continents* (1965)

O'Gorman, E., *Invention in the Americas* (1961)

Oswald, J. C., *Printing in the Americas* (1965)

Picon-Salas, M., *Cultural History of Spanish America from Conquest to Independence*, trans. I. A. Leonard (1963)

Priestley, H. I., *Coming of the White Man* (1929)

———, "Old University of Mexico," *University of California Chronicle*, XXI, No. 4, 369–385

Robertson, D., *Mexican Codices* (1959)

Royer, F., *The Tenth Muse, Sor Juana Inés de la Cruz* (1952)

Sanchez, G. I., *Development of Higher Education in Mexico* (1944)

Schons, D., *Book Censorship in New Spain* (1949)

Shepard, M. L. B., ed., *Life in the Imperial and Royal City of Mexico—by Francisco Cervantes de Salazar* (1953)

Steck, F. B., *Education in Spanish North America During the Sixteenth Century* (1943)

Thompson, L. S., *The Libraries of Colonial Spanish America* (1963)

——, *Printing in Colonial America* (1962)

Torres-Rioseco, A., *The Epic of Latin American Literature* (rev. ed., 1946)

Vance, J. T., *The Background of Hispanic American Law* (1943)

Weisman, E. W., *Mexico in Sculpture, 1521–1821* (1950)

Wethey, H. E., *Colonial Architecture and Sculpture in Peru* (1945)

Wilgus, A. C., ed., *Colonial Hispanic America* (1936)

Zea, L., *The Latin American Mind* (1963)

Chapter 14

The Seventeenth Century:
An International Rivalry
and Frontier Expansion

EARLY CHALLENGES TO SPAIN'S POWER

"THE SUN SHINES FOR ME as well as for others. I should very much like to see the clause in Adam's will that excludes me from a share of the world," said Francis I, the scornful king of France, in contemplating the papal bulls establishing the Line of Demarcation. Francis proceeded to send out a Florentine named Verrazano to lay a claim for France to the northeast coast of the new continent in 1524. Across the channel was that other king of scornful jest named Henry VIII, whose father had laid a similar claim for England through the voyage of John Cabot. Neither of these nations limited its subjects to voyages along the northern coasts, however. Corsairs and privateers went out of the ports of Bristol or Saint Malo and harried the trade of Spain in the Canaries or the ships of Portugal in the Azores. In 1527 an English three-master sailed right into Santo Domingo harbor on Hispaniola; its officers were wined and dined by the governor; then, after clearing port next day, they returned secretly and laid waste the countryside.

Such illegal goings-on hardly disturbed the Spaniards at first, for they considered the New World their exclusive property in the sixteenth century. *Mare Nostrum*, the Caribbean as Spain's own sea, was "a pontifical and regal principle" under the Demarcation Settlement. It was out of the question for Spain to make any trade or navigation concessions to her rivals, France and England, who were not yet strong enough before 1580 to challenge the *Mare Nostrum* theory. Their alternative was to steal Spain's markets surreptitiously, to rifle her colonial treasure ships. As the sixteenth century progressed into the seventeenth there were often wars in Europe, and the battlefields were always extended to the Caribbean. Even when there was sweet peace at home between colonial rivals, there was "no peace beyond the line"; France, England, and Holland needed no excuse to attack Spanish shipping in the New World beyond the Line of Demarcation. They were determined to challenge Spain's monopoly there.

Thus the visit of the three-master in Santo Domingo was actually the beginning of a long series of intrusions by marauders, sea-borne bands who poached on the Spanish preserve. Sacking towns, plundering trade—all with the most pious reasons in the rivalry between Catholics and Protestants—English, French, and Dutch roamed the Caribbean, harried the West Coast, and sacked the Isthmus, often at the request of statesmen. After a century and a half Spain had gradually declined as a world power; her kings at home grew weaker, and by 1700 it was surprising that she had been able to hold her empire at all against her formidable enemies.

During the first half of the sixteenth century most of the attacks were carried on by French privateers, attacks which led the king of Spain to organize the convoyed fleets for New World trade. A peg-leg pirate named François le Clerc had a squadron of ten French vessels in the Caribbean in the 1550s and methodically plundered and pillaged, temporarily capturing Havana in 1555. French colonizers even attempted to found a settlement at Fort Caroline in Florida and another in Brazil. After a peace in Europe between France and Spain in 1559, the corsairs had no official French backing; they were obscure marine thieves living a hunted life, holing-in along the shores of unsettled Caribbean islands which they used as bases. Here the renegade Frenchmen gathered food by catching wild cattle escaped from unsuccessful Spanish expeditions and drying the meat. The French word for such beef is *boucan*, so free-rovers who stocked their illegal ships with such meat were called *boucaniers*, the buccaneers, who became the scourge of the Spanish towns in the Caribbean.

By 1570 England, in her period of "new" commercial expansion and Protestanism, was a formidable enemy of Spain in the New World. The Englishman John Hawkins of Plymouth had formed a prosperous trading company in secret collusion with Spanish officials in the West Indies, smuggling slaves into Santo Domingo in return for hides and sugar. On his third voyage two ships of his fleet were the personal property of Queen Elizabeth, archenemy of the Spanish King Philip II. A storm in 1568 drove the whole smuggling fleet into the port of Vera Cruz where they were caught by the viceroy. Only Hawkins' own ship and the one captained by his young cousin Francis Drake escaped Spanish vengeance. The days of Hawkins' peaceful smuggling were over with this action. From then on, for 150 years, England and Spain, whether or not they were at war in Europe, were always at war in the Americas.

Drake became Elizabeth's "legal pirate," attacking Panama, sailing round South America and invading the West Coast ports, taking possession of California, and continuing round the world to start new rumors of a mysterious strait somewhere on the California coast. In Europe he sneaked in to burn the shipyards in the harbor of Cádiz. When Philip retaliated by building the Spanish Armada as a means of attacking England at home, Drake was instrumental in helping Elizabeth and England defeat this massive invasion fleet before a single Spaniard could land in England. With this defeat in 1588 the sea power of Spain was weakened and her empire began to go on the defensive. Drake continued to be the nemesis of Spanish shipping until he finally died of a fever at sea in 1596; his body was cast into the bay off Porto Bello. Drake was not the only sea-dog; there were others, notably Cavendish, Cumberland, and Andrew Barker. Drake was followed by Sir Walter Raleigh who even dared enter the Orinoco on a long flatboat trip into the interior in search of *El Dorado* in 1595, who gave England later claim to the coast of British Guiana, and who attempted a colony in North Carolina.

FRENCH AND DUTCH CHALLENGES

Thus with Raleigh we close the sixteenth century, the day of Elizabethan "sea-dogs," and commence a period of official encroachment by England in the Spanish New World. Spain began an era of "aggressive defense" in the seventeenth, the so-called "forgotten century," often neglected by historians as a time of declining power, of stalemated institutions, of stupid kings. But in that forgotten century Spain advanced her frontiers and kept off her enemies by land and sea to hold what she had. It is true that at home there was inefficiency and corruption. Charles I had been a fine emperor and a great man; his son, Philip II, was a prudent king and an upright man. Among their successors in the Hapsburg line in the 1600s, Philip III and Philip IV were poor kings and mediocre men; Charles II was neither king nor man but an imbecile, yet he ruled for thirty-five years. His rule was characterized by cynicism on the part of political officials, hypocrisy on the part of religious leaders, and graft on the part of economic administrators. All Latin America passed through a period of vigor and prosperity up to the third decade of the seventeenth century and then went into a period of decline and corruption. Meanwhile France, England, and Holland supplemented piracy and smuggling with actual settlement in the New World in lands claimed but not occupied by Spain. There is a bright side to this picture for Spain; her "aggressive-defensive" policies held and even advanced the frontier in North America, and in the long run she lost only the island of Jamaica to her enemies.

The Lesser Antilles had been neglected by Spanish colonists as too small, too dry, or too far out of the way. By 1664 the French flag flew over fourteen of these islands, islands already serving as headquarters for buccaneers. Guadeloupe and Martinique had been made official French colonies by Cardinal Richelieu in 1635. Meanwhile the Spanish colonists on Hispaniola had allowed the western half of the island to be taken over by cattle and hogs gone wild. The buccaneers made the island of Tortuga, close to the north coast of Hispaniola, their headquarters. When a French governor, Levasseur, was sent to win them over as a part of the French island empire, he joined the pirates as their chieftain, defied the authorities at home, and founded a "pirates' union," The Brethren of the Coast. He and his successors swarmed over the Caribbean, flying the "Jolly Roger," burying their stolen treasure in hidden caves, and probably enjoying the secret complicity of the governors on the French islands.

Since many of these French renegades were originally outlawed Protestant Huguenots, and since they were joined by equally renegade Englishmen, they were all grouped by the Spaniards under the heading of heretics, or Lutherans, the *Corsarios Luteranos*, willing to despoil churches, rob altars, and even steal holy statues if they were sufficiently jewel-encrusted. In the 1660s the Brethren shifted their headquarters to Jamaica; by the 1680s they found their "sweet trade," as they called it, outlawed by both the English and French governments. The year 1702 brought a young French Bourbon king to the throne of Spain, and with him began a new Franco-Spanish policy of friendship. In the last part of the seventeenth century the successful French West Indies Company was formed; it established sugar-planting colonists on the Antilles and in Saint Domingue, as the French-controlled Haiti was then called. Many of the buccaneers now had no choice save to settle down and raise sugar; large fortunes were amassed in the cane plantations of Haiti in the eighteenth century.

Some of the most active smugglers and pirates of the seventeenth century were Dutchmen, for in Holland there was a deep-seated hatred of Spanish rule, as well as an intense clash of religious faith. When Holland revolted from Spanish rule, the Dutch "sea beggars" attacked the Spanish Empire wherever they could. In 1621, during their war for independence, the Dutch organized the prosperous Dutch West Indian Company, whose ships "legally" harassed the Spanish West Indian trade. One of the greatest single hauls in the history of piracy was made by Piet Heyn, formerly one of the Brethren of the "sweet trade" who had been captured by Spain and sent for four years to the galleys. Out of chains eventually, he came back to the pirate islands and became an admiral in the Dutch fleet. He took his revenge for the four bitter years by capturing the Spanish silver fleet in 1628 and making a profit of fifteen million Dutch guilders for himself and the West Indian Company. Holland's gain in this exploit and Spain's loss is said to have upset the international money markets for a decade. The Dutch West Indian Company founded New York, held the coast of Pernambuco, Brazil, for forty years, and permanently colonized the formerly neglected islands of Curaçao, Aruba, and

Buen Aire off the coast of Venezuela, as well as the Dutch settlement in Guiana. A parallel Danish West Indian Company founded a sugar-growing colony in the unclaimed Virgin Islands, which were held by Denmark until purchased by the United States in 1917.

ANGLO-SPANISH RIVALRY, 1600 TO 1700

Elizabeth of England and Philip II of Spain were both dead by 1604, and Elizabeth's successor was concerned with a scheme for trade and colonization rivaling Spain's in the New World. Raleigh's successors had organized a company which founded permanent colonies on St. Kitts and Barbados, again islands Spain had never bothered to settle. The Puritans, so important in English history in the first half of the seventeenth century, were active merchants interested in colonies in Massachusetts Bay and in the Caribbean as well. The Providence Islands off the coast of Nicaragua, a nest of freebooters, were seized by an English captain under the very nose of Spain 300 miles away at Darién. A Puritan colony of "planters, artificers, and indentured servants" arrived in 1631, not on the *Mayflower* but on the *Seaflower*. They soon gave up farm work and imported slaves from Dutch smugglers while they went privateering. Though Spain eventually drove them away, they did make a success of the logwood business. Later this success gave England the idea for a toehold for dyewood cutting on the Central American coast and led to the British colony of Belize or British Honduras.

Oliver Cromwell, British dictator in the 1650s, developed the idea of a "Grand Design" to capture the Caribbean for Puritan England. The encounter between his well-organized fleet and the Spanish was a fiasco, and the Puritans were merely able to capture Jamaica, a tropical paradise with only 1,500 Spanish settlers. This was the one Caribbean possession actually settled by Spaniards that any enemy of Spain was ever to hold permanently. Jamaica was strategically placed and became the headquarters for English activity. The legal settlers established sugar plantations with a Negro slave basis, and the island became one of the busiest slave markets of the world. The pirates used it as the center for the Brethren, and the Jamaica freebooters became as feared in the late 1600s as Drake and the sea-dogs had been in the late 1500s. Even the governor, Thomas Modyford, sent expeditions against Havana and Porto Bello.

With Modyford's connivance, his lieutenant, Henry Morgan, made the most spectacular raid of the time on the Isthmus of Panama in 1671. Heading 2,000 armed renegades of all nationalities, he surprised Porto Bello with his invasion fleet, crossed to the Pacific before any word could precede him, and took Panama City from the land side. In the orgy of looting and killing which followed, some Spanish citizens escaped to sea, while Morgan burned ships in the harbor, destroyed the city, and returned by himself with his closest associates, leaving the rest of the renegades marooned amidst the destruction. For his efforts he was knighted, served

Ruins of Old Panama City, sacked by the English pirate Henry Morgan in the late seventeenth century. *Photo by Helen Miller Bailey.*

as governor of Jamaica in his own turn, and died a natural death in 1688. It was after his raid that the site of Panama City was moved to a better harbor, and the forts and church towers ruined by Morgan were left standing as ghosts in the jungle.

Later English buccaneers did not fare so well at the hands of their own government. England's colonies were by now prospering overseas, as was her trade with Spain at home. The English Charles II, no imbecile, made peace with Spain in the hopes of procuring greater profits by legal means. There was to be a new alignment of European policies, and the Americas were to be brought within the realm of international diplomacy; the days of "no peace beyond the line" were to be over. In the Treaty of Madrid (1670) Spain acknowledged the existence of the British colonies in North America, and England promised to end government-sponsored piracy in the Caribbean. Morgan's raid the same year was the last of its kind. Thereafter pirates such as the famous Captain Kidd were dealt with summarily by English justice. Piracy declined because it was bad for commerce, because it menaced freedom of the seas. England proceeded to procure *asientos*—the legal rights granted by Spain to foreign ships to trade in slaves—and to make money for the Royal African Company by sending African natives to be sold to the Spaniards from the Jamaica market.

French privateering continued for another two decades after the Treaty of Madrid, but eventually the French government bought off the buccaneer leaders. However, England did not frown on smugglers and contraband traders, who continued to bite into Spanish colonial revenues for the next century. Individual English smugglers made fortunes out of Spanish commerce from Pánuco and Acapulco to Buenos Aires and Valdivia. There was even a Scottish Darien Company which established a short-lived settlement on the Isthmus in the hopes of growing rich off contraband trade and perhaps digging a canal.

What was Spain's reaction to this century of looting in *Mare Nostrum?* She had fortified her main Caribbean ports, building the fortifications that the tourist sees at Havana and Cartagena and the long sea wall at Porto Bello which still stands mouldering on the edge of the jungle. Santo Domingo, hard to protect because it was so open to the enemy-held islands of the Antilles, declined to a town of less than 500 Spaniards. Cartagena, on the other hand, was built up to be the best-protected city in the New World, with walls forty feet thick, a great fort commanding them, and the large end of the open channel artificially closed with sunken debris to guard the harbor. Here the Spaniards were to withstand an official English siege for many months in the 1700s.

In addition to her land forts, Spain improved her sea armaments and built better naval vessels. By these means, and by the division among her enemies, she held the Caribbean, so that the islands of the Greater Antilles, save the Haitian end of Hispaniola, remained and are still today Hispanic in language and civilization. Spain's colonies on the two continents had meanwhile advanced their frontiers north and south, and had stopped English and French encroachments on their farthest borders. It was Spanish "defensive aggression."

FRONTIER EXPANSION ON THE NORTH

The need for "defensive aggression" was also felt on the northern frontier. By the end of the sixteenth century, as we have seen, the northernmost Spanish line had reached a point stretching from below the Rio Grande mouth to the Gulf of Lower California. Oñate had organized New Mexico far up the Rio Grande, and Santa Fé had been founded in 1609. Lower California, still thought to be an island, contained no permanent colonies, Alta California had been explored but not settled, while the fort at Saint Augustine gave Spain one small toehold on the Atlantic seaboard. In Spain's declining century this expansion went on. The motives were still the desire for wealth and the pursuit of missionary activity, but now a new one was added at the top of the list—defense. This new century was to see northern Sonora colonized, missionary occupation of Lower California begun, the Chihuahua area and Coahuila settled, Pensacola permanently founded, and a border struggle carried on against the French in Texas. It was on this northern frontier that the missionary system as a civilizing institution played its function to the fullest, though the advance of the missionaries was slow and was accompanied by many Indian uprisings.

The Franciscan missionaries were working on the center of the northern frontier, in Nuevo León, Durango, and New Mexico. Western

Mexico was to see even more active mission work. From the frontier of San Felipe in Sinaloa on Mexico's west coast the Jesuits entered the area in 1591 and worked along the western Sierra Madre up one dry river bed after another through Sinaloa and Sonora into the Nogales Valley in southern Arizona. Here on this long frontier the Jesuits claimed to have baptized 50,000 people, while they taught them farming and crafts. Their work was accompanied by clashes with the primitive Yaqui and Sonora tribes. An Indian grammar was written so that the fathers could teach the Yaqui in their own language, but those fiercely independent people remained un-Hispanized into the 1900s. However, the Jesuit missions in Sinaloa and Sonora had become mining and stock-raising settlements by 1700, while the pearl-diving industry had brought a small "boom" to the region of La Paz on Lower California. The pearl-fishing interests were required to colonize the region at their own expense under monopolies granted by the Crown.

With one such concessionaire in 1679 arrived that most famous Jesuit missionary in Spanish North America, Eusebio Kino. He had received permission to work the area on the mainland west coast called Pimería Alta. Over twenty towns were personally established by Father Kino between 1687 and 1711; the missions of San Xavier del Bac and Tumacácori in southern Arizona, landmarks in the Southwest today, were his special charge. From his cattle ranches, vineyards, and orchards, pack trains went weekly to the settled area of Mexico; supplies from these missions helped in the permanent settlement of Lower California. Father Kino himself, busy writing the geography and history of the region, spent more than a third of his years in the saddle on exploring trips around the frontier, proving that the mouth of the Colorado was a fresh-water estuary and that there was no body of water separating Lower California from the mainland. His map to this effect was quickly copied by the great map-makers of Europe. Because of his work the frontiers of Spain had been extended to the Gila and the Colorado.

By 1620 New Mexico, last outpost of the sixteenth century, 600 miles north of Chihuahua, had thirty-five Spanish *encomiendas* centered around the town of Santa Fé among the civilized Pueblo Indians. From the time of Friar Marcos, who had preceded Coronado, these Indians were considered targets for missions. Father Alonzo Benavides of Santa Fé was also an historical writer, and his accounts report 250 Spaniards and 750 half-breeds in Santa Fé in 1630. In that year he claimed twenty-five mission stations serving ninety villages comprising 90,000 Pueblo Indians as the sum total for the New Mexico frontier. His story also tells of skirmishes with the Apaches, the wild marauders who swept down on the settled towns, stealing corn and cattle and destroying the mission buildings.

Many settlers who came into New Mexico were runaways from older settlements, thieves, and cattle rustlers. They joined restless officials and military men in making new searches for Gran Quivira; they fought off the Apaches; they flogged the Indians into working for them. Because of all this misrule the thousands of alleged converts were resentful of Christian influence, tributes, and forced labor. They became sullen toward their exploiters and secretly practiced their own tribal religion under medicine men. Feelings among the Indians throughout the area became so tense that the inevitable revolt occurred there in 1680, the most successful rebellion against Spanish rule of any Indian group north of Panama.

An Indian medicine man named Popé, from the Pueblo of San Juan, formed a well-organized "terror" against the Spaniards, gaining the cooperation of the nomad Apaches who were being sent as slaves down to the mines of Zacatecas. Popé was determined to drive out the whites forever and to re-establish the ancient tribal faiths, but word of the plot, hatched over sand-paintings in the *kiva* council, leaked out to the Spaniards. Then Popé called out his conspirators in full force. Up and down the Rio Grande they threw the Spaniards out of New Mexico. Twenty-one missionaries and 400 Spaniards were killed by the enraged Indians, and the remaining settlers fled for their lives. They retreated downriver to El Paso del Norte, the present site of the Mexican city of Juárez, where a mission had been established in 1659.

El Paso now became the "last frontier" town, site of a presidio and an *alcaldía mayor*. From El Paso, missions spread down the Rio Grande in the other direction and into Texas. From the New Mexican settlements the idea of revolt spread into northern Mexico, from Nuevo León to Sonora, and mining camps, missions, and towns were destroyed in the years from 1683 to 1690. New presidio garrisons had to be set up to defend the old frontier. The Pueblos remained independent for twelve years, resisting all invasions. Then in 1692 their leaders began to disagree among themselves, and a Spanish expedition from El Paso was able to re-invade their villages. In another four years the area was reconquered under Diego de Vargas and repopulated with Spanish and *mestizo* settlers; missionaries returned and, with a better administration, the Spanish occupation became permanent. Of all regions in the United States once under Spanish rule, New Mexico is today the most Spanish in culture.

Missionary groups had entered Texas on the northeastern frontier of Nuevo León. Beyond the Rio Grande there now arose a new danger, the French under the Sieur de la Salle, who had found the Mississippi River mouth in 1682 and set up an unsuccessful colony on Matagorda Bay on the Texas coast five years later, thereby creating a direct menace to Spain in the Gulf region. To answer the challenge Spaniards temporarily occupied eastern Texas, only to abandon it in 1693 when the French danger seemed to have receded.

A greater menace was the advance of the English along the Atlantic coast. The settlement of Jamestown in the face of the Spanish claim to exclusive ownership had brought a new wave of Spanish missionary activity in Florida and Georgia, with the town of St. Augustine serving as a base. Franciscan missionaries attempted to convert the hostile Indians as far north as the Carolinas. By the Treaty of Madrid in 1670 the English settlements to the north of the Savannah River were acknowledged by Spain, and further development there becomes part of the history of the United States, not of Latin America.

Thus, at the end of the seventeenth century, the extensive frontier of New Spain was held by a series of fortified points to stop either European or Indian encroachment. Farming and mining settlements followed the missions and the presidios in the continuing pattern of Spanish settlement. In similar fashion other parts of Spanish North America had been consolidated and defended in the seventeenth century. The thriving towns of Central America, ruled from Guatemala City, had only to worry about English logwood cutters and Caribbean pirates. The last native civilization in Central America, the domain of Canek, king of the Itzás in the Petén region between Yucatan and Guatemala, a dying Mayan town untouched by the Spaniards for two hundred years, had been conquered by 1697. These last of the Maya were then converted by the Franciscan friar Andrés de Avedaño y Loyola, who knew the Maya language. Guatemalan settlements in the seventeenth century lived off cattle raising, while the Costa Rican area developed around small farms owned by individual Spanish farmers.

The main centers of Mexico went through a period of depression in the seventeenth century. So many of the aborigines had died or been enslaved that agriculture and mining suffered from lack of free workers. Some farmland was abandoned and wheat cultivation fell off; livestock ranches replaced the great *haciendas*. Peons who had tilled the crops fled to the urban centers and joined the crowds of beggars in the epidemic-ridden cities. By 1650 the native population reached an equilibrium; the diet had changed from the Spanish wheat to the Indian corn for everyone, and prosperity slowly returned. With it, the physical face of Mexico changed back from cattle ranches to *latifundia* and debt peonage.

The viceroys of this century were weak and the social and political life was decadent. The last seventeenth-century viceroy (1696–1701) was the Count of Montezuma, a descendant of the line of the Aztec ruler on his mother's side. This man with Montezuma's blood in his veins saw the end of the Hapsburgs with the death of the imbecile Charles II and the ascendancy of the new Bourbon line to the throne of Spain. In New Spain, in spite of bad rule at home, foreign rivalry, and stultified trade, the colonial towns of Puebla, Guadalajara, Oaxaca, Valladolid, Guanajuato, as well as Mexico City, continued to grow and thrive.

FRONTIER EXPANSION IN SOUTH AMERICA

Whereas in North America a frontier line had moved generally northward, in South America the frontier population tended to fan out from established nuclei. All of South America save Lima, Quito, and Bogotá was a frontier in 1600. Panama, the crossroads of the Americas and the link between Spain and Peru, was most hurt by foreign rivalries in the 1600s. Panama City itself was forced to move after Morgan's attack. Bogotá, seat of Jesuit learning, with seventeen Jesuit colleges by 1767, spent its time in quarrels between civil and ecclesiastic authorities. New Granada was a leading mineral-producing area, though methods were backward and transportation was very poor. Cartagena, its main port, was connected by a shallow sea-level canal to the Magdalena for riverboat transportation inland toward Bogotá, while Barranquilla on the sandy, treacherous mouth of the Magdalena was a frontier fishing village. Venezuela had a real frontier, the Orinoco, to protect against English and French encroachment. Here Jesuits carried Christianity to the *llanos* while Capuchins worked inland from Cumaná. Neither group was very successful, for they were dealing with untamed descendants of the cannibal Caribs in a region where there are wild Indians yet today. From the Orinoco the Jesuits carried Christianity to the *llanos* of the Meta and the Casañare, while armed forces sent out from Bogotá had to subdue the ferocious Pijaos, the "Araucanians of the Colombian highlands," before missionaries could contact them.

A more typical frontier of South America in the seventeenth century was the silver-mining region of Potosí. In 1611 this Bolivian mining town had a population of 114,000, including 65,000 Indians and 42,000 creoles. Its standard of living, its prices, its history parallel that of the gold-rush towns of California. At the beginning of the century Potosí had fourteen dancing halls, thirty-six gambling houses, and one theater, for which tickets of admission cost the equivalent of forty or fifty dollars. There were duels over mine claims and over women, while flashy streetwalkers ruled society and Indian workers died like flies in the mines.

Lima, the "shining jewel of Spain's empire," continued the center of society; in 1680 it boasted 70,000 people of whom 10,000 were whites. The nobles lived in luxury, the church was of the richest, and the Lima branch of the Inquisition was the strongest in the Americas. University professors were honored. The élite society basked in its literary reputation, attended the theater, and considered itself as aristocratic as society in Spain. Most of the *mestizos* and all of the Indians and slaves were poverty-stricken. In Cuzco there were 40,000 people and a university as well, though the newer Spanish part of town had been shaken down by an earthquake in 1650. The port of Callao, a town of about 4,000 people, had to withstand numerous Dutch, French, and English raids. Peru, with its seat of the viceroyalty, its wide divergence between rich and poor, its wealth from the mines, its Indian masses, was in a state of constant "jitters" about foreign attack in the seventeenth century.

A few attempts were made in the 1600s to explore and develop the *montaña,* the region on the Amazon tributaries beyond the Andes. A few Jesuit missions among the half-savage Maynas Indians attempted to stop the work of Portuguese churchmen coming up the Amazon toward Peru. Samuel Fritz, a German Jesuit working under the Spanish flag, went among the Omaguas in the 1690s and made his way down the Amazon into Portuguese territory and back, mapping the river and studying the Indian language.

Chile was a never-resting frontier. Here the war against the Araucanians continued; in 1590 these Indians had killed a governor of Chile and fifty of his men. Early in the seventeenth century a Jesuit missionary, Luis de Valdivia, convinced the court in Spain that peace could be won by missions and by better treatment of the Indian communities, but this policy did not work with the already bitter Araucanians. Though the Pact of Quillín was signed with the Araucanians in 1641, the peace it set up was soon broken. In the long run, missionaries were never successful among the Araucanians. The line between the settlements and the Indians became a group of forts, and a permanent army was subsidized from Peru to defend the agricultural communities in Chile. A hundred thousand Christianized inhabitants were reported there at the end of the 1600s. With the southern frontier along the Bío Bío always an armed camp, the Chileans never colonized the Straits of Magellan.

The development of what is now Argentina and Paraguay, areas created roughly in 1617, was conditioned in the 1600s by the distance from Peru, the foreign smuggling, the pressure of the Portuguese to the north, and the neglect of the mother country. On the Plata frontier Spain faced a really aggressive enemy, the Portuguese. Here the Jesuit missionaries held the line at Candelaria in Misiones, a point to which they had retreated in 1632 from a group of successful missions in the Iguassú region which had been raided and destroyed by the Portuguese from São Paulo. The quarrels over this frontier were to continue well into the period of independence.

Buenos Aires, with its 400 houses, its 500 men bearing arms, its 854 Spanish inhabitants, and its 1,500 slaves, ranked as the most important frontier town in the Plata area in 1650. Beginning in 1620, Spain was finally willing to allow two ships a year to come in directly from the mother country, in the face of all the open smuggling that went on in the Plata mouth, but few luxuries came in and life was still hard, simple, and cheap. Córdova, far to the interior, had a university, founded in 1614 by Bishop Fernando Trejo, a true frontiersman, born in Asunción in 1554, and serving as bishop of Tucumán. His influence made these Argentine towns, Tucumán and Córdova, no longer raw frontier communities.

The cattle ranches on the pampas stretched less than a hundred miles south from Buenos Aires against the wild Pampa Indians until after independence; there was so much unused pasture land that the cattle ranchers had no need to go south. Thus Buenos Aires itself was the frontier of the south on the Atlantic side, the Bío Bío at the edge of Araucanian country on the Pacific, and the Jesuit missions among the Guaraní on the Brazilian border. There was little further expansion in South America during the colonial era. Instead, the process continued to be a filling-in and a developing of the areas conquered in the sixteenth century.

Though Spain was battered from without during this "forgotten century," Latin America still had tremendous vitality. If the colonies were weakened in their position, it was because Spain at home was weakened, for she slipped during this century to a third-rate status in Europe. It was remarkable that she kept her mainland empire intact and expanded it on the North. Spanish institutions continued to grow deeper roots during the seventeenth century. There was need for reform and rejuvenation, both at home and in the New World, and that rejuvenation became the keynote of the Bourbon century, the 1700s.

Readings

Andrews, K. R., *English Privateering Voyages to West Indies, 1588–1595* (1959)

Bailey, J. B., *Diego de Vargas and the Reconquest of New Mexico* (1940)

Bolton, H. E., *Rim of Christendom* (1936)

———, *Spanish Borderlands* (1921)

———, *Spanish Explorations in the Southwest, 1542–1706* (1916)

Burney, J., *History of the Buccaneers of America* (1949)

Burns, Sir A., *History of the British West Indies* (1954)

Carse, J., *Age of Piracy* (1957)

Castañeda, C. E., *Our Catholic Heritage in Texas* (6 vols., 1936–1950)

Chatelain, V. E., *Defenses of Spanish Florida, 1565–1763* (1941)

Corbett, J., *Drake and the Tudor Navy* (2 vols., 1898)

———, *Successors of Drake* (1933)

Crouse, N. M., *French Pioneers in the West Indies, 1624–1664* (1940)

———, *The French Struggle for the West Indies, 1665–1713* (1943)

Davies, R. T., *Spain in Decline, 1621–1700* (1957)

Dawson, T. C., *South American Republics* (2 vols., 1903–1904)

Diffie, B. W., *Latin American Civilization: Colonial Period* (1945)

Espinosa, J. M., *Crusaders of the Rio Grande* (1942)

Esquemeling, A. O., *The Buccaneers of America* (1924)

Folmer, H., *Franco-Spanish Rivalry in North America,* 1524–1763 (1953)

Galdames, L., *History of Chile,* trans. I. J. Cox (1941)

Hackett, C. W., ed., *Historical Documents Relating to New Mexico, Nueva Vizcaya and Approaches Thereto to 1773* (3 vols., 1923–1937)

———, ed., *Revolt of the Pueblo Indians* (2 vols., 1942)

Haring, C. H., *Buccaneers of the West Indies in the Seventeenth Century* (1910)

———, *Spanish Empire in America* (1952)

Henao, J. M., and G. Arrubla, *History of Colombia,* trans. J. F. Rippy (1938)

Kemp, P. K., and C. Lloyd, *Brethren of the Coast: Buccaneers of the South Sea* (1961)

Lanning, J. T., *Spanish Missions of Georgia* (1935)

Leonard, I. A., *Spanish Approach to Pensacola, 1689–1693* (1939)

Levene, R., *History of Argentina,* trans. W. S. Robertson (1937)

Means, P. A., *The Spanish Main* (1935)

Mörner, M., *Political and Economic Activities of the Jesuits in the La Plata Region: The Hapsburg Era,* trans. A. Read (1953)

Moses, B., *Spanish Dependencies in South America* (2 vols., 1914)

Newton, A. P., *European Nations in the West Indies, 1493–1688* (1933)

Priestley, H. I., *Coming of the White Man* (1929)

———, *France Overseas Through the Old Regime* (1939)

———, *Mexican Nation* (1923)

Scholes, F. V., *Church and State in New Mexico, 1610–1650* (1937)

———, *Troublesome Times in New Mexico, 1659–1670* (1942)

Thompson, J. E. S., ed., *Thomas Gage's Travels in the New World* (1958)

Tibesar, A., *Franciscan Beginnings in Colonial Peru* (1953)

Unwin, R., *Defeat of John Hawkins* (1960)

Wilgus, A. C., ed., *Colonial Hispanic America* (1936)

Williamson, J. A., *Age of Drake* (rev. ed., 1946)

Chapter **15**

Changes Brought by
the Eighteenth Century

A NEW WORLD DEVELOPING
SEPARATELY FROM THE OLD

> Yet, now, for those of you whom subtle genius has
> raised above the common herd,
> Put off the custom of yesterday,
> and clothe yourselves with the new.[1]

So sang a poetic priest named Rafael Landívar (1731–
1793) to the youth of the Valley of Tepic, north of Guadalajara, Mexico.
He was writing of the beauties of Mexican rural life in a long poem called
Rusticatio Mexicana, and had already described the "flowery countryside"
of Oaxaca and the lakes at Pátzcuaro and Chapala. The last canto of this
book-length literary classic brought him to Tepic, and there he exhorted
this beautiful New World to throw off the yesterdays and turn to the to-

---

[1] From the translation by Gusta B. Nance and Florence J. Dunstan in Carlos
Gonzáles Peña, *History of Mexican Literature* (Dallas: Southern Methodist University
Press, 1945).

morrows. Though written in Latin, as was the style at the time, the whole poem was soon translated into Spanish and is known and loved in Mexico as a Spanish classic and a vivid description of the beauties of the homeland.

But it was more than that; it was a clarion call! Throughout the eighteenth century all Latin America was changing from the old customs and "clothing itself with the new"; by 1800 many Spanish colonials were ready to think of their beautiful New World as a separate homeland. The century from 1700 to 1800 brought many changes—in the international scene, in the administration, in the economic field, and in the cultural pattern of "Enlightenment" of which the poet Landívar was himself a part.

A new line of kings, influenced by the more progressive French, came to power in Spain in 1702. Their accession was followed by a long series of wars in Europe which was reflected in the colonies. In the colonial wars of the eighteenth century Spain had to deal with an England no longer torn by Puritan strife at home, but unified, progressive, and rich in colonial possessions herself. This new England challenged France in Europe, in America, and in India, and world history of the 1700s is dominated by the Anglo-French colonial struggles. Spain often became involved as a weaker third party, but, for the most part, her loss of prestige in Europe made her concentrate on better rule in the colonies. By 1750 wiser rulers at home, less concerned with European alliances and more concerned with the New World, instituted a series of reforms in trade, in government, and even in teaching methods in order to maintain prosperity in the colonies. The result was a rapid change in economy—more industry, more commerce, more taxes paid, more wealth pouring in from mines, a trend towards city life with the increased incomes, a new well-informed middle class—till the New World cities were finer than Madrid, and the individual New World fortunes often bigger.

All this change taught the colonials that they could live without Spain. French influences at the court of Madrid brought French philosophies and writings into the colonies. These French ideas challenged all the old concepts; there could no longer be unquestioned obedience to one king, one Church, one rigid set of class lines, one system of commerce.

French "Enlightenment" reached the Spanish court and brought to Spain a few shallow changes in fashions, university subjects, and industrial methods. All earlier Spanish movements had eventually had a tardy and weaker reflection in the colonies, but they had been brought to America only through Spanish contacts. French "Enlightenment," however, came through many other contacts. Rich young creoles visited Paris and attended universities there. Under the wiser, broader policies of the French-blooded Spanish kings, French books and periodicals and even Frenchmen themselves—on scientific expeditions and as professors and tutors—came to the colonies. These Frenchmen preached a doctrine that questioned the established authorities, a doctrine of the equality of classes, the rights of free trade. The creole class was most receptive to such ideas. Eagerly, the young sons of the newly enriched merchants listened to arguments that they were equal to the *gachupines*. Meanwhile the century of wars proved to the colonials that they could defend themselves, survive successfully in a competitive commerce, and live very well without any dependence on Spain.

Thus the eighteenth century made the Spanish New World philosophically, commercially, and militarily able to live as a separate entity from the Old World. The creoles were ready and willing to take the poet's advice and "clothe themselves with the new."

INTERNATIONAL CONFLICT
AND THE NORTHERN FRONTIER

Dynastic and commercial wars and the struggle for control of the seas were the international keynotes of the eighteenth century. In all of these the ruling house of Spain and its Spanish colonies were involved. With the death of Charles II, that poor bewitched moron who had been the helpless tool of intriguing politicians, the rule of the Hapsburgs had come to a sad end in 1700. The nation was bankrupt, the army demoralized. The next heir in line was the young Philip V, grandson of Louis XIV of France, to whom Charles II, under pressure from his French wife's relatives, had willed Spain. Though Philip acceded to the throne, the other powers of Europe, England and Austria, challenged this controlling influence of the powerful French kings in Spanish affairs, and fought the War of the Spanish Succession. At its end in 1713 the Bourbon prince was accepted as ruler in Madrid, independent from Bourbon rule in Paris, though still influenced by French ideas and advisers. Spain was also forced to grant England a limited legal right to slave trading in the Caribbean, an agreement called the *asiento*. Thus Spain had been dragged into the bitter Anglo-French rivalry, a titanic struggle which lasted till the end of the Napoleonic period.

For a long time there had been various causes of dispute between England and Spain, the most important of which arose from English contraband trade in the Spanish colonies. Englishmen, bent on finding a new *El Dorado* in Spanish colonial trade and dissatisfied with their limited rights, tried to increase the smuggling. But under Philip V Spain was better governed and had a more efficient coast guard. Restrictions were tightened and contrabandists treated roughly. Spanish reprisals were made against the English smugglers and a number were caught. One Englishman, Thomas Jenkins, was so unlucky as to have his ear cut off; he carefully preserved it and claimed the Spaniards had committed the act, all of which fitted in with English conceptions of the Spanish cruelty and furnished a pretext for the rising imperialists of England.

Claims and counterclaims led to the renewal of warfare in the War of Jenkins' Ear in 1739, which soon merged in the great European conflict called the War of the Austrian Succession. But insofar as Spain and England were concerned, it meant the Caribbean would be the principal center of action. Fighting took place there and along the Florida-Georgia frontier. By now the energy of the Bourbon dynasty in Spain was beginning to show results, and Spain was able to fight off British attacks. Admiral Edward Vernon did take Porto Bello and Commodore Anson sailed a British fleet around the Horn, set fire to a Peruvian port, captured a prize ship off Panama, and held up the Manila Galleon. But the Spaniards had expended

Fortifications of Cartagena, built as protection against the English, still stand high above the city. *Photo by Helen Miller Bailey.*

huge sums on fortifying Cartagena, which was regarded as a principal bulwark of her colonial defense, so that when Admiral Vernon laid siege to that city with a large fleet, the brave townspeople held out and he was forced to evacuate.

The peace that ended this European war in 1748 was in reality only a truce, for it led directly to the Seven Years' War in Europe. In the uneasy years between the wars Spain had, in effect, tacitly accepted the rights of free navigation of the Caribbean: England had to give up the *asiento* and Spain abandoned her fleet system in 1748, admitting the "right of effective occupation." Where other powers held island or mainland territory she no longer made claims. She had ceased to be the "mother of the Caribbean" and was now only one of the "sisters," but she had successfully defended Cuba, Panama, and the northern mainland of South America.

The Seven Years' War, concerned in Europe largely with the ambitions of Prussia, was fought in America as the famous French and Indian War of 1754 to 1763. Spain had joined the French under the Family Compact between Bourbon cousins. It was in this war that France lost all her possessions in Canada and the Mississippi Valley and Spain suffered severely in the colonies in the loss of ships and men. To regain Cuba, conquered by England during the war, Spain gave up East and West Florida, but was compensated by the grant of New Orleans and its inland territory of Louisiana. However, the war was another step in the decline of Spanish prestige, for she no longer had France as an ally in the New World, and now faced England there alone.

The next international war took place mainly in the New World: the revolution of England's North American colonies. France and Spain both fought on the side of the colonies as a way to hurt England, but the independence of those colonies as a result of the war was more hurt than help to Spain, for such independence showed the Spanish American creoles that mother countries were unnecessary. Many noble words about equality and popular sovereignty were spoken in the English colonies during this period, words which were later translated into Spanish in Mexico City, Bogotá, Caracas, and Buenos Aires. Lastly, the French Revolution of 1789, itself a movement full of new ideas of equality and self-rule, quickly became an international war by 1792 and again involved Spain in further minor changes of territory in the colonies. Within a decade the French Revolution had expanded into a titanic struggle between Napoleon on the one hand and England on the other. As will be told in a later chapter, the alliance of Spain and England against Napoleon was a direct cause of the revolt of the Spanish American colonies.

As a by-product of the wars, Spain was forced into shifts on the frontier while she improved the whole colonial system. By the Treaty of Utrecht at the close of the War of the Spanish Succession in 1713, Spain had been forced to grant England an *asiento,* the right of selling 4,800 slaves a year into the Spanish colonies, as well as the privilege of bringing one 500-ton ship yearly with general cargo into Porto Bello, a legal entering wedge in the Spanish monopoly. Spain lost Georgia during the War of the Austrian Succession and the Floridas in the Seven Years' War, only to get the latter back in 1783. When England temporarily held Havana in the Seven Years' War, that port was opened to free trade—free trade which meant increased revenue and prosperity for the Cuban colonists and taught Spain to allow more intercolonial trade afterward.

Finally, through all this century Spain's policy of "aggressive defense" in the New World was forced to change gradually to one of "defensive defense." The empire had reached its farthest limits by 1790; in that year Spanish ships challenged English ships to rights on the remote northwest coast at Nootka Sound. Having no effective allies in the Nootka Sound Controversy, Spain was forced to abandon any exclusive claim to this unsettled coast, a humiliating moral defeat. At the same time Russian advances down the same coast from Alaska had brought a new enemy into the territory. After 1763 England and Spain had a common frontier in the Mississippi Valley, with no buffer of French colonies in between.

DEFENSIVE EXPANSION ALONG THE NORTH AMERICAN FRONTIER

All the international complications just described—the changes and exchanges of territory as a result of wars in Europe—meant more English, French, and Portuguese advances on Spain's frontiers, and pushed Spain to a strong defensive policy—"defensive aggressive." In the eighteenth century Spain advanced its frontiers in both North and South America and tried to forge a ring of defenses around its empire, to hold the sea lanes, and to keep out further encroachments by the enemy.

At the end of the seventeenth century the frontier was north of Chihuahua and Coahuila. New Mexico, reconquered after Popé's revolt, now had two centers, Santa Fé and Albuquerque. El Paso remained a thriving town, while silver mines were booming in Chihuahua. But the upper Rio Grande towns were threatened by Navajos, Utes, and Comanches from the north and by Apaches from the east. The French were expanding in Louisiana and their traders in the Great Plains would buy any horses and cattle these marauders would steal. Expeditions were sent out to stop the raiders at their source, and Spaniards reached to the Colorado-Kansas border. In 1720 the Spanish Captain Pedro de Villasur led a well-equipped expedition from Santa Fé to oust the French, but the French traders and the Pawnees cut him to pieces on the North Platte. The first French traders from Louisiana pushed through to Santa Fé in 1739 and many other Frenchmen were arrested later for doing the same thing. Colorado itself was explored some fifty years later by Rivera and Anza, and Escalante visited the Great Basin in an effort to find a route to Monterey, California, in 1776. In spite of the roaming Indian enemies, New Mexico had 7,600 Spaniards in fourteen settlements by 1760.

More important was Texas, that vast area separating the French in Louisiana from the Spaniards in Coahuila. The temporary occupation of Eastern Texas by the Spaniards from 1690 to 1693, as a direct result of La Salle's ill-fated colony, has already been noted. As more French traders came into the Louisiana-Texas border, Spain began to settle Texas in earnest. The presidio and the Alamo mission in San Antonio were founded, and Texas was permanently occupied by troops under the Marquis de Aguayo in 1720. This was during a period of open border conflict with the French, despite the royal family friendship at home. The entire Gulf coast from Tampico northward had been made the new colony of Nuevo Santander in 1746, and over twenty settlements were thriving along the coast. Border rivalry continued with the French there until the Seven Years' War gave Louisiana to Spain and eliminated the Franco-Spanish border.

Louisiana was small source of pride or pleasure to Spain during the forty years she ruled it. The French settlers in New Orleans threw out Antonio de Ulloa, the first Spanish governor, and his ninety soldiers; in 1769 a sterner governor, Alejandro O'Reilly, forced the Frenchmen to accept Spain. The king then established lieutenant governorships at St. Louis and Natchitoches and ordered the adoption of Spanish law. Louisiana was regarded principally as a buffer against the English; after 1790 it was attached to the captaincy-general of Havana. Trade in furs, horses, and mules took place between Spanish frontier posts in New Mexico and Texas, along the Arkansas borders, and with Frenchmen from St. Louis. Spain adopted French methods in dealing with the Osage and Comanche Indians, giving them presents and maintaining trade with them, rather than attempting conversion through established missions. Fur traders were licensed and French traders, such as the successful Athanase de Mézières, were enlisted by Spain.

During the American Revolution Spanish Louisiana, under the energetic

Bernardo de Gálvez, aided the rebels. When Spain entered the war Gálvez drove the British from the Lower Mississippi Valley and conquered Pensacola and Florida. But economically Spain lost out to the English in the upper Mississippi Valley, for British traders invaded the Missouri area. To counter all this British activity and reassert Spanish claim to the entire territory west of the Mississippi, Spain chartered a private trading group, the Missouri Company, whose traders worked the Missouri, and even ascended as far as the Yellowstone, but never reached the Pacific. Thus the northeastern frontier of New Spain reached the Upper Missouri River in the interior of North America, at least temporarily. The idea of ringing the whole northeastern and northwestern frontier with a line of forts via the Missouri across to the Pacific was Spain's dream. However, by a secret deal in Europe, Spain retroceded Louisiana to France and the latter sold it to the United States in 1803.

On the west coast Sinaloa and Sonora had ceased to be the frontiers by 1750. Lower California and the Sonora coasts were held by the forts and missions of the Jesuits, started in the days of the great missionary, Father Kino, who had died in 1711. As a part of the defensive policy against both England and Russia on the Pacific, the wise Bourbon king Charles III had appointed an equally wise organizer, José de Gálvez, to make recommendations as to the strengthening of the frontier. Gálvez went to Lower California to see to it that the Jesuits left their missions intact when the expulsion of their order was decreed. From Loreto he looked to the north, felt instinctively the foreign menace, and ordered the occupation of San Diego and Monterey Bay by permanent settlements. Thus in 1769 Spain began her last great spurt of empire extension.

Gálvez felt he had reason to fear the Russians. Vitus Bering had found his strait, and by 1765 there were Russian fur traders in the Aleutians and Alaska. Against their possible southward advance by sea Gálvez ordered the occupation of Alta California. In 1769 a military expedition under Gaspar de Portolá, accompanied by a missionary leader, Father Junípero Serra (described in Chapter 11), traveled via Lower California to San Diego. From this base twenty-one missions were eventually founded, many of them the nuclei for modern California cities. An overland route back through Yuma to Mexico was pioneered by Juan Bautista de Anza, and settlers were brought over it to help found the presidio and mission of San Francisco in 1776. Once Alta California was occupied, exploration was undertaken up the northwest coast to counter the English and Russians, a movement that was stopped by the Nootka Sound Controversy. By treaties of 1790 and 1794 Spain was forced to admit the legality of exploration and settlement by other nations into territory which she had not yet effectively occupied above San Francisco.

Spain's North American frontier on the Atlantic side, the Florida line, shifted back and forth in the eighteenth century when Florida changed hands as a prize of war. No other nation held it permanently and it was finally sold by Spain to the United States in 1819 during the last years of the wars of Spanish American independence. Thus, in the long run, the results of the century of warfare, as they affected the border area, had little effect on the story of the modern Latin American nations and their civilization. The expansion beyond the Rio Grande was to give Texas and the southwestern third of what is now the United States to Mexico when she became an independent nation.

FRONTIER CONFLICT AND CONSOLIDATION IN SOUTH AMERICA

Expansion in South America in the eighteenth century consisted chiefly of Spanish-Portuguese border warfare north of the Plata. Here again Spain's "aggressive defensive" policy was in play. The Treaty of Tordesillas had divided the world between Spain and Portugal, though no one knew just where the line was. Throughout the first two centuries of expansion neither side came near enough to building up its assigned territories to run a counter claim to the other side. By the mid-1600s, however, Brazilian slave raiders from São Paulo had entered the area of the Jesuit missions in Paraguay and Misiones and had forced the missionaries south of the Iguassú. On the Amazon the Portuguese had advanced beyond the most extreme measuring of the Line of Demarcation, had founded Manáus in 1674, and had destroyed the missions which the Spanish Jesuit Father Fritz had founded among the Omaguas. The *Banda Oriental*, or eastern strip of Uruguayan coast across the Plata from Buenos Aires, became the most important bone of contention between the two nations; contraband trade into the Plata region was a profitable business for foreigners, Portuguese as much as English.

The hub of this illicit commerce was a Portuguese station just across the estuary from Buenos Aires, a station which the Portuguese called Colônia do Sacramento, or merely Colônia. Here a permanent town with settled streets and garden plots was laid out in 1680, just in time for its smuggler-inhabitants to begin the eighteenth century with a constant harassment of Spanish port authorities at Buenos Aires. Imports from Europe came in free; cities in the interior could buy these smuggled Portuguese wares at much cheaper prices than those asked on goods that came legally overland from Lima. The citizens of Buenos Aires were torn between their desires to wipe out Colônia as a foreign intrusion against Spanish power, or to urge its growth as a source of bargains. England, France, and Holland also participated in the trade and gave the Portuguese a tacit protection. On more than one occasion the governor of Buenos Aires protested that Spanish commerce, even in cattle and charcoal, might be permanently stifled by the existence of the Portuguese base. When he received no answer to his protest, the governor finally went over and burned the town.

Thus a long controversy began. Despite the fact that Spain captured Colônia a number of times, Portugal, usually with the aid of English pressure, was able to force her to give it back. The town remained a center for illicit English and Portuguese activity. The treaty of 1750, settling other Spanish-Portuguese difficulties, set up a border commission to agree on a line. The Uruguayan coast was ceded to Spain, in return for which Portugal received the Misiones area in the interior, so coveted by São Paulo slave raiders. It was in opposition to this transfer of territory that the Jesuit missionaries there defied the king's order by forcefully opposing the exchange and eventually found themselves and all other Jesuits expelled from the New World. As for the treaty, its provisions were unenforceable in the wilderness. The Colônia coast remained a Portuguese center till it was made permanently Spanish in 1777, when Portugal's ally England was busy with the American Revolution. This permanence was sealed by the Treaty of San Ildefonso in the same year in which Spain retained the Misiones territory as well. Thus, in the long Spanish-Portuguese frontier quarrel, the Spaniards stopped the Portuguese advance south of Rio Grande do Sul, though Spain lost territory and missions in the Upper Paraguay and Paraná regions.

The Portuguese attempt to make the Plata the natural southern boundary of Brazil had induced Spain to settle the Montevideo area just outside of Colônia in order to keep both sides of the Plata Spanish. In 1726 a few families from the Canary Islands were given free transportation, free land, cattle, and sheep to induce them to come to Montevideo; there were enough colonists to set up a *cabildo* in 1728. Liberty-loving from the outset, the Montevideans quarreled constantly with the military governor, and entered the contraband trade themselves as go-betweens for Colônia and Buenos Aires. To further consolidate Spain's power and make control easier, the wise King Charles III created the viceroyalty of La Plata at Buenos Aires in 1776. This new governmental unit included Cuyo, Tucumán, Buenos Aires, Uruguay, and Paraguay, and was to be a defense against Portugal and a protection against smuggling. Buenos Aires was now to be a port with direct trade with Spain, and the days of the long hauls across the Isthmus and over the Andes were ended. The new viceroys opened the port and thus gave a new impetus to the growth of Buenos Aires after decades of stagnation. They also planned to expand the Spanish frontier into the South toward Patagonia and into the Gran Chaco on the north, but except for Río Negro their settlements in both directions failed. No longer afraid of the Portuguese, Spanish settlers encroached on Portuguese lands in Rio Grande do Sul, and more than 4,000 Spaniards were living in Southern Brazil when a final boundary was set in 1800.

There were also some small advances in the Cauca valley in Colombia. The only other frontier in South America that saw any marked change in the 1700s was along the Orinoco and beyond, where missions and cattle ranches were established in the 1730s and '40s. The Jesuits on the Meta and the Casañare were subject to Bogotá, the Capuchins in Guiana were subject to Caracas. Here Spanish missionaries came into conflict with the Dutch, for the missions of the Capuchins harbored runaway slaves who had escaped from Dutch Guiana. On the Orinoco the town of Angostura was founded in 1764; it soon had twenty *haciendas* and many herds of cattle pasturing on the grassy *llanos*. Angostura was to become immortal in the story of independence, when Bolívar set up a government there on this last "new frontier" to carry out the challenge of the eighteenth-century poet to "clothe himself with the new."

ECONOMIC CHANGES
OF THE BOURBON CENTURY

The poet Landívar appealed for change among those "whom subtle genius has raised above the common herd." The Bourbons of the 1700s—Philip V and Ferdinand VI, his elder son—had infused a new spirit and brought some "subtle genius" into the administration of decadent Spain. Interested still in the prosperity of the mother country and the ruling class, they nevertheless felt that such prosperity depended on improvements for all, at home and in the colonies. To reorganize and rehabilitate the decadent Hapsburg monarchy, Philip V had remodeled the entire home government, bringing all administration and finance directly under the Crown. French absolutism was the model and imperial aggrandizement the ultimate end. Unfortunately, Philip V had his eyes on Spain's European interests and was willing almost to bankrupt Spain to hold them. Ferdinand VI, less involved internationally, gave Spain a breathing spell and left a treasury surplus. True to the "benevolent despotism" of the times, both these kings hoped to keep the people satisfied, but they made little attempt to bring this new spirit to the colonies.

Now came Charles III (1759–1788), a man of true genius who stands with Isabella and Philip II among the great rulers of Spain. Little concerned with the fashionable French life now at court, he devoted himself to government. He aimed to win revenge for the defeat Spain had taken from the English as an ally of the French in the Seven Years' War; he hoped to increase the military power and revive the trade of the empire. In order to strengthen the navy and fortify a new frontier he reformed the tax system, and cut graft and corruption and brought efficiency into imperial rule. In the previous reign a general survey of conditions in Spanish America had been undertaken, based on a report made by official though secret observers, Jorge Juan and Antonio de Ulloa, who had gone on a long tour of all the colonies in the 1740s. Now their recommendations and those of Charles' own agents were taken up, and a number of "visitors-general" was sent out to inspect conditions and take appropriate administrative action. The most famous of these were the "visitations" of José de Gálvez to New Spain, which led to many reforms within Mexico and the empire and to the settlement of Upper California, and the work of his opposite number, José de Areche, in Peru.

In economics as well as politics Charles III saw the need for change. Spanish economists Bernardo Ward and José del Campillo, products of the "Enlightenment," served as strong influences on the monarch. Charles saw that he must recover the trade of the colonies by enforcing the laws against contraband, while at the same time liberalizing commerce to and within the colonies and adding to the revenue of the Crown. Besides giving this encouragement to commerce, Charles hoped to expand colonial agriculture and revive mining. These economic reforms failed from Spain's point of view, owing to her own industrial weakness at home, the insecurity of shipping during the international wars, and the competition of cheap textiles and other wares from northern Europe. But from the American point of view the reforms succeeded by increasing trade, especially from one colony to another, by enhancing the prosperity of the merchants, and by giving the creoles a taste of freedom.

In the fields of commerce, therefore, Charles broke the monopoly of the Cádiz merchants, allowed all ports in Spain to trade with the colonies, opened up many ports in the New World, instituted a money-making monopoly on tobacco, and ended trade monopolies in the empire. The Crown had instituted monopolistic trading companies under the earlier Bourbons, especially in places where foreign smuggling had been heavy. A typical example was the Guipúzcoa Company of Caracas, which in 1728 had received exclusive rights to the Venezuela import trade along with special privileges and exemptions and control of the cacao market. This company of ambitious Basques had helped finance the defense of the Spanish Main against the English and had maintained the coast guard at its own expense, although the aristocratic landowners of Venezuela had staged an unsuccessful rebellion against its powers and exorbitant profits. Mail delivery had been granted as a monopoly to a single family, and other parallel companies operated in the Caribbean islands. By the 1780s Charles III had ended these private monopolies and brought the companies under the Crown. Mail was delivered on a systematic schedule by packet boats and there was an intercolonial postal delivery.

The traditional fleet system of convoyed merchantmen had become obsolete—a hindrance to legal trade by individual merchants and an invitation to smugglers. During the century of wars fleets had seldom been able to make the trip safely, and the whole convoy system was abolished definitely with the last one to Vera Cruz in 1778.

Profiting by the lesson learned from the increased shipping in Havana during the period of English occupation in the Seven Years' War Charles allowed a bimonthly trading ship to Buenos Aires. All West Indian ports were opened to individual private Spanish ships. No longer was it necessary to have a special license to sail with the fleet. The many taxes were consolidated into one import tax, which was then efficiently collected. The profits to the Crown increased so quickly that trade was next allowed directly between Peru and Mexico. Guatemala could trade with Caracas, Valparaiso with Buenos Aires. Between 1730 and 1740 less than 200 legal ships had come into Vera Cruz; between 1785 and 1795 more than a thousand came in. Because goods from Europe were more abundant, prices went down. Smugglers and monopolistic merchants in Spain went out of business and a new class of creole merchants began to prosper.

Trade between colonies by land was easier, for roads and trails were improved as the regular mail service from town to town was instituted. Ideas on freedom spread with the prosperity and with the mail, and thoughts of free trade with all nations began to occur to creole merchants and shipowners. Prosperity came to the individual towns in South America. Ten times as many hides were shipped from Buenos Aires in 1790 as in 1770. The population of Buenos Aires doubled; her hinterland prospered also, for there was more market for hides, tallow, and salted meat. Tucumán made a thriving business of textiles; Mendoza sold wine and brandy into Buenos Aires. Paraguay sent out *maté*, tobacco, and lumber.

Chile now had over thirty cities, with a total population of more than 150,000 creoles and mestizos; its rich lands and large herds of cattle enhanced the prosperity brought by the freer trans-Andean and intercoastal trade. Only Peru was hurt, for Lima now lost the monopoly on South American trade and merely shipped out the gold and silver from her own hills. Fewer and fewer ships came and went through Callao harbor now; gone was the lush trade, and with it much of the viceregal pomp of the old Lima, for there were viceroys now at Buenos Aires and Bogotá as well. Cartagena achieved a new prosperity as the center of an enlarged Caribbean trade; Havana and Vera Cruz thrived on the increased prosperity of Caribbean South America. Acapulco on the Pacific coast could now trade freely with Santiago or Lima or Guayaquil.

Everywhere the population increased with the exports and the subsequent buying power. It was the merchant class—creoles and even *mestizos*—who gained new wealth and felt little loyalty to the mother country because of it. Landowners felt a new prosperity because of the growing European demand for sugar, coffee, and hides, though land became more concentrated in the hands of the few. Mine owners made almost as much new profit, for, though the king's taxes were now carefully collected, mining methods had been greatly improved under royal experimentation. Young creoles could attend the new Schools of Mines in the colonies and there learn scientific mining methods. New mines were opened and with their output Mexico surpassed Peru in silver production. In general, Spain in the later eighteenth century did much to improve economic conditions in the colonies, but in the long run it was not enough.

BOURBON ATTEMPTS AT POLITICAL REFORM

Reform in political administration was also badly needed in the colonies. At home in Spain the Bourbon monarchs curtailed the powers of the Council of Indies and of the *Casa de Contratación*, and most of their functions were delivered over to a minister of the Indies appointed by the king. The first Bourbon king, Philip V, had sensed the need for greater decentralization and efficiency in the colonies; in 1717 he had created the viceroyalty of New Granada, putting control of Caracas, Panama, Cartagena, Popayán, and Quito in the hands of a new viceroy at Bogotá. Though temporarily abolished in 1724, the post was recreated in 1739 because British attacks on the Spanish Main made the area of greater importance to Spain. Venezuela was made a separate captaincy-general in 1777, as was Chile in 1778. More *audiencias* were created, with those at

Caracas in 1786 and at Cuzco in 1787 among the new ones. The creation of the viceroyalty of Buenos Aires put all the provinces east of the Andes under one unit.

In North America, Louisiana and the Floridas were included in a new captaincy-general of Cuba; at the same time, Mexico lost direct control over Central America when Guatemala was made a captaincy-general in charge of that whole area. In accordance with a recommendation made by Gálvez, the *Provincias Internas* were established as a commandancy-general in 1776 to consolidate the frontier. This new unit strengthened and protected the farthest northern provinces of New Spain, centered at Chihuahua and extending from Texas to California. Charles III's reforms thus continued the territorial decentralization within the empire. At the same time, this efficient monarch made plans to bring a high degree of centralism into its actual governing.

The colonial minister José de Gálvez, already mentioned as suggesting many specific economic and other reforms to Charles III as a result of his own investigation in New Spain, instituted a new type of official, the intendant, who was to be sent to the colonies to further Gálvez' suggestions. An intendant was a powerful new governor who did the work of the *corregidores, alcaldes-mayores* (which were abolished), tax collectors, and financial auditors, and even shared the powers of the viceroy. The idea of intendancies was a French institution brought into Spain earlier in the century. The new system aimed at centralizing administration, giving greater efficiency, increasing the royal revenues from the colonies, and strengthening the defense of the empire.

This new institution corrected abuses in the tax system, the treatment of the Indians, and the distribution of goods. By 1782 Gálvez himself was Colonial Minister in Spain in charge of the intendants. New Spain was divided into twelve of the new districts, Peru and the Plata into eight each, while smaller regions such as Cuba and Guatemala made one each. These units were subdivided into districts headed by subdelegates. In general intendants were superior individuals, but their subordinates, who were not, became notorious for some of their oppressive practices. Local administration improved somewhat under Charles III though *cabildos* lost power. Taxes were actually collected more scientifically.

Gálvez gave the colonials more experience by reorganizing the colonial armies and creating colonial militias, which had a brace of creole officers— a new recognition for the creoles in the army. New presidios were created on the frontiers. Militias were established with urban and provincial infantry, cavalry, lancers, artillery, and dragoons. They were recruited from all classes except Negroes and Indians. The upper class furnished the officers; the lower class filled the ranks; merchants and landowners provided the money. By 1804 there were 25,000 regulars in Spanish America and 127,000 militiamen. Some of these smartly uniformed creole lieutenants, whose fathers disliked the strict new customs control, became revolutionary colonels and generals in the next generation.

As a political reform tending toward centralization, the expulsion of the Jesuits (described in Chapter 11) should be noted. Perhaps recommended because the Jesuit missions seemed so independent of central authority, this expulsion decree had repercussions for Spain in the struggle of the colonies for independence.

The results of all the other administrative changes were very noticeable under Charles III. Revenues were increased, government strengthened and centralized, some abuses corrected, and the caliber of appointees markedly improved. With the tax collection centralized, peculation and petty graft were reduced, especially in the customs houses. The *mita* was legally abolished, the last *encomiendas* passed into history, and the empire was extended. Thus the eighteenth century produced changes in the field of government, and through them in mining, in commerce, and in agriculture.

The new viceroys who tried out these reforms, though still Spanish-born, were now required to be intelligent administrators. Don Pedro de Cevallos, the first viceroy of Buenos Aires, was a good example—a "career man" promoted up through the colonial service rather than a "political appointee" coming out to the new post direct from court. In his down-at-the-heels little capital he created a buzz of reform. He tried to break the evils of a one-crop economy—in this case hides—by forcing the cultivation of wheat, vegetables, flax, and hemp. The second viceroy, a creole born in Mexico, laid plans for a university at Buenos Aires, built a public theater in the central market, paved the two principal streets of Buenos Aires with cobbles, established secondary schools, founded a shelter for beggars, a home for orphans, and a hospital for women, set up a printing press, and even lit the main square with street lanterns containing tallow candles. Thus did Charles III's viceroys create a new Buenos Aires, just in time to lose it to a new Argentina in the next generation.

That Spain now chose executives from among those best fitted, rather than from among Spain's old families, is proved by the story of the colorful viceroy at Lima from 1796 to 1801, Ambrosio O'Higgins. Born plain Ambrose in County Sligo, Ireland, he found his way to Spain, where in an atmosphere friendly to anti-English Catholics he went into business and arrived in Peru as a "salesman" under the laxer immigration policies of the Bourbons. Later he became an engineer in the improvement of the pack trail between Chile and the pampas. Charles III spotted a good worker and made him a field marshal in charge of suppressing an Araucanian rebellion. Soon he was captain-general of Chile; then, under Charles' successor, he became Viceroy at Lima. O'Higgins' Chilean mistress bore a child named Bernardo who was destined to free Chile from the rule of viceroys forever.

All these improvements, this "clothing oneself in the new" as the poet urged, resulted in betterment for the colonies but an ultimate loss for Spain, since the reforms, despite their merits, did not cure the dissatisfaction of the colonials. Abuses by the local and provincial officials were corrected, but already creole *cabildos* had begun to correct abuses themselves without asking the crown officials. What advantages accrued to Spain under Charles III were all lost under his weak son and successor, Charles IV. In all his long-range plans as a benevolent despot, Charles III had neglected to educate his heir to responsibility.

EIGHTEENTH-CENTURY "ENLIGHTENMENT" IN SPANISH AMERICA

Manuel Belgrano, Argentine independence leader, who was to spend his middle age fighting up and down the pampas to create a republic of Buenos Aires, wrote of his youth, "As I was in Spain in 1789 and the French Revolution was then causing a change of ideas, especially in the men of letters with whom I associated, the ideals of liberty, equality, security, and property took a firm hold on me, and I only saw tyrants in those who opposed man's enjoying wherever he might, those rights with which God and Nature endowed him." To many other creole leaders besides Belgrano the ideas of "Enlightenment" stemming from France and Europe became a tremendous force. They were weary of European absolutism and of the political discrimination it brought against their own class. The concepts of natural rights, of liberty, of equality, justified their hatred of the *gachupin* "superiority" and of their own inferior position. Thus the "'Enlightenment" led them to form literary and patriotic societies, to demand more liberalized university courses, and eventually to oppose the Spanish government.

The Enlightenment movement itself stemmed from the writings of Rousseau who talked of social equality, of Locke and Montesquieu who believed in popular sovereignty, of Newton who was formulating his laws of nature, of Descartes who said that science should be based on proof through experimentation rather than on Aristotelian logic, of Adam Smith who said that economics could be scientific, and of Voltaire who challenged the authority of the Church.

Some of these ideas had reached Charles III, who read history and economics, entertained philosophers and playwrights at court, watched physics experiments conducted in the salons of the intellectuals, and is said to have secretly read some of the new books placed on the Church Index. His economic and political reforms for the colonies were "enlightened" in that they were utilitarian and efficient and were based on "experimentation" by means of new organizations and new policies. Spain itself saw many reforms at home. Officials were appointed for their merits and their services rather than for their blood and lineage. The credo of the Enlightenment, the "Doctrine of Progress," was manifest in the new courses at the University of Salamanca, where physics, astronomy, and medicine were encouraged by Charles III, and in the many new scientific institutes, businessmen's societies, and intellectual clubs which flourished during his reign. On the other hand, progress was hampered by the "paternalistic" basis of these reforms, which were all handed down from the top and had no democratic basis, as well as by the continued censorship of books and limitations on public education.

Such restrictions and paternalism tended to retard any spread of the Enlightenment spirit to the colonies. But if Spanish policy delayed the intellectual awakening of Spanish America, the creole interest in such ideas, once they came to the colonies, tended to accelerate the Enlightenment there. While the University of Salamanca was modernizing its curriculum, so was the University of Mexico. The Universities of San Marcos and of Chuquisaca set a pace for liberalism in higher education. Many of the professors supplanted memorization by scientific experimentation. British science, French philosophy, and American political ideas were being discussed by student groups. The revolutionary attack on authoritarianism and the introduction of doubt was thoroughly achieved in the universities in Latin America during the last half of the eighteenth century. Colonial leaders corresponded with European scientists and with such Americans as Benjamin Franklin.

This new thinking, plus the examples of the American and French Revolutions, brought on a literary and scientific revival in Latin America despite the rigid Spanish censorship. There was a gradual intellectual reorientation away from Spanish leadership, a growing receptiveness to new ideas, and a willingness to question the validity of the old ones. Officials and merchants traveled to Europe, colonial students went abroad to study, scientists and travelers from Europe came to the New World. Books and newspapers from revolutionary France and the new United States were smuggled in. Botanists studied under Mutis in Bogotá in the 1770s and a medical and scientific journal, the *Mercurio Volante,* was printed in Mexico.

Influenced by all this ferment, young creoles were taking more university courses, reading more books, entering the professions in the growing colonial cities, and joining the lodges of Free Masons. They enrolled in the Schools of Mines and of Fine Arts and in the classes in engineering, astronomy, and navigation which liberal-minded professors were offering. Jesuit domination of education had been ended with the expulsion of the Jesuits in 1767—thus probably removing a major obstacle to the entry of democratic ideas into the colonies. Within twenty years the colonial universities had recovered from the shock of the expulsion of many of their classical professors; now more and more lay teachers, intellectuals not trained in the church, were leading educational developments. The scientific expeditions and projects described in Chapter 12 were a part of the Enlightenment movement. Scientists measured the size of the earth, identified tropical plants, and encouraged the use of vaccine to cure smallpox.

The New World produced its own philosophical and liberal writers in this period. In Mexico, José Joaquín Fernández de Lizardi, best known as "The Mexican Thinker," led other restless creole minds in discussing "radical" new ideas—popular education, abolition of Negro slavery, Indian reform, free trade, and freedom of religion and the press. In the University of Chuquisaca, in today's Bolivia, students read a study by Victoriano de Villava of the economic ineffectiveness of the *mita* system of forced labor in Peru. Solórzano Pereira's *Política Indiana* and the French Abbé Raynal's *Philosophical and Political History of the European Colonies and Commerce in the Two Indies* were also studied in the new university classes. Though written by travelers from Europe, not by colonials, they gave criticisms of the Spanish government and foretold the inevitability of revolution and self-government.

Newspapers and magazines appeared during the Enlightenment to encourage such "advanced political beliefs" on the part of all their readers. A literary *Diario de Mexico* was started, ran eight months, and was suppressed by the viceroy in 1768. In 1790, on the other hand, the viceroy in Peru was very literary minded, and was willing to support authors and poets in his court as the enlightened French despots had been doing in Europe. Under his encouragement Peru was soon issuing a very "cultural" review, half literary and scientific journal, half newspaper—the *Mercurio Peruano*. For actual dailies with news and political comment, all Latin American capitals waited till the 1800s. Paper was scarce, of course, and news from Europe was weeks old when it was printed. These early newspapers and magazines carried essays on literature and the classics, locally written poetry, notices on agriculture, trade, and current improvements.

Those who wrote for these new journals formed literary societies. In Bogotá they called themselves the *Buen Gusto* or Good Taste Club; the members wrote poetry, studied botany, and perhaps talked of independence. The Lima society, called *Amantes del País,* Lovers of the Nation, limited its membership to thirty members, as exclusive as the French Academy. In these societies everyone was a poet, but no one seems to have been an outstanding one. Of the hundreds of verse-writers in Mexico City, Landívar, the priest and classical scholar whose verse heads this chapter, is one of the few still remembered. Books written in Spain continued to come into the New World in greater numbers than ever. French books came too; many copies of Voltaire, Rousseau, or the Encyclopedists were to be found in private libraries or even bookshops, though the violence of the French Revolution had frightened the Spanish Crown into stricter censorship.

Social life was changing also. The last decades of the eighteenth century saw notable improvements in comforts and elegance. Mexico City and Lima were both paved with cobbles and lighted with candle-lanterns. Stagecoach roads connected cities. Recreation showed new influences. Spanish bullfighting as a stylized spectacle now held the attention of Sunday crowds, and the *paseo* or evening walk around the plaza—girls in one direction, young men in the other—had been imported from Madrid as a correct pastime; it is still so today in most provincial Latin American towns. The risqué French waltzes and two-steps were frowned on by Charles III, but *boleros, fandangos,* and *jotas* had been brought from Spain as country dances. City people attired in powdered wigs danced French minuets. Gambling had become a secret sport under Charles III and was openly enjoyed by his son Charles IV; its popular form in the colonies is said to have given rise to the national lottery, an institution which supports government charities in many Latin American countries today. The French influence in general had made society less strict and formal, less prone to accept authority, more broadminded in its interests in the late 1700s than it had been in the late 1600s.

At the end of the eighteenth century there were between fourteen and seventeen million inhabitants in the Spanish colonies, perhaps 20 per cent of them creoles, the class which became most enlightened and most discontented. Because it caused the creoles to challenge authority and offered no solution to social and economic problems, the movement of the Enlightenment in Latin America was more destructive for Spain than constructive. It "tore away the curtain of superstition and ignorance," undermined the authority of Church and empire, and produced the "will to rebel." Thriving commercially, improving culturally, the colonies were reaching maturity. As the eighteenth century drew to a close so did the colonial period.

Readings

Aschman, H., *The Central Desert of Baja California* (1959)

Bannon, J. F., *Bolton and the Borderlands* (1964)

Bernstein, H., *Origins of Inter-American Interest, 1700–1812* (1945)

Bobb, B., *Viceregency of Antonio María Bucareli in New Spain, 1771–1779* (1962)

Bolton, H. E., *Athanase de Mézières and the Louisiana-Texas Frontier* (2 vols., 1914)

———, *Kino's Historical Memoir of Pimería Alta* (2 vols., 1914)

———, *Outposts of Empire* (1939)

———, *Pageant in the Wilderness* (1951)

———, *Palou's New California* (4 vols., 1926)

———, *Rim of Christendom* (1936)

———, *Spain's Title to Georgia* (1925)

———, *Spanish Borderlands* (1921)

———, *Texas in the Middle Eighteenth Century* (1915)

———, and M. Ross, *The Debatable Land* (1925)

Brown, V. E., "Anglo-Spanish Relations in America—the Closing Years of the Colonial Era," *Hispanic American Historical Review*, V, 327–483

Cambridge History of the British Empire, Vol. I (1929)

Carter, H., *Doomed Road of Empire: The Spanish Trail of Conquest* (1963)

Castañeda, C. E., *Our Catholic Heritage in Texas*, Vols. II–V (6 vols., 1936–1950)

Caughey, J. W., *Bernardo de Gálvez in Louisiana, 1776–1783* (1934)

Chapman, C. E., *Founding of Spanish California* (1916)

———, *History of California: Spanish Period* (1921)

Dawson, T., *South American Republics* (2 vols., 1903–1904)

Diffie, B. W., *Latin American Civilization: Colonial Period* (1945)

Dunn, W. E., *Spanish and French Rivalry in the Gulf Region of the United States* (1917)

Dunne, P. M., *Black Robes in Lower California* (1952)

Englekirk, J. E., *et al.*, *Outline History of Spanish American Literature* (3rd ed., 1965)

Fisher, L. E., *Background of the Revolution for Mexican Independence* (1934)

———, *Intendant System in Spanish America* (1929)

———, *Viceregal Administration in Spanish American Colonies* (1926)

Floyd, T. S., *The Bourbon Reforms and Spanish Civilization* (1966)

Folmer, H., *Franco-Spanish Rivalry in North America, 1524–1763* (1953)

Ford, L. C., *The Triangular Struggle for Spanish Pensacola, 1698–1739* (1939)

Galdames, L., *History of Chile*, trans. I. J. Cox (1941)

García-Calderón, F., *Latin America: Its Rise and Progress* (1913)

Gayarré, C., *History of Louisiana* (4 vols., 1903)

Griffin, C. C., ed., *Concerning Latin American Culture* (1941)

Hackett, C. W., *Historical Documents Relating to New Mexico, Nueva Vizcaya and Approaches Thereto to 1773* (3 vols., 1923–1927)

———, ed., *Pichardo's Treatise on Limits of Louisiana and Texas* (4 vols., 1931–1946)

Hamilton, E. J., *War and Prices in Spain, 1651–1800* (1945)

Haring, C. H., *Spanish Empire in America* (1952)

Henao, J. M., and G. Arrubla, *History of Colombia*, trans. J. F. Rippy (1938)

Henríquez-Ureña, P., *Literary Currents in Hispanic America* (1945)

Herr, R., *The Eighteenth Century Revolution in Spain* (1958)

Hill, L. F., *José de Escandon and the Founding of Nuevo Santander* (1926)

Houck, L., *History of Missouri* (3 vols., 1908)

———, *Spanish Regime in Missouri* (2 vols., 1909)

Howe, W., *Mining Guild of New Spain and Its Tribunal General, 1770–1821* (1949)

Humphrey, R. A., and J. Lynch, *Origins of the Latin American Revolution, 1808–1826* (1965)

Hussey, R. D., *The Caracas Company, 1728–1784* (1934)

Kinnaird, L., ed., *The Frontiers of New Spain: Nicolas de Lafora's Description, 1766–1768* (1958)

———, *Spain in the Mississippi Valley* (3 vols., 1949)

Kroeber, C. L., *Growth of Shipping Industry in the Río de La Plata* (1957)

Lanning, J. T., *Academic Culture in the Spanish Colonies* (1940)

———, *Diplomatic History of Georgia* (1936)

———, *The Eighteenth Century Enlightenment in the University of San Carlos de Guatemala* (1955)

Levene, R., *History of Argentina*, trans. W. S. Robertson (1937)

Lockey, J. B., *East Florida, 1783–1785* (1949)

Lynch, J., *Spanish Colonial Administration, 1782–1810: The Intendant System in the Viceroyalty of the Río de La Plata* (1958)

Madariaga, S. de, *Fall of the Spanish American Empire* (1948)

Manning, W. R., *Nootka Sound Controversy* (1905)

McAlister, L. N., *Fuero Militar in New Spain, 1764–1800* (1957)

McLachlan, J. O., *Trade and Peace with Old Spain, 1667–1750* (1940)

Means, P. A., *Fall of the Inca Empire and the Spanish Rule in Peru, 1530–1780* (1932)

Morfi, J. A., *History of Texas, 1673–1779*, trans. C. E. Castañeda (2 vols., 1935)

Morner, M., *Expulsion of the Jesuits from Latin America* (1965)

Moses, B., *Intellectual Background of the Revolution in South America* (1926)

———, *Spain's Declining Power in South America, 1730–1806* (1919)

———, *Spanish Colonial Literature of South America* (1922)

Mottem, C. G., *Mexican Silver and the Enlightenment* (1950)

Murdock, R. K., *Georgia-Florida Frontier, 1793–1796* (1951)

Nasatir, A. P., *Before Lewis and Clark* (2 vols., 1952)

Nichols, M., *The Gaucho* (1942)

Pares, R., *War and Trade in the West Indies, 1739–1763* (1936)

Petrie, Sir C., *The Spanish Royal House* (1958)

Pfefferkorn, I., *Sonora: A Description of the Province,* trans. T. Treutlein (1949)

Pierson, W. W., *Studies in Hispanic American History* (1927)

Pons, F. R. J. de, *Travels in South America* (2 vols., 1807)

Priestley, H. I., *Coming of the White Man* (1929)

———, *France Overseas Through the Old Regime* (1939)

———, *José de Gálvez, Visitor-General of New Spain* (1916)

Roberts, A., *The French in the West Indies* (1942)

Robertson, J. A., *Louisiana Under Spain, France and the United States* (2 vols., 1911)

Shaeffer, R. J., *Economic Societies of the Spanish World, 1763–1820* (1958)

Simpson, L. B., *Many Mexicos* (3rd ed., 1952)

Spell, J. R., *Rousseau in the Spanish World Before 1833* (1938)

Te Paske, J. J., *The Governorship of Spanish Florida, 1700–1763* (1964)

Thomas, A. B., *After Coronado* (1935)

———, *Forgotten Frontiers* (1932)

———, *Plains Indians and New Mexico, 1751–1778* (1940)

———, *Teodoro de Croix and the Northern Frontier of New Spain, 1776–1783* (1941)

Thompson, J. E. S., ed., *Thomas Gage's Travels in the New World* (1958)

Treutlein, T. E., ed., *Missionary in Sonora* (1965)

Ulloa, J. J. and A. de, *Noticias Secretas de America* (2 vols., 1826)

———, *Voyage to South America* (5th ed., 2 vols., 1807; abridged ed. in English, 1964)

von Humboldt, A., *Personal Narrative of Travels to the Equinoctial Regions of America During the Years 1799–1804* (7 vols., 1814–1829)

———, *Politcal Essay on the Kingdom of New Spain* (4 vols., 1811)

Whitaker, A. P., *The Huancavelica Mercury Mine* (1941)

———, ed., *Latin America and the Enlightenment* (1942)

———, *Mississippi Question, 1795–1803* (1934)

———, *Spanish American Frontier, 1783–1795* (1927)

Wilgus, A. C., ed., *Colonial Hispanic America* (1936)

Chapter 16

Colonial Brazil

PORTUGUESE INTEREST IN
AND SETTLEMENT OF BRAZIL TO 1600

THE PORTUGUESE MARINER Cabral, following the route around Africa pioneered by Vasco da Gama, had landed in 1500 far off his course on the shoulder of Brazil—either by design on orders from the king of Portugal or by chance wind. Thus the part of the New World which lay within the area granted Portugal under the Line of Demarcation and the Treaty of Tordesillas was claimed by a Portuguese explorer while Isabella was still working to make a permanent colony on Spanish Hispaniola. Therefore, from the first year of the sixteenth century this easternmost portion of South America had a separate history from that part explored by Spaniards. The great modern nation of Brazil, Portuguese in language and custom, differing from Spanish America even more than Portuguese Iberia differs from Spanish Iberia, began its individualistic course in the earliest colonial times. Portugal had spent its strength and gained its wealth in Africa and the East Indies; hence it neglected Brazil, where there were no wealthy civilized Indian tribes. The colonists who came to Brazil, in contrast to those in Spanish America, felt little centralized control and lived as a peaceful, feudal patriarchal group, controlling their own affairs.

The king of Portugal had been mildly interested in the report of Cabral's discovery, in the hope of finding a halfway station for ships on the long passage to India. He therefore granted permission to some merchants to explore and trade along the Brazilian coast. They found there the valuable red-colored dyewood which was called "brazil" and which remained the coast's only important article of commerce for a generation. Amerigo Vespucci perhaps sailed for these merchants. By 1510 French merchants as well as Portuguese were working unhindered in the dyewood trade and were bringing back Indian slaves, parrots, and monkeys. *Degredados*—a word used for escaped convicts, exiled heretics, sailors marooned for insubordination, deserters, and minor criminals—stayed in the dyewood cutting camps or roamed in the forests. One of these "squaw men," a Portuguese of noble birth named Diogo Álvares, became the patriarch of a large community of his Indian wives and his half-breed children and grandchildren. He had frightened the Indians with his musket when he was first stranded on the beach at the present site of Baía; they called him "Man of Lightning," Caramarú. His presence on the coast when an official Portuguese governor arrived in 1531, nearly three decades later, was of great help to the new colony. He lived to be more than a century old, and many proud Baíans were glad to claim descent from him.

Thirty years elapsed before there was formal settlement, for the coast had proved of no value on the route to India; Portugal's kings considered the Brazilian colony a "wretched business" and concentrated instead on the East Indian trade. In contrast to the opulence of the East, with its jewels, temples, and sumptuous textiles, Brazil had nothing. The real history of Brazil as a Portuguese effort begins in 1526. The ambitious John III grew alarmed at profits being made on the Brazilian coast by Frenchmen. He was also fearful of Spanish encroachments east of the Demarcation Line, now that the stories of Inca gold were being told in Spanish America, so he decided to hold the fine bay at Baía against foreign encroachment. He knew he must establish fortified, self-sustaining posts if Portugal expected to retain the territory.

John appointed Martim Affonso de Sousa, a thirty-year-old member of the nobility and a prudent and able statesman, to head the new colony. With five vessels and 400 men he arrived on the Baía coast in January 1531 to work out a program best adapted for colonization. Chronicler and explorer with him was his brother Pero Lope de Sousa. Caramarú, patriarch Man of Lightning, and his sons helped the expedition destroy the French logging interest and lay a permanent settlement. Ships sent out by the Sousas started another town called São Vicente near the site of modern Santos where they were helped by other *degredados*, notably one João Ramalho.

John III now instituted the second period in Brazil's early history, that of the *Donatários*. When Martim Affonso de Sousa returned to Portugal with his report, the king organized a system of grants under which Brazil was governed and settled for the next two decades. Large tracts of land, *capitania-donatários*, were granted to individuals who had economic backing. The *donatário* had rights similar to those granted to proprietors in the English colonies—jurisdiction stretching fifty leagues along the coast and inward as far as the Demarcation Line, wherever that might prove to be. He could found towns, levy taxes, hold monopolies. In return, the *donatário* had to bring settlers, organize a militia, pay a fifth of his profits to the king, and meanwhile pay all expenses. The financial outlay had to be immense, for many of the vast tracts had little economic value, the Indians were hostile, and the proceeds from such a raw country slight. Of the fifteen "middle-class noblemen" who took out the grants between 1534 and 1536, several never came to Brazil at all, and few made profits. A lasting effect was the decentralization caused by this system of private settlement, many Brazils, not one united colony, were created, and Brazil remains regionalistic to this day.

Most of the grantees or captains embarked on their Brazilian adventure in earnest, however, mortgaging their possessions in Portugal in order to set up towns, churches, and sugar plantations. The most successful was Duarte Coelho, who had already made a fortune in India and had large sums to risk on his grant of Pernambuco. A well-selected group of colonists sailed at his expense to settle at Olinda to raise sugar. Even Caramarú's help did not bring financial success to Francisco Coutinho who had been granted Baía. Though the town itself thrived, Coutinho expended his entire fortune and was reduced to poverty. The king had to learn the hard lesson that few private fortunes were capable of standing the strain of opening up a new country, although the system did accomplish the settlement of parts of the coastline at little royal expense. By 1548 there were sixteen towns with several fortified harbors, and the colonists were raising livestock, planting European-type crops, exporting dyewood, sugar, cotton, and tobacco, and profiting from the labor of both Indian and Negro slaves.

But politically the *donatários* failed. There was no bond uniting the regions, and efforts expended were dissipated. Many of the colonists were lawless; they revolted against the captains, joined bands of Indians, or quarreled among themselves. To cope with the widespread anarchy it was imperative to establish a common code, both administrative and penal, to be organized by a superior official representing the Portuguese Crown. This decisive step was taken in 1549, when the king issued a decree limiting the power of the *donatários* and creating a governor-general for the whole of Brazil. Conformity must be brought to the region, French and Spanish dangers met with a united front, and boundary difficulties between the *donatários* settled. To produce such unity another member of the Sousa family, Tomé de Sousa, was appointed first governor-general. An able and virtuous man having political judgment and administrative experience in Africa and India, he set up his capital at Baía and made it a direct royal colony, succeeding where the donatários had failed. Eventually all the *capitanias-donatários* reverted to the Crown, though in general, these subdivisions remain the modern states of Brazil.

Tomé de Sousa came to Baía with six ships conveying 1,000 people—mechanics, civil servants, and missionaries. He had been instructed to build a fleet and to encourage sugar as a crop for export. He soon had a hundred new houses built in the colony. One of his successors as governor, Mem de Sá, an experienced judge in Portugal, prepared workable laws for all the captaincies, set the vagabonds to work, stamped out cannibalism among

Olinda, Pernambuco, one of Brazil's oldest towns. The church here is a good example of colonial Brazilian architecture. *Photo by Helen Miller Bailey.*

the coastal Indians, encouraged the Jesuit missions, founded Rio de Janeiro by driving a group of French settlers away, and remained in Brazil for the rest of his life. Pero de Magalhães, an historian, described Baía in 1576 as being big enough to have sixty-two churches and forty-seven sugar mills, and containing both the lower town on the seashore and the upper town on the bluff, the two regions of Baía today connected by the famous public elevator. In addition Magalhães mentioned the growing communities at São Vicente, today's Santos, and Olinda and Recife in today's Pernambuco. Olinda was so prosperous that many wealthy men "ate their meals with a fork and set their tables with silver and fine porcelain." By 1600 there were probably 25,000 Portuguese inhabitants in this New World, nearly a hundred sugar mills shipping crystallized sugar back to Portugal, and 14,000 Negro slaves to do the work. Perhaps 18,000 Christianized Indians were in the missions or working for the plantations.

EXPANSION INLAND

The sixteenth century had dotted a few towns along the coast. The seventeenth century was to show long strides toward a stable society both in the towns and by the defeat of all foreign invaders. It also brought the penetration of the interior behind the settled towns, the exploration of the Amazon Basin, the extension toward Spanish lands to the south, and the conquest of the São Francisco River area. This expansion was heightened in the eighteenth century when gold and diamond mines were developed—a development which brought inflation, corruption, depopulation of the maritime areas, and increased vulnerability to foreign attack. São Paulo and Minas Gerais, modern Brazil's richest provinces, were opened in the early 1700s, and even Goiás and the Mato Grosso, still one of the world's frontier areas, were tapped. The lines of inland development for modern Brazil were set by 1750.

There would seem to be few incentives to push the settlers inland. Desert stopped them behind Pernambuco; mountains crowded the sea behind Rio de Janeiro and Santos; the unnavigable river of São Francisco kept Baíans on the coast. However, if the government was not concerned with exploration for conquest, slave raiders, cattle ranchers, gold prospectors, and missionaries were sufficiently interested in the interior to cover thousands of square leagues, thereby opening a frontier for later comers.

Portuguese renegades had gone into the plateaus beyond the north-south axis of the São Francisco, taking cattle with them into the rich grazing grounds there. Their descendants became rich ranchers, holding hundreds of square miles in single family holdings, and sending their *vaqueros* out to drive back the Indians. To the north in the Amazon area *donatários* failed miserably. Hostile cannibalistic Indians and French and Dutch renegades limited settlement to only a few hundred families in Maranhão and Belém at the mouth of the river by 1700. In the region behind Brazil's shoulder, the semi-desert or *sertão* of Ceará, and the treeless plains of Piauí provided slave raiders with a steady source of Indian slaves for the market farther south. The provinces of Rio Grande do Norte and Ceará were founded from slave-trading centers. To the north of the Amazon there remained a colonial no-man's land.

Just as the population filtered back from Baía and Pernambuco to occupy the inland valleys, and moved along the northern coast and up the Amazon, so there came from Santos far to the south a similar and much more significant expansion. Martim Affonso de Sousa, the great colonizer, had ordered settlers inland from Santos to the high plateau. Here they founded a village called Piratininga, which was soon combined with a Jesuit school and a mission for the nearby Indians and renamed São Paulo. Since natural features of the region made São Paulo the key to a new frontier of rolling and extensive plains, the people moved onward instead of stopping to raise sugar.

From the "crossroads" town of São Paulo, rivers led south and west into the Spanish colony of Paraguay, and northwest into the Mato Grosso, Goiás, and Minas Gerais areas. Indian slaves, gold, diamonds, and rich pasture lands waited for the pioneers in all these directions. Thus the men from São Paulo, the *Paulistas* of Brazilian history, a hardy, energetic and courageous mixture of races, spread out as frontiersmen to double the size of Portuguese Brazil. These raiders were the founders of the three modern Brazilian states of São Paulo, Minas Gerais, and Goiás, but they left few written records, since most of them could not write. Organized into raiding groups under their private banners or *bandeiras*, they were called *bandeirantes*. Not relying on the woods and Indian villages for food, these frontiersmen often drove cattle with them; many of them became frontier cowboys and later cattle farmers. Their trails into the interior were even followed by prospectors. It was they who made war on the prosperous and peaceful Spanish Jesuit missions of Paraguay, enslaving the Indians by the thousands, though most of the·*bandeirantes* were themselves half-breeds, or *mamelucos*, as Portuguese *mestizos* were called in southern Brazil. Portuguese Jesuit missions to the north of São Paulo were not safe from their raids. When the governor of Pernambuco hired a famous São Paulo *bandeirante* to come to the coast and lead a raid against fugitive Negro slaves, the bishop there described him as "one of the worst savages I have ever encountered; except that he is a Christian, he is not different from the most barbarous Indian." The activities of slave raiders were excused on the basis of hostility against any Spanish settlement, and of the "prevention of cannibalism." Government and Jesuits combined to oppose the Indian slave trade, but the law allowed Indians to be captured if they were cannibals. The *Paulistas* said that all Indians were cannibals; the Jesuit missionaries from Portugal said that all Indians had souls to be saved; thus there was a century of dispute between frontiersmen and missionaries.

That the Brazilian boundaries were set far to the west of the Line of Demarcation was due largely to the *Paulistas*. One *bandeirante* leader reached Peru on an Indian raid; there are authenticated reports of two explorers who had gone up the Amazon tributaries into Ecuador in the 1630s. They also went to the south, inspiring the founding of Colônia do Sacramento on the Uruguay coast and causing the fighting and negotiations concerning Misiones, the Paraguayan missions, and the north shore of the Plata. There were Portuguese governors and settlements at Santa Catarina and at Porto Alegre in Rio Grande do Sul by 1750; both of these settlements are the southernmost capitals of Brazilian provinces today.

When the *bandeirantes* discovered precious metals around 1700, they created a whole new colonial region of Brazil called Minas Gerais, the "general mines." This was to be a region as different from the plantation-sugar-slave life of Baía as a California mining camp in 1850 was different from Charleston, South Carolina. At the news of the discovery of gold, settlers rushed into the backlands. There was no food, and malaria and starvation killed off the miners, but still they came. Negro slaves were brought into the mines; sometimes their masters sold the sugar plantations in Baía or Olinda and brought the slaves to the mines with them. Immigrants from Portugal, runaway slaves, and half-castes from the coastal towns swelled the population. The miners chose their own leader until 1720; then Minas Gerais was made a separate province and given a government which brought a measure of order into the mining camps.

The central town grew up from straggling mining camps on two sides of a ravine. Here pure, dark gold was washed out in nuggets, called "black gold" or *ouro preto* in Portuguese. The *Paulistas* ruled by lynch law over this Ouro Preto mining camp, with its excesses in vice, its brazen women, and its smart gamblers which made it the "Potosí of Brazil." Newcomers from Europe, called by the Brazilians *emboabas*, and settlers from the plantation towns of the coast resisted the rule of the *Paulistas* in armed warfare for seven years until the newcomers won equality in the "diggings." Commerce flourished on the new trade routes to the coast. By 1780 Ouro Preto was no longer a tough mining camp, but an ornate city, a center of the Enlightenment, with churches on both hills and fine houses filling in the ravines. When the mines gave out, Ouro Preto stagnated on grazing and agricultural pursuits, changing so little that today the town has been declared a national monument of colonial architecture, to remain unaltered as a living museum, the "Williamsburg" of Brazil.

Defeated in the control of Minas Gerais, the *Paulistas* pushed almost a thousand miles inland, opening cattle trails through to Goiás, which is today as remote a frontier as any in the twentieth-century world. There were new gold mines in Goiás and the Mato Grosso by 1730, and diamonds had been discovered in northern Minas Gerais in 1728. By 1735 40,000 people were in the new town of Diamantina, working the diamond mines and living in lush style in stately houses. To serve all this new area, Rio de Janeiro, a port established by Mem de Sá on a former French site in 1567, became the most prosperous harbor on the Brazilian coast, and finally the center of government. To improve regional government, Goiás was made a captaincy in 1744, Mato Grosso in 1748, and Piauí in the north in 1750.

Thus it might be said, in summary, that the sixteenth century had been one of neglect and experimental colonization on the coast, the seventeenth century one of sugar plantations and coastal settlement in a lazy prosperity, and the eighteenth one of interior development, gold and diamond "rushes," and new frontiers. Brazil continued to carry on a "Westward Movement" similar to that of North America. The frontiers were held and expanded against the Spaniards. A mining, pastoral, democratic Brazil centering in São Paulo had developed in contrast to the sugar-planting, slave-holding north with its capital at Baía.

FOREIGN RIVALRIES AND INTERVENTIONS

All this expansion did not take place without exciting the envy of the foreigner. From the first cutting of brazil wood for dye, the French were rivals of the Portuguese in Brazil and tried to maintain trading posts in spite of Portuguese resistance and coast guards. When the struggle between Protestant Huguenots and Catholics in France led to ideas of an "Antarctic France" as a haven for the Huguenots, the Catholic French king granted "permission" to Nicolas Durand de Villegagnon for the founding of a French colony at the Bay of Rio de Janeiro. This fine harbor had been explored and then neglected by the Portuguese. When the French first came, the Portuguese settlers to the north and south had been too weak to drive them away; then the French leader himself abandoned his quarrelsome and impractical colonists in 1559, and Governor Mem de Sá determined to take the area for Portugal. After two attempts the governor's forces, in command of his nephew Eustacio de Sá, were able to drive the surviving French north for good, and to establish Portuguese Rio de Janeiro in 1567. The remaining Frenchmen, outlawed by all governments, joined other French outlaws to set up trading posts at Maranhão near the mouth of the Amazon. With the Portuguese founding of Belém, this last French outpost was destroyed, and the French menace was gone from the Brazilian coast.

English rivalry was not a serious problem for Portugal during the colonial period, for in the century of greatest colonial warfare the English and the Portuguese were fast friends. During the period from 1580 to 1640, however, when the Portuguese king had died and Philip II, claiming to be an heir to the throne, had annexed Portugal, English privateers pillaged Portuguese colonies as fair game to any enemy of Spain. Except for the Spanish king on the throne of Lisbon, there was little other change for Brazil during the years of joint Spanish rule. In 1640 the Duke of Braganza led a revolt in Lisbon which ousted the Spanish ruler and put the Braganza family on the throne of the Portuguese empire, where they were to remain until the twentieth century.

During the Spanish period, however, Brazil had acquired the enmity of the Dutch, whose clever ship captains went directly to India and the East Indies by the Portuguese trade routes and won Java and other eastern posssessions. After three attempts along the Brazilian coast the Dutch "Sea Beggars" were able to capture and hold the whole area of Pernambuco in 1630. Since the Spanish rulers of Portuguese possessions at that time had no spare troops to send to Pernambuco's aid, the Dutch remained in control of the northern coast of Brazil for twenty-four years, until 1654.

Actually, not Holland itself, but the Dutch West Indies Company ruled Pernambuco, though the governor from 1637 to 1644, Count Maurice of Nassau, was a prince of the royal house of Holland. An unusually well-educated, liberal man, interested in science, literature, and efficient government, Prince Maurice gave Pernambuco its best years. Migration of other creeds and nationalities was encouraged, and the count called a legislature in which Portuguese and Dutch settlers were both represented. Unfortunately, the company was not interested in democracy, nor in the botanical specimens the count was collecting, but wished to revive the sugar industry, make more money, and expand its holdings. In a clash with the company over policy, the good count resigned, even though a European settlement at the time of the Braganza revolution recognized nearly a third of the settled coast of Brazil as a Dutch possession.

After the resignation of Count Maurice, the Portuguese and mixed-blood settlers developed an intense nationalism against the Dutch. Mixed-bloods, freed slaves, Indians, and Portuguese citizens combined in a red, white, and black revolt to drive out the now-legal Dutch overlords. With no help from Mother Portugal they fought the Dutch for thirteen years from 1641 to 1654. Finally a fleet came from the home country to help them, and the Dutch were forced to leave, in return for which they received money indemnities and trading privileges. The Dutch withdrew all claims to Brazil in 1661. The whole episode served to show northern Brazilians an example of good government. Their revolt from the Dutch taught them local pride in their courage against a common enemy without help from home, a pride which is considered the beginning of Brazilian nationalism.

POLITICAL AND ECONOMIC CONDITIONS

Portuguese lack of concern over the Dutch in Pernambuco was typical of the whole policy of government. Unlike the Spaniards, the Portuguese had not created special governing bodies for control of the colonies; they ruled the American territories through the existing political machinery in Portugal, which had seemingly worked well enough for the early Portuguese government in India. Administrative organization never proceeded according to any uniform plan. Until the control of Portugal by Spain in 1580 there was not even a council or minister in Portugal charged with the entire responsibility of colonial affairs. Government of the colonies, as well as that of the home country, was concentrated entirely in the hands of a Chancellor, a Royal Registrar, and a secretary of the king. An Inspector of Finance for Portugal, India, and Brazil supervised the *Casa da India*, which prepared cargoes for all colonies and enlisted soldiers for colonial affairs. Only an ecclesiastical council, *Mesa da Consciencia é Orden*, exercised some authority over officials sent to Brazil; the authorities for local government which were sent out from Portugal consisted of the viceroy at Baía and the provincial governors.

Philip III improved on this situation, setting up a Council for the Indies in 1604 similar to that of Spain, and dividing its work into two branches, one for the East Indies and one for Brazil and Africa. Efficiency was so much enhanced that with the independence of Portugal under the Braganzas, the Spanish-founded institutions were maintained. In the seventeenth century Portugal suffered an even greater decline than Spain. Rule in Brazil became an entirely personal one, depending on the casual whim of the monarch with little organization or body of laws for Brazil. There was corruption and graft in the highest places, and venality reached its peak under John V.

After 1750 a new turn was given the Portuguese administration by the Marquis of Pombal, the great minister of "enlightened despotism" who was virtual dictator of Portugal for twenty-seven years. Government agencies in Brazil were improved, royal authority was more centralized, inefficiency and corruption were reduced, taxes and revenues for the Crown were increased, and trade and commerce more strictly controlled for the mother country. Trading companies and monopolies were established. In the line of social reform, Pombal was influenced by the French Enlightenment. He ended the political inequalities of Brazilians and Portuguese, abolished Indian slavery, and encouraged Portuguese immigration to Brazil. In his effort to reduce the importance of the Church, he expelled the Jesuits. The administration of justice, always a weak part of Portuguese colonial rule, was strengthened by the establishment of a second supreme court at Rio in 1751 to supplement the existing one at Baía.

As for government in the colonies themselves, Baía's governor-general had ruled with little interference from the days of Tomé de Sousa in 1549. Such a governor was called a viceroy after the Braganza revolution; under him served an attorney-general, a treasurer, and other royal officials.

Various captaincies in the provincial capitals of Brazil with royal officers were created as the frontier expanded. Finally, the viceregal capital itself was moved from Baía to the rapidly growing south and set up at Rio de Janeiro in 1763. Rio itself had grown from a thatched-roof town to a fair-sized city because of the flood of precious minerals leaving its port from Minas Gerais in the 1700s. The economic balance of the colony had shifted away from the sugar-producing north. Theoretically all the governmental posts, as well as judgeships and lesser administrative positions, could be filled by native-born Brazilians as well as by Lisbon-born Portuguese. There was no legal discrimination against creoles in Brazil, though actually, royal favorites close to the king's ear received most of the lucrative appointments.

Regionalism, still today one of Brazil's biggest administrative problems, flourished as a by-product of the laxity of central control. The Crown did not adequately support its representatives and did not provide sufficient military forces, so an independent spirit was to be expected in the provincial town councils and governors' offices. Captains-general ruled the provinces; plantation-owners were kings on their own lands; missionary fathers were the law in the mission compounds. The *câmaras* or city councils in the provincial towns were more active and democratic than the similar Spanish *cabildo*s. Though members were appointed, or were hereditary officials serving for life, they were leaders in their communities and took pride in their services. In these councils Brazilians dealt with shipping laws, customs duties, army maintenance—many such things which in the Spanish colonies were ordained from Spain. The church got its principal support from the municipalities. When, during wartime, communications with Portugal were weak, local *câmaras* took charge, even temporarily filling a vacancy in the governorship. In the interior, local militia bosses, assistants to the provincial governors, called *capitão mor*, recruited small armies and became political bosses. Since Brazilians were not in general very civic-minded, and there was no widespread culture and little self-reliance, no actual democracy developed.

The Crown made money from the colony of Brazil, though nothing to compare with the money Spain made from Spanish America. The customs duties, the royal monopolies, the *quinto* or fifth-part value on precious metals and stones brought in sufficient revenue to keep the kings interested, though taxes were farmed out to private tax collectors who kept their full share. After the discovery of gold and diamonds every attempt was made to collect taxes on these rich diggings. Entry and exit to the mining area were licensed; gold had to pass through royal smelting houses, and bullion and diamonds could be shipped only in royal craft. Smuggling, especially in the diamond fields, was rampant, and the Crown probably lost more than it gained during the eighteenth-century mining boom.

Portugal's commercial policy toward Brazil was never as comprehensive as Spain's toward her American possessions. It was chiefly directed toward increasing the government's revenues, preventing competition with Asiatic goods, obtaining benefits for privileged interests in the home country, and encouraging sugar planting and mining. Commerce was free to Portuguese ships only, for free trade was inconsistent with the mercantilist theories of the time.

The homeland maintained her colonial trade by means of convoys to and from Brazil, set up by a law of 1571 when Brazil was fast being recognized as a place of some value. The Portuguese convoys had something of the same irregular history throughout the seventeenth century as did the Spanish *flotas*, until they were finally completely abolished by 1800. Meanwhile trade was carried on through monopolistic companies, the first of which had been set up to protect the Pernambuco trade and expel the Dutch. These companies received grants for twenty years at a time to trade in tobacco, slaves, or dyewoods. All the trade north of Pernambuco was carried on in this way, and the mother country never hoped to make a large income there. In the southern colonies trade thrived. Staples from Portugal were exchanged for rice, sugar, coffee, vanilla, indigo, hides, and tallow, as well as gold and diamonds, though sugar export far exceeded all other trade throughout the colonial period.

Commodities used in the colony were manufactured there in handicraft industry on the plantations and in the missions, though wealthy plantation owners imported European-made luxury goods. As in Spanish America, simple farming and mining tools were forged in the New World, textiles were made on the plantations, and ships were built in coastal yards.

It was the plantation or *fazenda*, the great sugar-growing establishment, which was the essential feature of Brazil. "Sugar is King" was the motto. The sugar crop encouraged slavery, led to large holdings, and discouraged small tenancy. Sugar needed many unskilled hands in harvest time and required little intelligent management on the part of the owner, who could let his paunch grow fat while he lived idly in the big plantation house, keeping most of his slaves busy only a few months of the year.

Sugar had been deliberately introduced from the Madeira Islands as a quick money crop in the tropics. The sugar cane was crushed in mills and then crystallized into brown cakes or distilled into rum. A mill called an *engenho* became a symbol of wealth; since handling the crushing, entailed a large investment needing fifty slaves and twenty yoke of oxen, only the "sugar barons" could maintain one. In 1711 a report listed 146 such mills in or near Baía. To handle this sugar the *fazendeiros*, the plantation owners, were each allowed to buy from the Africa traders 120 slaves a year. More than 50,000 Negroes were brought in yearly to each sugar port to provide the labor supply for Brazil's agriculture. Indian laborers, still being captured in large numbers by the *Paulistas* in the 1700s were inferior to the Negroes as workers, and were used on cattle ranches rather than on the "sugar coast." There were few free artisans in such a colony; most labor was colored and involuntary. By the end of the colonial period slaves in Brazil outnumbered the whites by 50 per cent The other agricultural exports from Brazil were hides, which came from the backlands in great numbers, and tobacco, of which 25,000 "twists" a year were sent to Portugal. Planting coffee, which was to mean Brazil's wealth in the twentieth century, had little importance at this time.

The population of Brazil had grown enormously in the wake of all this prosperity. In 1776 there were almost 2,000,000 "civilized" people in

Brazil, in 1800 nearly 3,000,000. Of these perhaps 800,000 were whites, 300,000 were Indians, almost a million and a half were Negroes, and the remainder half-castes of all types. The captaincy of Baía had 530,000 people, Pernambuco 480,000, Rio 380,000, and Minas Gerais 600,000 in 1800. Though mining was producing $4,000,000 a year by then, agriculture, the real mainstay of Brazil, was bringing in triple that amount at the end of the colonial period.

BRAZILIAN COLONIAL SOCIETY

Negro slaves made the coastal economy possible and they worked along with Indian slaves in the interior. More Negroes came to Brazil, it is estimated, than to all the rest of the Western Hemisphere combined. There they were eventually absorbed as freemen, much as the Indian peons have been absorbed into the life of modern Mexico. The Indians of Brazil faded away into the jungle, died working for the *Paulistas*, refused to live in the sedentary villages where the whites placed them, or melted their bloodstream in with the large *mameluco* or *mestizo* class on the frontier. Negro slaves had long been used in Portugal, where they had been treated affectionately in Lisbon households, and had been considered as creatures with souls to be saved by religious teaching, rather than as draft animals. Portuguese ships had explored the coast of Africa and had a monopoly on the slave trade. When the young colony of Brazil needed strong, docile hands to plant and harvest cane and cotton, to drive oxen in the cane crushers and stoke the refining furnaces where the molasses boiled, what could be more natural than to bring in Negroes from Africa in large numbers?

Negroes who survived the Portuguese slave ships—those "floating coffins" —were herded into the warehouses around the slave markets, fed on mandioca flour, and offered for sale in groups. They were lucky ever again to be with anyone from their own village in Africa. It was because of their life in those villages in Africa that they were better workers than the Indians; with the exception of some tribes captured in the Congo, the Negroes brought to Brazil had lived a more civilized life than the Brazilian Indians. They had lived in stone huts, had domesticated cattle, knew how to plant crops and tend orchards, and were accustomed to hard field labor in the heat. They had been a people happy by nature and cooperative within their tribal groups. Many Negroes in Brazil kept their own native customs and religious beliefs; some of them were even Mohammedans from the semicivilized Sudan who could read and write Arabic. Slave groups developed a common language called Nâgo, a mixture of Portuguese words and African dialects, and many of its words are in use today.

There were instances of successful Negro villages in the backlands, settlements called *quilombos*. During the Dutch occupation of Pernambuco, for example, many slaves escaped into the wild northeast and there set up an independent "republic" called Palmares, after the palm forest in which the "capital" was situated. This capital was one of a group of well-fortified villages in an area almost as large as Portugal. They elected their own head, set up a judicial system, and allotted agricultural land to families. Perhaps 100,000 Negroes lived here by 1660; so strong was their republic that the Portuguese did not capture it until 1697. At that time, when a large force finally wiped the settlement out, more than half the adults had been born in the freedom of Palmares and had known no other life.

Those slaves who stayed docilely on the plantations received better treatment than they would have found elsewhere in the New World. Negro toddlers were pets in the Big House; masters and slaves joined in festivals on religious holidays. Portuguese men, long a seafaring band who traveled without women to lands where dark-skinned beauties could be had for the asking, always mated freely in the New World with both Indian and slave. Now their mulatto children by slave women were often freed at birth, grew up as overseers or artisans, and were sometimes even sent to study in Lisbon. All Brazil in general felt no antagonism toward black people as such; anyone with a little white blood was white, in contrast to the United States plantation-life development in which anyone with a drop of Negro blood was Negro. There were many laws and customs protecting the rights of slaves, the holidays granted them, the privilege to earn private money, the rights to inherit land and shops, to complain against unjust treatment, and to form protective and religious brotherhoods with other slaves.

The slaves lived in the patriarchal villages around the Big House, the *Casa Grande*, the master's manor house of fifteen or twenty rooms and a private chapel. The establishment contained elements of a social center, a hospital, fortress, school, commissary, and army corps kitchen. It was an isolated, patriarchal, self-sufficient village. Beyond the scores of slave huts would be the sugar refinery, the distillery, and the stock pens.

Here on the manor the *fazendeiro* had complete authority, often kept his own militia, and lived independent of any city rule. In the manor houses the ladies would live in almost Mohammedan seclusion, marry very early, go out only to church, and then be smothered in bejewelled cloaks up to their eyes. At home they grew fat on sugar-sweets and inactivity, their every wish anticipated by a slave. The daughters were married to other *fazendeiros* in early adolescence. According to an eighteenth-century French traveler, many Brazilian girls preferred the life of a nun to such early marriage and the secluded life and heavy childbearing that followed it. Wealthy families left their land to the eldest son, sent their second to college in Portugal so he might be a lawyer or enter the government service, and were apt to "give their third to the church" at fifteen.

In general, *fazendeiros* did not congregate in cities as did the Spanish colonial aristocracy, though they often kept town houses. The towns were more apt to be filled with middle-class Portuguese immigrants. In most towns unpaved streets ran past the Moorish-tile dwellings of the rich. Negro women washed clothes in the public fountains and mule trains and oxcarts trundled by, loaded with sugar and rum or hides from the interior. At night the streets were so dark that wayfarers were preceded by a slave carrying a fish-oil lantern. But let fiesta time come, Carnival or Saint John's Day, and the streets were full and gay, while social classes mixed freely in the parades and street dances, celebrating with greater abandon than did the population of any Spanish colonial city.

The social class lines were not so marked as in Spanish America. At the top were the *donatários*, the aristocrats or *fidalgos*. Though this was the small ruling class from Portugal, the creoles, called in Brazil the *masambos* or native-born, were not excluded from it as they were in Spanish America. Below the *fidalgos* came the *fazendeiros*, who owned the plantations, and the middle-class merchants who ran the businesses. In both these groups many mixed-bloods could be found by 1800. White peasants from Portugal, Jewish merchants and peddlers, Azores Islanders in business and on land, made a middle class. Then came the *caboclos* and *mamelucos*, the white-Indian mixtures, the mulattoes, and the *cafusos* or Indian-Negro hybrids; next the free Negroes and the free Indians, and at the bottom both Indian and Negro slaves. In these last groups there was much crossing over, with an ever-present opportunity to rise into a higher class in the second generation seldom found in Spanish America.

RELIGION AND CULTURE
IN PORTUGUESE AMERICA

Church organization had come to Brazil with the first centralized government at Baía and remained in a dominant position through colonial times. There was little cultural activity outside it. The Church grew with Brazil, maintaining four bishops and an archbishop by 1700. There seems to have been little effort made by the authorities to keep Brazil "pure" in the accepted faith; the Inquisition stayed in Lisbon and heard very few cases from the colonies. The Church in Brazil was never as wealthy or as powerful as it was in the Spanish colonies, and it was not an obstacle to political development after independence. The most important record of religious activity is that of the missionary workers among the Indians.

A leader among the Jesuits who came out with Tomé de Sousa was Father Manoel de Nobrega, one of the truly great men of all the colonies, a fearless, tireless champion of the Indians against enslavement by whites. He worked in the São Paulo area where he learned Indian languages, wrote dramas and music in those dialects, and personally taught thousands of young Indians in his mission schools. He and his successors founded mission villages to protect the natives from the *bandeirantes*.

"Graduates" of these missions found their way into the economy of the colony, took half-breed or mulatto girls to wife, and helped to create a new Brazil. A co-worker with Nobrega in the mission field was José de Anchieta, a sort of "Saint Francis Xavier of the New World." As famous as a geographer and historian of the early days of Brazil as he is as a devoted missionary, he is sometimes called the "Father of Brazilian Literature." Another outstanding Jesuit writer and leader in the seventeenth century was Father Antônio Vieira, who persuaded the king to put the Indians under exclusive Jesuit control. Thus the Jesuits ran all the missions in Brazil; in this they fought openly with the other colonists and finally clashed with the kings in Europe. The Marquis of Pombal, dictator minister of Portugal, had all members of the Jesuit order expelled from Brazil in 1759.

As in the Spanish New World, Jesuits in Brazil founded the secondary schools, ran the hospitals and carried on the charity. But in every town there was a parish priest and a church building. Never as concerned with political life as the Spanish American Catholic Church, the Brazilian church seemed closer to the peoples' lives. Church practice was never as stiff and formal; Christianity had more of friendliness, tolerance, and affection in Lisbon and Baía than in Seville and Lima.

Jesuits had controlled education even more completely than in the Spanish colonies, however. By the time of Nobrega's death there was a "school of elementary education" in every coastal town and at São Paulo. When the Jesuits were expelled two centuries later, they were maintaining nine advanced secondary schools and three seminaries. Plantation children learned to read and write from the house chaplain, were sent away to boarding schools, or grew up illiterate like their easygoing fathers. If one son of a rich family was to be sent to the university he had to go to Coimbra in Portugal; throughout the colonial period there was never a university in Brazil.

Thus Brazil approached the "Age of Enlightenment" with few educated people. There was no successful printing business in Brazil till after 1808. Brazil was behind Portugal in enlightenment, and Portugal was behind Spain. There is a spotty history of feeble little academic societies and literary clubs, especially in Ouro Preto, but few of them were able to hold more than twenty meetings or to last more than three or four years.

The Portuguese language was itself a tongue of seafarers and explorers rather than of classical scholars, and with the exception of histories and travel stories very little literature was produced in Brazil. Anchieta on the frontier was preaching in Tupi-Guaraní; priests among the freedmen in the north spoke to their flocks in Nâgo. For two centuries more town and plantation people spoke these two languages than spoke Portuguese. By 1750, when Portuguese finally dominated, it was a new language differing from "Lisbonese" as the language of Texas differs from that of London. The people who wrote for Brazil wrote of the land itself, its history and its resources—Anchieta, the missionary, Pero de Magalhães, the historian, and Father Antonil, the economist, from all of whose works much of the life and economic progress of colonial Brazil is known to modern scholars.

The 1700s at last saw formal stories of adventure and dramas written by people who set out to be writers. One such dramatist, Antônio José da Silva (1705–1739), had his satirical plays produced in Lisbon—a questionable honor, for he was burned at the stake there for heretical practices. A poet who died at the end of the seventeenth century, Gregório de Mattos Guerra (1633–1696), also wrote sarcastically about the authorities, singing with a guitar, as the gay young man-about-town, of the "fat cats" in the Portuguese colonial service. For thus lampooning society he was sentenced to several years in the prison colony in Angola, but was soon back in Brazil singing more scornful songs until his death. Two long epic poems are remembered today in modern Brazil, and both are concerned with the life of the Indians—*O Uruguay*, by José Basilio da Gama (1741–1795) and *Caramarú* by José de Santa Rita Durao (1722–1784).

The common people, with their Negro and Indian blood, never forgot the legends of their own people, and told the folk stories of the rivers and jungles of two tropical continents to their children and their children's children. Slave "mammies" told them to the white children; such stories of backwoods lore, of animal cunning, of moon magic were better known to most colonial Brazilians than the poems and stories in Portuguese published about Brazil in Lisbon.

Of all the colonies in the New World, only the Portuguese produced a real artist of world fame. He was Antônio Francisco Lisboa, born to a Negro mother of a white father and freed by his father on his baptism in Ouro Preto in 1730. His father, an architect, apprenticed him out to craftsmen to learn woodcarving. Soon he was the best known of Minas Gerais' church decorators. At the height of this local fame he was attacked by leprosy which disfigured his fingers and stunted his height. He came to be known as "Aleijadinho," the Little Cripple; under that name he is remembered as a dedicated artist. With his two devoted slaves he spent his last decades, chisel tied to his fingerless hands, carving the realistic and tragic statues of the life of Christ which adorn churches in Ouro Preto and Baía. The churches also reflected other art—fine colonial architecture, religious paintings, beautiful gold filigree on the altars, elaborate tile decorations—but it is all considered mediocre today compared to the work of Aleijadinho. The colony produced one famous musician, also a mulatto,

Carving of the prophet Isaiah, by "Aleijadinho," in the Church of Bom Jésus do Matozinho, Congonhas, Minas Gerais. *Courtesy Pan American Union.*

José Mauricio (1767–1830), who composed more than 300 musical works during his lifetime as a leader of the musical services in the Rio cathedral.

If José Mauricio was the only well-known composer, Brazil had thousands of creators of Brazilian music in the slaves, the principal sources of Brazilian folk music. Their dances are still copied in the great Brazilian carnivals today; they were Africa with a veneer of the New World. Dances and names of song types could fill many pages; some could be analyzed as having their roots in the Tupi-Guaraní, some in the Congo.

Culturally Brazil was not the equal of the Spanish colonies. There were no universities or institutions of higher learning, few private libraries, and no printing presses. But there was no censorship over the importation of books, and there existed a much greater freedom of discussion than in Spanish America, and a toleration of races and ideas which stemmed from the absence of a powerful Church and a strongly centralized government.

Individually, Portugal's writers, missionaries, soldiers, and empire builders were on a par with the Spaniards, but Portugal lacked the lawyers and the political theorists of Spain. Therefore, the Crown never had the strength in Brazil, the Portuguese bureaucracy was never as entrenched, the viceregal pomp was never as imposing as in New Spain and Lima. Less loyal to things Portuguese, Brazil already had a separate "nationality" by 1800. But Portugal had been successful in her empire. In three centuries, her claims covered half of South America, a region eighty times the size of the mother country and twice as much as the Treaty of Tordesillas had allowed her. The great republic of Brazil today is a testimonial to the intrepid colonists who laid the solid foundation on which the modern nation rests.

Readings

Arciniegas, G., ed., *The Green Continent* (1944)
Bandeira, M., *Brief History of Brazilian Literature* (1958)
Boxer, C. R., *The Dutch in Brazil, 1624–1654* (1957)
——, *Four Centuries of Portuguese Expansion, 1415–1825: A Succinct Summary* (1961)
——, *Golden Age in Brazil, 1595–1750* (1962)
——, *A Great Luso-Brazilian Figure, Padre Antônio Vieira, S.J., 1608–1697* (1957)
——, *Portuguese Society in the Tropics: The Municipal Councils of Goa, Macao, Bahía and Luanda, 1510–1800* (1965)
——, *Race Relations in the Portuguese Colonial Empire, 1415–1825* (1963)
——, *Salvadore de Sá and the Struggle for Brazil and Angola, 1602–1686* (1952)
Brown, R., *Land and People of Brazil* (1960)
Burns, E. B., *Documentary History of Brazil* (1966)
Calmon, P., *History of Brazil* (with de Mendeiros, 1939)
Calogeras, J. P., *History of Brazil*, trans. P. A. Martin (1939)
Castedo, L., *The Baroque Prevalence in Brazilian Art, Seventeenth to Twentieth Centuries* (1964)

Da Costa, L. E., *Rio in the Time of the Viceroys*, trans. D. H. Momsen (1936)
Dominian, H. G., *Apostle of Brazil: The Biography of José de Anchieta* (1958)
Freyre, G., *The Masters and the Slaves*, trans. Putnam (2nd ed., 1956)
——, *New World in the Tropics* (1959)
Fritz, S., *Journal of Travels and Labours of Father Samuel Fritz in the River of the Amazons between 1686 and 1723* (1922)
Furtado, C., *Economic Growth of Brazil* (1963)
Goldberg, J., *Brazilian Literature* (1922)
Goodwin, P. L., *Brazil Builds: Architecture New and Old, 1652–1942* (1943)
Greenlee, W. B., *Voyage of Pedro Alvares Cabral to Brazil and India* (1938)
Hill, L. F., ed., *Brazil* (1947)
Kiemen, M. C., *Indian Policy of Portugal in the Amazon Region, 1614–1693* (1954)
Lima, M. de O., *Evolution of Brazil Compared with That of Spanish and Anglo-Saxon America* (1914)
Livermore, H. O., *History of Portugal* (1947)
——, *Portugal and Brazil, an Introduction* (1954)
Magalhães, P. de, *Histories of Brazil*, trans. J. B. Stetson (2 vols., 1922)
Marchant, A., *From Barter to Slavery: Economic Relations of Portuguese and Indians in the Settlement of Brazil, 1500–1580* (1942)
Maria de Jesus, C., *Child of the Dark* (1962)
Medina, J. T., *Discovery of the Amazon* (1934)
Moog, V., *Bandeirantes and Pioneers* (1964)
Morison, S. E., *Portuguese Voyages to America in the Fifteenth Century* (1940)
Morner, M., *Expulsion of Jesuits from Latin America* (1965)
——, *The Political and Economic Activities of the Jesuits in the La Plata Region* (1953)
Morrill, P., *The Gold Rushes* (Chapter on Brazil, 1940)
Morse, R., *The Bandeirantes* (1965)
Nash, R., *Conquest of Brazil* (1926)
Nist, J., *Brazilian Poetry: An Anthology* (1962)
Nowell, C. E., *History of Portugal* (1952)
Parker, J., ed., *Tidings out of Brazil* (1957)
Pierson, D., *Negroes in Brazil: A Study of Race Contact at Bahía* (1942)
Polmentary, H. C., *The River of the Amazons—Its Discovery and Early Exploration, 1500–1743* (1965)
Prestage, E., *Portuguese Pioneers* (1933)
Ramos, A., *The Negro in Brazil* (1939)
Southey, R., *History of Brazil* (3 vols., 1810–1819)
Wiznitzer, A., *Jews in Colonial Brazil* (1960)

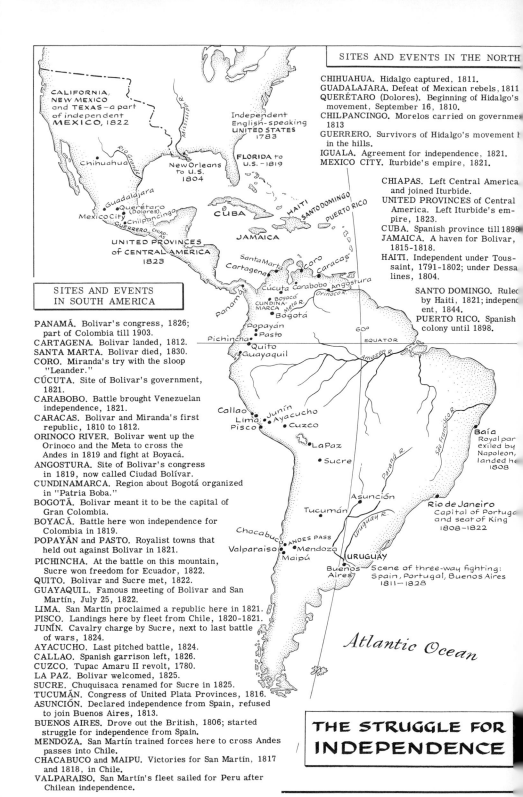

CALIFORNIA, NEW MEXICO and TEXAS—a part of independent MEXICO, 1822

Independent English-speaking UNITED STATES 1783

New Orleans to U.S. 1804

FLORIDA to U.S. 1819

Chihuahua

Guadalajara

Querétaro (Dolores)

Mexico City

Chilpancingo

GUERRERO, CHIAP.

UNITED PROVINCES of CENTRAL AMERICA 1823

CUBA

HAITI

SANTO DOMINGO

PUERTO RICO

JAMAICA

Santa Marta

Cartagena

Coro

Caracas

Cúcuta Carabobo Angostura

Boyacá

CUNDINA-MARCA Meta R. Orinoco R.

Bogotá

Panamá

Popayán

Pasto

Pichincha

Quito

Guayaquil

60°

EQUATOR

Amazon R.

Callao

Lima

Pisco

Junín

Ayacucho

Cuzco

La Paz

Sucre

São Francisco R.

Asunción

Tucumán

Paraná R.

Uruguay R.

Bahía. Royal par exiled by Napoleon, landed he 1808

Rio de Janeiro Capital of Portuga and seat of King 1808-1822

Chacabuco ANDES PASS

Valparaiso Mendoza

Maipú

URUGUAY

Buenos Aires

Scene of three-way fighting: Spain, Portugal, Buenos Aires 1811-1828

Atlantic Ocean

SITES AND EVENTS IN THE NORTH

CHIHUAHUA. Hidalgo captured, 1811.
GUADALAJARA. Defeat of Mexican rebels, 1811
QUERÉTARO (Dolores). Beginning of Hidalgo's movement, September 16, 1810.
CHILPANCINGO. Morelos carried on governme 1813
GUERRERO. Survivors of Hidalgo's movement f in the hills.
IGUALA. Agreement for independence, 1821.
MEXICO CITY. Iturbide's empire, 1821.

CHIAPAS. Left Central America and joined Iturbide.
UNITED PROVINCES of Central America. Left Iturbide's empire, 1823.
CUBA. Spanish province till 1898
JAMAICA. A haven for Bolivar, 1815-1818.
HAITI. Independent under Toussaint, 1791-1802; under Dessa lines, 1804.

SANTO DOMINGO. Rulec by Haiti, 1821; independ ent, 1844.
PUERTO RICO. Spanish colony until 1898.

SITES AND EVENTS IN SOUTH AMERICA

PANAMÁ. Bolivar's congress, 1826; part of Colombia till 1903.
CARTAGENA. Bolivar landed, 1812.
SANTA MARTA. Bolivar died, 1830.
CORO. Miranda's try with the sloop "Leander."
CÚCUTA. Site of Bolivar's government, 1821.
CARABOBO. Battle brought Venezuelan independence, 1821.
CARACAS. Bolivar and Miranda's first republic, 1810 to 1812.
ORINOCO RIVER. Bolivar went up the Orinoco and the Meta to cross the Andes in 1819 and fight at Boyacá.
ANGOSTURA. Site of Bolivar's congress in 1819, now called Ciudad Bolívar.
CUNDINAMARCA. Region about Bogotá organized in "Patria Boba."
BOGOTÁ. Bolivar meant it to be the capital of Gran Colombia.
BOYACÁ. Battle here won independence for Colombia in 1819.
POPAYÁN and PASTO. Royalist towns that held out against Bolivar in 1821.
PICHINCHA. At the battle on this mountain, Sucre won freedom for Ecuador, 1822.
QUITO. Bolivar and Sucre met, 1822.
GUAYAQUIL. Famous meeting of Bolivar and San Martín, July 25, 1822.
LIMA. San Martín proclaimed a republic here in 1821.
PISCO. Landings here by fleet from Chile, 1820-1821.
JUNÍN. Cavalry charge by Sucre, next to last battle of wars, 1824.
AYACUCHO. Last pitched battle, 1824.
CALLAO. Spanish garrison left, 1826.
CUZCO. Tupac Amaru II revolt, 1780.
LA PAZ. Bolivar welcomed, 1825.
SUCRE. Chuquisaca renamed for Sucre in 1825.
TUCUMÁN. Congress of United Plata Provinces, 1816.
ASUNCIÓN. Declared independence from Spain, refused to join Buenos Aires, 1813.
BUENOS AIRES. Drove out the British, 1806; started struggle for independence from Spain.
MENDOZA. San Martín trained forces here to cross Andes passes into Chile.
CHACABUCO and MAIPU. Victories for San Martín, 1817 and 1818, in Chile.
VALPARAISO. San Martín's fleet sailed for Peru after Chilean independence.

THE STRUGGLE FOR INDEPENDENCE

Part III

LATIN AMERICA
STIRS AND REVOLTS

I{N FEBRUARY OF} 1806, an American named James Biggs wrote a letter home from the sloop *Leander* in the British West Indies. Nearly 200 souls were aboard this tiny ship, most of them soldiers-of-fortune. They had been persuaded to "commit themselves to the chances of an enterprise at once extraordinary and dangerous." Wrote Biggs mysteriously, "Generally, I can say that we are engaged in an expedition to some part of the Spanish dominions, probably in South America, with a view to assist the inhabitants in throwing off the oppressive yoke of the parent country and establishing a government for themselves," for which, according to the *Leander's* commander, a Venezuelan named Francisco de Miranda, "the Spanish colonials have resolved and for which he says they are entirely disposed and prepared." Biggs concluded his letter, "We may be plucking a thousand dangers on our heads, but we presume our Conductor knows what he is doing, and will lead us to great exploits and splendid fortunes."

The "Conductor" misled them. His little "expedition,"

financed to the tune of \$20,000, was filled out with only 582 muskets and a few small cannons; with this equipment he had planned to take ports near the city of Caracas, and thus set off an entire South American revolution. But the Spaniards on the Venezuelan coast got news of the coming "attack" and captured two smaller vessels which had been added to the expedition in the West Indies. Though Miranda got control of the town of Coro, where he flew a flag of red, blue, and yellow which he had designed for independence, and though he made a call-to-arms to the populace, there was no mass uprising. No one seemed very interested. The town was easily retaken within ten days. The survivors of his expedition, with Miranda himself, got away to the British West Indies, and Biggs and his friends, disgruntled at receiving no wages for their time, probably drifted into other "extraordinary enterprises." The plan "petered out," but it was symbolic of the plans of several creole leaders at the time, who were willing to ask outside help in a blow for independence. The disaffection was there, the leaders were there, but the time itself was not quite ripe, as Miranda himself, great "precursor of the revolution," should have known.

The fundamental causes of the wars of the revolution were the oppression of the colonial system, the growing resentment of the creole class against restriction, the dissemination of the ideas of the Enlightenment and "foreign ideas against the Spanish system," and the successful examples of the French and American Revolutions.

At first the Spanish colonial revolutionists were not so anxious to break with Spain; the revolt began, not as a deliberate separatist movement, but as a reform of the bad governmental system and a protest against the questionable legal position of the Bonapartes on the throne after Napoleon had conquered Spain. Once under way, the movement turned against Spanish authority, rapidly in some localities, more slowly in others. Peninsular Spaniards still hoped to keep the colonies subordinate; the colonists themselves, meaning to remain loyal to the Crown, increasingly felt themselves the equals of the Spaniards at home in their common fight against the Bonapartists. When local committees took over the powers of the viceroys and the captains-general throughout the colonies, what had begun as an assertion of freedom from French control ended as a war of independence. The enormous and prosperous colonies would no longer submit to being treated as mere colonials. They were either to be part of the Spanish monarchy or, when the French were defeated, they would withdraw from the Spanish empire.

Thus the Spanish empire disintegrated. The revolutions began as local revolts, and ended ultimately in independent republics. There was no one single movement, no one single hero. The leaders differed among themselves over the ultimate aim, the type of government to be set up, the concept of freedom and individual liberty they actually fought for, the position of the Church and the landed aristocracy once the freedom was to be achieved. There was practical civil war between patriots and loyalists—that is, between the men loyal to Spain (both those already resident in the New World and those coming with the disciplining armies from the mother country) on the one hand, and the group of enlightened quick-witted creole leaders on the other hand. Indians and *mestizos* and slaves, now fighting on one side, now on another, varied in their confused loyalties from region to region, with little idea that independence might mean equality for them also. When independence was won it was a political change at the top only, with some economic improvements for the merchant class. The Latin American revolutions stopped short at the point where they might have evolved into social revolutions.

There was lack of unity from the beginning—no centralized staff, no general plan of revolt, no coordination of action by various groups of revolutionaries. Venezuela and Colombia constituted one area of localized revolt, Argentina and the other areas of South America below the Tropic of Capricorn a second. Peru remained the seat of the loyalists and the last stage of operations, the only area of centralized planning. Meanwhile, in Mexico and the Central American states, the war for independence, though happening simultaneously with the South American revolts led by Bolívar and others, was a separate movement.

In all areas, events in Spain called the tune. From 1808 to 1810 the colonies carried on a struggle for redress of grievances, for self-defense against Napoleon, and for the return of the Spanish king, Ferdinand VII. Broken in spirit by Ferdinand himself when the Bonapartists withdrew and he returned to power in Madrid in 1814, the colonies had no choice but sullen acquiescence till a liberal party again came to the front in Spain in 1820. The victories that then came to the colonials led on to final defeat of the Spaniards in spite of Ferdinand's return to power at home.

Chapter **17**

Backgrounds of Independence

DISAFFECTION WITHIN THE EMPIRE

THE THREE CENTURIES of Spanish colonialism were rapidly coming to their inevitable end. The discussions, the agitations, the rebellions, and the military campaigns of the eighteenth century gave evidences of widespread dissatisfaction. The very colonial system itself, with its social discrimination against creoles and *mestizos,* was a major factor. Ten generations had grown up in America, generations which were increasingly resentful of the arrogance and exclusiveness of Spanish policy. The feeling of patriotism and loyalty among Latin races is very strong, and the devotion to the Crown, taken as seriously as personal honor, tended to prevent complaints by the masses against the *status quo.* When laws seemed foolish and administrators corrupt, the people never blamed the Crown. "Long live the King, but death to bad government!" was the battle cry of several abortive revolutionary movements. The people tended to disregard or even openly disobey laws that were laxly enforced; when force was used to bring obedience to the laws, it was to be met in turn by a new force of resistance. This resistance was largely creole, for the creoles were the intelligentsia, and they were the ones who felt the discrimination most keenly and determined on action when the time came.

Economic reasons for disaffection there were in abundance, similar to the "trade and navigation" disputes between the Thirteen Colonies and England. When trade barriers were lessened by Charles III, the colonists had a new taste of commercial freedom, which made them love Spain even less. When taxes were collected, under the fiscal reforms of Charles III, riots occurred against the tax collectors in Quito, Bogotá, and Vera Cruz. The high fees collected by the Church, combined with increasing resentment on the part of "enlightened" young colonials against the "thought control" of the Inquisition and against the control of upper church positions by the *gachupines*, made the Church seem the ally of the restrictive colonial government. The Church, therefore, was plunged, voluntarily or otherwise, into the class struggle; many of the lower clergy were later to become leaders in the wars for independence.

The administrative reforms of Charles III had come far too late to be effective, and were not given a chance because of the weakness of Charles IV and his reversion to the old system. When this change of kings came in 1788, the creoles were already conscious of their powers and their demands. Both creoles and *mestizos* were better off than they had been a half century before, but they were also better informed—revolutions do not take place among ignorant people unaware of their possibilities. Some "radical" young creoles stood ready to furnish leadership, *mestizos* swelled the army ranks and helped pay the bills, and Indians and Negroes supplied the brawn. The town councils, the *cabildos*, the creoles' only chance for a voice, began to demand more power, to ask that their members be locally chosen; these requests for local control in the 1790s were coming at a time when Spain was a second-rate power, when her merchant fleet and her navy had less than one-tenth the power of that of England and one-eighth that of Holland. But even all these causes for disaffection might never have broken loose in the Spanish empire, bound by the Latin chains of patriotism and loyalty, if it had not been for the temporary destruction of Spanish power by Napoleon in the first decade of the 1800s. Other movements and other leaders, less dramatic than Miranda on the *Leander*, but reaching more people, had failed.

There had been such revolts against Spanish authority in Paraguay in the 1730s, in Caracas in the 1750s, in Peru and Bogotá in the 1780s— revolts against monopolistic companies, against Jesuit control of mission Indians, against continued Indian exploitation by Peruvian authorities— against taxes on tobacco to pay for colonial wars—a wide variety of small local causes. Leaders were anxious to save themselves money, to oust a particular government official, to improve conditions for their entire class in one locality, to bring wealth and power to themselves. None of these revolts became a widespread interregional affair, and each was handled as a separate instance by Spanish authorities.

In Paraguay a judge named José de Antequera, sent to settle a local quarrel, made himself dictator for four years in the late 1720s after a dispute over Indian workers with the legal governor, who backed the Jesuit missionaries in protecting the Indians from landowners. The landowners in the *cabildo* supported the ambitious judge and elected him governor in defiance of the Peruvian viceroy's appointee. When Antequera was captured and taken to Lima for execution, he chose a successor who continued the rebellion for another ten years. Their followers considered themselves independent of Spain; they called themselves *comuneros* after rebellious communities that staged a famous revolt in Spain against the royal government in the 1500s. Although the rebellion in Paraguay was put down on orders of the viceroy by an army from the Plata, this outbreak of disorder was typical of later revolutions in Latin America: ambitious leaders, a parliamentarian *cabildo*, the influence of the Church, the readiness to decide issues by force rather than by compromise.

In Caracas landowners revolted for another reason—anger at the monopoly of the Basque-owned Guipúzcoa Company, which held the trade of Venezuela in a vise. An army of creoles marched in force on Caracas to appeal to the *cabildo* to expel the Basque company. Though crushed by Spanish troops, this was considered a "loyal" revolt—"Long Live the King! Death to *chapetones!* Death to bad government!"—and its leaders were granted amnesty by Spain, while the company continued to control trade until all such monopolies were broken by Charles III.

In Quito in the 1760s, in Bogotá in the 1780s, there were revolts in which the rebels called themselves *comuneros*. In Ecuador a creole-*mestizo* party protested against the government alcohol monopoly. Fifteen years later Bogotá saw a much more widespread *comunero* revolt against the strict enforcement of sales taxes by the new intendant in order to pay for the war against England. The war-tax was resisted with especial fervor in a community of tobacco growers called Socorro. Though the leader was executed and many of the Indians who had staged a simultaneous revolt were killed, some of the grievances of this armed uprising were alleviated. In it the New Granadans had learned to make protests for redress of grievances and to revolt when they got no redress.

The Indians had joined the Socorro *comunero* revolt because they heard of the great uprising among the Indians in Peru. Long abused by the *mita* system and the *corregidores*, the work in the mines and the weaving establishments, the Indians in Peru had rebelled three times in the 1740s in the hopes of ousting the Spaniards and re-creating an Inca empire. In 1780, as the *comuneros* were protesting taxes in Bogotá, an educated man from a college in Cuzco, a dignified, well-dressed young gentleman named José Gabriel Condorcanquí, who read Latin and spoke Spanish, not Quechua, was serving as the Indian agent and tax collector in an Andean valley. His forefathers had been recognized as lineal descendants of Tupac Amarú, last of the Incas, and he himself had been granted the title of marquis by the royal *audiencia* before he was twenty. As Indian agent he had tried peacefully to alleviate the conditions of the Indians. Now in protest against the conditions of the *mita*, the forced labor in the mines, he formed an Indian army, claimed to be true ruler of Peru, and called himself Tupac Amarú II. When he went to the authorities at Cuzco to plead for reform, he received a disdainful reply; in answer, his Indians seized and killed the local Spanish governor. All the native villagers living near Cuzco rallied to his banner, and an actual war broke out from the Ecuadorean border down through Tucumán to the pampas. It took several months and 15,000 Spanish troops to quell the revolt. Tupac Amarú II was cruelly put to death when the Spanish troops captured him; his body was torn apart by horses pulling in opposite directions, but his followers kept on fighting. One of his cousins laid siege to the city of La Paz with an Indian army of 40,000. Though the army was disbanded, the wise Charles III followed the rebellion with reforms. A new viceroy made a study of the causes of the revolt, and recommended the abolition of the *mita* system. Tupac Amarú II accomplished little for the sons of the Incas; people of Indian blood live under conditions of extreme poverty in Peru today. However, the revolt taught the Indians to join with the creoles in the independence movement against Spain.

Other regions of Latin America stirred. There were disorders and uprisings against the taxation system in Mexico, Cuba, and Peru. Salta and Jujuy, in the Andean foothills of present-day Argentina, revolted against their governors in 1724 and again in 1767. The Argentine town of Corrientes rose against its local governor in 1767, imprisoned him, and replaced his power with a committee from its own *cabildo*. A baker named Jacinto Canek proclaimed himself King of the Maya in Yucatan and raised the Indians in protest against the heavy taxes and the lack of justice they received in the courts. In the same period there were separatist plots in Chile. In Caracas in 1797 José María España and Manuel Gual planned a similar conspiracy to overthrow Spanish rule, hoping for aid from British forces from Trinidad and encouraged by the governor of the island. The movement was imbued with French Revolutionary ideas and had many friends, for the creoles of Venezuela were well informed, aware of world trends, and angry at Spain; but the revolution in its turn was betrayed, and many leading creoles hanged as a result.

In Bogotá, by this time a center of intellectual activity, a young cacao exporter named Antonio Nariño, a French encyclopedist in philosophy and a typical creole in his opposition to Spain, had received a copy of the French Declaration of the Rights of Man, that stirring plea for equality. Nariño translated it into Spanish equally as stirring, had copies printed on a secret press in Bogotá, and distributed them widely. For promulgating such ideas the viceroy sentenced Nariño to ten years' imprisonment in Africa. Fortunately for the independence movement in Colombia, he escaped by jumping into a small boat when his prison ship lay in the harbor of Cádiz, and he returned to serve his native land again after 1810.

The writings of North American revolutionists had also been found among Nariño's papers. Franklin and Jefferson corresponded with leading Latin Americans; Hamilton, Knox, and others were in contact with Miranda. By 1800 the United States of North America was a going concern, economically as well as politically, and creole leaders had visited it. The revolution there influenced Spanish America in that it had proved that a rebellion against a mother country could succeed, that a republic could be a practical working entity. Members of the creole intelligentsia like Nariño had read Montesquieu, Rousseau, and Voltaire. Secret Masonic societies were formed in Spain itself, anti-Church and anti-Crown though they were. One of the most active Masonic groups in Spain and Spanish America was named the Lautaro Lodge in honor of the Araucanian Indian youth who had revolted against the first white men in Chile. Joining in the Masons' dislike of Spanish autocracy were the exiled

Jesuits, thousands of them back in Europe from their missionary and educational work in the colonies, and well organized as pamphleteers and conspirators against Spanish power in the Indies.

Forces working toward individual freedom and against Spanish control of the empire were thus very strong from the outside—the liberal philosophers, the American and French Revolutions. Propaganda concerning them came in through smugglers, through travelers and foreigners in the colonies, to add to the dissatisfaction already felt by the creoles.

THE FRENCH REVOLUTION IN THE CARIBBEAN

The workability of popular sovereignty in North America, and the French Revolution, with its ideas of "Liberty, Equality, and Fraternity" and its success in overthrowing a monarch, were both watched by Spanish America's creoles. In another region of the New World the French Revolution was taken even more seriously—the French West Indies.

The Haitian end of the island of Hispaniola was a thriving French colony by 1700, known to the homeland as Saint Domingue. It had been organized under a French governor and its largest town, Port-au-Prince, had been made the capital. A report of 1779 showed the colony to have 40,000 whites, 25,000 mixed-bloods and freedmen, and 480,000 slaves. Great fortunes were made in the sugar plantations and mills, where the few white overseers dominated the rural slaves. Mulatto slaves were treated

Independence Monument to Haitian Heroes, **near Cap Haitien. Toussaint stands first among the figures with Dessalines and Christophe behind him. Soldiers and flag bearers are on each side. The figures are of life-size bronze on a natural hillside.** *Photo by Helen Miller Bailey.*

as confidential servants in the plantation houses, and *mulata* mistresses were kept by most white men, with their quadroon children being freed at birth. Half the population of the towns of Port-au-Prince, Cap Haitien, and Aux Cayes were freed mulattoes. In these towns the handful of ruling whites lived a life of luxury; French plays and concerts were given, French novels read. The slaves, however—the majority of them African-born and recently purchased in Jamaica's slave market—worked on the plantations in chain gangs, died under the overseers' lashes, and were replaced by more new purchases in spite of a supposedly humanitarian French legal code.

In 1789 the Haitians—Negro slaves, free mulattoes, and white planters —all heard about "Liberty, Equality, Fraternity," and reacted each in his own way. White planters thought that now they would be represented in Paris; freedmen thought "equality" referred to all colors; Negroes thought that slavery was ended forever. A delegation of free mulattoes went to Paris in 1789, led by the prosperous Vincent Ogé, and brought back word from the National Assembly there that all tax-payers in the colonies could vote in new colonial legislatures. When Ogé attempted to prove himself qualified as a "voting taxpayer," he was executed in Port-au-Prince by being broken on the wheel in a gala public display. Three black slaves saw the mulatto Ogé die proclaiming liberty. They were Toussaint L'Ouverture, a coachman from a hill plantation, a slave boy named Henri Christophe, belonging to an innkeeper, and the third, an African-born member of a gang of stevedore slaves, a sullen, bitter illiterate named Jean Jacques Dessalines and called "The Tiger." The three of them were to bring death to a great number of whites and independence to mulattoes and Negroes on both the French and Spanish halves of the island before any other Latin American nation was independent. But freedom was to be accompanied by fifteen years of bloodshed and massacre such as no other colony was ever to know.

A visitor to the island colony, one Abbé Raynal, had just written a book of his travels, *Philosophical and Political History of the European Establishment and Commerce in the Two Indies,* in which he wrote with horror of the treatment of slaves in the French West Indies and of the inevitability of their revolt. "All that they need is a brave leader. Who will he be? There is no doubt that he will appear; he will come and raise the sacred standard of liberty." These words were read by Toussaint L'Ouverture, son of an African-born Negro, educated by Jesuit priests to whom his father had been a slave, trained as a coachman by an indulgent and liberal-minded master who was early interested in the wiry, intelligent little boy. Other slaves in Saint Domingue—speaking only African dialects, practising voodo rather than Christianity since the overseers felt it dangerous to teach them too much of white ways—knew little of the French Revolutionary doctrines for which Ogé had died, but Toussaint, the educated, the well-treated, did know; he remembered Raynal's words and Ogé's death. He was determined to liberate the slaves.

On the night of August 22, 1791, five months after Ogé's death, Negro voodoo priests aroused the slaves to the first widespread rebellion in island history. Plantations were destroyed, whole families massacred; mulattoes and freedmen joined one side or the other; Dessalines and Christophe became guerrilla leaders. Toussaint bided his time for two months, his own plantation home untouched in the holocaust. Then he helped his master to safety, organized his fellow slaves, and joined the rebels, where he soon became commander in chief.

At first loyal to the French king, who, he had been told, really wanted freedom for all the slaves, Toussaint refused to deal with French commissioners who opposed the royal power. When Toussaint heard that Louis XVI had been executed, he took his well-trained guerrillas across the mountains to Santo Domingo to preserve that colony for kings against the Republican commissioners then in Cap Haitien. A new commissioner representing the Directory persuaded him that the French Republicans were his true friends. In 1798 he was called Lieutenant Governor under the French Governor, and was made commander in chief of the colonial army—in which the soldiers were all former slaves. Soon, on one legal pretext or another, he had the officials of the French Republic sent home, and ruled the island alone in their name.

As an administrator there seems to be nothing but praise for Toussaint. His problems were stupendous: to produce food in a disorganized society with all owners and all overseers gone, to encourage ex-slaves to do any work at all for their own self-preservation. Toussaint had drafted a constitution proclaiming Saint Domingue a self-governing French protectorate, with himself as governor general. He made friends with the strong mulatto leaders at Aux Cayes in the south; he took progressive white leaders into his government, enlarged agriculture, and aided commerce. Visitors described him as a true leader, far ahead of his time, intensely just and upright, inspiring respect and devotion by his character. Meanwhile he made war on Spanish Santo Domingo and controlled the whole island by 1801.

Meanwhile in Paris, a new authority with less sense of justice, Napoleon Bonaparte, was now called upon to approve Toussaint's constitution. Napoleon had grandiose schemes for controlling the Caribbean from the island colony, including in his wide empire Louisiana which he had just wrested from Spain. Hearing from his colonial advisers that the white-owned plantation system had brought great revenues to France, he sent his own brother-in-law, General Charles LeClerc, with 20,000 well-trained troops to crush Toussaint. "I will not leave an épaulette upon the shoulders of a single black," he told LeClerc. The reconquest was to be accomplished in three phases—first, Toussaint was to be lured into friendship; secondly, LeClerc's troops were to take the island; thirdly, Toussaint was to be arrested on any type of pretext and sent to France, while LeClerc made himself dictator and restored both the French owners and the sugar-cane profits for France. Phases one and two were immediately impossible, for Henri Christophe, Toussaint's general in charge of the town, would not let LeClerc land. While he delayed, Toussaint reorganized his army, inflicted heavy losses on the French as they landed, and then played hide-and-seek, waiting for the rainy season to come and bring him a stronger ally.

That ally, which killed LeClerc and 18,000 of his men, and brought victory for the Negroes, was the yellow fever. In a virulent epidemic it took a hundred deaths among the susceptible Frenchmen daily, and left the immune Negroes victors in three months' time. LeClerc made peace, won over Dessalines and Christophe by making them officers in his army, and showered Toussaint with compliments and favors. When, in good faith, the Negro leader, now fifty-eight years old, rode unarmed to a dinner meeting with the whites, he was thrown into chains—phase three of Napoleon's instructions—and taken to Europe. There Napoleon refused to see him, and sent him to a bleak prison in the Alps, where he died of tuberculosis. His last words as he left Haiti had been, "In overthrowing me they have only felled the tree of Negro liberty in Saint Domingue. It will shoot up again, for it is deeply rooted, and its roots are many."

Shoots grew from the roots before Toussaint was dead. By November of 1802 LeClerc himself was dead of yellow fever. Dessalines and Christophe, hearing that Napoleon had re-instituted slavery in Guadeloupe and Martinique, deserted the French army and began again raising guerrillas in the hills. Napoleon now turned his attention to renewed war with England, sold Louisiana, his other Caribbean-area possession, to the United States, and the remaining handful of French soldiers sailed home. Jean Jacques Dessalines, "The Tiger," stood on a rock before his troops when the French left, took the French tricolor in his hands, and tore

Jean Jacques Dessalines, first ruler of an independent nation in Latin America, who declared Haiti free of France, January 1, 1804. *Courtesy Pan American Union.*

the white stripe out of it to trample under his boots. Thus would he trample the whites out of the French half of the island forever. He had a declaration of complete independence written in his name on January 1, 1804, using the old aboriginal word Haiti for the nation for the first time. He, and after him Christophe, ruled Haiti as absolute dictators. The French masters never came back; Haiti, with few white men left in the entire province, was the first Latin American state to win independence. This whole drama had been watched anxiously by the Spanish colonials; events in Haiti frightened many aristocratic creole landowners, but also proved that a small force of "Americans," in hills and valleys they knew, could fight off seasoned European troops unfamiliar with the tropics.

ENGLISH INTERVENTION VERSUS SPANISH AUTHORITY

England was involved in the struggle for Spanish American independence. She encouraged and financed revolutionary agents like Miranda and she tried to capture the port of Buenos Aires. In the confusion of the wars in revolutionary Europe, England was an enemy of Spains' again for a period after 1796. Still active in the Caribbean, England enlarged her anti-Spanish activities by making an attempt to invade southern South America and by encouraging anti-colonial agents and movements in the Spanish empire. War or no war, it would be to England's commercial advantage to have the Spanish American ports completely free, ruled by weak new republics that would look to England for all their trade relations.

Through the years of Spanish neglect Buenos Aires had been served by illegal English shipping. Under the more liberal trade policies at the turn of the century there were more than a hundred English vessels coming into the Plata by 1800. English colonial planners were not satisfied—in the light of the wars against Napoleon raging in Europe, and with the position of Spain there undecided—merely to steal the trade of Buenos Aires away from the Spanish homeland. An English fleet had captured Capetown; from South Africa in 1806 its commander sent William C. Beresford with six vessels and 1650 men across the South Atlantic to take the Plata estuary. There were no regular troops in Buenos Aires, and there was a very cowardly viceroy, Rafael Sobremonte, who hastily retreated inland to Córdova when the English landed.

> At the first gunshot and the soldiers' shout
> Sobremonte and his kin cleared out.

Thus the humiliated townspeople are supposed to have sung while watching as the British flag went up over their plaza and their public treasury moneys were shipped off to London. Word of the easy landing reached England together with the money, and plans were made there to consolidate the gains by sending more English troops inland and by making an attack on Chile. Meantime, the English held the port for two months, opened the harbor to free trade, and gave the creoles a touch of real commercial independence, while they guaranteed the rights of private property and the Catholic religion.

But the citizens of Buenos Aires were not taking the foreign occupation of their city without protest. Free commerce, yes, but foreign rule, no! Secretly they drilled and trained a local militia, some of whom under Juan Martín de Pueyrredón escaped from the city. The cowardly viceroy remained in hiding in Córdova, to the disgust of the loyal Spanish inhabitants. After two months a reconquest, the famous *Reconquista* of Argentine history, took place dramatically under Santiago de Liniers, a Frenchman by birth but a loyal servant of Spain, who had worked with Pueyrredón in organizing the militia. An army of young creoles from Montevideo and from the pampas met outside the city on a stormy night, marched into the bullring at dawn, forced the English to surrender, and made Buenos Aires again a Spanish city less than sixty days after the viceroy had fled.

The viceroy soon returned, but the gallant creoles, having tasted liberty, changed his power and that of the *gachupín audiencia.* They convened a *cabildo abierto,* deposed the viceroy, and made Liniers viceroy in his place, an appointment confirmed by Spain. Meanwhile Liniers resumed charge of the militia—the idea of a locally trained, locally supported militia of townspeople and volunteers was a new one in Spanish America —and drafted 8,000 men into his raw army. They were ready to meet the British when they came again in 1807. This time the English War Office sent twenty warships, ninety transports, and 12,000 men under General John Whitelocke to make the Plata area a permanent English colony. They landed first at Montevideo, while the creoles in Buenos Aires organized every block and every house for defense. After weeks of preparation across the river, the large English forces marched into Buenos Aires, and then the citizens did their duty. They blocked every street, they poured hot water from the housetops, they dropped stones on English heads. When the English general was court-martialed in London for the defeat which followed after a few hours of such fighting, he protested that English soldiers had never been faced with "such resolution and perseverance on the part of an enemy." The British removed themselves permanently from Montevideo and Buenos Aires; the viceroy returned to quarrel with the people and with Liniers. But things were never to be the same again. The citizens of Buenos Aires had learned to scorn their viceroy and rally to their own leader; they had learned to raise and train their local militia; they had learned to carry on free trade with the world. Though they had scorned their English "guests," at first their captors and then their prisoners, the "propaganda" those guests disseminated concerning free trade under British protection did not fall on deaf ears.

The English War Office was also interested in financing the anti-Spanish agent, Francisco de Miranda. Called by South American historians "the Morning Star of Independence," he spent thirty years of his life as an "agitator" in the cause of Spanish American revolt, and served as a link between the North American and the Latin American Revolutions. Unfortunately, most of these years were away from his native Caracas, where he was born in 1756, and where he had grown up among the aristocratic Venezuelan families and received the standard classical education. His family had purchased him a captaincy in the Spanish Army, and, because of his military ability, he was promoted in rank. While Spain was fighting England during the American Revolution, Miranda participated and was raised to a full colonelcy. But he was accused of smuggling and threatened with court-martial, so he became embittered against Spain and ran away. By 1784 he was a fugitive in the new United States. Here he talked to Thomas Paine and even to the aristocratic Alexander Hamilton, and evidently formulated plans for freeing the Spanish colonies with English or American help, though Hamilton later called him an intriguing adventurer. He was indeed involved in intrigue. After traveling widely in Europe for four years, he took his schemes for revenge against the Spanish army, added to them the idealism of the revolutionary creoles, and presented a definite plan to the English Foreign Office. England was to finance and staff an invasion led by Miranda himself; the Spanish colonials would rise up to join it, and great would be the strategic and commercial advantages accruing to England.

The English listened to him seriously enough to put him on an English pension and keep his ideas dangling on a string in case the British government decided on a blow against Spain. On English money he traveled to the continent, visited other royal courts, and became an intimate of Catherine the Great of Russia, for he was a handsome figure of a man. After years of adventure in revolutionary France, he was back in England in 1798, renewing connections with the British Foreign Office, and working on his plans for English help in an invasion. His modest rooms in London became the headquarters for young Spanish creoles on visits to Europe. Simón Bolívar met him there, as did Chile's future liberator, the young Bernardo O'Higgins. A secret lodge of Masons, with both English and Spanish creole members, centered around Miranda; branches of this lodge met in colonial cities and even in royal Cádiz, where they pledged colonial independence. The exhilaration of the London meetings and the correspondence with the young creoles after their return home undoubtedly led the volatile Miranda to believe that all South America was anxiously awaiting his English-financed liberating expedition. He dubbed himself "agent for South American independence."

Miranda was again in the United States in 1805. There he hired advertising agents to recruit help for an initial expedition to take Caracas. He consulted with Jefferson and Madison and got help from the Collector of the Port of New York. Only the small "spark plug" of one vessel was needed to set off a revolution, he was sure. Hence, the *Leander* and its two small escorts, its 200 adventurous volunteers, its "secretive conductor." When he reached the Venezuelan coast his young creole friends were not there to meet him and no spontaneous force arose to help him. Venezuelan officials had been forewarned. Miranda's name was better known in England than in Caracas. How could South Americans who never heard of him be expected to rally to his standard when he appeared unannounced in one small boat? Sadly he returned to sulk in England, and to inspire creole visitors. The creoles at home would have to feel a reasonable confidence in their ability to beat Spain, and the right moment had to come before revolution could be successful. Meanwhile Napoleon began to influence English policy far more than did any hopes for trade with Spanish America. A force under Wellington which had been raised to implement Miranda's plan once Venezuela was free, was sent to help Spain fight Napoleon at home in the Peninsula instead. It was that very Peninsular War which was to be the "spark plug" for independence in Spanish America, rather than any of Miranda's schemes.

EVENTS IN EUROPE LEADING
DIRECTLY TO THE REVOLUTION

A small percentage of creoles wanted independence; some merchants wanted freedom from the empire. A large percentage of all Spanish colonials were loyal to their king. But Napoleon changed that loyalty by his attempt to control the Spanish throne.

It must be remembered that Napoleon and his agents did not have to deal with a fine king and upstanding man of the Bourbon line such as Charles III. His successor, Charles IV, was completely under the control of the prime minister Manuel Godoy, who was the queen's paramour. The son and heir, Ferdinand, was also a weakling and a reactionary. Their vacillating foreign policy of Spain's government lost Trinidad to the English; the Louisiana colony with its port at New Orleans, Spanish since 1763, went to Napoleon in a treaty. After Nelson's victory at Trafalgar Napoleon completely distrusted the unstable government and decided to put an end to the Bourbon rule of Spain.

To accomplish this, Napoleon resorted to trickery. Hostile to Portugal as a long-time ally of his enemy England, he sent an army through Spain with Godoy's connivance and into Portugal from the east. This force captured Lisbon, while the English navy helped the Portuguese royal family escape to Rio de Janeiro, an escape on which the whole subsequent history of Brazil hinged. Godoy had been promised a share of the Portuguese spoils, but now Napoleonic troops were pouring into Spain, and Godoy saw he had been duped. The terrified Charles IV abdicated, and then recanted to save his favorite Godoy, while Godoy's mistress the queen made plans to flee Spain. Then the Crown Prince Ferdinand declared his father, who had abdicated and then recanted to save his favorite Godoy, a traitor and threatened to take over the government. The wily Napoleon invited both father and son to meet him as arbitrator in southern France. Thus both the Spanish Bourbons became Napoleon's "house guests," which they remained, practically as prisoners, until the death of Charles IV and the return of Ferdinand to the throne of Spain in 1814 after the defeat of Napoleon. Napoleon's brother Joseph was made king of Spain, and kept himself in power by means of 100,000 French troops who overran the Peninsula.

Now those Spaniards loyal to their king had no Spanish king. They armed themselves as guerrillas and, with help from the English, kept Napoleon's soldiers busy for seven years in the Peninsular War. They tried to run the government first through regional *juntas* or revolutionary committees and then, by September of 1808, through a central *junta* of thirty-five members which moved from Madrid to Seville to Cádiz as the French advanced, and which tried to rule the entire disrupted empire in the name of Ferdinand VII. Napoleon was now fighting the whole nation.

And what of the colonies in all this confusion? Joseph Bonaparte had sent agents to the various Latin American cities—at least sixty different Frenchmen—who were scorned, exiled, or imprisoned. He appointed pro-Bonaparte Spaniards as viceroys in Mexico and in New Granada, but his appointees refused the honor. Meanwhile the *junta,* taking refuge at Cádiz, chose a regency to arrange for the calling of a congress, a *cortes,* which included a small group of Spanish colonials then resident in Spain. This congress, under the influence of French revolutionary ideas, wrote a very liberal, limited-monarchy type of constitution for Spain in 1812.

The Constitution of 1812 declared the colonies an integral part of Spain, but did not end the restrictive system of colonial trade. Apart from allowing a small representation, the *cortes* merely demanded money from the colonies to fight Napoleon but did nothing to win colonial loyalty. Colonials who went before the *cortes* for consideration of specific New World problems received scant attention. Most colonials had no reason to feel that the Cádiz government was an actual substitute for the king.

In fact, the colonials did not want a substitute for the king. They set up their own *juntas* in the name of Ferdinand VII, proclaiming "The old king or none." Public opinion was not yet ready for independence, but throughout 1808 and 1809 Spanish prestige in the New World began to totter. At La Paz and at Quito there were armed revolts against the Spanish troops still in the New World to protect the now "un-legal" viceroys—revolts which declared independence yet protested loyalty to Ferdinand VII. Bogotá, Caracas, and Valladolid in Mexico saw revolutionary movements under local *juntas*. Their leaders claimed that if Seville or Cádiz could set up interim ruling *juntas* so could any Spanish American city. Not knowing what the imprisoned Ferdinand thought, and having found out that the *cortes* of Cádiz still considered the colonies as colonies, the New World cities proclaimed for Ferdinand and against the Cádiz government. This was actually the moment that began the Revolution. Under the flag of Ferdinand the creoles struck for independence in 1810.

The wars that achieved that independence are the exciting story of the next chapter. However, events in Spain between the proclamation of the liberal Constitution of 1812 and the winning of independence must be here summarized for the reader, as they had so many repercussions on the progress of the Spanish American revolutions. With Wellington's ousting of French troops from the Iberian Peninsula and the defeat of Napoleon in Europe in 1814 and 1815, his brother Joseph was forced off the Spanish throne, and the wily Ferdinand VII returned. Raised as a reactionary, he immediately declared the liberal Constitution of 1812 null and void and all the actions of the Cádiz *junta* and the *cortes* illegal. Members of those bodies were arrested, even though they had acted in Ferdinand's name and in hopes of his return. Most areas in the New World that had proclaimed their independence were again reconquered.

Liberal citizens of Spain were no happier over this turn of events than their counterparts in Spanish America, and the next five years saw revolt after revolt. However, the general tenor of the times in Europe, under the reactionary policies of Prince Metternich of Austria, made liberal successes impossible. Finally in 1820, when Spanish soldiers, assembled on the docks at Cádiz to be sent to fight Bolívar and other independent leaders to "save the empire," revolted against their own officers, a revolution against Ferdinand and for the Constitution of 1812 broke out under the leadership of Rafael Riego. Ferdinand was powerless before the storm and promised to summon a *cortes* to return to the liberalism of the Napoleonic period and the Constitution of 1812. During the three years of the government by this "limited monarchy" there were many victories for the South American patriots. Spain could not attempt reconquest in the Americas because of her own internal difficulties. This "rosy" period ended with the invasion of Spain by reactionary troops from France and Austria who restored Ferdinand to absolute power.

The next decade was a period of terrorism and confusion at home in Spain. First this group and then that prevailed with the weak Ferdinand, and various possible heirs plotted to take over the throne. In 1829 he surprised the plotters by marrying again. On his death in 1833 the child of this late marriage, the infant princess Isabella II, became Queen of Spain. By 1836 the advisers of this child ruler began tardily to recognize the New World daughter nations, who had, for all practical purposes, been independent a decade. Thus the rise and fall of the fortunes of King Ferdinand from 1810 to 1833, and the acceptance or rejection by the Spanish monarchy of the principles of constitutionalism, were as much factors in the successes of the Latin American patriots as were their own fierce battles in mountain and jungle.

Readings

Alexis, S., *Black Liberator: The Life of Toussaint Louverture* (1949)

Belaunde, V. A., *Bolívar and the Political Thought of the Spanish American Revolution* (1938)

Benson, N. L., *Mexico and the Spanish Cortes, 1810–1822* (1966)

Bernstein, H., *Origins of Inter-American Interest, 1700–1812* (1945)

Biggs, J., *The History of Don Francisco de Miranda's Attempt to Effect a Revolution in South America* (1808)

Costa Peers de Nieuburg, E., *English Invasion of the River Plate* (1937)

Davis, H. P., *Black Democracy: The Story of Haiti* (rev. ed., 1936)

Dawson, T., *South American Republics* (2 vols., 1903–1904)

Fisher, L. E., *Background of the Revolution for Mexican Independence* (1934)

———, *Champion of Reform—Manuel Abad y Queipo* (1955)

Griffin, C. C., *The United States and the Disruption of the Spanish Empire* (1937)

Humphreys, R. A., *Liberation in South America, 1806–1827: The Career of James Paroissien* (1952)

———, and J. Lynch, *Origins of the Latin American Revolutions, 1808–1826* (1965)

Kaufman, W. W., *British Policy and the Independence of Latin America, 1804–1828* (1951)

Leyburn, J. G., *The Haitian People* (1941)

Lovett, G. H., *Napoleon and the Birth of Modern Spain* (2 vols., 1966)

Lynch, J., *Spanish Colonial Administration, 1782–1810* (1958)

Madariaga, S. de, *The Fall of the Spanish American Empire* (1948)

Masur, G., *Simón Bolívar* (1948)

McAlister, L. N., *The "Fuero Militar" in New Spain, 1764–1800* (1957)

Mecham, J. L., *Church and State in Latin America* (rev. ed., 1966)

Miranda, F. de, *New Democracy in America* (1960)

Moses, B., *Intellectual Background of the Revolution in South America* (1926)

———, *South America on the Eve of Emancipation* (1908)

———, *Spain's Declining Power in South America* (1919)

Peers de Nieuwburg, E. A. J. C., *English Invasion of the River Plate* (1937)

Robertson, W. S., *France and the Independence of Latin America* (1939)

———, *Iturbide of Mexico* (1952)

———, *Life of Miranda* (2 vols., 1929)

———, *Rise of the Spanish American Republics* (1918)

Rydjord, J., *Foreign Interests in the Independence of New Spain* (1935)

Shafer, R. J., *Economic Societies in the Spanish World, 1763–1821* (1957)

Shepherd, W. R., *Hispanic Nations of the New World* (1920)

Spell, J. M., *Rousseau in the Spanish World Before 1833* (1938)

Thorning, J. F., *Miranda: World Citizen* (1958)

Waxman, P., *The Black Napoleon: The Story of Toussaint L'Ouverture* (1931)

Whitaker, A. P., *The United States and the Independence of Latin America* (1941)

———, *Western Hemisphere: Its Rise and Decline* (1954)

Wilgus, A. C., ed., *Colonial Hispanic America* (1936)

Chapter **18**

The Wars for Spanish
American Independence

VENEZUELA THE PROTOTYPE
AND BOLÍVAR ITS HERO

WITH THE COMING of Napoleon's troops into Spain, the stage
was set and the fuses were sputtering, ready to set off the series of explosions known as the Wars for Independence in Latin America. The movements toward rebellion had broken out simultaneously in many places.
Events in the Plata were speeded by the English intervention there. Then
in 1809 the Plata uprisings were reflected in La Paz and Chuquisaca and
even in loyalist Peru, where a serious revolt was put down by the Spanish
troops. Between April and September, 1810, revolutionary *juntas* or provisional governing committees set up in the name of Ferdinand VII were
formed in Santiago, Quito, Bogotá, and Caracas, beginning with the last.
None of these were hypocritical maneuvers to deceive the masses concerning a false loyalty to the king, but they were attempts to avoid obedience
to the Bonapartists. Creole leaders who joined in these *juntas*, however, were
determined never again to return to a purely colonial status. Thus in 1810
revolutions broke out almost simultaneously in all parts of Spanish America
—municipal outbreaks which became regional and national by extension.
   Venezuela is a prototype of the new nations that struggled under these

conditions. The methods used there were in general followed elsewhere. It is on the movement there and along the Spanish Main, where Bolívar became the heroic figure, that attention must first be centered, that area in which Miranda had tried to land the *Leander*, when he was the "Morning Star."

When in July of 1808 Napoleon had sent a special captain-general to Caracas, Venezuela, the people had rioted, carrying Ferdinand's picture through the streets with the label *Fernando El Deseado*, Ferdinand the Desired One. Within a year, however, they had to bow to the strict rule of a Spanish "stooge" of Joseph Bonaparte named Vicente de Emparán. A small group of patriots, driven underground, now met secretly in the home of the young Simón Bolívar. These patriots welcomed the news that a central *junta* had been set up in Seville. Then when word came that Seville had fallen to the Bonapartists, they assumed that there was no government left in Spain, and they decided to force the issue when agents arrived demanding recognition of the regency as supreme in Spain. They called a *cabildo abierto* in April, 1810, deposed the false captain-general, and established for themselves in the name of Ferdinand a *junta* composed of Bolívar's secret society.

The *junta* issued a clarion call to other cities in northern South America, but it did not even have all of Venezuela behind it. Followers of the Archbishop of Caracas were devoted to the old regime; Maracaibo and Coro to the west were jealous of the leadership of Caracas; out in the plains of the Orinoco the *llaneros* were to remain loyal to the government of Spain for years. Meanwhile, the Caracas *junta* debated in fine-sounding words and sent three of its members to England for recognition and aid. The rich young Simón Bolívar, aristocratic plantation owner, led the delegation. His errand in England was futile but, needless to say, he got in touch with Miranda in his same old London lodgings. The "Morning Star" had been busy writing articles which were sent out secretly to the new presses of South America; he had a blueprint for government in Caracas based on the writings of Locke and Rousseau. Bolívar was then twenty-seven, Miranda fifty-four. "Why not come home with us to Venezuela? The time has come!" said the younger man.

So Miranda arrived in Caracas on a British ship in December, 1810, and this time Caracas was ready to receive him. He soon got himself elected to a new congress called by the *junta*. His wide experience, soldierly bearing, and shock of white hair gave him great prestige, as did his now-popular stories of the *Leander* expedition; he was elected commander in chief of the rebel armies and put in charge of finances. Also influential in the congress was Simón Bolívar, now returned himself from London and appointed as military leader.

The *junta* and the congress were busy with reforms. A federation of the seven eastern provinces was set up. Indian tribute was abolished, the *alcabala* tax discontinued, the importation of slaves forbidden. Federalism won out over the strong objection of Miranda and Bolívar. Independence was voted at the insistence of the Patriots' Club, July 7, 1811, creating the First Venezuelan Republic. The flag used by Miranda on the *Leander* was adopted for the United Provinces of Venezuela. The constitution for these United Provinces, emphasizing the regional differences and local rivalries, weakened the new nation from the beginning, and began the Federalist versus Centralist quarrels that plagued all Spanish America for a century. Not only jealous regions, but also colored elements among the poor who were hostile to the creoles, as well as church leaders and the strong Spanish army contingent were all against the new government. Nature itself turned against the revolutionists. On the day before Good Friday in 1812, March 26, a terrific earthquake hit Venezuela, all along a fault line, bringing greatest destruction to the very towns that had been most active against Spanish authority. Priests who supported the Spanish government headed by the Archbishop of Caracas shouted that it was the judgment of God on the sinful republicans. "Down with the Republic! Acknowledge our King!" they told the frightened crowds. Simón Bolívar, working to free victims from the ruins, yelled back, "If nature opposes herself to us, we will wrestle with her, and force her to obey!"

But nature had given Miranda's republic a death blow. Congress quit quarreling and accepted Miranda as dictator in the emergency, but it was too late to save the government. Royalist soldiers made rapid progress against the rebellious sections of the country; the ports had been blockaded by Spanish ships; the patriot armies were undisciplined and many deserted; the congress was quarreling over the constitution; the lower classes, frightened by the earthquake, became hostile to the revolution. The popular young Bolívar, actually jealous of Miranda, had been put in command of the key fort of Puerto Cabello, and as the republic weakened, Bolívar had to give up the fort without a fight because of heavy desertions among his men. Thus the military situation was completely lost for the patriots. Miranda knew he had lost the confidence of the people also, and believed the whole Venezuelan republic hopeless for the time being. In desperation he made a treaty with the commander of the Spanish forces, General Domingo de Monteverde, in July 1812. All patriots were to be pardoned, and Miranda and the other leaders would be allowed to leave the country.

Then the perennially optimistic old soldier took the funds of the republic, planning to go to New Granada to use the money to further the more successful revolution that had started there—at least so his friends later insisted. An English ship awaited him in the harbor, but he delayed on shore one night too long. The Spanish commander had broken the treaty and was arresting patriots, cruelly persecuting civilians, and confiscating their property right and left. The younger leaders considered Miranda to blame; they thought he had sold out for the money. Led by Bolívar, they took Miranda prisoner in his lodgings and turned him over to the Spanish commander, listing him among the rebels as a traitor to his cause. Miranda was taken to a prison in Spain where he was kept in chains until he died four years later. The last attempt of the "Morning Star" had not been in vain, however, for his Venezuelan Republic was to be permanently revived within a decade.

Bolívar, with a passport from the Spanish commander, perhaps as a price for the arrest of Miranda, was permitted to go to Curaçao in August

Portrait of Simón Bolívar in the Pan American Union Building. *Courtesy Pan American Union.*

of 1812; from there he, rather than the "Morning Star," went to join a group of revolutionists who were seemingly succeeding in Cartagena, and to accept from their new governor a commission as colonel in the New Granadan army. Thus ended the First Venezuelan Republic.

What manner of man was Simón Bolívar—idealist, patriot, or, as one of his biographers calls him, "The Passionate Warrior"? How could he thus send his revered older leader to the dungeons? His treatment of Miranda is still unexplained, and is one of the few blots on an otherwise spectacular career of service and self-sacrifice. A very wealthy young creole born in 1783 in Caracas, heir to a four-million-peso estate, he had been orphaned at an early age and was raised by uncles and tutors. As a youth of great intellectual ability he had watched with interest the French Revolution and the rise of Napoleon. After an early and very romantic marriage he had lost his young bride in an epidemic. To ease his sorrow he traveled extensively in Europe, accompanied by Simón Rodríguez, a wise old tutor and scholar of the Enlightenment. On the Aventine Hill in Rome, after he and his tutor had spent the afternoon discussing South America's problems, Bolívar suddenly fell on his knees and made a solemn oath to "never allow my hands to be idle nor my soul to rest until I have broken the shackles which chain us to Spain."

A short man with irregular features, Bolívar had such "alert and pene-trating eyes" as to inspire all who met him. Though he never remarried, he was a favorite with the ladies. The girls of Caracas threw roses ahead of his horse's feet when he came triumphant into the city; ladies in Quito rivaled each other in giving him parties, and his devotion to a mistress or two did not deter other ladies from patriotic adulation. On the trail and the battlefield his skill in handling arms and horses won men's admiration also. The war was his whole life; his personal fortune was spent for the cause, his plantations were ruined by the fighting; he himself freed all his slaves.

It is difficult to follow his activities from his betrayal of Miranda in 1812 to the surrender of the last Spanish army in South America in 1826, while he wrote and made speeches, danced and made love, crossed rivers and mountains and fought in the thick of battle. We left him en route by British ship to Cartagena after the fall of Venezuela in 1812. He arrived there, an unknown young upstart, full of a dream of a great federation of Gran Colombia, a free union of all northern South America.

WINNING NORTHERN SOUTH AMERICA

New Granada, today's Colombia, had meanwhile followed a very com-plicated course, corresponding to the rough and mountainous character of the land and the confusing variations of population. Bogotá and Cartagena each had a separate revolution, while the towns on the passes into Ecuador, Popayán and Pasto, remained hotbeds of royalist feeling. Bogotá, the center of science and intellectual pursuits, with a vivid memory of the *comunero* revolts against excessive taxation in the 1780s and the secretly printed French revolutionary literature of Nariño, was quick to respond to Caracas' example. On July 20, 1810, influenced by the stirring writings of an idealistic Bogotá lawyer named Camilo Torres, the Bogotá creoles set up their own *junta*, "loyal to Ferdinand VII and to no other." Cartagena went further and on November 11, 1811, declared independence. But each town wanted to head a confederation of New Granadan cities. Cartagena called its organization the United Provinces of New Granada, while Bogotá pro-claimed the independent republic of Cundinamarca—the name of the province around Bogotá—on July 16, 1813.

Under Camilo Torres and the fiery Nariño, now returned from prison, the idealists of Bogotá argued endlessly over a model constitution. At the critical moment when a compact union was required, petty details involved the parochial civilians to such an impractical extent that Colombians call the following five-year period of Bogotá history *La Patria Boba*, the Foolish Fatherland. Its idealistic laws were never carried out, its fine speeches never listened to, while Nariño fought the republicans of Cartagena in a civil war on one hand and the Spanish loyalists on the other. He was captured and sent to Spain in chains, while New Granada was being reconquered by the royalists.

Bolívar, exile from the First Venezuelan Republic, had been made first a colonel and then a general in the Cartagenan forces. While the two New

Granadan cities fought each other, he issued a famous manifesto to the people of New Granada, appealing for their aid to liberate Venezuela. Then, after campaigning brilliantly along the lower Magdalena and ridding the area of loyalists, he proclaimed "War to the Death" and took Cartagenan troops into Venezuelan territory. After ninety days of unexpected victories he entered Caracas in triumph a second time on August 6, 1813, and had his first taste of flower-strewn streets. Given the title of "Liberator" he soon became dictator of the Second Republic of Venezuela which was set up.

This republic was as short-lived as the first. Many Venezuelans were blindly loyal to the king, including poor Indian cowboys from the Orinoco who joined an army under a savage cowboy general named José Tomás Boves. Boves then made a counter declaration of "War to the Death" against the rebels from Cartagena. It was brother against brother, without mercy to prisoners, wounded, or noncombatants on either side. Running from the half-savage army of *llaneros* and Spanish regulars, taking with him 10,000 of the terrified population in a dismal column of half-naked and starving people, Bolívar abandoned Caracas, found refuge for his people in the villages in eastern Venezuela, and escaped alone to Cartagena.

It was September, 1814, and Napoleon had already been defeated in Europe. New troops of the now-reinstated King Ferdinand were on the way to the Cartagena coast. Back in New Granada Bolívar had succeeded in an expedition to force Cundinamarca and Bogotá into confederation with Cartagena, but his short-lived success there was ended by the arrival of 10,000 new Spanish troops. In May of 1815 the "Liberator" had no choice save resignation and ignominious flight to Jamaica. Cartagena stood 106 days of bitter siege and fell to the new royalist troops. The year 1815 was a black one for the patriot cause. Ferdinand's most capable general, Pablo Morillo, occupied Venezuela, by then mainly royalist, and went on to Cartagena and up to Bogotá. All northern South America was again a "loyal" Spanish colony, while the stauncher patriots of *La Patria Boba* went underground.

In exile in Jamaica, the Liberator wrote letters, made plans for model governments and large-scale South American confederations, and seethed with ideas of reconquest of the mainland to win the liberty of the Americas. After other defeats in Venezuela his plans changed. His hopes centered on the Orinoco Valley, where the cowboy *llaneros*, such fierce fighters for the king three years before, had turned in wrath against their cruel General Boves and now craved excitement on the patriots' side. A rebel army of 1,500 of them was formed under their own illiterate and colorful leader, José Antonio Páez. In the spring of 1818 Bolívar joined Páez at Angostura, today called Cuidad Bolívar, on the Orinoco. There the Liberator called a congress and set up the Third Venezuelan Republic. He eloquently addressed the tiny group of patriots who attended his congress and announced plans to cross the Andes and liberate New Granada. At that congress which met on February 15, 1819, Bolívar was elected president and dictator of the war areas.

Bolívar's real success started from Angostura. Leaving Páez to command in Venezuela and harass Caracas from the rear, he took 1,300 infantrymen and 800 cavalrymen and set out on his daring scheme. Unbelievable as it seems, for no explorer would start such a trip on foot today, he took his little army of ragged plainsmen from the tropics up to the headwaters of an Orinoco tributary, then into the Andes and up to 13,000 feet elevation across a snow-covered plateau at the top, and then down upon the surprised Spanish garrison outside Bogotá. His losses had been high, men had slipped to their death in the narrow passes or frozen in the snow, but the clash with the Spanish troops at Boyacá on August 7, 1819, was brief and overwhelmingly victorious, a turning-point in the struggle for independence in northern South America. New Granada was free. In seventy-five days he had "marched a thousand miles and emancipated a nation." Leaving his lieutenants in charge in the now exuberant Bogotá, he himself went back to Angostura via Cúcuta in the foothills, to report to his little government still existing there and to create the Union of New Granada and Venezuela.

To Angostura had come help from Britain, the long-awaited result of that first mission of Bolívar's to London. Perhaps 5,000 foreign legionnaires, veterans of Wellington's Napoleonic campaigns and now unemployed in postwar London, were glad to go to fight in South America. American privateers had joined in the struggle and helped free the Caribbean of Spanish ships. Now with Bolívar's victory at Boyacá the Angostura congress was a successful government; it proclaimed the creation of the Republic of Gran Colombia, Bolívar's idealistic federation of all northern South America. In 1821 the congress was moved to a new capital, Cúcuta, near today's Colombia-Venezuela border.

The congress of Cúcuta proceeded to make a new constitution for the larger nation. Bolívar was chosen president with command of the army, while an ambitious Colombian civilian leader, Francisco de Paula Santander, was made the vice president in Bogotá, to do the actual governing. Bolívar was now ready to take his combined new army—the veterans of Boyacá, the *llaneros* of Páez, the foreign legionnaires—on to liberate the heart of Venezuela and then to Quito or Lima. For a few months it seemed that he would not have to; the liberals at home in Spain, under Riego, had revolted against Ferdinand and wished to pacify the colonists. There was to be a six-month truce while commissioners came from Spain to set up the new arrangements. Not liking to make a truce, Morillo resigned and was succeeded by General Miguel de la Torre. Bolívar had been suspicious of the truce and its proponents; his followers had lost their loyalty to Ferdinand and yearned for the complete independence they had fought for. When the visiting commissioners asked for an oath of allegiance to the Spanish constitution and merely promised that delegates from South America should sit in the Spanish *cortes*, Bolívar broke the truce. His troops fought a last decisive battle against the Spanish garrisons of Venezuela at Carabobo, June 24, 1821, and freed Venezuela from Spain forever.

Now the Spanish Main was one united state, and Bolívar turned his attention southward. Cities in Ecuador had tried to establish *juntas* in 1809 and 1811, but their revolutions had been wiped out by troops from loyalist Lima and the independence movement had remained quiescent.

Between Colombia and Quito lay the staunchly loyalist towns of Popayán and Pasto. Bolívar planned to win over these towns with his own personal persuasion, and set out overland through them with a small army. Fortunately, he sent a trusted lieutenant and military genius, José Antonio de Sucre, down to Guayaquil by sea with another army. Sucre proceeded to win and lose and win again in the country inland from Guayaquil, and then to move his troops up the Andes toward Quito. While Bolívar was meeting one of his most serious personal reverses in the narrow passes approaching Pasto, Sucre lined up what troops he had on the side of a volcano overlooking Quito, and won a decisive victory for the Colombian forces at Mount Pichincha on May 24, 1822.

When Bolívar arrived three weeks later he proclaimed the annexation of Quito and Guayaquil to his Gran Colombia republic. Thus Boyacá had won Colombia; Carabobo, Venezuela; and Pichincha, Ecuador—a firm foundation of victories upon which lasting independence could be built. Peru, most loyal of Spanish colonies, remained for the patriots to attack, but this was eventually done with aid from Argentina and Chile, where similar movements had been taking place from 1810 to 1820, and other heroes had been crossing the Andes and liberating cities.

INDEPENDENCE IN SOUTHERN
SOUTH AMERICA

The creoles in Buenos Aires had already learned to fight independently of Spain, for in 1807 they had beaten off the second English expedition against the Plata colony. The hero of that victory, Liniers, had served as viceroy, and had then been replaced by the unpopular Baltazar de Cisneros. The creoles were already plotting against him when they received news that Napoleon had overrun Spain. The patriots then arranged for a *cabildo abierto,* which soon appointed a creole *junta* and ousted the viceroy, this in front of a cheering crowd gathered in the Plaza de Mayo in the autumn drizzle of May 25, 1810, one of the celebration days of today's Argentina. Henceforward, loyalty to the imprisoned Ferdinand was forgotten, and the Plata region was the one colony that was never again to revert to Spanish rule after 1810.

The wars in southern South America now divided into three phases. Colonials there had reason to fear invasion from Brazil. The Portuguese royal family had escaped from Napoleon to come to Rio, and had brought with them the wife of the prince regent, the Spanish princess Carlota Joaquina, Ferdinand's sister and the only member of the royal family not in the clutches of Napoleon. As the Spanish heir she was trying to carve out a kingdom in the Plata and might be able to back her claim with Brazilian troops. To the northwest, Spanish royalist troops were entrenched in Lima and threatened the pampas from the Bolivian Andes. Thirdly, and in all directions, the jealous and ambitious port of Buenos Aires tried to bring all other Spanish colonies on the various Plata tributaries, the old viceroyalty of the Plata, under the direct control of that city. Actually more troops and funds were expended in this effort than in any fighting against Spain and Brazil.

While thus involved in a three-pronged fight, the people of Buenos Aires proceeded to conduct a quarrelsome government similar to Colombia's *Patria Boba*. Mariano Moreno, enthusiastic newspaper editor and admirer of the United States, held out for the formation of a republic. His bitter disputes with conservative leaders who favored inviting a European prince to serve as constitutional monarch in a "Kingdom of the Plata" disrupted efforts at real government. Moreno's enemies were pleased when he died en route on a mission for help from England and was buried at sea. "It took all that water to put out so much fire," they said. His death brought no peace to Buenos Aires and one government followed another in confusion, while men and resources were drained off to fight elsewhere.

General of these armies fighting the other colonies was Manuel Belgrano. From 1811 to 1813 he was busy in the foothills leading to Bolivia. He subjugated a separatist movement in Córdoba and fought on up into the *altiplano* as far as Lake Titicaca. After meeting varying fortune, he was turned back out of Upper Peru by the firmly entrenched Spanish loyalists. Then they followed his ragged troops on down into the pampas where the Spaniards were stopped and pushed back. After 1815 the royalists were stopped from invading modern Argentina by a gaucho guerrilla band under a local chieftain named Güemes, who fought them for two years in the foothills and so scorched the earth there as to keep them out of the fertile lowlands throughout the rest of the independence period.

Belgrano had meantime turned the attention of Buenos Aires and its armies to Paraguay in 1811. Creole sentiment there was as strongly separatist as that of the port, but the Paraguayans, always considering themselves superior to the pampa colonists, were determined not to be dominated by either port or mother country. Paraguayan troops defeated Belgrano when he invaded their river territory; then the Paraguayans combined under a fantastic lawyer, Dr. José Gaspar de Francia, to set up their own *junta* and make their own declaration of independence on October 12, 1813. "These are the arguments which I bring against the supremacy of Ferdinando Séptimo," Dr. Francia said as he laid two loaded pistols on the table at a *junta* meeting. No one brought loaded pistols to bear against his own supremacy, and he became the dictator of Paraguay till his death in 1840, keeping it an isolated hermit kingdom, and calling himself *El Supremo*, the Supreme One.

More complicated were the events on the eastern shore of the Uruguay River, along the Eastern Strip, the *Banda Oriental*, that was to become the modern nation of Uruguay. A four-sided struggle took place there till 1821. Belgrano and his troops from the port again entered the picture. Opposed to him were three factions. The first was a loyalist force under Elío firmly entrenched in Montevideo. Brazilian troops, invited to relieve Spanish troops besieged in Montevideo by patriotic forces, made up the second faction and later laid claim to the Eastern Strip. Finally, as a third force, there was a band of ardent gauchos from the interior under a romantic leader named José Gervasio Artigas, who wanted a Uruguayan state independent of both Spain and Buenos Aires. Spain withdrew by 1814; quarrels at home brought disgrace to Belgrano; but Artigas and his ragged army of gauchos and their families continued a guerrilla campaign until only a few fighting men were left alive. Then Artigas escaped to live out a lonely exile in Paraguay. Meanwhile, the Brazilians again occupied the area in 1816 and formally annexed the *Banda Oriental* in 1821. The gauchos and the Montevideans alike were to wait for independence until another series of three-way fights in 1825.

Some semblance of unity in the Plata without Bolivia, Paraguay, and Uruguay had been achieved by the Buenos Aires government. The Plata cities of Córdoba, Tucumán, Mendoza, and Santa Fé had little choice save to join with Buenos Aires in the face of the constant threat of Spanish invasion from Upper Peru. Buenos Aires conceded to the idea of a loose federation without agreeing on a constitutional principle. Thus a congress met at the city of Tucumán to decide on a government for the entire pampas region. They failed to agree on a constitution, but independence for the whole area was actually declared here for the first time on July 9, 1816, and the United Provinces of South America was proclaimed. This was a union in name only, however. Each province maintained an army, as much to keep down Buenos Aires as to ward off a re-invasion by Spain. A state of anarchy persisted, and the quarrel between Buenos Aires and the hinterland colored Argentine affairs for many decades.

Now the real hero of South America enters the story, José de San Martín. He was born an Argentine creole in 1778, but had gone to Spain as a very young cadet and had served faithfully as an officer in the wars against Napoleon. In 1812 he returned to his native land, determined to work for freedom there. Though only thirty-four years old, he could claim twenty-two years of military experience in the Spanish army. As a member of the Lautaro Lodge of the Masons in Buenos Aires, he came to the attention of the *junta* by offering to help train patriot soldiers in the methods he had learned in Spain. By 1814 he was commander in chief in charge of patriot troops fighting in the foothills north of Tucumán.

Suddenly San Martín resigned this post on the excuse of ill health and asked to be made military governor of the community of Cuyo province on the edge of the Andes across from Chile. All this was part of his long-range plan, which eventually freed South America from Spanish troops. San Martín knew that as long as any part of South America was in royalist hands, independence was in jeopardy. He had decided that Lima, the Spanish stronghold, could not be approached through well-fortified Upper Peru. With Mendoza as a base, "to cross into Chile with a small well-disciplined army is my course, there can be no other." Combined forces from the pampas and Chile could then go on to Peru.

At Mendoza he set about steering that course. All western Argentina helped him, the men training in the army, making special shoes for mules and horses to cross the mountains, casting cannon and shot, while women spun and wove uniforms and prepared compact rations for the army which was to cross over the Andes at over 12,000 feet. Down in Buenos Aires Supreme Director Juan Martín de Pueyrredón, from 1816 to 1819 head of government and San Martín's personal friend, knew his plans and sent him sporadic help of men and money, as well as endless

José San Martín, by the Argentine painter Bouchet. *Courtesy Pan American Union.*

unnecessary instructions. But the citizens of Mendoza bore the bulk of the costs.

What had taken place in Chile meanwhile? Throughout the summer of 1810 Chilean creoles had agitated against the Spanish authorities and finally threw them out in a mass meeting on September 18, 1810, today Chile's principal national holiday. In the *junta* and the congress which proceeded to meet, two parties developed, the radicals led by the young Bernardo O'Higgins, natural son of a former Irish-born viceroy, and the landed aristocrats, led by the Carrera family. While the two factions bickered, Spanish forces from Lima met the "army" of creoles led by O'Higgins at Rancagua in October of 1814 and put them completely to rout. The *junta's* rule was ended; leaders of both factions escaped to Mendoza, where San Martín listened to each side and conferred his trust on O'Higgins' party.

Now with reinforcements from O'Higgins, San Martín had 2,500 foot soldiers and 700 mounted men ready for the mountain passes. The artillery pieces went by a special pack train which carried a cable bridge, anchors, and grapnels to get the cannon over narrow bridges and rough precipices. Nearly half the 2,000 mules and horses were lost en route, but the men got through; within three weeks they were in the fertile valley of Chile. Here a decisive victory was won against the Spanish soldiers at Chacabuco on February 12, 1817. The troops entered Santiago the next day, where a *cabildo abierto* soon declared O'Higgins "Supreme

Dictator." One more battle, on the plains of Maipú a year later, April 5, 1818, had to be fought to make Chile forever free of Spanish royalists. Chilean independence was declared February 12, 1818; then Bernardo O'Higgins joined with San Martín in making plans to get their joint armies up to Lima.

THE CONQUEST OF PERU, LAST SPANISH STRONGHOLD

A sea-borne attack was the only solution, but how was it possible without ships? After Chacabuco and again after Maipú, San Martín had returned across the Andes and the pampas to Buenos Aires for help and money. An agent sent to the United States was able to procure two vessels with Buenos Aires money and dispatch them around the Horn to Valparaiso, but this was the last help San Martín was to get from his native land. The current dictator blamed him for wasting lives and funds in Chile, and "recalled" the Argentine army. San Martín resigned his Buenos Aires commission and he and his soldiers henceforth were in the employ of Chile.

That nation meanwhile had joined with English commercial interests and purchased a frigate, renamed the *Lautaro*. This and the American ships, together with two captured Spanish frigates, made the "Chilean Navy," the first in Latin America. To turn the navy into an "invasion fleet" O'Higgins hired a brilliant English naval officer in bad repute at home, Lord Thomas Cochrane. Cochrane captured more Spanish ships on forays up the coast, converted several fishing boats, and had a total of twenty-four ships and 1,600 sailors by August 1820. The soldiers totaled 4,430, 1,805 of them Chileans, 2,313 of San Martín's original men from Mendoza, and 332 soldiers of fortune—Irishmen, Englishmen, and Americans. With San Martín in command this motley fleet, carrying additional supplies to outfit the 15,000 volunteers he hoped to organize among the patriots of Peru, set sail from Valparaiso. Through widespread propaganda San Martín wanted to stir the Peruvians to win their own independence.

In Peru there were Spanish armies totaling over 16,000 men. A weak little independence movement led by poets and college professors had come to nothing, for Lima was full of Spanish aristocrats, and the Spanish viceroy during the Napoleonic period had been a strong and aggressive man. An uprising in Cuzco in 1814—a replica of the former Tupac Amarú revolution—had been suppressed. Creole leaders had been executed while the revolt was young. Thus there had been no independent government in Peru, no *junta* supposedly acting for Ferdinand during his imprisonment, though there was increasing unrest.

San Martín and Cochrane came at an opportune moment. Many Indians joined their armies; towns along the southern Peruvian coast welcomed them. A new viceroy sent from Spain was willing to dicker rather than fight. San Martín suggested a deal by which independence would be declared and then a young prince of the royal Spanish house would become the constitutional monarch of South America, such a scheme having

Bolívar met San Martín at the port of Guayaquil whose people built this monument at the dock where they first clasped hands. *Courtesy Pan American Union.*

probably been part of San Martín's philosophy from the first. The viceroy stalled the proceedings, evidently hoping for reinforcements from Spain. They never came, because of that revolt of the soldiers in Cádiz.

San Martín was not willing to be lulled by a truce as Bolívar had been. He came up the coast, landed south of Lima, won many converts without much fighting, and scared the most conservative loyalist families into fleeing to the interior. Now Lima rushed to invite San Martín in. The wild demonstration that met him there on July 12, 1821, touched the heart of even this very austere and selfless man. He told the Peruvians simply that "all I wish is that this country should be managed by itself alone." When a suitable government had been established by the Peruvians, "I shall consider that I have done enough, and leave them." He participated in a Peruvian declaration of independence on July 28, 1821, and then, as Protector of Peru, proceeded to worry over driving the strong Spanish forces out of the Andes valleys. He had quarreled with Lord Cochrane, who took many of the sailors and went back to Chile. The royalists in the interior mountains were gaining strength. There was criticism of San Martín in Lima. San Martín knew he would need help from other patriot forces in order to liberate Peru.

Meanwhile, a rival "Liberator" had appeared to the north. Bolívar's forces had conquered Ecuador, and that northern leader was now dancing and dining in Guayaquil, and glancing southward toward the last Spanish royalist stronghold. Most historians think that Bolívar was very jealous of San Martín; in his writing he claimed to be afraid of San Martín's plans for an over-all constitutional monarchy. San Martín himself knew the two should cooperate and get this Spanish business finished; he announced early in 1822 that he would sail up to Guayaquil to work out some plan with Bolívar. Quite a correspondence between the two resulted, all very flowery and mutually congratulatory. Then San Martín arrived in Guayaquil, on July 25, and was welcomed to "Colombian soil" by Bolívar.

There followed two days of meetings between the two at a house near the waterfront in Guayaquil, now marked as a shrine of South American history. No one else was present; no minutes were kept. Did they discuss a joint command? a plan of campaign? a future government for all South America? Did Bolívar refuse to join his forces for the victory unless he had supreme command and San Martín was completely out of the picture? At any rate, it was one of the most dramatic meetings in history and it resulted in one of the most unselfish acts. Next day, July 27, San Martín took ship and returned to Lima. From there he wrote Bolívar that the loyalists in the mountain strongholds outnumbered him two to one, but that some immediate action should be taken and he would be willing to resign his command to Bolívar and return to Chile if the northern forces would come to Peru. A Peruvian congress met in September 1822, to take over the government of Lima. In an eloquent speech before it, San Martín resigned to return home as a civilian leaving all behind him. In both Chile and Buenos Aires he found himself unpopular as an ill-advised waster of public funds. Already in ill health, he went quietly to live in Paris on a small pension he received, ironically enough, from a former companion-in-arms in the fight for Spain against Napoleon. Only after San Martín's death in 1850 did this self-effacing hero receive honor from the South American nations as a patriot and liberator.

After waiting for an "urgent" invitation from Peru which did not come immediately, Bolívar sailed to Callao in September 1823, and was given supreme command of the weakening Peruvian situation. Again Sucre, the able lieutenant, planned the campaign. With 6,000 Venezuelans and Colombians who had come to Peru with Bolívar, combined with 4,000 Argentines and Chileans, he prepared to meet the Spanish host of 16,000. In a dramatic charge on August 6, 1824, on the Plains of Junín, Bolívar's own horsemen, without firing a shot and fighting only with swords and lances like medieval knights, routed the cream of the Spanish cavalry and drove them back to Cuzco. *Mestizos* and Indians deserted from the Spanish forces, soon leaving less than 10,000 royal troops, of which only 500 were regulars from Spain.

With Bolívar busy organizing the government and attending social functions in Lima, Sucre took the initiative after Junín and brought his whole army to a well-chosen narrow valley at Ayacucho. Here on December 9, 1824, after a single morning's battle, the entire Spanish army together with the viceroy himself surrendered to the patriots. This battle is considered the final victory in the wars for independence.

Only Upper Peru, the towns of Chuquisaca, Potosí, and La Paz, remained unorganized. They had tried for liberty and independence three times in the period from 1808 to 1822, but had never succeeded. In the spring of 1825 both Bolívar and Sucre, with peace established everywhere, came to La Paz to create a separate nation. Independence was declared in La Paz on August 6, 1825. The citizens, not Bolívar himself, named the state Bolivia, but Bolívar had practically a free hand in writing its constitution throughout 1826. He created a strong executive presidency, elected for life, and left Sucre to fill the post. But the young Sucre did not get along with the high-altitude dwellers of La Paz, and after a short, stormy regime he resigned to go back to Quito. The city of Chuquisaca was renamed Sucre in his honor, so that his name as well as Bolívar's is preserved on the map. Bolívar himself went back to Gran Colombia in 1826 to report to the congress that the Spaniards were gone from South America forever. Once peace was established, Bolívar found no place for himself. Gran Colombia was to disintegrate within a very few years into the states of Venezuela, Colombia, and Ecuador, while Bolívar died of tuberculosis, alone and in poverty. But at least South America was freed from Europe.

THE INDEPENDENCE MOVEMENT IN SPANISH NORTH AMERICA

In Mexico, royalist control was stronger throughout the independence area than in South America and it held separatistic revolutions in check more successfully, so that when independence did come for Mexico it came as a conservative compromise in the form of a short-lived empire. However, the movement there contained two civil wars—Peninsular versus creole and white versus Indian—to a larger extent than in South America. The first revolution, under Hidalgo, was more of a social and racial revolt and was led by lower clergymen in the name of religion and the lower classes; the creoles opposed and crushed it, only to complete the work of independence themselves after the liberal revolution in Spain in 1820 rather than join in with that constitutional movement.

The news of Napoleon's invasion of Spain caused confusion in Mexico and became an excuse for each faction to claim the right to take over the government. The creole-dominated *ayuntamiento* rejected Napoleon, declared for a *junta* in the name of Ferdinand, and wanted popular sovereignty and equality with the people and provinces of Spain. The *gachupín*-dominated *audiencia* also rejected Napoleon, declared for a *junta* in the name of the king, and refused to accept any idea of popular sovereignty and equality with Spain. The viceroy José de Iturrigaray, an ambitious and opportunistic creature of Godoy, thought that he could not lose in such a situation, that if he worked with Napoleon, he might even become king of Mexico. He was flattered by the creoles and fell into their trap—thinking himself safe when on their side.

When the creoles threatened to act first, the *gachupín audiencia* staged a *coup d'état* led by Gabriel Yermo. The viceroy was deposed, a puppet placed in his office, and a new viceroy awaited from Spain. Outwitted and outplayed by the *gachupines*, the creoles organized "literary" and secret societies and went underground. In August 1810, Francisco Xavier

Father Miguel Hidalgo, who gave the first cry, the *grito,* **for Mexican independence.** *Courtesy Pan American Union.*

Venegas, the viceroy, arrived from Spain, and quiet reigned in the capital.

Not so in the northern cities. In Querétaro a secret group was led by Miguel de Hidalgo y Costilla, a gentle old creole parish priest of the nearby village of Dolores. An intellectual of "enlightened" ideas, he had often clashed with his superiors over improvements for his Indian charges. He and other conspirators in Querétaro, discouraged at the acceptance of the new Spanish viceroy by Mexico City liberals, decided to declare Mexico independent at a large regional fair set for December 1810. Unfortunately, the plot leaked out and a young captain named Ignacio Allende, a fellow conspirator, dashed through the night of September 15 out to the village of Dolores to warn Hidalgo of his threatened arrest.

Awakened at midnight, Hidalgo tolled his church bells, and before the startled Indian parishioners who assembled he proclaimed "Long live religion, long live America, down with bad government!" This was the famous *Grito de Dolores,* or Shout of Independence, enacted by a leading official in towns of Mexico at midnight on every September 15, to this day. After that first *Grito,* Hidalgo, his parishioners, Allende, and the troops under his command set out with the banner of the Virgin of Guadalupe to capture the city of Guanajuato. This was a social revolution in the name of religion, backed by the lower classes, led by a priest, and opposed by the Church and both the *gachupines* and creoles as well. Hidalgo's army amassed before Guanajuato within the week numbered a rabble of 50,000

Indians and *mestizo* peons, unarmed save for farm tools, and expecting Hidalgo to lead them to a better economic life. When the undisciplined army took the city they looted the homes of the aristocracy and killed many creole families.

As they advanced on other cities, as far as within sight of the capital, Hidalgo and Allende quarreled over disciplining the "army" and over planning military strategy. In Guadalajara by November, Hidalgo tried to form a government, set up a printing press, and formulate a policy. He was not so concerned about actual independence from Spain, but wanted to free the peons, procure lands for Indians, abolish Indian tribute, and give legal encouragement to native crafts and industries. The old priest had no time to work out this program peacefully—Indians were not to receive such recognition until another century had passed. On January 17, 1811, near Guadalajara, his forces met a complete defeat at the hands of trained regulars, when their munitions wagon exploded and set fire to the dry grass all around them. Both Allende and Hidalgo were captured as they fled northward. As a priest, Hidalgo went through a "defrocking" ceremony; then he and Allende were executed like common criminals.

The revolution did not die with them. Another parish priest, José María Morelos, had been sent by Hidalgo with a patrol of twenty-five men to plan some way to capture the port of Acapulco. There he had escaped the slaughter of the revolutionary leaders, and with 9,000 volunteers formed a guerrilla army in the hills of southwestern Mexico. A much better military planner and organizer than Hidalgo, Morelos continually harried the Spaniards and then slipped through their noose. While Napoleon fought in Spain, Morelos was able to hold a great part of southern Mexico. He had time, which Hidalgo never had, to form a government, to declare independence on November 6, 1813, at the town of Chilpancingo on the Acapulco road, and to frame a constitution at the village of Apatzingán in October, 1814, which set up a republic and abolished slavery and social and racial distinctions.

After 1814 more soldiers came from Spain to fight Morelos. On one occasion he was defeated while encamped on a rocky height by a young creole officer in the royalist army named Agustín Iturbide, who scaled the rocks and surprised the patriots. Who was to foresee that when independence came six years later, it was to be Iturbide, turncoat that he was, who would get the credit? Defeat followed defeat for Morelos. Determined to maintain the legal basis of the revolution, he sacrificed himself to save the congress. When his whole government was surrounded, he sent the best of his army to conduct the congressional delegates to safety, while he allowed himself to be captured in a delaying action.

Morelos in his turn was defrocked and executed on December 22, 1815, still thinking that his congress was saved and that his government would live. But the congress disbanded and many patriots were captured. Although the royalists held Mexico firmly until the Revolution of 1820 in Spain, an Indian named Vicente Guerrero held a group of guerrillas together in the hilly country south of Acapulco—today called the State of Guerrero; and a *mestizo* leader, Félix Fernández, who renamed himself

Guadalupe Victoria in honor of Hidalgo's revolution, lived for many years as a starving hermit, surviving to become the first president of the Mexican Republic.

To the conservative in Mexico City, members of the *audiencia*, landed aristocrats, and upper clergymen, the constitutionalism of the 1820 revolt in Spain, with its radicalism, anticlericalism, and ideas of popular sovereignty, was more dangerous than an independent Mexico. Thus we have the anomaly of independence being achieved by the very men who fought Hidalgo and Morelos. They looked for a military leader to help them achieve such "conservative" independence, and found him in the self-seeking creole officer Agustín Iturbide, who for some time had been in disgrace for grafting off the silver trains from northern Mexico which his troops had been sent to guard. He ingratiated himself with the right people through Church connections and soon found himself in command of the Spanish imperial forces, supposedly the tool of the new conspiracy.

As a first step he got in touch with the one remaining guerrilla leader of the former revolution, the Indian Guerrero. With him he formulated the "Plan of Iguala." Mexican history for the next century was to be dominated by plans and proclamations of axioms or principles by the leaders of a rebellion, hatched in and named after some obscure village, and backed by an armed force. This first Plan was to set up an independent monarchy in Mexico, to offer the throne to Ferdinand himself if he would like to come to the New World, or to any young prince he might suggest. A congress was to meet and a constitution to be written making "Three Guarantees"—independence, equality of all races, and the established position and privileges of the Catholic Church.

This Plan, backed by the Army of the Three Guarantees commanded by Iturbide, quickly won victories, both military and political. The viceroy resigned and went to Spain; a new viceroy, Juan O'Donojú, sent by the constitutionalists in power at home, bowed to Iturbide's forces and signed a treaty with the Mexicans at Córdoba on August 24, 1821. This treaty incorporated all the ideas of the Plan of Iguala, except the insistence on a Spanish prince. By now the wily Iturbide was suggesting that if no European prince could be had, then a Mexican congress could appoint one of its own choosing. He dominated the interim *junta* and paraded his soldiers down the main avenues of Mexico City, while the Treaty of Córdoba was being rejected by the Spanish government. Soon Iturbide and congress quarreled over making the constitution. Some loyal soldiers in the army staged a planned barracks *coup d'état* and cheered for Emperor Agustín Iturbide the First. A purchased "rump" congress rubber-stamped this home-town choice, and Emperor Agustín was crowned in Mexico City's cathedral, July 25, 1822.

While Iturbide set up an elaborate court with pomp exceeding that of any viceroy, leaders on all sides grew scornful of him. Guadalupe Victoria, now out of hiding, and the old Indian Guerrero were disillusioned; the creoles had no more power than before; the lower classes were living as poorly. When congress opposed Iturbide's expenditures, he dissolved it, jailing many of its members.

A young creole officer named Antonio López de Santa Anna, who was to dominate Mexican politics for three decades, took advantage of the disaffection to join with Guerrero and Victoria in a new Plan, this one formed at Casa Mata. This Plan accomplished the abdication and exile of the now unpopular Iturbide before his empire had lasted a year. In the fall of 1823 a new congress assembled, a new constitution providing for a federal republic was written, and Guadalupe Victoria became president. Nevertheless, there was to be no peace, for the army was controlled by the ambitious Santa Anna. Mexico was an independent republic, yes, but the old colonial creole class still ruled.

Iturbide's "revolt" against Spain was being closely watched in Central America. There had been short-lived *juntas* in 1810 in most of the Central American cities. Disaffection continued through the period of wars elsewhere; Panama held a *cabildo abierto* and joined Gran Colombia in 1821. When a *cabildo abierto* in Guatemala City declared independence on September 15, 1821, apparently forecasting a Central American republic, Iturbide sent an armed force to bring that area also under his power. The leaders in Guatemala voted in favor of Iturbide's empire. Before this union could be organized, however, his empire fell, and a congress called in Guatemala in July of 1823 voted to create the republic of the United Provinces of Central America. This federated republic, with its capital at Guatemala City, ruled the areas of Nicaragua, Costa Rica, El Salvador, Honduras, and Guatemala until it broke up into separate republics in 1839. Chiapas, a northermost province ruled from Guatemala, stayed with the 1824 Republic of Mexico, and remains a state of Mexico to this day.

Santo Domingo, ruled from Haiti since 1795, had become restive under French Negro rule and expelled those invaders in 1814. In 1821 a revolt proclaimed independence for the Spanish-speaking part of the island and voted to join Gran Colombia; but Boyer came in, conquered it, and joined it to Haiti. It was twenty-two years later, in 1844, that Santo Domingo became a republic, an independence scarcely challenged by the homeland. In fact, nothing remained of the Spanish empire in the New World after 1825 save the islands of Cuba and Puerto Rico, which waited under the European yoke until the Spanish-American War of 1898.

Readings

Anderson, R. C., *Diary and Journal, 1814–1826* (1964)
Angell, H., *Simón Bolívar* (1930)
Arnade, C. W., *Emergence of the Republic of Bolivia* (1957)
Beals, C., *Eagles of the Andes* (1963)
Belaunde, V. A., *Bolívar and the Political Thought of Spanish American Revolution* (1938)
Benson, N. L., *Mexico and the Spanish Cortes, 1810–1822* (1966)
Bushnell, D., *The Santander Regime in Colombia* (1957)
Caruso, J. A., *The Liberators of Mexico* (1954)
Craine, E. R., *United States and the Independence of Buenos Aires* (1961)

Davis, T. B., *Carlos de Alvear* (1955)

Fisher, L. E., *Background of the Revolution for Mexican Independence* (1934)

Galdames, L., *History of Chile*, trans. I. J. Cox (1941)

Graham, G. S., and R. A. Humphreys, eds., *The Navy and South America, 1807–1823* (1962)

Grahame, R. B. C., *José Antonio Páez* (1929)

Hall, B., *Extracts from a Journal* (2 vols., 1824)

Hamill, H. M., Jr., *The Hidalgo Revolution: Prelude of Mexican Independence* (1965)

Hasbrouck, A., *Foreign Legionaries in the Liberation of Spanish South America* (1928)

Henao, M. M., and G. Arrubla, *History of Colombia*, trans. J. F. Rippy (1938)

Humphreys, R. A., ed., *British Consular Reports on Trade and Politics of Latin America* (1940)

———, "The Historiography of the Spanish American Revolutions," *Hispanic American Historical Review*, XXXVI (1956), 81–93

———, *Liberation in South America, 1806–1827: Career of James Paroissien* (1952)

———, and J. Lynch, *Origins of the Latin American Revolutions, 1808–1826* (1965)

Keen, B., *David Curtis DeForest and the Revolution of Buenos Aires* (1947)

Koebel, W. H., *British Exploits in South America* (1917)

Lecuna, V., and H. A. Bierck, eds., *Selected Writings of Bolívar* (2 vols., 1952)

Levene, R., *History of Argentina*, trans. W. S. Robertson (1937)

Lloyd, C., *Lord Cochrane* (1947)

Madariaga, S. de, *Bolívar* (1952)

Manning, W. R., *Diplomatic Correspondence of the United States Concerning the Independence of the Latin American Nations* (3 vols., 1925)

Masur, G., *Simón Bolívar* (1948)

Mehegan, J. J., *O'Higgins of Chile* (1913)

Metford, J. C. F., *San Martín, the Liberator* (1950)

Mitre, B., *Emancipation of South America*, trans. W. Pilling (1893)

Munro, D. G., *Five Republics of Central America* (1918)

Noll, A. H., and A. P. MacMahon, *Life and Times of Miguel Hidalgo y Costilla* (1910)

Parkes, H. B., *History of Mexico* (2nd ed., 1950)

Peterson, H. F., *Argentina and the United States, 1810–1960* (1964)

Priestley, H. I., *Mexican Nation* (1923)

Robertson, W. S., *Iturbide of Mexico* (1952)

———, *Life of Miranda* (2 vols., 1929)

———, *Rise of the Spanish American Republics* (1918)

———, *France and the Independence of Latin America* (1939)

Rojas, R., *San Martín: Knight of the Andes*, trans. H. Brickell (1945)

Schoellkoph, A., *Don José de San Martín* (1924)

Shepherd, W. R., *Hispanic Nations of the New World* (1920)

Sheridan, P. J., *Francisco de Miranda, Forerunner of Spanish American Independence* (1960)

Sherwell, G. A., *Antonio José de Sucre* (1926)

Simpson, L. B., *Many Mexicos* (3rd ed., 1950)

Sprague, W. F., *Vicente Guerrero, Mexican Liberator* (1939)

Street, J., *Artigas and the Emancipation of Uruguay* (1959)

Timmons, W. N., *Morelos of Mexico: Priest, Soldier, Stateman* (1963)

Trend, J. B., *Bolívar and the Independence of Spanish America* (1948)

Turnbull, A. D., and N. R. Van der Veer, *Cochrane the Unconquerable* (1929)

Webster, C. K., *Britain and the Independence of Latin America, 1812–1830* (2 vols., 1938)

Wilgus, A. C., ed., *Colonial Hispanic America* (1936)

———, *South American Dictators* (1937)

Wise, G. S., *Caudillo: A Portrait of Antonio Guzman Blanco* (1951)

Worcester, D. E., *Sea Power and Chilean Independence* (1962)

Chapter 19

The End of an Era;
the Beginning of a New One

PROBLEMS OF THE GREEN
YOUNG NATIONS

ALTHOUGH THE WARS that won independence for Latin America were essentially political movements, they left a changed hemisphere. Areas had been devastated in the long period of fighting. The cattle industry was ruined where marauding soldiers had slaughtered the herds for food. Mining had been handicapped by loss of laborers and damage to installations. Plantations had suffered when the freed slaves had wandered away or been drafted into the armies. *Gachupín* owners of property had gone back to Spain. The wars had broken up families, driven people from place to place, siphoned off the leaders among the young men, disrupted the lives of cities, driven away the trained bureaucrats who carried on the public work, and left taxes uncollected and government obligations unpaid. Even church organization had broken down, since most bishops and archbishops had been loyal to Spain, and anticlerical feelings became a factor in subsequent politics. As after any long destructive civil war, society itself was partially destroyed. The wars for independence opened the way for most of the changes of the nineteeth century.

Now the new republics, the "Green Young Nations"—sixteen of them by 1830—had to rebuild. They had to be recognized in the eyes of the world as political entities, and they had to set up governments at home that had a legal basis and that were accepted by the people. The heroic leaders had spoken and written many fine words as to how these governments were to be run. But when their philosophies came up against hard realities, even while the wars were being fought, differences arose between classes and between regions. Constitutions were framed, sometimes before any fighting took place, and the idealistic documents were immediately ignored. Political parties in the modern sense did not evolve during the decade of the wars, but already conservatives and liberals lined up bitterly against each other. Where winning the fighting was the important thing, the military leader became the government leader; as peace came, he often remained the dictator. Meanwhile the financial situation remained chaotic and the lack of trained administrators increased the chaos. The removal of the mother country left a vacuum which the new republics were hard pressed to fill. The story of the nineteenth century in Spanish America reflects all these difficulties. One of the earlier problems solved was that of recognition by the other nations of the world. Without recognition the weak and indeed unformed nations in Latin America would have labored under political and economic handicaps.

THE FOREIGN PROBLEMS OF THE NEWLY INDEPENDENT COUNTRIES

No daughters are really footloose and fancy-free until mother admits they are; the Spanish colonies, having proclaimed their own independence, wanted recognition of that fact from Spain. Since continental Europe sympathized with Spain, European powers would not recognize the new nations if the mother country did not. As late as 1827 the Spanish foreign minister proclaimed Ferdinand's "unalterable resolution never to abandon his rights, and to refuse all offers of mediation or of amicable intervention which should contemplate an acknowledgment of the independence of the new states." Nearly ten years later, under a young new queen, Isabella II, a liberal-minded *cortes* was able to consider the question again. The members were told by the delegate who introduced the bill that "Spain should act generously in this important affair, and considerations unworthy of her noble character should not be involved in the emancipation of the former colonies." A bill was sent to the Queen, and she proclaimed the independence of Mexico in December 1836. This was tardily followed by the recognition of the other republics; by this time, most of the revolutionary leaders were dead, and the countries had been living without Spanish direction and advice for fifteen years and more.

And what of the United States, whose revolution had inspired the Latin American independence movement in the first place? As a young nation, America could only express sympathy, watch the struggles that went on during the Napoleonic Wars, and fight her own War of 1812 against the English. After the return of Ferdinand in 1814 the United States needed his friendship in order to settle the western boundary of the Louisiana Purchase and acquire Florida. The United States had declared its neutrality; now it raised the revolting colonies to the status of belligerency, tightened its neutrality laws, and sent commissioners to gather information. Individual Americans, sympathetic to revolutions against tyranny, had already gone adventuring with Miranda, had served under Bolívar and Lord Cochrane, had filibustered on Mexico's borders, and had financed privateers in the Caribbean.

Because of this participation by American citizens and for commercial reasons, the government began to take a more open interest. Joel Poinsett, a wealthy South Carolinian destined to be the first American minister to independent Mexico, had been an American agent in Buenos Aires and Chile from 1810 to 1814. At home Henry Clay led the agitation for recognition of the states to the south, and remained their consistent friend in the American Congress. Secretary of State John Quincy Adams opposed any official step to anger Spain, until the United States could be absolutely sure that the Latin American states could exist permanently and maintain law and order within their boundaries. The motives of the American government were mixed, confused by the conflict between its ideological sympathies and its commercial interests, between its fear of Europe and its hopes for neutrality. A commission which Adams sent to South America to check on conditions disagreed as to whether recognition was deserved or not.

When the Spanish American revolts promised success by 1820 and Florida was safely purchased, the stiff-necked American attempt to remain strictly neutral within international law seemed no longer necessary, and Latin America was clamoring for recognition. San Martín was in Lima in 1821; Iturbide had won independence for Mexico. Thus in January of 1822 Monroe urged recognition, and on June 19, 1822, Manuel Torres, a *chargé d'affaires* from Colombia, was formally received by President Monroe. The recognition of other states followed in rapid succession.[1] Not only were representatives received formally in Washington, but ministers from the United States were sent in exchange, and commercial and friendship treaties were signed.

British recognition was more important to the Green Young Nations than was acceptance by the weak new country to the north. Though English mercantilist interests had long been anxious to make money off Latin American trade, Spain was England's ally in the Peninsular War; after the British sea victory at Trafalgar, the colonial trade was open to British ships anyway, and there was no need to antagonize the Spaniards by recognizing the colonies. Then came the restoration of Ferdinand and the strict enforcement of trade regulations against English ships. However, the government in London could not openly condone interference in anyone's colonial empire, so England gave no direct official assistance, but played a double game of maintaining friendly relations with Spain and yet carrying on illegal commerce with Spanish America and permitting private participation in the wars by individual Englishmen. English bankers openly made loans to the patriot governments, while the members of the British foreign legion in Bolívar's army as well as the Chilean exploits of Cochrane and other navy men were widely publicized in England.

[1] The United States recognized Colombia and Mexico in 1822; Buenos Aires and Chile in 1823; Central America and Brazil in 1824; Peru in 1826.

Then came 1820, the revolts at home in Spain, and the attempt of Metternich's system, the Quadruple Alliance, to put them down with French troops and Austrian money. Britain had withdrawn from the Alliance at the Congress of Verona and feared the extension of such powers to the New World; at the same time she noted Bolívar's successes, America's recognition of South America, and its issuance of the Monroe Doctrine. British commercial interests brought increasing pressure toward English acceptance of the new states; agents and commissions sent out by Parliament reported back favorably. Accordingly, the only logical step was British recognition, which occurred for most of the nations established by 1826.

France remained under the domination of Metternich's system, which was so opposed to republics anywhere, until she threw off that yoke by the Revolution of 1830 which put Louis Philippe on the throne. Recognition of the Latin American republics followed, beginning with a treaty with Venezuela signed November 12, 1832. Papal recognition came by August 1831, when Pope Gregory XVI announced his intention of entering into relations with the then *de facto* governments of Spanish America; he finally recognized Colombia in 1835.

The most important by-product of the Quadruple Alliance (Metternich system) and its attempt to put down revolts against Spanish *legal* government was the Monroe Doctrine, important not so much for what it did at the time as for what it later became. When the French and Austrians first threatened intervention, the British foreign minister, George Canning, suggested joint aid in opposing it. John Quincy Adams, then Secretary of State in the United States, did not wish to join England in any declaration against the European continental powers; he was jealous of American prestige and wanted to "go it alone," knowing that such a declaration would have the protection of the British navy anyway. Accordingly he influenced President Monroe to include in his message to Congress on December 2, 1823, the famous statement that "any attempt to extend the political system" of the European powers "to any portion of this hemisphere is dangerous to our peace and safety." The New World was no longer open to further colonization by European powers; although the United States itself had no intention of interfering with the existing colonies, it would brook no interference with the new governments which had established their independence. In effect, the United States said that it would not tolerate the intrusion of Old World political systems in its hemisphere. This also was meant to apply to the Russians in the North Pacific.

At the time Metternich called the doctrine "indecent." England welcomed it with mixed feelings, for she was tacitly included in the doctrine, in spite of the fact that it was not jointly issued. In the new Latin American states where it was noted at all it was received with pleasure. Santander, then in charge of Colombia during Bolívar's absence in Peru, called it a "policy consolatory to human nature." A leading Mexican political philosopher, Lucas Alamán, was alarmed by it and saw already that it might be a "possible threat of North American imperialism." Actually, at the time, its major importance was that it allowed Latin America to work out

Meeting room of Bolívar's first Pan American Congress, maintained as an historic site in Panama City.
Courtesy El Halcon-Panama.

its own destiny. Up to the time of the Monroe Doctrine, Latin America had been a frontier of Europe; now it was part of the independent American continent, free to organize itself without the danger of intervention.

In a sense, one result of the Monroe Doctrine was the calling of the first Pan American Congress in 1826, at the instigation of Bolívar. He had had this idea as early as 1814. "How beautiful it would be if the Isthmus of Panama were to be to us what Corinth was to the Greeks, the site of a world capital. God grant some day an august congress of three quarters of the world may meet there," he had written. Accordingly he invited the new states to send delegates to Panama, just before the battle of Ayacucho. "Treaties of mutual cooperation will be made there," he wrote, "treaties which after a hundred years will be recalled with respect."

Alas for Bolívar's dreams of a Pan American federation! He himself did not go to the meeting; he was still in Lima. Of all the nations he invited, only Mexico, the new Central American Federation, Colombia, and Peru sent delegates. Brazil, Chile, and Bolivia accepted the invitation but their delegates never arrived. Two representatives were appointed by the United States; one died en route, the other arrived too late. The British and Dutch sent observers. The plan for a confederation suggested by the Peruvians was opposed by the Colombians. A proposal to submit boundary disputes to arbitration was accepted by the delegates, but was ratified only by Colombia. It was tragic that these nations did not accept a method for peaceful adjustment of boundaries; the century ahead was to see so many bloody wars on this subject between sister republics. On other matters also the Panama meeting accomplished nothing. In spite of the dreams of Bolívar, each Latin American nation tried to work out its own problems.

PHILOSOPHICAL IDEAS OF THE LEADERS

Other ideas of Bolívar also came to nothing. Eloquent in speech and writing, he had found time in the midst of constant activity to plan a government for all South America. His political program was set down in memorials from here, letters from there, *pronunciamientos* from another place. When he had landed in Cartagena in 1812 after the fiasco in Caracas, he had already analyzed why his first republic had failed. In a "Memorial to the Citizens of New Granada" of December 1812, he said of the Venezuela government, "We had philosophers for governors, philanthropy for legislation, dialectics for tactics, and sophists for soldiers." People who had known only the colonial rule of Spain were incapable of a prudent and orderly exercise of the right of suffrage. Thus Bolívar foresaw that complete democracy was to be difficult in Spanish America.

Three years later, an exile on the island of Jamaica, he wrote the famous "Letter from Jamaica" further analyzing the possibilities of the new states. Spanish-Americans, he said, had been lifted suddenly from their low status "without previous training, without practice in public affairs." They would not know how to be the legislators, magistrates, fiscal administrators, and diplomats that comprise "the hierarchy of a regularly organized state." Until "our compatriots acquire the political talents and virtues which distinguish our brothers of the North, entire popular systems, far from being beneficial, will, I very much fear, come to be our ruin." This clear conception of the future of Spanish America was surely an accurate prediction of the political confusion to come.

If real democracy was to be impossible, what other solution was available? Again, in a speech made at the Congress of Angostura in 1819, Bolívar stated that "social perfection and perfect systems of government are noble ideals but legislators deal with men, not angels." Therefore the new states should have a strong executive power; senators should serve for life; voting should be for the well-prepared only and should be closely safeguarded. The Congress of Angostura followed his advice in providing for a limited suffrage and a strong executive as well as a lifetime term for senators. When, in 1826, Bolívar was asked to make a model constitution for Bolivia, his interest in strong executive power and his distrust of universal suffrage were apparent. The president, as planned for Bolivia, was to be simply a monarch in disguise, chosen for life—this though Bolívar had been afraid of San Martín's ideas of having a limited monarch brought over from some royal house of Europe. When challenged to defend his plan for a strong presidency, he said that "Spanish America contained neither great wealth nor powerful ecclesiastics nor an ambitious clergy nor great nobles. Without these to support them tyrants could not be permanent, and any who aspired to become king or emperor would be deterred by the fate of Dessalines and

Christophe and Iturbide," all of whom had fallen before the creation of Bolivia. "Men need have no fear that monarchs will be established in America." In this Bolívar was both wrong and right; some of the powerful dictator chieftains, the *caudillos* of Latin America's nineteenth century, were as powerful as kings, but only in one instance, that of the López family in Paraguay, did they attempt to pass power to their sons, and that instance brought tragic results to the nation.

Bolívar was afraid of the idea of one big state, but equally fearful of the South American continent's breaking up into many small states. If the Spanish possessions were made into a single monarchical state, "the clumsy colossus would die of convulsion." There should be one republic for northern South America—the idealistic scheme of his for Gran Colombia—and perhaps an equally large unit for southern South America. These big, strong republics were to be based on "the sovereignty of the people, the division of power, civil liberty, the prohibition of slavery, the abolition of monarchy and of privileges." He always opposed federalism as providing too weak an executive.

The ignorant citizenry, the inexperience in government, and the dissolution of Gran Colombia under his eyes brought Bolívar bitterness before his death. "Those who have worked for the cause of Latin American freedom have ploughed the sea!" he wrote in 1829, as his hopes were collapsing all about him. "We have tried all systems; nothing has proved effective. Mexico has fallen; Guatemala is destroyed; there are new revolutions in Chile. In Buenos Aires they have killed the president. Bolivia had three presidents in two days, and two of them have been murdered." Latin America is "a turmoil, a chaos of passions, difficulties and disorders." In the newly freed nations he found "neither faith nor truth, whether it be among men or among nations. Treaties are mere scraps of paper, constitutions are books, elections are battles, freedom is anarchy."

The anarchy had driven him out of the leadership in his own Caracas, then had deposed him as president at Bogotá after the federation of Gran Colombia he set up fell to pieces. He was only saved from a planned assassination plot when he was warned by a faithful mistress, Manuela Sáenz, in time to jump out of a window and hide under a bridge. A victim of tuberculosis contracted during his last campaigns in Ecuador, he caught another cold en route to Cartagena in 1830, whither he had made his weary way downriver to help stop a rebellion. Penniless and ill, he found a meager lodging on a plantation in Santa Marta. Attended by a French doctor a few days before his death, he asked,

"What brought you to the New World?"

"The wish to find liberty," the doctor replied, "and I have found it."

"You have been more fortunate than I, doctor, for so far I have not."

San Martín, more conservative from the start, was perhaps never so completely disillusioned. He had felt that "a federated republic can never be established." Though he spoke of the war in Peru as "a war of new and liberal principles against prejudice, bigotry, and tyranny," he seems to have always preferred a constitutional monarchy with an imported European prince as the way to peace and the end to civil strife. "Public opinion is a mechanism but newly introduced to this country," so that elected executives would not be able to run republics successfully. Argentina, or the United Provinces of the Plata, "without art, sciences, agriculture, inhabitants, and with a large extent of territory which may properly be called a desert," could not survive in competition with the Brazilian monarchy next door. Never anxious to make himself the permanent leader, San Martín had retired from Peru, had found himself unwelcome in Chile and his native Argentina, and had gone to Paris to live out a quiet life in exile. His death in 1850 went unnoticed in Buenos Aires, though its centenary was celebrated there for an entire summer in 1950.

Other leaders had proclaimed philosophies of liberty, democracy, and republicanism, and had in turn met death without gratitude from the countries they helped found. Miranda, who had always thought in terms of monarchy for his ideal new countries and was not concerned with democratic procedures beyond the establishment of independence, had died miserably chained in a dark Spanish prison. Mariano Moreno, that fiery writer for independence and republicanism in the first days of Buenos Aires' new government, had died at sea en route to England. O'Higgins died after being exiled from his beloved Chile by the ambitious politicians of the new state. Sucre, having been elected the lifelong president of Bolivia under the Liberator's model constitution, wrote to Bolívar of "the anarchy, the confusion, and the ingratitude which surround me." When he retired in disillusionment to find a quiet life in Quito, his Bolivian enemies sought him out and assassinated him. The fiery Nariño, who had circulated the writings of the French Revolution, languished like Miranda for many years in a Spanish prison, escaped to fight in Colombia, and eventually even to serve as vice-president of that state, only to be accused of having misappropriated funds entrusted to him during the colonial period. He died penniless, leaving "my children my memory, and my country my ashes." Iturbide was captured and shot when he dared to return secretly from exile in 1824; Artigas died alone in Paraguay with only an old Negro servant at his bedside. Vicente Guerrero, Indian follower of Morelos in Mexico, served one term as president and was then executed by his successor. In fact, only the tough *llanero* Páez, of all the heroic leaders, actually died of old age, and even he was in exile in the United States, though in his eighties.

Those who wanted complete idealistic democracy, those who helped write the many flowery constitutions full of liberal guarantees, those who planned for constitutional monarchies or impractical republics, those who dreamed of great federations, and those who fought city against city—all these fighters and philosophers could say with Bolívar, "We who have worked for the cause of Latin American freedom have ploughed the sea!"

THE FINE POLITICAL PHILOSOPHIES IN THE HARD LIGHT OF REALITY

All the makers of constitutions and the framers of governments would find something in the philosophies of Bolívar, San Martín, Belgrano,

O'Higgins, Mariano Moreno, Sucre, or the others, to fit their ideas. But all wanted independent nations, and at least they got that. By 1826 the entire Western Hemisphere except Canada and the Caribbean colonial possessions was independent. The new nations owed something to European rivalries and to foreign aid, but all were products to some extent of New World factors.

Many of these nations had been attempting to organize governments for a decade or more before their independence was recognized. In that period all had run into the same problems. One of the largest issues facing the new governments was "centralism versus federalism." Should their new constitutions be patterned after the United States, allowing each province a governor, a legislature, and a maximum of self-rule? Or should constitutions be written that provided for a strong central government in a single national capital? It seemed natural for the four viceroyalties that existed at the end of the colonial period—Mexico, Peru, the Plata, and New Granada—to form four large new nations, in which the seats of *audiencias* might be state or provincial capitals. But soon the viceroyalties began to fall apart as units. Chile, one of the first sections to proclaim a republic, seemed naturally separate from royalist Peru, divided by a long desert, though formerly ruled from Lima. The Plata viceroyalty had included Upper Peru, which stayed loyal to Spain and Peru till after Ayacucho and then became the new republic of Bolivia. Uruguay and Paraguay were lost to the United Provinces of the Plata before they could be federated at the Congress of Tucumán in 1816. Even the regions there which remained loosely joined to Buenos Aires resented its domination and were engaged in constant strife with the port.

The viceroyalty of New Spain seemed destined to existence as an empire intact from Texas to Costa Rica, under Iturbide. But the Central American provinces soon left the "empire" to form their own federation, which in turn split into five quarrelsome little states before 1840. Mexico itself, ousting Iturbide and setting up a republic in 1824, proceeded to establish a federation modeled almost exactly on that of the United States to the north. Though the artificially created nineteen states held together in the long run, there was much dissension and civil war. The viceroy of New Spain had ruled Central America and the Caribbean from Mexico City, but the islands each followed a different pattern of history and never joined in any great federation. Geographic differences, bad roads, and difficult terrain still acted against the New World. So also did the lack of homogeneity in social and racial groups which made any unity impossible.

It was Bolívar's dream confederation of Gran Colombia that most completely shattered to pieces. He meant to include Venezuela, the Popayán region, the Quito and Guayaquil regions, Cartagena, and Panama, as well as Bogotá. When Bolívar resigned as president of this unwieldy union, Páez had already made himself dictator of an independent Venezuela; a general named Juan José Flores had united Guayaquil with Quito in an armed revolt against the forces of Bogotá. Even Cartagena planned to form a separate republic. Each faction accused the other of violating the federal constitution Bolívar had arranged at Cúcuta in 1821; yet each group left to form its own independent republic. Brazil's history is similar, for each region felt itself separate from every other region. However, monarchy, not republicanism, held Brazil together in the nineteenth century. In spite of the high hopes and fine words for unity, and against the wishes of most of the leaders of the revolution, Latin America was formed into sixteen nations and the empire of Brazil by 1830. With the exception of the latter, all were republics—at least in form.

North Americans, pleased with the successful long life of their own Constitution, are prone to think that writing a constitution solves a new nation's problems then and there. But constitution-making has been a favorite literary pastime of Latin America's heroes; nowhere are constitutions more elaborate. The constitutions put into effect in the 1820s all contained provisions for elected or at least nonhereditary executives, legislatures elected by at least partial manhood suffrage, and a system of judicial tribunals—all this in a region long ruled by a country that had never developed such traditions at home. The constitutions contained guarantees of personal freedom, Bills of Rights composed by well-meaning visionaries, students of the American and French Revolutions. The same rights had to be guaranteed by army leaders and strong men, who had no idea of putting them into actual practice. When adherence to the letter of the law bothered such a "strong man's" conscience, he could easily call a constitutional convention of his followers and have a new constitution written to suit his pleasure. The people, who were thus "guaranteed" empty sovereignty and hollow rights, did not have sufficient loyalty to the idea of a nation to understand a national constitution; they had loyalty only to a leader or a small region. Latin American government throughout the nineteenth century was to be a perpetual conflict between practice and theory.

Constitutions and Bills of Rights also contained other concepts unrelated or unacceptable to nineteenth-century Latin Americans. A society much more stratified into social classes than that of North America could not immediately believe in high-sounding pronouncements of the equality of all mankind. A region unused to voting could not peacefully hold an election and expect the losers, if well armed, to accept defeat cheerfully. A whole people accustomed to a state-supported Church that proclaimed all dissenters heretics could not understand references to freedom of religion and separation of Church and state.These things came slowly to Latin America with industrialization and increased contact with 'the outside world.

Some peaceable division into two main political parties is a necessary adjunct of a democratic state. In most Latin American states two such parties arose, often calling themselves simply the Liberals and the Conservatives. The people who hoped to carry out the glowing promises of the constitutions were in most countries the liberals. They were the townspeople, merchant class, intelligentsia, interested in trade and commerce, ambitious for education, suspicious of a dominating, tax-supported Church, often active members of Masonic lodges. They were opposed by the aristocracy, the old landlord class who needed no foreign commerce, who wanted the slow life of colonial times unchanged, whose eldest sons inherited the land and younger sons became leaders in the conservative, established Church, or privileged officers in a conservative army. In Argentina, for example, these conservatives were more apt to be federalists, rather than centralists or *unitarios*, because they could continue to dominate the provincial cities and agricultural regions as the nineteenth century progressed, while the capital became more sophisticated and industrialized under the centralist liberals.

In economic matters, liberals were willing to spend tax money freely for education, public works, and city and harbor improvements. Conservatives held the purse strings in tightly, and insisted on low taxes, especially on real estate. There were even differences in international policy, liberals being much more nationalistic and aggressive, while conservatives held to a cautious foreign policy, looked toward European powers with sympathy for monarchy and aristocracy there, and took no great pride in their nationhood. Socially and culturally, liberals were interested in reason, science, and the new philosophies of change, while conservatives wanted to preserve the *status quo* and the old classical culture—the old colonial regime. The two groups quarreled over the secularization of education, the separation of the Church and state, the extension of suffrage, the break-up of the large estates, and the superiority of civilian over military government. In some of these nations the disputes still go on today. The two parties might have been called *Blancos* and *Colorados* as in Uruguay, *Pelucones* and *Pipiolos* as in Chile, but their fundamental beliefs remained parallel throughout Latin America. Since even the liberals could not envisage universal suffrage and completely fair and open elections, both groups rallied around individual personal heroes in every country, and rule by an individual, be he benevolent patriarch or malevolent tyrant, became the nineteenth-century pattern in Latin America.

This pattern was inevitable because of the Spanish colonial heritage. In the sharply separated social caste system, individualism was exaggerated. Local chieftains or *caciques*, feudal landlords, and oligarchic societies in the cities were the government agents to be respected with a respect that bowed to the leadership of a person rather than an idea. Thus the people were habituated to what the Latins call *personalismo*, the loyalty to a leader. Combined with this was the strong local loyalty to one small region that the distance from Spain and the long years of war had encouraged. A people with such prideful loyalties, based on ignorance of the outside world and acceptance of the close and the known, a people who had no experience in government except the limited activity of *cabildo* and revolutionary *junta*, could not break away from personalism and localism in one generation.

The wars of independence demanded that the personal leaders be military heroes. Fifteen years of warfare had destroyed whatever government did exist and had shackled militarism on the people. The economic basis of society was destroyed, fields went untilled, labor forces had been conscripted for the various armies. The soldier bands, in their turn, had lived off the country, killing the livestock, looting the towns, and terrorizing the people. Once the wars were over all experienced governmental administrators—being *peninsulares* or *gachupines*—had either left for Spain or lost their lives in the struggle. The change from royal absolutism to formal democracy, even in theory, was too abrupt. The victorious generals who took over administration during the fighting refused to accept the obscurity of private life once the regions returned to civilian stability. The soldiers themselves, accustomed to plunder and adventure, were unwilling to return to shop and fields. The common people had been led by the fancy words of the idealists to expect a Utopia once Spain was vanquished. Now they saw the chaos all around them, and the brilliant uniforms of the generals were the only appealing thing left. It was far more heroic to gain control of government by saber and musket than by congresses and constitutional decrees. The division into classes, with its accompanying conflict of interests, only gave the military leaders the opportunity to pit one class against the other. Coercion by armed force often appeared as the only bulwark against anarchy, the only method of achieving social change in a land 95 per cent illiterate.

Already by Ayacucho, rule by military dictatorship had begun to evolve. Such an ideology is known to historians as *caudillismo;* the Spanish word *caudillo,* chieftain or leader, had been used early to describe the local chieftains of the Plata who were at war with Buenos Aires, and eventually the word came to be universally applied. The illiterate masses saw little difference between the revolutionary liberators and the later *caudillos;* each earned or lost his hero-worship on personal grounds. A *caudillo* was not an hereditary ruler; he never asked for loyalty by divine right. *Caudillismo* moved into the vacuum left by colonial government before colonial government was completely dead, and was to last well into the beginning of the twentieth century. It was a product of social and political conditions. As a pattern of life throughout Latin America it is discussed in the introduction to Part Four, following this chapter.

ECONOMIC AND SOCIAL CONDITIONS
AT THE TIME OF INDEPENDENCE

What had the revolution accomplished then, for the common people, if it brought them neither unity nor democracy nor orderly government? Of what use all the various declarations of independence, the "Plans" of this and that, the impassioned speeches before inexperienced congresses, the editorials in young news sheets? Of what avail the long marches over swamps and snow, the stealthy guerrilla-warfare, the firing squads, the secret meetings, all the loss of life and the devastation, and the heartache through fifteen years up and down a hemisphere? For the creole class it was a victory; now all offices were open to them and the new republics were organized and run by them. For the small middle class of merchants and mineowners, there was freedom from the restrictions of colonial Spain, but long decades of reconstruction lay ahead. For the town-dwelling *mestizo* there came some improvement; he moved up to the position second from the top where the creole had been before, but gained little improvement in his living conditions.

Throughout the fighting and the subsequent *caudillismo* it was the mass of the Indians, inert and apathetic, illiterate and tied to the land of the same aristocratic creoles as before, who continued to suffer. Blood, the more of it white the better, remained the basis of class stratification. Debt slavery, peonage on the *hacienda* where the Indian's father and grandfather had worked, replaced the *encomienda* and the *mita* of the Spanish colonial day, and the Indian seldom sensed the difference. In general, the poorer classes were no better off under the republic than they had been under Spain. Much as the idealists of the independence had made heroes of the "noble Indians" famous in the first struggles against Spain, much as they glorified Lautaro, Cuauhtémoc, or Atahualpa, these sentimentalists had no thought of the living Indians of their own contemporary period.

Negro slaves were probably better off. For most of them the revolutions brought legal freedom. In 1821, Bolívar's Congress of Cúcuta had declared the sons of slaves henceforth to be born free. The next two decades saw a worldwide antislavery movement headed by the Englishman Samuel Wilberforce. The statements about freedom for slaves written into many constitutions of the independence period were actually enforced.

The position of the Catholic Church had been both strengthened and weakened by the independence movement. Free from the *real patronato*, the Church now looked directly to the Vatican, which soon made Concordats, or formal treaties, with the new governments. Control by the Inquisition was over also, as well as the missionary urge from Spain which had meant the heavy expense on the frontier. The Church kept most of its New World lands until the twentieth century, continued as a money lender, and needed no support from a mother country. On the other hand, many key leaders had returned to Spain, the hierarchy was for a time disorganized, and the rank and file of parishioners were becoming more susceptible to new ideas.

The long war, the devastation to crops and grazing lands brought by the locustlike armies which had lived off the country, and the lack of any tax basis for the new governments brought a bankrupt economy and made little improvement of living conditions possible. The new industrialism, rapidly bringing changes to the United States after 1820, was unknown to Latin America in these decades. Plantations were not producing, mines were flooded and abandoned, roads were neglected, harbor facilities had fallen into decay. Each nation had economic chaos as well as political upheaval on its hands in the brave new era. Establishment of a stable government is a first requisite for social and economic progress, and stable government was decades away.

On the credit side economically, the landowners had been freed from royal taxation, and they were able to build a new prosperity for themselves, maintaining their old colonial caste and dominating the government. Merchants found profit in free trade outside the Spanish empire. To increase the middle class, foreign merchants filtered into the new nations, and with them came foreign capital. England dominated Latin American commerce and became the creditor of the new republics, making loans to the bankrupt republics and investing private capital in mines and industries, providing a total of over $100,000,000 before the middle of the century. Such foreign money kept the middle class alive and helped it to become dominant by the twentieth century.

The wars of independence had been accompanied by a fresh wind of cultural development in the urban centers. On Bolívar's return to Bogotá from the wars he had found the city flourishing. Rossini's new music from Italy was played in the capital. Harpsichord concerts were being held, to which Colombia's new élite came in elegant fashions already out of date in France. But the members of this society now had other ideas than merely aping European fashions. They were interested in universities, libraries, and collections of natural history specimens. They wanted to establish botanical gardens. Their most popular learned figure was Dr. Félix de Restrepo, a pupil of Mutis, a native of Antioquia, who taught mathematics, geography, and astronomy rather than the old-fashioned classics, and insisted that his lectures be given in Spanish—no more Latin.

His students, like the intellectuals of most of the revolutionary period, read newspapers and magazines that Latin America had not known before. Bogotá had a regular newspaper and a literary journal, while Mexico City had a periodical publication for each of its two political factions, Centralists and Federalists. There were printing presses in Caracas, Guayaquil, Santiago, Angostura, Arequipa, Cuzco, and Panama where there had been none before. From these presses flowed pamphlets, literary journals, and poetry to carry the new doctrines of "freedom" to all literates. This was part of a new nationalistic culture.

In this writing, rather than in any social and economic changes, we find the real revolutionary spirit, stirring hymns for the new nations calling the Spaniards "vile invaders," "bloody tigers," "insolent despots." The essays and the poetry must not follow European classical patterns, wrote the young hopefuls, though actually the writing did just that. Poetry was supposed to describe the glories of the battles and the geographic wonders of the New World. The writers of the 1820s and 1830s were not outstanding literary lights; rather, they are revered today as symbols of the new freedom.

The two best-known writers were products of no one region. José María Heredia, most widely read poet of the decade, was born in Cuba, which remained a loyal colony. But Heredia was not a loyal colonial. As a student in Havana he had been sentenced as a revolutionary to perpetual exile. Teaching in New York, or wandering in parts of Latin America, he wrote of the beauties of nature and the traditions of Indian civilization. A famous prose writer who helped develop a new South American literature of the independence period was a Venezuelan-born Spaniard named Andrés Bello. He had known the German scientist von Humboldt in Caracas, and had spent ten years in England on missions for Bolívar. Bello is claimed by Chile since he spent the last years of his life there, founded the University of Chile, and published the most widely accepted grammar of the Spanish language while living in Santiago.

Poets glorifying the independence battles and heroes of their own area were legion. Every issue of the contemporary literary journals was filled with their poems. The best-known poem was written by José Joaquín Olmedo, a native of Guayaquil and good friend of Bolívar, representative of the city of Guayaquil at the first Spanish *cortes* of 1810 and first vice-president of Ecuador after independence. He seems to have lived out his life naturally into old age, honored as the author of the poem on the battle just before Ayacucho, his famous "Ode to Junín." It is long and heroic, and school children learn it by heart throughout Latin America today, so that the spirit of the wars of independence shall be in their hearts forever. His ode and his life bridged the end of the old era and the beginning of the new.

Readings

Anderson, R. C., *Diary and Journal, 1814–1826* (1964)

Arnade, C. W., *Emergence of the Republic of Bolivia* (1957)

Belaunde, V. A., *Bolívar and the Political Thought of the Spanish American Revolution* (1938)

Bemis, S. F., *John Quincy Adams and Foundation of American Foreign Policy* (1949)

————, *Latin American Policy of the United States: An Historical Interpretation* (1943)

Bernstein, H., *Origins of Inter-American Interest, 1700–1812* (1945)

Brooks, P. C., *Diplomacy and the Borderlands: The Adams-Onís Treaty of 1819* (1939)

Chandler, C. L., *Inter-American Acquaintances* (2nd ed., 1917)

Chapman, C. E., *Republican Hispanic America* (1937)

Coester, A., *Literary History of Spanish America* (rev. ed., 1928)

Englekirk, J. E., *et al., Outline History of Spanish American Literature* (3rd ed., 1965)

Garcia-Calderon, F., *Latin America: Its Rise and Progress* (1913)

Griffin, C. C., *The United States and the Disruption of the Spanish Empire, 1810–1822* (1937)

Hamill, H. M., Jr., *Dictatorship in Spanish America* (1965)

Hasbrouck, C., *Foreign Legionaries in the Liberation of Spanish South America* (1928)

Henríquez-Ureña, P., *Literary Currents in Hispanic America* (1945)

Humphreys, R. A., *British Consular Reports on the Trade and Politics of Latin America, 1824–1826* (1940)

————, *Evolution of Modern Latin America* (1947)

Jane, C., *Liberty and Despotism in Spanish America* (1929)

Kaufmann, W. W., *British Policy and the Independence of Latin America, 1804–1828* (1951)

Keen, B., *David Curtis de Forest and the Revolution in Buenos Aires* (1947)

Lecuna, V., and H. A. Bierck, eds., *Selected Writings of Bolívar* (2 vols., 1952)

Lockey, J. B., *Pan Americanism: Its Beginnings* (1920)

Manning, W. R., *Diplomatic Correspondence of the United States Concerning the Independence of the Latin American Nations* (3 vols., 1925)

Martineau, H., *A History of the Thirty-Years Peace, 1816–1846* (4 vols., 1877–1878)

Mecham, J. L., *Church and State in Latin America* (rev. ed., 1966)

————, "The Papacy and Spanish American Independence," *Hispanic American Historical Review*, IX, 154–75

Moses, B., *Intellectual Background of the Revolution in South America, 1810–1824* (1926)

Parton, D. M., *Diplomatic Career of Joel Roberts Poinsett* (1934)

Paxson, F. L., *Independence of the South American Republics* (1903)

Perkins, D., *The Monroe Doctrine, 1823–1826* (1933)

Peterson, H. F., *Argentina and the United States, 1810–1960* (1964)

Rappaport, A., *The Monroe Doctrine* (1964)

Rippy, J. F., *Joel R. Poinsett, Versatile American* (1935)

————, *Rivalry of the United States and Great Britain over Latin America, 1808–1830* (1929)

Robertson, W. S., *France and Latin American Independence* (1939)

————, *Hispanic American Relations with the United States* (1923)

Shepherd, W. R., *Hispanic Nations of the New World* (1920)

Spell, J. M., *Rousseau in the Spanish World Before 1833* (1938)

Stevenson, W. B., *On the Disturbances in South America* (1830)

Tatum, E. H., *The United States and Europe, 1815–1823: A Study in Background of the Monroe Doctrine* (1936)

Temperley, H. V., *The Foreign Policy of Canning, 1822–1827* (1925)

Webster, C. K., *Britain and the Independence of Latin America, 1812–1830* (2 vols., 1938)

————, *Foreign Policy of Castlereagh, 1815–1822* (2nd ed., 1924)

Whitaker, A. P., *The United States and the Independence of Latin America, 1800–1830* (1941)

Wilgus, A. C., ed., *South American Dictators* (1937)

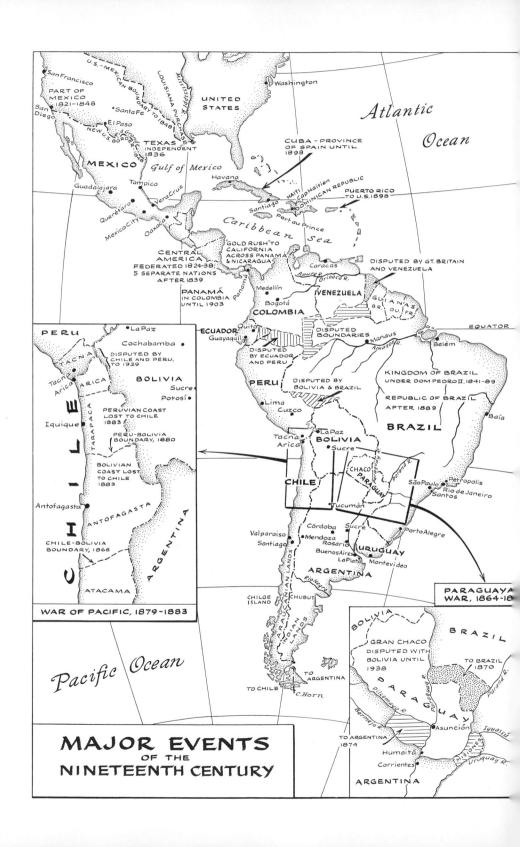

MAJOR EVENTS
OF THE
NINETEENTH CENTURY

Part IV

NINETEEN NATIONS EMERGE
IN THE NINETEENTH CENTURY

THE ENGLISH LORDS of the Admiralty, more than a century
ago, fitted out a sailing ship named the *Beagle* and sent it
on a five-year scientific expedition from the Cape Verde Islands
around South America to Tahiti. On it as zoologist and collector went a young man named Charles Darwin. His English
readers found his journal, *The Voyage of the Beagle,* as interesting for its picture of the world of the pampas, the Plata
River, the Southern Andes, and the newly independent countries there, as for its stories of the world of new biologic species,
both equally unknown to Europeans of the 1830s.

Darwin first saw the flat pampas country when the *Beagle*
anchored at Montevideo, then a town of 15,000 people, "whose
government was very undetermined," capital of a region of
"landowners and cattle herders, with occasional forlorn quiet
little towns." To see this back country he traveled inland "together with a troop of about a dozen riding horses, which were
driven ahead to provide constant changes of mount." He was
put up overnight at "any country farm without charge or ques-

tion," farms whose owners lived in adobe huts; "though rich to the point of possessing thousands of cattle and sheep and unlimited acreage, these people were ignorant of the use of maps and compasses and uninformed as to the existence of England." He admired the cowboys of the Argentine pampas, who were "generally speaking tall and handsome, but with a proud and dissolute expression of countenance," with their heavy mustaches and their "long black hair curling down their backs, their brightly colored garments, great spurs clanking about their heels and knives stuck as daggers at their waists."

When the *Beagle* went down the coast to a small settlement 500 miles south of Buenos Aires, Darwin again disembarked and proceeded by horseback to the port capital, across country unmarked by trails, covered only with grass, tall thistle plants, and an occasional lonely *ombú* tree. Within 200 miles of Buenos Aires he came into an encampment of wild Indians who were fighting the army of Buenos Aires, Indians who were living much as the Sioux or Comanches lived at the same time west of the Mississippi. They let him pass, and even provided him with fresh horses from among their limitless herds of Argentine ponies. Eighty miles out of the city he again came into adobe villages of Spanish-speaking rural folk. After such a trip, Buenos Aires seemed a fine place. "The outskirts of the city looked quite pretty, with *agave* hedges and groves of olive, peach and willow." He remarked on the "great corral on the edge of town . . . where animals are kept to supply food to this beef-eating population."

He was also impressed by the general equality among the people. There was "a member of the legislature who kept a common shop, officers of the army who cannot read and write and yet meet in society as equals." All this was "what could be expected in a new country," but it was "also lamentable how their lives are lost in trifling quarrels."

In 1832 in a camp outside the city Darwin met Manuel Rosas, the famous Argentine dictator, and described him as "a perfect horseman who can drop from a crossbar above a gate on to the back of a wild horse plunging through, and keep his seat without saddle or bridle." By his showmanship and by conforming to the dress and habits of the gauchos, "he has obtained an unbounded popularity in the country." Darwin asked a murderer that he met about his murder victim and his trial. "He spoke disrespectfully of General Rosas, so I killed him!"—this had also been his plea in court, and he "had been at liberty at the end of a week."

The naturalist then went on a wagon trip for fifty days along the Paraná. He found a stable government in Santa Fé, owing to the "tyranny of the local governor or *caudillo* as they call him who has now been seventeen years in power," and he philosophized, "Is tyranny as yet better adapted to these countries than republicanism? . . . The governor's favorite occupation is hunting Indians; a short time since he slaughtered forty-eight."

The next year found Darwin and the *Beagle* off the coast of Chile. He was delighted with Santiago and Chile's central valley: "these singularly fertile agricultural lands so easily irrigated." Here he found more stability of society, more class difference between owners and cowboys—the latter had "a more humble attitude." In Chile's northern desert he saw Indians and *mestizos* working in the nitrate, "the salt-petre works." In 1835 he left the west coast for the islands of the Pacific, having seen and recorded South American life at four cultural levels: gauchos on the pampas, rich landowners in fertile valleys, city dwellers in various growing towns, and miners in the Andes and the deserts. All four were to take part in the "evolution" of the new nations and to bring about a better life for themselves before 1900. Like the species studied by Darwin, some phases of Latin American life remained almost fossilized while others evolved toward modernism.

Not all Latin America was as wild and free as Darwin found southern South America. Lima, Mexico City, and Bogotá were the same large settled cities of colonial days, their populations growing with independence, and their governments the scene of clashes between liberals and conservatives typical of the first years of independence. Bankrupt governments plunged into civil wars which kept the economy backward for a half-century. Eventually the cattle business Darwin saw in Argentina and the nitrate works he saw in Chile brought prosperity—partially because they tempted new immigrant blood in the late 1800s. Germans, Italians, and Swiss farmers came to Argentina and Chile; English businessmen ran the railroads and lighted the cities with the new electricity. Italians, Portuguese, Spaniards, and even Japanese came to help build the coffee industry of the new Brazil. This new vigorous labor supply, leaving the Old World in search of a better future for itself, built a better future for the ABC countries, Argentina, Brazil, and Chile.

Economically these countries became the prosperous ones in the last few decades of the nineteenth century because each was developing a staple product which the industrializing world wanted. Argentina was producing meat and wheat, Brazil, coffee and rubber, Chile, nitrates and copper. With the immigration of peoples had come an immigration of foreign capital to develop these resource-rich regions. To ship the materials out, better communication facilities had to be established. Thus was the old colonial pattern broken.

To a more limited extent, one-crop tropical countries also saw some economic development in the last decades of the nineteenth century, as foreign capital came into other areas of Latin America. Unfortunately, profits from such developments remained in the hands of the old ruling class or were siphoned away to London or New York. In other areas, Latin America remained fossilized throughout the nineteenth century and into the twentieth in the same economic pattern as in the eighteenth century. Agricultural crops were produced by peon labor on large estates, consumed by the immediate locality or transported over bad roads to regional capitals, still carried by oxcart or on muleback for a century after independence.

The landowners maintained the privileges of their old colonial caste, paid out little in taxes, and did not help build up budgets for social improvements at all. The agrarian economy kept the Indians in their old subservient place till after 1900. Political control remained in the hands of a small minority; even the members of the liberal parties seldom worked for Indian betterment. The creole rulers of independent Latin America remained as scornful of manual labor and those who lived by it as the *peninsulares* had been. Every traveler to Latin America in the mid-1800s described the Indians as beggars in the cities or as ignorant peasantry on the land.

After the nations were recognized as independent republics, literary figures became heroes on the local scene only, and can best be considered as part of the local scene described in the following chapters. The break with the Spanish classical modes continued as the fervent young nationalistic writers turned to the French and English romanticists for models. The romantic spirit was applied to descriptions of the diverse and breathtaking landscapes of the New World; scenes of jungle, pampas, and Andes appeared in the new novels. Latin American exploration, conquest, and colonial history were romanticized. Finally, as 1900 approached, the saccharine writing with its European styling began to give way to social novels and modernistic poetry. Latin America slowly worked toward cultural emancipation throughout the nineteenth century.

Darwin had visited during the age of *caudillismo,* and the *caudillos,* such as General Rosas, whom he saw, were to control much of Latin America in the nineteenth century. *Caudillos* themselves were generally military men, literally "Men on Horseback," although there were a few civilian political bosses. Many were ignorant adventurers who waded through blood to power, and even were guilty of personal murders. In the latter part of the century they tended to become more respectable, to ally themselves to the conservative forces of Church and moneyed interests. If they needed elaborate shows of pomp and splendor to hold the masses, they arranged them at great expense, no matter how empty the treasury. Hardly ever were they displaced by a peaceful election. They remained in power till they died, often by assassination, or were defeated in an armed uprising by another military leader who in turn made himself a dictator. Such an armed uprising became the formula for change of ruler. A revolution with a "Plan," or program for reform, would take place against a *caudillo* in power. As soon as the forces of the revolution took over the capital and the army barracks, the words and the suggested reform were forgotten, and another *caudillo* would emerge, backed by his own "personalist" followers, and the vicious circle would begin all over. When a *caudillo* was able to hold the power against the attempts of his enemies for any long period of time, some stability and prosperity would emerge. Under all these *caudillos* there was a mild growth toward democracy in spite of the repression of speech and press, the violations of the constitution, the imprisonment of minority leaders.

Because of the vicious circle of *caudillismo,* revolutions have played an important part in Latin American history since independence. The social stratification produced by racial castes made those at the bottom willing to risk life in one adventure after another, since there was no way to change status by slow upward climbing. Even the poorest could get an army commission or a government job if his hero gained control of the government. The ignorant masses could know nothing of real freedom when there was little education and no free press; they could see only the hopes of being on the right side in a new revolution. Though this hope spurred all races and classes into constant civil war, actually the creoles remained in control, and successful Indian or *mestizo* generals became *caudillos* only when they allowed the creole landowners and merchants to continue as the aristocratic class. Creoles within a nation did not preserve this unity of creole loyalty from one town to another; leaders of society in Guayaquil made war on those of Quito; León and Granada fought each other in Nicaragua; the provinces of La Plata attacked Buenos Aires. *Caudillos* from the countryside fought bloody battles with demagogues from the cities. Peasants and city poor called their generals by heroic names—protector, saviour, deliverer, liberator, regenerator; in turn they were called *Rosasistas* or *Porfiristas* or *Gomezistas*—the Men of Rosas or Díaz or Gómez. Persons were valued more than programs and parties.

The end of the nineteenth century saw the decline of the obvious form of *caudillo* in most of South America. Through all the violence and the insecurity, *caudillos* had curbed anarchy and frightened away foreign intervention, and peace at last reigned. There were still examples of the *caudillo* type in the twentieth century, but there had been a gradual evolution away from violence. A new wealth based on trade and industry, a new wave of immigrants from Europe who had grown up without the old loyalties, a new intellectual class who honored more democratic ideas, a new sophistication brought by railroad and steamship contact with the outside world—all these were spelling the end of *caudillismo* by 1900. Urbanization, industrialization, education, and world contacts were the enemies of personal dictatorship in Latin America.

The endless civil wars in each nation were complicated by border conflicts between nations, brought on by the lack of definite boundaries between units of the Spanish empire. Thus for upward of a century the new republics struggled to maintain themselves against despotism and anarchy at home, invasion from their neighbors, and even—on two occasions—invasion from Europe. Bolívar's sad words, "We ploughed the sea," held true till after the turn of the century.

From such a general overview we must turn to consider first the larger nations—Mexico, Brazil, Argentina, and Chile, each so different and yet so important today—and then the smaller nations, region by region, tracing the events by which this general pattern developed in each area until 1900.

Chapter 20

Nineteenth-Century Mexico;
a Tragedy in Three Acts

LAUNCHING THE NEW REPUBLIC

Thou, Calderón, shalt be the worthy symbol
Of grateful reunion, of eternal friendship,
Which has already changed, in both worlds,
Insane discord into concord and fraternity.[1]

So, WITH MANY MORE verses and choruses, sang the enthusiastic street crowds in Mexico City, two days after Christmas in 1839. They were singing a specially composed hymn as a serenade to Señor Calderón de la Barca, the first minister from Spain to Mexico. His arrival in the city that Christmas season announced the decision of the mother country to recognize Mexico as an independent nation, twenty-nine years after Hidalgo's *Grito* at Dolores. The élite society of Mexico City was in the streets that night in open carriages; crowds of government leaders and their families were listening to the "serenade" from balconies. Madame Calderón de la Barca, the American wife of the new Spanish minister, has

[1] As translated by Madame Calderón de la Barca in her book *Life in Mexico* (New York: E. P. Dutton & Co., Inc., 1946).

described the scene in her century-old travel book, *Life in Mexico*. The greeting the crowd gave the minister showed the nation's delight at recognition: *"Viva la España! Viva la República de Mexico!"*

"Long life to the new Republic!" the singers chanted. But a year later the same lady visitor wrote about the discordant conditions in that republic: "One government has been abandoned, and there is none in its place, one revolution follows another, yet the remedy is not found." She spoke of one revolution as "more noise than slaughter." Mexico had seen a half-dozen such revolutions in its fifteen years since independence, and was well launched in the era of *caudillismo* by the time Madame Calderón de la Barca wrote her book.

The bulk of Mexico's population was illiterate at the outset of independence; the Indians and *mestizos* had never been given the opportunity to learn to read and write. Peonage continued to exist well into the twentieth century, and in spite of the plethora of "rights-of-man" *pronunciamientos*, there remained a wide gulf between the aristocrats and the masses. In such an atmosphere *caudillismo* thrived. Down to 1910 Mexico's history may be told through the lives of three famous leaders—a creole *opéra-bouffe* figure named Santa Anna, an unsmiling Indian lawyer of high integrity named Juárez, and a benevolent and paternalistic tyrant of *mestizo* blood named Porfirio Díaz. In and around the story of these three, other figures rose and fell in brief presidential terms, only two completing their term, of office.

The story began, as told in Chapter 18, with Agustín Iturbide, who, after fighting on the Spanish side, placed himself at the head of the independence movement in 1821, presided over the separation from Spain, and set himself up as Emperor Agustín I in 1822. Later in that year Antonio López de Santa Anna, commander of Vera Cruz and a former soldier in the Spanish service in Mexico, started a revolution for a republic in conjunction with the old liberal revolutionists and forced the already unpopular Iturbide to abdicate. The latter was given a pension on condition that he would go into exile and never return to Mexico again. When he violated this agreement a year later, he was promptly shot.

Now the liberal republicans were to have their first real chance. Santa Anna stood back to let Vicente Guerrero, Guadalupe Victoria, and the intellectual creoles who were with them make the constitution of 1824, modeled after the government of the United States. But the United States had states to unite, whereas Mexico was a single unit which had always been ruled by one viceroy. The constitution-makers arbitrarily created nineteen separate states. It was to prove difficult to run such a federation. Liberals, in the sense of the liberalism described in Chapter 19, wanted a decentralized, Jeffersonian-type republic. They were anti-Church and anti-army; they believed local self-government could be successful. They were opposed by the Centralists, who had behind them the money of the merchants of Vera Cruz and the silver mines of the North, as well as the prestige of the leaders of the Church party. The Centralists wanted the élite of Mexico City to run the nation. Santa Anna sided with them, but the brilliant lawyer and historian Lucas Alamán was their spokesmen.

The liberal Federalists had their chance from 1824 to 1828. Though they brought four years of peace, they had difficulties with finances, with foreign recognition, and with an inadequate and untrained civil service. Guadalupe Victoria, surviving leader of the days of Morelos, was the first president, and the only one for decades to come to last a straight, legal, four-year term. As if stabilizing a new nation was not problem enough, Victoria had to face disputes between two branches of Free Masons, both very active in the new government—the Scottish Rite Masons of the Centralists, backed by the British minister, and the York Rite Masons supported by Joel Poinsett, the American minister. In the election of 1828 the Scottish Rite and Centralist candidate won, but the Federalists protested the elections, and with the backing of Santa Anna and his Vera Cruz garrison they put Vicente Guerrero, that other survivor of the days of Morelos, into the presidency. The next four years were chaotic; Guerrero was overthrown, tried for treason, and executed; the vice-president who succeeded him was ousted by Santa Anna, for the time being a Federalist. Under a new plan Santa Anna got himself elected in 1833.

Since there was no money in the treasury and the two parties were hopelessly split, Santa Anna realized that any president would have an unpopular time. He temporarily retired to his lush plantation at Manga de Clavo in the hills above Jalapa, allowing the Federalist vice-president to govern for him and face the unpopular issues. This man, Valentín Gómez Farías, was one of the most intelligent liberal leaders and the first to attack the neo-colonial order. He tried to institute basic reforms and to run the government efficiently. But the creole aristocracy and church groups opposed his government, just as Santa Anna knew they would, for, despite independence, the colonial regime had simply lived on in Mexico. When cholera broke out in 1834, Santa Anna came out of retirement to quell the riots its spread had caused in Mexico City; Gómez Farías, who had even been blamed for the cholera, quietly took himself into exile in New Orleans. Santa Anna now proclaimed himself a Centralist and organized a new constitution. Mexico was to be dominated by Santa Anna till 1855, while the nation fought a powerful neighbor and lost half its territory.

THE AGE OF SANTA ANNA AND THE AMERICAN WAR

Santa Anna himself was hardly of heroic proportions. At eighteen he was a lieutenant in the crack Spanish regiment of Vera Cruz, with little sympathy for Hidalgo. Sent with troops in 1821 to fight against Iturbide's move for independence, he and his men clashed with the Mexican rebels at 4:00 A.M. on March 29. At 2:00 P.M. the same day he joined the rebels; before midnight they made him a colonel. For another generation Santa Anna was always quick to change his plans or even his nation's plans if such change seemed to his advantage. When Iturbide failed to promote him a year later, he was one of the first to proclaim for the Republic, "a word, of which, as he admitted afterwards, he scarcely knew the meaning." His military exploits in the next two decades were almost comic. He followed his troops in the war against Texas, taking with him an elaborate retinue including a carriage full of fighting cocks. Later in Mexico he took part in skirmishes against French troops trying to take the Vera Cruz customs house in payment of debts, and lost his leg. Then he proceeded to have the dismembered limb buried with pomp and a funeral discourse said over it. Santa Anna always used his wooden leg to arouse sympathy and to publicize his patriotism. Years later angry crowds dug up the bones of the lost leg and dragged them through the streets. Under his Constitution of 1836, the so-called Seven Laws with its *Poder Conservador*, and his later one of 1843, the *Bases Orgánicas Políticas*, sometimes called constitutional despotism, he ruled as virtual dictator, taking on mistress after mistress, while he is said to have maintained a large bodyguard to protect himself from his previous mistresses or their families.

In December 1844 Santa Anna's personal enemies and earnest patriots of all factions drove him to exile in Cuba and returned to the federalist principles of the Constitution of 1824. But the war with the United States, which so many feared, now came upon them and, for lack of a better general, Santa Anna was brought back into the limelight.

A major cause of the "War with the United States" lay in the frontier region of Texas. More sparsely populated than either New Mexico or California at the time of Mexican independence, Texas had settlements only at San Antonio, La Bahía, El Paso del Norte, and a few mission stations among the Tejas Indians. American cotton growers were tempted by the well-watered lands around San Antonio. Moses Austin and his son, Stephen, had planned to found colonies of Catholic Americans in Texas before Mexico's independence. Stephen carried out the plan by getting the consent of the new Mexican government in 1821. Three hundred families of non-slave-holding Catholic Americans were to get 177 acres apiece for farming. Men of the families were to be " of good character" and were to become Mexican citizens. Austin's colonists were welcome because they would be a buffer against both Indian and Yankee to the north, but they only encouraged more Yankees to come—slave-holding Protestants determined to stay American citizens. With no strong Mexican army in Texas to stop them, at least 12,000 Americans had entered by 1827.

Naturally Mexicans interpreted this migration and the attitude of the colonists who came after Austin as acts of aggression, and took steps to correct the situation. Laws were passed to prevent further immigration; Texas was no longer considered a separate governmental unit, but was combined with the state of Coahuila, making a majority of the citizens in the state thus created Mexican and forcing Texas to deal with government officials at Saltillo, hundreds of miles away. The original American settlers, who felt they had come in good faith with the promise of autonomy under a Federalist regime, joined with the many newly arrived squatters, the bad element of border "roughnecks," and the determined slave importers, who proceeded to violate the laws recently passed in Mexico City to emancipate the slaves.

The results of this Texas trouble are well known to most Americans. The Texans declared their independence, formed a provisional government, created a Texan army, and asked aid from the United States. A group of Texans was besieged in the Alamo Mission station at San Antonio and killed to the last man; the Mexican army under Santa Anna was defeated by the Texans in 1836 on the San Jacinto River. The Texans captured Santa Anna and most of his army and forced the opportunistic general, as a price for his liberty, to recognize their new nation with the Rio Grande as boundary. They then set up the "Lone Star" Republic and waited nine years for the United States to annex the territory as a part of the union. Mexico repudiated Santa Anna and announced that Texas was still a state of Mexico and annexation by the United States would be a cause of war. Mexican leaders even attempted to get the aid and friendship of European nations. Activities of American warships on the California coast made the Mexicans frightened for the safety of their entire frontier. The United States also felt she had grievances. There were large unsatisfied claims of many American citizens for forced loans and loss of life and property in the disorders of the continuous revolutions of the Santa Anna period. However, from the Mexican point of view, the war that followed was due to direct aggression. An official book of "Lessons in Mexican History," written for use in Mexican primary schools, says of the cause of the war with the United States: "That country wanted to enlarge its territory at all costs, and chose as the only method to do this the most unjust method, that of conquest."

When the United States Congress voted to annex Texas, the Mexican minister asked for his passport and went home. A bitter boundary dispute had arisen over the exact Texas line. General Zachary Taylor had troops on the Nueces River; when he advanced to the Rio Grande and crossed into the disputed territory along the border, war started. Taylor's troops won an easy battle at Matamoros, then were almost stopped by the patriots at Monterrey. Santa Anna was returned from exile on an American warship and was passed through the American lines so he could offer the Mexican president a negotiated peace. Finding himself in popular favor, he announced that he would shed his last drop of blood for the mother country; he made no attempt at negotiations, but led a poorly armed and underfed group of Indian conscripts northward. These troops fought to a stalemate at Buena Vista, but Santa Anna himself got away in a carriage and came back to Mexico City and again proclaimed himself a hero.

Meanwhile Americans had invaded elsewhere. Troops under Stephen Watts Kearny and John C. Frémont and sailors under John D. Sloat and Robert F. Stockton took New Mexico and California. Other American forces under Winfield Scott had landed at Vera Cruz and climbed up to the plateau, fighting their way through the hill towns. In Mexico City there was no strong leadership, no unified government. The American troops stormed Chapultepec Castle, then a military training barracks. The boy cadets who were left to defend it have become Mexico's real heroes of the "War with the United States." Nine of them, averaging about fifteen years of age, jumped over the precipice at the foot of the castle rather than be captured. They are called the *Niños Héroes*, the heroic children, and there is a great monument to them in Mexico City, while many towns have named streets for them.

At the fall of Chapultepec American soldiers occupied Mexico City, while their generals made peace. By the Treaty of Guadalupe Hidalgo of February 2, 1848, Mexico lost all her frontier region, and not only all claim to Texas, but California, Arizona, and New Mexico as well. However, payment of $15,000,000 was made by the United States into the impoverished Mexican treasury, and all claims that American citizens had against Mexico were settled by the northern republic.

Santa Anna, in disgrace over his defeat, was exiled to Venezuela. The war had left Mexico exhausted; the government had been annihilated; economic conditions were chaotic. Any semblance of national unity had been destroyed. A liberal party of antiprivilege and anticlericalism began to grow, led by the writer Dr. José María Luís Mora. The conservative ruling class, still rallying around that other political writer, Lucas Alamán, actually asked Santa Anna back as "dictator." He was recalled in lieu of anyone else who could hold the difficult presidency for more than a few weeks at a time. This time Santa Anna called himself "Serene Highness" and ruled with an elaborate court and a complete disregard of finances. He had to sell the area called the Gadsden Purchase to the United States for $10,000,000 in order to get funds. He soon squandered this money and in 1855 the liberals threw him out for good in a revolution called the Plan of Ayutla. In 1872, forgotten and poverty-stricken, he returned from nearly two decades of exile, and four years later died unnoticed in Mexico City. The first act of Mexico's tragic nineteenth-century drama was over as its "hero" went off into the wings.

What was the stage setting for Mexico's dramatic story? Madame Calderón de la Barca had found Vera Cruz "desolate and deserted," with the Spanish trade gone and the yellow fever rife as ever. Then she had journeyed from the port to the plateau in nine days in an eight-horse coach. Once in the capital she found the city delightful. The Alameda was a "fine public park," as it still is today, and the fashionable ladies, so "gracious and charming," drove around it in their carriages. On the streets she saw the bright dress called the *china poblana*, originally used by girls from Puebla and still worn at fiestas as the national costume of Mexico. During Holy Week there was "so much parading, and religious dancing," such crowding of society carriages and poor mountain Indians and gay *poblana* girls and barefoot soldiers, such elaborate church expense as to upset Madame Calderón de la Barca's concept of a religious Easter.

The Mexico City in which she saw the Easter parade was a city of 150,000 or 200,000 people. It was still in the center of marshland, though the drainage of the city was again being undertaken in 1840 on a small scale. A four-mile-wide Lake Texcoco still existed, and the villages along its edges oppressed all visitors by their shabbiness and squalor. Fruits and vegetables came into the market via the canals, as they had in Montezuma's time. Other traffic was borne into the city "on mules and donkeys, or on the backs of the lower order of inhabitants." Around the square in front of the cathedral Madame Calderón de la Barca found French tailors and hatters, Spanish wig-makers, German and English shopkeepers—a beginning of the cosmopolitanism that is Mexico City today.

Away from the city, life still revolved around the *hacienda.* The owner was "king amongst his farm servants and Indian workmen." Production on such an *hacienda* was poor. The *haciendas* were too remote from market, transportation was difficult, Indian labor apathetic. Corn and cattle were raised on this type of *hacienda,* but the money made was sent to the landlord in the city, or used by a general in his private army for a revolution. On such *haciendas* lived the Indian and *mestizo,* as they had lived in colonial times, for the "revolution" had not touched them. Madame Calderón de la Barca noted the blanketed Indians of Xochimilco poling their boats among the well-dressed and bejeweled visitors on Sundays, selling poppies. "Watching this scene," she wrote, "one might think Mexico a happy and peaceful land; but there is hardly a link between the blankets and the satins, the poppies and the diamonds."

Those who wore the blankets, however, were still nine-tenths of the population in 1850. Away from Mexico City regional differences among the Indian tribes gave the smaller towns separate color. Madame Calderón de la Barca bought lacquered work in Uruapan from the Tarascans and admired the hand-woven, embroidered blouses and black, pleated skirts worn in the region for a millennium. If she had visited Oaxaca and Tehuantepec she would have seen more striking costumes and more unchanged ways, preserved with the native language by half a million Zapotecans. Oaxaca was then a city of about 10,000 people, with a small veneer of the Spanish-speaking ruling class. Puebla, second city of the Republic, had a population of about 60,000 at mid-century.

To the north, Guanajuato, San Luis Potosí, and Zacatecas were still the silver-mining centers they had been in colonial times, though they were being rehabilitated by English capital in the 1840s after years of neglect. Beyond the mining centers, and the rich valley of Jalisco around Guadalajara with its 40,000 people, lay the country of the cattle ranges, as opposed to *haciendas.* Sonora, Coahuila, Nuevo León still were almost deserts; only a few cattle could be raised. Here, and in the frontier provinces of New Mexico and California which Mexico lost in the 1840s, developed the ranch life of nineteenth-century Mexico, the life of the *rodeo,* the *corral,* the *lasso,* the *vaquero*—the words themselves are a direct heritage from Mexico. In 1845 there were approximately 75,000 Spanish-speaking people in what we call the American Southwest, living an isolated ranch-type life. With the treaty of Guadalupe Hidalgo these were no longer a part of Latin America.

THE ERA OF BENITO JUÁREZ

The years following the fall of Santa Anna gave rise to a period of social revolution known as the Era of Reform. When the liberals, under the Plan of Ayutla, had ousted Santa Anna for the final time, the old Indian Juan Álvarez, illiterate *caudillo* of the state of Guerrero who had had served under Morelos, had been put into the presidency by a group of creole intellectuals. His cabinet included two anticlerical leaders, Miguel Lerdo de Tejada and Benito Juárez. Each of these reformers gave his name to a law: the *Ley Lerdo*, which broke up the large agricultural estates of the Church and offered them for sale in smaller tracts, and the *Ley Juárez*, which abolished the special courts and privileges of churchmen and military officers. Both of these laws were departures from the established mores of the creole aristocrats who had continued to rule Mexican affairs in colonial fashion. The resultant rift between political factions led to the resignation of Álvarez and the transfer of power to the vice-president, Ignacio Comonfort. Meanwhile a constitutional convention had been meeting throughout this stormy year of 1856, and it eventually produced the famous Constitution of 1857, a basic for much of the legal procedure in Mexico today. The principles of the *Ley Lerdo* and the *Ley Juárez* were included in this idealistic document, which became the "banner of liberalism" and the target of conservatives.

Who were liberals and who conservatives at the midpoint of nineteenth-century Mexico? The conservatives were the creole landed aristocracy, changed only from colonial times by the removal of the *gachupines,* or Spanish-born. By 1850 the sons and grandsons of these landlords had become spoiled playboys living in Mexico City or Paris, while overseers despoiled the Indian peons. Added to this class were the privileged and entrenched clergy, still in most cases the second and third sons of the wealthy families. Clerical and military leaders were never brought before the common civil courts but were tried in separate courts, where they were not exposed to stringent punishment. Throughout the next half-century these groups joined every military leader who would preserve for them their vast landed estates, their special position in society, and their *fueros,* or privileges in the eyes of the law.

Opposed to them were many creole intellectuals who had been educated in the philosophies of Rousseau and the political idealism of Jefferson. The Indian leader Benito Juárez joined them in the hopes of a greater equality of races and classes. Since the Church encouraged the aristocracy and was the stronghold of wealth, the liberals considered the land-rich Church their real enemy. The *Ley Lerdo*, designed to break up the estates of the Church and offer them for sale to private owners, meant to end the economic position of the Church. Unfortunately it was so worded as to allow also the private sale of communally owned Indian lands which speculators proceeded to grab cheaply. Church lands, too, fell into the hands of already-rich buyers who could afford them, and the law failed in its attempt to create a class of small farmers. Then came the law to abolish the legal privileges of Church leaders, advanced by Benito Juárez who as Chief Justice of the Supreme Court was now, under the new constitution, next in line for the presidency.

Benito Juárez is the hero of the second act of Mexico's nineteenth-century tragedy, a real hero to most Mexicans today. In a poor village of the non-Spanish-speaking Zapotec Indians in the Sierra of Ixtlán, still five mule-pack days from the city of Oaxaca, Juárez was born in 1806. Orphaned at three by the death of his parents, he could only say of them with pride, "They were Indians of the Zapotec Nation." And old uncle took him for his keep; he slept on the dirt floor of the uncle's adobe shack and earned a handful of tortillas for a day's sheep herding. Of the Spanish language, of the arts of reading and writing, of the mysteries of Oaxaca City, he heard only vaguely from muleteers passing through the Sierra. But when a sheep was stolen and he was held accountable, he ran away, walking all the long distance to see Oaxaca City for himself. He was then twelve years old. A kind family, well-to-do, and of Italian origin, without the prejudice of the Spaniards against the Indian, took him in as a servant boy; a priest, a close intimate of the family, adopted him and sent him to school. He grew up to take a degree in law and to marry the daughter of the family where once he was cook's assistant. As a brilliant young lawyer he served in the Oaxaca legislature and later became governor of the state. He is said to have had the highest integrity known at that time in Latin American politics. A short, dark Indian, morose and silent, he is revered as an "Abraham Lincoln" by most Mexicans today, for he held his nation together through a bitter civil war as well as a foreign invasion.

After his prominence in Oaxaca Juárez spent a period of exile, at Santa Anna's request, working as a cigar maker in New Orleans, and then rose to national prominence as Chief Justice. In 1857 when Ignacio Comonfort, who had attempted an about-face, had been forced to resign and an armed conservative force backing the opportunist General Félix Zuloaga took over Mexico City, the liberals withdraw to Querétaro and proclaimed the Chief Justice president in accordance with the new constitution. Mexico now had two presidents, and plunged into the three years of civil war called the War of Reform. The conservatives had the money and the trained army officers on their side; the liberals were merely bands of guerrillas. Juárez was forced to escape with his cabinet to the Pacific coast, to take ship there to Panama, and to cross the Isthmus and eventually reach Vera Cruz. There he was able to entrench himself, to proclaim it the real Mexico under the true constitution of 1857, and to control the proceeds of the customs house in order to carry on the war. He also decreed more anticlerical reforms, proclaiming the complete separation of Church and state, religious tolerance, the legality of divorce, the secularization of marriage and burial and the end of high clerical fees for them, as well as the establishment of public schools as opposed to Church schools.

Meanwhile in the other regions of Mexico liberals fought bitterly against conservatives, both sides containing many opportunists, both sides committing massacres, destroying opposing villages, and robbing churches. The conservatives lost the final battle in 1860, and the side of anticlerical revolution won the day with Juárez. The losers had made it a holy war, for *"religión y fueros,"* and its bitterness left a deep mark on a devout nation.

The war over, tired Mexico settled down to enjoy an era of reform, with Juárez elected president in 1861 in his own right. But Mexico was prostrate; the treasury was empty; the monthly deficit of the government ran to 400,000 pesos. His nation was heavily in debt to European governments and European banking houses, and many European citizens had claims against Mexico for losses during the War of Reform. It was impossible to pay even the interest on these debts after the war; Juárez could only declare a moratorium for two years. Spain and England were righteously indignant, and willing to join in an effort to collect the debts from the customs at Vera Cruz. But France had other plans. A series of bonds floated by a French-Swiss banker named Jecker made up a large part of the Mexican debt. France was at that time ruled by the ambitious Napoleon III, anxious to win popularity at home by a spectacular foreign policy. He acquired the Jecker bond claims and through them saw a chance to make a puppet state out of Mexico.

The tripartite endeavor to hold the Vera Cruz customs house as a way to collect debts ended in Juárez' promise to pay and the withdrawal of England and Spain. But France remained and sent 6,000 troops inland to intervene in Juárez' government. The French were driven back at the gates of Puebla on May 5, 1862, by the ill-armed but fiercely patriotic Mexicans. One of the young officers defending Puebla that day was named Porfirio Díaz. So complete was the French rout that May 5, *El Cinco de Mayo*, has become one of the most important Mexican national holidays, though this victory only brought a larger-scale French intervention.

Exiles from Mexico and adherents of the Church and the conservative party had sold Napoleon and his devout wife on the alleged popularity a strongly Catholic European monarch would have in Mexico, the need for such stability to "save the persecuted Church," and the chance to build up a strong monarchy to check the expanding United States. The French emperor offered the throne to a young Austrian archduke, Maximilian of Hapsburg, and his wife Carlotta. They were to come to Mexico as monarchs of an independent empire, to be backed by French troops. They were led to believe that all classes of society would welcome them, that a plebiscite in favor of such an empire had been held, and that Juárez and his government comprised a small, unpopular faction.

Maximilian and Carlotta—young, eager, ambitious—were doubtless sincere; they were certainly much more liberal-minded than their Mexican backers, and were anxious to do something to ease the peonage of the Indians, to reform Church procedure, to make themselves popular with all levels of Mexican life. But they had been raised in the hothouse of European royal palaces; they were "benevolent" in the tradition of Divine Right Kings; they were in absolute ignorance of Mexican ways of life and thought and of the new Mexican liberalism growing out of the War of Reform. The polite society which Madame Calderón de la Barca had seen in Mexico City received them in style. They created a "court," an elaborate and expensive one; they remodeled Chapultepec Palace as an ornate royal dwelling; they affected ways of Mexican dress and Mexican food. Without children of their own, they adopted the young grandson of Agustín Iturbide as heir to this "phantom crown."

Meanwhile Juárez, recognized by the United States but harried by the French soldiers, retreated northward until the president himself was living in El Paso del Norte, which is now called Cuidad Juárez, barely inside the territory of Mexico. Down in Mexico the whole project was costing more French lives and money than Napoleon III had anticipated. Maximilian could not balance his budget. He made no debt payments; he trained no army of loyal Mexicans to replace the French soldiers; what popular en-

Detail of the mural of Benito Juárez and the Constitution of 1857, painted by the modern Mexican artist Orozco for the Mexican National Museum of History·
Courtesy Pan American Union.

thusiasm he had aroused soon waned. Meantime, Napoleon III needed his soldiers at home, anticipating trouble with the Prussians. Once the American Civil War was over, Secretary of State Seward wrote notes to Napoleon III about this violation of the Monroe Doctrine. Soon all French troops were withdrawn from Mexico.

Maximilian grew desperate. Informed in October 1865 that Juárez had crossed into El Paso on the American side, he declared all followers of Juárez outlaws, to be shot as rebels. Many of them were executed when captured by Maximilian's small conservative army. Such action turned the scale. Mexican sympathies were now with Juárez. Carlotta sailed to France to urge Napoleon not to abandon them. When, after frantic appeals to the papacy, she realized the hopelessness of their position, she lost her mind, and lived sixty years in a European castle incurably insane, never realizing that Maximilian had reached an equally tragic end. For he had decided to lead his small remaining forces himself, met the Mexican nationalist army at Querétaro, was captured with two of his Mexican generals, condemned to death by a quickly organized Republican "court," and shot on June 19,

1867. The three years of his "empire," though well known in world history, comprised a mere incident in the struggle of Mexico toward liberal constitutional government. But the intervention had created a new consciousness of "Mexicanism." The land-owning Church leaders were discredited by their aid to the foreigners. Juárez, himself a deeply religious Catholic, had won his fight against the Church in politics and in economic power, though the national economy was again prostrate.

In July of 1867 Juárez came back into the city without fanfare, dressed in a black business suit, sitting in a small middle-class carriage, which can still be seen in the museum at Chapultepec among the splendid furnishings brought by Carlotta. Though his term under the Constitution of 1857 had expired, he was elected again in 1868, and tried for four years to carry out his aims: balanced budget, free education, encouragement to manufacturing, democratic elections, and tolerance to all faiths. In 1872 he ran for re-election; his victory was tarnished by an unsuccessful military revolt in favor of the younger Porfirio Díaz; death by heart attack took him suddenly soon after the election, his work unfinished.

THE AGE OF "DÍAZ-POTISM"

Now comes Porfirio Díaz to the center of the stage, carrying with him the banner of reform at first, becoming conservative as he entrenched himself in power. This central figure in the third act of Mexico's tragedy had come from somewhat the same background as Juárez. His widowed mother, an innkeeper of Indian blood in Oaxaca City, had labored hard to keep up a hostelry which muleteers would frequent when they came in from the Sierra. She was able to send Porfirio to the small public school of Oaxaca in the 1830s; he went on to attend the college which Juárez had attended, and even to take classes in law taught by the latter when he was director of the law school and governor of Oaxaca. But Juárez was a man of civilian legality; Porfirio Díaz, though on the Juárez side against Santa Anna, in the War of Reform, and in the Maximilian episode, came to prominence as a military leader. From the underprivileged class as a boy, he became an *hacendado* between military uprisings, making enormous profits on sugar plantations. Though he came to power because of his righteous promises for democratic popular government, he did all but kill it in Mexico.

When Juárez' well-meaning successor tried to succeed himself after a four-year term, Díaz "pronounced" against "re-election" as the greatest sin in Mexican politics. With a private army behind him, he proclaimed another Plan (of Tuxtepec) and made himself provisional president in November 1876. He also arranged his "constitutional election" shortly thereafter. At the end of his four-year term he gracefully kept his promise of no re-election and had his friend, Manuel González, serve in his stead from 1880 to 1884. But Díaz' appointees remained in all important positions, and when they went out for corruption on a large scale, the legal president took the blame for the scandal, just as Díaz had planned he should. Thus Díaz was easily elected again on a "reform" ticket in 1884. He remained president through constant "re-elections" until 1911.

This was the Age of Porfirio Díaz. After years of disorder and civil war Mexico enjoyed a long period of comparative stability under the strong rule of one man, who was nearly always "unanimously" re-elected. In the half century before him, Mexico had lived under two emperors, thirty-six presidents, nine "provisional presidents," twelve "regents," and five "supreme councilors." Now Díaz was the government; there existed only rubber-stamp congresses and courts and his personally appointed state governors to approve his every action.

Yet for years Díaz kept many kinds of people loyal to him. He won the conservative landlords by hushing all talk of dividing estates, for of course he was a large estate-owner himself. The clerical creoles were pleased with him, for though he made much of honoring the Constitution of 1857, he tacitly consented to do nothing to change the position of the Church—a policy in which he was abetted by his very devout young second wife, on whom the clerical class had a strong influence. Díaz held the ambitious intellectual creoles by giving them honorary positions in the government. The educated *mestizos* were the civil servants in his widespread bureaucracy; on him they lived, and without him they starved. Only the Indians gained nothing, but slid ever farther down the social and economic scale. Rival generals had been given offices in the Díaz troops, the *Federales*, or in his mounted police squads, the *Rurales*. On all those who dared voice political protest, Díaz' army used the *Ley Fuga,* the law of flight. The political discontents were taken prisoner on one pretext or another, and then "killed while attempting to escape." *Pan o palo*, bread or the club, was his watchword; and those who wisely decided to accept "bread" in the form of jobs or concessions fared well.

However, Díaz himself had a clear conscience; he was personally honest and he considered himself Mexico's greatest benefactor. Under the *Ley Lerdo*, which had subdivided Indian villages and estates owned by Church groups, foreign investors came into Mexico with millions to spend in acquiring oil lands and cattle-grazing grounds, in developing mines and building railroads. The millions they made from these investments seeped rapidly out of Mexico, for Díaz was a good friend to all foreign companies. They were allowed to exploit Mexican laborers as they pleased, take over unsurveyed Indian lands in open "steals," and pay little or no taxes as they siphoned all the profits to their shareholders in the United States, England, or Germany. Díaz was called "the father of the foreigners and the stepfather of the Mexicans." No one can deny the great material prosperity of the country; the mileage of railroads was expanding every year, the port of Vera Cruz bustled with activity such as it had never seen in the heyday of the Spanish Empire. Textile factories hummed in Mexico City and Guadalajara. Mines were in full production; mine smelters worked silver with new methods at San Luis Potosí and Zacatecas; henequen plantations in Yucatan made twine for all the world; and the famous Blue Hole in the Tampico oil fields produced more oil than any single strike of oil in history up to 1910. Mexico City was served by trolley lines, lit with gas lights, connected by Pullman line via two routes to the United States. And all this in a country that had known no industrialization whatsoever before Díaz' second term in 1880.

But it was all at the expense of the lowest classes of society. The Indians remained tied to the land by imaginary debts kept on the overseers' books from one generation to another, and thus they were never able to leave. In Yucatan the henequen plantations were worked by the grueling labor of the Maya Indians, who were practically enslaved. When they began to die off, the proud, independent-spirited Yaquis of Sonora were rounded up by the *Rurales* police and sent to plantation "prisons" in Yucatan. The peons received such low wages they could not buy shoes and so were ostracized in the towns; barefoot people could not walk the main streets nor sit in the public plazas, according to laws passed to "raise the standards of decency." Through it all rode the mounted police, the famous *Rurales* in their silver-decorated sombreros and their grey uniforms with red ties—splendid on their fine horses, busy "putting down banditry and giving confidence to travelers." They made Mexico "one of the safest countries in the world for all except Mexicans."

Equally famous was another group of Díaz' friends, the *Científicos*, educated creole intellectuals, lawyers, and economists, who influenced him in his old age. Led by the financial genius José Ives Limantour, who balanced the budget and stabilized the Mexican peso in world commerce, these scientifically minded politicians agreed that if the native Mexicans could not run the country efficiently and use the nation's natural resources, the foreign companies were the logical ones to do so. These young creoles honestly believed that dictatorship was the only possible government for their country and they did their utmost to modernize it. They themselves became a new class of rich men in the early 1900s, while Díaz and most of the members of his senate and cabinet were growing old and fossilized. In many ways the rule by 1910 was a type of colonialism with Díaz as the doddering but all powerful viceroy, but without the checks of the laws of the Indies and the royal inspectors. In spite of the great material progress and a thin veneer of sophisticated city culture, the "Peace of Don Porfirio" was a calamity for Mexico. He headed an irresponsible autocracy, a neo-colonialism under the dictatorship of the creoles.

In 1910, when Díaz celebrated the centenary of the Hidalgo revolt with the largest street fiesta ever held in Mexico City, and several carloads of champagne, the nation hailed him as the *Tata,* a kind grandfather. But the growing undercurrent of dissatisfaction was to bring ten years of violent civil war in the new twentieth-century Mexico. The curtain goes down on Don Porfirio, ending the last act of the nineteenth-century drama.

CULTURAL MEXICO
AS SCENERY FOR THE MAIN STAGE

During years of dictatorship and war the Mexicans had difficulty throwing off the cultural pattern of Spanish colonialism. For years the creoles continued to educate their children in the traditional fashion, to ape

European customs, manners, and tastes in art and literature, and to send their sons to study in Paris. Juárez, with a strong interest in a practical education for the masses separate from Church authority, expressed his hopelessness at bringing any change:

> Even though the schools multiplied and be well endowed and teachers well paid, there would always be a scarcity of pupils, so long as the cause which prevents the attendance of children persists. That cause is the widespread misery under which our people live. The man who cannot supply his family with food views the schooling of his sons not merely as something remote, but actually as an obstacle in his daily struggle for existence, since it takes from him his assistants.[2]

This sad commentary summarized the obstacle that still faces education in Mexico today. Juárez as president did, however, liberalize education at the upper level by broadening the curriculum of Mexico City's few secondary schools. Mexico's public schools, as an expression of a true noncolonial *Mexican* culture, came only after 1920.

There was a feeble new literature in the 1800s which attempted to express Mexicanism. From the early days of the Republic, nationalistic poets had written of preconquest days, the truly Mexican story. The poems of King Nezahualcoyotl quoted in Chapter 4 were translated and popularized in the 1830s, and there were sad epics about "The Vision of Montezuma" and "The Prophecy of Cuauhtémoc," written by Ignacio Rodríguez Galván (1816–1842), while the contemporaneous Indians of Aztec blood were scorned in the streets. Though lyric poets were still copying French patterns in 1860, a true Mexican beauty in poetic expression came after the French intervention when there was more desire to publish personal feelings that were not copies of things said in Europe. Two outstanding poets of the 1890s, whose spirit the Díaz regime did not crush, were Justo Sierra (1848–1912), son of another poet by that name, and Manuel Gutiérrez Nájera (1859–1895), who wrote lyrical love poetry. At the turn of the century came a modernist movement, a magazine devoted to *modernista* poetry paralleling the work of young poets in Central and South America. Except for this late blooming, the culture of nineteenth-century Mexico reflected Díaz' own envy of European society. Few writers of the time are even worthy of attention today.

No one single novel is listed among the great pieces of Spanish literature of the ninteenth century, though there are several that are popular reading today—novels that tell of romantic love in the midst of the War of Reform or the battle against Maximilian, of heroes in jail for their political belief, or dying in the armies of the Republic. Their authors almost without exception fought in such armies themselves, and often wrote fiery political articles as well as novels. *La Parcela* (*The Plot of Ground*) is the name and the theme of one of the first unromanticized novels about the Indian love of the land. It was written in the nineties by

2 Quoted in Ernest Gruening, *Mexico and Its Heritage* (New York: Appleton-Century-Crofts, Inc., 1928).

José López Portillo y Rojas (1850–1923), and was a forerunner of the many "land-hungry" novels of the 1920s.

Life itself was so exciting and tragic in Mexico during this period that novelists and political leaders both turned to writing history. Vicente Riva Palacio (1832–1896), a commander in the Juárez army, wrote historical novels—some of them written from a jail cell when the liberals were "out"—founded a literary magazine, and wrote a clever series of biographies of his contemporaries. His "novels" are so accurate as to be almost history. A prolific journalist named Francisco Bulnes (1847–1924), a political and social leader among the *científicos,* wrote complete, though pro-Díaz, histories of the period during which he lived.

The two political leaders of the opposing parties in Santa Anna's time are also remembered for their historical writings. José María Luís Mora (1794–1850), born in Guanajuato in 1794, fought with his pen through the "independence," defied Iturbide, and advocated the Republic. His many liberal articles in the papers of the early 1830s made him the cultural leader of the liberals. Lucas Alamán (1792–1853), the conservative political philosopher and exact opposite of Mora, was also a meticulous but partisan historian and a fine prose writer. Newspapers, though in existence from the time of these opponents, were, throughout the century until 1910, never more than political tools for the party in power. They could not be classed as a cultural influence.

In artistic endeavor the Mexicans of the nineteenth century fell far behind their Aztec forebears. The beautiful Indian handicrafts, sold to tourists in any Mexican center today, were not considered art objects of beauty a hundred years ago. Villagers made them for their own pleasure and use and had to wait for the Indian Renaissance of the 1930s to have them considered "art" and to receive encouragement in their preservation. The Fine Arts Academy in Mexico City, which had been described in the late colonial period by the traveler von Humboldt, had fallen into decay. Though the stability of the 1870s saw 700 students of fine arts in Mexico City, the art taught in the academy, discussed in cultured cities, and hung in drawing rooms was a provincial reflection of Europe. Only in folk art, in saloon paintings, "the people's murals," and in the political cartoons was a native art expression evident.

Music has always been Mexico's great love. Madame Calderón de la Barca went to the Italian opera in Mexico City. Native opera troupes appeared in Guadalajara, in the silver-mining towns, and even went by ship to Spanish California. Family life centered around music. Madame Calderón de la Barca saw pianos in every upper-class Mexico City house, heard daughters of every family play, and listened to singing by family circles every time she went to call. All young men learned to play the guitar, whether for "courting purposes" or not. Tea parties called *tertulias* centered around music—not a formal program as at a reception, but group singing by all. Popular songs were printed as *corridos,* running-ballads, and sold as penny sheets. True to Mexican spirit, they were often concerned with campaigns for the presidency, with the War against the United States, and with the "empires" of Santa Anna or Maximilian:

they were forerunners of the many famous ballads of the Revolutionary period from 1910 to 1920. The popular Mexican "folk songs" sung in staged fiestas in California and New Mexico today, such as *Cielito Lindo* and *Rancho Grande*, were sung in Mexico in the 1840s and 1850s. Throughout all three acts of the nineteenth‑century drama, the color, the music, the native charm of the people were there on the stage, year in and year out, no matter how confusing the plot of the play.

Readings

Barker, E. C., *Life of Stephen F. Austin* (2nd ed., 1949)
———, *Mexico and Texas, 1821–1835* (1928)
Beals, C., *Porfirio Díaz, Dictator of Mexico* (1932)
Bells, A. H., *Rehearsal for Conflict: The War with Mexico, 1846–1848* (1947)
Bernstein, H., *Modern and Contemporary Latin America* (1952)
Bernstein, M., *Foreign Investments in Latin America* (1966)
Bert, V. M., *Central Banking in Mexico: Monetary Policies and Financial Crises, 1864–1940* (1957)
Binckley, W. C., *Texas Revolution* (1952)
Blasio, J. L., *Maximilian, Emperor of Mexico: Memoirs of His Private Secretary* (1934)
Callcott, W. H., *Church and State in Mexico, 1822–1867* (1926)
———, *Liberalism in Mexico, 1857–1929* (1931)
———, *Santa Anna* (1932)
Calderón de la Barca, Mme., *Life in Mexico During a Residence of Two Years in That Country* (many editions)
Callahan, J. M., *American Foreign Policy in Mexican Relations* (1932)
Caruso, J. A., *Liberators of Mexico* (1954)
Castañeda, C. E., ed., *Mexican Side of the Texas Revolution* (1928)
Corti, E. C., *Maximilian and Charlotte of Mexico*, trans. C. A. Phillips (2 vols., 1928)
Cosío-Villegas, D., *United States versus Porfirio Díaz* (1963)
Cotner, T. E., *Military and Political Career of José Joaquin de Herrera, 1792–1834* (1949)
———, and C. E. Castañeda, eds., *Essays in Mexican History* (1958)
Crawford, W. R., *Century of Latin American Thought* (1961)
Dabbs, J. A., *The French Army in Mexico, 1861–1867* (1963)
Dawson, D., *The Mexican Venture (French Intervention)* (1915)
Flandrau, C. M., *Viva Mexico* (1908)
Garber, P. N., *Gadsden Treaty* (1923)
Gardiner, C. H., "Survey: Foreign Travellers' Account of Mexico, 1810–1910," *Americas*, III (1952)
Glick, E. B., *Straddling the Isthmus of Tehuantepec* (1959)
Gonzalez Pena, C., *History of Mexican Literature*, trans. G. B. Nance and F. J. Dunstan (2nd ed., 1943)
Gregg, R. D., *Influence of Border Troubles on Relations between the United States and Mexico, 1876–1910* (1917)
Gruening, E., *Mexico and Its Heritage* (1928)
Hamill, H. H., Jr., *Dictatorship in Latin America* (1965)

Henry, R. S., *The Story of the Mexican War* (1950)

Johnson, R. A., *The Mexican Revolution of Ayutla, 1854–1855* (1939)

Knapp, F. A., *The Life of Sebastian Lerdo de Tejada, 1823–1889* (1951)

Maissin, E., *The French in Mexico and Texas, 1838–1839* (1961)

Manning, W. R., *Early Relations between the United States and Mexico* (1916)

Matias, R., *Mexico and the United States* (1898)

McBride, G. M., *Land Systems of Mexico* (1923)

Mecham, J. L., *Church and State in Latin America* (rev. ed., 1966)

Morton, V., *Terán and Texas* (1948)

Parkes, H. B., *History of Mexico* (3rd ed., 1960)

Pike, F. B., *Conflict of Church and State in Latin America* (1964)

Portes Gil, E., *The Conflict between the Civil Power and the Clergy* (1935)

Priestley, H. I., *Mexican Nation* (1923)

Purcell, A., *Frontier Mexico, 1875–1878: Letters of William L. Purcell* (1963)

Ramirez, J. F., *Mexico During the War with the United States*, trans. W. V. Scholes (1950)

Read, J. L., *The Mexican Historical Novel, 1826–1910* (1934)

Relyea, P. S., *Diplomatic Relations between the United States and Mexico under Porfirio Díaz, 1876–1910* (1928)

Rives, G. L., *United States and Mexico, 1821–1848* (2 vols., 1913)

Rippy, J. F., *Joel R. Poinsett, Versatile American* (1935)

———, *United States and Mexico* (rev. ed., 1931)

Roeder, R., *Juárez and His Mexico* (2 vols., 1947)

Romanell, P., *Making of the Mexican Mind* (1952)

Ruiz, R. E., *An American in Maximilian's Mexico* (1959)

Sartorius, C., *Mexico about 1850* (1961)

Scholes, W. V., *Mexican Politics during the Juárez Regime, 1855–1872* (1957)

Sierra, J., ed., *Mexico—Its Social Evolution* (2 vols. in 3, 1900–1904)

Simmons, M. E., *The Mexican Corrido as a Source for Interpretive Study of Modern Mexico, 1870–1950* (1957)

Simpson, L. B., *Many Mexicos* (3rd ed., 1952)

Smart, C. A., *Viva Juárez* (1963)

Smith, J. H., *Annexation of Texas* (1911)

———, *War with Mexico* (2 vols., 1919)

Sprague, W. F., *Vicente Guerrero, Mexican Liberator* (1939)

Stevenson, R., *Music in Mexico* (1952)

Thompson, W., *Recollections of Mexico* (1846)

Tischendorf, A., *Great Britain and Mexico in the Era of Porfirio Díaz* (1961)

Ward, H. G., *Mexico in 1827* (2 vols., 1829)

Wyllys, R., *French in Sonora* (1932)

Chapter 21

The Waxing and Waning
of the Brazilian Empire

THE PEACEFUL BREAK
BETWEEN BRAZIL AND THE HOMELAND

A POOR BOY of mixed Portuguese, Indian, and Negro blood named Antônio Gonçalves Dias (1823–1864) was sent on a scholarship by the ruler of Brazil, the wise Emperor Pedro II, to study at the University of Coimbra in Portugal. There in 1843 he dreamed of the palm trees of Rio and the musical *sabiá* bird of Brazil's tropical woodlands. His famous *Song of Exile* has been set to music to become almost a folk song of the people:[1]

> Land of mine with waving palms,
> The sabiá is singing there.
> Birds do not warble as sweetly here,
> Not here, nor anywhere.

[1] Translated in Samuel Putnam, *Marvelous Journey: A Survey of Four Centuries of Brazilian Writing* (New York: Alfred A. Knopf, Inc., 1948).

Our meadows have more and fairer flowers,
More stars in the heavens above.
There is more life within our woods,
Within our lives more love.

The popularity of this poem shows a Brazilian patriotism which had not existed in 1800, when Brazil was a few sprawling cities of mixed peoples, stretching a thousand miles along a tropical coast and only 200 miles inland. Baíans knew or cared little for the people of Rio or Pernambuco and vice versa. That there grew up a nationalistic feeling at all, that an exiled student could sing of the universal appeal of Brazilian birds, flowers, and woods, is partially due to the same Emperor Pedro II who sent the poet to the university. The Emperor was a grandson of the ruler of Portugal of Napoleonic times. How did it happen that he governed an independent Brazil in the 1840s, and indeed the 1880s?

In such a sprawling colony as Brazil, with a population of 3,617,000, less than one-fourth of whom were white and about one-half Negro slaves, there had been no strong movement for independence. A few literary discussion clubs, a few educated intellectuals talked of the French Enlightenment and the North American independence movement. There was a small plot to establish a republic in Minas Gerais, a mining area in the interior. Here young Joaquim José de Silva Xavier, known to history as Tiradentes, "the Toothpuller," led an abortive revolt and drafted a constitution in 1789, but this "precursor" was soon executed. The independence for which he suffered martyrdom was to come gradually and under the leadership of the royal house of Braganza from Portugal. True, Brazil had many of the grievances against the homeland that were felt in Spanish America, but the Brazilians escaped the bloody revolution and the harrowing travail of rebirth as an independent nation that were experienced in other parts of South America.

The colonial period in Brazil, as elsewhere in Latin America, ended with the chaos incident to the Napoleonic era. In 1807 and 1808 Portugal found herself in the same position as Spain, faced with invasion by Napoleon. In a dramatic flight, however, the Portuguese royal family got out of Lisbon by sea in time to escape Napoleon's troops. The ruler of Portugal was the mentally ill Queen Maria I, whose middle-aged son John acted as regent for her. On November 29, 1807, convoyed by British naval vessels, the Queen, the Prince Regent, his wife, his two little sons, and a staff of valets, secretaries, and lesser noblemen amounting to over 10,000 persons sailed out of Lisbon harbor while the cannons of Napoleon's general could be heard within the outskirts of the city. Though library, archives, and furniture were brought along, the packing was incomplete; many of the wardrobe trunks were left on the dock. With only evening dresses and little soap and water this motley court set sail for Portugal's colony in the New World. After six weeks of rough Atlantic weather the courtiers hove to off the port of Baía, January 22, 1808, where the surprised Brazilians loaned them all the velvets and lace available in the backward colonial city and, after the first shock at having royalty in their midst, welcomed them effusively to the New World. Prince John, the regent, an easygoing, plump, intelligent man, had been something of a laughingstock in Portugal. Here he felt warmed and welcomed. He offered the Baíans any favor. They asked that their port be opened to the ships of all nations; John easily granted this request to apply to all ports on the coast, since this would help his English allies anyway. Thus he removed with one smiling word a cause of friction which had embittered the other New World colonies against their mother countries. Prince John's coming, in the long run, was to make a Brazilian war for independence unnecessary.

In his borrowed velvets he went on with his whole entourage toward Rio, where word of his coming had preceded him, and where he arrived on March 7, 1808. All the best houses in town were turned over to the royal court. The demented queen mother was ensconced in a Rio convent, where she died eight years later. In those eight years her son had made Rio de Janeiro the capital of the whole Portuguese empire and the largest city in South America. He had raised Brazil to a position of equal status with Portugal; it was a kingdom and no longer a colony. On March 20, 1816, after his mother's death, Prince John was crowned in Rio, although Napoleon had been for many months in exile on St. Helena. Brazilians were heavily taxed to support the Portuguese court, and some Brazilians never got their houses back, to say nothing of their laces and velvets, but the country prospered as it never had as a colony. The harbor was improved and running water was brought into the city. Rio became a center of society; King John established schools, libraries, and printing presses, started an institute of fine arts, set up botanical gardens, and invited scholars and scientists to Brazil. Happy in Brazil as he had never been in Lisbon, he perhaps heard the *sabiá* singing himself.

The Portuguese who had come with the king remained the aristocracy and received the favored jobs in government, while they treated the rich Brazilians with arrogance and regarded their own stay in Brazil as a temporary exile. John's wife, Carlota Joaquina, the witchlike woman who was the Spanish King Ferdinand's sister, involved him in difficulties with the Brazilians as well as with the Argentines. In the wars with Buenos Aires which followed, John gained Uruguay, which he called the Cisplatine Province. He had only one Brazilian revolution to quell, a revolt in Pernambuco; the Brazilians soon rallied again in loyalty to King John.

Finally conditions at home in Portugal changed John's successful rule in Brazil. Napoleon's troops had long since evacuated, and there was the postwar depression and unrest in the mother country. The absence of the court and the king contributed to the instability, and Portuguese leaders were demanding that John come back to make Lisbon again the capital of the empire and Brazil once more a colony. It was feared that "republicanism" might rear its ugly head in the homeland; revolution had broken out in Portugal and liberals had called a constitutional convention, influenced by the 1820 revolt in Spain; and several Brazilian states had elected delegates to go to it. If the monarchy was to be preserved on both sides of the Atlantic, John must return. Reluctant to do so after his thirteen years of contentment in Rio, nonetheless, for patriotic and dynastic reasons, he left for home on April 26, 1821, taking with him his hag of a wife and 3,000 Portuguese courtiers, who emptied the treasury before they left and took everything else of value they could lay their hands on. John's eldest son, Prince Pedro, was left in Brazil as regent.

Both John and his son knew that the spirit of independence was making gains in the neighboring Spanish colonies; they could foresee an ultimate break between Brazil and Portugal. Two years later, Dom Pedro was to write to his father in Portugal: "I still remember and shall always keep in mind, what Your Majesty told me in the ship's cabin two days before sailing—Pedro, if Brazil must break away, I would rather see you, of whose respect I am certain, take it, than some unknown adventurer!"

Events had moved rapidly in those two years. True to the liberal attitude he meant to maintain, John VI on his return to Lisbon had met with a congress or *côrtes* in Portugal. Soon he quarreled with its members about the status of Brazil. The *côrtes* members wanted Brazil subservient to Lisbon. They abolished the institutions set up by John in Brazil, renewed the Portuguese monopoly on commerce with the "colony." They ordered Pedro, known to be poorly trained for the European throne, to be brought to Portugal to finish his education. When these orders were known in Brazil, Pedro was flooded with requests to remain in Rio.

Pedro himself was torn between allegiance to his family and allegiance to his followers in Brazil. The "Patriarch of Brazilian Independence," José Bonifâcio de Andrada e Silva, an intellectual scientist who had been educated at Coimbra in Portugal, was the strongest influence on Pedro. He believed that a constitutional monarchy under the young monarch separate from Portugal was the best solution of all Brazil's difficulties. On January 9, 1822, Pedro disobeyed the order to go to Lisbon, and sent a reply to his many petitioners—"*Fico!*"—I will remain.

Now Pedro was in the difficult position of defying the homeland. The Portuguese garrison in Rio had tried to force Pedro and his family on board a ship bound for Lisbon, but a local militia was raised which got control, first of the hills and then of the city, and forced the Portuguese garrison itself, not Prince Pedro, to go home. Meanwhile Pedro appointed a new cabinet in which his mentor José Bonifâcio was prime minister, hoping to unify the varying factions in all the provinces. During the spring he made a tour of Minas Gerais and received enthusiastic support there. In May he took the title of "Perpetual Defender of Brazil"; in June he issued a call for an assembly to draft a constitution. Then he went for a horseback tour of another of his provinces—São Paulo.

Here on September 7, 1822, as his horseback party was halted on the little stream of Ypiranga near São Paulo, couriers caught up with him to bring him a message from Portugal abolishing his new cabinet and ordering the prosecution of its members. It had been forwarded from Rio with a note from his intelligent and popular young wife: "The apple is ripe; harvest it now or it will rot." He knew what "harvest" meant. Standing up in the saddle, he unsheathed his sword. "Comrades," he yelled in the famous *Grito de Ypiranga,* "the Portuguese *côrtes* wishes to reduce Brazil to slavery; we must forthwith declare her independence. Independence or death! We are separated from Portugal!"

On his return to Rio he was proclaimed "Constitutional Emperor of Brazil," and soon after crowned as Pedro I, December 1, 1822. Thus revolution had come from the top without violence and with little real support or knowledge on the part of the masses. Political and social reforms were no part of it. In striking contrast to Spanish America, Brazil had won its independent position without a battle; Portugal was in no position to make war on her giant colony. Besides, Pedro soon acquired an experienced naval commander, the ubiquitous Lord Cochrane, and had army enough to continue the fight in the three-cornered wars in Uruguay. England recognized the new state—a good place to promote British trade—and the mother country had no choice but to yield to the pressure of her long-time British allies and confer recognition also. This was done in 1825; United States recognition had already come the year before. The wars for independence in Spanish America had lasted fifteen years; Brazilian independence was accomplished in little more than fifteen months.

The new emperor had promised to call an assembly, and elections were held for it immediately. Church dignitaries, plantation owners, and mining prospectors met in Rio, May 3, 1823, a motley crowd symbolic of the mixed groups which were to run Brazil. They discussed humanitarian ideas, and disagreed with the obstinate and strong-minded young ruler. José Bonifâcio and his two brothers resigned from the government in July of 1823, and founded an anti-Pedro newspaper. By November, Pedro had exiled the Andrada brothers, dissolved the assembly, and appointed a new Council of State to draft his own constitution. This document, drafted in 1824 and remaining in effect till 1891, provided for a constitutional monarchy, a bicameral legislature elected indirectly, a ministry responsible to the emperor and not to the legislature, and a Council of State. Though it guaranteed freedom of press and religion, it declared Catholicism the religion of the state, and the person of the emperor sacred. It did provide that the ruler could not meddle in Portuguese affairs.

Immediately the popularity of the young monarch began to decline. He did not call the legislature which his constitution had provided until 1826; when it met he quarreled with it and governed without regard to a parliamentary majority. On his southern frontier he lost the Cisplatine Province of Uruguay after a three-year war; in the north Pernambuco revolted again and formed a Federal Republic of the Equator with three other northern states, which took six months and Lord Cochrane's fleet to put down. Within another two years there were riots against him in Baía and demands for his abdication in Minas Gerais, for he was turning more and more toward his old Portuguese friends, and was shocking Rio society as well.

Pedro's own personal life brought him as many critics as did his arbitrary government. He had been only twenty-three years old in 1822, handsome and warm-hearted, with little formal education. As the problems of government became too heavy for him he picked up many "undersirable" friends on the outer rims of society, and caused his pleasant and popular wife, the Austrian Princess Leopoldina, a mortal sickness by openly establishing a São Paulo girl in Rio as his mistress. Even though he married a Bavarian princess when his empress died, and forsook his mistress for the new bride, he had lost what little remaining loyalty the people had for him.

Meanwhile, his father had died in Lisbon, and the Portuguese throne was once more empty. Though Pedro had arranged that his oldest child, his seven-year-old daughter Maria da Gloria, be crowned Queen of Portugal, he feared the plans of his own younger brother and his scheming Spanish-born old mother back in Portugal. By 1830 he was so concerned in Portugal's affairs as to create the "Portuguese Question" in Brazil. His critics accused him of being unconstitutional and anti-Brazilian. There were street brawls in Rio, defection in the army, and indiscipline in general. Return to Portugal seemed the Emperor's only way out. His arbitrary government, the loss of his popularity with all classes including the commercial leaders, the antagonism of the army, and his loyalty to the Portuguese forced his abdication, in spite of the progress toward individual liberty and constitutional government made under him.

On April 7, 1831, Pedro wrote out his abdication in favor of his second child, a five-year-old son. José Bonifâcio had been allowed back from exile in 1828; now Pedro, once his enemy, named him tutor for the little prince. Then Pedro sailed back to Lisbon, his birthplace, to live the remaining three and a half years of his stormy life fighting for his daughter's right to the Portuguese throne. The little son, guided by José Bonifâcio, was to rule as a constitutional monarch, Don Pedro II, a true native-born Brazilian without any "Portuguese Question" in his life.

There followed a period known as the regency, a time of stress for Brazil through the 1830s. The abdication did not solve Brazil's problems, and they could not be solved by a five-year-old boy. There were revolts up and down the coast for the next ten years. In Rio a board of three regents ruled in the child's name for three years, 1831-1834, with the child's former tutor, José Bonifâcio de Andrada, on the board, aided by the able Minister of Justice, Father Diogo Antonio Feijó. This governing group was backed by the moderates and by the liberal friends of Pedro I. But disorder in the provinces and lawlessness in the city continued. In 1834 congress amended the constitution to give the provinces more authority, and abolished the triple regency. Father Feijó then became the sole regent. After two years of strong government in the name of the young monarch, Father Feijó was replaced by the conservative Pedro Araujo Lima. The regency period taught the Brazilians that a strongly centralized power was essential to maintain order and preserve the union. During this period political parties began to form, and the leaders received training in parliamentary government. Tired of a conservative regency, a group of liberals formed a coalition in July 1840 to declare Prince Pedro king in fact as well as name. The constitution had required that he be eighteen years old, and he was only fifteen, but the General Assembly overrode this unconstitutionality. The prince declared himself "willing to rule," and on July 11, 1841, he was crowned Emperor Pedro II.

PEDRO II, A REMARKABLE BENEVOLENT DESPOT

The boy prince—his father and his pretty new stepmother gone forever to Portugal—had been reared scientifically by tutors. His mother Leopoldina had had scholarly interests unusual for her time. At six he had been a "rare and unusual child," who could read and write Portuguese and English and was taking lessons in French. This precocious interest in languages persisted into old age; at sixty he was eagerly learning to speak ancient Hebrew. The cultural history of Brazil from 1840 to the 1880s is bound up with this remarkable emperor. He was to rule with a firm hand, but in a soft velvet glove. The "Age of Pedro II" was Brazil's Golden Age.

Ruler in his own right at fifteen, he was married at eighteen to a plain-faced Italian princess, three years his senior, who bore him four children, two sons and two daughters. Both sons died in early childhood; his oldest daughter, Isabel, became his heir and was strictly trained in the responsibilities of the throne. The royal family remained happy in its domesticity, democratic in manner and dress, and never kept elaborate court. The emperor was interested in education, read widely in educational philosophy, and visited schools on trips to America and Europe. He was the best-educated person in Brazil in his lifetime. He also accomplished so much in the way of international improvements, unification, and foreign relations as to compare favorably with any enlightened European ruler of the last two centuries. A dignified, reserved, handsome man six feet four inches tall, he was described, even in his old age, as a "library on top a locomotive."

His first task as emperor was to wipe out the heritage of civil war left over from the regency, the so-called Ragamuffins' (*Farrapos*) War which had been raging in Rio Grande do Sul for years, and revolts in other regions as well. One by one his armies controlled these separatist movements. By 1848 all such splinter rebellions were permanently settled and unity achieved in the decade of the "*sabiá's* song." This had meant the development of a centralist government in which the emperor and his advisors chose the provincial governors. Pedro II used his personal power wisely; he had maintained his father's constitution of 1824, in which the cabinet was responsible to the ruler not the legislature, but he believed in the British cabinet system, and aimed to choose most of his ministers from the majority party in the Chamber. The Chamber of Deputies was elected indirectly by manhood suffrage, limited by property and literacy restrictions on voting. Pedro himself chose the members of the Senate, but showed care and rare impartiality in his choice. Although the indirect election system kept the power in the hands of the land-owning and slave-holding class, while the masses of free laborers and slaves had no voice in the government, the political stability and the long years of progress and economic development improved conditions gradually for all classes. Two parties existed side by side—conservatives who believed in keeping the power in the central government and controlling the provinces from Rio and in high suffrage qualifications, and liberals who stood for subordination of executive to legislative powers, autonomy in the provinces, and progressive social and economic measures with a broader suffrage basis. In the latter part of the reign, by 1871, a Republican Party emerged, but the first thirty-five years of Pedro II's rule were without serious party strife.

In foreign affairs, the pacifistic-minded emperor had few war troubles on his hands, once all his provinces were brought into satisfied union with the center. Since revolutions were constantly occurring in the eight Spanish American countries bordering on Brazil, there were bound to be repercussions. Pedro II intervened in such revolts only twice, however. He sent troops to aid in the overthrow of the Argentine dictator Rosas, and he was one of the allies in the war against the dictator Francisco Solano López of Paraguay in the 1860s. Brazil won this five-year war and gained thousands of square miles on the Paraguay border. But the Brazilians suffered 50,000 casualties and spent $300,000,000; Pedro himself was never so popular in military circles again. Brazil learned from this war to settle difficulties by arbitration while concentrating on internal improvement.

In Pedro's dealings with the United States, he was a highly honored figure and visitor of state, though his slave-minded subjects sympathized with the South in America's Civil War and invited Confederate leaders to migrate to Brazil after 1865. He traveled in France as a scientist and a poet and spent some days with Victor Hugo. He was welcomed on several occasions in Portugal where the son of his sister, Maria da Gloria, was ruler. Tolerant and open-minded abroad, he also believed in real religious tolerance at home. His government aimed to help all religions and encourage European immigration by maintaining ministers of any sect to which groups of new immigrants might belong. He had laws passed recognizing the civil marriages of all non-Catholics, and allowed the maintenance of Protestant and Jewish chapels and burial grounds, a practice in opposition to that of most Spanish-speaking countries of South America in his time. Though he was a practicing Catholic himself, Church authorities began to rise against him near the end of his reign because of his leadership in the Masonic lodge in Rio which was regarded as anticlerical by the leading bishops, and because of his belief in separation of Church and state. This came at the same time as the crisis over slavery and helped lead to the downfall of the empire. Before that can be discussed, some mention must be made of economic and social progress in the "Age of Pedro II."

ECONOMIC, CULTURAL, AND SOCIAL GROWTH IN THE DAYS OF DOM PEDRO

In 1820 Rio de Janeiro stretched a half mile along its bay and had 100,000 people. In 1853 it extended three miles and boasted 350,000 people, though a traveler called it "an unsanitary and bad copy of Lisbon." The same traveler returned in 1869 to see the bay shore settlement "a circuit of many miles," and a home for 600,000 people. It was still a city of narrow streets, pink, blue, and yellow tile houses, and singing street merchants. Well-to-do ladies traveled through the streets in sedan chairs carried by liveried slaves. A traveler considered the Brazilian ladies "too fat and overdressed" and always several years behind the Paris fashions, a cruel remark that can no longer be made of the ladies of São Paulo and Rio. Most of the women stayed at home as they had done in colonial times, were married very young, gave birth to twelve or fifteen children, and were "withered or corpulent at twenty-five."

The home was the center of life; family birthdays and saints' days were celebrated with enthusiasm. Married sons brought their brides home, and several families, all related, lived under the same roof. During Carnival everyone was in the streets, however, for the Rio Carnival was as hilarious then as now. Easter itself was more boisterous than in Spanish America, with rocket explosions all day on "Halleluja Saturday," indicating the same love of fun and celebration that persists in Brazil today.

In spite of the hilarity, Rio, like other cities in the tropics before the discovery of the causes of disease, was an unhealthy place in which to live. Pedro called medical conferences as early as 1846 to discuss the high rate of infant mortality. One traveler was informed by a sugar grower near Rio that "not half the Negroes born in this estate live to be ten years old." Swamps behind the city of Rio remained undrained and mosquitoes filled the air, although an elaborate aqueduct project was constructed to bring pure water into the central Carioca Fountain—that fountain from which modern "Cariocas" take their nickname as residents of Rio. Pedro II built a summer resort at Petropolis, in the hills where mosquitoes did not come, to get his family away from the epidemics of yellow fever that so often hit the city.

The sick in the city were cared for by orders of nuns or by "brotherhoods" of laymen similar to the *hermandades* of Spanish America. Because of the charities of such brotherhoods, begging was not very necessary for the poor of Rio, and after 1855 was only done by "licensed" beggars whose claims the authorities had investigated. As to danger in the streets, a Protestant missionary reported in 1855, "I have found few cities more orderly than Rio de Janeiro; and the police are so generally on the alert, that in comparison with New York and Philadelphia, burglaries rarely occur. I felt greater personal security at a late hour of the night in Rio than I would in New York."

In the provinces there was little of the city life of Rio. Country life was the same as in the colonial period, the plantation life of master and slave. Baía impressed travelers in 1855 with its commercial houses on the upper level, "edifices which would adorn the business portions of London, Paris, or New York." But the lower town was "old and wretched" even then, crowded with peddlers, "and at times as filthy as the streets of New York." No wheeled vehicles could be used in Baía because of the steep ascent from the lower town.

Baía lived on sugar, and sugar was still considered Brazil's staple crop in the 1870s. The Imperial Agriculture Institute of Rio cultivated twenty-one varieties of sugar cane on Dom Pedro's model plantation, distributed large numbers of new experimental plants, and was constantly recommending new methods. Brazilian tobacco was also exported and "competed well with Havana," while the cotton of Pernambuco was "being substituted in Europe for that of New Orleans."

Coffee plantation, or *finca,* **near São Paulo. Coffee was introduced by Pedro II in 1872 as an experimental crop to be cared for by European immigrants.** *Photo by Helen Miller Bailey.*

We are so accustomed to thinking of Brazil as the coffee country that we forget that coffee was never planted in Brazil until 1727, and then only when a few plants were smuggled out of French Guiana. Rio de Janeiro's plantation owners planted it as a crop toward the end of the colonial period, and between 1800 and 1860 increased its production a hundredfold. A frontier town, home of the historic *bandeirantes,* São Paulo slumbered in the 1860s with 25,000 inhabitants. It stood fourteenth among cities in a nation not given to cities. In 1872 coffee began to be planted in this cool upland state, tended by immigrant laborers from Europe and not by slaves. The real "boom" of São Paulo occurred under the Republic after 1890 and not during the Empire. Coffee had small "booms" in other areas, particularly in the region of Vassouras.

Rio Grande do Sul was England's chief source of hides, dried beef, and tallow before the development of freezing facilities in Argentina. It was a country of independent spirit, threatening to join Uruguay, and later Paraguay. Descriptions of life there among the hard-riding *vaqueros* sound like stories from Argentina more than from tropical Brazil, for the area is geographically an extension of the pampas. Dom Pedro had an interest in the cattle country from boyhood, and he encouraged European immigration there, exhorting the farmers to take up small personal holdings and produce dairy cattle, sheep, hogs, corn, and flax.

The story of the Amazon area in Dom Pedro's time is the story of a "boom" leading to a "bust." Explorers in the 1700s had seen the Indians carrying rubber bags, had learned the Indian process of making latex, and sent out rubber to be used in galoshes, pencil erasers, and raincoats. In 1844 Goodyear patented vulcanized rubber in the United States. Now the balls of latex, smoked from the sap of the Hevea tree, found a world market. In 1840, 400 tons were shipped out of Belém; in 1860, 3,000 tons. Around Belém, an old colonial city in the sugar business, all cultivation of sugar, corn, or mandioca stopped. The rubber trees grew wild upriver; the Indians knew how to find and tap them, and were soon enslaved by rubber merchants. In the 1860s the Amazon was opened to steam travel and in 1867 to world commerce; by 1870, a fleet of English steamers took the rubber directly to Europe. Manáus began to grow as the center 1,000 miles upriver, when Dom Pedro's last years saw a new market for pneumatic rubber tires. By that time, however, the Brazilian monopoly on rubber had been lost. Though it was forbidden to take rubber tree seeds or cuttings out of Brazil, British botanists managed to transplant some to the East Indies and Malaya, in cultivated plantation orchards which stole the world market from Brazil's wild rubber.

Transportation between the regions of Brazil, still Brazil's great economic problem today, was far more difficult a century ago. Dom Pedro, king at five, had yet seen no other city except Rio when he was twenty-five. From Rio to Baía, one went by sailing vessel; to Minas Gerais or São Paulo by horseback. No wonder Pedro welcomed the ideas of an engineer named Mauá who built ten miles of railroad from Rio toward the new resort of Petropolis in 1854.

Baron Mauá, who had been a poor orphan boy apprenticed to a British grocer, was responsible for most of Brazil's economic development. He had quickly learned British accounting methods and larger British companies employed him, sent him to England on business, and encouraged him to build Brazil's first foundry in 1854. He was instrumental in sending a line of steamers to Europe and brought gas lights to Rio. Through him industrialization and banking increased, and immigration began to come to Brazil. Post roads and railroads inland from Rio were built with government money by immigrant labor and not by slaves, a reform idea of Dom Pedro's; he felt that no such public improvements should bear the stigma of having been built with slave labor. With British capital other short railways were constructed in Dom Pedro's time, from São Paulo to Santos, from Rio to Minas Gerais. By the end of the empire there were 6,000 miles of railroad and about 12,000 miles of telegraph line in Brazil, though in the late 1950s there was still no continuous north-south railway to connect Rio to Baía or Pernambuco. Dom Pedro, the paternalistic ruler, meanwhile created every new thing he could for Brazil—a scientific agricultural committee to fight famine in the dry region of Ceará, a regular line of coastal steamers, a smallpox vaccine institute, a silkworm-rearing establishment, a cable connection to the Transatlantic cable.

Though society in the empire was still predominantly rural and politics were controlled by the large landholding and slave-owning families, all this new industrialization and scientific interest had great significance for Brazil. Foreign commerce, immigration, and business capital were creating a new generation on a new basis of wealth in the 1880s.

Dom Pedro and his father had both been concerned with schools for their people. Under the constitution every village or town was to have a public school, though laws passed do not automatically build schools. The central government did not control or pay for elementary schools in the provinces; the capital merely passed laws, hoping that schools would be set up by localities. Only schools in Rio were supported by the imperial government, and in that city in 1844 there was one primary school for every 900 children, schools to each of which perhaps only thirty or forty students went. Education remained the prerogative of a gentleman; only sons of the aristocracy went beyond primary school. By 1886 Brazil had 6,605 public primary schools and many private and Church schools, libraries, and museums.

Dom Pedro did all a man could, single-handed, to alleviate this situation. He was a true schoolteacher at heart. At the age of twelve he had been made a "Protector of the Colégio Dom Pedro," a public secondary school for boys, and he maintained a lifelong interest in it, supporting many needy boys who came to his attention and paying their way through college after they finished high school. He established teacher-training schools at imperial expense, and he tried to standardize examinations for teachers. Through his unfailing efforts for elementary and secondary schools, education in Brazil was ahead of that in most Spanish-speaking countries, though illiteracy still stood at 90 per cent of the population at the end of his reign. As for higher education, in the last years of the empire Brazil had two faculties of medicine, two academies of law, a school of nurses, a school of fine arts, a music conservatory, an observatory, and a naval academy and a war college. In the secondary schools, new egalitarian philosophies were openly taught, and the new generation which learned them was ready to abolish slavery and favor political and educational reform.

In spite of the great mass of Brazilians who were illiterate, a native Brazilian literature was developing. The poetry of the time reflected Europe's romanticism, but some of it grew out of the intense love of country, exemplified by the singing *sabiá*. Several novels on native themes were popular during Pedro II's reign. One of the first South American "best sellers" was called *The Little Brunette,* written by Joaquim Manoel de Macedo (1820–1882). The story would seem very sentimental to us today, but most older Brazilians now alive read it and wept over it in their youth. A rock in Rio Bay, which has become famous as a lovers' suicide leap, is named after the heroine. The romantic life of the Indians came into fiction in the books of José de Alencar (1829–1877). The hero of his *O Guarany* is a noble Indian who risks his life to save the daughter of a plantation owner from death in a flood. So famous is this Indian character that South America's best-known opera was written around his story by the Brazilian composer Carlos Gomez for a debut in Milan in 1870. Alencar's masterpiece, *Iracema*, was published eight years later. Later novelists wrote more realistically about life as it was. Joaquim Maria Machado de Assis (1839–1908), a poor mulatto boy who became a literary genius, wrote short stories and novels about human troubles. He lived into the twentieth century, but his best writing was done in Pedro II's time. He has been called the "Brazilian Somerset Maugham." His *Don Casmurro* has been proclaimed the best Brazilian novel, and his *Jacob and Esau* has been translated into English and became a best-seller in America.

Dom Pedro's own personal interests encouraged scientific writing. When his mother, the Empress Leopoldina, came as a bride, she brought a European botanist with her who had started a compendium of Brazilian flora. It eventually filled forty volumes and identified and described 20,000 species of Brazilian plants; many native scientists worked on it, for it took forty-six years to complete. The American naturalist, Louis Agassiz, came to Brazil to confer on it as the guest of Dom Pedro, and gave a scientific lecture in Rio, an event of the social season. On August 18, 1838, a "committee of twenty-seven illustrious Brazilians" had met to organize the Brazilian Historical and Geographical Institute. Dom Pedro turned a room of the palace over to the society and was one of its most serious members, serving as chairman at 506 of its meetings. Today, this society is the most active of its kind in South America, rivaled in the Western Hemisphere only by the National Geographic Society of the United States. There were many other scientific and literary societies. The interest in botany, geology, and zoology led to the development of a National Museum. The Public Library founded by John VI had grown during his grandson's reign to fill a twelve-room structure, housing 171,000 volumes.

Opera houses were built in Rio and São Paulo, but only foreign compositions were played. In 1839 in a village in the state of São Paulo a "natural" musician named Antônio de Carlos Gomes (1839–1896) was born. Apprenticed early to a tailor, he studied by himself, but attracted a wealthy *Paulista* who financed him at the conservatory branch of the Rio Fine Arts Academy, where Dom Pedro II, the "fairy godfather," heard his work and sent him to Italy to study. His native Brazilian *arias* were difficult for Italian orchestras to perform; they could not get the jungle effects with regular instruments. But he it was who set Alencar's romantic story, *O Guarany*, to opera music; it was performed at La Scala in Milan in 1870, a great musical triumph for a Brazilian. Verdi heard it and proclaimed that the Western Hemisphere had produced his own equal. More than fifty other operas were composed by Brazilians in mid-century, many of them with native Brazilian themes. The imported European culture provided the "tone," however, when music and drama were performed at the ten theaters and opera houses of Rio.

All this culture and society were described daily in the *Jornal do Comércio*, Rio's largest newspaper. It had been founded in 1821, and was printing 15,000 six-page copies every morning by the 1870s. The year 1876 saw the beginning of "a very cheap daily paper," the *Gazeta de Notícias* which had the large staff of twelve reporters to get out its morning edition. There were then several other journals in Rio, and many more in Baía, Pernambuco, and São Paulo.

THE SLAVERY ISSUE
AND THE DOWNFALL OF PEDRO II

Of the nearly ten million people in Brazil a century ago, only 400,000 belonged to the landowning, slave-owning class, and only 142,000 of these qualified as voters. A third of the people were slaves. Some worked on the docks at Rio and Baía, many were house servants in the cities, and some acted as burden bearers on the city streets and country roads. The great majority of them were slaves on plantations growing sugar or coffee. Life there in 1850 was very much as that described in Chapter 16 for 1650. The Negroes in Brazil—the Bantus, the Sudanese, the Minas, the Angolas, the Guinea natives, all with their varying degrees of agricultural and handicraft skills from African villages and their native folk ways—had largely been mixed into a homogeneous group.

On the plantations and in the homes, slaves were not often mistreated and manumission was common. Since there was no color prejudice, freed slaves could go to the cities and enter business, so that their descendants often became men of importance. A British committee investigating slavery in 1847 found that slaves in Brazil were much better treated than those in the West Indies, and that they had thirty-five holidays a year in which they could celebrate or earn money to free themselves. Many plantation owners allowed them to work their own plots of land and buy their freedom with the profits. There was a growing abolition movement, however; clubs were organized, propaganda printed, and a political issue was being created.

England, which had wide influence in Brazilian politics because of her heavy investment of capital there, had assumed world leadership in ending the slave trade, making a treaty with Brazil that ships carrying slaves could be stopped as contraband on the high seas. When Brazilian ships were slow in cooperating, the British vessels threatened to enter Brazilian ports and rivers to apprehend the slaves. Dom Pedro and his congress decided to avoid this affront to sovereignty by passing a Brazilian law abolishing the slave trade in September 1850. After this law was enforced, all slaves brought in had to be smuggled.

By the 1870s abolition had become a subject for speeches, essays, poems, and politics. A young idealist named Antônio de Castro Alves (1847–1871), called the Harriet Beecher Stowe of Brazil, "wept with shame" that Brazil still carried on the buying and selling of slaves. His poem *The Slave Ship* describes conditions under which slaves were shipped clandestinely from Africa. As an answer to the abolitionists Viscount Rio Branco, the conservative prime minister, drafted a law called "Freedom of the Unborn Child," or the Rio Branco Law of 1871. Every child born to a slave mother henceforth was to be free. Rio Branco planned to have all slaves over sixty-five liberated as the next step, though the rural aristocracy, a powerful vested interest and largely in the conservative party, was naturally opposed to all liberation.

Dom Pedro had a long-term solution for Brazil's work-force problem. He had freed the slaves on the royal plantation; he forbade any of the modernizing public work to be built with slave labor. On his visits to the United States he had seen the labor problem being solved by hundreds of thousands of European immigrants. Already Dom Pedro had had the Petropolis railway built by German immigrants, and had settled them in villages afterward, while he supported their Lutheran minister. So successful was this venture that Dom Pedro brought more Germans to work his

Pedro II in 1887. *Courtesy Pan American Union.*

plantation with modern German farming methods. In 1840 there were 15,000 European immigrant colonists in Brazil; between 1874 and 1888, 600,000 had come in. Especially after 1870, Italians by the thousands had settled in São Paulo state alone, under a sharecropping system which was to make possible São Paulo's coffee industry.

For the immigrants there was a good future in trade, commerce, and handicrafts, for the freed men were largely untaught, and the plantation owners and educated classes, as in other parts of Latin America, did not want to enter trade. Portuguese, Italians, and Germans became grocers and peddlers, shop keepers, mechanics, or small farmers. The Brazilian government offered through its consulates in Europe to pay the difference between passage to the United States and to Brazil so that prospects would make the southern choice. If the newcomers went to one of the government colonies, they received forty-eight acres of cleared land, as well as seeds and implements, and were promised ninety days of paid employment in public works. By these methods, as well as by improved health standards, the population of Brazil tripled during the reign of Pedro II, and a large strain of European blood came to mix with the older racial strains.

With an increasing substitute source of labor, the opposition to slavery increased, and the abolition movement grew more powerful than that in the United States, inspired by the poems of Castro Alves. The William Lloyd Garrison of Brazil was Joaquim Nabuco, scion of an aristocratic family of Pernambuco and a young protégé of the emperor. Elected to the Chamber of Deputies in 1878, he devoted his impassioned speeches to the cause of immediate abolition, reading Castro Alves' poems aloud, and arousing sympathies with stories of cruelty under the slave system. Defeated in the Chamber, he founded an Anti-slavery Society, with branches all over the country, wrote a powerful book, *O Abolicionismo,* in 1883, and was soon re-elected. Dom Pedro himself paid Nabuco's expenses on an extensive speaking trip for the cause of abolition throughout the empire. The propaganda bore fruit, for two states passed local abolition laws, the law freeing slaves over sixty-five was approved, and when younger slaves deserted by the thousands, the army refused to catch them.

It was Joaquim Nabuco's movement, strangely enough, that helped bring about Dom Pedro's fall from power. Physically, the Emperor's gigantic frame was beginning to give out. Forced by diabetes to withdraw from his active life, Dom Pedro went to Europe in 1887 for treatment, leaving his middle-aged daughter Isabel to act as regent. Never as popular as her father, Isabel was married to the very unpopular Frenchman, Count d'Eu. She was sincere and impulsive, however, and intensely pro-abolitionist. On May 13, 1888, she signed the law which the Chamber and then the Senate had passed freeing the slaves in one stroke with no compensation to owners. In 1870 there had been 1,700,000 slaves in Brazil, but the law of 1888 freed the 750,000 who still remained slaves after eighteen years of gradual emancipation. Dom Pedro, very ill in Italy, immediately rallied when told of the emancipation act and sent cables: "My blessings and congratulations, to everybody, what a nation! What a people!" He was soon well enough to come home, and received a warmer welcome than usual.

But Pedro II did not realize the undercurrent of feeling against the monarchy in general—the strength of the republican movement, the impatience at some of Dom Pedro's high-handed ways. Many liberals had intended to bide with Dom Pedro until his death, and then establish a republic rather than accept Isabel. Now, with her impulsive act freeing the slaves, she had lost the support of the conservatives as well. The most reactionary slave-owners and landlords were willing to work with the most ardent young republicans. Army leaders joined the strange alliance. The young lieutenants had been indoctrinated in the war college by a remarkable mathematics teacher, Colonel Benjamin Constant, a fanatical republican. There was also a clique in the army in sympathy with the disgruntled plantation owners, led by General Deodoro da Fonseca. Many other politicians thought that a republic controlled by the army would be preferable to Isabel.

Other changing conditions were working against the monarchy. An electoral reform law, widely heralded in 1881, had set up direct elections for deputies, but had limited the vote to the well-to-do, and kept the same class of society in power. A conservative prime minister had used the law to restrict the budding Liberal Party, so the emperor had lost much liberal-minded support. He had never had the support of the new industrialist class. At the other extreme the clergy, fearing Pedro's Free-Masonry, opposed the separation of Church and state. When the press supported the Republican party factions on the one hand and the slave-owning nobility on the other, it needed only the defection in the army under Deodoro da Fonseca to bring about the end of the empire.

Hatching an intrigue very similar to the "palace revolutions" so common in Spanish America in the 1800s, Fonseca was able to take control of the city. The revolutionary clique asked for Pedro's resignation and got the confused old gentleman on shipboard and off to Europe with his family before he could actually realize what had happened, or before the rest of the country knew the empire was dead. Many people who witnessed the "revolt" thought it was merely another parade. The Republic of Brazil was proclaimed under army auspices on November 15, 1889. Dom Pedro himself was brokenhearted; he died in Europe two years later without any chance to see a vindication of his reign, though it was two generations before Brazil was so well governed again. Thirty years later his remains were brought back to Rio on a battleship and buried in state, the ashes being officially accompanied by the same Frenchman, Count d'Eu, the unpopular husband of Isabel. He and his sons stayed in Brazil, and their descendants are among the aristocratic "younger set" of Petropolis.

Brazil today appreciates Dom Pedro. He had been the cohesive force that held the nation together. His liberal constitutional monarchy had given Brazil experience in parliamentary government at the same time that Spanish America was going through the chaotic period of *caudillismo*. His ability, patriotism, and rugged honesty had meant a half-century of almost continual peace and material prosperity, a high place in international affairs, and an advance in culture and education.

Readings

Agassiz, L. A., *Journey in Brazil* (1868)

Armitage, J., *History of Brazil, 1808 to 1831* (2 vols., 1835–1836)

Azevedo, F. de, *Brazilian Culture*, trans. W. R. Crawford (1950)

Bernstein, H., *Modern and Contemporary Latin America* (1952)

Bettancourt Machado, José, *Machado of Brazil* (1962)

Box, P. H., *Origins of the Paraguayan War* (2 vols., 1929)

Burns, E. B., *Documentary History of Brazil* (1965)

Calmon, P., with C. de Medeiros, *History of Brazil* (1939)

Calogeras, P., *History of Brazil*, trans. P. M. Martin (1939)

Camacho, J. A., *Brazil: An Interim Assessment* (1954)

Correa da Costa, J. C., *Every Inch a King* (1950)

Cruz Costa, João, *History of Ideas in Brazil* (1964)

Duncan, J. S., *Public and Private Operation of Railways in Brazil* (1932)

Freyre, G., *The Masters and the Slaves*, trans. S. Putnam (1946)

Furtado, C., *The Economic Growth of Brazil* (1963)

Gauld, C. A., *The Last Titan: Percival Farquhar, Entrepreneur in Latin America* (1964)

Goldberg, I., *Brazilian Literature* (1922)
Goodwin, P. L., *Brazil Builds Architecture New and Old, 1652–1942* (1943)
Harding, B., *Amazon Throne: The Story of the Braganzas of Brazil* (1941)
———, *Southern Empire: Brazil* (1948)
Haring, C. H., *The Empire of Brazil* (1958)
Herring, H., *Good Neighbors* (1941)
Hill, L. F., ed., *Brazil* (1947)
———, *Diplomatic Relations Between the United States and Brazil* (1932)
Humphreys, R. A., and J. Lynch, *Origins of the Latin American Revolutions, 1808–1826* (1965)
James, P., *Brazil* (1946)
Kelsey, V., *Seven Keys to Brazil* (1943)
Livermore, H. V., ed., *Portugal and Brazil—An Introduction* (1953)
Manchester, A., *British Preeminence in Brazil* (1933)
Marchant, A., *Viscount Mauá and the Empire of Brazil* (1965)
Morse, R. M., *From Community to Metropolis, a Biography of São Paulo* (1958)
Nabuco, C., *Life of Joaquim Nabuco*, trans. R. Hilton *et al.* (1951)
Normano, J. F., *Brazil, A Study of Economic Types* (1925)
Oliveira Lima, M. de, *The Evolution of Brazil* (1914)
Pierson, D., *Negroes in Brazil* (1942)
Putnam, S., *Marvelous Journey: Four Centuries of Brazilian Literature* (1948)
Ramos, A., *The Negro in Brazil* (1939)
Sanceau, E., *The Perfect Prince: A Biography of Dom João II* (1959)
Schurz, W. L., *Brazil, the Infinite Country* (1961)
Smith, T. L., *Agrarian Reform in Latin America* (1965)
———, *Brazil: People and Institutions* (2nd ed., 1954)
———, and A. Marchant, *Brazil: Portrait of Half a Continent* (1951)
Stein, S. J., *Brazilian Cotton Manufacture* (1957)
———, *Vassouras: A Brazilian Coffee Country, 1850–1900* (1957)
Thornton, M. C., *The Church and Freemasonry in Brazil, 1872–1875* (1948)
Torres-Rioseco, A., *Epic of Latin American Literature* (rev. ed., 1946)
Turner, C. W., *Ruy Barbosa: Brazilian Crusader for the Essential Freedoms* (1945)
Veríssimo, E., *Brazilian Literature: An Outline* (1945)
Wilgus, A. C., ed., *Argentina, Brazil, and Chile Since Independence* (1935)
Williams, M. W., *Dom Pedro the Magnanimous* (1937)
Wythe, G., *et al.*, *Brazil: An Expanding Economy* (1949)

Chapter 22

Argentina as a Gaucho Nation

THE NEW CREOLE STATE
IN THE PLATA PROVINCES

GOD AND NATURE conspired to make the Argentines into a great Latin American nation," say today's citizens of that leading Southern Hemisphere republic, but they followed a tortuous path to achieve that eminence. Endowed with great economic resources on the land surface, but none below, they had been treated as stepchildren by the metal-hungry Spaniards. Since the wide pampas contained only isolated nuclei of creole and *mestizo* cities having strongly individualistic and localistic feelings—Córdoba, Santa Fé, Rosario, Mendoza, far across the plains from Buenos Aires and up into the foothills—little feeling of nationalism developed. Not only did Argentina have the usual troubles of the newly independent nations—the inadequately trained leaders, the militaristic *caudillos,* the lack of financial basis—but there ensued the most dramatic struggle between city and country, centralists and federalists, to take place in any New World nation. In the attempts to work out the relationship between Buenos Aires and the provinces almost every theory of government, every type of state and constitution was tried.

After Buenos Aires ousted the viceroy and set up an independent *junta* on May 25, 1810, Spanish rule was never re-established. For the next six years, however, confusion in the government of the city and quarrels with the pampas provinces postponed any declaration of independence.

While Manuel Belgrano, as the *junta's* military commander in chief, spent the resources and men of the port fighting the interior provinces and trying to force them into union with Buenos Aires, at home the *junta* changed its personnel and shifted its policy repeatedly between conservatives and liberals. The conservatives consisted of the rich landowners, whose descendants were to be known as the "oligarchs" of Argentine history, combined with the wealthy merchants of Buenos Aires and the clergy. If they must break with Spain, they wanted the old regime continued. There were such conservative "oligarchs" both in Buenos Aires and in the interior, but they found no agreement, for those of Buenos Aires wanted to dominate the entire area and control all revenues, while the rich landowners of the provinces objected. The conservatives gave an impetus to federalism in the early days in order to frustrate the reformers. For the same reason they also permitted the growth of *caudillos* in the interior. In the cities there were also liberals, who hoped to abolish tithes and ecclesiastic *fueros,* establish religious tolerance, public schools, and freedom of the press, and create a prosperous, solvent republic able to coin its own money and pay its own bills through efficient customs collection. In the period between the establishment of the May 1810 *junta* and the declaration of independence in 1816, the government of the port changed twelve times.

Finally the various towns consented to meet at the northern town of Tucumán in March of 1816. Buenos Aires, Córdoba, Cuyo or Mendoza, Salta, Rosario, and Tucumán were there. Already the conference split on the issue that was to tear Argentine politics apart for generations: the *Unitarios* from Buenos Aires wanted a strong central government centering on the port, and the Federalists wanted each region autonomous. Independence for the entire region was proclaimed after weeks of deliberation, of quarreling over various suggestions for a limited monarchy, and of postponing plans for a definite form of government. The congress did say the country should be ruled from Buenos Aires by a "Supreme Director," and appointed Juan Martín de Pueyrredón to that position.

Pueyrredón served as director for a harassed three years, moving toward centralized authority too fast to please the interior *caudillos.* After his resignation, anarchy reigned in the port city. The following year, 1820, is called "The Terrible Year Twenty" in Argentine history because of the many revolutions and changes in the government. Chieftains in the hinterland remained practically independent—for example, an Indian chieftain in the province of Corrientes, and a cowboy politician in Santa Fé who used the head of a donkey, ears sticking up, as his military headgear. The government in Buenos Aires drained itself white fighting such gaucho chieftains.

Out of this confusion emerged a wise leader with a strong hand. Bernardino Rivadavia, who had spent some years in England, served as Minister of Foreign Affairs from 1821 to 1824 and as President in 1826–1827. He was imbued with ideas of democratic government and separation of Church and state. During his administration the Argentine National University was founded, public schools were opened, primogeniture abolished, and the regions of the pampas were brought into a more friendly federation.

He envisioned the elements of Argentina's greatness: immigration, foreign capital, and public education. He improved the harbor, introduced sheep-raising into remote Patagonia, and built a national library.

However, his well-meaning plan for the distribution of public lands to farmers through long-term leases, a program called emphyteusis, was to produce later land scandals and create a stronger, more wealthy oligarchy and *latifundia*. By 1827 over 6,500,000 acres had been granted to or rented by only 112 individuals or companies, of whom ten received more than 130,000 acres each. This lavish distribution of land to the wealthy few continued after Rivadavia. Meanwhile, war with Brazil over Uruguay brought Rivadavia disgrace and exile in 1827. He was followed in 1829, after a period of great anarchy, by Argentina's strongest and most colorful dictator, Manuel Rosas. Thus, by the end of the chaotic 1820s the personal rule of a military chief was generally accepted as a natural form of government.

THE ERA OF A GAUCHO DICTATOR

The years from 1816 to 1830 had been years of disorganization and violence with *caudillismo* rampant and little semblance of national government. But they were also years of growth. The isolated provinces had developed a feeling of nationality they did not have at the time of the Congress of Tucumán, in spite of the power of the local *caudillos*. The population of the Plata area increased from 508,000 in 1818 to 630,000 in 1826; some legislation to encourage immigration had been passed. Foreign trade, possible through the port since 1810, had increased by leaps and bounds; there was prosperity in the shipment of hides, tallow, and grain to Europe. Two incompatible types of society continued to exist side by side. There was, on the one hand, an increasing number of urbanized town-dwellers. But the aristocrats of the new Argentina were still the cattle ranchers, whose animals ran free on the wide pampas and produced hides in unlimited quantity. For them on the unfenced prairie lands worked the gauchos, who provide the color and the legends of the middle half of the nineteenth century.

The gaucho's hero in the 1830s was the dictator Manuel Rosas. As a boy, this colorful character had run away from his father's ranch and his mother's discipline and had become a famous "bronco-buster." But he had not been satisfied with the aimless gaucho life and had become a handler of meats and hides. Backed by his private gaucho force, he served as governor of Buenos Aires province for three years. When Indians threatened the settlements on the southern edge of the province, he set out to quell them, while his wife kept political contact in Buenos Aires for him. It was in the south that Darwin saw and described him in camp in 1832. He was ruling the whole nation three years later.

President Rivadavia had been forced to resign in 1827 because of dissatisfaction over the outcome of war against Brazil in Uruguay; his successor, Manuel Dorrego, was ambushed and shot because of the same issue. Again there ensued civil war in the Plata provinces, with *Unitarios* in the capital opposing Federalists from the interior—a civil war led by General Rosas, who called himself a Federalist. Churchmen and landowners, alarmed by Rivadavia's centralist reforms, were glad to back him. Elected president, he also remained the governor of Buenos Aires province. By 1835 he was in actuality dictator of the country.

Rosas first consolidated his power. While he talked federalism and persecuted the city politicians, the *Unitarios,* he slyly built up control in every interior province. He "eliminated" the lesser chieftains, and though *caudillos* remained in Santa Fé, Tucumán, Mendoza, and Entre Ríos, Rosas allied himself with and controlled them. Thus the country was "unconsciously" being unified around Buenos Aires, while the sincere patriots who worked for that end were tortured in jail or exiled to Montevideo or Chile. Rosas, true to the colorful meaning of his name, required everything about him—his saddle blankets, the waistcoats of his diplomats, the baggy pants of his gaucho soldiers—to be rosy red. The red sash worn across the vest of a gentleman's evening clothes would bear the printed words, "Federalism or death! Death to the filthy, loathsome, savage *Unitarios.*" Blue, the color of the "underground" *Unitarios,* was worn in public on pain of death or imprisonment. Rosas' private police, "an aggregate of cutthroats" who routed out the secret "blue wearers," were so closely knit together as to be called the *mazorca,* or corn on the cob, each kernel in its place in the dictator's service. Underground, it was whispered that this gang of cutthroats was really the *más horca,* which though pronounced the same as *mazorca,* means "more gallows." It has been estimated that during Rosas' power 3,765 people were garrotted, 1,393 shot, 722 assassinated, 14,920 killed in battle, and 1,660 forced into exile.

Argentina took seventeen long years of Rosas with little objection. He maintained some degree of internal peace in spite of a number of revolts which broke out against him. Meanwhile he negotiated a treaty with England which abolished the slave trade, organized a provincial bank which forced the collection of taxes sufficient to support the federal government, and even introduced vaccination against smallpox. He controlled the Church, forcing out any Church leaders who opposed him, while the priests were forced to extol him from the pulpit. Pictures of the dictator and his influential wife Encarnación were carried in religious parades side by side with holy images.

Unsympathetic with even elementary education, Rosas regulated the courses taught at the University and withdrew his financial support when he thought the professors were too impractical in their teaching or in the slightest degree unfriendly to him. Literary and liberal-minded Argentines lived out his years of rule in exile in Uruguay or Chile. Any newspaper or book printed in Buenos Aires during his rule was directly approved by him. Even the Church hierarchy became his abject tool. The estate owners, the *estancieros,* supported him for he continued the land policy that allowed them to acquire even larger holdings. Though all his oppression did nothing to promote the country culturally or economically, he did hold Argentina together, by brutal force, and saved the Plata area from being cut up by the gaucho *caudillos*—a sort of "negative nation-building."

Eventually Rosas wore out his hold on the people by an inept foreign policy. In 1837 he had engaged in a costly war with the dictator of Bolivia. In 1838 and 1839 he was embroiled with a French fleet which attempted to block the estuary. In 1843 he launched a nine-year war of intervention in the chaotic affairs of Uruguay and here became involved with both France and England who were backing Uruguayan politicians in a long siege of Montevideo. Because of Rosas' activity across the Plata, the estuary was closed to upriver trade. The continued trade monopoly of Buenos Aires, the blockades caused by his wars, turned the interior against him. The dictator of independent Paraguay, the *caudillo* of the river province of Corrientes, and his former friend Justo José Urquiza, wealthiest landowner in Entre Ríos, all joined to oust him.

Urquiza received the backing of Brazil, which did not want to see Rosas control Uruguay. Encouraged by a society of young intellectuals called "Young Argentina" whose members lived in exile in Montevideo, and by the *Unitarios* still living in Buenos Aires, Urquiza "pronounced" against Rosas on May 25, 1851. Brazil made a formal alliance with Urquiza on May 29, and with soldiers from Entre Ríos and Corrientes, joined by the Brazilian army, Urquiza was able to defeat Rosas at the battle of Caseros on February 3, 1852. The dictator resigned and took his young daughter with him to England, where he died in genteel poverty in 1877. With Rosas gone, the oligarchy consolidated its power under the Constitution of 1853.

ARGENTINA UNDER THE CONSTITUTION OF 1853 TO 1900

Justo José Urquiza, *caudillo* of Entre Ríos province, was not openly for strong central power, but he did promise to organize the nation under a constitutional government and to bring greater economic prosperity by opening the Plata river system to the trade of the world. He accomplished the latter by negotiating eleven treaties with Europe and America. In an attempt to arrange for constitutional government he invited the governors of the provinces to a conference at the town of San Nicolás on May 31, 1852, where the "Agreement of San Nicolás" was made. Its nineteen articles, ratified by thirteen provinces, renewed the federation, called for a constitutional convention whose delegates were to be elected, and granted control of the army and of foreign affairs to Urquiza. However, both the city and province of Buenos Aires, which comprised the most powerful part of Argentina, were fearful of Urquiza and his provincial backing, resented his triumphal entry at the head of his troops three months before, felt no gratitude to him for ending the dictatorship, and so rejected the Agreement of San Nicolás.

Urquiza then laid siege to Buenos Aires, but the river boats he hoped to use in the blockade went over to the port faction. Urquiza himself barely escaped in a neutral vessel, the *U.S.S. Waterwitch*, so he abandoned hopes of ruling Buenos Aires for the time being, withdrew to his estates in Entre Ríos, and set up headquarters for his new government in Paraná.

Urquiza's congress proceeded to meet and call a constitutional convention to plan a stable federated government, while Buenos Aires province went ahead and made its own centralized constitution as if it were an independent nation. The federalist constitutional convention met at Santa Fé without any Buenos Aires delegates, and drafted a constitution similar to the federal plan of the United States but providing more power to the president. Much of the thinking behind the document was based on the works of the Argentine writer Juan Bautista Alberdi, especially his *Bases and Points of Departure for the Political Organization of the Argentine Republic*. Thus was produced the Argentine Constitution of 1853, which was ratified by thirteen of the interior states, and which was to last with few changes until the Perón era in 1949. Under it the central authorities would have power to maintain order and national unity without killing provincial autonomy. Still considered a "federalist plan," it was unacceptable to Buenos Aires, so that Urquiza, as constitutional president of the Confederation, had to maintain an uneasy truce with the port city while he ruled from far upriver. Well-educated, courteous in diplomacy, a great hand with ladies, temperate in eating and drinking, and withal an efficient administrator and true patriot, Urquiza was a break with Argentina's past of the rough gaucho *caudillos*. He especially encouraged education and immigration and initiated steamboat service upriver to Rosario.

He could not keep the peace with Buenos Aires, however. All products of the interior had to go out through the port; treaties with England, France, and the United States providing for the free commerce up the inland rivers availed him nothing, for customs were still collected at the port where the oceangoing vessels had to halt. Urquiza retaliated by charging duty on Buenos Aires goods sold inland. In 1859 war finally broke out between the forces of Urquiza and the forces of General Bartolomé Mitre, commander for Buenos Aires. The defeat of Mitre in the battle of Cépeda forced Buenos Aires into the confederation, though the government still remained under Urquiza's control at Paraná. The rich port taxes, best income of the nation, remained in Buenos Aires control, and neither faction was happy, while Urquiza served out his six-year term and was succeeded by Santiago Derqui in 1860.

When delegates from Buenos Aires came to the congress at Paraná a year later, they were refused recognition because they had not been elected under the true federal constitution. Insulted, they returned home and their leader, General Mitre, prepared for war again. This time Mitre won at the Battle of Pavón, September 7, 1861, and was declared national as well as provincial leader while Derqui was removed. Thus in 1861 the idea of a federation with the capital at Buenos Aires finally won out. General Mitre, a hero from Buenos Aires, a symbol of the port or *porteño* spirit, began a constitutional term as president in 1862. For the first time the newly coined term Argentine Nation was used, as opposed to Provinces of the Plata, or Republic of the Plata—*argentum* being the Latin word for silver as *plata* was the Spanish.

Bartolomé Mitre, a *Unitario*, is one of the first really modern sons of Argentina. A literary liberal exiled by Rosas, he was a statesman, a military general, an historian, an essayist, and a journalist, founder of the great newspaper, *La Nación,* which was to become a force for social betterment in later years. As a writer Mitre produced a history of independence, biographies of San Martín and Belgrano, a study of ancient Indian dramas, and a translation of Horace. To promote prosperity, Mitre continued railroad building which had been begun on a small scale under Urquiza. He invited in British capital, opened public elementary schools, and encouraged the university. Meanwhile he tried to placate all factions, for his objective was to foster national unification as well as to develop the country economically. The Constitution of 1853 was now actually in force, though Buenos Aires city was still the capital of both the province of Buenos Aires and of the nation. Mitre kept his dual position as governor of Buenos Aires and president of the nation, and served out his term as president from 1862 to 1868.

Unfortunately, after three years of constructive work, he was forced to waste thousands of lives and millions of dollars on the tragic Paraguayan War of the 1860s, a grandiose effort which ended in the devastation of Paraguay. (See Chapter 24.) Mitre himself headed the Argentine army which invaded Paraguay toward the close of the war. The election of 1868 was held during the war, and Mitre refused to run again. Returning victorious, with much of southern Paraguay added to Argentina by treaty, Mitre retired to civilian life and the editing of his newspaper, and became one of Argentina's distinguished elder statesmen, intervening several times in politics before his death in 1906.

The election of 1868 was won by one of the most progressive literary men South America had produced, Domingo Faustino Sarmiento, who first came to fame as a writer urging sophistication instead of the gaucho life. Sarmiento was a poor boy from the interior. His ambitious mother, whose tireless work with the loom supported the family, made sacrifices so that he could be educated, and at fifteen he was already teaching in a small rural school. He was even then a *Unitario.* Barely escaping imprisonment by Rosas' local *caudillo,* Facundo Quiroga, Sarmiento crossed the Andes to become a rural teacher in Chile. Ten years later he was supporting himself by writing for a Chilean paper. By 1845, owing to his articles on education and his intellectual contest with the old sage Andrés Bello, Sarmiento became the director of the new Chilean normal school. Chile sent him abroad to study schools; he observed Horace Mann's educational methods, received honorary degrees from American universities, wrote a biography of Lincoln, whom he had met personally, and founded a two-language review called *Both Americas.*

Welcomed to Buenos Aires after Rosas' fall, Sarmiento became a successful newspaper writer and political leader in his native land. He was to serve as director of schools, governor of San Juan, and Minister to the United States. His rise to the presidency was a new departure, a president of a united Argentina who was neither a local *caudillo* nor a successful general nor a rich cattleman, but a poor schoolteacher. His term was a period of great social and political evolution in Argentina. As president and leader of the *Unitario* party his first thoughts were for schools, for he was a passionate believer in democratic institutions and insisted that "to govern is to educate." "An ignorant people will always elect a Rosas," he said. During his six years as the "Schoolmaster President" the school enrollment increased from 30,000 to 100,000. In almost every schoolroom in Argentina today there is a portrait of Sarmiento, "Father of Education." He doubled the number of European immigrants who came in to farm the pampas; he began modernization of the port and built a sanitary water supply and sewer system for the city. To enhance the new trends in shipping beef for meat he planned an even more extensive system of railroads than Urquiza and Mitre had dreamed of. He imported American teachers to conduct his teacher-training institutions, English technicians to build the railroads, and German and Swiss colonists to build up the cooler provinces in the unsettled south. Perhaps he tried to hurry his native land too much. The old *caudillos* rose against him, and he had armed revolt on his hands twice in the province of Entre Ríos.

Meanwhile the port did not love Sarmiento, a native of San Juan in the interior. A test of strength between the provinces and the port, headed by the retired General Mitre, occurred in the election of 1874 when Sarmiento backed his Minister of Education, the Córdoban, Nicolás Avellaneda. When Avellaneda won, Mitre came out of retirement to lead an armed revolt in opposition. Mitre was disarmed in a brief encounter, and the leniency with which he was pardoned after a very short prison term shows the general improvement in stormy Argentine politics. National order was now consolidated under the progressive regime of Avellaneda. Sarmiento continued in the government, as a senator and as Minister of the Interior. When, under a series of weaker presidents in the 1880s, he saw his hopes for democratic elections fading away, he left politics and devoted his time to literature, leaving fifty-two volumes of published works at the time of his death in 1888. The administration of Mitre had moulded the nation; that of Sarmiento continued Mitre's work. By 1880 Argentine society had been transformed by education, immigration, railroads, and foreign capital.

During all this period Argentine expansion to the south was hindered by those same Indian tribes on the southern pampas who had changed little since Darwin's time. In 1878–1879 General Julio Roca, a sort of Argentine Custer, led an army of gauchos—actually the last militia in Argentine history that was costumed in gaucho fashion—in a war of extermination against the savages. As the Sioux and the Comanche, the Apache and the Pawnee were driven out of the fertile lands of the Mississippi Valley onto reservations in the semidesert, so the pampas hunters were driven into bleak Patagonia, or were transported into work colonies in semitropical Sante Fé and Entre Ríos. The campaign opened the area above the Indian frontier in southern Chubut for colonization, though the land so acquired was recklessly squandered in scandalous speculation. The gauchos themselves, in drifting back from this last Indian war, were giving up the old "hell-for-leather" existence and becoming settled tenant farmers or hired cow hands.

The successful Indian campaigns made Julio Roca the presidential candidate of the Federalist and interior party in 1880 on the old issue of the port versus the pampas. The provincial politicians had formed the Córdoba League, determined to maintain their supremacy and make Buenos Aires a capital detached from its powerful province. The agreement under Mitre had been a five-year truce under which Buenos Aires city was to be only temporarily the capital of both nation and province. Year after year the problem of a permanent capital had been fought over in the elections. When Roca won the election because of the backing of the Córdoba League, winning all the electoral votes but those of Buenos Aires and Corrientes, the *Unitarios* challenged the election with arms and another civil war resulted. With Roca's victory in the war a compromise was worked out which holds to this day. A new town, La Plata, was created to serve as capital of Buenos Aires province, a province which has since had little more influence in national affairs than other large provinces. Buenos Aires city, with its great port, was separated from the province, as the constitution writers of 1853 had suggested, and made into a federal district which included only the city and its suburbs.

All political troubles in Argentina were not solved by this formula, however. Both port and pampas were controlled by the oligarchs, the established old families of rich cattlemen. Provincial governors controlled the legislatures at home and their delegations to the national congress at Buenos Aires, and were in turn controlled by the great landed families. Whoever was president had to work through this "machine" to get his policies approved and enforced. Voting was restricted to a few, and there was no secret ballot. Reformers from the two old parties regrouped in various ways and tried to force fair electoral practices, honest use of local and federal funds, and representation in office of the rapidly growing urban working class. They were powerless against the oligarchical families who faked the elections and monopolized political appointments.

Roca himself, once returned from the Indian wars, was a conservative who promoted national prosperity and railroad building only to improve the fortunes of the landowning classes. To help them he encouraged overspeculation, and his paper money became almost worthless. His party was a regrouping of conservative forces which controlled the elections and was *the* government of Argentina for a generation. This was the era of the "generation of the 1880s"—a generation of men born in turmoil and civil war, whose fathers had been exiled or murdered and who wanted domestic peace, with prosperity for themselves and their rich agricultural lands. They were afraid of true democracy, but encouraged immigration, trade, and commerce under the *status quo*.

After General Roca's term expired in 1886, there followed a period of graft in government under his corrupt brother-in-law, Miguel Juárez Celman. Business struggled with inflation as the rapidly modernizing country tried to readjust itself to the change from a nation of wide-open prairies. The whole world faced a financial panic in 1891 which was quickly reflected in Argentina with its dependence on British financial houses. Liberal-minded citizens had organized a nationwide revolt against the oligarchs, calling themselves the *Unión Cívica*. When a middle-of-the-road compromise candidate, Luis Sáenz Peña, was elected to the presidency in 1892 as a way to settle both revolt and scandal, the *Unión Cívica* split in two, and its more liberal faction, the *Unión Cívica Radical,* destined to be famed as the Radical Party of the twentieth century, plotted to overthrow the compromise. Again there were revolts, which ended in 1895 when José Evaristo Uriburu took over the presidency upon the resignation of the president. He redeemed the paper money at 44 per cent of face value in gold, refunded the national debt, and helped business and agriculture resume their former growth. In 1898, during a war scare with Chile, the privileged few voters again chose the old General Roca, still the tool of the oligarchs. Their heyday was passing, however, for the Radicals were to come to power after one decade had passed in the new century. Roca's second term, 1898 to 1904, was an effective oligarchic dictatorship, with frequent interventions in the provinces. But commerce increased, the port was improved, and the Drago Doctrine was issued against intervention in Latin American affairs by foreign creditor nations.

Boundary disputes troubled the 1890s also. Argentina and Brazil both claimed part of the province of Misiones west of the Uruguay River, a dispute settled when arbitration by President Cleveland awarded the area to Brazil. Not so simple was the dispute with Chile over the boundary line in Tierra del Fuego and in the Andes passes. The question was whether the Andes line should be the watershed or the line of highest peaks—for in the Andes the two are not the same. Here again the dispute was arbitrated, though war threatened at the turn of the century. The United States minister decided the northern end of the line; King Edward VII of England established the southern. In honor of this peaceful settlement the statue of Christ of the Andes was erected on the highest peak of the boundary, a symbol of peace between Argentina and her neighbors.

THE GAUCHO IN NINETEENTH-CENTURY
ARGENTINE LIFE

In the first half of the nineteenth century the gauchos were the lowest class of society, the raw materials for the *caudillos'* armies. By the second half of the century, as the cities and the pampas both filled with immigrant peoples from Europe, their life had become as legendary as the life of the cowboy in America. The gaucho was the national hero, the central figure in drama, poetry, dance, and novel, a mixture of Buffalo Bill, Daniel Boone, and Robin Hood.

> A son am I of the rolling plain,
> A gaucho born and bred;
> For me the whole great world is small,
>
> Believe me, my heart can hold it all,
> The snake strikes not at my passing foot,
> The sun burns not my head.[1]

---

[1] From Walter Owen translation, José Hernández, *The Gaucho Martín Fierro,* (Farrar and Rinehart, 1936), p. 4.

Thus sang the most famous of all gauchos, Martín Fierro. Martín seems a real person to most Argentines, but he was actually a fictitious character created in a long rollicking poem by José Hernández (1834–1886), an Argentine born on a cattle ranch near Buenos Aires a decade after Darwin's visit. He lived to edit a Buenos Aires newspaper and to serve in the Argentine legislature, but today no one remembers his political activities. During his own lifetime he was always identified with Martín Fierro himself.

The unlettered gauchos came to know the whole of Martín's story in rhyme, for their own singers, their *payadores,* sang just such songs of their own lives and adventures. The pampas were "brown with the grazing herds" in the days Martín sang of. All the gaucho needed beside his rope and saddle was "the plain below and sky above, a horse, and a thatch and a bit of love." At the end of the story Martín became an outlaw and went south to live with the Indians. But the gauchos were not content to have Martín go off like that; Hernández had to bring him back years later in 1879 in *The Return of Martín Fierro,* and have him describe his further adventures as a wandering minstrel in a complete new edition of the verses.

Another such guitar-playing cowboy was named Santos Vega, who may perhaps have actually existed. Even before Hernández' time his compatriot, Hilario Ascasubi (1807–1875), had written down a series of poetic adventures of cowboys, supposedly told by this singer. Every *pulpería,* or country saloon, had its guitar ready for the wandering *payador.* If two *payadores* showed up, there was a singing contest; each one extemporized in producing verses; a dispute as to who was best could become a free-for-all fight. Sometimes the *payadores* would join small companies of traveling players and sing their verses while stories of gaucho deeds were acted out. Thus a native theater, the *dramas criollos,* grew up, a theater that traveled by wagon from town to town giving these famous "horse operas." The character of Santos Vega was in many of them, as well as several characters of the Jesse James type whose escapes from the law made them frontier heroes. At the turn of the twentieth century the gaucho plays moved into the cities and were given more formal staging and complicated plots in the theaters of Buenos Aires. They set the style for gaucho stories that would become the literature of a nation, while dance forms and art centered around this theme in the entire Plata region.

Literature, music, and art were not the only fields influenced by the gauchos in the life of Argentina. They supported Rosas, fought the wars in Uruguay, kept the Indians away from the cities on the Plata. They cared for the cattle which provided the food, and dried the hides to make the chief export. Their homes were rude; a bed made of hides and a few steer skulls for stools were the only furniture. But the true gaucho seldom sat anywhere save astride a horse, and horses were so numerous that any traveler could rope one for his use and not be called a horse thief. The women, once won by the *payadores* songs, were kept busy shearing the sheep, milking cows, weaving coarse cloth, planting Indian corn in small patches, and rearing the children, who in turn took to the saddle as soon as they were able to walk. It was a life that ended by the 1880s with the fencing in of the great estates,the coming of that same barbed wire that changed America's own West, the introduction of placid pedigreed cattle fattened in stalls on corn and alfalfa.

ARGENTINE LIFE AS IT MOVED
FROM THE PAMPAS TO THE CITIES

While the gaucho pined for his vanishing freedom, he was working indirectly to bring prosperity via the beef business to the cities he scorned. Trade statistics for the 1850s indicate an increase in exportation of hides out of Buenos Aires by 50,000 each year. Sarmiento wrote in 1845, "Buenos Aires is destined to some day become the most gigantic city of the two Americas . . . because she is the mistress of navigation of a hundred rivers . . . the outlet of thirteen provinces." At that time the once neglected port had a population of about 100,000, more than did Lima in its colonial heyday. By 1890 it was a luxurious city of 668,000 with parks and boulevards, already "illumined by electricity." Well-to-do families, grown rich on the pampas, were building marble villas in the new suburbs, but the city poor, descendants of gauchos combined with half a million European immigrants who did the work of docks and packing houses, lived in crowded tenements and one-room shanties.

In the 1850s Sarmiento had been distressed that there were so few other urban centers. "The grazing provinces sometimes have no towns at all save their capital cities," he wrote, "and with some of those the open plains end at the city streets." In the province of Córdoba, "of 160,000 souls scarcely 20,000 dwell in its only city." Rosario, with 8,000 people in 1850, had started a regular stagecoach service by 1860, as well as a boat service on the Paraná to attract trade from Asunción. Few of the sophistications Sarmiento admired found their way into the back country. Wagon-freight charges were added to the price of city-made goods; in turn, the inland farmers received 30 per cent less profit on their hides, tallow, and horsehair than the farmers near Buenos Aires. No wonder they hated the power of the port in politics.

As both port and inland towns expanded, education and culture grew with the gaucho's decline. Two hundred and five public schools were reported for all Argentina in 1850, with 12,000 pupils and 241 teachers. Thirty-five years later there were 1,900 schools, 4,080 teachers, and 164,600 students. There had been 78.8 per cent illiteracy in 1868; 1893 figures show only 54.4 per cent. The leading Argentine university was still the old colonial one of Córdoba, but the University of Buenos Aires soon rivaled it. Sarmiento traveled from one to the other by a newly opened railroad in 1870 to dedicate an astronomical observatory he had presented to Córdoba. Gauchos did not dominate the city theater; Buenos Aires had fifteen modern theaters and concert halls by 1890, in which European and local troupes gave the most sophisticated of current plays and the most classical of operas which would have delighted the progressive soul of Sarmiento a generation before.

Domingo Faustino Sarmiento (1811–1888) himself ranks as the best prose writer of the period. Most of his fame rests on his biographical study of a corrupt gaucho politician in whose province Sarmiento was born, *The Life of Juan Facundo Quiroga*, published in 1845. Subtitled *Civilization and Barbarism*, this book contains much of Sarmiento's progressive philosophy, his criticism of the backward though colorful gaucho day, and his forecast of Buenos Aires' great future.

It was Esteban Echevarría (1805–1851) who introduced romanticism in Argentina in his *La Cautiva*, although his unfinished novel, *The Slaughterhouse*, is considered his masterpiece. Another romantic story called *Amalia*, though its heroine is too sweet and its villains too black, courageously describes the conditions in Buenos Aires under Rosas, and earned for its author, José Mármol (1817–1871), the title of "Rosas' Poetic Hangman" because of its influence in aid of the opposition party. Juan Bautista Alberdi (1810–1884) is remembered as the philosopher behind the Constitution of 1853, and one of South America's most profound political thinkers.

And there was always poetry—poetry about politics, poetry against dictators, written surreptitiously and circulated in the "underground." But with more stable conditions there seemed less poetic urge. Poets of the latter half of the 1800s seem merely to have tried to copy European writing fashions without any of the "breath of the New World." A notable exception is the poem by Luis L. Domínguez (1819–1898) called *El Ombú*, in praise of the one tree that grows natively on the pampas, a poem today loved and memorized by schoolchildren.

> Every territory on earth has a conspicuous feature:
> Brazil, its glowing sun, Peru, its mines of silver,
> Montevideo, its hill.
> Buenos Aires—my beautiful country
> Has its magnificent pampas,
> The pampas have the *ombú*.
>
> . . . There are no leafy groves there,
> But sometimes there appears on the top of a little hill,
> Which rises so that it can be dimly seen,
> The *ombú*, solemn, lonely, of elegant, graceful growth,
> Which rises to the clouds like a light house of the sea.[2]

The cities grew into the pampas, and other trees were planted which dwarfed the native *ombú*. Railroads were being built across the pampas; blooded cattle were introduced to produce tender steaks; by the latter part of the century refrigerated ships were being developed to preserve and ship such steaks to the world market. The change in agriculture and shipping by 1900 is the true "Revolution" of Argentina.

[2] Translated by Alice Stone Blackwell, in *Some Spanish American Poets* (New York: Appleton-Century, 1929), pp. 338–39. Reprinted by permission of the University of Pennsylvania Press, copyright owners.

Round-up on the pampas. *Courtesy Pan American Airways.*

In 1872 a system of artificial refrigeration had been invented; in 1882 a meat-freezing plant was built in Buenos Aires. By 1900 these freezing plants were slaughtering more animals than the old salt-meat and hide works had handled. Salting plants had needed thick-hided cattle whose poor flesh salted easily, and whose hide was the greatest value. Freezing plants wanted high-grade meat, tender and fat. A new type of steer was already being raised on the pampas to meet this need, steers bred from Hereford and Angus stock brought in from England. In the same decade wire fencing came to herd the purebreds in. Alfalfa was planted to feed them; the open range was reduced to farming land. Not gaucho riders but tenant farmers were needed, tenants who would settle down to raise corn and alfalfa for the fat cattle and wheat for the new flour mills of Buenos Aires. To handle the trade in meat and wheat Buenos Aires built new docks in 1889 and dredged the channel of the Plata to meet them. From the port 6,000 miles of railroad stretched across the pampas by 1890, calling for a capital investment of $53,000,000, much of it British capital, much of it contracted under the guidance of an American engineer named William Wheelright. The towns of the hinterland were now connected with the port and the long wagon hauls ended.

Who were the people doing all this new work, ploughing land, building railroads, planting alfalfa, freezing beef carcasses? Leaders like Alberdi, Sarmiento, and Mitre knew that thrifty, hard-working farmers and artisans must come to these sparsely settled temperate lands of South America from temperate Europe. In 1876 a law was passed in the Argentine congress providing for "the organizing of immigrants, payment of their passage, and substantial aid after their arrival." There was never free homestead land on the pampas as there was in North America—the great estate owners wanted docile tenant workers, not freeholding neighbors—but for many south Europeans, Italians especially, a Catholic land, without a hard winter, offered more inducement than did the Dakotas or Nebraska. Many Italians came as harvest hands when the wheat lands opened up; they were called *golondrinas*, swallows who went home when summer was over. But two or three harvest seasons decided them: they would stay in the new country and farm the pampa lands as tenants, land so much more fertile than their hilly tenant farms in Italy. More than a million Europeans came to Argentina to settle between 1857 and 1898. Swiss and Germans also went to the southern provinces where they liked the brisk winter. In Buenos Aires is 1890, as in New York or Boston, 25 per cent of the people were foreign-born. Foreigners far outnumbered Argentines in commerce and industry, and contributed to the stable new middle class.

Thus in the latter half of the nineteenth century an economic revolution had begun to transform the pampas. Industrialization and urbanization were to be the keynotes of the coming twentieth century. The European immigrants who had already displaced the gaucho made Argentina in 1900 seem more like the United States of the same period than like any other part of Spanish-speaking South America. A cowboy tradition was passing, a prairie being fenced in. Scattered nomadic Indians had been sent to remote reservations. Farmlands were offered to immigrants and a European immigrant population was pouring in. Swiftly expanding railways were crossing the nation. A temperate-climate prairie produced wheat and beef by new scientific agriculture. All these things make the story of the changing Argentina. By 1900 the pampas had been transformed by a new all-white population raising cereals and wheat to meet increasing European demands. Is that the story of some tango-dancing, gaucho-singing Latin nation, or is it a repetition in the Southern Hemisphere of the Yankee's own story? Darwin, apostle of evolution, could have seen no more surprising evolution than that of Argentina, had he been able to visit there again in 1892 as he had in 1832.

Readings

Arciniegas, G., ed., *Green Continent* (1944)
Bernstein, H., *Modern and Contemporary Latin America* (1952)
Box, P. H., *Origins of the Paraguayan War* (2 vols., 1929)
Bunkley, A. W., *Life of Sarmiento* (1952)
———, ed., *A Sarmiento Anthology* (1948)
Burgin, M., *Economic Aspects of Argentina Federalism, 1820–1852* (1946)
Cady, J. F., *Foreign Intervention in the Rio de La Plata, 1838–1850* (1929)
Cochrane, T. C., *Entrepreneurship in Argentine Culture* (1962)
Coester, A., *Literary History of Spanish America* (rev. ed., 1928)
Correas, E., *Sarmiento and the United States* (1961)
Cowles, F., *Bloody Precedent* (1952)
Crawford, W. R., *Century of Latin American Thought* (1961)
Criscenti, J. T., *Argentine Constitutional History, 1810–1852* (1961)
Darwin, C., *Charles Darwin's Diary of the Voyage of H.M.S. "Beagle,"* ed. N. Barlow (1933)

Davis, T. B., *Carlos de Alvear, Man of Revolution* (1955)

Dennis, P., *The Argentine Republic* (1922)

Ferns, H. S., *Britain and Argentina in the Nineteenth Century* (1960)

Ford, A. G., *The Gold Standard, 1880–1914: Britain and Argentina* (1962)

Gibson, H., *History and Present State of the Sheep-Breeding Industry in the Argentine Republic* (1893)

Haigh, S., *Sketches of Buenos Ayres, Chile and Peru* (1831)

Hamill, H. M., Jr., *Dictatorship in Latin America* (1965)

Hanson, S. G., *Argentine Meat and the British Market* (1938)

Haring, C. H., *Argentina and the United States* (1941)

———, *South American Progress* (1934)

Hernández, José, *The Gaucho Martín Fierro*, trans. Walter Owen (1936)

Herring, H., *Good Neighbors* (1941)

Hudson, W. H., *Far Away and Long Ago* (1918)

———, *Green Mansions* (1943)

———, *Tales of the Pampas* (1939)

Humphreys, R. A., *Evolution of Modern Latin America* (1947)

Ireland, G., *Boundaries, Possessions and Conflicts in South America* (1938)

Jefferson, M., *Peopling the Argentine Pampas* (1926)

Jeffrey, W. H., *Mitre and Argentina* (1952)

———, *Mitre and Urquiza: A Chapter in the Unification of Argentina* (1952)

Jones, T. B., *South America Rediscovered* (1949)

Joslin, D., *A Century of Banking in Latin America: Bank of London and South America Limited, 1862–1962* (1962)

Kennedy, J. J., *Catholicism, Nationalism and Democracy in Argentina* (1958)

Kirkpatrick, F. A., *History of the Argentine Republic* (1931)

Kroeber, C. L., *Growth of Shipping Industry in the Rio de La Plata, 1794–1850* (1957)

Levene, R., *History of Argentina*, trans. W. S. Robertson (1937)

Lichtblau, M. L., *Argentine Novel in the Nineteenth Century* (1959)

MacDonald, A. F., *Government of the Argentine Republic* (1942)

McGann, T. F., *Argentina, the United States and the Inter-American System, 1880–1914* (1957)

Nichols, M., *The Gaucho* (1942)

———, *Sarmiento* (1940)

Pendle, G., *Argentina* (3rd ed., 1963)

Peters, H. A., *The Foreign Debt of the Argentine Republic* (1934)

Peterson, H. F., *Argentina and the United States, 1810–1960* (1964)

Phelps, V. L., *The International Economic Position of Argentina* (1938)

Rennie, Y. F., *The Argentine Republic* (1945)

Rowe, L. S., *The Federal System of the Argentine Republic* (1921)

Sarmiento, D. F., *Facundo*, trans. Mrs. Horace Mann (1st publication, 1845); many editions)

Scobie, J. R., *Argentina: A City and a Nation* (1964)

———, *Revolution on the Pampas: A Social History of Argentine Wheat, 1860–1910* (1965)

———, *The Struggle for Nationhood: Argentina, 1852–1962* (1964)

Taylor, C. C., *Rural Life in Argentina* (1948)

Tinker, E. L., *The Horsemen of the Americas* (1953)

———, *Life and Literature of the Pampas* (1961)

Torres-Rioseco, A., *Epic of Latin American Literature* (rev. ed., 1946)

Turner, T. A., *Argentina and Argentinians: Notes and Impressions of a Five Years' Sojourn in the Argentine Republic, 1885–1890* (1892)

Whitaker, A. P., *Argentina* (1964)

———, *Nationalism in Latin America* (1962)

Wilgus, A. C., ed., *Argentina, Brazil and Chile Since Independence* (1935)

———, *South American Dictators* (1937)

Williams, J. H., *Argentine International Trade Under Inconvertible Paper Money, 1880–1900* (1920)

Chapter **23**

Chilean Progress
and Leadership to 1900

A NEW NATION IN THE MAKING

SANTIAGO, CHILE, had delighted Charles Darwin in 1833, perhaps because there were many English merchants there with whom he could talk his own language; besides, the scenery in that land of contrasts was so much more beautiful than at Buenos Aires, the "people happier, the farms more prosperous." This land with its northern deserts, its beautiful central valley, and its prosperous farms was to reach stability and modernization more rapidly than its near neighbors.

As in most other parts of Spanish America, the revolution that won independence was a creole revolution. The creoles supplanted the *chapetones* but retained their characteristics throughout the nineteenth century. At the close of the colonial period Chile had about half a million inhabitants, among them perhaps 100,000 usually hostile Araucanian Indians. At the top was the oligarchy of conservative creole landowners who made Chile almost a feudal society. Nearly everyone else was dependent upon them, in a life that was based chiefly on agriculture with the central valley dominant. Santiago, the capital, had about 30,000 people, and no other city of over 5,000 existed. Industrious Basques and northern Spaniards began to immigrate in large numbers before 1830, rising to be shopkeepers and merchants. Though more liberal-minded than the rural landlords, they did not like anarchy, and they joined with the conservatives to keep the peace with a strong, stable government. Thus the white creole landowners and the merchants worked hand in hand, and there was less city-versus-country difficulty in Chile than elsewhere.

The stability did not come with independence, however. Chile, too, had its years of chaos and *caudillismo,* though they were over by 1831. Torn between the two conflicting influences of successful revolt in Buenos Aires and the ultra-royalist feelings of Lima, the isolated frontier province of Chile had had its creole rebels and its royalist factions in the period from 1810 to 1814. In 1818, a year after San Martín won the battle of Chacabuco, Chilean independence was proclaimed. Now Bernardo O'Higgins, who fought for San Martín, was the accepted provisional ruler of Chile, while Chilean troops and ships went north to fight in Peru.

In the emergency O'Higgins called himself Supreme Dictator and ruled with a cabinet or "advisory senate" of five members, which he himself appointed from the various regions of Chile. He continued this rule even after a "constitution" was written in 1822, for that document extended his personal dictatorship for another ten years. O'Higgins forbade cockfighting, gambling, religious processions, and games of dice. Determined to break the power of the old Spanish aristocrats, who had never accepted him as the legal son of Ambrosio O'Higgins, he launched a campaign against the inheritance of land by primogeniture, the unbroken holding of the vast estates of Chile by the eldest son of the eldest son, and abolished titles of nobility. Sternly enforcing safety of travel on Chile's roads, he created a strong centralized police force, which further antagonized the old aristocracy. With very progressive ideas for education, newspapers, schools, and the construction of a drainage canal outside of flood-threatened Santiago, O'Higgins still planned to achieve these things by personal power alone.

Soldiers in the army had not been paid for months. Their leader, Ramón Freire, led a revolt against O'Higgins when the news of his plan for a ten-year extension of power reached them. The aristocratic landowners joined the disgruntled soldiers, set up a new *junta,* and forced O'Higgins to resign rather than face a civil war. He went into permanent exile in Peru, where he was given an estate as a reward for his part in defeating the Spanish loyalists. Thus the father of independent Chile joined the other great leaders of South American independence, dying in exile, unappreciated by his own countrymen.

The seven years after the fall of O'Higgins are usually looked upon as Chile's age of *caudillismo,* the briefest such experience in any of the Spanish American countries. The "stormy petrel" of the period was the military leader, Ramón Freire, whose soldiers had won the revolt against O'Higgins. He served as chief executive, Supreme Dictator, from 1823 to 1826, and ruled as high-handedly as O'Higgins before him. Successful as a general, Freire captured Chiloé Island, the last stronghold of the Spaniards on the Chilean coast. But he did not solve the financial and political difficulties of the country and was forced to resign in 1827. From 1827 to 1829 there were five revolutions and two more attempts at constitution-making; by

1830 the country was in a state of social and economic as well as political chaos. Finally, at the battle of Lircay, April 17, 1830, a conservative faction under Joaquín Prieto won the country and the presidency. The attempt to impose democracy on Chile had failed, and the period of political experimentation was at an end. Henceforth the executive represented the aristocracy; his government was an oligarchy. But within this ruling class his subjects had equality before the law, taxes were collected and the budget balanced, and the country continued to progress. Thus Chile gained government stability earlier than any other Spanish American country and was the first to be placed firmly upon the road to economic and intellectual progress.

DECADES OF PROGRESS IN MID-CENTURY

Now began a period of the "ten-year presidents," each serving two five-year terms under a constitution of 1833, a practical document which was to last longer than almost any other Latin American constitution. These presidents were not *caudillos* like the military dictators elsewhere, but were conservative statesmen representing the landowning aristocracy and the growing commercial and mine-owning class, the high clergy and the military. They often consciously adopted progressive ideas in promoting industrialization, and they preserved order. The party these leaders represented was called in Chilean history the "bigwigs," the *pelucones*, while their organized opponents, the intellectual liberals, city newspapermen, school leaders, and advocates of religious tolerance, were called the "beardless young ones," the *pipiolos*. As the century advanced, *pelucones* became more modernized in their attitudes, while *pipiolos* became less aggressive, and were to give way eventually to workmen's leaders among the miners and factory laborers.

The actual leader of the generation of the 1830s in Chile was not the President Joaquín Prieto, who had won the civil war of 1830, but his Minister, jointly of Interior, Foreign Relations, War, and Navy, the businessman Diego Portales. Portales has been called the Alexander Hamilton of Chilean history, for he brought honesty into government, stabilized Chilean finance, protected national industries and agriculture by tariffs, and welcomed English merchants who made Chile into a popular investment area for other Englishmen. His was a regime of authority and fórce; he gagged the extreme opposition and exiled its leaders, and then with "firmness and tact" he kept the milder *pipiolos* and *pelucones* all in line. A codification of Chilean law was completed in 1855 by the great South American scholar Andrés Bello who spent thirty-six years in Chile and helped found Chile's National University. Valparaiso was improved as a harbor, for Portales meant to make it the chief port of South America's west coast.

When he became involved in a tariff war with Peru over the duties charged by Chile on Peruvian sugar, and by Lima on Chilean wheat, Portales sent ships into open warfare in 1836 against the dictator of Peru. Chilean merchants feared the combination of Peru and Bolivia which dictators of both nations were planning, and were anxious that the Bolivian dictator Santa Cruz should not extend his power into Lima as a rival to Chile's prospering trade. Though *pipiolos* at home opposed the war, Portales and Prieto won it in a series of successful sea battles in the next three years. It was a costly war for the Chileans, however, as they not only lost men and supplies, but Portales as well; he was shot by some Chilean troops who were revolting against the president. Prieto staged a great public funeral for Portales, and in the wave of popular sentiment managed to stay in power himself, successfully ending the war after the decisive victory at Yungay, January 28, 1839. Chile's reputation abroad as a well-organized fighting nation was established by this victory.

The decade of the 1840s was dominated by Manuel Bulnes, a hero of the war, under whom Portales' conservative-progressive ideas were continued. The American engineer William Wheelwright, who built English railways across the Argentine pampas, helped plan such a railroad in Bulnes' administration, as well as to promote steam navigation on the coast of Chile by means of coal mined in Chile itself. As president, Bulnes extended Chile to the Straits of Magellan. The period of the 1840s was one of progress in all lines. Agriculture developed through the introduction of machinery and the formation of a National Society for Agriculture.

At the same time as railroads and steamboats arrived on the scene, a religious controversy developed in this progressive new nation. The financiers and industrialists were Englishmen; Englishmen were Protestants and wanted to hold open Protestant services and be buried in their own Protestant graveyards. *Pelucones*, deeply fanatic in matters of the Church as were conservatives all over Latin America, opposed these "heretics"; and the Church-state issue in Chile became involved in the dispute over the hillside used as a cemetery for Englishmen in Santiago. This holy ground for Protestants was not actually declared legal until 1875. The decades from 1840 to 1870 saw disputes settled amicably over the establishment of civil marriage, the abolition of compulsory tithes for Church support, and the end of *fueros* for Church officials. The Church remained rich and powerful in its ownership of vast agricultural lands, but had to remove its influence from education when the Chilean school system was reformed along North American lines.

During the 1850s Manuel Montt, supported by a revolt of active young liberals, served as president, staying in power for a decade of continued progress of the Portales pattern. Montt was a poor boy who had been educated on a scholarship; one of his chief interests was education. Thirty years after O'Higgins' first attempt, Montt was able to abolish primogeniture as a first step in dividing the great estates, though by so doing he won the hatred of the oligarchy. His era was a time of economic progress, for Chile was suddenly on a main world trade route. Gold had been discovered in California and the ports of Chile were on the direct sea lane around the Horn to the gold fields. A railroad across Panama soon ended the thriving trade with the California coast, but Chile remained on the world map and English vessels continued to call in great numbers for nitrate of soda. Immigrants came in to work on Wheelwright's Santiago-to-Valparaiso railway and Germans settled in the cool regions below the

Bío Bío which seemed so like northern Europe. Political agitation against Montt's high-handed methods was so strong by the end of his "decale," however, that after a revolt in 1859 the administration named José Joaquín Pérez as a "coalition" and compromise candidate. By this time the forces of liberalism were growing more insistent on reform and a new aristocracy of wealth in mining and urban pursuits was developing which aligned itself on the side of the liberals against the landed aristocracy.

Pérez proceeded to rule during a new "era of good feeling" in which the only outbreaks were the seemingly endless troubles among the Araucanian Indians, who remained almost as unpacified as in the days of Lautaro. Pérez himself was the "last of the decenniates," the ten-year presidents. His inauguration began a period of more liberalism within the oligarchical type of government. In his time political parties became well-organized groups, built around philosophies of conservatism and liberalism in the modern sense, rather than around the personalism of individual leaders. The issue of religious freedom dominated the later years of Pérez' regime. In 1871 the constitution was amended to permit complete freedom of private religious worship. At the same time, the presidential term was limited to one five-year period.

The almost equal balance between conservative and liberal factions gradually brought about other liberalizing measures. The ecclesiastical courts were restricted, the non-Catholic cemeteries legalized, though Church and state were not yet separated. Other liberalizing measures—removal of municipal government from presidential control and increases in the power of the legislature—brought greater democracy to bear against the strong executive.

In the 1870s Chile's presidents became involved in a full-scale war with Peru and Bolivia, the War of the Pacific. Apart from the war interest, political life in this period centered on the struggle between the president and congress for the ascendancy. The increased clamor for complete universal suffrage was carried on by miners and city workers. This clamor won recognition for a growing proletarian class who hoped for actual representation in the legislature, decades before their counterparts in other parts of South America were politically conscious. Under Federico Errázuriz (1871–1876) the long and hotly disputed policy of widening the powers of the state over Church was pushed forward. During a serious depression he gave way to Aníbal Pinto (1876–1881), and he in turn, during the War of the Pacific, to Domingo Santa María (1881–1886), under whom the War was ended and the anticlerical program reached its climax. By 1891, the end of the war era, the party of congressional control, as opposed to the supporters of a strong presidency, had won the government, but that is part of the story of the War of the Pacific.

WARS IN CHILE, FOREIGN AND DOMESTIC

Of all the Spanish American nations, only the two west coast nations, Peru and Chile, ever went to war with Spain again after independence. Spain had never recognized Peru, and in the 1860s a serious controversy arose between Peru and its former mother country. Peru refused to pay the reparations demanded by the Spaniards and the latter declared war. Chile, sympathizing for once with the usually scorned neighbor, agitated against Spanish demands, and there was a demonstration in the streets of Santiago which threatened the person of the Spanish minister. A Spanish naval commander, just driven out of Callao harbor by the Peruvians, demanded an apology and a salute from Chile. Chile refused to be so "insulted." Forgetting bitter internal politics, all Chile joined in a "defensive and offensive" alliance with Peru, Bolivia, and Ecuador, declaring war September 24, 1865. Though the Chilean navy had only one usable war vessel, Chile stole the Spanish flagship and fought the Spanish navy to a draw, only to have Spain bombard Valparaiso to the tune of $10,000,000 damage. England forced Spain to pay for damages done the British-owned docks at Valparaiso and the affair ended in a moral victory for Chile. But Chileans had learned the necessity of building a powerful navy if they were to be a power on the west coast.

Many more Chileans died in the ceaseless war against the Araucanian Indians in the south throughout the second half of the century than died in the "war with Spain." A native rebellion of 1859, led by powerful *caciques* among these "Apaches of South America," produced two years of guerrilla fighting. When peace was restored, the government set the policy of permanently occupying the Indian country through the erection of forts and the building of towns. European settlers founded communities further and further inside the Araucanian frontier. But the Araucanians were not subdued; they rose up again in the Pérez administration, led by a fanatical French trader who called himself King Orelie Antoine I. In his name, revolt flamed along the frontier until the border guards brought him in as a captive; the courts declared him insane and expelled him from the country. A "treaty" between the Araucanians and the Chilean government in 1883 recognized the tribal government and traditions and held the Indian lands in reservation. Later the Araucanians were given representation in the Chilean congress, but their lands slowly "melted away" and became small patches, crisscrossed by railroad and telegraph lines and separated by the new towns of the European settlers.

The northern border along the nitrate deserts brought aggressive warfare on the part of the Chileans against their erstwhile allies in the naval war with Spain. The exact frontier line between the coastal lands of Chile and Bolivia had never been decided. When nitrates from that desert region came into demand in world trade, an agreement on the 24th parallel was reached, with a share of all proceeds from mines between the 23rd and 25th parallels to be divided between both countries. Chile had the engineers, the capital—borrowed from British firms—and the workers; they went in and made the desert profitable. When Bolivia protested, Chile gave up her claims above the 24th parallel, while Bolivia promised not to add any new taxes on the Chilean firms already there. In 1878 a Bolivian *caudillo* taxed a Chilean company in violation of the treaty and the war was on.

The course of the ensuing War of the Pacific, from 1879 to 1883, is more a part of the story of Bolivia and of Peru than of Chile, since it was fought almost entirely in their area, and influenced their history. Chile was a much more modernized nation with better-trained and better-equipped forces, and she soon had the mastery on land and sea. Chilean troops captured Arica early in 1880; the Chilean fleet blockaded the Peruvian coast and carried out destructive naval raids on Peruvian coastal towns. Chile was so determined on a complete victory that she refused terms set up by an American board of mediators and continued the war in 1881. In January of that year Lima itself was captured and sacked by the victorious Chilean army. Two more years of naval blockade and occupation ensued before the Peruvian government would admit defeat. The peace was finally signed at Ancón on October 20, 1883. Tarapacá was ceded to Chile; Tacna and Arica were to be controlled by Chile for ten years, until a plebiscite would decide which country should have ultimate sovereignty. Such a plebiscite was not held, and Chile continued in possession of the nitrate workings. A separate truce signed with Bolivia in 1884, made into a formal treaty in 1904, gave Chile the Bolivian seacoast on the Pacific and cut Bolivia off from a port entirely, except for the rights of access by railroad. This railway right and the Tacna-Arica question remained open sores in Latin American diplomacy for almost half a century.

Chile emerged from the War of the Pacific one of the richest and most powerful of the South American republics, prosperous from her conquests and exploitation of mineral resources of the north as well as from new markets for her agricultural products to the south. But the *inquilinos*, as the peasants were called, and the *rotos* or proletarian workers, who continued to eke out only a bare subsistence, had achieved no recognition, and the country was not yet a modern democracy. Bribery, fraud, and strong-armed methods were used by the presidents, especially Santa María, to maintain control of congress. However, an alliance of liberal factions brought José Manuel Balmaceda, an able diplomat and cabinet member, to the presidency in 1886.

Balmaceda started a five-year term as president with every chance of success. The nitrate income was assured, new public works were begun, a sanitation and pure drinking-water campaign started. Who would have thought the fine beginning would end in tragedy? But public improvements cost money; the country was in debt because of the War of the Pacific; congress opposed the president's policy. Thus, in order to put his democratic measures into effect, Balmaceda the reformer, on behalf of the inert masses, became an unconstitutional dictator. Over a budget dispute in 1891 the conservative majority of congress revolted, was joined by the navy, and fought in the name of liberalism and constitutionalism. The army rallied to Balmaceda's side; fierce fighting resulted, the most serious civil war in Chilean history. The navy captured first the nitrate coast and revenues and then Valparaiso. Balmaceda was defeated and took refuge in the Argentine legation. There he ended the bitter struggle by committing suicide, September 19, 1891, one day after the termination of his legal term of office. He is remembered as the man who struck the first blow in behalf of the masses against the oligarchy in preparation for a social revolution which was to come to fruition after 1920.

One last "foreign fracas" of the nineteenth century took place as a result of the civil war. During the fighting a ship named the *Itata*, carrying

Harvest time on a Chilean *fundo* **of the Central Valley, where meat from Europe replaced Indian corn.** *Courtesy Pan American Union.*

arms for the congress party, was seized by the United States Navy, an act considered unneutral by the Chileans. Shortly afterward the American warship *Baltimore* was in Valparaiso, and the anti-American Chileans became involved in a brawl with the "liberty-happy" sailors. When two sailors were killed, America forced Chile to pay an indemnity and to apologize, an act which hurt the ambitious Chileans and augured no good-will for the United States.

Jorge Montt, leader of the successful conservative forces in the Civil War of 1891, was chosen president in that year and instituted a new era of pseudo-parliamentary government which lasted until 1920. Domestic peace had come to Chile by the election of 1896; economy budgets had cleaned up the deficits the civil war produced; freer elections were the order of the day. Federico Errázuriz, son of a former president, the winner of the fair and hotly contested 1896 election, was declared president by a margin of two votes in congress, and this close a tie brought no armed revolt on the part of the losers. Chile faced the 1900s with a stable equilibrium between congress and president which was to last till 1920.

INTELLECTUAL AND SOCIAL ADVANCES
IN PROSPEROUS CHILE

Chile's land tenure system seemed even more "oligarchical" than did the great *estancias* on the open range of the pampas to the east. The *fundo* owners, similar to the *hacendados* of Mexico, were the ruling class their sons studied law in Santiago and became the leading politicians among the *pelucones*. The tenant farmers, the *inquilinos*, worked for the landlords in payment for the small plots of ground they were allowed to cultivate for themselves. When European immigrants came in large numbers they went to the southern frontier, or became miners in the rapidly developing nitrate workings of the north, or stayed in the cities, where there was a new aristocracy of commerce and mining. Thus the cities grew while the *fundos* remained unchanged.

Santiago and its suburbs had 250,000 inhabitants by 1890, among whom a middle class was rapidly developing. British merchants were accepted in Santiago society and encouraged beautification of the city. Santiago had a school of architecture as early as 1850; soon there was a School of Fine Arts and a National Conservatory of Music. The University of Chile had been founded in 1842 with Andrés Bello as its first rector. The Argentine statesman Sarmiento, exiled in Chile by Rosas, had started a teacher-training school and had set a pattern for elementary education while he lived there. By 1890 there were many provincial and city high schools, both public and private. One child in four went to school, an average better than in most European countries at the time; and Chile also had many libraries and museums. Many young lawyers, doctors, dentists, engineers, and pharmacists were being trained. In 1860 there were two daily newspapers in Chile; in 1890 the rapid spread of education had provided enough readers for seven newspapers in Santiago alone, and for twenty more throughout the country. Cultural societies of literary-minded people flourished, conducting scholarly contests and holding public lectures.

In 1885 a census taken in Chile showed a population of two and a half millions, one-third urban and two-thirds rural. Many of these people were members of a new class of society for South America—industrial workers and miners, with some elementary education and some political consciousness. Chile had long since excelled at mining. She was the leading copper producer of the world from 1850 to 1880. The nitrates so easily obtainable on the coast along the Atacama desert had been known as a source of gunpowder; discoveries in the mid-1800s led to their use as fertilizer also. A process of extracting the chemicals easily was worked out in 1886, soon after Chile acquired the richest beds from Peru in the War of the Pacific. By 1900, nitrates comprised 75 per cent of Chile's exports. The boom in the nitrate business sucked agricultural laborers from the farms in the south. Workers received five or six times as much in Antofagasta or Iquique as in the central valley. When they returned to the farms, they would not again work for so little; they demanded and got higher wages; already they had the suffrage. Thus nitrates brought even the *inquilinos* a measure of prosperity at the turn of the century. Agriculture also increased with the addition of more land under cultivation, land worked with machinery. Many landlords felt a strong enough interest in education to provide a schoolmaster to teach the children of the *inquilinos* during the less busy months on the *fundo*.

Intellectually, Chile was more Europeanized than the nations to her north. Andrés Bello (1781–1865), the great Venezuelan man of letters, had spent three decades in Chile and shaped the intellectual life there, greatly influencing her writers and philosophers. The young Argentinian Sarmiento engaged Bello in a lively controversy between classicism and the new ideas, as a result of which Chilean literature was emancipated from eighteenth-century form. Sarmiento won by converting José Victorino Lastarria (1817–1888), who became the guide to the new generation. Chile produced a group of historians worthy of the title in competition with any European, especially Benjamín Vicuña Mackenna (1831–1886), revolutionist, journalist, politician, and diplomat, who authored and edited nearly 100 volumes. He, together with Miguel Luis Amunátegui (1828–1888) and Diego Barros Arana (1830–1907), form a trio of outstanding historians. The second half of the nineteenth century saw the rise of a true Chilean national literature. Perhaps the most famous Chilean writer of the period was Alberto Blest Gana (1830–1920), who is called the Balzac of South America, so realistic are his stories of Chilean life. In his novel *Martín Rivas*, written in 1862, the hero seems a very human person, a middle-class young man trying to "crash" aristocratic Santiago society. In his descriptions of the parties of the aristocracy, the church ceremonies, and the popular festivals, Blest Gana's characters seem typical members of the middle class anywhere. Actually Chile, like Blest Gana's hero, was becoming a rising middle-class nation. By the end of the nineteenth century it was beginning to be a country of wealth and splendor. The Chilean government had made improvements in political, social, and economic life, but the advances were not equally or justly distributed. Such distribution became the twentieth-century problem.

Readings

Bernstein, H., *Modern and Contemporary Latin America* (1952)

Bowman, T., *Desert Trails of Atacama* (1924)

Burr, R. N., *By Reason or Force: Chile and the Balance of Power in South America, 1830–1905* (1965)

———, *Stillborn Panama Congress: Power Politics and Chilean-Colombian Relations during the War of the Pacific* (1962)

Butland, G., *Chile* (3rd ed., 1956)

———, *Human Geography of Southern Chile* (1958)

Campbell, M. V., *Development of the National Theatre in Chile to 1842* (1958)

Chisholm, A. S. M., *Independence of Chile* (1911)

Coester, A., *Literary History of Spanish America* (rev. ed., 1946)

Davis, W. C., *Last Conquistadores: The Spanish Intervention in Peru and Chile, 1863–1866* (1950)

Dawson, T. C., *South American Republics* (2 vols., 1903–1904)

Dennis, W. J., *Tacna and Arica* (1931)

Edwards, A., *The Dawn* (1931)

———, *My Native Land* (1928)

Elliot, G. F. C., *Chile, Its History and Development* (1927)

Evans, H. C., *Chile and Its Relations with the United States* (1927)

Fergusson, E., *Chile* (1943)

Fetter, F. W., *Monetary Inflation in Chile* (1931)

Galdames, L., *History of Chile*, trans. I. J. Cox (1941)

Hancock, A. U., *History of Chile* (1893)

Hanson, E. P., *Chile: Land of Progress* (1941)

Haring, C. H., *South American Progress* (1934)

Herring, H., *Good Neighbors* (1941)

Johnson, J. J., *Pioneer Telegraphy in Chile, 1852–1876* (1948)

Kaempfer-Villagran, G., *Bloody Episodes of the Workers' Struggle in Chile, 1850–1925* (1962)

Lindsell, H., *Chilean-American Controversy of 1891–1892* (1943)

Markham, C. R., *War Between Peru and Chile, 1879–1882* (1883)

McBride, G. M., *Chile: Land and Society* (1936)

Millington, H., *American Diplomacy and the War of the Pacific* (1948)

Pendle, G., *The Land and People of Chile* (1960)

Pike, F. B., *Chile and the United States, 1880–1962* (1963)

Roberts, S. A., *José Toribio Medina, His Life and Works* (1941)

Shaw, P. V., *The Early Constitutions of Chile, 1810–1833* (1931)

Sherman, W. R., *Diplomatic and Commercial Relations of the United States and Chile, 1820–1914* (1926)

Subercaseaux, B., *Chile: A Geographic Extravaganza* (1943)

Subercaseaux, G., *Monetary and Banking Policy of Chile* (1922)

Torres-Rioseco, A., *Epic of Latin American Literature* (rev. ed., 1946)

Wilgus, A. C., ed., *Argentina, Brazil, and Chile Since Independence* (1935)

———, *South American Dictators* (1937)

Chapter 24

Chaos in Uruguay and Paraguay

URUGUAY, A TURBULENT LAND
ON THE EASTERN PLATA

Uruguay is often called the Denmark of the Western Hemisphere because of its flat lands, agricultural basis of society, dependence on one large city, democratic government, and lack of distinct social classes. This is remarkable when one realizes that as a Spanish colony it was a "late comer," and that its development in the nineteenth century is one of party strife and civil war, so chaotic as to be mere confusion in the telling. But more than most other Latin American states, it has a sharp division into two chapters between nineteenth and twentieth century, with a complete about-face for the better as of 1903.

Montevideo had been founded as late as 1726, as a frontier against Brazilian encroachment on the *Banda Oriental*, the eastern shore. After years as a bone of contention between the Spaniards and Portuguese, the area emerged as a buffer state between Argentina and Brazil. When Buenos Aires became independent, the whole Uruguayan area had a population of perhaps 70,000, about one-fifth of them residents of Montevideo, the rest being either ranchowners, wandering gauchos in the backlands, or wild Charrúa Indians. From 1811 to 1816 the Uruguayans were involved in a four-way struggle: royalist Spaniards, Buenos Aires armies, Uruguayan patriots, and Brazilians. José Artigas, the Uruguayan national hero, had saved Montevideo from Buenos Aires domination, only to lose it to

José Gervasio Artigas, *gaucho* **founder of Uruguay, in whose name the Thirty-Three Immortals fought Brazil for the** *Banda Oriental. Courtesy Pan American Union.*

the Brazilians under John VI. After 1822 the area became a part of the Brazilian empire under Pedro I and remained such until it achieved its own independence in 1828.

Many of the Montevideans, irked at Brazilian rule, had gone into exile to Buenos Aires. In that exile, Juan Antonio Lavalleja organized a small group of patriots, the Thirty-three Immortals, and slipped across river to meet another small band led by Fructuoso Rivera on the other side. These "Immortals" of Uruguayan history took and held an area of backland, where they called an assembly to declare all-out war on Brazil in 1825. There ensued an indecisive three-year struggle, the War of the Thirty-three Immortals, between Brazil and Lavalleja, with Argentina fighting on Lavalleja's side. England, with an eye to trade, intervened in the war on behalf of Uruguay as a separate nation. Finally on August 28, 1828, Brazil and Argentina signed a peace treaty recognizing Uruguay and guaranteeing its independence for five years. The two nations then withdrew, though they continued to cast covetous eyes on the *Banda Oriental.*

Uruguay's subsequent instability as a nation led to further intervention by both rivals, while Montevideo quarreled with its own backlands for the next fifty years. There were at least forty revolutions before the end of the century. Of the twenty-five different governments in power till the turn for the better in 1903, nine were forced out by military power, two

Montevideo's monument to the nineteenth-century Uruguayan patriots—the statue by Belloni called *La Carreta*. *Courtesy Pan American Union.*

were "liquidated by assassination" and one by "grave injury," while ten resisted successfully one or more revolutions during their periods in office, and only three were free from serious disturbances. Lawless frontiersmen, rival *caudillos*, a psychology of endless fighting, and continued foreign influence and intervention combined to make chaos in Uruguay.

Trouble had begun right away among the leaders of the Thirty-three Immortals; former guerrilla leader Rivera, as inspector general of the new army, did not accept the leadership of governor Lavalleja. As head of the army, Rivera, who was to dominate politics through thirty-four years of feuding, got himself elected first president under the Constitution of 1830 —a centralistic constitution, incidentally, which was in force to 1919, in spite of the chaos of the country. Gaucho, patriot, and warrior, three times president, Rivera founded the Colorado party, a name applied to the more liberal-minded city dwellers who followed him. Through this party he left the impression of his personality on nineteenth-century Uruguay. Since his strength lay in riverbank and coastal centers, regions associated with the trade and commerce of La Plata, he feared Argentine domination, and therefore was more pro-Brazilian in outlook. He tried to govern a country in which Brazilian coins were the only ones in circulation, actual slavery was still the order of the day, ownership of ranches in the backlands was in constant dispute, and the Charrúa Indians roamed at will, pillaging the frontier. Furthermore, the country had no financial credit whatsoever.

In 1835 Rivera peacefully gave way to his successor, Manuel Oribe, and retired as head of the army, only to lead another revolt when his financial accounts were questioned. For seven years a feud continued between Rivera's Colorados, with Brazilian troops on their side, and the party called the Blancos, organized among the back-country landowners by Lavalleja's supporters with help from the Argentine dictator Rosas. This conservative Blanco party of the landowning aristocracy looked to Argentina as a counterweight against the possibility of Brazilian domination. The long fight in the backlands came to the doors of Montevideo in 1843. Thus began the so-called Great War—the conservative rural Blancos and Argentina's Rosas on one side, the Colorados, the Montevideans, and the Brazilians on the other, while Montevideo withstood a nine-year siege.

Strange to say, it was not the city-dwellers who suffered. Supplied by the French and British navies, which were blockading Rosas' Argentina, they ate well, went to the theater, and maintained their normal life. It was the backlands, the estates and villages of the Blancos, which were to feel the hurt, cut off as they were from imported supplies and city trade. Bandits from both sides and from the allied countries stole the cattle and horses; gauchos left the plains and went into the armies. No schools and no roads were built. The war itself wavered first to one side, then to the other. Rivera was first exiled, and then was in and out of the besieged Montevideo through the next four years as he broke his exile, and was finally released legally when the siege was lifted. The Great War was over and the Argentine dictator Rosas was defeated at home in Buenos Aires in 1852.

Before a stable government could be established in Uruguay, however, Rivera and Lavalleja had died, both of them, strangely enough, from natural causes or sheer exhaustion. The peace made with Brazil gave that aggressive nation a large section of the northern frontier. The Colorado government which opposed it fell from power and a Blanco government, with 4,000 Brazilian soldiers behind it, tried to rule the country. Peace finally came when the Brazilians withdrew and left the Blancos, the country ranchowners, to rule the city for a stormy decade. The leader of the suppressed Colorados, Venancio Flores, was able to work up a revolt from exile. He gained support from both Brazil and Argentina, both of which countries feared that the increasing chances for stability under the Blancos would end their hopes for territory. By 1863, when Flores reinvaded his homeland, there was an ambitious dictator in neighboring Paraguay, Francisco Solano López, who hoped to add Uruguay to his "empire" by aiding the now friendless Blancos against these new enemies. By such intervention Paraguay became involved in the Great Paraguayan War which lasted from 1864 to 1870. The war was fought outside of Uruguay, and is a story in itself. Uruguay was simply the pawn over which that war was started, but when the war ended Argentine-Brazilian intervention in Uruguay ended also.

Flores, whose plan to take over the presidency from the Blancos had brought Paraguayan intervention in the first place, served as president and actual dictator in Montevideo while the war raged. His power was brought to an end by assassination in February 1868. He is usually considered the last of the gaucho *caudillos*. Later presidents were professional soldiers who brought gradual peace and a softening of the Colorado-Blanco bitterness.

Tranquility did not come for another decade, however. Blanco fought

Colorado for two more years after the Paraguayan War was over in 1870, until Argentina arranged a negotiated peace. This strange agreement gave the Blancos $500,000 and the police control of four interior provinces, but left the capital and the presidency in the hands of the Colorados; the device of bribery was a less costly solution for party rivalry than was civil war. The Blanco landlords seemed satisfied with control of their backlands, and this "deal" set a pattern for later agreements.

A new kind of "president," Colonel Lorenzo Latorre, came to power in 1875, suppressed disorder between the parties for the first time in fifty years, reformed the army, controlled the wasteful finances, and channeled the money thus managed into schools and internal improvements. When he came to power a financial panic threatened the nation, for its growing city industries could not support its endless wars in the backlands. But his financial measures did not solve this unexpected new problem, and he resigned in disgust in 1880, refusing to rule longer because, as he said, "Uruguay is ungovernable." Another "military first magistrate," Máximo Santos, followed him with the same policy: strict control of finances, placation of both parties, end of internal warfare. After the next adminis-tration, that of Máximo Tajes, the political influence of the army, which had ended the constant guerrilla fighting, was allowed to diminish. Uru-guay was at last growing up. A civilian lawyer, the first city-educated, nonmilitary president in Uruguay's stormy history, Dr. Julio Herrera y Obes, came to the presidency in 1890, and after suppressing a revolution gave way peacefully to his elected successor, Juan Idiarte Borda, in 1894.

Uruguay was to revert to adolescent tantrums once more. These military and civilian reformers had all been Colorados. But the Blancos were not dead; they still sat on their prosperous cattle ranches in the interior and watched the city jealously. When they saw that the congress was a tool of the new president Borda, they revolted, in 1897, under a wealthy but uneducated *estanciero* named Aparicio Saravia, who remained a powerful Blanco leader for a decade. President Borda was assassinated in the melee. Now came a compromise leader, Juan Lindolfo Cuestas, who made another of those "'deals" with the Blancos. This time they were to have control of six provinces and a payment of $200,000 "for the expense of pacification." Cuestas then became president until 1903, when the mature little country was able to shake off its bad heritage in one last revolt of the Blanco leader Saravia, and to march steadily toward prog-ress.

The real key to the increasing maturity and the decline of civil strife after 1870 is economic and social advance. The population increased from 70,000 to 900,000 in eighty years. British who had come to intervene stayed to go into business. Italians, Germans, and Spaniards came to farm the pampas or to settle in Montevideo, uninformed and unconcerned about traditional party feuds. They and their descendants created a middle class of lawyers, doctors, and merchants. A railway line was begun in 1867; the first meat-packing plant was built by a German firm in 1861. Gauchos could find jobs in such plants or in the well-run ranches which supplied them; they did not have to look to a private armed band for employment.

Landowners and merchants, in their turn, became more interested in developing their properties than in the wars of Blancos and Colorados. The bitterness between those parties, though it did not die out, became less acrimonious in the third and fourth generation away from the Thirty-three Immortals, and aroused no interest among the newly arrived immigrants to whom the rich land looked so good.

One of the fathers of progressive modern Uruguay was José Pedro Varela, a youth who lived only 34 years, but who in his short life had known Sarmiento and Horace Mann. He organized the "Friends of Popular Education" in the 1870s and got the dictator, Colonel Latorre, to create the position of "Inspector of Primary Education and Instruction" for him to fill. His new ideas on free, compulsory education, liberalized curriculum, and improved teaching methods grew more popular after his death.

Montevideo, growing in sophistication in spite of endless civil wars and long siege, was not without culture. There had been a national university there since 1849; the National Library dates from 1816. The Ateneo, which dates from 1880, gives recitals, conferences, and lectures open to the public. Uruguayans had been writing poetry even during the Great War, and gold medals had been awarded for nationalistic and romantic poetry as early as the 1850s. By 1865 *La Revista Literaria* was being published in Montevideo; many of its successful poetry contributors were revolutionists and soldiers as well as writers, but they wrote of romance rather than realism. A famous epic poem of Indian life, called *Tabaré*, was published by Juan Zorilla de San Martín (1855–1931) in 1888, and is considered a masterpiece of Uruguayan literature. Other "masterpieces" dealt with the life of the colonial aristocracy—for example, the versified novel called *Celiar*, written by Alejandro Magariños Cervantes (1825–1893). Today Magariños' best-known book is his novel of gaucho life, *Caramarú*.

The new peace between political parties brought out a flowering of intellectual accomplishment among the bright young men of Montevideo who could turn their attention away from the Colorados and Blancos and toward arts, letters and sciences. The 1890s saw backward Uruguay produce a novelist worthy of international attention, Eduardo Acevedo Díaz (1851–1924), whose trilogy of novels about the Uruguayan ranchers and their part in the many wars between factions are full of descriptions of landscapes and manners as well as understanding of the bitterness of the strife. *Estancia* owners, beautiful relatives from the city, gauchos, Charrúa Indians, and Brazilian soldiers take part in the interwoven plots of the three novels, but it is the characters and the vivid description of them that are important in the literary history of South America.

PARAGUAY: ISOLATED UNDER ITS FIRST DICTATORS

Paraguay, inland country to the northwest of Uruguay with a name so similar, had started out more auspiciously than its coastal sister. Its history had been fascinating, though of third-rate importance. Isolated in the heart of the continent, almost completely an Indian country, with

Asunción the oldest Spanish city in the Plata area and the center of the greatest Jesuit successes, the whole nation had no access to the sea except through Argentina. Saved by a powerful, unchallenged dictator from the usual costly civil war after independence, and building up an isolated but self-sufficient agricultural economy, this inland nation of Guaraní-speaking *mestizo* peoples had every chance for peace. If Uruguay was torn by constant political war between two factions in which no one person stands out to be remembered, Paraguay remained a one-party state under three dictators, the second succeeding the first at his death from old age, the third chosen by his father the second, as his rightful heir. But with the succession of this "crown prince" in the 1860s Paraguay's peace ended, and the little nation was plunged into such a war as the Blancos and Colorados had never known, a war against three other nations which practically annihilated the Paraguayan people.

Independence had come to Paraguay as a by-product of the movement centered at Buenos Aires. General Belgrano had tried to force Paraguay under the sway of the *junta* of Buenos Aires of 1810. Dr. José Gaspar Rodríguez Francia, who led the Paraguayans, was able to rid his country of both Spanish and Argentine interference. An assembly called in Paraguay made him "first consul" and finally perpetual dictator, which he remained for twenty-nine years, longer than anyone else in South American history. Dr. Francia declared complete independence in 1813, refused to participate in the Congress of Tucumán in 1816, and kept his country in splendid isolation until his death in 1840.

Dr. Francia was an educated man, one of the few in Asunción, with a degree from the University of Córdoba. As a young man he practiced law but never mixed socially with the handful of Asunción elite. As dictator he ruled without congress, ministers, or tribunals, although he refused any salary, made no attempt to enrich himself, and hired watchers to keep a close tab on the national treasury. His foreign policy was one of complete isolation; no visitors came in save for two or three scientists who were under constant surveillance during their brief botanical forays. No Paraguayans went out. Traffic downriver was all but closed.

A lean, haughty man, misanthropic but devoted to peace and prosperity in Paraguay, Dr. Francia does not follow the pattern of cowboy or soldier *caudillos*. His people called him *El Supremo*, and took off their hats when he passed; for this his law required that every Paraguayan wear a hat to take off, even though he might wear little else. Death, torture, and exile came swiftly to anyone who opposed Dr. Francia. As he isolated Paraguay from the rest of the world, so he isolated himself from humanity, living alone with four servants, sleeping in a different room of his rambling house every night so that no enemy could know where to come and stab him in his sleep. He even set spies to spy on his spies.

Dr. Francia made long-range plans for his backward state; he avoided the holocaust of civil war experienced by most other new Latin American nations and he forced economic self-sufficiency. When Argentina charged a heavy duty on river traffic, Dr. Francia quit foreign trade and insisted that the Paraguayans raise their own corn and cane, cotton and tobacco, *yerba maté* and beef, rather than depend on Argentine crops for food. Only munitions to fortify the frontiers and arm the secret police came from abroad; the people did without everything else. Livestock increased; local trade between villages was encouraged by fairs. Money was unnecessary when every trade was made by barter. Jesuit missionaries would have seen little difference in the way of life in Paraguay from 1640 to 1840. The only outside enemy that Dr. Francia had to fight was a great army of locusts; he drafted all males from fourteen to sixty to replant the half-grown harvest the locusts had destroyed. Legend has it that thus Dr. Francia learned that two crops of wheat and corn would grow in a year in this semitropical land, and ordered that such be planted henceforth.

The Asunción of Dr. Francia's last years had only 20,000 people, but it was Paraguay's only city. There were very few two-story houses, and "sand still substituted for pavement," according to one of the few visiting scientists. "Ravines continued their errant ways, and served as efficient sewers in wet weather" and the "shops were miserable stores like those of the countryside in Argentina."

The Paraguayan natives did not let such criticism bother them. More generous, happy natured, and possessing more individual dignity than the far-away Buenos Aires sophisticates or the trade-minded Montevideans, Paraguayans went barefoot, but wore the embroidered white drawers of the Argentine gauchos below their baggy pants and tied them with scarlet sashes. Though the majority of these Paraguayans were *mestizo* stock, all spoke the Guaraní language, which had been written down by the Jesuit missionaries. When some Paraguayans were taught to read and write under Francia, it was Guaraní they learned first before Spanish, for Dr. Francia was very much pro-Guaraní, and at one time had forbidden Spaniards to marry other than Indians or mulattoes. A few well-to-do families in Asunción aped the styles of Buenos Aires—their meagre contact with the outside world, two weeks travel downriver. In such a nation no literature developed. Church authority was limited strictly by the anticlerical *El Supremo*, but no other social force arose to take its place.

At the age of seventy-four *El Supremo* rode in his formal carriage past his reverential subjects for the last time. On September 20, 1840, he was dead, though the people could not believe he would ever die. He left no heir and no tradition of electing one. Francia's secretary Patiño, after hiding the news of *El Supremo's* death as long as he could, called a *junta* to govern, with himself as secretary. The *junta* threw the secretary into jail, where he committed suicide. After six months of government by a confused *junta*, a congress was called in March 1841 which proceeded to set up the same type of "consul" government Dr. Francia had started in 1811. Chief consul was Carlos Antonio López, who served in that capacity three years. In 1844 he called a congress to adopt a constitution making himself president for ten years; this "election" process was repeated ten years later and signified "approval" of his rule until his death in 1862.

There could not be two *El Supremos*, so Carlos López was called *Excelentísimo*. López was a huge, corpulent, pear-shaped man, mild mannered and "respectable looking"; his regime was one of stability equal to that of Dr. Francia and of much greater modernization and material prosperity. He reorganized the judicial system, collected taxes on a fair basis, brought in the first newspaper, abolished slavery, and tried to encourage primary education. Sixteen young Paraguayans were sent at his own expense to study in Europe. A railroad fifty-five miles long was built from Asunción toward the Uruguayan border, bridges were built across the Paraná, and ferry service was established between towns. Trade upriver was permitted to all nations, if and when Argentine dictators allowed it through.

Carlos López meant to establish a place in foreign affairs for Paraguay, a reversal of Francia's policy. He arranged for his country's recognition by Argentina for the first time, but he was not as successful in other forays into foreign relations as he had hoped. Paraguay's boundaries with Argentina and Brazil remained unsettled, a problem his son was to use as a reason for war. He quarreled with the United States over an American steamship company formed to commence regular steamship traffic and whose first cargo was wrecked on the Brazilian coast. England also had an altercation with López and forced the release of a captured British subject by blockading a Paraguayan ship which was in Buenos Aires harbor. France was also angered by López when promises to French settlers induced to settle the frontier were not kept. All these clashes hurt Paraguay's prestige abroad at a time when the nation was definitely hoping for importance and position. At least Carlos López did not involve the nation in any foreign debt; he had developed the country's resources, opened it to foreign commerce, and left to his son and successor an economically prosperous land.

THE PARAGUAYAN WAR
OF FRANCISCO SOLANO LÓPEZ

Carlos López' most serious mistake was in the choice of his son as successor. Francisco Solano López was a boy of fourteen when his father came to power, untrained, ignorant, and barefooted. Soon he was given a commission in the army, assigned special tutors, and taught to speak French and to ape the manners of the small colony of diplomats in Asunción. Long before he was thirty he was the commander in chief of the armed forces and built a large military machine in order to play politics against his strong neighbors, Brazil and Argentina. Francisco, the "crown prince" who by now imagined himself the "Napoleon of the New World," went to Paris to buy ships and arms for a Plata River empire and to make an impression on Parisian society. Already bored with the half-Guaraní girl of Asunción, he acquired a mistress in Paris, a footloose Irish girl named Elisa Lynch. She shared his plans for a South American Napoleonic empire and returned with him to lead Asunción society. Carlos López persuaded his subservient congress a month before his death to proclaim Francisco his legal successor. When his *Excelentísimo* died, Paraguay's slow and peaceful life came to an abrupt end, for Francisco, his mistress, and his army immediately took control of the government. On October 16, 1862, he was declared Supreme Chief and General of the Armies.

Francisco Solano followed his father's internal policies and actually made some improvements in communications and transportation. He established the first telegraphic line in South America and dreamed of making Asunción a great city so that his paramour would not feel so downcast at having left Paris. But his foreign policy was so ambitious as to be disastrous. To push it, he built up in two years the largest, best-trained army that South America had ever seen.

Meanwhile Argentina and Brazil skirmished over the Blancos and the Colorados in Uruguay. When Brazil supported the Colorados in Uruguay, López supported the Blancos—sufficient excuse for war. In November 1864 López seized a Brazilian steamer which had heretofore been allowed peaceful transit up the Paraguay River as the only route by which Brazilians could reach their undeveloped province of Mato Grosso. Then he sent an army into the Brazilian area. In order to attack the Brazilian troops in Uruguay as soon as war was openly declared the next month, Francisco López invaded the Argentine province of Corrientes. Though Argentina and Brazil had been traditional enemies in the long disputes in Uruguay, they now united against Francisco López; he was not to have the pleasure of fighting them one at a time. Indeed, his side lost out in Uruguay, and that small nation then joined the Triple Alliance fighting against Paraguay.

Historians are prone to put all the blame for the ensuing war on López, but this is a misinterpretation of fact. The war had its origins in Brazilian encroachments upon Paraguayan territory, in Brazilian and Argentine meddling in Uruguay, and in Paraguayan desires to play a decisive role in the politics of the Plata area. It is true, however, that Francisco López precipitated the war, and upon him rests the responsibility of the tragic results for Paraguay. The costly and bloody war lasted nearly six years.

The Paraguayans fought with fanatical bravery throughout, though the odds against them were overwhelming. Once López' troops had lost the offensive, the combined enemy troops fought right up the Paraguay River toward the heart of the nation. Brazil sent her naval squadron up the river to win Brazil's only naval engagement among the water hyacinths. Pedro II's son-in-law, the Comte d'Eu, fought in this useless war, as did the great Argentine statesman Bartolomé Mitre, wasting his ability and Argentina's resources when he was the elected president. Paraguayans swam out into the river to attack Brazilian ships, or stole along in canoes camouflaged with the water hyacinths. Three thousand Paraguayans held muddy trenches along the river against 15,000 invaders, and, with but a handful of soldiers, maintained a fort at Humaitá on the Paraguay River for months against the allied fleet. Six thousand howling Guaraní attacked 40,000 allied soldiers in a narrow pass and were almost entirely wiped out. No individual Paraguayan would admit defeat. Francisco López had taught each of his Guaraní soldiers to consider himself worth six of the enemy.

But they were doomed to defeat because of the lack of adequate leadership, the inferiority of numbers and resources, and the extreme isolation of Paraguay.

After four years, every male in Paraguay from eleven to sixty was at the front on the river approaches above Corrientes; women and children worked without wages behind the lines. Elisa Lynch is said to have led a women's battalion into the last days of fighting. Francisco López himself escaped with 2,000 survivors when the enemy occupied Asunción. In the wilderness 150 miles north of the city the allies tracked him and cut him down, leaving his body to rot in the sun, where Elisa found it and covered it with dirt dug with her own bare hands.

The conquering allies set up a provisional government, then signed a peace treaty with this new government in June of 1870, a treaty which exacted a heavy indemnity. The prostrate Paraguay was unable to make any such payments, so the allies kept occupation troops in Paraguay for six more years. Argentina and Brazil each wanted territory from Paraguay; she was forced to grant 55,000 square miles of land northeast of the Paraguay River to Brazil and all claim to Misiones and the region beyond the Pilcomayo to Argentina. Some of this territory has not yet been surveyed. The border disputes concerning frontiers set by the treaty dragged on. Eventually Argentina's dispute was settled by the arbitration of President Hayes of the United States in November of 1878, who gave the disputed Pilcomayo Chaco lands to Paraguay.

When the allies withdrew they left chaos in the government of the devastated country. After the Paraguayan War, when other nations were settling into stability, the era of palace revolutions, changing *caudillos*, and upset constitutions had only begun in Paraguay. Twenty-two presidents were to serve Paraguay in the forty-two years between 1870 and 1912, a year in which some stability began. It would be pointless to list the names of the individuals involved in these uncertain administrations and of the rebellions that overturned them. The Constitution of 1870 had intended a centralized government. The Colorado party, which was founded under the aegis of General Bernardino Caballero in 1874, remained in power until 1904, when the Liberal Party, founded in 1887, came to power in one of the more "popular" revolts. There was no real party government, however, and gunplay, not ballots, changed the administration. Not until 1912 was a president elected who filled out a full four-year term in office. However, the period did witness the coming of a group of intellectual leaders to power and the birth of a Paraguayan culture, despite the fact that Paraguay is still today in the age of *caudillismo*.

Socially, the Paraguayan War, the War of Francisco Solano López, was even more of a disaster. It is estimated that there were 525,000 people in Paraguay when Francisco López came to power. In 1871 the victorious allies counted 221,079, of whom 106,254 were women, 86,079 children and 28,746 adult men. Such a shortage of men led to promiscuity, to large numbers of illegitimate children, and to a race of lazy males in a land where the women did all the work. Also, the land which the women now had to farm was devastated, the orange orchards were neglected, the horses and cattle dead. Schools were closed and newspapers unprinted for a generation. There were no writers, for people had forgotten how to read.

Readings

Barrett, W. E., *The Woman on Horseback* (1938)
Box, P. H., *Origins of the Paraguayan War* (2 vols., 1929)
Browning, W. E., *The River Plate Republics* (1928)
Cady, J. F., *Foreign Intervention in the Rio de la Plata, 1838–1850* (1929)
Coester, A., *Literary History of Latin America* (rev. ed., 1928)
Decoud, J. S., *History of Paraguay* (2nd ed., 1902)
Dombrowski, K. von, *Land of Women* (1935)
Elliot, A. E., *Paraguay* (1931)
Fitzgibbon, R. H., *Uruguay, Portrait of a Democracy* (1954)
Gordon, R., *Argentina and Uruguay* (1916)
Graham, R. B. C., *Portrait of a Dictator, Francisco Solano López* (1937)
Hanson, S. G., *Utopia in Uruguay* (1934)
Hudson, W. H., *The Purple Land* (1885)
Koebel, W. H., *Paraguay* (1917)
———, *Uruguay* (1911)
Kolinski, C. J., *Independence or Death: Story of the Paraguayan War* (1965)
Murray, J. H., *Travels in Uruguay* (1871)
Pendle, G., *Paraguay—A Riverside Nation* (2nd ed., 1956)
———, *Uruguay* (3rd ed., 1963)
Raine, P., *Paraguay* (1956)
Rengger, J. R., and M. Longchamps, *The Reign of Doctor Joseph Gaspard Roderick de Francia in Paraguay* (1827)
Robertson, J. P. and W. P., *Francia's Reign of Terror* (1839)
———, *Letters on Paraguay* (2 vols., 1838)
Ronde, P. de, *Paraguay, A Gallant Little Nation* (1935)
Warren, H. G., *Paraguay: An Informal History* (1949)
Washburn, C. A., *History of Paraguay* (2 vols., 1871)
White, E. L., *El Supremo* (1916)
Wilgus, A. C., ed., *South American Dictators* (1937)

Chapter 25

Three Struggling Republics
of the Higher Central Andes

A COMMON HERITAGE OF "CAUDILLISMO"

THE AMERICAN MINISTER to Ecuador in the 1860s, Mr. Frederick Hassaurek, traveling by mule train from Guayaquil to Quito, could find no food for sale along the road. "Many a time when I stopped to buy eggs or other provisions, the people told me, 'We have nothing to sell, sir; the soldiers were here and took all we had.'" The troops would be loyal either to the outgoing dictator or his outlawed opposition, for all Andean revolutions, to be successful, "must originate with or be supported by the soldiery." Such soldiers, according to the minister, were poorly paid and ill-clad, and usually supported themselves by requisitioning supplies from the villagers. Any revolutionary leader "resorts to the customary mode of Spanish American warfare . . . featuring forcible impressments, forced loans and contributions; in addition they seize all the horses, mules, cattle, provisions, Indians and other property they can lay their hands on. . . . The government party is meantime acting in the same way." The ordinary commerce of the Andean republics "is periodically paralyzed by such troubles. Agriculture is continually interfered with by the recruiting officers, who carry away farm laborers and beasts of burden. The middle classes always become poorer, the poor remain poor, and the number of wealthy families is diminished."[1]

In such an atmosphere Bolívar's dreams of confederation had evaporated; the nations which he had founded had forsaken him. The subsequent history of the three Central Andean countries is summarized by the above story from the American visitor. The nations that formerly made up the Inca empire are grouped together easily, for there is more unity than meets the eye. All have a large majority of *mestizo* and Indian people, a large area of tropical lowland which is undeveloped, a need for foreign capital to develop resources, and a small white caste which ruled through a series of *caudillos* during the nineteenth century.

ECUADOR, AN ULTRA-RELIGIOUS STATE

Ecuador is one of the smallest of today's South American nations in area, and is nearly the smallest in population and in amount of exports and imports. She has not always been so small, for she has lost half of her original territory as the result of boundary disputes. Much of this lost land has been in the *Oriente*, that jungle-covered area of the eastern slope of the Andes where the sources of the Amazon rise. Ecuador's capital of Quito and most of her larger towns are in the central Andean valley. One-fourth of Ecuador's territory is the tropical coast, source of her exports of bananas and cacao, and site of her port city Guayaquil.

Guayaquil, the progressive port, was always at odds with Quito, the conservative and very religious mountain capital. The influence of Bolívar and Sucre had kept the two cities united in one nation, aided by a very young lieutenant from Venezuela, Juan José Flores. This uneducated but charming twenty-six-year-old won the loyalty of the Ecuadorians after Bolívar and Sucre left the country. In 1829 he led Ecuadorian armies to victory over the Peruvians, who had tried to annex Quito. In 1830 Flores called a *cabildo abierto*, which on May 13 declared Ecuador an independent state, completely separate from any control by Bogotá. "That day, May 13, 1830, was the last day of despotism and the first day of the same thing." Thus Flores was Ecuador's first *caudillo*. Though in the long run he lost Popayán and Pasto, those old loyalist towns in the passes north of Quito, to Colombia, in the boundary settlement he gained the Galápagos Islands far out to sea.

Flores dominated the nation for fifteen years through a political alliance with the conservatives of Church and army and the wealthy class of the Quito area. Liberal leaders at Guayaquil, opposing Flores as a Venezuelan and his regime as arbitrary, organized a series of revolts under Vicente Rocafuerte, a leader who represented those Latin American liberal intellectuals opposed to the political power of the Church. By 1845 these liberals had written a new constitution, Flores had been exiled to Spain, and *Florianismo* was ended. Not in Flores' mind, however, for he persuaded

[1] F. Hassaurek, *Four Years Among the Spanish Americans* (New York: Hurd and Houghton, 1868).

the Spanish queen to let him have ships to retake the west coast colonies and to establish monarchy in the Andean region. It was only British intervention that ended this disgraceful attempt of a vengeful ex-*caudillo* to bring back Spanish power. The forgiving Ecuadorians, who had loved Flores as a young lieutenant when he first came with Bolívar, allowed him to come back as a subaltern government official in the 1860s.

At home Rocafuerte served till 1849, quarreled almost to the point of war with Colombia over the Popayán boundary, and retired by request of the conservatives, having accomplished no lasting liberal reforms for the country. The years down to 1860 were tumultuous ones, with many short-lived *caudillos* rising and falling, some exiling the Jesuits and some bringing them back. Some even tampered with Church schools and replaced them— explosive acts in this religious-minded nation. The period was marked by foreign wars with Peru and Colombia, internal revolts, and civil wars. As many as eleven different men were in and out of office. The last of this group of *caudillos,* the liberal Guillermo Franco, set up his capital in Guayaquil. He was driven out by a conservative army under Gabriel García Moreno, assisted by the returned Flores, which broke the power of the liberals for a long time. The battle won, a convention was called in September 1860, which named García Moreno president. Thus began the "Golden Age of García Moreno."

García Moreno, the first statesman Ecuador produced, is considered Ecuador's greatest hero, and is still hailed by conservative Catholic South Americans as the champion of religion. A young poet and newspaper editor and lawyer of Guayaquil, he had traveled to Europe during the revolutions of 1848 there, and was imbued with the idea of progress. According to his philosophy, progress was not possible without civil peace; peace was not possible without national unity; national unity was not possible without a strong religious influence. "Liberty and Equality," to him only synonyms for anarchy, were evil. He himself was so deeply devout as to believe he had divine guidance in everything he did for Ecuador. Calling himself "The Catholic President," he said, "The Church must march side by side with the civil power under conditions of true independence." He then organized the finances, broke up the army, founded an auditing system for government expenses which he himself supervised, and, according to a contemporary, "waged a pitiless war upon smuggling and speculation" as well as corruption within the government itself. He was responsible for two constitutions, one in 1861 setting up a strong executive, and a later one in 1869, which his enemies called "the Charter of Slavery to the Vatican," so strong did it make the ties to the Church, and so powerful the religion-dominated president. But he strengthened the civil law also, making it superior to the military; he brought some modernization and material progress and increased trade to the country. Not until García Moreno's term was there any road between Quito and Guayaquil save the mule trail traveled by the critical American minister—which had been passable only in the four driest months. García Moreno made it wide enough for carriages and oxcarts and maintained it passable the year around. The schools, though all Church-managed, were increased threefold. As strict with priests as with civil servants, he insisted on an eager and devout clergy and made many changes in Church leadership.

Wealthy through his own creole aristocratic family in Quito, García Moreno turned his salary as president over to Church charities as a part of his program of "virtue, faith, and order." Congress, which had approved his constitution giving him a six-year term and allowing re-election, was influenced by his personality to the extent of voting overwhelmingly, in 1873, to consecrate the nation to the "Sacred Heart of Jesus" and to place it under the moral authority of the popes. His devotion to the Church did not prevent some scientific interest on his part; he introduced the Australian eucalyptus tree to the barren slopes of the Andes where they grow today in native profusion; he modernized the Ecuadorian school of medicine, and he founded an astronomical observatory.

García Moreno's re-election to a third term, to start in 1875, caused a revolt among his enemies. As he came out of the cathedral onto the main Quito plaza on August 6 of that year, he was stabbed to death. The little nation was right to mourn him deeply for he was an unselfish leader of devoted purpose, though an opponent of free suffrage, religious toler-ance, and public education. His domineering, impetuous, and violent char-acter had provoked much opposition and his intolerant religious despotism clashed with the slowly growing liberalism of the country. He left no heir among his advisers, no one trained to carry on. Ecuador "floundered" through civil war, economic depression, and organized brigandage for twenty years, writing two more constitutions, bringing to eleven the total number of such documents for the little nation between 1830 and 1895.

Only Guayaquil, in spite of the recurrent yellow fever epidemics that made it one of the world's most feared pestholes, made some progress, for it was linked with world markets through the port. A real Liberal party gradually grew up to dominate local politics there. These port people, the *costeños,* opposed the feudalistic, religious, mountain-girt capital and its people, the *Quiteños.* The awakened Liberals had no leader in the nine-teenth century, and thus could not win over the government. In the twentieth century, Eloy Alfaro, a *mestizo* born in a coastal village, was a true liberal leader and brought an actual revolution in government, and a relaxing of the religious conservatism. Though he came to the presidency in 1895, he controlled Ecuador for the first decade of the twentieth century, and is actually the herald of a new age. The story of nineteenth-century Ecuador, therefore, actually ends in 1895, when the period of new liberalism commenced.

PERU: DETERIORATION FROM THE DAYS OF THE VICEROYALTY

Peru had been the flower of the colonial regime, but its transition from colonial society to a modern state was a long and perilous one. Life in Lima, Arequipa, or Cuzco in the nineteenth century was less comfort-able, held more of insecurity and danger for all classes of society, than in the eighteenth or even the seventeenth century. For Peru declined after independence to the position of a very "second-rate" area of South America, the domain of petty *caudillos*, several of whom often claimed power at once, staging forty revolts in less than fifty years after Ayacucho. Added to the internal chaos and helping cause it were wars with Bolivia, Spain, and Chile. In these wars Peru was to suffer territorially as well as politically.

Big in size, fourth among the Latin American republics, Peru lies in not one but three geographic areas—the arid coastal plain which contains the capital and the major port, the sierra with its irrigated plateaus and valley, and its Indian population little changed since Inca time, and the *montaña* jungle, like Ecuador's *Oriente*, which contains a fourth of the area and very little of the population. Climate and geography—little rain on the coast, difficulties of transportation in the mountains, lack of good land for agriculture—made progress difficult. Even the wealth of natural resources brought trouble for Peru; the guano and nitrate deposits caused war with Chile; the silver declined with the departure of the Spaniards; the copper and oil waited for development till the twentieth century. Nineteenth-century independence was no blessing for Peru.

Actually, Peruvians had not wanted independence as desperately as had other South Americans, and freedom was imposed by outsiders. Aristocrats and Indians had combined to support the last of the Spanish soldiers before Ayacucho. Many Peruvians had not considered Bolívar a Liberator, but a meddling northerner. In fact there was bitter sporadic warfare between Colombian and Peruvian forces for three years. Indeed, Peru's chief problem of the 1820s was to get rid of foreigners. When all Colombian soldiers were withdrawn, the patriotic Peruvians could not agree among themselves and gave way to a series of "small-time" tyrants very confusing to follow. Most of them were soldiers, the so-called Marshals of Ayacucho, veterans of the campaigns against Spain. One of them was an aristocratic *mestizo* named Andrés Santa Cruz, who helped drive out Bolívar's Colombians, and then hoped for a federation of Bolivia and Peru. In this he was opposed by General Agustín Gamarra. In the struggle between their forces in the high Andes plateaus Sucre's government set up by Bolívar in La Paz was ousted; Santa Cruz took control there, forced Gamarra out of Bolivia, and remained as dictator himself. Then Gamarra went back to Lima, where he was elected president in 1829. His four-year term became a chaos owing to the agitation of Santa Cruz in Bolivia for a port on the Peruvian coast, and to the intrigues at home in Lima.

The mid-1830s saw a three-way struggle in Lima and its interior Andean valleys for control of Peru. One of the three leaders, with no legal army of his own, asked help of the well-entrenched Bolivian dictator Andrés Santa Cruz, who had sat waiting for a chance to control Peru. Santa Cruz' forces soon defeated the two other opponents in the three-way struggle and he was able to found a Peru-Bolivia federation, made up of Bolivia, North Peru, and South Peru, with its capital at La Paz. Popular with very few of its citizens, the federation was a cause of alarm to Portales in Chile and Rosas in Argentina. Chile won its side of the ensuing small war, curtain-raiser to the much more serious War of the Pacific. But in the subsequent strife at home, Chile lost its leader, Diego Portales.

Rosas was driven back to Tucumán by the Bolivians, though Santa Cruz was completely defeated elsewhere in the Andes and driven out of Peruvian politics for good. Peru meanwhile splintered into sections.

In 1838 at the time of Santa Cruz' defeat there were eight different presidents claiming power in various regions of coast and mountains. The old warhorse Gamarra held power briefly in Lima itself, but he proceeded to make a new war on Bolivia. In the war's one battle at Ingavi on November 18, 1841, Gamarra himself was killed. Evil as he may have been, he was the one military dictator of the age of *caudillos* "to have had the saving grace to die on the battlefield." Three thousand of the 5,000 soldiers with him were killed or captured. Gamarra's chief of staff, Ramón Castilla, was the one surviving Peruvian officer.

By 1844 Castilla had seized power in Lima and in 1845 he was named president, but Peru was a shambles. The Indians were still the half-starved peons and burden-bearers; Negro slaves were still bought and sold; Lima was a dirty, backward, decaying city. Castilla, a military man with little education, was able to suppress anarchy and to push Peru along the path toward stability while he dominated the country from 1844 to 1862. Well-meaning and fair-minded, probably Peru's ablest nineteenth-century ruler, Castilla granted amnesty to his political enemies. In the realm of economics he planned railroads and telegraph communications, consolidated the chaotic finances of the country, and developed the fertilizer industry. The deposits of guano, or seabird dung, on the small barren islands offshore were being developed as a national monopoly. As long as the supply held out, Peru prospered. Castilla, who had been elected for a six-year term, gave way in 1851 to a puppet who spoiled the record with scandal and graft in the guano business, and Castilla finally returned for a second term to last till 1862. Not until this second term of Castilla's in the 1850s were the Negro slaves emancipated in Peru and the Indian villages freed of the tribute collected since early colonial times. Castilla's constitution was to remain in force for fifty-nine years. But a war with Spain, bankruptcy over the fertilizer business, and the long tragic dispute with Chile over the nitrate beds during the period called the War of the Pacific erased all Castilla's gains. The stories of these wars and of this economic difficulty are told in the last sections of this chapter.

The war with Spain occupied Peruvian politics until 1867. In a revolution that followed it Castilla himself, though no longer president, was involved in the fighting and was killed. The governments that came after him exploited the guano business, wasted the funds gained from its monopoly, and went deeply into debt to English and French bankers. Some needed improvements were made in railroads and harbors, and Lima was modernized, but extravagance and financial mismanagement bred revolt, and liberalism increased its strength. In the scandals one president, José Balta, was jailed and later murdered. The one bright spot was the presidency of Manuel Pardo, 1872–1876, the first civilian president of Peru, who followed the murdered Balta, and whose backers called themselves the *civilista* party. Pardo reorganized and reformed the government, gave offices to lawyers and businessmen, established schools, and reduced the army. However, the civilian leaders faced bankruptcy, for soon the guano deposits became exhausted; artificial fertilizers made from nitrates were at the same time being developed by Chilean and English companies on Peruvian and Bolivian desert lands. When the Peruvian government tried to nationalize these deposits and make the nitrate business a government monopoly as the guano business had been, Chile went to war as is told below. During the war the current president, Mariano Prado, went to raise funds in Europe and never returned; Chilean troops entered Lima in 1881, and there was no Peruvian government. In the vacuum various generals continued the war with their own private armies, generals who fought over the presidency once the peace was signed with Chile.

Andrés Cáceres, one of the surviving generals, served as president a legal four-year term from 1886 to 1890, but he could accomplish little in a country demoralized by war, burdened with foreign debt, and bankrupted by the loss of the nitrate provinces—the only revenue-producing section of the country. English bondholders helped him bring stability by organizing an advisory Peruvian Corporation of economic experts, who took over the management of the remaining guano deposits, the railroad, and the port, and worked out plans for payment of the debt over a period of sixty-five years. Under control of this corporation Peru started on the road to economic recovery, renewed prosperity, and a new flowering of arts and letters. Political stability was not achieved so easily, for military and *civilista* parties came to blows in the election of 1890. The military party won, but peace was not achieved until 1895 with the election of Nicolás Piérola, who served as president till 1903. An improved economy brought more political freedom also, for the granting of full suffrage made the administration give concessions to the vote-laden civilian party. Piérola had organized the Democratic Party, rallying the democratic forces against the military. He established a new monetary system, permitted civil marriage, reformed the army. For thirteen years, 1895–1908, Peru had peace and the *civilista* party was successful in electing candidates.

Thus Peru in 1900 was at least peaceful as a nation, with its budget balanced and its debt financed, its merchants prospering and the war destruction rebuilt. For people in Lima it was doubtless by 1900 a better nation in which to live than it had been in 1830. For the descendants of the Incas, who comprised 80 per cent of the population in the Andes, the century had brought no changes whatsoever.

BOLIVIA: THE CHILD OF SIMÓN BOLÍVAR

Upper Peru, with its cities of La Paz and Chuquisaca, later to be called Sucre, and its unexhausted silver mines of Potosí, was a Spanish colony till after Ayacucho. At that time it had 900,000 square miles, twice as much territory as it has now. It lost half of its area and all of its seacoast to its neighbors—the nitrate provinces and the Pacific to Chile, large regions to Argentina and Paraguay, and 190,000 square miles of jungle verging on the Amazon Basin to Brazil. With its remaining 412,777 square

Andean mountain trail, Viloco, Bolivia; no roads in the Andes nations were better than this until the 1870s.
Courtesy Pan American Union.

miles it still ranks fifth in size in South America, though landlocked in the heart of the continent, its Andean plateau and mining areas separated from the Pacific coast by a high western *cordillera*. Actually the country consists of three violently divergent regions: the *altiplano*, or high plateau on which are the central cities, the *yungas* or deep narrow valleys to the east which produce the foodstuffs for the cities and the mines, and the *selvas*, Bolivia's name for the eastern jungle area sloping down into the Amazon drainage basin. Spain had used all this area only as a source of silver; the Aymará Indians either worked in the silver mines or lived in the bleak farming villages they had always known. The whites remaining in 1826 were the "hangers-on" of colonial days, who were to mislead the ignorant masses in no less than sixty civil wars in seventy-three years. Bolivia was to have the saddest history of the age of *caudillismo*, while she struggled under ignorant, hard-drinking tyrants, seven of whom met death by assassination. Issues of centralism and federalism, Church and state, liberalism and conservatism, though they existed in Bolivia, played little part in the story. Bolivia's history in the nineteenth century is almost exclusively a tale of dictatorial domination.

Sucre was Bolivia's first president and one of its few well-meaning ones. He had entered La Paz at the request of Bolívar in February 1825, a month after the victory of Ayacucho. Chile and Argentina both hoped for a slice of the silver-producing colony; Bolívar pulled a clever *coup* when he arrived there himself and declared the area an independent state, separate completely from even Bolívar's Grand Confederation. An assembly called in August named the whole area of Upper Peru *La República de Bolívar* "in honor of its father and protector of the people." Bolívar himself was given supreme executive power and declared "Protector and President."

Then the Liberator wrote a model constitution for Bolivia, the famous *Constitución Vitalicia*, which incorporated his ideas for a strong central government and a lifelong president. This was of little actual concern to the Bolivians, who changed their constitution many times in the next century. Under the model constitution José de Sucre, who stayed in La Paz to carry out Bolívar's plans, was elected first constitutional president in December 1826. Bolivia immediately became involved in the Peruvian war to drive Bolívar's Colombians out of the central Andes areas. After a mutiny among Sucre's Colombian troops, Peru's generals, the Marshals of Ayacucho, Santa Cruz, and Gamarra, came up into the *altiplano* and forced Sucre out of office and back to Ecuador. In the ensuing confusion between Peru and Bolivia, Gamarra, it will be remembered, became president of Peru, and Santa Cruz was to be for years the dominating power in Bolivia, taking office as president in La Paz on May 24, 1829— the first in a long list of dictatorial *caudillos*.

Andrés Santa Cruz, one of the outstanding nineteenth-century South Americans, was born near La Paz in 1792 soon after the revolt of Tupac Amarú, a son of a Spanish colonial official and a wealthy Indian woman of Tupac Amarú's family who claimed to be an Inca princess. Santa Cruz took the legends and destinies of his mother's people very seriously. He had grandiose plans for re-establishing the Inca empire in a great west coast nation, and for humbling Chile, that aggressively modernizing neighbor. On the other hand, Santa Cruz showed respect for law and order, arranging a codification of law for both Peru and Bolivia, commencing public works, and proudly proclaiming Bolivia as the "only country in America without a foreign debt." In La Paz he established seven institutions of higher learning, including schools of medicine and fine arts.

All this was to be wasted, for like his Inca forebears Santa Cruz believed in paternalistic government, in efficiency more than in democracy. In 1836 his well-trained army took over Peru, and Santa Cruz was legally elected president of both countries. Rosas in Argentina and Diego Portales in Chile watched his rise with apprehension and started hostilities against him. Though he quickly defeated Rosas, he took defeat after defeat from the Chileans in this war of the 1830s, and finally fell from power himself, forced into exile by both Peruvians and Bolivians in 1839. It is sad to note that he spent many years before his death in Europe trying to interest Spain and France in a reconquest of South America.

The fall of Santa Cruz initiated a long period of anarchy and civil war and a series of brutal despots. The Peruvian Gamarra had attempted to conquer Bolivia, but was defeated in a single battle in 1841. The hero of the battle, General José Ballivián, ruled till 1847 under a new constitution. He tried to do a good job, emancipating the Negro slaves and attempting to develop the resources of the country, but the infuriated oligarchy threw him out. Within a year after his overthrow the demagogue Manuel Isidoro Belzú came to power. His name produced the noun *belcismo*, a new word for selfish dictatorship and venal opportunism, for during his regime "rapine, robbery, and riot" were the normal state of affairs in the land. Even Belzú had to resign after eight years and declare Bolivia ungovernable. Attempted reform and civil wars bring Bolivian history up to a barracks revolt in 1864, typical in every way of many other Andean changes of president.

Mariano Melgarejo, an illegitimate *mestizo* who had been an army packboy at nine, was Bolivia's president as a result of this latest barracks revolt. During it he seized the palace, slew the president and turned the palace over to his soldiers to loot. Melgarejo ruled for the next six years. He has been called the "Dictator of Dictators," for he did his country more damage than fifty years of progress could rectify. He suppressed municipal councils, sent home the Bolivian senate, made rules concerning the duties of bishops and priests, executed his enemies as traitors. As for himself, wining and dining and sporting various mistresses kept him busy while he fleeced his subjects. In order to gain personal funds which he senselessly squandered, the dictator made private deals with Chilean nitrate companies to work the beds on the coast, deals which led directly to the War of the Pacific, in which Bolivia lost all the nitrate coast. Melgarejo was defeated and driven out in January 1871, and shortly thereafter he was assassinated, eight years before the war began—killed in a personal quarrel with the brother of one of his mistresses.

The war with Chile was started by a second "Hero of Bolivia," Hilarión Daza, who was destined by nature to be a pickpocket but became president of Bolivia in 1876. An ignorant and drunken reprobate, he seized lands and raised the taxes on the Chilean companies granted the concessions by Melgarejo, thus precipitating the War of the Pacific. When Chile fought for the companies, Daza performed so poorly as a general and strategist that Bolivia lost the nitrate area entirely. He was ousted in December 1879, when the war was hardly begun; his successor continued the fight but was not even asked to the peace negotiations, so overwhelming was his defeat. The story of the war itself is told below. The war and the loss of the seacoast had a chastening effect on Bolivia. A new constitution was promulgated in 1880; presidents of the Conservative party ran a centralized government, encouraged the revitalization of the old silver-mining industry, and, just before 1900, opened up the tin mining that was to bring Bolivia some material progress and importance in the two world wars of the twentieth century. At the close of the century General José Manuel Pardo and the Liberals came into control and set the capital permanently at La Paz.

WARS AND INTERNATIONAL DISPUTES THAT RETARDED THE ANDES NATIONS

Because the boundaries of the unsurveyed lands in the *Oriente*, the area of the Amazon headwaters and tributaries, had never been settled in colonial times, "incidents" were created between Colombia and Peru, Peru and Ecuador, and Bolivia and Brazil which remained bitter disputes into the twentieth century. Shooting wars broke out over equally unsurveyed acreage in the waterless deserts on the Pacific side of the Andes, where the lands were not "mere chunks on the map" but sources of valuable nitrates discovered in the 1840s and worked inside Peruvian and Bolivian boundaries by Chilean companies. This situation made the three high Andean nations natural enemies in spite of their common background.

This common heritage brought the three uneasy neighbors into an alliance in the decade of the 1860s for a brief "war" against the mother country. The Spanish Crown had never recognized Peru, its most loyal viceroyalty, as an independent nation. Spanish intrigue, urged on by such plotters as the exiled Flores of Ecuador and Santa Cruz of Bolivia, had centered on recapturing these west coast countries. Suddenly difficulties arose over the question of recognition and over a Spanish attempt to collect on old "damages" from the War of Independence. Meanwhile some Basques, Spanish citizens, had been murdered while at work on a *hacienda* at Talambo. The agent of Spain who demanded compensation had instructions from Spain implying that Peru was still a colony. When the current Peruvian dictator, Juan Antonio Pezet, refused to deal with him, a Spanish fleet seized the guano-bearing Chincha Islands off the coast. Pezet then gave in and was ousted by Mariano Ignacio Prado. It was he who declared war on Spain and brought on Spain's blockade of the coast and bombardment of Callao. On this occasion Chile, less meek than Peru, leaped to her neighbor's defense. "The American Union," a military alliance consisting of Chile, Peru, Bolivia, and Ecuador, declared war on Spain in January 1866. The city of Valparaiso suffered heavy casualties in the naval war and bombardment, but the distance from Spain and the long coastline to be attacked made Spain's position untenable and she withdrew. In 1871 the belligerents signed a truce at Washington, D.C. During the subsequent peace Peru was recognized as a nation in 1879, the Chincha Islands were recognized as Peruvian soil, and the Chilean merchants of Valparaiso, including many Englishmen, were paid damages for the destruction.

Meanwhile, at home on the west coast, the allies had fallen apart. In the days of Santa Cruz in the 1830s Bolivia and Peru as a joint nation had lost a small-scale war to Chile. Chile, whose gunboats had done most of the fighting against Spain, was now a military, self-confident nation. Peru began to fear Chilean poaching in the nitrate industry and proclaimed that nitrates in Arica and Tarapacá, Peru's southernmost provinces where the Chilean companies had been most successful, were to be a Peruvian government monopoly. At the same time, Bolivia broke the agreement made by Melgarejo, increased her taxes on the Anglo-Chilean companies, and cancelled some of the concessions. The powerful Antofagasta Company refused to pay the tax; Bolivian dictator Daza ordered the company sold for taxes. On the day the tax sale was to be held, February 14, 1879, Chilean armed forces seized the Bolivian port of Antofagasta.

Peru, allied to Bolivia, intervened, and Chile declared war on both nations. Thus began the notorious War of the Pacific, which had many repercussions for South America. Historians are inclined to blame an aggressive Chile, whose industry and efficiency were far ahead of her more backward enemies. It was a "strange war of contrasts." The "slingshots of the Incas" were used side by side with the most up-to-date Krupp-made field artillery. Chile controlled the routes around Cape Horn; the only supplies for the northern allies had to be bought in the United States and smuggled across Panama, then a province of the rigidly neutral Colombia. When the battles in the desert became frenzied, however, both sides simply knifed the wounded on the field; water was too scarce to waste on them. Only the Bolivian Indians could fight long without water, but since they fought with Stone Age equipment, the Bolivian army soon lost Antofagasta and the whole nitrate coast.

Peru, a weak ally, had no way to hold Tarapacá and Arica, her provinces north of the 21° line, and had no navy equal to Chile's. The Chilean troops proceeded to invade the Peruvian capital; American observers were "horrified at the shameful treatment of Lima" by the conquering Chilean troops. Libraries, universities, private homes, and even the menagerie were looted. Peru's condition was so chaotic that there were several factions claiming to be the government. Chile recognized one faction and forced a difficult peace in the Treaty of Ancón, October 20, 1883, by which she got Tarapacá and a ten-year occupation of Tacna-Arica, the coast provinces up to the 19° line. At the end of that period an international commission was to hold a plebiscite. Chileans moved into the profit-producing provinces; attempts to hold the plebiscite failed and the dispute lasted into the 1920s as the explosive "Tacna-Arica Problem."

Bolivia, thrown out of the fighting early in the war when Daza's government fell, signed a truce with Chile in 1889. Its provisions were incorporated into a treaty ratified in 1904 by which Bolivia lost her entire seacoast. Save for the right to ship goods to the ports of Arica and Antofagasta, where eventually railroads were to be built, Bolivia remained a landlocked country. Damaging as the War of the Pacific was to Bolivia, she had lost almost as much territory by the treaty of 1867 with Brazil. The ignorant Melgarejo, hoping to gain advantages in commerce, had ceded nearly 200,000 square miles on the right bank of the Paraguay and the Marmoré to Brazil's Emperor Pedro II. This area almost led to bloodshed in 1903, when the Treaty of Petropolis gave this still disputed rubber-bearing area to Brazil, in return for a railroad to be built out to a navigable Amazon tributary. Thereby hangs a tale of difficulty and broken promises in the twentieth century.

ECONOMIC AND SOCIAL BACKWARDNESS IN THE ANDES

While dictator followed dictator, the descendants of the Incas—the Ambatans and Otovalans of Ecuador, the Quechuas of Peru, the Aymarás of Bolivia—spun and wove the same patterns of textiles as had their Inca ancestors, and lived in their ancestral villages in the mountains under the same type of local *cacique*, hardly realizing the government had changed.

If they were free from the *mita* and other oppressions of the Spanish viceroys, they were raided and impressed into the armies by the dictators, as noted by the American minister in Ecuador quoted at the beginning of this chapter. *Mestizos,* usually called *cholos* in the Andean countries, were the poor of the cities and the farm workers on the large estates owned by the aristocrats and politicians nearer to town. In Peru and Bolivia Indians continued to work the silver mines; by mid-century they had been drafted into the guano and nitrate industries. In none of these countries were the Indians given any education or voting rights, though they comprised more than three-fourths of the population.

They had little chance to see more than their own villages because of the lack of transportation. García Moreno had dreamed of a Quito-Guayaquil railroad, and an American company received a concession to carry out this difficult project in 1896. Because it had to be built by the same methods as the cart road of the 1860s, it was not completed until 1908, though only 290 miles long.

Before the War of the Pacific Peru had contracted for a railroad with an engineer named Henry Meiggs, a "promoter" from California's gold rush days who had left there after a political scandal, but who was acceptable in South America as a nephew of the William Wheelwright who put rails across the Andes from Chile to Argentina. In 1868 Meiggs began a railway from the coast at Mollendo up to Arequipa, the second largest town in Peru. In the 1870s this line was continued by Meiggs on the difficult run to Puno on Lake Titicaca, and thence to Cuzco. Meanwhile Meiggs started in Lima and built a line to the silver country of Huancayo, later to be one of the copper centers of the world. Meiggs himself told the Lima papers that this railroad would cross on over and meet the navigable Amazon, a feat which no west coast railroad had done by mid-twentieth century. La Paz connected with the Puno railhead by carriage and Lake Titicaca sailboat; she had no rail connection to the sea till after 1900.

These few rail lines did not bring nineteenth-century prosperity to the Andes. Quito still lived as it had in 1800, on agriculture and Indian hand labor. Guayaquil, center of a "province which abounds in timber for ship and house building, and an exuberant growth of fruit, especially cacao and and plantains," according to a visitor, lived on ship trade, with its port improved by García Moreno. But both cacao and bananas had little value in the nineteenth century, and waited for the Panama Canal to shorten Guayaquil's routes to any world markets. At the time the Canal was begun this port city of Ecuador had only 40,000 inhabitants.

Peru and Bolivia had lived off the silver mines since colonial days. Then in the 1840s, as described in the outline of Peruvian politics, private companies began to dig the guano, off the Chincha Islands. These rainless rocks had been bird-breeding grounds for untold millennia; the dung lay sixty to a hundred feet deep. It had but to be shoveled off, loaded into ships, and sent round the Horn to Europe for the manure-starved fields of England and Germany. Indians from the highlands died at the job, so the new millionaires of the guano bonanza imported more than 80,000 Chinese coolies who worked off their passage in practical slavery in the guano beds. Other islands and coastal areas proved to be just as rich; Peru's dictators lived well by simply laying monopolistic high taxes on the guano industry. Twenty years of digging practically exhausted the original beds; the seabirds were scared away; bankruptcy faced both the newly rich millionaires and the spendthrift government. In the two decades of the manure boom more value was gained from it at $80 a ton than from all the gold collected by Pizarro, but as far as the development of Peru was concerned, both were wasted. Peru's and Bolivia's nitrate business fell into the hands of Chile very early in the "nitrate era." Unable or unwilling during the guano boom to raise her own food, the city of Lima let the surrounding valleys neglect their irrigation system and began to import all her cereals, fruits, and vegetables from Ecuador, and her meat from Chile, a condition continuing as late as 1910.

Dwellers in Lima, La Paz, or Quito had little interest in literature during this stormy century. Manuel González Prada (1878–1918), a political and social philosopher, was Peru's best-known author in the 1890s. Courageously he wrote essay after essay of bitter satire against the power of Lima's old aristocracy, corruption in government, and the oppression of the Indians, and in favor of land reforms, improvement of labor, and more representative government. Later reform movements in Peru owe much to him. A woman writer in Peru, Clorinda Matto de Turner (1858–1909), had the vision to think of the Peruvian Indians as a contemporary social problem rather than as Incas who died gloriously against the early Spaniards. In her novel *Birds Without Nests*, written in 1889, she wrote with compassion about the injustices done the mountain Indians by her own generation of whites. Ricardo Palma, born in 1833 and still writing poetry just before his death in 1919, is considered Peru's most famous nineteenth-century poet. He also preserved much of colonial Lima's social history in his ten volumes of *Peruvian Traditions*. Having suffered in his own house from the vandalism of the Chileans when they took Lima in the War of the Pacific, Palma is remembered with gratitude for his work of restoring the national library after the invasion and recovering many of its treasures scattered by the Chilean soldiers.

Writers in Ecuador who partook of the religious mysticism of the nineteenth century are scarcely remembered today. A novel of Indian life, *Cumandá, a Drama Among Savages*, treated the Amazonian Indians of Ecuador's *Oriente* as lofty, idealized figures of the James Fenimore Cooper style. Its author, Juan León Mera (1832–1894), writing in 1871, was interested in Indian folklore and natural science, however, and his passages describing the *Oriente* and the daily rituals of its inhabitants are authentic. The most famous Ecuadorian writer was the well-known philosopher Juan Montalvo (1832–1889), "implacable enemy of tyrants" and uncompromising liberal in the face of the conservatism of García Moreno. Writing caustic articles on García Moreno and his Church policy from exile in Panama, Montalvo rejoiced when he heard the news of the dictator's assassination. "My pen has killed him," he is reported to have cried.

University life in Quito, and even in Guayaquil, was limited to Church schools run as they were in colonial times. Chuquisaca, renamed Sucre, cultural center before Córdoba, to which young residents of the pampas went to school in the eighteenth century, had ceased to have any intellectual activity; Melgarejo and Daza stifled what Santa Cruz had hoped to encourage there and in La Paz. The University of San Marcos in Lima, once the academic center for South America, had been sacked and looted in the civil and foreign wars and no longer could compete for prestige with newer schools in Chile and Argentina. When many of the dictators themselves could scarcely read or write, what hope was there for education and culture?

Readings

Adams, A. A., *The Plateau People of South America* (1915)

Agle, W. C., *Eastern Peru and Bolivia* (1901)

Archaud, C., and F. Herbert-Stevens, *The Andes: Roof of America*, trans. E. E. Smith (1956)

Arnade, C. W., *Emergence of the Republic of Bolivia* (1957)

Bernstein, H., *Modern and Contemporary Latin America* (1932)

Blanksten, G. L., *Ecuador: Constitutions and Caudillos* (1950)

Bowen, J. D., *Land and People of Peru* (1963)

Bowman, I., *The Andes of Southern Peru* (1916)

Browning, W. C., *The Republic of Ecuador* (1920)

Bulnes, G., *Chile and Peru, Causes of the War of 1879* (1920)

Chapman, C. E., "Melgarejo of Bolivia," *Pacific Historical Review*, VIII, 37–45

Cleven, N. A. N., *Political Organization of Bolivia* (1940)

Coester, A., *Literary History of Spanish America* (rev. ed., 1928)

Davis, W. C., *The Last Conquistadores* (1950)

Dawson, T. C., *South American Republics* (2 vols., 1903–1904)

Dennis, W. J., *Tacna and Arica* (1931)

Duffield, A. J., *Peru in the Guano Age* (1877)

Duguid, J., *Green Hell* (1931)

Enoch, C. R., *Ecuador* (1914)

———, *Peru* (1908)

Ford, T. R., *Man and Land in Peru* (1955)

Franklin, A. B., *Ecuador, Portrait of a People* (1943)

Guise, A. V. L., *Six Years in Bolivia* (1922)

Hassaurek, F., *Four Years Among Spanish Americans* (1868)

Kirchoff, H., *Bolivia: Its People and Scenery* (2nd ed., 1944)

Kubler, G., *The Indian Caste of Peru, 1795–1940* (1952)

Leonard, O. E., *Bolivia* (1952)

Linke, L., *Ecuador, Country of Contrasts* (3rd ed., 1960)

Markham, C. R., *History of Peru* (1892)

———, *War Between Peru and Chile, 1879–1882* (1883)

Maurtua, V. M., *The Question of the Pacific* (1921)

Mecham, J. L., *Church and State in Latin America* (rev. ed., 1966)

Millington, H., *American Diplomacy During the War of the Pacific* (1948)

Niles, B., *Peruvian Pageant* (1937)

Osborne, H., *Bolivia: A Land Divided* (3rd ed., 1964)

Palma, R., *The Knights of the Cape*, trans. H. de Onis (1945)

Pike, F. B., *Conflict between Church and State in Latin America* (1964)

——, *History of Republican Peru* (1966)

Reid, W. A., *Bolivia, the Heart of the Continent* (1919)

Stewart, W., *Chinese Bondage in Peru* (1951)

——, *Henry Meiggs—Yankee Pizarro* (1946)

Stuart, G. H., *The Governmental System of Peru* (1925)

Torres-Rioseco, A., *Epic of Latin American Literature* (rev. ed., 1946)

Walle, P., *Bolivia* (1914)

Whitaker, A. P., *The United States and South America: The Northern Republics* (1948)

Wilgus, A. C., ed., *South American Dictators* (1937)

Chapter 26

Colombia and Venezuela to 1900

GRAN COLOMBIA: A DISAPPOINTMENT TO BOLÍVAR

SIMON BOLÍVAR, who dreamed of a great federation of northern South America, knew the terrain of the Spanish Main, the modern states
of Colombia and Venezuela, better than perhaps any man has since, for
he had personally traveled over so much of it on foot, on horseback, in
river boat and canoe. He knew every hill between Caracas and La Guaira
or Valencia or Coro; he had fought over the rough country from Coro to
Cúcuta. Landing at Cartagena he had been up and down the Magdalena
on the way to Bogotá, and doubtless he had also been many times in the
lower Cauca Valley. Then he came into the Orinoco Valley from Jamaica
and led his forces up the Apure and over the high Andes to Bogotá,
a trip made only by explorers for geographic societies to this day. In fighting
for the freedom of Ecuador he had gone through the mountain passes
south of Cali on the upper Cauca and had won Popayán and Pasto
from the royalists. But as he lay dying he felt that he had "ploughed the
sea"; he knew that this region he loved would never hold together, that it
was already torn by local civil wars fought by ambitious leaders. He
had predicted that if the regions became separate stable states, Colombia would be "the university," the intellectual center, Venezuela would
be the "barracks," the land dominated by the military, while Ecuador
would be the "convent," the religion-dominated state. These prognostica-

tions came true in the course of the nineteenth century, while transportation remained just as difficult as in Bolívar's lifetime, and regionalism just as strong.

STORMY COLOMBIAN POLITICS TO 1903

Bogotaños considered themselves literary lights, and their city the "Athens of South America." It is true that in their approach to the ensuing bloody civil wars between conservatives and liberals they were more "intellectual" than were other South Americans, and their quarrels were more idealistic and less bound up with personal loyalties to leaders. In her first century of existence Colombia, or New Granada as she was called until 1850, witnessed ten civil wars that were national in scope, and lived under eight constitutions. "Yet no national president has been assassinated," an eminent historian reminds us, and "only two legitimate governments were overthrown by revolution in the entire hundred years." The Colombians were opposed to military dictators; they were concerned about the relation of the Church to politics, the secular control of education, the power of the provincial capitals as opposed to Bogotá. And they were concerned enough to fight each other to the death on the two major issues of Centralism versus Federalism and Church power versus freedom of religion. Nearly 100 insurrections and civil wars resulted from the efforts to settle these two questions, which very soon became interrelated.

The first republic in Bogotá had been so "philosophical" and impractical as to be called *La Patria Boba*. It was easily destroyed by the returning Spanish forces in 1815, and the country had to wait for Bolívar to come to Boyacá over the Andes from the Orinoco to be freed in 1819, after which the New Granadan leader, Francisco de Paula Santander, was given the civil administration of the provinces of New Granada—comprising only one province in the Gran Colombian federation according to Bolívar—while Bolívar went off to fight elsewhere. Santander was a very serious, legalistic person, who was called "The Man of Laws." He was thin, strait-laced, and unsmiling, the opposite of Bolívar and never his personal friend. He believed in enforcing the constitution to the letter. Although a democratic Federalist, he was realist enough to make Bogotá, and not the provincial capitals, the center of all financial and cultural matters. Partially owing to Santander's quarrels with the Venezuelan cowboy leader Páez, Venezuela was the first nation to leave the federation, and the triumphal return of Bolívar himself after Ayacucho did nothing to bring the regions together. The quarrel between Federalism and Centralism waxed stronger; at the Convention of Ocaña in 1827 the Federalists were ousted and Bolívar became a dictator. His opponents even plotted to assassinate him, and as a result of this plot, among other things, Santander was exiled. When Bolívar gave up and went downriver to his death in Cartagena, his scheme of Gran Colombia was dead also.

In 1832 Santander was called back from exile, given a great ovation, and elected president. Now he could make plans for his government of laws and lay the foundations for the subsequent development of liberalism in New Granada. The tradition left by Bolívar made all government seem personal, however, and all financial and administrative troubles in the chaotic new republic were blamed personally on Santander. In retaliation for this criticism Santander stifled all opposition, insisting that the opposition was delaying the progress his Liberal followers hoped for. The Church and its lay supporters in congress, who represented the Conservative provinces of Popayán and Pasto, opposed his plans for secular education and development of the economy. Santander was faint and ill; he gave his last speech before congress in defense of his forward-looking policies, withdrew, and died shortly afterward, in May 1840, the last Colombian survivor of Bolívar's co-workers in the Gran Colombian dream. After his death, opposition by the Church and army led to civil war and the accession as president of Pedro Alcántara Herrán. Herrán and his successor, Mosquera, brought the Conservative party to power under the new constitution of 1843.

The Conservative party, now identified with the Centralists and the Church leaders, produced a dictator-president by 1845. This was Tomás Cipriano de Mosquera—author, scientist, soldier, and statesman of remarkable versatility, whose term of office was a period of enlightened progress. Although a Conservative born in Popayán, he secretly had many liberal ideas, he introduced steam navigation on the Magdalena, approved a liberal education program in the university, encouraged foreign trade, and signed a treaty allowing United States interests to build the railroad across the Isthmus of Panama. His outstanding cabinet member, Mariano Ospina, a native of Medellín, helped build that city and its province of Antioquia into a rich coffee-producing area. Disputes with the strong and well-educated Liberals over religious issues caused a split in his party and put these Conservative leaders out by 1849. This change produced a very liberal anticlerical federalistic constitution in 1853. But the separation of Church and state provided by the new document could not come peaceably in this tense nation of clashing idealisms, and the resulting civil strife brought an army dictatorship to Colombia in 1854.

When the Liberals split, with their right wing combining with the Conservatives against army dictatorship, four former presidents converged on Bogotá with their "personal" armies to oust the "national army" from political power. Though Colombian Liberals were industry-minded and thus were Centralists, and the Conservatives represented the far-flung provinces and were Federalists, the progressive developer of Medellín, Mariano Ospina, became the Conservative president from 1857 to 1860. Deeply devout as well as interested in commerce, Ospina drafted a new constitution—the Granadine Confederation—providing for alliance between Church and state again. This extremely federalistic instrument gave opportunity for local *caudillos* to become strong again, and in 1863 the confederation was overthrown by the private army of the former dictator Mosquera. His administration was signalized by a vicious attack on the Church. His constitution of 1863, using the name United States of Colombia, was one of extreme states' rights and anticlericalism, and lasted until 1886. Guerrilla warfare continued, valley against valley, province against capital. While busy fighting on the Ecuadorean border in an attempt to recreate Gran Colombia, Mosquera was unseated in the capital by a barracks revolution and sent into exile in 1867. Although he had started his career as a patriotic Conservative, he is remembered for the autocracy of his old age. During the next thirteen years the Liberals held power but with many revolts and civil wars.

Strange that during all this chaos Colombia made more progress toward economic modernism than did the other Andean Republics. A group of young politicians who believed in complete freedom of worship, free education, and limitations on any strong executive created a new party, the Radicals. They found supporters among the small shopkeepers and working people in the cities, and among the professional classes, but their mild "radicalism" so aroused Church leaders, who actually felt that the faith was dying, that Colombia was racked by one of her worst armed uprisings in 1876. The old Liberal party was hopelessly split between radicals and moderates. Making friends on both sides—the more conservative shopkeepers and the more liberal landowners and Church leaders—the moderates won the day, formed a coalition, and ruled the country for a decade and a half of comparative peace and considerable material progress. Part of the debt from the civil war was paid with the sum of $10,000,000 received from the French concern, led by Ferdinand de Lesseps, which had contracted to build the Panama Canal.

Rafael Núñez, a poet and a scholar in his own right, a social philosopher, a keen intellectual, and one of South America's great nineteenth-century figures, was leader of the reorganized party, now called the Nationalists. Very much inclined toward radicalism as a young man, he had become more conservative as he grew older. In his most famous poem, *What Do I Know?*, he worries about the difference between good and bad. "They are so inextricably mingled that a poet cannot separate them." Perhaps this poem explains his willingness to lead the Liberals while he carried on the Conservative party's program. After years of experience in congress and in the foreign service, Núñez had been elected to the presidency in 1880 with much Conservative and Church backing. Civil war was still imminent; his strong-arm methods of stopping it made him the darling of the Conservatives, and he is called the "Regenerator." He brought about order and stability, and then went on to abolish the constitution and break the autonomous power of the provinces, while providing nationwide tax support for the Church. He muzzled the press, restricted suffrage, and exiled Liberal leaders, while he remained personally popular with a host of Liberal and even Radical friends. His pro-Church, strongly centralistic constitution of 1886 lasted until 1936; he himself served as president until his death in 1894. So powerful was his influence that he ruled, not from Bogotá, but from his own plantation outside Cartagena far away on the coast. He remains a literary name in Colombia for his writings on philosophy and political science. His influence was felt in recent times in Colombia where the issues of Church and state in education, and of the free practice of missionaries of other than the Catholic faith have been very controversial questions.

At his death, the long repressed left-wing Liberals and Radicals broke

Stern-wheel steamers on the Magdalena, first introduced in 1852. *Photo by Helen Miller Bailey.*

out again in open warfare. There was no peace, only truces from month to month, and finally, in 1899 to 1902, the famous "Thousand Days of Civil War." So chaotic was the entire country by that time, so powerful the provinces against the capital, that the remote little ·state of Panama was actually ruled by the port of Cartagena rather than by the inland capital of Bogotá. This situation made it easy for the United States to encourage a revolt in Panama during the Canal crisis of 1903; the shock of this loss led to a more stable Colombian government by 1904.

ECONOMIC AND CULTURAL DEVELOPMENT OF COLOMBIA TO 1900

Economically Colombia still held to the colonial patterns until after 1850. There was livestock raising, subsistence agriculture, some wheat production in the savanna of Bogotá, some tobacco culture, and some coffee planting on the coast near Santa Marta. Medellín and Cali in the Cauca Valley became boom towns of the coffee business at the same time that São Paulo began to emerge as a coffee center in Brazil. European immigrants came into the Cauca province of Antioquia ready to work as sharecroppers in the coffee lands or as small shopkeepers or artisans in the new towns. The workers in the small industries became an articulate classs in the struggle between the right and left wings of the Liberal party just before the days of Núñez. It was one thing to make good cigars or produce finer-flavored coffee beans than São Paulo; it was another thing to get them out to the world. In Colombia the problem was river transportation. In the days of Rafael Núñez the dictator preferred to stay at Cartagena, rather than take the long sternwheeler trip to Bogotá. From Bogotá the forty miles across the savanna to towns on the other side of the valley were not traversed by a carriage road until after 1850.

In Bolívar's last days the upriver trip on the Magdalena was made in canoes. Two steamers of the Mississippi River type were making the trip in the rainy season by 1852. As late as 1875 there was no accommodation for women; the paying gentlemen brought their own hammocks to sling on the deck; the sailors tied up every night and fished for their dinner. At the overnight stops they got off and cut wood for fuel. At the end of the boat trip the travelers had to buy their own mules for the trip to Bogotá. In 1887 a railroad was begun to Girardot, the head of navigation on the Magdalena. There had been a railway across the Isthmus of Panama, the remote Colombian province, since the California gold rush, but it was of no value to Colombia's domestic development. President Núñez had dreams of connecting Bogotá by rail to the port of Buenaventura on the Pacific; he dredged parts of the Cauca and made it navigable into Antioquia province. By mid-nineteenth century, however, little improvement in the ground transportation to Bogotá had been made; it was still impossible for travelers from the capital to reach the Caribbean by road or rail.

Bogotá, isolated as it was, nevertheless was an intellectual center. Its dictators wrote history and poetry; its young liberals read John Stuart Mill and admired paintings by the French impressionists. In 1851 only 30,000 people lived in Bogotá; both Cartagena and Popayán were larger. By 1880 Bogotá had doubled in population; 1900 gave her more than 100,000, with "many fine hygienic new houses" and a tramway. The streets were of mud and cobblestone, which the pedestrian long had to share with the mules, as there were no sidewalks till the 1880s. *Bogotaños* praised their national library, though it was so small as to boast only one librarian who closed it during his frequent illness. In their much-lauded scientific museum were still the specimens collected by Mutis and von Humboldt, and very little that was new. Notable progress was made in Colombia in the fields of jurisprudence and historical writing, however.

And what did the poets write—anything new at all? Poems of the 1850s dwelt on the scenery of Colombia, the rivers, the mountains, the "strange and varied flora." Several concerning the beautiful Falls of Tequendama near Bogotá were published in the literary journals. In the single year 1854 more poetry and more prose was published than in a decade before or after; one product was a poetic drama in five acts written by Felipe Pérez, telling the story of the explorations of Gonzalo Pizarro. So numerous are the Colombian writers on nationalistic themes—history, scenery, patriotic fervor—that it is impossible to list them. Many, like Rafael Núñez (1825–1894) himself, produced a wide variety of works and were active in public life as well. For example, Manuel María Madiedo (1817–1900) wrote "whole volumes on social science, logic, and law." Editor of a paper, widely versed in European philosophy, acquainted with several languages, Madiedo wrote well-known poems on the "Great River Magdalena, free and strong, beautiful and rebellious," and on "the ocean before the walls of Cartagena," as well as odes to Bolívar, Sucre, and the battle of Ayacucho. At the turn of the century Rafael Pombo (1833–1912), then sixty-seven years old, was Colombia's best-known poet. In his lines *To Bolívar*, Pombo wrote of the shortcomings of his own time as compared to the heroics of the independence era:

> Hero, thy last antagonist is Time.
> Thy triumph waxes as the years decay.
> For even our errors and our meannesses
> Make thee stand out still greater every day.[1]

Most famous literary work of this period in all northern South America is Jorge Isaacs' novel *María*. Isaacs (1837–1895) was the son of a Jamaica planter of English-Jewish origin, who married a Colombian girl and came to live on a plantation in the Cauca Valley near Cali. After attending boarding school in Bogotá, Isaacs supported himself by writing, and in 1867, before he was thirty, had produced one of the best-known love stories of the Spanish language. Though its author failed in business and died in poverty, his book is still widely read in Spanish, French, and English. It is almost autobiographical; the heroine María is a cousin of a Jewish plantation-owning family in Jamaica who is adopted by them. When the hero Efraín returns from boarding school he falls in love with his beautiful cousin; their touching love story, opposed on religious grounds, ends in the death of the heroine. But it is the description of Colombian life, the views of the Cauca River, the hero's trip home across country from Bogotá, the warm stories of family life, that make the novel alive. A modern critic has said that the scenes in María are "real countryside thinly veiled by words."

Nineteenth-century Colombia laid the foundations not only for dictators like Mosquera and Núñez, and for interregional strife and religious fanaticism, but also for the respect of culture in all its forms.

VENEZUELA: THE AGE OF PÁEZ

Venezuela in the nineteenth century was even more turbulent than Colombia, and its turbulence lasted longer. Civilian executives, who made so many contributions to Colombian life, made no such gains for Venezuela. Soldiers of Indian blood controlled the Andes and the *llanos*, with one spectacular city-dweller from Caracas varying the pattern in the 1870s. An ignorant populace in an area devastated by the War for Independence had no experience in good government. Seldom were the geographic regions of the country unified; the very difficulty of transportation bred military control. As Bolívar had said, Venezuela was to be "the barracks."

[1] Translated by Alice Stone Blackwell, in *Some Spanish American Poets* (New York: Appleton-Century, 1929), p. 394. Reprinted by permission of the University of Pennsylvania Press, copyright owners.

There were perhaps a half million people in Venezuela at the end of the devastating wars for independence. Of these perhaps a quarter were whites, and a hundred thousand were pure-blooded Indians—either the peon farmers of the Andes or the uncivilized tribal groups beyond the Orinoco. Along the coast were almost as many Negroes, the heritage from the slavery of colonial days. Many of them were still held in bondage until freed by the tardy government in 1830, though the first constitution had abolished the slave trade. The remaining inhabitants were mixtures of white, Indian, and Negro, divided by class line drawn according to wealth and land ownership. By the time of independence Venezuela was a land of poverty, ignorance, and illiteracy, sparsely settled with few large towns. The landowning creole class had been largely wiped out in Bolívar's War to the Death; only in the cities did any number of wealthy conservatives remain, and the recently freed masses opposed their control. From 1810 to 1888 there were forty-two important revolutions, a figure which does not include riots or minor coups. Seven dictators and eleven constitutions governed Venezuela during the nineteenth century. Venezuelans could say, "A constitution is just a yellow-backed booklet to be found in the archives."

In the light of such general disorganization and lack of unity, it is not strange that Venezuela was the first state to break away from Bolívar's Gran Colombia confederation. In doing so, the Venezuelans were following a *llanero*, their cowboy hero of independence, José Antonio Páez. Born in 1790 and involved in a murder at seventeen, this illiterate youth ran away to the Apure, where he worked as a wandering cattle herder and horse breaker till he joined Bolívar's army. While Bolívar was busy in Bogotá, Quito, Guayaquil, and Lima, Páez had acted as the actual dictator of the Venezuelan area in Bolívar's name. Members of the congress in Bogotá accused him of high-handed methods in violation of the new Gran Colombia constitution and asked him to resign his leadership in Caracas. When his actions were approved by a convention of his henchmen, he declared Venezuela a "sovereign state" and himself responsible only to Bolívar. Soon Bolívar faced troubles of his own in Bogotá, while a citizens' assembly in Caracas called for a constitutional convention to draft a government for Venezuela alone. This congress met in April 1830 at Valencia, and as a consequence of its actions Páez became Venezuela's first president. His new constitution "freed" the slaves and guaranteed "civil rights" and free public education, but it restricted citizenship and suffrage. In all his years as dictator Páez found little time to really carry out these noble commitments.

Thus began the Age of Páez, which lasted with occasional interruption until 1863. The Indians and *mestizos* from the *llanos* were devoted to their cowboy leader and called him "The Lion of the Apure"; his rough sense of humor and his skill at horsemanship delighted his illiterate followers. He realized that he knew little about government, and was anxious to take suggestions; the only trouble was that he could not distinguish good suggestions from bad. Opposed at first by the white aristocracy, he was able to make friends with the Caracas leaders after he became personally very wealthy from confiscated cattle. The records indicated that his regime was honest as compared with those of other *caudillos* in South America. He handled the "Church Question" without antagonizing the clerical leaders, although he abolished tithes and special privileges for the clergy. This cowboy of the open ranges, turned cattle rustler, turned general, made a "none-too-bad" president.

Páez' first term was over in 1835, and he retired gracefully in favor of his elected successor, but he was back in the presidency by 1838, as the constitution had forbidden only direct succession of a president by himself, but had made no mention of a return to power after an interim presidency. The next four years were the period of Páez' greatest success. Páez felt that he personally was so popular that he did not have to maintain a large army, so he used tax money to build more roads and to improve the economy of Venezuela. When his term expired again he continued in the background; by now he was the strong friend of the dominating creole aristocracy of landowners, and the humble *llaneros* were neglected and forgotten.

But a liberal group was in the making. An opposition newspaper had been founded in 1840, edited by Antonio Leocadio Guzmán, who appealed to the masses, demanding universal suffrage and improved conditions for the freed slaves. During a suit for libel Leocadio Guzmán defended himself eloquently, became a popular hero, and joined a plot to overthrow the Páez regime in the elections of 1846. After this first organized movement against Páez had failed and its leader Guzmán was thrown in prison, the old dictator retired to his ranch. He was sure that the conservatives were strongly enough entrenched in the congress and allowed the party of two brothers, José Tadeo and José Gregorio Monagas, a coalition group, to dominate the presidency. The Monagas family ("liberal-oligarchy") soon split with Páez (ultra-conservative) and stayed in control for more than a decade. The liberal Leocadio Guzmán was released from prison and together with his son Antonio Guzmán Blanco formed a liberal-federalist coalition against the centralist conservative army. Thus started the Federalist War, which went on for several years up and down the western Andes and across the *llanos*. It brought to a head thirty years of unrest and discord and gave rise to new class conflicts. It ended only when Páez, who had been taken from his ranch by the army faction and sent into exile, returned to make himself dictator again in 1861.

The Lion of the Apure returned, an old man, to a Venezuela torn by years of civil war. The two years during which he remained in Venezuela on his return from exile were years of constant guerrilla fighting. He eventually made an agreement in 1863 which allowed a regime under Juan Cristomo Falcón to come to power, and which provided for Páez' own permanent retirement. As a cattle buyer for an American company the old dictator journeyed to Buenos Aires, where he was lionized as the last surviving lieutenant of Bolívar—in fact, the only one who had the opportunity to survive into old age. After a triumphal tour of other South American countries he died in exile in New York at eighty-three, his fortune intact, after having authored his autobiography. Under Falcón and the federalists the name "United States of Venezuela" was adopted, but this regime was not peaceful and the country was torn by revolution.

VENEZUELA : THE AGE OF GUZMÁN BLANCO

With Páez out of the way, two new political groupings were formed. These were called, for a change, the *Azules*, the Blues, and the *Amarillos*, the Yellows. The leaders were the same enemies as before: the army for the Blues, Antonio Guzmán Blanco for the Yellows. As was to be expected, civil war raged for two years, and Blues and Yellows alternated in the shaky government. But Antonio Guzmán Blanco was destined to come out on top. On April 27, 1870, he entered Caracas at the head of an army, took the oath as president on July 20, made himself dictator, and spent the next two years putting the armed bands of Blues to rout. Either he or one of his henchmen served as "president" from then until 1888. This era of peace and, by Venezuelan standards, of culture and prosperity is known as the Age of Guzmán Blanco. Its colorful and refined dictator does not follow the pattern of the rough soldiers, cowboys, or Andean peasants who have ruled Venezuela for the greater part of her history. Caracas-born and trained, he at least had the best education that city could offer, and he followed in the footsteps of his father, that able journalist and lawyer among the more liberal creoles.

Guzmán Blanco has been described by any number of varying adjectives: intellectual, ingenious, virile, pompous, ridiculous, extravagant, poetic, artistic, versatile, and vainglorious. He was lavish in bestowing honors on soldiers, scholars, and public-spirited citizens. (These honors were always medals with his own profile and name on them.) Anxious for scholastic recognition beyond his own education in law, he sought every possible degree that any learned man anywhere could earn or receive as an honor, and eventually he was awarded every one save that of Doctor of Divinity. Each literary and learned society in Venezuela—and he sponsored and encouraged all existing ones and founded new ones—made him an honorary member, and he made scholarly addresses to each. Every book published during his administration—and he prided himself on the literary output of his state-financed scholars and writers—bore his name on the flyleaf: "Published in the administration of Antonio Guzmán Blanco." Time after time the congress declared him president, then chose a puppet when his term expired, then ousted the puppet and returned Guzmán Blanco. During the reigns of the more docile puppets he traveled abroad with his family and became a well-known literary light and patron of the arts in the best circles in Paris. His beloved daughter married a well-born Frenchman, and Guzmán Blanco, that man of the world, considered her home on the Champs Elysées his secondary headquarters. While he commuted between Paris and Caracas, his rubber-stamp congress voted him "Illustrious American, Regenerator, and Pacificator."

Venezuela itself, its *llanos*, its rugged Andes, and its unexplored jungles, did not fare too badly under this "cultured" Pacificator, so seemingly foreign to its own spirit in every respect. He increased the taxes, collected them fairly enough, and reduced the debt. With the revenues he built roads into the Andes, and even a railroad from La Guaira to Caracas. As Grand Master of the Masonic Lodge of Venezuela he opposed the economic and political powers of the Church, secularized education, proclaimed civil marriage, and invited foreign Protestant missionaries into Venezuela. Primary education was made free and public and, in the written law at least, compulsory. Secondary schools and technical institutes were established in the leading towns. He encouraged industry and codified laws, and he gave Venezuela a period of peace and order. All this constructive work was done by "decree legislation," however; when Guzmán Blanco was in Paris, he regularly sent home "laws" to be enacted by the interim puppets for the "good of the people." Through it all, he maintained himself and his friends in the utmost luxury. With his intensely personal and arbitrary government he was as much a *caudillo* as was any other South American tyrant, albeit a benevolent and refined one.

Venezuelan literary historians point with pride to the writings published in Venezuela in this Age of Guzmán Blanco, but none of the many writers whose works were published with Guzmán Blanco's administration credited on the flyleaf is considered important enough to be listed in the standard Spanish American anthologies. In fact, Venezuela produced no great literary figure after Andrés Bello until the turn of the twentieth century. The writers of the time, 1870–1890, were so anxious to please the dictator in his love for all things French, that they were almost academic in aping the romantic style of Victor Hugo. When Zola became more popular in Paris, young Venezuelans became less romantic and more realistic. In any style they won fame if Guzmán Blanco liked them. The most widely read novel of the period necessarily appeared after Guzmán Blanco's prizes were no longer offered. It was *Peonía*, written in 1890 by Manuel Romero García (1865–1917). Its plot centers on a dictatorial father whose sons and daughters cannot rebel against him because of Venezuela's unjust laws; it treats of the social conditions in Venezuela. *Peonía* is considered the first of the nationalistic or creole novels of Venezuela. Under the artificiality of Guzmán Blanco, in spite of his sponsorship of liberalistic courses in the university and his organization of the Academy of Social Sciences and Fine Arts, frank, critical, or naturalistic literature had no chance.

Artificial or not, literary efforts and cultural societies went into a decline with Guzmán Blanco's own decline of power. When he went for another "vacation in Paris" in 1887, his current puppet was faced with an uncontrollable uprising. The dictator was too old, he was absent too much, his old generals were dead. This time Guzmán Blanco sensed the turn of events and remained in Paris, where in 1899 he died at seventy, peacefully in bed amidst luxurious surroundings. Strife in Venezuela between his possible successors lasted from 1887 to 1892. On October 6 of that year, Joaquín Crespo, former puppet president (1880–1881), came into Caracas at the head of a victorious army championing *"legalismo,"* as had Guzmán Blanco before him. Crespo was called "The Hero of Duty" and had a large popular following. His national assembly drew up another constitution under which Crespo held power as an able and efficient dictator, though without Guzmán Blanco's dramatic flair and without continuing his encouragement of the arts.

Crespo's administration, peaceful at home, was involved in the first serious external problem ever faced by Venezuela. Great Britain claimed that the western boundary of British Guiana extended into Venezuelan territory—an old boundary dispute going back to 1844 when English prospectors had crossed the vague line in search of gold. During his presidency Crespo requested that the dispute be submitted to arbitration and appealed to Grover Cleveland, the American President. Under the Monroe Doctrine—in fact in one of its early applications in South America—the United States threatened war on England if she did not submit to arbitration. American Secretary of State Richard Olney declared that "the United States is practically sovereign on this continent and its fiat is law upon the subjects to which it confines its interposition." England tacitly agreed by accepting arbitration. The rulings of the boundary commission meant a defeat for Venezuela, however, since a lion's share of the territory in dispute went to British Guiana. Much of this area, as well as the entire third of the Venezuelan nation that lies south and east of the Orinoco, remained completely unexplored into the twentieth century.

The turn of the century saw the end of Crespo, last of Guzmán Blanco's lieutenants, who was killed in a battle over his successor. This opened the way for a new dictator, General Cipriano Castro, neither a *llanero* like Páez nor a cultured *Caraqueño* like Guzmán Blanco, but a hard-riding cowboy from the western mountains. As the "Lion of the Andes" he rode into power in October 1899, became provisional president until July 1902, and "full constitutional president" until 1909. His ruthless regime began a thirty-year period of rule by Andean soldiers and peasants which characterizes the first quarter of the twentieth century. That century, though still marked by military dictatorship, was to bring a new gushing prosperity, the "Age of Petroleum," an era of its own.

Readings

Allen, H. J., *Venezuela: A Democracy* (1940)
Bernstein, H., *Modern and Contemporary Latin America* (1952)
——, *Venezuela and Colombia* (1964)
Bushnell, D., *The Santander Regime in Gran Colombia* (1954)
Coester, A., *Literary History of Spanish America* (rev. ed., 1928)
Crist, R. E., *The Cauca Valley, Land Tenure and Land Use* (1952)
Davis, H. D., ed., *Economic Development of Venezuela* (1961)
Dawson, T. C., *South American Republics* (2 vols., 1903–1904)
Dennis, A. L. P., *Adventures in American Diplomacy, 1896–1906* (1928)
Fergusson, E., *Venezuela* (1939)
Galbraith, W. O., *Colombia—A General Survey* (1953)
Gibson, W. M., *The Constitutions of Colombia* (1948)

Gilmore, R. L., *Caudillismo and Militarism in Venezuela, 1810–1910* (1964)

Graham, R. B. C., *José Antonio Páez* (1929)

Grummond, J. L. de, *Caracas Diary, 1835–1854; Journal of John G. A. Williams* (1954)

————, *Envoy to Caracas—The Story of John G. A. Williams, Nineteenth-Century Diplomat* (1951)

Henao, J. M., and G. Arrubla, *History of Colombia*, trans. J. F. Rippy (1937)

Lieuwen, E., *Petroleum in Venezuela—A History* (1954)

————, *Venezuela* (1961)

Mack, G., *The Land Divided: A History of the Panama Canal and Other Isthmian Canal Projects* (1944)

Marsland, W. D. and A. L., *Venezuela Through Its History* (1954)

Masur, G., *Simón Bolívar* (1948)

Mecham, J. L., *Church and State in Latin America* (rev. ed., 1966)

Moron, G., *History of Venezuela* (1964)

Niles, B., *Colombia, Land of Miracles* (1924)

Parks, E. T., *Colombia and the United States, 1765–1934* (1935)

Parsons, J. J., *Antioqueño Colonization in Western Colombia* (1949)

Perkins, D., *History of the Monroe Doctrine* (new ed., 1955)

————, *Monroe Doctrine, 1826–1867* (1933)

————, *Monroe Doctrine, 1867–1907* (1937)

Radcliff, D. F., *Venezuelan Prose Fiction* (1933)

Rippy, J. F., *The Capitalists and Colombia* (1931)

Romoli, K., *Colombia: Gateway to South America* (1941)

Scruggs, W. E., *Colombia and Venezuelan Republics* (1905)

Spence, J. M., *The Land of Bolívar, or War and Peace and Adventure in the Republic of Venezuela* (2 vols., 1878)

Torres-Rioseco, A., *Epic of Latin American Literature* (rev. ed., 1946)

Watters, M., *A History of the Church in Venezuela, 1810–1930* (1933)

Whitaker, A. P., *The United States and South America: The Northern Republics* (1948)

Wilgus, A. C., ed., *South American Dictators* (1937)

Wise, S. G., *Caudillo: A Portrait of Antonio Guzmán Blanco* (1951)

Wohlube, R. A., *Land and People of Venezuela* (1959)

Chapter 27

The Caribbean

and Central American Areas

in the Nineteenth Century

TWO AREAS WITH MUCH IN COMMON

COLUMBUS HAD DISCOVERED Hispaniola, had skirted Cuba, and had seen the Caribbean coasts of Central America. Today these regions contain nine separate nations, colorful countries anxious for the American tourist trade, influenced by the American interest in the Panama Canal, and largely a part of the United States' economic sphere. These tropical climate countries, lands of sugar, coffee, cacao, bananas, and tobacco, lands of many mixed races, have much in common. Each was to change its status from part of a union or an empire to separate existence sometime during the nineteenth century; each was to see quarrels between liberals and conservatives, centralists and federalists, and to fight off intervention by outsiders. But each story is different and contains plots, intrigues, heroes, and villains worthy of the most romanticized fiction.

CUBA, A COLONY AND A REPUBLIC

Cuba had lain dormant during the wars of independence; it and Puerto Rico were the only remaining Spanish Colonies in the New World. Spanish society dominated Havana life and Spanish-born officials held the government jobs. The governor's post was refilled every few years, as soon as the Spanish incumbent had made a fortune at it. Taxes were heavy on all necessities; many commodities were government monopolies. Slavery was still the system of labor, and Spanish families owned the vast sugar plantations worked by the slaves. In 1840 Havana was a neglected and disorderly city, with thousands of footloose vagabonds and with muddy streets filled with homeless starving dogs, while a thin veneer of Spanish society attended poetry reading salons aping Europe.

Cuban patriots today remember the poetry of a poor Negro, Gabriel de la Concepción Valdés (1809–1844). Brought up in an orphanage, self-taught, a carver of tortoise-shells by trade, this Cuban of the mid-nineteenth century wrote under the pen name of Plácido. In his verses he promised to be "the tyrant's restless foe"; then he could with clear conscience "face the rifles, freed from bondage." In 1844 he did face the rifles, having been arrested on a charge of conspiring to free his fellow Negroes. His death helped fan the smoldering embers of revolt.

Cuba did not get independence in Plácido's lifetime, but her history, with its plots and conspiracies against Spain, shows dissatisfaction with Spanish colonial policies. Spain herself was alert for the safety of this last American colony, because France, England, Mexico, and Colombia all showed interest in helping free it for various reasons. The pro-slavery American South was anxious to annex slave-holding Cuba, and individual Southerners backed three filibustering expeditions to the island. In 1848 Narciso López, the Venezuelan who had fought both with the patriots and royalists in his own country and in Spain, became an adopted Cuban. After he had planned a rebellion there which failed in 1848, he escaped to the United States and organized three unsuccessful filibustering expeditions. On his fourth he "landed an army of soldiers of fortune," but no Cubans rallied to him and he was captured and executed. In his hope for annexation to the United States, López had been aided by the pro-slavery men of the American South.

On October 10, 1868, a group of patriots within Cuba, relying on no adventurers from the outside, declared Cuban independence on the plantation of Yara. Carlos Manuel de Céspedes was the civilian leader among them and was chosen president. There followed a decade of guerrilla warfare known as the Ten Years' War. Its strategist was General Máximo Gómez, a gloomy old *mestizo* who had had experience fighting with the Spanish army in Santo Domingo. Under him the half-breed and Negro soldiers, ill armed and barefooted, fought a guerrilla campaign and freed the eastern half of the island. Second in command was Cuba's most famous soldier, Antonio Maceo, an enormous mulatto who rode a horse like a centaur, sustained many serious wounds, and even won respect from his enemies. At the head of his guerrillas Maceo slashed through jungles, burned storehouses, and harried the Spanish landowners out of the provinces. The Spanish forces, including many Havana society youths, met fire with fire, and in 1875 the open hostilities were ended with the Peace of Zanjón, a "no-victors" peace. The war had won freedom for the slaves as a concession from Spain, but its leaders, still fearing the other lukewarm Spanish promises regarding amnesty for the rebels and administrative reforms, remained in hiding. General Calixto García maintained an outlawed army in the eastern mountains. Maceo and Gómez went into exile. Tomás Estrada Palma, who had succeeded de Céspedes as patriot president, went to teach Spanish in a private school in New York. None of these leaders considered the war ended or thought of the peace as other than a truce.

Meanwhile in 1854, as part of the expansionist spirit known as Manifest Destiny, the United States ministers in several European capitals had announced that the United States should offer to buy Cuba for as much as $120,000,000, and if Spain were to refuse, she should be threatened with war. This is the statement known as the Ostend Manifesto. Ridiculed by the European powers, the United States declared it "unofficial." With the end of the Civil War, Southern attempts to annex the slave-holding island ended, although New York and Florida remained the headquarters for Cuban agitation for freedom. During the Ten Years' War money was raised to help García and supplies were sent on a Cuban ship flying the American flag. When this ship was captured in 1873 and the American as well as the Cuban patriots on board were shot, American public opinion was aroused—an interest which continued until 1898.

All this time the Spanish governor maintained the same dictatorial powers of life and death in Cuba as before the Ten Years' War. There was widespread graft and oppression; taxes were siphoned off to Spain; there were still many trade restrictions. Moreover, Cuba was by now an important factor in United States trade. American capital was invested in Cuba and American machinery saved the Cuban sugar-cane industry in its competition with beet sugar. Higher prices for sugar in the United States had brought a new prosperity to Cuba, but it was counterbalanced by the necessity of paying wages to sugar workers once the slaves were free, and by the high United States tariffs in the 1890s. Even the conservative Cuban merchants and sugar planters began to hope for a free Cuba which would have access to worldwide markets. By 1895 the war cry of *"Cuba Libre!"* was again on the lips of the majority of Cubans.

The war that freed Cuba was for three years (1895–1898) a struggle of Cubans against Spaniards, and for 100 days a series of land and naval engagements between Spain and the United States. On July 15, 1895, the revolutionists in exile had adopted a declaration of independence; Estrada Palma had formed a *junta* in New York and was raising funds; Maceo, who had been in Jamaica since the Ten Years' War, soon joined him; and with them was José Martí, the young poet who organized the revolution and who remains the national hero of Cuba.

Martí was born in Havana in 1853, and in his early youth he was involved in sporadic protests against the government. He was sent to prison at hard labor at seventeen, and his fetters formed scars which he carried to his death. Released and exiled, he became a typical Caribbean cultural figure, wandering in Central America and Mexico, supporting himself by writing. Cuban schoolchildren know many of his ringing words for freedom. He comforted those who lost everything in the Ten Years' War with, "To many generations of slaves must succeed one generation of martyrs." He insisted that the war for freedom was inevitable; he soon became the best-known Cuban patriot, founding clubs among Cuban cigar workers in Florida, and raising arms for Palma's *junta*.

In February 1895 Martí and Maceo set out for the Caribbean. By April General Gómez had joined them. Martí, the inspirational leader, was betrayed by a guide and killed from ambush a few days after landing; Maceo, the brilliant mulatto leader of the Ten Years' War, was killed in a skirmish. The Spaniards rejoiced: the weak little revolution would die without its beloved leaders. The plan was to crush it quickly and avoid the long guerrilla warfare of the previous insurrection.

Spain thus sent 200,000 soldiers to Cuba to stop the 25,000 patriots who had joined Gómez. At their head was General Valeriano Weyler who launched a scorched-earth policy to beat the patriots at their own guerrilla game. He held the key cities, herded the country people into great fenced areas called *reconcentrados*, where they could not farm and where thousands starved or died of disease. The cities were caught with no food, as General García held the eastern end of the island and kept food from reaching the starving capital; 52,000 died in Havana alone. The desolation caused repercussions even in Spain, and General Weyler was recalled, while Madrid promised greater measures of self-government. The patriots meanwhile had written a second declaration of independence and again chose Tomás Estrada Palma as their provisional president.

Sympathies were now aroused in the United States. Newspapers vied with each other in printing stories about the *reconcentrados*. American investments in sugar plantations were being destroyed; trade was being cut off. When the battleship *Maine*, sent to protect Americans in Havana, mysteriously exploded in February 1898, and 260 men were killed, American public opinion blamed it on the Spaniards. At the same time a letter written by the Spanish minister in Washington criticizing President McKinley was discovered and printed in a New York paper. Calmer leaders in Spain and the United States tried to avoid hostilities, but the public aroused Congress to declare war in April 1898.

The story of the next three months is famous in America. Theodore Roosevelt's Rough Riders on San Juan Hill, the message carried by an American foot soldier to the guerrillas under García, the defeat of the Spanish fleet under Cervera, the battle of Manila Bay are taught to every school child. Few Americans, however, know of the brave fighting of Gómez' troops, also at Santiago, of the long Cuban campaigns which made the quick American victory possible. In the minds of Cubans their independence was won by the fighting of their own patriots over a thirty-year period.

Under the peace treaty Puerto Rico, Guam, and the Philippines became United States possessions, and America was launched as a world power which was to influence Latin American affairs in the twentieth century. Cuba was recognized as independent by both Spain and the United States, but her foreign affairs were hampered by the Platt Amendment, which allowed American intervention, and by the treaty which gave the United

States military bases on Cuban soil. The arrangement also included tariff-free trade for Cuban sugar shipped into the United States, a provision readily acceptable to American and Spanish planters alike, who hoped to build up their plantations in Cuba after years of devastation.

American troops occupied the island for three years at the turn of the twentieth century. The American military government, under General Leonard Wood from 1899 to 1902, restored order and granted financial aid. Food was distributed to the people who had been in the *reconcentrados*; cattle, seed, and cane stock were sent in under the arrangements made by Calixto García on a mission to Washington. General Wood's interim government rebuilt towns and villages, installed water and sewage systems, set up hospitals, cleaned streets, and rebuilt roads. Elections were held and Cuba drafted a constitution.

An American doctor with Wood, Walter Reed, also declared a second "War to Free Cuba"—this time from yellow fever. He contacted a Cuban scientist named Carlos Finlay, who had experimented with its causes. No one had listened to Finlay's theory that mosquitoes carried yellow fever; the Cuban war had kept his experiments from being known. Dr. Reed's assistants tried to produce yellow fever by all known types of contacts, but only the patients bitten by mosquitoes who had fed off yellow fever cases contracted the disease. Armed with this proof, the American army began to kill mosquito larvae by draining swamps and pouring oil on breeding places. Thus Cuban-American cooperation made possible the end of yellow fever and led to disease-free work on a large scale in many parts of the tropics, including the panama Canal Zone.

Dr. Carlos Finlay, the Cuban who discovered the cause of yellow fever. *Courtesy Pan American Union.*

To help prepare Cuba for a democratic society, more than 3,000 schools were founded under the American regime, where before there had been only a few inadequate private schools. More than a thousand young Cubans went to the United States in the summer of 1900 to attend a special summer school at Harvard to be trained for teaching in the new republic. With this American help, Tomás Estrada Palma started as president of the Cuban Republic, May 20, 1902. But years of war, colonial misrule, racial inequality, extremes of wealth and poverty, and lack of experience in government had ill-prepared the new island republic for life in the dawning twentieth century.

HAITI'S FIRST CENTURY AS THE FRENCH-SPEAKING NEGRO REPUBLIC

Hispaniola, the first land to be cultivated by Europeans and the first Latin American country to win independence, contained two small unstable republics during the nineteenth century while Cuba remained a Spanish colony. Unlike its sister republics, Haiti is a French-speaking Negro republic; its story has been different from the beginning. The reader will remember the revolt of Toussaint L'Ouverture and his fellow slaves against the French owners of Haiti.

Jean Jacques Dessalines, illiterate and bitter against the whites, was the first independent ruler of this devastated land which had few whites left and few educated ex-slaves to help organize a government. He declared the independence of Haiti on January 1, 1804, but this declaration included only the western part of the island. The eastern portion remained under French and later Spanish forces. In an elaborate coronation Dessalines crowned himself Jacques I, Emperor of Haiti. He held formal court while the ground lay uncultivated, ex-slaves went to the hills to live in primitive villages, and commerce remained at a standstill. The emperor let Henri Christophe, that other ex-slave lieutenant of Toussaint's, rule for him in the north of the island, while Alexandre Pétion, an educated, liberal-minded mulatto, governed in the south at Aux Cayes. Occasionally Dessalines rode to one or the other camp with his bodyguard to issue proclamations and maintain stern army discipline. On one such occasion his own dissatisfied troops ambushed and killed him.

Now it was Henri Christophe's turn. He was perhaps twenty years younger than Toussaint, tall, straight-featured, coal black, and very proud. Nothing is known of his ancestry, save that he was born a slave in the British West Indies, was taught the stonemason's trade at eight years of age, and ran away to be a cabin boy at twelve. The ship captain sold him in the harbor of Cap Haitien to a French naval officer going to fight for North American freedom. His master sold him on his return to Haiti to a free mulatto hotel keeper to serve as a waiter and stable boy. Here he saw the mulatto Ogé, harbinger of Haitian freedom, tortured to death. When Toussaint's army came into the city he joined as a sergeant.

At the death of Dessalines, Christophe called an election for an assembly to write a constitution and choose a president. The northern provinces around Cap Haitien, known as the "State of Haiti," picked Christophe; the south, dominated by the mulatto freedmen, made a separate "Republic of Haiti" under Alexandre Pétion. There were skirmishes between the two areas for a decade. Henri Christophe at first called himself chief governor, but at the end of a four-year term he had himself made president for life, and then crowned as Henri I on June 2, 1811.

Christophe tried to follow Toussaint's example rather than Dessalines'. When he came to power, there had been no cultivation since before Napoleon's troops came; ex-slaves on the sugar plantations were living in straw huts built inside the roofless ruins of old mansions. There was no money in circulation and all trade was by barter. The West Indian jungle was moving in on the towns. Using military force, Christophe established order and put the field hands back to work. Coffee was picked on the abandoned plantations and sold to England for cash to start a treasury. In the docks at Cap Haitien a small merchant marine was built to trade with other islands. English artisans were imported to start a weaving mill. Sea captains who handled Christophe's trade reported 10,000,000 pounds of sugar and equal quantities of coffee, cacao, and cotton exported each year in 1812 and 1813.

Christophe prospered personally and lived in splendor, hiring English physicians to care for him and English secretaries to handle his correspondence, for he never learned to read and write well enough to do the latter for himself. Besides a fancy personal palace, "Sans Souci," he built a great citadel on a hilltop, Laferrière, the strongest single fortification in the New World, and still a curiosity to tourists. He created an elaborate nobility with dukes, duchesses, and counts. Using his childhood stonemason's training, Christophe worked tirelessly on the construction projects himself. School buildings were begun in the town of Cap Haitien, and teachers from France and the United States were invited to teach there. "While I live I shall try to build the pride we need," said Christophe. "No one is indolent and dirty, for indolence and filth are forbidden by the emperor!"

Haitians chafed under his rule; they felt that they had not fought the French only to become the slaves of Christophe. In Pétion's southern republic villagers sat lazily in the sun and grass grew in the markets of Port-au-Prince, but the subjects of Christophe envied the life there. In 1820 Christophe had a paralytic stroke; his army deserted to Pétion and his people came to Sans Souci to kill him. "We dreamt so much, Toussaint, the Tiger and I, and we have done so little," he said, as he blew his brains out with a special silver bullet he had cast just for that purpose.

Alexandre Pétion, born free to a mulatto woman, educated in France at the expense of his white father, had long dreamed of an ideal republic. He was twice elected president and in 1816 he wrote a constitution which lasted till 1867, providing for lifelong presidency and forbidding foreign ownership of property in Haiti. He had distributed the lands near Aux Cayes in small plots, leaving it up to the new owners whether they cultivated the plots or not. He was harassed by Christophe's northern men and by internal dissension and civil war. Of all these hard-fighting Haitian leaders he was the only one to die a natural death, in the midst of his indolent people. During his last illness he designated another free-born mulatto, Jean Pierre Boyer, to succeed him in 1819. Boyer's men took over Christophe's army and united Haiti again into one state. They inherited the empty treasury and the uncultivated fields of the south, the growing caste system between educated mulattoes and the black sons of slaves, which had developed under Pétion, the anger against the government which had developed in the north under Christophe, and the lawless bandits and primitive villages of the interior.

Boyer ruled Haiti from 1819 to 1843. Not contented with his own disorganized area, he moved into the vacuum left by the removal of Spanish troops from Santo Domingo, the Spanish-speaking eastern half of the island, and ruled that part also. He was able to win final recognition from France, but at the expense of an enormous indemnity payment for the years of rebellion, and thus was saddled with a French debt which was never paid off. When he distributed more land in small plots, his people quit growing the things for export that they had produced under the forced labor in Christophe's time. The few educated mulattoes of Boyer's own class became a new aristocracy, the elite, but there was no progress among the ex-slaves at the bottom. As time went on Boyer became more arbitrary, and he was overthrown and sent into exile in 1843. There followed four years of confusion and "barracks revolts" during which Haiti lost Santo Domingo, which broke away in 1844. Four different leaders, all Negroes, attempted to maintain the helm by military force. Out of the melee an illiterate ex-slave named Faustín Soulouque crowned himself Emperor Faustín I in 1847. He remained the ruler for twelve years, breaking with the mulatto aristocracy and governing through a Negro army.

After Soulouque's fall in 1859 Haiti averaged one new dictator every two-and-a-half years for the next half century. Efforts were made to reconquer Santo Domingo, to establish a sound currency, to improve agriculture, to start elementary schools—all to no avail. Ninety per cent of the people remained illiterate. Black presidents, often illiterate, were backed by the army in throwing out mulatto presidents, often educated in Paris but concerned only with their own upper-class mulatto friends. A dark mulatto, Nicolas Geffrard, a compromise ruler between the two racial groups, held office from 1859 to 1867. He saved funds for elementary schools by cutting the army in half, and he aided agriculture. He won recognition from the United States, made a Concordat with the Vatican, and established an organized French priesthood on the island for the first time since independence. In 1867 he too was forced to flee and give way to chaos.

The administration of Paris-educated president Lysius Salomon from 1879 to 1888 was a time of real progress. He created a national bank and stabilized the currency, encouraged import trade, opened some schools in country villages, and brought teachers of Parisian French from France to improve the almost unintelligible Haitian *patois* dialect. Haiti gained some stature as a nation and became a member of the International Postal Union. But Salomon was ruthless to his opposition. Of his successors, only Florvil Hyppolite (1889–1896), a tyrant who brought some order in finances, and Tiresias Augustin Simon Sam (1896–1902), under whom some railroads were introduced and commerce increased with German investments, served longer than a few months in office. In both cases fear of foreign complications eventually sent them into exile. The first threat of foreign intervention came in the 1890s, when German warships appeared in the harbor threatening to collect by force some of Haiti's confusing debts.

In all these years nothing had been done to relieve the poverty, malnutrition, and ignorance of the masses. Public funds were never spent on public works but always on the ruling class. Inflation of paper money, unpaid foreign debts, and chaotic government led directly to United States intervention in the twentieth century. The only roads were mule trails unrepaired since Christophe's time. The only real workers were the farm women, who brought produce into town on their heads, then sat and sold it in the markets as their forebears had done in the villages of West Africa. Coffee was the only cash crop, but both coffee and sugar lands were "left in a wild state." "At least two-thirds of the population do not speak any language recognized by the civilized world," said a visitor. Yet some excellent verse had been produced in the Haitian *patois*, called "creole," the most noteworthy of which was the work of Oswald Durand (1840–1896), whose love poem *Choucone* is well remembered today. The French bishop who came after the signing of the Concordat with the Pope found little pure practice of Christianity in the "cities" of Port-au-Prince and Cap Haitien, for the entire rural populace practiced the superstitious rituals of voodoo. Cut off from the rest of the French-speaking world, out of tune with the Spanish culture and tradition of most of Latin America, failing to develop a new middle class from among the descendants of an enslaved people, Haiti, for all the brave dreams of Toussaint, remained the most backward Caribbean country till the twentieth century.

SANTO DOMINGO: A SPANISH-SPEAKING APPENDAGE OF HAITI

The eastern end of the island, Spain's first colony in the New World, had been the loyal province of Santo Domingo in 1820. Twice as big as the French-settled area in the west, it had less than half as many people in the mid-nineteenth century, and its history is clouded by the shadow of its more spectacular neighbor. Toussaint had held Santo Domingo temporarily, but the French-speaking Haitians had been ousted by the Spaniards. Then, a year after a weak republic had been declared there in 1821, Haitian forces of Pierre Boyer had conquered it.

The Dominican people, perhaps 20 per cent Negro, had no pride in Negro blood and resented Haitian dominance; Haitian rule was considered worse than Spanish colonial rule. Their young men were forced into the Haitian army, their university was closed, their church officials were shut off from access to papal authority. What little there had been of culture and religion, of trade and city life in the decadent Spanish colony deteriorated under the Haitian foreigners. Naturally a "youth society," the *Trinitaria*, dedicated to "God, Fatherland, and Liberty," planned rebellion. The rebels succeeded when Boyer was exiled and they declared independence in 1844; they were also strong enough to expel Faustín Soulouque in the 1850's when he attempted a reconquest. The struggling little republic continued to suffer raids from the Haitians, and had little success in self-government at home.

For the three decades after Faustín's defeat, Dominicans were dominated alternately by Buenaventura Báez, who would like to have annexed his country to the United States and even dickered with President Grant over the possibilities, and Pedro Santana, who actually brought Santo Domingo back under Spanish control. While the United States was busy with her own Civil War, Queen Isabella II, the weak Spanish queen, was proclaimed the guardian of Santo Domingo, and her "governor," Santana, ruled in her name with an iron hand. The Dominicans, who hated the price they had to pay for Spanish domination—reduction to colonial status —went underground. These Dominican guerrillas proved too costly to Spain, and after the "War of Restoration" Spain withdrew. Now the pro-American Báez was in again, but he was to be out of power five times before 1878.

The 1880s brought a Christophe-type dictator to power in Santo Domingo; he was Ulises Heureaux, the illegitimate son of former slaves from Haiti and the Virgin Islands. Well educated and shrewd, he was "an Apollo in physical build, courageous and of extraordinary stamina." In 1882 he began a seventeen-year military dictatorship, cowing all opposition by bribery, bullying, and murder. He was an able administrator in things domestic but a child when it came to finances. He turned the finances over to the "Santo Domingo Improvement Company," which helped itself and Heureaux personally but sank Santo Domingo further into debt, though agriculture and commerce prospered as American capital ventured in sugar. Shortly after the end of his rule the government owed various foreign countries over $30,000,000, a debt which brought foreign intervention early in the twentieth century. Heureaux himself did not live to reap the whirlwind his poor finance had sown, for he was assassinated by a political enemy in 1899.

Santo Domingo, however, had maintained a higher standard of culture than its near neighbor. The plantation owners and the city creoles had not been driven out or killed as had the French whites next door. From these creole families sprang some writers known to all Latin America. Señora Salomé Ureña de Henríquez (1850–1897) had founded a high school for girls and encouraged teacher-training and public elementary education; she also found time to write sad poetry on Dominican history, which was widely read in other Spanish-speaking countries. Though she died in 1897, her husband, a noted physician, was president of Santo Domingo in the early 1900s and both her sons achieved a literary fame as great as her own. Santo Domingo also claims one of the advanced political and social philosophers of the 1890s, Eugenio de Hostos (1839–

Small holder's cabin, Port Limón, Costa Rica. Thus lived most rural Middle Americans in the nineteenth century. *Photo by Helen Miller Bailey.*

1903) ; born on the then-Spanish island of Puerto Rico, he came to Santo Domingo as an exile from Spanish rule in the 1880s. While devoting himself to teaching in Santo Domingo he found time to write prolifically in the cause of Cuban and Puerto Rican independence.

CENTRAL AMERICA'S ATTEMPTS AT A FEDERATION

Conditions on the mainland of Central America were as unstable politically as on the islands. When Mexico became independent under Iturbide he had attempted to hold Central America as part of his empire. But the former Spanish provinces of Nicaragua with its cities of Granada, León, and Managua, Guatemala with its capital and *audiencia* seat of Guatemala City, El Salvador with its one city of San Salvador, and the more remote regions of Honduras and Costa Rica all were anti-Mexican. They spurned Iturbide and upon his downfall they again declared independence (July 1823), setting up a federation of states, the independent United Provinces of Central America.

Of all travel stories of the nineteenth century one of the most fascinating is called *Incidents of Travel in Central America, Chiapas and Yucatan,* the account of a trip made by John L. Stephens of New York, who represented President Van Buren on a mission to that federation in 1839. He landed at Belize, now called British Honduras, and held by England as a mahogany-producing colony to this day. Hiring mules and native packtrain guides, he and an artist friend found their way to

Guatemala City, traveling on unused trails, staying in Indian huts, or slinging up their hammocks in the crude *cabildo* buildings of unpaved mountain towns. In a trip of ten months Stephens visited all five of the regions that are today's Central American republics, met dictators and generals, watched frontier-type congresses at work, argued himself out of border difficulties and jail terms owing to constantly changing regulations against strangers.

Stephens ended up enthusiastic about the scenery and the ancient Mayan ruins, mildly tolerant of the backward people, and pessimistic about the unstable government. In fact he wasted considerable time trying to contact the federal authorities, as "it was incumbent upon me to look around for the government to which I was accredited." Where was the national capital? Was it Guatemala City—which impressed him as a new town—since the earthquake of 1776 had destroyed the old capital? No, Guatemala City was in the control of an Indian named Rafael Carrera, a despot supported only by the Guatemalan conservatives and abjured by the other regions. Was the capital at Quetzaltenango, Guatemala's second city, which had just declared itself a separate province in the federation? No, just before Stephens' arrival a mob of frenzied women had stoned to death the federal vice-president who had come to collect federal taxes there. The federal military commander maintained his headquarters in San Salvador, but only the people of that city themselves considered it the federal capital. In Nicaragua and Costa Rica Stephens met independent dictators who had left the federation the year before his visit.

In short, he found only confusion in Central America, its towns as far apart as the island capitals in the Caribbean, the mountains and forests between them more difficult to cross than the Caribbean Sea between the islands, and much less frequently traveled. The fine federation, the *Provincias Unidas del Centro de América*, founded with such idealism in 1823, suffered from disunity from the first. The smaller capitals resented the power of the federal capital, Guatemala City; the government of the state of Guatemala could not live happily side by side with the federal government. It was the typical struggle between centralism and federalism, combined with the standard Latin American struggle between liberalism and conservatism, in an area where the Indian masses were living as in pre-Columbian times and the Church was unusually powerful. Manuel José Arce, elected first president of the federation, was caught in the crossfire of liberals and conservatives, and in attempting to please everyone succeeded in satisfying no one. When a church group in El Salvador, disappointed at not having El Salvador created a separate diocese, started a revolt against the federal government, civil war ensued. A young Honduran creole, Francisco Morazán, won a victory for the combined Honduran and Salvadorean liberals and was elected president of a temporarily pacified federation in 1830.

Morazán, then only thirty years old, is the hero of Central American federation. So great was his threat against the conservatives, however, that they went to every length to turn the people against him. They told the ignorant mountain Indians of Guatemala that Morazán and the liberals would upset the true religion. One such Indian, a pig driver of nineteen named Rafael Carrera, roused the Indians against Morazán, raised a rabble horde, and marched on Guatemala City, telling the poor that he was the Archangel Rafael. Morazán came up from El Salvador with liberal troops and drove out Carrera, who melted back into the cornfields and mountain tops with his Indians, only to rise up again with conservative backing and retake Guatemala City a year later.

When Stephens visited the city, he was anxious to meet Carrera, whose name had been mentioned in hushed tones by everyone he had met. Carrera was then twenty-three years old, a small dark Guatemalan Indian like many the tourist sees trudging to market today. He had learned to read and write since coming to power, but though he had issued the cry "Long Live Religion and Death to Foreigners!" Stephens was the first foreigner he had ever seen and one of the last. Carrera was destined to be the tool of conservative influences, and he ruled ruthlessly, backed by a well-paid army and the religious devotion of the Indian masses. But he constantly improved as an administrator and brought peace, albeit the peace of death, to Guatemala for a quarter century. Often the target of attempted assassinations, twice temporarily exiled, Carrera ruled for many years in the separate republic of Guatemala and died of natural causes in bed in 1863.

The federal power, so diligently searched out by Stephens in 1839, itself died in that year of his visit. He was present at the last meeting of the federal congress, when a small group of hostile delegates, in a dark gloomy room, with no other visitor save himself and two small urchins, argued over the methods of forced collection of church tithes from the Indians, a practice that had been legally abandoned in the first brave days of 1821. Three years afterward, when he attempted to oust a current Costa Rican dictator, Morazán, the federal leader, was defeated with his Honduran and Salvadorean army and executed in Costa Rica. The subsequent record of Central America is the story of five different republics.

Attempts to reunite Central America after Morazán's downfall were uniformly unsuccessful. In Guatemala the great families and the Church preferred their own local government; Costa Rica, even more isolated geographically, had no stomach for civil wars and federation. The other three countries, however, did at various times attempt federation.

In Guatemala political parties were divided on real issues. Lines were sharply drawn between the Conservatives made up of the clergy, nobility, and many great landowners and merchants, and the Liberals composed of the *mestizo* and creole professional men and other less privileged groups. It was the former led by Rafael Carrera who overthrew the federation and dominated Guatemala until Carrera's death in 1865. Carrera intervened several times in the neighboring states to knock over Liberal regimes and substitute Conservative ones.

The Liberals gained control in Guatemala in 1871 and came under the shadow of their Liberal dictator, Justo Rufino Barrios, an industrious and forward-looking man who, during his presidency, 1873–1885, destroyed the political influence of the Church and the aristocracy. He developed the production of coffee and bananas, proposed public improvements, including road building and schools, and separated Church and state. In his time all large Guatemalan towns with Spanish-speaking rather than Indian population had a primary school supported by tax funds. Barrios himself, in his capacity as president, made trips to the United States and Europe, talked of inviting factories and railroads into his country and connecting the capital with the Caribbean port which today bears his name. His dominant ambition was to head a Guatemala-dominated Central American federation; to that end he announced a one-sided decree in 1885 declaring the union re-established. This time it was the armies of El Salvador that opposed the Guatemalan federation. In the ensuing battle between the two countries Barrios himself was killed, and Central American union was again laid away.

By this time the Liberal regime was so entrenched in Guatemala that the death of its leader did not upset it. His policies of continued growth of trade and agriculture were continued under two regimes until the assassination of president José María Reyna Barrios, the great leader's nephew, gave rise to the long-term, notoriously corrupt dictatorship of Manuel Estrada Cabrera, at the close of the century in 1898.

In Guatemala City there were enough sophisticated creoles to provide real parties and an understanding of the issues between liberals and conservatives. In Barrios' time the capital had 5,000 houses, but Quetzaltenango, second town of the nation, was still a half-Indian village. In these two "cities" and a few lesser ones lived the 30 per cent of the population who were at all Europeanized, while in the villages of the western highlands lived the 70 per cent who were Indians, little changed since Maya times, speaking variations of the Maya dialect but subject to the heavy taxes and the forced-labor draft by which Barrios paid for his country's progress.

In contrast to *mestizo* and Indian Guatemala, Costa Rica, at the other end of Central America, was inhabited by some 600,000 prosperous, hard-working farmers of an almost pure Spanish strain. It had been the first region to make a complete break with the idea of federation. Stephens had enjoyed his stay there. "San José, I believe, is the only city that has grown up or improved since the independence of Central America." He was impressed with the well-cultivated coffee acreage, held in small ownership, the "progressive women of the country," and with the current dictator, a simple businessman, "short, stout and plain, not a general," who lived in the same small house "in which his wife had a little store," and in which he had "three clerks writing for him" caring for the government business. This simple prosperity lasted through various congress-chosen liberal and conservative "dictators" till the twentieth century.

Costa Rica started its separate and progressive history under Braulio Carillo who laid the foundations of Costa Rican stability. Land was parceled out in small units of ownership. Costa Rica's first really constitutional president was José M. Castro. Under Juan Rafael Mora at mid-century,

Costa Rica underwent a decade of order and economic advance, followed by a decade of dictators dominated by the conservatives. In 1870 Tomás Guardia rose to power—power that was chiefly military. Even such dictatorship gave peace and economic improvement to the little country, bringing the building of railroads and the development of the banana industry. This new crop, in addition to coffee, promoted Costa Rica's foreign trade and prosperity. Guardia's rule was followed by attempts to arrange fair elections and some more effective voice of the people in affairs of government. Freer elections became the vogue as the twentieth century began—with Costa Rica a well-governed, peaceful, and well-educated community, despite its small area and population.

El Salvador and Honduras were not faring so well. Honduras remained underdeveloped because its population, made up largely of Indians and descendants of slaves, lived so widely separated in such small communities. Agriculture was difficult in the tiny infertile valleys. Other governments continually interfered with Honduran political affairs. Consequently, at the time of the breakup of the Central American federation there ensued a long, sustained era of civil wars, foreign wars, and interventions from neighboring states—an uninterrupted narrative of disorders. Guatemalan intervention was behind most of the changes of the *caudillos* in Honduras. Marco Aurelio Soto's regime (1876–1883), together with that of his successor Luís Bográn until 1891, gave Honduras brief intervals of stability. In 1894 the ardent Liberal Policarpo Bonilla was imposed on Honduras by Nicaragua. A Liberal rule ensued until the turn of the century and in 1903 the Conservative faction forced their way into office. Honduras contained an abundance of mineral wealth, but the mines worked in colonial times were neglected for two generations after independence. Until foreign investment began to develop the gold-washings in the 1880s, the capital was a country village, connected by mule trails to the rest of the nation.

El Salvador, center of the strong Church group which had started the disruption of the federation in the first place, was more progressive, more thickly settled, and had a more productive agriculture than Honduras. Having an ideal climate and altitude for coffee production, it would have shown great economic improvement by 1900 if the Salvadoreans had been free of dictators and palace revolutions. Family rule by benign dictators under constitutions which breathed democratic idealism may have looked good, but the rival families were supported by powerful rival armies, and this meant autocratic rule, interrupted by revolutions and party strife. There was almost constant border conflict with and intervention by El Salvador's neighbors, especially Guatemala and Nicaragua.

NICARAGUA: CENTER OF INTRIGUES FOR ISTHMIAN CONTROL AND HOME OF ONE FAMOUS POET

Nicaragua had withdrawn from the Central American union in 1838, and was the scene of bitter internal fighting till the 1850s. But this disorderly little nation suddenly came to world attention, while the other nations remained isolated, because of the discovery of gold in California in 1848. Gold-seekers from the east coast of the United States could reach San Francisco by taking ship to Greytown on the Caribbean coast, then by paddling upriver to Lake Nicaragua. After crossing the lake by sail to the cities of central Nicaragua, the traveler had only a forty-mile stage coach trip across the range to reach a tiny port on the Pacific where he could wait for a sailing ship to San Francisco—altogether a much shorter journey than crossing the United States in a covered wagon.

Soon the American promoter Cornelius Vanderbilt organized a successful company to care for all stages of this trip. He met opposition not from the Nicaraguans but from the British, who considered the area their own sphere of influence owing to their possession of British Honduras. The result of the ensuing negotiations was the Clayton-Bulwer Treaty of 1850, in which Britain and the United States agreed that neither nation would obtain or maintain exclusive control over the proposed canal, nor occupy any part of Central America, nor give exclusive privileges. Vanderbilt's company made the crossing until a railway was built across Panama.

Vanderbilt's success seemed to provide an open invitation for other individual American adventurers to make a strike in Nicaragua. In June 1855 William Walker, most famous of "land pirates" or filibusters, landed in Nicaragua with fifty-eight followers from the California mining towns. A Tennessean who had already taken a bunch of fellow adventurers on an unsuccessful "invasion" of Lower California, Walker felt destined to carve a pro-American empire out of the region of Vanderbilt's route. Arriving in Nicaragua, he and his "army" became Nicaraguan citizens so they could help a revolutionary faction oust the current government. In 1856 he had himself elected president of Nicaragua, and drew hundreds of adventurers from the United States to help him "win an empire." Soon he was in control of Vanderbilt's steamers and stage coaches and was dictator of the country. He was not satisfied till he tried to control all Central America, financed by a group of New Yorkers who were jealous of Vanderbilt, and assisted by Southerners who dreamt of extending the slave states. A gentlemanly little man, not at all the pirate-type, Walker inspired a new fear of federation in all the neighboring republics. Now Central America rallied to save Nicaragua, and even Great Britain made moves to oppose Walker. Juan Rafael Mora, a far-sighted Costa Rican president, attacked and defeated Walker's troops. An epidemic of cholera laid the American volunteers low when the Walker troops "holed up" in the Nicaraguan city of Granada. While the allies laid siege to the city, Walker escaped on the lake, then went downriver to an American vessel in the Caribbean.

Now Granada lay in smoking ruins; cholera raged unchecked in many Central American towns; the steamers and the stage coaches were damaged; American "enterprise" was the object of fear and hatred in Central America for years. Walker persisted in his "destiny," however. Landing as a hero in New Orleans, he soon found new followers, and made two subsequent attempts to control Nicaragua and Honduras. He was finally caught by the British navy off the coast of Honduras, turned over to the government at Tegucigalpa, and executed in September 1860.

Nicaragua's own problem was to settle disputes as to which of its cities should be the capital. León was a city of liberal politics; Granada, rebuilding after the war against Walker, was the Church and Conservative stronghold. In between lay a sleepy village called Managua, which became the capital after a generation of disputes. In 1863 Nicaragua ended its long era of chronic civil war when a period known as the "Thirty Years of Peace" was inaugurated under conservative rule, marked by some national progress. The year 1881 saw a railroad built along the Vanderbilt stage road to connect the lake cities with the Pacific. The route itself brought some small business to Nicaragua until the canal was built at Panama, a region which throughout the century was a province of Colombia.

The Central American republics, sleeping between their revolutions, had small interest in things intellectual in their undeveloped little capitals, and would hardly deserve a section on "culture" in so short a study. But León, Nicaragua, home of the strongest liberal party of the region and a center of culture in colonial times, produced the "father of modernism" in Latin American literature, Rubén Darío. Darío was born a mixed-blood of Spanish, Indian, and Negro stock in a Nicaraguan village in 1867. Educated by an uncle in León, he wrote poems at the age of sixteen which attracted the attention of well-to-do citizens of that town. Before the age of nineteen he visited the other Central American capitals, had poetry printed in their newspapers, and was writing lovesick poems in Paris. In 1888, his twentieth year, he won a poetry contest in literature-conscious Chile, while writing for a Santiago newspaper. In that year a volume of his *modernista* poems entitled *Azul* appeared in Chile, a volume called by critics "Art for Art's Sake." Although he spent time in Spain, Colombia, Cuba, and his native Nicaragua, Darío's greatest influence was on the literature of Argentina, where he wrote for several newspapers during a period of twenty-six years. Restlessness and alcohol wrecked his personal life; he returned to León to die in 1916, having tried unsuccessfully to support himself by lecturing, writing, and serving as consul.

His book *Prosas Profanas,* the collected works published in 1896, is called the "zenith of the *modernista* movement." His *Songs of Life and Hope* is his greatest collection of poems. Much of his sensuous poetry has been translated into English. There is color in his verses in any language. The sight of a girl he loves brings him the inner "sight of orange flowers"; a shell found on the shore is a "golden" message murmuring of azure mines of hidden treasure beneath the sea. There is his description of pines: "Oh, sunny pines, all bathed in charm, in glory, in blue air...." When he threw a rock into the sky it was "a pebble of pure gold"; when he saw a bird, "its flight on high with ruby streaked the sapphire sky." Today's modern travel books call Central America "the rainbow republics." Rubén Darío, their famous poet, was the rainbow poet. When Chileans, Colombians, Argentines think of Central America at the turn of the century, they do not always think of petty dictators or lost federations or canal plans. They perhaps often think of Rubén Darío, poet of all Latin America, who was born and who died in Nicaragua.

Readings

Adams, R. N., *Cultural Surveys of Panama-Nicaragua-Guatemala-El Salvador-Honduras* (1957)

Alexis, S., *Black Liberator—Life of Toussaint L'Ouverture* (1949)

Arciniegas, G., *The Caribbean: Sea of the New World*, trans. H. de Onis (1946)

Baily, J., *Central America* (1850)

Bancroft, H. H., *History of Central America* (3 vols., 1883–1887)

Biensanz, J. and C., *Costa Rican Life* (1944)

Blanchard, P., *Democracy and Empire in the Caribbean* (1947)

Bumgartner, L. E., *José del Valle of Central America* (1963)

Burgess, P., *Justo Rufino Barrios* (1926)

Caldwell, R. G., *The López Expedition to Cuba, 1848–1851* (1915)

Callcott, W. H., *Caribbean Policy of the United States, 1890–1920* (1942)

Carr, A. Z., *The World and William Walker* (1963)

Chamberlain, R. S., *Francisco Morazán—Champion of Central American Federation* (1950)

Dana, R. H., *To Cuba and Back*, ed. C. Gardiner (1965)

Davis, H. P., *Black Democracy—The Story of Haiti* (rev. ed., 1936)

Deutsch, H. B., *The Incredible Yankee: The Career of Lee Christmas* (1931)

Fergusson, E., *Guatemala* (1937)

Follick, W. M., *The Twelve Republics* (1952)

Foner, P. S., *History of Cuba and Its Relations with the United States* (2 vols., 1962–1963)

Fortier, A., and J. R. Ficklin, *Central America and Mexico* (1907)

Gray, R. B., *José Martí: Cuban Patriot* (1962)

Griffith, W. J., *Empire in the Wilderness* (1965)

Holleran, M. P., *Church and State in Guatemala* (1949)

Howland, C. P., ed., *American Foreign Relations in the Caribbean* (1929)

Ireland, G., *Boundaries, Possessions, and Conflicts in Central and North America and the Caribbean* (1941)

Jenks, L. H., *Our Cuban Colony* (1928)

Johnson, S. H., *The Negro in the New World* (1910)

Johnson, W. F., *History of Cuba* (5 vols., 1920)

Jones, C. L., *Caribbean Backgrounds and Prospects* (1931)

———, *Costa Rica and the Civilization of the Caribbean* (1935)

———, *Guatemala, Past and Present* (1940)

Karnes, T., *Failure of Union: Central America, 1824–1960* (1961)

Kelsey, V., and L. de J. Osborne, *Four Keys to Guatemala* (1929)

Kemble, J. H., *Panama Route, 1848–1869* (1943)

Kepner, C. O., and J. H. Southill, *The Banana Empire* (1935)

Leyburn, J. G., *The Haitian People* (1941)

Lizaso, F., *Martí, Martyr of Cuban Independence* (1953)

Logan, R. W., *Diplomatic Relations of the United States with Haiti, 1776–1891* (1941)

Manach, J., *Martí: Apostle of Freedom*, trans. C. Taylor (1950)

Martz, J. D., *Central America: The Crisis and the Challenge* (1959)

———, *Justo Rufino Barrios and Central American Union* (1963)

May, S., *et al.*, *Costa Rica: A Study in Economic Development* (1952)

Millis, W., *The Martial Spirit* (1931)

Montagu, L. L., *Haiti and the United States, 1774–1938* (1940)

Munro, D. G., *The Five Republics of Central America* (1918)

Osborne, L. de J., *Four Keys to El Salvador* (1956)

Parker, F. D., *Central American Republics* (1964)

———, *History and Historians of Central America to 1850* (1951)

———, *José Cecilio del Valle and the Establishment of Central American Confederation* (1954)

Perkins, D., *The United States and the Caribbean* (1947)

Rauch, B., *American Interest in Cuba, 1848–1855* (1948)

Roberts, W. A., *The Caribbean* (1940)

Rodman, S., *Quisqueya: A History of the Dominican Republic* (1962)

Rodriguez, M., *Central America* (1965)

———, *A Palmerstonian Diplomat in Central America: Frederick Chatfield* (1964)

Scherzer, C., *Travels—Central America* (2 vols., 1857)

Scroggs, W. O., *Filibusters and Finances: The Story of William Walker* (1916)

Slade, W. F., *The Federation of Central America* (1917)

Smith, R. F., *What Happened in Cuba? A Documentary History* (1963)

Squier, E. G., *Nicaragua* (2 vols., 1852)

———, *Notes on Central America* (1855)

———, *Travels in Central America* (2 vols., 1853)

Stephens, J. L., *Incidents of Travel in Central America, Chiapas and Yucatan* (new edition; 2 vols., 1949)

Stewart, W., *Keith and Costa Rica* (1964)

Stokes, W. S., *Honduras: An Area Study in Government* (1950)

Stuart, G. H., *United States and Latin America* (5th ed., 1955)

Tansill, C. C., *United States and Santo Domingo, 1798–1873* (1938)

Underwood, E., *The Poets of Haiti, 1782–1934* (1934)

Vandercook, J. W., *Black Majesty* (1928)

Welles, S., *Naboth's Vineyard* (2 vols., 1928)

Whetten, N. L., *Guatemala: The Land and the People* (1961)

Wilgus, A. C., ed., *The Caribbean Area* (1934)

Williams, M. W., *Anglo-American Isthmian Diplomacy, 1815–1915* (1916)

Wilson, C. M., *Challenge and Opportunity: Central America* (1941)

———, *Empire in Green and Gold* (1947)

———, *Middle America* (1944)

SOUTH AMERICA
THREE MAJOR POWE

ARGENTINA, BRAZIL, CH

Part V

MAJOR LATIN AMERICAN NATIONS LOOM LARGE IN TODAY'S WORLD

IN THE SPRING OF 1956 one adobe hut in the vast area called the Federal District of Brazil on the 4,000 foot plateau of Goiás had been provided as the home of a new federal capital for the Brazilian nation under the Constitution of 1946. In the spring of 1966, 250,000 people were living there in the fabulous new city of Brasilia. President Kubitschek of Brazil had promised in 1957 that he would build a new federal capital in three years' time, a capital which would help create a strong national feeling among the many jealous regions of Brazil. He announced an international competition among architects and city planners for the design of a new city in the wilderness. The prize was won by a Rio de Janeiro architect, Lucio Costa, whose design called for an arrangement of city streets, government buildings, and government workers' apartments which would resemble an airplane. It was to be encircled by a winding lake twenty-five miles long, and to contain sufficient modern housing units for a capital city of 300,000, all to be built within three years. A bond-selling agency called NOVACAP (for New Capital) was set up to finance the building program.

Kubitschek hired a former student of Costa's, Oscar Niemeyer, a Brazilian of Swiss ancestry who had helped design the United Nations in New York, to work out plans for the individual government buildings. Neimeyer worked on a scale model of the entire Brasilia area in his Rio studio, setting up small blocks of modeling clay to represent buildings to fill Costa's plan. When Kubitschek enthusiastically approved the model, Neimeyer and his family moved to a shanty in the trackless federal district. He arrived by truck from the nearest hamlet eighty miles away, following the bulldozers which were building a road. The first project was to bulldoze an airport so workers and supplies could be brought in by air. The second item was to dam up the two local streams to make the lake.

Then the concrete mixers came to pour Niemeyer's buildings in the shapes he had planned on the scale model—two tall shafts of green glass for the Senate and House office buildings, an upturned saucer for the meetings of the Senate, an overturned saucer for the meetings of the House, a glass-enclosed block for the president's house, rows and rows of model apartments for the government workers, each with its school and playgrounds. On April 1, 1960, the anniversary of the death of Tiradentes, an early martyr for Brazilian independence, the Brazilian congress met in the new buildings. Kubitschek was already living in the president's mansion. By 1965, all the departments of government save the foreign affairs section were in Brasilia, and Niemeyer was busy building embassies for the major nations in Brasilia. The spring of 1966 saw the city blooming at the end of its ten years as if it had been there twenty.

But as in many other fabulous modernized cities of Latin America, Brasilia had troubles behind its glass and aluminum façade. Politically, the governors of the powerful Brazilian states were accusing the president of military dictatorship. Economically, the Brazilian unit of money was worth less than a tenth of a cent. Though Brasilia's housing projects were all full of people, the white-collar workers could not pay their rent because of inflation. Schools did not have enough trained teachers. The new university did not have enough students because there were too few free secondary schools. Construction workers who had poured in by the thousands were running out of work as the building program slackened after Kubitschek's term. Refugees from drought-stricken rural areas came to Brasilia and found no work and no housing. They built shanties for themselves along dirt trails in the uncleared brush outside the limits of Brasilia city, in slums which soon held many more people than the housing projects. In these slums there was no running water, no electricity, no schools. Transportation was still woefully inadequate: there was only one through road out to anywhere and no railroad came near Brasilia. Reformers challenged the government for spending so much on the dazzling, half-used capital. While social problems went unsolved, the birthrate in Brasilia, as in the rest of Latin America, outran the increase in the productive economy by 2 or 3 per cent every year.

But Brasilia does represent a new modernization carried on by an emerging middle class, and as such is symbolic of a New Latin America. In São Paulo, Buenos Aires, and Mexico City there are hundreds of new buildings of chrome, aluminum, and glass. Along with these new buildings, the social problems of Brasilia—shanty towns of the newly urbanized poor, inadequate education, low literacy rate, high birthrate, lack of skilled labor—are to be found in these other cities. But with the new buildings has emerged a dynamic new Latin America.

Leaders in these cities are the middle class—the architects, the bankers, the factory owners, the engineers. Their hands hold the new wealth, shifted away from the owners of rural estates who once held the wealth and power. Such leaders are conscious of social changes and realize that political stability rests on a satisfied proletariat and some workable arrangement between freedom in private enterprise and foreign trade on the one hand and government planning on the other.

The rise of this middle sector in the great urban centers has meant a vastly broadened political base. The white-collar workers and the industrial laborers have become a force in politics. In recent years even dictators, where there were any, had to win the approval of the masses. The old politico-religious controversies have been replaced by socio-economic issues. The "state" is not merely a system for keeping power in the hands of a landed oligarchy or a military clique; it is a new "vital state" which builds

The Congress buildings at Brasilia, designed by Oscar Niemeyer. *Photo by Helen Miller Bailey.*

housing projects, owns and operates railroads, oil wells, refineries, and electric power projects. Such a state has a "development" division for controlling agriculture and industry, sets up Five-Year Plans, runs Tennessee Valley-type area projects, works through state-controlled labor unions. The army has been increasingly professionalized and agriculture more diversified. These projects are so tremendous that the big Latin American nations today, though they have more world prestige than ever before, are more concerned with internal problems than with the international situation.

Indeed nationalism—the drive for economic and political independence—is a major objective. Internal problems, like the problems of Brasilia, are by no means fully solved: labor is often restless; farm workers want immediate land reform. The now "urbanized" families in big city apartments have lost some of the traditional Latin American "family feeling," while the family members have turned away from Church-dominated activities toward the movies, television, and commercialized sports. Public education, with its goal of reaching every family, and government assumption of charity and welfare work have also limited the Church as a force in the twentieth century. Thus, as we study the large nations, Mexico, Argentina, Brazil, and Chile, and their dynamic cities, we will find ourselves talking about social legislation, rising living standards, education programs, or middle-class growth, rather than about gaucho *caudillos*, barracks revolutions, and struggles of Church versus state. Industrialization and urbanization are the keynotes as, in the fourth century of their life, all these nations seek to catch up with world leaders.

Chapter 28

Mexico from Civil War
to Modern Democracy

TEN YEARS OF REVOLUTION
WITH A CAPITAL "R"

PORFIRIO DÍAZ had been president of Mexico for three decades. But "Díazpotism" was destined to go, and for the next years the *corridos*, the folk songs of Mexico, were to be about the violent manner of its going.

>All the streets of Zacatecas
>Were piled high with Federal dead,
>And the few that were not slaughtered,
>Early in the day had fled.
>
>For some Federals were so frightened
>That they hid in women's skirts,
>Pulling them up over trousers,
>And mantillas over shirts.

So sang the ballad-makers to their guitars when the great Revolution against Díaz was in progress. General after general was to rise and fall, little

461

generals on the local stage, bigger generals—Huerta, Villa, Zapata, Carranza, Obregón—on the national stage. The soldiers sang:

Oh, Oh, my beloved general!
He made a sharp advance against the peasants' land.
He became rich and famous after six months in command,
And owned more farms than ever he had planned.
Oh, Oh, my beloved general!
But not content wth his lot, against the government he rose
Taking part in a plot;
A court-martial tried him and had him shot,
And that was the end of my general![1]

And not until ten years after the fall of Díaz could the tired soldiers sing:

Pancho Villa has surrendered
In the city of Torreón
We are tired now of fighting,
And now cotton will be grown.

Now we are all one party,
There is no one left to fight.
The war is ended, *compañeros*,
Let us work, it is our right.[2]

The Revolution, spelled with a capital "R", which came to Mexico a century after Hidalgo's revolt against Spain, began as a struggle for political reform and evolved into an era of social change which is still in progress. Its root causes had been accumulating for a century—the abuses of the workers and the voiceless Indian masses, the anger of the outraged intellectuals, the dislike of foreign economic domination. Díaz brought it on by failing to build up a native Mexican middle class, by not allowing his prosperity to trickle down to the masses, by holding his power until he and his friends grew too old to function. His fall was to be followed by two years of attempted housecleaning under Francisco Madero, who sparked the revolution but whose political objectives were too narrow for the spark to catch fire. Then came two years of counterrevolution under Díaz' own followers, and four years of chaos as three generals fought each other for control. Finally a period of stabilization under the dictatorship of generals from the northern state of Sonora evolved into a clear-cut social revolution.

Out of these ten years, during which men of various degrees of idealism struggled for mastery, came a remarkable new constitution, a new national feeling, and a new prestige for those who were of Indian blood. Those

[1] Ernest Gruening, *Mexico and Its Heritage* (New York: Appleton-Century-Crofts, 1928), p. 650.
[2] Anita Brenner, *The Wind That Swept Mexico* (New York: Harper & Row, Publishers, 1943), p. 57.

who followed the new constitution became a powerful, all-controlling party, still governing Mexico in the late 1960s, but little by little bringing about all the things the Revolutionists yearned for. The Mexican Revolution was of importance throughout Latin America as the first major effort to uproot the system of great estates and peonage, to curb foreign control over natural resources, and to raise the living standards of the masses.

THE RISE AND FALL
OF FRANCISCO I. MADERO

In 1908 Francisco I. Madero, the younger son of a very rich family of landowners, a starry-eyed, five-foot-tall idealist with little knowledge of economics or of the weaknesses of human nature, had written a book called *The Presidential Succession in 1910*. Immediately a sellout, the book was printed in a second edition which urged Don Porfirio to hold an election for a vice-president who would then take over the old man's duties. Shortly before it was published, Don Porfirio himself had given an interview to an American reporter named James Creelman, telling the American public that Mexico was now ready for democracy, that he would welcome an opposition party, and that the election of 1910 would be open and free. Don Porfirio was surprised to learn that the Mexican public read the American article and took his word as truth. Opponents of Díaz now rallied behind Madero, the author of the increasingly popular book, urging him forward as a candidate in a campaign of "effective suffrage and no re-election."

In January 1909 the Democratic Party was openly organized and Madero was nominated. When Don Porfirio saw that the opposition party was being taken seriously, he reverted to his old tactics and threw Madero in prison. Then he held his largest fiesta, the centennial celebration of September 16, 1810. When the celebration was over, Madero was allowed to escape to San Antonio, Texas; Díaz held the "election" and proclaimed himself winner of the presidency for another term.

In protest, the exiled Madero issued the Plan of San Luis Potosí on October 5, 1910, declaring the election fraudulent, asking for new elections, and calling Mexicans to arms against the dictator. He had little hope for an armed insurrection, but the people of the state of Chihuahua rose up and took the city of Ciudad Juárez in the name of Madero on May 10, 1911. Limantour, Díaz' efficient financial adviser, recognized the growing revolt and could see that Díaz' cause was lost; he persuaded the old man to resign. Tortured by an infected wisdom tooth, nagged by his imperious young wife, the aged Don Porfirio was put safely on a boat for Paris, where he lived on his foreign investments in peace and plenty until 1915.

On June 7, 1911, Madero came into Mexico City as a hero, and won the subsequent elections without challenge. His supporters soon fell out among themselves: each group thought that it alone was destined to regenerate Mexico. Madero's Plan of San Luis Potosí had contained little actual planning, no recognition of the land hunger of the peasants or of the opposition of the middle class to the power of foreign capital. Madero never understood the issues and grievances that had made him the hero of Mexico. He did not realize that he had stirred the masses to new hope against the creole landowners and the *científicos*. "Effective suffrage" was still a dream in a largely illiterate nation, and "no re-election" simply made it impossible for Madero to insure his own power.

With his lack of common sense and civil service experience, his small stature and squeaky voice, his mystic belief in spirits and destiny, Madero, found the situation hard to control. His rich relatives, especially his brother Gustavo, who had millions invested in mines, became so powerful in the government that Madero by association seemed just another aristocrat. When he tried to call a congress, he found that his Democratic Party did not even have a titular majority. For the proponents of direct action he was too mild and polite; for the land-hungry peasants his devotion to mere election reform seemed traitorous. Less than a month after Madero's inauguration, the peasants under an Indian leader named Emiliano Zapata revolted in Morelos, declaring in the Plan of Ayala that they would fight for redistribution of the landed estates. Their slogan was *"Tierra y Libertad!"*—Land and Liberty. Cried their ballad singers:

> But no land was being given; "And if now Madero fail us,
> We'll fight on," declared Zapata, "we the people of Morelos,
> We, the suffering *campesinos*, who have lived till now in squalor,"
> And he thereupon proclaimed revolt, the Plan of Villa Ayala.[3]

While the landless peasants revolted against Madero on the left hand, the conservative army and the forces of "Díazpotism" made trouble for him on the right. A drunken ex-Porfirian army officer named Victoriano Huerta had been sent to put down an anti-Madero revolt in Chihuahua, but later, with an army behind him, joined the anti-Madero forces in Mexico City. Meanwhile Don Porfirio's nephew Félix Díaz, backed by the Church, pronounced himself master of Vera Cruz. Unwilling to punish any of these rebels by death, the trusting Madero allowed all segments of his enemies to rally against him.

Into this confusion was injected the reactionary meddling of the American ambassador, Henry Lane Wilson, a Taft appointee and no relation of the liberal-minded Woodrow Wilson, who had just been elected in the United States but had had no time to change his foreign representatives. Henry Lane Wilson represented the colony of rich American businessmen in Mexico City who considered Madero an insane radical and who longed for the *status quo* which favored American capital. When the army of Huerta began bombarding the forces of Félix Díaz in Mexico City, the ambassador invited both leaders to the American embassy on February 16, 1913, urging them to make peace and join in asking for Madero's resignation. At the same time that this Pact of the Embassy was being

[3] Gruening, *Mexico and Its Heritage*, p. 648.

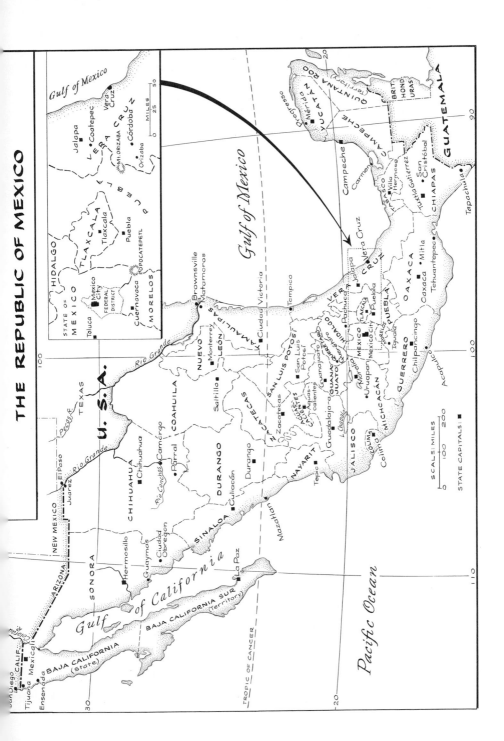

THE REPUBLIC OF MEXICO

Gulf of Mexico

STATE OF MEXICO

MILES
50
25
0

Gulf of Mexico

Jalapa
Cootepec
Vera Cruz
VERA CRUZ
Mt. ORIZABA
Córdoba
Orizaba

HIDALGO
TLAXCALA
Tlaxcala
Puebla
P U E B L A
POPOCATEPETL

Mexico City
FEDERAL DISTRICT
Cuernavaca
Toluca
MORELOS

QUINTANA ROO
Progreso
Mérida
YUCATAN
CAMPECHE
BRIT. HOND. URAS.
GUATEMALA

Campeche
Carmen

Villa Hermosa
TABASCO
Tuxtla Gutiérrez
San Cristóbal
CHIAPAS
Tapachula

Jalapa
Vera Cruz
VERA CRUZ
Puebla
OAXACA
Caxaca
Mitla
Tehuantepec

U. S. A.

TEXAS
Pecos
Rio Grande

Brownsville
Matamoros

Gulf of Mexico

Ciudad Victoria

TAMAULIPAS

NUEVO LEÓN
Monterrey

Tampico

SAN LUIS POTOSI
San Luis Potosi

VER.
Pachuca
HIDALGO
TLAXCALA
MEXICO
Mexico City
MORELOS
PUEBLA
Iguala
GUERRERO
Chilpancingo

Acapulco

NEW MEXICO
El Paso
Juárez
Rio Grande

Rio Conchos
Camargo

COAHUILA
Saltillo

ZACATECAS
Zacatecas

AGUAS. CALIENTES
Aguas-calientes
GUANA-JUATO
Guanajuato
QUERETARO
Queretaro
Morelia
MICHOACÁN
Uruapan
L. Chapala

ARIZONA
CHIHUAHUA
Chihuahua
Parral

DURANGO
Durango

JALISCO
Guadalajara
COLIMA
Colima

SONORA
Hermosillo
Guaymas
Ciudad Obregón

SINALOA
Culiacán

NAYARIT
Tepic

Mazatlán

San Diego CALIF.
Tijuana Mexicali
Ensenada
BAJA CALIFORNIA (State)

Gulf of California

La Paz

BAJA CALIFORNIA SUR (Territory)

TROPIC OF CANCER

Pacific Ocean

SCALE: MILES
0   100   200

STATE CAPITALS: ■

discussed, the Huerta faction had just captured and tortured to death Madero's wealthy brother Gustavo. During these Tragic Ten Days (February 9–18) of street fighting deliberately caused by the two factions opposing Madero, the president felt himself helpless and his cause lost. Thus Francisco Madero and his vice-president resigned. They were taken into the "protective custody" of Victoriano Huerta, and were "shot while attempting to escape" during the night of February 22, 1913. Ambassador Wilson was recalled by the State Department for supporting the men who murdered the president, but the drunken, conscienceless Huerta declared himself the provisional president of Mexico. The *Porfiristas* were again in control; the army supported the perpetually intoxicated dictator, while terrorism ran rampant and the treasury was rifled.

Woodrow Wilson refused to recognize this government and attempted to influence Mexico toward a liberal constitution. He was willing to intervene and sell arms to Huerta's opponents, a group of anti-*Porfiristas* in the north rallying to the standard of Venustiano Carranza and calling themselves "Constitutionalists." Huerta was thus able to gain support for his unpopular rule by claiming to be the victim of American aggression. This claim was almost proven true when an unfortunate and confusing incident took place at Tampico in April 1914. American sailors landing in the town for supplies were temporarily taken into custody. Though they were released "with regrets," their commanding officer asked for an apology in the form of a twenty-one-gun salute. Huerta refused and thus became the champion of Mexican sovereignty against the foreign aggressor. Unable to get arms from America to fight his northern enemies, Huerta was dealing with German agents at a time when world opinion was anti-German. The United States, offended by the refusal to salute in apology, and determined to prevent the delivery of guns from a German vessel, unwisely occupied Vera Cruz harbor. In the sharp street fighting which ensued, lives were lost on both sides. "The Vera Cruz incident" further popularized Huerta and his "anti-American" regime. Only by accepting the mediation of Argentina, Brazil, and Chile could Wilson prove that he did not intend to occupy Mexico for the sake of "Dollar Diplomacy." His insistence that "Huerta the Murderer" must go, combined with the victories the "Constitutionalists" in the north were winning with smuggled arms, led to the forced resignation of Huerta on July 14, 1914.

CHAOS WHICH LED TO A CONSTITUTION

> Hah, you drunkard Victoriano,
> Your bad heart will skip a beat,
> When you hear of Zacatecas
> Where your troops have met defeat![4]

At Zacatecas and at other towns in the northern mining region Victori-

---

[4] Gruening, *loc. cit.*

Guerilla bands led by Emiliano Zapata fought the Revolution of 1910 to 1920 for *"Tierra y Libertad!"* *Courtesy United Press International.*

ano Huerta's troops had met defeat at the hands of the soldiers of the north, led by Pancho Villa and Álvaro Obregón. Singing marching songs about the beautiful Valentina, or the sweet Adelita, or about *La Cucaracha,* the cockroach, and calling themselves the *Constitucionalistas,* they fought together until they had defeated Huerta; then they quarreled among themselves, causing a three-way civil war, until, in 1917, as one sad song said, "only four cornfields are left."

Venustiano Carranza, the leader under whom the present remarkable constitution of Mexico was drafted, was a dignified old man with a white goatee who had been civilian governor of Coahuila under Díaz, and was responsible for bringing that state into the Madero fold. His state had refused to recognize Huerta, and in 1913 he had combined with the revolutionists in Chihuahua under the slogan "Return to the Constitution of 1857." Then he began to call himself First Chief of the Constitutionalist Army.

New Álvaro Obregón, boss of the state of Sonora, brought that region and its Yaquis into the Constitutionalist camp. Obregón had been a mechanic in the Americanized north and had prospered enough to become a small landowner. Intelligent, concerned for the common people, practical-minded, cognizant of the problems of the rising class of industrial workers, and a personable leader of men, Obregón stood sincerely for Madero's principles and was capable of making long-range plans to assure their success. He understood the economic problems of the Revolution and was willing to bide his time and cooperate with Carranza.

Not so the leader of the forces from Chihuahua and Durango, the notorious bandit Doroteo Arango, the Robin Hood of the North, who called himself Pancho Villa. Chief of a band of outlaws and cattle thieves, he had brought his personal army of 40,000 ex-cowboys into the Constitutionalist camp. He and Carranza were both ambitious for the presidency and were potential enemies. Villa's presence in the Constitutionalist leadership brought further American intervention, when he became personally angry at the whole United States because of United States favoritism to Carranza, crossed the border, and "shot up" the town of Columbus, New Mexico. In retaliation United States cavalry forces under Pershing chased him through the sagebrush of northern Mexico in an open violation of Mexican sovereignty. Villa himself kept up his private war with Carranza until Carranza was legally ensconced as president, then retired to a big-scale ranch and some small-scale banditry, until he was murdered in a private quarrel in 1923. The cause of the Revolution was to gain little from him. But in the mid-1960s Mexican writers began to give more credit to this picturesque Robin Hood as a really inspirational revolutionary force.

The leader of the rural masses in the south, Emiliano Zapata, had no personal ambition whatever. Zapata himself was an illiterate tenant farmer of Indian blood whose ghost is said still to ride on his swift white horse through the hills of Morelos and Guerrero, restless till every peon owns his plot of land. His ideals were formulated by the intellectual Antonio Díaz Soto y Gama, to whom the Revolution meant the division of the great estates into small holdings, the return of the Indian lands to the villages robbed by Díaz, and the creation of *ejidos* or community-held lands for landless Indian villages. The peasants of southern Mexico followed Zapata in the belief that the equal distribution of land was the solution of all problems. Willing to fight on Carranza's side if the Constitutionalists were the most likely to guarantee such distribution, Zapata's forces— feared like the scourge as they burned *haciendas*, killed the landlords, and proceeded to farm the land themselves—fought their way to Mexico City by the winter of 1914 and the spring of 1915. There they found the army of Villa coming down from the north; the two "outlaw" leaders met amicably and posed for photos in the empty national palace, while Zapata's Indians begged and Villa's cowboys roamed the city streets engaging in drunken rapine.

Meanwhile, after an abortive convention and a futile plan for compromise with the more "respectable" Constitutionalists, the opportunist Carranza decided to set himself up as a Revolutionary "savior" to outdo the "outlaws." He issued a series of proclamations in 1915: under his leadership Indian lands would be restored, foreign capital ousted, workers' conditions improved, free public education made compulsory, and Church influence removed from politics. Many liberal leaders now joined him, and his combined forces under Obregón ousted Villa from the capital, whence he returned to cattle rustling and began to harass the United States. Another Carranza general, the brutal Pablo Gonzales, defeated Zapata and drove him back to his own mountains, where his forces continued to fight for land distribution till Gonzalez' agents had him assassinated in 1919.

By March of 1915 Carranza was provisional president in Mexico City. Popular now for his liberal promises, he gained further favor by quarreling with the United States over damages done to Americans during the three-way fighting in Mexico City and other towns, and over Pershing's "invasions" of Mexican soil in pursuit of Villa. Calling Woodrow Wilson—who was extremely embarrassed by the whole situation during his 1916 re-election campaign—an "imperialist" leader of the "Colossus of the North," Carranza gained friends at home from all sides. During World War I he remained anti-United States, though technically neutral.

But the land of Mexico was in a terrible plight after years of internecine fighting. Paper money was worthless; land lay untilled; guerrilla bands roamed the provinces. Once in power, Carranza had meant to forget his proclamations for agrarian and industrial reforms, but the intellectuals in his camp were not to let him. Under pressure from them he called a constitutional convention at Querétaro which was to produce the ultra-modern Constitution of 1917, a document far ahead of its time. Labor leaders, land reformers, opponents of foreign capital, and leaders for public education came to Querétaro and put their stamp on the new document.

A federal government that preserved the states but gave very strong powers to the central executive, a president elected for a four-year term but ineligible for re-election, a representative assembly and a senate—these things were to be expected in a modern Latin American constitution. But Articles 3, 27, 33, 123, and 130 were new departures in constitutions, and brought in anticlerical, antiforeign, and socialistic ideas. Articles 3 and 130 were a declaration of independence from the clergy. They aimed to drive the Church out of politics and confine its program to religion. The activities of priests were limited, marriage was re-emphasized as a civil contract according to the Constitution of 1857. The schools were removed from Church control and elementary education was declared free and compulsory for all children. Though Article 14 guaranteed the right of private property, under Article 27 the nation was to be the legal owner of all oil and minerals under the soil. "The subsoil rights" could never be granted to private parties, but only leased. Community Indian lands, *ejidos*, were always to belong to the villages. Under this provision later presidents confiscated the holdings of foreign petroleum companies, broke up foreign-owned cattle ranches, divided hundreds of large estates among Indian villagers, and gradually worked toward the ideals of Zapata, even at the risk of American intervention. Article 33 hurt the idea of foreign ownership even more by giving the president power to deport foreigners at his discretion and to forbid foreigners from meddling in politics.

Article 123 was to be the Magna Carta of Mexican Labor, a rising class of Mexican society which grew up during the Revolution. Labor's friends wrote right into the constitution the eight-hour day, the minimum wage, the abolition of child labor, the end of peonage for rural workers, the obligation of employers and landowners to provide adequate schools and decent housing, industrial accident and unemployment compensation, and the recognition of union organizations and the rights of collective bargaining. In 1917 no other country in the world, including many nations much more highly industrialized than agricultural Mexico, had such laws written into their constitutions. But the laws were a statement of aspirations rather than of facts. Articles 27 and 123 were promises to the landless poor and the underpaid city laborers and were designed to bring all the peasants and workers of Mexico into the Revolutionary camp. For the next four decades the history of Mexico was centered on the struggle to put this new constitution into effect, the struggle against the same old enemies which reform in Mexico had faced since Iturbide. Although reform was a painfully slow process and its achievement was at times imperceptible, this twentieth-century reform was to be genuine.

Carranza accepted the reforming articles but had no intention of enforcing them. Mexico had three years of "peace" under Carranza after his inauguration as legal president in March 1917. During those years no progress was made. The insincere old man broke his promises to the peasants by giving out only a tiny percentage of the free land hoped for by the *Zapatistas.* He reneged on his promises to labor by breaking a strike called by the labor leader Luis Morones. Morones himself escaped arrest and went to Saltillo. He formed a new federation of labor at a convention there in 1918, the *Confederación Regional Obrera Mexicana,* to be known for a decade in politics as the powerful CROM. Leaders of this federation. calling themselves the *Grupo Acción,* entered politics for the purpose of defeating Carranza and installing Obregón in office.

Meanwhile education was neglected, foreign debts were unpaid, and corruption was as bad as in the days when Díaz ruled Mexico. Unable to run for re-election in 1920 because of his own constitution, Carranza attempted to stay in power through a puppet, but the disappointed intellectuals joined with the *Grupo Acción* to raise an "Army of Sonora," oust Carranza, and accept Obregón as president. It was hardly necessary for this army to fight any battles, for all elements were disgusted with the waste, corruption, and insincerity under Carranza. When Obregón marched into Mexico City in May of 1920, Carranza attempted to escape with five million pesos from the treasury, and was murdered while he slept in a mountain hideout.

By November 1920, under Obregón's leadership, Mexico had found a real peace, and was more nearly united than at any previous time in its history. The first phase of the Revolution had ended.

THE NORTHERN DYNASTY

Whoever was to bring stability to Mexico in 1920 must rehabilitate the country, refill an empty treasury, reconstruct agriculture and industry, work out relations with the Church, establish an educational system, and set up some more workable political machinery, as well as secure Mexico a respected position abroad and sovereignty at home. At the same time the promises of the Revolution must be fulfilled and the hopes of the idealists realized. A large order! Because it was undertaken with some success for fourteen years by men who came from Sonora, this period is called the time of the Northern Oligarchy. Northern Mexico, less populated and far from the center of control and conservatism in the south, was always a land of Revolution and liberalism.

Álvaro Obregón, leader of the Men of Sonora, who brought internal peace to Mexico by 1920.
Courtesy Pan American Union.

Álvaro Obregón, the Sonora leader, was elected under the Constitution of 1917 and inaugurated in November 1920. Something of a dramatic hero because he had lost an arm fighting Villa, the popular, plump, and peaceable Obregón knew that true democracy was still impossible; he hoped only to be a practical and able dictator. Never an ardent believer in "land for the Indians," he soothed the *Zapatistas* by allowing free villages to apply to an Agrarian Commission for land. However, since this was to be done on the Indians' initiative, and little favorable publicity was given the program, the requests were very modest; less than 3,000,000 acres were distributed. Depending from the first on the labor movement, Obregón backed Luis Morones and made him a labor czar. The CROM, Morones' labor federation, handled all labor disputes; no rival unions arose; the union treasury and Morones himself waxed rich and wasteful, but labor achieved a slowly rising standard of living. Obregón also permitted the peasants to form an organization under Zapata's mentor, Soto y Gama. Obregón sincerely believed in schools and appointed an eminent educational philosopher, José Vasconcelos, as Minister of Education. With Vasconcelos the well-known movement for rural education described in the next chapter got its start. A thousand elementary schools were built in the four years of Obregón's administration, 1920–1924. The problems of land reform and Church-state relationships were left for Calles to solve in the next decade. Obregón prepared the ground by consolidating his power over the army, the agrarians, and the workers, setting the course the Revolution was to take for the next fourteen years.

Obregón's greatest difficulty was in foreign affairs. Recognition by the United States was an important factor in the stability of Mexican government. The United States had recognized Carranza before the promulgation of the Constitution of 1917, which proclaimed that foreign companies could not own land or mining concessions in Mexico. Naturally, the Harding administration elected in 1920 did not wish to recognize Obregón, who had ousted Carranza with military force. The United States disapproved of Obregón on all the traditional old issues, the unpaid debts, the defaulted bonds, the injured American citizens. To these problems was added the anxiety of American companies, who had half a billion dollars invested in oil wells and mines, most of it in lands granted by Díaz, and who faced confiscation if Article 27 were enforced. Mexico argued that old Spanish law had always given the subsoil rights to the king and that the modern Mexican government was his legal heir, that mining codes throughout the nineteenth century had held to the same principle of government ownership of natural resources, and that the whole issue was simply the "right of eminent domain." In addition, if the laws for labor in Article 123 were enforced, American companies would have to pay American wages to Mexican oil workers, and would lose their margin of profit. When Obregón's agents asked Secretary of State Charles Evans Hughes for recognition, Hughes wanted assurance that the 1917 law would not apply to holdings granted before the Constitution was written. When the Mexican Supreme Court, acting on Obregón's advice, settled several law suits concerning Americans in a manner indicating good will and fair-mindedness, Hughes was willing to accept a "verbal agreement" that Article 27 would never be retroactive. Finally, on August 30, 1923, the United States recognized Obregón.

Obregón had appointed another Sonoran, Plutarco Elías Calles, as his Secretary of *Gobernación*, or internal affairs, a position which for three decades was to be a stepping stone to the presidency; it was understood among the Sonora clique that Calles was to succeed Obregón. An election was held and Calles was duly elected; Obregón turned over the office on December 1, 1924, and the "stabilization of the Revolution" went on.

Calles, formerly a primary teacher in a northern desert town, was not actually a well-educated man, but he was ardently interested in public education and opposed to the Church as a power in politics. He was an able administrator and perfected the Obregón system. Lacking Obregón's geniality and tolerance, he was at first a bitter Revolutionary; when he grew wealthy and entrenched in power he became much more conservative. His era was a time of commercial prosperity and the beginning of financial stability. Anxious to hold the support of the agrarians, he had pronounced himself the heir of Zapata; during his four-year term some 8,000,000 acres were distributed to more than 1,500 villages. As is to be explained in the next chapter, compulsory rural education, land reform, campaigns of sanitation and hygiene, irrigation projects, road construction, cooperative rural banks, agricultural schools, vaccination, and anti-malaria programs began to get under way by 1925, made possible by the new stability under Obregón and Calles. At last those who fought the Revolution were to get some benefits. Agrarians and laborers were strongly *Callista*.

Calles needed their help, for he was out to break his more serious opposition, the power of the Church. The Catholic hierarchy had opposed the Madero revolution, had refused to recognize the Constitution of 1917, had tried to organize Catholic unions in opposition to labor boss Morones, had kept the now illegal parochial schools open, and had urged the people to boycott the new public elementary schools. In 1926 the well-entrenched Calles struck back, enforcing the provisions of the Constitution forbidding alien priests, closing many religious schools, and ordering priests to register with civilian authorities so that their political activities could be checked. In protest the priests left the churches, and no Catholic services, marriages, baptisms, or burials were held. The resulting three-year strike on the part of the clergy, discussed as a social problem in the next chapter, had serious political consequences. Deeply religious people organized rebel bands called *Cristeros*, under the motto "Long Live Christ the King and Death to the Heretics!" Soon such rebel bands became rallying points for all enemies of Calles; the *Cristeros* burned government schools, stoned the teachers sent out under Calles' zealous new rural school program, and even blew up trains. In retaliation Calles' armies committed parallel atrocities; some Catholic groups in the United States were distressed enough to urge American intervention.

Calles was having other difficulties with the United States. He had passed a new petroleum code and a land law saying that corporations holding land in Mexico must be 50 per cent Mexican-owned. His law also ordered all companies holding grants of land dated before 1917 to take out fifty-year leases, implying that the real ownership still lay with the Mexican government. As this seemed to violate Obregón's verbal agreement, American oil and mining interests joined with Catholic groups to urge drastic action against Mexico. Calles profited, however, by the sudden disrepute of the United States oil companies because of the Teapot Dome scandals at home. Coolidge sent the understanding and pro-Mexican Dwight W. Morrow to Mexico, the first ambassador to mix with the Mexicans socially. Morrow did much to help the United States and Mexico understand each other. Two months after the arrival of this influential new ambassador in 1927, the Mexican Supreme Court altered Calles' petroleum code to take the sting out of the fifty-year lease law, and the Americans were satisfied.

Now came the election of 1928. It had been evident for some time that Obregón and Calles intended to rotate the presidency between themselves. While Calles amended the constitution to set up a six-year presidency but allow intermittent terms, two other candidates, both generals, "pronounced" against the Calles-Obregón deal, with Plans of this town and that. Obregón, who had been quietly raising chickpeas on his northern ranch and amassing a fortune, rallied the agrarian reformers and put an end to these "Plans." As the only candidate, Obregón was "elected," and the Northern Dynasty seemed assured, for Obregón was widely trusted and respected as a democratic leader. In spite of such trust, however, a fanatic Catholic youth, pretending to draw a sketch of him at a political luncheon after the election, drew a gun from out of the sketch materials and assassinated him.

This left Calles alone in control, but he was prohibited by the constitution from succeeding himself and filling out Obregón's term. However, he was able to remain the strong man of Mexico, called *Jefe Máximo* (the chief boss), for the next six years by organizing a well-knit political party called the *Partido Nacional Revolucionario*, or PNR, and keeping himself as the party boss. "When Calles spoke, no dog barked." Calles dictated from his home in Cuernavaca while three different "stooges" of various shades of liberalism served in the *zócalo* as presidents until 1934. In local and congressional elections only the PNR-nominated candidates were elected; if there was opposition its ballots were not counted.

However, the PNR had to have a popular base; it could not completely betray the Revolution. The old slogans of *"Tierra y Libertad"* and "land, education, free elections, no re-election" were mouthed more loudly than ever. The Church, actually broken from its political power, made peace with the Calles regime in 1932, though religious education was not declared legal until a decade later. The agrarian program looked successful; land was continually being distributed to peons and village schools were being founded on just a large enough scale to make a constant stream of newspaper stories. The six-year term starting in 1928 was over; another Calles stooge was to be elected by the well-oiled machinery of the PNR. To pacify the left wing in his party Calles chose his liberal cabinet minister, Lázaro Cárdenas, expecting his own rule to continue while his cronies drove limousines and built palatial country homes.

The ruling group considered the "Revolution" at an end. It had gone around a full circle. The men of the revolutionary generation were now older, wealthier, and conservative. After 1928 a distinct "hardening" had taken place in the "new capitalism" among the new set of millionaires. There was a single political party which included many opportunists as well as sincere reformers.

THE CÁRDENAS REGIME

Cárdenas, if Calles had but known it, was to mean a change in the policy of the party, the end of the Northern Dynasty and of the Calles dictatorship. Calles should not have been surprised at the changing tenor of the nation, the impatience at his own "new-rich" complacency. The depression had brought new forces into play, for the reformers were calling for a "Mexican New Deal." On May 30, 1933, Calles himself had made a speech at the convention of the National Revolutionary Party in which he spoke of a "Six Year Plan" to develop the country industrially, improve and enforce the labor laws, build new highways and ports, accelerate the land division program, and give 20 per cent of the federal budget to new schools. He and his chosen successor were promising to do all this by 1940. Pressure was upon him from agrarian leaders and from a new far-left labor organizer named Lombardo Toledano, whose movement had discredited the now rich and fat Morones and his CROM. Calles had to talk about some popular program to show he was still with the people.

Lázaro Cárdenas, the "puppet" chosen to keep up the talk about the Plan, had already improved conditions in exactly the manner outlined by the Plan in his own state of Michoacán when he was governor. Born May 21, 1895, one of eight children in a poor family of Indian blood, he had gone off to join the army of Zapata at the age of eighteen. Here he drank deep of the real Revolutionary spirit, and he never forgot his determination to carry out the hopes for land and schools. Serving afterward under Villa and Carranza, he rose to the rank of general by the age of twenty-five. Honest, able, and good at political strategy, Cárdenas carried on enough anticlerical activity as governor of Michoacán to bring him to Calles' attention; he became party leader of the PNR and then secretary of *Gobernación*, the post which always seemed to lead to the presidency. He had enemies within the party and among the conservatives—they said he "smelled of *petate*," the Indian's straw-mat bed—but in Mexican politics by 1934 that was as valuable a piece of propaganda as for an American of a century ago to run for election because he "had been born in a log cabin." Cárdenas' adoption of the Six Year Plan described in Calles' speech signified the most advanced and active stage of the Revolution.

Cárdenas was completely devoted to the common people; he took his campaign to the grass-roots, traveling on foot and burro-back to listen to the complaints of the peons. He was the first president to visit the rural areas. Inaugurated in December 1934, Cárdenas was the first president since Díaz who did not come from the north, the first to be elected peacefully for a regular six-year term, the first not to have his election challenged by an armed rebellion, the first to serve out his six years and retire into a secondary position when the six-year term ended.

He was still faced with all Mexico's old problems, however. As to his attitude toward them, this story was currently told to show that he meant to be president of all the people of Mexico.

> One morning while the President was transacting business in the capital, his secretary laid a list of urgent matters and a telegram before him. Here is the list and the comment Cárdenas wrote nonchalantly on each item.
> Bank reserves dangerously low—tell the Treasurer.
> Agricultural production falling—tell the Minister of Agriculture.
> Railroads bankrupt—tell the Minister of Communications.
> Serious message from Washington—tell the Minister of Foreign Affairs.
> Then he opened the telegram—"My corn is dried up, my burro died, my sow was stolen, my baby is sick. Signed, Juan Pablo, village of Huitzipituzco."
> "Order the presidential train at once," said Cárdenas, "I am leaving for Huitzipituzco."[5]

5 Anita Brenner, *The Wind That Swept Mexico* (New York: Harper & Row, Publishers, 1943), p. 85. The anecdote as told here is paraphrased and shortened.

This concern for the peon's problems had not been a part of Calles' plan. Cárdenas purposely made a breach with the *Callistas* and their whole corrupt set of military leaders and millionaires who had allowed the Revolution to die. He closed up their sources of corruption and graft and backed an anti-Calles labor group in a series of strikes. By June of 1935 labor was united behind Cárdenas; Congress had split into a pro-Cárdenas and a pro-Calles faction within the party; and Cárdenas had ousted Calles' friends from his cabinet. Cárdenas also made friends with leading churchmen in a move toward greater tolerance, so that now Church, labor, peasantry, and politicians were on his side. Calles was soon isolated and exiled to the United States. Then Cárdenas had only to deal with a local *caudillo* in San Luis Potosí, whose revolt was put down by arms—the last private-army rebellion in Mexican politics.

To develop mass support and forestall the threat of conservative reaction, Cárdenas proceeded to reorganize the one strong party, changing its name to *Partido Revolucionario Mexicano*, the PRM. Its basis was made functional and regional; it was to be primarily a workers' and peasants' party. Cárdenas armed the peasants, won over the rank and file of the army, and organized labor. The day of labor czar Morones was gone, and he followed Calles into exile. The new labor leader, Lombardo Toledano, was a very controversial figure, perhaps a Communist and certainly a troublemaker afterward among labor groups throughout the Western Hemisphere. But at this time Toledano was a friend of Cárdenas and was willing to organize all Mexican labor behind the Cárdenas movement. His powerful union, the *Confederación de Trabajadores Mexicanos*, or CTM, demanded that the Six Year Plan be put into effect, and was to remain a strong influence in the politics of the 1930s and 1940s.

Cárdenas' measures to help the peasantry are more adequately described in the next chapter, as they mark a turning point in the social and economic progress of the Mexican people. However, it is politically important that 47,000,000 acres of land were distributed among nearly a million peasants in more than 12,000 villages, and often with the land came a new piped water supply and a new rural school. Cárdenas himself was often present at the ceremonies of distribution. He strongly supported the program of *ejidos* or communal village holdings, and organized cooperative *ejidal* banks, crop and machinery loans, and irrigation projects.

Education had prospered under Calles; Cárdenas was to take Mexican rural schools so far toward modernization as to make them an example for the world. The school program became famous for its integration of the Indian in the national life of Mexico. When the Church continued to fight Cárdenas' school policy, he relaxed the enforcement of the anticlerical laws. On the economic front, the world was recovering from the depression, and the standard of living began to improve in Mexico under Cárdenas' New Deal measures. Prices rose, but consumption rose with them, as state revenues increased and a flood of tourists began to pour money into Mexico. Meanwhile Cárdenas decreased foreign capital through expropriation of agricultural lands and other holdings, reducing United

States investments by one-third. Mexico was strong enough and prosperous enough to challenge the power of foreign capital, the largest remaining problem Cárdenas had inherited from the Revolution.

In November 1936 Cárdenas signed a forceful expropriation law, allowing him to take over any property "held and monopolized to the exclusive advantage of a few persons," if justifiable "for public and social welfare." At first used to take over land for agricultural projects, the law was applied by Cárdenas to industries which refused to conform to the labor laws of Article 123. Since railroads and oil were key factors in Mexico's economy, he wanted the government to control both. In June 1937 he nationalized all railroads with over 700 miles of track and gave them to the railway workers' cooperative. Mining and oil companies had to watch their step in dealing with labor; if their workers complained of constitutional violation, it might be a cause for confiscation. The large American and English oil-drilling companies had been quarreling with the government and the workers for twenty years. In 1937, faced with a sharp rise in the cost of living, a new petroleum workers' union, affiliated with the strong CTM federation, demanded higher wages and better working conditions and even a share of the management in the Mexican oil fields. The government ordered the dispute settled by the Industrial Arbitration Board set up under the Constitution of 1917. The Board examined the financial record of the companies and ordered the pay raise, giving the companies six months to comply. The companies refused and appealed the case to the Supreme Court, which turned them down.

When no settlement of the strike was reached at the end of the six months, Cárdenas simply "nationalized" the oil fields on March 18, 1938, a day still celebrated in Mexico. It was the beginning of Mexico's economic independence. Backed by popular enthusiasm, Cárdenas turned the oil fields over to an Administration for National Petroleum and created the Pemex agency, which still produces and sells all petroleum products in Mexico. The rising generation of trained Mexican technicians learned to handle the drilling and refining, and the World War II demand for petroleum products made nationalization an economic success.

Though there was some agitation at home for American intervention, it was now the heyday of the Good Neighbor Policy. The days of Henry Lane Wilson were gone forever. Franklin Roosevelt insisted that the oil companies arbitrate their dispute with Mexico on the understanding that the Mexican government pay a "fair price" for the expropriated properties. The English company *El Aguila* was also forced to arbitrate. The negotiation meetings continued for several years until finally, during the administration of Ávila Camacho, Cárdenas' successor, a settlement was reached under which the Mexican government paid about $24,000,000 for the petroleum land being worked by Pemex. This amount was paid in full by the end of another decade. Thus Cárdenas emerged victorious in the most aggressive "foreign affair" ever launched by Mexico.

As the world divided between pro-Fascists and anti-Fascists, Cárdenas sided with the Spanish Republicans against Franco. Forced to sell oil to the Nazis as his only possible customer, he broke with them when they paid him only in barter, and when England severed relations over the affair. When World War II began, he threw his support to the Allies.

At home Cárdenas became a legendary hero of Zapata-status to the Indians, and a leader of successful labor groups. Ready to retire in 1940, he allowed the more conservative elements of the PRM to choose the next president. He had never pleased the rising new industrialists, a grow-ing class of small businessmen who hoped for a lull in the Revolutionary program. Party action, with Cárdenas' blessing, settled on Manuel Ávila Camacho, a colorless army general and devout Catholic who, true to pattern, had been in Cárdenas' cabinet. Conservatives of many types—a strange mixture of Morones' old labor leaders, fanatical Catholics, and big businessmen—opposed this choice. Add to them the neo-Fascist or-ganizations of young terrorists financed by Italian and German Fascist agents and called variously Gold Shirts and *Sinarquistas,* which were mak-ing a strong appeal to young urbanites in 1939 and 1940. Together these groups formed a new party and backed a millionaire general named Juan Andreu Almazán, who had been a Huerta supporter during the Revolu-tion. Sure of the power of the PRM as a smooth-running political machine, Cárdenas allowed the Almazán party to run a free campaign of criticism, held an open election, and, in spite of some fraudulent voting and a little violence here and there, could truthfully say that Ávila Camacho won the election. Almazán went into retirement, for his Fascist friends were soon in disrepute as Mexico joined the United States in the war effort. Thus Cárdenas ended his remarkable six-year term, having rescued Mexico from the *caudillismo* of Calles, and having served his nation as a con-structive builder of great popularity.

PRESIDENCIES AND POLITICS SINCE 1940

By the end of Cárdenas' regime the term Revolution had come to mean the party. The first of the purely party presidents was the honest, dogged conciliator, Manuel Ávila Camacho; fat, slow, and pompous, he did not undo the Cárdenas Revolution, but merely slowed it up. He meant to consolidate Mexico's gains and his motto was moderation. Mexico settled down to an internal peace it had never known before, while Mexican na-tional resources were channeled into the United Nations' effort against the Nazis. Ávila Camacho displeased labor by ousting Lombardo Toledano from power and allowing Calles, in late years an antilabor man, to come back from exile. However, wartime wages kept the growing urban labor class happy and social security benefits and other labor measures became law under Camacho while war expansion nurtured a new young capitalism at home. A new class of farmers, small private owners wealthy enough to clear untilled land and work it by machinery, came into being. A campaign to teach adult illiterates, the "each one teach one program," was launched by the Secretary of Education, Jaime Torres Bodet, as explained in Chapter 29. Ávila Camacho took the army out of politics and made it professional and efficient. A Mexican air force was trained under American tutelage. The Pan American Highway was extended with American cooperation during the War; Mexican laborers, the *braceros*, came by the thousands to help the United States harvest its wartime crops.

Lázaro Cárdenas came out of retirement to head Mexico's war effort after the declaration of war against the Axis on May 30, 1942. Differences with the United States were settled, trade treaties signed, and lend-lease granted to Mexico. Under a mutual defense agreement, strategic materials from south of the Rio Grande poured into the United States' war effort. *Sinarquismo* and other Latin American Fascist groups were crushed by the president. Avila Camacho is remembered as the president who enhanced Mexico's international prestige and wartime industrial growth at home during World War II. His *Secretario de Gobernación* was a modern-minded planner interested in expanding industry, an able former governor of Vera Cruz named Miguel Alemán.

Camacho's six-year term ended in 1946; his nominee was Alemán. The national party was now strongly institutionalized. Military influences were removed; the party bases had become agrarian, labor, and popular. This new party met in convention in January 1946 to change its name to *Partido Revolucionario Institucional*, PRI, and to make a Plan Alemán for increased agricultural production and industrialization. The Plan denounced foreign ideologies and declared that its followers would "make Mexican institutions work better." When Alemán announced it as his platform, Ezequiel Padilla, the popular secretary of Foreign Affairs and delegate to the United Nations, bolted the party to run against Alemán. The election of July 7, 1946, was probably quite fair, as the announced returns gave Alemán only 77 per cent throughout the nation, and only 52 per cent in sophisticated Mexico City. Under the successful Alemán the election law itself was improved, women were granted full rights of voting, and the populated northern part of Lower California came in as a state. Fascist *Sinarquistas* and Communist followers of Lombardo Toledano were reduced to ridiculous positions. No longer was the PRI an exclusive lodge for Revolutionary generals; it had become at mid-century a middle-of-the-road combination of labor, agrarians, and the new middle class; the Revolutionary generation was dying out.

Miguel Alemán was a young civilian, a member of a new generation which had not taken part in the 1910–1920 Revolution. He launched a well-integrated program to make industrialization the heart of the Mexican economy under government direction. Alemán's presidency was a period of grandiose public works—irrigation projects, highways, enormous new public buildings like the National University, river control, valley-wide programs for hydroelectric projects in Michoacán and Vera Cruz states. Much of this development was accomplished with loans from the United States; much of the money was dribbled away in waste; many of Alemán's friends and, it is said, Alemán himself became a great deal richer than before. But thousands of acres of previously uncultivated land were added to Mexico's skimpy arable regions; factories run by electricity sprang up in Monterrey, Mexico City, Guadalajara; trucks displaced mule-train transportation everywhere on the new roads of Mexico. The PRI continued strong enough to win elections without resort to fraud or force. In 1952 party leaders chose the winning candidate, the austere, sixty-one-year-old accountant, Adolfo Ruíz Cortines, Alemán's *Secretario de Gobernación*, and they felt sufficiently confident to enter him openly in a field of five other candidates. Mexico was growing up politically. Ruíz Cortines had the support of laborers, peasants, and the growing middle class; he pledged to reduce the cost of living and modernize agriculture to increase the food supply.

In 1952 at the time of Ruíz Cortines' peaceful election, Mexico was industrially a hundred years ahead of its position in 1932. Cárdenas had distributed the land, Ávila Camacho had brought economic peace, Alemán had hastened industrialization. If Alemán took many *mordidas,* or bribe bites, out of the new wealth, Ruíz Cortines pledged himself to an administration that would end graft and corruption in the government. He proceeded to take direct action against price gougers and to curb monopolies. He said, "There is nothing wrong with Mexico which honesty, diligence, and intelligent use of available resources won't cure." When in 1953 and 1954 the industrial boom began slowing down, inflation had set in, and Mexico faced a recession, Cortines devalued the peso in a swift move and the whole nation tightened its belt. Gold reserves picked up by 1956, foreign capital made new investments, and prosperity was on the increase.

Ruíz Cortines attacked the major problems of Mexico with firmness. These were the fundamental problems of balancing food production and agriculture with industrialization, and of providing prosperity for the rapidly growing population, which topped 31 million in mid-1959. On November 4, 1957, the PRI with Ruíz Cortines' blessing nominated the popular Secretary of Labor Adolfo López Mateos for the July 1958 presidential elections. López Mateos, forty-seven years of age and a moderate leftist, was the choice of ex-president Cárdenas, still a powerful elder statesman with millions of labor and farm supporters.

López Mateos, the son of a small-town dentist, had worked as a teacher to pay for his law degree. As Labor Minister he had handled 13,382 labor disputes, of which only thirteen had developed into strikes. Both management and labor considered him a "square shooter." He promised to maintain Mexico's "maturing democracy and fast-developing economy." Active in negotiations concerning "wetback" labor, he had gained a friendly feeling toward the United States. When the election was held in July 1958, with an unprecedented turnout owing to the first woman suffrage in Mexican history, López Mateos received 80 per cent of the vote. A candidate named Luis Héctor Álvarez, of the right-wing National Action Party which held six seats in the Senate, received the other 20 per cent in a fair election in which only one death occurred in the whole nation. In December 1958 López Mateos was inaugurated for six years of "smooth bossing of the current combination of state and private enterprise." Said López Mateos at the time of his inauguration: "Mexico must create national wealth from capital, outside capital if necessary, to make jobs for an additional 1,000,000 Mexicans a year. The human factors involved, that is, whether the worker gets enough to eat and whether his malaria is cured, are the responsibilities of modern capitalism."

The new president had not been in office four months when thousands of workers on the nationally owned railways struck for a 16 per cent wage increase plus fringe benefits. Train service was held up all over Mexico during the first week of April 1959. López Mateos, supposedly so deft at handling strikes, blamed this one on the Communists, and asked two Russian embassy employees to leave the country. He then took drastic action against the strikers, declaring their action illegal and using the army to force restoration of railroad service. Unions headed by extreme leftists were forced to choose other leaders. To offset this action against the extreme left, López Mateos also took steps against the extreme right, outlawing the remnant of the old *Sinarquistas*. To hasten industrialization, meanwhile, he placed the still popular Lázaro Cárdenas in charge of increasing steel production.

The young and vigorous president then moved ahead in fields that had been recently neglected. He vastly increased land distribution, dividing up 35,000,000 acres, a third of the total land distributed since 1915. He realized, however, that *ejido* cultivation of marginal lands was uneconomical. An agriculture depending on individual ten to twenty acre holdings, as envisioned by Zapata, could never feed an industrialized urban Mexico. He encouraged the clearing of virgin lands by machinery and the development of large-scale planting by corporations in which the government had a financial share. Whole communities were assisted in moving from unproductive *ejido* lands in the arid Laguna region of North Central Mexico to moist newly-cleared lands in Campeche and Quintana Roo.

For the city workers López Mateos set up a plan for compulsory profit schemes in industry and pushed public housing in Mexico City in an attempt to outdistance the growth of shanty-towns around the new factory districts. To help Mexican industry López Mateos enforced the "Mexicanization" program under which a majority of the stock of companies doing business in Mexico must be held by Mexican nationals. All businesses in Mexico were subject to fairly collected income tax. An increasing portion of the budget thus balanced was spent on education. López Mateos will be remembered in coming generations as the president who paid for three school books apiece for every rural school child in Mexico.

In foreign affairs López Mateos maintained an independence without isolation. Mexico was the only country which recognized Fidel Castro's Cuba, yet Mexico became no open refuge for Latin American Communists, who made few headlines in Mexican affairs during López Mateos' term. Mexico refused to back the Organization of American States in the military action of 1965 in Santo Domingo, yet cooperated completely in every other Pan American activity. "Mexico," said López Mateos, "insists on national sovereignty, non-intervention in internal affairs of other states, and juridical equality of states."

Though disagreeing with the United States on Cuba and Santo Domingo, López Mateos' own relations with the United States were exceedingly friendly. An old dispute about the land inside the city of El Paso along the

President López Mateos of Mexico greeting President Johnson of the United States in Los Angeles in 1964. Señora López Mateos, Mrs. Johnson, Secretary of State Rusk and his wife, and Senator Kuchel of California join the applause. *Photo courtesy of the Los Angeles County Board of Supervisors.*

bed of the Rio Grande, an area called Chamizal, was settled by an agreement with President Kennedy, giving Cuidad Juárez, Mexico, the disputed city blocks. In March of 1965, President Johnson signed a treaty guaranteeing the desalinization of irrigation water from the Colorado River which reached the eastern side of Baja, California. In December 1964 both nations agreed to end the *bracero* program as no longer necessary for the economy of either side. López Mateos met both Kennedy and Johnson several times, and came to speak jointly with President Johnson at Charter Day ceremonies at the University of California at Los Angeles, where both received honorary degrees.

In the traditional pattern, the PRI party chose López Mateos' Secretary of *Gobernación* as his successor. In a fair election, with opposition candidates openly campaigning, Gustavo Díaz Ordaz was elected in July 1964 for a term to run until December 1, 1970. The son of a postal worker in Puebla, Díaz Ordaz, a middle-class lawyer and more conservative than López Mateos, inherited a prosperous and united nation facing no major problems. He was Mexico's sixtieth president since 1824. He meant to "put economic growth over doctrinaire politics," to make the increase in the gross national product come to 4 per cent annually, and thus exceed the 3 per cent annual growth of the birth rate. "Work and concord" was his motto. In April 1966 he welcomed President Johnson to Mexico City for a brief visit and made further plans with him to review the success of American financial help under the Alliance for Progress. Díaz Ordaz also meant to emphasize domestic economy, and the Mexicans expected years of good government into the 1970s.

Mexico was no longer a rigid one-party state by 1967. Even in 1963 the PRI felt secure enough to accept a constitutional reform which granted bonus votes to opposition parties in the Chamber of Deputies. For the term 1964–1967, the Chamber held 175 PRI members and 35 opposition party members. Thus a "loyal opposition" may be developing with "genuine debate" taking place—steps toward democracy.

Mexico is fast becoming a westernized capitalistic society and few Mexicans are objecting to it. "Sustained and balanced economic growth" now characterizes Mexico's development. All interest groups have benefited in the 1960s, some merely more than others. Thus, in the long run, the Mexicans won the Revolution of 1910–1920 as they had not won the Revolution of 1810. This last Revolution was a home-grown product—the result of a people's hunger for land, for bread, for justice, and for liberty. Through science, industrialization, technology, and strident nationalism, the Mexican nation painfully inched its way toward the satisfaction of those hungers in a democratic fashion. The Mexican Revolution is a significant phenomenon in Latin American history. Let us examine the effects of the Revolutionary era on present-day social conditions, economic life, and culture south of the Rio Grande.

NOTE: Readings for this chapter are combined with those on social and economic problems at the end of Chapter 29.

From Indianism to Industrialization in Present-Day Mexico

THE LAND AND THE PEOPLE WHO LIVE ON IT

IN THE HILLS above the state capital in the province of Oaxaca in southern Mexico lies the village of Santa Cruz Etla; thirty families, comprising about 150 people, live along two ridges and in the ravine between. These poor farmers own less than five acres of land apiece, plowing it with oxen to raise barely enough corn and beans to feed the children. For cash to buy city-made articles the young men cut wood in the communally owned forests of the distant *sierra*, burn it into charcoal, and sell it in the kitchens of the distant city. There has never been a resident priest, and a generation ago only one man there could read and write. Then, in 1929, this one literate man procured blueprints from the Mexican federal school authorities and led his fellow townsmen in building a two-room adobe schoolhouse. A year later they hired a young girl from the Oaxaca Normal School as teacher.

One of the present authors has known this village well over the years since the school was started, and has seen the community make other advances with the first literate generation taught in the school.[1] The death rate among children has been lowered by almost 30 per cent because of the

[1] See Helen Miller Bailey, *Santa Cruz of the Etla Hills* (Gainesville, Florida: University of Florida Press, 1958).

new teaching about sanitation and diet and the government anti-malaria and vaccination campaigns. With better seed and iron tools the farmers are growing more corn per acre. In the campaign against illiteracy in the 1940s every adult in the village had the opportunity to learn to read. The community water supply has been improved and deep wells dug for the dry season, while the burro trail to the city has become a road wide enough for heavy trucks.

All is not optimism in Santa Cruz Etla, however, for the depletion of the forest land by centuries of charcoal burners has reduced the woodcutters' livelihood and eroded away the farmland below. By the 1960s many of the young men of the first literate generation had left the poor land. They went to work on the new highways or on the Oaxaca city waterworks project. Several of them migrated to that far-off Mecca, the national capital, where they found occupation in the new industries, in textile plants and foundries. The oldest son of that first literate man who built the school found work in a tile factory, sent for his younger brothers, and put one of them in business college to learn typing, bookkeeping, and English, while he himself through his labor union and social security was guaranteed more pesos per week than any family had earned per year back in the hills. Several whole families had moved to Mexico City by 1966, although three of them found no place to live save in crowded shanties in Mexico City's new slum fringe. Their children found no school to attend there, while the children back at home were using fine new free textbooks sent to them by López Mateos and Díaz Ordaz.

The story of this village, its improvements at home and the changes coming to the young people, can be repeated in many other regions of

The recent Mexican campaign against adult illiteracy reached to every corner of the land. Women of Santa Cruz Etla, Oaxaca, make their mark to enroll. *Photo by Helen Miller Bailey.*

Mexico. In 1921 Mexico had 14,000,000 people; in the late 1960s, 43,000,000. Of these people 65 per cent still live in communities of less than 2,000. Highly industrialized Mexico City, center of wealth and culture, has grown almost tenfold since the abdication of Díaz in 1910, when it had less than half a million inhabitants. In fabulous modern Mexico City and its metropolitan area live nearly five million people. There is more urbanization in Mexico than in any other area of Latin America: sixteen cities each have more than 100,000 people. Charming, sleepy Guadalajara has suddenly become an industrial center of 750,000 with many multi-storied office buildings and a great complex of textile factories. Monterrey, the Pittsburgh of Northern Mexico, has 700,000 people, and Puebla, with its scores of colonial churches, now boasts industry enough to occupy 350,000 people. In 1910, 77 per cent of the population had been engaged in rural occupations; in 1966 only 50 per cent were still living in rural areas in marked contrast with the rising urban city class, although more than a million rural families still lived on a subsistence level, with less than 100 dollars in cash a year. The yearly population growth rate in the late 1960s was 3.3 per cent.

The problem of illiteracy is yet to be solved; in 1965 Díaz Ordaz reported that 28 per cent of Mexico's people were still unable to read and write. Of the illiterates, more than 500,000, or about 3 per cent, are non-Spanish-speaking Indians, speaking 33 different languages, pre-Columbian tongues never written down. Another 27 per cent of the population are of pure Indian blood though living in Spanish-speaking communities; 60 per cent are *mestizo* and 10 per cent white. The Indian people in the remote mountains and the *mestizos* in the villages like Santa Cruz Etla create a cultural and social problem for modern Mexico. However, in the four decades after the fighting stopped the Revolution has attempted to solve that problem by a new agrarian program.

For an agricultural nation, Mexico's tragedy is lack of fertile land; one-half of the surface is mountainous; of the other half, only 14 per cent has enough natural water for agriculture. Only a little more than half of that is actually sown to crops; the rest lies fallow or is grazed by livestock. The Constitution of 1917 gave the government the right to break up big estates, and by the end of 1926 land had been returned to more than 2,000 villages that had lost their communal lands under the Díaz regime. It was not until 1932, however, that Mexican courts ruled that the government could give new lands to villages that had never owned acreage; finally, the law was also interpreted to allow villagers who lived on estates as feudal peons to receive land, either as private owners or as members of a cooperative or *ejido*.

President Cárdenas increased the pace of *ejido* distribution; he provided financial assistance to these cooperative agricultural projects through the National Bank of Ejidal Credit, together with technical assistance in improving the seed stock and handling the newly financed farm machinery. Cárdenas' most ambitious project was at Laguna in the area of Torreón, an important cotton-growing district. Thirty thousand families were resettled there and were taught the methods involved in a new widescale irrigation project. Similar projects were undertaken in Sinaloa, Morelos, and Sonora.

At the end of the Cárdenas regime big owners still held three times as much land as the cooperative villages, though Mexicans revered Cárdenas as the "Father of the *Ejido*."

For twenty years after Cárdenas the land distribution program lagged. Without adequate irrigation the Laguna project could not support the natural increase of population on its cotton lands. There were inadequate methods of financing small farmers outside the *ejido* system. Small family plots of less than ten acres could not produce enough, by hand and oxen labor, to send surplus to the growing cities. Then came López Mateos, who gave away more land than any previous president save Cárdenas. Further-more, his grants were larger, and many of them were on newly irrigated land. The excess population at the Laguna project were given the oppor-tunity to move to tropical lands cleared by bulldozers and drained by new canal systems. Between 1915 and 1965, 50 per cent of all productive land in Mexico was distributed among 2,200,000 peasants. There were 18,000 *ejidos* in 1965, 4,000 of them collectives producing cotton, sugar, rice, and hemp. But in 14,000 *ejidos* each family cultivated its own land, sharing machinery and marketing and credit facilities with other families. The agricultural production had increased 350 per cent. Where there were 56,000 individual land owners in 1910, in 1965 there were 3,600,000, two-thirds in *ejidos* and a third in separate holdings. In the meantime the acreage under production had grown from 26,000,000 to 36,000,000. As can be seen from the above figures, Mexico in the mid-1960s was moving away from the communal ownership pattern so ardently desired by the revolutionaries.

The *ejidal* banks have survived financially and have expanded their capital; in the year from September 1964 to September 1965 133,000 in-dividual *ejido* members had received a total of a billion dollars in loans from the bank for seed, machinery, or water conservation projects and had cleared the loans or were making regular payments. More than 500 of these communities are on former large estates in which the whole *hacienda* was expropriated as a unit and is now being worked cooperatively. There are today very few enormous estates; more than 250 acres in a single holding is theoretically forbidden by law. Even though Mexico has so little arable land to balance the increase in population, with the help of irrigation, swamp drainage, and farm machinery, Mexican farmers today are actually feeding the city population, and little food needs to be imported. Agicul-tural self-sufficiency has been a major goal of the last two decades.

Cooperation with the American government in the use of the Rio Grande water supply is making more acres available in the desert north. New irrigation projects have been built, including the great new Falcón Dam finished in 1957, the Amistad Dam on the northern border in 1965, the Lerma Chapala project in Jalisco, and the Culiacan-Yaqui River project in Sinaloa. Two valley regions, the Papaloapan and the Tepalcal-tepec, both in southern areas of heavy rainfall, were developed under President Alemán on the pattern of the Tennessee Valley Authority for long-range flood control, swamp reclamation, transportation improvement, and resettlement of whole villages from dry and eroded areas. Millions of pesos are also being spent on reclaiming the Durango "dust bowl" where rainfall has been so slight that many families had to become migrants. To increase the corn crop for both *ejidos* and small owners a Maize Commission has been set up to study why Mexico's corn yield per acre should be only one-sixteenth that of Iowa.

Land newly cleared or newly irrigated often must be fertilized, as must worn-out or eroded land. Artificial fertilizer plants have been financed by the Mexican-style Reconstruction Finance Corporation, called the *Nacional Financiera,* a typical modern Latin American *Fomento* or government development agency, partially financed by the American Export-Import Bank. The endemic hoof and mouth disease among cattle was attacked by a joint American-Mexican campaign which sent veterinary scientists throughout the infected areas of Mexico to slaughter the diseased animals.

It is of interest to trace the accomplishments in the presidencies following that of Cárdenas. Ávila Camacho succeeded in producing more food for the World War II economy, making the lowland tropical coast fertile as a result of a movement called the "March to the Sea." Wartime inflation was partially balanced by Ávila Camacho's insistence on the production of agricultural crops for export: corn, wheat, cotton, sugar, beans, rice, and cacao. Under Alemán the railroads, oil industries, and hydroelectric projects had their biggest boom, as he spent large sums to industrialize Mexico at the expense of agriculture. However, more cropland was created, an Erosion Control Commission was set up, electricity was brought to rural areas, and marginal villages were resettled. Ruíz Cortines continued Alemán's "Tennessee Valley" projects and placed him in charge of the one at Papaloapan, as a retired president. Ruíz Cortines, anxious to concentrate on industry, did, however, take over a 647,000-acre American-owned holding near the Arizona line at Cananea, the last big foreign cattle ranch in Mexico.

President Díaz Ordaz, in his first message to congress in September 1965, said, "I have signed 294 decrees, distributing 213,428 hectares of land among 27,763 farmers. But at this rate there will not be enough land available to all. Thus we are faced with the problem of creating new sources of wealth."

Modern Mexican leaders, no longer Revolutionary, realize that improved agriculture will not solve the over-all problems of a large and rapidly increasing population on poor soil. More research, farmer education, better agricultural methods, more industrialization and mechanization of agriculture, more water on the lands in the north, more flood and erosion control on the lands in the south, all are needed and are being developed more rapidly than in most other parts of the world. Thus the land distribution of Mexico, though it brought free holdings to a great many people who had wanted them, has not increased the food supply commensurate to the higher standard of living an industrialized people want. It has not been enough to answer the cry of Zapata by giving *tierra y libertad* to the peasants. When they have the land they must learn to improve their methods of using it. Industrialization is also a partial answer.

THE NEW INDUSTRIALIZATION

Anyone who knew Mexico three decades ago, and then drove down either route of the Pan American Highway today, through such thriving communities as Monterrey on the east or Hermosillo and Guadalajara on the west, would not believe he was in the same country. Factories, filling stations, garages, motels, truck assembly plants, housing projects with running water in each unit and schools in the center—all these things so unlike the colonial towns and adobe slums of yesteryear—hit his eye as he drives south, while traffic becomes congested and buses and trucks almost push him off the road. It is Mexico City with its factories and new suburbs and ultra-modern freeways that surprises him most, capital of a nation that owns its own oil industry and railroads, that is building up its consumer-goods manufacturing, and that hopes to be self-sufficient in all but the heaviest industry.

The tourist driving south has been able to purchase nothing but government-produced gasoline called Pemex. The controversy over oil in the 1930s has been solved; payments from profits on the government monopoly were made in the amount of $24,000,000 to eleven American companies whose property had been expropriated, and $81,000,000 to British interests. In 1950 the Mexican wells had doubled their 1932 production figures; new oil fields and pipelines were developed under Ruíz Cortines. The Pemex distributors had found a new market for Mexican gasoline and fuel oil in the local industries and the cars and trucks within Mexico itself. By 1960 Pemex had become Mexico's biggest business and biggest taxpayer. Laborers in oil field and refinery had profited in proportion. New wells are being tapped yearly. Mexico, in 1921 the world's second largest oil producer, is today using as many barrels at home at it was sending abroad in those days of large exports. It also had the highest developed petrochemical industry in Latin America by 1966. "Mexico for the Mexicans" was the cry of the Revolutionists against foreign concerns, and Mexican oil is fulfilling that promise by helping make Mexico self-sufficient. Meanwhile there are other sources of power for industry; the hydroelectric projects of the Alemán regime, though using only a fraction of Mexico's potential, are providing power for home industries. To provide iron and steel for the new consumer-goods industries using this power and employing the men migrating to the cities, Mexico is developing steel foundries in Monterrey and Colima. Mining, once the mainstay of the Mexican economy, is today producing 23 per cent of the total exports of Mexico and employing 2 per cent of the working public. There is more wealth in the new coke industry, the diesel motor plant in Mexico City, the plastic and paper factories financed by the *Nacional Financiera*.

There are two things which Mexico needs in this program—technical skills and more capital. Technical education is more easily available in Mexico today than it was two decades ago; young Mexicans are graduating from Mexico City's Polytechnic Institute, are earning scholarships to

United States' technical schools, or are being given in-service training in both Mexican and American-owned factories. As in other parts of Latin America, engineering has become an honored profession in which sons of all classes are finding opportunity. Local Mexican capital has been inadequate for the ambitious new program; water and sewage systems for the new growing cities alone, for example, needed $10,000,000 of new capital in one recent year. Large, long-term loans from foreign agencies—the Export-Import Bank, the International Bank for Reconstruction and Development—have gone very largely into public works developed by the government. Financing is now made easier through the Alliance for Progress developed since 1963.

Government money has been poured into the railways of Mexico. All privately owned lines have been expropriated and their owners paid in full; the lines originally built by the government in the Díaz regime have been expanded. In the cabinet sits a Secretary of Communication and Public Works, one of whose jobs is to run the railways as a paying proposition. Of the loans from the United States Export-Import Bank, $15,000,000 went into improved track and new rolling stock; the *Nacional Financiera* built new lines to open Yucatan in the south and Lower California in the north to direct contact with the mainland. Three paved highways run down from the United States border to Mexico City; the central route continues on to the Guatemalan border to meet Guatemala's section of the Pan-American Highway. Local road improvement has also been emphasized, so that every village could be brought closer to a market center, so that even Santa Cruz Etla could be reached by truck.

Nacional Financiera is actually a corporation in which the government owns a majority of the stock. Joining with other government agencies, it has arranged a series of "six-year plans" following the pattern laid down by Calles. These plans for industrialization are dominated by the New Group, the modern-thinking new businessmen growing out of the northern oligarchy. Under them foreign capital as well as local businessmen have prospered. The New Group has made foreign companies welcome in the last decade; the restrictions put upon their profits and their labor relations are not nearly so strongly enforced as the Constitution of 1917 implied. Most new capital is going into smaller ventures, into assembly plants, into manufacturing with Mexican materials and Mexican skilled workers, rather than into the extractive industries of a bygone age. The need for expanded credit goes on; in the mid-1960s Mexico needed another billion for roads and new trucking, six billion for irrigation, additional billions for public sanitation and education projects.

Article 123 of the 1917 Constitution and subsequent legislation have provided for the high standards Mexican labor has expected—the eight-hour day, equal pay for men and women, natives and foreigners, no child labor, no peonage, safe and sanitary working conditions, accident and sickness benefits, old age pensions, adequate housing and schooling for the working class, the right to organize and to strike, severance pay as a guarantee against unfair layoffs. These were far-fetched utopian visions in 1917. But under their impetus, Luis Morones founded the CROM, a craft union like the AFL which later gave way to Lombardo Toledano and his more industrialized CTM. Lombardo Toledano soon became a famous left-wing "labor rouser" throughout Latin America and brought down the suspicion of Communist domination on his labor organization in Mexico. When Ávila Camacho became president, he ousted Lombardo Toledano from the CTM, bringing that labor group into the National Revolutionary Party and the government into greater control of the labor movement. Alemán and Ruíz Cortines stepped firmly on labor only when the occasion demanded. Ruíz Cortines had the CTM call off a general strike in 1954, saying that the government would take care of wage and labor problems separately for each industry. In fact, no strikes occurred during Cortines' regime, owing largely to the effective work of his Labor Minister López Mateos, who was to be elected president in 1958 as Ruíz Cortines' successor. López Mateos himself had to break a serious railway strike in the spring of 1959, which he blamed on foreign left-wing agitation.

Government-sponsored unions now claim upward of 2,000,000 members in the rapidly industrializing new Mexico. The larger industrial firms had long remained hostile and foreign capital hesitated to invest in labor-dominated industries, afraid of Morones' type of labor racketeer and Lombardo Toledano's type of ultra left-wingism. However, by 1945 the Mexican National Manufacturers' Association joined with the CTM to back the National Revolutionary Party and to further labor-management plans for Mexican economic development. Mexican labor no longer screams for the nationalization of industry under the "People's Revolution" but concentrates on asking for fair treatment and higher wages.

The first law to carry out the Social Security provisions of 1917 was not passed until 1939; no actual inclusive coverage was provided until 1943. Today there is a Mexican Social Security Institute, with a head-quarters building covering two blocks in modern Mexico City. More than a million persons are being benefited by the medical, old age, and unemployment insurance programs. Year by year hospital and clinical services are being established in all urban centers. Before this government-controlled health program was put into effect, there was no medical service available for the families of workers in Mexico; now the law provides free medical treatment and medicine to all workers who contribute a percentage of their wages to the fund. Federally financed low-rent housing projects surround Mexico City and other growing towns. Just to give one example, the *Centro Urbano Presidente Alemán* in Mexico City, a 3,000,000-peso project completed in 1950, has room for 6,000 occupants and is a complete city in itself, with recreation facilities, schools, and clinics.

Mexico probably ranks near the top, next to Chile and Argentina, in the living standards of its workers. But the younger sons of the *ejido* members and the small owners, unwilling to share with their older brothers the meager living in the rural homes, come to the city in increasing numbers. Their families are surrounding Mexico City with shanty-town slums where there are inadequate water, sanitation, and schooling. For these in-migrants, Mexico's cities must provide 3,500,000 new jobs by 1975, as well as decent housing and good schools for their children.

A problem concerning laborers, peculiar to Mexico alone, was the situation regarding "wetbacks," those who illegally cross the Rio Grande to work in America, and *braceros,* those who come legally under contract. Urgently needed in the United States during World War II, when 2,000,-000 Mexican nationals were at work in America, and still desired by some types of American agricultural interests as cheap labor, Mexicans were tempted to cross the border by the hundreds of thousands. Meanwhile the newly irrigated fields of Sonora and Sinaloa needed 100,000 more farm laborers. In December 1964, by common consent between Mexico and the United States, the *bracero* agreements were ended, and such use of Mexican workers in the United States became illegal.

Meanwhile, looking toward the 1970s, Mexico's industrial production was rising. "Growth has become Mexico's normal condition," said President Díaz Ordaz in 1965. In 1967, economic growth promised to top 7%, while the gross national product reached nineteen billion. A cooperation between government and industry has been possible in Mexico because there was no vested interest of native private industry in Mexico to speak of before the 1910–1920 Revolution. Thus industry and the "Revolution" have gone along hand in hand, building a home-grown revolution.

Mexico has the most diversified economy in Latin America today. Cotton provides 20 per cent of her exports, coffee 10 per cent, and minerals 30 per cent. In the one year 1965, Mexico's steel production was up 5 per cent, truck manufacture up 10 per cent, crude oil processing up 10 per cent, gasoline refining up 8 per cent, and electric energy output up 10 per cent. The Mexican stock exchange was booming with foreign investment. Mexico was the first Latin American nation to invest in Early Bird Tel Star communication. Tourism has been a major industry enhanced by the 1968 plans for the Olympic Games to be held in Mexico City, where new stadiums and hotel accommodations comprised an investment to make Mexico City a permanent sports center. Woolworth, Sears Roebuck, Ford, and Chrysler not only have large retail outlets in Mexico, but also manufacturing and assembly plants. In 1965 General Motors of Mexico built a 32 million-peso plant to produce 50,000 automobiles a year for local Mexican sale. Such a diversified economy made strides toward creating the 3,500,000 jobs Díaz Ordaz called for.

EDUCATION IN TWENTIETH-CENTURY MEXICO

The followers of the Revolution of 1910–1920 wanted free public education as a part of their program equal in importance to the free distribution of land. Article 3 of the 1917 Constitution goes beyond any requirement for education in other modern constitutions of the world, providing as it does for education as a government trust, limiting parochial education, and making all plans, programs, and methods of teaching the responsibility of the state. To carry out this heavy responsibility in a land with few teachers and little tradition of state-supported education, Obregón appointed José Vasconcelos, a Revolutionary leader in his student days and by then director of the National University, to be the first Administrator of Federal Education in 1921. His pioneer efforts were carried on by Möisés Sáenz under Calles, who attempted to carry out the promise to found rural schools in all villages. By 1930 there were more than 3,500 new village schools such as the one in Santa Cruz Etla.

These rural schools were the epitome of the Revolutionary doctrine, built by the people themselves, staffed by very young idealists who could hardly be trained fast enough for the demand, serving as health, cultural, and recreational leaders for the new order. Some of the teachers met with violent opposition; a few were even attacked, in the religious upheaval of the *Cristero* movement. In Cárdenas' time every new *ejido* grant obligated the villagers to build a school; 1,600 new schools went up by Cárdenas' order on large ranches, and additional hundreds were started in factory communities financed by the owners of the industrial development. In the mid-1940s it could be said that in proportion to per capita income, Mexico was now spending a larger share for education than the United States.

In the 1960s there were more than 30,000 public elementary schools in Mexico with more than four million students. For each of these schools a teacher had been recruited and trained and was being paid well by Latin American standards, two-thirds from federal funds, one-third from local. Though much credit is due Cárdenas, actually Avila Camacho and Alemán founded more schools than he, and under later presidents public secondary and technical training showed rapid improvement. Dedicated and sincere men have served in the position of Minister of Education.

Only areas of very sparse population, or Indian-speaking tribal communities in the more remote mountain areas, do not now have public schools; only one-tenth of Mexican children are now in private or church-supported elementary schools. However, since laws for compulsory attendance are not enforced, no penalties are visited on parents who keep their children out of school; and, since teachers and classrooms are still in short supply as well, 2,500,000 children throughout the nation are deprived of elementary education. Most rural and village schools only offer four grades, each grade requiring more factual and advanced material than the corresponding grade in the United States, and ordinarily taking two years to finish. Because a sixth-grade certificate is required for admission to the city secondary school, most rural children have no opportunity for any advanced education.

But formal advanced education has not been the goal for the agricultural population. Simple reading and writing have been augmented with such a wide social program that the elementary rural schools in Mexico have become a model for other parts of Latin America. Scientific agriculture, better care of livestock, improved feeding of infants, control of public health, purification of water supply—these are the things about which simple textbooks have been written and which the teachers have been trained to emphasize. Vasconcelos and Sáenz had to push the normal training-school program rapidly to get teachers prepared for such service; Santa Cruz Etla and thousands of other communities waited from one to three years after their building was finished for a trained teacher. Boys and girls from the villages, especially in areas of Indian culture, have been granted liberal scholarships to encourage them to go to normal schools and return as teachers in their own communities. The rural teachers of Mexico have been a zealous, dedicated group, actual "missionaries" in a non-religious sense.

Their work was from the first augmented by "cultural missions." Since the young teachers sent out to the hill communities in the 1930s were so poorly trained and the communities themselves so unused to schools, groups of trained specialists were sent on circuit to help them. Nurses, gardeners, art-craft workers, recreational leaders, and musicians were formed into units which traveled with mobile libraries and craft rooms from community to community. Successful from the first, cultural missions became a permanent feature of Mexican life, and their example has inspired educators in other parts of Latin America.

To reach the non-Spanish-speaking tribes, the cultural mission program was augmented by bringing promising young Indians into Mexico City for advanced education and training in leadership. The success of these young tribal Indians in the city schools convinced many skeptical Mexicans of the great potential lying dormant in the Indians. But this program failed when the young people so trained did not want to go back and serve the communities they had come from; schools were then founded out in the Indian-speaking regions where teachers were trained on their own home grounds. Today there is a school teaching Spanish in most large Indian-speaking communities. Thus, eventually, all village centers of Indian-speaking groups—the Otomí, the Mixtec, the Zapotecans, the Tarascans, the Huichols, the Chamulas, the Yucateca Maya—will be "Mexicanized" and literate in the Spanish language.

Among the Spanish-speaking people in town and country in the 1930s 60 per cent did not know how to read and write. In 1944 in a wartime emergency, Ávila Camacho decided to launch a program to teach illiterate adults to read. Doctor Jaime Torres-Bodet, afterward chairman of UNESCO and again Minister of Education for López Mateos in 1959, was appointed in charge of this program. A primer was prepared to teach adults letter by letter in a very simple way, a primer with which any person who knew how to read and write was able to teach any illiterate person. This "each one teach one" plan was widely publicized throughout Mexico and inspired another "missionary movement" on the part of hundreds of thousands of literate people. Those who could read taught more than a million others to read between 1944 and 1946. Recent presidents have launched a new campaign, using regular trained teachers and granting them extra pay for after-hours work with adults. Today the plan is being copied, through UNESCO by other underdeveloped areas of the world. In 1967, Díaz Ordaz even drafted American companies into the literacy campaign. For example, out of a total of 15,568 "literacy centers" in 19 states, 70 were set up in that year by the Coca Cola Company and its local bottling agencies.

One of the aims of the literacy program has been to give information about malaria, tuberculosis, and venereal disease. To thousands of villages an improved water supply, piped into the village plaza and made free of typhoid contamination, came hand in hand with the new rural school. The Department of Education has cooperated with the Department of Public

Health in giving teachers courses in rural medicine. There is a campaign against malaria, a campaign against tuberculosis, a campaign against venereal disease, just as there is a campaign against illiteracy. Other Latin American nations come to Mexico for information about the anti-malaria campaign, and the Pan American Sanitary Bureau has been working closely with it.

Medical students are few in comparison with the number needed, partially because so few students have adequate secondary school training. Even in the city elementary schools, of the six years of free public education offered, 37 per cent of the pupils are in the first grade, 21 per cent in the second grade, and 1 per cent in the six grade. Without a sixth-grade certificate secondary education is impossible. Since the demand is still small, the government builds 3,000 elementary schools for every ten secondary institutions of any kind. Though public high schools have been improved, secondary schooling has remained largely a private enterprise, and in the final "live and let live" policy which the government worked out with the Church under Ávila Camacho it has been an accepted fact that more than two-thirds of the secondary education is done by Church authorities. There are also the Latin American-type *colegios* or privately run secondary schools, with varying standards of subject matter and instruction.

This whole secondary school set-up brings only the cream of the brilliant and the sons of the well-to-do into the institutions of higher learning. However, Mexico has become famous in Latin America for her splendid new university buildings. In 1952 the National University of Mexico, eighty-five years older than Harvard, was given a $15,000,000 campus, a beautiful University City in a new suburb some twenty miles outside Mexico City. This plant, with its startling and ultra-modern functional

Mosaic decoration on the main library of the new University of Mexico. *Courtesy Pan American Union.*

architecture and its Aztec motif, its capacity for 25,000 students, and its library, laboratory, visual education, and sports facilities—certainly one of the finest physical plants for a university in the Western Hemisphere— replaced a great many scattered units throughout Mexico City, which had the medical school here, the law school there, the teacher-training schools elsewhere. The university was filled to capacity in the late 1960s in spite of the lack of secondary school graduates.

There are also an 8,000,000-peso Polytechnic City which houses a technical school, a National School of Agriculture, a School of Tropical Medicine, a Workers' University, and the University of the Americas, an international institution on the American plan, as well as a smaller university in each state capital. The Monterrey Technical Institute, founded in 1942, is the Cal Tech of Mexico. American students who go to school in Mexico find student life quite different from that in the United States. They miss the sociability of college life in America. Though there are now some full-time faculty salaries for the out-of-town campus, university professors often teach part-time and sometimes have to make their real living by means of their law practices, their government jobs, or their journalistic activities. Therefore, they do not feel themselves a part of campus life. Campus life itself is almost nonexistent; there are few residence groups or undergraduate organizations, and athletics are only now becoming a part of Mexican student life. The courses, however, are very strict and scholarly; advanced degrees which are given are accepted throughout the academic world.

The University of Mexico is coeducational, and many women study for the professions. The position of women in politics, in law, and in medicine has improved enormously since the Revolution. There is also a Women's University, to which it is increasingly stylish for women to go. The members of the Association of University Women are leaders in public affairs in Mexico City. There are also many colleges which are run by the Church. They maintain the high scholastic standards and much of the prestige they had in colonial times, and today they have no opposition from the government.

As in many other parts of Latin America, college students in Mexico were restless and frustrated in the late 1960s. A student riot in Mexico City forced the rector of the University and twenty-five of his staff to resign. Disorders broke out among students in seven other areas of Mexico in 1966 and 1967. But university life seemed to go right on, and standards of teaching and of scholarship consistently improved.

"INDIANISMO" AND A "NEW CULTURE"

More than any other Latin American nation Mexico is now proud of her Indian blood and Indian tradition. When José Vasconcelos was Education Minister in 1921, he arranged a handicraft exhibition which emphasized the Indian folk art, music, and folklore. He and his associates in the "Renaissance" of Mexico said, "We wish to make Mexico the cultural center of the Western Hemisphere as the United States is the industrial

Diego Rivera, creative and controversial Mexican mural painter. *Courtesy Pan American Union.*

center." Vasconcelos' interest in regional crafts brought a whole new industry to Mexico, as tourists hurried to buy the blue blown glass of Guadalajara, the textiles of Oaxaca, the leather craft of Toluca, the silver filigree from Taxco, the lacquer from Michoacán. The work of Aztec, Tarascan, and Zapotecan craftsmen was revived. Hand in hand with this interest went the revival of pride in the Indian heritage. Indian symbolism in literature, and Indian themes in music expression became almost a fad in Mexico City. In the upsurge of national pride brought by the Revolution, Mexico was one place in the Western Hemisphere in which a person was proud of his Indian ancestry.

Indianism was best shown in the art of the 1920s and 1930s. Its leader, Diego Rivera (1885–1957) became the best-known Western Hemisphere artist in the eyes of the world. When Madero was president, Rivera was a young artist studying French expressionism in Paris; José Clemente Orozco (1883–1949), the second great Mexican artist, was busy painting scenes of poverty in Mexico City; and David Siqueiros (1898–   ), the third Revolutionary art leader, was drawing cartoons to illustrate Revolutionary song sheets. By 1919 a congress of soldier-artists had been held to discuss ways of using art in the new Revolutionary program, and from this congress Siqueiros and Orozco were sent abroad. In Paris they met Rivera; moving on to Barcelona they published a "manifesto" proclaiming the Western Hemisphere art of the future to be a true Indian art. Returning to Mexico after studying alfresco mural painting methods in Italy, Rivera and his young colleagues joined with Vasconcelos in the Indian-based movement. An art teacher, Adolfo Best-Maugard, originated a system of teaching drawing in the new public schools, with simple elements of design to be taught to every rural student. The new trends in art, music, and folk dancing were popularized in a great cultural fair in Chapultepec in 1921.

Meanwhile Rivera put his study of alfresco methods to use in painting spectacular murals on the new public buildings of the Revolutionary Party, using a palette of ten bright earth colors in wet plaster. Central motif of each of these enormous murals was the Indian, an Indian with crude face, large feet and hands, and dark earth-red skin color. The three-story Department of Education building was covered with almost an acre of mural paintings of Indian groups of every region. The Cortés Palace in Cuernavaca, used as the state legislature for Morelos, has Diego Rivera's concept of the entire history of Mexico painted across the outside wall facing the town.

Orozco,[2] Rivera, and Siqueiros, though differing sharply in style and approach, all felt a need to put across a social message. They were not satisfied with simply making paintings of Indians; they criticized the clergy, made cartoons of public characters, showed Justice as a debauched drunken person, and the Father God surrounded by harpies instead of angels. Polite society in Mexico City was scandalized; conservatives protested the defiling of public buildings, while Rivera took delight in shocking people even more by playing around with the political philosophy of Communism. At the time of his death in December 1957, Rivera and his work were still controversial; his gigantic underwater design for the Mexico City reservoir caused anger and confusion when it was created, and some smug amusement when its colors began to wash away. But Rivera had succeeded in bringing the Indian element into modern art, and recent Mexican artists of a milder school have continued his work of making Mexican art a distinctive New World force. Miguel Covarrubias (1904–1959), in illustrating American books, has made readers conscious of Zapotec culture. Sculpture is also using Aztec motifs, and the name of Manuel Centurión is known among world sculptors.

By the 1960s the *Indianismo* which the Revolutionary artists set out to promote had been left behind, and seemed almost a forgotten cause. David Siqueiros, long held in jail for his communist activities, was busy in 1960 and 1965 painting "the largest mural in the world" in a Cuernavaca hotel. Its subject was the "whole history of humanity emerging into the modern world." Rufino Tamayo, Mexico's leading painter in the late 1960s, painted with the flamboyant Mexican colors, but chose themes common to all humanity. He considered El Greco and Picasso his masters rather than Rivera and Orozco. Busily painting into his seventh decade, Rufino Tamayo was considered an artist "of the Americas and of the world," more than was Rivera, the artist of Mexican "Indianismo." Today all Mexico is very art-school conscious and has become a Mecca for art-minded tourists and students.

2 See the photograph of the Orozco mural featuring Benito Juárez, p. 342.

In the meantime, several Mexican classical musicians had also followed the new pattern, starting with the Indian folk tune and creating from it a sophisticated modern music form which is wholly Mexican and not European. The first Revolutionary compositions were the camp songs quoted at the beginning of the previous chapter, still popular as folk songs in Mexico. But Carlos Chávez (1899–   ), son of a Spanish father and an Indian mother, a brilliant composer at the age of fifteen and founder of the Mexico City Symphony, brought both Indian and revolutionary themes into his works. As Director of the National Conservatory of Music he started many young students working in the same direction. He has conducted in the United States, much of his music is played there, and the Pan American Union has considered him one of the foremost musicians in Latin

Carlos Chavez, Mexican composer, preparing for recording of native-theme music. *Courtesy* Américas *Magazine.*

American history, second only to the great Brazilian, Villalobos. The contemporary school of Mexican music presents a wide variety of styles, from the academic through the Indian to the ultra-modern.

A new popular Mexican theater was born during the Revolution. Called at first "crude, improvised, and disreputable, but alive," this drama, given in tent shows which followed the armies, was entertainment for the common people. Now such plays have come into their own in a musical theater in the downtown area. Musical reviews caricaturing political evils of the day are very popular in Mexico, some of them handed down from the Revolution itself. More important than any play today is the motion picture, for the movies are a big industry in Mexico. Mexican-made movies are shown throughout Latin America, play to packed houses in the Spanish-speaking theaters of Southern California and the American Southwest, and are often shown in New York. Three-quarters of the films deal with Mexican historical subjects, with the great era of the Revolution and with the story of the Spanish conquest. The stars who play in them are better known in Venezuela or Argentina than are many American actors. Best known of all has been the comic character and pantomimist Cantinflas, whose films have been praised in Spain as samples "of the highest form of a dramatic art possible with one essential character."

Mexico is still interested in its Indian culture. Cárdenas founded an office of *Asuntos Indígenas,* things Indian, to keep the customs and culture of indigenous groups alive. Alemán established the National Institute of Fine Arts, whose prime objective is to "become guardian and permanent judge of what is purely Mexican throughout the coming generations, to preserve that combination of Indian and Spanish which makes Mexican culture today." *Indianismo* and the Revolution have been kept alive in literature. Gone is the popularity of lyric poetry, so much a part of Latin American literary life through the centuries. The Revolution, more interested in strong, deep feelings than in light lyrical ones, produced a new type of literature, the Revolutionary novels concerned with the masses. Three novelists, Gregorio López y Fuentes (1895–   ), Mariano Azuela (1873–1952), and Martín Luis Guzmán (1887–   ) are outstanding in the cultural history of all Latin America.

López y Fuentes, born of a well-to-do family in 1895, was writing novels in 1910. In the days of Obregón he worked as a journalist and produced a daily column of sketches of common people in the Revolution. A series of these columns became his first novel, *Campamento,* the disorganized adventures of a band of Revolutionary soldiers. His second novel, *Tierra,* is actually the life of Zapata; it has kept the Indian hero a shining figure in the eyes of a non-Revolutionary second generation. In the novel *El Indio* the main character is the Indian village, a community like Santa Cruz Etla, which is brought from semibarbarism into contact with the world by means of a school, a new road, and a church. López y Fuentes had served as a rural teacher in order to get material for this famous novel. Its style is like that of his other books—an incident here, an incident there, the setting of atmosphere and mood rather than plot.

Guzmán was a journalist with the forces of Villa and Carranza and wrote of his experiences in *The Eagle and the Serpent* and in *La Sombra del Caudillo (Shade of the Chieftain)*; though meant to be narrative history, they have the dramatic quality of novels. By the mid-1960s Guzmán was considered one of Mexico's most noted historians. He published the memoirs of Pancho Villa and did much to make Villa's memory seem heroic. Azuela, the third great writer of this group of novelists, was a young doctor who served for several months in 1915 as head of a guerrilla band.

With Carranza victorious, the more liberal Azuela fled to El Paso, Texas, and there published in serial form in a Spanish-language paper a novel based on his life as leader of a Revolutionary band. After he returned to the practice of medicine in post-Revolutionary Mexico City, his novel became popular as *Los de Abajo* (*The Underdogs*). The chief character in this most famous of all modern Mexican novels is a humble Indian from Zacatecas who becomes the leader of a guerrilla band. His men follow him into the army of Villa, where they fight, kill, love, drink, and sing in a manner completely convincing to the reader, whether former Revolutionary soldier or not. When Carranza fought Villa, these men were forced to retreat and were boxed up in a canyon, where they, *Los de Abajo*, those below, were wiped out by soldiers on the hills above. The novel shows the spirit of the Revolution, but at the same time much of its aimlessness and futility. It is today one of the most widely read twentieth-century Spanish literary works.

Writers in the late 1960s were less interested in *Indianismo* and the Revolution. The leading poet, Octavio Paz (1914–   ), said, "We want to be contemporaneous with all mankind." His own poems and essays deal with many subjects: art, mysticism, religion, and psychology. He has been widely translated into English and other European languages, and he in turn has translated Japanese, Portuguese, and Swedish poets into Spanish. He has "exercised an enormous influence on the young writers of the whole hemisphere," according to the *Americas* magazine. Paz is a career diplomat who lived in France for several years as the counselor of the Mexican embassy in Paris. In 1965–1966 he was Mexican Ambassador to India, where he had a chance to enhance the worldwide view of modern Mexican poetry by learning Hindi.

The Mexican novel of the 1960s, also had a broader appeal than the mere "Spirit of 1910." Juan Rulfo (1918–   ), whose famous novel *Pedro Páramo* was written in 1955 and published in English in 1959, has reached the top of popular modern writers in Latin America. Though his story is about peasants in his native Jalisco where he himself was once a homeless orphan, it has a universal appeal to all who have known homelessness and hunger. His more recent works have the same psychological approach, which was copied by Carlos Fuentes (1929–   ) in his *The Death of Artemio Cruz* (1962) and other social novels.

A very competent present-day generation of Mexican literary critics and historians continue in the tradition of writing in well-rounded prose. The Institute of Anthropology and History and the Colegio Nacional de Mexico are outstanding centers of advanced study. The literary critic Alfonso Reyes and the philosophic writer Alfonso Caso should be mentioned, as well as the anthropologist Manuel Gamio. Poetry is still a literary hobby of many public figures; the world-renowned Education Minister Jaime Torres-Bodet, who headed UNESCO and was the Mexican delegate to the Pan American Conference at Bogotá in 1948, likes best to be remembered for his six novels and his seventeen published volumes of poems. Where reading matter for the masses is concerned, Mexico vies with Argentina in the publication of cheaply bound books and in the variety of newspapers and magazines.

Thus modern Mexican culture is interwoven with Mexican public life. When the violence of the Revolution was over, the fires of creation were rekindled out of the Indianist-*mestizo* social force to produce educational movements, aesthetic influences, and literary styles which have been among the most significant developments in modern Latin America.

READINGS

Adams, R. N., *et al.*, *Social Change in Latin America Today* (1960)

Alexander, R. J., *Organized Labor in Latin America* (1965)

Alisky, M., *State and Local Government in Sonora, Mexico* (1962)

Azuela, M., *Two Novels of Mexico: The Flies, The Bosses,* trans. L. B. Simpson (1956)

———, *The Underdogs* (various editions)

Bailey, H. M., *Santa Cruz of the Etla Hills* (1958)

Baklanoff, E. N., ed., *New Perspectives of Brazil* (1966)

Banco Nacional de Comercio Exterior (Mexico), *Mexico 1963: Facts, Figures, Trends* (1963)

Beals, C., *Porfirio Díaz, Dictator of Mexico* (1932)

Bennett, R. L., *The Financial Sector and Economic Development: The Mexican Case* (1965)

Bermudez, A. J., *Mexican Petroleum Industry* (1963)

Bernstein, H., *Modern and Contemporary Latin America* (1952)

Bernstein, M., *Mexican Mining Industry, 1890–1950* (1965)

Bett, V. M., *Central Banking in Mexico: Monetary Policies and Financial Crises, 1864–1940* (1957)

Blaisdell, L. L., *The Desert Revolution—Baja California, 1911* (1962)

Booth, G. C., *Mexico's School Made Society* (1941)

Born, E., *et al.*, *The New Architecture of Mexico* (1937)

Braddy, H., *Cock of the Walk: The Pancho Villa Legend* (1955)

Brand, D., *Mexico: Land of Shadow and Shade* (1965)

Brandenburg, F. R., *The Development of Latin American Private Enterprise* (1964)

———, *Making of Modern Mexico* (1964)

Brenner, A., *Idols Behind Altars* (1929)

———, *The Wind that Swept Mexico: History of the Mexican Revolution, 1910–1942* (1943)

Brothers, D. S., and L. Solísm, *Mexican Financial Development* (1966)

Brushwood, J. S., *Mexico in Its Novels* (1966)

———, *The Romantic Novel in Mexico* (1954)

Callahan, J. M., *American Foreign Policy in Mexican Relations* (1932)

Callcott, W. H., *Liberalism in Mexico, 1857–1929* (1931)

Castaneda, J., *Mexico and the United Nations* (1958)

Charlot, J., *Mexican Art and the Academy of San Carlos, 1785–1915* (1962)

———, *The Mexican Mural Renaissance, 1920–1925* (1963)

Clark, M. R., *Organized Labor in Mexico* (1934)

Clendenen, C. C., *The United States and Pancho Villa* (1961)

Cline, H. F., *Mexico: Revolution to Evolution, 1940–1960* (1962)

———, *The United States and Mexico* (rev. ed., 1962)

Coe, M. D., *Mexico* (1962)

Corwin, A. F., *Contemporary Mexican Attitudes Towards Population, Poverty and Public Opinion* (1963)

Cosio-Villegas, D., *American Extremes* (1964)
———, *Change in Latin America: The Mexican and Cuban Revolutions* (1961)
———, *United States versus Porfirio Díaz* (1963)
Crawford, W. R., *A Mexican Ulysses* [Vasconcelos] (1963)
Cronon, E. D., *Josephus Daniels in Mexico* (1960)
Crow, J. A., *Mexico Today* (1957)
Cumberland, C. C., *The Mexican Revolution: Genesis Under Madero* (1952)
———, *Social and Economic History of Mexico* (1966)
Daniels, J., *Shirt Sleeve Diplomacy* (1947)
Davis, M. L., and G. Pack, *Mexican Jewelry* (1963)
Ducoff, L. J., *Human Resources in Central America, Panama and Mexico, 1950–1980* (1960)
Dulles, J. W. F., *Yesterday in Mexico: A Chronicle of the Revolution, 1919–1936* (1961)
Dunn, F. S., *Diplomatic Protection of Americans in Mexico* (1933)
Dunn, H. H., *Crimson Jester: Zapata of Mexico* (1933)
Englekirk, J. E., et al., *Outline History of Spanish American Literature* (3rd ed., 1965)
"The Eye of Mexico," *Evergreen Review*, 1959
Feller, A. H., *The Mexican Claims Commission, 1923–1934* (1935)
Fergusson, E., *Mexico Revisited* (1955)
Gaither, R. B., *Expropriation in Mexico* (1940)
Gill, T., *Land Hunger in Mexico* (1951)
Glades, W. P. and C. W. Anderson, *Political Economy of Mexico* (1963)
Glick, E. B., *Straddling the Isthmus of Tehuantepec* (1959)
Gonzalez Pena, C., *History of Mexican Literature*, trans. G. B. Nance and F. J. Dunstan (1943)
Gordon, W. C., *The Expropriation of Foreign Owned Property in Mexico* (1941)
Great Britain, Board of Trade, *Overseas Economic Survey—Mexico* (1949)
Green, G., *Another Mexico* (1939)
Gros, B., ed., *National Planning, Power, Purpose, Performance* (1965)
Gruening, E., *Mexico and Its Heritage* (1928)
Guzmán, M. L., *Eagle and the Serpent*, trans. H. de Onis (1936)
———, *Memoirs of Pancho Villa* (1965)
Hackett, C. W., *The Mexican Revolution and the United States, 1910–1926* (1926)
Hancock, R. H., *Role of the Bracero in the Economic and Culture Dynamics of Mexico* (1959)
Hanke, L., *Mexico and the Caribbean* (rev. ed., 1966)
Herring, H., and H. Weinstock, *Renascent Mexico* (1935)
Houston, J. A., *Latin America in the United Nations* (1956)
Howland, C. P., ed., *Survey of American Foreign Relations* (1931)
Hunley, N., *Dividing the Waters* (1966)
Inter-American Committee for Agricultural Development, *Information Basic to the Planning of Agricultural Development in Latin America: Mexico* (1964)
International Bank for Reconstruction and Development, *Economic Development of Mexico* (1953)
James, Daniel, *Mexico and Americans* (1963)
Johnson, J. J., *Military and Society in Latin America* (1964)
———, *Political Change in Latin America* (1958)
Johnson, M. C., *Education in Mexico* (1956)
Kelchner, W. H., *Latin American Relations with the League of Nations* (1930)
Kneller, G. F., *Education of the Mexican Nation* (1951)

Lewis, O., *Children of Sanchez: Autobiography of a Mexican Family* (1961)

——, *Life in a Mexican Village: Tepoztlan Reconsidered* (1951)

——, *Pedro Martínez, A Mexican Peasant and His Family* (1964)

Link, A. S., *Wilson: Confusion and Crises, 1915–1916* (1964)

López Mateos, A., *The Economic Development of Mexico during a Quarter of a Century, 1934–1959* (1959)

López y Fuentes, G., *El Indio* (various editions)

MacCorkle, S. A., *American Policy of Recognition Towards Mexico* (1933)

Madariaga, S. de, *The Eagle and the Bear* (1962)

Maddox, J. S., *Mexican Land Reform* (American Universities Field Staff—1957)

Maier, J. and R. W. Eatherhead, eds., *Politics of Change in Latin America* (1964)

Martin, P. A., *Latin America and the War* (1925)

Mayer, B., *Mexico As It Was and As It Is* (1944)

McBride, G. M., *Land Systems of Mexico* (1923)

McGavran, D. A., *Church Growth in Mexico* [Protestantism] (1963)

McNeeley, J. H., *The Railroads of Mexico: A Study in Nationalization* (1964)

Mecham, J. L., *Church and State in Latin America* (rev. ed., 1966)

Merrill, J. C., *Gringo: The American as Seen by Mexican Journalists* (1963)

Moore, W. E., *Industrialization and Labor: Social Aspects of Economic Development*, Chapters 9, 10, 11 (1951)

Morton, W. M., *Woman Suffrage in Mexico* (1962)

Mosk, S., *Industrial Revolution in Mexico* (1950)

Myers, B. S., *Mexican Painting in Our Time* (1957)

Myers, S. D., ed., *Mexico and the United States* (1938)

National Planning Association, *Sears Roebuck de Mexico* (1953)

Nicholson, H., *Dwight Morrow* (1935)

Orozco, J. C., *José Clemente Orozco: An Autobiography*, trans. R. C. Stephenson (1962)

Padgett, L. V., *The Mexican Political System* (1966)

Pan American Union, *Materiales para el Estudio de la Clase Media en la America Latina* (6 vols., 1950–1951)

Papers on Mexico and Central America (Eighth Conference of Rocky Mountain Council on Latin American Affairs, 1961)

Parkes, H. B., *History of Mexico* (3rd rev. ed., 1960)

Partido Nacional Revolucionario, *Mexican Government's Six Year Plan, 1934–1940* (1934)

Partido de la Revolucion Mexicana, *The Second Six Year Plan, 1941–1946* (1940)

Paz, Octavo, *An Anthology of Mexican Poetry* (1960)

——, *The Labrynth of Solitude: Life and Thought in Mexico* (1962)

Phipps, H., *Some Aspects of the Agrarian Question in Mexico* (1925)

Pike, F. B., *Conflict Between Church and State in Latin America* (1964)

Pinchon, E., *Zapata the Unconquerable* (1941)

Poleman, T. T., *The Papaloapan Project: Agricultural Development in the Mexican Tropics* (1964)

Potash, R. A., "Historiography of Mexico since 1921," *Hispanic American Historical Review*, XL (1960), 383–424

Powell, J. R., *The Mexican Petroleum Industry, 1938–1950* (1956)

Powelson, J. P., *Latin America: Today's Economic and Social Revolution* (1964)

Pozas, Juan, *The Chamula: An Ethnological Re-Creation of the Life of a Mexican Indian* (1962)

Priestley, H. I., *Mexican Nation* (1923)

Quirk, R. E., *Affair of Honor* (1964)

——, *The Mexican Revolution: 1914–1915* (1960)

————, *The Mexican Revolution and the Catholic Church* (1963)
Ramos, S., *Profile of Man and Culture in Mexico* (1962)
Read, J. L., *The Mexican Historical Novel, 1826–1910* (1939)
Reed, N., *The Caste War of Yucatan* (1964)
Reyes, A., *Mexico in a Nutshell* (1964)
Rice, Sister E. A., *Diplomatic Relations Between the United States and Mexico as Affected by the Struggle for Religious Liberty in Mexico, 1925–1929* (1959)
Rippy, J. F., *United States and Mexico* (rev. ed., 1931)
Rivera, D., and B. O. Wolf, *Portrait of Mexico* (1937)
Romanell, P., *Making of the Mexican Mind* (1952)
Ross, S., *Is the Mexican Revolution Dead?* (1965)
Ross, S. G. and J. B. Christenson, *Tax Incentives for Industry in Mexico* (1959)
Ross, S. R., *Francisco I. Madero* (1955) (1963)
Ruiz, R. E., *Mexico: The Challenge of Poverty and Illiteracy* (1963)
Rukeyser, M., trans., *Selected Poems of Octavo Paz*
Sanchez, G. I., *Mexico: A Revolution in Education* (1936)
Schmeckebier, L. E., *Modern Mexican Art* (1939)
Schmitt, K. M., *Communism in Mexico* (1965)
Scott, R. E., *Mexican Government in Transition* (1959)
Shafer, R. J., *Mexico: Mutual Adjustment Planning* (1966)
Sherman, W. L. and R. E. Greenleaf, *Victoriano Huerta: A Reappraisal* (1960)
Shipway, V. and W., *The Mexican House, Old and New* (1960)
Simpson, E. N., *The Ejido: Mexico's Way Out* (1937)
Simpson, L. B., *Many Mexicos* (3rd ed., 1952)
Smith, T. L., *Agrarian Reform in Latin America* (1965)
Spratling, W., *A Small Mexican World*, ed. L. B. Simpson (1964)
Stevenson, R., *Music in Mexico* (1952)
Stewart, V., *Forty-five Contemporary Mexican Artists* (1951)
Strode, H., *Timeless Mexico* (1944)
Tannenbaum, F., *The Mexican Agrarian Revolution* (1929)
————, *Mexico: The Struggle for Peace and Bread* (1950)
————, *Peace by Revolution* (1933)
Thord-Gray, I., *Gringo Rebels (Mexico, 1913–1914)* (1960)
Toor, F., *A Treasury of Mexican Folkways* (1947)
Townsend, W. C., *Lazaro Cárdenas: Mexican Democrat* (1952)
Tucker, W. P., *The Mexican Government Today* (1957)
Turlington, E., *Mexico and Her Foreign Creditors* (1930)
United Nations . . . , *The Population of Central America (Including Mexico), 1950–1980* (1954)
United States, Department of Commerce, Bureau of Foreign Commerce, *Investments in Mexico—Conditions and Outlook* (1956)
Verissimo, E., *Mexico* (1960)
Vernon, R., *Dilemma of Mexico's Development* (1963)
————, *Public Policy and Private Enterprise in Mexico* (1964)
Weyl, N. and S., *The Reconquest of Mexico, the Years of Lazaro Cárdenas* (1939)
Whetten, N., *Rural Mexico* (1948)
Whitaker, A. P., ed., *Mexico Today*, in *Annals of American Academy of Political and Social Sciences*, No. 208 (1940)
Wilgus, A. C., ed., *Carribbean: Mexico Today* (1964)
————, ed., *The Caribbean at Mid-Century* (1951)
Wionczeh, M. S., *Public Policy and Private Enterprise in Mexico* (1964)
Wood, B., *Making of the Good Neighbor Policy* (1961)
Zea, L., *Culture and Man of Our Times* (1959)

Chapter **30**

Modern Brazilian Politics:
Regionalism Versus Unity

TWENTIETH CENTURY BRAZIL, LAND OF THE FUTURE

I hear all Brazil singing, humming, calling, shouting!
Hammocks swaying,
Whistles blowing
Factories grinding, pounding, panting, screaming
   howling and snoring,
Cylinders exploding,
Cranes revolving,
Wheels turning,
Rails trembling,
Noises of foothills and plateaus, cattle bells, neighings,
   cowboy songs, and lowings,
Chiming of bells, bursting of rockets, Ouro Preto, Baía,
   Congonhas, Sabará,
Clamor of stock-exchanges shrieking numbers like parrots,
Tumult of streets that seethe beneath the skyscrapers,
Voices of all the races that the wind of the seaports
   tosses into the jungle! . . .
But what I hear above all. . . .
Is the song of thy cradles, Brazil, of all thy cradles, in
   which there sleeps, mouth dripping with milk, dusky,
   trusting,
The Man of Tomorrow! [1]

[1] Translated in Dudley Fitts, ed., *Anthology of Contemporary Latin American Poetry*. Copyright 1942 and 1947 by New Directions. Reprinted by permission of New Directions.

Rio from the Sugarloaf cable car, in the mist of early morning. *Photo by Helen Miller Bailey.*

So wrote Ronald de Carvalho (1893–1935), a Brazilian diplomat and writer, who in the 1930s envisaged a Brazil of the future, a country of great industrial potential, of vast natural resources, of mixed peoples and a democratic basis. Political developments from the fall of the empire in 1889 to the second half of the twentieth century sometimes encouraged that future, sometimes retarded it. That the land itself and the people who lived on it had that future there was no doubt as Brazil approached the last quarter of the twentieth century.

THE STRUGGLING YOUNG REPUBLIC

The old emperor, the remarkable Pedro II, had been forced to abdicate in the autumn of 1889. The empire was overthrown without a struggle and practically without bloodshed. The new government was engineered by the army leaders, the former slave owners, and the liberal-minded Republicans. In the new Republic of Brazil the European immigration and the coffee and rubber booms which were started under Pedro II continued and, although the government was often chaotic, the modernization of Brazil went ahead apace. In fact, the Republic was a reflection of the shift in economic weight from the sugar of the north to the coffee of the south with its need for free immigrant laborers. The republican *coup d'état* was followed by fifteen months of confusing provisional rule and then by a period of military-dominated governments. The military was supported by an oligarchy of the wealthy landowners. The sincere and likeable Deodoro da Fonseca, general and former loyal friend of Pedro II, found himself in charge of the new republic on November 16, 1889. His first decree was to create the United States of Brazil, a federal republic. Then he set up a commission of five to prepare a draft for a constitutional convention, secured recognition of his regime by foreign powers, and kept peace under martial law until the constitution was written fourteen months later.

The new constitution, modeled somewhat after the imperial constitution of 1824 and somewhat after the federal plan of the United States, was adopted in 1891. It provided for the twenty states that had existed under the empire, with Rio de Janeiro in a federal district, and a new federal district mapped out on the Goiás plateau. The constitution granted central powers to the federal government, including rights to intervene in the states. The states had many self-governing rights, however, but these rights have often been violated by powerful presidents. Election of the president and the federal congress was to be by a direct majority of all males who could read and write, perhaps ten per cent of the population at the time. The Senate was to represent the states; the Chamber of Deputies was to be chosen on a basis of population; Church and state were to be separated and all religions tolerated.

The fine constitution did not bring stability to the new republic. Deodoro himself—for modern Brazilians call their politicians by their first names—was elected first president with General Floriano Peixoto, a cold, efficient military man, as vice-president. Within six months of the election Floriano's army officers were quarreling with the new civilian congress and with Deodoro himself. When the President acted arbitrarily and sent congress home, revolts in favor of the congressmen broke out in the provinces. Deodoro himself sadly resigned, blaming "the ingratitude of those for whom I sacrificed myself," and turned the government over to Floriano, giving way to a military dictatorship less than two years after the Republicans had so hopefully taken over the country. This was a testing time for the survival of the new republic, while military *caudilhismo* overweighed civilian control at the same time that finances were in a state of chaos.

As might be expected, there was soon widespread revolt against the cold Floriano because of his praetorian regime, his intervention in the states, and the bad state of his finances. This time the fight turned into another navy-versus-army siege. The gauchos of Rio Grande do Sul, some still loyal to Pedro II, were on the side of the dissatisfied and neglected navy; Rio city was on the side of the army and the president. The navy and merchant fleet revolted on September 3, 1893, and attempted to close Rio harbor and keep supplies out of the city; foreign warships came to the city's aid, and it was the sailors, not the city dwellers, who almost starved without supplies. The fleet finally escaped south to join the Rio Grande ranchers and to fight there in a last effort to restore the monarchy in June 1894. Defeated by soldiers from São Paulo, the rebels escaped into Uruguay; the republic was destined to survive under civilian rule.

The whole affair had consolidated the majority of Brazilians behind the President. He was allowed to serve out his term in peace, and give way in

1894 via a peaceful election to a distinguished civilian lawyer from São Paulo, Dr. Prudente José de Moraes Barros. But the treasury was empty, and the army officers, though successful against the monarchist navy, were jealous of the new civilian leaders and determined to embarrass them if possible by accusing them of monarchist sympathies. They found an excuse for such accusation in Brazil's outer fringes to the north.

The *sertão*, that region of the northeast in Ceará, in behind Baía and Pernambuco, had gone through drought after drought. Among the poor farmers of the region a mentally unbalanced religious fanatic named Antônio Maciel, called Antônio the Counselor, began to preach against all organized authority. He wandered from town to town urging "sinners" to join him and his throng of ragged believers. Expelled from the settled coastal area, he took his followers, now numbering in the thousands, to the far western edge of the state of Baía where he set up a religious state which he named Canudos. Thousands of huts were built; the frenzied population did just enough farming to feed themselves, and they augmented their colony by means of forays along the coast for food, livestock, and new converts. Their destructive raids produced just the scandal the military leaders and been looking for. They persuaded the people in Rio that Canudos was a dangerous antirepublican movement. Division after division of federal troops were sent over the foot trails of the dry *sertão* to "conquer" Canudos, but the city-bred soldiers died from lack of water or were picked off by guerrillas. Finally artillery was hauled in by oxen, siege laid to the straw and adobe town, and the religious leader killed in the siege. Canudos had held out more than a year until nearly every defender had died. When the handful of survivors surrendered, starved and pitiful, the Rio military leaders looked absurd. How could these ragged back-countrymen have been a menace to the republican government, a secret conspiracy to restore the monarchy? Today the incident is looked upon as an heroic event in Brazilian history; Antônio the Counselor is a sort of poor man's hero. The only good that came out of the episode is Euclides da Cunha's greatest of Brazilian regional studies, *Os Sertões*, translated into English under the title *Rebellion in the Backlands*. From the point of view of economic history, Canudos belongs to a long series of events leading to the opening of the interior. The incident, together with the dastardly attempt on the life of the president in 1897, brought to a close an era marred by the twin evils of factionalism and militarism.

AN ERA OF PEACE AND DEVELOPMENT

The year 1898 ushered in a dozen years of reconstruction and progress, the longest period of comparative peace and undisturbed material prosperity since the abdication of Dom Pedro. "King Coffee" was bringing wealth and political power to planters in São Paulo. Mining and industrialization made Minas Gerais almost equally powerful. As a result of this balanced equation, Brazilian politics under the republic began to revolve on the axis of "São Paulo versus Minas Gerais." Between 1898 and 1914 the peculiarities of national politics faded away before the economic and social changes to be discussed in the next chapter.

Factionalism and militarism as the controlling influences in Brazilian politics had lost ground. The next three presidential terms were devoted to peacetime developments. The first of these presidents was Manóel Ferraz de Campos Salles of São Paulo, under whose administration (1898–1902) finance-minded leaders negotiated loans in Europe to fund the national debt caused by the revolts and the debacle at Canudos. The national credit was stabilized through an increased tariff and economies in government spending. In 1902 Francisco de Paula Rodrígues Alves, a capable, well-equipped civilian *Paulista*, was elected to the presidency in an uneventful contest. Energetic and scientific-minded, he has been called Brazil's most able civilian leader; he is famous for beautifying Rio, developing natural resources, building railroads. It was in his regime that the world renowned scientist Dr. Oswaldo Cruz was given full government support to rid Rio of the yellow fever, as described in the next chapter. In 1906 a *Mineiro*, Affonso Augusto Moreira Penna, continued both the civilian rule and great material progress.

Baron Rio Branco, son of the author of the antislavery law, was appointed as minister of foreign affairs by Rodrígues Alves in 1902 and served under four administrations until his death in 1912. With increased Brazilian prestige and strengthened continental solidarity as his objectives, Rio Branco became one of the best-known Brazilians abroad and made Brazil a leader in peace movements at the Hague and at Pan American meetings. The third Pan American conference was held in Rio in 1906 and the American Secretary of State attended personally. The foreign service was reorganized and strengthened, and in 1905 Brazil obtained the first cardinalate in South America. Twenty-nine different arbitration treaties were negotiated during Rio Branco's years of service. In some of these treaties he acted as arbitrator; in others he represented Brazil or negotiated settlements of boundaries long disputed with her neighbors—the border with Argentina's Misiones territory and the boundaries with Holland, England, and France in the Guianas. Bolivia, fronting on the southwest in a little-known region of wild rubber trees, claimed a section of the Amazon drainage basin called Acre and revolts occurred there; Rio Branco negotiated the Treaty of Petropolis in 1903 which gave this area to Brazil. Rio Branco guaranteed to build Bolivia a railroad from her border around a falls and out to a navigable Amazon tributary, the Madeira; a route at long last made available by highway construction in 1967.

FACTIONALISM THROUGH WORLD WAR I

The presidency continued to be shuttled back and forth between *Paulistas and Mineiros,* until death of the *Mineiro* president in 1909 interrupted the pattern, although his vice-president served out his term to 1910. Brazilian politics were dominated by regional loyalties; there were no political parties as such, and each outgoing president had been able to pick his successor. Now in 1910 two groups each held nominating conventions, unprecedented in Brazilian history. Actually they were still regional groups and their party strife ushered in another era of *caudilhismo* versus republicanism which lasted more than two decades. One of these 1910 parties, backed by the vice-president, was dominated by a local *caudilho* from the cowboy country of Rio Grande do Sul, a sports-loving, hard-riding cattle rancher named Pinheiro Machado, who had bossed politics in the south for fifteen years. His convention chose Hermes da Fonseca, military leader who bore the magic name of his revered uncle and first president, Deodoro. São Paulo, Minas Gerais, and Baía boycotted this convention and called another one, nominating the publicist and former popular finance minister Ruy Barbosa, who had written much of the 1891 constitution. There followed a spirited campaign with all the fanfare of party politics.

After seventy-four days of vote-checking by congress, Hermes da Fonseca was declared elected, in spite of protests of fraudulent balloting. With Pinheiro and the southern cattle barons bossing the job, and with other regions fiercely opposing him on the basis of local loyalties, Hermes served to 1914. He was a decided retrogression from the caliber of presidents Brazil had had since 1898, and brought corruption, inflation, and military control into the saddle. True, economic gains had been made by the whole nation, the valorization of coffee described in the next chapter had been attempted as a price-control system, and immigration had poured in from Europe, but the coffee price scheme failed in the long run as did the attempt to boost the rubber market in the face of the new Far Eastern competition. World War I, which came just as Hermes' presidency ended, had repercussions for Brazil both in the trade of these commodities and in politics.

World War I is of greater importance in Brazilian history than in that of any other Latin American nation, for Brazil is the only one actually to participate in it, and her participation brought her into world affairs. The war coincides with the presidency of Wenceslau Braz, a *Mineiro* and a great improvement over Hermes. In this semicolonial country, dependent on world prices for the sale of her raw materials, restrictions on international trade in the first two years of the war almost brought economic disaster. After 1916 the situation began to improve as the Allies purchased more food and raw materials, and Brazilians were exporting other things besides coffee and rubber. Actually, the later years of the war brought a brief boom in Amazon rubber also.

Always sympathetic to the Allied cause, even through the first months of declared neutrality, the Brazilian people enthusiastically espoused the cause of the Allies when Italy joined them, for São Paulo had grown to be practically a city of Italian ancestry owing to the immigration of Italian coffee workers. Finally in April 1917, shortly after the United States entered the war, Brazil severed relations with Germany. Forty-six German ships interned in Brazilian waters were leased to the Allies. When German submarines continued to sink Brazilian shipping, an actual declaration of war was made on October 26, 1917. Some aviators and some medical units were sent to the European front; the Brazilian navy was active in patrolling the South Atlantic. More important was the increase in the production of foodstuffs—beans, refrigerated beef, and sugar flowed out from Brazil into Allied storehouses.

This new emphasis on more diversified agricultural staples was a good thing for Brazil at home. She was also forced to start making some manufactured articles locally when she could no longer get them from Europe, and a healthy new industrialization began. Politically, the current president, Wenceslau Braz, had to act under martial law to control the large sections of German population in Rio Grande do Sul, Paraná, and Santa Catarina. German newspapers were suppressed and some 700 Germans were interned; German businesses were taken over by the government. The German population remained more loyal than had been expected, however, and no serious trouble broke out. Conscription was enacted on a nationwide basis; young Brazilians from the provinces came to Rio for military training. In general, World War I served as a unifying force in the regional-minded Brazilian nation.

Equally important was the new attitude in Brazil toward world affairs. As a belligerent she was invited to the peace conference, was able to keep some of the requisitioned ships, received pay from Germany for confiscated shipments of coffee, and won some prestige at the peace conference by insisting on these points. Since the United States did not join the League of Nations, Brazil was the leading American nation in League affairs, and worked closely with the powers of Europe in the restoration of peace and order. However, her seat on the League Council was not considered one of the permanent ones, and when Brazil was refused such a permanent seat after the Locarno settlement, she left the League of Nations in protest.

Four days after the Armistice, the popular Rodrígues Alves had been elected again, the first president in Brazilian history to serve a second term. However, the splendid old financial expert was dead within a year, and by that time Brazil was beginning to face a postwar slack. The whole era of 1918 to 1930 was to be one of politico-military intrigue and revolutionary ferment. Industrial growth and labor unrest were to produce economic political conflicts leading to a complete revolution under Vargas in 1930. Meanwhile, regional conflict continued. São Paulo and Minas Gerais had rotated the presidency between the politicians of their two states for so long that other states had little chance. Unexpectedly the small northern province of Paraíba won the interim election with the compromise choice of its leader, Epitácio da Silva Pessôa, an earnest progressive interested in public works, who served out Rodrígues Alves' term as the postwar slump worsened.

São Paulo was not to let the leadership of a small state go unchallenged. When *Paulistas* tried to resume control of the central government in time for the election of 1922, they found opposition from the rancher leaders of Rio Grande, from the mine workers of Minas, and from the army officers who opposed the civilian cabinet members Silva Pessôa had put in charge of the military. The election campaign which followed was filled with recriminations, stories of forged letters, and open rebellion in the military camps. Behind all this fraudulence and armed revolt was Hermes da Fonseca, who tried for years to be the "kingmaker" in Brazilian politics. A *Mineiro*, Arthur da Silva Bernardes, won the election, while the price of coffee sank and São Paulo resorted to an open revolt, a costly affair which had to be put down in 1924 with federal troops. Without funds in the worldwide slump, Bernardes had to stop the public works begun by his predecessor. Meanwhile depression on the coffee plantations was reflected by unemployment in the city. For the first time, the inarticulate workers and immigrant agricultural tenants found a spokesman in the frankly left-wing, Moscow-oriented Luiz Carlos Prestes, a rabble-rouser who made a two-year trek of the *sertão* and organized many party cells in restless Brazil. His cells were broken up by federal police and he was exiled to Argentina, but he reappeared in Brazilian affairs to harrass the government for decades.

São Paulo won the ascendency again with the election of 1926, which— true to the rotation plan—went to a *Paulista*. Washington Luiz Pereira da Souza, whose election was uneventful and unchallenged, was a former governor of São Paulo state, a rich coffee planter with the "coffee first" philosophy of the *Paulistas*. In spite of his efforts to keep the price up, to the neglect of many other economic problems in Brazil, coffee continued its downhill slide, as the whole world plunged into the depression of the 1930s. Washington Luiz could do little to stem the tide of dissatisfaction when he could not even help his own backers, the coffee planters. World depression left the one-crop regions of Brazil helpless. The landowning system was still feudal, labor in city and country was destitute and illiterate, and commerce and finance were foreign-controlled and dependent on the outside world which was rapidly going to pieces financially. Brazil was ripe for a change in politics and leadership, and the only successful revolution in the history of the republic took place in 1930.

THE ERA OF VARGAS

From 1889 to 1930 the Republic of Brazil had gone through an era of military dictatorship, an era of prosperity under civilian presidents coming alternately from São Paulo and Minas Gerais, and now an era of economic depression. Political parties as such hardly existed, in spite of occasional nominating conventions. Each state had its own political machine, run by rubber kings or coffee planters or rich mine owners or sugar barons or cattle ranchers as the case might be, but always a small, closed oligarchy. The people themselves had little part in any of them. In the fifteen weaker and smaller states there was little interest in the federal government. In the five big states, few participated in the elections, either for federal or for local officials. Regional rivalries dominated politics in the capital; the governors of each state were *caudilhos* at home and strong powers in Rio when the president came from their region.

Washington Luiz, leaving office in 1930, had the chance, as was the custom for outgoing presidents, to "suggest" his successor, provided he, a

Paulista, chose a *Mineiro.* His mistake was that he chose instead the governor of São Paulo, Júlio Prestes. This action threw the politicians of Minas Gerais into the camp of the ambitious leaders in Rio Grande do Sul who had been hoping for a chance at the presidency. Liberals and even radicals of Luiz Carlos Prestes' "cells" joined the Rio Grande group to oppose Washington Luiz' pro-planter regime; army men also threw their weight toward Rio Grande in opposition to Washington Luiz' policy of ignoring the army in politics. All these factions formed a new liberal alliance, which proclaimed a reform program. The alliance sounded two mottoes: "no choice of a president by his successor" and "attention to other crops and to industry equal to that given coffee." Its members wanted protection of industry, compulsory and secret voting, and public education for the children of laborers. The man on whom all concentrated to defeat the *Paulista* was Getúlio Vargas, a lawyer and a cattle rancher from the pampas of South Brazil. When the election returns showed a majority for the *Paulistas,* the self-confident Júlio Prestes took a tour of the United States as president-elect, while economic disorder continued at home, coffee prices fell to the bottom, further foreign loans were refused, and many planters were ruined. The succession of *Paulista* presidents was blamed. The election of 1930 brought the social and political discontent into full force.

João Pessôa in the north, Oswaldo Aranha, a leader in Rio Grande affairs, and many *Mineiros* entered into a plot to put Vargas into power. Completely in control of a "revolution" to make him president in Rio Grande, Vargas began a triumphant march north; cities along the way welcomed him as "conquering hero and liberator." There was little military resistance. In Rio a handful of generals brought the army to Vargas' side. Only outgoing president Washington Luiz opposed, and he was held in prison till his legal term of office was over a month later, then sent to Europe in exile. On November 3, 1930, Vargas entered Rio as the provisional president.

The year 1930 marked a turning point in Brazilian history as dramatic as the change from empire to republic had been. Politically, the easygoing federalism of the old republic succumbed to a powerful trend toward centralism and executive domination. Economically, the drive for diversification and industrialization had almost swept coffee from its lofty perch while mining and manufacturing made tremendous gains. Socially, the neglected laboring classes were to find in Vargas a champion whose coming had been long delayed.

This champion, Getúlio Vargas, was born in 1883 on a large cattle ranch on the Rio Grande do Sul frontier, where he worked with the gauchos on his father's estates. As a boy "he grew up with a lasso in his hands and a horse between his knees." Enemies were to say that he still used the lasso a half century later, but that Brazil, not the horse, was then between his knees. After a turn in the army, he took a law course and then founded a newspaper in Porto Alegre. Soon he was in state politics and was serving in the legislature, but he maintained his army officer's status and rose to the rank of lieutenant colonel through participation in the recurring revolts in volatile Rio Grande. By 1926 he was federal minister of finance in Rio

Getúlio Vargas, World War II dictator of Brazil. *Courtesy Pan American Union.*

de Janeiro, then governor of Rio Grande do Sul state, a meteoric rise for such a small, unassuming man of friendly word and ready smile. After his inauguration in 1930 he posed as the "poor man's president," living simply as a devoted family man, keeping up with his love of horses and riding, but working sixteen hours a day at the presidency and expecting his advisers to do likewise. Interested in the study of the English language and of American business methods, he became a warm friend to the United States in spite of some flirtation with the Axis. As a politician he was clever and shrewd, playing state against state and group against group and holding no grudges. During the fifteen years of power in his first "reign," he was untouched by scandal. He was unassuming, tolerant, and modest; most Brazilians thought of him as "our Getúlio."

Politically, Vargas kept control of the situation and survived from one four-year period to the next. From 1930 to 1934 he was called "interim or provisional president" and was given dictatorial powers. He had dissolved congress and the state and local legislative bodies and had changed the government officials in all the states, an action which comprised a ruthless and complete purge of the old aristocratic elements on which the blame for Brazil's economic ills was laid. Though his rule under these "abnormal conditions" was completely autocratic, he meant to broaden the economic and political base of Brazil. He inaugurated a sort of New Deal, helping agriculture by limiting sugar and coffee and encouraging diversified crops like grain, citrus fruits, and silk. He particularly tried to bring crop improvement into the drought-ridden northeast. He helped manufacturers by setting up an international protective tariff while at the same time encouraging commerce by abolishing interstate tariffs and state export taxes—a step taken in the United States in 1787. He instituted exchange controls. His supporters among the laborers received minimum wage and child welfare laws. However, all civil rights had been suspended. In São Paulo the friends of Júlio Prestes, the legally elected president, staged a serious armed revolt, a last stand for states rights and the old aristocracy, which lasted three months and had to be crushed by hard-fighting federals.

Under pressure about the São Paulo revolt, Vargas called a constitutional convention in May 3, 1933; most of the members of this convention were elected by secret ballot cast by all literate men, and by women as well, while a small portion of the delegates were chosen by labor, trade, and professional organizations. The constitution, which was produced in 1934—the first Brazilian constitution since the early days of the republic in 1891—gave the president and the central government wide economic powers in an effort to solve the depression. The legislature was to have specific representation from industries and professions. Subsoil resources were to belong to the nation; the federal government was authorized to regulate and control the mines, to form national corporations in various industries, and to own banks and insurance companies. Various social measures were incorporated into the constitution. A president was to be elected by a direct secret ballot, to serve for four years, but not be eligible for immediate re-election. Dom Getúlio's friends had helped make the constitution; he was legally elected to the presidency by its authority and inaugurated for his first actual "term" on July 20, 1934.

Now began Vargas' period of constitutional government. Under his increased national intervention and control over industry, the country slowly recovered from the depression. Coffee went up in price; the Amazon Valley was opened to development. Steel plants were built and road and railroad mileage increased. A reciprocal trade treaty was made with the United States in 1935. Such activity took up most of Dom Getúlio's time, and he allowed the growth of radicalism and fascism to become pressing problems. Luiz Carlos Prestes, the Communist leader, staged a revolt which Vargas crushed in 1935. The far right gave him more trouble than the far left, however. Hitler had come to power in Germany; Mussolini worked on the loyalties of the thousands of Italians in Brazil and a noisy "Young Fascist" group called the Green Shirts, or the *Integralistas*, entered politics.

As these four constitutional years began to approach their end, Vargas felt himself destined to stay in power. Using the dangers of uprisings on both left and right as his excuse, he staged a *coup d'état* against the 1934 Constitution and made himself again the dictator on November 10, 1937. Anxious to remain "constitutional," he announced the new Constitution of 1937. This one set up "the corporate state of Brazil," the *Estado Novo*, supported by the army. Under it Vargas could rule by decree through a National Economic Council. Gone from it were all pretenses at parliamentary liberalism and representative government. Dom Getúlio took over education from state and local authority; he censored the press, banished labor conflicts through the creation of government-controlled labor syndicates, abolished political parties.

In short, the *Estado Novo* was a dictator-controlled, planned economy, an economic nationalism, with executive centralization which aimed at an integrated society under a personalized control. Vargas had promised to subject this constitution to approval by national plebiscite. While he delayed, the green-shirted *Integralistas*, still unjailed, got out of hand again. A group of these German-financed young men tried to take the Guanabara Palace, Brazil's White House, in May 1938. Getúlio and his daughter fired shots into the intruders from behind the curtains of the reception room. The assassination plot was thus foiled by Getúlio personally, the *Integralistas* were jailed or banished, and the German influence in Brazilian politics brought to an abrupt end. The incident more than ever endeared "our Getúlio" to the masses, and he never felt the pressure to put the *Estado Novo* to a plebiscite. He maintained his "amiable despotism" and called his rule a "disciplined democracy." His rule was by decree as there was no congress and there were no elections. "Don't speak; Getúlio will do it for you; don't think—the DIP [the propaganda bureau] will do it for you."

Though the Brazilian people paid this price of dictatorship, they gained in economic progress and a higher living standard. The three years between the *Estado Novo* and Pearl Harbor were years of progress and development for Brazil, especially in industrialization. A National Economic Council, a Five Year Plan of 1940, and a central education ministry all helped Vargas improve as well as control his country. The decade of 1930 to 1940 saw the number of children in secondary school increase from 60,000 to 300,000. The number of elementary school buildings throughout the country was exactly doubled. Road mileage was increased 100 per cent, airports multiplied tenfold. The Volta Redonda plan for steel production, the São Francisco Valley Authority described in the next chapter, the search for petroleum, the drought control in Ceará, the system of coffee quotas—all these were once little ideas in Vargas' own head, worked out by his able henchmen. Labor had him to thank for an eight-hour day and a minimum wage (even though he forbade labor unions to organize) and for vocational and technical education. Poor farmers thanked him for opening up the frontier to free settlement. Poor city dwellers thanked him for new housing projects and for workers' restaurants where cheap food was served in balanced rations. The whole program of the *Estado Novo* was a gigantic public welfare plan imposed from the top like Mussolini's prewar projects in Italy. Undoubtedly he raised the standard of living and brought greater national unity. Brazilians had been accustomed to say first, "I am a *Paulista*, I am a *Mineiro*, I am a *Baiano*"; during the epoch of Dom Getúlio they learned to say on first thought, "I am a Brazilian," and to think of their region only secondarily.

Meanwhile the world and the German element in Brazil were still being wooed by the powerful Nazi propaganda machine. The large Italian population was also a target after Hitler's alliance with Mussolini. To help ease the depression, Vargas had undertaken barter trade agreements with the Germans in 1934, and became deeply involved as Hitler tried to control the world coffee market. Plínio Salgado's *integralista* putsch was the last straw. When Vargas realized how the trade agreements were being broken by the Nazis, he asked the German ambassador to leave. He outlawed the German language press and clubs, proclaimed Portuguese as the only language to be taught in all Brazilian elementary schools, and made a reciprocal trade treaty with the United States to bolster the economy which Hitler's program had depressed—all this in 1937–1938, two years before Europe went to war. In addition, Hitler's increasing racial discrimination angered the easygoing and racially tolerant Brazilians. They turned more and more toward the United States.

The United States was attacked by the Axis on December 7, 1941; Brazil declared "continental solidarity" on December 8, froze Axis funds on the 9th, and suspended pro-Axis newspapers on the 13th. January of 1942 brought Brazilian leadership in the Rio conference to defend the Western Hemisphere, and by August 22 Brazil was openly at war. In the early years Brazil's help was of great importance to the Allied cause, for the route to Africa from the bulge of Brazil at Natal was the one free step to North Africa and Mediterranean Europe until 1943. The United States Fourth Fleet was based at Recife, while Brazilian aviators and naval men were trained by American officers for the defense of the Hemisphere. The Brazilian navy helped in patrolling the South Atlantic and in convoy duty. A Brazilian infantry force fought under Mark Clark in Italy in 1944, the only Latin American land forces to fight abroad in World War II. Meanwhile raw materials—rubber, mica, beryllium, quartz, iron ore, copra, vegetable oils, and foodstuffs—poured from Brazil into the Allied coffers. The United States rather than Europe became the center of Brazilian diplomatic and cultural interest. Brazil's war efforts can be expressed in concrete terms—strategic bases, air forces in the North African campaign, soldiers in Europe, war materials for defense plants, strict control of Axis propaganda and seizure of Axis properties at home in Brazil. The great demand for Brazilian goods brought unprecedented prosperity and seemed completely to vindicate Vargas' economic dictatorship, though the war had brought inflation, an active black market, and a great deal of "profiteering."

From 1930 to 1945 Dom Getúlio so dominated the political scene that few other leaders stand out. However, with Brazil so active in World War II and in the United Nations affairs which followed, the Secretary of Foreign Affairs became a world figure, also; he was Oswaldo Aranha, that old friend of Getúlio's from Rio Grande. As a thinker and statesman he was ahead of his fellow gaucho. He had studied for three years in Paris as a youth but had returned to fight in the endless rebellions of Rio Grande. From local leadership he came to Rio with Vargas. As ambassador to the United States he had been called "the most popular Latin American ambassador who was ever in Washington," "the essential link between Brazil and North America." After World War II he became a leader in the United Nations Security Council.

Minister of War under Vargas was Eurico Gaspar Dutra, a quiet army man born in Cuibá, a town in Mato Grosso. He worked behind the scenes, holding the army together in support of Vargas. The world was surprised in February, 1945, to read that " our Getúlio," that permanent president, was at home on his ranch in Rio Grande, a retired farmer, and that this quiet Eurico Gaspar Dutra was suddenly president of Brazil. Vargas himself had been well aware of the criticism against his dictatorial methods, and had begun as early as 1943 to promise postwar elections. With the war in Europe almost won, Vargas announced in February 1945 that he would retire before the end' of the year. Behind this action was the pressure of the army, which feared another Vargas *coup d'état*, and took over the government in October 1945. Vargas then returned to his home in Rio Grande and successfully ran for the senate. Dutra had already been announced as the army's candidate; in the elections held December 2, he won and was inaugurated January 31, 1946, the first inauguration of a popularly elected president since 1926.

THE POST-WORLD WAR II PERIOD

The mediocre Dutra took over peacefully and promised to sweep away the fascist overtones of Vargas' regime, to restore the rights of states, to call a new constitutional convention, and to cooperate with the United States. The constitution written in 1946 was essentially conservative. It provided for a five-year presidency with never a second term, made the legislature a real law-making body, reasserted the local direct election of state governors who had all been appointed by Vargas in recent years, and granted individual rights and guarantees. At the same time it assured the continuation of Vargas' social and economic reforms. The quiet, colorless, but strongly nationalistic Dutra made few other changes. His army party had little control in congress. Luiz Carlos Prestes' Communists, free now of wartime censorship, had 10 per cent of the assembly seats, but were later outlawed. In the senate, Dom Getúlio himself now sat for Rio Grande as a Labor Party senator, endeavoring to embarrass the administration. Nevertheless, Dutra served as president till 1950, in a world trying to control inflation and reconstruct itself after World War II. During his term economic nationalism and promotion of industrialization continued and business leaders became powerful in the government. Nationally controlled TVA-type development plans were begun, and railroads and highways built, though the lower classes felt increasing hard times under inflation.

Two candidates emerged at the close of Dutra's term, an army man and a lawyer from Minas Gerais. There were no national issues and, save for local squabbles, there was little to choose between the two. Suddenly "our Getúlio" emerged as the candidate of the new Labor Party, supposedly an unwilling candidate answering an irresistible popular demand. He spoke to crowds, making sweeping promises to better economic conditions and appealing to the masses. With no other issue save who was the most popular and colorful personality, the elections of October 3, 1950, brought Vargas back to the presidency, his first actual election by a free democratic choice in open competition. Members of his new Labor Party were not all elected to the congress, however, and Vargas was forced to use a more conciliatory spirit in governing in this second session than he had in his fifteen years as dictator. Getúlio's own education, welfare, and health programs had so improved Brazil that political democracy was the next logical step. But Vargas was not his old self—he was older and in ill health; he did not choose able men, and graft and corruption surrounded him. Brazil was itself different in outlook, for political and economic nationalism was much stronger than in Vargas' earlier years. The army acquiesced in Vargas' election but later opposed him in his new reforms and his concessions to labor.

Vargas pledged himself to a policy of continental solidarity and cooperation with the United States to get loans. His chief domestic policies were the further industrialization and development of natural resources in Brazil. He hoped to integrate the Amazon region in the national economy and to extend social and other benefits to labor. But those policies required money and technical training while the financial condition of Brazil was deteriorating sadly. Clearly Vargas was unable to solve Brazil's economic problems, and discontent mounted.

Vargas had been elected president for the second time at what seemed on the surface a time of great expansion and prosperity. Coffee prices had been stabilized and profits were pouring into São Paulo in the 1950s. Vargas returned to the presidency in a Brazil with a great future, and with new middle-class consciousness of that future. A "deal" with the governor of São Paulo had necessitated his taking as his vice-president João Café Filho, an editor from northern Brazil. The two of them faced a five-year term and a challenge to stop Brazil's serious inflation and the general leniency among Brazilians toward gradual Communist infiltration.

Vargas did not stop the inflation. Two years after he had promised to reduce food prices, living costs had gone up another 30 per cent. In São Paulo 250,000 factory workers had staged hunger strikes. The price at which Vargas' economists pegged coffee almost drove it off the American market and reduced sales to the extent of $2 million deficit in overseas trade. Meanwhile, he quarreled with the army over appointments in the war ministry and over a controversial Minister of Labor who closed his eyes to a high-pressure Communist campaign among the dissatisfied workers. In the spring of 1954 army and conservative leaders were asking Vargas to resign.

Matters came to a head when supposedly pro-Vargas assassins attempted to take the life of a militantly anti-Vargas editor, Carlos Lacerda, whose paper was crusading to get Vargas out of office. Lacerda was injured in the foot, but an air force major talking with him in front of his home was killed. In air-minded Brazil, the army and the navy might be out of politics, but the air force is a strong power. Vargas' former political opponent, Brigadier Eduardo Gomes, headed a group asking Dom Getúlio to resign. Deputies in congress joined the military men; people in the streets carried signs saying "Down with Vargas."

Vargas seemed to scorn his opponents. Then on the last Tuesday in August 1954, more than a year before his five-year term was to expire, he called his cabinet into meeting shortly after midnight. Next morning he wrote out his resignation and shot himself. He left a note, "To the wrath of my enemies I leave the legacy of my death. I take the sorrow of not having been able to do for the humble all that I desired." The masses of Rio, if not the air force, mourned "Our Getúlio" in a sorrowful public funeral. In spite of his domination of Brazil for a quarter century, Dom Getúlio's dramatic death at the age of seventy-one did nothing to cure the inflation or to solve Brazil's other fundamental problems, domestic and international. However, he had laid the basis for a new and greater Brazil.

João Café Filho unwillingly and unhappily took over a restless nation. Knowing that the constitution forbade him to succeed himself, he set about restoring order. The congressional elections returned a right-of-center majority to congress; the price of coffee in the United States went down and Brazilian trade picked up. Honesty in government, exemplified by Café Filho's own simple personal life, seemed a new spirit in contrast to the corrupt last days of the Vargas regime. Café Filho, an even warmer friend of the United States than Getúlio had been in his last term, received economic help for his deflation plans in the form of large loans. But although he tried economy and austerity he could find no solution to the very urgent problem of inflation.

Meanwhile, politicking for the presidential elections of 1955 had been going on since 1953. By February 1955 there was a strong and active Social Democratic Party, which entered a three-candidate race and nominated the governor of Minas Gerais, a popular personality of Slavic immigrant ancestry named Juscelino Kubitschek, with controversial João Goulart as his vice-presidential candidate. Kubitschek proceeded to launch the biggest campaign in Brazilian history; on the slogans "Power, Transportation, and Food," he made 1,215 different speeches. In a fair but close election, held under tense conditions in which 10,000,000 Brazilians voted, the Social Democrats were elected by a 36 per cent plurality.

The Latin American tradition of bullets instead of ballots could not be so easily submerged, however. Army men were bitterly opposed to Kubitschek and threatened to prevent his inauguration. Then Café Filho had a heart attack and was unable to run the government in the interim. His Minister of War, Henrique Texeira Lott, took over the capital by force in the name of the constitution and the legal electoral mandate, and avoided a seizure of power by the dissatisfied army officers. Kubitschek, unworried by all this tension, took a pre-inauguration trip to the United States, thus preparing the way for greater friendliness and more loans to curb the rising inflation. When he was inaugurated, peacefully enough, at the end of January 1956, he had three major and two minor parties behind him and a coalition control of both houses of congress. A poor boy from Diamantina in the frontier, who worked as a telegraph operator to put himself through medical school, a Vargas man through years as mayor of Belo Horizonte, delegate to the Chamber of Deputies, and successful governor of the rapidly industrializing state of Minas Gerais, the personable and "Americanized" Kubitschek represented a new class of society in the presidency. His promise to "advance Brazil fifty years in a five-year term" could be carried out with a combination of his middle-class and labor supporters, and with the development of Brazil's great potentialities by larger foreign capital investment and government loans.

In his first year in office Kubitschek had control of the political situation, though he was pressed on one side by the army and on the other side by the restless labor unions led by João Goulart, his vice-president. Under his five-year plan of "Power, Transportation, and Food" development, Kubitschek wished to improve the "poorhouse northeast" and the interior. His special pet was the building of a new capital in a federal district in the uncleared bush on the Goiaz Plateau, a model city to be called Brasilia. The project was dear to his heart in spite of the heavy financial outlay it required during stringent times. He meant to complete building his city in three years and agreed to remain neutral in the 1960 campaign if the capital was officially moved to Brasilia by the date he set. On April 21, 1960, Kubitschek opened Congress in the new capital building in Brasilia, surrounded by plowed ground and uncleared brush. Many departments of government, including the diplomatic corps, stayed in Rio.

On the Hemisphere scene, Kubitschek became a Pan American leader by suggesting "Operation Pan Americana," a joint development with United States funds that would counteract the anti-Americanism evident when Vice-President Nixon visited South America in May 1958. His plan was to come to fruition in the Alliance for Progress.

But Brazil's chronic inflation and deficit spending threatened the country with bankruptcy, especially as raw materials and coffee entered a period of falling prices. Kubitschek attempted to offset the crisis by increasing production. He combatted the social and economic unrest by explaining to the people over the radio the causes of the rising cost of living. In his fourth annual state of the union message, he apologized for his inability to check the raging inflation, which had caused a 100 per cent rise in the cost of living since he became president. Industrialization and foreign investment were slowing down because of the lack of a sound agricultural base and the shortage of skilled laborers.

The bleak economic situation in Brazil was reflected in the rise of a new figure in the October 1958 congressional elections, Jânio Quadros. In 1959 Quadros announced his 1960 candidacy for the presidency. With interest in the election seething, economic difficulties unsolved, and Kubitschek constitutionally unable to succeed himself, old-line Communist leader Luiz Carlos Prestes said in March 1959 that the dangerous economic situation could cause Kubitschek's government to fall before the new election. However, Kubitschek remained personally very popular, and gave way legally when the newly elected Quadros was inaugurated with great ceremony at Brasilia in January 1961.

Jânio Quadros was brilliant but temperamental, a self-made man in São Paulo politics, with badly crossed eyes due to a childhood injury, and an unprepossessing appearance. His election symbol was "a new broom" to sweep Brazil clean of corruption. Accustomed to hard work and complete honesty on the job himself, he demanded these attitudes in those who worked under him. He had hoped to reorganize Brazil's lax civil service, cure inflation by price and wage controls, and stop the endless printing of paper money with which Kubitschek had tried to control the economy. Quadros' ideas of strict discipline on the part of government workers were not welcomed by João Goulart, Kubitschek's left-leaning labor minister, who, by the chance of Brazil's presidential election system, had become Quadros' vice-president. Goulart had no intentions of helping solve inflation by an austerity program, and went off on "economic and cultural mission," first to Moscow and then to Peking.

So Quadros struggled against odds to solve the rising discontent. Forty-three billion *cruzeiros* in unbacked paper money had been printed under Kubitschek. When Quadros ordered the printing stopped, a wave of strikes broke out in the industrial centers where living costs were far outrunning wages. In the northeast drought had hit five years in succession, and there were many cases of actual starvation. A "voice of the people," Francisco Julião, arose in the northeast; Julião organized peasant leagues, urging the farm tenants to take farmland away from the landlords by force. The influence of Cuba's Fidel Castro was strong, both among the landless peasants and the drought refugees, who poured into the city slums where living was expensive and jobs scarce. In the São Paulo coffee area, where there was no drought, bumper crops had brought a glut of coffee on to the world market. Coffee prices fell, bringing depression to São Paulo as well as to the northeast.

Quadros served as president for seven months during this economic chaos. Suddenly on August 25, 1961, he resigned and took a freight boat to England. Some Brazilians thought he had become mentally unstable. Others said he hoped that this dramatic move would force the public to accept his belt-tightening reforms and "woo" him back. The majority in congress were afraid of the leftist influence of Vice-president Goulart, who quickly returned from the Far East to take over the government. Officers in the powerful armed forces refused to accept him as president. In September 1961 a compromise was reached; congress passed a law establishing a Council of Ministers, composed of members of congress, its chairman to act as a prime minister. This was similar to the British cabinet system; under it Goulart would be a "limited monarch."

In spite of plans for financial help from the new Alliance for Progress —plans to be carried out in the distressed northeast under an agency called SUDENE—neither Goulart nor congress accomplished anything for the next two years, for they remained bogged down in a "parliamentary quagmire." No laws were passed. The value of the Brazilian *cruzeiro*, formerly worth twenty to the dollar, fell to 1,100 to the dollar, and then to 1,500 by the spring of 1964. Goulart did nothing to check the urban strikes and the rural revolt. When a group of enlisted men in the navy mutinied and staged a sit-down strike, their officers had them jailed. Goulart freed them and ordered them restored to their regular status. By this move, the president lost what little support he had had in the military.

Officers, businessmen, members of congress, local leaders in Rio, São Paulo, and Minas Gerais, all united in March of 1964 to overthrow Goulart. This was done in a bloodless "coup" backed by army units in Rio, São Paulo, and Paraná. Goulart fled to his ranch in Rio Grande do Sul, where he had acquired vast holdings during the thirty-one months of his presidency, perhaps with public money. His brother-in-law Leon Brizzoli, governor of Rio Grande do Sul, had angered Americans by confiscating the American Telephone Company there. Now both branches of the family fled into Uruguay, taking their fortunes with them and leaving their leftist supporters embarrassed and disillusioned.

The military officers persuaded the civilian congress to choose Army Chief of Staff General Humberto Castello Branco as interim president to serve out the term of Goulart until 1966. Castello Branco had been in charge of the Brazilian forces in Italy in World War II, but was comparatively unknown to civilians. The military forces behind him declared an *Ato Institucional*, or Act of Institution, on April 4, 1964, declaring "Revolution is a profound constitutional power." All measures advocated by this group which were not passed by Congress within thirty days were automatically to become law.

Evidently Castello Branco did not intend to create a military dictatorship, for he pushed a land reform bill through the landlord-controlled senate, making it legal for the government to pay for confiscated tracts of farm land with government bonds, rather than cash, and to distribute the land to needy tenants on a long-term credit basis. The activities of SUDENE, the irrigation and social improvement agency for the northeast, were increased, for American investors trusted Castello Branco to maintain stability. The Communist sympathizers Julião and Luiz Carlos Prestes were deprived of their rights to vote and participate in politics, as were 400 other politicians, including former leaders such as Kubitschek who were accused of having profited personally from public office. Meanwhile Castello Branco pushed 237 laws through congress in two years' time, improving the election system, equalizing tax collecting, and allocating federal funds to public secondary and college education.

Many Brazilians praised Castello Branco for having brought on a "real revolution." Perhaps he did avert a more violent one from the "left." However, local political leaders were not under the control of his government, now firmly based in the new Brasilia, and his supporters lost governorships and congressional seats in the elections held in ten of Brazil's twenty-two states in October 1965. Several of the winning governors were friends of Kubitschek, who returned to Brazil from a self-imposed exile. Carlos Lacerda, dynamic governor of Guanabara state, formerly the capital district of Rio de Janeiro city, also veered away from support of Castello Branco. Quickly Castello Branco issued a second *Ato Institucional*, actually an executive decree apart from any action of congress. He ordered Kubitschek back into exile, and threatened Jânio Quadros with a trial for graft during his presidency.

In 1964 there had been fourteen political parties in Brazil. After the 1965 election of anti-Castello governors, Castello Branco ordered that all parties which had not elected at least twelve state legislators in at least seven states would have to disband. This party reform left only two groups legally active, Castello Branco's own National Alliance for Renovation, or ARENA, and a "loyal opposition" called Brazilian Democratic Movement or MDB. ARENA had to assist in financing this synthetic opposition and "enroll" congressmen into it to make up a third of Congress' membership. Congressmen who would not join it were "suspended" from exercising their political rights.

Under this political set-up, Castello Branco "decreed" an election for September 3, 1966, to choose governors in the remaining twelve states.

ARENA governors won with little opposition. Next followed a "decree" for choice of a new president by Congress in a vote taken October 3, 1966. Castello Branco had always said he would retire in March of 1967. The hand picked candidate, another tough old soldier, Artur da Costa e Silva, was easily the winner. The outgoing president next decreed a new congressional election on November 22. With his ARENA friends and his approved MBD "opponents" neatly reelected, he turned Congress into a constituent assembly, sent it a new constitution, and had it accepted on January 22, 1967.

This new Brazilian constitution, together with a very strict control of the press by the presidency, changed the name from the United States of Brazil to simply Brazil, included a plan to put public employees on a tight civil service system, and provided for the collection of all taxes save those on property by the federal government and their reallocation to local units. The executive, to be chosen every four years by Congress, maintained the power to initiate all legislation concerning public finance and national security, to suspend civil rights for individuals, and to impose military law in a "state of siege" if necessary.

Such undemocratic and high-handed procedures were perhaps not all bad. Castello Branco himself issued a new unit of money, curbing inflation by stabilizing it at 2.20 to the dollar. He enforced a tough universal income tax law. He expropriated unused land from large estates dating from colonial times, and encouraged "homestead" type colonization. He could point with pride to the civilian activity of his army men; both officers and privates were building schools, teaching in them, launching road building and community sanitation campaigns. He sincerely did not consider himself a "military dictator," and felt that only his type of government could have slowed down inflation, controlled corruption, and brought economic order out of the chaos of the early 1960s. With the peaceful inauguration of Costa e Silva on March 15, 1967, Brazilians could look forward to four years of the same kind of rule. Meanwhile industrialization went rapidly ahead toward a Brazil of the 1970s.

"I hear all Brazil singing—factories grinding . . . cylinders exploding . . . wheels turning, rails trembling" said the poet of modern Brazil quoted at the head of this chapter. Loudest of all, the poet heard the voice from the cradle of the "Man of Tomorrow." There will be many men in this rich and industrialized Brazil of tomorrow. In 1830 Brazil had 5,000,-000 people; in 1950, 50,000,000; in 1966 over 80,000,000. Economists think she could support 500,000,000. She is only cultivating two-fifths of her land area, only using 1.5 per cent of her electric potential, has whole solid mountains of iron ore unmined, whole petroleum-producing regions not yet tapped. Brazil is the "frontier country," the nation with perhaps the greatest economic future of any in the world. Some analysis of these potentialities and of the work and social life of the "Men of Today" in Brazil is given in the next chapter.

NOTE: Readings for this chapter are combined with those on social and economic developments at the end of Chapter 31.

Brazilian Economic
and Social Development
in the Twentieth Century

THE COFFEE INDUSTRY IN SÃO PAULO

IN THE NEW middle-class Brazil, the city of São Paulo is the leader. In the 1960s it was the fastest growing city in the world. When Dom Pedro II fell from power the little town of 30,000 on the "frontier" had begun to look forward to a great future in coffee. Portuguese, Swiss, and German farmers, and especially the hard-working peasants of northern Italy, came to replace the freed slaves in the newly created republic. On arrival they were given a small plot of land, usually planted to a thousand coffee trees, to be cared for on a sharecropping basis. For the European immigrants this development was better than the peasant status and the poor land they had known in Europe; for São Paulo it was the beginning of the boom. Not 100,000 people lived in the whole province in 1890; by 1963 over 10,000,000 people, more than half of them of Italian descent, lived in São Paulo state, 4,300,000 in the city. Brazil's day as a "sugar" country was over; coffee was king and his throne was São Paulo. One of the most important Brazilian government agencies in the past decade has been the Coffee Institute, which supervises the coffee industry, sets prices, arranges quotas, and promotes research.

On the red-soiled rolling hills of São Paulo state, in June and July, whole families of sharecroppers down to the six-year-olds are busy picking the bright red coffee berries—joined by hundreds of seasonal workers. Other workers pour the berries out on the central drying grounds and rake them endlessly in the sun. Every large plantation has a cleaning plant where the dried coffee is brought, the dried hull floated off, and the small brown beans graded. Then commission merchants come to take the sacks of graded beans to Santos, the adults turn their attention to care of the orchard for next year's picking, the children go back to the *fazenda* school, and the migrants go back to the city. In such a work cycle, nearly one-third of the world's coffee supply is grown in a single region of 100,000 square miles. Brazil grows 58 per cent of the world's coffee, and São Paulo state grows almost half of Brazil's export crop, with 25 per cent more coming from Paraná and another 20 per cent from Minas Gerais. Of all this coffee, the United States takes 58 per cent.

In the many *fazenda* colonies of São Paulo state each family of *colonos,* or European-descended sharecroppers, usually lives in a neat little cottage in the central village near the drying yard, the cleaning mill, the commissary, and the large house of the *fazendeiro;* members of the family go out into the rolling hills to tend their 1,000 trees, and care for their own garden plot and livestock nearer the village. The *colonos* live better than agricultural workers in most parts of the world; they can move off as they please to start small farms of their own on cheap new lands on the frontier.

São Paulo has often overproduced coffee; beginning in 1906 the Brazilian government made its first attempt to keep prices up. All prices soared again during World War I, but the 1920s saw one desperate price drop after another. By 1929, the bumper crop was of no value in world markets. Attempts to destroy the crop by burning it in kerosene-soaked piles, or dumping it out at sea caused only extra expense. Growers and pickers were living on government bounty to produce a crop just to be destroyed, and even in spite of this control—"valorization" as it was called —prices continued to drop. A series of conferences in the late 1930s between Brazil and other coffee-producing nations set up a quota system, under which Brazil was to sell about 65 per cent of the world's supply, and all countries would cooperate to keep the price up. World War II and the postwar inflation kept the price up anyway, and the early 1950s brought boom years to São Paulo. Then the world price went too high, and the United States began to cut its consumption. Today many *fazendeiros* have diversified their crops; they are producing materials for São Paulo's own factories and food for São Paulo's own people and hope to survive any future slump in world coffee prices. In the mid-1960s several Brazilian companies were experimenting with the factory production of soluble coffee concentrate to seek new world markets.

São Paulo city, prospering first from the coffee boom and the immigrant tide, is growing even more rapidly in the era of the new diversification. Not only does the coffee production center there, but the city is responsible for over one-half of the industrial production of Brazil. The city government has constructed viaducts, freeways, and tunnels to handle the traffic.

Electric power was produced cheaply by damming up two rivers on the plateau and creating artificial lakes thirty miles long. Factories of all types are being built in São Paulo because of the cheap power, the skilled labor, the supply of prosperous consumers. To house its business offices, the city boasted 1400 "skycrapers" in 1967. Members of the lower middle class can own their own homes, for new subdivisions are constantly offering houses in the suburbs which can be purchased on the installment plan. There are also many smaller boom towns throughout the region, with new ones springing up every year. These new towns show how the small farmers prosper when they can "homestead" their land on long-term loans.

Most of the state's products come out to the world through the harbor of Santos, the leading coffee port of the world. In 1920 it had 50,000 inhabitants; today it has 300,000. Trucks and railway cars bring São Paulo's coffee to Santos at the rate of a million bags a month. Santos itself, warmer than São Paulo because it is at sea level, also ships 12,000,000 stems of bananas a year. To São Paulo city dwellers Santos is as important today as a beach resort as it is as a port. Jealous of Brasilia and anxious to grow faster, the whole region typifies the new South America looking toward the 1970s.

RUBBER AND THE AMAZON RIVER

A thousand miles to the north of bustling São Paulo lies another great economic region which rose to a boom on a single crop—the Amazon River Valley with its rubber. The turn of the century saw rubber used for tires on the new horseless carriages, as well as in the waterproofing of cloth. To get the raw material Brazilian middlemen kept Indian rubber collectors in debt slavery, sending them out in the forest to tap the wild rubber trees. Manáus was the center of this boom, a jungle town a thousand miles up the Amazon. Money flowed freely; huge mansions and even an elaborate opera house were erected, streets were paved, extensive docks built—all on the one product, rubber. The peak year was 1912; almost as much rubber was exported that year as coffee.

But the bubble burst. British botanists who had smuggled out rubber-tree seeds in violation of Pedro II's monopoly had started plantations in Malaya, where a steady supply of patient hand labor waited to care for the trees. Plantation rubber of uniform quality stole the Brazilian market; the Manáus boom ended in 1915 and with it the livelihood of many hundreds of Brazilian Indians and half-breeds from the coast who had settled the little river towns along the Amazon.

In the 1930s the American industrialist Henry Ford hoped to revive the Amazon rubber industry, thus making the Western Hemisphere independent of Malayan rubber. Ford developed experimental plantations in the Amazon basin at Belterra and on the Tapajós and planted more than two million trees of carefully grafted, disease-free stock. Much was expected of this venture when World War II cut off the supply of Far Eastern plantation rubber, but the war ended before Ford had begun to clear any profit. When Malayan rubber again entered world markets in 1946, Ford turned over his experimental plantations to the Brazilian government, which has continued the project of improving the native rubber stock through the work of the Agronomical Institute of Northern Brazil. The botanists in charge hope that the Amazon Valley, which is 40 per cent of the land of Brazil, will break the tyranny of a single-crop system, and are experimenting with rice planting and jute for burlap sacking, as well as with Ford's rubber stock, working out plans for drainage and flood control. To grow rice and jute in commercial quantities Brazil needs machinery and workers, which the Amazon does not yet have.

Meanwhile, World War II's rubber boom put Manáus back on the map. Goodyear and Firestone established branch factories in Rio and São Paulo using Amazon rubber. The end of the war did not bring a collapse, because the rising standard of living in Brazil's cities and the "boom" in São Paulo brought more automobiles for Brazilians. Today Manáus is a cosmopolitan little city of 180,000 people. Through it and its Atlantic port of Belém, with its 400,000 people, stream thousands of tons of other Amazon products —mahogany, carnauba wax, rotenone roots for insecticides, Brazil nuts, babassu oil, and coconuts. Timber and other forest products, mostly from the Amazon, are the fourth most important export of Brazil.

AGRICULTURE IN OTHER ECONOMIC REGIONS

In the northeast of Brazil, Baía, and Pernambuco, sugar had been king until the slaves were freed just before the establishment of the republic. In 1889 there was already more coffee and more rubber produced than sugar; by 1936 sugar comprised only 2 per cent of the total export. But all sugar consumed in Brazil is grown there, so that Baía and other sugar-cane regions produce 25,000,000 sacks a year. The old sugar mills on each plantation in the northeast had been replaced by *usinas*, sugar refining factories, in the early days of the republic. Soon these factories had bought out the sugar plantations of slave days; the trend toward small landholdings in São Paulo's west has been reversed in the north. But Pernambuco no longer needs to live by sugar mills alone. The area grows quantities of cotton, and its capital, Recife, now a city of almost 2 million, is a cotton textile-mill center.

Baía is today a port for shipping cacao, the chocolate-producing bean. Brazil is one of the world's chief exporters, sending 200,000,000 pounds of cacao beans to the United States a year. The crop is sold in world markets through a cooperative called the Cacao Institute of Baía. The trees which produce cacao beans in large pods hanging from the limbs and trunk can be grown either in plantation formation or in anyone's back yard; both small and large landowners therefore can belong to the Baía cooperative. Baía is also the center of Brazil's tobacco and cigarette trade. Still a proud city, Baía has more than 600,000 people and is much more than a museum piece, being the center of the musical culture contributed to Brazil by people of Negro blood.

A special problem exists farther north, in the interior of the bulge, the *sertão*. Here the land is unusable because of recurrent drought. In 1956 Kubitschek established the Northeastern Social and Economic Development

Agency, called, from the initials of the words in Portuguese, the SUDENE. Its plans for irrigating unused acreage, producing electric power from irrigation dams, and dividing unused land into small holdings to be paid for on longterm credit have continued into the late 1960s under other presidents with financial help from the U.S. under the Alliance for Progress. This is the overcrowded poverty-striken area where the pro-Communist organizer Julião gained so many recruits in 1962 and 1963 as to cause fears that Fidel Castro's influence would make Brazil's northeast another Cuba. Castello Branco hoped to satisfy Julião's followers through SUDENE's activities, while he had their leader put in jail. Under SUDENE 500,000 restless northeasterners were offered better farm lands in the irrigated areas or in Amazonas and Mato Grosso. The new roads, school buildings, and irrigation ditches have employed more than 100,000 construction workers. More than 2,000 miles of roads have been built in an area in which twenty years ago there were no roads at all. The capital of the area, the port of Fortaleza, now has over 500,000 inhabitants.

The beef industry makes the state of Rio Grande do Sul largely a one-export region. Life on the beef-cattle ranches of Southern Brazil is very much like that in Argentina. There are more than 14,000,000 head of cattle in Rio Grande do Sul, much of it of fine quality for producing frozen or refrigerated meat. Brahma stock has been used to breed hybrids, and their resultant fine hides, unscarred by ticks, make Brazil the second source of hides in the world. Porto Alegre, meaning "Happy Harbor" in Portuguese, is the meat capital of Brazil and lies 700 miles south of Rio; its 640,000 inhabitants seem to live more in the manner of Argentines than Brazilians.

The four C's—cacao, cotton, cattle, and coffee—combine to make Brazil a great agricultural nation. Since the coffee-caused depression there has been tremendous diversification in agriculture. Cotton is the nation's second export, and Brazil is the largest cotton producer in Latin America and fifth in the world. Brazil also raises most of its own food, all its beans, manioc, and maize; three-fourths of its wheat requirement is produced in the states south of São Paulo. Even today less than 5 per cent of all the area of Brazil is under cultivation, so the nation has great potentialities as a world food basket in the twenty-first century.

With all this agricultural development, the mass of Brazil's population still lives within 100 miles of the coast. Under Vargas the government made an organized attempt to settle the interior. Exploring parties composed of botanists, doctors, agriculturists, and engineers surveyed routes into the Mato Grosso and western Goiás, the two great undeveloped regions of Brazil whose rivers feed both the Plata and the Amazon. There is other urban development in Goiás besides Brasilia. Goiâna, the new capital of Goiás, was founded in 1942 and had 133,000 inhabitants by 1965. Other nearby towns are booming. The new town of Anapolis, called a "hamlet" when Brasilia was first planned, is now an important trading center of 60,000. Cattle thrive in this "West" of South America's center, and corn, cane, and cotton will do as well as cattle. Goiás and Mato Grosso are to South America in the second half of the twentieth century what Iowa,

Missouri, and Texas were to North America in the first half of the nineteenth. The most spectacular development of the interior, of course, is the new capital of the federal republic, Brasilia, seventy-five miles from Goiâna, described in the introduction to Part V as being a symbol of Latin America today.

URBANIZATION, MINING, AND INDUSTRY

About 32 per cent of the population in Brazil is urban. The ten largest cities in Brazil hold 13 per cent of the population, while there are twenty-nine cities with over 100,000 population. Rio de Janeiro was the capital and is the principal port of this far-flung, widely divergent "empire," reaching its fingers out to control plateau, river valley, and jungle. Of itself it is a beautiful place, situated on one of the most spectacular harbors in the world. In general, Rio, with a population of about 3,800,000, is disappointingly modern to anyone looking for "quaintness." There are more ultra-modern apartment houses in daringly new architectural

Rolling mill, *Volta Redonda,* **the largest steel-producing complex in South America.** *Courtesy Brazilian National Steel Company.*

styles in Rio than in Brasilia. Where there was not room enough against the hills for the city to expand, engineers reclaimed land from the bay. There are large theaters, imposing government buildings, and traffic congestion unparalleled in Latin America. Rio residents call themselves *Cariocas,* and are very proud of being "moderns." Above the city, the *favelas* or hillside shantytowns, comprise some of the worst slums in South America, without streets, schools, electricity, or running water. In the very heavy rainy seasons of both 1966 and 1967, hundreds of these crowded shanties were washed down hill into the streets below with great loss of life among the occupants.

Brazil's greatest city of São Paulo has already been described. Minas Gerais has a new state capital to replace the colonial city of Ouro Preto; this is Belo Horizonte, Beautiful Horizon, which was started as a model community in 1905 in a wild virgin area. Then it was just a diagram on a draftsman's table. Today it is a city of 700,000, well planned for modern living. Home of the gold and diamonds of colonial times, Minas Gerais is still the richest state of Brazil in mineral output. Its towns have enormous blast furnaces and rolling mills producing pig iron, sheet steel, wire, rods, and galvanized iron. There is one whole hill, Itabira Peak, which is said to be solid iron ore, of the highest grade known in the world. The United States Export-Import Bank loaned the Brazilians money to develop this ore deposit and to build a railroad 360 miles to the port of Vitória to ship it out. With improved equipment this Rio Doce or Sweet River Mine is producing a million tons of iron ore a year.

The deep mine of Morro Velho, Old Hill, scene of a gold rush in 1705, is producing gold yet, and diamonds are still an exciting lure which brings prospectors to Minas. A great part of the finds are "industrial diamonds," of use only as drills in machinery, but nevertheless worth $3 million a year in the export trade. Manganese to the amount of 150,000 tons a year is exported from Minas Gerais to the United States. Quartz, mica, chromium, tungsten, nickel, lead, titanium, and bauxite are mined in Minas Gerais.

Dom Pedro, that good emperor, had helped start 903 "industrial establishments" in Brazil before he abdicated in 1889. Today Brazil is the most highly industrialized country of Latin America; there are nearly 100,000 such establishments in Brazil which manufacture consumer goods, process foods, and weave textiles. Four hundred and forty cotton mills produced 1,200 million meters of goods in a recent year, mostly in São Paulo. Wool knitting and silk and rayon manufacture are growing industries. Millions of shoes, suits, hats, a hundred thousand tons of glass, and a half-million inner-tubes are manufactured yearly. The list could go on and on— the Cinderella story of the modern Brazilian economy as it builds itself into self-sufficiency. The best single example of the new industry is the steel mill at Volta Redonda, ninety miles south of Rio. Here ore is brought from Minas Gerais by rail via Vitória, and coal comes from one of the few mines of Brazil in Santa Catarina. The 20,000 Volta Redonda workers, employed under the best social welfare scheme in South America, live in model houses, with electricity and running hot water. By 1949 this government-run plant was returning 6 per cent on the investment, and it has been expanded since that time. A similar government promotion is the TVA-type electric development which is changing the São Francisco Valley, one of the few north-south river valleys near the coast, into a well-farmed area, where a series of dams are making the river navigable all the way. Erosion is to be controlled and quantities of power produced.

This latter valley, like all areas away from the coast, has been under-developed because of poor transportation. There is today no north-south railroad line at all; the track that runs from São Paulo inland to the Paraguay River to tap the Mato Grosso is the only actual line into the interior. The "road out" promised to Bolivia was begun under Dutra, working from Corumbá on the Paraguay River, and was continued toward Santa Cruz, Bolivia, by Kubitschek. In 1965 the Maurico Joppert Bridge across an Amazon tributary, one-and-a half miles wide, was opened to complete a 1,900 mile long highway to the Peruvian border, thus allowing cars to cross South America from east to west 10° south of the equator. However, one still travels from Rio to Baía or Recife by sea or by one of the twenty airlines operating in aviation-conscious Brazil. In addition to American lines and the several European services which fly in from Rome or Lisbon or Paris, locally owned companies maintain "milk runs" into all parts of the interior.

Vargas, Dutra, Kubitschek and Castello Branco all had five-year plans, long-range programs for economic improvement. Fuel and power, still Brazil's greatest needs, are developed by increasing hydroelectric projects and by exploration for petroleum. Under the government geological research agency called Petro-Bras, some oil has been found in the Amazon Valley.

Brazil's greatest need today is capital. In the late 1800s all capital was from foreign companies, mostly English. Today's foreign capital in Brazil is about 54 per cent American and 29 per cent British. Under Vargas the Brazilian government itself went into business as a sort of partner of local and private capital. Today the government owns the National Steel Company with its plant at Volta Redonda, the telegraph system, a National Motors Company, and the Lloyd Brasileiro Steamship Company, which has a monopoly on coastal traffic. Many other companies have been nationalized by the government, which also subsidizes many new industries by loans, gifts of land, or freedom from taxes. This whole development is part of the economic nationalism common to all of Latin America today.

Today Brazil encourages international capital. In 1948 a joint United States-Brazil Economic Development Commission, known as the Abbink Commission, recommended a continuation of the five-year-plan type of agricultural, industrial, and mineral development, and a guarantee of fair treatment of American capital by the Brazilian government. On the basis of this report and under the later Alliance for Progress, American public and private capital came to Brazil by the hundreds of millions in spite of inflation under the Goulart regime of 1962–1963. As Brazil approached the 1970s such development was continuing, and capital was still forthcoming. The industrialization had perhaps been too fast, for it brought deficit budgeting, inflationary prices, extensive paper money, shortage of exchange, and a skilled labor and power shortage.

RACIAL GROUPS AND SOCIAL LIFE
AMONG THE BRAZILIANS

To be Brazilian is to be black or white or any mixture in between. In the United States, to have one-sixteenth Negro blood is to be Negro; in Brazil, to have one-sixteenth white blood is to be white, and it makes very little difference anyway. Three hundred years of tolerance toward slaves and acceptance of mulatto freedmen in colonial times produced a mixed race which prides itself on a nearly complete absence of discrimination. Most Brazilians have no sympathy with Americans who talk of "race consciousness" or "racial problems."

Visitors who go to Brazil expecting to see pure democracy at work in this regard are disappointed to note few very dark-skinned people among the well-to-do or the professional classes and to watch the heavy menial labor done by markedly Negroid and Indian types. Brazilian sociologists claim that this is *class* prejudice, not race prejudice. The landowning class is still wealthy. Its members are the descendants of the wealthy Portuguese colonists and they never marry outside their class. Their sons get a classical university education and then go into the professions.

As new fortunes are being made in industry, these old class lines are breaking down. The members of the new commercial middle class have little race or economic prejudice. Recently an estimate on colors in the population was made, although meaningful figures are difficult to ascertain in Brazil where color differences are seldom considered. About 60 per cent were judged to be predominantly white, 15 per cent predominantly black, and 20 per cent "brown" or obvious mixtures of the three races, with the remaining 5 per cent being pure Indians, the wild tribal Indians of the Mato Grosso and the Amazon.

Modern Brazil is attempting to "Brazilianize" all her people, and to attract many new people to fill in her vast areas. By 1960, 40 per cent of the residents of São Paulo were of Italian origin. More Portuguese farmers and city laborers came to Brazil in the last half-century than were left in Lisbon. Slavic people, especially Poles, also came in large numbers to take up farmland of their own. In Paraná, Santa Catarina, and Rio Grande do Sul Germans, Poles, and Italians became the backbone of the new agriculture. Today there are also groups of Poles in the back country in Mato Grosso; these people have brought European farming skills and managerial abilities to the new frontiers.

Willing to encourage all groups who would be absorbed in the bloodstream and help make the new hybrid type, Brazil welcomed 250,000 Japanese farm workers, but they were legislated against during World War II when it was claimed that they had remained clannish. Since 1946 they have again been welcome, and their numbers now total more than 500,000. Displaced persons from the European refugee camps came to Brazil in large numbers after World War II. Immigration has been encouraged by departments within the government since Dom Pedro's day.

The Indian people of Brazil constitute a special problem. Except for those who have come into modernized villages in recent times to work as rubber gatherers in the Amazon or as woodcutters and stevedores for the little river launches, the Indians of the remote interior are among the earth's most primitive people. On the Rio das Mortes, the River of Death, live the warlike Chavantes, for example, who have caused the disappearance of many an explorer, including the British Captain Faucett in the 1920s. To improve the Indians' health and protect them from exploitation by the white man, the Brazilians have organized an Indian Protective Service. The Service has been the life work of General Cândido Mariano Rondon, himself of Indian blood, who went into the Indian country as a young Brazilian army major with Theodore Roosevelt's expedition in 1913. His policy of placating and helping rather than frightening the Indians brought the Chavantes in to make a treaty in 1946. Now the Indian Service has an advanced base among the Chavantes. Land was cleared for model farm settlements to teach agriculture to these forest dwellers as a part of Rondon's long-range program.

In this plan of settling nomadic Indians on agricultural reservations, the Brazilian story resembles that of the United States. There are many other similarities: slave blood concentrated in one region where slaves were first owned, immigrants filling in farmland and rising to success in industry. But social customs remain quite different from the North American pattern. This is particularly true of family life. As in Spanish-speaking America, the family is the social unit and includes all the aunts and uncles, cousins to the third and fourth degree, and the families of godparents. In the tall modern apartment houses in Rio several floors are taken up by one family and all its relatives.

Brazilian women are more active in politics and go more freely to play golf or tennis, to swim or to attend the theater with other women than they do in Bogotá or Lima. There are women in government positions of importance. Brazil has more trained women engineers than all the rest of Latin America put together. In the election for Dom Getúlio's constitutional assembly held in May 1933, women voted for the first time and soon a woman was elected to the Chamber of Deputies. There are several outstanding women writers.

A generation ago men as well as women of the aristocratic class did not concern themselves with business or estate management, but the new industrializing spirit is changing this. Heads of families and their sons manage the business now, invest money in factories, and bring their whole families into this new interest. The old pattern of social life is being altered.

So also is the attitude toward religion. With few exceptions the Brazilians are Catholics, but there is complete tolerance of anyone else's point of view, and Protestantism enjoys more freedom than elsewhere in Latin America. The Catholic Church itself seems not as serious and grave an affair as in Peru or Colombia. One religious holiday, the Carnival or last days before Lent, as celebrated in Rio, has become famous all over the world. The songs from Rio's Carnival become hit tunes for the year. During the four days of the celebration the streets are a mass of happy, friendly people. Costumed *Cariocas* dance in and out of strange houses and shoot each other with squirt guns full of perfume. No one does any work; the entire population is in the streets. The whole festival is less "organized" than any Mardi Gras in New Orleans, and has little of the "promotion" and advertising of Pasadena's Tournament of Roses.

Although the working people enjoy Carnival, their daily life in the cities is on a very low standard. The white-collar workers have a hard time making ends meet, as a pair of shoes costs a clerk's weekly salary, and bookkeepers or teachers make far less proportionately than they would make in the United States. The day laborers and factory workers find it very expensive even to buy shoes. The hills of Rio are covered on one side with fancy hotels or luxuriant tropical vegetation; on the other side, the shanties of the poor fill the entire hillsides with communities called *favelas*. There are 232 separate *favela* communites totaling more than a million inhabitants on the hills of Rio, each with its own governing council. The councils cannot provide schools or running water or electricity, and cannot control the criminal element, but they do try to keep up the stone steps and the "goat trails" that connect the hillsides with the city streets. Even in progressive, bustling São Paulo there are back streets of tenements where workers live on less than a dollar a day. Such a low standard of living, with its accompanying diet deficiencies, produces an unproductive work force in a nation whose rapid industrialization demands efficient labor.

The Brazilian government has not let these conditions go unheeded. Vargas won popularity among the people by providing old-age pensions for workers, child-welfare programs for dependent children, safety inspection in dangerous industries, and model housing for labor near the new industries. Dom Getúlio, for all his political motives, had set the pattern of workingman's security as a part of government obligation. Article 157 of the post-Vargas Constitution of 1946 lists seventeen "rules for workingmen which legislation shall observe," including plans for profit-sharing, paid vacations, and maternity benefits, as well as rights of collective bargaining and industrial accident compensation. Any visitor to Brazil can see these laws for workers unenforced in many ways. Nevertheless they are there in the supreme law of the land, a goal for Brazil to work for, improving human resources as she develops natural resources.

Rural life in Brazil varies with the area. Sharecroppers on the coffee *fazendas* are controlled by the *fazendeiro*, living in "company" houses and buying at "company" stores, while the migrant workers who help with the coffee picking wander back to the city slums when the harvest is over. Polish villagers in the interior of Paraná or Santa Catarina live in neat wooden houses, carry on diversified farming, and travel by bus four or five days on dirt roads to reach a city. Towns on the São Francisco or the Amazon are built of wood and thatch, with perhaps one main front street on the river composed of neat houses of brightly painted plaster or colorful mosaic tile. Here live the store owner, the teacher in the government-supported elementary school, the members of the country government council. The towns support themselves on "thatch and patch" agriculture or on the river traffic, live on beans, rice, and mandioca flour, and pay little attention to color lines between their "upper-class" citizens in the painted houses and the rubber gatherers or cattle herders in the forests.

Such towns have one great problem in common with the cities: the poor health of their people. Statistics collected in 1947 proved that the birth and death rates were both high, that the life expectancy of the Brazilians in general was so short that almost half of the population was under fifteen, and that people were not surviving into middle age. One-third of the rural population was afflicted with malaria and one-fifth with hookworm; tuberculosis and syphilis claimed a very high rate in the urban population, while dysentery was endemic in both city and country. Fewer than 10 per cent of the houses had running water or sanitary facilities; 75 per cent of the houses were not connected to a sewer system. Forty per cent of all nurses and doctors in the nation lived in Rio and São Paulo, so the countryside and the smaller towns went without.

Into this depressing picture came the *Servicio Especial de Saude Pública*, an outgrowth of World War II and American interest in making friends in Latin America. Through the Nelson Rockefeller Committee described in Chapter 41, North American public health specialists came to Brazil as part of a joint two-nation project. They worked out a plan for rural health and sanitation, financed at first by the United States, but paid entirely by Brazil for the last two decades. After experiments with water-filtering systems, nursing programs, mass inoculations, and many small clinics in an area of Minas Gerais, the program was started in the Amazon Basin. Here thirty health centers were set up, seventeen launches fitted out as "healthmobiles" to serve the river towns, and a fifty-bed hospital built at Santarém, a town halfway up the river to Manáus. Girls with elementary school diplomas were trained as visiting nurses and midwives. Engineers from the *Servicio* organized improved water supply systems for many towns. Educational campaigns have encouraged more balanced diets. Young doctors from several different regions of Brazil come to the United States for a year's study at Johns Hopkins or other centers for the study of tropical diseases. Endemic diseases are being diminished in incidence and intensity. The *Servicio*, cooperating with the Ministry of Health, has also made a great stride forward in the treatment of lepers, of which there were some 3,000 in north Brazil alone as recently as 1940.

The Oswaldo Cruz Institute has made other spectacular contributions to public health. It is because of the existence of this Institute that Rio de Janeiro is today so free from mosquitoes and there is no yellow fever or malaria in the city. In the early 1900s yellow fever killed tens of thousands in Brazil's cities every year. Then in 1903 a young Brazilian doctor, Oswaldo Cruz, was appointed to head a Brazilian Bacteriological Institute, in charge of a public health program pledged to wipe out yellow fever of Rio in three years. Dr. Cruz carried on a drastic campaign to make the death of every mosquito the goal for Rio dwellers. By 1913 his health program had stopped malaria and yellow fever in the capital and had concentrated on a pure water supply, thus cutting down typhoid. As an organizer and leader, Oswaldo Cruz trained younger men to work after him, and set up research laboratories. Today Rio's health problem is one of malnutrition and organic disease. The three killers—malaria, yellow fever, and typhoid—are gone from Rio, it is to be hoped, forever.

EDUCATION AND CULTURE IN BRAZIL

Unfortunately, Brazil's interest in education has not been as great as her interest in public health. As soon as the republic was established a Ministry of Education was created and Benjamin Constant, that idealistic mathematics professor, was given the job. Interested in higher learning, he developed the technical college course in Rio but neglected primary schools. The Constitution of 1891, the republic's first, put the responsibility of primary education on the shoulders of the new state governments, where it was largely neglected. Finally in 1930 Vargas' new Ministry of Health and Education reorganized the system and campaigned for compulsory primary schools in all regions. At that time more than half the children of elementary age were not in school. President Vargas took education under the wing of the federal government and made education free and obligatory. Today there is a school building of sorts in every Brazilian village large enough to be called a town. But as 1970 approached there were still four million children in rural areas who had no school to attend, and the nation remained more than 50 per cent illiterate. In Rio, that fine modern city of the *Cariocas*, 14 per cent were unable to read and write.

Brazil is as understaffed for teacher personnel as she was for nurses and doctors. The public health program bogs down when the people at whom it aims its clever pamphlets on disease and sanitation cannot read them. The Constitution of 1946 provided that 10 per cent of federal and 20 per cent of state tax revenues were to be spent on education. However, the Brazilian government in the 1960s was spending only 9 per cent of its budget on education, and this included both local and national budgets. But the new middle class, growing so rapidly in the cities, is now demanding better elementary schools for its children, and high school education as well. Today the Ministry of Education and Culture is tackling the problem. Its national Institute for the Study of Education is doing research on elementary methods and maintaining a central office to help localities. Though the curriculum is "federal," the teacher-training institutes are state-maintained and are neither uniform nor free.

The secondary education situation is still completely inadequate for a practical, industrialized modern nation. The senior high school, the *Colégio or Preparatório*, offers only academic courses preparing directly for college. A bare minimum of such schools is provided by the government, and most secondary schools are private ventures, making profit on tuition. Naturally, secondary education becomes a luxury for the children of the upper classes only. To have a secondary school diploma brings more prestige today in Brazil than a bachelor's degree in America. A new interest in trade schools has developed a second type of senior high school.

In 1937 there were only 30,000 students in commercial, "business-college type" high schools, trade-technical schools, or vocational schools of any kind, in all of Brazil. By 1965 there were 700,000. Both São Paulo and Minas Gerais now have agricultural secondary schools offering courses in tractor repair, soil conservation, care of dairy herds, and control of plant diseases.

University education, of the traditional academic type, is of a high standard in Brazil. So respected is an advanced degree that the title of "doctor" has become traditional to use in addressing any well-educated person in the cities. In 1930 the Schools of Medicine and of Law and the Polytechnic School were legally united to form the University of Rio de Janeiro. To this group were added the Schools of Mines, of Dentistry, and of Fine Arts, and the Institute of Music. This whole combined institution is now called the University of Brazil and offers degrees in such "untraditional things" for a Latin American university as engineering, veterinary medicine, architecture, metallurgy, and political science. State Universities are being modeled after this national pattern; that at São Paulo with its new School of Agriculture is considered one of the best universities in all South America. By 1966 the entire nation could boast forty-two separate institutions of higher learning, including the new glass and chrome University of Brasilia.

All university students and most secondary school graduates are required to have a reading knowledge of English, and there is a brisk demand for technical books in all fields written in the English language. Young teachers of English by the dozens have come to the University of Michigan to study "language lab" methods of teaching English as a foreign language and have returned with model "language labs," records, and tape recorders to bring spoken English into Brazilian college and high school classrooms. Many students speak French also and, like the Argentine students, have spent a year or two in Paris. Student life as a whole is much more like European university life than like North American. Though there is a great interest in soccer, and the enormous new Maracaña Stadium, one of the largest in the world, was built in Rio in 1950, the players who cause the delirious enthusiasm are not college students but paid professionals.

The Brazilian college system has produced some eminent scientists. In the fields of geology, soil erosion studies, hydrographic surveys, and other modern applications of soil sciences the faculty of the School of Mines of Ouro Preto in Minas Gerais has been outstanding. Dr. Emil A. Goeldi has worked in the field of Brazilian zoology, and the museum of Amazonian wild life in Belém is named for him. A new interest in the science of sociology is developing. Arthur Ramos produced a great work on the Negro in Brazil; Gilberto Freyre is the leader of the sociological writers and his works on Brazil's social problems have been translated into English, as have also those of Hermane Tavares de Sa and of the Brazilian cultural historian Fernando de Azevedo. The science of aviation has a famous Brazilian on its roll of honor, Alberto Santos-Dumont, who, Brazilians claim, antedated the Wright brothers in the first flight.

Provisional President Castelo Branco greeting American Fulbright Summer Seminar Teachers in Brasilia in 1964. Dr. Eloisa Barbosa Fuiza, University of Ceará, stands at far right as interpreter. *Photo by Helen Miller Bailey.*

For applying the scientific work of its researchers Brazil deserves special mention among Latin American countries. Mosquito-borne diseases have been controlled; serums have been developed to cure poisonous snake bites. Serums which are produced in the famous snake farm of the Butantan Institute of São Paulo are sent out all over South America. Contributions have been made to sea navigation and radiology. The Biological Institute of São Paulo has pioneered in the control of plant diseases, and employs eighty-eight scientists and 200 laboratory technicians to care for its experimental gardens, while the Brazilian National Observatory makes astronomical observations for the whole Southern Hemisphere.

It is as fashionable to write for publication in Brazil as it is in Spanish America, and the twentieth century is producing new authors with a new spirit, many of whose works are now being translated into English and receiving worldwide attention. Perhaps the modern concern of Brazilian writers with social problems was forecast by the famous book, *Rebellion in the Backlands*, or, as it was called in the original Portuguese, *Os Sertões*, the name given the drought-stricken region behind Baía and Fortaleza. The revolt against republican authority led by the religious fanatic Antônio the Counsellor had occurred here in 1896 and 1897, and the author, Euclides da Cunha (1866–1909), was a civil engineer with officer's training

Gilberto Freyre, the famous Brazilian sociologist, on the porch of his home in Recife. *Photo by Helen Miller Bailey.*

working on a public project when a São Paulo newspaper sent him to accompany the federal troops and write up the story of the rebellion. In 1907 he made public his detailed and analytical story of the campaign. Brazilian writers formerly interested only in classical themes were influenced to write of the regions of Brazil by this new "classic." A thrilling story, *Os Sertões* reads like a novel, but a novel filled with sociological implications and revealing the psychology of the rural poor.

Other authors followed his lead. Graça Aranha (1868–1931), the "apostle of Brazilian modernism," wrote a novel in the 1920s about Brazil's new "melting pot" for European races, a book called *Canaan*. In São Paulo in 1922 some young intellectuals put on a Modern Art Week, at which, after viewing exhibits, the participants sat around discussing the new freedom in European literature after World War I and deciding that Brazil should have a new freedom in literature, in Brazil, by Brazilians, and about Brazilian themes. In the 1950s writers who participated in that famous "week" in São Paulo were still writing. Erico Veríssimo (1905–   ), whose books are translated into English, wrote a novel, *Crossroads*, bringing his home town Porto Alegre into world literature for the first time. His *Of Time and the Wind* began an epic of a south Brazilian family, of which a recent volume is called *The Archipelago* in popular English translation. Veríssimo became the "dean" of Brazilian novelists, has spoken and taught in the United States, and has served as a cultural coordinator for the Pan-American Union. Regional interest, sociological themes, and modernist style have brought other novelists to attention, particularly Jorge Amado (1912–   ), José Lins do Rego (1901–1957), Graciliano Ramos (1892–1953), and the woman Raquel da Queiroz (1910–   ). Most of those mentioned are novelists of the northeast—creators of the new Brazilian novel. Popular as novels are, the vicissitudes of the publishing business make it very difficult to make a living at writing. Brazil's best writers augment their incomes by translating modern North American novels. In Hemingway and Faulkner modern Brazilian writers find their models—frank, earthy descriptions of life as it is when people are poor. This earthy theme was startlingly used by a São Paulo woman, Carolina Maria de Jesus, in the 1960s, in a stark description of her own life in the shanty town *favelas*. Translated into English as *Child of the Dark*, her book became a "must" for students of sociology everywhere.

Poetry, like the novel, has made an impressive showing, and proves that literary Brazil has come of age. The modern trend was begun with João de Cruz e Sousa (1862–1898) whose *Last Sonnets* were published in 1905. A Negro, son of slaves, Cruz e Sousa wrote indignantly of the wrongs done his race. His poems were nationalistic and modernistic, and their pattern was followed by young poets of the São Paulo Art Week movement. With these poems and novels, Brazil ceased to be an outpost of European letters and became the leading center of Portuguese thought and writing.

The São Paulo cultural week movement continued in the 1960s as an "Art Biennial" at which nations throughout the world were represented by "non-objective" art entries. In 1963 the winner of the modern-art first prize was an American, of the second prize a Venezuelan. In 1964 São Paulo was the scene of a "battle" between the French and the Italian schools of modern artists, at which the Brazilian judges gave the prize to a young Italian who "pressed heavy doses of paint on rough burlap." Poets are still attending São Paulo's "week," selling a little magazine called *Street Singers' Guitar*, full of "the best current poetry for the masses, written with a social purpose." Poets in Belo Horizonte have their own modern poetry movement, called *Tendency*, which prints the poetry of "the stream of Belo's younger poets." Even the famous sociologist Gilberto Freyre has printed a book of modern verse called *Poetry Perhaps*. An archivist in the Ministry of Education in Rio named Carlos Drummond de Andrade is such a well-known writer of philosophical verse as to be called "the most admired intellect of this generation." He opposes modern mechanical development "for fear personalities will be lost in the great blob," but enjoys living in the present for "time is my master, time *now*, life *now!*"

Apart from the "life now" abstractionists in art, Candido Portinari (1903–1962), a world-renowned muralist, remains Brazil's best known modern artist. Commissioned to make a series of murals for government buildings showing the "spirit of Brazil," Portinari drew a long frieze of muscular, sweating coffee plantation workers, to the horror of those who had commissioned him. Portinari himself was born to humble Italian immigrants on a coffee plantation and worked his way through the Academy of Fine Arts, an unusual thing to do in Brazil. Now he has murals in the Library of Congress in Washington, D.C. In architecture, Rio de Janeiro itself, even more than Brasilia, is a modernist's delight, as it contains some of the most "futuristic" buildings in the world. The Swiss architect Le Corbusier influenced those young Brazilians, Lúcio Costa and Oscar Niemeyer, now of Brasilia, who applied the designs of Frank Lloyd Wright to fit into the hills and bays of Rio, thereby creating what amounts to a school of modern tropical architecture.

Heitor Villa-Lobos, Brazilian composer, the Western Hemisphere's most famous musical leader. *Courtesy Pan American Union.*

Brazil has a host of distinguished musicians of high talent and originality, who have made a valuable contribution to Western Hemisphere music. Leader in the field was Heitor Villa-Lobos (1894–1960), who was another strong advocate of the use of the poor common people of all racial strains as an inspiration to cultural creation. One of the world's best-known recent composers, Villa-Lobos used native Indian and Negro folk music as his inspiration. He wrote over 1,500 compositions of all types, from simple piano solos to symphonies and operas. Many of his followers could be mentioned, among them Camargo Guarnieri (1907–   ), who, like Villa-Lobos, has conducted as a guest artist in the United States. The folk music of Brazil, with its slave and Carnival themes, has also become popular in modern America, as have the Carnival dance steps of Rio and Baía. Considering the Brazilians' fondness for poetry, pageantry, music, and the dance, it is small wonder that there is a very active theater in Brazil, interested in folk plays and native music. In the Ministry of Education and Culture there is a National Theater Service whose director is himself a playwright. He has established a National School of the Theater as a part of the university. Brazil is also producing art films and won the film festival at Cannes in 1963 with a film on life in Rio.

All Brazilians are very music- and rhythm-conscious. It is the musical program that has made the radio so popular in Brazil today, rather than the political broadcast or the variety show. Today there are more than 300 radio stations and several television networks in Brazil, while 490 magazines and 252 newspapers are published regularly. These media are doing more to bring together the diverse elements of Brazilian life than all the politicians described in the previous chapter.

READINGS

Adams, R. N., *et al.*, *Social Change in Latin America Today* (1960)
Alexander, R. J., *Communism in Latin America* (1957)
———, *Labor Relations in Argentina, Brazil and Chile* (1962)
Avila, F. B. de, *Economic Aspects of Immigration: The Brazilian Immigration Problem* (1954)
Azevedo, F. de, *Brazilian Culture: An Introduction to the Study of Culture in Brazil*, trans. W. R. Crawford (1950)
Baer, W., *Industrialization and Economic Development in Brazil* (1965)
Baklanoff, E., *New Perspectives of Brazil* (1966)
Bandeira, M., *Brief History of Brazilian Literature* (1958)
Bello, J. M., *History of Modern Brazil, 1899–1964* (1965)
Bernstein, H., *Modern and Contemporary Latin America* (1952)
Brazil Election Fact Book (1965)
Brazil, Ministry of Foreign Relations, *Brazil: 1960* (n.d.)
Brown, R., *Land and People of Brazil* (1960)
Burns, A. B., *Documentary History of Brazil* (1966)
———, *The Unwritten Alliance: Rio Branco and Brazil-American Relations* (1966)
Calmon, P., with R. C. de Medeiros, *History of Brazil* (1939)
Calogeras, J. P., *History of Brazil*, trans. P. A. Martin (1939)
Camacho, J. A., *Brazil: An Interim Assessment* (1954)
Cooke, M. L., *Brazil on the March* (1944)
Costedo, L., *Baroque Prevalence in Brazilian Art* (1964)
Cruz Costa, J., *History of Ideas in Brazil* (1964)
Cunha, E. da, *Rebellion in the Backlands*, trans. S. Putnam (1944)
Cunha, L. de A., *Art in Latin America Today: Brazil* (1960)
Danbaugh, L. M., *Coffee Frontier in Brazil* (1959)
de Azevedo, T., *Social Change in Brazil* (1963)
Denis, P., *Brazil* (1911)
Dos Pasos, J., *Brazil on the Move* (1963)
Driver, D. M., *The Indian in Brazilian Literature* (1942)

Dulles, J., *Vargas of Brazil: A Political Biography* (1966)

Ellison, F. P., *Brazil's New Novel* (1954)

Faust, A. F., *Brazil: Education in an Expanding Economy* (1959)

Form, W. H., and A. A. Blum, eds., *Industrial Relations and Social Change in Latin America* (1965)

Free L. A., *Some International Implications of the Political Psychology of Brazilians* (1961)

Freyre, G., *Brazil, An Interpretation* (1945)

———, *Mansions and the Shanties: The Making of Modern Brazil* (1963)

———, *The Masters and the Slaves*, trans. S. Putnam (2nd ed., 1956)

———, *New World in the Tropics* (1959)

Furtado, C., *Development and Underdevelopment* (1964)

———, *Diagnosis of the Brazilian Crisis* (1965)

———, *Economic Growth of Brazil: A Survey from Colonial to Modern Times* (1963)

Gauld, C. A., *The Last Titan: Percival Farquhar, Entrepreneur in Latin America* (1964)

Geiger, T., *General Electric Company in Brazil* (1961)

Goldberg, I., *Brazilian Literature* (1922)

Goodwin, P. L., *Brazil Builds: Architecture New and Old, 1652–1942* (1943)

Gordon, L. and E. Grommers, *United States Manufacturing Investment in Brazil: The Impact of Brazilian Government Politics, 1946–1960* (1962)

Hambloch, E., *His Majesty the President* (1935)

Harris, M., *Town and Country in Brazil* (1956)

Havighurst, R. J., and J. R. Moreira, *Society and Education in Brazil* (1965)

Herring, H., *Good Neighbors* (1941)

Hill, L. F., ed., *Brazil* (1947)

———, *Diplomatic Relations Between the United States and Brazil* (1932)

Hirschman, A. C., *Journeys Towards Progress* (1963)

Horowitz, J., *Revolution in Brazil: Politics and Society in a Developing Nation* (1964)

Houston, J. A., *Latin America in the United Nations* (1956)

Hughlett, L. J., ed., *Industrialization of Latin America* (1946)

Hunnicutt, B. H., *Brazil, World Frontier* (1949)

Hutchinson, H. W., *Village and Plantation Life in Northeast Brazil* (1957)

Irwin, R. D., *Industrialization and Economic Development in Brazil* (1965)

James, H. G., *Brazil After a Century of Independence* (1925)

———, *The Constitutional System of Brazil* (1923)

James, P. E., *Brazil* (1946)

Jobim, José, *Brazil in the Making* (1943)

Johnson, J. J., *Military and Society in Latin America* (1964)

———, *Political Change in Latin America* (1958)

Joint Brazil-United States Economic Development Commission, *Brazil Technical Studies* (1945)

———, *Development of Brazil* (1958)

Kelchner, W. H., *Latin American Relations with the League of Nations* (1930)

Kuznets, S., W. E. Moore, and J. J. Spengler, eds., *Economic Growth: Brazil, India, Japan* (1955)

Le Corbusier (pseud. of Jeanneret-Gris, C. E.), *Creation Is a Patient Search: A Self Portrait* (1960)

Levine, R. M., *Brazil: Field Guide in the Social Sciences* (1966)

Lieuwen, E. *Arms and Politics in Latin America* (rev. ed., 1961)

————, *Generals vs. Presidents* (1964)

Lowenstein, K., *Brazil under Vargas* (1942)

Luper, A. T., *The Music of Brazil* (1943)

Macedo Soares, J. C. de, *Brazil and the League of Nations* (1928)

Maier, J., and R. W. Weatherhead, ed., *Politics of Change in Latin America* (1964)

Manchester, A. K., *British Preeminence in Brazil: Its Rise and Decline* (1933)

Mariz, V., *Heitor Villa-Lobos Brazilian Composer* (1963)

Martin, P. A., *Latin America and the War* (1925)

Maurette, F., *Some Social Aspects of Present and Future Economic Development in Brazil* (1937)

Mecham, J. L., *Church and State in Latin America* (rev. ed., 1966)

Mindlen, H. E., *Modern Architecture in Brazil* (1956)

Morse, R. M., *From Community to Metropolis: A Biography of São Paulo* (1958)

Mosher, A. T., *Case Study of Agriculture Program of ACAR in Brazil* (1955)

Nash, R., *Conquest of Brazil* (1927)

Nist, J., *Modern Brazilian Poetry: An Anthology* (1962)

Normano, J. F., *Brazil: A Study of Economic Types* (1933)

Phelps, D. M., *Rubber Development in Latin America* (1957)

Pierson, D., *Negroes in Brazil* (1942)

Putnam, S., *Marvelous Journey: Four Centuries of Brazilian Literature* (1948)

Ramos, A., *Negro in Brazil*, trans. R. Patten (1939)

Robock, S. H., *Brazil's Developing Northeast: A Study of Regional Planning and Foreign Aid* (1963)

Rodriques, J. H., *Brazil and Africa* (1965)

Sa, H. T. de, *The Brazilians: People of Tomorrow* (1947)

Sayers, R. S., *The Negro in Brazilian Literature* (1956)

Schurz, W. L., *Brazil, The Infinite Country* (1961)

Silva, C. M., *Public Functionaries and Brazilian Constitution* (1954)

Simonsen, R. C., *Brazil's Industrial Revolution* (1939)

Skidmore, T., *Brazil Since 1930* (1966)

Smith, T. L., *Agrarian Reform in Latin America* (1965)

————, *Brazil: People and Institutions* (rev. ed., 1963)

————, and A. Marchant, eds., *Brazil: Portrait of Half a Continent* (1951)

Spiegel, H. W., *The Brazilian Economy: Chronic Inflation and Sporadic Industrialization* (1949)

Stein, S. J., *The Brazilian Cotton Manufacture, 1850–1950* (1957)

————, *Vassouras, A Brazilian Coffee Country, 1850–1900* (1957)

Torres-Rioseco, A., *Epic of Latin American Literature* (rev. ed., 1946)

Turner, C. W., *Ruy Barbosa: Brazilian Crusader for the Essential Freedoms* (1945)

United Nations, Department of Economic and Social Affairs, *Economic Development of Brazil* (1956)

United Nations, Economic Commission for Latin America, *Economic Development of Brazil* (1956)

————, *Recent Developments and Trends in the Brazilian Economy* (1951)

United States, Department of Defense, Army Department, *U.S. Army Handbook for Brazil* (1964)

United States Department of Labor, Bureau of Labor Statistics, *Labor in Brazil* (1962)

Verissimo, E., *Brazilian Literature: An Outline* (1945)

Wagley, C. *Amazon Town: A Study of Man in the Tropics* (1964)

————, *Brazil, Crisis and Change* (1964)

————, *An Introduction to Brazil* (1963)

————, ed., *Race and Class in Rural Brazil* (2nd ed., 1963)

————, *Social Science Research in Latin America* (1964)

Webb, K., *Brazil* (1964)

Wilgus, A. C., ed., *Argentina, Brazil and Chile Since Independence* (1935)

Wythe, G., R. A. Wight, and H. M. Nordkiff, *Brazil, An Expanding Economy* (1949)

Young, J. M., *Brazil: Government and Politics* (1966)

Zweig, S., *Brazil, Land of the Future* (1941)

Chapter 32

Twentieth-Century
Argentine Politics

THE STAGE SETTING AT THE TURN OF THE CENTURY

Temperate-climate, European-blooded, agriculturally rich
Argentina! How similar it seems at first glance to the United States, how
different in many respects from the colorful, tropical Latin America of
mid-hemisphere! The fat pure-blooded cattle on parade at the stock
shows, the thousands of square miles of wheat acreage, the meat-packing
plants and the frozen-beef industry, balanced by the sophisticated modern
metropolis with its chic little stenographers strolling past the smart fashion
shops at their noon hour, the highly unionized stevedores working the busy
port and living in model housing, the preponderance of European immigrant stock with little trace of the Indian—all these things make Argentina
and its capital seem a mixture of Chicago, Kansas, and New York. Where
is the gaucho with his guitar, the tango dancers with their Latin rhythms?
Usually one finds them only in the night clubs and on the Buenos Aires
television.

These trends had been apparent when the twentieth century opened,
as the beef industry, and with it the nation, rushed toward modernization.
Argentina by 1900 had become one of the world's greatest suppliers of
food. An economic revolution had come first to the pastoral industries, and
then to the agricultural, brought about by better methods of breeding,
planning, and shipping, and accompanied by the increase of foreign capital

and the wave of immigration. But with the subsequent industrialization and urbanization had come a growing disparity between the wealthy few and the needy masses. The tide of European immigration had brought about a change in the racial composition of the population and had built up a large minority which had no effective defense of its interests through labor unions or political parties until the twentieth century. Immigration had given a great stimulus to the development of both a proletariat and a middle class, but the growing middle class of itself was not stable enough to form a political party of its own which could put up a united front of opposition. Thus the oligarchy of landowners, with an element of "new-rich" commercial leaders added, continued to rule as the twentieth century opened. But these very forces of economic and population change were gathering to produce a new political force, and to give Argentina the best political party system in Latin America.

Already in 1895 a census showed that one-half of the population could read and write, that railway lines, mostly financed in England, had doubled in mileage, and that foreign immigrants, many of them trained in commerce and mechanical trades, were ploughing up and fencing the open pampas as tenants, or building a new commercial class in the cities. Though many of the provinces were backward frontier areas which felt the pinch of rural poverty, Buenos Aires was a city of wealth—wealth which was no longer concentrated in the hands of the estate owners but was being amassed by the sons of the commercial-minded immigrants. Along with the immigrant factory workers and stevedores, these new-rich leaders were soon to press for a voice in the government. A new liberal party, the *Unión Cívica*, had already formed during the periods of revolt in the 1890s to challenge the entrenched political party of the estate owners, the "oligarchs."

There was a protest vote against the oligarch's power in the election of 1904, a protest which was spread over five weak candidates, and which allowed Manuel Quintana, the official oligarch candidate, to win the plurality. Opposing this choice was a new left-wing group called the Radicals which had split off from the moderately anti-oligarch *Unión Cívica* in the election of 1891. Its leaders were Leandro Além and his nephew Hipólito Irigoyen. When the oligarchs continued to rule Argentina through the 1890s, Além, who had hoped for a direct frontal attack on conservatism by leading an unsuccessful revolt in 1893, committed suicide in bitter disillusionment in 1896. The younger Irigoyen retired to teach in a private girl's school. From this seclusion he held the Radicals in a tightly knit opposition group, who protested by the indirect methods of "abstaining" from holding government jobs and from voting in elections.

In 1905, to challenge the minority president, Irigoyen left his teaching job and his undercover leadership of the quiescent Radicals and groomed himself as champion of the new laboring class of factory, dock, and railway workers. While the revolt stalemated, President Quintana died; in the same year the last of the elder statesmen, Bartolomé Mitre, also died. The generation that had ruled the stormy Argentina of the last two decades was passing. The congressional elections of 1906 brought a well-organized group of Irigoyen's followers and a few Socialists into the legislative body, where

Plaza del Congreso **and the Capitol building, Buenos Aires.**
Courtesy Braniff Airways.

they carried on a violent struggle with the able vice-president. In 1907 the
vice-president, José Figueroa Alcorta, is credited with the first feeble beginnings of social legislation—laws forbidding factory work on Sunday, limiting
the work hours for women and children, and creating a labor office.

Against the growing influence of the Radicals, oligarchs cooperated with
the new commercial class to win the presidency in 1910 with a compromise
candidate, Roque Sáenz Peña. It was an era of social pressures on politics,
and Sáenz Peña was ready to do more than merely "compromise."

THE ERA OF IRIGOYEN AND HIS RADICAL PARTY

Irigoyen's party was not "radical" by today's English connotation of
the word; he said little about land division and economic rights for labor,
and asked only for political rights—universal suffrage and fair elections.
Immigrant farmers, small tradespeople, and factory workers joined his
party and achieved some representation in the Congress. The general level
of political education was rising. The newspaper, *La Prensa*, though usually
representing the landed aristocrats, and *La Nación*, representing the middle
class, agitated for actual constitutional two-party government, fair elections,
and free trade. Trade unionists were interested in social reform. The

University of Buenos Aires had become the bulwark of academic freedom and secular liberty and a center of research and inquiry. All these forces rallied behind Irigoyen and helped him form a political machine, the powerful and growing Radical Party.

Roque Sáenz Peña, with experience as Minister of Foreign Affairs and as an ambassador in Europe, knew that the forces of democracy must be heeded and that a wider suffrage would encourage more immigrants to become naturalized citizens. He believed that reforms should come from the top. In 1912, through his personal insistence, the famous Roque Sáenz Peña Law was passed. It required that every man at the age of eighteen enroll his name for military service and register as a voter. Ballots were to be secret and only people who had actually registered were to vote, both ideas heretofore unknown in Argentina. Voting was made compulsory, with a fine of twenty pesos for failure. A little enrollment book was given each voter, containing identification, record of military service, and space for recording attendance at the polls for every election. The oligarchy yielded grudgingly to the Radicals on this law.

The Sáenz Peña Law was the magic "open-sesame" for Irigoyen's party. The first elections under the law, the congressional elections of April 1912, saw the Radicals turn out to vote in large numbers. They won many seats in the Chamber of Deputies, and soon also had three important provincial governorships, while the Socialists won a majority in the municipal government of Buenos Aires. More than 640,000 people voted in 1912; 745,000 in 1916; 1,461,000 in 1928. Argentina seemed headed for true democracy.

Roque Sáenz Peña died during his term, respected and honored by all factions, and his vice-president peacefully served out his term to 1916. Argentina was by then the richest country in Latin America, with a population of 8,000,000 and a capital city of 1,500,000 serving as one of the great agricultural shipping ports of the world. Social legislation was expanded. Employers were now responsible for accidents in industry; a national commission had been set up to provide cheap housing for industrial workers; laborers' wages could not be attached by creditors. World War I, which temporarily dislocated the Argentine economy, created boom demands for pampas meat and wheat by 1916.

The election of 1916, its votes counted with "scrupulous impartiality," brought Hipólito Irigoyen to the presidency with a large popular vote, ushering in a period of Radical rule to last until 1930. He was one of the most unusual characters in Argentine history, such a colorless, shabby-looking hulk of a man as to be called *El Peludo*, the mole, and his followers the *Peludistas*. Neither an inspiring orator nor a flamboyant writer, with no private fortune to spend and no family loyal to him in his lonesome life, he seems the antithesis of Latin American demagogic leaders. Born in 1853, he was the son of an illiterate Basque stable boy and a well-educated Buenos Aires woman. Together with the idealistic brother of his mother, Leandro Além, Hipólito devoted himself to the struggle against the oligarchy; he was in and out of various jobs but always active in the new *Unión Cívica Radical* party. As a teacher, he found time to translate liberal German philosophers into Spanish. His own words were

Hipólito Irigoyen. Photograph sent to the Pan American Union on his inauguration as president of Argentina, October, 1916. *Courtesy Pan American Union.*

always deeply philosophical, and his followers, who seldom understood him, considered him a saint. After his uncle's suicide the nephew kept on, exerting a mystical leadership, plotting endless intrigues against the oligarchy, now in the provinces and now in the city.

At first in 1916 he had declined the nomination made by the lesser leaders of his own party. All he said he wanted was victory for his ideals of equality and justice. The exuberant Radicals, meeting in an openly recognized political convention, persisted: if Irigoyen would not accept the nomination, the loosely joined party would disband. To the convention's emissaries, he finally said in the quiet of his study, "Do with me what you will." Then he went out into the country, refusing to campaign or to open his mail. Even at the inauguration he would not make a speech and tried to slip away from the hysterically joyful crowd.

Irigoyen was right, however, in saying he would not be a good administrator. Congress, which still contained a large minority of oligarchs, failed to respond to him. The Radical party consisted of a heterogeneous middle-class core, but with many diverse elements. Once in power the party had many "hangers-on" who were as selfish and corrupt as the worst of the opposition. Irigoyen's program of "honesty and equality" was so abstract as to accomplish little that was concrete. The new laboring class in Buenos Aires city profited from his philosophy, for he persuaded Congress to recognize the right of labor to form unions, and passed a more liberal code of wages and hours for factory workers. He also improved public health and brought running water and sewers to all large towns. World unrest after the European War of 1914–1918 was reflected in Argentina in mass uprisings among Buenos Aires labor, in spite of Irigoyen's laws, and in 1919 the city saw a "week of blood" in which many people were killed. Irigoyen claimed to be puzzled that his labor code, so poorly enforced, should result in so much bloodshed, and quelled the riots with military force like any other dictator. He ran the nation as he ran the party, as a dictator without any trust in subordinates. He intervened in the provinces, and the press was critical of him.

During the war he had been faced with an unexpected foreign problem. There were many Germans in Argentina, but sympathy in the nation was almost wholly with the Allies, who were buying Argentina's food products. German submarine warfare hit Argentina hard; it became very difficult for neutral food-laden ships to trade with England. In the fall of 1917, when two Argentine vessels were sunk, it was discovered that the German ambassador in Buenos Aires had acted as informer for his government as to the whereabouts of the ships. He had advised his government to either permit Argentine ships to get through or sink them without a trace, and had characterized the Argentine president as "a notorious ass." Irigoyen, determined to remain neutral, simply asked the ambassador to leave and accepted an apology from Germany, without severing diplomatic relations, declaring war, or taking any direct part in aiding the Allies. This strict neutrality was bitterly opposed by a pro-Allied Congress which passed nearly unanimous resolutions to sever relations with Germany. The pro-Allied members of the cabinet resigned in disgust at Irigoyen's neutrality. Meanwhile, food prices became inflated because of the overseas wartime demand; there were hardships and food riots at home, which diminished still further the popularity of Irigoyen.

The Radical party, with all its segments, was still strong enough for Irigoyen to handpick his successor, for the Constitution of 1853 had provided that no president could succeed himself until after a six-year interval. Thus in 1922 Marcelo T. Alvear, a Radical party leader, became president. A more practical man than Irigoyen, familiar with world conditions from his post as ambassador to France, he faced a difficult administration because of the postwar depression and the collapse of Argentine beef markets abroad. Alvear proved to be no puppet of Irigoyen and broke away to form a new anti-personalist faction of the Radical party. Under him inheritance taxes and taxes for schools were enacted, and rapid advances in labor rights were gained. He also became involved in a long dispute with the papacy because he interfered with Church appointments. Relations with the papacy were severed for two years, until a solution was reached in 1926 under which Catholicism was recognized as the "official" religion, the president had no power to make Church appointments, and all other faiths were to be freely tolerated.

Alvear had some difficulties with the United States, which had just passed the high Fordney-McCumber Tariff Act, tending to close the markets of America to Argentine meat and wheat. There was also bad feeling caused by the exclusion of Argentine beef from the United States market because of the supposed taint of hoof and mouth disease, which is discussed as an economic problem in the next chapter. At the Pan American conference at Havana in 1928 Argentine delegates protested American unwillingness to consider tariff reform, though to no avail till the Good Neighbor Policy of tariff reciprocity in the mid-1930s. Alvear had, however, "stood up to" the United States, as an example for later presidents.

At the end of Alvear's middle-of-the-road term in 1928, Irigoyen suddenly decided to run again. Now he was seventy-six years old, a senile hermit, though still a popular memory. The combined conservative factions could not prevent his election. His second term was a tragedy for the old man, a farce for Argentina. The workers were disillusioned with his leadership, as costs of living and unemployment both rose. He was easily controlled by a corrupt staff who charged visitors a high price for appointments with him. After two years of budget deficits, corruption in government, unsolved labor disputes, and loss of prestige abroad, the restless workers and critical middle classes were willing to follow a military clique led by the oligarch general José Uriburu, which threw the ineffectual Irigoyen out in a "spontaneous" revolution in 1930. The plot, which was hatched by the army, was assisted by rioting university students. In and out of prison for the next three years, Irigoyen died friendless and alone on July 3, 1933. Now the party remembered him—in death he was the symbol of democracy, though in life he had been the despised old "mole." Thousands jammed the street before the cheap little flat where he had died; people stood bareheaded for hours with tears running down their faces.

In the two years of this second term Irigoyen, or his henchmen in his name, had quarreled with Congress, interfered in the provinces far beyond the power of the president, and had split the Radical party. Even so, the military revolt was a shock to Argentines, who had considered their country too mature for barracks revolutions. Constitutional government, which had been making strides since 1900, came to a halt in Argentina with the revolution of September 6, 1930.

ARGENTINE THROUGH WORLD-WIDE DEPRESSION AND WAR

The *coup d'état* of 1930 was made by an army *junta* which took over the entire government, removed every Radical from office, postponed elections month after month, and threatened repeal of the Roque Sáenz Peña fair-election law. This was the first violent overthrow of government under the Constitution of 1853, and it succeeded only because of the world economic situation, and the desperate position of Argentine agriculture with the loss of foreign markets. With the failure of the Radicals, the country had no place to turn save to the Conservatives. Head of the *junta* was General José Uriburu, member of an old landlord family. Pledged to cut taxes on the landlords, he had to make many government economies, and even so faced a decline in the value of the peso and an unbalanced budget. At home the army controlled the government; the city of Buenos Aires lived as if in a state of siege, with Congress dissolved and the municipal government not functioning. Uriburu intervened in the local governments of twelve of the provinces, called off or postponed elections, and kept all opposition leaders in prison. The nation accepted all this because Irigoyen's last term had been so chaotic; the Conservatives, hoping to return to power in spite of the Radical majority in the country, accepted Uriburu's martial law until they could manage a Conservative election.

Eventually civilian opposition and division in the army forced Uriburu's hand, and the election, a one-sided rigged affair of the 1890 type, was held in November 1931, after thirteen months of promises. The Radicals, the majority of the voters in the nation, were not allowed to present candidates and boycotted the elections. Augustín P. Justo, supposedly leading a new party called the National Democrats, a combination of the old oligarch landowners, the city industrialists, and the anti-Irigoyen Radicals, was elected president to serve until 1938. Justo was a retired general, an ex-Minister of War, and a wealthy rancher from Entre Ríos province. Though he was responsible for a return of autonomy to the provinces, being a provincial himself, in the capital he simply maintained a continuation of Uriburu's military *de facto* government. Justo broke with Uriburu personally in 1932, but the idea of military dictatorship remained under the surface. Yet his first two years showed some awareness of social responsibilities when he passed income and inheritance tax laws and allowed the formation of more powerful unions. During his last two years the Radicals threatened control of Congress and so he dissolved it. The Conservatives behind him were determined that Argentina should never return to Radical rule. Under Justo the Conservatives ended laissez-faire and introduced a controlled economy. Guided by an able Finance Minister, Frederico Pineda, exhange controls, protective tariffs, bilateral agreements, and other measures brought Argentina out of the depression. But the prosperity benefited only the oligarchy, through the cattle industry and foreign trade. The middle and lower classes were worse off.

In Europe it was the age of military dictatorship, of fascism. In Argentina, the landlord families who feared ruin with the loss of the world market for beef, the Argentine army which had backed the Uriburu revolution, and even many of the intellectuals and clergy who were dissatisfied with the failure of Irigoyen democracy all dabbled with the idea of fascism. From 1934 to 1937 German Nazis came in large numbers into Argentina as "immigrants"; they learned Spanish and married Argentinians. In 1939 Hitler could claim 1,300,000 German "nationals" in Argentina, though the census showed only 43,626 newcomers born in Germany. Buenos Aires had 131 Nazi organizations and 203 German-language schools. Meanwhile Franco had won the Spanish Civil War and had a *falange* in Argentina. Justo did little to discourage the Fascists, who supported his government and spread their influence among army officers and young Conservative nationalists. An ineffectual commission was merely appointed to list such anti-Argentine agencies. Meanwhile the well-known Argentine diplomat, Carlos Saavedra Lamas, was a leader in foreign affairs, working for the "solidarity of the American states under Argentine guidance." At home and abroad Argentina was building up a strongly militaristic nationalism.

The left-wing Radicals had no leader after the death of Irigoyen, and by 1937 democratic politics had reached a new "low" in Argentina. In that year Congress passed only three laws, one to authorize expenditures and the other two to permit the president to take vacations. Not even a budget for the year was passed. The Radicals had won control of Congress in 1936 and were strong enough in the election of 1938 to force Justo to suggest a coalition compromise, a Liberal president and a Conservative vice-president. With many voters boycotting the polls and preferring to pay a fine rather than vote, with many employers and big ranchers collecting their employee's voting booklets and voting them all at once on election day, Justo's choices were naturally elected.

Roberto M. Ortiz, who had been in Alvear's cabinet, was chosen as the "front man," the man with liberal following who was to lull the masses into acceptance of the continued dictatorship. But Ortiz was not content merely to be a "front"; he staunchly opposed Nazis and Fascists and was sympathetic to the Allies although maintaining neutrality. He interfered in several "rigged" election in the provinces, and he insisted on fair elections for Congress in 1940. Anti-Nazi coalition groups made plans for socio-economic reforms, which, ironically enough, were to become the basis of Perón's promises six years later. The candidates of this coalition gained control of the lower house though the Senate remained in conservative control. Ortiz himself, a diabetic, lost his eyesight and the conservative vice-president, Ramón Castillo, favorite of army and landlords, had to act for the blind president. When Ortiz died in 1942, the brief interlude for democracy was over as Castillo took full control.

Castillo's sympathies had been pro-Axis, and now the repercussions of World War II were strongly felt in Argentina. Castillo made a feint for American aid to secure lend-lease military equipment in exchange for strategic tungsten. Then he used the equipment to enforce a strong military dictatorship. The anti-Castillo forces had no voice in the government after 1942. Castillo rigidly censored the press in favor of the Nazis, prohibiting pro-Allied meetings and openly encouraging pro-Axis propaganda. The Conservatives, who had lost much of their prewar trade in agricultural products with the British, were lulled into thinking that Hitler would win, and that Argentina's future lay in commercial relations with a victorious Germany. Popular sentiment was still strongly pro-Allied, however— especially since Germany continued to sink Argentine ships and to use the the German consulates in Argentina as bases for propaganda aimed at all Latin America. At home Castillo, backed by police force, represented the Conservatives. His government was one of fraud and repression while the cost of living went on up. Army leaders began to fear the rising tide of public anger. When Castillo attempted to impose his handpicked successor, a colorless sugar plantation tycoon, a group of army generals quietly drove Castillo from office in June 1943, and engineered an army revolution to "avoid bloodshed," with pro-Allied Arturo Rawson in as a 48-hour president.

June 7 saw a "permanent" president, the more pro-Axis General Pedro Ramírez, representing the victorious army faction. He dissolved all political parties, outlawed the Confederation of Labor, recessed Congress, and canceled elections, while he ruled ruthlessly by decree and with the backing of the Catholic Church. Military interventors were sent into all fourteen provinces to assume control from the elected governors, and even the mayors of large cities were replaced by army officers. The cabinet members who favored the Allies were replaced by friends of the Axis. Nazi propaganda continued to pour out of Argentina; especially the newspaper *El Pampero* carried daily criticism of England and the United States. Ramírez asked the United States for more military supplies under Lend-Lease, but was sharply rebuked by Hull, the American Secretary of State who refused to "put weapons into the hands of enemies of the United States." When enthusiasm for the Allied cause broke into demonstrations in the street, the pro-Axis government of generals and admirals quickly clamped down, padlocked the democratic newspapers, sent student rioters and striking meat-packers to jail, and continued its pro-Axis rule by decree.

But the next decade was to be an age of "colonels," not of generals. The army group which had ousted Castillo in 1943 realized that the monopoly of power in the hands of the landowning oligarchs was out of date. The *estancieros* could not satisfy the needs of a modern state. Now the "middle-class" military leaders made plans for a more popular backing among the lower classes, while they remained strongly pro-Axis in foreign affairs. Closest to the soldiers and strongest in policy-making among the military were a group of colonels, led by Colonel Juan Domingo Perón, then serving as Under-Secretary of War. Month by month President-General Ramírez became the tool of the colonels; pro-Axis tyranny became even stronger as university professors and government workers who signed a pro-United Nations manifesto published in the press were jailed without a hearing. Meanwhile Ramírez, angry at his puppet status, tried to accomplish an "about-face," hoping that by severing relations with the Axis he would save himself and would receive military help from the United States. But he was forced to resign in February 1944 and turned over his colonel-controlled seat to former Minister of War Edelmiro Farrell, puppet of the colonels' clique.

England and the United States ignored the government of Farrell and Perón; America called home her ambassador, and shipments of gold to Argentine banks were cancelled. The colonels still did not respond to Allied pressure and in February of 1945 sent no delegate to the inter-American conference at Chapultepec Castle in Mexico City. There the other Western Hemisphere nations resolved that any country that did not join the war against Germany could not join the United Nations to be formed the next month at the Charter Meeting in San Francisco. Only then did the Argentine government conform and declare war on Germany and Japan, March 27, 1945, when American and Russian soldiers were well inside the borders of Germany and marching on Berlin. Then Argentina was admitted to the good graces of the inter-American group and soon became a respected member of the United Nations.

Argentina's troubles with the United States about Nazi activity were not over, however. Ambassador Spruille Braden openly opposed Perón in Buenos Aires, while the United States State Department prepared a "Blue Book" showing in detail how Buenos Aires had been the headquarters of Nazi activity. Braden was recalled and his criticism only served to make Perón more popular at home. It was April 1946 before the United States welcomed Argentina into postwar friendship, accepting Argentine pledges to clean up Axis influences. By this time the Axis issue was dead, and Perón had won the February 1946 elections.

A DECADE OF PERÓN IN THE SADDLE

At home Perón called himself neither pro-Allied nor pro-Nazi, but pro-Argentine. Argentina was by now enjoying unprecedented prosperity, selling her foodstuffs to the victors. She claimed to be "the one spot in the Western World unbothered by the war." There was a building boom going on in Buenos Aires; well-dressed shoppers went in and out of the smart shops on Calle Florida where displays were rich and plentiful. Meat prices were high abroad; other South American nations, cut off from Europe, were buying the new industrial products of Buenos Aires' factories. Workers in the port and out on the pampas were better paid than ever before. All Argentina was willing to back any general, or even any colonel, who preserved this prosperity.

And Juan Domingo Perón was more than a mere colonel. At first not a "headliner" in the military government, he soon got himself promoted from Under-Secretary of War to Minister of War, Labor, and Welfare, and finally in 1944 under Farrell he called himself Vice-President. By then he had begun a policy of social and economic revolution. Three thousand of his opponents were in prison camps, and he was in control of the labor unions. As Labor Minister he had created a civilian army of backers, the new basis of power the "colonels' clique" had planned. Born October 8, 1895, Perón was one of many bright young lieutenants graduated from the Argentine military academy at eighteen; he was famous as a skier, a boxing champion, an expert swordsman, and a crack pistol shot. In 1930 he was teaching at the academy; in 1936 he was military attaché to the embassy in Chile; in 1939 he was sent on a special mission to Italy where he learned to admire and copy Mussolini's methods. Early in the colonels' regime he settled a widespread meat-packers' strike by a quick personal tour of the factories and workers' quarters, where he soon made friends with the labor leaders by treating them as honored equals and greeting them with the warm Latin embrace. Stubborn labor leaders found themselves in exile in Tierra del Fuego; "cooperative" labor leaders helped the Minister of War and Labor to found puppet unions. A widower, charming in manner, tall and prepossessing, Perón was full of vitality at fifty in the spring of 1945.

In October 1945 army leaders decided Perón was too powerful and had him imprisoned on a pretext. A parade of union members, led by his current girl friend, a radio actress named Eva Duarte, protested his arrest. In a few days Perón was out of prison; the day of his return was a labor holiday for the next decade. Within the week he and Eva were married. By October 17 he was the complete dictator of Argentina. In 1946 he was the candidate for the presidency of both army and labor; his one opponent, a Dr. Tamborini of the weak old Radical party, had little chance. The big landowners, the oligarchs, opposed him because of his promises to the poor that he would break up the large estates; they had no candidate of their own and were forced into a weak coalition behind the colorless Dr. Tamborini.

Perón's greatest power lay in the working masses in the large cities. For a half century each Argentine city worker's dream was to have a job or social position calling for the wearing of a white shirt, a *camisa*. We would call it "the urge to be in the white-collar class," to be among the *camisados*, the wearers of starched shirts. Perón told his followers among the laborers to scorn all this; they were the "unshirted ones," the *descamisados*, the men in work clothes, the real future of Argentina. It was not necessary to rig the election of February 1946. Perón was the friend of the masses, the champion of social justice, the enemy of the "imperialistic Yankees" who had written that critical Blue Book. The Church, the army, and the pro-Axis foreign groups were all on his side. Everyone voted in the secret ballot booths, each on his own registration enrollment book, perhaps for the first time. Impartial observers considered 1946 the fairest election in Argentina since 1916. Perón was not afraid to announce openly Dr. Tamborini's 44 per cent vote in the light of his 56 per cent. The Congress was composed of 90 per cent of his followers, the Radical opposition was weakened, governors of his own choosing were in the provincial capitals, and his own personal enemies were in exile in Montevideo or in work camps in Tierra del Fuego. Perón thus moved into six dramatic years of power.

The drama was enhanced by the beautiful Eva Duarte, now the First Lady. It was unprecedented for an Argentine president to marry an actress of unknown origin. But Eva Duarte was an illegitimately born adventuress playing for high stakes; blond, intelligent, and charming, she did not fear social ostracism by the wives of the oligarchs. Her appeal to the women of the *descamisados* brought her husband more popular support than any social "freeze-out" would have taken away. As shrewd as Perón, she defied tradition still further by entering politics as the Minister of Social Welfare and was only stopped by the army when the *descamisados* wanted to nominate her for vice-president. The money voted her department by Congress was put in the Eva Perón Foundation. With it and millions from private "contributions," she founded orphanages, homes for working girls, and cheap chain groceries where food was supposedly sold at cost. "I never keep book," she said, "I just work from the heart." Her portrait, six feet high, was on every public building, in every clinic and relief center. She became Secretary of Labor also, managing labor unions, calling strikes on and off at will when they seemed good publicity for Perón, and making large profits from the three newspapers which she bought on forced sales. She controlled the labor unions, the radio, the theater, and the newspapers in Argentina. "Eva is the soul of the workers! Perón is the father of the people!" announced the posters, while Eva proclaimed the emancipation of Argentine women and organized a *Peronista* Women's Party. Theatrical as the regime seemed, its base was its popularity among the working class, a new thing in Argentine politics. *Peronismo* was actually a political party opposed equally by the conservative old oligarchs and the remnant of Irigoyen's Radicals.

In 1947 a Bill of Rights for Workers was passed by Perón's Congress, later to be incorporated in his new constitution of 1949. Perón's *descamisados* got vacations with pay at new beach resorts for workers, higher wages, sickness benefits, tenure on the job, and bonuses at Christmas—at a time when the free unions under their own leaders had gained little or nothing for their members in the forty years since Roque Sáenz Peña. Rights of Labor, yes—but not the right to strike. In all this love song there was an undercurrent of tension and bitterness. Several strikes started without the Perón approval and were ruthlessly put down; there was quiet sabotage on the trains because of the railway workers' dislike of *Peronismo*.

Still labor leaders did not openly oppose Perón and the Argentine workers in general waxed fat. The old Radical party still existed, with a token number of seats in Congress, but it was the only "opposition" permitted. New parties could not organize; any existing party could be dissolved for "endangering the social peace." Perón meanwhile consolidated his own power by purging the Supreme Court and the university faculties, controlling elementary education, and organizing his own personal political party, the *Partido Peronista*. He was bent on preserving his totalitarian power and stopping all possible incipient revolt. For this purpose he proclaimed a law of *desacato* (don't be "disrespectful" or you will be arrested); he maintained a large police force against mob action, and kept tight control over the army.

Boldest opposition was from the eighty-year-old newspaper *La Prensa*. The rich and powerful *La Prensa* had always criticized what it pleased in every administration, meanwhile achieving world fame for its excellent coverage, and local prosperity for its circulation and fat advertising. It continued to criticize what it didn't like about the Peróns, though the government cut its newsprint paper supply, and called a strike of its employees. Finally in 1951 the newspaper was accused of being "foreign-bossed" because it carried dispatches from the United Press. *La Prensa's* owner, Gainza Paz, escaped to Uruguay. An editor was borrowed from *La Democracia*, one of Eva's papers, and the new editions began to sing Perón's praises as the circulation dropped.

Perón's economic policy was to convert Argentina into a powerful and self-sufficient modern state. He wanted to break the *estanciero* class and its hold on the food export trade, and to end Argentine dependence on foreign markets. He proposed to make Argentina the industrial giant of South America, economically independent, and launched a Five Year Plan to achieve that end, an elaborate blueprint for industrial progress filling 128 pages. There were to be sixty-nine hydroelectric plants, steel foundries, port improvements, and irrigation projects; some manufacturing and an expanded merchant marine were included. The agricultural crops of the Argentine pampas were to be bought from the producers at a fixed price by the government, then sold abroad at gouging prices in a starved world market. Money thus made was to pay for the grandiose industrialization schemes.

By 1949 the schemes had begun to bog down. The world market for Argentine food fell off as Marshall Plan funds made war-torn Europe more nearly self-supporting. International prices for beef dropped, while the purchases of heavy machinery abroad for the new industry overbalanced the sale of the food exports. Meanwhile large and small farmers alike began to complain of the differential between Perón's price to them and Perón's price abroad. Rural workers left the farms and came to the cities for the high wages being paid factory workers. Perón had to reverse himself and turn his attention to agriculture. Argentina lacked the coal and iron necessary for industrialization; what Perón needed to import first were not expensive oil drills and dynamos and Bessemer converters but "90,000 tractors, 20,000 combined harvesters, and 100,000 gang plows."

Perón's new industry was to be financed with Argentine, not foreign, capital. For a century English capital had controlled Argentina's banks, meat-packing plants, railways, and small manufacturers. Perón's rise was contemporary with the worldwide decline of English capital. The English railway companies sold to Perón outright, as they were not realizing $1\frac{1}{2}$ per cent on their billion-dollar investment. For little more than half this investment Perón received thousands of miles of track, a great deal of it obsolete, much outworn equipment, and responsibility for 150,000 employees. For months Perón's railway cost him $300,000 a day and the public was bitterly disappointed at the result of this much-touted venture into national ownership.

So Perón's six-year term went by. During that period he had carried his revolution into every branch of national life. He had expanded manufacturing, set prices, brought many social gains to labor, controlled the press, cut down the power of the oligarchy, and tried to eliminate foreign financial influence. Now he determined to entrench himself in power. According to the constitution in force since the fall of Rosas in 1853, no president could succeed himself. Copying Mexico's Porfirio Díaz, Perón called a constitutional convention in 1949, which meekly amended the law of presidential succession. The new "Perónized" constitution allowed indefinite re-election of the president by popular vote including woman suffrage, abolished the electoral college, expanded the economic power of the government, and included his own social program. Now Perón could run again in 1951. However, a plan to have Eva elected vice-president met with chilly opposition from Perón's own army officers, traditional in their views when it came to the position of Argentine women in society. Eva's name was withdrawn under pressure, at the same time that she became suddenly critically ill. When her illness was diagnosed as incurable cancer, the presidential campaign turned into a sad and muted affair. The Radical party put up Ricardo Balbín and Arturo Frondizi as their candidates, but they were given little opportunity to present the issues to the people, for Perón owned the press and radio and could send his police to harry opposition meetings. It was unnecessary for the army to supervise the election; it was easily rigged and as easily won by Perón. The surprising fact was that despite all this, the Radicals won a third of the votes cast.

For this second six-year administration—unprecedented since the days of Rosas, to whom many of Perón's enemies compared him—there was an equally unprecedented austere inauguration. Eva was ill unto death; Argentine economy was equally weak. An ambitious second Five Year Plan got off to a bad start. Beginning in February 1952 there were "meatless days" weekly in every restaurant, this in a land where the poorest families were accustomed to juicy steaks. Owing partly to Perón's overemphasis on city workers and manufacturing, partly to unwillingness of farmers to plant crops or sell young steers in the face of Perón's low fixed prices, partly to a two-year drought, the meatless days were a shock to well-fed Argentinians. Throughout 1952 and 1953 this austerity continued.

In 1952 Argentina's living costs were skyrocketing, her peso was devaluated, her foreign trade balance was unfavorable. In the midst of this economic dilemma, Eva died, July 26, 1952. Multitudes of *descamisados* mourned hysterically at her funeral; all streets, towns, plazas, and school rooms named for President Mitre, long since forgotten, were declared by Congress to be renamed for Eva Perón. Her body was to be embalmed in an open glass shrine.

Throughout the decade Perón had considered himself a world power. Calling Argentina the "Third Force which would inherit the world's ashes," Perón's newspapers had loudly proclaimed the Korean episode in June 1950 as the "Great Russo-Yankee War." Perón thought of his nation as the future leader of the Western Hemisphere; he had spent money lavishly to help his friends get elected in Ecuador, Chile, and Bolivia. He had made Argentine embassies in the smaller Latin American nations headquarters for the distribution of anti-American literature, some of it identical with that distributed by the Communists. Arms manufactured in Buenos Aires turned up in revolutions in the Caribbean. Argentine movies and radio programs, Argentine books and papers actually made Argentina seem a world force to be reckoned with. Perón renewed the Argentine claim to the Falkland Islands, long held by Britain, and "incorporated" them into the Argentine nation; he also published maps which showed Antarctica as Argentine territory.

Perón's chief problems in the second administration were to put the national economy back on a sound footing and to promote its further development. He was forced to reverse some of his policies and to shift emphasis from "social justice" to "sound business." He attempted to prove he could rule without Eva, and he ousted her favorites in the government and the labor organizations. After November 1952, when productivity lagged and economic difficulties increased, he adopted a policy of "get along with the oligarchs, go back to the beef industry and to agriculture as the basis of national wealth." Plans for Eva's glass burial place were quietly changed; names of places called after President Mitre were quietly *not* changed. Let Argentina forget Eva and the new industrialism, while workers from the congested city were urged to return to the land and increase agricultural production. Peron played off one factor against another, *descamisados* and industrialists against landowning oligarchy and army officers, shopkeepers and employers against workers. A deflationary policy was instituted and imports curtailed. But as clever and shrewd a demagogue as Perón was, he saw his schemes beginning to fail and his devoted minions in the army and the unions beginning to doubt him.

Then in 1954 in the mistaken hope of stirring up liberalistic loyalties, Perón quarreled with the Catholic Church. Taking advantage of labor discontent the Church formed a Catholic labor party. He accused the priests of meddling in politics and opposing his regime. When Catholic leaders criticized him in return, he imprisoned them, closed Catholic papers, prohibited religious processions, raided Catholic students' clubs at the university, and dismissed religious teachers. To further spite devoted Catholics he legalized divorce and prostitution and legitimatized illegitimate children. "It is Christ or Perón!" cried the Church leaders. By 1955 the Church had organized a strong opposition, the first anti-Perón movement that had ever been able to survive and grow.

When the Church quarrel had weakened the last popular hold the dictator had, he tried to arm his labor followers to stop the pending rebellion. Army, navy, and air force officers reacted by joining with the underground liberal intellectuals and their small following in Congress. They rallied behind a military man, Eduardo Lonardi, who had been jailed for opposing Perón in an abortive plot. This combination succeeded in an army *coup* which threw Perón out of the Casa Rosada in September 1955. The mobs had broken into Perón's several private houses, found evidences of enormous hidden wealth and luxurious living at public expense, of mistresses kept in the place of Eva of the now tarnished memory. It was evident that Perón had been a large-scale grafter. He left Argentina with over $1,200,000,000 debt and an internal debt of 70 billion pesos. He was fortunate to escape upriver to Paraguay. Soon he went to live in a high-priced hotel in Panama, then showed up a year later organizing racetrack betting in Caracas. In 1959 he was a guest of Trujillo in Santo Domingo, though at home in Buenos Aires members of his organized labor unions continued to cast large blocks of votes as he directed them from afar. No matter how bad his regime had been, he had brought a social revolution to Argentina which was irrevocable, with the shift in political power away from the oligarchs.

THE NEW DIRECTION OF ARGENTINE POLITICS

Pleased as most Argentines were to be rid of Perón, they had reason to be dismayed by the problems he had left and to question the ability of the new government to deal with them. Perón had left a wrecked economy and the inheritors of that wreckage were to be plagued for a generation or more. For *Peronismo* could not be denied; the Argentines had been caught up in the revolution of rising expectations. They had reached an intermediate stage of economic development and thus, unlike most Latin American countries, had passed out of the underdeveloped stage. Yet they experienced economic crisis, social ferment, and political instability. Though an agricultural nation, Argentine hoped to skip to the next stage, that of industrialization, without paying for the interlude of Perón.

To run Argentina in the vacuum left by Perón was difficult for anyone. Lonardi, the "middle-of-the-road" man with no plan save to oust the dictator, lasted only fifty days. When he refused to "crack down" on the *Peronistas*, he was himself ousted by another palace *coup*, November 13,

1955, which installed a little-known infantry officer named Pedro Eugenio Aramburu. Aramburu's government, which could only be a "caretaker's" government, faced major problems. It first had to keep itself in power for its allotted term until elections could be held, allowing no violent revolution among the many dissident Argentine factions. In December of 1955, June of 1956, and November of 1957, outbreaks had to be put down by armed force. Secondly, it had to solve the problem of "de-Peronization," a large task of cleaning out ten years of favoritism and corruption. Thirdly, it had to avoid economic chaos in a country whose cost of living index went up 34 per cent in 1957. This Aramburu attempted to do by keeping wages frozen, thereby controlling inflation to some extent but increasing his own unpopularity among the laboring class.

Economic problems were left unsolved, but politically Aramburu acted wisely and well. He called a constituent assembly of 205 delegates to meet at Santa Fé in August 1957. These delegates set up a plan for elections of a president, a congress, and all provincial governors to be held on February 23, 1958. Aramburu himself said, "Remember always that political decisions are not to be made in barracks, air bases, or naval ships. . . . Whatever candidate promises a paradise for indolents will be lying, and if he should win, the country will be in danger."

The active anti-*Peronistas* were members of the old Radical party, who had put up a presidential candidate, Ricardo Balbín, and a vice-presidential candidate, Arturo Frondizi, as recently as 1951, and had been allowed a few seats in Perón's congress. Now the Radicals split, the more conservative following Balbín, and the more liberal nominating Frondizi and calling themselves Intransigent Radicals. Frondizi, one of fourteen children of an Italian immigrant who had settled in Corrientes, had been a leftist in his law-school days, but was now willing to work with foreign capital. He won the votes of industrial leaders by promising high tariffs. The Church rallied to him when he took "free divorce" out of the Radical platform. The socialists of his youth were promised the nationalization of electric power and telephone companies. In world affairs, the coolly intellectual Frondizi guaranteed to line up Argentina strongly with the West.

Only one of his promises backfired; he had offered amnesty to imprisoned *Peronistas*. When Perón from exile ordered 1,500,000 Perón followers to vote for Frondizi, he won easily, but when *Peronistas* held an enthusiastic street celebration at the Frondizi inauguration, Frondizi broke it up with tear gas. He did put the promised general amnesty bill through his majority-controlled congress, saying that he had always been the anti-Perón leader but had "a deep personal belief that no one should be persecuted for his political ideas." The further leniency of his congress in giving unions large measures of autonomy kept several strong Perón backers in control of labor, and allowed Perón to brag from his borrowed villa in Ciudad Trujillo in 1958 that he could paralyze the nation with a strike at any time, and thus control seven million votes. When his followers tried such a strike, however, Frondizi ended six months of pussyfooting with the *Peronistas,* and broke it up by armed force. Many Argentines were willing to join the strikers in protest against Frondizi's austerity regime.

Frondizi kept administrative spending down in the face of the huge national deficit, cut wages in an attempt to bring down inflated prices, and warned the military that they could expect no bonuses and few favors. Tackling the trade deficit, he tried to build Argentina's own oil production by importing foreign capital to prospect for further petroleum deposits and thus eventually end the $300 million yearly import item for gasoline and oil alone. By so doing, he made a frontal assault on the economic nationalism rooted in Argentina for a generation. On a trip to Washington in 1959 he made an appeal for American capital investment. At the same time, the International Monetary Fund announced a $329 million loan to Argentina, the largest to any single Latin American nation up to that time.

Frondizi had been elected because of his promises to please everybody. Soon he found it impossible to please anybody. Walking a tightrope between the army and the working-class *Peronistas*, he failed to help the big Argentine middle class fill the power vacuum left when the landowning oligarchs lost control of politics. He tried to make himself personally popular in Argentina as a great South American leader by his visit to the United States and subsequent trips to Europe and other Latin American nations. In 1960 he joined the newly-formed Latin American Free Trade Association, a common market plan, and broke relations with Communist Cuba in 1962.

But at home he faced crisis after crisis—thirty-two threats against his presidency and his life. In the congressional election held in 1960, *Peronistas* cast more than a million blank ballots, on orders from Perón in exile. Frondizi's party received fewer votes than the *Peronistas* cast blanks. So Frondizi decided to reform the election law, allowing many small parties and splinter groups to put up candidates and to receive proportional representation in Congress. This so-called "reform" brought twenty-six parties into the Congress in the congressional elections of March 1962, including a large bloc of *Peronista* backers. In panic lest the *Peronista* working class control the Congress, the army declared the election invalid. A group of officers arrested Frondizi and held him under house arrest in the southern resort of Bariloche for fourteen months.

Again democracy had failed in Argentina and the army was in control of the capital. An army puppet, José Guido, president of the senate, was next in line to the presidency. He declared congress in recess until elections scheduled for the summer of 1963. The government seemed almost to have returned to the chaos of the Reds and the Blues of Rosas' time, as warring factions within the army leadership called themselves the Reds and the Blues.

Senate chairman Guido struggled along for fourteen months till the elections arranged by the army for July 1963. Twenty-four different parties put up candidates for Congress; seven different persons were nominated for president. The winning candidate, Dr. Arturo Illia, of the more conservative wing of the old Radical party, received only 27 per cent of the popular vote. But coalitions with minor parties won him a majority in Congress, over both the Frondizi and the Perón factions.

Dr. Illia, a physician from Córdova, came to the presidency in 1963, hopefully, for a six-year term. So relieved were the Argentines to have a "stable, mature moderate" in the presidency that the Buenos Aires Stock Exchange posted its biggest trading day in history the day Dr. Illia's election was proclaimed. Foreign trade seemed to be picking up, the peso was rallying from its all-time low under Frondizi, and the skyrocketing upward curve of the cost of living seemed to be flattening out.

But, alas, Dr. Illia's popularity was shortlived. A successful country doctor, he knew little of politics. His philosophy was "to sit quietly back and let the land of beef and wheat run itself." His only positive action in the foreign field was to cancel the contracts for petroleum prospecting granted to foreign companies by Frondizi. Thus oil production came almost to a halt, and Argentina began to import oil again at high prices. Illia did have some success in satisfying the *Peronista* workers with higher pay and more jobs—attempting thus to get the *Peronista* group out of politics. It had become a working-class party which no longer had a leader. Perón himself, by this time a "playboy" in the international social set, came to visit in nearby Rio. When Illia refused him a visa to come to Argentina, the labor leaders made no great outcry. His pretty young third wife, a Spanish girl named Isabelita, came to Buenos Aires to lead the *Peronistas* and to hold rallies in his name in 1965, and drew very small crowds. Perón himself was politically a dead issue by 1966. But the working-class voters had gained a political power under Perón greater than that of any other Latin American laboring group save that in Mexico. Still calling itself *Peronista*, the Labor party won 35 per cent of the total vote in the congressional elections of 1965. It could be said as the 1970s approached that Perón had made a great and lasting impact on Argentina despite his faults. His real achievement had been to better the lot of the workers.

The presidency of the well-meaning Dr. Illia had brought stalemate by 1966. His commander-in-chief of the Argentine army was a tough polo-playing cavalry officer named Juan Carlos Onganía, a quiet "strong man" with no political experience. In May, 1966, the army charged the Illia government with doing little to advance the economy and of having permitted the growing social unrest to threaten the foundation of society. Illia's party members attempted to divide the army but failed, and on June 28 the army surrounded the *Casa Rosada*, the "Pink White House," with 400 troops and ousted the ineffective Dr. Illia. On June 30, 1966, Onganía was simply declared Argentina's thirty-first president. The United States and other New World nations grudgingly recognized him within a month.

Throughout the fall and winter of 1966, Onganía clamped down on all vestiges of democratic government. He dissolved the Congress, disbanded all political parties, ended local self-government and sent his own army officers to govern the states, and abolished the National Election Board, declaring himself president for an indefinite term. The constitution, last approved in 1956, was thus completely invalidated.

In November, 1966, Onganía told business groups that he had taken over "to pull the country out of stagnation, against the adversaries of inefficiency, outdated structures, vested interests, and indolence." A thin man himself, he criticized the "obesity" of the meat-fed Argentines, and set rigid price controls to channel food stuffs into the export trade. He ended Dr. Illia's toleration of *Peronista* labor unions and threatened to end any strike with military force in twenty-four hours. A general walk-out in protest in February, 1967, lasted only two hours. He devalued the peso and interfered in the nine state universities. As of mid-1967, Onganía's rule seemed one of the harshest dictatorships in Argentine history.

Facing the 1970s, Argentina was far from solving its historical problems. It was still ruled by military men. The working people could not forget the bonuses and favors they had been promised under the demagogue Perón; the rich landowners still owned the fertile hinterland in large estates and showed no sign of accepting any land reform program. Thus Argentina, which in 1920 had seemed the most modernized, educated, and democratic nation in Latin America, had retarded its own progress by 1965. But the Argentines themselves, like the cattle grazing on their rich pampas, remained for the most part plump and happy.

NOTE: Readings for Chapter 32 are combined with those for Chapter 33.

The Argentines—A Sophisticated, Prosperous People

WHEAT AND MEAT: THE BASES
FOR ARGENTINA'S PROSPEROUS FUTURE

IF ARGENTINE STATESMEN turned away from the new industrialization and back to agriculture for political and economic stability, it was because therein lay the destiny of the nation. True, one-fourth of Argentina's population lives in Buenos Aires, but that fourth lives off the agriculture of the pampas and the foreign exchange earned from exporting it. No matter how well the cities pay their workers, no matter how fast the cities are growing, they cannot absorb of themselves the products of the rich and fertile pampas. Argentina must sell meat and wheat abroad or "die on the vine."

The pampas produce so much more than ever before—300 pounds of beef a year per capita, in contrast to 145 pounds per capita in the rich United States; there are thirty head of cattle per person in Argentina compared with five head per person in the United States. Argentina has contributed 75 per cent of all beef eaten in England over the last three decades, and meat is being sent in cheaper cuts to France and Germany, in Kosher form to Israel, and in cans of corned beef to even the beef-rich United States. Beef-raising creates a social problem of tenant farmers and large

Judging prize beef at the National Livestock Fair Buenos Aires. *Courtesy Pan American Union.*

estates, a social hierarchy of beef-raisers, a cultural tradition of stock shows and cattle judging, a cultural heritage of gaucho song and story.

The steers themselves are oblivious to all this; they are among the world's most "contented" animals. The 1900s saw the "revolution" on the pampas—the fenced-in pastures, the growing of alfalfa for a year-round food supply to keep the beef fat, the coming of windmills and watering troughs so that pampered cattle never had to wander far for water. After refrigerated ships were developed in the 1890s, a new kind of animal was needed for a new world market, one that developed tender steaks and roasts where stringy muscles had been before. The Rural Society, really a closed corporation of the oligarchs, was formed to develop the scientific breeding of beef cattle, to import Shorthorns, Durhams, Herefords, and Aberdeen Angus from England. To compete in the grand championship shows so popular by 1900, an estate-owner's entries had to have pure blood lines and pedigrees registered in the records of the Rural Society. Out of these blooded lines come the prize bulls of the yearly livestock shows, where winning animals bring 50,000 to 150,000 pesos apiece at exciting public auctions attended by the highest society. The weight of individual animals increased 50 per cent in five decades; the use of the land to provide rich pasturage had improved so much that 4,000 head are pastured on ten square miles where 1,000 had been pastured in 1900. One-third of the cattle today are in the province of Buenos Aires, always the richest of Argentina's provinces, where grass is green the year around and the weather so mild that the cattle live outdoors all year, and no frostproof barns have to be built.

Nature itself upset this cattleman's paradise in the last decade. The years 1961 and 1962 brought unprecedented drought to the pampas. Four million cattle died of thirst and starvation, one in every ten in the entire nation. To keep up the exports of beef needed for foreign exchange, Buenos Aires city people, who ordinarily eat 200 pounds of meat each year, had to go on a diet of two meatless days a week till the end of 1963. Thousands of city meat packers were out of jobs till the pampas herds gradually built up again by 1966. Then Onganía again rigged the prices of foodstuffs at home so that the diet went down and the reports went up.

To the north, in the provinces of Misiones, Corrientes, and Entre Ríos, *criollo* cattle, the stock descended from the cows brought by the Spaniards, are raised in abundance for local consumption. In these regions, the hoof and mouth disease is endemic in a mild form. This cattle scourge, in its highly contagious form, broke out in the United States beef-producing regions in 1924, and the frantic American cattle-owners persuaded Congress to clap a quarantine on all raw beef imports from mildly infected Argentina. The quarantine—persisting because of American beef-producers' fear of the competition of cheaply raised Argentine beef imports—has produced more hard feeling against the United States in Argentina than any so-called acts of "imperialism."

Argentines are ahead of all the rest of Latin America in the consumption of fresh milk, butter, and cheese for there are many dairy farms close to the port city. Fresh fruits and vegetables for the Buenos Aires markets are grown in such well-kept truck gardens as to make the area seem like rural New Jersey and Maryland.

Today Argentina, whose aborigines never learned to plant the corn of the Maya and Aztecs, leads the United States in corn export. Wool exports and frozen mutton from Argentina are second in world trade only to those from Australia and New Zealand. To the wind-swept territories of Patagonia and Chubut have come Basque and Scottish shepherds to care for thousands of head of the best wool-producing breeding stock, with all this development occurring since 1902 when a territorial dispute over Patagonia between Argentina and Chile was finally settled. Argentina is second only to Canada as a wheat-exporting country. The wheat ranchers, whose work is done by tenant farmers, form the powerful "oligarchy" of the district around Rosario; Rosario itself, with its docks on the Paraná accessible to steamers of 10,000 tons, and its 620,000 population, is Argentina's second city and one of the world's chief wheat-shipping ports. In the wheat and corn belts, rice and barley are grown, as well as flax for seed oil. Of the linseed oil used in the world's paint industry, 80 per cent comes from Argentina.

North and west of the Plata area sugar and cotton thrive; the Tucumán region, a one-crop area, produces sugar for the urban population, while the Argentine Chaco, an unincorporated territory on the Paraguay border, is now producing enough cotton to feed Buenos Aires' new textile mills and to export considerable quantities to English mills as well. Here in the north are vast national forests where hardwoods and *quebracho* for tanning are produced under state control. Mendoza, that irrigated mountain valley where San Martín's men trained more than a century ago for the Andes crossing, is now a pretty foothill city of over 130,000 people, in the center of the "Garden of the Andes," with its thousands of acres of wine grapes. Italian and Spanish wine producers immigrated to Mendoza in great numbers, and today their Italian-type red wines are seen on many South American tables.

In the southern Andes and the northern semitropics there are still forests, which comprise 32 per cent of Argentina's over-all acreage. Another 14 per cent consists of unproductive regions of the Chaco or the middle Andes. Ten per cent of Argentina is in planted crops to produce the enormous tonnage of exportable corn and wheat and other foods. This leaves 41 per cent of Argentina as the great pasture of the pampas. Of Argentina's total foreign exports, 44 per cent are meat products, and 50 per cent are grain, vegetable oils, wool, and cotton.

ARGENTINA'S HOPES FOR INDUSTRIAL IMPORTANCE

Despite the lack of fuel and iron, Argentine industrialization has progressed steadily since its first few factories opened in the 1890s. Today industry employs more people than does agriculture. The major industry is, of course, connected with the preparation of meat. Here in Buenos Aires are meat-packing plants as large as any in Chicago. In fact, to the grief of many nationalistic Argentines, the three largest are owned by the same firms as are those in Chicago—Armour, Wilson, and Swift. Anglo-Argentine, an English company, owns the fourth largest, and the single large plant that is Argentine-owned ranks only fifth. In these giant *frigoríficos*, as the packing plants are called, the meat must be prepared for shipment overseas, so the most modern techniques are used. Since World War II the whole beef-packing industry has changed over from emphasis on chilled beef to "deep-freeze beef"; no longer is it necessary to have the carcasses on board the British refrigerated boats within a few days after they have been slaughtered. Frozen beef can be held for higher prices, can be shipped in Argentina's own "deep-freeze" fleet. Some of the beef cuts are still canned as corned beef; Argentine corned beef, cooked under high pressure and thus free of hoof-and-mouth contagion, enters freely into the United States, where there is no large canned-beef industry to be hurt by it. From the 8,000,000 beef carcasses slaughtered every year, 5,000,000 beef hides, mostly wet-salted rather than dried as in the days of the gaucho, enter into the export trade and reach the shoemakers of the world.

Of the Argentine factories which produce machinery, 500 plants are busy putting out agricultural machinery, plows, harvesters, tractors, windmills, and even silos. Foreign investments have helped build Argentine industry. The railroads and docks were built largely by English capital, though sold at a loss to Perón and running rather inefficiently in the mid-1960s under government ownership. The Chicago meat-packers investment is worth $50,000,000; other manufacturing plants absorbed a hundred million, and assembly lines for automobiles and farm machinery have accounted for a hundred million more. Prosperous *porteños*, tired of using American vacuum cleaners, American Ford cars, American plows and electric refrigerators, and resentful of the beef "quarantine," enthusiastically accepted Perón's Five Year Plan to industrialize Argentina and make the nation self-sufficient in both heavy industry and consumption goods.

In some fields Argentina did fulfill Perón's Five Year Plan quotas within the decade of the 1960s. Textile manufacturing was up 300 per cent over 1940, the manufacture of leather, ceramics, processed and packaged foods, chemicals, medicine, cement, furniture, paper, tires, and rubber goods made from Brazilian raw rubber also increased rapidly. As English capital was bought out in the purchase of the railways, so a great deal of American capital was "squeezed out" by Perón-aided local industries, and by the "tussle over red tape" that Perón's government created for foreign capital, as well as by his demand that profits made in Argentina be kept in pesos and ploughed back in Argentine development. In the early 1960s American investors were "afraid of getting burned." Perón's successors' reversed his "anti-American capital" policy and began to woo United States investors. A loan negotiated to build a steel plant at San Nicolás was completed by Aramburu. Dr. Illia made a great show of material self-sufficiency but welcomed Alliance for Progress loans to build for industry.

Hard coal is not mined in Argentina; hydroelectric projects must be developed in the Andes 600 miles away. Recent plans to deconcentrate the new industry depend on the tardy development of such power. Meanwhile geologists searched for oil in Patagonia, as the Chaco nationally-owned oil wells could not produce one-fourth of Argentina's yearly needs.

President Frondizi felt that the whole nation was desperate for oil, so he made contracts with ten American and British companies in 1958 to continue the search for oil, while at the same time developing the existing oil wells and setting up refineries. Within five years under these contracts, Argentina was producing enough oil for local use and saving the burden of spending $300,000,000 a year on imported oil. But the unpopularity of this grant to foreigners helped to lead to Frondizi's downfall. One of Dr. Illia's first acts as president was to cancel these contracts and turn the producing wells and the refineries over to a group of inexperienced civil servants. Dr. Illia undertook to pay the foreign companies for all money spent in fruitless prospecting, as well as in developing production. An agreement as to payments was accepted by the companies in September 1965, and Argentina had to import oil again. Dr. Illia briefly became a hero to the ardent Argentine nationalists, but faced a long, difficult debt-payment scheme, without the great resources in oil that had made Mexico's petroleum nationalization a success.

Argentina still depends on foreign trade, no matter how successful she is at developing home-consumption industries. Long centering their trade on England, Argentines have shifted since 1939. Today the United States is the source of most of Argentina's imports and ranks second in consuming

Argentine goods, but much of this trade is now carried in Argentine owned ships.

THE OPEN PAMPAS OF THE GAUCHO, NOW FILLED-IN

> Welcome all nations, to the new promised land!
> Here is the region of El Dorado,
> Here is the terrestrial paradise.
> Here the longed-for good fortune,
> Here the golden fleece![1]

Thus sang the world-famous Latin American poet, Rubén Darío, who, though born in Nicaragua, had made Argentina his "second motherland." He was writing a "Hymn to Argentina," in honor of the 1910 centenary of Argentina's independence. He cried to dissatisfied Italians, Jews, Spaniards, Swiss, Germans, "all the disinherited of the earth," to come to "Plata's shores, a mystic Eden," to come to the Argentina that offered a full life. How like North American poems about the Statue of Liberty! And there are stories in Argentina of immigrants who came penniless and made millions, just as there are in the United States.

To balance such success stories there were a hundred thousand stories of tenant farmers on the pampas, or of city factory workers. Perhaps a million Italian and Spanish farm workers came as *golondrinas,* swallows, for three months of harvest labor in the corn and wheat during the season of Europe's own winter, and returned in the cheap steerage. But there were the millions who stayed, who filled in the pampas, built the new barbed-wire fences, planted the alfalfa now so necessary for the pedigreed steers, and replaced the picturesque gaucho of the nineteenth century. The immigrants changed Buenos Aires to a fast-growing, industrialized metropolis; they stimulated both the middle class and the proletariat; they altered the whole face of Argentina and made it the commercialized modern leader of the Southern Hemisphere, adding greatly to the social and cultural diversity of the nation.

The population doubled every twenty years. In 1914 it was ten times that of 1852; of the inhabitants in 1914 those of the part-Indian, typical Latin American *mestizo* stock numbered only 5 per cent. Sixty-five per cent were descendants of pure Europeans, while 30 per cent were themselves European-born. Immigration, slack during World War I, boomed in the 1920s when postwar conditions at home in Italy were particularly hard. Nearly two million Italians had chosen to stay in Argentina, as well as nearly a million Spaniards and hundreds of thousands of Swiss, Austrians, and Russians, almost all of these farm and city laborers. English businessmen and engineers in the thousands live in Buenos Aires today; German technicians came in great numbers to this land of opportunity; Scotch, Welsh, and Basque sheep farmers found success in Patagonia.

---

[1] Isaac Goldberg, *Studies in Spanish American Literature* (New York: Brentano's, 1920), p. 177.

Though 40 per cent of Argentines have Italian blood, there has emerged an Argentinized type, product of the melting pot as is the "Americanized" type of the United States. Immigrants are still coming, now encouraged again by Argentine government agents in Europe. In the late 1960s Argentina was about 90 per cent white, 8 per cent *mestizo*, and 1 to 2 per cent Indian. In 1965 an unofficial estimate put the total population at just under 22,000,000. Of the 8,000,000 Argentines gainfully employed in 1966, 21 per cent worked in agriculture, 36 per cent in industry, 20 per cent in transportation, and 22 per cent in permanent service.

Though all the governments since Roque Sáenz Peña had talked about free lands for colonizers, and about cheap small holdings on the pampas, those immigrants who came to find such lands were almost always disappointed. The land was already owned, in the large holdings of the cattle barons who saw no advantage in selling off small acreage. Railroads, built by British capital to serve the large ranchers, did not need to bring in small freeholders to settle new lands as did the railroad builders of the United States. Italian immigrants, used to tenancy at home, were satisfied with the larger tenant farms, the better crops, the greater freedom of movement, and the unlimited meat rations they found on the pampas.

The great estate owners heard few complaints against their system. For them the new refrigeration, the better transportation, the improved stock, and the cheap labor had turned the wild pampas of 1850 into one of the world's richest gardens, and they themselves had become one of the world's most prosperous classes. "As rich as an Argentine" became a by-word on the French Riviera, where many Argentine estate-owning families had villas—families who also maintained houses in Buenos Aires, and who visited the palatial mansions on their pampas lands once a year. The hundred wealthiest families owned more than ten million acres among them; 272 individuals and corporations owned one-sixth of Buenos Aires province, 2,000 owned about one-fifth of the total area of Argentina. Many of these *propiedades* or holdings are still held today by family "corporations," interlocked complexities of inheriting sons and cousins, many of whom never see the land. Recent governments have done almost nothing about land distribution.

In the center of such an estate, or *estancia*, is a palatial mansion house, surrounded by thousands of trees artificially planted on the treeless pampas two or three generations before, and now further surrounded by swimming pools, tennis courts, and polo fields. Here an expert overseer maintains a staff of servants in preparedness for the rare occasions when the owners visit, and supervises the villages of the tenants who care for the hundreds of thousands of head of beef and dairy cattle and sheep, and perhaps a thousand race horses and polo ponies on the stud-farm.

In this feudal organization, the day laborers received in the 1960s the equivalent of about $40 a month in cash—a ranch hand's wage three generations ago in the American West. Planted crops are cared for by tenants or sharecroppers, who use the owners' machinery, receive meat rations, garden plots, small adobe dwellings, free horses, and elementary education for their children from the owners—a life better than that of most European peasants or that of peon farmers in several other parts of Latin America. Such alfalfa land was often broken in from native grass pasture by hiring tenants to plow and plant wheat for four or five seasons. Then alfalfa, which has to be replanted only once in six or seven years, would replace the wheat, and day laborers the tenants. These tenants, now footloose, might move on into the corn belt to farm 150 acres for another owner. Always living in adobe houses, usually comfortless and dirt-floored, never feeling any pride in or love for the land, the tenant feels little need to improve his community, no civic interest in schools or good roads. His women are tied to drudgery in the fields beside him; his children seldom rise above his station. The increased wages made compulsory by the Perón government were counterbalanced by the increased cost of clothing and city supplies. Unless he is content to live little better than did Martín Fierro in the days of the gaucho riders on the open pampas, the tenant has no "out" save to migrate to the city as an industrial laborer. Tenant migration has caused a farm labor shortage and forced recent governments to urge city workers back to the country. But some agricultural workers have achieved success in the city and have joined the middle class. This class of shopkeepers, small owners, clerks, and professional people is rapidly growing in post-Perón Argentina and is estimated to include about 45 per cent of Argentines today. At the top the rich landowners, their estates still undivided though their political power is largely ended, remain Argentina's aristocracy.

URBAN LIVING CONDITIONS

Do not think that all life away from the rich port is one of cow herds and wheat farmers. There are towns on the pampas, grown far beyond the *pulperías* of Martín Fierro's day, towns built on the rail lines and along the new highways. Of the more than 21,000,000 Argentines, over 5,000,000 live in the modern Buenos Aires metropolitan area, making it the largest Latin city in the world. Six million live in the "rural areas" and another 6,000,000 in towns of 10,000 or more away from the Plata mouth. Thus even the provinces of Argentina are more urbanized than most other Latin American countries, though none of the other cities is more than 15 per cent as large as Buenos Aires. Córdoba, seat of Spanish colonial culture before Buenos Aires was born, center of the cloistered university life, and now heavily industrialized with 500,000 inhabitants, still feels itself superior to the "port." Even the language sounds different in the two cities. The nineteenth century rivalry between port and provinces continues to exist, though in milder form.

The families who own the largest estates have set the style in Buenos Aires for fifty years—200 families which have intermarried to a confusing degree, families of old creole stock with a sprinkling of Italian or English names. Devoutly Catholic, yet cosmopolitan in their interest in things European and in their knowledge of French language and literature, they have held to social castes and have controlled politics and politicians, save only Irigoyen and Perón. They maintain exclusive clubs, set fashions, and promote horse racing and particularly polo, a rich man's game even in Argentina, that land of wiry horses. A "new-rich" class has come into being with the recent industrial development. Its members do not play polo with the oligarchs, but support the many soccer teams which play in international competition with the soccer-minded Brazilians and Uruguayans. They maintain swank apartments in town, villas on the local beaches near Mar del Plata, and buy the automobiles now finished in the Argentine assembly plants from American-made parts.

The white-collar workers of Buenos Aires never own cars; they are the commuter class, living in the suburbs and riding daily in and out of the city on the crowded, government-run buses and the new subway trains, now propelled by Japanese-made electric engines. This class of society was caught between the aristocrats and the Perón-pampered *descamisados*. It is traditional that a white-collar worker be a *camisado*, that he wear a white shirt and a neat black business suit to his poorly paid job, even though he takes off coat and shirt for a white smock as soon as he gets to work, for he can afford but one suit every two years. Though he can pay for two trips a day back and forth in order to have his three-hour lunch at home, though he can afford American movies, good books, a radio, or even a television, he still lives in substandard housing; the high city rent is his biggest problem. Perón added to this class by creating a very large number of positions for new bureaucrats, and thus tied many of the white-collar workers to him. To cut down this heavy expense of civic workers has been one of the problems of the post-Perón presidents. The cost of living and inflation continued to spiral in 1967 in spite of attempts to freeze rents and prices, and the peso continued to fall in value.

In La Boca, slum section of Buenos Aires, there used to live as crowded and underprivileged a mass of stevedores and factory workers as in any city in the Western Hemisphere. In the 1950s these workers, numbered among the *descamisados*, were the political tools by which Perón's government remained in power, and hence they were privileged above other Latin American workers. Higher-paid than any other workers in Latin America, save those in the Venezuelan oil fields, workers took vacations at the seashore at Mar del Plata for the first time. They also began paying for social security, for pensions, health and accident benefits—not receiving as much at Perón had promised, but more than they would have dreamed of a decade before.

Buenos Aires, in 1880 a big provincial town, sprawling, unsanitary, and unattractive, is today one of the ten largest cities of the world—the Paris of the Southern Hemisphere. One Argentine in every four lives there. The city, in which the culture is still Spanish and Catholic to the core, has not kept pace with the population growth, the drift of rural workers to the cities, and the influx of postwar immigrants. There are dwelling units enough to provide one for every four people; large families are no longer the general rule, and young married couples are less prone to live with the old folks. But city planners have been trying for three decades to bring the city up to date. Today the creation of parks and the widening of streets, begun in the 1880s by far-sighted municipal authorities, has continued, making Buenos Aires a rival of Washington, D.C.

The outskirts are changing too. Thirteen new industrial areas, each centered around one or more new factories, sprang up in the 1950s. Such decentralization goes a long way toward solving the problems of this fast-growing city; workers housed in adequate dwellings near their own factories can go home for their long lunch and yet pay rents within their means. But there are slums in Buenos Aires as in all big Latin American cities. La Boca district itself has been replaced by model housing, but new in-migrants to the cities since the drought of 1962 settled in new shanty towns now called *villas miserias*.

Downtown Buenos Aires still does its sophisticated shopping in the street called simply Florida, a street closed to all but pedestrian traffic. For a century it has been the headquarters for Argentina's most aristocratic shoppers, its shops as exclusive as those of Paris, for the lady of Buenos Aires is one of the world's fashion plates, dressed in chic black. Apart from the select stores, department stores excel those of most American cities, while the food stores have a more luxurious display at cheaper prices than in any other city of Latin America. Argentines are famed as heavy eaters; they live in the nation of cheap, plentiful food.

Beyond the busy city, across the park of the Plaza Colón, lies the port, through which flows 80 per cent of all the trade of Argentina. The days of landing in the mud flats in high-wheeled oxcarts seem a millennium ago, not a mere century, at this most modern of harbors, with its electrical equipment and installations worth more than $100,000,000. Ships of all nations and of all sizes come into Buenos Aires; Argentina's own merchant fleet now serves all South America. Railroads and highways from the entire pampas, from Mendoza, from the Bolivian border and from Asunción, Paraguay, route the freight into Buenos Aires port.

This busy and glittering cosmopolitan city has its ordinary share of social problems. For generations social work was done by the ladies of the aristocratic class, or their employees, through charity organizations with Church backing. And then, when Eva Perón was not accepted by the ladies of the aristocracy, she founded her own charity organization backed so lavishly by public money. Today modern procedures have brought other more efficient innovations—care of the aged through union benefits or employees' pensions, treatment of child delinquents in juvenile courts and "cottage-village" institutions. Pitiful beggars, abject poverty, child criminals are not seen on the streets of Buenos Aires. A National Director of Public Health presides over advanced methods in epidemic control, water and milk inspection, and maternal and child health programs, so that life in the *villas miserias* is better than life in the *favelas* of Rio de Janeiro.

Women themselves have changed. In 1947 women were granted the right to vote as a symbol of the new era. Daughters of the oligarchs go to the theater with their fiancés unaccompanied by family chaperones. Daughters of the new rich go to the university and become lawyers and doctors and social workers. Daughters of white-collar and *descamisado* workers learn to be stenographers; they walk through the city streets unmolested and uncriticized in their new freedom. Though legalized by Perón, divorce was suspended again under Lonardi, and is still unacceptable in a deeply Catholic country, but marriages themselves are happier, no longer made entirely by parents for family convenience. Young people are much freer in their friendly association with each other than in most Latin American countries.

The Church itself, never ostentatious in Buenos Aires, where Carnival and Holy Week parades of the Seville type are seldom seen, has always been a behind-the-scenes force in society. However, it has not had the control over education customary in other Latin American countries; Argentina has been a public-school nation since the days of Sarmiento. After Church officials backed the Colonels' Revolution of 1943, Church control was allowed to spread into the schools to an unprecedented extent. Perón kept Church leaders on his side by allowing them a larger share in affairs, especially social and educational. Then in 1954 he began to quarrel with them. Perón finally fell from power because, as a last straw, he antagonized Catholic opinion and the Church.

ARGENTINE CULTURAL LIFE

Buenos Aires considers itself a highly cultured city, a center of university life, of museums, of symphony orchestras. This is a culture reminiscent of Europe, not of the New World. In Argentina the modern visitor finds no *Indianismo* like that of Mexico; Argentines are chic and sophisticated with their eyes on whatever is the cultural trend in Paris. They consider themselves a "white race," and their cartoonists lampoon the darker-skinned nations of Latin America. Many Argentines feel a superiority to Brazilians or Cubans or Mexicans or Paraguayans, and often teach this superiority from the primary grades up. They are interested in French modernism in art and music; to some Argentines North American culture patterns are those of "crass barbarians."

It is true that Argentine high society seems more interested in well-performed classic-style European music than does the American wealthy class. The reversal of summer and winter makes it possible for the finest soloists, opera troupes, and orchestras, through with their European bookings, to appear in Buenos Aires for the brilliant musical season. Many European artists prefer a Buenos Aires appearance, with perhaps side performances at Montevideo and Rio de Janeiro, to a schedule in the United States. The Argentines call their great Colón Theater "the most important opera house in the Western Hemisphere."

A modernist group, interested in writing contemporary classics and in the creation of "absolute music," formed a *Grupo Renovación* in 1929, copying new music trends in Paris. Two brothers, José María and Juan José Castro, led in this musical revolution. Juan José Castro (1895–   ), the conductor of the Buenos Aires Philharmonic Orchestra, came as a guest conductor to the United States, and not only composed all types of music save opera, but launched many young modernists by playing their works. His brother, José María Castro (1892–   ) was a leader of a chamber music society in the 1940s and 1950s and composed works for the cello, which he played. An early co-founder of the *Grupo Renovación*, Juan

Carlos Paz, is called "the most advanced contemporary composer of South America." He left that group in 1936 to found his own group devoted to ultra-modern music. The students of the Castro brothers and Juan Carlos Paz progressed away from classical European music styles and from ultra-nationalist themes. Mario Davidovsky, Armando Krieger, and Antonio Tauriello are "turning Buenos Aires into the most important center of musical creativity in Latin America."

Best known as a world figure in this group is Alberto Ginastera. His first compositions were nationalistic pieces called *The High Plains* and *The Estancia*. More recently he has composed pieces titled simply *Second Quartet for Strings* and *Concerto for Piano*, written with "dodecaphonic hues and universalist trappings" to "mark a milestone in New World composition." In 1964 he produced an opera, written with a grant from the city of Buenos Aires, the first operatic work out of Latin America to receive worldwide attention. It was called *Don Rodrigo*, and is concerned with a medieval Spanish king. But the musical score, calling for many new types of instruments, including pealing bells strung throughout the theater and operated electronically, set a new pattern for opera music. Ginastera was head of the Latin American Institute for Advanced Musical Studies in the late 1960s, where he trained in composition twelve "music fellows" a year from other Latin American countries. All music published by these composers is printed in Buenos Aires for no other Latin American capital has adequate music publishing houses.

Partially for this reason, many other Argentine composers of the serious "new" movement are well known in Europe, and Spain's greatest modern composer, Manuel de Falla, spent many years in Buenos Aires where some of his best works were first played, and died in Córdoba in 1946. The love of music in daily life came to Argentina with the Italians. American jazz dance music came also via Paris and has monopolized the time of many of the little café orchestras. To find real gaucho music, the songs of the *payadores*, the visitor has to search out places catering to tourists. The tango still remains Argentina's best known dance form, but has been replaced in local popularity by two-steps and even "rock and roll."

Perón encouraged nationalistic music by ordering every radio musical program to play at least one piece by an Argentine composer. He also started a national theater movement in 1946 and decreed that each legitimate theater company present two native Argentine plays for every foreign play given. Aramburu removed such controls, and today the Argentine theater flourishes. Both it and the very prosperous movie industry do a great deal with gaucho themes from Argentina's history, though the practice is no longer "Perón-ordered."

Nostalgia for the pampas life was kept alive into mid-century by the Walt Disney of Argentina, Molina Campos, whose humorous drawings of gauchos and horses helped him become financially the most successful artist in Buenos Aires. Bernalde de Quirós is known as a formal painter of the old-time gaucho, in his baggy trousers, with the white lace *chiripás* and the bright red poncho of the Rosas period. Another phase of Argentine life, that of the poor stevedores of the La Boca slums, has been immortalized on canvas by Benito Quinquela Martín, himself a foundling who grew up to be a coal heaver. Self-taught in art as well as in letters, Quinquela Martín painted his own people to bring prosperity to himself and to his street in La Boca. Today there is a free art school there; any children of the stevedores who show talent are trained free in the waterfront studio founded by Quinquela Martín. From the world point of view, he was Argentina's best artist. Many other Argentine artists have copied the French modernists, have turned their eyes on the Paris patterns, and have forgotten Argentina's own rich heritage. "Pop-art" became fashionable in 1964 and 1965, and a group of "pop-artists" from Argentina entered international art shows.

The newspapers of Buenos Aires have been mentioned in the dramatic story of Argentine politics, so that the reader already feels familiar with *La Prensa* and *La Nación*. Founded in 1869 by José Carlos Paz, *La Prensa* remained in the hands of his family, financially successful, pro-democratic and pro-United States, resembling the *London Times* in its neat conservative appearance and the *New York Times* in its prestige and coverage. Then Eva Perón forced it to close. It was returned to Gainza Paz, current member of the founding family, at the fall of Perón, and resumed publication in 1956. Bartolomé Mitre, the year after retiring from the presidency, founded a rival paper, *La Nación*, which was curtailed but not closed out by the Perón policy. Counting these two giants, twenty newspapers are published daily in Buenos Aires. In variety and number of magazines for sale, Buenos Aires newsstands seem as full as those of the United States. There are literary reviews like *Nosotros*, feminine magazines like *Saber Vivir* ("Know How to Live") and *Selecta*, the local *Vogue*, and a serious and widely read review called *Sur*, edited by Victoria Ocampo, who is described as "the foremost feminine intellectual of Argentina." A staunch democrat, Señorita Ocampo was once imprisoned by the Peróns. Many professional magazines and reviews are published in Argentina, particularly in the field of history.

As for books, "Buenos Aires is now the leading publishing center of books in Spanish," writes the president of the Argentine Publishers' Association. Only the United States, in all the world, published more books in the last decade. Argentina is one country of Latin America in which a writer of books can support himself by writing, and need not hold a teaching or clerical government job on the side. Most Argentine books come out in paperbound editions, but these same little volumes are seen in book stores from Chile to Southern California and Texas. Argentine films, like those of modern Mexico, are also seen throughout the Hemisphere.

The culture of the Argentine masses is reflected in the steady reduction of the percentage of illiteracy—from 78 per cent in the first census in 1869 to less than 13 per cent in 1965, and only 7 per cent in Buenos Aires. Public education is free and compulsory for all children from six to fourteen years of age. Though *Peronismo* soft-pedaled the veneration of Sarmiento in the elementary classroom, since he was considered too strong a democrat, Sarmiento's methods of free public elementary education make Argentina's school system one of the best in Latin America. Six compulsory grades are given; entrance into most trades requires a certificate of completion. Secondary education corresponds more to the English and French type, being entirely college preparatory or technical. The 250 secondary level schools accommodate only a small percentage of those who finish the 11,135 elementary schools in Argentina. Perón's interference in and strict control of the schools for a decade caused a lowering of standards, and created another problem for the post-Perón leaders.

The universities of Argentina are a far cry from the one small classical university at Córdoba a century ago. Today there are six of them, all nationally owned, the largest at Buenos Aires, the second at La Plata, then smaller institutions in the provinces of Tucumán and Cuyo, as well as at Santa Fé and Córdoba. The student body is even more tensely interested in politics than the average American student body in the late 1960s. Traditionally Argentine students have had a large part in campus policy-making. But Onganía, in early 1967, after street fights between police and students and faculty groups, stopped all self-government in the universities. In protest, half the faculty of the University of Buenos Aires resigned.

Each subject-matter division is still in a separate building, perhaps across town from other "faculties." In fact, the six universities have thirty-six different campuses. As in other Latin American nations, professors are usually part-time lecturers and part-time practicing lawyers or even members of Congress. Argentina has developed an intellectual elite whose voice is heard in non-academic as well as academic circles at home and abroad. Its ranks contain second-generation Argentines from many backgrounds—for example, the Italian José Ingenieros, sociologist; the German, Alejandro Korn, philosopher; the French literateur-historian, Paul Groussac.

Many literary critics feel that Argentine literature leads the Spanish-speaking world. As Martín Fierro, the gaucho, stood out as a literary figure in the nineteenth century, so in the twentieth Argentine readers remember best another gaucho, Don Segundo Sombra, hero of a novel by that name by Ricardo Güiraldes (1866–1927). The author himself was the son of an *estancia* owner and lived among the gauchos as a youth. The central character of his famous 1929 novel was a footloose singer and horse-breaker, prototype of all gauchos; the narrator of the story is a young boy who worships him, a sort of Argentine Huckleberry Finn. The two of them wander on the pampas, breaking horses for hire, working cattle on long drives, while Don Segundo soliloquizes constantly about his philosophy, his store of folklore of the days of the unsettled pampas, until the boy comes into an inheritance and learns city ways. The boy seems to symbolize the modern Argentina, nostalgic for its gaucho past, its democratic adventure on the open road, its free life among the horse and cattle, and in maturity turning away from that life. Thus *Don Segundo Sombra* typifies modern Argentine literature, realistic and down-to-earth, an Argentine rather than a European product.

The gaucho theme was the dominant note in literature and drama in 1900 and still is in evidence today. The stage success *My Kid*, by the well-known playwright Florencio Sanchez (1875–1910), the story of a struggle between a gaucho father and a city-educated son, is the best remembered of all dramas of the decade 1900 to 1910. Boisterous gaucho novels were popular in the 1920s; the gaucho and rural-life novels of Benito Lynch (1885–1951), tough and brutal as the rough life might make them and with nothing of the "folk nostalgia" in them, were being read while their author's classes in literature were being censored at the University of La Plata by Perón's agents. Hugo Wast, a pen name for an ultra-conservative political leader, Gustavo Martínez Zuviría, born in 1883, was a veritable Zane Grey of Argentina in producing fiction about horses, cow hands, cattle farms, and Argentine frontier life. His novels have more literary merit than their American counterparts, more actual realism. By reading them in translation—the *House of the Ravens, Black Valley, Stone Desert*—the North American gets the "feel" of the Argentine back country.

Realistic novels of social problems in city and country are predominant today. Many authors and titles could be mentioned. Manuel Gálvez, born in 1882, for instance, was listed as the outstanding Western Hemisphere candidate for the Nobel Prize in literature on two different occasions. The subject matter of his novels ranges from rural teachers, to the Church influence on university education, to the life of prostitutes in Buenos Aires slums. In the mid-1950s the novelist Eduardo Mallea (1903–   ), a pessimistic writer of psychological novels, was rated Argentina's "best" by literary critics for *Américas* magazine.

A Buenos Aires newspaper recently took a poll on reading tastes in the city and found that "poetry occupies the lowest place on the list. Only four-tenths of 1 per cent of the readers want it." Continued the paper, "This seems almost incredible, because most people remember many acquaintances who write verses; consequently it would appear that there are more poets than readers of poetry!" It is true that, as in all Latin America since the sixteenth century, Buenos Aires statesmen, journalists, teachers, and priests like to write verses. But, as in France and in Spain, there arose a school of poets for poetry's sake, young writers who believed in the Ultra, the "Absolute" in poetry, and called themselves *Ultra-istas*. They were influenced by the great Nicaraguan poet Rubén Darío, who after the turn of the century practically considered himself an Argentine. His closest Argentine friend was Leopoldo Lugones (1874–1938), an avowed socialist and ardent nationalist, who is listed as Argentina's finest poet. He headed Argentina's National Council on Education and served as the Latin American on the League of Nations Committee on Intellectual Cooperation. His poems in translation lose their music and novelty of form and seem very abstract to the American student.

After Darío's death Jorge Luis Borges (1899–   ) became the leader of the *Ultra-istas*. As an editor and literary critic he urged others to "see poetry" in their own city; because of his influence many of the younger Argentine poets are nationalists. The works of young writers who follow the Darío tradition are published in little poetry review magazines. Their contributors include many other well-known Argentine writers and public figures. The *Ultra-istas* who publish these little magazines are struggling to "create a new realm of being" in describing their native country. Some have even condemned all the current Argentine literature as too European, as "lacking the flavor of the soil." The spirit of the city streets was captured by Argentina's most famous woman poet, Alfonsina Storni, born in 1892. She felt that the big port city so crushed the individual, and that she herself was so "lost in the spiritual poverty of the century," that she took her own life in 1938.

Miguel Grinberg, editor of one of the "little" poetry magazines, author of novels published in both Buenos Aires and Mexico City, and scenarist for several of Argentina's "short art films," wrote for *Américas* (October 1964, page 16) magazine that it is now "habitual for Buenos Aires citizens to expect dynamic cinema and theater productions, . . . many thin little literary magazines edited by young people, a . . . flame of enthusiasm in modern dance techniques, and . . . an interest in electronically composed music and the experimental theater." The Argentine was "he who creates" artistically in the late 1960s.

Thus, creative modern Argentines do not agree with the depressed suicidal poetess of 1938. In spite of spiraling living costs under Frondizi and Illia, and the dictatorship of Onganía, the Argentines are a people confident of their future.

Readings

Adams, R. N., ed., *Social Change in Latin America Today* (1960)
Alexander, R. J., *Communism in Latin America* (1957)
——, *Labor Relations in Argentina, Brazil and Chile* (1962)
——, *Perón Era* (1952)
Amadeo, S. P., *Argentine Constitutional Law* (1943)
Arciniegas, G., ed., *The Green Continent*, trans. H. de Onis (1944)
Bank of London and South America, *The Prebisch Plan* (1955)
Bernstein, H., *Modern and Contemporary Latin America* (1952)
Blanksten, G. I., *Perón's Argentina* (1953)
Bruce, J., *Those Perplexing Argentines* (1954)
Cochrane, T. C., and R. E. Reina, *Entrepreneurship in Argentine Culture* (1962)
Cowles, F., *Bloody Precedent* (1952)
Crawford, W. R., *A Century of Latin American Thought* (1944)
Denis, P., *The Argentine Republic: Its Development and Progress* (1922)
Díaz-Alejandro, C. F., *Exchange-Rate Devaluation in a Semi-Industrialized Country—Experience of Argentina, 1955–1961* (1965)
Englekirk, J. E., *et al.*, *Outline History of Spanish American Literature* (3rd ed., 1965)
Fillol, T. P., *Social Factors in Economic Development: The Argentine Case* (1961)
Fitts, D., ed., *Anthology of Contemporary Latin American Poetry* (1942)
Flores, M., *The Woman and the Whip* (1952)
Gordon, W. G., *The Economy of Latin America* (1950)
——, *Political Economy of Latin America* (1965)
Greenup, R. and L., *Revolution before Breakfast: Argentina, 1941–1946* (1947)
Hamill, H. M., Jr., *Dictatorship in Latin America* (1965)
Hanson, S. G., *Argentine Meat and the British Market* (1938)
Haring, C. H., *Argentina and the United States* (1941)

Henríquez-Ureña, P., *Literary Currents of Latin America* (1945)

Houston, J. A., *Latin America in the United Nations* (1956)

Hudson, W. H., *Green Mansions* (1943)

———, *Tales of the Pampas* (1939)

Ireland, G., *Boundaries, Possessions and Conflicts in South America* (1938)

Jefferson, M., *Peopling the Argentine Pampas* (1926)

Johnson, J. J., *Military and Society in Latin America* (1964)

———, *Political Change in Latin America* (1958)

Joseph, R., *Argentine Diary* (1944)

Kelchner, W. H., *Latin American Relations with the League of Nations* (1926)

Kennedy, J. J., *Catholicism, Nationalism and Democracy in Argentina* (1958)

Kirkpatrick, F. A., *History of the Argentine Republic* (1931)

Levene, R., *History of Argentina*, trans. W. S. Robertson (1937)

Lieuwen, E., *Arms and Politics in Latin America* (rev. ed., 1961)

———, *Generals Vs. Presidents: Neomilitarism in Latin America* (1964)

Luper, A. T., *Music of Argentina* (1942)

Macdonald, A. F., *Government of the Argentine Republic* (2nd ed., 1954)

Main, M. F., *Woman with the Whip: Eva Perón* (1952)

Martin, P. A., *Latin America and the War* (1925)

McGann, T. F., *Argentina: The Divided Land* (1965)

McGann, T. M., *Argentina, United States and the Inter-American System, 1880–1914* (1958)

Mecham, J. L., *Church and State in Latin America* (rev. ed., 1966)

———, *Survey of United States-Latin American Relations* (1965)

———, *The United States and Inter-America Security* (1961)

Owen, F., *Perón: His Rise and Fall* (1957)

Paita, J. A., *Argentina, 1930–1960* (1961)

Paz, A., and G. Ferrari, *Argentine Foreign Policy, 1930–1962* trans. J. Kennedy (1966)

Peffer, E. L., *Foot and Mouth Disease in United States Policy* (1962)

Pendle, G., *Argentina* (3rd ed., 1963)

Perón, E., *My Mission in Life* (1953)

———, *Writings of Eva Perón* (1955)

Perón, J. D., *Theory and Complete Doctrine of General Perón* (1946)

———, *Voice of Perón* (1950)

Peters, H. E., *The Foreign Debt of the Argentine Republic* (1934)

Peterson, H. F., *Argentina and the United States, 1810–1960* (1964)

Phelps, D. M., *Migration of Industry to South America* (1936)

Phelps, V. E., *International Economic Position of Argentina* (1938)

Rennie, Y. F., *Argentine Republic* (1945)

Richardson, R. L., *Florencio Sánchez and the Argentine Theatre* (1933)

Rippy, J. F., *Latin America and the Industrial Age* (1944)

Ronning, C. N., *Law and Politics in Inter-America Security* (1963)

Romero, J. L., *History of Argentine Political Thought* (1963)

Rowe, L. S., *Federal System of the Argentine Republic* (1921)

Scobie, J. R., *Argentina: A City and a Nation* (1964)

———, *Revolution on the Pampas: A Social History of Argentine Wheat, 1860–1910* (1965)

———, *The Struggle for Nationhood: Argentina, 1852–1962* (1964)

Shea, D. R., *The Calvo Clause* (1955)

Silbert, K. H., *The Conflict Society: Reaction and Revolution in Latin America* (1961)

Smith, O. E., *Yankee Diplomacy: United States Intervention in Argentina* (1953)
Taylor, C. C., *Rural Life in Argentina* (1948)
Torres-Rioseco, A., *Epic of Latin American Literature* (rev. ed., 1946)
Waldo, F., ed., *Tales from the Argentines,* trans. A. Brenner (1950)
Wedell, A. W., *Introduction to Argentina* (1939)
Weil, F., *Argentine Riddle* (1944)
Whitaker, A. P., *Argentina* (1964)
————, *Argentina Upheaval* (1956)
————, *Nationalism in Latin America* (1962)
————, *United States and Argentina* (1954)
White, J. W., *Argentina, the Life Story of a Nation* (1942)
Wilgus, A. C., ed., *Argentina, Brazil and Chile Since Independence* (1935)
Wythe, G., *Industry in Latin America* (2nd ed., 1949)

Chapter 34

Twentieth-Century Chile:
A Progressive,
Europeanized Nation

PROLETARIANS AND ARISTOCRATS IN CHILEAN POLITICS

"Something like a synthesis of the planet is fulfilled in the geography of Chile," writes Gabriela Mistral, famous Chilean poetess and Nobel Prize winner for literature. "It starts in the desert, which is like beginning with sterility that loves no man. It is humanized in the valleys. It creates a home for living beings in the ample fertile agricultural zone," she continues in her poetic description; "it takes on a grandiose sylvan beauty at the end of the continent as if to finish with dignity, and finally crumbles, offering half life, half death, in the sea."[1] It is this range of geography which created Chile's modern political and economic life. The sterile desert has produced nitrates and copper which in turn have created a politically conscious mining proletariat and an investment of foreign capital; the "ample fertile valley" provides the setting for Latin America's standard struggle between landowners and peasants; the "sylvan beauty at the end of the continent" has been a new frontier for European coloni-

[1] Gabriela Mistral, "My Country," *United Nations World* (May, 1950), p. 51.

zation and the attendant problems. The combinations and interplay of these three social and economic groupings have given Chile a progressive outlook, a modern spirit, an urge forward, confined as she is by her geography, by the coast and narrow valleys and steep escarpment.

The workers confined in the desert and in the valley were not able to move forward, to express themselves as a political force, until the era of World War I. At Balmaceda's death in 1891 the party of the Chilean Congress had won the "revolution," and for many years no strong president monopolized the scene. This period of parliamentary government was unstable, however. The multiplication of political parties made congressional responsibility impossible. Conservative landowners, heirs to the *pelucones*, held a large block of parliament seats. The old liberals, the *pipiolos*, progressive-minded industrial leaders, with their interest in railways, mines, and urbanization, had become more conservative, and were willing to continue blocs in the Chilean parliament to make a "right-wing liberal plus left-wing conservative combination." This party grouping kept the presidency in the background, and served to prevent the working people from participation in the government for twenty-five years; electoral fights were simply fights between wealthy aristocrats. Politics, it seems, was an aristocratic sport—controlled through bribery and fraud.

The landholding and merchant-class oligarchs had kept the peace well in the nineteenth century through the complete submission of the lower classes. But like many other dominant social groups, the Chilean oligarchs had lingered on beyond their time. By the early 1900s their rule was inadequate; they had become hopelessly inefficient and corrupt. The broad education program, made compulsory in 1913, had led to a gradual awakening of the masses. Foreign immigration and the colonization of south-central Chile had created a small class of independent farmers. Now the million or more city dwellers were willing to unite with them and with the downtrodden peasants and miners against the inefficient and corrupt oligarchy. The friction of the twentieth century was caused chiefly by the exploitation of the *inquilino*, the peasant on the land, and by the abuses heaped on the industrial laborers.

The nitrate industry, unique in Latin America, had produced an alert, organized laboring class. Santiago and Valparaiso, temperate-climate cities, were filled with *rotos*, laborers poor in earthly goods but conscious of their voting power. These workers were not afraid, in the democratic climate of Chile, to call a general strike when the worldwide panic of 1907 brought depression in the nitrate region. City workers combined with small property owners in a new and truly liberal Democratic Party. Miners formed a Socialist Labor Party. By the election of 1915, the bloc formed by these two parties was strong enough to challenge the conservative coalition in a bitterly fought election won by Juan Luis Sanfuentes in which the social plight of the people was an issue. In spite of violations of her neutrality Chile remained neutral during World War I while both sides sought her rich nitrates. When the conservatives again won the presidency, only the prosperity brought by the War and the opening of the Panama Canal kept the new parties from revolt. The conservatives were frightened into passing

South America's early social legislation—workmen's pensions, accident compensation, and railroad workers' retirement laws—in the period from 1916 to 1919. These were the first gains made by Chile's now class-conscious workers, but they had no voice and no leader. When peace in Europe brought a nitrate slump, the desert provinces themselves brought forth a leader of the people in the pèrson of the senator from Tarapacá, Arturo Alessandri.

Alessandri, a tall man with "an enormous leonine head sunk deep in hulking shoulders"—the Lion of Tarapacá—was to dominate politics in Chile for two decades, one of South America's "great men" of recent times. Elected with a majority of one electoral vote by a combination of all liberal parties in 1920, he was the first president of the people and was committed to labor and middle-class demands for social and economic reforms. Alessandri had already had experience in "cleaning-up" local politics in the nitrate provinces, and in working with immigrant laborers—his own father had come from Italy to work in the mines. He pledged to separate Church and state, not yet accomplished by 1920, even in progressive Chile, to lay income taxes on the rich, to control the nitrate industry through a government bureau, to increase the welfare benefits for labor, to expand public education, and even to allow women to vote.

In order to do all these things Alessandri needed strong executive power, so he forced the passage of a new constitution. The Diego Portales Constitution, in effect since 1833, had given the real power to the president and to the upper house controlled by the landowning senators. When Alessandri was blocked by Congress and forced to use arbitrary methods, his supporting coalition fell apart. All these political difficulties were increased by the great economic depression which hit Chile and brought unemployment, unrest, and lowering of government revenues. Forced out temporarily by a military *junta* which opposed him, threatened by the loss of the labor groups to more radical Marxian leaders, he spent some months in exile in Italy. Then he was invited back by a younger military group and finally effected his constitutional changes in 1925. This new document, approved by a plebiscite, gave a more powerful president, directly elected, a six-year term. It advanced the chamber of deputies above the senate in importance, and it created provincial assemblies with more autonomy, thereby giving Chile its first semblance of states in a federal system. In religious matters the new constitution completely separated Church and state and made a strong statement guaranteeing the freedom of all religions. Labor's right to social improvements was recognized and the government assumed protection of trade unions. This constitution ended the rule of the oligarchs and prepared the way for further development of democratic institutions. Alessandri saw the constitution ratified, called new elections under its provisions, initiated some banking and budget reform measures, and was then forced to resign again by the powerful groups opposing him. He turned his power over to a colorless new president and went back to Italy.

One of the younger army officers who had invited Alessandri to return the first time had been a typical *caudillo* type, a twentieth-century "man on horseback" named Carlos Ibáñez del Campo. An admirer of Mussolini's new Italian government, Ibáñez promised all things to all men—stability to the conservatives, social security to the *rotos*. Ibáñez served as Minister of War for two years under the new constitution, was appointed vice-president, and then took over the presidency himself while the leading liberals went into exile. A 1927 election confirmed Ibáñez, for many Chileans were alarmed at the threat of class warfare and were willing to support a military government. The now powerful army pushed through modernization budgets and encouraged industrialization so that armament materials could be locally made. When the nitrate market continued to slump as synthetic substitutes were developed in Europe, Ibáñez borrowed abroad to keep his army well supplied and to keep his supporters among the laborers quiet by giving them jobs on foreign-financed public works. To maintain employment in the mines he formed a government-controlled nitrate corporation, the *Compañía de Salitre de Chile*, or COSACH, Chile's first experiment in government ownership. Ibáñez passed some advanced labor laws, started a modest agrarian reform, extended education, and ended the long Tacna-Arica dispute. Repressive dictator though he was from 1925 to 1931, Ibáñez was efficient and might have been successful, had it not been for the worldwide depression, which hit hard at a one-export country like nitrate-producing Chile. His popularity collapsed when prosperity ended.

When opposition to Ibáñez increased among all factions, he tightened his military control until students, professors, workers, and sailors joined in a bloody riot and threw him out in July 1931. There followed eighteen months of utter political chaos. Within that period nine different governments rose and fell, some of them conservative conspiracies, some military *coups*, and one a socialist government which lasted 100 days. The liberals were split in every way; there were two general strikes and a fleet mutiny. But eventually the armed forces demanded that efficient, legal government be restored. Political parties regrouped in the midst of the depression, and by popular demand held a constitutional election in October 1932.

POLITICS THROUGH DEPRESSION AND WAR
TO THE PRESENT

In the election of 1932 Alessandri staged a comeback, pledging constitutional rule, law, order, stability, and a semisocialistic program. Alessandri was overwhelmingly elected from a field of five candidates, and his second presidency lasted the full legal six years. He himself had become more conservative. That he was less the workingman's friend than during the 1920s, and more the supporter of the nitrate companies, can be explained by his attempt to stabilize the nitrate industry. With decreasing demand for the product abroad, prices had to be kept up by the government. The COSACH of Ibáñez' time had become the tool of the big nitrate companies who owned half the stock of the government company. Alessandri abolished it and returned ownership to private hands, setting up instead a government marketing and price-setting agency. Each company had its quota of the shrinking world market; soon no one was satisfied and wages went down while food prices went up. Alessandri, busy trying to preserve economic stability, sponsored no further social legislation. In 1936 he actually used the army to stop a serious railway strike. He and his Finance Minister, Gustavo Ross, pulled Chile through the serious depression of the 1930s in spite of high living costs and unemployment. His second term was an era of industrial improvement, though he undertook no social reform and never tackled the land distribution problem.

So the masses turned to a new leader, Pedro Aguirre Cerda, a man sincerely concerned with land reform, public health, education, and the unemployment caused by the nitrate slump. He had been one of eleven children of a poor farmer, had gone to school with the *rotos*, had earned a law degree and become Minister of Education, building up an investment in vineyards on the side. Thus the landowners did not hate him, while the intellectuals were his best friends. "If I had the power, I would strew Chile with schools as a farmer sows wheat on rich land," he said.

Aguirre Cerda, elected in a very close vote by a coalition of parties in October 1938, called his government a Popular Front, a term being used for the multiparty anti-Nazi governments in Europe at the time. This popular front called for *"pan, techo y abrigo"* (bread, clothes, and shelter) for every Chilean; it was a coalition of the Radicals with labor and the left, with leadership in the hands of the middle class and business elements of the Radical Party. By 1941 Aguirre Cerda's government was a Radical Party government. But because Aguirre Cerda compromised with Communist labor leaders on the one hand, and served as president of the Wine Growers' Association on the other, he pleased no one. Caught in the middle, he attempted to devote himself to public health and child welfare. Meanwhile the German immigrants in southern Chile were forming a very strong pro-Nazi party as the world entered World War II. Ignoring the world situation, Aguirre Cerda planned to expand the Chilean social program. When a disastrous earthquake killed more than 20,000 people, Aguirre Cerda's welfare funds were so depleted that he formed a Development Corporation, the *Corporación de Fomento*, or CORFO, for long-range industrialization and for WPA-type employment to improve the balance of trade and increase effective production. Too strong for the conservatives, too pro-Chilean for the Nazis, too weak for the labor leaders, the CORFO only brought dissatisfaction. Bewildered and disappointed, Aguirre Cerda died in November 1941, having served only half his term.

Both Alessandri and Ibáñez, as well as a Nazi leader, all hoped for election to succeed Aguirre Cerda. Juan Antonio Ríos, wealthy friend and follower of Aguirre Cerda and leader of the right wing of the Radical Party, took advantage of the confusion and won the election, while much of the Western Hemisphere was plunged into war following Pearl Harbor. Ríos kept a precarious balance between the loud Nazi minority and the strongly pro-American sympathies of the majority. This majority popular opinion was able to force a break in diplomatic relations with the Axis powers in January 1943; by such a break, though an act short of actual belligerency, Chile became eligible for the same type of United States financial aid which American wartime policy was extending to direct Allies in the Hemisphere. Meanwhile the Allies were also making heavy purchases of nitrates and copper. On February 12, 1945, just before the Hemisphere Meeting at Chapultepec, President Ríos declared war against Germany and Japan and signed the United Nations declaration, though the Chilean Congress did not approve his action until April 12, only a month before the United Nations met to frame the charter at San Francisco. However, the German element in Chile, so much more New-World-minded, never constituted the threat to the Allies which the smaller Nazi group did in Argentina. At home Ríos conducted an intelligent, businessman's administration, and encouraged industrialization.

When Ríos died in June of 1946, another leader from the nitrate regions, Gabriel González Videla, leader of the Radicals, won the bitterly fought special election. A friend of the United States who was widely acclaimed as a charming and popular figure when he visited President Truman in the White House, González Videla was a well-known Western Hemisphere figure in 1948. With a flashing smile, and a chic wife who was one of Santiago's leading social workers, González Videla was an informal president. He was available to all citizens, danced at rural fiestas, and was willing to "wait in line at the movies." Called by his own admirers a "clever tightrope walker" in his treatment of postwar Fascists, Communist sympathizers among the dissatisfied labor leaders, and estate owners afraid of land reform, González Videla served out his six-year term. But he could not control postwar inflation and lost his labor support when the cost of bread went up 30 per cent. With the help of industrialization programs financed by the successful CORFO, González Videla had achieved comparative prosperity by 1949. The *fundo* system with its feudal *inquilino* peasants continued to exist side by side with a democratic government and a strong city labor movement. In 1950 González Videla's Chile was praised for "remaining the bright spot for parliamentary republicanism and democracy in Latin America." John Gunther, American news writer, said of Chile's progress, "She will never have a tyrant like Ibáñez again."

What a surprise, then, when Ibáñez was returned to office in the fair and peaceful elections to choose González Videla's successor in September 1952. His campaigning, perhaps financed by Argentina's Perón who had been a close friend of Ibáñez in the 1940s, came at a time when "strong men on horseback" were winning elections elsewhere in Latin American. Ibáñez, who had created the Agrarian-Labor Party in 1949, courted every kind of dissident group, made appeals to workers in an inflation-wracked Chile in which the cost of living had increased 900 per cent since his first term, and promised strong orderly government to the Conservatives. Elected when the weak, traditional parties were rejected by the voters, Ibáñez could not make himself absolute dictator of democratic-minded Chile, for he was faced with a hostile congress. As a man in his mid-seventies he tried to grapple with the continuing economic ills of a country which produces one item for export, which has an outmoded landholding system, but an alert electorate. When the voters began to suspect that he was working closely with Perón, his government nearly fell. Ibáñez had to keep his promises of making administration more efficient, developing industries, promoting electrification and land reclamation schemes, and building roads. The cost of living was still high and labor was restive while Ibáñez changed his cabinet eighteen times in five years. The American firm of Klein and Saks made economic recommendations to fight the chronic upward cycle of inflation. Ibáñez attempted to halt inflation by austerity, economies, and controls, and turned the tide until mid-1957. Then his attempts were thwarted by one of the worst droughts in the history of Chile's central valley, floods in the north, and at the same time a 40 per cent drop in the price of copper on the world market. Ibáñez' programs of land reclamation, irrigation, electrification, and new small industries, as well as his balanced budget and his efficient tax system did not quite overbalance these catastrophes. Politics upset Ibáñez' sincere efforts and in 1957 the Radical Party and rightest groups, which were anti-Ibáñez, gained control of Congress. A fair and open election was held on September 15, 1958, at which, according to constitution and tradition, the people would choose a president by plurality vote whom the Congress would then approve. There were five candidates, including the supposedly popular socialist, Salvador Allende.

Both Ibáñez and the radical Allende lost the election to a moderate right-winger with a magic name, Jorge Alessandri, the austere but enlightened son of Arturo Alessandri, the old Lion of Tarapacá. Jorge was a manufacturer who controlled Chile's papermaking business, and had been a conservative senator in the 1950s. He attempted to "govern above party," and disciplined private-business monopolies as well as wasteful public utilities to control inflation and keep the cost of living down. But it was not that easy in the early 1960s. The economy was still dependent on exports of nitrates and copper, and there was heavy unemployment in both those industries. The unproductive feudal agricultural system was a century out of date. The peasants left the land to find work in the crowded cities where there was no work. The value of the Chilean peso had fallen so low as to call for a new currency called the *escudo*. The Communist party, legally recognized in politically tolerant Chile, had a wide appeal. It claimed more than 100,000 members by 1960, and the socialist leader Salvador Allende curried their support, as the severe earthquakes of the early 1960s added to the misery of the urban and rural poor.

Jorge Alessandri passed Chile's first agrarian reform law in November 1962, but the law applied only to land which was not currently being worked. This reform law only helped farm families with some captial to invest in developing unused marginal lands. It helped very few *inquilinos* gain passession of their own land. An income tax to pay for new urban housing units on a government-supported building plan called CORVI brought Jorge Alessandri little popularity or support. In his last address to Congress at the end of his term in May 1964 he claimed that industrial production had increased by 33 per cent in the six years of his administration, but did not add that the cost of living had increased 190 per cent in the same period.

So the election of 1964 brought out two candidates urging greater social progress, both of them to the left of Jorge Alessandri. Salvador Allende led a large group of leftists called *Frente de Acción Popular,* or FRAP, asking for complete nationalization of the copper and nitrate industries. His opponent Eduardo Frei, born in Santiago of Swiss parents in 1911, had been a university professor. His devout Catholic faith called for social and economic reform through Christian leadership, he felt. He organized a Christian Democratic Party similar to Catholic Action parties in Europe, the first such liberal religious party in the Americas. He planned to achieve his reforms by acting as a strong executive through a congress controlled by Christian Democrats. He hoped to create a "mixed society in Chile of private, public, and cooperative ownership."

In the historic Chilean election of September 4, 1964, women voted for the first time in Chile, and they voted two to one for Frei. He received a majority of 400,000 votes in a very fair election. But votes for Frei were not merely anti-communist. They were votes against the landed oligarchy and the foreign control of business as well, "anti-communism with constructive alternatives." Frei's slogan was "Revolution in Liberty."

Frei's alternatives were to buy up large shares in the nitrate and copper companies for the Chilean government. Let these companies be privately managed but let the government sit on the board of directors. Let locally-owned smaller industries have some government management and invite in new foreign capital as well. Let the money earned by the government in these new "participation" endeavors be used to buy up more and fertile lands from the oligarchy with small down payments and settle a million *inquilinos* on the land. Let 100,000 urban housing units, not a mere 20,000, be built. In the congressional election of March 1965, Frei's party won the majority in the Chamber of Deputies.

Frei's biggest obstacle came from his failure to win control of the senate. His enthusiastic majority in the house passed his bill to buy into the copper industries, and the American and British companies, vastly preferring such a plan to nationalization, set up committees to work with government agents. New jobs were created by the thousands. Finally the oligarch-controlled senate passed his plan to purchase copper shares, but stalled on other reforms. Meanwhile he personally went on "good-will" trade missions, was welcomed in Italy, France, England, and West Germany, and came home with promises of several big investments in electric power production and in diversified industries. "The world has faith in our country," Frei reported when he returned to Chile in August 1965. He was also receiving full support from Alliance for Progress financing in the spring of 1966. Some of the funds thus loaned were to build up agricultural industries so that Chile would no longer have to import $140,000,000 worth of food yearly. A report to American financing firms in October 1965 said that President Frei was "maintaining democracy while promoting cooperatives," in "Savings and Loan" housing, small businesses, and new farm processing plants.

As a substitute for communism in solving some of Latin America's ills, Frei's Christian Democratic Party was being watched with interest throughout Latin America as the 1970s approached. In foreign affairs Chile opposed the United States in Santo Domingo, renewed relations with Russia, and allowed the Communist Party legal status at home. Frei himself hoped to become a leader in economic integration in the Western Hemisphere and planned a presidential summit conference to push the Latin American Common Market. His wings were clipped by his enemies in the senate, led by Salvador Allende, when they spitefully used an old law to forbid him to go to Washington in February 1967 to help plan such a meeting. But his popularity with the people seemed to guarantee a successful six year term from 1964 to 1970.

THE VARIEGATED ECONOMY IN THE REGIONS

Nowhere in the world was there such a nitrate deposit as in the west coast regions of Tarapacá, Antofagasta, and Atacama. Chile had fought and won the War of the Pacific to acquire the richest nitrate beds from Bolivia and Peru; Chilean and foreign investors began to develop refineries there, which brought a surge of labor into the region, both Chilean and immigrant. Heavy investment eventually caused overspeculation and it seemed in 1914 that the industry and its golden stream of revenue might collapse. The world needed fertilizer, but not at the high prices Chile was charging. World War I brought a boom demand for nitrates as explosives; that same war almost ended the Chilean nitrate business when German chemists, isolated from the Chilean product by England's blockade, developed methods of fixing nitrogen from the air. By 1926, 80 per cent of the world's nitrates were made by synthetic plants in Europe and the United States. Chile's exports were cut to 10 per cent of the 1914 total. Many nitrate-producing centers became ghost towns; the ragged workers flooded the ranks of the unemployed in the cities.

Meanwhile the Guggenheim Company of America, knowing that cotton in the United States South would grow better in Chilean nitrate than in synthetic fertilizers, invested millions in new plants near Antofagasta. There followed various government attempts to equalize the profits from big and little companies, maintain employment and social improvements for the workers, and keep both Chilean and foreign capital happy. In 1965 the quantity of nitrate exports, in spite of efficient new methods, the discovery of new beds, and a fertilizer market in such rapidly developing regions as Israel, was only slightly higher than the amounts exported in 1900.

The easily decomposed masses of nitrate ore lie just below the surface, and can be "mined by steam shovel." In a wetter climate the nitrates would have drained into the ocean ages ago; only the rainless climate of the Atacama coast saved the ores for Chile. Enormous steam shovels have replaced the *roto* workers and their oxcarts of thirty years ago. With ten such shovels in operation at the great Guggenheim workings called the *María Elena*, an acre of ground is cleared of ore in a week, a square mile in ten years. Though the nitrate deposits will thus last indefinitely, 15,000 tons are hauled to the cleaning plant daily from these ten shovels. The ore needs only to be pulverized and washed in a stream of hot water. The nitrates and the valuable by-product iodine are dissolved, and the waste materials are spewed out in endless piles over the empty desert. The nitrate solution is then cooled to form crystals for shipment.

In between the shovels and the piles of waste lies the company town of María Elena. Living in houses much better than those of peasants on Central Valley estates, the workers send their children to modern schools, attend workers' clubs and recreation centers. They also attend union meetings, for the nitrate workers are articulate and highly organized and have been an extremely left-wing force in Chilean politics. They are completely dependent on the company for life, however. Water is piped from the snow of the Andes 200 miles away; food and even green potted plants come in by ship; fuel oil for the refinery water heaters comes down from Peru. Another equally large plant is called the *Pedro de Valdivia*. The government has concentrated its control and quota system on these two large plants so that there should be no overproduction.

Today Chile ranks next to the United States in world copper production. The 1950 copper export brought in 70 per cent of the foreign exchange to bolster the inflated peso and paid a very large share of the nation's taxes, so the fall in the price of copper hurt Chile badly. Here as in the nitrate business foreign capital dominates. The Chuquicamata, not a hundred miles above María Elena in the mountains, is the world's largest copper mine; it is owned by America's Anaconda Company. The living conditions for the copper miners were inferior to those for the nitrate workers, because their unions have only recently been active. In the 1950s these workers were receiving a pittance compared to wages paid copper miners in Montana or Arizona; the foreign companies were at loggerheads with the Chilean government over insurance for indemnities, expensive safety precautions, and the large government royalties imposed. The monopoly of the copper business in the hands of American companies led to bad feelings against the Yankees. President Frei's plans for partial government ownership of the Anaconda and Kennicott Companies went peacefully into effect in the spring of 1967 with the Chilean government purchase of 51% of the stock by long-term bonds.

Tungsten has been discovered in Chile and the iron ore deposits at El Tofo feed the new steel mills at Huachipato. Coal, from Lota in the south near Concepción, is not mined for export, but only for local fuel and power. Oil will rapidly replace coal in the Chilean economy if the new wells being developed in the Straits of Magellan area come into heavy production. Since World War II government encouragement has doubled the output of hydroelectric power; streams from the Andes entering the agricultural valleys are a greater hope and have a tremendous potential for power development in the future and bring more promise of industrialization than do coal and petroleum.

As a long-range method of raising the standard of living and curing social unrest, the Chilean Development Corporation, or corfo, was founded in 1939. It made loans to private business in order to improve balance of trade, to promote a new steel industry, to coordinate industry with agriculture, mining, and fishing, to stabilize employment, and to develop oil wells. It has made electric power a main feature of its program. corfo's steel plant was financed partly by a loan from America's Export-Import Bank, and is large enough to provide steel for Chile, Bolivia, and

Ecuador. Cotton and woolen mills, fruit canneries, and cement plants built by CORFO make home-consumption industries an important element in the economy of Valparaiso, Santiago, and Concepción. The factories are powered by electricity and provide employment for the *rotos* displaced by machine methods in the nitrate and copper regions to the north. This development helps make Chile less dependent on mineral exports.

The political influence the workers exert stands behind all this government effort to raise the standard of living. The first Chilean strikes had taken place in the 1880s; by 1916 miners' and nitrate workers' unions were active enough to get laws passed making employers liable for accidents on the job, and providing for one free day in seven. Because of the better education and increased industrialization of Alessandri's time, Chile's labor accomplished more and accomplished it earlier than did unions in other parts of Latin America. The Chilean Workers' Federation (CTCH) had over a quarter of a million members by 1946. The unusual conditions of work in the ore-extracting industries of the northern desert contributed to the political power of labor. Workers had to be induced to come and petted into staying; here was no problem of humble peasants tied to the land.

Alessandri's labor code legally recognized the growing unions. In the following decade they achieved a large measure of social security for their members. Under the Preventive Medicine Law, 80 per cent of Chile's population gets some form of medical insurance. Workers' *cajas*, a word meaning cash box, are organized in every occupation, with the worker, the employer, and the government paying into the fund. The money thus raised not only provides pensions and unemployment benefits similar to those under the United States Social Security, but also sets up cooperative shops, maintains a rotating loan fund, and provides facilities for buying homes as well.

City workers' health programs have lowered the infant mortality rate, cut tuberculosis deaths, and, since 1920, have raised the life expectancy among city workers and miners from thirty-one years at birth to forty-four years, an increase of thirteen years in the four decades since Alessandri's labor code set out to raise the standard of living for workers. Two people out of every twenty-five in Chile still have tuberculosis, but the rate is upped by malnutrition in rural areas. Factory workers in Santiago or nitrate workers in María Elena were faced with the same problems in the late 1960s as were their counterparts in the United States. Their salaries had doubled in the previous decade, but food, clothes, rent, and transportation costs had trebled.

All this talk of unions and *cajas* and model housing has scarcely reached the agricultural countryside, where the *inquilino* works the landlord's *fundo* or estate, and the *huaso* or Chilean gaucho herds the rancher's cattle. The poverty of the Chilean *inquilinos* is an affront to the democratic faith of the Chileans. They use the same methods, eat the same diet, wear the same style *poncho*, and probably live in the self-same houses as did their ancestors at the time of Darwin's visit, for there has never yet been a "land" revolution in Chile. Half of Chile's population lives on the land, but that land is held in big estates. In the Central Valley, less than 400 families hold more than half the cultivated land, with some single estates exceeding 250,000 acres. The estate owners have remained a closed class, those conservatives in politics who controlled the senate, and through it the government, from 1891 to 1920. A little more modernized than Argentina's oligarchs, they have recently been offering some estates for sale in small holdings while they invest the family fortunes in new industries. Also there exists a homestead law, under which lands on the southern frontier and in the submarginal, hard-to-irrigate areas are offered as homesteads, but the large holdings and the attendant inefficient methods and depressed peasantry are still Chile's major farm problems. In December 1966 Frei finally got an agrarian reform through both houses of congress, redistributing land to 100,000 landless families in a six-year program.

The agriculturally rich Central Valley is fairly level, with a gradual western slope down from the Andes that makes irrigation easy from the surging rivers of melted mountain snow. It supports wheat, orchards, vineyards, and pasture. Three-fifths of Chile's lands are in wheat—south of the 35th parallel it can be grown without irrigation—for Chile was always a wheat-bread-eating, not a corn-*tortilla*-eating Spanish country. Small farmers must thresh the wheat on the threshing floors with oxen; the more modernized larger *fundos* use American combine harvesters. Chileans are prouder of the fruits—citrus and deciduous—which make Chile's Central Valley the rival of California's central valley. Wines from Chile compete with those from Mendoza on the tables of Lima or Rio. Apples, peaches, and pears from Chile are served as dessert in many less productive regions of South America. On the irrigated pastures graze cattle as fat as those of Argentina's pampas. In the cool south sheep raising has become a very specialized industry, managed by Scotchmen and Basques.

Fundo agriculture has not caught up with the machine age; it is still run by oxen. Reapers and tractors were not introduced until the 1940s. President Ríos did propose a plan of small farms aided with machinery which by 1945 increased agricultural production. The *fundo* house, less palatial than that on the Argentina *estancia*, is usually a one-story Spanish-style building around a series of patios. Behind it are acres of family orchards, gardens, and vineyards, and the granaries, wineries, workshops, implement sheds, and stock corrals. Beyond lies the village of the tenants, the *inquilinos*, and the day laborers, who comprise 40 per cent of the Chilean population; they remain the submerged class as urban Chile moves rapidly ahead. The *inquilinos* have a small plot of land assigned for food for their own families and animals, while they work the master's land for the equivalent of less than 50 cents a day. Rural schools, to be supplied by the landlord, are inadequate compared with those provided at nitrate plants, and most of the social legislation does not apply to *inquilinos*. The Communists found the *inquilinos* willing listeners to their talk of radical unions for agricultural laborers. To counteract their activity, the landowners accepted a bill forming unions of all field workers who could read and write. Since there is 90 per cent illiteracy among adult *inquilinos*, effective organization may have to wait a generation. Some enlightened *fundo* owners have forestalled unrest by creating workers' cooperatives, clinics, loan agenices, and adult classes in their own *fundo* villages.

The difficulties of transportation across the Andes and the desert have delayed Chile's industrialization as much as have feudal estates. There are five railway lines linking Chile with her neighbors today, as well as an internal spinal column of longitudinal rails. Most railroads are now government-owned. Today an all-weather section of the Pan American Highway runs to La Paz, Bolivia. Chile's trade had been seaborne via the Pacific rather than over the Andes. The real difficulty is the long haul the length of Chile, the 2,000 miles from Puerto Montt on the far south to Pisagua on the Peruvian border, for much domestic commerce has to go this long way by steamer. The government owns a fleet of cargo and passenger vessels and by law coastal trade is confined to Chilean vessels.

The country south of the Bío Bío River, Valdivia's own last line of settlement, has been Chile's "western frontier." Beyond Concepción was the forest, the beautiful lake region of today's new tourist interest, and the Araucanian Indian reservations. In 1928 President Ibáñez opened much southern land for small-farm settlement under an Institute of Land Colonization. In this region more than two-thirds of the people were of German ancestry, for the German had for fifty years been attracted to the fir trees and the cold winter of the lands beyond 38° south latitude. It was among these people, increasing by 6,000 new German migrants a year in the 1920s, that the Chilean pro-Nazi parties which harassed President Ríos during World War II developed, though the hard-working immigrants stayed loyal to Chile for the most part. Near the straits of Magellan lies Punta Arenas, Chile's and the world's southernmost city, which supports itself by shipping out the wool grown in the region.

The territory between 40° and 50° south latitude is still largely Araucanian Indian territory. There are 170,000 of these Indians, descendants of Lautaro's brave bands who have themselves never been conquered by force of arms. Lautaro is a great national hero to the Chileans, but his descendants are simply poor Indians on marginal lands. Many of the Araucanians are fiercely anxious to preserve the old ways and the independence that was guaranteed by "treaty" with the Santiago government in 1883, but they are finding their large communal land holdings melting away. Some of the lands have been granted out in small shares to individual tribal members who want them, but unfortunately non-Indian Chilean citizens can also homestead some of this land. Araucanian handicrafts and strikingly designed wool textiles are sold to tourists as typical of "native" Chile, but the Indians themselves are scarcely a factor in Chilean life, though they comprise 4 per cent of the population.

CHILEAN CULTURE:
A EUROPEAN AND YANKEE MIXTURE

Santiago is as sophisticated as Buenos Aires, in a more beautiful setting. Fourth largest city in South America, capital of a nation of over eight million people, Santiago with its suburban area has a population of

Valparaiso, Chile, port city rebuilt after the disastrous earthquake of 1906. *Courtesy Pan American Union.*

two and a half million. Its big, new civic center has been called by a modern authority on city planning "the finest group of public buildings in Latin America, in that it achieved dignity without monumentality." Santiago is famous for its parks and gardens, including the beautiful Santa Lucía Hill, once the despised Protestant cemetery. Santiago's business and shopping center is as modern as that of Buenos Aires or São Paulo. Even the slums, the old unsanitary courtyards, a family to each room, have been torn down by the *cajas*, the workers' social security agencies, and thousands of cooperative workers' apartments have been built. Containing about 54 per cent of Chile's new manufacturing industry, Santiago continues to grow rapidly as her industrialization tempts the *inquilinos* in from the farms to taste the higher standard of living in the city. As in other Latin American capitals, the newcomers have crowded into "mushroom" towns or *callampas*, where 80,000 slum-dwellers lived in 1965.

Valparaiso, with a population of over 300,000 and a position of importance as the main harbor and greatest commercial center on South America's west coast, has had more of a struggle to become a large modern city. An earthquake which hit the port in 1906 was one of Latin America's major disasters and caused greater loss of life than that of San Francisco a few months earlier. Like San Francisco, the city rose again in greater prosperity and beauty than before. Fifteen minutes' drive away is the west coast's best-known beach resort, Viña del Mar, for which even many wealthy Argentines cross the Andes.

The beautiful valleys of southern Chile were hit by the most severe South American earthquake in modern times in 1960, killing 5,000 people. The loss of life was almost repeated by another series of earthquakes in April 1965, with damages ·totaling $300,000,000. Homes and schools destroyed in 1960 had not yet been repaired when the quake struck in 1965. Frei's government had to call for worldwide aid for the stricken people in the cold south Chilean winter.

In normal years, the Andes and the beautiful lakes of the southern national parks make Chile one of the world-famous summer vacation and winter ski areas. The cities abound with movie palaces showing pictures from the American, Argentine, and Mexican film industries. Many *zarzuelas* or short musical comedies are given in the regular theater, and for traditional legitimate drama Chile is tops in Latin America. It boasts a well-known dramatic school, a large playwriters' group theater, and annual government prizes for the best new plays. Meanwhile the *inquilinos* give local village fiestas in traditional Spanish colonial style, dance the *cueca*, the pigeon-strutting courtship dance of the seventeenth century, and stage yearly rodeos with a "wild west" flavor.

Schools in Chile, as elsewhere in Latin America, do not come up to the hopes of democratic people. Elementary education is provided free by the central government, but although the system is "compulsory," hundreds of thousands of Chile's school-age children get no opportunity to attend. Secondary schools offer college preparatory work for the most part. Some practical progress is being made in Chile to break this classical European pattern. There are nurses' schools, schools for social workers, and vocational and technical high schools. More than in most Latin American nations, Chilean young men are eager to take mechanical and engineering courses, to specialize in practical science applicable in the new industry. In Santiago the Institute for Rural Education, started by a group of socially conscious city women and similar to Mexico's cultural missions, sends out literature and materials to the poorest *inquilino* schools. University life is among the most active in Latin America. Chile's large universities include the National University of Chile, with its 6,000 students, the Catholic University, the University of Concepción, and the Santa María Technical University in Valparaiso. All these good developments were enhanced by Frei's law of 1966 which promised free education for every Chilean child through the university level.

The Chilean university students, although anti-United States in their treatment of Robert Kennedy in November 1965, nevertheless turned away from the student Communist movement in their support of President Frei. Instead of taking summer vacations, they went out by the thousands as a "domestic peace corps" to build 5,000 rural classrooms and teach 150,000 people to read in one summer.

The students and their fellow Christian Democrats had a long way to go to satisfy Chile's demands for a good society. Dr. Eduardo Molina, President Frei's Finance Minister, reported to the Inter-American Development Bank in October 1965 that though Chile was much better off than other Latin American countries, of very 100 youngsters entering elementary schools, only thirty reached sixth grade, only five completed high school, and only two would enter college. Meanwhile 90 per cent of the rural population lack potable water and sanitary facilities. "The population increases 3.7 per cent every year," said Dr. Molina, "but one child in three receives no medical attention in the first year of his life. Over 30 per cent of the population still live in unhealthy and subhuman conditions."

In spite of these sorry statistics, 80 per cent of the Chilean people are literate and are sophisticated enough to read newspapers. Santiago's daily *El Mercurio* ranks among the Western Hemisphere's best. There are five other papers in Santiago with varying and uncensored political opinions; in the provinces local papers are influential because of the great distance from the capital. The weekly magazine *Ercilla* and the clever political satirical magazine *Topaze* are often quoted in American papers.

Reading *Topaze*, running the workers' *cajas*, building the new factories is a rising middle class whom Yankees can really understand. Among Chilean women, modern educated American career women feel at home. There are Chilean women doctors, newspaper writers, and political organizers. The director of the National School of Social Work is a woman; a woman doctor has been in charge of public health work in Santiago. Chile was the world''s fifth country to appoint a woman diplomat, sending a lady minister to the Netherlands in 1946. A Chilean woman lawyer served as Chief of the United Nations Division on the Status of Women. Señora González Videla, herself a social worker, led the successful campaign to carn Chilean women the right to vote in presidential elections, a right which they exercised for the first time in the election of Frei in September 1964.

A Chilean woman, Gabriela Mistral (1889–1957), was one of the modern world's best-known poets. Her poetic thoughts on the geography of Chile were quoted as an introduction to this chapter. Having served as cultural attaché in the Chilean embassies in Paris and Rome, and on committees for the League of Nations, as a guest advisor in Mexico's rural education program in 1922, and as exchange professor at Vassar and Columbia in New York, Gabriela Mistral was also one of the world's most widely known women before her death in 1957. Born Lucila Godoy, she spent a girlhood of privation and struggle for self-education. As a young adult she wrote verse under the pen name Gabriela, signifying "angelic annunciation," and Mistral, the name for a warm spring wind. Love of nature and of children mingles in her writing with philosophy about death, hopes for humanity, and her own ideal of service. Hundreds of her poems are well known to all Chilean schoolchildren, while she continued in her old age to visit other Latin American countries as a consultant on educational progress. In 1945 she received the Nobel Prize for literature.

Meanwhile Chile was producing many writers who became well known at home. Chilean poetry had been strongly influenced by Rubén Darío, who had lived in Chile in the 1890s, and by the great Chilean novelist of the nineteenth century, Alberto Blest-Gana (1830–1920), who was still writing satires on Chilean family life when in his eighties. In 1915 the poet Pedro Prado (1886–1952), heir to these great writers, founded a literary and artistic circle called *Los Diez*, "The Ten." A writer of symbolic novels, he is also known for a long poem about the resurrection of Lazarus, "one of the finest poems in Spanish of the modernist era."

Chilean poetess Gabriela Mistral, reading poetry at the Pan American Union, at the time of her Nobel Prize award, 1946. *Courtesy Pan American Union.*

The third best-known Chilean contemporary poet calls himself Pablo Neruda, but he is really Neftalí Reyes (born in 1904), the leader of Chile's Communist party, who was active in Congress against González Videla in 1949. Regardless of his politics, he won Chile's national prize for literature in 1945. His poems are difficult to understand and reflect the mood of the ultra-modern, but he has many imitators throughout Latin America.

Novels have been a marked Chilean contribution to recent Spanish literature. The typical Chilean novel is *El Roto*, a powerful description of the life of the city worker in Santiago's slums, written by Joaquín Edwards Bello (born in 1888) in 1920. That such a novel, and *Esmeraldo's Cradle* by the same author, should be so popular is typical of the socially conscious attitude of Chile's readers. The best-known short stories are by Manuel Rojas (born in 1896), and are concerned with migratory field hands and railroad workers. Rojas wrote from experience, having worked as a youth on the Trans-Andean Railway, though his journalistic writing brought him the post of manager of the University of Chile Press. His *Lanchas en la Bahía*, written in 1932, stamped him as a worthy novelist as well.

As outstanding as its fiction has been the Chilean contribution to fact; Chile's great historian and bibliographer, José Toribio Medina (1852–1930), wrote, compiled, and edited more than 200 volumes of historical material. His name is well known to any serious student of Latin American history. All these works are printed inside Chile, which has a booming publishing business and produces thousands of cheap, paperbound books, including translations of modern American writing, for its literate workers.

The University has its own Faculty of *Bellas Artes* which joins with the National Conservatory of Music and the National Academy of Fine Arts to foster a new Chilean art and music. The dean of the *Bellas Artes* faculty, Domingo Santa Cruz Wilson (born in 1899), was Chile's best-known composer. He won the prize offered in 1941 for music written in honor of the four-hundredth anniversary of the founding of Santiago. His work was a symphony in three parts based on praise of the "mighty mountain stream Maipó, the giant mountain Aconcagua, the beautiful lakes of the South." Chilean folklore, with Araucanian themes, was used by the "original and colorful" Carlos Isamitt (born in 1885) to create ballets and symphonies which have been performed in America. Isamitt was also a painter and recorded Araucanian faces as well as songs. Juan Orrego-Salas came to the United States for subjects for ballets, cantatas, and piano compositions, studied in New York on a Rockefeller grant, and was welcomed home with his works as Chile's finest young composer. The world-renowned ballerina Margot Fonteyn danced in Santiago in 1960 and created a new interest in Chilean native ballet. Based on folklore from northern Chile, the ballet *Candelaria*, composed by Carlos Riesco and produced by the Chilean dancer Octabio Cintolessi, brought an "integration of the arts in an authentic national ballet idiom."

There has been an active Chilean school of sculpture for more than a century; one of the best modern sculptors was the great-granddaughter of Andrés Bello, Rebecca Matte de Iñíquez, who died in 1929. The Faculty of *Bellas Artes* gives prizes for painting—the Chilean Congress itself votes 100,000 pesos as the yearly budget for art premiums. The prize-winners have most often been landscape artists who painted the color of Chile, the light in her valleys, the perpetual snow on the Andean summits. Geography has given a special quality to Chilean art, as well as to its music, literature, and politics.

Readings

Alexander, R. J., *Communism in Latin America* (1957)
———, *Labor Relations in Argentina, Brazil and Chile* (1962)
Bernstein, H., *Modern and Contemporary Latin America* (1952)
Bowers, C. G., *Chile Through Embassy Windows, 1939–1953* (1958)
Butland, G., *Chile: An Outline* (3rd ed., 1956)
Clissold, E., *Chilean Scrapbook* (1952)
Cohen, A., *Economic Changes in Chile, 1929–1950* (1960)
Edwards, A., *My Native Land* (1928)
Elliot, G. F. S., *Chile, Its History and Development* (1927)
Ellsworth, P., *Chile, An Economy in Transition* (1945)
Englekirk, J. E., et al., *Outline History of Spanish American Literature* (3rd ed., 1965)
Evans, H. C., *Chile and Its Relations with the United States* (1927)
Fergusson, E., *Chile* (1943)
Fetter, F. W., *Monetary Inflation in Chile* (1931)
Finer, H., *The Chilean Development Corporation* (1947)
Galdames, L., *History of Chile*, trans. I. J. Cox (1941)
Gil, F. G., *Genesis and Modernization of Political Parties in Chile* (1962)
———, *Political System of Chile* (1966)
———, and C. J. Parrish, *The Chilean Presidential Election of September 4, 1964* (1965)
Halperin, E., *Nationalism and Communism in Chile* (1964)
Hanson, E. P., *Chile: Land of Progress* (1941)
Haring, C. H., *South American Progress* (1934)
Herrick, B. H., *Urban Migration and Economic Development in Chile* (1966)
Herring, H., *Good Neighbors* (1941)
Hirschman, A. O., *Journeys Towards Progress* (1963)
———, *Latin American Issues, Essays and Comments* (1961)
Houston, J. A., *Latin America and the United Nations* (1956)
Hughlett, L. J., *Industrialization of Latin America* (1946)
International Bank for Reconstruction and Development, *Agricultural Economy of Chile* (1952)
Jefferson, M., *Recent Colonization in Chile* (1921)
Johnson, J. J., *Political Change in Latin America* (1958)
Kaempfer-Villagran, G., *Bloody Episodes of the Workers' Struggle in Chile, 1850–1925* (1962)
Kelchner, W. H., *Latin America and the League of Nations* (1926)
Mamalakis, M., and C. W. Reynolds, *Essays on the Chilean Economy* (1965)
Martin, P. A., *Latin America and the War* (1925)
McBride, G. M., *Chile, Land and Society* (1936)
Mecham, J. L., *Church and State in Latin America* (rev. ed., 1966)
———, *Survey of United States-Latin American Relations* (1965)
Mistral, G., *Selected Poems*, trans. L. Hughes (1957)
Pan American Union, *Gabriela Mistral, 1882–1957* (1958)
Pendle, G., *Land and People of Chile* (1960)
Pike, F. B., *Chile and the United States, 1880–1962* (1963)
Poblete Troncoso, M., and B. G. Burnett, *Rise of the Latin American Labor Movement* (1960)

Silvert, K. H., *Chile: Yesterday and Today* (1965)
———, *The Conflict Society: Reaction and Revolution in Latin America* (1961)
Smole, W. J., *Owner-Cultivatorship in Middle Chile* (1963)
Stevenson, J. R., *The Chilean Popular Front* (1942)
Torres-Rioseco A., *Epic of Latin American Literature* (rev. ed., 1946)
Wilgus, A. C., ed., *Argentina, Brazil and Chile Since Independence* (1935)

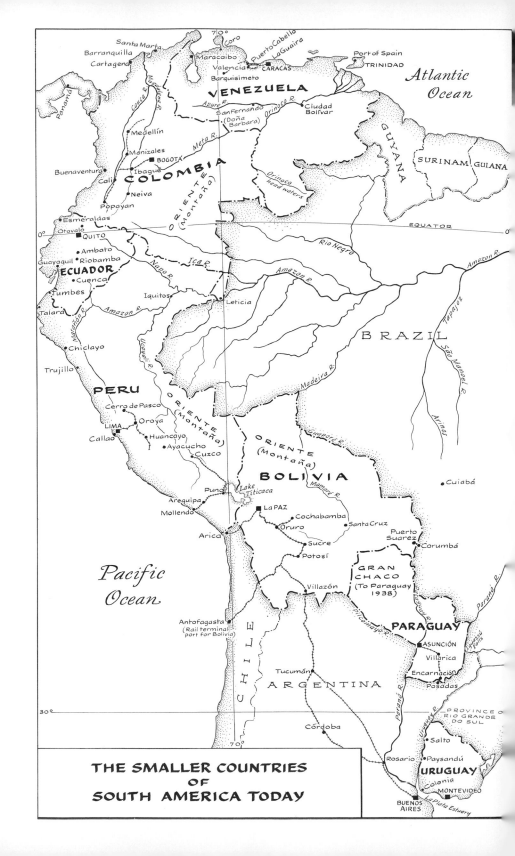

THE SMALLER COUNTRIES
OF
SOUTH AMERICA TODAY

Part VI

SMALL NATIONS BUFFETED BY
TWENTIETH-CENTURY FORCE

O NE OF THE PRESIDENTS of modern Venezuela was a writer
named Rómulo Gallegos, more famous for one single great
novel than for his political failure. This book is called *Doña
Barbara*; one of the three or four most widely read novels in
Latin America, it was made into a popular movie by both Mexican and Argentine film companies. It has been called "a starkly
realistic allegorical novel of the struggle for freedom and progress." Its hero, a product of the *llanos*, Venezuela's wide, flooded
Orinoco plains, returns from the university in Caracas to take
over the cattle land he has inherited. He finds the attempt to
modernize the back-country ranch a seemingly hopeless task.
His foreman tells him—

> The *llaneros* [the cowboys] have done nothing to improve the
> cattle industry . . . because this 'land is a grindstone that dulls
> the edge of the hardest-tempered will. We'll begin just where we
> were twenty years ago. And in the meantime the breed is
> degenerating from lack of crossing and the plagues that kill a

tenth of the herds. . . . Now that you mention crossing, try it. . . . In the end the revolutionists will eat the cattle . . . The minute the meat gets a little better, there'll be more revolutions.[1]

Perhaps the novelist meant by "the breed" not only the cattle but the people of the Andean and Caribbean areas, who were "degenerating" for lack of scientific care, better industry, broader education, and more democratic government. The people of the smaller Latin American nations are today worried by "plagues that kill a tenth of the herd," not so much yaws or malaria as old-fashioned *caudillismo*, one-crop economies, poverty and illiteracy. How many times in this current century, from Paraguay to the Dominican Republic, "the revolution has eaten the cattle," while the local "cowboys" did little to improve conditions.

The picture is not all that dark. In Uruguay, with which our story of the smaller nations starts, and in Costa Rica, living conditions are pleasant and modern. Lima, Caracas, Havana, Bogotá, Guatemala City are splendid modern capitals with a politically powerful laboring class and a growing middle class. In areas of one-product economy, foreign owners like the oil companies in Venezuela and the United Fruit Company in Honduras have agreed to plough large shares of their profits back into the land. Most of these nations in the past two decades have set up national Development Plans, *Fomento* Departments, in the conscientious desire to industrialize the economy and improve the output of the small farms.

As the 1960s approached, feuds between just such *caudillo*-type dictators stirred the waters of the Caribbean area and upset the small nations. In 1959 the Cuban hero Fidel Castro, with his own *personalista* following, threatened invasion of the Dominican Republic, controlled by *caudillo* Trujillo. Trujillo in turn tried invasion of Cuba, with neutral Haiti caught in the middle, and in addition urged opposition leaders in Venezuela to revolt against their new democratic government. Trujillo was assassinated by members of his own army staff in 1963 but no internal peace came to Santo Domingo. Cuban-based guerilla bands attacked Panama and Nicaragua, and were blamed for causing an abortive revolt in Honduras. Thus seven small nations reverberated from the "People's Revolution" in Cuba. Meanwhile, these underdeveloped small states of tropical America continued to focus world attention on their political methods, their interfeuding, their land reforms, their soaring birthrate and their treatment of investment capital.

Each of the nations to be considered—Uruguay, Paraguay, Bolivia, Peru, Ecuador, Colombia, Venezuela, six Central American countries and three Caribbean island nations—has its own characteristics, and in seeking generalizations about them we are in danger of oversimplifying.

[1] From Rómulo Gallegos, *Doña Barbara*, trans. Robert Malloy (New York: Cape and Smith Co., 1931), p. 286.

Chapter 35

Uruguay and Paraguay:
Contrasting Nations
in the Twentieth Century

A DICTATORSHIP AND A DEMOCRACY

TWO SMALL NATIONS, each with a population less than that of Buenos Aires, each with only one city, each with more "head of live-stock" than "head of humans," each with a stormy history of dictatorship, war, or revolution up to 1900, each named the Indian word for a great river, each overshadowed by the same large neighbor, Argentina—how similar Uruguay and Paraguay seem on the map, how confusing their names. And yet the similarity ends there. After 1900 the two countries developed on such different patterns that the above few notes of comparison are the only ones that can be made. Paraguay is still a tight dictatorship with little popular support, while Uruguay is a modernized urban nation with a generous social security system and a population 97 per cent literate.

THE MARCH OF DEMOCRACY IN URUGUAY

A nation so uniform and modern as to lack appeal for American tourists seeking the picturesque or quaint, Uruguay has been described as "an uninteresting place to visit but a fine place to live." It is a self-conscious, proud, independent, and democratic nation. Uruguayans themselves say, "Everybody here talks, writes, works, drinks, smokes, relaxes, and prospers about as he pleases." A rich agricultural land located entirely within the Temperate Zone and in an area of sufficient year-round rainfall, a land with a coastline of 120 miles on the Atlantic, and 235 miles along the Plata, Uruguay is favored among South American nations. No longer the crossroads of international turbulence and civil strife after 1900, Uruguay had left *caudillismo* behind and progressed through social evolution, not military revolution.

A great Uruguayan statesman, José Batlle y Ordoñez, often referred to as the "Founder of Modern Uruguay," was responsible for much of the "revolutionary" legislation from 1903 to 1920. Born in 1856 during the years of active Blanco-Colorado fighting, he had been sent by his well-to-do Colorado family abroad to study in a different environment; when he was not yet thirty he had founded the great modern newspaper *El Día* which brought a new kind of liberalism to the Colorado party. After service in Congress, this newspaper editor was elected to the presidency in 1903. He was immediately faced with a Blanco uprising which had to be quelled with military force, but Batlle was soon bringing the Blancos into the government. At the end of his term one of his associates, Claudio Williman, was elected president in a fair election, while Batlle went abroad to represent Uruguay at international conferences at The Hague, and to study the government of Switzerland. He was elected president again on his return in 1911.

Dr. José Batlle y Ordònez, "Grand Old Man" of Uruguayan politics to 1929. *Courtesy Pan American Union.*

A great lion of a man with an enormous head and a shock of unruly hair, Batlle had a forceful personality. As a member of Congress after his second presidency, as editor of *El Día,* as a leader of the National Council of Administration after 1920, Battle continued to stamp his personality and his progressive ideas on the wax of Uruguay until his death in 1929. In his lifetime Uruguay emerged as a nation socially ahead of any other small Latin country.

Batlle, true friend of democracy, believed the basic problems of Uruguay had stemmed from dictatorship and instability. "Reform" to him meant three things: (1) improving politics by compulsory suffrage, mass public education, and wide representation of all parties and classes; (2) controlling the national economy by state operation of banks, public utilities, and some industries; and (3) raising the standard of living by all types of social security and labor legislation. He saw his first principle bring about free elections during his own lifetime; on the second and third he fought a bitter fight with gradual success, aided by popular opinion and by his ability to influence the policies of his successors in the office of presidency. Batlle was contemporaneous with Scandinavian leaders in urging government competition with private industry, with Theodore Roosevelt in breaking the power of monopolistic companies, with the more progressive state governments in the United States of Wilson's time in setting minimum wages and establishing the rights of unions to strike.

All was not smooth sailing for the Utopia. Uruguay remained neutral in the World War I conflict then raging, but the little nation had to fix prices and control exports in order to avoid inflation in the upset of world trade. In 1917 an Uruguayan ship was torpedoed by the Germans and Uruguay severed relations with the Central Powers, though there was no actual declaration of war. Trade with the Allies kept Uruguay prosperous.

In the tide of peace and prosperity, Batlle had suggested a plural executive, a cabinet government by committee rather than by a powerful president. Much of Batlle's program was incorporated in a new constitution which went into effect in 1919, the first since 1830. The president was to be directly elected, but his powers were cut to those of a mere chairman, sharing executive power with an elected nine-member Council of Administration, serving six years on a staggered plan. The minority party was always to have a third of the members, elected by a system of proportional representation. The new constitution called for compulsory voting, separated Church and state, provided for government participation in industry, and included much labor legislation.

The president had responsibility for foreign affairs. The first to hold office under the new plan, Baltasar Brum, a former Minister of Foreign Affairs during World War I and a close associate of Batlle, brought Uruguay to world attention. He is famous in Latin America for having issued in 1920 his Brum Doctrine, proposing that the Monroe Doctrine be made a multilateral pact of all the Americas in keeping out aggression, and not a mere policy of the United States. He also made Uruguay an active member of the League of Nations. Agreeing with Batlle that the president should not be a power in domestic affairs, he and his successors after him up to 1931 all turned more power over to the Council.

Prosperity ended for the world in 1929, and for Uruguay as well. Depending on world markets for meat, hides, and wool, Uruguay's Administrative Council found it difficult to control the unemployment of the depression years. Gabriel Terra, a lukewarm Batlle man serving as president, quelled disturbances with repression. When he was opposed by the National Council and by Congress, he dissolved both institutions and made himself dictator. Opposition newspapers were closed, opponents arrested. Terra was forced to call a new constitutional convention in 1934; the resulting plan of government returned to a strong presidential government and abolished the Administrative Council. Though the conservative property-owning class had more influence with the Terra regime than in the previous two decades, Terra did not abandon the social and economic reforms of his predecessors. His political policy was more repressive, yet minority rights were still protected. One-half of the new senate and one-third of the cabinet posts were to be filled by the president's opponents. To prevent the two traditional parties from splitting up into several "fragment parties," the law provided that each party could run as many candidates as it pleased, but that "all ballots cast for any of a party's candidates are credited to the one who received the largest number of votes." Thus the most popular candidate within the most popular party won. Terra stepped down from the presidency in 1938; his successors, beginning with his brother-in-law Alfredo Baldomir, returned to the Batlle tradition.

World War II involved Uruguay in an unexpected way. The Declaration of Panama had declared the waters of the Western Hemisphere "out of bounds" for the belligerents, and Uruguay had joined in it. Uruguay then acted belligerently herself when British cruisers drove the German battleship *Graf Spee* into refuge in Montevideo harbor. When the great ship overstayed her limit in neutral waters, she was scuttled, perhaps by the captain, in Montevideo Bay, and her crew interned; Uruguay answered international protests by announcing that her action was in accordance with the Declaration of Panama. Uruguay was then one of the first Latin American nations to sever relations with the Axis powers after Pearl Harbor, conceding the use of bases to the United States and securing military equipment through lend-lease, as opposed to the pro-Nazi attitude of "big neighbor" Argentina. In February 1945, in time to qualify for membership in the United Nations, Uruguay declared war on the Axis.

Luis Herrera, the aging Blanco leader, was an old political warhorse, pro-Nazi and proclerical in opinion though an intellectual historian on the side. He ran for the presidency in 1942, and again in 1946, but a series of political "coups," minor constitutional changes, and Colorado winnings kept him from office. In 1946 Herrera won a plurality of votes as a person but was forced to concede to the Colorado candidate with a lesser total vote because the combined Colorado party vote was greater—the law being that "the highest candidate in the highest party wins." Of the three Colorado candidates in 1946, one was Batlle's own son, editor of the family paper *El Día*, and another was Batlle's favorite nephew and heir-apparent in politics, Luis Batlle Berres. Though Tomás Berreta, the third candidate, won the plurality, Batlle Berres became vice-president, and succeeded to the presidency on the death of the aged Berreta.

Again in 1950 the law of "the highest candidate in the highest party" defeated Herrera and elected Andrés Martínez Trueba. The new president bent all his efforts to restore the Batlle type of government which was contained in a new constitution ratified by a plebiscite in 1951. Under it there was again a nine-member federal executive council, but this time with no president at all. Instead the council ruled Uruguay as the federal council of seven rules Switzerland, the chairmanship rotating among the members by the year. There was also a cabinet, which depended on the majority within the assembly and rose or fell with that majority according to the English system. The council was put into operation with Trueba as its first chairman.

That literary-minded old warhorse Herrera got a seat on the executive council at last in 1952 and again in 1954, but his chance to serve as chairman, and thus as national president, was blocked by the political make-up of the body. Luis Batlle Berres, José Batlle's nephew, and Cesar Batlle Pacheco, José Batlle's son, both served on the council and became bitter rivals within the Colorado party. When acting as the chairman in 1956, the nephew Luis came to visit in the United States; he was described as a "mild, chubby, rather sad-eyed little man," famous for his constant support of a losing soccer team and for his concern with child welfare projects.

However, the inflation and the competition in world markets that all one-crop Latin American nations faced sent up prices of manufactured articles in Montevideo and brought down the real value of fixed pensions. Uruguay, the most welfare-minded economy in Latin America, had difficulties. There were strikes and unemployment; the wool market dropped; nationalized industries were being mismanaged. In the elections of December 1958 a new rural leader, Benito Nardone, a folksy radio star who had taken to the country precincts to arouse political support of Herrera's long-losing Blanco Nationals, was able to win a majority vote for the Blancos on the nine-man council, a break for the Blancos after ninety-three years of Colorado control. Blanco Herrera, by then eighty-five, was leader-emeritus of an aging faction of the old Blancos which bickered with Nardone's' more modern-minded Blanco friends. The Batlle cousins continued to split the Colorado or urban party. In the 1962 elections Blancos won the National Council, but the Colorados held the Congress.

The Colorados had not realized that their cozy little welfare state was good for city workers only, and that the countryside, source of the nation's wealth, was a century behind. Not only did farm workers receive few social benefits, but the rich farm land itself was being used to only one-third of its possible capacity. In the ten years from 1956 to 1966, Uruguay's share in the world meat market had fallen from 9 per cent to 7 per cent, in wool from 16 per cent to 10 per cent. Without the foreign exchange brought into Montevideo by meat and wool exports, the city itself was declining. A government facing bankruptcy could not afford the generous pensions at fifty-five and the high unemployment insurance and yearly wage increases the city workers wanted. Pension payments fell three years in arrears by 1965, and the value of the peso had plunged. Meat prices were so much higher across the border in Brazil that farmers drove their cattle into Rio Grande do Sul and let the Montevideo *frigoríficos* work on half time. To people in the city, unpaid and out of work, Cuban *Fidelismo* began to look good. Anti-United States feeling mounted and crowds heckled official American visitors. President Nardone had to beef up an army of 10,000—the first efficient military force in Uruguay in the twentieth century—to deal with rioters. A thousand army men ran the electric and telephone services when the electric workers' union went on strike, and thus proved that most of the 12,000 striking workers in the government-run industry were "feather bedding."

In the midst of this economic chaos, both Batlle Berres and Benito Nardone died in 1964. In March of 1965 Washington Beltrán, fifty-one-year-old editor of the Batlle newspaper *El Día*, became president of the council. By this time the council seemed no more than a third house of the legislature. Beltrán hoped to strengthen the executive power. In August 1965 he sent a commission to the United States for advice and financial help. A plan was made to refund $500,000,000 of Uruguay's national debt in Washington, in return for austerity at home. This meant cuts in wages and pensions, so 500,000 members of the National Confederation of Workers went out on strike. Beltrán, assuming executive authority, declared a "state of siege" and got the workers back on the job. Meantime Uruguayan economists, with help from the *Alianza para Progreso*, announced a ten-year development plan of 3,600 printed pages, which called for a "reorganization of the country's social security system, sharp restrictions on imports, and increased agricultural production for export."

In spite of the development plan, Uruguay was tottering on the brink of bankruptcy by 1966. The National Council was stalemated between the Colorados and the Blancos. In the midst of strikes and inflation, the Council asked for a vote to return to a single executive. On November 27, 1966, the voters cast a big majority for a new constitution providing for a single strong president for a five year term, and elected retired Air Force general Oscar D. Gestido. He took office on March 1, 1967. With this reform Uruguay's record of democratic institutions showed that the little nation would be able to "pull itself up by its own bootstraps."

URUGUAY AS AN ECONOMIC AND CULTURAL UNIT

Uruguay's economy, more so than that of Argentina, is dependent on the two tyrants, wool and meat. Helpless when world prices in these commodities fluctuate, Uruguay has attempted to overcome the handicap of the one-crop economy by social and economic experimentation through government ownership in industry. The state owns the Bank of the Republic, the Mortgage Bank, and the State Insurance Bank, which has a monopoly on all forms of insurance—life, fire, marine, and accident. The State Electricity Board controls all light, power, and phones; a government corporation runs the harbor and manages all fuel and alcohol, and even all cement in this treeless country where building is seldom done with wood. A government-run *frigorífico* processes a quarter of the nation's meat for export. Radio stations, beach hotels, ballet troupes are government business. A fishing fleet and a fish cannery, a truck and bus line, a taxicab concession, all are owned by the state. Uruguay points with pride to the fact that little foreign capital has been necessary in her development. Though the number of government employees is top-heavy, the program has achieved a good deal of success, perhaps because the country is so small. Only one city is involved, and it would have been difficult to build up any large private capital in a country without coal or iron. Uruguay weathered the depression, the effects of World War II, and the postwar boom, but her welfare state has been expensive, and she was in financial difficulties in the mid-1960s, as described above.

Meanwhile the people have happily supported themselves, aided by many types of social security from the government. Batlle's personal enemies had bitterly opposed his 1911 plans for social legislation. "Why should we," they wrote in their own paper, "an underpopulated country hardly known abroad, continually astonish the world with the radicalism of our laws?" "You have not seen anything yet," the editor of *El Día* snapped back, "We may be a poor and obscure little republic, but we can have forward-looking little laws." These words became so famous they were used in pushing legislation for two generations. Maximum work hours, minimum wages, unemployment and accident insurance, and workmen's compensation were the order of the day. The year 1916 saw an old-age pension law. The Spanish word used for "retired" in Montevideo is *jubilado,* and older workers have happily looked forward to *jubilación* for

Nursery school in Montevideo workers' district being visited by an Uruguayan civic committee. *Courtesy Pan American Union.*

more than a generation. A modern "Children's Code" is concerned with all children, legitimate and illegitimate, from conception through high school.

When the term "city" is used, only Montevideo is meant. With its wide boulevards and fine beaches, its million people, it dominates the little country just as Providence dominates Rhode Island. Paysandú, second urban center, has less than 100,000 people collected around plants for canning corned beef and for processing leather. Steamers go up the Uruguay River to the farming center at Salto where orange and tangerine groves cover thousands of acres and honey is produced in quantity for export. Railroads and modern highways radiate from Montevideo and into Paraguay, Argentina, and southern Brazil. The Pan American Highway connects towns from Montevideo all the way to São Paulo.

Between the Uruguay River on the west and Montevideo on the east lie the rolling grasslands, home of the old Blanco aristocrats. Still wealthy today, these estate owners live much more simply than do the Argentine *estancieros* or the Chilean *fundo* owners. There is little need of farm buildings around the rambling estate houses, for in the mild climate on the edge of the subtropics cattle live outside the year round, and feed never has to be stored. Owing to the use of so much land for grazing, there has been little opportunity for small freeholding farmers, and the government has to subsidize a wheat-planting program in order to get enough flour for Montevideo's bakers without importing it. High wages in the city and machine methods on the estates have driven the agricultural workers off the land; most of the social legislation refers to city laborers. One of Uruguay's greatest economic needs today is the counterbalancing of excessive urbanization by mechanized, improved agriculture. Meanwhile the population has continued to grow as European immigration flows into this already predominantly white country, which by 1967 had a population of 2,800,000.

Across the rolling Uruguayan pampas, there are very few small village units around a rural school and church as there are in Mexico or Brazil. The Basque shepherds and their staff of riders contact other communities only at lambing or shearing time. Though mutton and wool from the Merino, Lincoln, and Romney strains of purebreds brought in from Europe are of a high grade, Uruguayan beef is considered inferior on the world markets because of the absence of special care and feeding methods on the open ranges. Uruguayan economists are concerned that Argentine beef and Australian wool bring higher prices than Uruguayan, and wonder whether some of the advanced social thinking spent on improving conditions for city workers should not have been applied also to improving the care and diet of the livestock and thus bringing in more money from world markets.

Since, in spite of the limited economy, Uruguayan life is easy and pleasant, it is not surprising that Uruguayan writers are among the best in Latin America. The essayist José Enrique Rodó (1872–1917) has been called the "greatest modernist prose writer," second only to Rubén Darío as a Latin American literary light. He died in 1917, but not before he had written a thin little book called *Ariel*. The refined and cultured spirit of the aristocratic Latin American—not of the gaucho or the Indian—is the true Ariel of Shakespeare's play, *The Tempest,* while North American materialism, which Rodó considered an evil menace, is the crude gorilla-like Caliban, villain of the play. Thus Latin Americans should be proud of their own culture; there should be a "spiritual unity" among the Spanish-speaking people of the New World; they are the true Americans. Since Rodó was editor of a literary review widely read in all Spanish-speaking countries, his influence in arousing intellectuals against the United States is felt to this day.

Another Uruguayan "greatest in Spanish America" in the twentieth century was the short story writer Horacio Quiroga (1878–1937), who knew the jungle country of the Argentine province of Misiones and spent several years in the Chaco. His jungle stories made the outdoors a popular subject for story material. The backlands world of the gaucho was still the central theme of several well-known Uruguayan works at mid-twentieth century. As in all Latin American countries, Uruguayan poets are as numerous as journalists or politicians—young "ultraists" who write obscurely and live the Bohemian life, such as Julio Herrera y Reissig (1875–1910), and more serious public figures who write poetry as an avocation, among whom are several women. Uruguayans are active in literary criticism and have some well-known literary periodicals. Markets for books being small, the authors must finance their writings, but the Ministry of Public Instruction offers prizes and purchases a number of copies.

Opera and drama are so good in Montevideo that the discriminating Argentines cross the long ferry route to see the state-sponsored Uruguayan shows. All Montevideo theater activity comes under a government agency called SODRE, the initials for Official Service of Radio and Culture Diffusion. SODRE takes summer stock into the backlands, operates schools of opera and ballet, manages the symphony, and conducts art competitions and art classes. "High-quality, low-priced entertainment and artistic training" is SODRE's motto. One of South America's greatest artists was the Uruguayan painter Pedro Fegari (1861–1938). The more recent Uruguayan painter, Joaquin Torres García (1874–1949) went to Spain as an art student and worked with the Spanish abstractionists Miró and Picasso. He returned to Montevideo to introduce Picasso's style to South America. Called the "Latin American artist who did most for universal painting," he founded a studio and gallery in Montevideo which bears his name and from which current Uruguayan artists send traveling exhibitions to New York.

Uruguay is a literate nation, a nation of newspaper readers. Education is the highest single item on the national budget, since Uruguay feels no need for armament spending. Actual compulsory attendance is enforced, not merely written into beautiful law as in other small Latin American lands. All Uruguayan schools are tuition-free, including the university, and there are thousands of high school graduates who continue on to college. Uruguayan college life seems very much like that of the United States, with an intense interest in school sports. The Uruguayans in general are very sports-minded, and they follow international soccer with the zest common to baseball fans in the United States. Say "Uruguay" in other

Latin American countries, and the natives think immediately, not of sheep or of social legislation, but of world-champion soccer teams.

PARAGUAY: A TWENTIETH-CENTURY VICTIM
OF ITS NINETEENTH-CENTURY TROUBLES

John Gunther, ubiquitous American correspondent, found Paraguay "the most remote and picturesque state in the Americas, a kind of forlorn and almost forgotten fairyland with overtones of brutal and contemporary reality . . . a country where no one knows who anybody's grandfather is, where every Paraguayan speaks Guaraní as well as Spanish," where though "all the people are *simpáticos,* the political situation is called *confusionismo.*"

Paraguay is an isolated country with no access to the world save through other nations' territory. Naturally this landlocked nation of a million and a half Indians and *mestizos* is predominantly rural. The average Paraguayan lives amongst the bounty of his own little farm, goes to the sagging colonial church in the middle of his town's weedy little plaza, and does not worry about politics. He is likely to own his little farm of about ten acres, planted in corn, mandioca, beans, and garden vegetables. Perhaps five or six acres will be planted in cotton, the one crop that ever gets to a city market. His family may own a run-down cow or two, some donkeys, pigs, and chickens. His women sit at home or in the village market place making the famous *ñandutí* lace or some other local handicraft specialty. His hut is made of bamboo poles and adobe, with little furniture inside, and kitchen utensils all outside. The family sits outside also to drink *yerba maté,* the Paraguayan tea, from the *bombilla,* or tube stuck in a gourd, and to eat the *puchero* or stew made from boiled beef, vegetables, and mandioca root.

Several years ago the Rockefeller Foundation made a health survey in a district of such family farms. More than 30 per cent of the people had malaria; bad water brought frequent typhoid epidemics; lack of mineral content in the water produced a high incidence of goiter. There was one case of leprosy for every 500 people, seventeen cases of tuberculosis for every thousand. The Rockefeller Foundation workers were looking particularly for hookworm, and they found more than 80 per cent of the rural population infected in the area studied. Illiteracy also ran 80 per cent.

Naturally, there are Paraguayans for whom life is neither so unhealthy nor so simple. Reporting 305,000 people in 1965, one-sixth of all Paraguayans, Asunción was more in touch with the world than ever before in the mid-1960s. Airplanes now come in and out every day; steamers dock twice a week, at the end of the three-day trip up the Paraguay from Buenos Aires. The train across eastern Paraguay runs the 230 miles to Encarnación on the Alto Paraná, and on across the Argentine province of Misiones to connect with Montevideo and Buenos Aires once a week. A modern paved highway has been built 475 miles across the Chaco to the Bolivian border. Asunción itself has electricity and a modern water and sewer system, financed with an American loan. Along one bank of the river is a fine residential district; banks and government buildings seem imported from a good-sized North American city, but ladies who want to shop in big department stores must go downriver to Buenos Aires. Though hovels along the waterfront are mere country-type straw huts, and 60 per cent of the city dwellers are illiterate, the city has enough soccer fans to support a league of fifteen different teams, and to back a national team which is skillful enough to compete with the invincible Uruguayans. Villa Rica, a good-sized town, lives off sawmills and sugar refineries; Concepción with 34,000 inhabitants has meat-packing plants and a tannery. Encarnación on the Alto Paraná facing Argentina at the end of the railway is considered a port, but it seems no more than a country village without an actual main street save the railway tracks, although it has a population of 35,000.

North and west of Asunción are wild lands of the Chaco, a region where "there is not even a tree without thorns." On the far side of the Chaco are the foothills of the Andes, but the rivers which rise there are lost in lagoons and marshes during the flood season, February to April, while the marshes turn into hard-packed dry beds during the rest of the year. In spite of the new highway, only a vast development program with millions in modern capital to spend could preserve the water through the dry season for livestock and humans. Oil is hoped for in the Chaco. Many of the Indians of the Chaco are primitive migrants, who move from water hole to water hole as the dry season advances. Temperatures vary from almost freezing in the fierce winds of July and August to around 115° in December, the highest temperatures recorded in South America. Such conditions dominate three-fifths of Paraguay's actual area.

There has been some settlement in the Chaco, especially a group of 1,700 Mennonites from Canada, whose cooperative agricultural colonies prospered after bitter years of drought. Sixteen hundred more Mennonites came to the colony in 1929 from Soviet Russia, and another 2,300 from displaced persons' camps in 1949. The success of this latter group led the International Refugee Organization to send a large number of Ukrainians to the area north of Asunción on the edge of the Chaco; individual European settlers, artisans, and independent farmers have not come to any part of Paraguay in any great numbers. The rush of Italians, Basques, Germans, and Swiss to southern South America stopped far downriver on the pampas. On the Paraguayan continuation of the pampas, the Gran Chaco, the only successful inhabitants are the Indians, most of whom have seen no white men, wear no clothes, paint their bodies with geometric designs, and hunt game with bow and arrow. President Stroessner was hoping in the mid-1960s to build up the equally undeveloped northeast on the Brazilian border, where he opened a $30,000,000 hydroelectric project.

The Chaco produces some tanning extract from the hard wood called *quebracho*, which is logged by private concerns—the principal one Argentinean—having their own railways and logging camps. From the more wooded area of Paraguay, timber for beams, girders, and railroad ties is shipped downstream to treeless Argentina to make up the major export. The wild forests of Paraguay also produce the *yerba maté*, the Paraguay tea so popular in Argentina, but plantation-type development within Argentina itself has stolen most of the market from the wild leaf. Cotton farming in the populated southern area of Paraguay has to fight locusts and a special tropical "pink boll worm" and can hardly compete with Argentina and United States cotton. Paraguay's tough, lean, tick-bitten cattle are descended from the cattle brought upriver by Irala, with little admixture of improved breeds. Only meat concentrates and canned beef are exported, since neither flesh nor hides are of a quality fit for world trade. Oranges brought to the Guaraní missions by the Jesuit fathers have flourished almost in a wild state; during the 1920s and 1930s boatloads of them, gathered piecemeal from each tiny ranch, went downriver to Buenos Aires. Then Argentina began to refuse the scrubby little seedlings as inferior to her own navel oranges. Paraguay grows enough food to feed herself and, in addition to those products already mentioned, exports tobacco and petit-grain oil. Thus it can be seen that Paraguay depends upon agriculture, livestock, and forest products.

Small wonder that during World War II when Paraguay was given a chance by the United States Coordinator of Inter-American Affairs to choose some type of technical aid, she chose scientific agricultural advice. By 1950 a fourfold program had jointly been worked out to be partially financed by the Paraguayans: kill orange blights and improve tree stock by grafting, augment cattle diet by grain feeding, raise milk production, and preserve stored crops from rats and weevils by means of underground silos. Botanists, plant pathologists, dairy and livestock experts started the pilot project. Farmers in villages reached by truck roads were brought to the model farms in groups by bus. More than 11,000 farmers also received loans from the *Servicio Técnico Inter-americano de Cooperación Agrícola*, or STICA, as the joint agency was called. At the time, the plan was considered a pattern for other Point Four projects, but it would take another generation of interested farmers before these methods influenced Paraguay greatly.

It is not surprising that a nation which for so many years devoted its energies to war should still be backward in education. Though the law says primary education is free and compulsory, elementary schools are inadequate and the law is not enforced. In Asunción and the larger towns the "educated classes" are increasing, however; the university has 2,000 students and there is now an agricultural school as well as the medical and law schools. The Guaraní language, a source of much national pride, is actually a cultural drawback. Though there is some fine literature in Guaraní, it has no circulation outside Paraguay. Spanish itself is twisted by the Paraguayans, and many suffixes and prefixes of Guaraní origin make new words in the Spanish of even Asunción's elite.

Transportation remains the great hindrance. In spite of the dawning air age the rivers are still the main through freight routes. Vessels of seven-foot draft, most of them belonging to an Argentine company, come up to Asunción; vessels of five-foot draft go on up to Corumbá in Brazil's Mato Grosso, 1,800 miles from the Atlantic, and maintain a service from Corumbá to Asunción and thence to Buenos Aires every three weeks. All Paraguay reaches the outside world only through Argentina or the new roads which join those in the interiors of Bolivia and Brazil.

POLITICAL "CONFUSIONISMO" IN PARAGUAY'S TWENTIETH CENTURY

An isolated nation, a poor economy, a crippling war in the 1860s, military occupation for nearly a decade, a decimated population, thirty years of changing presidencies—what hopes were there for Paraguay in the early 1900s? A popular revolution in 1904 threw out the long-entrenched Colorado rule and ushered in Liberal party rule. But the change did not produce stability, and Paraguay continued to be ruled by a rapid turnover of *caudillos*. From 1870 to 1932 there were twenty-nine different presidents. The barracks-room revolutions, the *cuartelazos*, continued. Often they boiled out of the *cuarteles*, the soldiers' quarters, into the streets. A major and ten companions captured the artillery barracks to make one such revolution, "mounted guns at street corners to command approaches to public buildings, and waited till sunrise to start the shooting," according to Paraguayan history. Another change in government was brought by a politician who imported 200 farmers from a town forty-five miles away, farmers who knew nothing about the government in the city, but fought hard for the fun of it. An outgoing president quelled a revolution against his successor by mounting a naval piece on a railway car. His opponents won by "seizing a locomotive, packing it with high explosives, and sending it careening madly down the rails." This particular little by-play took place in 1911. The year 1912 saw a peacefully elected German-Paraguayan, Eduardo Schaerer, come to the presidency, bringing a short respite of peace, prosperity, and progress to Paraguay, and actually serving out his full term, the first president since the López family to do so.

It is strange that the presidents of this early part of the new century were intellectuals; they are called the "Generation of 1900," and their era, the "Golden Age of Paraguayan Culture." Dr. Cecilio Báez (1862–1919), leader of the liberals who ushered in Liberal party rule, was a college teacher who occupied the highest posts in state and University, a leader in the fight for religious tolerance, and a prolific writer in both French and Spanish on Paraguayan history and diplomacy. His contemporary, Manuel Domínguez (1867–1935), served as vice-president and foreign minister, while he also spent his spare time writing lyrical poems and patriotic essays on Paraguay's past. A third outstanding figure of the literary-political "Generation of 1900" was Manuel Gondra (1871–1927), expert on the problems of the Chaco, and twice president, who was also an historian of note and a literary critic.

Though the "Generation of 1900" established a bank, chartered the steamship company from Buenos Aires, and built the railway to Encarnación, their Golden Age cannot in any way be compared to the era of Sarmiento in Argentina or of Batlle in Uruguay. Their literary works were only read by each other; their music was performed in the parlors of the tiny group of elite; their art gallery, founded in 1910, was visited by their own wives and children and a few diplomats. All these gentlemen presidents were intellectuals in the sense of nineteenth-century liberal principles; they discussed philosophies the world had gone on to prove in practice a century earlier elsewhere. One of the last "literary presidents" was Eligio Ayala (1879–1930), whose term from 1924 to 1928 was another period of progress. As a group, these presidents never engaged in any drastic economic and social reforms; they had no interest in the masses and thus the masses had no interest in them or in the government in Asunción, for it concerned the mass of the people not at all. With such a limited economy and with such small-scale *cuartelazo* revolutions, Paraguay remained uninfluenced by the troubles of other nations—no involvement in any foreign war, no banking crises, labor troubles, unemployment, or revolts for land subdivision. When the world depression cut off Paraguay's foreign markets after 1930, there was some city unemployment and political agitation among intellectuals for reform, but Paraguay's attention was soon directed elsewhere.

For 1932 brought Paraguay a second devastating foreign war, this one over the uninhabited Gran Chaco. Bolivia, another poor country with backward Indian peoples ruled by dictators, had claimed the Chaco since 1810, saying that it had been a part of the jurisdiction of the *audiencia* of Charcas and, as such, Bolivian property since independence. After Bolivia lost her seacoast in the War of the Pacific in 1883, she strove to get a footing on the Paraguay River and a trade route out by that river to the Atlantic. By 1927 there were border clashes in the Chaco. Then, when the Tacna-Arica dispute was settled in 1929 and hopes of reclaiming the Bolivian seacoast were dead forever, Bolivia began to press Paraguay through diplomatic channels. There was a series of conferences in Buenos Aires to adjudicate the claims; neither side would give an inch. An "incident" at a frontier fort occurred in 1928, a half-hour's fight in which five Bolivians were killed, and soon national popular indignation was whipped up in both countries. Argentina and Brazil joined with a commission of inquiry of the Pan American Union to try and stop impending disaster, but they only postponed it for four years.

In 1932 two thousand Bolivian troops were in the Chaco in January when all was an immense swamp. They were still there six months later when the earth lay baked and cracked. Paraguay had one division to every six from Bolivia, one general to every five Bolivian, sixteen cannons to Bolivia's more than a hundred, 12,000 rifles to Bolivia's boasted 100,000. Paraguay's soldiers went barefoot because no shoes were ever issued to them to wear in the coarse grass or across the thorny brush or the rough ground. But her soldiers fought upriver from home. The Bolivian commander in chief was a Nazi-trained German imported for the job; he had ideas of a *blitzkrieg* to be fought with modern war machines, but he had to bring machines and men down from the Andes by narrow mountain trails. His privates were Aymará and Quechua Indians, used to life at 12,000 feet altitude. All Bolivian tactics came to naught when the Indians died like flies in the low, oppressive, hot Chaco. The Western Hemisphere sat back horrified at the gruelling conditions of this fighting, in which Indian fought Indian in "that Hell of green and gray." Says an historian of Paraguay, "Then let their masters gather around and draw lines on maps, on maps that will never show where brown men died for nothing!"

A truce attempt was made in 1933, and the League of Nations set up a Chaco Commission, but neither side accepted its decision. By September 1934 Paraguay had captured 22,000 square miles of the territory beyond Bolivia's line of forts, and the German commander of Bolivia's forces resigned. Both countries agreed to the request of the Argentine foreign minister to talk peace terms in Buenos Aires in June 1935, while a tense truce hung over the Chaco. The final boundary was set in July 1938, ten years after the first border incident. Paraguay received the territory she had fought for; Bolivia was given the right to come down to the Paraguay River by a railroad, which was not yet built twenty years later. Paraguayan progress had again been retarded by a senseless war.

Any political leader who agreed to the privileges granted Bolivia in the settlement could not be popular in postwar Paraguay. A new revolutionary movement, not a mere *cuartelazo*, called itself the New Paraguay, and in 1936 gained control of the presidency for its leader Rafael Franco, thus bringing to an end the Liberal party government. Franco attempted to institute some social and economic reforms, and announced a fine modernizing program from which all his successors have drawn ideas. But he failed to fulfill his promises and fell from power. After three years of more *confusionismo*, the social reform was taken up again by General José Félix Estigarribia, hero of the long campaign of attrition in the Chaco. Estigarribia came to the presidency in 1939 hoping to procure loans from the United States to build up the country, expand university education, and improve marginal lands. He helped frame the new constitution of 1940, which provided for a strong president elected for five years. Estigarribia set to work eagerly under this document, but unfortunately for Paraguay, who needed his vitality so badly, this handsome, progressive president was killed in an airplane accident after one year in office.

The hero of the Chaco was followed in the presidency by Higínio Morínigo. He was not of a pattern of the intellects of the Golden Age; his Indian mother is reported to have said that if she had known her son was to become president, she would at least have sent him to school. His only advantage was the boom trade of World War II, in which he played Argentina against the Allies for financial favors. While he joined the United States in a declaration of war and thus made Paraguay a member of the United Nations, he extracted every possible economic advantage out of friendship with the United States and Brazil, at the same time staying on the best of terms with pro-Nazi Argentina. At home the press was taken over by him, and his jails and concentration camps were full of his enemies. He did develop Paraguay economically, stimulating food production, aiding agriculture and some industry. But laborers, students, journalists, and intellectuals who opposed him and dared to strike in 1948 were ruthlessly repressed. When *cuartelazo* after *cuartelazo* tried to overthrow him, he placed the city under five months' siege. This sort of thing went on till 1947. In February of 1948 with Asunción tired of such civil war, Morínigo, after eight years of tyranny, allowed his Finance Minister, Natalicio González, to be elected. With Morínigo's retirement *confusionismo* returned to Paraguay, which had five presidents in the next seventeen months. Then the army placed the aged Frederico Chávez in the presidency with the backing of Perón in Argentina. Chávez was the equal of Morínigo as a dictator and held the Colorado Party under his heel until overthrown by the head of the army, General Alfredo Stroessner. Stroessner, who came in via *cuartelazo* in 1954, was also a Perón man, and helped the strong man in Buenos Aires to "escape" upriver to "visit" him, on his way to exile.

In November 1957 Stroessner was nominated by the party for another five-year term, beginning with the "election" held in February 1958. Paraguayan labor remained the poorest paid in Latin America, but when its leader dared to call the first strike in twelve years in September 1958, Stroessner had his army quickly stop it.

In 1963 Stroessner called an "election" in which an opposition candidate ran, but Stroessner was neatly elected for another six years. In the fall of 1966 heavy-handed Stroessner had stayed in power longer than any other Latin American ruler then living, and remained as one of the few real *caudillos* left in South America. Meanwhile, his poverty-stricken Paraguayans still suffered—not only from the same malnutrition and lack of schooling, but now also from a new inflation. There has been some economic progress with the improvements in scientific agriculture, health, and education; exchange has been made free and money stabilized. There are new rail links to Brazil and new oil pipelines from Bolivia, as well as two new hydroelectric projects, but the masses feel such improvements little as yet. Stroessner's country is still 90 per cent illiterate, though he has provided jobs on the new roads and electric projects, and was hoping to welcome foreign investments and new industries. To build up a good image abroad, he denounced "Cuban Communism," sent soldiers to join the American marines in Santo Domingo in 1965, and backed United States policies in the Western Hemisphere. To continue legally in office Stroessner called a convention to modernize the Constitution which met in March, 1967. In the late 1960s, Paraguay was what it had always been, a poverty-stricken, backward, isolated, dictator-controlled country. It has the potential to become the paradise of Guaraní legend, but the tragedy of this natural Arcadia is that it can neither live in idyllic solitude in the twentieth century nor compete with the great nations that surround it.

Readings

Aguirre, A., ed., *Uruguay and the United Nations* (1958)

Canon, M. M., *Social and Labor Problems of Peru and Uruguay: A Study in Contrasts* (1945)

Coester, A., *Literary History of Spanish America* (rev. ed., 1928)

Craig, C. W. T., *Paraguayan Interlude* (1935)

Crawford, R. W., *Century of Latin American Thought* (rev. ed., 1961)

Davis, H. E., *Social Science Trends in Latin America* (1950)

Elliot, A. E., *Paraguay: Its Cultural Heritage, Social Conditions and Educational Problems* (1931)

Fenwick, C. G., *Inter-American Regional System* (1949)

Fernandez Artucio, H., *Nazi Underground in South America* (1942)

Finot, E., *Chaco War and the United States* (1934)

Fisher, F. R., *et al.*, *Investments in Paraguay* (1955)

Fitzgibbon, R. H., *Uruguay: Portrait of a Democracy* (1954)

Fretz, J. W., *Pilgrims in Paraguay* (1953)

Gordon, W. C., *Economy of Latin America* (1950)

——, *Political Economy of Latin America* (1965)

Hanson, S. G., *Economic Development of Latin America* (1951)

——, *Utopia in Uruguay: Chapters in the Economic History of Uruguay* (1938)

Harris, C. G., *Uruguay: Economic and Commercial Conditions in Uruguay* (1950)

Harris, S., *Economic Problems of Latin America* (1944)

Henderson, I. L., *Paraguay: Economic and Commercial Conditions* (1952)

Henríquez-Ureña, P., *Literary Currents in Hispanic America* (1945)

International Bank for Reconstruction and Development, *Uruguay* (1951)

Ireland, G., *Boundaries, Possessions and Conflicts in South America* (1938)

James, P., *Latin America* (rev. ed., 1950)

Johnson, J. J., *Political Change in Latin America* (1958)

Josephs, R., *Latin America: Continent in Crisis* (1948)

Klein, M. A., *A Forest Survey of Paraguay* (1946)

Koebel, W. H., *Paraguay* (1917)

Krause, A. E., *Mennonite Settlement in the Paraguayan Chaco* (1952)

La Foy, M., *The Chaco Dispute and the League of Nations* (1946)

Lindahl, G., *Uruguay's New Path: A Study in Politics during the First Colegiado, 1919–1963* (1964)

Macdonald, A. F., *Latin American Politics and Government* (2nd ed., 1954)

Martin, P. A., *Latin America and the War* (1925)

Mecham, J. L., *Church and State in Latin America* (rev. ed., 1966)

Pendle, G., *Paraguay: A Riverside Nation* (3rd ed., 1963)

——, *Uruguay: South America's First Welfare State* (3rd ed., 1963)

Peterson, S. E., *Forest Products of Paraguay* (1945)

Raine, P., *Paraguay* (1956)

Reh, E., *Paraguayan Rural Life: Survey of Food Problems, 1943–1945* (1946)

Rodó, J. E., *Ariel*, trans. F. J. Stimson (1922)

Ronde, P. de, *Paraguay: A Gallant Little Nation* (1935)

Service, E. R. and H. S., *Tobati: Paraguayan Town* (1954)

Smith, H. L., and H. Littell, *Education in Latin America* (1934)

Taylor, P. B., *The Executive Power in Uruguay* (1951)

——, *Government and Politics of Uruguay* (1962)

Thompson, R. W., *Germans and Japs in South America* (1942)

——, *Land of Tomorrow: A Story of South America* (1937)

Torres-Rioseco, A., *Epic of Latin American Literature* (rev. ed., 1946)

United Nations, Department of Economic Affairs, *Economic Survey of Latin America, 1948* (and for later years; for example, 1955, 1956, 1957)

United Nations, Economic Commission for Latin America, *Economic and Legal Status of Foreign Investments in Selected Countries: Paraguay* (1951)

United Nations, Food and Agriculture Organization, *Agricultural Development of Uruguay* (1951)

University of Texas, Institute of Latin American Studies, *Political, Economic and Social Problems of the Latin American Nations of Southern South America* (1949)

Uruguay Institute of International Law, *Uruguay and the United Nations* (1958)

Vanger, M. J., *José Batlle y Ordoñez: Creator of His Times* (1963)

Warren, H. G., *Paraguay, An Informal History* (1949)

Wood, B., *The United States and Latin American Wars, 1932–1942* (1966)

Wythe, G., *Industry in Latin America* (2nd ed., 1949)

Ynsfran, P. M., ed., *Epic of the Chaco: Marshal Estigarribia's Memoir of the Chaco War, 1932–1935* (1950)

Ysita, E., ed., *National Economy of Uruguay, 1941–1946* (1948)

Zook, D. H., *Conduct of the Chaco War* (1960)

Chapter 36

The Three Andean
Nations Today

GEOGRAPHIC LIMITATIONS
AND ECONOMIC DEVELOPMENTS

> Over the whole continent, the Andes run,
> Braiding their mighty knots in the shining air,
> Lifting a shield of granite in the sun,
> And crowned with silver helmet gleaming fair.[1]

THUS WROTE the Peruvian poet José Chocano (1875–1934) in the early twentieth century, himself a lover of natural beauty, little concerned with the problems "the mighty knots" of the Andes brought to the modern nations who rested upon them. But Ecuador, Peru, and Bolivia, each with a central core of Andes ridges towering over none-too-fertile valleys or plateaus, separating them from vast undeveloped areas to the east, have been slow in economic development because of their difficult geography and their Indian masses still living in crannies in the "shield of granite in the sun." In order to understand political developments in these nations,

[1] From Isaac Goldberg, *Studies in Spanish American Literature* (New York: Brentano's, 1920), p. 283.

we require some explanation of the problems common to all in the economic and social fields.

Ecuador is the "Tale of Two Cities." Over one-third of her people live on the verdant stretch of coastal plains which supports the port of Guayaquil, largest city in Ecuador, and its 515,000 people by producing bananas and cacao for export. Three-fifths of the nation's people live in the *sierra* and its highland valleys, where lie the nation's capital at Quito, with its more than 360,000 people, the white and *mestizo* towns of Ambato, Riobamba, and Cuenca, and the scores of little villages of unchanged Andean Indians. Five per cent of the Ecuadoreans live in the Amazonian *oriente*, many of them uncivilized savages.

Peru is also three separate worlds. Lima the sophisticated capital, fifth largest city in South America, with nearly two million people, is dominated socially by the same oligarchic families as in the eighteenth century, though its modern culture seems Parisian. In the 1960s Lima contained one of the worst shanty towns in Latin America, as its rainless climate made life possible in hovels roofed with matting. Four hundred thousand of Lima's 2,000,000 people lived this way when President Belaúnde-Terry started projects for streets, sewers, and running water in 1964. Peru's coast contains a few irrigated valleys and the oil fields near the port of Talara. Two million Peruvians, 27 per cent of the total population, live in these coastal areas; the rest of the coast is parched desert. Five and a half million Peruvians, 60 per cent, live in the Sierra of the Andes, most of them Indians who take no part in Peru's modern "money economy." Thirteen per cent of the Peruvians live in the Amazon area, the *montaña*, containing 60 per cent of the area, centering on the large river port of Iquitos which ships rubber and mahogany out down the Amazon, and serves a region bigger than Texas. Few people from Lima ever went to Iquitos, which was accessible only by plane, or by a long sequence of truck-road and river-launch trips consuming two weeks' travel. President Belaúnde-Terry's Peruvian road building plan with Alliance for Progress funds was to have Iquitos connected to Lima by road in 1970.

Bolivia also has its three regions: (1) the *altiplano* of the Aymará Indians, the capital cities, and the silver-mining centers, (2) the *yungas* or area of deep narrow valleys which are the garden and granary of Bolivia, centering on Cochabamba, and (3) the *selvas*, the tropical plains of the Department of Santa Cruz, thinning out at its southeastern edge into the Paraguayan Chaco. Transportation from one of these Bolivian regions to another has only recently been improved. In January 1955 a railroad was finally opened to Corumbá, the Brazilian port on the Paraguay River, from which Bolivian products can make rail connections to São Paulo. The rail and highway route east via the Madeira River and the Amazon, provided for in the Treaty of Petropolis with Brazil in 1903 and worked on with great loss of life in the 1914–1915 period, was finally opened in 1955. A railroad from La Paz out of the Andes and down to Buenos Aires was opened in 1925. To reach the cities of Peru from La Paz it has been necessary to cross Lake Titicaca on a little biweekly steamer, which was transported into the Andes in pieces and assembled on the lake in the 1920s. In the 1950s there was finally a macademized road around the lake connecting the two countries as a part of the Pan American Highway system.

In Ecuador and Peru, the railways built by Henry Meiggs and Archie Harmon are the rail lines today. One reaches Cuzco by rail by taking a ship from Callao to Mollendo, then taking Meiggs' rail line to Arequipa and Cuzco. A rail line connects Quito to Guayaquil and a long-delayed line was completed from Quito to the port of Esmeraldas in 1957. The Simón Bolívar Highway comes into Ecuador from Colombia via Popayán but it has only become possible to drive from Guayaquil on into Peru in the last few years. Other bad effects of climate and geography have hurt these two countries; earthquakes brought destruction to the Ecuadorean town of Ambato in 1949 and to Cuzco in 1950. Guayaquil had to fight the yellow fever and the plague, insect-borne diseases which gave the port a reputation as a pest-hole quarantined to American sailors, until an international commission in the 1930s cleaned up the city's sanitation system.

Peru and Bolivia depend largely on the extractive industries for export trade. In 1895 a first shipment of Bolivian tin was sent out on a new railroad to Chile's Antofagasta into a world suddenly interested in preserving food in tin cans. Today Bolivia produces 30 per cent of the world's tin. The old silver mines are worked for tin, and the Glory Hole of Potosí has 742 tunnels for tin extraction. There are ten mining centers, developed by three big companies, Patiño, Hochschild, and Aramayo, which were nationalized by the Bolivian government in 1952.

Simón Patiño, founder of Bolivia's tin economy, was a poor Indian from a remote village who went to work as a clerk in a company store at the Oruro silver mine. When he grubstaked a prospector from store funds, he lost his job and was left with only the worthless claim of the prospector for his trouble. He went out alone with his Indian wife to work it into the most fabulous of the tin mines. By 1930 Patiño owned 70 per cent of the mines of Bolivia, controlled a world tin cartel, and enjoyed a personal income greater than that of the Bolivian government. Never socially accepted by the creole aristocracy of La Paz, he took his fortune abroad and "crashed" society on the French Rivera, while he exploited his fellow Indians in the mines at home. On his death his playboy sons took little interest in the Bolivian nation.

The world price of Bolivian tin has been high, owing to the cost of transporting the ore down out of the mountains to smelters in Europe. During World War II the United States built smelters in Baltimore and Texas to refine the product in the Western Hemisphere. The need for tin kept America concerned about Bolivian production and tranquility in the mines, and forced the United States to cooperate with the Bolivian political leaders who nationalized tin in the 1950s. When nationalization brought severe losses owing to inefficiency of management, American economic missions worked out plans to keep the mines operating, to build smelters in Bolivia itself, and to improve the means of shipment. For two generations the Indian tin miners had been mercilessly exploited by all three companies; eventually a radical union movement entered politics and pushed through the nationalization, as described below.

Peru has the fabulous copper mine at Cerro de Pasco, owned by an American copper company which has invested $30,000,000 there. The Indian miners at Cerro de Pasco have been better treated than the Bolivian miners, and have schools and sanitary housing provided by the American company, though their wages are pitifully low compared to those paid copper miners in Montana or Arizona. Oil production in Peru, fourth in South America, has built new centers of population around the oil-port of Talara. Foreign companies now ship out 12,000,000 barrels annually, under strict control from Belaúnde-Terry's government which threatened them with nationalization of the oil reserves. Fearing that the Talara fields might soon become exhausted, Peru was exploring for oil in the *montaña*, and was developing iron mines and other mineral resources in the late 1960s. Bolivia has developed oil in her nationalized properties, and is now shipping out many thousands of barrels daily above her own consumption. Some oil has recently been found in the Santa Elena Peninsula in Ecuador.

Except in the irrigation projects of northern Peru which produce cotton and sugar by machine methods for export, and the new projects which clear land for settlement in Peru's *montaña*, agriculture in all three nations is little different from what it was in colonial times. Ecuador's cacao groves, which produce abundantly with little attention on the warm moist coastal plain, provide the business of the port of Guayaquil. The cacao pods grow on the tree trunks and on large limbs like canteloupes sprouting from a giant vine stalk. Inside the pods the pulp-covered seeds contain rich brown centers which provide chocolate bars for the world. Guayaquil is one of the world's cacao centers; in its side streets one sees the pods spread out to dry during the shipping season, while town traffic is routed through other thoroughfares. Ecuador's economy has risen and fallen with world chocolate prices, and with the control of leaf disease on the plantations. Bananas are also an important export from Guayaquil. Balsa wood, of use in airplane parts, and *cinchona* bark, the basis of quinine, come into world markets largely from Ecuador. Ecuador has no mineral exports, but silver mining is still important to both Peru and Bolivia, in spite of the emphasis on copper and tin.

TODAY'S "INCA EMPIRE" SOCIALLY AND CULTURALLY

All three of these nations have large Indian populations, with high infant mortality and illiteracy rates and very low per capita income. A million Aymará and a million and a half Quechuas in Bolivia, nearly four million Quechuas in Peru, as well as a half-million "cousins" of the Quechuas in Ecuador provide the "masses" of these nations. Direct descendents of the Incas, still speaking the ancient tongues, they cling to the mountain farms, work in the mines, and let the stream of modernism go around them. To the tourist, who looks at the brilliant hand-woven costumes, watches the llamas on the trails, and sees the women sitting selling gnarled potatoes in the markets at Huancayo or Cochabamba while they

Extension agent from the Antiplano Experiment Station, Bolivia, encouraging Indian farmers to plant lettuce and other green vegetable crops. *Courtesy Inertnational Cooperation Administration.*

spin endless wool thread on a hand distaff, all this seems picturesque, a living archeology. The Indian, with his short, broad physique, his great endurance at high altitudes, his stoic attitude toward misfortune and exploitation, seems impervious to the effects of cold and hunger.

The Indian persists in his farming methods, owning on the average about two acres and ploughing with the hand-operated digging stick of the Incas when not fortunate enough to own oxen, for the temperamental llama has never been harnessed to plough. Sheep are grazed on the bleak hills and kept for wool and meat; burros are seen occasionally as beasts of burden. Save for the wheat, the sheep, and the donkeys, agricultural life has changed not at all. Houses remain typically Inca—stone or adobe walls, tile roofs, crudely fashioned stools and benches, with no way to provide warmth against the winds of the Andes. Village headmen learn only enough Spanish to deal with tax collectors and other government officials from Lima or La Paz. Most villages have no resident priest, and the villagers perform the rituals of the Catholic faith in bare stone churches, with little more depth of understanding than did their forebears in the early colonial days. Indians have a very high sense of morals in their own groups, and only become degraded when their tribal customs are broken down in contact with whites. Playing on the young Indians' dissatisfaction with this treadmill of life, Communists trained in Cuba are organizing some Andean villages to take the land into their own hands.

For centuries the Indians have been made apathetic to reform or self-help by the continuous chewing of coca leaves, the raw material from which the drug cocaine is made; this practice is considered by some sociologists a source of degradation, and by others a necessary protection for the Indian against the rigors of his life. Originally a wild Andean plant, coca plants today are grown from seed in the *yungas* area of Bolivia and have become one of the most profitable crops of the Andes. Undoubtedly great quantities of Bolivian and Peruvian coca leaves are smuggled out through Argentina and Chile into the illegal cocaine markets of the world.

Indians at work in the mines need all the "tranquilizing" they can get. Though the mines are at 12,000 feet, they are near the equator, and the heat in the interior is terrific. Few Indians stay at the mines throughout the entire year, but go and come with the agricultural seasons. At the mines the Indians are actually better fed and housed than in the villages, but their tribal patterns are broken and nothing is substituted. Here, under white bosses, Indians seem debauched and stupid, but in recent years they have been organized into powerful unions in Bolivia. Many Bolivian city and mine laborers are *cholos* or Bolivian *mestizos*, who speak Spanish but maintain Indian costumes and customs.

Ecuadorian Indians fare better than Peruvian or Bolivian, in a pleasant climate on more fertile, better-watered land. Near Ambato and Otovalo, Indian village groups own thousands of rich acres in communal holdings, and bring in their produce to those two colorful market towns for weekly fairs. Farm workers in the central highlands and on the cacao plantations of the coast are more apt to be *mestizos* working for cash wages than Indians tied to the land.

The new interest in Inca archeology has created an aesthetic and literary interest in the Indians of these Andes countries. Dr. Julio Tello, himself of Indian blood, created a department of archeology in the Peruvian government and founded the Inca and Pre-Inca museum in Lima. Such modern writers as Jorge Pando Gutiérrez and Franz Tamayo have popularized sociological writings about the living archeology of Indian villages today. The "reform party" in Peru called APRA, described below, became the champion of Indian education; in 1947 experimental schools were founded among the Quechuas on the plan of the Mexican rural schools to teach the children first the Spanish language and then reading, writing, sanitation, and better agriculture. United Nations pilot projects have taught the Ecuadorian Indians of Otovalo the commercial weaving of tweeds on their native looms, a project which has brought cash money and a higher standard of living into the Ecuadorian valleys. Various cooperative groups in Peru have revived the old handicrafts of silver work, and variegated pattern-weaving for the tourist trade. Peru and Bolivia have improved their elementary school systems, built secondary schools on the American style for city children, and revised the curriculum in their classical old universities, but it is the very rare and unusual Indian who finds his way into these schools. The problem of bringing the Indians, the masses of the poor of the

Andean nations, into the full stream of the political and economic life of these nations remains unsolved.

All three of these Andean countries are controlled by small white elements, European and Spanish, with no middle class save perhaps in Peru. Although all have organized labor confederations, they all need more diversification of their national economies to strengthen and stabilize them and raise standards of living. All have small industries of textiles and food processing. All have extremely wide gaps between "white" city and "Indian" country, but urbanization is increasing, especially in Peru. Even mountain Indians have taken up the life of urban workers as an escape from the *latifundia* and the failure and overpopulation of rural agricultural villages.

Consciousness of the Indians has not permeated the social and cultural life of the Andes nations as has the pride in Aztec tradition in Mexico. However, it has contributed much of what is new and vital to the cultural developments there in the last three decades. The best-known novelists from each country are those who have analyzed the problems of the Indian masses. A prize-winning novel, *The Serpent of Gold,* was written by the leading contemporary novelist of Peru, Ciro Alegría (born in 1909) in 1935. It tells the story of the life of Indian people in the Peruvian Amazon and their exploitation by lumber and rubber companies. Alegría's better-known 1941 Indianist novel was another prize-winner, *Broad and Alien Is the World,* which is the culminating work of the modern *novela indiana.* Alcides Argüedas (1879–1946) of Bolivia wrote a semifictional account of Indian problems in *The Race of Bronze,* published in 1919. A contemporary Ecuadorean, Jorge Icaza (born in 1906) has received national prizes for novels about the problems of Indians and *cholos,* especially his *Huasipungo,* published in 1934. Apart from Jorge Pando Gutiérrez and Franz Tomayo (born in 1899), the Bolivian writers mentioned in the section on modern sociological studies of the Indians, few Bolivian writers are known outside La Paz and Sucre. Only within the last two decades were Bolivian literary works printed inside the country; manuscripts were usually sent to Europe or to Buenos Aires for preparation in book form.

In Peru the movement toward an interest in the Indians was manifested in the formation of a Society of Amateur Artists in the 1940s which produced little-theater plays, wrote radio dramas, and printed poetry on the Peruvian Indian problem. This group also held exhibitions of native crafts and has promoted an interest in the paintings of Indians. In Ecuador, Oswaldo Guayasamín (born in 1918), a young *mestizo* of Quito, has exhibited over a hundred paintings on Indian themes and the sufferings of the village and city poor. Similarly, Antonio Sotomayor (born in 1904) of Bolivia, whose work has been shown in the United States and who has studied both there and in Europe, has made Bolivian Indian life a subject for sympathetic and popular canvasses. Though the United States was made conscious of Inca themes by the Peruvian singer Yma Sumac, in music at home the three Andean countries have followed the same European classical forms they did in the nineteenth century.

Political writings, essays, histories, editorials have done most to produce "Indianism" in Peru, where the interest in Indians has been a part of a general reform movement. The most famous Peruvian writer at the opening of the twentieth century was the essayist and reformer Manuel González Prada (1848–1918), mentioned before as a fiery nineteenth-century writer. He became milder in middle age and was a member of congress, but he remained critical of the veneer of culture in upper-class Lima, the concern with empty poetry and beauty of form in writing. If there was any intellectual ferment in the 1930s and 1940s, it was due in great part to his influence on younger writers. José Carlos Mariátegui (1891–1930) picked up the torch from Prada and carried it far beyond any liberal ideas into a radical Marxism. A young *mestizo* from the slums of Lima, he went to work at twelve, but by chance in a printing shop. Here he handled manuscripts of liberal writers in Prada's group and began to write himself at sixteen. His writings came to the attention of a newspaper and he was sent abroad as a young correspondent, visiting post-World War I Europe. His first book, *The Contemporary Scene*, published in 1925, was a bitter criticism of American imperialism in Latin America. At home in Lima he edited a journal of radical thought called *Amanta*. His editorials from it were published in 1928 under the title *Seven Essays Interpreting the Realities of Peruvian Life*, essays calling for a worldwide state of the workers, in which the South American Indians would become a section of the new proletariat. Luis Alberto Sánchez (born in 1900), literary historian and leftist politician, bridges the gap between literature and current history in his writings. The Peruvian political reformer Haya de la Torre (born in 1895), who founded the reform party APRA which so stirred Peruvian politics, was a close friend of Mariátegui in his youth, though he broke with Mariátegui on the issue of Communism as a cure-all. Haya himself was a prolific writer; both his works and Mariátegui's more radical *Seven Essays* were very widely read throughout South America and Mexico.

Unlike the prose writers, poets did not write about Indians, for they saw little that was poetic in such limited lives. The best-known poet of the Andes nations was also a Peruvian, José Santos Chocano (1875–1934), whose verse introduces this chapter. A contemporary and a rival of the great Rubén Darío, Chocano lived twenty years longer and had many more published works. He is more concerned than Darío with the beauties of Latin America, and with the idealistic hopes for the future of the Latin American people, including the Indians. José María Egurén (1882–1942), Peruvian poet and artist of worldwide recognition, made no further contribution to "Indianism" but only to musical, lyrical verse.

In these nations with their poorly managed budgets and their domination by a few extractive industries there is litle money to spend on schools. The University of San Andrés in La Paz has a fine fourteen-story building, but few full-time paid professors. San Marcos University in Lima, oldest in South America, continues to give a limited classical education to a chosen few, though its students have often taken part in radical demonstrations. In Ecuador there are four classical-type universities, and elementary and secondary schools are still dominated by the Church. Under UNESCO guidance there has been a campaign against illiteracy and an "each one teach one" program on the Mexican pattern, but progress has been slow. Guayaquil, more cosmopolitan and modern than Quito, has a group of young intellectuals who call themselves the "School of Guayaquil" and encourage the publication of books within Ecuador.

All three countries faced twentieth-century social upheavals in the course of their political progress, which we shall next consider.

PERUVIAN POLITICS: RISE AND FALL
OF THE APRA MOVEMENT

Peru had been badly defeated in the War of the Pacific, but presidents from 1895 to 1908, though very conservative, had brought some stability and civilian control. The most outstanding personality in the early twentieth century was Augusto B. Leguía, a vigorous leader, and at the same time a small, tactful, unassuming little gentleman. Leguía served two terms with an eight-year period in between, was elected in an open election in 1919, and then maintained an army-and-conservative-backed dictatorship till 1930. Though a successful Lima businessman and a smart financier, Leguía actually represented the same oligarchic elements of army, church, and landlords that had always ruled Peru—coast, mountain, and jungle—from Lima. During the interim between his terms Peru passed through the crisis of World War I by severing relations with Germany after the United States entered the war. The trade the war brought helped create a prosperous new merchant class.

In the postwar period of the 1920s Leguía, always the financier, borrowed nearly a hundred million dollars from English and American banking houses, some to be used on internal improvements—highways and irrigation projects and railroads—but some to be used for himself and his friends, and all of it to be defaulted on during the depression. For the Indians and city workers Leguía did nothing. On paper he appeared to be an enlightened and progressive ruler, but "his practices belied his protestations." Though he did lay the foundations for the modern Peru, only the settlement of the long-festering Tacna-Arica dispute seemed a permanent gain during this period.

In protest against Leguía's undemocratic methods a student strike in the University of San Marcos was led by a young "hot-head" named Victor Raúl Haya de la Torre. As a result, martial law was clamped down on Lima for three days, and Haya de la Torre was exiled. But he had come to public attention, and for more than twenty-five years he was to be a world figure in the fight for political and social equality against dictatorship.

While in the university, Haya de la Torre had been influenced by philosophical socialistic writers, especially José Mariátegui, who afterward turned all the way toward Communism. Haya in exile moderated his own views; travel in Russia disillusioned him; a year in Mexico fired him with enthusiasm for the "Indianism" revolution. He made converts among young liberals in Argentina and Chile, and called his movement the *Alianza Popular Revolucionaria Americana*, or APRA. His ideas came to be called *Aprismo*—land reform for the Indians, social legislation for city workers, public improvements in irrigation, electrification, and transportation that actually served the people, industrialization as a prerequisite to improved living standards, nationalistic socialized development of natural resources as opposed to development by foreign capital. Through all its later difficulties APRA served as the vehicle for the spread of democratic ideas within Peru's feudal structure.

Leguía was overthrown in 1931 by the army, which revolted and placed Colonel Luis M. Sánchez Cerro in power. Opposition to Leguía by all elements in Peru had already brought Haya de la Torre back from exile in 1930 as head of an accepted APRA party. Allowed to campaign and speak openly, he was the most popular presidential candidate in 1931, and probably won the election, but the vote was counted by the government and the *caudillo* Sánchez Cerro was declared president. APRA did win many seats in congress and Haya de la Torre remained a powerful party leader. To deflect domestic unrest Sánchez Cerro seized Leticia, thereby causing trouble with Colombia. Then in April 1933 the president was assassinated and the APRA was blamed. Haya de la Torre and twenty-seven of his party members in congress were forced into exile and his party outlawed. Congress chose Marshall Oscar Benavides as president, and he soothed the people by actually passing some of APRA's reforms into law— workers' housing and clinics, mild social security plans on the Chilean pattern—and settling the Leticia question. However, he ruled as a dictator in the manner of Leguía, while no *Aprista* could run for office.

In 1939 Benavides allowed a one-sided election in which Manuel Prado Ugarteche came to power. Though wealthy, he was conciliatory and national-minded. In 1942 he severed relations with the Axis, and in 1945 declared war, meanwhile bringing a wartime boom to encourage Peru's industrialization. With the pro-American policies of most worldwide liberal movements in World War II against Nazism, APRA reversed its "anti-Yankee capitalism" stand and became a party for immediate domestic reforms—the secret ballot, universal suffrage, control of absentee-landlordism, separation of Church and state, education for the Indians. Haya de la Torre was again returned from exile by mild President Prado and became a champion for the Allied cause. A coalition of factions brought a liberal, Dr. José Luis Bustamante y Rivero, into the presidency in a regularly held election in 1945, and gave three cabinet posts to APRA men, while Haya de la Torre remained the "power behind the throne." The Democratic Front coalition had also gained control of congress; but cleavages soon appeared. The reforms began: rural schools, housing projects, surveys for new government-financed irrigation and power projects. But it was to be slow. "A short, careful step is better than a brilliant audacious hop," said Bustamante. "The reactionaries irrigated the country with blood; we will irrigate it with water," answered Haya de la Torre.

Because of the shedding of one man's blood, Haya's whose program came to discredit. In January 1947 a powerful conservative newspaper editor was murdered. Other newspapers blamed an APRA man; in the ensuing scandal, the coalition cabinet fell and Conservatives in congress blocked the government; Bustamante ruled without congress and tried to join with the military and the old established Peruvian oligarchy. One of the new cabinet members was the fanatical rightist, General Odría, who insisted that APRA be outlawed again. Bustamante stalled, but slowed down on APRA's program; "I believe in social reform and in improving living standards, but APRA wanted to do in a day what should be done in a year." APRA was not only slowed down but knocked out when a naval revolt at Callao in October 1948 was also blamed on Haya's followers. A far better-organized revolt of the army at Arequipa a few weeks later resulted in the fall of Bustamante. The army's leader, General Odría, became president in the ensuing upset, and he soon established himself as an oppressive military dictator. Haya de la Torre escaped arrest by taking refuge in the Colombian embassy, where he stayed as a "house guest" for four years, while the legality of such "right of asylum" was bandied about by international lawyers. He was eventually allowed to take a plane to Panama in 1954 and went on to spend three years in Europe supporting himself by teaching and writing. When Haya was allowed to return to Peru in 1957 under a later liberal regime, much of his program had already slowly evolved into acceptance, and he seemed merely a "leader emeritus."

Odría, serving from 1948 to 1956, determined to exterminate all APRA organizations but did not dare to abolish the APRA-inspired new schools, public clinics, and social security of the Bustamante coalition. The Peruvian economy was bolstered by the demand for copper, cotton, and oil during the Korean War. Odría's government put no restrictions on the new foreign companies, and they have taken out profits at will without the royalties demanded by the Venezuelan government from the oil companies. However, the American Export-Import Bank has helped finance new copper mines and new smelting works; exports have doubled in cotton and wool, and with such revived export trade the government's income has tripled. Some of this new income was spent on schools, hospitals, and roads in the interior and on expansion of social security. Odría meant to be a "benevolent dictator," responsible for the industrialization of Peru, including even steel production. He allowed the open election of his successor in June 1956. The moderate former president, Manuel Prado, won in a close but fair enough election in which women voted for the first time.

President Prado served out his six-year term to 1962. He legalized the APRA party and included many of APRA's ideas in the mild reforms which he accomplished with the cooperation of the APRA men elected to congress. In the 1962 campaign in a close three-way election, the tired old leftist leader Haya de la Torre won a plurality after all those years of frustration. But the Peruvian army was never going to let Haya be president of Peru. The generals "sent tanks crashing through the gates of the presidential palace," nullified the election, and while ruling with a four-man *junta*, called another presidential election.

This time the election was won by a more active reformer than the old Haya de la Torre. A Lima architect who had become interested in the city's growing shanty slums through his work on public housing designs, Fernando Belaúnde-Terry had run for the presidency in 1962 and emerged a high runner-up in the three-way race. Now he concentrated on forming a new political party called *Acción Popular*, or "Self-Help." Though he belonged to the old aristocracy and was the great grandson of a former president, he had studied architecture at the University of Texas. He was determined to arouse the Lima slum dwellers and the Andean Indians to a self-help program, for which the government would provide the technical assistance and the tools. He toured every one of the 140 provinces of Peru by car, truck, mule, or launch, campaigning for "Reconquest of the difficult geography of Peru by the Peruvians themselves." A new Christian Democratic party, similar to that of Frei in Chile, joined in a coalition to get Belaúnde-Terry elected by a narrow vote in a new election called in 1963. Feeling sure of a six-year term Belaúnde-Terry forged ahead in 1966, accomplishing more than most leaders of the larger Latin American countries. He pushed a projected network of roads up over the Andes to meet a common trunk road to parallel the Amazon through Brazil and out to the Atlantic. His land reform program paid large owners for inefficiently farmed lands with a small down payment and a twenty-year bond program. Since this released comparatively little land, he planned to open new lands in the 62 per cent of Peru's cultivable surface which is in the eastern *montaña* and to resettle sharecroppers there. Students and army officers were sent out on "work years" to teach in Indian schools and show villagers how to construct their own roads. Navy gunboats were fitted out with crews of doctors, nurses, and technicians and sent to ply the Amazon, constructing clinics and schools. Figures on the numbers of new pupils, new rural schools, and new mountain roads seemed fantastic by 1966. American Alliance for Progress advisers who were helping Belaúnde-Terry carry all this out expressed pleasure at his success. Though 1,700 known Communists were trained in Cuba in 1964 and 1965 and sent into Peru's backland to carry on guerilla tactics and urge Indians to take over farm land as squatters, Belaúnde-Terry claimed to have this problem solved by his resettlement schemes. Peru's Communist party leader, Gernaro Checa, one of the most prolific Communist writers in South America, had often been in and out of Lima's prisons, but Belaúnde-Terry insisted that his own program would solve Peru's social problems faster. He was trying to promote social and agrarian reform within the framework of democracy. The weakened APRA joined with the far right to try to clip his wings in the congressional elections of November 1966, and he almost lost his working majority. But his popular follower, Luis Bedoya Reyes, won a sweeping majority as mayor of Lima, and thus had hopes that he might continue Belaúnde-Terry's program in the presidency in 1969.

Meanwhile the gross national product grew from a yearly increase of 3.5 per cent in 1963 to 8 per cent in 1965, as new mineral deposits of iron, zinc, and antimony were developed, new irrigation projects on the west coast brought cotton and sugar land under production, and the *montaña* opened up to lumbering and farming, with hope for direct roads out for these products both west and east. Peru in 1966 seemed to be returning to the prosperity of the Inca empire.

BOLIVIAN POLITICS AND TIN NATIONALIZATION

In 1899 Bolivia's only internal dispute was between the cities of La Paz and Sucre as to which should be the capital; a half-century later the country was torn over the issues of nationalizing the rich mineral resources of the Andes and the part the awakened Indian miners should play in the government. The capital dispute was settled by holding the supreme court in Sucre and keeping congress in the more accessible La Paz. The La Paz faction, a middle-class business group which won the dispute, held the presidency afterward until 1920. They avoided bloody revolts by rotating the administration among the conservative business and tin company "Liberals," chief among whom were José Manuel Pando (1899–1904), Ismael Montes (1904–1909; 1913–1917), and Eliodoro Villazón (1909–1913). Middle-class economic reforms were instituted until halted by World War I. This was also the period of the tin boom during World War I, the development of the three giant tin companies, and the increasing company domination of the Bolivian government.

The Liberals were overthrown in 1920 by the so-called "Republicans," who ruled for more than a decade. Presidents Bautista Saavedra and Hernando Siles floated large loans from private American investors to the tune of $60,000,000, and spent it on personal graft and enormous military expense. The tin bonanza slackened off with decreasing world trade in the period following World War I. While her ignorant peasants and miners toiled on, and the world depression hit Bolivia hard, tension increased at home and coalition governments rose and fell. Then the expensive army was almost annihilated in the senseless War of the Gran Chaco against Paraguay.

When the long and confusing peace meetings to settle the Chaco War had been concluded in 1937, Bolivia had only acquired a strip along the Upper Paraguay River which was of little worth to her as a shipping point for years to come. During the unpopular war, which had disrupted the Bolivian economy even more than the depression had done, revolutions had taken place at home—new alignments of discontented returning veterans and students were created, while laborers formed a new confederation. One strong man had emerged, a half-Indian, half-German hero of the Chaco War named Germán Busch, who had been born on the edge of the eastern jungle. Though himself a liberal, he inherited a defeated country with an empty treasury. Meaning to improve conditions for the miners, he was forced to stop strikes by military action when they got out of hand. Meaning to take over the Big Three tin mines, he could only weakly try to limit their power and profit. His Constitution of 1938 set a precedent for improved education, rights of labor, rural cooperatives, and national ownership of minerals, but its measures were side-tracked for a decade. Unable to enforce any program, Busch became neurotic and died by gunshot, probably a suicide, in August 1939.

His death brought no peace to Bolivia, for campaigns against the tin companies were now well started. A radical party called the PIR, or Leftist Revolutionaries, wished to confiscate all tin interests for the workers, while an ardently nationalistic and socialistic Movement of National Revolution, or MNR, with its leaders Gualberto Villarroel and Victor Paz Estenssoro, wanted all foreigners thrown out of the tin industry. In the 1940 election the conservative *cholo*, Enrique Peñaranda, supported by labor, middle-class and conservative landowners, and the army, was elected president with the army probably counting the ballots. The administration of

Peñaranda was pro-American, and brought Bolivia and its tin into World War II on the Allied side in 1943, keeping the flow of tin going to American smelters. Peñaranda also settled a long-standing dispute with the Standard Oil Company of New Jersey which had been forced out of its explorations and prospecting schemes for oil in the Chaco by an antiforeign regime under David Toro at the time of the Chaco War. Peñaranda did nothing to alleviate the wretched condition of the tin miners and broke strikes with a heavy hand. One such "strike-breaking" produced a number of deaths, the infamous "Cataví Massacre" of 1942. Taking advantage of the situation, the nationalist MNR leaders, who had been exiled in Argentina, came home, overthrew the Peñaranda administration in December 1943, and made Villarroel president.

Tin was still ruler in Bolivia; when prices fell in the post-World War II slump the dictatorial new president, Villarroel, was powerless to stop the street riots. University students, workers, and businessmen violently revolted against hard times and Villarroel. In July 1946 he himself was ambushed in the government buildings, dragged out into the street, and hanged to a lamppost. The other MNR leaders went into exile again, changed from the pro-Perón, pro-Nazi emphasis, grouped around the more democratic Paz Estenssoro, and concentrated their antipathy on the tin interests. The more radical PIR had meanwhile founded articulate unions for the first time among the miners under Juan Lechín, an ex-soccer player of Syrian ancestry, whose sympathies were on the Communistic side. In the tension between the business and tin-interest party, on the one hand, and the exiled MNR and the vociferous PIR on the other, ineffective compromise presidents kept Lechín in jail and tried to handle the many riots and strikes. They held the balance of power up to 1951, while tin again rose and fell and with it inflationary food prices owing to the Korean War.

A legal election was held in May of 1951, in which all literate males could vote, though the literacy requirement limited the possible voters to 200,000. The MNR was allowed to campaign openly; Paz Estenssoro, six years an exile in Argentina, undoubtedly received a large share of the votes. When he was not proclaimed president, students, liberal intellectuals, and labor leaders combined in a well-organized but bloody revolt of April 9, 1952, to put him into the presidency. This was not a *cuartelazo*, a barracks and palace revolution, but a mass protest against dictatorship and for an elected candidate, a new thing in the Andes.

Victor Paz Estenssoro was a quiet, intelligent economics professor who talked like an American businessman. He felt that there was little chance at reform until the tin mines were owned by the government, but he wanted financial support from the United States and recognition from Washington. This latter he gained on the promise that he would refuse to take orders from Moscow. Inviting Juan Lechín, now released from jail, into his cabinet as Minister of Mines, Paz Estenssoro went ahead with his long-range plan to really improve Bolivia.

The major ingredients in this peaceful change were six: land reform, economic independence, nationalization of the tin industry, social improvements through education, enlarged suffrage, and increased security benefits.

The Bolivian land-reform scheme of 1953 was being watched by all of South America, for 70 per cent of the arable land had been owned by great landed proprietors, half of them absentee landowners. Enough land was expropriated to create more than two million new small landholders. The land was paid for in national bonds, while the new owners were given twenty-five years to pay off the debt. Each plot of land, depending on the use, water available, and crop grown, was judged to be sufficient to support a family. Land was offered to cooperatives as well, and attempts were made to colonize Indians in the hot lowlands. Every effort was being made to fill the chief need, an increase in the food supply.

As for the tin nationalization, Paz Estenssoro's followers were convinced that the tin companies were bigger than the state, and that the second generation of tin barons had no concern for Bolivia at all. He proceeded to assess the mines at a figure smaller than the back income taxes the companies owed the government, then passed a decree of nationalization with great ceremony in October 1952. Again all Latin America watched Paz Estenssoro. The United States was more concerned with the supply of tin than with the fortunes of the large international companies, and continued to send Point Four help for other public improvements, and to encourage private American capital in various minor industries. Paz Estenssoro, an economist, pegged the price of tin at what seemed to him the most feasible economic figure, carried out for the miners as many reforms as he speedily could manage, and let a peaceful election in 1956 replace him with another reform president, Hernán Siles Zuazo. The latter, young and popular, was inaugurated August 5, 1956.

The program for economic self-sufficiency in Bolivia depends on the development of other products besides tin. To achieve such self-sufficiency recent governments have built up the Cochabamba valleys and the eastward transportation facilities via the Amazon and the Paraguay and the Plata; they have also explored for new oil and developed the known oil reserves. Meanwhile, the suffrage has been enlarged to include every adult, no matter what the sex or state of illiteracy. More than half of the budget for routine government expenses above the cost of tin and land programs went for new primary schools and campaigns against illiteracy. To aid in balancing Siles Zuazo's budget the United States sent an economist, George Jackson Eder, to head the National Monetary Stabilization Council of Bolivia. To augment his efforts to control inflation, keep tin moving, and still diversify the country, the United States granted aid to the extent of one-third of Bolivia's annual budget. Bolivia also received technical cooperation from the United States for health, education, agriculture, and road building. The popular Siles Zuazo, determined to make this program work and bring Bolivia out of economic feudalism, has made many personal sacrifices, visiting remote villages, going down into the mines, and even undertaking hunger strikes to win his points. When world tin prices were depressed due to the dumping of Soviet tin, unemployment hit the inefficiently run Bolivian mines, and Siles Zuazo resettled thousands of miners on the new agricultural lands or sent them as *braceros* to work in Argentina. Though United States aid had provided almost as much money in recent years as had the tin mines, half the Bolivians did not know it, and the United

States was not popular. Leftist riots against United States journalists almost lost Siles Zuazo his North American support in the spring of 1959.

Meanwhile the miners who remained expected high wages, short hours, and jobs for all, and could not understand the necessity of introducing new machinery and efficient methods into the tin industry. Juan Lechín, radical leader of the miners' unions, joined with past president Paz Estenssoro in a triumvirate with Siles Zuazo, forming a coalition to run the country and the MNR, or National Revolutionary Party. The tin industry was organized as a government corporation called COMIBOL, which in 1959 froze any increase in wages or additional employment and made efforts to push scientific management and satisfy American economic advisers.

Siles Zuazo, under the Bolivian constitution, could not succeed himself, but the coalition stayed together and Paz Estenssoro came back to the presidency legally in 1960, having skipped a term in between. For two years Bolivia seemed to be making rapid progress. The tin mines began to show a small profit. But the miners became restive when they saw machinery introduced to replace men on the job. Miners' unions became private armies, using dynamite to destroy the mine tunnels and hold the police and regular army at bay, capturing newspaper men and detectives as hostages. Farmers sent to farm the new lands in Cochabamba destroyed the tractors clearing the land, deserted the new towns, and walked back by the thousands to the highlands.

In this hornet's nest Paz Estenssoro saw no solution save to have congress amend the constitution and allow him to run for a consecutive term. The coalition behind him broke up violently at this announcement. Juan Lechín regrouped the PIR party, ran for the presidency himself, and urged the miners to more violence. A conservative army party nominated a young general, René Barrientos Ortuño. Each party printed ballots of a separate color so the illiterate voters could make their choice. Paz Estenssoro won a plurality by agreeing to take Barrientos as his vice-president. Disillusioned and ill, Lechín went into exile in Paraguay.

The miners did not take this defeat of the PIR sitting down. Their violence increased, as Cuban-trained communists infiltrated into the union leadership. Paz Estenssoro, supposedly the working man's friend, declared martial law. In November 1964 Vice-President General Barrientos set the army on Paz Estenssoro and took over the government himself. The "state of siege" against the miners and the martial law over the whole country continued under General Barrientos into 1966. Violence continued also at the mines and in the city streets. Such martial law of course did not solve Bolivia's problems. After a period of twenty months under a revolutionary *junta*, with the very able General Alfredo Ovando Candia serving as president during the last few months of the provisional regime, General Barrientos was elected to the presidency on July 3 and was inaugurated as Bolivia's 47th president on August 6, 1967 to serve for a four-year term.

Hopes for the success of Bolivia's genuine social and economic "Revolution of the 1960s" seemed to rest with the left of center movement. The "Revolution" had been trying since 1955 to bring the Bolivian Indian, either in the mines or on the land, into full citizenship in the government, to operate the tin mines effectively as a national resource with help from foreign investors such as the Alliance for Progress and the Inter-American Bank, to diversify the country's economy by developing the eastern interior, and to break the power of the old elite by building up peasants' and miners' unions. The totalitarian rule of Barrientos seemed a backward step, while all Latin America watched Bolivia struggle to achieve economic and social transformation without following Castro's Cuba.

THE POLITICAL COURSE OF EVENTS IN ECUADOR

Ecuador had been an intensely religious, conservative little country until 1895. Then "liberalism" emerged as the governing clique, with the accession of Eloy Alfaro, head of an anti-Church group. He and his bitter rival within the party, Leonidas Plaza Gutiérrez, rotated the presidency until 1916. Though dictators, they created a civilian, secular government and separated Church from state. The Quito-Guayaquil railroad was completed, the tax system stabilized, and attempts were made at establishing sanitary systems and public secular education.

Succeeding presidents stayed in power by a combination of the Quito landed aristocracy and a growing class of financiers and shippers in Guayaquil dependent on the cacao trade. Post-World War I and depression years in the one-crop country caused hardship to workers at the port and to the landless peasants. They formed a left-wing party which actually held the presidency for a few months in 1926. With the deepening depression, however, military *juntas*, often backed by Quito bankers, ruled Ecuador in the stormy thirties. Since 1925 Ecuador has had thirty-one different presidents.

During this period changes also took place in political alignments and issues—the appearance of a laboring class, the growing importance of a small but slowly increasing middle class. The depression brought tremendous hardships which, added to loss of territory, were some of the causes for political instability. But despite all, attempts were made to tackle the economic problems. Some social labor legislation was enacted; production of food was increased, trade expanded, and women's suffrage granted.

In 1940 an alliance of liberals held a "legal" election, which an Ecuadorean historian calls "normally fraudulent," and Carlos Arroyo del Río, a wealthy corporation lawyer from Guayaquil, became president. The boundary dispute described below, which led to war with Peru, and the subsequent loss of Ecuadorean territory in the *Oriente* soured his term. So also did the inflation brought on by the World War II boom in balsa, cacao, and rubber from the *Oriente*, even though Arroyo del Río declared war on the Axis and granted bases to the United States. In retaliation against the dissatisfied workers' group Arroyo del Río gagged the press and exiled the opposition leaders, in the hope of assuring his election in 1944. But the opposition combined behind Velasco Ibarra, one of the exiles, and when the president refused to allow his opponent to return from Colombia to campaign, he suddenly found himself in exile, August 1944, and his opponent in the presidency. By 1946, however, the changeable Velasco Ibarra, a mere opportunist, had deserted the liberals, thrown the Arroyo del Río men in jail, canceled local elections, and announced a switch to the right, in spite of his campaign promises of "peace, work, and freedom." In such an explosive situation, the typical *cuartelazo* revolt so common in Ecuador was inevitable. When Velasco Ibarra himself took flight again in 1947, four different presidents followed in quick succession.

A coalition of labor, intellectuals, and liberal businessmen called the National Civic Democratic Movement found a leader in Galo Plaza Lasso, a six-foot son of a former president who had put himself through the university in the United States by working in a factory when his land-rich father disapproved of his modern ideas. Imbued with scientific American methods, particularly the use of agricultural machinery, he returned to Quito to make his ancestral acres the finest modern farm in Ecuador. Now in 1948, after defeating the Conservative candidate by a very narrow margin, and with a coalition of liberals behind him, he had his chance to make all Ecuador a "modern farm." Encouraging foreign capital, founding development associations for the tropical areas, opening highways, starting self-supporting Indian handicraft industries, Galo Plaza was a busy and good-humored president. He showed by example that Ecuador could be governed freely and democratically through constitutional institutions. His enemies were free to print what they pleased and organize as they wished. Ecuador was to be a United States-style democracy, proclaimed Galo Plaza, while he went on good-will tours as the guest of Alemán in Mexico and Truman in Washington. At home, production for export doubled and the standard of living began to rise.

In the election of June 1952, with all campaigning open and free, Galo Plaza's personal enemy, the mayor of Guayaquil, supported the supposedly discredited Velasco Ibarra. Velasco Ibarra controlled the powerful Guayaquil newspapers, and openly said, "Give me a balcony in each town, and I shall again take possession of Ecuador." Since Galo Plaza refused to back any candidate as his successor, it is not surprising that Velasco Ibarra, that smooth turncoat, was president of Ecuador for a third time, filling out his full term, 1952–1956, for the first time. He was elected in a fair but three-cornered election, winning about 42 per cent of the 351,000 votes cast. Galo Plaza went back to his own farm, and later served as a UN inspector in a Near Eastern border trouble, while many of his "development schemes" lay neglected in Ecuador. Actually, however, he had started his little country toward stability.

In 1957 the Conservative Party candidate, Camilo Ponce Enríquez, was elected by a small plurality after Velasco had successfully completed his full legal term. President Ponce improved Ecuador to some extent by scientific agriculture, mining and small industries, and highways, backed by loans from the United States. Then 1960 brought the quarreling leaders back to campaign again. Galo Plaza ran against Velasco Ybarra, but Velasco was the more spellbinding orator. His narrow margin of victory brought tension;

the rightists were concerned at Velasco's friendliness toward Castro's Cuba; the landlord class refused to pay taxes he laid on the wealthy. When his vice-president Carlos Arosemeña opposed him, Arosemeña was thrown in jail. The air force and the navy, with no military problems to solve for Ecuador, interfered, threw Velasco out of the presidency, and put in Arosemeña in November 1961.

Soon the military became dissatisfied with Arosemeña, a playboy who embarassed his backers by being drunk at official receptions. On July 11, 1963, the combined armed forces replaced Arosemeña with a military rule by a *junta* headed by Admiral Ramon Jijón. The admiral remained in power into 1966. His government pushed the reform schemes of Galo Plaza, actually collecting a graduated income tax, and using the funds to pay professionally trained government workers hired by Ecuador's first civil service, and to bring some degree of work limits and elementary schooling to the highland Indians.

With the hope of returning to democratically elected government in the latter part of 1966, Ecuador seemed to be achieving some modernization as it moved toward the 1970s. But on March 29, 1966, student riots against government intrusion in the university resulted in the resignation of the *junta*. A sixty-six-year-old economist, Clemente Yerovi Indaburu, a "progressive moderate," was named provisional president. The military rule of the *junta* had not been very harsh. Hundreds of decrees were issued, including workable projects for agrarian reform. An institute had been set up to administer funds for recolonization of landless peasants on unused land. This program involved confiscation of large tracts, although well cultivated and productive land has not been touched. In the first year of operation, this land reform movement made a good start toward correcting some of the evils of the Ecuadorian agricultural problem. On October 16 seventy-nine delegates to a constituent assembly were elected to draft a new constitution. On November 3 they elected Otto Arosemena Gómez to serve as president until constitutional order had been resumed.

BORDER DISPUTES AS A COMMON PROBLEM

Limited in cultural progress, slow in solving social problems, racked by political troubles, the Andean nations made their own existence more complicated by continuing border disputes which left unsettled feuds both among themselves and with their neighbors to the north and south. The War of the Gran Chaco of 1932–1937, described in the chapter on modern Paraguay, left deep scars on Bolivia. The War of the Pacific of the 1880s left its unsettled problem of Tacna-Arica.

These provinces of the nitrate-bearing desert had been occupied by Chile at the close of the war in 1883, until a plebiscite could be held to decide which nation, Chile or Peru, was to have permanent sovereignty. In 1898 diplomats of both sides agreed to let the Queen of Spain organize the plebiscite, but this plan was defeated in the Chilean congress. After a decade of delay, Peru broke off diplomatic relations with Chile in 1910. Eventually an agreement was reached between Peru and Chile in Washington, D.C., in 1922 to accept North American mediation. Since the provinces were now inhabited by a majority of Chileans, the North American commissioners decided that only those born in Tacna or Arica could register for the voting. When the process of registration was completed in March 1926, it was found that only Chileans had registered, since the Peruvian sympathizers boycotted the whole attempt at arranging for a plebiscite and charged Chile with intimidation. Therefore, no election was held, and the discouraged commission could only urge the two countries to resume diplomatic relations so they could negotiate directly. This they finally did in 1929, accepting President Hoover's plan which divided the area almost equally, giving Tacna to Peru and Arica to Chile. Since the latter had the port and railway developments, Chile paid Peru $6,000,000 and opened the port of Arica to Peruvian commerce. Thus the "Question of the Pacific" was decided forty-six years after the close of the war that had raised it.

Peru continued to quarrel with other neighbors over boundaries. As is told in the chapter on modern Colombia, 300 Peruvian soldiers from Iquitos attacked the Colombian settlement of Leticia on a branch of the Amazon in 1932. The League of Nations settled the dispute in 1934, with the return of Leticia to Colombian sovereignty. The next decade, the 1940s, saw Peru at variance with Ecuador, again over undeveloped and unsurveyed areas in *Oriente*. In 1904 Ecuador had been forced to cede a large chunk of the map to Brazil; the same year commenced a long quarrel with Peru over the remaining country to the east of Quito, where Ecuador claimed a triangle between the Marañon and the Napo. Franklin Roosevelt was attempting mediation when actual warfare broke out in 1942, the war that brought the downfall of President Arroyo del Río. The following year Argentina, Brazil, and Chile joined the United States in urging both nations to agree to a settlement made by neutral boundary commissioners in a meeting at Rio. The line accepted in 1942 cut Ecuador's *montaña* back to the Andes foothills, but gave her free access to river navigation eastward. The boundary there is not yet settled, owing to disagreements on what was meant by certain articles in the Rio protocol, and border warfare has flared up several times since. From 1954 to May of 1956 Peru and Ecuador went so far as to sever diplomatic relations.

Earlier in the century Bolivia suffered losses equal to Ecuador's. In addition to the lands lost in the War of the Pacific, she lost further areas in the Amazon to Brazil, on the upper Paraguay to Argentina, and on the northern border to Peru, all between 1903 and 1909. In the mid-1960s Bolivia had border difficulties, leading to a rupture of diplomatic relations with Chile.

Readings

Ache, J. V., *Art in Latin America: Peru* (1961)
Adams, R. N., *et al., Social Change in Latin America Today* (1960)
Alexander, R. J., *The Bolivian National Revolution* (1959)

————, *Organized Labor in Latin America* (1965)

Arnade, C. W., *Emergence of the Republic of Bolivia* (1957)

Beals, C., *Fire on the Andes* (1934)

Belaúnde-Terry, F., *Peru's Own Conquest* (1965)

Bernstein, H., *Modern and Contemporary Latin America* (1952)

Blanksten, G. I., *Ecuador, Constitutions and Caudillos* (1951)

Bushnell, G. H. S., *Peru* (1964)

Cardenas, M., and G. C. Cutler, *Chicha, A Native South American Beer* (1941)

Carey, J. C., *Peru and the United States, 1900–1962* (1964)

Carter, W. E., *Aymará Communities and the Bolivian Agrarian Reform* (1965)

Coester, A., *Literary History of Spanish America* (rev. ed., 1928)

Crawford, R. W., *Century of Latin American Thought* (rev. ed., 1961)

Dion, H. G., *Agriculture in the Altiplano of Bolivia* (1950)

Duguid, J., *Green Hell* (1931)

E.C.L.A., *Economic Development of Bolivia* (1958)

Ferguson, J. H., *The Revolutions of Latin America* (1963)

Ford, T. R., *Man and Land in Peru* (1955)

Form, W. H., and A. A. Blum, eds., *Industrial Relations and Social Change in Latin America* (1965)

Franklin, A. B., *Ecuador: Portrait of a People* (1943)

Goodrich, C., *Economic Transformation of Bolivia* (1955)

Gordon, W. C., *Economy of Latin America* (1950)

————, *Political Economy of Latin America* (1965)

Hammel, E. A., *Wealth, Authority and Prestige in the Inca Valley, Peru* (1962)

Hanson, S. G., ed., *Economic Development of Latin America* (1951)

Heath, D. B., *Contemporary Cultures and Societies in Latin America* (1965)

————, *Land Reform and Social Revolution in Bolivia* (1966)

Henríquez-Ureña, P., *Literary Currents in Hispanic America* (1945)

Hudson, M. O., *The Verdict of the League: Colombia and Peru at Leticia* (1933)

Hughlett, L. J., *Industrialization of Latin America* (1946)

Ireland, G., *Boundaries, Possessions and Conflicts in South America* (1938)

James, P., *Latin America* (rev. ed., 1950)

Kandell, T. L., ed., *Education in the Latin American Countries* (1942)

Kantor, H., *Ideology and Program of the Peruvian Aprista Movement* (1953)

Kirchoff, H., *Bolivia: Its People and Scenery* (1944)

Kubler, G., *The Indian Caste of Peru, 1795–1940* (1952)

La Barre, W., *The Aymará Indians of the Lake Titicaca Plateau, Bolivia* (1948)

La Foy, M., *Chaco Dispute and the League of Nations* (1946)

Leavitt, S. E., *Tentative Bibliography of Bolivian Literature* (1933)

————, *Tentative Bibliography of Peruvian Literature* (1932)

Legg, H. J., *Bolivia: Economic and Commercial Conditions in Bolivia* (1952)

Leonard, O. E., *Bolivia: Land, People and Institutions* (1952)

————, *Canton Chullpas: A Socio-Economic Study of an Area in Bolivia* (1948)

————, *Pichilingue: A Study of Rural Life in Coastal Ecuador* (1947)

————, *Santa Cruz: A Socio-Economic Study of an Area in Bolivia* (1948)

Lieuwen, E., *Generals vs. Presidents* (1964)

Linke, L., *Andean Adventure: A Social and Political Study of Colombia, Ecuador and Bolivia* (1945)

————, *Ecuador: Country of Contrasts* (3rd ed., 1966)

Lockwood, A. N., *Indians of the Andes* (1956)

Lynch, J. V., and P. J. Ferell, *Agricultural Economy of Bolivia* (1961)

Macdonald, A. F., *Latin American Politics and Governments* (2nd ed., 1954)

Marsh, M. A., *Bankers of Bolivia* (1928)

Martin, P. F., *Peru in the Twentieth Century* (1911)

Mautner, H. E., *Doctor in Bolivia* (1960)

Mecham, J. L., *Church and State in Latin America* (rev. ed., 1966)

Meggers, B. J., *Ecuador* (1966)

Monge, C., *Acclimatization in the Andes*, trans. D. F. Brown (1948)

National Planning Association, *Casa Grace in Peru* (1954)

Needler, M., *Anatomy of a Coup d'état: Ecuador, 1963* (1964)

Nelson, R. H., *Education in Bolivia* (1949)

Ogilvie, A. G., *Geography of the Central Andes* (1922)

Osborne, H., *Bolivia: A Land Divided* (3rd ed., 1966)

————, *Indians of the Andes: Aymarás and Quechuas* (1952)

Ostria Gutiérrez, A., *A People Crucified: The Tragedy of Bolivia* (1958)

Owen, R. J., *Peru* (1963)

Palmer, T. W., *Search for a Latin American Policy* (1957)

Pan American Union, *Peruvian Economy* (1950)

————, *A Statement of the Laws of Bolivia in Matters Affecting Business* (3rd ed., 1962)

Patch, R. W., *Peru's New President and Agrarian Reform and Other Studies* in *American Universities Field Staff Reports Service* (1964)

Payne, J. L., *Labor and Politics in Peru* (1965)

Pike, F. B., *History of Republican Peru* (1966)

Platt, R. R., *Ecuador* (2nd ed., 1962)

Plaza, G., *Problems of Democracy in Latin America* (1955)

Poppino, R., *Communism in Latin America* (1964)

Rippy, J. F., *Latin America and the Industrial Age* (1944)

Robinson, D. A., *Peru in Four Dimensions* (1964)

Saunders, J. V. D., *The People of Ecuador* (1961)

Smith, T. L., *Agrarian Reform in Latin America* (1965)

Stuart, G. H., *The Governmental System of Peru* (1925)

Torres-Rioseco, A., *Epic of Latin American Literature* (rev. ed., 1946)

Tudela, F., *The Controversy between Peru and Ecuador* (1941)

United Nations, *Economic Development of Bolivia* (1957)

————, *Economic Survey of Latin America* (1957)

United States Army, *Handbook of Bolivia* (1963)

United States, Department of Commerce, Office of International Trade, *Investments in Peru* (1957)

Urquidi, C., ed., *A Statement of the Laws of Bolivia* (3rd ed., 1962)

Violich, F., *Cities of Latin America* (1944)

Von Hagen, V. W., *Ecuador and the Galapagos Islands* (1949)

————, *Ecuador the Unknown* (1940)

Whitaker, A. P., *United States and South America: The Northern Republics* (1948)

Wood, B., *The United States and Latin American Wars, 1932–1942* (1966)

Ybarra, Y. T., *Lands of the Andes, Peru and Bolivia* (1947)

Zook, D. H., *Conduct of the Chaco War* (1960)

————, *Zaramulla-Marañon: The Ecuador-Peru Dispute* (1965)

Chapter 37

The "Spanish Main" Countries in the Last Half-Century

COLOMBIAN POLITICS IN THE TWENTIETH CENTURY

THROUGHOUT THE HISTORY of Colombia her political life has been handicapped by the inaccessibility of the inland plateaus which stand at the head of those river valleys into which the country is split by the three ranges of the Andes. Caribbean ports have been connected to the capital by highway only within the last decade, and two-thirds of the country remains practically empty—the Caribbean lowlands, the vast area south of the Andes in the Amazon Basin, and the cold high mountain tops. Of the more than 15,000,000 modern Colombians, 90 per cent live on one-third of the land. Though there is no racial and little class rivalry, the separateness of the regions prolonged provincial rivalry, and the lack of outside contacts kept the issue of Church versus state alive long after it had been settled elsewhere. Essentially a democratic country, traditionally opposed to dictatorships, Colombia has had such intense party strife that she has often been torn by civil war, though only two of her presidents have been thrown out by violence in the last half-century. Indeed, the period after 1949 was one long guerrilla fight between two parties, and did not seem true to form for modern Colombia.

Her first misfortune in the twentieth century was the loss of Panama. Under Rafael Núñez, regionalism had developed in that isolated province before 1900. When the United States was anxious to negotiate for the Panama area in 1901 to 1902, Colombia was torn by the War of the Thousand Days, and was lacking any strong leadership. The United States, which had pledged with England in the Clayton-Bulwer Treaty of 1850 that no nation would maintain exclusive control over any canal to be built, had looked askance at Colombia's concession to de Lesseps' French firm in 1878. Forced by the tropical conditions to abandon the site, the French firm arranged to sell its rights to the United States. Then the American government made a treaty with Colombia's foreign minister Herrán, arranging for the use of a six-mile-wide zone for a cash payment and an annual fee. Regional elements in the disorganized Colombia senate blocked the passage of the treaty. Meanwhile, in 1901 the Clayton-Bulwer Treaty was abrogated and Theodore Roosevelt tacitly encouraged the incipient revolt in Panama. On November 2, 1903, the province of Panama became an independent nation. Its loss was a shock to Colombia and became a cause of dissent and disunity. Finally, in 1922, American oil companies anxious to begin drilling in Colombia brought pressure to bear on Harding to improve relations. The United States paid Colombia $25,000,000 for her loss and the matter was closed.

Rafael Reyes, the president active in the attempt to secure redress for loss of Panama, had emerged as strong man from the civil strife of 1903, and held the presidency from 1904 to 1909. Famous for explorations on foot over hundreds of miles in the Colombian Amazon, Reyes later made a career in the army, then won the presidency as leader of the Conservatives. Reyes was actually an unconstitutional dictator, but he rehabilitated Colombia economically, supported by a landowners' and army officers' bloc. He improved communications by building railroads from the highland cities to Buenaventura on the Pacific, and by dredging the Magdalena River route. He stabilized the currency and restored Colombia's foreign credit. In 1909 his handpicked National Assembly extended his term in office, at the same time that he arranged a first, unpopular settlement with the United States over Panama. These two steps produced so much popular resentment that Reyes was forced to resign and to go into exile.

The disappearance of Reyes opened the way for the Conservatives to bring in a more traditional regime, through which that party ruled Colombia till 1930. Under a constitutional provision for minority representation, the Liberal party opposition enjoyed full democratic rights and was invited into coalition cabinets. Meanwhile Colombia prospered from the opening of the Panama Canal, as both her coasts could be visited by ships from either ocean. World War I brought increased trade to neutral Colombia. Once the Panama controversy was settled and American oil prospectors came to Colombia after 1922, the new oil boom commenced which today brings millions in revenue to Colombia. Under Pedro Nel Ospina (1922–1926) and his successor Miguel Abadía Méndez (1926–1930), Colombia's small industries were expanded, her whole economy improved, and coffee production encouraged. The Cauca Valley, with its industrial center of

Medellín, became a leader in the nation, and contributed statesmen to the Conservative party. Cali, former stronghold of clerical conservatism, became a center of liberalism.

Worldwide depression, the rise of an articulate laboring class, the fall in the price of coffee, and a strike of the banana workers against the United Fruit Company plantations on the coast all combined to change parties by 1930 and bring the Liberal leaders into power. Enrique Olaya Herrera, former minister to the United States, was elected by a large majority, after a vigorous campaign against a split Conservative party replete with promises of social reform and betterment of living conditions. In 1934 a completely Liberal administration succeeded him under Alfonso López. Thus the Liberals ushered in the period 1930–1946, and gave Colombia a new deal. They guided the nation through economic recovery, reorganization of national education, war with Peru, settlement of the Church question, and the Constitution of 1936. The period encompassed an era of increased economic nationalism, industrialization, cooperation with the United States, and a swing back to conservatism. The Liberals weathered World War II even though Colombia had been a target for Nazi business operations and home of one of the major German-owned airlines in South America, the SCADTA. The line was nationalized as a threat to the Panama Canal as soon as Colombia broke relations with Germany after Pearl Harbor. Colombian newspapers and public opinion were all pro-American, and actual war was declared in November 1943. The war period even saw a feeble revival of the old idea of Gran Colombia, when Ecuador and Venezuela conferred with Colombia on several common problems in 1942 and 1943. It was a time also of expanded Colombian agriculture and industry, increased education, and advanced labor laws.

During the 1930s and the 1940s visitors praised "cultured, progressive Colombia, the true democracy." The Liberal presidents of the 1930s, Olaya Herrera and Dr. López, were newspaper editors and writers in the field of history and economics. However, Dr. López had instituted a new constitution in 1936 which, together with various pieces of legislation, stirred up old religious resentments by placing government inspectors over Church schools and making charities government-regulated. The constitution, setting up a unitary government, also provided for social security, income and real estate taxes, and some government control over business. It did much for labor and education. After a term under another Liberal newspaperman, Eduardo Santos, from 1938 to 1942, Dr. Alfonso López was elected a second time. But in ultra-devout Colombia the anticlerical president could not hold his cabinet together in his second term. López was forced to resign in 1945, and his term was completed by the moderate Alberto Lleras Camargo, who was later to serve as a leader in the Organization of American States. By this time the Liberals had split widely into two factions, thereby enabling the Conservatives to gain control in the 1946 election, as many Liberals abstained from voting in protest at the growing Conservative power and at their own party dissension. By plurality vote in a three-cornered election the Conservative and devout Mariano Ospina Pérez was easily elected to serve to 1950.

All this time Liberals and Conservatives alike had appealed only to a relatively small educated minority. Long before 1946 among the left-wing Liberals there had arisen a champion of the people, of the city workers and the landless peasants of Colombia—Jorge Eliécer Gaitán, Minister of Education. As a self-made young lawyer, he had represented a group of banana workers on strike. In spite of the restrictions of the Conservative president, Gaitán became a popular orator, in Conservative opinion a rabble-rouser. His own position became so dangerous that he asked for— and failed to receive—personal police protection. Then, when dignitaries of all Latin American states were meeting in Bogotá on April 9, 1948, to hear General George Marshall, American Secretary of State, the meeting was suddenly interrupted. Gaitán had just been assassinated on a Bogotá street! The screaming pro-Gaitán crowd lynched the assassin, while the embarrassed government moved the foreign delegates to the suburbs. The matter did not end there, however; mobs burned anti-Gaitán newspaper offices, and ran riot for several days, while government leaders put the blame on the very small Colombian Communist Party. Thus began the *violencia*, the banditry which, until recently, was not politically motivated.

Fear of civil war and internal danger shocked the parties into coopera-tion, and the Conservatives and Liberals combined to support a coalition government, but only for a very short time. By autumn armed clashes in the provinces had grown into a guerrilla campaign which lasted for years. Gaitán was more powerful in death than in life. The underfed masses, to whom no one had appealed so strongly before, could not forget him, while the archconservatives feared further disorder. President Ospina Pérez turned reactionary, and the year 1949 was one of disorder and tension. As police control tightened, Liberals again boycotted the polls, and Laureano Gómez, an archconservative, pro-Spanish, and Catholic news-paper editor whose press had been burned by the rioting mobs of April 1948, was elected almost "unanimously" for the term beginning in August 1950. There followed three years of terror. Protestant groups, tolerated by the Liberals and hated by Conservatives, were attacked; a Perón-type army was built up by Laureano Gómez. The Conservatives themselves rioted in September 1953 when religious fanatics and youths from the "best Bogotá families" destroyed a Liberal newspaper plant and even burned the home of the revered past president, Dr. Alfonso López. Laureano Gómez declared a nationwide "state of siege"; armed bands on both sides took to the hills. Each side called the other Communists or Fascists. In the single year of 1952 the guerrilla fighting caused 12,000 deaths. A new constitution gave Laureano Gómez "supreme power in military emergen-cies." The dominant Conservative party split, and despite widespread oppo-sition, the country turned to the army for relief from atrocities and a rapidly spreading civil war.

In June of 1953 a coalition was formed between the right-wing Liberals and the more progressive Conservatives to try to bring some sort of peace into chaotic Colombian affairs. General Gustavo Rojas Pinilla, endorsed by the Church and leading a moderate element within the army, made a truce with the guerrillas in the provinces, lifted the press censorship, and became head of a provisional government on June 13, 1953. Within two years Rojas Pinilla became a more oppressive military dictator than Laureano Gómez had been, while the rural areas maintained their guerrilla warfare and attacks on Protestant missionaries continued. Whereas before 1950 Rojas Pinilla had lived in a modest rented house, by 1957 he was a multimillionaire and Colombia's number one cattleman and had exported millions for his own future use (which were to be needed in May 1957, when he was exiled). His iron rule was shot through with graft, while Colombia faced a huge debt and a fall in the value of the peso.

Colombia's traditional faith in democracy and opposition to military rule finally turned against Rojas Pinilla when he made a barefaced attempt to perpetuate himself in power in the spring of 1957. A banking and commercial strike forced even the army to oppose him. University students rioted against his "re-election by his handpicked assembly. On May 10, 1957, Rojas Pinilla was forced to resign. A military *junta* appointed by Rojas Pinilla chose as provisional president Gabriel Paris, who later added a civilian advisory committee to the military *junta*. The Liberal Dr. Alberto Lleras Camargo, active in foreign affairs and first Latin American Secretary General of the Organization of American States, who had remained the real leader of the Liberals, was called in for consultation. Meeting with the Conservative leaders in August of 1957, Lleras Camargo drew up a formula for alternating national and local offices between Conservatives and Liberals for the next four four-year presidential terms. The first such term was to begin under an openly elected president in August 1958. The plan was accepted by the weary Colombians with "cautious optimism" in an 18-to-1 vote in December 1957. Each party agreed to make its own choices in a sort of "party primary" for the 50 per cent of national, provincial and local offices it was allowed. With the evenly divided congress chosen, Lleras Camargo was elected president in May 1958. In August the *junta* peacefully resigned; Lleras Camargo was inaugurated August 18, 1958, in the midst of nationwide celebration. Lleras Camargo's policy called for a severe monetary and stabilization program, a higher standard of living in the rural areas, the development of raw materials and local manufacturing—all under an austerity program to check inflation. Lleras Camargo worked hard to bring some semblance of order to the country.

The coalition plan held together through Lleras Camargo's legal term and brought the fair election of a mild Conservative in 1962. The most pressing problem, the violence in the backlands, became less political and more a matter of local banditry and crime. Well-trained Colombian army men were sent into remote villages to teach school, organize local self-help groups, and alleviate the fear of bandit gangs. This program was continued by the Conservative president from 1962 to 1966, Leon Valencia, the son of a well-known poet. He continued the well-organized campaign against rural terror, cutting the number of deaths by two-thirds. He did have to face falling coffee prices, urban unemployment, and a 45 per cent increase in the cost of living. In the 1966 elections, there were splits in both parties which threatened the system of alternating the presidency for

1966–1970 which had been worked out so well by Lleras Camargo. But a distant cousin of his, Carlos Lleras Restrepo, peacefully gained the presidency and was inaugurated for a four-year term on August 7, 1966. There is good reason for future optimism for Colombia; the human and economic resources of the area are surely leading towards increasing self-improvement of the Colombians in the 1970s.

A good part of the Colombian tension had been due to religious difficulty, which, in Colombia of the 1950s as in Mexico of the 1920s, has to be discussed as a political rather than as a social issue. Colombians are deeply and sincerely Catholic with an almost medieval fervor. Under the early Liberals, Protestant missions were established among the rural mountaineers, where the Catholic Church had had no social program. Several Protestant sects gained converts in the cities, and a YMCA was founded in Bogotá. But in such a strongly Catholic country, Protestantism still seemed as antisocial as heresy had in medieval times; Protestant mission schools which used "foreign money" to "win away" children already baptised Catholic, by means of attractive picture books and recreation programs, were considered actually wicked. After 1948, mob outbreaks against such Protestant establishments increased; there were more incidents of violence against Protestants in the early 1950s in Colombia than in all the rest of Latin America in a whole century.

The Protestants themselves showed poor judgment, carrying on street services in front of Catholic churches on Sunday morning, loudly attacking Catholic dogma and institutions, and disagreeing among their various sects. Priests led children in stoning Protestant meetings; the lives of native Colombian converts were not safe. Modern-minded Catholic leaders, distressed at the situation and the bad publicity it brought to Colombia, proposed compromise plans of limiting Protestant missionaries to a quota and in turn guaranteeing police protection of those already there, while other forward-looking Catholic laymen advocated Catholic social action and welfare programs as a countermeasure to the spread of Protestantism. In the increasing industrialization of Colombia and in the rise in the standard of living taking place throughout this stormy period lay the hopes for more tolerant attitudes. The coalition government of 1958 ended the persecution of Protestants in Colombia and again granted visas to Protestant missionaries.

Losing Panama at the beginning of the century and frightening Pan American delegates with street riots at the mid-point, Colombia had a minor international fracas in between. The "Leticia Affair" in the 1930s was a small-scale war with Peru over a remote jungle outpost on the Amazon, a group of galvanized iron warehouses and thatched huts at the tip of the wedged-shape territory which Colombia owns there. In 1932, when a Peruvian dictator sent soldiers to try to expel the Colombian inhabitants, war between Colombia and Peru resulted; in the eyes of the world this was a senseless war, for both nations had defaulted on foreign-held bonds in the depression and yet spent millions of dollars in the fight. Finally the League of Nations arbitrated the dispute and gave the river town back to Colombia. In the late 1960s the Colombia government was building roads towards the Amazon and developing the Leticia area.

Other Colombian foreign relations have been very successful. Colombians had been active in the League of Nations—a Colombian had served as president of the League Assembly—and Colombia was one of the first nations to support the United Nations. A token force of Colombian troops fought in Korea; Colombian troops served with Scandinavians in a UN police patrol in the Suez dispute of 1956. Foreign investors have had no unhappy time in Colombia. American oil interests built one of the world's famous pipelines, the Barca; the United Fruit Company developed large holdings in the Santa Marta area, and, when the company had labor troubles, the Conservative government backed the American company.

DICTATORSHIP PATTERN BROKEN
IN OIL-RICH VENEZUELA

Venezuela, seventh in area in Latin America, supports more than eight million people. The *llanos* in the Orinoco Basin which figured so dramatically in Bolívar's campaigns are still sparsely settled and under-developed. The plains on the coast around Maracaibo are often stricken by drought; the foothills of the eastern Andes facing the Orinoco are covered with humid jungle. South and east of the Orinoco, in the Guiana Highlands, lies a jungle area still not explored. The grazing lands of the *llanos* are too dry in the dry season for the stock, too flooded in the wet. Only in the cooler valleys near the coast where lie Caracas and other modern towns is life really pleasant. Geography, which treated Venezuela so badly, still left billions of dollars worth of oil beneath her hills and tidelands. The people who live in this "poor-rich" country are 60 per cent illiterate. The *Caraqueños*, those fortunates who live in Caracas, inhabit ultra-modern apartment houses and ride on freeways paid for by the oil royalties in a country with the highest per capita income of Latin America, but the mountain Indians and the Orinoco *llaneros* live just as they did in Bolívar's time. The age of *caudillos*, up to the 1950s, went right on in the spectacular new buildings of the capital.

The twentieth century had dawned in Venezuela with a cruel, vindictive, and irresponsible military *caudillo*, Cipriano Castro, in power—power he held for nine years, during which he bankrupted Venezuela and built up a tremendous personal fortune outside his native land. When finally exhausted from debauchery, he went to visit a kidney specialist in Germany, leaving a trusted henchman, Juan Vicente Gómez, in control. Castro never got back into Venezuela, for Gómez took over and kept him an exile.

Thus commenced the "Age of Gómez," a time of tyranny and cruelty, although not without some material progress. It lasted twenty-seven years. Illegitimate son of a poor mountain Indian woman, himself a peasant who never learned to read and write, Gómez had risen to prominence as one of Castro's army of cattlemen and by 1900 was a wealthy rancher. By 1910 all Venezuela was his ranch. He never married, but fathered scores of illegitimate children who lived around him on fat government jobs. His personal holdings were fabulous; he was said at his death to be worth $30,000,000, but none of his good fortune ever trickled down to the Indian masses. He maintained order by force and cruelty; common people called him *El Brujo*, the sorcerer, and could not believe he would ever die. When his death from old age in bed was announced in December ber 1935, the city of Caracas literally went on a drunken spree of celebration.

But Gómez' rule, like that of Porfirio Díaz in Mexico, was not all bad. As a benevolent despot he was interested in promoting public works and sanitation, though he frowned on mass education. He employed smart, scientifically trained young men to do the actual work of government. His foreign relations were harmonious and he preserved a prosperous neutrality during World War I. Most important for the future, oil was discovered in Lake Maracaibo during his rule, and Gómez was smart enough to turn it to his own profit. Foreign capital was allowed to develop the petroleum, but an eighth-part of all oil produced had to be turned over as taxes to his government. Maracaibo turned out to be a fabulously rich field; Gómez' government paid off the national debt, reduced domestic taxes to a minimum, and lived fat off the oil revenues. He gave some material prosperity to Venezuela in agriculture, stock raising, and industry, although they were monopolies. In sharp contrast to the rest of Latin America, Venezuela was hurt very little by the depression, and the prosperity of the government from the oil taxes has persisted to the present day.

Into the orgy of celebration at the dictator's death came Gómez' Minister of War, General Eleazar López Contreras, to bring peace and order; the congress declared him president for the next five years. López Contreras served his country well; a new constitution was made providing for a national labor office and some social insurance. Under it López Contreras broadened the franchise slightly and formed a new liberal government, but in reality he was a continuation of the rule of Venezuela's masters of great estates and businessmen. He organized a Three Year Plan to use the fat revenues for the improvement of transportation, water works, and schools. Though World War II cut into the flow of oil revenues, he maintained Venezuela's prosperity and peacefully designated his successor, General Isaías Medina, in a rigged election in 1941.

Isaías Medina continued Contreras' policy, cooperated with the Allies in World War II, and declared war in February 1945. He completed Contreras' Three Year Plan and adopted a Four Year Plan of public works and agricultural production; he improved harbors and developed low-cost housing. Meanwhile a liberal faction called *Acción Democrática* was growing into a political party of middle-class professionals and businessmen, with some labor support. Convinced that Isaías Medina was planning to dictate the next election, the liberals joined with a group of dissatisfied young army men. Consolidating behind Rómulo Betancourt, who became provisional president, a military *junta* overthrew Isaías Medina in October 1945. As provisional president from October of 1945 to February of 1946, Betancourt established democratic government under a new constitution. He also attempted social legislation, expanded education, started land reform, and tried to lower the cost of living. Rómulo Gallegos, beloved leader of *Acción Democrática* and a famous novelist, was elected president in February 1946, in the first honest election in Venezuela.

A Caracas school teacher under whom many of the young men in his government had studied history, Rómulo Gallegos was recognized as one of the great writers in the Spanish language. Now at sixty-five, he tried his hand at the presidency under a new constitution with great plans for improving the country. In July 1948 he came to the United States to dedicate a statue of Bolívar, calm in the belief that the Age of *Caudillos* was over in Venezuela. But a group of corrupt older army officers, stopped in their customary graft during Gallegos' administration, were not content to let it be, and precipitated a *coup d'état* on November 23, 1948. This palace revolution, about which the populace first heard over the radio that morning, set up a three-man *junta* which soon sent the idealistic Rómulo Gallegos to exile in Cuba.

The three-man *junta* called their revolt "a democratic necessity in the face of Communist influence." Then they put 4,000 opponents in jail, outlawed the *Acción Democrática*, and disbanded congress. Newspapers were censored; the university was closed. One member of the triumvirate was assassinated in November 1950, the second retired from active administration, and the third, Marcos Pérez Jiménez, was proclaimed provisional president and then actual president by 1953.

Pérez Jiménez was a dictator in the old *caudillo* tradition. Son of a small coffee planter, he had been educated in the War College in Lima and had taught at Venezuela's military academy. His urge to oust the democratic Rómulo Gallegos government stemmed from his dissatisfaction with a major's rank. As president he was a model family man, staging parties and pageants for the public, and shunning the fancier society of oil-rich Caracas. Slated to finish his "legal term" in 1958, he had his congress "declare for a plebiscite to be held on December 15, on his continuing in office for another term to begin in April 1958." Because of his advantageous "deals" with the oil companies, the middle- and upper-class people of Caracas lived well indeed, attended school in streamlined glass buildings, inhabited model apartment houses which excelled those of Rio, and enjoyed a prosperity unparalleled elsewhere in Latin America. The slums of Caracas, the *llanos*, and the Andes remained much the same as in Bolívar's time, however, as far as the masses of the inhabitants were concerned. The Pérez Jiménez government ran an "orderly" administration and pointed with pride to many improvements in Caracas. But its opposition was in exile and it showed no respect for human dignity. Thus it rated as one of the worst dictatorships in South America as of January 1958.

Early that month a group of air force officers rose in revolt against Pérez Jiménez, and when other branches of the military failed to join them, thousands of air force personnel were crowded into jail. By January 10 Pérez Jiménez had jailed a group of liberal priests also, and thus came into sharp conflict with the Church. Now the army generals lost their timidity and forced the dictator to name a new chief of police to replace his hated "stooge" Hector Estrada. Estrada fled precipitately to join Perón with Trujillo in Santo Domingo, but the crowd in the streets had now lost its timidity also. Church leaders rang the church bells continuously on February 1; students left classes to swarm in the streets; the "underground" against Pérez Jiménez came out above ground. At 2:00 A.M. February 2, 1958, the dictator and an eleven-car caravan of friends drove to the airport and to refuge on a "visitor's visa" at Miami. Venezuelans rioted twenty-four more hours, then settled down to rule by a five-man *junta*—four civilians and only one military officer. Head of this group was a rear-admiral, Wolfgang Larrazábal, who governed throughout the summer of 1958 and supervised a legal election on December 7, 1958. Larrazábal, himself a candidate, had the support of the left-wing, anti-United States faction and of the vociferous though small Communist party.

It was the *Acción Democrática* of Rómulo Gallegos' day, out from hiding since the exile of Pérez Jiménez, which won the election. Its candidate was one of its founders, Rómulo Betancourt, provisional president in 1945 and 1946, who had been spending years of exile observing democracy at work in Costa Rica and Puerto Rico. Imprisoned with ball and chain in his student days by Juan Vicente Gómez, Betancourt had worked for democracy in Venezuela through thirty years of adulthood, twenty-one of them spent abroad. Now he was president after a fair election, and was inaugurated February 14, 1959. Pérez Jiménez had left the country with nothing but disorder. Now Betancourt—honest, hard working, socially conscious, but economy-minded—brought some stability to his nation.

One of his first problems was to work out a new arrangement with the oil companies, whereby a fairer share of their profits came directly to the Venezuelan people, but in which the oil companies themselves had a chance to negotiate. His opponent Larrazábal did not allow him this chance, but led the retiring *junta*, in the last days before Betancourt's inauguration, to "slap" a 67 per cent tax on oil profits, without any negotiations. Accused already of "too much friendliness to United States oil," Betancourt could not reverse the *junta's* decision, though he hoped to encourage foreign investment. He needed additional funds to attack unemployment, build schools for the 600,000 Venezuelan children crowded out, and fulfill the promise of better living held tantalizingly before the people by the grandiose freeways, housing projects, and half completed hospitals which Pérez Jiménez and Larrazábal's *junta* had built with the 50-50 oil royalties.

Four years later Betancourt, though harassed throughout his term by the strongest *Fidelista* Communist party outside Cuba, by "cloak and dagger" spies and secret arms caches from nearly Havana, was able peacefully to turn over his office to Raúl Leoni in February 1963. This was the first time in 152 years that one legally elected president served out his entire term of office and turned over his job to a legally elected successor.

The military had not intervened in politics from 1958 to 1966. This period under Betancourt and Leoni was one of the principal challenges to totalitarianism in Latin America. The new president had been a revolutionary against Gómez in his youth, had been imprisoned, tortured, and exiled, but in the presidency he seemed a placid, plodding man, bald and portly at fifty-eight. However, he formed coalitions between the *Acción Democrática* and three other moderate parties, and thus pushed a reform program faster than had Betancourt. In 1964 he inaugurated a Four Year Plan with financial backing from the American Alliance for Progress, and immediately began irrigation projects in the dry land south of Maracaibo. That same year he distributed farm land in other areas of Venezuela to more than 60,000 families, including settlers in 700 new cooperative farm villages. Although 350,000 families were still waiting for lands promised them in Betancourt's 1960 Agrarian Law, this progress seems rapid in a nation in which two per cent of the population had always owned 70 per cent of the farm land. The Four Year Plan also included the building of 380,000 new housing units and the diversification of industry in one-product, oil-rich Venezuela. Later plans of Leoni included collecting higher taxes from the oil companies and even hopes for eventual government ownership of the oil industry.

Venezuela had begun the century with the fear of foreign invasion. Cipriano Castro, the Lion of the Andes, who became dictator in 1899, soon earned himself the name "International Bad Boy" because he made no payments on debts contracted by his predecessors. In 1902 British, German, and Italian warships set up a blockade along the Venezuelan coast to force payment on these debts, an incident known as the Second Venezuelan Crisis. Again the United States exercised the Monroe Doctrine. Theodore Roosevelt persuaded England and Italy to settle the matter by arbitration, and threatened the Germans with armed force. The subsequent arbitration awarded a compromise amount to the three powers. Actually, Castro never paid it, and Venezuela remained in bad repute until the matter was settled by Gómez, who, though more crude at home than Castro, was more suave abroad.

In World War I Gómez pursued a policy of neutrality, selling oil rights to whoever could come and pay for them. As the world's needs for oil increased after 1920, he granted leases to Dutch, American, and British companies. American companies, in an oil-conscious world, deliberately made friends in Venezuela by their fine housing projects for workers in the oil fields, and their policy of hiring as many Venezuelan citizens as possible.

By World War II this happy economic friendship between the United States and Venezuela was bearing fruit. Reciprocal trade agreements had been signed in November 1939. When the Nazis took Holland the next year and threatened the Dutch Caribbean islands so near Maracaibo, the two nations were jointly responsible for their defense. The United States granted Venezuela lend-lease funds to train her army and replace her tankers sunk by German submarines. A German-owned railway in Venezuela was expropriated by the government. Thus Venezuela played her full part in inter-American defense, broke with the Axis, declared war, and joined the United Nations. Her relationships with the powers whose companies own the oil concessions have remained friendly and cooperative under every presidency since.

However, resentment flared against the United States because she had "maintained such comfortable relations with the dictator" and had welcomed him in exile. In the recession of 1957 and 1958, oil imports to the United States were cut, and with them much of Venezuela's tax money. When Vice President Nixon arrived on a visit to Caracas in May of 1958, this resentment boiled over and he was spit upon and stoned in the street. Communists and rightists combined in using the latent anti-United States feeling as a whip against Rómulo Betancourt's government. Leoni continued Betancourt's foreign policy of support for self-determination and political democracy. In the 1960s Venezuela's most serious foreign problem was to stop infiltration of Communist terrorists and their armaments from *Fidelista* Cuba. However, she was able to get the Organization of American States to condemn such arms shipments.

MODERN ECONOMIC CONDITIONS
ALONG THE SPANISH MAIN

That the standards of living are rising in both Columbia and Venezuela is partially due to the petroleum industry. In 1907 a concession to exploit petroleum deposits in Lake Maracaibo was granted by the Venezuelan dictator Castro to an American company. By 1917 the company at Maracaibo exported 60,000 barrels; in 1965 the production of Venezuela ran to nearly three-and-a-half million barrels a day. About two-thirds of Venezuelan oil comes from the Maracaibo, and one-third from the Orinoco region. Standard Oil has considered the Venezuela holdings a very valuable property, contributing two-thirds of Standard's production outside the United States.

Refined at first in the Dutch West Indies, Curaçao, and Aruba, just off the Maracaibo coast, a large part of the oil is now refined in three coastal refineries, bringing employment and profit to Venezuelans, and more good will to the companies. In the last decade the American companies made a two-billion-dollar profit, of which they re-invested more than a billion right back into Venezuela; the Venezuelan government received more than two billion itself from all these operations.

Perhaps learning a lesson from Cárdenas' anti-oil company action in Mexico, the American management in Venezuela's fields determined to promote good relations. "The oil in Venezuela belongs to Venezuela," says a public relations announcement of an American company. "'By means of an arrangement that is mutually profitable to Venezuela and ourselves, we are converting the country's greatest natural resource into the country's greatest source of income." To carry out these fine words, the company not only paid the high royalty, but employed 94 per cent native personnel, even in skilled technical positions, for which they trained young Venezuelans on scholarships. Oil camp communities provided better housing and better schools, hospitals, and recreational facilities than were available to most other Venezuelan working people.

On the other hand, the oil workers' high wages and the government's high profits produced inflation in a nation otherwise economically poor. Since the country did not produce sufficient foodstuffs, and very little consumer goods, prices on such things skyrocketed with the higher wages and more sophisticated demands. Living costs for the workers and the city white-collar classes almost wiped out the advantages of high wages. Presidents through the 1930s and 1940s adopted a policy of "sow the petroleum profits back into the nation." A *Corporación de Fomento*, or Development Corporation, was set up to use the money in public works, housing projects, hydroelectric plants, and agricultural training and soil and livestock improvement for the *llanos* and the mountain farms. Whole blocks of model tenements were built in Caracas, hospitals erected, compulsory health programs started, and better highways into the backlands built.

Colombia, the second largest petroleum producer in South America, also shares in the oil bonanza, with her deposits lying in the same geologic formation as those of the Maracaibo Basin. The fields which have been developed at the bend of the Magdalena nearest the Venezuela line are producing 5 per cent of Colombia's exports. Most of this oil is carried to the coast at Cartagena by means of the Barca pipeline, a spectacular project through the jungle, eight inches in diameter and 335 miles long. Agricultural exports, bananas and coffee, loom larger in the Colombian economic pictures than do such products in Venezuela.

Iron ore reserves in Venezuela are placed at one billion tons, usable for the outside world because they are accessible to year-round navigation on the Orinoco. In 1940 Bethlehem Steel staked out a concession to open up this area, using open-pit mining with electric shovels and thirty-ton diesel trucks in the jungle wilderness. United States Steel has also gone into the region above Ciudad Bolívar. This new iron and steel development was a boon to the Leoni administration in its attempt to diversify the economy. If, as some petroleum authorities prophesy, Venezuelan oil reserves are exhausted by 1980, the slack will be taken up by this boom on the Orinoco. By 1965 a pre-planned town on the Orinoco, Santo Thomé, had 70,000 inhabitants; the Guayana Development Corporation on the Orinoco had built a hydroelectric project on the Caroni River, an Orinoco tributary, to provide power to process the ore. In its first year the steel complex, the "Ruhr of Venezuela," produced 70,000 tons, in its second year, 1964, 300,000 tons. Nickel deposits are also being worked in the area. Colombia has built its own steel refinery at Paz del Río, 280 miles northeast of Bogotá, second in production only to Brazil's Volta Redonda steel plant throughout all South America, and capable of satisfying Colombia's own increasing manufacturing needs.

True to the *Conquistadores'* dreams, gold, diamonds, and emeralds are still being mined along the Spanish Main. Diamond mining in the Venezuelan highlands southeast of the Orinoco is on the increase. Colombia is producing fifteen million dollars' worth of gold from the central *cordillera* annually, and is today the world's chief source of emeralds.

In local manufacturing—textiles, cement, printing, food industries, chemicals, building materials, soap, aluminum products, refined sugar— the two countries are not self-sufficient, though Colombia may be so in another decade. More than 50,000 such establishments are listed, but few of them employ large numbers of people. Foreign trade—in oil, ores, coffee, and bananas—has trebled fqr the whole region in the last three decades, helping the countries cushion themselves against worldwide fluctuations. Each nation has since established a Department of *Fomento* or Development, which has loaned money to local consumer-goods industries.

Industrialization of agricultural countries produces a new class of industrial laborers, and with them social and political tensions. Though oil workers fared well in Venezuela, the whole policy of the military government was very repressive against trade unions there. Identifying labor unions with the outlawed *Acción Democrática*, the Pérez Jiménez *junta* dissolved the unions. While still active in the 1940s, labor had been able to write into law the eight-hour day and the forty-eight-hour week. However, these measures have not been enforced outside the oil industry. Dr. Alfonso López, as liberal president of Colombia before 1946, was very pro-labor; his congress passed a basic wage-hour-vacation law in February 1945. During his day the Colombian Federation of Labor held the balance of power in elections. Strongly behind Gaitán, labor went into an eclipse politically under the governments which followed his death.

The typical Colombian laborer is not a city dweller, but rather is a coffee plantation worker living in the Cauca Valley near Medellín or Cali under much the same conditions as his counterpart in São Paulo, though more often eventually owning his own small acreage and becoming a freeholder, not a laborer. Two-thirds of the working population of Colombia are in agricultural, pastoral, and forestry pursuits. Coffee, specially labeled for flavor as "Colombian Coffee" in the world's markets, comprises over 70 per cent of the nation's exports by value. Tuning in on the quota system for world coffee production devised under Brazilian leadership in 1940, Colombia kept up her trade during World War II and did not suffer from Brazilian competition. The sloping highlands in which Colombian coffee is grown do not lend themselves to large plantation methods; some producers must get their product down to the river freighters by muleback as they did thirty years ago. The coffee planters, long an entrenched aristocracy in the Cauca Valley, remain the backbone of the Conservative party, and do not take to new methods, although Medellín, capital of the Cauca state of Antioquia, is a center for urban Liberal ideas. Bananas, developed by the American United Fruit Company on the Caribbean around Santa Marta, account for 10 per cent of Colombia's foreign trade.

Agriculture in Venezuela employs about half of the population. Long neglected and backward, it has profited from the "sow the petroleum revenues back into the soil" policy. This operates through trained agronomists and veterinarians who are part of an "extension service" to improve methods of planting and breeding among Venezuela's depressed farmers and cattlemen. Schools of practical agriculture have been opened, with active clubs organized for farm youth on the 4-H pattern. Both Colombia and Venezuela need to put more land under cultivation; in Colombia in the last two decades the population has increased twice as fast as the amount of new land planted. There is need for more diversified farming, for taking land out of grazing and putting it into crops, for mechanization and technological development of agriculture to feed the growing cities. To help in such improved agriculture, Colombia has an Institute of Colonization and Immigration to colonize government-held lands cooperatively. Venezuela has also brought in a number of immigrants, both for agriculture and as artisans, under the National Agrarian Institute Colonization Program.

Much potentially usable acreage is accessible via the Orinoco, which could be a lifeline for a new Venezuela, reaching the vast undeveloped grassland region. Though long navigated by boats from Trinidad to Ciudad Bolívar, the Orinoco is only now open to scheduled transportation farther inland. Colombia's rivers are more useful to her, as the valleys of the Magdalena and the Cauca and the plateau of Bogotá comprise the principal settled area of the country. A new network of highways connecting the Caribbean with Bogotá, and Bogotá westward to the Cauca Valley and on to the Pacific at Buenaventura was finished in the 1960s. At its mouth the Magdalena is so shallow that only in the last twenty years has it been deepened to make Barranquilla a real ocean port. It is possible to travel by car or bus on the all-weather Simón Bolívar Highway, a section of the Pan American Highway though an unpaved and winding mountain road, from Caracas to Bogotá to Popayán to Quito. Venezuela has even less highway and even fewer miles of railway. In 1952 a new superhighway, built with oil revenue, was opened from Caracas to La Guaira, the modernized Caribbean port; other roads into the Venezuelan interior were built in the 1960s.

Aviation is the answer to northern South America's transportation problems. AVIANCA, the national Colombian aviation company, carries commuters on one-hour trips from Bogotá to Medellín or from Cartagena to Cali. Industrial leaders, politicians, coffee planters, and the growing middle class use planes as North Americans would use interurban trains.

THE GENERAL LATIN AMERICAN CULTURAL AND SOCIAL PATTERNS IN THE SPANISH MAIN COUNTRIES

Racially there is more of an admixture of Negro blood in these two countries than in any other South American nation save Brazil. Of the 15,000,000 Colombians, about 20 per cent are pure white, another 2 per cent pure Indian, living as tribal groups in remote areas, perhaps 46 per cent *mestizo*, and 32 per cent Negro or mulatto, many of them dockworkers in the ports where their slave ancestors were the stevedores of the Spaniards. Venezuela with its 8,800,000 inhabitants has much the same pattern, except that there are more primitive Indians in remote sections, descendants of the Caribs. There is so much mixture that there is little racial prejudice, though the large and rapidly growing capital cities are mostly white or *mestizo*. Caracas, with only 250,000 people three decades ago, now has more than 1,000,000 inhabitants in its metropolitan area. About half as many people live in all Venezuela, which is four-fifths as large as Colombia. All administrations in Venezuela have encouraged immigration since World War II; thousands of Italian·artisans and farmers came to settle, as did other European groups, including many displaced persons sent by the International Refugee Organization after 1946.

Playground at a public housing project, Bogotá, Colombia. *Courtesy Pan American Union.*

Bogotá, now a city of over a million-and-a-quarter, high in the mountains, gray and chilly the year round, has had its face lifted in recent years by careful architectural planning under the French designer Le Corbusier. Housing projects and a new government center show a different face to the city than it had before it was looted and burned at the time of the Gaitán murder. Housing loan cooperatives have been founded, patterned after those of Chile. A modern slum clearance project of 12,000 units was dedicated by John F. Kennedy on his 1962 visit to South America and is named Kennedy City.

The growth of Medellín, the "Manchester of South America," with a population of 700,000, has been so phenomenal that, as in São Paulo, all the buildings seem new. "Everyone in Medellín makes good money and lives well," say the Colombians. Manizales, a town just over a century old, already has a population of over 176,000, and thrives on the new highway across the ridges to Buenaventura on the Pacific. Cali, in the upper Cauca, is the third city with 600,000. It seems new and bustling also, as does Barranquilla, with a population of 520,000—an important port since the dredging of the river mouth. Only in Cartagena, sleeping behind its walls built to keep out the buccaneers, does the visitor see much of the old Spanish colonialism of New Granada.

Caracas has a new face too—skyscrapers downtown, lines of apartments with curving balconies of the Rio-Copacabana Beach type, new homes in the suburbs, four-level traffic ways downtown, and a fabulous new university that rivals that of Mexico for its ultra-modern campus. But the shacks on the sides of the surrounding hills, housing the poorest workers, are still as bad a slum as anywhere in South America. Maracaibo, Venezuela's second city, has 325,000 people, with its many oil workers and technicians, its busy port with tankers lined up at the wharf.

Education at the elementary level in both countries is behind that of Chile, Argentina, or Mexico. Alfonso López in his first term in 1934 had tried to modernize Colombia's primary school system and free it from religious domination. A decade later, only one child in two was in any school at all, and of those who finished elementary school, only one in four went to secondary schools, most of which were run by the Church. A school Finance Law of December 1949 required that 30 per cent of the national budget be devoted to primary education, and that local governments provide adequate buildings and hire trained teachers at a standard salary, but because of the continuing guerrilla warfare this has been impossible to enforce in the rural areas. Venezuela has made some valiant efforts recently to increase its schools and to spread elementary and adult education. However, rural schools are practically nonexistent, though Caracas schools have been recently reorganized by an Uruguayan educator imported for the purpose. Illiteracy is unusually high among Venezuela's poor, although Betancourt and Leoni doubled the number of children in school.

In university education, both capitals have a proud tradition. Their long-established national universities have both moved into "University Cities"—large campuses with fine buildings in the suburbs. Though the young men of Bogotá are said to go back into the center of the city to do their homework, where they can sit at the sidewalk cafés and discuss politics or recite poetry while they are trying to study, the "all-one-campus plan" is tending to give faculty and students alike more of a feeling of identification with what North American students would call "real campus life." Venezuela has two other university-level schools; Colombia has fourteen, including the new free University of the Andes founded in 1948. However, none of these college-level schools carries on the training of primary teachers, which is one of the greatest professional needs of both countries. There has always been a high standard of education in Bogotá and Caracas for the sons of the wealthy and professional classes at the top, who are often not interested in training for jobs as technicians, engineers, or commercial leaders. Professional "student" Communists organized riots on both national campuses in late 1966, causing the governments to cut down on university autonomy.

Meanwhile, the black-suited, earnest, upper classes of Bogotá take their culture seriously. In Bogotá, the "Athens of South America," even mechanics enter union-run poetry contests. Classical music is taken equally as seriously. Though Colombia has produced no Heitor Villa-Lobos, Guillermo Uribe-Holquín (born in 1880) has been Colombia's outstanding composer, a violinist and long-time director of the National Conservatory of Music in Bogotá. There are symphony orchestras in Bogotá, in Cali, Medellín, and Barranquilla. Music is important in the social life of Caracas, also; that city's "oil-supported" symphony has almost a hundred members, and has won recognition throughout South America. Caracas is regular host to an all-Western Hemisphere music festival and symphony competition. Most of this musical interest is centered in European-style music, however, and has little of the folk spirit of the music of Brazil, where Negro peoples are also important segments of the population.

Poetry, the cultural interest of all Bogotá citizens, the subject of whole sections of the Sunday newspapers, of hours of special radio programs, of many small magazines, is European-classical in type, with little of the modern spirit or of the native pulse. For all Bogotá's love of poetry, the one well-known poet of these northcoast countries is the Venezuelan, Rufino Blanco Fombona (1874–1944), a writer in many fields—history, essay, literary criticism and, unfortunately for him, political satire. Blanco Fombona, like his friend Rubén Darío, was a citizen of all Latin America. Forced into exile by Gómez after several periods of imprisonment in Gómez' foul prisons, he supported himself in other Latin American capitals by editing anthologies and writing editorials attacking the United States for its Caribbean intervention program of the early 1900s. Blanco Fombona's *criollo* novel, *A Man of Gold*, a bitter satire on the politicians of Caracas who had kept him in prison, was widely read outside Gómez' Caracas.

Colombia's most widely read novel of the 1900s—there has been no second *María*—is a true native picture of Colombia's Amazonian backlands called *The Vortex*, a severe criticism of the exploitation of the rubber workers. It was written in 1924 by José Eustacio Rivera (1889–1928), who was a member of a Colombian-Venezuela Boundary Commission in that area, and who himself became lost in the jungle, traveled with river Indians, and almost died of malnutrition.

Poets and novelists of Colombia joined in a school of thought called *Los Nuevos*, the New Ones, after World War I, and attempted to modernize Colombian literary expression. Present-day novelists, historians, and literary critics are members of this modernist group. Best known in the United States is Germán Arciniegas (born in 1900), who writes popular biography and fictional history of the romance of colonial Spanish America, and who has brought his own country to the attention of world readers.

In Venezuela, other novelists have been overshadowed by the former president Rómulo Gallegos (born in 1884), whose novel *Doña Bárbara*, quoted in the introduction to this section of the text, remains the greatest novel of the region in the twentieth century, famous for its descriptions of the *llanos*, and ranking with Isaacs' *María* and Güiraldes' *Don Segundo Sombra* among South America's greatest novels. Its symbolic hero returns from his city education to the ranch he inherited, filled with progressive new ideas, and finally succeeds in driving out Doña Bárbara, a wicked woman who had usurped land and demoralized the countryside. Rómulo Gallegos, himself typifying the hero when he served briefly as president of a Venezuela demoralized by the Doña Bárbara-type dictators, spent years in exile while his book was widely read.

Philosophers, literary critics, and historians are very popular in both countries. Baldomiro Sanín Cano, born in Colombia in 1861, has been acclaimed as one of Latin America's greatest teachers, literary critics, and philosophers. His Venezuelan contemporary, José Gil Fortoul (1862–1943), has written the best constitutional history of Venezuela. Both countries have been interested in their history and have published much documentation concerning their heroes. Writers in these countries, as in most Latin American countries, cannot live solely by their pens, but must supplement their writing by other occupations.

Readings

Alexander, R. J., *Organized Labor in Latin America* (1965)
———, *Prophets of Revolution* (1962)
———, *Venezuelan Democratic Revolution* (1964)
Arcaya, P. M., *The Gómez Regime and Its Background* (1936)
Arciniegas, G., *Caribbean: Sea of the New World* (1946)
———, *Green Continent: A Comprehensive View of Latin America by Its Leading Writers*, trans. H. de Onis (1944)
Allen, H. J., *Venezuela: A Democracy* (1940)
Bernstein, H., *Modern and Contemporary Latin America* (1952)
———, *Venezuela and Colombia* (1964)
Callcott, W. H., *Caribbean Policy of the United States, 1890–1920* (1942)
Coester, A., *Literary History of Spanish America* (rev. ed., 1928)
Crist, R. E., *Cauca Valley, Land Tenure and Land Use* (1952)
———, *Venezuela* (1959)
Davis, H. D., ed., *Economic Development of Venezuela* (1961)
Eder, G., *et al.*, *Taxation in Colombia* (1965)
Fals-Borda, O., *Peasant Society in the Colombian Andes* (1955)
Fergusson, E., *Venezuela* (1939)
Fluharty, V., *Dance of the Millions: Military Rule and Social Revolution in Colombia, 1930–1956* (1957)
Friedman, J., *Regional Development Policy: A Case Study of Venezuela* (1966)
———, *Venezuela—From Doctrine to Dialogue* (1965)
Galbraith, W. O., *Colombia: A General Survey* (1953)
Gibson, W. M., *The Constitutions of Colombia* (1948)
Gordon, W. C., *Economy of Latin America* (1950)
Henao, J. M., and G. Arrubla, *History of Colombia*, trans. J. F. Rippy (1938)

Hirschman, A. O., *Journeys Towards Progress* (1963)

Holt, P. M., *Colombia Today and Tomorrow* (1964)

Hudson, M. O., *The Verdict of the League: Colombia and Peru at Leticia* (1933)

Hunter, J., *Emerging Colombia* (1962)

Inter-American Development Bank, *Economic Development of Venezuela* (1961)

———, *Fiscal Survey of Colombia* (1965)

International Bank of Reconstruction and Development, *The Basis of a Development Program for Colombia* [Currie Report] (1950)

Jankins, A. P., and N. M. Malloy, *Venezuela, Land of Opportunity* (1956)

Jones, C. L., *Caribbean Since 1900* (1936)

Lazardo, R., *Venezuela, Business and Finance* (1957)

Leavitt, S. E., and C. Garcia-Prada, *Tentative Bibliography of Colombian Letters* (1934)

Lieuwen, E., *Generals versus Presidents* (1964)

———, *Petroleum in Venezuela: A History* (1954)

———, *Venezuela* (1963)

Marsland, W. D., and A. L., *Venezuela Through Its History* (1954)

Martz, J. D., *Acción Democrática: Evolution of a Modern Political Party in Venezuela* (1965)

———, *Colombia: A Contemporary Political Survey* (1962)

Mecham, J. L., *Church and State in Latin America* (rev. ed., 1966)

Miner, D. C., *The Fight for the Panama Route: History of the Spooner Act and the Hay-Herran Treaty* (1940)

Moron, G., *History of Venezuela* (1964)

National Planning Commission, *Creole Petroleum Corporation in Venezuela* (1955)

Parks, E. T., *Colombia and the United States, 1765–1934* (1935)

Parsons, J., *Antiqueno Colonization in Western Colombia* (1949)

Public International Development Financing in Colombia (1963)

Ratcliff, D. F., *Venezuelan Prose Fiction* (1933)

Rippy, J. F., *The Capitalists and Colombia* (1931)

———, *Latin America and the Industrial Age* (1944)

Roberts, W. A., *Caribbean: Story of Our Sea of Destiny* (1940)

Romoli, K., *Colombia: Gateway to South America* (1941)

Rourke, T., *Gómez: Tyrant of the Andes* (1936)

Royal Institute of International Affairs, *Venezuela: A Brief Political and Economic Survey* (1956)

Serxner, S. J., *Unión Democrática of Venezuela: Its Origin and Development* (1958)

Taylor, P. C., *A Case Study of Relationship between Community Development and Agrarian Reform* (1961)

Torres-Rioseco, A., *Epic of Latin American Literature* (rev. ed., 1946)

Traba, M., *Art in Latin America Today: Colombia* (1959)

United States, Department of Commerce, Office of International Trade, *Investments in Colombia* (1953)

———, *Investments in Venezuela* (1953)

Watters, M. A., *History of the Church in Venezuela* (1933)

West, R. C., *The Pacific Lowlands of Colombia* (1957)

Whitaker, A. P., *United States and South America: The Northern Republics* (1948)

Whitbeck, R. H., *Economic Geography of South America* (rev. ed., 1940)

Wilgus, A. C., ed., *Caribbean Area* (1934)

———, *Caribbean: Contemporary Colombia* (1962)

————, *Caribbean: Venezuelan Development* (1963)
Wohlrabe, R. A., *Land and People of Venezuela* (1959)
Wood, B., *The United States and Latin American Wars, 1932–1942* (1966)
Wurfel, S. W., *Foreign Enterprise in Colombia: Law and Policies* (1965)
Wythe, G., *Industry in Latin America* (2nd ed., 1949)
Ybarra, Y. T., *Young Man of Caracas* (1941)

Chapter 38

Central America
in the Twentieth Century

COMMON PROBLEMS OF MIDDLE AMERICA

CENTRAL AMERICA consists of six tiny republics, the five which had broken apart from the Central American Federation of a century ago, and Panama which became independent of Colombia in 1903. Combined, the six republics cover about 218,000 square miles, less than half the area of Peru; a great part of the entire region is undeveloped mountain or jungle. The total population of the six Central American states in the late 1960s was estimated at 12,700,000, half the population of Argentina. In the export of important raw materials Central America in no way approaches either Peru or Venezuela; in industrial production it is where Argentina was a century ago. Its largest city, Guatemala City, has some 400,000 people. San Salvador with 236,000 people, and Tegucigalpa, Honduras, and San José de Costa Rica, with just over 100,000 people apiece, are national capitals. Over one-half of the Guatemalans, perhaps 20 per cent of the Hondurans, and at least 10 per cent of the Panamanians are non-Spanish speaking Indians whose way of life has changed little since 1492.

Why then the importance of this area? It is close to the United States, it stands between that country and South America, it is the Hemisphere at its narrowest point. There the United States built a canal, negotiated for the unilateral right to build on another route, plans to build on still a third route, and intervened to keep other nations from gaining influence. Secretary of State Philander Knox said in a speech in 1912, "Our tremendous national interest created by the Panama Canal make the safety, the peace, and the prosperity of Central America and the Caribbean of paramount interest to the government of the United States." For that reason, he said, the United States must "apply a remedy in these regions where the malady of revolution and financial collapse is most acute."

A single nation, a united federation, had seemed the solution for these "acute maladies," but the attempts to form it had failed throughout the nineteenth and early twentieth centuries. In 1906, when El Salvador and Honduras combined to fight a current dictator of Guatemala, Manuel Cabrera, Mexico and the United States intervened, fighting stopped, and a conference was held at San José de Costa Rica to formulate treaties which would help avoid such wars in the future. All attended except the Nicaraguan dictator Zelaya, who wanted a federation under his own leadership. In the following year, after two more interventions to preserve the peace, the five Central American nations sent representatives to meet at Washington to plan some way to avoid these little wars. A Central American Court of Justice was established, before which all future border controversies were to be heard. The Court was given a chance, in 1916, to settle controversies concerning the rights of El Salvador and Costa Rica in any future Nicaraguan Canal. Though the Court recognized these two claims, Nicaragua and the United States paid no attention and denounced the convention which had set up the Court. After this feeble beginning the Central American Court of Justice never met again. The Washington meeting in 1907 had set up the Central American International Bureau to deal with common cultural and economic problems. Six conferences were held under its auspices from 1909 to 1914, but its many conventions were never ratified, and the Bureau ceased to function in 1921.

On the downfall of the ambitious Cabrera in Guatemala in 1920, four of the Central American states attempted union again. El Salvador, Honduras, and Costa Rica accepted a plan for a unified plural executive representing all the states equally, but another revolution in Guatemala brought in a faction opposed to it. In 1923 a second conference in Washington resulted in a treaty of peace and eleven conventions on various subjects, signed by the five nations. No mechanism to preserve this peace was set up, and the treaties remained empty expressions. However, the five nations worked together during World War II, all declaring war against the Axis; all were active in the United Nations and the Organization of American States after 1945. Within the framework of the OAS, five of the Central American states formed a regional "League of Nations" called the ODECA. It did not establish a political union, but organized a common Supreme Court in 1962 and maintains a permanent secretariat. It has held several conferences of foreign ministers and educational ministers, and its economic successes led to the Common Market described below.

Economically, the nations have lived off coffee, bananas, or "patch and thatch" farm plots. The North American-owned United Fruit Company developed the banana industry for which Middle America is famous. Cultivated bananas were not native in the Americas, but roots from West African stock were taken to Santo Domingo by a priest in 1516. Slow-moving sailing ships could not bring such a perishable product to the United States, but by 1900 refrigerated ships made the popularization of bananas possible. Soon the United Fruit Company was clearing jungle land along the Caribbean coasts of Costa Rica, Honduras, and Guatemala, building ports and wharfs, and operating its own ships.

Botanists experimented with the plants, improved the root stock, and worked out efficient methods of planting, for this was all a new industry. Banana plants produce only one bunch of bananas; cutters must watch the green fruit for the exact day of cutting since it is never to be cut after ripening. The plant which has produced the one bunch then withers away, and the root stocks must be carefully cultivated so that a second plant will spring up and produce another bunch in eight or nine months. Thousands of square miles of "banana coast" are covered with rows of these self-perpetuating plants where two generations ago there was jungle.

It has not all been simple. The poor laboring classes of the Central American countries were *mestizos* and highland Indians, unaccustomed to and uninterested in heavy daily wage work in the tropics, so the company imported Negro laborers from the West Indies. This caused discrimination in an area where there had been few slaves in colonial days. Negroes, most of them underprivileged and uneducated, became the poor people of Puerto Barrios, Guatemala, of Port Limón, Costa Rica, and of Puerto Cortés,

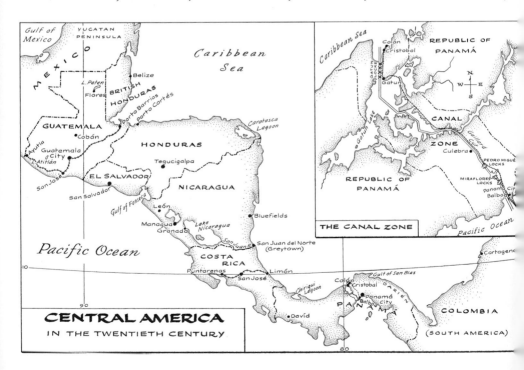

CENTRAL AMERICA
IN THE TWENTIETH CENTURY

Honduras. Any blight or disease of the banana plants, any political upheaval between the dominating company and a nationalistic-minded government meant economic upheaval for the workers. Abandoned plantations left the workers destitute while the company went on to develop new plantings elsewhere, perhaps near Santa Marta, Colombia, or Davíd, Panama.

In later years the reorganized United Fruit Company took better care of its employees. It taught them diversified farming, provided primary education and even several fine vocational and experimental agricultural schools. The company worked with the new unions of banana plantation laborers and allowed the governments to set wage and housing standards without interference. As a second crop, coffee is important in Guatemala and is the one crop of El Salvador; grown on small farms, with hand methods, it finds a ready market in America because of its flavor.

One of the main problems in Central America is that of transportation and communication, which the broken terrain makes difficult. Railroads are not numerous and generally run from the capitals to the coast. The Pan American Highway, built with United States aid, has recently connected the capitals of the Central American republics.

Foreign capital has also developed the forest extractive industries, hardwood lumber and chicle gathering. Mahogany was the reason for the British colony at Belize in the first place, and still provides revenue there and in Guatemala and Honduras. Chicle trees grow wild in the Petén region of Guatemala, where native and West Indian workers tap them. Used as a basis for chewing gum, chicle makes up a third of Guatemala's exports. Guatemala also draws a large revenue from the increasingly popular tourist trade. Its Maya ruins are accessible by plane, and its highland lakes are breathtakingly beautiful. Each of its mountain Indian villages specializes in a different weave and pattern of bright colors now being popularized by art- and craft-conscious Americans.

Isolation, a per capita income of $275 per family, a dependence on coffee and bananas for foreign exchange, a lack of modern industry and its products—all these things the five nations had in common. The political meetings of the ODECA led to the signing of five trade agreements from 1955 to 1962 to improve the area economically. Then in November 1962 the Latin American Common Market, an economic union, came into effective being. A Guatemalan economist, Dr. Pedro Abelardo Delgado, its first secretary-general, said, "Our five nations, averaging two million people each, cannot possibly find the resources to develop their economies if they work separately. So we combine." A common monetary unit, the Central American peso, was set up on a par with the United States dollar, and by 1966 all the paper transactions among the five nations were carried out in this unit, which by 1970 was to be in actual circulation, replacing the *colones, cordovas, lampiras,* and *quetzales* of the separate countries. The paper work was handled by the CABEI, the Central American Bank for Economic Integration, which, with United States aid, financed 60 per cent of any approved local industry—such as tire plants in Guatemala, cement in Costa Rica, refrigerated meat in Guatemala, automobile assembly in Salvador—which would cut the areas dependence on coffee and bananas.

In the former United Fruit company town of San Pedro Sula in Honduras, sixteen such new factories were in operation by 1966. Inter-Central American trade leaped from $32,000,000 in 1960 to over $130,000,000 in 1966. The growth rate of the gross national product of the region grew from 4.5 per cent a year in 1963 to almost double that figure in 1966, the best growth rate in the Western Hemisphere.

By 1966 the common market was still employing only Dr. Delgado and six secretaries, housed in a six-room house next to a grocery store in Guatemala City, but its activities had spread to other fronts. In 1965, 850,000 Central American school children had received free copies of first and second grade school books printed by the common market's educational committee. Ministers of agriculture had met to set minimum prices on corn, rice and beans from country to country. A thousand miles of village-to-market roads had been started. Laborers crossed borders freely to go where workers were needed, using a common passport to travel. "Persons born in the member states of the Central American Common Market shall be considered in any of the states as nationals of that state," read a resolution of the common market board in issuing such passports. This free movement of workers brought in the political ODECA again to establish plans for a single diplomatic corps, a common citizenship, a single graduate-level university, a regional telecommunications network, and a joint public health plan. The Central American Common Market was surprising the Hemisphere in the late 1960's.

Socially, there are still great contrasts and inequalities. The major part of Central America is *mestizo*. There are the Negro workers from the West Indies on the Caribbean coast. There are the half-naked primitive Indians in Honduras and in Panama, the picturesque and isolated San Blas Indians off the Panamanian coast. Of all pure Indian groups in Latin America today, the spinners and weavers of Guatemala's hill towns are best known to North Americans. Tourists have seen the elders of Chichicastenango, in hand-embroidered black wool, burning pagan incense on the steps of the church of Santo Tomás, or the men of San Martín Chile Verde in red-striped clothing walking the long mountain miles to market in Sololá on Lake Atitlán. Anthropologists study their religious beliefs, sociologists their land ownership systems, artists their textile designs. They still constitute a very large majority of Guatemala's total population. Bringing them modern schooling is difficult, as their language is Maya-Quiché, or Zutuhile, or Cakchiquel. Only the men who go to market know any Spanish. An increasingly large group of semi-urbanized Spanish-speaking Indians and *mestizos* in Guatemala are called *Ladinos*.

El Salvador, Nicaragua, and Honduras are *mestizo*, while the highland area of Costa Rica away from the coast is almost entirely European white. Culture patterns in the towns seem similar to those of many other parts of Latin America. Central America at the turn of the century produced one great cultural "hero," the Nicaraguan poet named Rubén Darío, who had such a profound effect on Latin American literature that he has already been mentioned in several other chapters. No figure anywhere near his equal has appeared in the divided little countries in the twentieth century.

Gatun Locks on the Caribbean side of the Panama Canal. *Courtesy Panama Canal Company.*

One poet, Joaquín Pasos (1905–1947), reflects the Central American environment in recent times. Guatemala has a modern-style university, and a National Library, whose director, Rafael Arévalo Martínez (born in 1884), has achieved some fame as a novelist, writing on themes connected with nature. Carlos Mérida (born in 1893) and Humberto Garavito have painted the Indian life of Central America and earned some recognition in the United States. The Costa Rican Joaquín García Monge is the world-famous editor of a literary review, *Repertorio Americano*, published in San José and considered one of the most important cultural periodicals in today's Latin America and a consistent voice for democracy.

THE PANAMA CANAL
AND THE NATION AROUND IT

> Hail, prodigy of human effort!—
> Hail to you, Inter-Oceanic Canal,—
> Magnificent reality!
> My country bears in her breast
> The deep wound that opened this artery of the dark sea.
> It rends her entrails; and, with emotion,
> She offers herself nobly to the sacrifice
> To exclaim: "For the good of the world!"[1]

[1] Alice Stone Blackwell, *Some Spanish American Poets* (New York: Appleton Century, 1929), p. 526. Reprinted by permission of the University of Pennsylvania Press, copyright owners.

So wrote Benigno Palma (1882–1930[?]), Panamanian poet, when the Canal was opened to world traffic in 1915. It had been the dream of Spanish explorers and kings that there be a passage through Panama. As American Secretary of State, Henry Clay had asked for a report on its possibilities in 1825; by the Clayton-Bulwer Treaty of 1850 England and America had stalled each other's ambitions there by agreeing that neither nation would build a canal to the exclusion of the other. The United States conquest of California and the gold-rush crossings of the 1850s had re-emphasized the need for a ship passage. Finally, in the 1870s such a project had apparently been proved possible by the construction of a canal through Suez. Ferdinand de Lesseps, builder of the Suez Canal, had received a charter from Colombia, of which Panama was then a province, and in 1879 had financed a stock company and begun digging. Here, however, he did not have the flat, sandy isthmus he had at Suez, but an area of mountains, swamps, and yellow fever. In the eight years de Lesseps' Company worked at the diggings, 40,000 laborers and engineers died of the fever, and the company went bankrupt before two-fifths of the work was done.

When the forceful Theodore Roosevelt became President of the United States, he determined to promote the completion of the canal. First, the Hay-Pauncefote Treaty with England gave the United States the right to build a canal by itself. Then the agent of the defunct French Company, Philippe Buneau-Varilla, agreed to sell all the French rights as well as the abandoned machinery to the United States for only $40,000,000. Secretary of State Hay next arranged with the Colombian foreign minister Herrán to lease a zone across the isthmus for the American project. The Colombian senate, torn by factionalism, turned this treaty down in the hopes of a higher price.

The impatient Roosevelt, the anxious Buneau-Varilla, and a small group of independence-minded Panamanians were in no mood for further treaties. When the Colombian government sent 500 soldiers to Panama's Caribbean port to quell any possible revolt, the American-owned Panama Railway refused to transport the "army" across the Isthmus to Panama City, the center of "revolt." On November 3, 1903, with the American gunboat *U.S.S. Nashville* conveniently in the harbor, the republic of Panama was proclaimed, after a street fight in Panama City in which one life was lost. Naturally, Theodore Roosevelt recognized the new country immediately, and made plans for a canal treaty with the young republic. Roosevelt's act was acclaimed in the United States, but Colombian pride was hurt, and Latin Americans everywhere were affronted at the "rape of Panama."

But the "dirt began to fly," as Roosevelt himself said. Disclaiming any protectorate of Panama, the United States leased a zone ten miles wide for 99 years. Here a corps of engineers arranged for the drawing of plans, the hiring of laborers, the maintenance of spur railways, the allocation of supplies and machinery, all on a scale unprecedented in any human undertaking up to that time. Yellow fever had just been conquered by the Cuban Carlos Finlay and American doctors in Havana after the Spanish American War; United States Army Surgeon William Crawford Gorgas wiped the mosquitoes out of Panama so vigorously that the last yellow fever case reported on the canal workings was in 1906. Thus the jungle enemy which had defeated de Lesseps was in turn defeated by the American builders.

Colonel George W. Goethals of the United States Army Engineers was in charge of building the canal—forty-five feet deep, through thirty-five miles of locks, upland lakes, and newly created highland ditch, with fifteen miles of approaches dredged out at sea level, to make a total of fifty miles of ship passage. Three locks were built to raise ships a total of eighty-five feet from the Atlantic, three more to lower them to the Pacific on the other side. The ditch between the locks was blasted out of the mountains; the Chagres River was controlled and its water made available for the locks and the new cut.

For all this, thousands of unskilled workers from the Negro populations of the West Indies were brought in, creating a social problem of segregation and discrimination inherited later by the Panamanian Republic. At last on August 15, 1914, a warship used in the construction made the first transit. The following spring regular freight and passenger traffic was begun, ships from all the world paying toll equally at $1 per ton, averaging $4,500 per ship and saving 8,000 miles over the Round-the-Horn route.

A ship coming in from the Pacific enters Panama Bay along six miles of dredged channel and proceeds through Balboa Basin to the Miraflores Locks. Here, by means of two stair-step locks; the vessel is lifted fifty-five feet to the level of Miraflores Lake, eight miles from the Pacific. The artificially created Miraflores Lake, two miles across, ends at the Pedro Miguel Lock, where the vessel is again raised thirty feet. Now the ship is in the true canal, the Gaillard Cut, a quiet channel cutting through the hills of the Isthmus. It opens out into the old course of the Chagres River, where the waters were dammed up to create the twenty-three-mile long Gatún Lake. After crossing the lake, the ship reaches the Atlantic port of Colón, and is lowered through three Gatún locks the eighty-five feet to the level of the Atlantic. The whole journey takes about eight hours, and increasing world trade calls for a clearance of this bottleneck by a second canal.

In the ten-mile leased strip called the Zone, the town of Balboa grew up on the Pacific end, Cristobal on the Atlantic. In these towns the American colony has kept itself isolated, shopping at government commissaries and discriminating against colored employees. Panama City, with a population of more than 350,000, is contiguous to Balboa on the Pacific side; its *mestizo* and Negro population has had good reason to resent the exclusive American colony. Most of the remainder of the Panamanians live at the Atlantic port, Colón, with about 60,000 people, connected to Panama City by highway and rail, or in the coconut and banana plantations around David, a town of 15,000 to the north on the Pacific plain. The great part of the interior has not been developed. Though the Pan American Highway has been pushed in the north to the Costa Rican border, the Darien region southeast of the Canal was as impenetrable in the late 1960's as in Balboa's day. Panamanians exist on interoceanic transportation, and on the export of small amounts of cacao, coffee, rubber, sugar, bananas, and mahogany.

When the canal was being built, the United States had agreed to pay Panama $10,000,000 in payment for the lease, and $250,000 annual rental for use of the watercourse. Though greatly benefited by American sanitary control and yellow fever eradication, and by the enormous business boom the canal brought, Panamanians have often resented the United States. The United States continued to control Panamanian foreign affairs, under a treaty arrangement like the Platt Amendment in Cuba.

The domestic history of Panama as a nation closely follows the pattern of other Caribbean nations, including fraud and violence in elections, and revolutions stopped by United States intervention. A growing spirit of nationalism and anti-American feeling developed during the depression. At the same time, politics waxed hot as rival families tried to hold the presidency. Harmodio Arias was elected in 1932 on a platform of changing the treaty binding Panama to the United States. A new treaty was ratified in 1939, several years after Arias fell from power; in it the United States gave up the right to intervene in Panamanian affairs and upped the yearly rent payments for the Canal Zone to $430,000 in return for the right to build strategic air bases near the Canal. This arrangement was soon disrupted by the election of Harmodio Arias' brother Arnulfo Arias, an ardent pro-Nazi, in 1940. He had little long-term influence, for an attempt to increase his power by changing the constitution brought his downfall.

Pearl Harbor brought Panama back to the side of the United States, with Ricardo Adolfo de la Guardia inaugurated as a pro-American president. Good working relations were reached between the United States and Panama over air bases and canal defense throughout World War II, but the "American Question" has remained a big issue of Panamanian politics. The election in 1952 of the very popular pro-American president, José Remón, promised a future of cooperation with the United States and economic and social improvement of Panama. But this rare political stability was rudely smashed when Remón was assassinated in January 1955, and his immediate successor was held for trial for the murder. Panamanian politics promised to remain turbulent, to follow the pattern that in a half-century of history had given the new state twenty-eight presidents, only five of whom have finished their term in office. In a hectic election in May 1956, another member of the de la Guardia family, Ernesto Jr., was elected, to become Panama's twenty-ninth president. His Arias family rival attempted to take the government in the spring of 1959 by landing a handful of Cuban adventurers, but la Guardia wisely applied to the Organization of American States, formerly the Pan American Union, which quickly voted to send "investigators," and the comic opera invaders surrendered.

Remón's pro-American policy had paid off in a new arrangement with the United States which was completed after his death. In 1956 the Canal Zone rental was to be upped again to $1,930,000 a year. The United States agreed to end its enforcement of sanitary measures, its monopoly on railroad construction, its special commissary privileges for its own employees, its discrimination against Panamanians in employment. This treaty went into effect in 1956. In June of 1955 the United States agreed to extend Point Four aid to Panama until 1960, and to work jointly to improve health, education, and diversified agriculture in the undeveloped backlands. A Panamanian Institute of Economic Development was set up to continue road building, to search for new sources of wealth, to improve-the backlands, and to develop balanced agriculture.

These new arrangements were given no time to succeed. The sensitive Panamanians wanted some immediate recognition of their independent status. On November 3, 1958, the fifty-fifth anniversary of their independence from Colombia, a parade of floats, girls in national costume, and children bearing flags marched through the streets of Panama City and attempted to take their Panamanian flags across the dividing street into the Canal Zone at the Balboa city line. The paraders were turned back by American soldiers and a riot ensued. Bad feeling continued throughout the next year until President Eisenhower ordered the Panamanian flag to be shown equally with the American flag in Shaler's Triangle, a public garden inside Balboa. The Independence Day parade in November 1959 came peacefully into the park and both flags flew together. This conciliatory gesture was repeated in 1960.

Meanwhile, in May 1960, a peaceful election was held in which the moderate businessman, Roberto Chiari, was elected. He was to be the first Panamanian president in twenty-five years to complete his full term. President John F. Kennedy ordered that the United States flag was not to be displayed in the Canal Zone unless accompanied by an equally large Panamanian flag at the same level. With this reassurance, Chiari backed his reputation on his friendly relations with the United States.

But in January 1964 an American high school boy in the Canal Zone High School insisted on flying the American flag from the school balcony in the face of a marching group of Panamanian students. In the three days of rioting which ensued, twenty-three people were killed, including four American soldiers. The Johnson administration temporarily called home its ambassador from Panama City.

During the same year American experts were considering the need for a new canal through the Isthmus. Many military and merchant ships were too large to use the Panama locks; ships waited two days for a turn to pass through the bottle-neck of slow locks. By 1990 the canal would be completely inadequate for world trade. New atomic blasting methods could perhaps build a sea-level canal elsewhere in Central America. Panamanians were alarmed at such talk. Any increase in traffic should be in a widened canal in the old bed, or in less populated areas elsewhere in Panama. Eleven thousand Panamanians were working in the Zone; a hundred million dollars a year poured into Panama yearly from canal business. Panamanian nationalists began to call the canal "Our Natural Resource." The United States was "morally obligated" to maintain it, they said.

Meanwhile a peaceful election was held in May of 1964 and a cousin of Chiari, Marco Robles, was elected—a plurality president in a field of seven candidates. He was inaugurated in October 1964 with a platform of "make a new treaty about the canal, abolish the privileges of the Zone, but keep any new canal in Panama." The United States had sent commissioners to sound out Colombia on the use of a ninety-five-mile, near-sea-level route through the jungle country at the base of the Isthmus, and to talk with Costa Rica and Nicaragua about a sea-level canal to run 139 miles parallel to their common border. President Johnson announced that a new canal would be begun before 1970 on a sea-level route, and would cost two billion dollars.

Faced with the fear of losing the new canal, Panamanians backed President Marco Robles to reach an agreement with the United States. Negotiations were begun in October 1965. The new treaty was to "effectively recognize Panamanian sovereignty," to "grant Panamanian participation in Canal operation," and to cover any new sea-level canal built anywhere in Panama. Johnson allocated $17,500,000 for a three-year survey of two additional routes in Panama as well as the other Central American routes, and the possibility of widening and deepening the 1903 canal.

President Robles then concentrated on internal development with Alliance for Progress funds. Panama showed an 8 per cent gross national product increase in 1965, ahead of most of the rest of the Hemisphere. The value of shipments in and out of Panama was rising 20 per cent a year in the late 1960s, and Panamanians were maintaining the Colón Free Zone, neither joining the Central American nor the Latin American Common Market, but acting as a fulcrum between the two trading areas. The interracial slums of Panama City, such an eyesore to canal visitors, were being cleaned up under Robles' development program. With a fair canal settlement reached, the little country of 550 square miles and a million and a quarter people seemed headed for a better future in the 1970s.

GUATEMALAN POLITICS:
COMMUNISM OR "CAUDILLISMO"

Guatemala, largest of the Central American republics and one of the prime tourist attractions of the Western Hemisphere, is listed in guidebooks as "the most fascinating spot within a night's flight of the United States." But here in the ancient land of the Maya, the food on which Communist doctrine thrives is ever present—underprivileged masses of people, exploitation by a few foreign companies, class and race discrimination, a peonage system of land tillage, a high rate of illiteracy—and was present under *caudillismo* throughout the first half of the twentieth century.

Manuel Estrada Cabrera had been vice-president when President Reynosa Barrios was assassinated in 1898. Though a civilian, Cabrera proceeded to set up a military despotism which kept him in power for twenty-two years. Old age was his only serious enemy; in 1920 his own congress voted him mentally incapacitated to hold office, and a revolution threw him out. Guatemala had profited not in the least by his long tenure. Four presidents and eleven years later, he was followed by another dictator.

Jorge Ubico was Guatemala's second *caudillo* of the twentieth century. Though acting as absolute ruler, he improved the lot of the Indians to such an extent that they called him "Tata" or grandfather. He legally ended their peonage on the land, enforced better treatment for plantation workers, and built some schools for their children in the larger hamlets. He also balanced the budget and had money left over for schools for the

Spanish-speaking children in every large town, and for roads connecting the towns with the capital. Ubico was a friend of Central American cooperation and joined in conferences with his fellow-dictators in neighboring countries. Though there was a German majority in the coffee-rich town of Cobán and the province of Alta Vera Paz, Tata Ubico maintained strong sympathies with the Allies, declared war against Germany right after Pearl Harbor, and allowed American troops to use Guatemalan bases; thus wartime prosperity came to Guatemala.

During a world war to end dictatorship, Ubico's repressions of speech and press caused repercussions among the students and laboring people in his own capital. Though comprising a very small percentage of the Guatemalans, this new group put on a general strike in 1944 which paralyzed all business in the modern little city. Tata Ubico was not to see the end of the war, for the strikers got him out of power in July, a year before VE Day. An interim triumvirate—Committee of Liberation—took over the government, held elections in December of 1944, and chose Juan José Arévalo as president for a six-year term. The new group tackled the problems of Guatemala in a new constitution in 1945 which granted unusually broad social reforms. Here began the faint suspicions that the Communist party was becoming a strong influence in Guatemala.

The Indians, though emancipated from ties to the land, still did not own the farmland themselves, and had not improved their condition. The newly politically conscious labor group in the city listened to any rabble-rouser. Many people were angry at North American companies, especially the United Fruit, which had exerted so much influence on Ubico. While the radicals yelled at "Yankee imperialism, colonialism, and monopoly," the North American companies made offers of adjustment and improved labor relations, calling attention to their fine housing and hospitals for plantation workers, but Arévalo, out of touch with things after years of exile in Argentina, answered all these pros and cons with a vagueness he called "mystic socialism." This went on for six years of speechmaking and little other activity, while Communist infiltration gained control of the city workers' group.

In the election of 1951, the left-wing groups backed Jacobo Arbenz Guzmán, who had been a personal friend of Arévalo, his Minister of Defense, and the boss of the Guatemalan army. Though not personally a Communist, Arbenz, a half-Swiss military career man who had risen to dominance of the army under Ubico, was radical in his sympathies with Indians and labor, but so ambitious personally for his own power as to use such sympathies to his own ends. His wife, who was educated abroad, was an idealistic Marxist. One of their closest associates was an avowed Marxist named Fortuny, who dominated the Labor Party. With Arévalo's tacit support, Arbenz won the election easily and was inaugurated March 15, 1951.

Arbenz had promised his followers "action." Within the next year his government had nationalized the United States-owned electric company, had expropriated 234,000 acres of the Pacific holdings of the United Fruit Company, and was threatening the 174,000 acres on the Atlantic.

Private landowners, coffee plantation holders, and any other large estate owners who kept land out of cultivation were in danger of government confiscation. Arbenz promised to redistribute this land to small owners and to Indian villages. No actual Communists were in the Arbenz cabinet, but the party controlled the Guatemalan newspapers and wrote scurrilous articles against the United States in the press. Their party had control of Congress by 1953, holding forty-six of the fifty-seven seats, and gained control of press and radio. Moscow radio programs were heard loud and clear throughout the country.

What could the United States do? To intervene on behalf of the United Fruit Company was to bring down on its head all the old charges of imperialism the Good Neighbor policy had so hoped to silence. When enemies of Arbenz were given refuge in the neighboring states, Guatemala threatened armed reprisals. Reaction in other countries gave the United States the hope of using joint public opinion pressure rather than direct intervention. At the Caracas meeting of the Organization of American States early in the spring 1954, Secretary of State Dulles pushed through a resolution condemning Communist activity in the Western Hemisphere. In May of 1954 Arbenz received a shipload of armaments from Communist Poland. Somoza, the dictator of Nicaragua, as well as leaders in Costa Rica and Honduras where anti-Arbenz exiles were active, feared the direct use of such arms in a big Central American melee. The United States could now send arms and planes to these smaller neighbors under new mutual assistance agreements without fear of too much criticism.

At this tense moment, *caudillismo* came to the front again. On the border in Honduras a former Secretary of War under Ubico, Carlos Castillo Armas, who represented the rightist army faction, was collecting arms and training a band of peasants for an invasion. In Guatemala City only the very small minority of factory workers knew what Communism was all about anyway, and Arbenz' hold on the populace was weakening. The army was ready to desert him and join Castillo Armas, who had planes and pilots to fly over and drop leaflets on the capital. While the United Nations and the Organization of American States viewed this menace of Communism with alarm, and called for a meeting in July, the ragged rebel army crossed the border into Guatemala.

Now there did not need to be any international investigation of the activities of the Communist party in Guatemala, because Castillo Armas' forces came triumphantly into the city. Arbenz finally found exile abroad, and the two leading Communists, José Manuel Fortuny and a writer named Carlos Manuel Pellecer, disappeared into Europe behind the iron curtain. In October, Castillo Armas, who had been in military control of the city since summer, was elected by a 99 per cent vote, and started a term supposedly to run until 1960.

First Castillo Armas had to settle the confusion in the land relocation affair. He allowed small holders who had been given lands to maintain them if they had been planted, and then announced a long range, five-year rural improvement program, including regulations for installment buying of small farm plots. The plans for developing undeveloped lands and for finishing the Pan American Highway from Mexico to bring in more dollar-spending tourists all needed time. Castillo Armas himself, a career army man with no administrative experience, brought only disappointment to his backers who hoped for efficiency and democracy rather than mere military *caudillismo* as an answer to the problems which had aroused Communist sentiment in the first place.

Meanwhile the United Fruit Company agreed to pay taxes on the Standard Oil Company pattern for Venezuela, and to turn over more unused land for distribution. This land, however, is in the tropics, and not in the highlands where the Indians live so poorly.

Castillo Armas was in power long enough to promulgate a new constitution, a "model of good intentions." No one was to ever know if Castillo Armas intended to be a "constitutional president" and hold a legal election at the end of his term, for he was assassinated by a pro-Arbenz army guard in August 1957. A military *junta* took control until an election could be held in November 1957. Miguel Ydígoras Fuentes, ambassador to London and delegate on UN committees, though described as a "crusty old soldier," won the city vote, but his opponent claimed a victory by fraudulent counting of rural votes. Three days of street fighting followed the announcement of Ydígoras' defeat until another military *junta* took control and cancelled the election. The *junta* then held an indecisive second election and tossed the choice to congress, which arranged a truce of the two factions. Ydígoras was peacefully inaugurated in March 1958.

As the 1960's approached Guatemala's population neared 4,500,000. But the Maya-Quichés, the Zutuhiles, the Cakchiqueles, and all other descendants of the Maya—who are the majority of all Guatemalans—still lived in their thatched villages at the bases of the volcanoes around the shores of azure-blue Lake Atitlán and in the deep *barrancas* and high ridges of Alta Vera Paz and Huehuetenango. In all such communities, the local tribal *alcaldes* are the only government that touches the people. Most of these picturesque Indian people never have heard about Communism at all, and doubtless did not realize they could have held an election in 1964.

Ydígoras was not to serve out his six-year term. A moderate, he concentrated on activating the new Central American Common Market agreements and hoped to rally support by quarreling with England over Belize. He was ardently anti-Communist, and allowed Cuban exiles to train for the Bay of Pigs landings on Guatemalan soil. When the Bay of Pigs attempt failed, Guatemala City student leftists rioted and Ydígoras proclaimed a state of martial law. By 1963 moderates were joining leftists in opposition. Former-president Arévalo headed this opposition in preparation for the 1964 elections. But the conservative army had pledged never to allow Arévalo to be president again. Defense Minister Enrique Peralta Azurdía, an austere career officer, staged a *coup*, Ydígoras went into voluntary exile, and Colonel Peralta ran the country by military decree under a new constitution. This was the fourth constitution for Guatemala in twenty years.

Finally, in February 1966, after three years of military government, Peralta permitted a free and open election. In a three-cornered fight between two colonels and a civilian, the civilian won by a plurality. He was Julio César Méndez Montenegro, a quiet, moderate dean of the University of Guatemala Law School. He did not win an absolute majority, and the election was decided in the newly elected congress in May of 1966. By November, 1966, Communist guerillas in the back country and rightists in the army gave Méndez Montenegro such trouble that he declared a "state of siege"—canceling civil rights—which lasted into early 1967. Still he hoped to maintain his basically civilian rule for a six-year term to 1972, a feat accomplished by only one civilian president since Guatemala's independence. Meanwhile former-president Arévalo, once considered a dangerous leftist, was devoting himself to a UNESCO program to set up a television set in every village which had electric power, in order to teach literacy in the Spanish language to Guatemala's Maya-speaking Indians.

EL SALVADOR: POCKET-HANDKERCHIEF
COUNTRY IN THE COFFEE BUSINESS

Facing on the Pacific side only, at midpoint in Central America, lies the tiny country of El Salvador, no bigger than Maryland. It is the smallest, most industrialized, most prosperous, and most densely populated of the Central American republics, with a total population of 2,800,000. To the confusion of most North Americans, the nation is really named El Salvador, "the Savior," while its capital and only large town is named San Salvador, "Holy Savior." This city has 256,000 people; the small towns and open farming country and the two tiny ports have enough population, very thickly settled, to make over two-and-a-third million. The farmland is almost perfect for coffee, of a certain flavorful type which brings high prices in the United States. Thus El Salvador is prosperous when coffee prices are high, but suffers from all the difficulties of a one-crop country. Its coffee *fincas* are small, owned by small native landholders; no powerful estate owners, no foreign banana company dominates El Salvador. El Salvador came into existence in the first place because of her quarrels with Guatemalan dictators inside the Central American federation. Much of her history has been concerned with avoiding or being dominated by Guatemalan leaders. She has always been a friend of Central American federation; in the 1950s her President Osorio took the lead in bringing about the Organization of Central American States, the ODECA, set up as a regional arrangement under the OAS in 1951. El Salvador also encouraged the free trade "common market" for Central America. She has faithfully followed a policy of nonintervention in other neighbors' business, though her presidents have maintained large armies, chiefly to keep themselves in power. Many of the army conscripts are given practical instruction in agriculture and real steps have been taken to improve health, sanitation, and literacy.

Twenty families have usually rotated the presidency and joined in the typical *cuartelazo* or barracks revolt to throw opponents out of office. The Meléndez family held the reigns from 1913 to 1927, Carlos Meléndez being succeeded by his brother and then his brother-in-law. The Meléndez presidents kept El Salvador neutral during World War I and brought prosperity to the coffee business. Shortly after they fell from power, depression hit the one-crop country and riots ensued. The army took over the government and its candidate Maximiliano Hernández Martínez became dictator with a ruthless control that lasted from 1931 to 1944. However, he did tackle some of El Salvador's problems, building roads, promoting scientific agriculture, and parceling out land grants to small owners. During World War II Martínez changed from admiration of Hitler to full cooperation with the Allies, declaring war and receiving United States aid.

Before the war was over, Martínez' own people had turned against him in a general strike, which caused his fall and brought years of political chaos. The liberal-minded commercial class in the capital combining with the army finally was able to control the situation and make Oscar Osorio president in 1949. Copying the successes of larger nations, Osorio, under a new and liberal constitution which granted women suffrage and offered protection to labor and small farmers, launched a five-year plan and an Institute for Development. This Institute helped him build up diversified agriculture and industry with the assistance of American experts. In September 1956 his friend José María Lemus peacefully succeeded him and continued to carry out his development plans.

The "Cuban Communism" issue led to Lemus' downfall, however, for he openly backed Guatemala's efforts to help train the Cuban exiles for the Bay of Pigs attempt. Leftists took this action as indicating Lemus' intention to make no social reforms at home. Their strikes and riots brought the army into control again through a military *junta*. The *junta* backed the new common market, however, and carried out the reforms required by it and the Alliance for Progress.

In July 1962 Colonel Alberto Rivera was inaugurated with the backing of the *junta*, under a new constitution which extended his term to July 1967. A young man from the poorer classes, Rivera continued the common market reforms, used the new Central American textbooks to found 926 new reading-teaching centers staffed by literate army men. With full employment and with science applied to diversified crops, El Salvador's gross national product increased by 8.1 per cent in 1965, the fastest increase in Latin America. Rivera is devoted to progress, and has set up a program of broad and meaningful social and economic reform which should push El Salvador toward greater prosperity by the mid-1970s. Colonel Fidel Sanchez Hernandez was inaugurated in July 1967 and will carry on the enlightened policies of the Rivera military administration.

HONDURAS: LAND OF THICK FOREST AND SPARSE POPULATION

Today Honduras is the most backward nation of Central America. Its soil is not good for coffee; it has no good port on the Caribbean and only the tiny port of Amapala on the Gulf of Fonseca facing the Pacific. It has the greatest deposits of mineral wealth between Mexico and Colombia, but few good roads to transport the ores out if they were mined. Even so, silver and gold make up nearly a fourth of Honduran exports, and mahogany and other hardwoods equal another fourth. Forty-six per cent of the export trade is in bananas; Honduras is the country most often thought of when the term "banana republic" is used and is the nation whose politics have been most closely controlled by the United Fruit Company. Tegucigalpa, the capital and largest city with 137,000 out of the small total population of just over 2,000,000, is not on the Pan American Highway, nor on any rail line to anywhere, although there is a new paved road which runs from the port of Amapala across the highway and into the capital

The air age has brought this isolated little country together. A small air company called TACA, organized on a shoestring in the 1920s with American World War veterans as pilots, began to build landing fields in every Honduran town, and even flew out the gold ore being mined by primitive methods in the hills. Later taken over by the Pan American Airways, this pioneering air venture put Tegucigalpa in touch with the world.

In politics Honduras has been a century behind the times, remaining in the "age of *caudillos*." Any detailed description of small-town dictators, *cuartelazo* revolutions, and "permanent presidents" in Honduras is of little importance in the whole history of Latin American civilization. An ignorant soldier, Tiburcio Carías Andino, became the power behind the throne in 1923, making and unmaking presidents. He became president himself in a fraudulent election held in 1932, and lasted until old age forced him to resign in 1948. Though he ruled by force, allowed no free speech, and kept the jails full of his political enemies, he maintained a stable government and developed mining and aviation. When he stepped down, he still controlled his personal political party and arranged the election of his successor, Juan Manuel Gálvez.

During his term, 1948 to 1954, Gálvez attempted real constitutional government, and took the first steps to modernize the nation's economy. One of his changes was the encouragement of organized labor and the limitation of foreign companies. He made a new contract with the United Fruit Company, which included the payment of 30 per cent of the company's profits in taxes to the government. The contract did not include enough rights for the workers, and there was a serious strike, which gave rise to a labor party which in turn has brought new candidates as well as confusion and violence into recent elections. Strikes in the banana plantations combined with devastating floods and leaf disease brought about the abandonment of the Honduran plantings by the United Fruit Company for new fields elsewhere. In its later years of Honduran activity, the company did much for its workers in the way of sanitation, housing, and education.

Insisting on free elections, Gálvez held one in 1954, but the three-cornered electoral campaign resulted in no majority and in political uncertainty. Taking advantage of the impasse, vice-president Julio Lozano Díaz assumed executive power and acted as a dictator while concentrating on economic and social development and engineering his election in October 1956. But the army ousted him in Honduras' 135th revolution. Elections were held for a constituent assembly in September 1957. In November the constituent assembly elected Liberal Party leader Ramón Villeda Morales as president and brought to an end the regime of the military *junta* which had been in power since October 21, 1956.

The six-year term of Villeda Morales approached its end in peace and progress, with the president signing an agrarian land reform bill and attempting to put Alliance for Progress programs into effect. But Honduras' 136th military coup ousted him sixty days before his term was up in October 1963. He was replaced by Colonel Osvaldo López Arellano, who seemed set to continue military rule as an old type *caudillo*. However, elections were held for a constituent assembly on February 16, 1965, and the assembly thus elected converted itself into a national congress, promoted Osvaldo López Arellano from colonel to general, and made him president for a six-year term to last until 1971.

Throughout the entire twentieth century, Honduras has been at peace with her neighbors, and, having the least to lose from union, has always been the most favorable toward united action of all kinds in Central America. With the spurt brought to Honduras by the common market, with Alliance for Progress help in promoting new industries in San Pedro Sula, and new roads between towns, Honduras had made some progress toward the 1970s in spite of confused government.

NICARAGUA: CANAL RIGHTS, INTERVENTION, AND DICTATORS

Nicaragua, situated where the Isthmus begins to narrow down, is blessed with lakes and river connections which made it a possible route from Atlantic to Pacific. This fact warped its history in the nineteenth century and continued to be a factor in its intra-Hemisphere relations well into the twentieth. Larger than Guatemala, Nicaragua has a third as many people. Only a very small fraction of its population of 1,600,000 are primitive Indians; perhaps 10 per cent are Negroes on the Caribbean coast; the remainder are *mestizos*. Though the economy is based on agriculture— coffee, cattle, and a new interest in cotton predominating—a third of its people live in Granada, León, and Managua, the three cities—actually only large towns—which huddle in mountain valleys along the lake shore just a ridge from the Pacific. On the Atlantic side Nicaragua is as dense a jungle as is the Petén region of Guatemala. In 1900 it was a *caudillo*-ruled country, and still is today. But the possibilities of a canal and the necessity of preventing European nations from building it kept the United States involved there, rightly or wrongly, until the Franklin Roosevelt era.

At the turn of the century, José Santos Zelaya (1893–1909) had been dictator for seven years, coming at the end of a long period of Conservative rule. Unusually ruthless and selfish, he had done few things to promote the progress of his country and had made many personal enemies, especially among the governments of the neighboring countries with whom he constantly interfered. In the face of civil war and international complications, Zelaya resigned in December 1909 in favor of a short-lived puppet. When the leader of the anti-Zelaya revolt, Juan Estrada, came into Managua as president in August 1910, he found the country so disorganized, so deeply in debt to foreign powers, that he asked the United States for aid.

Thus began the United States' fiscal, electoral, and military intervention in this Latin American nation. Marines were to stay in Nicaragua from

1910 to 1934, save for a few months in 1925. Naval vessels were in the harbor, financial advisors in the customs house, guards at the legation. Technical experts supervised elections and drew up long-range plans for improved administration and debt payment. A national guard, the now famous *Guardia Nacional*, was trained by American Marine officers. All this was justified by American presidents and statesmen as necessary on strategic grounds, for it defended the canal route and protected future canal rights. Financially, such American military control prevented European intervention to collect debts and arranged their ultimate payment. In the first three decades of the twentieth century, however, the United States' employment of the Marines brought it enmity from the rest of the Hemisphere. Latin American critics scornfully called the program "Dollar Diplomacy" or, more often, *Imperialismo*.

The chronology of Nicaraguan developments is confusing. Estrada's government, coming into power by force when Zelaya left, fought a bloody civil war for two years. When the war was over, America supervised the next two elections, 1913 and 1917, and policed the country to ensure peaceful four-year terms for the winners. Since these winning candidates were leaders of the Conservative party, as anti-Zelayists in the first place, the United States had the reputation of automatically backing Conservatives.

Interest in possible canal rights was made secure through the Conservatives. The Bryan-Chamorro Treaty, ratified in 1916, gave the United States an option to build a canal along the San Juan River-Lake Nicaragua route, in return for an outright grant of $3,000,000. When the three million was used up—much of it paid on foreign debts under American supervision —Robert Lansing, Wilson's Secretary of State after Bryan, worked out plans for backing private American investment in Nicaragua through American customs control. A High Commission for Nicaraguan Finance, consisting of two Nicaraguans and one American, approved such loans, allocated the Nicaraguan tariff collections, and managed so efficiently that the private bankers, both American and European, were satisfied with payments by 1925, and consented to the termination of American controls.

Thus in 1925 everything seemed peaceful, American intervention was considered a success, and the Marines were withdrawn. A coalition government, consisting of a Conservative president, Carlos Solórzano, and a Liberal vice-president, Juan B. Sacasa, had been elected under the American-supervised election system, and had taken office in January. The Marines left in August; in October the recently defeated presidential candidate, Emiliano Chamorro, staged a revolution to return to power. Back came the Marines and the election supervision system. An American-approved congress chose a compromise candidate, while Mexico threw her weight on the side of the former vice-president Sacasa. Finally Sacasa withdrew while President Coolidge sent the distinguished Henry L. Stimson to work out an adjustment.

The Stimson Plan included Marine supervision of the 1928 elections as soon as both sides would lay down their arms. All agreed save one young lieutenant on the Liberal side. He was César Augusto Sandino, still today a hero in the eyes of many Latin Americans who fear the power of the United States. He and his followers took to the hills and jungles and carried on guerrilla raids for five years. Called a bandit in the conservative press of both Nicaragua and the United States, Sandino was considered a "symptom of resistance to Yankee imperialism" by the Liberals. He had sworn "never to leave Nicaragua alive as long as a Yankee soldier remained." Sandino also had a program of internal reform, advocating cooperatives to raise the standard of living, the creation of a small landowning class through the break-up of foreign-owned estates, and the development of the resources of Nicaragua. Meanwhile American Marines tried to be more impartial in Nicaraguan elections than they had appeared to be before; in the elections of 1928 and 1932 Liberal party candidates won under American supervision.

The same Juan B. Sacasa, titular head of a 1926 revolt when he was backed by Mexico in opposition to the United States, won the election of 1932. Sacasa's inauguration coincided with that of Franklin Roosevelt. Now came the Good Neighbor Policy, the end of armed intervention, which had varied from a large force to a legation guard of only a hundred, and which had left behind better schools, better roads, improved health, a balanced budget, satisfied creditors, but a resentful populace. When the United States withdrew electoral supervision and armed guards, military dictatorship and the *Guardia Nacional* took over the government.

Sandino, still at large, claimed a victory because the Americans had gone, and, with Sacasa in Managua as president, came out of the jungles into the city. But the chief of the *Guardia Nacional*, Anastasio Somoza, trained by the United States Marine Corps, was the famous guerrilla's personal enemy. He had Sandino shot when the rebel arrived for a peace-making dinner with Sacasa's friends. Throughout the next two decades while Somoza was unquestioned dictator, the friends of Sandino yearly threw red flowers on the airplane runway built over the site of Sandino's assassination, and let the departing planes crush the blood-red blossoms on the asphalt.

With Sandino dead and the American forces gone, the powerful army leader Somoza was able to eliminate all other candidates for the election of 1936; Sacasa himself resigned when his term was up. Since there was no other candidate, Somoza had himself returned to office by what he could claim was a completely honest election. Then for twenty years, until he was assassinated in 1956, he was "Nicaragua."

Anastasio—called Tacho—Somoza made millions on the side in his own cattle business, while controlling the beef sold in his capital. His sons were considered his probable heirs; one headed the *Guardia Nacional*, the other was president of congress and made First Delegate in 1955. The pictures of his favorite daughter Lillian appeared on the twenty-peso bills, which were called "Lillians." Owning 117 different business enterprises, Tacho was said to have learned his expansive business methods while he worked his way through a bookkeeping and advertising course in Philadelphia. On the other hand, many Nicaraguans praise him as a competent ruler, a benevolent despot who modernized agriculture, built roads, schools, and hospitals, and improved living conditions in his country.

Tacho had been a good friend of the United States through World War II and in the "cold war" incident in Guatemala in 1954. He expected the United States to reciprocate without too much criticism of his dictatorial methods or of his continuous running quarrel with Costa Rica's President Figueres. As president he returned in state to America to be a guest in the White House and to receive lavish enough entertainment to still some of the resentment in Nicaraguan hearts against the long United States intervention. Tacho, who learned his English as a busboy in Philadelphia, told a correspondent, "Now, as I told F.D.R., democracy down here is like a baby, and nobody gives a baby everything to eat right away. I'm giving them liberty, but in my own style. If you give a baby a hot tamale, you kill him." Tacho's personal enemies finally killed him in September 1956, and left his sons to quarrel with the Nicaraguan Liberals over control of the little nation.

Congress appointed Luis Somoza Bayle, leader of the Tacho-controlled assembly, to finish out his father's term to May 1957. Naturally Luis Somoza ran for the presidency himself when an election was held, and he won for a six-year term to last till 1963, supposedly by an 89 per cent vote. Luis Somoza realized that the family's feudal control of the country led to the spread of Cuban-type Communism. Though his younger brother "Tachito" remained head of the army, Luis started a literacy campaign, cut individual land holdings (other than those of his own family) to 1,200 acres (500 hectares), and bid for Alliance for Progress loans within the new Central American common market framework. His successor, René Schick Gutierrez, a personal friend of the family, succeeded him in an actual election, with a "conservative" candidate running a weak second. Luis Somoza remained a leader in the Senate and "Tachito" Somoza the commanding general, and thus the family, buoyed up by the new common market prosperity, planned to control the elections of 1967.

COSTA RICA: MOST DEMOCRATIC
CENTRAL AMERICAN STATE

Costa Rica has always bragged that it has more school teachers than soldiers. An organized army is forbidden by its constitution, and it has only a small police force. Its 1,400,000 inhabitants own more than 100,000 small farms. The people in its high central plateau, around and in its two small cities of San José and Cartago, are almost all of pure European stock, descendants of farmers who came from Spain in colonial times. As in the time of Stephens' visit a century ago, the president still lives in a small bungalow on a small salary. Throughout the nation there is 80 per cent literacy. Rail lines connect its port on the Pacific with its port on the Atlantic only 300 miles away, but over a 4,000-foot plateau in between. Against the Negro banana workers and stevedores at Port Limón on the Caribbean, descendants of West Indians brought in to build the port, there is discrimination to the extent that they are not welcomed in the central plateau.

In San José the 166,000 inhabitants live as well as do citizens of Montevideo. Cacao, bananas, and coffee bring in foreign exchange and with it prosperity, for no foodstuffs need to be imported; this is no one-crop economy. Progressive governments have developed hydroelectric power in abundance; roads from east to west are paved highways. Even the dairy industry has been encouraged in recent times, a thing little known in Latin America save in Buenos Aires or Montevideo. Better breeding sires have been imported and butter and dry milk manufactured—this in Central America where most children have never tasted butter. Pasteurized milk is now sold everywhere in the highland towns. Secondary schools are the accepted standard for all communities, schools which offer vocational training as well as the orthodox Latin American classical education.

From 1885 to 1944, with a few occasional flurries, easily settled to the general satisfaction, there was a new president for every term, and no violence in any election. Costa Rica earned the respect of the world for orderly government and democratic elections. Thus it was a shock to the Costa Ricans to have a real civil war, international intervention, and bitter fighting take place in this Shangri-La throughout the late 1940s and early 1950s. The retiring president in 1944, Rafael Angel Calderón García, picked Teodoro Picado as his successor with the long-range plan of securing the presidency for himself again in 1948. Costa Rican tradition is against such schemes, and the election of 1948, though marred by some bloodshed, was fairly won by Otilio Ulate, a liberal newspaper publisher. But the congress was controlled by Picado and it declared Calderón García elected anyway. Ulate himself was arrested.

Now came a new figure into this atypical Costa Rican situation, the civilian José "Pepe" Figueres, a follower of Ulate, who raised a volunteer army (the country has no standing army) and attempted to put the legally elected Ulate in by force. All this would have attracted no world attention if it had not been for the armed intervention of Nicaragua's Somoza. After a good deal of skirmishing, a *junta* chose Pepe Figueres himself to act as provisional president. The *junta* put in a new constitution including woman suffrage and containing unusual protections against the abuses of authority. Banks were nationalized, Communists outlawed, small businesses aided, and the army disbanded. In November 1948 Ulate returned to the presidency to fill out his legal term. Then Somoza's troops again entered Costa Rica; this time Figueres and Ulate appealed for help from the Organization of American States. Under prodding from the OAS, both countries signed a treaty of friendship, and the invading troops as well as the home army disbanded in February 1949.

After four years of progress under Ulate, Pepe Figueres, a graduate of Massachusetts Institute of Technology and a local Costa Rican small farmer on the side, became president in July 1953, in a legal election in which 92 per cent of the registered voters cast their ballots. He arranged with the United Fruit Company, formerly so powerful at Port Limón on the Caribbean, to pay 50 per cent of their profits to his government; he was also able to break United Fruit's monopoly on the cacao, hemp, and palm oil industries, and to force it out of the electricity and railroad businesses in Costa Rica. Thus he regained for the government an economic control of the country, but did not ruin the banana business.

He was not yet through with the unfriendly Nicaraguan dictator Tacho Somoza. In 1955 Tacho bought 25 "mustang" planes from Sweden, and so had the largest air force in Central America. In the spring of that year border skirmishes drew blood for eleven days until the OAS again intervened. Just as a five-man peace commission ended a long investigation and treaties were made, Tacho was shot down by a gunman in September 1956, and Pepe Figueres had time to restore Costa Rica to its Shangri-La status. As he ended his term in 1958, he was busy improving vocational and technical schools, promoting electric power projects, and trying to control inflation—a worldwide scourge in the late 1950s which also reached isolated Costa Rica.

The inflation helped produce a quarrel among the "heirs" of Don Pepe in the election of February 1958, and a conservative lawyer, Mario Echandí, won out over Don Pepe's choice by only 6,000 votes. However, it was a fair election, refereed by UN observers at the request of Don Pepe, the first national leader in the world to thus invite in an international election supervisory team. Conservative Echandí ran the country with the smooth civil service already set up, and gave way in 1963 to a member of Figueres' party, Francisco Orlich. Figueres, kept by the constitution from succeeding himself until eight years had passed, busied himself as a conciliator of Latin America, serving on OAS teams in Santo Domingo and elsewhere.

Costa Rica, bright spot in Latin America, had an unsuspected enemy in nature. In August 1962 the inactive volcano Irazú, near the capital city, began a continuous eruption which rained ashes on the city and the finest Central Valley farmland for two years. Livestock died, vegetation was ruined, city life almost impossible. This catastrophe threatened to destroy the social fabric of the little nation, though its economy was bolstered by the common market while the rain of ashes continued until 1965.

With economic standards normally well above the Latin American norms, Costa Rica was recuperating from catastrophe in 1966. Meanwhile, a hard-fought election in 1966 resulted in the choice of José Joaquin Trejos, a mathematics professor almost untried in politics, for a presidential term to last till the 1970s. Opposition parties had joined together in their anxiety to keep "Pepe" Figueres and his party from controlling Costa Rica again. However, Trejos' margin was so small that a stalemate could result. Figueres' popular party gained a majority in the elections for the unicameral legislature held the same day.

Readings

Adams, R. N., et al., *Cultural Surveys of Panama-Nicaragua-Guatemala-El Salvador-Honduras* (1957)
———, *Social Change in Latin America Today* (1960)
Adler, J. H., E. R. Schlesinger, and C. C. Olson, *Public Finance and Economic Development in Guatemala* (1952)
Alexander, R. J., *Communism in Latin America* (1957)
———, *Organized Labor in Latin America* (1965)
Arciniegas, G., *Caribbean: Sea of the New World*, trans. H. de Onis (1946)
———, *The State of Latin America* (1952)
Arévalo, J. J., *The Shark and the Sardines* (1961)
Baxter, R. and D. Carroll, *The Panama Canal* (1965)

Beals, C., *Banana Gold* (1932)

Bemis, S. F., *Latin American Policy of the United States* (1943)

Biesanz, J. and M., *Costa Rican Life* (1944)

——, *People of Panama* (1955)

Blackwell, A. S., *Some Spanish American Poets* (1929)

Bloomfield, L. M., *British Honduras-Guatemala Dispute* (1953)

Busey, J. L., *Latin America: Political Institutions and Processes* (1964)

——, *Notes on Costa Rican Democracy* (1962)

Bush, A. C., *Organized Labor in Guatemala, 1944–1949* (1950)

Carr, A., *The World and William Walker* (1964)

Checchi, V., *et al.*, *Honduras: A Problem of Economic Development* (1959)

Coester, A., *Literary History of Spanish America* (rev. ed., 1928)

Committee for Economic Development, *Economic Development of Central America* (1964)

Cox, I. J., *Nicaragua and the United States, 1909–1927* (1927)

Denny, H. N., *Dollars for Bullets* [Nicaragua] (1928)

Ducoff, L. J., *Human Resources in Central America, Panama and Mexico, 1950–1980* (1960)

Du Val, M. P., *Cadiz to Cathay* (2nd ed., 1947)

Ealy, L. O., *Republic of Panama in World Affairs, 1903–1950* (1951)

Fergusson, E., *Guatemala* (1937)

Fiscal Survey of Panama: Problems and Proposals for Reform (1964)

Grubb, K., *Religion in Central America* (1937)

Hill, H. C., *Roosevelt and the Caribbean* (1927)

Hill, R. R., *American Marines in Nicaragua, 1912–1915* (1942)

——, *Fiscal Intervention in Nicaragua* (1933)

Holleran, M. P., *Church and State in Guatemala* (1949)

International Bank for Reconstruction and Development, *Economic Development of Guatemala* (1951)

——, *Economic Development of Nicaragua* (1953)

Ireland, G., *Boundaries, Possessions and Conflicts in North America and the Caribbean* (1941)

James, D., *Red Designs for the Americas: Guatemala Prelude* (1954)

Johannessen, C. L., *The Savannas of Interior Honduras* (1963)

Jones, C. L., *Caribbean Since 1900* (1936)

——, *Costa Rica and the Civilization of the Caribbean* (1935)

——, *Guatemala, Past and Present* (1940)

Kantor, H., *Costa Rican Election of 1953: A Case Study* (1958)

Karnes, T., *Failure of Union: Central America, 1824–1960* (1961)

Kelsey, V., and L. de J. Osborne, *Four Keys to Guatemala* (2nd ed., 1961)

Kepner, C. D., *Social Aspects of the Banana Industry* (1936)

——, and J. H. Southill, *The Banana Empire* (1935)

Kilijarni, T. V., *Central America: Lords and Lizards* (1962)

La Barge, R. A., *Impact of United Fruit Company on the Economic Development of Guatemala, 1946–1954* (1960)

Lloyd, J., *Guatemala, Land of the Maya* (1963)

Lookley, L. C., *Guide to Market Data in Central America* (1964)

Macaulay, N., *The Sandino Affair* (1966)

Mack, G., *Land Divided: History of the Panama Canal and Other Isthmian Projects* (1944)

Martin, P. F., *El Salvador in the Twentieth Century* (1911)

Martz, J. D., *Central America: The Crisis and the Challenge* (1959)

May, S., *et al.*, *Costa Rica: A Study in Economic Development* (1952)

——, and Galo Plazo, *The United Fruit Company in Latin America* (1958)

McCain, W. D., *United States and the Republic of Panama* (1937)

Mecham, J. L., *Church and State in Latin America* (rev. ed., 1966)

Miller, H. G., *The Isthmian Highway* (1929)

Munro, D. G., *Five Republics of Central America* (1918)

———, *Intervention and Dollar Diplomacy in the Caribbean, 1900–1921* (1964)

———, *United States and the Caribbean* (1934)

Nunley, R. E., *The Distribution of Population in Costa Rica* (1963)

Osborne, L. de J., *Four Keys to El Salvador* (1956)

———, *Indian Crafts of Guatemala and El Salvador* (1965)

Padelford, N. J., "Cooperation in the Central American Region: The Organization of Central American States," *International Organization*, XI (1957)

Palmer, T. W., *Search for a Latin American Policy* (1957)

Pan American Union, *Foreign Trade of Nicaragua, 1945–1955* (1955)

Parker, F. D., *Central American Republics* (1964)

Perkins, D., *United States and the Caribbean* (1947)

Pincus, J., *The Central American Common Market* (1962)

Pippin, L. L., *The Remón Era: An Analysis of Events in Panama, 1947–1957* (1964)

Reina, R. E., *Chinautla: A Guatemalan Indian Community* (1960)

Rippy, J. F., *Caribbean Danger Zone* (1940)

Rodriguez, M., *Central America* (1965)

Rosenthal, M., *Guatemala, the Story of an Emergent Latin American Democracy* (1962)

Schneider, R. M., *Communism in Guatemala, 1944–1954* (1958)

Shepherd, R., and R. M. Kinne, *Central American Common Market: Opportunities Plus* (1964)

Silvert, K. H., *A Study in Government: Guatemala* (1954)

Slade, W. F., *Federation of Central America* (1917)

Stokes, W. S., *Honduras: An Area Study in Government* (1950)

Suslow, L. H., *Aspect of Social Reforms in Guatemala, 1944–1949* (1949)

Tax, S., *Penny Capitalism: A Guatemalan Indian Economy* (1953)

Torres-Rioseco, A., *Epic of Latin American Literature* (1959)

Tower, F. J., *Basic Data on Economy of Honduras* (1961)

Tuman, M. M., *Caste in a Peasant Society* (1952)

Turner, G. P., *An Analysis of the Economy of El Salvador* (1961)

United Nations, Bureau of Social Affairs, *Population of Central America Including Mexico, 1950–1980* (1954)

United States Bureau of Labor Statistics, *Labor Law and Practices in Costa Rica* (1962)

———, *Labor Law and Practices in Guatemala* (1962)

———, *Labor Law and Practices in Honduras* (1961)

Wallach, H. C., and J. H. Adlèr, *Public Finance in a Developing Country: El Salvador, A Case Study* (1951)

Whetten, N. L., *Guatemala, Land and the People* (1961)

Wilgus, A. C., ed., *Caribbean Area* (1934)

———, *Caribbean at Mid-Century* (1951)

———, *Caribbean: Central America Area* (1961)

Williams, M. W., *Anglo-American Isthmian Diplomacy, 1815–1915* (1915)

Wilson, C. M., *Challenge and Opportunity: Central America* (1941)

———, *Empire in Green and Gold: Story of American Banana Trade* (1944)

———, *Middle America* (1944)

Ydígoras Fuentes, M., *My War with Communism as told by Mario Rosenthal* (1963)

Chapter 39

Caribbean Island Nations Today

TWO ISLANDS, THREE SEPARATE NATIONS

THE FRENCH-SPEAKING Republic of Haiti, the Spanish-speaking Dominican Republic, and the sugar-producing Republic of Cuba comprise a total of 74,400 square miles, and contain fifteen million people. They constitute a strategically important area of the Caribbean, commanding the approaches to the Panama Canal and other possible canal routes. They are dependent on outsiders and have reason to nurture resentment toward these same outsiders. Their favorite target is the United States, which has had uneasy and unstable relations with these islands throughout their years of independence. The United States has done them immense good at times, and immense harm at others. By their proximity and their many common historical experiences, they should have been friends, but they have not been, and among their rulers there has been a tendency to meddle in the politics of each other. Their histories are as colorful and violent as their scenery is beautiful. Although comparisons and contrasts can be made, it is best in this context to treat each nation separately.

CUBA, THE PEARL OF THE ANTILLES

Cuba, the island of concentration camp and rebellion and yellow fever in 1898, the island of America's occupation at the turn of the century, was the center of American concern about Western Hemisphere Communism in the 1960s. Millions of American dollars were invested in its plantations and refineries; hundreds of thousands of tourists swarmed through Havana during the Prohibition era to visit the gay night clubs, watch the rhumba and the mambo, and gamble on the cockfights and the lottery. Its population is a mixture of races; Fulgencio Batista, dictator of the 1950s, had a Chinese grandfather, while his other forebears were mixed Spanish, Indian, and Negro. The degrees of wealth and poverty were as marked as in any area of the Hemisphere. The rural population lived in poverty while politicians lived handsomely and ended their terms with millions of pesos of profit above their legal salaries.

But the picture in the early 1950s was not all sordid. Elementary schools reached many rural children; health standards were high for the tropics. The Batista government kept the peace and raised the standard of living as well as maintaining very friendly relations with the United States. The mixture of races, all living side by side with no evidence of discrimination seemed to be producing a new cultural renaissance. Paved highways ran the 750-mile length of the island, connecting Havana, a city of over a million population at one end, with Santiago, a city of nearly 200,000 at the eastern end. Then this sophisticated Cuba of the 1950s came to a crashing end with Fidel Castro in the 1960s.

The story of Cuba in the nineteenth century had ended with the end of American occupation under Leonard Wood, the presidency of Tomás Estrada Palma, and the great hopes for the future promised by the democratic constitution. But when Estrada Palma's inexperienced people were granted local self-government, they did not know how to use it and soon various areas of Cuba became festering sores of revolution against the central power, each one encouraged by greedy generals. By 1906, Estrada Palma tried to get himself re-elected, but could not control the situation. Accordingly, he called on the Secretary of War, William Howard Taft, who sent Charles E. Magoon, a Nebraska lawyer, to restore civil government. Magoon supervised the election of José Miguel Gómez, candidate of a so-called Liberal Party, and withdrew the American occupation forces in 1909.

With Gómez began the series of presidents who all entered office poor and retired as millionaires, while Tomás Estrada Palma was forced to retire to a little ranch and end his days in poverty. In 1913 Gómez was willing to resign with his new private fortune, and Mario García Menocal was elected, to serve two terms until 1921. Menocal's second term included World War I, in which Cuba joined, and the boom in prices, the expansion of great estates, and the fantastic speculation that the era brought to Cuban sugar. His regime is referred to as "the dance of the millions"; a great part of these millions the President and all his family and friends acquired personally. Though Menocal's regime was unpopular with the "outs," American troops prevented any revolutions against it and preserved it through another term by backing Menocal against a liberal revolt in the fraudulent elections of 1917. Woodrow Wilson had propounded the Wilson Corollary of the Monroe Doctrine, which said "protect American lives and property" and refuse to recognize governments brought in by revolutionary change.

Under this Corollary the existing regime, no matter how corrupt, was maintained as long as peace and prosperity were preserved.

Menocal's own candidate, Alfredo Zayas, known as "the *peseta* stealer," was chosen in 1921 in an election supervised by an American commission headed by General Enoch Crowder. Now came the collapse of the World War I sugar prosperity. To avoid financial panic, General Crowder remained in Cuba to advise Zayas. The United States would loan the now-bankrupt Cubans $50,000,000 provided Zayas would carry out fifteen specific reforms laid down by Crowder's commission. There was to be control of graft, economy in the budget, reform of the national lotteries, auditing of the business of the national bank, appointment of an "honest cabinet." Cuba had recovered in the sugar market by 1923; Crowder became ambassador; Zayas fired his "honest cabinet" and returned to the normal "siege on the treasury." Since there had been charges of "imperialism" against the United States from other Latin American nations because of the Crowder commission, Harding's government refused to interfere. Though Zayas' government became a record-breaker for corruption, protection of organized vice, connection with United States gangsters of the prohibition era, and viciousness in his own personal relationships, the United States continued to support him under the "no successful revolutions" corollary.

Zayas was powerful enough to back his own candidate for the election of 1924 and have him inaugurated peacefully in 1925. This man, General Gerardo Machado, was to be the archetype of Caribbean dictators through the 1920s. By borrowing heavily from American banks he hoped to assure American protection and interest in his behalf; by amending the constitution, he hoped to stay in office for life; by imprisoning intellectuals and the liberal-minded university students in foul dungeons, he hoped to quiet opposition forever.

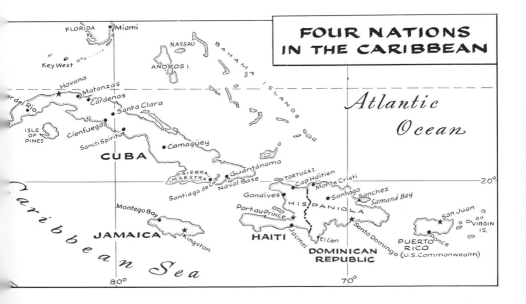

FOUR NATIONS IN THE CARIBBEAN

In 1933 this martial rule by a brutal general was suddenly brought to an end by a popular mass uprising and an attack on the presidential palace. Franklin Roosevelt, the Good Neighbor, sent the tactful Summer Welles to spirit Machado out by plane and help set up a provisional government. Within three weeks there was another street riot and Welles had to ask Washington for more protection. When several naval vessels appeared in answer to this request, Cuban resentment against the United States ran high. The provisional government fell and a new force came to power, a combination of a college professor, Ramón Grau San Martín, and a sergeant, Fulgencio Batista. Grau San Martín was the accepted president, anti-American demonstrations died down, and peace reigned, but only as long as the sergeant, Batista, the real power, wanted it so. When he disagreed with Grau, who had been denied recognition by Washington, Grau resigned in 1934.

During the next seven years seven presidents came and went, while the little sergeant wielded his puppets and the United States made no protest. This pudgy noncommissioned officer, who made himself a colonel by 1940, was still dictator in 1958. A barefoot boy from the canebrakes, of a family so underprivileged that his elder brother had died of tuberculosis and malnutrition, Fulgencio Batista had joined the army as an illiterate private at seventeen. Here he was issued shoes, taught himself to read and write. Eventually he learned to take stenographic dictation, to make himself a useful secretary to officers, and to organize a powerful political machine among the other "noncoms." The "noncoms" got the support of the enlisted men, seized the barracks at the time of Machado's fall, and put Batista in power.

Batista was content till 1940 to be "king-maker" and not "king." As part of the Good Neighbor Policy, his presidents saw the Platt Amendment, and with it the United States' legal rights in Cuba, canceled forever. Depression conditions were alleviated by loans from the American Export-Import Bank, by continued preferential treatment for Cuban sugar in the depressed United States market. To keep peace at home, Batista built up the strongest, best-paid, best-fed army of privates Cuba had ever known. Then, to keep them busy, he built primary schools throughout the island, and sent the now literate soldiers to teach in them. Cane workers were a little better paid, rural roads improved, and companies forced to improve working conditions.

The little sergeant finally tired of doing the planning while others received the credit. In 1940 he ran for president himself, allowed the weak opposition party to campaign, counted the ballots fairly enough, and declared himself by far the most popular candidate. During the next three years the great demand for sugar in World War II brought prosperity never known before, while Batista joined with the Allies, sold Cuba's sugar and minerals to them, and granted bases to the United States.

In 1944 Fulgencio Batista, again allowing a fair election, saw his own candidate defeated, and went peaceably to live the life of a millionaire in Miami. This time it was Grau San Martín, the college professor, who was elected. Supported by a coalition of anti-Batista men, including both conservative and labor-supported Communists, Grau had an uneasy hold on politics. During his four years until 1948 Grau was a very poor administrator and seemed helpless in the vacuum left by Batista and the end-of-the-war price boom. Grau's friends and supporters waxed rich at the public trough, while Communist influence grew among the workers. Grau attempted some reforms, trying to promote industrialization and diversified agriculture and attacking the problems of health and illiteracy, but Congress did not cooperate with him. A strong anti-Communist, Carlos Prío Socarrás, Grau's own candidate, was elected in 1948. Formerly a friend of Grau, Prío Socarrás found many evidences of misappropriation of funds in his predecessor's records. The result was an unprecedented thing for Cuba, a trial of an ex-president for graft in office. Grau was cleared, but the funds remained unaccounted for, and, for the record, it had become a public offense for a president to make a fortune while in office. This did not keep Prío Socarrás from retiring in 1952 with more money than he had had in 1948.

The elections of 1952 found the political situation very confused. It looked as if the friends of Prío Socarrás would take control of the government by force without a legal election. So in March of 1952, announcing that he must prevent a bloody revolution between the opposing factions, Fulgencio Batista eased himself back in the saddle. He carefully posted his old friends the noncommissioned officers in strategic spots in Havana and came riding into the city in a full-fledged *coup d'état*. Two hours and sixteen minutes later, Batista had imposed a complete dictatorship. The United States recognized this Batista regime, and continued to send technical and military aid to Cuba. In the actual election of 1954, Batista, as the only candidate, won a legal four-year term.

Meanwhile, the price of sugar was high, wages and working conditions were better than under Grau, and the schools full; fine cars, Paris styles, well-fed people were to be seen on the streets of Havana and Santiago. There had been much investment of private capital in new industries, electric power had been doubled, a housing program pushed—all under a Social and Economic Development Plan inaugurated in 1954. The United States, that strong neighbor who had cast her shadow across Cuba by her very nearness, was giving economic aid. It looked as if dictatorship by a sergeant was not necessarily all bad when compared to many eras of dictatorship by generals.

But an increasingly well-educated and enlightened populace did not remain satisfied with Batista's "benevolent despotism." Opposition parties increased their underground activities through the later 1950s and university students staged bloody riots. Those anxious for political freedom found a champion in the rebel Fidel Castro Ruiz. A visionary idealist from a well-to-do Santiago family, the young Fidel Castro had tried to take Batista's barracks in Santiago with a handful of friends on July 26, 1953, as a protest against Batista's return to power. Fidel and his brother Raúl had been captured in this fiasco, and given long prison terms. But they were freed and allowed to go into exile in Mexico during a general political amnesty declared by Batista in 1955. In Mexico they rallied other Cuban exiles into a closely knit group, and took lessons in guerrilla fighting from a veteran of the Spanish Civil War, while they were supporting their cause, now called the "26th of July Movement," on funds donated by exiled former president Prío Socarrás.

In November 1956 the Castro brothers and eighty-one other youthful enthusiasts landed on the shores of eastern Cuba from a sixty-two-foot boat. Escaping from Batista's troops, they found their way into the inaccessible Sierra Maestra hills, where they set up rebel headquarters. For two years they harassed Batista's soldiers, arousing worldwide sympathy and attracting many recruits, and much secret support from the villages and towns.

In the face of growing opposition, Batista had announced an election for June 1, 1958, but he canceled it when the Castro forces won several skirmishes. Then, by December 1958, the rebels began to advance with a great popular following. Normal life on the island stopped; Batista declared "a state of emergency." His real emergency was that his own soldiers were deserting by the thousands to the rebels. By New Year's Day, 1959, Batista was in flight to the Dominican Republic. Now the Castro brothers were in Havana while the crowd went wild with hysteria. The rebel soldiers had allowed their hair and beards to grow long in the mountains; the long black beard had become a symbol of the "People's Revolution." There was to be no immediate election in this People's Revolution, however. A little-known Judge Urrutia, friendly to the rebel cause, was declared provisional president while Fidel himself was called "premier," a title seldom used in Latin America; brother Raúl was commander in chief of the army and a fiery young Argentine Communist, Ernesto "Che" Guevara, was economic adviser. Soon a "puppet" named Osvaldo Dorticós Torrado was declared "legal" president. Public opinion in the United States and other democratic Western nations was turned against the bearded "26th of July" leaders, when their followers insisted on vengeance against Batista henchmen and held hurried "kangaroo court" type trials which ordered executions of more than 500 Batista policemen, secret service men, and army officers in the first three months of 1959.

On the international scene, the name "Fidel Castro" soon became synonymous with a new type of Western Hemisphere Communism. It was a movement to arm guerrillas among the poorest rural workers and landless peasants in other nations in order to hasten the "socialist revolution." The Dominican Republic, Venezuela, Peru's *montaña*, and Brazil's depressed northeast felt the presence of such armed bands. Panamanian street rioters yelling, "Fidel! Fidel!" protested United States' policy in the Canal Zone. Venezuela's liberal President Betancourt almost fell from power due to the activities of secret "Fidelistas." The United States had recognized Fidel's government on January 7, 1959, as soon as Batista had fled, and had made efforts to promote the same financial aid that had been extended to Batista, but Fidel made it clear that he resented such aid. Eventually the United States withdrew recognition in January 1961, as did all the Latin American states save Mexico. Cuba was not welcomed at later meetings of the Organization of American States, did not join in the Latin American common market or the Alliance for Progress, and tried to gain world attention by denouncing the United States at the United Nations, rather than protesting through the regional Organization of American States.

Meanwhile, at home in Cuba, Fidel formally announced that Cuba was a "socialist state," and that he himself would be a "Marxist-Leninist until the last day of my life." He now revealed that he had kept his Communist sympathy quiet in the Sierra Maestra for fear his guerrilla army would lose supporters. Fidel and the economic czar, "Che" Guevara, made visits to Moscow where they received the "red carpet" treatment. By the summer of 1960, Fidel had contracted to sell all Cuba's sugar output to Russia, and the Cuban government had confiscated most of the American sugar properties, investments totaling $850 million. The United States, in turn, canceled our country's contracts to purchase Cuban sugar giving the Cuban preferential quota to other sugar-producing areas.

In July 1960 the Russian leader Khrushchev said in the United Nations that Russia would defend Cuba if that island was invaded by the United States, an open threat against the Monroe Doctrine. Fidel Castro, speaking on radio and television for hours, night after night, castigated the United States for its "years of economic aggression" against Cuba. A meeting of the Organization of American States at San José de Costa Rica in August 1960 condemned the intervention of "outside powers," without mentioning Russia, in any Western Hemisphere state.

With this tacit anti-Russian, anti-Castro agreement behind them, Cuban exiles, by then in the United States in large numbers, attempted to organize a Cuban army-in-exile. Exile leaders received encouragement, equipment, money, and training from the United States Central Intelligence Agency under President Eisenhower. The army, about 1,500 strong, was trained secretly on Guatemalan soil. When Kennedy became president, he agreed to the plans for an invasion of Cuba by this army, as long as no Americans were directly involved. It was assumed that hundreds of thousands of Cubans would join such an anti-Castro invasion, once the invaders had a toe-hold on the island. Castro's own intelligence officers warned him of the plans, thousands of the exiles' possible supporters were jailed, and the planned landing place was alerted. The result was the Bay of Pigs fiasco on April 19, 1961. Three hundred of the exiles' army were killed and 1,200 were taken as prisoners, prisoners who were later ransomed by private individuals in the United States for $63 million worth of drugs and infant foods. The incident strengthened Fidel's hold on his own people and on the imagination of thousands of underprivileged people throughout Latin America.

The United States' seeming weakness in the Bay of Pigs led the Russians boldly to use Cuba as a base for missiles directly pointed at the United States ninety miles away. In October 1962 President Kennedy announced that photo reconnaissance planes had identified an elaborate system of nuclear missile launching-sites on Cuba. There followed a tense week of formal exchanges between Russia and the United States, in which Russia backed down and removed the missiles. In the eyes of Fidel's friends throughout Latin America this confrontation showed American strength and revealed Fidel's own weakness as a tool of the Russians. Further Castro attempts to shut off the water from the American naval base at Guantánamo hardly caused a tremor. An American-imposed quarantine of Cuba was reported to have lowered the Cuban standard of living by 15 per cent, although 748 merchant vessels called at Cuban ports in a three-year period, quarantine or no.

In the late 1960s Fidel seemed anxious to allow all dissatisfied Cubans to leave Cuba, save those eligible for military service or skilled in technical trades, perhaps because food and jobs were getting scarcer on the island. The United States undertook an airlift of 2,000 persons a month, to be flown to Miami with Castro's full consent—this in spite of the lack of diplomatic contacts and of any friendly exchange of visitors or correspondents.

American observers in early 1967 hoped that this indicated that the Cuban economy was in serious trouble. Cuba had always been a one-crop island, with the bright cane waving the length and breadth of it. In the pre-Castro era, one-third of the six million Cubans lived by the processes of cultivating and refining it. The *guajiros* or field hands, usually descendants of slaves who worked there before them, lived in huts on the plantations among the cane. They were employed only three months of the year, however. Guaranteed year-round wages for the *guajiro*, compulsory subsistence garden plots for families, and adequate schooling for the children might have solved many rural social evils, if Batista, the rich Cuban plantation owners and the American sugar refining interests could all have seen the way to forestall Cuban Communism.

The sugar refineries were called *centrales*, great complexes in the center of the plantations, for Cuba's sugar was a factory business. Oil-heated evaporators and centrifugal separators turned out the white crystals; assembly lines weighed and bagged them. Because this outlay of machinery called for heavy investment, 70 per cent of the Cuban sugar industry was owned by United States capital, so that North American industry often called the tune in Cuban affairs. Preferential treatment in the United States market, where Cuban sugar competed with Louisiana cane and Western beet sugar, had been an accepted fact since the "liberation" of Cuba from Spain. Meanwhile, sugar might be held responsible for the poverty of the mass of Cubans; it prevented small ownership, concentrated land in large holdings under absentee owners, either in Havana or in New York, kept land out of diversified cultivation, and cut down the production of food crops that would have made Cuba self-sufficient. Though beef and tobacco were grown for export, they formed only ten per cent of the foreign trade.

Fidel Castro launched his drastic land reform program in the summer of 1959. All large holdings, including those of American sugar companies, were expropriated in return for long-term bonds, on which no payments have yet been made. They were supposedly redistributed to small holders in sixty-seven-acre plots, though many of these were recombined into large state farms by 1965. Castro's Agrarian Reform Institute also confiscated the grazing lands of the rich cattlemen and made grandiose plans to improve cattle and plant seed strains and to help small farmers toward economic independence.

But by 1960, Castro turned his attention away from this agricultural development. Between 1960 and 1963 Fidel and "Che" Guevara had hoped to make Cuba an industrialized nation. Russian planners came to Cuba to work out a four-year development plan. Actually, by 1963, the plan had failed. Fidel went to Moscow a second time in 1963 to side with Russia in her quarrel with China, and returned with new plans to put Cuba back into a sugar-and-cattle-producing economy. Even small, privately owned farms were expropriated this time, as Fidel's new planners pushed for 90 per cent state control of a single vast sugar "factory-in-the-fields." City workers, soldiers, and students were sent out into the fields to harvest the cane. When the 1964 crop brought in as much sugar as Cuba had produced before 1959, world prices went down, and Russia paid only the equivalent of those lower prices. The Cuban economy became chaotic. The sugar refineries began to break down for lack of new parts. Russian specialists could not repair them, and supposedly went home in disgust, saying, "Marxist-Leninist principles were not meant to work with *these* people in *this* climate."

"Che" Guevara mysteriously disappeared in the summer of 1965. *Fidelismo* may have still been considered the "wave of the future" by many underprivileged Latin Americans in 1967, but his "wave" at home had seemingly stalled at the crest. He was still fabulously popular with the younger Cuban people, for whom he had provided schooling and technical training never before undertaken. These young people had a feeling of security in new jobs provided by Castro, and a feeling of self-importance in their service in Castro's "Youth Militia." No Western observers, as of 1967, were able to judge whether the *guajiros*, the poor cane-cutters at the bottom in the 1950s, were very much better off at the end of the 1960s. Most intellectual and middle-class Cubans had gone underground or into exile.

It may prove true that Fidel Castro brought a real social and economic revolution to Cuba. The ruling landowner class was dispossessed and the landless, jobless peasants have been given great psychological importance. But political life in the democratic sense is dead; there is complete dictatorship. The press and radio are Fidel's mouthpieces, education has been made the instrument of *Fidelismo,* with resentment against the United States one of the principal keynotes. Temporarily the economy has been wrecked, so that Castro's methods no longer seem so attractive elsewhere in the Hemisphere. To some extent Communism as it is exemplified by the *Fidelista* movement in Latin America has been counterbalanced by the Alliance for Progress described in Chapter 41.

Just before Castro's revolution in 1959, Cubans had been making a new contribution to Western Hemisphere culture. "Afro-Cubanism" was a modernist movement in poetry, in prose, in music, and in art. Wrote Cuban mulatto poet Nicholas Guillén (born in 1903):

Shadows I alone can see,
My two grandfathers guard me.
Lance with head of bone,
Drum of wood and leather:
My black grandfather.
Ruff, wide at the throat,
Gray warrior's armor:
My white grandfather.
Naked feet, rocky torso,
These from my black man:
Pupils of Antarctic glass,
These from my white man![1]

His song was typical of Cuba in the 1940s—the sophistication of the European influence, the music and rhythm of the black. Guillén's poems on Negro life, on his own personal sorrows, he called *sones,* and wrote them with the syncopated rhythm of the African dance. Cuban rhumba music, perhaps based on the old march of the chained slaves, four steps ahead and one sideways to throw the chain out of the way, had four straight beats and a half beat. So did Guillén's poetry. One of his famous *sones* was even named "Four Anguishes and One Hope." Other poets, not necessarily Negro, wrote of the lives of the cane cutters and the city poor on the streets of Havana, such as the white Emilio Ballagas (born in 1908), who spoke from an intimate knowledge of Negro folklore and psychology. Novels of the 1930s to 1950s dealt with the social problem of the poor field worker of Negro blood, such as Carlos Enríquez's (born in 1901) *Tilin García,* or with the hardships suffered by their ancestors in the slave trade, as in Carlos Montenegro's (born in 1900) *Men Without Women.* One of Cuba's best-known serious writers was the sociologist Dr. Fernando Ortiz, whose studies of African lore and its persistence in Cuba are widely read by anthropologists. Historians such as Carlos Manuel Trelles y Govín and international legalists such as Antonio Sánchez Bustamante y Soria enhanced the intellectual life of Cuba. After the Castro revolution in 1959, no Cuban literary contributions reached the Western world, and the literary journals and the five daily papers of Havana ceased to exist as far as the serious literary readers of the Hemisphere were concerned.

The Cuban music best known abroad is of the rhumba type, such as Ernesto Lecuona's (born in 1896) *Malagueña.* Even a serious musician like Amadeo Roldán (1900—1939) wrote his best-known *Variations on Cuban Themes* to bring out the rhumba influences. Alejandro García Caturla's (1906–1940) orchestra music has been often played in New York, particularly his *Berceuse Campesina,* a "combination of African rhythm and cane cutters' melody." Both Roldán and Caturla have set Guillén's Afro-Cuban poems to music. The Cuban painter whose work has received most acclaim in New York is Wilfredo Lam (1902–   ), a half-Chinese, half-Negro and *mestizo* leader in the Afro-Cuban art movement in Havana.

[1] From H. R. Hayes, editor, *Twelve Spanish American Poets* (New Haven: Yale University Press, 1943), p. 334.

Conga drum team in the Havana Carnival. *Courtesy pan American Airways.*

Cuban modernist painter Wilfredo Lam. In his veins flows the blood of four races, Spanish, Negro, Caribbean Indian, and Chinese. *Courtesy Pan American Union.*

Cuba's own "two grandfathers," the white and black, did not cause any great social problem in the first half of the twentieth century. Class lines were drawn by wealth, and since slavery had so recently been abolished, there had been little time for the sons of slaves to reach the upper classes. But a large percentage of the people have somewhere a slave or a freedman ancestor. Cuba's social problem was the grinding poverty of the rural workers, whose illiteracy brought the national figure up to 30 per cent in 1950. Fidel Castro's ardent supporters claimed that he was abolishing illiteracy, staging gigantic public health campaigns, and providing housing for rural and factory workers, though these were programs that looked good on paper only. If he could have brought a decade of peaceful democracy and such reforms with it, Cuba could be a tropical paradise.

HAITI: LATIN AMERICA'S FRENCH-SPEAKING NEGRO REPUBLIC

On the western half of the island of Hispaniola, the smallest independent area in the Americas, live the French- and "creole"-speaking natives, mulattoes and Negroes, who are the Haitians. In the mid-1960s there were 4,600,000 of them. Their three major population centers were Port-au-Prince, with 200,000 people, and the much smaller Cap Haitien, and Aux Cayes on the two opposite sides of the island. All the rest of the Haitians are rural people. In this all-Negro republic there has been, unfortunately, a rigid class division. Between the educated mulattoes, who live and speak like Parisians and comprise perhaps 3 per cent of the people, and the rural Negroes, 90 per cent illiterate, who speak a patois called "creole" and live like West African villagers, there was a deep rift. The Negroes have controlled the army, and through it the presidency, in the majority of the years since independence. The mulattoes controlled the congress, the courts, and the civil service. Herein has lain much of Haiti's trouble.

After some semblance of stable government in the last two decades of the nineteenth century, there came complete political and financial bankruptcy by 1908. From 1908 to 1915 eight different presidents held the office, each backed by a private army of *cacos*, illiterate mountain farmers. Where did the money come from to support these private armies? Some of it was left from loans made by French, English, American, and German bankers who had supported one president or the other in office, loans which were never repaid. In the spring of 1915, when Davilman Théodore was thrown out of the presidential palace by a new leader, Guillaume Vilbrun Sam, a new danger of European intervention seemed possible. American banking interests had been attempting to solidify Haitian finance since 1910; now they stood to lose the investments they had made and appealed to the American government for aid. With World War I raging in Europe, the United States could not afford to see European forces clash over Haiti, and although tensions from Europe lessened, the United States wanted guarantees against possibilities of future interference.

Meanwhile, President Sam attempted to throw out the American banking group, resorted to violence to keep himself in office, jailed his opponents, and had 167 of his political enemies assassinated. When this news was known, a mob attacked his palace and Sam took refuge in the French embassy. The street mob broke into the embassy, pulled the president out from under a bed, and tore him to pieces. The next day, July 28, 1915, the United States Navy landed American marines to protect the legation, and took over many of the public services and the control of the only source of revenue, the customs house.

The United States then arranged a treaty, by which the Haitians agreed to American intervention for ten years. American specialists were to supervise the finances, arrange payments to the creditors, and control elections. This arrangement made Haiti an actual United States protectorate. No Haitian territory was to be ceded to any other nation. Americans were to organize the police to end violence, and to improve education, health, sanitation, and trade. The Haitian senate had no choice but to approve this treaty. In 1917 it was extended to twenty years' duration, and in 1918 amended to include American approval of legislation and a veto power by the American financial adviser on all expenditures. United States experts drafted a constitution for Haiti in 1918 which allowed foreigners to own land, and encouraged foreign capital.

American "protection" was not popular. The city mulattoes disliked it because as civil service workers they were under American army bosses, and some of them were irked over the loss of supervisional jobs and the graft that went with them. In the rural areas American soldiers set up schools, drained swamps, and built the first real roads in the country. But they did this with forced black labor, the *corvée,* working the Negro farmers without pay, under American officers, many of them Southerners who treated the Haitians as inferiors. Sewage systems and pure water supplies were built for Port-au-Prince and Cap Haitien; electricity was brought into these towns for the first time, and telephones set up in public offices. Peace and order reigned, the financial system was stabilized, and efficiency increased. But all revenues went to retire foreign loans and little was done to alleviate the condition of the masses.

The resentful Haitians did not want to be "improved," anyway. They had a strong national pride in their own country, the New World's only Negro republic, left unmolested by the white man for more than a century. Now they had no say in the new regime, but were treated like little children who must be patiently taught new things. Resentment became rebellion among the country people on the road gangs, and a guerrilla war flared in the backlands for two years. A United States Senate investigation ended the worst abuses in 1922 and a new High Commissioner, General John H. Russell, was sent from the United States. Louis Borno, an intelligent and well-educated mulatto, was elected president, and served two terms, from 1922 to 1930, a period of some achievement and progress.

When Borno's second term came to an end, the anti-American agitation was renewed. Political demonstrations, general strikes, and mob violence endangered the American forces. President Hoover sent a civilian commission under W. Cameron Forbes to investigate the whole situation. The commission's plan was to arrange for withdrawal by 1936, and meanwhile send civilians in place of General Russell and his army officials to direct Haitian affairs. Under this plan free, fair, and honest elections under Marine supervision were held in 1930, and Stenio Vincent, a leader in the opposition to American occupation, was elected president.

By 1934 the Good Neighbor Policy, described in a later chapter, was being worked out in Washington. Franklin Roosevelt sent a United States Minister to Haiti as to an independent foreign state. The controls of the Haitian government—police, finances, customs collection, school program —were all turned over to President Vincent in 1934. By 1935 Haitian finance was considered sound, even in the midst of world depression. The American fiscal commission was withdrawn in 1941 and Haitian interests owned the national bank which had been American-run since 1910. Vincent changed the American-model constitution to provide for direct election of the president and to allow his own re-election through to 1941; however he proved a more capable administrator than any of his predecessors. He met the depression by public works projects and improved the domestic conditions as well as the world position of Haiti. He said that the Haitian people were not ready for democracy, however, so gave them little power in the government, controlling through the aid and support of the Haitian Guard, and showing no respect for the civil rights of his enemies.

His major enemy was the enemy of all Haiti, the Dominican dictator Trujillo next door. Seasonal laborers from Haiti often joined work crews to go to help with the sugar-cane harvest in the Dominican Republic across the mountains. In 1937 more than 60,000 Haitians were working in the Dominican Republic; with hard times at home many of them planned to stay. Trujillo, who did not want any more "black blood" in his own personal domain, sent his troops and aroused his people to stage a "pogrom," slaughtering more than 15,000 of the migrant Negro workers, whose bodies were then thrown to the sharks. The United States protested to Trujillo, and he paid damages to the Haitian government amounting to $550,000, thus implying a tacit admission of responsibility for the death of 15,000— in which case each Haitian was worth $37. Vincent lost popularity because he accepted such a cheap price; in 1941 he withdrew from the presidency and named his successor.

Vincent's choice for president, Elie Lescot, was a sophisticated Haitian who had been in Washington as minister to the United States. His five years of administration lasted until 1946; during this time he declared war on Japan and Germany just after Pearl Harbor, and kept Haiti from excess inflation and trade dislocation during the stress of wartime in the Caribbean. Haitian ports were turned over for use of the Allies, and Haitian workers found demand for their labor in new crops. The end of World War II saw a slump in this new importance for Haiti. Haitian workers came back to their little plots of land; wages went down, and prices for Haitian products dropped. The dissatisfaction forced Lescot out of the presidency at the end of one term, and put in Dumarsais Estimé in August 1946. Estimé was a Negro from the rural area, the first after thirty years of rule by the mulatto elite. He had been raised on a mountain farm, but had secured funds for a legal education by working for years as a rural school teacher. He had been Lescot's Minister of Education, and was known as a sincere idealist, a person interested in compulsory rural education and improved agriculture. In order to finance his public works he levied an income tax, the first in Haitian history. The last of the old pre-1922 foreign debts were paid off under this regime. He even was able to live in peace with strong man Trujillo next door.

In spite of his success, Estimé was not allowed to continue in office beyond his legal constitutional term as he had planned. The army which had brought him to power promptly threw him out, and turned over the presidency to a military *junta* headed by General Paul Eugène Magloire. Overriding a new measure against military presidents, Magloire was elected in 1951 by a nationwide popular election. A very dark Negro, son of a mountain peasant who had risen to be an officer of the army, Magloire had served in the capital as aide-de-camp to President Stenio Vincent, and had been chosen chief of police. He had made and unmade presidents who had preceded him. Born from the blacks, but serving his political apprenticeship under the mulattoes, Magloire was determined to end the long rift between blacks and mulattoes in Haitian politics. He meant to concentrate on long-range technological advances which would help both city and country. His currency was sound, his country unburdened by heavy debt, his people all small landowners with no large plantations and no foreign absentee owners. The problem of Magloire's Haitians was one of ignorance in the best use of the land.

The black "patch and thatch" farmer of Haiti owns his own land but resents outside teaching. These Haitian farmers have no contact with the outside world; their language has no written literature and is scarcely understandable to a Frenchman or a Port-au-Prince intellectual. The village and hill people, poor and illiterate like the Indians of the mountainous sections of Spanish America, kept their native religion—in Haiti's case, African animism—and combined it with a thin veneer of Catholicism. The result, a "fetishistic" religion called voodoo, is of great interest to anthropologists.

For these people, President Magloire announced a five-year plan for agricultural improvement in 1951. United Nations experts and technicians from the United States helped to develop the badly eroded Artibonite Valley on a TVA-like plan. Over a nine-year period 80,000 acres were to be reclaimed for use, producing diversified crops under small ownership. The plan also included more agricultural schools, the purchase and use of tractors by village cooperatives, cooperative banks for small-farm credit, and a system of county farm agents. Better breeding of cattle, better rural elementary education, better health campaigns—with the help of the United Nation's health agency—against the prevalent yaws and malaria—

all these were hopes for the late 1950s. Through all this improvement Magloire maintained a formal "court" with emphasis on balls and fancy uniforms to impress his people.

Magloire failed to impress all of them enough, however, and when it was evident he intended to prolong his legal term, he was forced out of office by a general strike in December 1956. In the next year, strife-torn Haiti had seven different governments. After eight months of anarchy, military *junta* rule, and near-bankruptcy, Haiti elected François Duvalier president in September 1957. Ironically, the president made his first major speech on the 151st anniversary of the assassination of Jean Jacques Dessalines, the founder of the republic. By mid-1959 President Duvalier, a doctor who had worked in the campaign to eliminate yaws, was threatened with invasion by Fidel Castro's Cubans and the opposition Duvalier himself had exiled, and he had clamped down with strong-arm, dictatorial methods.

In 1961 Duvalier declared himself re-elected for a six-year term, and in 1964 he proclaimed himself president for life. He asked the Haitians to vote on Haiti's twentieth constitution, which named him permanent president and gave him sweeping powers, but the ballot used for the vote was simply a piece of paper containing the one word "oui," yes. Duvalier himself said, "I am an exceptional man, the kind the country could produce once every half-century. I am the personifaction of the Haitian people, and only God can take my power from me." The uneducated country people loved him and called him "Papa Doc," while he controlled the educated city people with his fierce personal army of terrorists, called the *tonton macoute*. Thus Haiti faced the 1970s as a failure in democracy, the failure of its own people and of the outsiders who have intruded upon them to achieve modern civilization.

But the folk art, the music, and the dances of the Haitians are much admired. Modern Haitian artistic endeavor which has received recognition abroad has, like the Cuban, been built around the African slave theme. A *Centre d'Art Moderne* in Port-au-Prince provides art lessons and an exhibit gallery for Haitians who show interest in developing native themes. Prizes in Pan American novel contests have been won by two brothers named Philippe and Pierre Marcelin (born in 1904 and in 1908, respectively), whose works *Canapé-Vert* and *The Beast of the Haitian Hills* are novels of Haitian peasant life. Haitian art, in a brilliant primitive style graphically portraying native farm and market life in Haiti, became very popular in the United States and Paris in the 1950s. Several composers have developed an exotic native-type music with many African characteristics. The most original of these was Justin Elie (1883–1931), who found inspiration in voodoo chants. Alain Chérie was Haiti's most gifted composer in recent times.

The French-speaking mulattoes in the cities, not so interested in this renaissance of peasant art and literature, strive to orient themselves toward Parisian culture. They had always hoped to live a sophisticated life, go to the university in Paris, and read their well-edited daily newspapers and French-language Haitian reviews. But their writings were not taken seriously in France and are not known to the rest of the New World. By being French-speaking, even the elite Haitians cut themselves off from the mainstream of Latin American affairs. Duvalier's dictatorship silenced many of their publications, drove many of them into exile, and forced an even deeper rift between his Negro, voodoo-ridden following and the mulatto elite.

THE DOMINICAN REPUBLIC:
SPANISH-SPEAKING HALF OF HISPANIOLA

The Dominican Republic, the Spanish-speaking half of the island, contains 3,400,000 people, a million less people than does the Haitian section, while it is almost twice as large in area, with more land and less mountains. The Dominican people pride themselves on being descendants of the earliest Spanish colonists and have ambitions to be considered a white nation; though predominantly mulattoes they have no pride in Negro blood as do the Haitians. While there is no discrimination against those of Negro or mixed blood born in the Republic, there still is bitter hatred of the Negroes who have migrated in from Haiti to work on the sugar plantations. Dominicans consider themselves cultured in the Spanish tradition; they belong to poetry clubs and literary societies, read the best novels of Spanish America, and write novels in the same style. Only 370,000, 12 per cent of the total, live in the one large city, Santo Domingo, but they are, in general, much more attuned to modern life than the Haitians and their wealthiest people enter into international society as sophisticated Latins—all this in spite of the fact that their country, like Haiti and Nicaragua, was occupied by United States military forces during the first third of the twentieth century, and has been dominated by one of the most ruthless modern dictators during the great part of the second third.

They had ended the nineteenth century under the domination of an earlier picturesque Negro dictator, Ulises Heureaux. His assassination in 1899 had given rise to new revolutions. For the next five years there was nothing but anarchy. Money had been borrowed from European firms to such an extent that yearly payments, if made, would consume all but $100,000 of the national income. In 1903 and 1904 France and other nations threatened to collect the debt payments by force. By arrangement with the almost defunct Dominican government in October 1904, Theodore Roosevelt took over one of the customs houses and acted as receiver for the bankrupt nation. America agreed to recognize the territorial integrity of the republic, administer the finances, pay 55 per cent of the customs revenue on the debts, and give 45 per cent to the Dominican government. A new treaty of 1907 provided that customs receivership should continue as long as bonds were outstanding. Though many Americans, and Dominicans as well, opposed such intervention, it is true that the Dominican government actually received much more revenue under this regime than it had when the entire customs were turned over to the corrupt officials. More money was collected yearly than the creditors demanded, and much of it was available for local public works.

The United States was at first merely in charge of finances, with no military occupation. American interests seemed always to be on one side or the other, in the chaotic-political upheavals, so that the interference did more harm than good, politically. In 1915 a distinguished physician, Francisco Enríquez y Carvajal, was chosen interim president after an especially chaotic period of disorder. He was to make some arrangements with the United States acceptable to both nations and to supervise the next election. When the treaty suggested by the United States was not accepted by Enríquez' party, American financial agents refused his government any money. There ensued five months of deadlock. Finally, in November 1916, Captain Harry S. Knapp of the United States Navy landed, announced the military occupation of the Dominican Republic for "repeated violation" of Theodore Roosevelt's agreement, and established a direct military government under the United States Navy Department. This direct American rule was not carried out through puppet presidents as was done in Haiti. The proud Dominicans refused to serve as such puppets, so the subterfuge was maintained that this was "an independent state under temporary occupation."

The direct military government, with martial law and troops in occupation, lasted eight years. Much was accomplished in the way of material betterment; finances were efficiently administered, the bureaucracy trimmed to reason and trained in civil service, schools and sanitation improved, and a civilian police force organized. Streets were paved and the harbor facilities improved. During the occupation, however, even those who approved military action had reason to be ashamed. The United States was involved in World War I; the army withdrew the best officers and sent inefficient, prejudiced men and raw recruits into the occupation. None of these "rulers" tried to learn the Spanish language or Latin American customs. The Dominicans remained hostile and uncooperative. When a distinguished young poet, Fabio Fiallo, was jailed for denouncing the United States, resentment ran high. Woodrow Wilson himself was sympathetic and suggested withdrawing all American influence save the control of finances; for the Dominicans it was "all or nothing at all."

The Harding administration in 1922 sent Sumner Welles to work out a tactful plan for effective withdrawal. Welles' candidate, Horacio Vásquez, backed by a coalition of parties, was elected in a supervised but fair vote. He came to Washington, was greeted as an equal, and returned to be inaugurated for a four-year term. He was willing to allow American technical experts to remain quietly behind the scenes but American troops were all withdrawn by 1924. With the revenues thus stabilized, Vásquez continued the public works projects as a purely Dominican venture, and gained credit in the eyes of his people. At the end of a six-year term, a period of prosperity and relative political tranquility, he became ill and went to the United States for treatment, assuming that he would be re-elected. But as soon as Vásquez' back was turned, a group of generals attempted to take over the government. The chief of these generals was Rafael Trujillo. Vásquez, who had practically promised the United States that there would be no more bloody revolution, adjusted the matter when he returned from the hospital, and then resigned owing to "ill health." Backed by the army, Trujillo promptly took over the government, meanwhile holding an election in May 1930 in which he was elected himself.

Thus began, in 1930, "Year One" of the Era of Trujillo. A mixture of the opportunistic type of Somoza and the oppressive type of Machado, Rafael Leonidas Trujillo Molina, born in 1893, had been a cattle rustler like Venezuela's Gómez before he joined the army. Soon he became chief of staff and made the constabulary his private army. Now he was absolute ruler and remained so until his death in 1961. Santo Domingo, a city once ruled by Columbus, was renamed Trujillo, as were many villages, plazas, and streets. Twenty private residences belonged to the dictator, as well as a majority of all small industries, and one-fifth of all the agricultural land of the republic, for Trujillo was interested in cattle, "rustled" or legally confiscated. He served four times as president and had puppets in office between his own terms. His brother Hector served as president and on May 14, 1957, was "re-elected" for another full term. His six brothers, all his minor relatives, and his many children, legitimate and otherwise, had lucrative positions in the government. Over the entrance to hospitals appeared the inscription, "Only Trujillo Cures You." Those whose democratic idealism he did not "cure" were either dead or elsewhere. In fact, so bitter were his opponents in exile that they formed a powerful "Caribbean Legion" in 1948, and, failing to land on Dominican soil, collected sympathetic exiles fleeing from other dictators and fought for Costa Rica in a fracas with Nicaragua.

The hundreds of other political exiles could not be sure of returning even on Trujillo's death, for his twenty-eight-year old son and favorite, a pampered young playboy of the international "jet set" was slated as his "heir." Nearly 70 per cent of the Dominicans worked for Trujillo. Even the dictator's office-holding relatives actually worked long, strictly supervised hours at specific responsibilities. Trujillo himself was indefatigable, with a businessman's knowledge of his entire "estate," both public and private. The whole "republic" was his well-kept garden. He and his family busily salted away hundreds of millions in profit in Swiss banks, while he maintained lobbyists abroad to build up a favorable image.

Nevertheless, other Western Hemisphere peoples despised him. There was especially bad blood between Trujillo and Haiti. He encouraged his people's prejudice, begun in the days of Boyer, against the darker Haitians. Trujillo's anti-Haitian policy hit the world's headlines during the massacre of Haitian field workers in 1937. He balanced this adverse publicity by offering to take in displaced war refugees from Europe, though few ever arrived. He had declared war on the Axis powers right after Pearl Harbor, profited by the wartime trade, and paid his debts. American control of finances was ended by treaty in 1941. He claimed to be completely out of debt to any foreign nation, though gladly accepting American economic and military aid against "Communism" in the 1950s.

Sugar remained the major crop, and the world's largest sugar refinery, the Río Haina, was in the Dominican Republic. Exports of bananas, coffee, and cacao increased. Though a million or more Dominicans still lived on their tiny "patch and thatch" farms, the country as a whole was self-sufficient in food, and rural areas were more prosperous than in neighboring Haiti. The farms were more level and fertile and there was more water on level land for irrigation. Anyone who did not like the "patrón" system of farming under Trujillo's henchmen would have his farm taken over directly by the dictator.

Despite a general cultural backwardness, the Dominican Republic in the first part of the century did produce some well-known figures in art and literature. The two sons of Doña Salomé Ureña de Henríquez (1850–1897), the great woman writer and educator of the late nineteenth century, achieved wider fame than did their mother. One of the brothers, Pedro Henríquez Ureña (1884–1946) was a distinguished literary critic and anthologist of Latin American literature. Abelardo Rodriguez Urdaneta was a leader in Dominican painting and for twenty-five years director of the Dominican Academy of Fine Arts, widely advertised by Trujillo's lobbyists as a cultural center. But the three million Dominicans, 56 per cent illiterate, lived little better than they had in the sixteenth century.

By mid-1959, however, many Dominicans looked toward Fidel Castro in Cuba for some help against the dictator. Trujillo in his turn appealed to the Organization of American States for help against *Fidelista* infiltrators. Trujillo himself in those years was playing host to the exiled dictators, Perón, Pérez Jiménez, and Batista, who had been recently ousted from other Latin American countries. In 1960 there was evidence that Trujillo's agents had tried to assassinate Venezuela's liberal President Betancourt. Venezuela appealed to the Organization of American States to censure Trujillo, and a motion was made that its members break relations with the Dominican Republic and place an embargo on trade with Trujillo. With this opposition in the Hemisphere, Trujillo clamped down on what little opposition he had at home, and evidently planned to stay in power forever.

But younger officers in his own private army, angry at long delays in promotion, formed a plot against him, led by Colonel Antonio Imbert Barrera. In May 1961 three of them ambushed and shot the old dictator on a lonely road as he was driving to meet a current girl friend. Gone was the glory of "God and Trujillo", the "Benefactor of the Patria." There followed six months of tyranny and chaos in Dominican politics. The puppet vice-president, Joaquim Balaguer, vied for power with Trujillo's own brothers and the favorite heir, Rafael Trujillo, Jr., while American naval vessels stood far off shore to protect American citizens. In January 1962 all members of the Trujillo family and close intimates fled the country to live "happily ever afterward" on the Swiss savings.

A Council of Government was formed which ran the uneasy country throughout 1962 and called an election for December 20, to be supervised by the OAS. Eight political parties had mushroomed in the confusion, grouping around a conservative businessmen's party on the right and the

Popular Revolutionary Democrats, or PRD, a moderate left. The latter group, outlawing Castro-ite Communists from its midst, won the election with a 62 per cent vote. Their candidate was Juan Bosch, son of Catalan and German parents, a novelist and political science teacher, who had been working against Trujillo from exile for nearly two decades. He was a close friend of Betancourtis and of the Costa Rican liberal "Pepe" Figueres.

With a controlling vote in congress, Bosch started to push the inexperienced new "democracy" toward all types of democratic reforms as rapidly as possible. He tried to distribute the Trujillo farm lands to the peasants, only to meet the legal block of court action from the families who had owned the land before it was confiscated by Trujillo in the first place. Businessmen opposed his orders to nationalize all the Trujillo business enterprises, hoping to share in their profits themselves. Army men feared that Bosch would end the political power of the officers, who had staged the assassination of Trujillo. So, in spite of American backing, Bosch fell from power after only seven months. A military and civilian *junta* exiled him to Puerto Rico and took over the government in September 1963. Army leaders who led the *coup* were Colonel Imbert, who had killed Trujillo, and a fanatical anti-Communist of Lebanese descent, General Elías Wessin y Wessin, who thought every act of Bosch was Castro-inspired. A businessman of Scottish descent, Donald Reid Cabral, soon dominated the *junta* and ruled the country, with United States recognition and financial aid.

Reid Cabral's rule could not be tyrannical, with six of the political parties still active and protesting. It was only inept and corrupt, torn between active Communists, who fed on the disappointment of the masses in all the empty promises of the post-Trujillo governments, and the rightist military leaders. Reid set the date for elections on September 1, 1965, but the restless factions could not wait. A revolution led by Bosch sympathizers exploded on April 25, 1965, with wild violence in the streets of Santo Domingo. Junior officers, in the name of the exiled Juan Bosch, passed out arms to the street fighters, who threatened to attack embassies and hotels where there were hundreds of foreigners.

After an absence of 31 years, the United States Marines returned. President Johnson was anxious to prevent another Castro-type Communist Caribbean takeover. On the excuse that American lives were in danger, he quickly sent thousands of American marines and paratroopers. These American forces soon controlled the central part of the city. Another section was in the hands of the army officers under Colonel Imbert, and Wessin y Wessin, though the latter was forced to resign under American pressure as too "rightist" a figure. The other third of the city, the slums and the port, was held by an opportunist named Colonel Francisco Camaaño Deno in the name of Juan Bosch. It was feared that this group contained many Castro sympathizers, and it is true that somewhere they found arms and ammunition for 15,000 guerila street fighters.

Johnson was widely criticized for this quick, large-scale unilateral action in violation of treaties pledging no intervention without joint action. His attitude was called the "Johnson Doctrine," an attempt to stop the spread of Caribbean Communism by United States military action. By a narrow margin, the Organization of American States voted to send in a military force, the first vote of its kind in history. In the following weeks, Brazil sent 1,200 men and a general to command the entire military effort. Token contingents came from a few other Latin American nations. The combined force, still largely American troops, was being called the OAS Peace Force. Except for sporadic sniping, this force did bring about a stalemate in August 1965. Many different missions had tried to work out a democratic solution and prevent both a Castro takeover and further bloodshed—an OAS mission, Figueres and Betancourt as friends of Bosch, a papal nuncio, McGeorge Bundy as Johnson's personal representative. No one could ascertain how serious the actual threat of Communism had been.

Finally after four months of negotiations and gunfire, both Imbert and Camaaño resigned their "commands." Bosch and Trujillo's vice-president, Balaguer, had each returned to the island as private individuals. A compromise provisional president, Hector García Godoy, the Republic's forty-seventh president, took office September 3, 1965. Backed by the OAS Peace Force, he cleared both parts of the city of armed men and reinstated regular traffic and food sales as an uneasy peace settled on the oldest city in the Western Hemisphere.

Riots continued in smaller towns well into 1966. In the late spring only 6,500 United States soldiers remained, and they were to be withdrawn after elections scheduled for June 1, 1966. Both Joaquín Balaguer and Juan Bosch carried on active campaigns for the presidency, but in a peaceful, good-humored spirit. Balanguer won by a 140,000 vote margin out of 1,270,000 votes cast, and was peacefully inaugurated on July 1, 1966. In the following month, the last 8000 OAS troops, 6300 of them from the United States, were withdrawn entirely. Only a few United States officers remained as advisers for President Balaguer's national guard. Free from control by the Trujillo family, Balaguer proved a good administrator. Bosch supporters entered his coalition cabinet, as he promised to "operate with a scalpel on those old ulcers of Dominican progress, inflation, corruption, political favoritism, and inefficiency." The Castro leftists were so weakened by the spring of 1967 that they failed dismally in an attempt to call a nation-wide anti-Balaguer strike. On the day of the announced protest, more people came to work than usual.

As to the necessity of the United States and the OAS intervention of 1965, questions remained unanswered: whether the whole incident was another unpopular intervention in the Caribbean; whether an OAS Peace Force was a workable new institution; and above all, whether the strife-torn underprivileged island republic could achieve democracy at all in the first generation after Trujillo's long reign.

Readings

Alexander, R. J., *Communism in Latin America* (1957)
———, *Organized Labor in Latin America* (1965)

Arciniegas, G., *Caribbean: Sea of the New World*, trans. H. de Onis (1946)
Balch, E. G., *et al.*, *Occupied Haiti* (1927)
Beals, C., *Crime of Cuba* (1934)
Bemis, S. F., *Latin American Policy of the United States* (1943)
A Bilingual Report on the Dominican Republic Today (1964)
Blackwell, A. S., *Some Spanish American Poets* (1929)
Blanchard, P., *Democracy and Empire in the Caribbean* (1947)
Bosch, J., *et al.*, *The Dominican Republic* (1964)
————, *The Unfinished Experiment: Democracy in the Dominican Republic* (1965)
Buell, R. L., ed., *Problems of the New Cuba* (1935)
Burks, D. D., *Cuba under Castro* (1964)
Callcott, W. H., *The Caribbean Policy of the United States, 1890–1920* (1942)
Chapman, C. E., *History of the Cuban Republic* (1927)
Chester, E. A., *A Sergeant Named Batista* (1954)
Coester, A., *Literary History of Spanish America* (rev. ed., 1928)
Courlander, H., *The Drum and the Hoe: Life and Lore of the Haitian People* (1960)
Crasmiller, R., *Trujillo* (1966)
Davis, H. P., *Black Democracy: Story of Haiti* (rev. ed., 1936)
Dewart, L., *Christianity and Revolution: The Lessons of Cuba* (1963)
De Young, M., *Man and Land in the Haitian Economy* (1958)
Draper, T., *Castroism Theory and Practise* (1965)
————, *Castro's Revolution—Myths and Realities* (1962)
Dreier, J. C., *The Organization of American States and the Hemisphere Crisis* (1962)
Dubois, J., *Danger over Panama* (1964)
Espaillat, A., *Trujillo: The Last Caesar* (1963)
Fagg, J. E., *Cuba, Haiti, and the Dominican Republic* (1965)
Fergusson, E., *Cuba* (1946)
Fitzgibbon, R. H., *Cuba and the United States, 1900–1935* (1935)
Foner, P. S., *A History of Cuba and Its Relations with the United States, 1492–1895*, Vol. I (1962)
Foreign Policy Association, *Cuban Crisis: A Documentary Record* (1963)
Fox, A. B., *Freedom and Welfare in the Caribbean* (1949)
Gilly, A., *Inside the Cuban Revolution* (1964)
Goldenberg, B., *The Cuban Revolution and Latin America* (1965)
Goldwert, M., *The Constabulary in the Dominican Republic and Nicaragua—Progeny and Legacy of United States Intervention* (1962)
Gray, R. B., *José Martí, Cuban Patriot* (1962)
Halperin, E., *Castro and Latin American Communism* (1963)
————, *Castro's Cuba* (1966)
————, *The Ideology of Castroism and Its Impact on the Communist Parties of Latin America* (1963)
Hamill, H. M., Jr., *Dictatorship in Latin America* (1965)
Harris, S. G., ed., *Economic Problems of Latin America* (1944)
Henly, D. F., *The United States in Cuba, 1898–1902* (1963)
Herskovits, M., *Life in a Haitian Village* (1937)
Hicks, A., *Blood in the Streets: Life and Rule of Trujillo* (1946)
Howland, C. P., ed., *Survey of American Foreign Relations* (1929)
International Bank of Reconstruction and Development, *Report on Cuba* (1951)
Ireland, G., *Boundaries, Possessions and Conflicts in North America and the Caribbean* (1941)

James, P., *Latin America* (2nd ed., 1950)

Jenks, L. H., *Our Cuban Colony* (1928)

Johnson, H., *Bay of Pigs: The Leader's Story of Brigade 2506* (1964)

Jones, C. L., *Caribbean Since 1900* (1936)

Knight, M. M., *Americans in Santo Domingo* (1928)

Kurzman, D., *Santo Domingo: Revolt of the Damned* (1965)

Lago, C. M., and R. E. Hernandez Morales, *Social Security in Cuba* (1964)

Latortue, G. R., *Feudal Haiti: Caribbean Crisis* (1966)

Leyburn, J. G., *Haitian People* (1941)

Lieuwen, E., *Generals versus Presidents* (1964)

Lockmiller, D. A., *Magoon in Cuba: A History of Second Intervention, 1906–1909* (1938)

MacGaffy, W., and C. H. Burnett, *Cuba, Its People, Its Society, Its Culture* (1962)

———, *Twentieth-Century Cuba, the Background of the Castro Revolution* (1965)

Manigat, L. F., *Haiti of the Sixties* (1964)

Mathews, H. L., *The Cuban Story* (1961)

———, *Return to Cuba* (1964) [A reply to this was published by Association for Reconstruction of Cuban Economy, Miami University, 1964]

McCrocklin, J. H., *Garde d'Haiti, 1915–1934* (1956)

Mecham, J. L., *Survey of United States-Latin American Relations* (1965)

Meyer, K. E. and T. Sculc, *The Cuban Invasion: The Chronicle of a Disaster* (1962)

Millspaugh, A. C., *Haiti Under American Control, 1915–1930* (1931)

Monchon, J., and K. O. Gilmore, *The Great Deception* (1963)

Montague, L. L., *Haiti and the United States 1714–1938* (1940)

Morray, J. P., *The Second Revolution in Cuba* (1962)

Munro, D. G., *Intervention and Dollar Diplomacy in the Caribbean, 1900–1921* (1964)

———, *United States and the Caribbean* (1934)

Nelson, L., *Rural Cuba* (1950)

Niles, B., *Black Haiti* (1926)

Noyes, R., *Investment in the Caribbean* (1964)

Ortiz y Fernandez, F., *Cuban Counterpoint: Tobacco and Sugar,* trans. H. de Onis (1947)

Osorio-Lizarazo, J. A., *Birth and Growth of Anti-Trujillism in America* (1958)

Pachter, H. M., *Collision Course: The Cuban Missile Crisis and Co-existence* (1963)

Perkins, D., *United States and the Caribbean* (1947)

Phillips, R. H., *Cuba: Island of Paradox* (1960)

Political, Economic and Social Thought of Fidel Castro (1959)

Puech-Parham, A. de, *My Odyssey: Experience of a Young Refugee from Two Revolutions by a Creole of Saint Domingue* (1959)

Rippy, J. F., *Caribbean Danger Zone* (1940)

Rivero, N., *Castro's Cuba* (1962)

Roberts, W. A., *Caribbean: Story of Our Sea of Destiny* (1940)

Rodman, S., *Haiti: The Black Republic* (1954)

———, *Quisqueya: A History of the Dominican Republic* (1962)

Rubens, H. S., *Liberty—The Story of Cuba* (1932)

Seabrook, W., *The Magic Island* (1929)

Seers, D., ed., *Cuba, the Economic and Social Revolution* (1964)

Smith, R. F., *Background to Revolution: Development of Modern Cuba* (1965)

———, *The United States and Cuba: Business and Diplomacy 1917–1960* (1961)

———, *What Happened in Cuba* (1963)

Sobel, L. A., *Cuba, United States, and Russia, 1960–1963* (1964)

Stuart, G. H., *Latin America and the United States* (5th ed., 1955)

Tang, P. S. H. and J. Malmey, *The Chinese Communist Impact on Cuba* (1962)

Tondel, L. M., ed., *Inter-American Security System and the Cuban in Crisis* (1964)

Underwood, E., *The Poets of Haiti, 1782–1934* (1934)

United States Congress, Subcommittee on Inter-American Affairs of the House Committee on Foreign Affairs, Hearings March 14, 1963

United States, Department of State, *Events in United States-Cuba Relations: A Chronology, 1957–January 1963* (1963)

——, *United States Policy Toward Cuba* (1964)

United States Senate Committee on Foreign Relations and Committee on Armed Services, 87th Congress, 2nd Session, *Situation in Cuba* (1962)

University of Miami Cuban Economic Research Project, *Cuba: Agriculture and Planning, 1963–1964* (1965)

Urrutia, M., *Fidel Castro and Company, Inc.* (1964)

Wallich, H. C., *Monetary Problems of an Export Economy: Cuban Experience, 1914–1947* (1950)

Waxman, S. M., *Bibliography of the Belles-Letters of Santo Domingo* (1931)

Welles, S., *Naboth's Vineyard* (2 vols., 1928)

Wilgus, A. C., ed., *Caribbean Area* (1934)

——, ed., *The Caribbean at Mid-Century* (1951)

——, ed., *Caribbean: Contemporary Education* (1960)

——, ed., *The Caribbean: Contemporary International Relations* (1957)

——, ed., *The Caribbean: Contemporary Trends* (1953)

——, ed., *The Caribbean: Its Culture* (1955)

——, ed., *The Caribbean: Its Economy* (1954)

——, ed., *The Caribbean: Its Political Problems* (1956)

——, ed., *Caribbean: Natural Resources* (1959)

——, ed., *The Caribbean: Peoples, Problems and Prospects* (1952)

Williams, E., *Negro in the Caribbean* (1942)

Williams, J. J., *Voodoos and Obeahs: Phases of West Indian Witchcraft* (1933)

Williams, W. A., *The United States, Cuba, and Castro* (1962)

Wood, H. A., *Northern Haiti: Land Use and Settlement* (1964)

Wright, P. G., *Cuban Situation and Our Treaty Relations* (1931)

Zeitlin, M., and R. Scheer, *Cuba: Tragedy in Our Hemisphere* (1963)

INTER-AMERICAN COOPERATION
IN THE TWENTIETH CENTURY

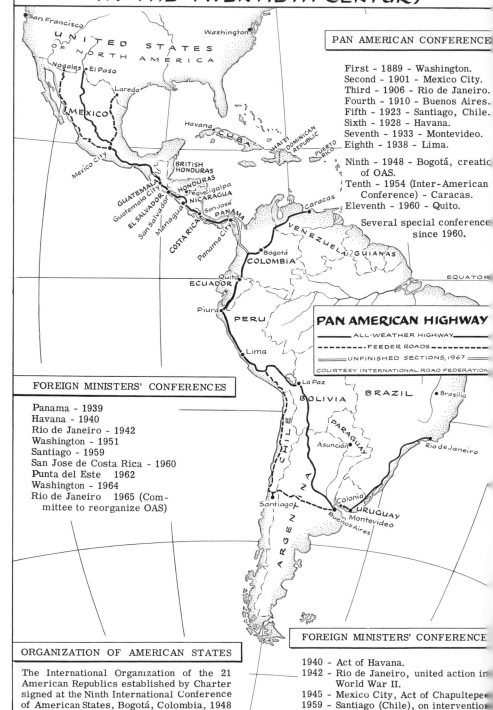

PAN AMERICAN CONFERENCE

First - 1889 - Washington.
Second - 1901 - Mexico City.
Third - 1906 - Rio de Janeiro.
Fourth - 1910 - Buenos Aires.
Fifth - 1923 - Santiago, Chile.
Sixth - 1928 - Havana.
Seventh - 1933 - Montevideo.
Eighth - 1938 - Lima.

Ninth - 1948 - Bogotá, creatio
of OAS.
Tenth - 1954 (Inter-American
Conference) - Caracas.
Eleventh - 1960 - Quito.

Several special conference
since 1960.

PAN AMERICAN HIGHWAY

———— ALL-WEATHER HIGHWAY ————
- - - - - - - FEEDER ROADS - - - - - - -
===== UNFINISHED SECTIONS, 1967 =====
COURTESY INTERNATIONAL ROAD FEDERATION

FOREIGN MINISTERS' CONFERENCES

Panama - 1939
Havana - 1940
Rio de Janeiro - 1942
Washington - 1951
Santiago - 1959
San Jose de Costa Rica - 1960
Punta del Este   1962
Washington - 1964
Rio de Janeiro   1965 (Com-
mittee to reorganize OAS)

ORGANIZATION OF AMERICAN STATES

The International Organization of the 21
American Republics established by Charter
signed at the Ninth International Conference
of American States, Bogotá, Colombia, 1948

FOREIGN MINISTERS' CONFERENCE

1940 - Act of Havana.
1942 - Rio de Janeiro, united action in
World War II.
1945 - Mexico City, Act of Chapultepe
1959 - Santiago (Chile), on interventio

Part VII

LATIN AMERICA ASSUMES
AN IMPORTANT PLACE
IN INTERNATIONAL AFFAIRS

To the Statler Hotel in New York in a recent spring came delegates from twenty-one nations to attend the Congress of the Pan American Association of Ophthalmologists, eye doctors who perform sightsaving surgery. Says the *Américas* magazine, journal of the Pan American Union, in describing this meeting, "Its announcement did not excite a flicker of surprise. Everybody takes Hemisphere cooperation more or less for granted and agrees that medical interchange is vital. Yet only a short twenty years ago such pooling of professional knowledge among eye specialists of North and Latin America would have been impossible."[1] This particular organization of doctors was spark-plugged by Dr. Moacyr E. Álvaro, a

[1] Betty Reef, "Battle Against Blindness," *Américas*, March 1957.

Brazilian specialist trained in Vienna and honored in the United States as an authority on glaucoma. His Ophthalmologists' Association has made the "first definite survey of blindness in the Western Hemisphere. Through Association offices, leading United States eye doctors have visited Latin American countries to give lectures. The compliment implied has led many to study Spanish or Portuguese so they can deliver their talks in the language of their hosts." A journal published by the society is put out in Spanish and English. Several American texts on eye treatment have been translated into Spanish and Portuguese by the Association staff. The Association members have also pledged themselves to set up examining boards to quality doctors in the home nations, and thus to raise standards of practice in the fight against blindness.

This improvement in eyesight on a Hemisphere-wide scale was made possible through the cultural and scientific activities of the Organization of American States and its Sanitary Bureau. It is watched with eager interest by the World Health Organization, the WHO of the United Nations. Like its counterparts in the fields of child health, slum clearance, scientific agriculture, control of tropical diseases, and a host of other specialities, the Pan American Association of Ophthalmologists exemplifies effective cultural exchange in a joint endeavor which breeds respect and understanding throughout the Hemisphere. In such endeavors the Pan American regional organizations are leading the world.

Such cooperative effort was not always possible among New World nations. For a century after independence the Latin American nations remained isolated from each other and from the United States. When Latin American nations contacted each other it was to quarrel over boundaries, or to go to war against Francisco Solano López in Paraguay, or to fight about nitrates in the War of the Pacific. Relations with England had centered in economic investments and trade while Latin American relations with other European countries during the nineteenth century had been of little importance. The United States meanwhile threatened the European nations with war under the Monroe Doctrine if they tampered with Latin American independence, and at the same time rattled the saber of Manifest Destiny at the nearby Latin neighbors. After 1900, Latin American nations spent thirty years fearing and hating the United States, thinking of the growing power above the Rio Grande as the "Colossus of the North," bent on "Dollar Diplomacy."

Then came the Good Neighbor Policy of the 1930s which changed this anti-American attitude for the better. It succeeded in guaranteeing a more united front in World War II; nevertheless the war provoked further ill-will toward the United States. The neglect of the Latin American area by the United States after the end of the war further weakened the friendships that had begun to blossom with the Good Neighbor Policy. In fact, if an ophthalmologists' conference could lessen "blindness" in the Hemisphere, it should have worked on the "glaucoma" that appeared in the United States policy toward Latin America in the 1950s. A blind neglect of Latin America's needs, together with their policies of economic nationalism, caused bitter reaction and produced the attacks on Vice-President Nixon in the spring of 1958. Subsequent events proved that the United States learned a lesson from Mr. Nixon's tour, and more attention was paid to Latin America's real problems.

Then in the 1960s the United States saw a new threat to its own security in the New World. ·Fidel Castro's Communism in Cuba was threatening to spill over into other Caribbean-centered nations. Should the United States act alone to stop it? At the Bay of Pigs in 1961 the United States saw itself involved in a fiasco. Eighteen months later, in the Russian missile confrontation, President Kennedy asked and, within twenty-four hours, got the support of the Organization of American States in his stand against Russia. Three years later fears of Communism's spread to the Dominican Republic brought American marines in alone, while President Johnson tardily asked for inter-American support.

On the economic front, the United States cooperated fully with all Latin America in a new, bold Alliance for Progress in 1961. It was a ten-year plan to stop the appeal of Communism by offering generous financial aid to those countries which would aid themselves. The countries who received help were pledged to increase democratic methods at home, collect taxes from their own rich classes, make well-planned efforts to educate and house their masses, institute land reforms, and modernize industrial and agricultural methods. As the New World faced the 1970s, the new approach of the Alliance for Progress seemed to have turned the tide toward optimism

Latin America's basic economic and social problems remained. Yearly per-capita income averaged $150 in nine of the nations, including tiny Honduras and vast Brazil. Mexico and Panama listed their per-capita average income at $250 in the mid-1960s, Uruguay and Chile at $400, Argentina at $550, and oil-rich Venezuela at $650. Meanwhile the population continued to increase at 3 per cent a year. Thirty per cent of Latin Americans lived in city "shanty slums." The food intake in calories was very low as compared to the United States. Only 5 per cent of the land surface was used for agriculture, and that 5 per cent was very inefficiently farmed.

With the Latin American nations producing 80 per cent of the world's coffee, 75 per cent of the world's sugar, 68 per cent of its meats, 64 per cent of its bananas, and 40 per cent of its copper, trade should be brisk and life good. But the oas, the un, the Alliance for Progress, and a friendly and generous United States could not produce diversification enough in a generation to balance the economic ills and local poverty produced by dependence on a few crops.

Latin American people tend to expect immediate solutions to political and economic problems as they pass from dictatorial to democratically elected governments. The worldwide "Revolution of Expectations of the 1960s" has led people to expect too much too quickly, and hence has provoked a phase of anti-American nationalism. All the Americas, north and south, need a mutual acceptance of each other's respective values.

Most of the individual stories of trade projects, wartime cooperation, and diplomatic relations have been told in the foregoing chapters. The remainder of the book aims to summarize activities from the Hemispheric and the world point of view. Of the two concluding chapters, the first focuses upon political and diplomatic developments. Such developments provided the structures within which other forces have begun to operate,— the forces of economic advance, cultural interchange, social improvement, and Western Hemisphere regional cooperation which are described in the last chapter. These forces form an optimistic hope for the future as the story of Latin American civilization is brought up to the immediate present.

Chapter 40

Latin American Relations with the United States and with the World

RELATIONS WITH EUROPEAN NATIONS

T HE "MEETING OF TWO WORLDS" after 1492 brought the European nations, Spain and Portugal, into contact with the Western Hemisphere. Later the Spanish colonies had reason to fear encroachments of other European nations, France and England. Today the virile young nations of the New World, such as Brazil, Argentina, or Mexico, can treat with England as an equal, and can feel themselves as stable as France and much more powerful than Spain or Portugal. During the century and a half since independence, Latin America's relationships with nearly every European nation have taken an almost complete turnabout. The newly independent nations in the 1800s, however, they either feared intervention from the European countries or asked for their help. Spain's position in today's world has become negligible and her interest in Latin America only cultural. England, in the 1800s the dominant world power and principal investor in Latin American industry and transportation facilities, has today become a lesser force and can afford to take only a minor interest. This is even more true of France. Germany, however, a power "on the make" from 1900 to 1940, became a serious threat to the Western Hemisphere in the 1930s, and more recently Russia has been something of a similar menace.

Ties with the mother country, Spain, had been abruptly broken early in the nineteenth century. Later Spain made some feeble attempts at friendship. In 1856 the Spanish minister in Washington contacted the ministers from the Latin American countries to discuss plans for union. But ill-advised officials in Madrid counterbalanced the movement by attempting to establish a monarchy in Ecuador. When the plot was discovered, diplomatic relations with Ecuador were severed in 1846. Spain continued to harass her former west coast colonies and made war against Peru and Chile in 1864 to 1866. Though a small naval fracas rather than a full-fledged war, it served to infuriate the west coast countries against the Spaniards, especially since Spain had not officially recognized them at the time. That Spain meant to maintain a foothold where she could was proven by her "reacceptance" of Santo Domingo as a colony under Santana in 1861, and her desperate hold in Cuba. When Cuba was lost in 1899, then Spanish attention was turned to holding Spanish America by ties of "loyalty" alone, and concentrated on a program of cultural *rapprochement* called *Hispanidad*. (See Chapter 41.)

France could never forget that the richest of all her colonies had been the sugar-producing island of Haiti. French rulers were willing to try a naval blockade on Vera Cruz in 1838 and an intervention in the affairs of Rosas and Uruguay at about the same time. France's investments in Mexico and the purchase of the Swiss Jecker bonds by a relative of Napoleon III gave that monarch the excuse for his famous attempt in Mexico, his sponsoring of the ill-fated Maximilian against Juárez. It was the last attempt to expand French colonialism in the New World. But French culture has continued to be a dominant force in Latin American life.

The colony-hungry German government made several "passes" at Latin America during these days of phenomenal economic growth. In 1897 two German naval vessels appeared in Haitian waters to demand the freedom of a German national who was being held for assaulting a policeman, and to present an ultimatum to the Haitian government. The United States declined to intervene under the Monroe Doctrine; Haiti accepted the ultimatum, freed the German, and made a formal apology. A year later, when the United States went to war against Spain in Cuba, the German Kaiser was openly sympathetic with Spain, as one monarchy to another. Because of the German threat to send forces to Venezuela to collect the debt incurred to German banks by the dictator Cipriano Castro, Theodore Roosevelt formulated the Roosevelt Corollary. He threatened the action of a United States naval squadron in Venezuelan water to prevent the landing of German troops. The dispute was settled by arbitration in 1904.

These incidents helped to build up fear of German expansionism in Latin America. When, in January 1917, the Zimmerman note—a cable from the German Foreign Secretary instructing the minister in Mexico to offer California, New Mexico, Texas, and Arizona to Mexico in return for an alliance with Germany if the United States should go to war—was intercepted and given publicity in America, these fears seemed realized. During World War I eight Latin American nations declared war; five others had sufficient belligerent status to sit in on the Versailles Peace Conference as contracting parties. Defeat ended German expansionism for the time being, cut her merchant fleet down to nothing, bankrupted her foreign investments, and brought her into the depths of depression ahead of the rest of the world. The Weimar Republic could afford no Latin American policy, save an attempt at mutual trade relations.

The Third Reich under Hitler had a more aggressive policy, with political overtones. Every German trader among the Indian tribes, every German storekeeper on the pampas, as well as German pilots with the airplane companies and German bank clerks in the cities all became potential Nazi agents. If such New World Germans were not ardent Nazis they were replaced by ones who were. Many Argentine radio stations and newspapers were controlled by the Nazis as propaganda tools for the whole New World. The German embassy in Buenos Aires was the center of such espionage. Though there were many more German immigrants living in Chile, with the city of Valdivia a center of German settlement and language, Chile remained more nearly neutral and less suspect to the democratic nations than did Argentina. After Pearl Harbor, only these two southern South American countries failed to break with the Axis.

The account of Latin American participation in World War II has been given in the account of individual nations as it affected their national history and economic situation. Fear of Nazi infiltration brought the Latin American nations into conferences in 1938 and 1939 to declare their "common concern" and to "quarantine" Western waters, as told in the story of the Pan American conferences. Twenty-one states joined in wartime agencies and boards after 1942. With the advice of these boards, Nazi firms in the Americas were eliminated, Nazi funds blocked. Only the 104 Axis-controlled firms in Argentina remained in operation. Even Argentina broke off diplomatic relations with Germany in the last few weeks of the war. The hatred of things German did not hold over into the 1960s, however, as West Germany, an economically rather than a politically active new state, proceeded to recapture and multiply the trade which all of Germany had held before the war.

Relations with the other Axis powers during World War II were never as dangerous or as unfriendly. Italy was a Latin country, center of the Catholic faith. Millions of people in Argentina and Brazil were of Italian origin. Italian investment was never large; Mussolini's propaganda agents were not very clever. Italy was out of the war by 1943, and few Latin Americans thought of her as a menace. Japanese relations were resumed after the war, and a thriving Japanese-Brazilian trade picked up where it had stopped in 1941. The Japanese merchant fleet was again visiting South American waters in the 1960s; Japanese colonists were being invited to the rice plantations Brazil was attempting to establish on the Amazon.

In the 1960s Latin America felt her interests were often inimicable to those of Europe. Attempting to launch a Latin American Common Market, the grain and meat producing states feared the rivalry of the

European Common Market, while banana, coffee, and sugar producing states feared British Commonwealth trade areas in Africa and Asia. Charles de Gaulle, wooing Latin American trade in 1964 and hoping to win Latin American sympathy for his Third Force against the United States, found a cool reception on his visit to South American capitals in 1964.

In the post World War II era, Russian infiltration became a danger. There were active Communist parties in several countries. Perón used Russian funds to propagandize against the United States; Guatemala was controlled in 1954 by a pro-Communist government with Russian money; the April 1964 the Castelo Branco revolution in Brazil ousted the Russian sympathizer Goulart. With the rise of Fidel Castro as the Communist leader in Cuba, Russian policy seemed to turn the training and financing of Western Hemisphere Communist groups over to him, under long-range Moscow direction. Appealing to workers, to peasants, and particularly to university students, Castro-type Communists made "Yanquis, No!" a youth cry, as much for national patriotism as for international Communism. By the mid-1960s the old-line Cuban Communist Party, loyal to Russia, was being elbowed out of importance in Cuba. Ché Guevara, a world-oriented Communist revolutionary, disappeared from the Cuban scene. Thirteen hundred Castro-trained guerillas were reported in the highlands of Peru in 1965, a hundred in Colombia, 150 in Guatemala, all under fiery, young native Communist leaders who had been to Havana, but not to Moscow. Moscow, still hoping to control these "native products" and to avoid any influence on them from Peking, called an Afro-Asian-Latin Communist Party Conference in Havana in January 1966. That the democratic Latin American governments were aware of this menace was proven by their cooperation with the Alliance for Progress in the later 1960s.

As for England, her participation in Latin American affairs was more economic than political and forms a portion of the next chapter. Occasionally England concerned herself with Latin American diplomatic affairs. In 1833 she seized the Falkland Islands while the Argentine dictator Rosas protested. In the Uruguayan difficulties she sent a fleet to blockade the harbor during the siege of Montevideo; in the Maximilian episode she joined with Spain and Napoleon III in an attempt to collect debts, then withdrew when she became suspicious of French plans. As the self-appointed conscience of the world in the fight against the slave trade, she enforced her blockade of the African coast. England exacted from Brazil a promise to end the slave trade as a price for recognition of Brazil as a nation in 1827. When it was later apparent that Brazilians took this promise none too seriously, English warships infringed on Brazilian sovereignty by entering Brazilian ports to stop the slavers. Only when Brazil made the slave trade illegal in 1850 was this problem finally solved.

Accepting the United States as the dominant power in the Caribbean area after the American Civil War, Britain was mainly concerned that any canal built should be neutral and free. In the Clayton-Bulwer Treaty of 1850 both powers pledged themselves to avoid dominating Central America and to assist in the building of a free canal jointly. With the British already holding a piece of Honduran coast at Belize, Britain challenged this treaty almost as soon as it was made by declaring the Bay Islands a British colony. American protests forced her to withdraw, and to give up the toe-hold on the Mosquito Coast of Nicaragua also. A half-century later the Hay-Pauncefote Treaty guaranteed America's right to build the Panama Canal, as long as it was open equally to ships of all nations. England remains a power in the Caribbean; she has an interest in the new self-governing Commonwealth nations of the British West Indies, including Trinidad, Jamaica, and British Guiana on the mainland. In the 1960s British policy in Latin America was completely tied in with that of the United States in promoting trade, preventing the spread of Communism, and helping raise the standards of living through the Alliance for Progress.

UNITED STATES RELATIONS
WITH LATIN AMERICA TO 1959

From the early days of independence until the eve of World War II there was little cordiality between the Latin American states and the United States. There were no genuinely equal bilateral dealings between the United States and even the larger Latin American states. The under-developed states were understandably fearful of anything that resembled economic colonialism. Latin Americans were culturally attracted to educa-tion and society in France, Spain, and Italy rather than to the more dynamic, but perhaps less "cultured" society of the English-speaking Protestant United States. All these factors produced little Hemispheric friendship. Loud talk of Manifest Destiny, followed by neglect for half a century, and later by Theodore Roosevelt's Big Stick policy, produced little friendship or affection for the United States. Though much of the detailed story of American diplomatic dealings with Latin America has been told chapter by chapter as a part of the national histories, it is of value to repeat it briefly here from the point of view of over-all United States policy.

The Monroe Doctrine, which had been promulgated in 1823, was as much a part of the United States' policy of isolationism and avoidance of entangling alliances at it was a reflection of sympathy with Latin America. Monroe's message to Congress declared to the mother countries, Spain and Portugal, that "we should consider any attempt on their part to extend their system to any portion of this hemisphere as dangerous to our peace and safety." It was its own peace and safety in the face of threatened intervention by the Metternich Alliance which concerned the United States. The Doctrine was practically forgotten once the power of that alliance weakened in Europe. The United States allowed England to take the Falkland Islands from Argentina in 1833 and to strengthen her foothold in Belize and the Honduras coast islands. When British en-croachments seemed closer to home in Texas and Oregon in 1844, President Polk made the first new interpretation of the neglected doctrine. England should not even try to "advise" the independent people of this continent who "alone have the right to decide their own destiny."

An actual invasion of an American state during an American war occurred nearly two decades later when Napoleon III's armies placed Maximilian on the throne of Mexico. Secretary of State Seward made only a mild protest against Maximilian in the name of the Monroe Doctrine in 1862 and 1863. When the Civil War was over, Seward took a stronger stand. President Johnson's message to Congress in 1865 considered that it would be a "great calamity to the peace of the world should any foreign power challenge the American people . . . to the defense of republicanism against foreign intereference." The American threat combined with the losses in Mexico to end Maximilian's career there.

The Monroe Doctrine was next reinterpreted to mean that disputes between an American nation and a foreign power must be settled by arbitration rather than by war. In 1895 President Cleveland used such an interpretation to force England to arbitrate a boundary dispute between British Guiana and Venezuela which had been causing bad feelings between the two nations for a half-century. Latin Americans had no cause to thank Cleveland for this interference. Cleveland's Secretary of State wrote to his ambassador in England, "Today the United States is practically sovereign on this continent [and] there is a doctrine of American public law . . . which entitles and requires the United States to treat as an injury to itself the forcible assumption by an European power of political control over an American state." Britain's involvement in the Boer War led her to come to terms with the United States on this issue and settle the boundary by arbitration in 1899.

All this amplification of the Monroe Doctrine did not go unchallenged. An Argentine jurist, Carlos Calvo, had written a treatise in 1868 saying that a sovereign nation was "immune from external intervention no matter what the state's degree of political stability or the quality of its courts." This Argentine statement was used in 1902 by Luis Drago, Argentine Minister of Foreign Affairs, in a note to Washington. "Failure of a state to pay its debts does not justify the use of armed force against it," said Drago. Since sovereign nations could brook intervention from no one, not even a sister nation in the same Hemisphere, all the American nations together should act jointly in "prohibiting the armed intervention by any European power in any American state for the collection of a public debt." Drago considered his proposal as his own Corollary of the Monroe Doctrine; but United States policymakers treated Drago coolly, and the Roosevelt Corollary followed two years later. Drago's own government, changing hands, repudiated his doctrine as "in conflict with Argentine foreign policy." Other Latin American nations, pleased to be asked as equals to the Hague Conference in 1907, brought into that body a wording of the Drago Doctrine which had been formulated at the Third Pan American Conference the year before. The South American bloc was able to get a weakened resolution passed at The Hague: "The Signatories agree not to have recourse to armed force for the recovery of contracted debts." To all intents and purposes this Drago Corollary became a part of the body of international law, a protection against aggression from creditor nations.

The assumption of Hemisphere leadership by the United States prepared the way for Theodore Roosevelt's Corollary to the Monroe Doctrine. Participation in Cuban affairs during the Spanish-American War and plans to build an Isthmian Canal made America conscious of the Caribbean. The Venezuelan dictator Cipriano Castro had incurred debts which the German Wilhelm II threatened to collect by force. Owing to the United States' new prestige, Germany warned the State Department in 1901 that such a step might be necessary, and Roosevelt answered via a message to Congress that the United States did "not guarantee any state against punishment if it misconducts itself, provided that punishment does not take the form of acquisition of territory by any non-American power." Castro was quick to ask the United States to arrange arbitration.

The story of American intervention in the political and financial affairs of the Dominican Republic, Haiti, and Nicaragua has been told from the point of view of those frustrated little nations. When the Dominican Republic threatened to default on its debts to European creditors and the national governments of those creditors made vigorous protests, Theodore Roosevelt sent another message to Congress on the Monroe Doctrine in 1904. "Chronic wrong doing may . . . ultimately require intervention by some civilized nation, and in the Western Hemisphere the adherence of the United States to the Monroe Doctrine may force the United States . . . to the exercise of an international police power." North Americans received this Roosevelt Corollary with patriotic enthusiasm; European creditors felt it guaranteed the payment of debts; but Latin Americans saw it as an excuse for American intervention, to them as bad as or worse than European forced debt-collection. Meanwhile Roosevelt insulted his neighbors even more by quoting his "favorite West African" proverb, "Speak softly and carry a big stick, you will go far."

A "Lodge Corollary" was developed in 1912 when Henry Cabot Lodge assumed that Japanese interests, in attempting to buy property in Magdalena Bay in Lower California, were violating the Monroe Doctrine. Lodge considered the Japanese group a "corporation or association which has a relation to another government, not America," which would give "that government practical power of control for national purposes." Thus foreign companies were discouraged from colonization schemes.

In time the Monroe Doctrine itself was softened in United States interpretations. Woodrow Wilson in a speech at Mobile in 1913 "scuttled" the Big Stick and Dollar Diplomacy policies. He hoped to use the Doctrine in support of worldwide self-determination of nations, spoke of it in the Fourteen Points as a successful regional agreement, and was instrumental in having mention of it included as "a regional understanding for securing the maintenance of peace" in Article 21 of the League of Nations Covenant. However, sadly enough, it was on the basis of the United States' own right to interpret the Monroe Doctrine unilaterally that Henry Cabot Lodge led the Senate's opposition to the Covenant. That the Doctrine was "distinctively the policy of the United States" and that the United States had the right to its "definition, interpretation, and application" was insisted upon by Charles Evans Hughes at the Fifth Pan American Congress at Santiago in 1923. Naturally such insistence did not ease Latin America's fears. Hughes and his colleagues did their best to assure Latin American critics that the United States only held such rights in the Canal area and the nearby Caribbean Islands. President Hoover, a good friend of Latin America, was opposed to the early twentieth-century interpretations of the Monroe Doctrine. After 1930 references to the Monroe Doctrine did not include the right of intervention.

To keep the peace in Central America, and possibly to avoid foreign armed intervention, the United States from time to time withheld recognition of governments that had come to power by violence. However, since delayed recognition often weakened a government which the United States opposed, it was considered a subtle type of intervention, and as such became an issue between Latin America and the United States. In 1913 the United States government declared that to receive recognition a nation must demonstrate: "The control of the administrative machinery of the state; the general acquiescence of its people; and the ability and willingness of their governments to discharge international and conventional obligations." Wilson called this the doctrine of "constitutional legitimacy," and attempted to use it to discipline the Revolutionaries in Mexico.

The United States has withheld recognition from governments in Central America with varying results. From 1907 to 1921 in Honduras, Nicaragua, Costa Rica, and Guatemala in five different cases United States recognition was withheld after a revolution, and in no case did it bring about a clear-cut change toward peace and stability. Since 1930 the United States has assumed that a *de facto* government was to be recognized. The statement of the Mexican publicist, Genaro Estrada, sometimes known as the Estrada Doctrine, that "any government which is actually in control of the country is to be acknowledged" is gradually becoming accepted Western Hemisphere practice.

One consistent long-time United States policy that influenced relations with Latin America was built around hopes for an Isthmian Canal. As early as 1846 the United States had signed a treaty with New Granada "conveying to the United States the right of or transit across the Isthmus of Panama, upon any modes of communication that now exist, or that may be hereafter constructed." In 1850 the Clayton-Bulwer Treaty established a partnership between England and the United States in case any canal should be built. With the United States' victory in Cuba in 1898, interest in an American-dominated canal grew. Secretary of State Hay arranged the Hay-Pauncefote Treaty of 1900–1901, in which Britain bowed to the growing power of the United States, accepted her promise of neutrality once the canal was built, and withdrew from the joint partnership of interest. A dispute between supporters of a Nicaragua route and backers of the Panama route was settled in the United States Congress. When Colombia refused to ratify the Hay-Herrán Treaty providing for an American canal project, the Panama Revolution resulted. Then by the Hay-Buneau-Varilla treaty with Panama, and the purchase of the rights of the defunct French company, the United States proceeded to acquire the Canal Zone, and to dig the "Big Ditch." Subsequent dealings with Nicaragua, such as the Bryan-Chamorro Treaty, though part of the "Dollar Diplomacy" policy of dealing with Central America during the Taft era, centered on the option to the Nicaraguan canal route. With this same policy in mind, the United States acquired the Danish West Indies in 1917, continued its protectorate over Cuba under the Platt Amendment, and maintained the Big Stick in the Caribbean.

It was time for some United States president or secretary of state to counteract all the strong anti-American currents. A trend in that direction had already started when Herbert Hoover, as President-elect, made a good-will trip to Latin America in 1928. He suggested a successful formula for settling the Tacna-Arica dispute and announced that "we have no desire for territorial expansion, for economic or other domination of other peoples." Under Hoover the United States withdrew from Haiti; the Marines left Nicaragua for good in the last month of Hoover's term in office, and a policy of recognizing *de facto* governments has been pursued up to the present. However, this policy of recognition of any established government brought criticism in the 1950s for supporting dictators.

Franklin Roosevelt first made the new attitude of nonintervention a specific policy in his inaugural address two months after the Marines left Nicaragua. "In the field of world policy," he said, "I would dedicate this nation to the policy of the good neighbor, . . . the neighbor who respects his obligations and respects the sanctity of his agreements in and with a world of neighbors." A month later, April 1933, he used the same words in a speech before the Pan American Union. Cordell Hull as the new Secretary of State went to the Pan American Conference at Montevideo in December of 1933, reiterated the Good Neighbor stand, and supported a pact to outlaw intervention. These brave words were soon followed by deeds. When disorders broke out in Cuba protesting the Platt Amendment it was withdrawn. Haiti and Panama received treaties guaranteeing more equal treatment. In 1936 Roosevelt himself went to a special conference at Buenos Aires. There, as a "traveling salesman for peace," Roosevelt called for united Hemisphere action in the face of any outside aggression, having in mind the Nazi infiltration which was apparent by then. At this meeting no new multilateral Monroe Doctrine was drawn up, but peace machinery between the various American republics was to be strengthened, and the principle of nonintervention was reaffirmed. When Mexico expropriated foreign-owned oil fields two years later, the Roosevelt government ignored the pressure to intervene by armed force, and eventually a satisfactory settlement was reached. Meanwhile, war clouds gathered in Europe, and the next inter-American meetings were concerned with mutual defense against dangerous outsiders.

As World War II changed the position of England and Germany in the world, so it brought further changes in the relationships between the United States and Latin America. By the time the Eighth Pan American Conference was held at Lima in 1938, Hitler had marched on Austria and was threatening Czechoslovakia. The Declaration of Lima, which bolstered the United States' neutrality stand, reaffirmed continental solidarity, and promised collaboration in the face of any forced intervention, showed a new respect for the American position. By September 1939 the foreign ministers of the Latin American nations were ready to come to Panama and declare with the United States that there was to be no hostile act committed by any non-American power in any Western Hemisphere territorial water. The actual steps in the achievement of this continental solidarity will be taken up shortly. The importance here of all these joint statements leading up to World War II is that they show the Latin American nations, with the exception of Argentina and Chile, willing to align themselves with the United States against an enemy who looked more like a colossus than did the power north of the Rio Grande.

When France and Holland fell in 1940 and the existence of England was threatened, the United States saw clearly the danger to the Hemisphere if the Caribbean possessions of those nations fell to the Nazis. Thus the Axis representatives were told in June 1940 that the United States "would not recognize any transfer, nor acquiesce in any attempt to transfer any geographic region of the Western Hemisphere from one non-American power to another non-American power." Even in this the United States did not wish to appear to be acting alone. At Cordell Hull's request a conference of the foreign ministers of all the American states met in Havana a month later, July 1940. At this meeting the Monroe Doctrine ceased to be a one-nation policy, for the Act of Havana, product of Hull's diplomacy at that meeting, proclaimed that "any European possession apt to change sovereignty" should be placed under provisional control by a joint committee, representing all the American states. This was to be called the Inter-American Commission for Territorial Administration, and was to act if Nazi action directly threatened any Caribbean island. Also, it was agreed that any attempt against the inviolability of territory of any American state "shall be considered as an act of aggression against the states which sign this declaration."

With the Act of Havana, the ideas of Calvo and Drago and their hopes for multilateral action under Monroe's Doctrine came to fruition. The series of joint conferences held on Western Hemisphere defense during World War II are described in greater detail in the section on Pan American action. Some analysis of this wartime activity must be given here, however, to explain United States policy toward Latin America during the war and since. The United States further demonstrated good will by cooperating with the new Inter-American Financial and Economic Advisory Committee to try to absorb and allocate the surpluses of Latin American products stranded by the blockade of Europe. United States finance helped in defense and security, built large sections of the Pan American Highway as a Hemispheric defense measure, sent technical groups of United States Army personnel to help train armies to the south, and often sent military supplies as well. Meanwhile the English bases in the Bahamas, St. Lucia, Trinidad, Antigua, and British Guiana were being maintained by the United States on a ninety-nine-year lease from England.

When war was declared on the Axis powers by the United States on

December 8, 1941, Haiti, the Dominican Republic, and all Central America—those states which had most feared "Dollar Diplomacy"—followed suit within a few hours. At another conference of foreign ministers held at Rio de Janeiro in January 1942, resolutions were passed calling on all American states to break relations with the Axis and to suppress sabotage. Only Chile and Argentina, the latter being by then very anti-United States, abstained from such action. An Emergency Advisory Defense Committee, which led to an Inter-American Defense Board, largely staffed and financed by the United States Army, grew out of this meeting. The United States set up bases—in Panama, to guard the Canal, and in Brazil to facilitate the shipping of supplies from Natal to Dakar in the early years of the war. Strategic materials—tin, copper, nitrate—were handled by the United States out of South American mines; a joint rubber effort was undertaken on the Amazon with American staff and money. Meanwhile, the Office of Coordinator of Inter-American Affairs, known as the Nelson Rockefeller Committee, was set up in the United States State Department as a way to "win friends and influence people."

Finally came the meeting described later which was held at Chapultepec Castle in February 1945, six weeks before the United Nations was organized at San Francisco. Here the Monroe Doctrine was expanded to "make all the American republics co-guardians of the Monroe Doctrine, even against an American aggressor." Only Argentina was absent from this meeting in Mexico City. So great was the pressure to join with the United States against the Nazis and sit in on the new United Nations, that Argentina herself accepted the Act of Chapultepec and declared war on March 27, 1945, seven weeks before Germany surrendered. The Monroe Doctrine was now a part of the entire Western Hemisphere relations. After 1945 the United States planned a clear-cut policy of handling relations with Latin America through the Organization of American States, an outgrowth of the Pan American movement.

It was not to be as simple as that, unfortunately. The United States suddenly found itself a major world power with heavy responsibilities. Its interests, attention, and economic aid had to be spread thinly around the globe. It had Marshall Plan funds to spend freely in Europe, but in so doing it did not fulfill Latin American expectations for the large-scale financial assistance tacitly promised during the war. In addition Latin America was antagonized by Spruille Braden's interference in the Argentine election of 1946. President Truman restored some of the wartime friendly feeling by visiting Mexico in 1947 and placing a wreath on the monument to the Niños Héroes of 1847. He also attended the Rio de Janeiro Pan American Conference of 1947.

By 1947 the newly aroused nationalistic Latin American states wanted "a greater share of the world's good things" *now*. They wanted United States assistance in improving health, providing practical education, and bringing material progress. They felt that the United States was so concerned with world Communism that it had forgotten them. They contrasted the attentions showered on them during World War II with the neglect of the postwar decade. A more generous loan policy was promised by the United States in a conference at Petropolis in 1954 and at a meeting of the Finance Ministers at Buenos Aires in 1957.

Just as these plans seemed to bring promise, the United States went into an economic recession at home. The raw materials it bought in Latin America declined in price while Latin American dollar reserves dwindled. At the same time as this economic pinch began to produce new bitterness, Pérez Jiménez, the hated dictator of Venezuela who had been receiving loans from the United States and royalties from American oil companies, fled for his life from infuriated mobs in Caracas, but found haven in Miami. "Tacho" Somoza, long-time dictator of Nicaragua, was shot by an assassin and the United States rushed him by army plane to an American hospital in the Panama Canal Zone. The playboy son of Trujillo, the autocratic dictator of the Dominican Republic, was acting like an "honored guest" at an officers' school in the United States. In critical Latin American eyes, the United States was causing a slowdown in economic progress in Latin America while it deliberately hurt the cause of democracy by supporting the most undemocratic dictators.

In 1953 President Dwight Eisenhower had sent his brother, Dr. Milton Eisenhower, president of Johns Hopkins University, on a fact-finding mission to Latin America. He returned to report the need for improvement in the economic condition of the area. He suggested steps to improve United States and Latin American relations, to cooperate more fully with the OAS, and to promote a common market. Then in 1958 Vice-President Nixon toured Latin America as part of a trip to attend the inauguration of President Frondizi of Argentina. He was heckled by students in Uruguay, stoned at the University of San Marcos in Lima, and barely escaped an angry crowd in Caracas, where mob action had run Pérez Jiménez out of the country only a few weeks before.

Following the Nixon episode, the President again sent his brother, this time to Central America. After his second Latin American visit, Dr. Eisenhower added a note of urgency to his reports, stressing the need for "a large program to meet a large problem."

The American people were shocked, but reacted with a searching survey of the United States' postwar Latin American policy. Juscelino Kubitchek, president of Brazil, took advantage of the United States' new attitude to suggest a stronger plan for economic assistance, a new Inter-American bank, and a series of more meaningful conferences. These ideas were to grow into the cooperative plan called the Alliance for Progress. President Eisenhower himself was well received on a good-will tour to southern South America in 1960.

Part of our neglect of Latin America in the 1950s was due to our concern with the "Cold War" against Russia. At every inter-American meeting the United States had hoped for forthright sentiments against Communist infiltration in the Hemisphere, while the Latins minimized this danger. John Foster Dulles, at the Organization of American States meeting in Caracas in 1954, asked for a strong resolution expressing "solidarity against intervention by international Communism." The resolution received a narrow margin of approval from states who hoped for economic assistance. The

Latin American states actually did not intend to approve of *any* intervention—including intervention by the United States. Later in the same year an inter-Latin American investigating committee acted slowly to condemn Communist sympathizer Arbenz as president of Guatemala. Meanwhile the United States Central Intelligence Agency gave secret, unilateral help to Arbenz' Guatemalan enemies, and his regime fell. Although the resolution passed at Dulles' insistence was never invoked, the United States was criticized by the Organization of American States members for the action against Arbenz.

In dealing with Panama, the United States was forced to grant greater and greater concessions in connection with flying the Panamanian flag in the Canal Zone and with paying the Panamanians a larger percentage of the Canal tolls. When the concessions did not seem enough to the ultra-nationalist Panamanians of the 1960s, and riots in January 1964 killed twenty-four persons and injured 200, the Organization of American States sent a committee to investigate the United States' action. By the 1960s there seemed to be no action of the United States in Latin America which could avoid cooperation with the other Western Hemisphere states.

The Cuban revolution led by Fidel Castro had turned into a real Communist menace to established governments throughout the Western Hemisphere. The last one-country attempt by the United States to intervene in Communist Cuba, the Central Intelligence Agency's secret help to Cuban exiles, had ended in the Bay of Pigs disaster in 1961. Latin American tempers flared at this seeming intervention without the knowledge or consent of other Hemisphere states. Just over a year later, when it was evident that Russia was planning to use Cuba as a missile base, President Kennedy conferred immediately with the Council of the Organization of American States. Conscious by then of the actual Communist nature of Fidel's Cuba, the Latin American states backed Kennedy. When Johnson sent marines into the Dominican Republic in April 1965, public opinion and his own advisers forced him to consult with the Organization of American States within two days. In the later 1960s United States policy toward Latin America seemed to mean working through the oas, both in handling diplomatic problems and in counteracting the appeal of Communism by economic aid through the Alliance for Progress. To understand the influence of the Organization of American States on Latin America and on United States policy, it is necessary to trace the history of Latin American cooperation from the time of Simón Bolívar.

INTER-AMERICAN DEVELOPMENT
FROM THE PAN AMERICAN UNION
TO THE ORGANIZATION OF AMERICAN STATES

For a century after independence there was no regional cooperation within Latin America. Attempts at Central American union had failed; the Gran Colombian Confederation had broken up soon after independence. Argentina, Brazil, and Chile, calling themselves the abc Powers, proposed to act as a board of arbitration in regional disputes around 1915, but did not develop a regional union.

There were some few wars between Latin American nations, such as those against the dictator López of Paraguay, the War of the Pacific over Tacna-Arica, and the War of the Gran Chaco. There have been years of friction over unsettled boundaries, disputes over navigation of international rivers, military operations of political refugees across international frontiers, and "incidents" caused by ambitious leaders who coveted the territories and natural resources of their neighbors. But more impressive is the record of pacific settlement of disputes, often with the arbitration of one of the great powers.

That there should be need for arbitration over boundaries is not surprising. By the Doctrine of *Uti Possidetis* of 1810 the new nations were to establish their frontiers on the lines between various Spanish colonial administrative units at the time the independence movements began. The indefiniteness of these lines, some of them not even yet surveyed through jungles and over mountain ranges, produced many "incidents." Some of the possible pairs of nations with common frontiers have made arbitration treaties to settle border disputes; others have refused arbitration on such matters "affecting vital national interests." Through a century and a quarter of such disputes, European kings, American presidents, and international courts of justice have served as boards of arbitration. By the Gondra Treaty of 1923, an outcome of the Fifth Pan American Conference, a Permanent Diplomatic Commission of Investigation and Conciliation was set up, and its machinery further augmented by the Inter-American Treaty of Good Offices written at the Buenos Aires conference of 1936. Though some border disputes still simmer, the Pan American Union reports that

Council of the Organization of American States in session, November, 1958. *Courtesy Pan American Union.*

more than seventy-eight disputes have been settled since independence without resort to violence. No recent Latin American squabble has led to a full-scale war, and chances are small that there will ever be such a struggle between any group of Western Hemisphere nations again. This development is largely due to the rise of the Organization of American States.

A union of the American states was a dream of Bolívar's. In his letter from Jamaica in 1815, at one of his periods of deepest discouragement, the Liberator wrote: "Would to God that some day we may have the good fortune to convene . . . an august assembly of representatives of republics, kingdoms, and empires to deliberate upon the high interests of peace and war. . . . Then will we march majestically toward that great prosperity for which South America is destined. Then will those sciences and arts which . . . have enlightened Europe wing their way to a free Colombia which will cordially bid them welcome." When such a meeting was held at Panama City in 1826, its "Treaty of Perpetual Union, League, and Confederation" was ratified only by Colombia of the four nations which attended. Bolívar died, and his dreams disintegrated. The Spanish American states met in partial agreement three more times before the 1880s: the west coast countries in 1847 to draft "a comprehensive plan for peaceful settlement of inter-American disputes" in the face of danger from Ecuador's dissatisfied General Flores and his backers in Spain; Ecuador, Peru, and Chile in 1856 at Santiago; and the Central and northern South American states the same year at Washington, to make a "Continental Treaty." In 1864 a so-called Congress of Hispanic States met at Lima with eight states present to "devise measures of accomplishing Latin American union." All these efforts failed of ratification. Though other conferences met on cultural and social topics, the dream of an American family of nations was almost lost. By the 1880s, however, Latin America was looking for defensive safeguards, and the United States was looking for expanded trade and new places for investment. In 1882 the American President Chester Arthur and his Secretary of States James G. Blaine proposed a Pan American conference at Washington to discuss ways of settling disputes peacefully and to improve commercial relations, but delayed action on it, partially because of the War of the Pacific. Blaine became Secretary of State again under Benjamin Harrison; this time he pushed the idea of the Pan American meeting.

Representatives of eighteen nations came to Washington at Blaine's invitation in October 1889, spent six weeks touring the United States on a special train—which included Pullman cars with hot and cold running water in the washrooms—and then settled down to meetings lasting until April 19. After deliberating over the project of a customs union, suggesting resolutions on a plan of arbitration and on points of international law against conquest, the conference concluded by setting up a Commercial Bureau of the American Republics. Since the meeting was sponsored by the United States, this Bureau was to have permanent headquarters in Washington and to be "charged with the care of all translations and publications and with all correspondence pertaining to the International Union." It was to publish a "bulletin of useful commercial information."

This bureau was established in Washington in November 1890, and Mr. William E. Curtis became its first director. Up to this time, most Latin American leaders considered "Pan Americanism" merely a policy of United States aggrandizement. The Bureau continued under United States auspices, but was not to remain purely a commercial affair.

In the spirit of the peaceful pre-World War I world, the American states met again in Mexico City in the winter of 1901–1902. Here the Hague Convention of 1889 was signed by the Latin American delegates present, and questions of the collection of debts and the arbitration of disputes were discussed. Four years later in 1906 at Rio de Janeiro a Third International Conference was held to continue discussions of the Hague conferences and to request the second Hague meeting to consider "the question of the compulsory collection of public debts." The meeting at Rio, however, accomplished nothing more concrete than to set up a commission of jurists, who, it was hoped, would codify international law for the Americas, and include in the codification a statement against intervention for the collection of debts.

By 1910 the Pan American Sanitary Bureau of 1902 and the Commercial Bureau of 1890 were given a new name, the Pan American Union. The American philanthropist Andrew Carnegie donated funds for the Pan American Union building in Washington, D.C., which still houses all cultural and welfare activities of the Pan American movement. The year 1910 was also the centennial of the independence movement; as part of the celebration the nations met in the Fourth International Conference of American States in Buenos Aires. Here the entire organization changed its name to Union of American Republics, and adopted four treaties relating to copyrights, trademarks, and the collection of debts. The Bureau in Washington was enlarged and strengthened, and was to concern itself with cultural matters and sanitary improvement, as well as to serve as a commercial clearing house.

A Fifth Conference had been scheduled for 1914, following a four-year pattern, but it was postponed because of World War I. When the Fifth Pan American Conference finally met in Santiago in 1923, the Latin American states had emerged from World War I with increased status, and were more accustomed to joint action. The Fifth Conference set up four permanent commissions: on economic relations, on labor, on public health, and on intellectual cooperation. Whereas the United States Secretary of State had heretofore served as *ex officio* chairman of the Union, now there was to be a governing board with one member from each nation and an elected chairman and vice-chairman. The treaty for the pacific settlement of disputes, the Gondra Treaty, was signed. Here at Santiago, too, was made the first suggestion which led to the Pan American Highway.

The year 1928 saw the Sixth Conference meeting at Havana, for conferences were now to be held every five years. This sixth meeting voted to send special delegates to sit upon the Union's governing board, rather than merely have the current ambassador in Washington act in that capacity. Here at Havana the delegates organized the American Institute for the Protection of Childhood, and created new permanent divisions on agricultural cooperation and labor. This Havana meeting also set up a

Special Conference on Conciliation and Arbitration, which met at Washington in December 1929, and wrote several agreements for peaceful settlements of international disputes. By 1931 more than sixty technical and scientific conferences had been held on a wide variety of subjects. At the building in Washington the American Secretary of State continued to act as general chairman, even though now "elected" by the members.

By 1933 America was launched on the Good Neighbor Policy under Franklin Roosevelt, and his Secretary of State Cordell Hull went to Montevideo to the Seventh Conference to tell the other delegates so. From 1933 on, the Pan American movement gained greater prestige in Latin American eyes. The Seventh Conference, therefore, was able to accept unanimously a convention of the "Rights and Duties of States," establishing in treaty form the doctrine that "no state has the right to intervene in the internal or external affairs of another." New provisions for enforcing the compulsory arbitration agreements were passed in an effort to stop the war then raging in the Gran Chaco.

Montevideo showed concrete evidence of the spirit of cooperation. As war clouds gathered in Europe, a special Conference for the Maintenance of Peace was held in Buenos Aires in 1936 which produced an agreement that "a threat to the security of any American nation is a threat to all." The nations present also resolved that they would "consult together" on the procedure to follow when such a threat occurred. In 1938 the nations met at Lima, faced with the possibility of another world war into which Latin America might be drawn, and resolved on a series of meetings of the Ministers of Foreign Affairs of the twenty-one republics to provide concerted action. Thus, when war in Europe spread to America, and the regular meeting of the Ninth Conference had to be postponed in 1943, the foreign ministers had already held a series of meetings on the problem of maintaining neutrality and providing Hemispheric security.

World War II conferences have just been reviewed from the point of view of United States policy. The first of the foreign ministers' meetings was in 1939 at Panama. Here, by the Declaration of Panama, the delegates drew a line some 300 miles offshore around the American continents, and declared that belligerent ships were not to operate within that zone. They also created the Inter-American Financial and Economic Advisory Committee to solve the problems of trade dislocation brought by the war in Europe. By the time of the Rio de Janeiro meeting of the foreign ministers in January 1942, most nations of the Western Hemisphere were in the war, owing to the bombing of Pearl Harbor. The policy of "an attack on one is an attack on all" had "paid off." Plans were made for mobilization of resources to fight the Nazis, and for control of subversive activity. Argentina remained aloof from much of this joint action, but the activities of the remaining Latin American nations prepared them for a strong voice in the postwar deliberations and in the United Nations. When that time came, the Pan American movement was strong enough to be incorporated into the new Organization of American States.

World War II was practically over in February 1945, when delegates of all belligerent states were called to Chapultepec Castle in Mexico City for the Inter-American Conference on War and Peace. Secretary of State

Stettinius was sent to Chapultepec to make sure that the Latin American states were behind the United States in the new United Nations, and that Latin America would stay with the war until it was finished in Japan.

The most important decision made in 1945 at Mexico City, termed the Act of Chapultepec, provided that security within the Western Hemisphere depended on collective action of the American states, and would be solved by common corrective action. Such action was to be regional, in accordance with the special situation of the Western Hemisphere and the strength of the Pan American movement. However, such collective action was to be considered in harmony with the new United Nations. This Act made it possible for the Pan American Union to be reorganized as the Organization of American States, a "regional organization" within the United Nations, but actually an independent and almost equally strong body.

Soon the Act of Chapultepec was to be carried out in the formation of a strong new regional organization. In 1947 an Inter-American Conference for the Maintenance of Continental Peace and Security met at Rio. The "Rio Pact of 1947" forced its signers to unite against any aggression on a member state from the outside world, or from another American state, and was to be prominent in the 1960s in connection with Communism in the Caribbean.

Then in 1948 the Ninth Conference met in Bogotá, to form the Organization of American States. This was the first regional agreement signed under Article 51 of the United Nations Charter. A definite regional charter, which had never existed for the previous loose Pan American movement, was signed as a treaty. This charter set up six major organs: first, the Inter-American Conference, the supreme body of the new organization, to meet every five years to plan general policy and programs; second, the meetings of foreign ministers, such as that called in the Korean emergency; third, the Specialized Conferences to be called on technical matters of all kinds. The remaining three organs are permanent bodies which work throughout the year. They are, first, the Council of the OAS replacing the old Governing Board of the Pan American Union; second, the Pan American Union, a term now applied to the General Secretariat and the permanent clerical workers of all types, with headquarters in Carnegie's building in Washington; and, finally, the Specialized Organizations which had been set up from time to time by the early conferences, or had come into being to fill specific needs. By 1948 these covered a myriad of activities in health, agriculture, welfare, and economic betterment.

The opening article of this charter says that the signatory states mean "to achieve an order of peace and justice, to promote their solidarity, to strengthen their collaborations, and to defend their sovereignty, their territorial integrity, and their independence." Thus the OAS was more than a regional pact within the UN; it meant no sacrifice of sovereignty, and would continue to exist no matter what the future held for the world organization. To further carry out these purposes, the delegates at Bogotá signed an American Treaty on Pacific Settlement, which outlawed war in the Western Hemisphere, and bound the American republics to "refrain from the threat or the use of force, or from any other means of coercion

PRESENT AND PROPOSED STRUCTURE OF THE OAS

(For clarity in presentation the Specialized Conferences, Specialized Organizations, Special Agencies and Commissions, and Permanent Committees of the Councils are omitted.)

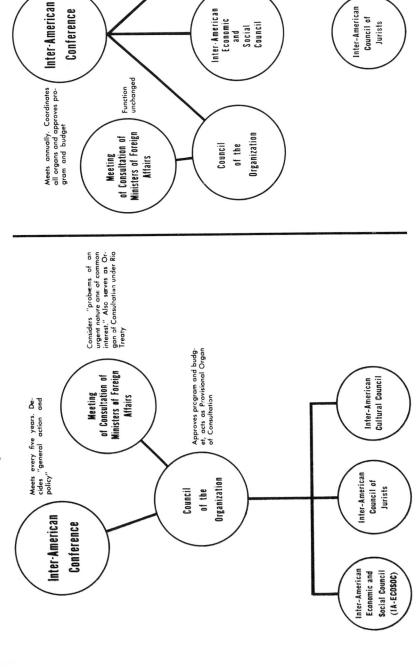

PRESENT
According to Charter of Bogotá

PROPOSED
According to Act of Rio de Janeiro

for the settlement of their controversies, and to have recourse at all times to pacific procedures." A Treaty on Reciprocal Assistance, signed at Rio de Janeiro the year before, had promised joint action in the event of aggression on any American state. The entire OAS plan was unanimously ratified by 1956.

The OAS under this charter soon became far more newsworthy than the Pan American Union. The Tenth Inter-American Conference at Caracas in March of 1954 is a good example. Its work is especially important today because its chief "Caracas Declaration" stated that "any time any American Republic falls under domination or control of international Communism an emergency meeting is to be convoked." Its meetings show the beehive of activity which goes on at such a conference. In the spectacular new University of Venezuela, the delegates met as the guests of the Venezuelan government, which had budgeted three million dollars to cover costs. Eighteen translators and nine reviewers were hired to keep things going in the four official languages of the conference, English, Spanish, Portuguese, and French. Twenty-eight different items appeared on the elaborate agenda. The hard-working delegates met for four weeks, and the product of their discussions ran to 117 different resolutions. Almost all of these concerned recommendations and implementations of projects already planned by the various workers in the field under the Specialized Agencies. None of them comprised any startling new development in policy, but it is the total aggregate of their subject matter that shows the ramifications of Pan Americanism. Resolutions were concerned with campaigns against illiteracy, seminars on university education, a Memorial Lighthouse to Columbus on the island of San Salvador, universal suffrage, modernization of penal systems, vocational education, migratory rural workers, civil and political rights of women, agricultural surpluses, completion of the Pan American Highway, racial discrimination, a continental tribute to Andrés Bello, and 105 other matters, some of them discussed in the next chapter. That many of these were mere brave resolutions there is no doubt. Still, on more than half the items some group within the Pan American framework was already taking positive action. Pledged in its 1948 charter to maintain peace and to promote human welfare, the OAS constantly expanded its program, enlarged its staff and its budget, and widened its scope.

THE UNITED STATES AND
THE ORGANIZATION OF AMERICAN STATES SINCE 1960

Still the United States was discouraged in 1960 because the Organization of American States was not sufficiently concerned about Communism in the Caribbean. United States Secretary of State Christian Herter had gone to a foreign ministers' meeting at Santiago, Chile, in the late summer of 1959, called because Trujillo had objected to Castro's interference in the Dominican Republic. A planeload of bearded Cuban soldiers who arrived in Chile during the meeting were treated like any other unwelcome visitors without visas. The sympathies of the meeting, however, were not with Trujillo, but were opposed to any kind of intervention, against dictators or against Communists. The oas was definitely not going to intervene in Cuba to discipline Castro for his subversive guerillas.

In June 1960 the United States made a formal report to the oas on all Fidel Castro's "excesses" in harassing and confiscating American investments in Cuba throughout 1959 and 1960; but expected no action and meant only to have the problem "on the record." Then Venezuela complained that Dominican dictator Trujillo had sent assassins to attack her liberal President Betancourt. Meeting in August 1960 as an "Organ of Consultation" on this specific problem, the Sixth Meeting of Ministers of Foreign Affairs at San José de Costa Rica applied the 1947 Rio pact against aggression for the first time. Member states were asked to break diplomatic relations with Trujillo, forbid the shipment of arms to him, and refuse to buy Dominican products. The United States agreed and withdrew its ambassador, in the hopes that oas members would then agree to the same kind of treatment against Communist Cuba. American promises to boycott Dominican sugar only led to embarrassment, for the United States Congress refused to cut down on Trujillo's quota of sugar sold in the United States. This was perhaps due to the activities of Trujillo's lobbies in Washington, perhaps to pressure from American firms with large Dominican sugar investments. At any rate, Latin American observers credited this joint action against Trujillo for the deterioration of his power in the Dominican Republic and the courage of his assassins the following year.

With the Dominican dictatorship seemingly out of the way as a Caribbean problem and United States' unilateral action discredited at the Bay of Pigs, the oas was willing to take some action against Cuba by January 1962. Finally, another Hemisphere state, Peru, had complained about subversive activity of Castro-trained guerillas inside her territory. Peru's complaint had been turned over to one of the agencies set up by the 1954 Caracas conference, the Inter-American Peace Committee. The well-documented report of that committee led to a meeting of Consultation of Ministers of Foreign Affairs in January 1962, the first meeting held at the resort of Punta del Este, Uruguay. Neither the oas charter nor the 1947 Rio Pact against aggression had clearly set down what could be done in such cases of subversion, but the oas showed itself flexible enough to devise a method of warning against Castro. The delegates resolved that the Castro Communist offensive was a "clear and present danger" and that the Americas are bound by "ties of democracy which make the present government of Cuba incompatible with the principles of the inter-American system." Seventeen nations voted that "Cuba has voluntarily placed itself outside that system." A resolution was also passed to "apply limited sanctions of trade" against Cuba—a mere gesture for Cuba was by this time sending all her sugar to the Soviet bloc and needed no imports from the Latin American states. Mexico, Bolivia, Uruguay, and Chile still maintained diplomatic relations with Cuba in the spring of 1962, but the United States had finally persuaded the oas to take a stand against Fidel Castro.

This oas stand served the United States in good stead when President Kennedy announced that Russia was setting up missile bases in Cuba. The President made this announcement at 7:00 P.M., October 22, 1962. Before mid-afternoon on October 23, the Council of the OAS had "unanimously called for the immediate dismantling and withdrawal of all missiles" and other offensive capabilites. Member countries were to take "all individual and collective measures necessary" to prevent more military supplies from reaching Cuba. Thus the OAS Council unanimously backed President Kennedy on the embargo of Russian shipping to Cuba which led to the removal of Russian arms from the island. The whole Russian missile incident gave both the United States and the OAS added prestige against Communism in the Western Hemisphere.

In July 1964 Venezuela complained to the OAS that Fidel Castro was making clandestine arms shipments to Venezuelan insurgents, trying to interfere with the peaceful end of Betancourt's presidency and the inauguration of Leoni. The Ninth Consultative Meeting of the OAS Foreign Ministers of Washington, July 26, 1964, accused Cuba of subversive aggression which, "though not an armed attack," called for "mandatory diplomatic and economic sanctions under the Rio Pact of 1947." As a result of this OAS condemnation Chile, Uruguay, and Bolivia called their ambassadors home from Havana. Only Mexico maintained an embassy there, but she did this more to tell the world that Mexico was not a puppet of the United States than to show any approval of Fidel Castro.

Though bands of Cuban-trained guerillas continued to appeal to peasants in various underprivileged areas of Latin America, most Latin American governments had ceased to fear the influence of Fidel Castro by 1966. The United States was answering Latin America's plea to counteract the Communist threat by means of massive economic assistance through the Alliance for Progress described below. Russia itself seemed disillusioned in attempting a foothold in the New World via Cuba. The Cuban economy seemed to be on the decline; Communism there had not been an immediate panacea for the ills of overpopulation, underindustrialization, and grinding rural poverty—a fact which seemed to be proven by Cuba's agreement with the United States to allow several thousand refugees a month to leave the island. On October 6, 1965, the OAS expressed its interest and desire to help this refugee effort multilaterally. President Frei's Christian Democratic Front in Chile, President Belaúnde-Terry's economic improvements in Peru, and even Castelo Branco's tight control against Communists in Brazil seemed to imply that Latin America hoped to control its own Communist parties.

But the Johnson administration still feared Communism in the Caribbean. American and OAS attempts to bring stability to the Dominican Republic after the assassination of Trujillo had come to nothing. The *junta* under Donald Reid Cabral in control there in the spring of 1965 was pressed on the right by Trujillo's old army officers, in the middle by a group of younger army officers, and on the far left by Communists— both a hard core of the old Russian-financed Communist underground from Trujillo's day and a new group of younger people inspired by Fidel Castro. These elements combined to overthrow Reid Cabral in April

1965, and left a vacuum of power, punctuated by street fighting and terror from both right and left. Claiming that a large number of Americans and other foreigners were in danger, President Johnson sent in a detail of marines on April 28 to guard the embassy, the downtown hotels, and an evacuation beach. When these marines were fired upon by the leftist rebels led by Camaaño Deno, more marines and paratroopers were sent in unilaterally by the United States, till the American troops numbered around 15,000. Assistant Secretary of State for Latin American Affairs Thomas Mann, a career diplomat with years of Spanish American experience, but one often accused of a businessman's "hard line" in Latin America, justified the presence of the troops. He said he had "clear information of the danger of Communists in the Camaaño movement." American troops must control the "clear and present danger" by holding the port and keeping an open corridor in the city "until the OAS can act." President Johnson was accused by Latin American observers of promulgating a new American policy, the Johnson Doctrine: "the United States will intervene unilaterally to prevent a Communist coup in any Latin American state without waiting for OAS action."

President Johnson immediately declared that he had no intention of invoking this "doctrine" elsewhere in Latin America. The legal counsel of the State Department published a defense of the United States action, saying, "We landed troops in the Dominican Republic in order to preserve the lives of foreign nationals. . . . We continued our military presence in the Dominican Republic for the additional purpose of preserving the capacity of the OAS to function in the manner intended by the OAS Charter" —that is, to secure a ceasefire, re-establish orderly political processes, and supervise a free election.

To bear out this defense of the United States' unilateral action, President Johnson had called the OAS into action on April 29. On May 6 the OAS resolved "to request governments of member states who are willing and capable of doing so to make contingents of their . . . forces available to the OAS . . . to form an inter-American force . . . with the sole purpose of cooperating in the restoration of normal conditions in the Dominican Republic." This historic resolution created a new body in Hemisphere history, an Inter-American Peace Force. By the middle of May 1965 forces from Brazil, five central American states, and a team of civilian doctors from Panama had arrived in Santo Domingo. A Brazilian general, Hugo Panasco Alvrim, was chosen to command the force. American marines were withdrawn, though regular army troops remained wearing the blue and yellow armband of the OAS and serving under the command of the Brazilian general. Dr. José Mora, an Uruguayan statesman who was then Secretary-General of the OAS, said at that time, "The purpose of this Inter-American Peace Force is clearly not one of intervention, but rather one of rendering assistance to people of a sister nation."

Ironically, the great mass of this Peace Force was made up of American soldiers. In August 1965, after three months of street fighting, a precarious truce in the city of Santo Domingo was achieved by the "OAS Force," which then numbered 13,820 men—1,110 Brazilians, 250 Hondurans, 175 Paraguayans, 164 Nicaraguans, 21 Costa Ricans, and 12,100 Americans. The Dominican slum dwellers were still yelling "Yanquis, no! Yankee go home!" Mexico and Chile still opposed the whole idea of the Inter-American Peace Force, the IAPF, as an American tool for intervention.

In the city of Santo Domingo itself a UN commission acting separately from the regional OAS made an investigation, as did officials representing President Johnson and even a papal nuncio, all with plans to keep the peace. Leaders of the OAS met with American ambassador Ellsworth Bunker throughout July and August in fifty-one different sessions. Thirty-one meetings had been held with the rightist factions and thirty-three with the leftist. By September both sides had laid down their arms and the OAS Peace Force held the entire city. The moderate Hector García Godoy was accepted as interim president until the election of Juan Balaguer in June 1966. Half the American troops had gone home in the fall of 1965, though the Latin Americans under General Panasco Alvrim stayed to protect Godoy's precarious position. Throughout the winter of 1965–1966, sniping continued in the city, buildings were occasionally blown up, and riots broke out in the smaller city of Santiago in the provinces.

After Balaguer's inauguration on July 1, 1966, all OAS troops went home and the incident was over. Had a Communist take-over ever really been a threat? Assistant Secretary of State Mann proclaimed in November 1965, "Nonintervention is the keystone of the structure of the inter-American system. American states have a treaty as well as a right to choose their political, social, and economic systems free of all outside interference." In the Dominican Republic, he said, the United States had not supported either one faction or another, but had kept the peace through the OAS. In other words, there was no "Johnson Doctrine."

In the face of these developments, a full-scale OAS Conference was planned to meet in Rio de Janeiro in 1965, the first such conference since that of Caracas in 1954. The regular meeting planned for Quito had never been convened, and the Rio Conference had been called to discuss the further development of the Alliance for Progress. But Secretary of State Dean Rusk and Assistant Secretary Mann hoped to use the increasing success of that economic alliance to gain an approval of the idea of a permanent Inter-American Peace Force. If there was to be no Johnson Doctrine, then the OAS should control Communist takeovers with multilateral action by a "ready-reserve" force. By the time the American delegation arrived at Rio, however, its members had felt the hostility of the Latin American states to the "permanent force" idea.

A House of Representatives Resolution of September 20, 1965, passed independently of presidential or State Department backing, had said, "Unilateral military intervention in the Western Hemisphere is proper if intended to block creeping communism." This created a storm of protest in Latin American capitals. A house Democrat had told the press, "I'm not particularly worried about public opinion in Latin America," for "opinion against us in this regard is merely Communist opinion." At the same time Congress was passing a new United States immigration bill, which liberalized immigration from all parts of the world, save from Latin America, whose citizens were restricted to a specific number for the first time in history. Faced with this Congressional activity, which seemed to prove that Americans talked with one voice at home and another at OAS meetings, Latin Americans organized opposition to the United States delegation.

Due to the strong voices of Chile and Mexico against the Inter-American Peace Force, Dean Rusk asked only for a "full-scale review" of the OAS charter at the Rio Conference held in November. There was to be special focus on ways of "speeding up and strengthening the Hemisphere's peace-keeping machinery to act effectually in emergencies." Chile, Peru, and Mexico also asked for charter revisions. They wanted annual meetings of the full-scale OAS conference, a new juridical council responsible for the maintenance of human rights, a stronger Economic and Social Council to implement the Alliance for Progress more quickly, a cultural and scientific council of equal status with the other subdivisions, and a decentralization of many of these agencies away from Washington. The United States had to be satisfied with the appointment of committees to draft such new provisions and the hope that the slow process of charter amendment might bring about new methods for faster action against subversion. The high point of the Rio Conference of November 1965 was Rusk's announcement that the United States was pleased with the cooperation evident in the first five years of the Alliance for Progress and would support it financially for another decade after 1971. Brazil strongly backed the American hopes for a peace force; Brazil's foreign minister said, "It will one day come into being; it's going to take time for the idea to sink in." Even OAS Secretary-General Mora warned the conference that "the Caribbean continues to be an area of potential danger, and joint action may again be necessary." The final Act of Rio, November 30, 1965, gave greater emergency "peace-keeping power" to the OAS Council itself, and voted to hold a conference in July of 1966 to pass on charter amendments.

Secretary Mora said in his closing speech at Rio in November 1965, "Three million Latin Americans reach voting age every year; in a few years their incorporation into the electorate will alter many prevailing political ideas. Leisurely and dispassionate analysis will be difficult. Our people have developed a taste for fast answers and urgent change."

That both the United States and the OAS were aware of these new pressures is evident in the monthly reports of OAS activity. The economic programs to be discussed on the Punte del Este agenda took up a great deal of space and time. But the OAS Council was also hearing reports on highway extensions in the Andes, the Amazon, and the Darién jungles, was concerned with electrification cooperatives, a budget for malaria and smallpox control, for safeguards against air and water pollution, and all the many projects described in Chapter 41. Due to the Alliance for Progress, United States relations with Latin America in 1966 were improved over those in 1956, in spite of the Bay of Pigs and the Dominican intervention.

Democracy itself was faring better. In 1954 there had been legitimate constitutional governments in only seven out of twenty countries; in 1966 there were fifteen elected constitutional governments, one provisional government planning an election, and only four military dictators. The

Johnson Administration had recognized the "Revolution of Expectations" exploding in Latin America, and "hoped to be on the winning side. Their interests lie parallel with ours," said Mann in 1966. Thus the United States was forced to keep the friendship and approval of the Latin American states, as the Americans themselves became deeply involved in Asia.

LATIN AMERICA'S PARTICIPATION
IN WORLD ORGANIZATIONS

Latin American states had been gravitating toward membership in some type of world organization even before the Pan American system had any strong influence. Only Mexico and Brazil had been asked to the first peace conference at The Hague, and Brazil had failed to send delegates. But all save Costa Rica participated in The Hague meetings in 1907, sending outstanding jurists as delegates and influencing The Hague conferences to incorporate "nonintervention" as part of international law. Latin American delegates voted unanimously for Red Cross rules of humanitarian war and accepted settlement of disputes as "obligatory in principle." Dr. Antonio Sánchez de Bustamente of Cuba became a member of the Permanent Arbitration Tribunal of The Hague, and was active two decades later in the League of Nations.

Eight Latin American nations had declared war against Germany in 1917 and five had severed relations; these thirteen states attended the Versailles conference. Eleven later signed the treaty, and all but Ecuador ratified it. Thus ten nations became charter members of the League of Nations, and all the others eventually joined. Part of the enthusiasm Latin America felt for the League of Nations was based on antagonism to the United States in the early 1920s; here was a new world organization, in which the Latin American states were equal to European nations, but from which the United States stayed aloof. Subsequently two Latin Americans served as president of the Assembly, Augustín Edwards of Chile and Cosme de la Corriente y Peraza of Cuba; two others became president of the Council, Dominico da Gama of Brazil and Alberto Guani of Uruguay. There was a bureau within the League framework to deal with Latin American affairs. As far as the Latin American disputes of the 1920s were concerned, the Chilean delegates opposed any consideration of the Tacna-Arica affair by the League Assembly. In the early 1930s the League, joined by the ABC powers, had unsuccessfully attempted to arbitrate the war in the Gran Chaco, and had successfully formulated a proposal acceptable to Peru and Colombia in the Leticia dispute. Meanwhile, however, the Pan American system was strengthened by the lessening fear of the United States under the Good Neighbor Policy, while the League itself at Geneva was dying on the vine.

At the meeting called at Chapultepec Castle in February 1945 as World War II came to a close, the Dumbarton Oaks proposals had been accepted by the Inter-American system as a basis for a new world federation. Thus the Latin American states went in a body to the San

Francisco charter meeting in April 1945, where they advocated the equality of small and large nations. Latin America has had a strong influence in the subsequent development of the UN. Germán Arciniegas, famous Colombian writer, said in the late 1940s, "Latin America was nothing thirty years ago. Now in the United Nations one third part is Latin America. The United States has one vote. Russia, with all its satellites, has maybe six. Latin America holds the balance of power."

The Charter had provided that of the six nonpermanent members of the Security Council elected every two years, two should always be Latin American nations. Thus leading Latin American statesmen have always served on the Council. Angel Zuleta of Colombia was chairman of the Preparatory Committee for the first Assembly, held in London in 1946. Of the fifteen judges elected by this first Assembly to serve on the International Court of Justice, four were Latin Americans, though the judges were chosen purely on the basis of ability, with no relationship to country represented. One-third of the chairmanships of Assembly committees also went to Latin Americans. The Chilean Benjamín Cohen became one of the seven Assistant Secretaries-General.

Outstanding Latin Americans have continued to serve the United Nations, many of them also having experience with the OAS. Ana Figueroa, a school teacher from Chile and one of the most active women in international politics, served for Chile on the Security Council. She was chairman of the Third Commission of the General Assembly in 1952. The Brazilian Minister of Foreign Affairs, Oswaldo Aranha, also served as president of the Sixth General Assembly. In 1958 Galo Plaza of Ecuador acted as chairman of the UN fact-finding team along the border between Syria and Lebanon in a seething Near East crisis.

At first the Latin American bloc of twenty nations in a total UN membership of fifty or sixty did "hold the balance of power," and Russia charged that this bloc made up a strong pro-United States vote. But Latin America has voted with the United States on some issues and against her on others. In general, these nations held a caucus on each important question before coming to the UN, just as they decided among themselves which of them were to be elected to the Security Council or other UN bodies. They have voted with the West on "Cold War" issues, pledging support for the UN stand in Korea. In 1957 a unit of Colombians was among the UN army standing guard to keep the peace in the Isthmus of Suez. Latin America divided on nuclear testing, on Palestine, and on membership for Red China. In other words, the Latin American nations have not formed a coherent bloc in the UN. With the increase in the membership of the UN to more than 115 nations, the Latin American "bloc" ceased to be so important. After 1961, with the defection of Cuba to the Communists, Latin America could at best have only nineteen or twenty votes.

What is the exact relationship between the United Nations and the Organization of American States? Article 51 of the UN Charter authorizes regional action in case of self-defense. The Treaty of Rio de Janeiro of 1947, which was accepted and incorporated into the Pact of Bogotá at the Ninth Conference in 1948, fully coordinates all its provisions with those of the Charter of San Francisco. Without specific mention of the Pan American system, the UN Charter's Articles 52 and 54 admit the existence of "regional arrangements." Article 1 of the OAS Charter of Bogotá says that "within the United Nations the Organization of American States is a regional agency."

Until 1954 the United Nations had no reason to question the regional powers of the OAS to settle disputes in the Western Hemisphere. When the Guatemalan situation in that year was brought before the UN Security Council, the UN was satisfied that the OAS was handling the problem satisfactorily. When Cuba protested United States actions in July and October 1960, the UN simply referred to "measures for pacific settlement of disputes established by the OAS."

Thus there was some surprise in May 1965, when the UN Security Council called for a cease-fire in Santo Domingo and sent a commission of its own to try to arrange a truce. Manuel Bianchi, the UN negotiator, talked to Dominicans, interviewed prisoners on both sides, and made himself more approachable and popular than the OAS committee members, who were trying to hold themselves aloof. Crowds in the streets of Santo Domingo were crying "UN, sí! OAS, no!" Adlai Stevenson, then American delegate on the UN Security Council, had to plead that the OAS was doing a good job, that OAS Secretary-General Mora was in constant touch with Stevenson, and that OAS action was entirely consistent with Article 52 of the UN Chapter. This had been the only occasion on which the UN and the OAS had seemed to clash. Acting on their own, but with the blessing of UN Secretary-General U Thant, twenty-one Latin American nations, including Trinidad, met in Mexico City in February of 1967. Their purpose was to approve a treaty banning nuclear weapons throughout Latin America. The United States, England, France, and Russia, the powers which possessed nuclear weapons, "expressed sympathy," but did not attend the meeting or approve the treaty. U Thant read a statement, February 13, 1967, saying that "This treaty has world-wide significance in curbing the nuclear arms race."

Meanwhile in the United Nations social and economic committees worked constantly with their OAS counterparts in health, education, and agriculture. These agencies have brought increasing improvements to backward areas of Latin America, providing an optimistic story for the last chapter of this book.

NOTE: Readings for Chapter 40 are combined with those at the end of Chapter 41.

Chapter 41

Latin American Cooperation in Economic, Social, and Cultural Matters

INTERNATIONAL ECONOMIC DEVELOPMENTS TO 1960

MORE IMPORTANT in bringing Latin America together today than conferences and diplomats are the truck and the airplane, for increasing travel and improving transportation are vital in Latin America. Trucks can now reach remote hamlets within each nation, and can travel from nation to nation. International motor transit has been made possible by the Pan American Highway system, on which plans were commenced before 1930. The United States government assumed part of the cost of construction under the Inter-American Highway Act passed by Congress in December 1941. American engineers have assisted in the planning and construction, but each section has been built under the direction of the local government involved, and has not been completed until the local government has hired the workers, pushed the work, and paid its share of the bills. When completed, the system will include nearly 16,000 miles of highway and will have cost half a billion dollars. The northern section, known as the Inter-American Highway, has three branches by which the motorist may enter Mexico and proceed to Mexico City. The paved road continues through Guatemala and El Salvador. An all-weather road runs through

Nicaragua into southern Costa Rica. One hundred fifty miles of difficult terrain in northern Panama has been cleared and the connecting link joining southern Panama with Colombia has been surveyed to connect this Central American road with the routes in northern Colombia. The highway in northern South America is called the Simón Bolívar Highway, and is completed from Caracas, Venezuela, through Bogotá and Quito on into Peru and Bolivia to connect with roads coming up from Argentina. Extensions from the Andes to parallel the Amazon out to the Atlantic were to be finished by 1971.

The highway is thus doing what railways never did: it is connecting groups of Latin American nations. There is no all-Central American rail line; the railroads pioneered in South America by Wheelwright and Meiggs seldom crossed national boundaries. Probably little further international rail building will take place in Latin America, as the airplane is a better answer to transportation problems.

There were commercial airlines in Latin America by 1920. Pan American Airways, a United States firm which held a virtual monopoly in some areas, has been forced to surrender its monopoly to nationally owned lines. There are today more than 200,000 miles of air routes in Latin America. A series of commercial aviation, airmail, and aerial navigation conferences has been held, the earliest as long ago as 1923. Modern trucking and cargo-carrying airlines have improved inter-Latin American trade.

The nations of Western Europe have made profits from Latin American investments for a century and a half. This is especially true of England. Most of the railroads of the nineteenth century were built by English capital, and England was the first nation to profit from Latin American independence. The value of British trade with Latin America in 1823 was $7,500,000, an increase of $2,500,000 over the previous year. Not only traders but investors saw such a rich field for profit that Britain was Latin America's investment banker throughout the nineteenth century. British interests built the railways across the pampas and into the Andes; they started the wool industry in Argentina and Uruguay, improved cattle by importing the best British herd sires. English companies started the tramways in both Buenos Aires and Rio de Janeiro, brought steamers to the Pacific coast, financed the Chilean nitrate industry, developed the silver mines in Mexico, and constructed the first *frigoríficos* in Buenos Aires.

By 1870 British investments totaled £85,000,000. By 1913, the peak year of British economic activity in Latin America, investment had reached £756,000,000, then more than $4,000,000,000. Of these funds, 32 per cent was in government bonds, 46 per cent in railway securities and shipping, and 18 per cent in agriculture and mining. By the beginning of World War I, British companies owned 118 railroads, forty-five port facility companies, 112 public utility companies, and thirty-five nitrate companies, as well as almost all the telephone exchanges, electric power distributors, and water works in Latin America. Since the over-all return was said to be under 5 per cent, it is true that Latin American countries obtained both their capital and their technical assistance at very cheap prices in their first century of growth. But two world wars in the twentieth century destroyed

England's economic leadership, in Latin America as well as in the rest of the world. By the 1950s English capital had been partially replaced by American investment and by new locally owned capital. French investment in Latin America has been very small compared with that of the British. French trade reached a peak of $323,000,000 worth of business in Latin America in 1928, most of it with Argentina and Brazil.

German activity before World War I was largely confined to promoting German commerce, investments, and immigration. German firms had investments worth $2,000,000,000 in trade yearly, while 700,000 German settlers in Latin America helped keep German companies prosperous. This economic machinery, revived in the 1930s, was of great use to Hitler, under whom it grew to startling proportions. It went through various vicissitudes during World Wars I and II, as described in the nation-by-nation analysis. Today the West German Republic is again making important investments in Latin America and stimulating trade relations by giving careful attention to the client's specifications, extending adequate credit, and providing practical technical aid.

Since 1900 it has been the United States that has loomed largest in the Latin American trade and investment picture. The monetary relations between Latin America and the United States can be divided into three categories: first, the investments made by private American interests; second, the trade relations, the balance of exports and imports between the two regions; and third, the economic aid and governmental loans made as a part of American foreign policy since the 1940s.

The United States was not an investing nation until the twentieth century, and American firms put little into Latin America before the Spanish-American War. By 1910 the banana companies had begun their plantations in Central America, and the American friends of Porfírio Díaz had started to drill for oil in Mexico. American firms are estimated to have invested perhaps $1,600,000,000 in Latin America by 1914. True, the Taft era was one of "Dollar Diplomacy," but most historians consider that the interventions in Central America and the Caribbean were as much a part of a new American continental strategy as they were a defense of "Wall Street profits." During World War I, American capital began to surpass European capital in the southern republics. The United States itself was a nation of surplus capital, looking for foreign investments.

In the 1930s 43 per cent of all investment abroad by American nationals was in Latin America. American banks had pressed Mexican loans, Bolivian bonds, or Peruvian municipal flotations on their home-town buyers, often without sufficient investigation, and millions of such bonds had been defaulted during the depression. Latin American dictators had often borrowed from American bankers in bad faith, and the money had been wasted. Though the United States was often blamed for "economic imperialism," it never used force to collect these defaulted debts. The United States State Department said "No economic reprisals." Bondholders' protective committees were private affairs, and the government took no responsibility for helping individual American losers. A total of more than $700,000,000 was thus defaulted during the depression.

Individual American companies had not always fared badly; in fact great fortunes were made—by the United Fruit Company, with its fabulous empire in the Caribbean; by the W. R. Grace company, which had a tight hold on shipping, transportation, and banking on South America's west coast; by the Guggenheims, who developed in Chile the largest supply of high-grade copper in the world. Manufacturing did not enter the picture until the new assembly plants of American factories were set up in the rapidly industrializing countries of Mexico, Chile, Argentina, and Uruguay after World War II.

The major part of the United States investments had encouraged the one-crop cultures of many lesser nations and had become monopolies which brought pressure on the weak governments, thereby promoting much ill-will. United States nationals working abroad as employees of American companies usually lived in exclusive American "colonies," seemingly "superior" to the "inferior" natives. They played golf with each other, their wives made no attempt to mix socially, and few such company representatives bothered to learn Spanish. Paid in United States dollars, such families lived well on "the exchange" and took very little interest in Latin American affairs. That United States companies also raised wages and living standards and improved public health in Latin American communities cannot be denied, though most of them neglected to hire local technicians or encourage the training of such among the native populations, and often paid ridiculously small taxes. These policies led in some cases to outright nationalization, as in the Mexican petroleum industry, and in others to government regulation. All except four Latin American countries have passed laws requiring a minimum percentage of nationals to be employed in any foreign venture; many countries have special tax laws which require foreign companies to receive the same tax treatment as local companies. Extractive industries, such as the copper in Chile and the oil in Venezuela, have had to accept a *modus vivendi* of paying high royalties to the government. Today the United Fruit Company and most American oil companies give the governments of countries in which they operate more than 66 per cent of their net profits.

In the post-World War II world, Latin America was as anxious to attract industrial capital as to discipline it. The Ninth Pan American Conference at Bogotá in 1948 passed a resolution: "The States shall take no discriminatory action against investments by virtue of which foreign enterprises or capital may be deprived of legally acquired property rights. . . ." Signatories could thus guarantee foreign investors fair treatment. American capital saw a green light by the 1950s. An Inter-American Investment Conference was held in New Orleans in 1955 to study additional means of making money in Latin America through the creation of a private International Finance Corporation, approving the floating $35,000,000 worth of loans in eighteen Latin American countries. Some of this was to be in bankers' loans to local Latin American companies, some to American firms with plants abroad. All this provided encouragement in a field which was prospering already. In the 1960s private United States investments in Latin America totaled more $9,000,000,000, while the yearly figures of exports and imports were approaching $8,000,000,000. The taxes American firms paid in Latin America totaled more than their profits, and the companies themselves provided seven hundred thousand jobs. There was bitterness against such companies, however, for they were largely in mining and petroleum, and the Latin Americans accused them of using up non-renewable resources.

Latin American businessmen fared well in direct trade with the United States. When the United States had passed the Smoot-Hawley Tariff in 1930, Latin American trade had been jolted. But by 1933, faced with worldwide depression, the United States was ready to take Cordell Hull's advice on reciprocity. At the Montevideo Pan American Conference in 1933, Hull advocated a resolution "calling upon the American republics to enter upon a program of reciprocal lowering of high tariffs to moderate levels, upon the principle of the unconditional most-favored nation formula by bilateral and multilateral reciprocity agreements." A law of Congress of June 12, 1934, gave the President of the United States the power to make such trade agreements; Hull set up the necessary machinery, and by 1943 had concluded sixteen such trade agreements with Latin American nations. In general, duties were lowered by almost 30 per cent. Today Latin Americans buy millions of dollars' worth of American-made machinery and consumer goods yearly. Sixty per cent of Latin America's imports come from the United States, and only 21 per cent from Europe. In return the United States is Latin America's biggest market, absorbing 44 per cent of their exports. By 1967 United States and Latin American exports and imports were almost equalling each other at about 40 per cent.

Government-to-government aid became a part of United States World War II policy. From 1941 to 1945 American government money poured into Latin America to build up supplies of strategic materials; 34 per cent of all loans made by the Export-Import Bank went to Latin America. After the war, when Marshall Plan money was being spent in postwar Europe and the stream of funds to Latin America trickled out, Latin American delegates protested at the 1948 conference at Bogotá. Here Secretary of State Marshall promised them more loans—though not direct grants— to built up transportation and hydroelectric and irrigation projects, as well as loans from the Export-Import Bank in greater amounts and assistance from private firms with government approval.

But a harvest of ill-will collected from the halfhearted way in which these post-World War II promises were kept. United States economic aid was being spread out over world areas seemingly less friendly to the United States. Though private American firms had invested the astronomical sum of $9,000,000,000, these dollars were in profit-making ventures, and only helped develop the economically backward regions as an incidental by-product. Though the Organization of American States and the UN launched scores of development projects in Latin America, as will be seen below, and though a fourth part of their cost was borne by United States public funds or private philanthropies, the actual amount spent by United States sources on such cooperative development programs from 1945 to 1960 was very small compared to that spent on military aid to Greece or Turkey or Nationalist China in any one year in the 1950s. Loans were made to Alemán in Mexico, Paz Estenssoro in Bolivia, and others for specific improvements, but the over-all amounts were small compared to the billions the United States spent elsewhere.

Meanwhile, Communist agents worked on Latin American disappointment with American promises, and Soviet trade with the individual Latin American States, though small, was growing. It was practically negligible before 1950, but in 1955 nineteen Soviet trade deals involving $500,000,000 worth of goods were made. A fourth of this trade was with Argentina, a nation which has subsequently carried on 13 per cent of her trade with Iron Curtain countries. By 1958 Russia was the largest single buyer of Uruguayan wool. Soviet trade commissions were visiting Caribbean and Central American countries; Poland and Czechoslovakia were underselling the West to get contracts from Brazil for shipbuilding and railway rolling-stock manufacture. The drop in copper prices brought on by the 1957 recession in the United States forced Chile to sell 15,000 tons of copper wire to Russia, while Red China was anxious to buy the Chilean nitrate fertilizer which American farmers do not use.

In June 1958 Brazilian President Kubitschek called for joint action to end some of the ill-will and ease the Communist threat by means of a cooperative development he called "Operation Pan American," to be carried out with American funds. Said he, "Washington has not shown equal interest in the serious problem of development in countries still with rudimentary economies. . . . The Western cause will unavoidably suffer if in its own Hemisphere no help comes. It is difficult to defend the democratic ideal with misery weighing on so many lives." Within two months after this report, Secretary of State John Foster Dulles had flown to Brazil for a talk with Kubitschek. The two leaders discussed "a ten-year program coordinated by a central agency to raise Latin American productivity and living standards, thereby throwing up a barrier against Communist penetration." By August 25, 1958, two weeks after Dulles' visit, the United States announced its willingness to cooperate in setting up a special new international bank for Latin American economic development, calling it "an inter-American regional development institution" supplementing the straight loans of the World Bank and the Export-Import Bank. President Kubitschek presented plans in September for a "Committee of Twenty-One" to meet in early 1959 to make the bank a joint operation of all twenty-one nations, using American capital. A charter for the Inter-American Bank was drawn up in Buenos Aires in 1959. However the new bank had a long way to go to combat ignorance and poverty in the growing city shanty-slums and the rural areas of Latin America.

THE ALLIANCE FOR PROGRESS AND
THE LATIN AMERICAN COMMON MARKET SINCE 1960

The Agency for International Development (AID) and the Food for Peace, United States programs for underdeveloped areas, were already pledging tens of millions of dollars to help Latin America by 1960, so the Eisenhower Administration was ready to consider a more unified program. Meanwhile Fidel Castro's success in Cuba and the appeal of his type of Communism in underprivileged areas of Latin America proved to American statesmen that "restricted or even moderate assistance would no longer suffice." In July 1960 President Eisenhower announced the American acceptance of Kubitshchek's Operation Pan American idea and Congress authorized the expenditure of $500 million to establish an inter-American socio-economic development fund. A special oas meeting in Bogotá in September 1960 produced a plan to use this half-billion dollars in cooperative projects—projects in which the Latin American states themselves promised socio-economic reforms in their own governmental system. This was called the Act of Bogotá.

In the fall of 1960 John F. Kennedy promised to enlarge this whole plan if elected president. He called it a "Marshall Plan to help the Latin American people help themselves." On March 13, 1961, after his election, President Kennedy pledged a billion dollars a year over a ten-year period and called his program an Alliance for Progress, "to satisfy the basic needs of the American people for homes, work and land, health and schools." After a planning meeting at Montevideo in July, the oas Council called a special meeting of the Inter-American Economic and Social Council in August 1961. With 440 delegates present, the meeting was held at Punta del Este, a resort in Uruguay, the second inter-American meeting held there in the early 1960s. The Alliance was incorporated in the Charter of Punta del Este. Its preamble is as follows:

> We the American Republics, hereby proclaim our decision to unite in a common effort to bring our people accelerated economic progress and broader social justice within the framework of personal dignity and political liberty. . . . Today, in ancient lands, men moved to hope by the revolutions of our young nations search for liberty. Now we must give a new meaning to that revolutionary heritage. For America stands at a turning point in history. The men and women of our hemisphere are reaching for the better life which today's skills have placed within their grasp. . . . The American Republics hereby resolve to adopt the following program of action.

Latin American history is full of documents that began with noble preambles. But this one went on to set up twelve conditions under which the nations could get the financial help. They agreed to: (1) improve democracy at home; (2) hasten social development; (3) carry out housing plans; (4) encourage farm improvement; (5) wipe out illiteracy; (6) improve health and sanitation; (7) assure fair wages and working conditions; (8) reform tax laws; (9) check inflation; (10) stimulate local private enterprise; (11) stabilize prices of basic Latin American exports; and (12) lower tariff barriers and hasten economic integration between their own states. This whole program was to raise the per capita wealth by 2.5 per cent every year for the ten years of the Alliance. This was the first time Latin Americans were called upon to aid in helping themselves.

The United States in turn agreed to contribute $1.3 billion a year, almost three times yearly the half-billion pledged at Bogotá in 1960. The money was to be deposited in the new Inter-American Development Bank, and granted out by a committee of the Economic and Social Council when proposed projects seemed to fulfill any one of the twelve requirements. In addition, $100 billion in investment capital was to be raised to encourage private industry and create urban employment. Of this money, $80 billion was to be raised by Latin Americans themselves, $10 billion by United States private sources with "non-confiscation" guarantees, and $10 billion by investors from other industrialized areas of the world. The whole arrangement was much more all-inclusive than the Marshall Plan or any other such scheme in history. It was a pledge, as a counteraction to the appeal of Communism, to wipe out adult illiteracy, provide primary education for all children, fight epidemics, reduce infant mortality, provide decent housing, water, sewage, and sanitation, expand jobs and fair wages, and reform outmoded agricultural tenancy—all within a framework of state financing and regulation, and of foreign and domestic capital.

The American attitude at Punta del Este in 1961 made many Latin American delegates feel that "the days of United States apathy are over." The United States delegation, led by Assistant Secretary of State Douglas Dillon, felt that Latin America sincerely meant to carry out administrative reform and end the rule of the oligarchies. Ché Guevara, who had come representing Cuba, was given no place on the agenda to tell how Communism would accomplish these goals faster. He did make a two-hour speech, raging against the United States, "that monster," but stormed out after hecklers interrupted him.

With such high hopes, the first years were bound to bring disappointments. In the heat of 1962, earnest committees, made up of specialists in the OAS-ECOSOC, staff members from the Pan American Union and the Development Bank, and an American staff headed by the Puerto Rican Teodoro Moscoso, set to work. There were soon six "special committees" for planning, for agriculture, for fiscal reform, for industrial development, for education, for health and housing. But by January 1963, of the billion dollars committed via the Development Bank, only one-fourth had been allocated. The promised local and foreign private capital had not materialized. Very few projects worthy of the committee's approval had been suggested. Moscoso had resigned and an American Assistant Secretary of State for Economic Affairs, Edward M. Martin, was appointed as American Administrator, with Carlos Sanz de Santa María as Chief Executive. The plans presented had not been specific enough and had included no tax reforms. "Compared to the real need, the 1962 effort is pitiful," said an American reporter. Latin Americans complained of the red tape necessary for approval, the requirement to "run all over Washington to different offices for signatures." The Ecuadorean liberal Galo Plaza had said that the program would take a long time. Latin American leaders were not conscious of the needs, he felt; no one wanted fiscal reform; the middle class was too small to make investments; the clerical class was only interested in creating more clerical jobs, making out reports, and setting up red tape matching that in Washington.

Naturally, there was disappointment in both Washington and Latin America that the Alliance had not achieved the momentum expected by 1963. Performance was uneven; some nations had "pitched in to cooperate with vigor," while some nations were "moving at a snail's pace." The program had been "oversold" at the beginning. It was expected to solve problems quickly which had grown up over centuries of time. It was started in the early 1960s, a time of great population explosion and unusual political upheaval. Private capital, always shy of political change and more than ever fearful of expropriation, was not flowing in from America at anything like the rate planned. Latin American investors seemed no more willing to invest capital at home than they had been before. The old oligarchic class viewed the whole Alliance scheme as a "socialist threat" to spend their private fortunes on public reforms they did not want. Thus the Alliance "antagonized the very groups whose help it needed most" if the "self-help" features of the plan were to be realized.

However, on the credit side of the balance was the changing United States' attitude. For the first time the United States "recognized the nature of what is going on in Latin America" in the way of eventual social revolution. The United States hoped to make this a more gradual evolution, while still helping it take place rapidly enough so that "people will not turn to totalitarian methods" to bring changes long overdue. The hope was to bring the social changes through political democracy and economic improvements.

President Kennedy was optimistic about these hopes. "This is not just a doctrine of development, not just a blue print for economic advance," he said in 1962. "Rather it is an expression of the noblest goals for our civilization." Kennedy himself seemed to embody the new American attitude in the eyes of Latin Americans. He was young, Catholic, part of a large loyal family group in the Latin American tradition. On a trip with him to Bogotá to dedicate a slum-clearance housing project as part of the Alliance plan, Mrs. Jacqueline Kennedy spoke to the crowds in flawless Spanish. When this handsome young couple were removed from the presidential scene by the assassination on November 22, 1963, Latin Americans wept openly on the streets. Hundreds of thousands put up wreaths and candles in their homes as the traditional signs of mourning for a member of the immediate family.

The Kennedy name still lingered over the Alliance for Progress and perhaps helped it to greater achievement from 1964 to 1966. Kennedy's appointee, the Puerto Rican Teodoro Moscoso, had returned to his own activities in San Juan. The "harder line" Thomas Mann headed the State Department Latin American Affairs division under President Johnson. Mann was transferred to be Under Secretary of State for Economic Affairs in February 1965, but was still in control of Alliance for Progress policies, having been replaced at the Latin America desk by John Vaughn. Soon Vaughn was in charge of that agency most appreciated in Latin America, the Peace Corps. Then former ambassador to Brazil, Lincoln Gordon, a career man with knowledge of the languages and histories of the Latin American nations, came back to Washington to head the State Department's Latin American desk in April 1966. These changes augured well for the whole Alliance concept.

So Kennedy's idealistic hopes seemed justified by 1966, the fifth year of the Alliance. The whole effort was by then coordinated in the *Comité Inter-Americana de la Alianza para el Progreso,* the CIAP, directly under the OAS Council. The United States had given out four billion dollars in specific loans, grants, and technical assistance to nineteen nations, ranging from $960 million for Brazil to $20 million for Haiti. Food allocated from the Alliance program had reached 25 million people in 1965. President Johnson had said in August 1965, "More than 1.5 million people have new homes; a million children have new classrooms, ten million textbooks have been produced." Nearly 1,200 water systems had been constructed, benefiting 27 million people. Eight thousand miles of road had been built. Credit unions and agricultural loans had reached 200,000 small farmers. Ten nations had "full-dress development programs" approved by the CIAP. Latin Americans themselves had invested $24 billion in development projects and private foreign lenders had added another billion. Nine nations had passed, and promised to enforce, graduated income tax laws. Eleven nations had undertaken agrarian reform under Alliance regulations.

Díaz Ordaz, President of Mexico, praised the Alliance for its help in irrigation projects, livestock improvement, rural credit unions, and "loans for projects which will increase our yield per acre.... The Alliance objectives are those of the Mexican Revolution," he concluded.

The United States, in 1967 deeply involved in Asia, was willing to continue financing Latin America as an anti-Communist measure. At the Rio de Janeiro OAS Conference in November 1965 Secretary of State Dean Rusk announced that the United States would continue to finance the Alliance for Progress for a second decade after 1971, with a total investment to reach another $20 billion.

The numbers and achievements still seem pitifully small when contrasted with the needs of the great Latin American masses, but "reform cannot happen in one afternoon." Thomas Mann, realistic United States Latin American expert, said that capitalistic America had recognized the need for "state socialism in underdeveloped Latin American areas. We can expect ten more years of their experimenting with their economies. I am anxious to see economic development with *any* kind of capital. They need capital."

Latin Americans themselves after many decades had begun a "systematic evaluation of their own development." Countries there knew a great deal more about formulating national economic plans in 1966 than they had known in 1956. They were aware of the "necessity of self-help and self-discipline." It is very likely that at least a generation will pass before the goals of the Alliance for Progress will be attained throughout Latin America. The American policy planners could also take hope from the fact that no other countries in Latin America had gone the way of Cuba by the summer of 1966. For this the Alliance for Progress was at least in part responsible.

Mann also recommended trade concessions to give Latin American manufactured goods easier access to the United States market, no matter how competitive, and assistance in keeping up prices on the raw materials that make up the bulk of Latin American exports. Eight South American countries and Mexico had faced the competition of the European Common Market and the British Commonwealth by forming a Latin American Free Trade Association, the LAFTA, at a meeting at Montevideo in 1960. They agreed to cut tariffs and promote trade among themselves, and by 1965 had listed 2,500 items on which the nine nations had regional free trade. They pledged to remove all trade restrictions in the region by 1973.

In 1966 trade among these nine nations had increased 85 per cent. However, only 10 per cent of the trade of the area was within the region. None of the nations were even self-supporting in manufactured goods, and all more or less produced the same raw materials for export. But Mexico's trade with South America had already improved 110 per cent in 1963. New companies were busy sending cement blocks from Monterrey to Montevideo and building ships for freight going from Vera Cruz to Porto Alegre. The eight South American members of LAFTA had not shown this much improvement. Their trade with each other improved less than 40 per cent. Ecuador and Paraguay hesitated in joining for fear that what little home industry they had would be swamped by manufactured articles from Argentina and Chile. However, the Central American Market described in Chapter 38 was much more successful by 1967. Its trade among the nations involved had increased 294 per cent.

The LAFTA had not raised the price of coffee, though at least it remained stable. But sugar, of which Latin America produces 75 per cent of the world's total, was kept at a twenty-five year low in price by the Cuban situation. Cacao was at its lowest ebb in twenty-four years due to world overproduction and large exports from the new African states. Copper, with Latin America responsible for 40 per cent of the world's supply, received little LAFTA or Alliance attention, but iron ore, of which Latin American produced 3 per cent of the world's supply, was marked for greater expansion. The LAFTA zone had 180 million people and an enormous potential for the 1970s. One of the aims of the Alliance for Progress was "regional economic integration" and the LAFTA was a step forward. In the spring of 1966 its members were holding committee meetings on common labor legislation and the free passage of laborers from one LAFTA nation to another. "It is certain that without integration there will be no economic development in Latin America," said Felipe Herrera, director of the Inter-American Development Bank.

EXCHANGE AND ASSISTANCE TO ATTACK ECONOMIC AND SOCIAL PROBLEMS

From the time of the first activities of the old Pan American Sanitary Bureau, agencies in the Western Hemisphere have worked toward raising the standard of living, improving health, and solving social problems. Though it must be admitted that the program in reality has not accom-

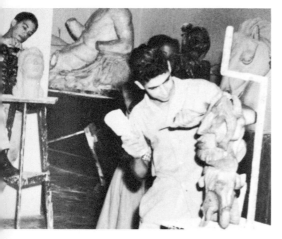

Specialized educational opportunities offered to young Latin Americans through international or United States agencies: Fine arts classes in the Dominican Republic, agricultural experiment station growing bell peppers in Haiti, radio technology class using United States equipment in Asuncion, Paraguay. *Courtesy International Cooperation Administration* and *Américas Magazine.*

plished as much as its outline on paper might indicate, nevertheless the spirit, the promise, and the organized committee work did exist.

Before World War II the Pan American movement consisted of a heterogeneous complexity of separate agencies, bound together by irregular conferences or by the inefficiently expanded old Commercial Bureau in Washington. Most of these activities were correlated with the OAS as specialized agencies by the 1950s. Their mass of paperwork and committee arrangements were headed by the Secretary-General, elected for a term of ten years. Such leading Latin Americans as the Colombian President Alberto Lleras Camargo, the Chilean former president Carlos Dávila, and the Uruguayan Dr. José Mora held this post after World War II. The organization worked on a budget of nearly $6,000,000, of which 66 per cent was provided by the United States as the wealthiest and most populous member, and the remainder prorated among the twenty other states according to their ability to pay. The specialized agencies—those concerned with the protection of childhood, with agricultural sciences, with Indian affairs —together with the Institute of Geography and History and, the oldest of all, the Pan American Sanitary Bureau—were all financed from special funds. So also was the OAS Program of Technical Cooperation, which received nearly $2,000,000 a year in the 1950s from its member nations and spent the greater part of it for agriculture, control of animal diseases, conservation, and rural education. One popular method of organizing technical cooperation under the OAS was through the creation of *Servicios* set up by the host country, which cooperated with the technical experts and joined in the financing. In 1955, there were forty-seven *Servicio* projects operating in Latin America.

A report on the specialized activities of the OAS for a five-year period, just before the more generous financing through the Alliance for Progress, filled 200 pages with descriptions of concrete activities. A list of the "Forthcoming Inter-American Conferences" for a single year announced eightyone projected meetings, to be held in various capitals, tropical institutes, rural education centers, or archeological sites throughout the Hemisphere. Preventive medicine, travel conditions, geodetic surveys, nutrition, population problems, tuberculosis treatment, weather prognostication, child psychology, prenatal care, and juvenile delinquency all served as topics for meetings. If such conferences accomplished nothing more constructive than a meeting of minds among the experts, the Hemisphere made progress. Such a meeting was the convention of eye-disease specialists described in the introduction to this unit. Another technical-cooperation project of the OAS dealt with providing low-cost, hygienic housing in the fast-growing cities. This project, called the Inter-American Housing Research and Training Center, was at Bogotá; it trained some fifty technicians a year in its courses. New housing within the range of young people of lower income groups, city planning, slum clearance, and building for earthquake resistance in the Andean countries all occupied the attention of the trainees at Bogotá.

Delegates to Pan American meetings were concerned with health problems as early as 1902. The revolutionary experiments to prove Carlos

Finlay's theories on yellow fever had just been finished, and the possibilities of making life safe and sanitary in the tropics appealed to all. There had been ten further meetings on health and sanitation by 1940. The Pan American Sanitary Bureau could report progress of interest to the whole world. The appallingly large figures on the incidence of malaria, yaws, hookworm, venereal disease, smallpox, and yellow fever, country by country, discouraged poorly developed nations with inadequate budgets for welfare projects. Thus the Pan American Sanitary Bureau's broad program of scholarships for doctors and nurses, improvement of hospitals, technical assistance in creating sanitary water supply and sewage systems, and quick service in fighting epidemics and providing relief during disasters such as hurricanes and earthquakes gave the Sanitary Bureau a very good reputation from the first, when other Pan American ideas were merely beautiful words. During World War II the United States undertook to expand this work under the direction of the Pan American Sanitary Bureau, financed by the funds of the Rockefeller Committee. More than 800 individual projects in public health were completed during the war years. In the 1950s the OAS committee had merely to carry on work so well and widely begun; by that time it had the help of the World Health Organization of the United Nations, whose regional office the Pan American Sanitary Bureau had become. Thus the Latin American health experts were well prepared in 1962 when the first Alliance for Progress health plans were presented for their approval.

Cooperation in the field of agriculture brought into being a specific agency of the Inter-American Institute of Agricultural Sciences maintained by the OAS at Turrialba, Costa Rica. Here research work on the growing of tropical products such as coffee, cocao, vegetable fats and oils, and fiber was carried on at a 1,250-acre site donated by the government of Costa Rica. Under the Institute of Agricultural Sciences of the OAS an *Aftosa* Center was set up in Brazil in 1951 to counteract hoof and mouth disease among livestock. A series of meetings on problems in the banana industry were held throughout 1955. Agricultural training centers were supported by the OAS in Cuba,. Peru, and Uruguay, all of which were branches of the training headquarters in Costa Rica.

"The OAS is a living and constantly growing organism," said José A. Mora, chairman of the OAS Council, writing in the attractive monthly magazine *Américas* for March 1955. It still needed more funds for all of its projects and more interest in them on the part of the American people. However, they were there, ready to provide a network through which Alliance for Progress funds could be distributed.

The agricultural, health, and social reform programs of the Pan American Union and the OAS have served as examples for the activities of the United Nations. Often there was official joint action; the OAS has signed agreements for cooperation with the International Labor Organization, UNESCO, the UN Food and Agricultural Organization, and the WHO, or World Health Organization. In all these fields, the Pan American specialists worked out methods of international action to teach the European specialists who came to work with them, and who in most cases had had no international experience. UN teams were then able to run "pilot projects" in backward areas. An example of such a project was a series of meetings on the improvement of the livestock industry—keeping records of milk production per cow, pasturage treatment, vaccines against cattle diseases, cross-breeding to improve cattle strains—held in Brazil in 1952 and attended by 150 delegates from European as well as Latin American nations. UNICEF has worked with the OAS agricultural institute in Costa Rica, hoping to formulate plans to improve dairying everywhere and thus make milk available to all children. The story of joint agricultural activity could fill many pages with reports on locust control, agricultural teaching, care of farm machinery, improvements in farm management—projects in training at the local level carried on with funds from the UN Technical Assistance Administration. There is a parallel and even more successful story concerning the work done through WHO in malaria control, development of insecticides, and large-scale vaccination programs.

After the Alliance for Progress was launched, UN agencies in Latin America were at first uncertain where they stood. The UN Economic Commission for Latin America, or ECLA, had observers who also worked on later organizing committees at the Punta del Este meeting in 1961.

The Punta del Este Charter, Chapter IV, paragraph 3, number C, provided that Alliance for Progress agents would always "seek technical advice" from and "work in cooperation with United Nations specialized agencies." The UN-ECLA itself was always short of funds. In the 1960s it was primarily a study group on over-all projects such as population control, forestry, communication, urban housing, and increased food production. Latin America was still a guide post of UN study in 1967, for population was outgrowing the food supply and the UN Food and Agriculture Organization reported that the next thirty-five years in Latin America would prove whether the world could solve its food problems or not.

That the United States itself, apart from OAS or UN cooperation, had an official policy of promoting improvement in Latin America is plainly evident from the list of agencies in Washington concerned with its neighbors to the south. In the Departments of Agriculture, Commerce, and Labor there are sections on encouraging scholarships for Latin Americans and on exchanging statistical studies. The Office of Education has a Division of Inter-American Educational Relations. Many agencies have assisted in financial matters and the State Department has carried on various types of cooperative effort. An interdepartmental Committee on Cooperation with the American Republics was created in 1938 to coordinate all such activities, and a "master plan" for seventy-four different projects was worked out. All such plans were transferred to the Office of the Coordinator of Inter-American Affairs during World War II, and were placed under the direction of Nelson Rockefeller.

Through the Coordinator of Inter-American Affairs, Latin American nations were offered programs in elementary education, in agricultural improvements, and in public health. Paraguay received a model dairy project with thirty head of Holstein cattle and three dairy experts from the University of Wisconsin, paid for by the State Department, as well as projects in silo building and orange-tree fungus control. With American assistance

Brazil founded nurses' training schools in the Amazon and São Francisco Valleys, sent out mobile clinics by launch, built purified water supplies in many Amazon towns. By 1950 the Brazilian government was paying 50 per cent of the expenses of this program. Such technical assistance was costing American taxpayers only $18,000,000 nine years after it was started; by 1955 it was being supported 80 per cent by local funds. In 1947 Congress had combined all these activities under a new Institute of Inter-American Affairs, but failed to vote adequate funds to support its activities to the extent set up in World War II.

American public health efficiency had always been admired by Latin Americans. Wheelwright had brought sanitary waterworks to Chile and Peru; the private Rockefeller Foundation had advertised American sanitation throughout the tropics. Even United Fruit spent $54,000,000 on disease control from 1914 to 1941. The Division of Health and Sanitation of the Office of Coordinator of Inter-American Affairs had undertaken 950 projects in seventeen different countries by the end of World War II: 325 "environmental improvement" projects which cleared malarial swamps and improved water supply and sewage control, 214 health centers and hospitals, 300 preventive services in clinics, and eighty-one doctors' and nurses' training schools. Some of this work was continued under assistance schemes or financed directly by the Export-Import Bank when the wartime funds were withdrawn from the Nelson Rockefeller Committee.

The period from 1941 to 1945 also saw many cooperative efforts to improve agriculture, such as the Paraguayan dairy mentioned above. Export crops such as *abacá, cinchona,* and kapok were experimented with in Honduras. Soil conservation service teams went up and down the Hemisphere; an American-Haitian Agricultural Development Society, with American public funds, undertook a long-term program of developing new crops—rubber, oils, seeds, spices, drug plants, and fibers—in the place of sugar and bananas. A group of sixteen Ph.D.'s working jointly for the Rockefeller Foundation and the Colombian government in 1958 had developed new seed strains on a model Colombian farm to double the per-acre production of wheat and barley. During one postwar year there were 650 technicians from the United States stationed in Latin America and an even larger number of Latin American technicians of various kinds studying in the United States. These technicians were not all doctors or teachers or agriculturists; many of them were engineers in industry, transportation, and hydroelectricity.

Not all the social work was done by government agencies. Most famous of all private agencies in the Latin American field is the Rockefeller Foundation, using the private funds amassed by Nelson Rockefeller's grandfather, which spent millions over the years on the control of hookworm and yellow fever through the tropical regions of the world. Of these vast sums, more than $10,000,000 was spent in the American tropics—Mexico, the Caribbean islands, and Central America—from 1913 to 1940. After World War II, the Rockefeller doctors and clinics continued to cooperate with the programs financed by the oas and the United Nations.

Into this well-planned set-up of programs of the oas, un, United States Federal Government, and United States private philanthropies came the greatly increased funds of the Alliance for Progress. In 1961 the Inter-American Economic and Social Council, or IA-ECOSOC, was already serving as the clearing house for UN, OAS, and privately financed efforts. Much of the money came from the American agencies, the Export-Import Bank and the Inter-American Monetary Fund, set up in Washington in the spring of 1959. The International Bank for Reconstruction and Development, founded at the Bretton Woods Monetary Conference in 1944 to help rehabilitate Europe after World War II and now known as the World Bank, had been a source of financing for Latin American projects under the UN-ECLA. Roads, hydroelectric projects, telephone lines, and irrigation systems were financed by the World Bank. In order to avoid depression-causing defaults of the kind that occurred in the 1930s, the Bank's agents made careful checks on the use of the money, and would never underwrite the entire cost of any project.

With all this talk of money, it seems surprising that Chapter 40 of this book was so full of references to Latin American hostility to the United States, and to various weaknesses in United States policies through the years that gave the Latin Americans reason to complain. Some of the persisting hostility could have been overcome by giving publicity to what the United States was doing through these various financing and development agencies. Most Latin Americans were not aware of United States efforts in their behalf, of the many government loans and private philanthropic efforts under which American dollars found their way "South of the Border." However, it must be remembered that the original sum suggested by the Eisenhower Administration for a new coordinated effort in answer to Kubitschek's Operation Pan America of 1959 was the then seemingly staggering sum of a half-billion dollars. The Alliance for Progress undertook to spend a total of 30 billion over two decades; and its first five years of expenditures had been considered "pitiful in the face of the need."

Some specific examples of what the Alliance accomplished in its first five years show how the extra money could be spent, given the requirement of local reform on the part of Latin American governments. The Mexican village of San Francisco Tepeyecac, less fortunate in its land and water than the Santa Cruz Etla described in Chapter 29, received a deep well, with a pump and motor and the pipes to provide irrigation water for ninety small farms. Thus able to double the corn yield, farmers were granted credit for seed, fertilizer, and small tractors from a new rural credit union, and technical assistance in how to use them. In a four-year period the crop yield could be multiplied four times and the excess sold for cash to buy a variety of food and clothing; the young people would stay on the farms and not move to Mexico City's urban slums. The improvement of this village, a type long hoped for by Mexico's rural planners, had been impossible under Mexico's own program due to lack of funds and personnel for such marginal land. It served as a pilot project for five Mexican marginal valleys by 1967. In these valleys, feeder roads, food storage and processing plants increased the economy of each central market town.

A cheap protein food from corn, cotton-seed meal, yeast, and sorghum, developed by a UN project in Panama, is being produced by the millions of pounds to add to the diet of underprivileged children throughout central and northern South America. Ninety thousand residents of one of the first Alliance projects, the slum-clearance housing development in Bogotá dedicated by President and Mrs. Kennedy, named their houses "Ciudad Kennedy." The last link in the Pan-American Highway, the difficult jungle stretch in Darién, was to be undertaken in 1966 with Alliance funds, while other Alliance funds carried on jungle road building and clearing for pasture in the Peruvian, Colombian, and Brazilian upper Amazon areas. Underdeveloped little Honduras received its first hydro-electric plant, as well as long-term credit for local industries. AID, with Alliance funds, granted credit to Federal Savings and Loan Associations to spend 1 per cent of their assets in model housing projects in Latin America; Baía, Brazil, long dependent on sugar, received credit for tapping iron deposits, building a 140,000-ton-capacity steel mill, and a wharf for shipping the ore. Air and water pollution control, mobile-health service in rural and city slums in Peru and Bolivia all received approval in the fall of 1965, after careful consideration of the promises for social improvement in the countries involved. These and hundreds more such projects gave the planners of the Alliance and all its network of banks and agencies the hopeful outlook they held for the 1970s.

INTER-AMERICAN CULTURAL MOVEMENTS

Culturally, the Latin American nations long felt themselves tied to Spain and to France, and have been scornful, throughout most of their history, of the "materialistic culture" of the "*Yanquis*." This feeling, combined with fear of "Dollar Diplomacy," has naturally crept into Latin American poetry. Some of the best writers of Spanish America wrote bitter denunciations of the "Colossus of the North." Rubén Darío, famous Nicaraguan poet, composed an uncomplimentary *Ode to Roosevelt* in the days of the presidency of Teddy the Rough Rider:

> You are the United States, you are the future invader
> Of that ingenious America of native blood,
> That prays to Jesus still and still speaks Spanish. . . .
> You hold that life is a fire, and progress an eruption;
> That where your guns can reach, there you control the future.
> No! . . . Beware! For Spanish America lives!
> The Spanish Lion has a thousand cubs.
> 'Twere needful, Roosevelt, to be, . . .
> The terrible rifleman and the hunter strong,
> Even to keep us in your iron grasp.[1]

Rufino Blanco-Fombona of Venezuela, an equally famous poet, novelist, editor, essayist, and historian who had visited the United States as a

[1] G. Dundas Craig, ed., *The Modernist Trend in Spanish American Poetry* (Berkeley: University of California Press, 1934), p 68.

haven of refuge in exile, called the northern country a "giant octopus, extending its sinuous tentacles toward the small republics to the south and strangling them one by one." Two other Latin American writers of almost equal stature have been leaders in the diatribe against the United States. Carlos Pereyra of Mexico wrote a scathing series of history books, most of them published in Madrid from 1915 to 1917, entitled variously *The Constitution of the United States as an Instrument of Plutocratic Domination; Bolívar and Washington as an Impossible Parallel;* and *The Crime of Woodrow Wilson.* Manuel Ugarte, son of a wealthy Argentine *estanciero,* took on a twenty-five-year personal campaign against the United States, at home in Buenos Aires, then in the European press, and finally on the lecture platform through half the Latin American capitals. Such writings and lectures, which proved very popular among intellectuals and students, were all influenced by the philosophy of the great Uruguayan writer Rodó, whose work *Ariel,* described in a previous chapter, had so criticized North American materialism. To Rodó, the Spanish American spirit was the true culture, and the North American spirit merely a crude materialism.

This attitude was encouraged by the movement called *Hispanidad,* or Pan Hispanism, a spirit of cultural solidarity with Spain. Spain had vainly hoped to maintain cultural ties with her former colonies in the early years of independence. Then the Spaniards began a positive attempt to recapture the imagination and devotion of the Spanish-speaking area overseas in the twenty-year period following the loss of Cuba in 1898, hoping for "a spiritual reconquest by Spain of her former empire." This was to be done by means of congresses, student exchanges, and cultural societies.

The first such congress had already been held in Madrid in 1892, honoring the fourth century of Columbus' discovery. October 12 thereafter became the *Día de la Raza,* or day of the Spanish race, even now a big celebration in Latin America, often called also *La Fiesta de Hispanidad.* During the next eight years Spanish newspapers were full of affectionate expressions of solidarity with the Hispanic American nations. A commercial and literary congress with Hispanic American delegates in Madrid was very successful in 1900; in 1912 the Spanish-speaking nations jointly celebrated the centenary of the Constitution of 1812. A *Casa de América* was set up at Barcelona, and an Hispanic American Academy at Cádiz.

World War I enhanced the movement. Primo de Rivera, dictator of Spain in the 1920s, called Hispanic American medical and aeronautical conferences. The crown prince of Spain was sent to Chile to celebrate the four-hundredth anniversary of the voyage of Magellan. All this was reflected in Latin America. Almost every city had a Spanish Club. The anti-American writers who opposed the United States in the Ariel-Caliban discussion joined with this Pan Hispanic movement, though the idea was criticized as artificial and reactionary by other Latin American writers such as Leopoldo Lugones in Argentina.

The Pan Hispanic movement might have remained a purely cultural tie of interest mostly to university professors, if it had not been turned into a new *Hispanidad* by the success of General Franco in the Spanish Civil War of 1936–1938. Latin Americans were sharply divided by this war—the liberals placing great hopes on the Loyalists; the conservatives and pro-Axis Argentines, as well as the Sinarquistas in Mexico, aiding Franco. Their loud talk was counteracted by the presence in many Latin American countries, especially Mexico, of numerous refugees from the Franco regime. As the Western Hemisphere was drawn into the war against the Axis, only Argentina listened officially to the siren call of *Hispanidad*. By the 1950s the movement was almost dead. Ties with Spain remained, but they were strong in the opposite direction; the best novels, the best movies, the good plays in the Spanish language were produced in the New World, and Spaniards were anxious to read and see them. In the new economic-minded Latin America of the 1960s, Franco Spain created a stir at the Rio meeting in November 1961 by offering the Alliance for Progress a billion dollars in credits to 1975. "We have always fraternally shared your sorrows and your hopes," said the Spanish "official observer" at Rio. As for cultural relations with Portugal, Brazil is today the unqualified leader of the Portuguese-speaking world, and has unquestionably replaced Portugal in the letters and science of the twentieth century.

Anti-*Yanqui* sentiment had continued through the period just before World War II. The *Unión Latino-Americana*, founded by José Ingenieros in Buenos Aires, that headquarters of anti-Yankee cultural sentiment, published an influential little review called *Nosotros*. After a visit and some sympathy from José Vasconcelos, the Mexican educator in the new Revolutionary Mexican movement, *Nosotros* branched out into a monthly called *Renovación*, which showed much Mexican influence, contained strong articles against United States' activities in Mexico, and was widely read in Spanish-speaking countries. A student group within Mexico which Vasconcelos founded considered itself international and was called the *Unión Juventud Hispano Américana*. The Ibero-American Student Confederation, with its headquarters at Mexico City, is another such anti-North American organization. In the 1960s many Latin American student groups no longer scorned the "materialistic culture" of the United States, joined student groups sponsored by the Pan American Union, with its Yankee tinge, and hoped for scholarships to come to the United States. But there was still much anti-Yankee sentiment in the late 1960s.

As the 1970s approached, many Latin Americans still felt themselves more cultured than English-speaking people, because of the unifying influence of the Spanish language and the increase of books, newspapers, journals of all kinds, and popular literature in Spanish which were reaching the masses as illiteracy declined. Argentina sends its locally printed books in cheap editions all over Latin America. Motion pictures made in Buenos Aires and Mexico City are shown in Mérida, Yucatan; or Cali, Colombia; or Antofagasta, Chile; or Ambato, Ecuador; or Camaguay, Cuba. Book fairs, international book prizes, and the Montevideo annual international film festival are held separate from the many cultural activities of the Pan American Union with its Washington headquarters. As Montevideo holds its Spanish-language film festival, so Caracas holds international festivals of music at which the best Latin American compositions are played and each nation sends its visiting orchestra conductor. A Chilean singer is enthusiastically acclaimed in Mexico City, a Bolivian artist shows in Buenos Aires, a Guatemalan exhibit of Indian weaving goes to Lima. Latin America is proud of its culture. The long-time cultural attachment of Latin Americans to France had been a pro-Latin unifying tie, and not necessarily an anti-Yankee sentiment. For every South American of any wealth and education, Paris was the Mecca. Sophisticated older people in Buenos Aires and Rio still speak French with ease. Franco-Argentine and Franco-Brazilian Institutes encouraged literary exchange. Bastille Day used to be celebrated with frenzy in Mexico City or Buenos Aires. With the decline of French prestige after World War II and the increasing respect for American technical education, students became as anxious to study in New York or Berkeley as in Paris. France served her turn as the inspiration of things liberal and modern in the eighteenth and nineteenth centuries; with her decline as a world power, her cultural influence is slowly waning in Latin America. She is no longer the "Mother Country" of the poets, philosophers, and literateurs. Today the tables are turned, as Paris sponsors shows of Mexican culture and art. But France still holds a lure for many Latin Americans, and French influence still survives in educational and university circles.

Contrary to current apprehensions in the United States, Latin America has not turned culturally toward Russia. In Latin America, communism never became a movement of the masses. Russian-inspired Communist parties have existed in most Latin American countries for over a half-century and none have ever come to power. Many Latin American countries have outlawed the Communist Party and relatively few recognize the USSR officially. Communist supporters have swung elections in vote-trading deals, joined "Popular Fronts," aroused students to riot, and influenced such labor and peasant leaders as Lombardo Toledano in Mexico and Francisco Julião in Brazil. But the hard-line Leninist-Marxists got old and tired. *Fidelista* movements inspired from Cuba after 1960 appealed to the young, but their efforts were weakened by clashes between Moscow and Peking. In the direct vote in Chile between Communists and Frei's Christian Democrats in 1964, Frei's mild state-socialism, inside a Catholic and democratic capitalistic framework, had the most appeal. Cuba had never been considered a highly "cultured" nation by the Mexicans or South Americans, and few Latin American intellectuals were attracted to *Fidelismo*.

Trade unionism had never been a strong inter-American movement, due to the slow development of industrialization. However, Labor has become increasingly active as a political force in those Latin American countries which are rapidly industrializing. A Pan American Federation of Labor was organized in 1916, and came to be dominated by Luis Morones and his CROM in Mexico. It took a stand against the treatment of laborers by dictators in Venezuela, Peru, and Cuba, and held several joint meetings with the AFL in the United States. Though it sent delegations to South American countries, it never had any influence there. Its influence died in Mexico and the Caribbean with the removal of Morones from politics and the death of Samuel Gompers in the United States. Labor movements in Argentina and Chile, influenced by international Communism in the 1920s, considered it pro-capitalistic.

More radical labor leaders came to the front with Lombardo Toledano in Mexico, and a new Confederation of Latin American Workers, the CTAL, was founded by him in 1938. When he retired as secretary of the Mexican CTM in 1941, he proceeded to give the CTAL all his time. Meanwhile labor leaders in Argentina representing the Argentine General Confederation of Workers met with Toledano's group in Mexico, and served in Argentina as an ardent anti-Axis element. However, all these labor groups were to some extent anti-American also; they feared the United States was trying to keep Latin America an economically "colonial country," exporting raw products forever, and never allowing it to industrialize in competition with the United States. Labor groups made surveys, held discussion meetings, and compared problems on many social issues—child labor, minimum wages, housing, conditions of women in industry. However, most such surveys and meetings were done under the auspices of larger movements, such as the Pan American Union or the International Labor Organization at Geneva. Perón attempted to create a "Latin American Labor Organization" but was unsuccessful.

Today some Latin American labor groups belong to the International Confederation of Free Trade Unions, a group formed after World War II by unions that withdrew from the Communist-dominated World Federation of Trade Unions. Its Latin American regional organization is known as the *Organización Regional Interamericana de Trabajadores,* or ORIT. Most Latin American unions have no international affiliation. At home, however, they are organizing into political parties, such as the Labor Parties in Brazil, Argentina, and Bolivia, and are pushing new labor and social legislation.

Russian influence on culture hardly materialized and French influence declined. What about American influence? For a half-century the Latin Americans had looked to the United States for loans, for advice on health, medicine, and farming, for engineers on roads and in industry. They had never considered their northern neighbor cultured enough to teach them anything about literature, art, music, or higher education. Then during World War II the United States made an all-out effort to limit German influence in Latin America. The Nelson Rockefeller Committee set up Divisions of Communications, of Press, of Motion Pictures, of Radio, of Publications, of Art, of Music, Education, and Travel. An inter-American radio program included a network of 100 stations and produced twenty-seven different programs in Spanish and Portuguese known as the "Brave New World" series. Slick-paper picture magazines, cultural institutes connected with the American embassies all openly wooed Latin American friendship. The more than fifty Cultural Institutes enrolled 75,000 students in free classes in English, the speech of the new technology.

Thus some of the prejudice against Americans was overcome. Exchange professors wrote histories of United States literature in Spanish; students came to study on scholarships in liberal arts colleges as well as in technical institutes. In the 1960s it was estimated that 60 per cent of the scholarships used in the United States by Latin Americans were in health and engineering, 30 per cent in public administration, child welfare, economics, and agriculture, and a good 10 per cent in art, music, and literature—fields in which no student would have considered an American university above a European one a decade before.

Meanwhile, translations of North American books took up half the lists of the new best sellers in South America, and Latin Americans were busy reading Hemingway, Steinbeck, O'Neill, Thomas Wolfe, and Edna Ferber as well as Mark Twain and Emerson. Heitor Villa-Lobos and Carlos Chavez conducted symphonies in the United States; American music critics have gone to South America and published histories of American music in the Spanish and Portuguese languages. Meanwhile GI's went to Mexico City College, to the University of San Marcos in Lima, to the University of Córdoba in Argentina to learn more about Latin America on their GI Bill education benefits. Many South and Central America universities offered summer sessions conducted in English for American teachers. Not only did the Latin Americans come to accept the existence of a North American culture, but North Americans began to have a wholesome respect for Latin American culture.

Meanwhile Americans at home were more interested in studying Spanish than a former generation had been in learning French or German. They learned Spanish to go as Fulbright scholars to South America, to visit Argentine or Chilean homes for college credit under the Experiment in International Living, to work in church-sponsored "community help projects" in mountain villages. A thousand young Americans in the Peace Corps served as teachers, recreation directors, nurses, and even brick makers in Spanish-speaking communities. More than 800 Peace Corps volunteers learned Portuguese and served in Brazil. Universities exchanged programs—Stanford with the new University of the Peruvian Andes at Iquitos, Cornell with Buenos Aires, the University of Kansas with the University of Costa Rica. The Carnegie Foundation established a program to assist such exchanges called the CHEAR, the Council on Higher Education in the American Republics.

With the increase of such exchanges, town to town, school to school, student to student, came a new interest in Latin American literature published in English. A sample recent year brought new English editions of the poems of Jorge Luis Borges, Rubén Darío, and Sor Juana Inés de la Cruz. *Don Segundo Sombra, Doña Barbara, The Eagle and the Serpent,* and other famous novels found their way into English in most college libraries. Classical works by Spanish explorers came out in paperback. Even the anti-American *Ariel* was available to English readers in their new efforts to understand Latin America.

At home in Latin America, national programs for education took 20 per cent of local budgets in the 1960s, according to Dr. José Mora of the OAS. The Alliance for Progress gave a spurt to elementary education in rural and urban slums, and to adult education everywhere. Four million dollars a year was set aside by the Alliance in 1965 for two regional translation centers for Spanish and Portuguese in Brazil and Argentina to make the literature of each nation available to the other. Another Alliance-financed agency, the Regional Technical Aids Center in Mexico City, translated technical materials into Spanish for use in the new vocational training in all parts of Latin America. The OAS and the Alliance continued the programs begun in the 1930s to train rural teachers, and joined with UNESCO in model schools for rural teachers from all over the New World at Patzcuaro, Mexico, and at Rubio, Venezuela. The "each one teach one" method worked out by Dr. Jaime Torres-Bodet for Mexico has been applied in classes for illiterates everywhere.

The OAS continued to sponsor art exhibits both in the Pan American Union in Washington and in Latin American capitals. An exhibit of 115 paintings, sculptures, and art photographs called "The World of Peru" was in Washington in the fall of 1965 and at the University of Texas in the spring of 1966. The "New Art of Argentina" exhibit was sent to Minneapolis one year, and on to Rio the next. Even the Inter-American Development Bank sponsored an art show by its own employees in 1965. An Inter-American Musical Festival was scheduled in Washington every four years, starting in 1958. There is worldwide interest in the spectacular modern architecture of Latin America, and shows of "South American Design" are often held in New York. In April 1964 the First Inter-American Poets Encounter was held in Mexico City, with fifteen nations represented. The old Pan American Union itself had sponsored such cultural activity, and the OAS has continued the effort. The Pan American Conferences of 1936 and 1938 adopted resolutions which led to the First Inter-American Conference for Intellectual Cooperation. Sunday afternoon concerts at the Pan American Union Building continued to feature Latin American performers and composers. Book fairs, international book prizes, awards for novels and poetry emanated from the Carnegie building. Geographers, historians, astrophysicists, bibliographers, geologists, journalists, and architects have met more or less regularly from 1920 to the present. The preservation of archives, the standardization of university courses and library filing systems, the publication of lists of fellowships and exchange professorships, the preparation of accurate maps, and the reduction of postal rates on educational materials occupied the time of these busy committees.

As a publishing venture, the Pan American Union has an old history. *The Hand Book of the American Republics*, a commercial guide 300 pages long, came out in 1891. The first *Bulletin of the Pan American Union*, a monograph on coffee production, was printed in 1893. By 1911, a meaty magazine, profusely illustrated and full of social and historical material was published monthly under the title *Bulletin of the Pan American Union*. Its post-World War II successor *Américas* contains stories, art and music criticism, book reviews, political articles, and much chatter about the comings and goings of personalities in the inter-American world. In addition, the Pan American Union's Department of Cultural Affairs publishes *Panorama*, a quarterly cultural review of inter-American affairs. There is also a regular music bulletin, a quarterly *Annals of the OAS*, a *Dictionary* of *Latin American Literature,* a *Guide to Public Collections of Art in Latin America,* and a quarterly *Inter-American Bibliographic Review.* The list of other printed materials available through the Pan American Union is itself thirty pages long.

That the Alliance for Progress meant to spend money on "culture" was shown in a series of meetings called "Inter-American Conferences of Cultural Directors." In the Final Act of the November 1963 conference, the Cultural directors agreed:

1. The principles and objectives of the Alliance for Progress constitute a position that the various aspects of cultural expression and cultural activity must be incorporated on both the national and regional levels into the joint efforts of the countries participating in the Alliance, and
2. To fulfill the aims of the Charter of Punta del Este, which states that "the men and women of our Hemisphere . . . are determined . . . to gain access to knowledge and equal opportunity for all, [and] to end those conditions which benefit the few at the expense of the needs and dignity of the many," we express our resolve to take steps to promote the adoption by our governments of the measures necessary to assure that cultural manifestations will receive the stimulus and support that they must have within the general framework and the individual projects of the Alliance for Progress.

The *Américas* magazine concluded its report of this meeting by saying, "With this fraternal pledge the representatives of the American republics put their seal on another chapter in the unfolding story of the race of men whose domain is called, and with reason, the New World."[1]

Readings

Adams, M., ed., *Latin America: Evolution or Explosion?* (1963)
Adams, R. N., and C. C. Cumberland, *The United States University Cooperation in Latin America* (1960)
Adams, V., *Peace Corps in Action* (1964)
Aguilar, A., *Latin America and the Alliance for Progress* (1963)
Aguirre, A., ed., *Uruguay and the United States* (1958)
Aiken, D., *The All-American Front* (1940)
Alba, V., *Alliance Without Allies: The Mythology of Progress in Latin America* (1965)
———, *History of Latin American Labor* (1966)
Alexander, R. J., *Communism in Latin America* (1957)
———, *Labor Relations in Argentina, Brazil and Chile* (1962)
Allen, R. L., *Soviet Influence in Latin America: Role of Economic Relations* (1959)
Alliance for Progress, Official Documents Emanating from the Special Meeting of the Inter-American Economic and Social Council at the Ministerial Level (OAS official records)
———, Committee of Nine, *Evaluation of the General Economic and Social Development Plan of Colombia* (1962) [other countries since]

---

1 *Américas,* November 1963, p. 4.

Alvarez, A., *The Monroe Doctrine* (1924)

American Universities Field Service Staff Reports—Latin American Reports

Arciniegas, G., *The State of Latin America* (1952)

Artucio, A. F., *Nazi Underground in South America* (1942)

Baer, W., and Kerstenetzky, eds., *Inflation and Growth in Latin America* (1964)

Baerresen, D., M. Carony, and J. Grunwald, *Latin American Trade Patterns* (1965)

Bailey, N., *Latin America: Politics, Economics and Hemisphere Security* (1966)

Ball, M. M., *Problems of Inter-American Organization* (1944)

Barber, W. F., and C. N. Ronning, *Internal Security and Military Power* (1965)

Beale, H. K., *Theodore Roosevelt and Rise of America to World Power* (1956)

Beals, C., et al., *What the South Americans Think of Us* (1945)

Beckett, G., *The Reciprocal Trade Agreement Program* (1941)

Bemis, S. F., *John Quincy Adams and Foundation of American Foreign Policy* (1949)

———, *Latin American Policy of the United States* (1943)

Benton, W., *Voice of Latin America* (1961)

Berle, A. A., Jr., *Latin America: Diplomacy and Reality* (1962)

Bernstein, M., *Foreign Investments in Latin America* (1965)

Bidwell, P. M., *Economic Defense of Latin America* (1941)

Bradley, A., *Trans-Pacific Relations of Latin America* (1942)

Brown, W. A., and O. Redvers, *American Foreign Assistance* (1953)

Burr, R. N., *By Reason or Force: Chile and the Balance of Power in South America, 1830–1903* (1965)

———, *Latin America's Nationalistic Revolutions* (1961)

———, *Stillborn Panama Congress: Power Politics and Chilean-Colombian Relations During the War of the Pacific* (1962)

———, and R. D. Hussey, *Documents on Inter-American Cooperation* (2 vols., 1955)

Callahan, J. M., *American Foreign Policy in Mexican Relations* (1932)

Callcott, W. H., *Caribbean Policy of the United States, 1890–1920* (1942)

Canyes, M., *Meetings of Consultation: Their Origin, Significance and Role in Inter-American Relations* (rev. ed., 1962)

———, *The Organization of American States and the United Nations* (6th ed., 1963)

Carey, J. C., *Peru and the United States, 1900–1962* (1964)

Carleton, W. G., *The Revolution in American Foreign Policy* (1963)

Castaneda, J., *Mexico and the United Nations* (1958)

Chase, A., *Falange, The Nazi Secret Army in the Americas* (1943)

Clark, J. R., *Memorandum on the Monroe Doctrine* (1930)

Claude, I. L., Jr., *Organization of American States, the United Nations and the United States* (1964)

Cline, H. F., *United States and Mexico* (1953)

Council on Foreign Relations, *United States in World Affairs, 1931–1941; 1947– to date*

Daniels, J., *Shirt Sleeve Diplomacy* (1947)

Davila, C., *We of the Americas* (1949)

Dean, V. M., *Nature of the Non-Western World* (1958)

DeConde, A., *Latin American Policy of Herbert Hoover* (1951)

Del Río, A., ed., *Responsible Freedom in the Americas* (1955)

Delwart, L. O., *The Future of Latin American Exports to the United States: 1965 and 1970* (1960)

Department of State, *Peace in the Americas* (1950)

De Vries, E., and J. Medina Echavarría, *Social Aspects of Economic Development in Latin America* (1963)

Dietrick, E. B., *Economic Relations of the United States with Latin America* (1941)

Dillon, D., *International Communism and Latin America: Perspectives and Prospects* (1962)

Donovan, J., *Red Machete: Communist Infiltration in the Americas* (1963)

Dozer, D. M., *Are We Good Neighbors?* (1959)

———, *Monroe Doctrine* (1965)

Dreier, J. C., *The Alliance for Progress: Problems and Perspectives* (1962)

———, *The Organization of American States and Hemisphere Crisis* (1962)

Dubois, J., *Operation America* (1963)

Duggan, L., *The Americas, the Search for Hemisphere Security* (1949)

Dyer, J. M., *United States—Latin American Trade and Financial Relations* (1961)

Eister, A. W., *The United States and the ABC Powers, 1889–1906* (1950)

Ellis, H. S., ed., *Economic Development for Latin America* (1962)

Ellis, L. E., *Frank B. Kellogg and American Foreign Relations, 1925–1929* (1961)

Fenwick, C. G., *The Inter-American Regional System* (2nd ed., 1961)

Ferns, H. S., *Britain and Argentina in the Nineteenth Century* (1960)

Fiscal Policy for Economic Growth in Latin America (1965)

Flores, E., *Land Reform and the Alliance for Progress* (1963)

Gantenbeim, J. W., ed., *Evolution of Our Latin American Policy: Documentary Record* (1950)

Gerassi, J., *The Great Fear: Reconquest of Latin America by Latin Americans* (1963)

Glick, P. M., *Administration of Technical Assistance: Growth in the Americas* (1957)

Goldman, R., ed., *Readings in American Foreign Policy* (1959)

Gordon, L., *A New Deal for Latin America: The Alliance for Progress* (1963)

Gordon, W. C., *Political Economy of Latin America* (1965)

Gross, F. B., ed., *The United States and the United Nations*, Chap. VII (1964)

Guerrant, E. O., *Roosevelt's Good Neighbor Policy* (1950)

Guggenheim, H. F., *Latin America Now or Never* (1963)

Hanson, S. G., *Economic Development of Latin America* (1951)

———, "The End of the 'Good Neighbor Policy,'" *Inter-American Economic Affairs*, X (1953) 45–96

Harbron, *Canada and Organization of American States* (1963)

Haring, C. H., *Argentina and the United States* (1941)

———, *South America Looks at the United States* (1928)

Hauch, C. C., *The Current Situation in Latin American Education* (1963)

Haverstock, N. A., *The OAS: The Challenge of the Americas* (1966)

Heath, D. B., and R. N. Adams, *Contemporary Cultures and Societies of Latin America* (1965)

Herrera, L. F., *Inter-American Bank* (1962)

Horn, P. V., and H. E. Bice, *Latin American Trade and Economics* (1949)

Houston, J. A., *Latin America in the United Nations* (1956)

Houtart, K., and E. Pin, *The Church and the Latin American Revolution* (1965)

Hull, C., *Memoirs of Cordell Hull* (2 vols., 1948)

Humphrey, J. P., *Inter-American System: A Canadian View* (1942)

Inman, S. G., *Latin America: Its Place in World Life* (rev. ed., 1942)

———, *Problems in Pan Americanism* (2nd ed., 1925)

Inter-American Conference, Official Documents

Inter-American Conferences of Foreign Ministers, Handbooks of Delegates of the United States of America and other materials prepared for each meeting

Inter-American Development Bank, *Account of by Tibor Masid* (1963?)

——, *Annual Reports* (2nd, 1963)

——, *Social Progress Trust Fund, Annual Reports* (2nd, 1963; 3rd, 1964)

International Bank for Reconstruction and Development, *World Bank Activities in Latin America: A Report for the Economic Conference of the OAS at Buenos Aires, 1957* (1957)

International Development Board, *An Economic Program for the Americas* (1954)

Ireland, G., *Boundaries, Possessions and Conflicts in Central and North America and the Caribbean* (1941)

——, *Boundaries, Possessions and Conflicts in South America* (1938)

Janowitz, M., *The Military in the Political Development of New Nations* (1964)

Johnsen, J. E., *Canada and the Western Hemisphere* (1944)

——, *Latin American Relations with League of Nations* (1930)

Josephs, R., *Latin America—Continent in Crisis* (1948)

Kelchner, W. H., *Latin American Relations with the League of Nations* (1930)

Kidder, F. E., *Latin America and Unesco: The First Five Years* (1960)

Latin America Tomorrow—Annals of the American Academy of Political and Social Sciences—Vol. 360, July 1965

Latin American Free Trade Association (LAFTA): see Wionczek and also U.S. Tariff Commission publication No. 60

Latin American Viewpoints—Annals of the American Academy of Political and Social Sciences (1942)

Lauterpach, A., *Enterprise in Latin America* (1966)

Laves, W. H., ed., *Inter-American Solidarity* (1941)

Lewis, C., *America's Stake in International Investments* (1938)

Lieuwen, E., *Arms and Politics in Latin America* (rev. ed., 1961)

——, *Generals Versus Presidents* (1964)

——, *United States Policy in Latin America: A Short History* (1965)

Lindsell, H., *The Chilean–American Controversy of 1891–1892* (1943)

Liser, M., *Organization of American States* (4th ed., 1949)

Lockey, J. B., *Essays in Pan Americanism* (1939)

——, *Pan Americanism: Its Beginning* (1920)

Logan, J. A., Jr., *No Transfer, an American Security Principle* (1961)

Macdonald, A. F., *Latin American Politics and Government* (2nd ed., 1954)

MacDonald, N. P., *Hitler over Latin America* (1940)

Madariaga, S. de, *Latin America between the Eagle and the Bear* (1962)

Madden, C. H., and L. Rall, *Latin America: Reform or Revolution* (1962)

Maier, J., and R. W. Weatherhead, eds., *Politics of Change in Latin America* (1964)

Manger, W., ed., *The Alliance for Progress: A Critical Appraisal* (1963)

——, *Pan America in Crisis: The Future of the OAS* (1961)

——, *The Two Americas: Dialogue on Progress and Problems* (1965)

——, *The War and the Americas* (1944)

Manning, W. R., ed., *Diplomatic Correspondence of the United States Concerning Latin American Independence* (3 vols., 1925)

——, *Diplomatic Correspondence of the United States: Inter-American Affairs, 1831–1860* (12 vols., 1932–1939)

——, *Arbitration Treaties Among the American Nations to 1910* (1924; Supplement to 1929)

Maritino, N., *Alliance for Progress* (1963)

Martin, P. A., *Latin America and the War* (1925)

Martz, J. D., ed., *Dynamics of Change in Latin American Politics* (1965)

Masters, R. D., *Handbook of International Organization in the Americas* (1945)

Mathews, H. L., ed., *United States and Latin America* (2nd ed., 1963)

McClellan, G. S., ed., *United States Policy in Latin America* (1963)

McGann, T. F., *Argentina, United States and the Inter-American System, 1880–1914* (1958)

Mecham, J. L., *Survey of United States–Latin American Relations* (1965)

———, *The United States and Inter-American Security, 1889–1960* (1961)

Morrison, D., *Latin American Mission: An Adventure in Hemisphere Diplomacy* (1965)

Motten, C. J., ed., *Latin America: Development Programming and United States Investments* (1956)

Munro, D. G., *Intervention and Dollar Diplomacy in the Caribbean, 1900–1921* (1964)

———, *United States and the Caribbean* (1934)

National Planning Association, *Studies in Technical Cooperation in Latin America* (Seven studies to 1957)

———, *Technical Assistance by Religious Agencies in Latin America* [by J. G. Maddox] (1956)

———, *Technical Cooperation in Latin American Agriculture* [by A. T. Mosher] (1957)

———, *The Role of the Universities in Technical Corporations in Latin America* (1955)

Nearing, S., and J. Freeman, *Dollar Diplomacy* (1926)

Nystrom, J. W., and N. A. Haverstrock, eds., *The Alliance for Progress: Key to Latin America's Development* (1966)

Onís, J. de, *The United States as Seen by Spanish American Writers, 1776–1890* (1952)

Organization of American States, Pan American Union: *Manual of Inter-American Relations* (1953)

———, *Report of the Activities of the Organization of American States, 1948–1953* (1953)

———, *Inter-American Treaty of Reciprocal Assistance Applications* (2 vols., 1964)

———, *The Act of Bogotá* (1961)

———, *Economic Survey of Latin America, 1962* (1964)

———, *The Flow of Capital from the European Economic Community to Latin America* (1963)

———, Inter-American Statistical Institute, *America en Cifras* (9 vols., 1961)

———, Secretariat-General, *Human Rights in American States* (1960)

———, *Applications of Inter-American Treaty of Reciprocal Assistance, 1948–1956* (1957)

Organization of American States, Economic Conference, Buenos Aires, 1957, *Final Act* (1957)

Padilla, E., *Free Men of America* (1943)

Palmer, T. W., *Search for a Latin American Policy* (1957)

Perkins, D., *A History of the Monroe Doctrine* (new ed., 1955)

———, *Monroe Doctrine, 1823–1826* (1927)

———, *Monroe Doctrine, 1826–1867* (1933)

———, *Monroe Doctrine, 1867–1907* (1937)

———, *United States and the Caribbean* (1947)

———, *United States and Latin America* (1961)

Peterson, H. F., *Argentina and the United States, 1810–1960* (1964)

Phelps, D. M., ed., *Economic Relations with Latin America* (1940)

———, *Rubber Development in Latin America* (1957)

Pinheiro de Vasconcellos, H., *World State: or New Order of Common Sense* (1959)

Plaza, G., *Problems of Democracy in Latin America* (1955)

Poppino, R. L., *International Communism in Latin America: A History of the Movement, 1917–1963* (1964)

Porter, C. O., and R. J. Alexander, *The Struggle for Democracy in Latin America* (1961)

Prebisch, R., *Towards A Dynamic Development Policy for Latin America* (1963)

Privitera, J. F., *Latin American Front* (1945)

Problems of Tax Administration in Latin America (1966)

Quintanilla, L., *A Latin American Speaks* (1943)

Rappaport, A., *The Monroe Doctrine* (1964)

Raushenbush, J., *The Challenge to the Alliance for Progress* (1962)

Ray, P. A., *South Wind Red—Our Hemisphere Crisis* (1962)

Redington, R. J., *The Organization of America States as A Collective Security System* (1960)

Rippy, J. F., *Caribbean Danger Zone* (1940)

———, *Globe and Hemisphere, Latin America's Place in the Post War Foreign Relations of the United States* (1958)

———, *Latin America* (1958)

———, *Latin America in World Politics* (3rd ed.,1938)

———, *Rivalry of the United States and Great Britain over Latin America, 1808–1830* (1939)

———, *United States and Mexico* (rev. ed., 1931)

Robertson, W. S., *France and Latin American Independence* (1939)

———, *Hispanic American Relations with the United States* (1923)

Ronning, C. N., *Diplomatic Asylum: Legal Norms and Political Reality in Latin American Relations* (1965)

———, *Law and Politics in Inter-American Diplomacy* (1963)

———, *Punta del Este: The Limits of Collective Security in a Troubled Hemisphere* (1963)

Rowe, L. S., *et al.*, *Latin America in World Affairs, 1914–1940* (1941)

Rowland, D. W., *History of the Office of the Coordinator of Inter-American Affairs* (1946)

Royal Institute of International Affairs, *Survey of International Affairs*, 1920/1923 . . . 1938; 1949 . . . to date

Rubin, J., *Your Hundred Billion Dollars: The Complete Story of American Foreign Aid* (1964)

Sands, W. F., *Our Jungle Diplomacy* (1944)

Schmid, P., *Beggars on Golden Stools: A Journey Through Latin America* (1956)

Schultz, T. W., *Economic Test in Latin America* (1946)

Schurz, W. L., *Latin America* (rev. ed., 1963)

———, *This New World* (1954)

Scott, J. B., ed., *International Conferences of American States, 1889–1928*, and a supplementary volume, 1933–1940 (1931 and 1940)

Shea, D. R., *The Calvo Clause* (1955)

Slater, J., *A Revaluation of Collective Security: The OAS in Action* (1965)

Smith, T. L., *Current Social Trends and Problems in Latin America* (1957)

————, *Some Educational and Anthropological Aspects of Latin America* (1948)

Snow, S., *The Pan American Federation of Labor* (1964)

Some Aspects of Postwar Inter-American Relations (1946)

Soward, F. H., and A. M. Marnlay, *Canada and the Pan American System* (1948)

Stetson, C., and B. Fairchild, *Framework of Hemisphere Defense* (1960)

Stoetzer, O. C., *The Organization of American States* (rev. ed., 1965)

Stuart, G. H., *Latin America and the United States* (5th ed., 1955)

Szulc, T., *The Cuban Invasion: The Chronicle of a Disaster* (1962)

————, *Latin America Today and Tomorrow* (rev. ed., 1964)

————, *The Winds of Revolution* (rev. ed., 1965)

————, *Twilight of the Tyrants* (1959)

Tannenbaum, F., *Whither Latin America?* (1934)

Thomas, A. V. and A. J., Jr., *Non-Intervention: The Law and Its Import in the Americas* (1956)

————, *Organization of American States* (1963)

Tomasek, R. D., ed., *Latin American Politics—24 Studies of the Contemporary Scene* (1966)

Tondel, L. M., ed., *Inter-American Security System and the Cuban Crisis* (1964)

Torres-Rioseco, A., *Aspects of Spanish American Literature* (1963)

Travis, M., and P. W. Buck, eds., *Control of Foreign Relations in Modern Nations* (1957)

Tyler, A. C., *Foreign Policy of James G. Blaine* (1927)

Ugarte, M., *Destiny of a Continent*, trans. J. F. Rippy (1925)

Unesco, *Social Aspects of Economic Development in Latin America* (2 vols., 1963)

————, *Urbanization in Latin America*, ed. P. M. Hauser (1962)

United Nations, *Economic Development of Latin America and Its Problems* (1965)

————, *Economic Development Planning and International Cooperation* (1961)

————, *International Cooperation: A Latin American Development Policy* (1905?)

————, *Multilateral Economic Cooperation in Latin America* (1962)

————, *Towards a Dynamic Policy for Latin America* (1964)

United Nations, Department of Economic Affairs, *Study of Prospects of Inter-Latin American Trade (Southern Zone of the Region)* (1954)

————, *A Survey of Trade Between Latin America and Europe* (1953)

United Nations, Economic Commission for Latin America, *Economic Review of Latin America, 1955*

————, *Agriculture in Latin America: Problems and Prospects* (1963)

————, *Economic Development of Latin America in the Postwar Period* (1964)

————, *Economic Development in Latin America Sociological Considerations* (by J. Medina-Echevarría) (1963)

————, *Economic Survey of Latin America, 1947–1957* (annual)

————, *Foreign Capital in Latin America* (1955)

————, *International Cooperation in a Latin American Development Policy* (1954)

————, *Latin American Common Market* (1959)

————, *A Measurement of Price Levels and the Purchasing power of Currencies in Latin America, 1960–1962* (1963)

————, *Social Aspects of Population Growth in Colombia* (1962)

————, *Towards a Dynamic Policy for Latin America* (1964)

United Nations, Food and Agriculture Organization (FAO), *Progress of Land Reform: Third Report* (1962)

————, *Report on Regional Land Reform Tenure for Latin America* (1961)

United States, Department of State, *Papers Relating to the Foreign Relations of the United States, 1861–to date* (annual)

————, *Inter-American Efforts to Relieve Tensions in the Western Hemisphere, 1959–1960* (1962)

————, External Research Staff—Various publications

United States Congress, House Committee on Appropriations, 88th Congress, 1 Session, *Economic Assistance Program*, Part IV (1963)

United States Congress, Senate Committee on Judiciary, Subcommittee on Administration of the Internal Security Act and Other Internal Security Laws, 88th Congress, 1 Session, *Documentation on Communist Penetration in Latin America* (3 vols., 1965)

United States Congress, Subcommittee on Inter-American Economic Relations of Joint Economic Committee, 88th Congress, 2 Session, *Hearings* (January 1964)

United States Congress, Senate Committee on Foreign Relations, 86th Congress, 2 Session, Document No. 125, *United States-Latin American Relations* (1960)

Urquidi, U. L., *The Challenge of Development in Latin America* (1964)

Uruguay Institute of International Law, *Uruguay and the United Nations* (1958)

Van Aken, M. J., *Pan Hispanism: Its Origin and Development to 1866* (1959)

Vernon, R., ed., *How Latin America Views the U.S. Investor* (1965)

Webster, C. K., *Foreign Policy of Palmerston* (1941)

Welles, S., *Time for Decision* (1944)

Whitaker, A. P., *Argentine Upheaval* (1956)

————, *Development of American Regionalism* (International Conciliation No. 442)

————, *Inter-American Affairs: An Annual, 1941–1945*, Vols. I–V

————, *United States and Argentina* (1954)

————, *United States and Independence of Latin America, 1800–1830* (1941)

————, *United States and South America: Northern Republics* (1948)

————, *Western Hemisphere Idea: Its Rise and Decline* (1954)

Wilbur, W. A., *The Monroe Doctrine* (1965)

Winkler, M., *Investments of United States Capital in Latin America* (1929)

Wionczeh, M. S., *Latin American Free Trade Association* (1965)

Wood, B., *Making of the Good Neighbor Policy* (1961)

————, *The United States and Latin American Wars, 1932–1942* (1966)

Wythe, G., *United States and Inter-American Relations: A Contemporary Appraisal* (1964)

Aids to Further Study

BIBLIOGRAPHICAL NOTE

THIS BIBLIOGRAPHY is not an exhaustive one, but is planned solely as an aid to the further study of Latin American history by students, teachers, and interested readers. It contains few magazine articles or foreign language publications, and consists mainly of books written in English. Naturally a knowledge of Spanish and/or Portuguese is essential for the undertaking of scholarly study in Latin American history, but beginning scholars must, of necessity, approach the field through English works. We have included here a small selection of titles on the general fields of colonial history, the modern nations, international relations, and cultural materials. The student is referred to the lists following the various chapters for more specialized studies. We have attempted to include only a few source materials in English translation to give "a touch of flavor" for the braver student. Parallel college textbooks, of which there are a number, are not listed.

GENERAL BIBLIOGRAPHIES

Albanel, M. N., *Cuba, Dominican Republic, Haiti and Puerto Rico—Selected Bibliography* (1956)
Alinsky, M., *Latin American Journalism Bibliography* (1958)
American Geographical Society, *Catalogue of Maps on Hispanic America* (4 vols., 1930–1932)
American Historical Association, *Guide to Historical Literature* (1961)
American Universities Field Staff, *List of Publications, 1961–1962* (1963)
———, *A Select Bibliography, Supplement on Latin America* by T. D. Long (1960)
———, *Bibliography of the Andean Countries* (1958)
Andrews, B. H., *Latin America: A Bibliography of Paperback Books* (1964)

Bayitch, S. A., *Latin America: A Bibliographical Guide to Economy, History, Law, Politics and Society* (1961)

Behrendt, R. F. W., *Modern Latin America in Social Science Literature* (1949)

Bemis, S. F., and G. G. Griffin, *Guide to the Diplomatic History of the United States, 1775–1921* (1935)

Bernstein, S. P., *Bibliography on Labor and Social Welfare in Latin America* (1944)

Bibliography on Public Administration in Latin America (1954)

Bibliography of Selected Statistical Sources on the American Nations (1947)

Boggs, R. S., *Bibliography of Latin American Folklore* (1940)

Borchard, E. M., *Guide to the Law and Legal Literature of Argentina, Brazil and Chile* (1917) [Other guides for most of the other countries have been produced under the auspices of the Library of Congress.]

Brown, L. C., *Latin America: A Bibliography* (1962)

Butler, R. L., *Guide to the Hispanic American Historical Review, 1918–1945* (1950)

Carroll, T. F., *Land Tenure and Land Reform in Latin America: A Selective Annotated Bibliography* (1962)

Chapman, C. E., "List of Books on Caudillos," *Hispanic American Historical Review*, XIII (1933), 143–46.

Chase, G., *Guide to Music of Latin America* (rev. ed., 1962)

Childs, J. B. (ed. for Library of Congress), *Guide to the Official Publications of the Other American Republics* (19 vols.—Latin American Series, 1945–1949)

———, *The Memorias of the Republics of Central America and Antilles* (1932)

Cox, E. G., *Reference Guide to the Literature of Travel*, Vol. II: *New World* (1938)

Daniels, M., *Sources of Information on Contemporary Caribbean International Problems* in A. C. Wilgus, ed., *Caribbean: Contemporary International Relations* (1957)

Davis, H. E., *Social Science Trends in Latin America* (1950)

del Toro, J., *Bibliography of the Collective Biography of Spanish America* (1938)

Doors to America [quarterly list of books] (since 1954)

Easton, D. K., *Sources for the Study of Caribbean Culture* in A. C. Wilgus, ed., *Caribbean: Its Culture* (1955)

Economic Literature of Latin America: A Tentative Bibliography (2 vols., 1936)

Education in Latin America: A Partial Bibliography (1958)

Englekirk, J. E., *An Outline History of Spanish American Literature* (3rd. ed., 1965)

Fleener, C. J., and R. L. Seckinger, *The Guide to Latin American Paperback Literature* (1966)

Gibson, C., *The Colonial Period in Latin American History* (1958)

———, *Index to the Hispanic American Historical Review, 1946–1955* (1957)

Goldsmith, P. H., *Brief Bibliography of Books in English on Latin America in English, Spanish and Portuguese, relating to the Republics commonly called Latin America* (1915)

Griffiths, W. J., "Historiography of Central America since 1830," *Hispanic American Historical Review*, XL (1940), 548–67 [There are many other historiographical articles in that publication, which also has valuable reviews of books and lists of books on Latin America.]

Grismer, R. L., *A Guide to the Literature of Latin America* (1939)

———, *New Bibliography of the Literature of Spain and Spanish America* (7 vols., AA–CEZ, 1941–1946)

————, *Reference Index to Twelve Thousand Spanish American Authors* (1939)
Grossman, George, *Bibliography on Public Administration in Latin America* (rev. ed., 1954)
Guide to the Official Publications of the Other American Republics (19 vols., 1945–1948)
Handbook of Latin American Studies, Nos. 1—(annual since 1936)
Hardoy, J. E., *Bibliography on the Evolution of Cities in Latin America* (1962)
Harvard Council on Hispano-American Studies, a series of bibliographies relating to the Belles-Lettres of the Latin American countries by various editors (14 vols., 1932–1935) [On Argentina, Bolivia, Brazil, Central America, Chile, Colombia, Cuba, Ecuador, Panama, Paraguay, Peru, Santo Domingo, Uruguay, and Venezuela.]
Harvard Guide to American History (1952)
Hespelt, E. *et. al.*, *An Anthology of Spanish American Literature* (1946)
Hill, R. R., *National Archives of Latin America* (1945)
Hilton, R., *Handbook of Hispanic American Source Materials and Research Organizations in the United States* (rev. ed., 1956)
Humphreys, R. A., *Latin American History: A Guide to the Literature in English* (1958)
Index for the Published News of the New York Times
Index to Latin American Periodicals (1961; a quarterly)
Inter-American Bibliographical Review (quarterly since 1951)
Jackson, W. W., *Library Guide for Brazilian Studies* (1964)
Jones, C. K., *Bibliography of Latin American Bibliographies* (2nd ed., 1942)
Jones, T. B., E. A. Warburton, and A. Kingsley, *Bibliography on South American Economic Affairs: Articles in Nineteenth-Century Periodicals* (1955)
Jones, W. K., *Latin American Writers in English Translation, a Tentative Bibliography* (1944)
———, *Spanish American Literature in Translation: A Selection of Poetry, Fiction and Drama Since 1888* (1963)
Keniston, H., *List of Works for the Study of Hispanic American History* (1920)
Ker, A. M., *Mexican Government Publications—1821–1936* (1940)
"Latin American Fiction in English Translation" in D. Dozer, *Latin America: An Interpretive History* (1962), pp. 580–82 [Many more English translations of Latin American literature have since been published.]
Latin American Research Review (three times a year, since 1965)
Lauerhaus, L., *Communism in Latin America: A Bibliography: The Post War Years 1945–1960* (1963)
Leavitt, S. E., *Hispano-American Literature in the United States: A Bibliography of Translations and Criticism* (1932)
Library of Congress, Hispanic Foundation, *Bibliographic Series* (since 1942)
———, *Latin American Series* (Many guides and bibliographies)
———, Law Library, *Index to Latin American Legislation, 1950–1960* (1961)
Ludwig, L., *Communism in Latin America, a Bibliography: The Postwar Years (1945–1960)* (1962)
Marchant, A., *Boundaries of the Latin American Republics, an Annotated List of Documents, 1493–1943* (1944)
Mecham, J. L., "Northern Expansion of New Spain, 1522–1822: A Selected Descriptive Bibliographical List," *Hispanic American Historical Review*, VII (1927), 233–76
Moses, B., *Spanish Colonial Literature in South America* (1922)

Mughiuddin, M. B., and B–J. L. Clark, *Cuba Since Castro: A Bibliography of Revolutionary Materials* (1963)

National Education Association, *Latin American Backgrounds: A Bibliography* (1941)

New York University, School of Law, *Bibliographies on the Law and Uses of International Rivers* (1960)

Nott, K. F., *San Martín—100 Years of Historiography* (1960)

O'Leary, T. J., *Ethnographic Bibliography of South America* (1963)

de Onís, H., ed., *The Golden Land* (2nd ed., 1961)

Okinshevich, L., *Latin America in Soviet Writings: A Bibliography* (2 vols., 1966)

Organization of American States, Pan American Union, *Bibliography of the Liberator Simon Bolivar* (rev. ed., 1933)

———, *Catalogue of Pan American Union Publications: Inter-American Review of Bibliography*

———, *Librarians, Editors, Authors* (*L.E.A.*)

———, *Pan American Bookshelf*

———, *Select List of Books in English on Latin America* (1929) [The Pan American Union has issued many lists of books and bibliographies.]

Pan American Union, *Bibliography of Latin American Culture in English Translation* (1963)

———, *Bibliography on Education and Economic and Social Development* (1962)

———, *Books and Libraries in the Americas, recommendations of the Inter-American Conferences, 1947–1962* (1963)

———, *Books in the Americas* (1960)

———, *Index to Latin American Periodical Literature, 1929–1960* (1962)

———, *Latin American Higher Education and Inter-American Cooperation* (1961)

———, *Surveys of Investigations in Progress in the Field of Latin American Studies* (1962)

———, *Theses on Pan American Subjects* (by F. E. Kidder) (1962)

———, Department of Economic Affairs, *International Organizations Active in the Field of Agricultural Development, Agrarian Reform and Rural Life in Latin America* (1964)

Paperbound Books in Print (annual—since 1955)

Paperbound Book Guide for Colleges (annual—since 1957)

Parker, F. D., *Histories and Historians of Central America to 1850* (1951)

Phillips, P. L., *List of Books, Magazine Articles and Maps Relating to Latin America* (1902)

Pierson, D., *Survey of Literature on Brazil of Sociological Significance Published up to 1940* (1945)

Pierson, W. W., *Hispanic American History: A Syllabus* (rev. ed., 1926)

Reader's Guide to Periodical Literature

"Recent Articles on Historiography" in L. Hanke, *Readings in Latin American History*, I, 309.

Select Bibliography of Trade Publications with Special Reference to Caribbean Trade Statistics—Annotated (1954)

Shelby, C., *Latin American Periodicals Currently Received in the Library of Congress and in the Library of the Department of Agriculture* (1945)

Simmons, M. E., *A Bibliography of the Romance and Related Forms in Spanish America* (1963)

Smith, R. C., and E. Wilder, *Guide to the Art of Latin America* (1948)

Spell, J. R., *Contemporary Spanish American Fiction Writers* (1944)

Steck, F. B., *Tentative Guide to Historical Materials on the Spanish Borderlands* (1943)

Stokes, W. W., *Causes of Inter-American Misunderstandings; a Selected Bibliography* (1957)

Taeuber, I. B., *General Censuses and Vital Statistics in the Americas* (1943)

Thompson, E. T., *The Plantation: A Bibliography* (1957)

Topete, J. M., *A Working Bibliography of Latin American Literature* (1952)

UNESCO, *Directory of Current Latin American Periodicals* (1958)

——, *International Bibliography of Social and Cultural Anthropology, of Economics, of Political Science and of Sociology* (annual—since 1955)

Union List of Latin American Newspapers in Libraries of the United States (1953)

United Nations, F. A. O., monographs and lists published yearly

United Nations, *Latin America, 1935–1949: A Selected Bibliography* (1952)

United States, Department of Agriculture, *Bibliography of Agriculture* (monthly since 1942)

United States, Department of the Army, *Latin America, Hemisphere Partner; a Bibliographical Survey* (1964)

United States, Department of State, Bureau of Intelligence and Research, *Studies in Progress: American Republics*

United States Military Assistance Institute, Library, *Selected Reading List on Latin America* (2nd rev. ed., 1963) [Supplements on individual country surveys are regularly issued.]

United States National Students Association, *Readings on: Latin American Student Movement and the Rise of the Latin American Left* (1965)

University of California at Los Angeles, Center of Latin American Studies, *Guide to Latin American Studies* (1966)

——, *Latin America in Periodical Literature* (monthly, 1962–1963)

——, *Master Directory for Latin America* (1965)

——, *Periodicals for Latin American Economic Development, Trade and Investment: An Annotated Bibliography* (1965)

University of California (Berkeley), *Spain and Spanish America in the Libraries of the University of California: A catalogue of books* (2 vols., 1928–1930)

University of Florida Library, *Caribbean Acquisitions* (annual since 1956)

University of Texas, Department of Sociology, *International Population Census Bibliography: Latin America and the Caribbean* (1965)

Violich, F., *Bibliography on Community Development Applied to Urban Areas in Latin America* (1963)

Wagley, C., *Social Science Research in Latin America* (1964)

Wagner, H. R., *The Spanish Southwest, 1542–1794* (2 vols., 1937)

Whitaker, A. P., *Latin America Since 1825* (1958)

Wilgus, A. C., *Histories and Historians of Hispanic America* (1942)

Work, M. N., *Bibliography of the Negro in Africa and America* (1928)

Zimmerman, I., *A Guide to Current Latin American Periodicals* (1961, 1962)

GENERAL WORKS ON MODERN LATIN AMERICA[1]

Adams, R. N., *Cultural Surveys of Panama–Nicaragua–Guatemala–El Salvador–Honduras* (1957)

---

[1] For Inter-American relations, see list at end of Chapter 41.

————, ed., *Social Change in Latin America Today* (1960)

————, and C. C. Cumberland, *United States University Cooperation in Latin America* (1960)

Aikman, D., *All-American Front* (1940)

Akers, C. E., *A History of South America* (rev. ed., 1930)

Alba, V., *Alliance without Allies; the Mythology of Progress in Latin America* (1965)

————, *Politics and the Labor Movement in Latin America* (1966)

Alderfer, H. F., *Local Government in Developing Countries* (1964)

Alexander, R. J., *Communism in Latin America* (1957)

————, *Labor Movements in Latin America* (1947)

————, *Labor Relations in Argentina, Brazil and Chile* (1962)

————, *Latin American Politics and Government* (1965)

————, *Organized Labor in Latin America* (1966)

————, *Prophets of Revolution* (1962)

————, *Today's Latin America* (1962)

Allen, R., *Soviet Influence in Latin America: Role of Economic Relations* (1959)

Almond, G., and J. S. Coleman, eds., *Politics of Developing Nations* (1960)

American Universities Field Staff, Staff Reports [continued as *Latin American Report*]

Anderson, C. W., *Politics and Economic Change in Latin America: The Governing of Restless Nations* (1967)

D'Antonio, W. V., and F. B. Pike, eds., *Religion, Revolution, and Reform: New Forces for Change in Latin America* (1964)

Arciniegas, G., *The Caribbean: Sea of the New World*, trans. H. de Onís (1946)

————, ed., *Green Continent* (1944)

————, *The State of Latin America* (1952)

Astrato, P., *Latin American Problems* (1964)

Baer, W., and I. Kerstenetzky, eds., *Inflation and Growth in Latin America* (1964)

Baerresen, D. W., M. Carnoy, and J. Grunwald, *Latin American Trade Patterns* (1965)

Bain, H. F., and T. T. Read, *Ores and Industry in South America* (1934)

Barber, W. F., and C. N. Ronning, *Internal Security and Military Power* (1965)

Barnes, W. S., *et al., Tax Policy on United States Investments in Latin America* (1963)

Basic Ecclesiastical Statistics for Latin America (*World Horizon Report* No. 25, 1960)

Baxter, R. R., *The Law of International Waterways* (1964)

Beals, C., *America South* (1937)

————, *Fire on the Andes* (1934)

————, *Latin America: World in Revolution* (1963)

————, *Pan America* (1940)

Behrendt, R. F., *Economic Nationalism in Latin America* (1941)

Benham, F., and H. A. Holley, *A Short Introduction to the Economy of Latin America* (1960)

Benjamin, H. R. W., *Higher Education in the Americas* (1965)

Benton, W., *The Voice of Latin America* (1961)

Bernstein, H., *Making of the Inter-American Mind* (1961)

————, *Modern and Contemporary Latin America* (1952)

Bernstein, M., *Foreign Investments in Latin America* (1966)

Blackwell, A. S., *Some Spanish American Poets* (1929)

Botsford, T., *Songs of the Americas* (1940)

Brandenburg, F. R., *The Development of Latin American Private Enterprise* (1964)

Bryce, J., *South America: Observations and Impressions* (new ed., 1914)

Burnett, B., *The Rise of the Latin American Labor Movement* (1960)

Busey, J. L., *Latin America, Political Institutions and Processes* (1964)

————, *Latin American Political Guide* (annual)

Cardozo, M., ed., *Higher Education in Latin America: A Symposium* (1961)

Carleton, W. G., *The Revolution in American Foreign Policy* (1963)

Center of Intercultural Formation (CIF), *Reports:* Cultures, the Church, the Americas (Published ten times a year.)

Chapman, C. E., *Republican Hispanic America* (1937)

Chilcote, R. H., *The Press in Latin America, Spain and Portugal* (1963)

Christensen, A. N., *Evolution of Latin American Government* (1951)

Clagett, H. L., *Administration of Justice in Latin America* (1952)

Clark, G., *The Coming Explosion in Latin America* (1963)

Cleven, N. A. N., ed., *Readings in Hispanic American History* (1927)

Clissold, S., *Latin America: A Cultural Outline* (1966)

Coester, A., *Literary History of Spanish America* (2nd ed., 1928)

Coleman, W. J., *Latin American Catholicism: A Self Evaluation* (1958)

Collver, O. A., *Birth Rates in Latin America: New Estimates of Historical Trends and Fluctuations* (1965)

Committee for Economic Development, *Economic Development in Central America* (1964)

Considine, J. J., ed., *The Church in the New Latin America* (1964)

Cosío Villegas, D., *American Extremes* (1964)

————, *Change in Latin America: The Mexican and Cuban Revolutions* (1961)

Crawford, W. R., *A Century of Latin American Thought* (rev. ed., 1961)

Crow, C., *Meet the South Americans* (1941)

Davis, H., ed., *Organized Labor in Politics* (1958)

Davis, H. E., ed., *Government and Politics in Latin America* (1958)

————, *Latin American Leaders* (1949)

————, *Latin American Social Thought: The History of Its Development Since Independence. With Selective Readings* (1961)

————, *Makers of Democracy in Latin America* (1945)

Dawson, T. C., *South American Republics* (2 vols., 1903–1904)

Del Río, A., *The Clash and Attraction of Two Cultures, the Hispanic and Anglo-Saxon Worlds in America* (1965)

De Vries, E., and J. Medina Echavarría, *Social Aspects of Economic Development in Latin America* (1963)

De Vries, H. P., and J. Rodriguez-Novas, *The Law of the Americas* (1965)

Diamond, S., ed., "Economic and Political Trends in Latin America," *Proceedings of Academy of Political Science, New York*, XXVII, No. 4

Dietz, A. G. H., M. N. Koth, and J. A. Silva, *Housing in Latin America* (1965)

Dillon, D., *International Communism and Latin America: Perspectives and Prospects* (1962)

Domville-Fife, C., *States of South America* (1920)

Donovan, J., *Red Machete: Communist Infiltration in the Americas* (1963)

Dozer, D. M., *The Monroe Doctrine: Its Modern Interpretation* (1965)

Dreier, J. C., *The Alliance for Progress: Problems and Perspectives* (1962)

————, *The OAS and Hemisphere Crisis* (1962)

Dubois, J., *Operation America: The Communist Conspiracy in Latin America* (1963)

Ducoff, L. J., *Human Resources in Central America, Panama and Mexico, 1950–1980* (1960)

Duggan, L., *The Americas: The Search for Hemisphere Security* (1949)

Duggan, S., *The Two Americas: An Interpretation* (1934)

Dunbaugh, F. M., *Marketing in Latin America* (1960)

Dunne, P. M., *A Padre Views South America* (1945)

Dyer, J. M., *United States—Latin American Trade and Financial Relations* (1961)

Edelman, A. T., *Latin American Government and Politics* (1965)

Eisenhower, M. S., *The Wine Is Bitter: The United States and Latin America* (1963)

Ellis, H. S., ed., *Economic Development for Latin America* (1962)

————, and H. C. Wallich, eds., *Economic Development for Latin America* (1961)

Englekirk, J. E., *An Outline History of Spanish American Literature* (3rd ed. 1965)

Ezekiel, M., *Economic Relations Between the Americas* (1941)

Fenwick, C. G., *The Organization of American States: The Inter-American Regional System* (2nd ed., 1962)

Ferguson, J. H., *Latin America: The Balance of Race Redressed* (1961)

————, *The Revolutions of Latin America* (1963)

Finer, S. E., *The Man on Horseback, the Role of the Military in Politics* (1962)

Fitts, D., ed., *Anthology of Contemporary Latin American Poetry* (1942)

Fitzgibbon, R. H., *Constitutions of the Americas* (1948)

Flores, E., *Land Reform and the Alliance for Progress* (1963)

Foerster, R. F., *Italian Emigration in Our Time* (1924)

Follick, W. M., *The Twelve Republics* (1952)

Forbes, R., *Eight Republics in Search of a Future* (1933)

Ford, G. S., ed., *Dictatorship in the Modern World* (1939)

Form, W. H., and A. A. Blum, eds., *Industrial Relations and Social Change in Latin America* (1965)

Franklin, J. H., *From Slavery to Freedom: A History of the American Negroes* (1947)

Friedman, W. G., and G. Kalmanoff, eds., *Joint International Business Ventures* (1961)

Fuentes, C., *et al.*, *Whither Latin America?* (1963)

Furtado, Celso, *Development and Underdevelopment* (1964)

————, *Economic Growth of Brazil: A Survey from Colonial to Modern Times* (1963)

Galenson, W., ed., *Labor in Developing Economies* (1962)

García-Calderon, F., *Latin America: Its Rise and Progress* (1913)

Gerassi, J., *The Great Fear: Reconquest of Latin America by Latin Americans* (1963)

Gomez, R. A., *Government and Politics in Latin America* (1960)

————, *Study of Latin American Politics* (1966)

Gordon, L., *A New Deal for Latin America: The Alliance for Progress* (1963)

Gordon, W. C., *Political Economy of Latin America* (1965)

————, *Economy of Latin America* (1950)

Griffin, C. C., ed., *Concerning Latin American Culture* (1941)

Guerra y Sanchez, R., *Sugar and Society in the Caribbean* (1964)

Guggenheim, H. F., *Latin America Now or Never* (1963)

Hague, E., *Latin American Music, Past and Present* (1934)

Hamill, H. M., Jr., *Disctatorship in Spanish America* (1965)

Hanke, L., *Mexica and the Caribbean* (rev. ed., 1967)

———, *South America* (rev. ed., 1967)

Hanson, S. G., *Economic Development of Latin America* (1951)

Harbron, J. D., *Canada and the Organization of American States* (1963)

Haring, C. H., *South American Progress* (1934)

Harris, M., *Patterns of Race in the Americas* (1964)

Harris, S. E., ed., *Economic Problems of Latin America* (1944)

Hauser, P. M., ed., *Urbanization in Latin America* (1961)

Heath, D. B., and R. N. Adams, eds., *Contemporary Cultures and Societies of Latin America* (1965)

Henríquez-Ureña, P., *A Concise History of Latin American Culture*, trans. G. Chase (1965)

———, *Literary Currents in Hispanic America* (1945)

Herrera, L. F., *Inter-American Bank* (1962)

Herring, H., *Good Neighbors* (1941)

Hespelt, E., et al., *An Anthology of Spanish American Literature* (1946)

———, *An Outline History of Spanish American Literature* (2nd ed., 1963)

Hirschman, A. O., *Journeys Toward Progress: Studies of Economic Policy-Makers in Latin America* (1963)

———, *Latin American Issues* (1961)

Horn, P. V., and H. E. Bice, *Latin American Trade and Economics* (1949)

Houtart, F., and E. Pin, *Church and the Latin American Revolution* (1965)

Howard, M., ed., *Soldiers and Government: Nine Studies in Civil-Military Relations* (1959)

Hughlett, L. J., ed., *Industrialization of Latin America* (1946)

Humphreys, R. A., *Evolution of Latin America* (1947)

Inman, S. G., *Latin America: Its Place in World Life* (rev. ed., 1942)

———, *Problems in Pan Americanism* (2nd ed., 1925)

Intellectual Trends in Latin America (1945)

Inter-American Committee for Agricultural Development, Meeting of High Level Experts on Agricultural Problems Held in Washington, D. C., October 9–13, 1961, *Report and Official Documents of Meeting* (1962)

Inter-American Development Bank, *Institutional Reforms and Social Development Trends in Latin America* (1963)

———, *Proposals for the Creation of Latin American Common Market* (1965)

———, Social Progress Trust Fund, *Annual Report, 1962–*

International Bank for Reconstruction and Development, *The World Bank Group in the Americas* (1963)

International Monetary Fund, *Central Banking Legislation* (1962)

Ireland, G., *Boundaries, Possessions and Conflicts in Central and North America and the Caribbean* (1941)

———, *Boundaries, Possessions and Conflicts in South America* (1938)

Jane, C., *Liberty and Despotism in Spanish America* (1929)

Janowitz, M., *The Military in the Political Development of New Nations* (1964)

Jenks, L. H., *Migration of British Capital to 1875* (1927)

Johnson, J. J., *The Military and Society in Latin America* (1964)

———, *Political Change in Latin America* (1958)

———, *Role of Military in Underdeveloped Countries* (1962)

————, ed., *Continuity and Change in Latin America* (1964)

Jones, C. L., *Caribbean Backgrounds and Prospects* (1931)

————, *Caribbean Since 1900* (1936)

Jones, E., *A Study of Rural Youth Groups in the Americas* (1962)

Jones, T. B., *South America Rediscovered* 1949)

Joseph, F. M., ed., *As Others See Us: The United States Through Foreign Eyes* (1959)

Kantor, H., *Patterns of Politics and Political Systems in Latin America* (1966)

Kautsky, J., ed., *Political Change in Underdeveloped Countries* (1962)

Keen, B., *Readings in Latin American Civilization* (rev. ed., 1967)

Kingsbury, R. C., and R. M. Schneider, *An Atlas of Latin American Affairs* (1965)

Latin America Tomorrow—Annals of the American Academy of Political and Social Sciences (July 1965)

Lauterbach, A., *Enterprise in Latin America: Business Attitudes in a Developing Economy* (1965)

Lee, T. F., *Latin American Problems: Their Relations to Our Investors' Billions* (1932)

Lehman, L., *Latin America Dances*

Lekis, L., *Folk Dances of Latin America* (1958)

Leonard, O., and C. P. Loomis, eds., *Readings in Latin American Social Organization and Institutions* (1953)

Levin, J. V., *The Export Economics: Their Pattern of Development in Historical Perspective* (1960)

Lewis, C., *America's Stake in International Investments* (1938)

Lieuwen, E., *Arms and Politics in Latin America* (rev. ed., 1961)

————, *Generals Versus Presidents* (1964)

————, *U.S. Policy in Latin America: A Short History* (1965)

Linton, R., ed., *Most of the World: Peoples of Africa, Latin America and the East Today* (1949)

Logan, J. A., Jr., *No Transfer, an American Security Principle* (1961)

Lower, M. D., R. R. Hannigan, and R. K. Jansen, *Some Aspects of Latin American Trade Policies* (1964)

Macdonald, A. F., *Latin American Government and Politics* (2nd ed., 1954)

MacEoin, G., *Latin America: The Eleventh Hour* (1962)

MacShane, F., *Impressions of Latin America* (1963)

Madariaga, S. de, *Latin America Between the Eagle and the Bear* (1962)

Madden, C. H., and L. Rall, *Latin America; Reform or Revolution* (1962)

Maier, J., and R. W. Weatherhead, *Politics of Change in Latin America* (1964)

Manger, W., ed., *The Alliance for Progress: A Critical Appraisal* (1963)

————, *Pan America in Crisis* (1961)

————, *The Two Americans: Dialogue on Progress and Problems* (1965)

Maritino, N., *Alliance for Progress* (1963)

Martz, J. D., ed., *Dynamics of Change in Latin American Politics* (1965)

Masur, G., *Patterns of Nationalism in Latin America* (1966)

May, S., and G. Plaza, *The United Fruit Company in Latin America* (1958)

McMillan, C., Jr., R. Gonzalez, and L. G. Erickson, *International Enterprise in a Developing Economy: A Study of U.S. Business in Brazil* (1964)

Mecham, J. L., *Church and State in Latin America* (rev. ed., 1966)

Medina-Echavarría, J. M., *Economic Development in Latin America: Sociological Considerations* (1957)

Meiss, M., *et al.*, *Latin American Art and the Baroque Period in Europe* (1963)

Messer, T. M., and C. Copa, *The Emergent Decade: Latin American Painters and Painting in the 1960's* (1966)

Mikesell, R. F., *Liberalization of Inter-Latin American Trade* (1957)

Millen, B. H., *The Political Role of Labor in Developing Countries* (1963)

Milliken, M. F., and D. Blackmar, eds., *The Emerging Nations* (1961)

Mudd, S., *The Population Crisis and the Use of World Resources* (1964)

Mulhall, M. G., *English in South America* (1878)

National Planning Association, *The Future of Latin American Exports to the United States, 1965 and 1970* (1960)

——, *Technical Cooperation in Latin America: Recommendations for the Future* (1956)

Needler, M. C., *Latin American Politics in Perspective* (1963)

——, ed., *Political Systems of Latin America* (1965)

Nehemkis, P., *Latin America: Myth and Reality* (1964)

Normano, J. F., *Struggle for South America: Economy and Ideology* (1931)

——, and A. Gerbi, *Japanese in South America* (1943)

Nystrum, J. W., and N. A. Haverstock, *The Alliance for Progress* (1966)

Okinshevich, L., and R. G. Carlton, *Latin America in Soviet Writings* (2 vols., 1966)

Onís, H. de, ed., *Golden Land—An Anthology of Latin American Folklore in Literature* (2nd ed., 1961)

Onís, J. de., *The United States as Seen by Spanish American Writers* (1952)

Organization of American States, Pan American Union, General Secretariat, Series on *Art in Latin America Today*

——, *Social Science Monographs*

Padilla, E., *Free Men of America* (1943)

Pan American Union, *Composers of the Americas* (3 vols., 1955–1957)

——, *Economic Survey of Latin America 1963* (1965) [An annual series, of which this is the latest volume.]

——, *The Flow of Capital from the European Economic Community to Latin America* (1963)

——, *Inter-American Treaty of Reciprocal Assistance Applications* (2 vols., 1964)

——, *Planning for Economic and Social Development for Latin America* (1961)

Pan American Union, Secretariat General, *Applications of Inter-American Treaty of Reciprocal Assistance, 1948–1956* (1957)

——, *Human Rights in the American States* (1960)

Parker, F. D., *Central American Republics* (1964)

Peffer, E., *Foot and Mouth Disease in United States Policy* (1962)

Pflaum, I. P., *Arena of Decision: Latin America in Crisis* (1964)

Phelps, D. M., *Migration of Industry to South America* (1936)

Pierson, W. W., and F. S. Gil, *Governments of Latin America* (1957)

Pike, F. B., ed., *Conflict of Church and State in Latin America* (1964)

——, *Freedom and Reform in Latin America* (1959)

Pincus, J., *Central American Common Market* (1962)

Plenn, A., *South America* (1948)

Poppino, R. E., *International Communism in Latin America: A History of the Movement, 1917–1963* (1964)

Porter, C. O., and R. J. Alexander, *The Struggle for Democracy in Latin America* (1961)

Powelson, J. P., *Latin America: Today's Economic and Social Revolution* (1964)

Prebisch, R., *The Economic Development of Latin America and Its Principal Problems* (1950)

——, *Towards a Dynamic Development Policy for Latin America* (1963)

Price, A. G., *White Settlers in the Tropics* (1939)

Price, Waterhouse and Co., *Doing Business in Mexico* (1960, with a 1966 supplement)

Problems and Progress in Latin America, special issue of *Journal of International Affairs*, IX, No. 1 (1955)

Radler, D. H., *El Gringo: The Yankee Image in Latin America* (1962)

Ray, P. A., *South Wind Red: Our Hemisphere Crisis* (1962)

Read, C., ed., *Constitution Reconsidered* (Chapter on "Federalism in Latin America" by C. H. Haring) (1934)

Reynolds, T. H., *As Our Neighbors See Us: Readings in the Relations of the United States and Latin America, 1820–1940* (1940)

Rippy, J. F., *British Investments in Latin America 1822–1949* (1959)

——, *Globe and Hemisphere* (1958)

——, *Latin America* (1958)

——, *Latin America and the Industrial Age* (1944)

Riquelme, M. A., *Student Movements in the United States and Latin America* (1963)

Riullet, A. S., *Contemporary Latin American Philosophy* (1954)

Roberts, W. A., *The Caribbean: The Story of Our Sea of Destiny* (1940)

Ronning, C. N., *Law and Politics in Inter-American Diplomacy* (1963)

Ryan, C., *The Church in the South American Republics* (1932)

Rycroft, W. S., *Religion and Faith in Latin America* (new ed., 1963)

——, and M. M. Clemmer, *Study of Urbanization in Latin America* (1962)

Saenz, V., *Latin America Against the Colonial Regime* (1945)

Sanchez, R. A., *Contemporary Latin American Philosophy* (1954)

Schmitt, K. M., and D. D. Burks, *Evolution or Chaos: Dynamics of Latin American Politics* (1963)

Schurz, W. L., *Latin America—A Descriptive Survey* (rev. ed., 1963)

——, *This New World* (1954)

Scott, J., *How Much Progress? A Report to the Publishers of Time* (1963)

Shepherd, R., and R. M. Kinne, *Central American Common Market: Opportunities Plus* (1964)

Shepherd, W. R., *Hispanic Nations of the New World* (1919)

Siegfried, A., *Impressions of South America*, trans. H. H. and D. Hemming (1933)

Sigsworth, J. W., *Openings and Opportunities in Latin America* [for Canadians] (1965)

Silvert, K. H., *The Conflict Society* (1962)

——, *Reaction and Revolution in Latin America* (1961)

——, ed., *Expectant Peoples: Nationalism and Development* (1964)

——, and F. Bonilla, *Education and the Social Meaning of Development: A Preliminary Statement* (1961)

Slater, J., *A Revaluation of Collective Security: The OAS in Action* (1965)

Slonimsky, N., *Music of Latin America* (1945)

Smith, R. C., and C. Wilder, *A Guide to the Art of Latin America* (1948)

Smith, T. L., *Agrarian Reform in Latin America* (1965)

Snow, S., *Pan American Federation of Labor* (1965)

Show, P. S., ed., *Government and Politics in Latin America* (1967)

Some Economic Aspects of Post War Inter-American Relations (1946)

Sommerfeld, R. M., *Tax Reform and the Alliance for Progress* (1960)

Soule, G. H., *et al., Latin America in the Future World* (1945)

Spell, J. R., *Contemporary Spanish American Fiction* (1944)

Staley, E., *The Future of Underdeveloped Countries: The Political Implications of Economic Development* (rev. ed., 1961)

Stark, H., *Social and Economic Frontiers in Latin America* (1961)

Stetson, C., and B. Fairchild, *Framework of Hemisphere Defense* (1960)

Stoetzer, O. C., *The Organization of American States* (1965)

Strausz-Hupé, R., and A. W. Hazard, eds., *Idea of Colonialism* (1958)

Szulc, T., *Twilight of the Tyrants* (1959)

———, *The Winds of Revolution: Latin America Today—and Tomorrow* (rev. ed., 1965)

Tannenbaum, F., *Slave and Citizen: The Negro in the Americas* (1947)

———, *Ten Keys to Latin America* (1963)

———, *Whither Latin America?* (1934)

Taylor, P. B., Jr., *Government and Politics in Latin America* (1966)

Teichert, P. C. M., *Economic Policy Revolution and Industrialization in Latin America* (1959)

Te Paske, J. J., and S. N. Fisher, *Explosive Forces in Latin America* (1964)

Thomas, A. V. W., and A. J. Thomas, Jr., *Non-Intervention: The Law and Its Import in the Americas* (1956)

———, *Organization of American States* (1963)

Tomasek, R. D., ed., *Latin American Politics: 24 Studies in the Contemporary Scene* (1966)

Torres-Rioseco, A., *Epic of Latin American History* (rev. ed., 1946)

Toynbee, A., *The Economy of the Western Hemisphere* (1963)

Troncoso, M. P., and B. S. Burnett, *Rise of Latin American Labor Movement* (1960)

UNESCO, *Social Aspects of Economic Development in Latin America* (2 vols., 1963)

———, *Urbanization in Latin America*, ed. P. M. Hauser (1962)

United Nations, *Economic Development of Latin America and Its Principal Problems* (1950)

———, *Economic Development Planning and International Cooperation* (1961)

———, *International Cooperation in a Latin American Development Policy* (1954)

———, *Multilateral Economic Cooperation in Latin America* (1962)

United Nations, Bureau of Social Affairs, *Population of Central America (including Mexico), 1950–1980* (1954)

———, *Population of South America, 1950–1980* (1955)

United Nation, Department of Economic Affairs, *Energy in Latin America* (1957)

———, *Study of Inter-Latin American Trade* (1957)

United Nations, Economic Commission for Latin America, *Central American Integration and Development* (1961)

———, *Economic Development in Latin America: Sociological Considerations* (1963)

———, *The Latin American Common Market* (1959)

———, *Economic Development of Latin America in the Postwar Period* (1964)

———, *A Measurement of Price Levels and the Purchasing Power of Currencies in Latin America, 1960–1962* (1963)

————, *Social Aspects of Population Growth in Colombia* (1962)

United Nations, Food and Agriculture Organization, *Progress in Land Reform: Third Report* (1962)

————, *Report of Regional Land Reform Tenure for Latin America* (1961)

United States, Department of Agriculture, *1963 World Agricultural Situation: Western Hemisphere Supplement No. 1* (1963)

United States, Department of Commerce, *Factors Limiting United States Investments Abroad: Part I* (1953)

————, *United States Investments in Latin American Economy* (1957)

United States, Department of Commerce, Bureau of Foreign Commerce, series entitled *Investments in...*

United States, Department of Labor, Bureau of Labor Statistics, series entitled *Labor Law and Practices in...and Labor in...*

United States, Department of State, *Inter-American Efforts to Relieve Tensions in the Western Hemisphere, 1959–1960* (1962)

————, Department of State, External Staff, Office of Intelligence Research, Papers on "Study of Causes of Hostility Towards the United States in Latin America" by Walter S. Washington—and others

United States, Tariff Commission, *Latin American Investments* (three parts in four vols., 1940)

United States, Treasury Department, *Census of American Assets in Foreign Countries* (1947)

United States Congress, Senate Committee on Foreign Relations, 86th Congress, 2 Session, *United States Latin American Relations: Compilations of Studies* (Document No. 125, 1960)

United States Congress, Senate Committee on Judiciary, 88th Congress, 1 Session, *Documentation of Communist Penetration in Latin America* (3 vols., 1965)

University of California at Los Angeles, Committee on Latin American Studies, *Statistical Abstract of Latin America* (1956) [annual publication.]

Urquidi, V. L., *Challenge and Development in Latin America* (1964)

————, *Foreign Trade and Economic Integration in Latin America* (1964)

————, *Free Trade and Economic Integration in Latin America* (1962)

Vernon, R., ed., *Latin America Views the United States Investor* (1965)

Violich, F., *Cities of Latin America, Housing and Planning to the South* (1944)

————, *Low Cost Housing in Latin America* (1949)

Von der Nichden, F. R., *Politics of Developing Nations* (1964)

Ward, B., *The Rich Nation and the Poor Nation* (1962)

Weisbord, A., *Latin American Actuality* (1964)

Wendt, H., *The Red, White, and Black Continent: Latin America* (1966)

Whitaker, A. P., *Nationalism in Latin America* (1962)

————, *et al.*, "Pathology of Democracy in Latin America," *American Political Science Review*, XLIV, 100–49

————, and D. Jordan, *Nationalism in Contemporary Latin America* (1966)

Whithers, W., *Economic Crisis in Latin America* (1964)

Wilgus, A. C., *The Caribbean Area* (1934)

————, ed., *Argentina, Brazil and Chile Since Independence* (1935)

————, ed., *Caribbean Series* (published annually since 1951)

————, ed., *Modern Hispanic America* (1933)

————, ed., *Readings in Latin America Civilization* (1946)

————, ed., *South American Dictators* (1937)

Wilkinson, J. R., *Latin America and the European Economic Community: An Appraisal* (1964)

William, E., *The Negro in the Caribbean* (1942)

Wionczeh, M. S., *Latin American Free Trade Association* (1965)

——, *Latin American Economic Integration: Experiences and Prospects* (1966)

Woytinsky, W. S., *United States and Latin America's Economy* (1958)

Wythe, G., *Industry in Latin America* (rev. ed., 1949)

——, *An Outline of Latin American Economic Development* (1946)

——, *The United States and Inter-American Relations: A Contemporary Appraisal* (1964)

GENERAL WORKS ON THE COLONIAL PERIOD

Acosta, J. de, *Natural and Moral History of the Indies*, trans. C. Grimstin (2 vols., 1880)

Bannon, J. F., *Bolton and the Spanish Borderlands* (1964)

——, *Indian Labor in the Spanish Indies* (1966)

——, *The Spanish Conquistadores* (1960)

Beals, C., *Eagles of the Andes* (1963)

——, *Nomads and Empire Builders* (1961)

Benitez, F., *A Century After Cortes* (1965)

Bernstein, H., *Origins of Inter-American Interest, 1700–1812* (1945)

Bolton, H. E., *Spanish Borderlands* (1921)

——, and T. M. Marshall, *Colonization of North America, 1492–1783* (1920)

Bourne, E. G., *Spain in America, 1450–1580* (1904; new ed., 1962 by B. F. Keen)

Boxer, C. R., *Four Centuries of Portuguese Expansion, 1415–1825: A Succinct Survey* (1961)

——, *Portuguese Society in the Tropics, 1510–1800* (1965)

Burns, A. B., *Documentary History of Brazil* (1965)

Burr, R. N., *By Reason or Force: Chile and the Balance of Power in South America, 1830–1905* (1965)

Bushnell, G. H. S., *Ancient Arts of the Americas* (1965)

Church, G. E., *Indians of South America* (1912)

Cleven, N. A. N., *Readings in Hispanic American History* (1927)

Cortés Society, *Documents and Narratives* (2 series, 9 vols., 1917–1942)

d'Anghiera, P. M., *De Orbo Novo*, trans. F. A. MacNutt (2 vols., 1912)

Dawson, T. C., *South American Republics* (2 vols., 1903–1904)

Diffie, B. W., *Latin American Civilization: Colonial Period* (1945)

Dockstader, F. J., *Indian Art in Middle America* (1964)

Driver, H. C., *Indians of North America* (1964)

Duran, D., *Aztecs: History of the Indies of New Spain* (1964)

Dusenbury, W. M., *The Mexican Mesta: The Administration of Ranching in Colonial Mexico* (1960)

Espinosa, A. V. de, *Compendium and Description of West Indies*, trans. C. U. Clark (1942)

Esquemeling, J., *Buccaneers of America* (1929)

Foster, G. M., *Culture and Conquest: America's Spanish Heritage* (1960)

Frederick, C. J., *Age of the Baroque 1610–1660* (1952)

Gage, T., *The English American: A New Survey of the West Indies*, ed. A. P. Newton (1929), new ed. by J. E. S. Thompson (1958)

Garcilasso de la Vega, *The Inca* (1961)

[Gonzalo, Fernández de], *Natural History of the West Indies* (1959)

Graham, G. S., and R. A. Humphreys, *The Navy and South America, 1807–1823* (1962)

Greater America: Essays in Honor of Herbert Eugene Bolton (1945)

Hakluyt Society, *Works* (2 series, .206 vols.) [original narratives and documents]

Handbook of South American Indians, ed. J. H. Stewart (6 vols., 1946–1950)

Hanke, L., *Aristotle and the American Indian* (1959)

———, *Do the Americas Have a Common History?* (1964)

———, *Mexico and the Caribbean* (rev. ed., 1966)

———, *South America* (rev. ed., 1966)

———, *Spanish Struggle for Justice in the Conquest of America* (1949)

Haring, C. H., *Buccaneers in the West Indies in the Seventeenth Century* (1910)

———, *Spanish Empire in America* (1952)

———, *Trade and Navigation Between Spain and the Indies* (1918)

Harney, M. P., *The Jesuits in History: The Society of Jesus Through Four Centuries* (1941)

Helps, A., *Spanish Conquest of America* (4 vols., 1900–1904)

Herrera, A. de, *General History of the Vast Continent and Islands of America*, trans. J. Stevens (6 vols., 1725–1726)

Hispanic American Essays: A Memorial to Juan Alexander Robertson (1942)

Horgan, P., *Conquistadors in North American History* (1963)

Humphreys, R. A., *British Consular Reports on Trade and Politics of Latin America* (1940)

———, and J. Lynch, *Origins of the Latin American Revolutions, 1808–1826* (1965)

James, P. E., *Latin America* (2nd ed., 1950)

Keen, B., *Readings in Latin American Civilization* (rev. ed., 1967)

Keleman, Pal, *Baroque and Rococo in Latin America* (1951)

Keller, A. G., *Colonization* (1908)

Kemp, P. K. and L. C., *Brethren of the Coast: Buccaneers of the South Seas* (1961)

Kirkpatrick, F. A., *Spanish Conquistadores* (1946)

Kubler, G., *The Art and Architecture of Ancient America* (1962)

———, and M. Soria, *Art and Architecture in Spain and Portugal and Their American Dominions, 1500–1800* (1959)

Lanning, J. T., *Academic Culture in the Spanish Colonies* (1940)

Las Casas, B. de, *Historia de las Indias* (5 vols., 1875–1876)

Lea, H. C., *Inquisition in the Spanish Dependencies* (1908)

Leonard, I. A., *Baroque Times in Old Mexico* (1959)

———, *Books of the Brave* (1949)

Lothrop, S. K., *Treasures of Ancient America: The Arts of the Pre-Columbian Civilizations from Mexico to Peru* (1964)

Lynch, J., *Spanish Colonial Administration, 1782–1810: The Intendancy in the Viceroyalty of La Plata* (1961)

Madariaga, S. de, *Fall of the Spanish American Empire* (1947)

———, *Rise of the Spanish American Empire* (1947)

Means, P. A., *The Spanish Main, Focus of Envy, 1492–1700* (1935)

Merriman, R. B., *Rise of the Spanish Empire in the Old World and in the New* (4 vols., 1918–1934)

Morner, M., *The Expulsion of the Jesuits from Latin America* (1965)

Morrison, S. E., and M. Obregon, *The Caribbean as Columbus Saw It* (1964)

Morse, R. S., *The Bandeirantes* (1965)

Moses, B., *Establishment of Spanish Rule in America* (1898)

———, *Intellectual Background of the Revolution in South America, 1810–1824* (1926)

———, *South America on the Eve of Emancipation* (1908)

———, *Spain's Declining Power in South America* (1919)

———, *Spanish Colonial Literature of South America* (1922)

———, *Spanish Dependencies in South America* (2 vols., 1914)

Nettl, B., *Folk and Traditional Music of the Western Continents* (1965)

New Spain and the West. Historical Contributions Presented to Herbert Eugene Bolton (2 vols., 1932)

Newton, A. P., *European Nations in the West Indies, 1934–1688* (1933)

O'Gorman, E., *Invention of America* (1961)

Oswald, B. J. C., *Printing in the Americas* (2 vols., 1965)

Parry, J. H., *Sale of Public Office in the Spanish Indies Under the Hapsburgs* (1953)

———, *Spanish Theory of Empire in the Sixteenth Century* (1940)

Penrose, B., *Travel and Discovery in the Renaissance* (1952)

Picon-Salas, M., *A Cultural History of Spanish America from the Conquest to Independence,* trans. I. A. Leonard (1963)

Pike, F. B., *The Conflict Between Church and State in Latin America* (1964)

Prescott, W. H., *History of the Conquest of Mexico* (many editions)

———, *History of the Conquest of Peru* (many editions)

Prestage, E., *The Portuguese Pioneers* (1933)

Priestley, H. I., *Coming of the White Man* (1929)

Quivira Society, *Publications* (13 vols., 1929–58)

Richman, I. B., *Spanish Conquerors* (1919)

Rippy, J. F., and J. T. Nelson, *Crusaders of the Jungle* (1936)

Robertson, W., *History of America* (3 vols., 5th ed., 1788)

Robertson, W. S., *Rise of the Spanish American Republics* (1918)

Rodrigues, J. H., *Brazil and Africa* (1965)

Sauer, C. O., *The Early Spanish Main, 1492–1512* (1966)

Schurz, W. L., *This New World* (1954)

Shaeffer, R. G., *Economic Societies of the Spanish World, 1763–1820* (1958)

Shields, W. E., *King and Church: The Rise and Fall of the Patronato Real* (1961)

Smith, R., *The Spanish Guild Merchant: A History of the Consulado, 1250–1900* (1940)

Stewart, J. H., ed., *Handbook of South American Indians* (6 vols., 1946–1959)

Tannenbaum, F., *Slave and Citizen, the Negro in the Americas* (1947)

Thompson, G. A., *Geographical and Historical Dictionary of America and West Indies* (5 vols., 1812-1815)

Thompson, L. S., *The Libraries of Colonial Spanish America* (1962)

———, *Printing in Colonial Spanish America* (1962)

Ulloa, J. J. and A. de, *Voyage to South America* (abridged ed., 1964)

Vance, J. T., *The Background of Hispanic American Law* (1943)

von Humboldt, A., *Personal Narrative of Travels to Equinoctial Regions of the New Continent—1799–1804,* trans. H. M. Williams (7 vols., 1814–1829)

———, *Political Essay on the Kingdom of New Spain,* trans. J. Black (4 vols., 1811)

Watson, R. G., *Spanish and Portuguese South America during the Colonial Period* (2 vols., 1884)

Wauchope, R., *They Found the Buried Cities* (1965)
Whitaker, A. P., ed., *Latin America and the Enlightenment* (1942)
——, *Western Hemisphere Ideal: Its Rise and Decline* (1954)
Wilcox, R. T., *Folk and Festival Costume of the World* (1965)
Wilgus, A. C., ed., *Colonial Hispanic America* (1936)
——, ed., *Readings in Latin American Civilization* (1946)
Zavala, S., *New Viewpoints on Spanish Colonization of America* (1943)
——, *Political Philosophy of the Conquest of America* (1955)
Zea, L., *The Latin American Mind* (1963)

COLLECTIONS OF READINGS

Arciniegas, G., ed., *The Green Continent: A Comprehensive View of Latin America by Its Leading Writers* (1944)
Beckett, S., trans., *An Anthology of Mexican Poetry* (1963)
Bierck, H. A., *Readings in Latin American History* (1967)
Blackwell, A. S., *Some Spanish American Poets* (1929)
Burr, R. N., and R. D. Hussey, *Documents on Inter-American Cooperation* (2 vols., 1955)
Cleven, N. A. N., *Readings in Hispanic American History* (1927)
Colford, W. E., *Classic Tales from Spanish America* (1962)
Craig, G. D., *The Modernist Trend in Spanish American Poetry* (1934)
Cranfill, T. M., *The Muse in Mexico* (1959)
Fitts, D., *Anthology of Contemporary Latin American Poetry* (rev. ed., 1947)
Flakoll, D. J., and C. Alegria, *New Voices of Hispanic America* (1962)
Flores, A., *An Anthology of Spanish Poetry* (1961)
——, and D. Poore, *Fiesta in November: Stories from Latin America* (1942)
Frank, W., ed., *Tales from the Argentine* (1930)
Fuentes, P. de, *The Conquistadores—First Person Accounts of the Conquest of Mexico* (1963)
Gantenbein, J. W., *Evolution of Our Latin American Policy: A Documentary Record* (1950)
Green, E. S., and H. Von Lowenfels, *Mexican and South American Poems* (1892)
Hanke, L., *Mexico and Caribbean* (rev. ed., 1967)
——, *Readings in Latin American History* (2 vols., 1966)
——, *South America* (rev. ed., 1967)
Haydn, H., and J. Cournos, *A World of Great Stories* (1947)
Hayes, H. R., *Twelve Spanish American Poets* (1943)
Heath, D. B., and R. N. Adams, *Contemporary Cultures and Societies of Latin America* (1965)
Hespelt, E., *An Anthology of Spanish American Literature* (1946)
Johnson, M. A., *Swan, Cygnets, and Owl: An Anthology of Modernist Poetry in Spanish America: Translations* (1956)
Jones, W. K., *Latin American Writers in English Translation* (1944)
——, ed., *Spanish American Literature in Translation: A Selection of Poetry, Fiction and Drama Since 1888* (1963)
Keen, B., *Readings in Latin American Civilization, 1492 to the Present* (rev. ed., 1967)
Leonard, O., and C. P. Loomis, *Readings in Latin American Social Organizations and Institutions* (1953)

Mandel, O. S., *The Theatre of Don Juan: A Collection of Plays and Views, 1630–1963* (1963)
Nist, J., *Brazilian Poetry: An Anthology* (1962)
Onís, H. de, *The Golden Land: An Anthology of Latin American Folklore in Literature* (2nd ed., 1961)
———, *Spanish Stories and Tales* (1956)
Patterson, H. W., trans. and ed., *Poetisas de America* (1960)
Paz, O., ed., *Anthology of Mexican Poetry* (1958)
Poor, A. B., *Pan American Poems* (1918)
Reynolds, F. H., *As Our Neighbors See Us* (1940)
Three Spanish American Poets: Pellicer, Neruda, Andrade (various trans.) (1942)
Torres-Rioseco, A., ed., *Short Stories of Latin America* (1963)
Translations from Hispanic Poets (1938)
Underwood, E. W., *Anthology of Mexican Poets* (1932)
United States National Students Association, *Readings on: Latin American Student Movement and the Rise of the Latin American Left* (1965)
Walsh, T., *The Catholic Anthology* (rev. ed., 1942)
———, *Hispanic Anthology* (1920)
Wilgus, A. C., *Readings in Latin American Civilization* (1946)

(NOTE: There are many collections of readings on special topics; these have been listed in their appropriate places.)

STANDARD REFERENCE WORKS

American Universities Field Service—*Staff Reports* (continued as *Latin American Report*)
Busey, J. L., *Latin American Political Guide* (annual)
Fitzgibbon, R. H., *Constitutions of the Americas* (1948)
Foreign Trade of Latin America (rev. ed., 4 vols., 1942)
Foreign Trade of Latin America Since 1913 (1952)
Grismer, R. L., *A Reference Index to Twelve Thousand Spanish American Authors* (1939)
Hanson, E. P., ed., *New World Guides to Latin American Republics* (3 vols., 1950)
Hilton, R., ed., *Who's Who in Latin America* (3rd ed., 7 vols., 1945–1951)
Kingsbury, R. C., and R. M. Schneider, *An Atlas of Latin American Affairs* (1965)
Manual of Inter-American Relations (1953)
Martin, M., and G. Lovett, *Encyclopedia of Latin American History* (1956)
Organization of American States, *Economic Survey of Latin America, 1963* (1965)
Slonimsky, N., *Music of Latin America* (1945)
Smith, R. C., and E. Wilder, *A Guide to the Art of Latin America* (1948)
South American Handbook (annual)
United Nations, Economic Commission for Latin America, *Economic Survey for Latin America* (annual)
University of California at Los Angeles, Center of Latin American Studies, *Master Directory for Latin America* (1966)
———, *Statistical Abstract for Latin America* (annual publication, to be bi-annual beginning with 1964; the latest edition is for 1963—published in 1965)

Yearly reports of Organization of American States, International Monetary Fund and Inter-American Development Bank

Hanson, E. P., *Index to Map of Hispanic America* 1 : 1,000,000 (1945)

Palmer, R. R., ed., *Atlas of World History* (1957)

Shepherd, W. R., *Historical Atlas* (rev. ed., reprint 1956)

Wilgus, A. C., *Latin America in Maps* (1943)

PERIODICALS TO KEEP THE STUDENT UP TO DATE

Alliance for Progress: A Weekly Report on Activities and Public Opinion (Washington, Pan American Union, No. 1, September 7, 1962—April 29, 1963; continued as *Weekly Newsletter* since May 27, 1963)

American Journal of International Law (quarterly since 1907)

Américas (quarterly review of inter-American cultural history since 1944)

Américas (monthly of oas since 1949)

Annals of the Organization of American States (quarterly or semi-annually)

Annual Reports of Carnegie Corporation of New York, Ford Foundation, Rockefeller Foundation, John Carter Brown Library, Creole Petroleum Company, Standard Oil of New Jersey (also periodical), Organization of American States, International Monetary Fund and Inter-American Development Bank

Bank of London and South America, *Fortnightly Review*

Brazil Culture

Brazilian-American Survey

Brazilian Business

Bulletin of Hispanic Studies

Bulletin of the Pan American Union (monthly 1893–1948, superseded by *Américas* and *Annals*)

Business Conditions in Argentina (quarterly since 1918)

Business History Review (Winter 1965 issue devoted to Latin America)

Business Week

Carnegie Endowment for International Peace, *International Conciliation*

Center of Intercultural Formation, *Reports: Cultures, the Church, the Americas* (published ten times a year)

Central American Bulletin

Chase Manhattan Bank of New York, *Latin American Business Highlights*

Colombia Today (monthly since November 1965)

Current History

Doors to Latin America (quarterly) [bibliographic]

Economic Bulletin for Latin America (semi-annual—un)

The Economist

Embassy of Uruguay News

Encounter

Evergreen Review

Export Trade

First National Bank of Boston, *Situation in Argentina* (Buenos Aires, monthly since 1925)

First National City Bank of New York, *Foreign Information Service Bulletin*

Foreign Affairs (quarterly)

Foreign Commerce Weekly (U. S. Office of International Trade)

Foreign Policy Bulletin (bi-weekly)

Hanson's Latin American Letter (weekly)
Hispania
Hispanic American Historical Review (quarterly since 1918, with a hiatus of five years) [Numerous articles and monographs, book reviews, bibliographical notes, and news.]
Hispanic American Report (monthly, 1948–1962)
Hispanic Review
Inter-American Economic Affairs (quarterly since 1947)
Inter-American Labor Bulletin (monthly, O.R.I.T.)
Inter-American Municipal Review (Havana, 1950–   )
Inter-American Review of Bibliography (quarterly since 1951)
Inter-American Statistical Institute Estadística (quarterly bulletin since 1943) [*Consumer Price Indexes*]
International Affairs (Royal Institute of International Affairs, 1922–1939; 1944–   )
International Commerce
International Financial Statistics (International Monetary Fund)
International Labor Review (I.L.O., Geneva, 1921)
International Legal Materials: Current Documents 1962–   (continuation of sections in *American Journal of International Law*)
International Organization (World Peace Foundation, quarterly since 1947)
Journal of Inter-American Studies (quarterly since 1959)
Latin America—New Orleans (monthly)
Latin American Embassies in Washington issue regular publications, e.g., Brazil, Chile, etc.
Latin American Business Review (Chase Manhattan Bank, New York, monthly)
Latin American Report (International Trade Mart of New Orleans, bi-weekly)
Latin American Research Review (three times a year since 1965)
OAS Chronicle—(bi-monthly, began August 1965)
Luso-Brazilian Review (semi-annually since 1963)
Mexican Life
Mexico This Month
Mid America (quarterly)
Modern Language Notes
Monthly Review
News from Chile
New York Times, *Latin American Economic Review* (semi-annual)
Noticias: A Weekly Digest of Hemisphere Reports (since 1945)
OAS Chronicle—(bi-monthly, began August 1965)
Odyssey Review (quarterly since 1961)
Publications of Modern Language Association
Review of the River Plate (Buenos Aires)
Revista Iberoamericana (Iowa City, semi-annual)
Romantic Review
Royal Institute of International Relations (London), *International Affairs* (quarterly)
——, *World Today* (monthly)
South American Journal (London)
Studies on the Left (quarterly)
Texas Quarterly
Times of the Americas (weekly)
World Oil (Houston, Texas)

United Nations Review
United Nations, *Economic Bulletin for Latin America* (semi-annual, 1956–   )
————, *Monthly Bulletin of Statistics* (1947–   )
United States Chamber of Commerce in Argentina, *Economic Survey* (Buenos
    Aires, 1941–1951; 1956 to date—weekly)
Vision (weekly in English', New York since 1964)

Many banks and companies issue reports and magazines (e.g., United
Fruit Company; W. R. Grace and Company; Creole Petroleum Co., etc.
See D. M. Phelps, "Sources of Current Information on Latin America" in
Handbook of Latin American Studies, No. 3).

For newspapers: the best available are the *New York Times,* the
Christian Science Monitor and *Washington Post.* Some of the more standard
magazines have regular Latin American departments as in *Time, Newsweek,*
and *U.S. News and World Report.*

OFFICIAL PUBLICATIONS IN ENGLISH
United States

> Bureau of the Census
>> *Census Atlas,* maps of Latin America
>
> Department of Agriculture
> Department of Commerce, Office of Business Economics (Bureau of Foreign
>> Commerce)
>> *Economic Reports*
>> *Foreign Commerce Weekly*
>> *Handbook on Investments*
>> *International Commerce* (periodical)
>> *Investments in Colombia*
>> *Investments in Peru*
>> *Investments in Venezuela*
>> *Overseas Business Reports* (formerly *World Trade Information Series*)
>> *Quarterly Summary of Foreign Commerce of U. S.*
>> *Survey of Current Business*
>> *Survey of International Travel*
>> *United States Investments in Latin American Economy*
>
> Department of Health, Education, and Welfare
> Department of Labor
>> *Foreign Labor Information Bulletin*
>
> Department of Labor, Bureau of Labor Statistics
>> *Directory of Labor Organizations—Western Hemisphere* (1964)
>> *Labor Digest*
>
> Department of State
>> Publications at various times on Latin America
>> *Bulletin* (weekly)
>> *Conference Series*
>> *Diplomatic Papers* (papers concerning the Foreign relations of the United
>>   States, 1861–   )
>> *International Organization and Conference Series* (American Republics)
>> *Treaties and Other International Acts Series*
>> External Research Staff—American Republics: *Papers*

Export-Import Bank, *Annual Reports to Congress*
United States Tariff Commission
> *Latin America as a Source of Strategic and Other Essential Materials*
> (1941)

United Nations [2]

> *Annual Reports of ECLA* (Economic Commission for Latin America)
> *Central American Integration and Development* (1961)
> *Demographic Yearbook*
> *Directory of International Trade* (monthly)
> *Economic Bulletin*
> *Economic Survey of Latin America* (annual since 1947)
> Many monographs: e.g., *Program of Land Reform; Study of Trade Be-*
> > *tween Latin America and Europe; Inter Latin American Trade;*
> > *Foreign Capital in Latin America; Population of Central America*
> > *(including Mexico), 1950–1980* (1954); *Population of South Amer-*
> > *ica, 1950–1980* (1955)
> *Statistical Papers*
> *Statistical Yearbook*
> *Yearbook of International Trade Statistics*

UNESCO

> *Analysis and Prospectus of Economic Development*
> *Economic Bulletin for Latin America* (semi-annual; annual supplement
> > on statistics is now separately published)
> *Economic Development, Planning and International Cooperation* (1961)
> *Economic Development of Latin America in the Post War Period* (1964)
> *Economic Survey of Latin America* (annual)
> *International Political Science Abstracts*
> *International Yearbook of Education*
> *Latin American Common Market* (1959)
> *Multilateral Economic Cooperation in Latin America* (1962)
> *Statistical Bulletin for Latin America*, Vol. I, No. 1, March 1964 and
> > issued quarterly
Economic Commission for Latin America
> Annual Economic Surveys; semi-annual economic bulletins
Food and Agriculture Organization
> *Bulletin of Agricultural Economics and Statistics* (monthly)
> *Production Yearbook*
> *Prospects for Agricultural Development in Latin America* (1953)
> *Trade Yearbook*
> *Yearbook of Food and Agricultural Statistics*
International Labor Organization
> *Yearbook of Labor Statistics*
Technical Assistance Commissions
> *Report of United Nations Mission of Technical Assistance in Bolivia*
> > (1951); *Report of United Nations Mission of Technical Assistance*
> > *to the Republic of Haiti* (1949)

[2] All United Nations publications are available from the Columbia University
Press.

Organization of American States
and Pan American Union [3]

Actualidades: A monthly bulletin of education developments in Latin America, beginning September 1965

America en Cifras (8 vols., 1960)

Américas (monthly)

Annals of OAS

Annual Reports of Secretary General

Ciencias Sociales series

Economic Development of Brazil, 1949 (1950)

Economic Survey of Inter-American Agriculture (2 vols., 1949)

Economic Survey of Latin America, 1963 (1965)

Forthcoming Inter-American Conferences and Meetings (quarterly)

Inter-American Juridical Yearbook

Inter-American Labor Bulletin

Inter-American Peace Committee report to the Second Special Inter-American Conference of the Committee on the activities of the Committee since the Tenth Inter-American Conference, 1954–1965

Inventory of Information basic to the planning of agricultural development in Latin America, by the Inter-American Committee for Agricultural Development (One volume on Mexico and one on Panama published in 1964–1965.)

Monographs: e.g., *Selecciones Económicas* (on Latin American economic subjects)

Provisional Listing of Alliance for Progress Projects (March 1963, and addendas issued irregularly thereafter)

Union List of Latin American Newspapers in Libraries of the United States

Inter-American Economic and Social Council of the OAS
Various monographs and annual reports

Inter-American Development Bank
Annual Reports on Social Progress Trust Fund
Proposals for the Creation of the Latin American Common Market (1965)

Inter-American specialized conferences, various reports

Pan American Institute of History and Geography, various monographs and reports

Caribbean Commission

Statistical Digest, Economic Review, various other publications, available from the University of Florida Press

Great Britain

Board of Trade, Commercial Relations and Export Department
Overseas Economic Surveys

[3] Publications of the various agencies of the OAS and the Pan American Union are available from the Pan American Union, Washington 6, D.C.

Economist Intelligence Unit (London) publishes a series of economic reviews concerning economic development of Latin America and a yearly review of the countries

Foreign Office
> *British and Foreign State Papers*, 1841–
> *Diplomatic and Consular Reports*, 1886–

United Kingdom, Export Promotion Department (formerly Department of Overseas Trade) publishes reports on economic conditions in Latin American countries

LITERARY AND CULTURAL MATERIALS OF GENERAL INTEREST

The student can have no real understanding of the life of the Latin American peoples until he has read some of their great novels and literary works, at least in English translation. Güiraldes, *Don Segunda Sombra*, telling the life of the gauchos; da Cunha, *Os Sertões* (translated as *Rebellion in the Backlands*), Brazil's famous literary work telling of the rebellion in the 1890s; Isaacs, *María*, the story of life in Colombia's Cauca Valley; Rómulo Gallegos, *Doña Barbara,* concerned with the *llanos* of Venezuela; Veríssimo, *Of Time and the Wind*, which describes a century of life in southern Brazil; Azuela's *Los de Abajo* (translated as *The Underdogs*), and López y Fuentes, *El Indio*, which tells of the Mexican Revolution and the new life of the Mexican Indians; Fernández, *The Gaucho Martin Fierro*, Argentina's epic in verse—all these have appeared in English translation and sometimes in "easy reading" abridgments in their original language for the beginning foreign language student. More and more of Latin America's novels and poetry are being translated into English, many appearing in paperbound editions. One can no more understand Latin America without knowing them than one can understand the nineteenth-century United States without reading Mark Twain. Also to be recommended are collections of poetry, such as that of Blackwell, *Some Spanish American Poets* (1929) and Fitts, *Anthology of Contemporary Latin American Poetry* (1942). The student is also referred to the preceding sections on general works for recommended reading in the history of Latin American art, music, architecture, and general literary criticism. Recently a large program of translating Latin American classics and literature into English was undertaken, and several University Presses are quite active in publishing such translations—e.g., the presses of the Universities of California, Texas, and Indiana.

A NOTE ON PAPERBACKS AND CHEAPER EDITIONS

The recent tendency of publishers to put out paperback reprints is a great boon to students. Latin American materials have in recent years fared quite well. An increasing number of general works and some classics and specialized studies have been published. Among some of the early paperback editions may be listed: W. H. Prescott, *History of the Conquest of Mexico and History of the Conquest of Peru* (both combined in Modern

Giant Library Series); G. C. Vaillant, *Aztecs of Mexico*; J. A. Mason, *Ancient Civilizations of Peru*; H. H. Hart, *Venetian Adventurer: Marco Polo*; Bernal Diaz del Castillo, *Discovery and Conquest of Mexico*; J. B. Brebner, *Explorers of North America, 1492–1806*; B. Flornoy, *World of the Incas*; V. W. Crane, *The Southern Frontier, 1670–1732;* Von Hagen, *Realm of the Incas*; Euclides da Cunha, *Rebellion in the Backlands*. An increasingly wider market has been created for original contemporary accounts and translations of Latin American literary works.

Recently a number of publishers have undertaken many new publications relating to Latin America in paperbound editions, some simultaneously with hard back editions. For example, Houghton Mifflin Company is publishing a series of paperback books on the Political Systems of the Latin American governments—e.g., Frederick G. Gil's *The Political System of Chile*—most of them by political scientists. Prentice-Hall, Inc. has begun a series of histories of the Latin American countries emphasizing the twentieth century written by eminent historians; Oxford University Press, Inc. has a series on Latin American histories. D. Van Nostrand Co. also has a series of histories and in addition several other studies on Latin American subjects. Another tendency in paperback books is exemplified in the Borzoi series on Latin America of the Alfred A. Knopf company which consists of collections of readings on a spectrum of Latin American subjects under the editorship of Lewis Hanke; no less than sixteen of these have already appeared. Frederick A. Praeger, Inc., Free Press of Glencoe Inc. (Macmillan), Alfred A. Knopf, Inc., Crowell–Collier & Macmillan, Inc., Penguin Books, and others have published many Latin American subject books in paperback editions. Several University presses have begun to reprint many studies on Latin American subjects and translations of Latin American classics, a number of them in paperback editions. The reader is referred to *Latin America: A Bibliography of Paperback Books* compiled by David H. Andrews and edited by T. J. Hillmon, and published in 1964 under the imprint of the Hispanic Foundation of the Library of Congress and Charles J. Fleener and Ron L. Seckinger, *The Guide to Latin American Paperback Literature* published by the Center for Latin American Studies of the University of Florida in 1966. There is also an annual *List of Paperback Editions in Print.*

It should be noted that Latin American nations print more books in paperbound editions than does the United States. The valuable studies published by the University of California in its scholarly *Ibero-American* series are published in paperbound editions.

Glossary of Unfamiliar Terms

This glossary aims only to help the reader understand the Spanish, Portuguese, or Indian words which have become a part of Latin American history. Quite often the definition of the same term changes from country to country. A word in Portuguese seemingly very similar to the Spanish will have a different meaning in Brazil. Words with one connotation in colonial times have come to mean something different in the twentieth century. Recent decades have brought a new type of confusing term, the use of capital letters—initals from the Spanish or Portuguese name of a government agency, political party or program—to form a completely new term, in the same way that the United States has used GOP, HEW, or UNESCO. Not all such terms have been included, only those in which the series of letters has developed into an expression of historic importance.

A

abrazo—an embrace, the customary Latin American greeting of welcome and farewell among close friends and relatives, a greeting of cordiality.

Acción Democrática—a middle-class democratic party in Venezuela since the 1940s.

Acción Popular—President Belaúnde-Terry's political party in Peru in the 1960s.

acuerdo—an agreement or resolution; *real acuerdo*—an agreement made with or by parties representing the Spanish crown in colonial times.

adelantado—a private individual given royal permission to explore territory at his own expense, found a colony there, and govern it for the Spanish king; governor of a frontier district during the colonial regime.

aftosa—Spanish word for hoof-and-mouth disease among cattle.

agave—a kind of cactus, similar to the maguey or century plant.

AID—Agency for International Development, United States economic aid agency.

alcabala—a tax on sales levied within the Spanish colonies.

alcalde—a magistrate of local government in the Spanish colonies, a justice of the peace; mayor, head of a municipal district.

alcalde mayor—a Spanish colonial regional governor in a frontier district; *alcaldía mayor* refers to the Spanish colonial regional government, centering on a frontier municipality and based on a European settlement.

alguacil—a constable

Alianza Para Progreso—the Alliance for Progress, to promote the development of Latin America in the 1960s.

altiplano—the high plateau country above La Paz, Bolivia.

almojarifazgo—an export and import tax charged against colonial trade by the Spanish government.

APRA—The *Alianza Popular Revolucionaria Americana*, or reform party in Peru led by Haya de la Torre after 1930. *Aprismo* is the name of the movement which it represented; members were called *Apristas*.

Armada de Barlovento—the windward fleet, the coast guard of the Caribbean.

asesor—an assessor, an adviser.

asiento—a contract granted by the Spanish king to ship owners or foreigners allowing them to import slaves into the colonies. Such an *asiento* was granted to England for importing 4,800 slaves a year into the Caribbean colonies of Spain in 1713.

Asuntos Indígenas—Indian problems, hence a government Department of Indian Affairs in modern Mexico.

Ato Institucional—a constitutional act, amendment, or supplementary act in Brazil, such as occurred in 1834, and the one which gave power to Castello Branco in 1964.

audiencia—a group of judges sent from Spain to colonial administrative centers, who had some executive as well as judicial powers; the highest colonial court in Spanish America; also applies to the territorial division over which the *audiencia* has jurisdiction.

auto da fé—public punishment or execution of heretics condemned by the Inquisition.

ayuntamiento—a local town council, sometimes also applied to the city hall. See also *cabildo*.

B

La Banda Oriental—the eastern strip of the Uruguayan coast across the Plata from Buenos Aires; Uruguay.

bandeirantes—groups of men who traveled the interior of Brazil in small, organized "traveling cities." Brazilian frontiersman; Portuguese gold and slave hunters in the interior of Brazil.

barranca—a deep canyon.

batata—the New World sweet potato, different from the yam.

belcismo—a word for corrupt and selfish dictatorship, derived from the nineteenth century Bolivian demagogue Belzú.

bolas—a type of lasso made with stones tied at the end of long strips of rawhide, used by gauchos to trip up cattle on the Argentine pampas.

bolero—a country dance from Spain, also a sleeveless jacket worn at such a dance.

boucaniers—French term for men who lived on dried beef or *boucan* in the Caribbean area, thus eventually buccaneers, freebooters, or pirates. *Boucaner* is the French word meaning to smoke meat on a wooden frame.

braceros—literally "those with arms," similar to field "hands," referring to farm workers from Mexico under contract to harvest crops in the United States.

C

caballero—mounted horseman, hence a Spanish knight or gentleman.

caballería—a Spanish land grant, or land measure equal to 33½ acres.

Caballeros-Racionales—secret revolutionary societies in Mexico during the war of independence.

cabildo—a town council, or the building where such council meetings were held. See *ayuntamiento*.

cabildo abierto—an open meeting of a *cabildo* or municipal council to consider gravely important matters, attended by prominent men of the town. Such meetings were a vital factor leading to the wars for independence.

caboclo—Brazilian Indians or mixtures of white and Indian; in recent times any poor farmer in northern Brazil.

cacique—an Indian tribal chieftain, often maintained as a constable or local authority after the Spanish conquest; in recent times a local "boss" or "ward heeler."

cafuso—in Brazil, a person of mixed Indian and Negro ancestry.

cajas—cash boxes, applied to workers' cooperative credit unions in modern Chile.

callampas—shanty-town slums in Chile in the 1960s.

calpullec—the principal civil officer of the Aztecs.

câmaras—Portuguese town councils in Brazil, similar to Spanish *cabildos*.

camaya—a provincial governor in the Inca empire.

campesinos—peasant farmers in Mexico, sometimes called *peones*.

capitania-donatários—tracts of land granted to large-scale proprietors in sixteenth-century Brazil.

capitão mor—boss of local militia in colonial Brazil.

caracas—hereditary chiefs of vassal governments within the Inca empire.

Carioca—a person who lives in Rio de Janeiro.

Casa de Contratación—the Spanish House of Trade which regulated commerce in the New World.

Casa da India—the Portuguese agency for supervising colonial Brazil.

casa grande—a manor house in Brazil.

Casa Rosada—literally the Pink House, home of presidents of Argentina.

catedrático—a university professor.

Caudillo (*caudilho* in Portuguese)—the Spanish word for chieftain or leader, hence a military leader who had a group of followers loyal to him personally; later a military dictator and political "boss." The noun *caudillismo* (*caudilhismo* in Portuguese) refers to military dictatorship and/or "bossism."

centrales—a term for sugar refineries in Cuba.

chapetones—"tenderfeet," a term applied by the Spanish colonials in South America to Spaniards born in Spain.

charro—a Mexican "dude" horseman in colorful costume.

CHEAR—the Council on Higher Education in the American Republics, financed by the Carnegie Foundation.

china poblana—a native costume trimmed with China silk worn by the girls of colonial Puebla, today the national costume of Mexico.

chiripá—a long fringed shawl, part of the costume worn by the old-style Argentine *gauchos*.

cholos—the Bolivian expression for *mestizos*, persons of mixed Indian and Spanish strain.

chunca—an Inca village which held land in common.

científicos—advisers and political supporters of Porfírio Díaz, dictator in Mexico, who made a fetish of scientific efficiency in government administration.

cimarrón—a person of Negro descent or Negro and Indian blood who ran away from a plantation to "go native" in the interior of Brazil or colonial Spain.

cinchona—the Indian term for the bark of the quinine-producing tree.

Cinco de Mayo—"The Fifth of May," a Mexican national holiday honoring a temporary victory over Napoleon III's troops at Puebla on May 5, 1862.

civilista—an adjective referring to civilian rather than military rule.

colegio—a Latin American secondary school, usually privately financed.

colonos—immigrants from Europe settled in São Paulo state, Brazil, to care for coffee plants; also Andean highland farmers, enjoying use of land in return for labor.

COMIBOL—the Bolivian government corporation to control the tin industry in the 1960s.

comuneros—rebellious communities which opposed the colonial Spanish royal authorities.

confusionismo—chaos in government.

conquistadores—the general term used for the early Spanish explorers and conquerors.

constituyentes—a constituent assembly convoked to formulate the constitution and basic laws of the land.

consulado—a merchants' guild or "chamber of commerce" representing Spanish merchants in Spain and in the chief colonial cities.

continuismo—continuous, one-man government; extension of tenure in office.

cordillera—the Spanish word for backbone, referring to the entire chain of the Andean mountains.

CORFO—the *Corporación de Fomento*, a Chilean economic development agency in the 1940s.

corregidor—a special liaison officer between the Spanish king and Spanish towns; later used in the New World for governor of a frontier area based upon Indian settlement, an area called *corregimiento;* also sometimes a *corregidor* was a royal representative for the Indians.

corrido—during the Mexican Revolution, a street ballad about politics, with real and imaginary characters; a folk song.

cortes—(Portuguese: *côrtes*) a parliament or congress in medieval Spain, also applied to the Spanish "underground" meetings held in Cadiz against Napoleon.

COSACH—the *Compania de Salitre de Chile,* the government-controlled nitrate mining development in Chile.

creoles (Spanish: *criollos*)—a term meaning "born of European descent in the New World," never used in colonial times to indicate racial mixture.

criollismo—"nativism."

Cristeros—an anti-revolutionary, pro-Catholic party in Mexico in the 1920s, carrying on underground terrorism.

CTM—the *Confederación de Trabajadores Mexicanos,* new name for Mexico's strong labor organization after 1936.

cuartelazo—a "bloodless" revolution starting in the barracks or soldiers' "quarters," similar to a *coup d'état.*

Cuba Libre!—"Free Cuba!" the war cry for independence among the Cuban guerrillas in 1895.

cueca—a Chilean folk dance.

D

degredados—outlaws or exiles living in the forests of colonial Brazil; castaways on Brazilian shores in colonial days.

desacato—defiance and disrespect of authority; a law of *desacato* was passed by Perón to allow arrest of his political enemies on the excuse of "disrespect."

descamisados—"the shirtless ones," hence the "non-white-collar" workers, the urban proletariat, refers especially to those workers who followed Perón in Argentina.

diezmo—the ten per cent of income pledged to the church in Spanish colonial times; a tithe.

donatários—proprietors of original land grants in early Brazil who founded colonies at their own expense.

dotación—grant of land to an individual in accordance with Mexican agrarian law; literally, an endowment, gift, or dowry.

dramas criollos—gaucho folk plays, given by wandering troubadours in the pampas towns of nineteenth-century Argentina.

E

ECLA—the United Nations' Economic Commission for Latin America.

ejido—a community-owned farm in Mexico, originally Indian village or tribal lands; *ejiditario*—a farm worker on communal land.

El Dorado—"the Gilded Man" or gold-dust-covered king, hence a myth about such a person in the Colombian Andes.

El Supremo—"The Supreme One," a title referring to Dr. Francia, dictator of Paraguay.

emboaba—a Portuguese settler newly come to Brazil; especially a derisive term applied to newcomers in the mining regions in colonial Brazil.

empleomanía—"job mania."

encomienda—a tract of land granted to a settler by the Spanish kings, including the Indians living there who were to do the work; grant given to an individual in recognition of distinguished service.

engenho—a sugar mill in Brazil; sometimes also a plantation including such a mill.

Estado Novo—"The New State," a term used by Getulio Vargas in Brazil to describe his government in 1937.

estancia—a large agricultural estate in the Argentine area; *estanciero* is the term used for the owner of a large cattle ranch in Argentina, member of Argentina's nineteenth-century ruling oligarchy.

F

falange—a unit of the followers of Franco in the Spanish Civil War of 1936.

fandango—a formal Spanish group dance.

Farrapos—"Ragamuffins," a term applied to rebels in the state of Rio Grande do Sul against the Brazilian emperor in the 1830s and 1840s.

favelas—shanty-town slums in Brazilian cities in the 1960s.

fazenda—large plantation or estate in Brazil; *fazendero* is the term applied to the man who owned such a plantation, a member of the Brazilian oligarchy.

Federales—national militia kept by Porfírio Díaz to maintain his dictatorship in Mexico.

fico—Portuguese verb meaning "I will remain," proclaimed by the Brazilian emperor Pedro I, January 9, 1822, when he disobeyed orders to return to Lisbon.

fidalgo—Portuguese word for an aristocrat, similar to a Spanish *hidalgo.*

Fidelismo—the Latin American Communist movement of the 1960s, centered in Cuba; *Fidelistas* are the followers of Fidel Castro, Cuban dictator of the 1960s, hence Latin American Communists.

fiesta—the celebration of a public or religious holiday.

finca—a coffee plantation in Central America.

flota—a fleet of cargo ships sent from Spain to Vera Cruz annually during the colonial regime.

fomento—governmental internal development; usually done through a government corporation.

FRAP—*Frente de Acción Popular,* a socialist communist "Popular Front" in Chile in the 1960s.

frigoríficos—meat packing and freezing plants in Buenos Aires and Montevideo.

fuero—a privilege to claim exemption from the civil or common law in Mexico.

fundo—a rural estate in Chile.

G

gachupín—"He who wears spurs"; a person born in Spain, residing in New Spain; the Spanish ruling class hated by the colonials in the independence period.

galeones—the fleet of Spanish cargo ships sent to Cartagena and Puerto Bello in colonial times.

guanaco—a wild species of llama in the Chile area.

gazeta—a newsletter, term applied to the first colonial newspapers.

gente de razón—people with "ability to reason" in the colonial period, as opposed to slaves and Indians.

Gobernación—cabinet office of internal affairs in several Latin American nations.

Godos—a sarcastic term for blond or Gothic Spaniards, hence all newcomers from Spain just before the independence period.

golondrinas—the Spanish word for swallows, hence migratory workers from Italy who came to Argentina to do harvest work in the Southern Hemisphere summer.

GOU—*Grupo Officiales Unidos,* a group of united officers in Argentina.

gremio—a craft guild of skilled artisans in colonial times.

Grito de Dolores—the "cry" or "shout" made by Father Miguel Hidalgo at the town of Dolores, September 16, 1810; hence the Mexican movement for independence.

Grito de Ypiranga—the "cry" or "shout" for independence made at the stream of Ypiranga near São Paulo by the Emperor Pedro I, September 7, 1822, to announce Brazilian independence.

guajiros—Cuban sugar plantation workers.

guanaco—a wild species of llama in the Chile area.

guano—the dung of sea birds, collected off the coast of Peru; a valuable fertilizer.

Guaraní—name for Paraguayan and Brazilian Indians, hence also the language spoken by the Guaraní tribes.

guardia nacional—a national guard or police force.

H

hacienda—a large, feudal, agricultural estate in Mexico; **hacendado,** owner of a *hacienda*, a powerful landowner in Mexico.

hamaca—Caribbean Indian word for a hammock.

hermandades—brotherhoods of laymen in Catholic society which undertook municipal jobs such as police patrol.

hidalgo—Spanish term for a nobleman, an *hijo de algo*, or son of "somebody."

Hispanidad—an attempt on the part of modern Spain to promote cultural ties with Latin America.

Hispaniola—the name of the island including Haiti and the Dominican Republic.

hondo—deep ocean areas near the Central American coast.

huaso—a Chilean cowherd or *gaucho*.

huna—an Inca tribal group, or family council.

IA-ECOSOC—The Inter-American social and economic council of the OAS.

imperialismo—the Spanish term for United States' "imperialism."

Inconfidência—the revolutionary movement in Brazil in the pre-independence period, of which the principal leader was Tiradentes.

Indianismo—the term applied to the cultural interest in Indian backgrounds in modern Mexico.

inquilino—a peasant or tenant farmer in Chile.

Integralistas—pro-German Fascists in Brazil in World War II; the "greenshirts."

Intendencia—a French political institution introduced into the Spanish colonies by the Bourbons in the eighteenth century.

IPAF—the Inter-American Peace Force in the Dominican Republic in 1965–1966.

J

Jefe Máximo—absolute leader of party government; "Chief Boss," the nickname given to Calles in Mexico in the 1920s.

Jefe Político—governor of a district.

jota—a regional or country dance from Spain.

junta—a provisional committee to take over political authority during a revolutionary period.

justicialismo—a term used by Perón to describe his Argentine regime; literally, a "doctrine of justice."

Juzgado de Indias—port authority which controlled shipping from Cádiz during the colonial regime.

Juzgado de Indios—a special court to hear complaints of Indians, created in 1573 to protect the aborigines in the Spanish empire.

L

labrador—farm worker.

Ladinos—modernized Spanish-speaking people of Indian descent in Guatemala.

LAFTA—Latin American Free Trade Association, a trade-promoting agreement in the 1960s.

latifundio—a large landed estate worked under feudal conditions; hence also *latifundismo*, the system of land tenure.

Lautaro—password, name for secret societies opposed to the Spaniards in 1810, from the name of the Araucanian Indian who killed Valdivia.

Lépero—Vagabond, disorderly element in colonial New Spain.

Ley de fuga—"Law of flight," hence justification of "shot while trying to escape," as used by Porfírio Díaz to justify the killing of political prisoners.

liceo—a secondary school.

llanero—a cowboy on the plains of the *llanos* or Orinoco Valley.

llanos—the grasslands of the Orinoco Valley.

Luteranos—"Lutherans," hence all Protestants in Spanish colonial times, including especially British pirates.

M

machismo—from the adjective *macho*, or masculine, virile, hence the popularity of masculinity or virility in politics and society.

malambo—a type of folk dance in the Argentine area.

mamelucos—Portuguese half-breeds, mixed European and Indian blood.

mandioca—a root in tropical America providing a starchy food.

maravedi—a little-used Spanish coin.

Mare Nostrum—Latin for "Our Ocean," used by Spain to mean the Caribbean.

masambo—Brazilian word for creole or person born of European stock in the New World.

mas horca—"more gallows," a term used by the Argentine underground against the dictator Rosas and his special police units called *Mazorca*.

maté—a wild plant originating in Paraguay; a popular tea drink is made from the leaves.

mayor domo—administrator of a landed estate.

mayorazco—the right of primogeniture, or inheritance by the eldest son.

Mazorca—an Argentine term for "corn on the cob"—used by the police of the dictator Rosas to imply the closeness and unity of their organization. Pronounced by his enemies as *mas horca*, or "more gallows."

Mesa da Consciencia é Ordens—a Portuguese church council created in 1532 to regulate officials and handle Indian affairs in Brazil.

mesta—a guild of livestock breeders in medieval Spain and in the New World.

mestizo—a person of mixed Spanish and Indian descent (feminine, *mestiza*); *mestizaje,* the culture and way of life in a *mestizo* society.

milpa—a plot of land in Mexico on which Indians grow corn.

mita—forced labor, periodic conscription of Indian labor in Spanish colonies.

mitamaes—Inca colonists sent to newly conquered territories to consolidate control; the Inca military forces encamped within the empire.

MNR—The Movement of National Revolution in Bolivia, less radical than the PIR.

mocambo—fugitive slave settlement in Brazil.

Modernista—"Ultra-modern," referring to the type of poetry written by Rubén Darío.

montaña—the areas of Ecuador, Peru, and Bolivia lying in the foothills of the Andes east of the divide on the edge of the Amazon Basin.

mordidas—"bites," a slang word for bribes to government officials.

mulato (feminine, mulata)—person of mixed Negro and Caucasian stock (English, mulatto).

N

Nacional Financiera—A Mexican government financing agency for agricultural and industrial loans.

Noche Triste—"The Sad Night," during which Cortés and his followers escaped from the Aztecs on June 30, 1520.

NOVACAP—The Brazilian project for the new capital at Brazilia in the late 1950s.

O

OAS—Organization of American States.

obraje—a textile factory or work shop in the Spanish colonies employing Indian laborers.

ODECA—the federation of Central American States in the 1950s and '60s.

Oficiales Reales—Royal Officials of the Treasury (tax gatherers).

Oidores—judges in the Spanish colonial courts or members of the *audiencia*.

ombú—a bushy tree growing on the Argentine pampas.

Oriente—the eastern slope of the Andes leading out to the Amazon, sometimes called the *montaña*.

ORIT—Inter-American regional organization of labor, a Latin American branch of a worldwide trade union movement.

Ouro Preto—black gold (Portuguese), hence a dark colored ore of high gold content; hence the name given to the Brazilian town near a rich strike of such ore.

P

padre—Spanish word for father, hence a missionary or parish priest.

palmos—"hands," about eight inches, as used in measuring the height of horses or, in the Spanish empire, the height of slaves.

pampas—the level grasslands of Argentina, inland from Buenos Aires; beef and wheat producing area.

pan ó palo—bread or the club, the guiding principle of Porfírio Díaz' dictatorship.

pan, techo y abrigo—bread, clothes, and shelter, the slogan of the Chilean "Popular Front" in 1938.

pardo—mulatto or Negro.

paseo—a walk or stroll, such as through a park, hence often a street near a park.

patio—a central garden or courtyard in a Spanish-style house; also a method of crushing ore under stones by mule-power.

patois—the dialect of French, with many African words added, which is spoken in rural Haiti, sometimes called *creole*.

Patria Boba—"The Foolish Fatherland," referring to the chaotic government in New Granada from 1810 to 1815.

patria chica—the "small fatherland," attachment to local region.

patronato real—a Spanish pact with the papacy; right of Spanish kings to dispose of all ecclesiastical benefits and make church appointments.

Paulistas—people from São Paulo, hence early explorers of the Brazilian interior.

payadores—wandering folk minstrel singers on the Argentine pampas.

pelota—Spanish game of handball.

pelucones—"big-wigs," hence a Chilean political party of older conservative leaders in the nineteenth century.

peninsulares—people born in the Iberian peninsula, i.e. in Spain or Portugal rather than in the colonies.

peón—an agricultural worker tied to the land; an indigent agricultural worker.

peonía—a small land grant made to a Spanish foot soldier.

personalismo—a political policy of loyalty to personal leader, rather than to a political philosophy; *personalista* refers to the follower of a dictator for reasons of personal loyalty.

pieza de Indias—a valuable African slave in the "prime" of life.

pípiolos—"beardless young men," hence a Chilean political party of young progressives in the nineteenth century.

plan—a platform or political program, usually advanced by revolutionary leaders.

Plata—the Spanish word for silver, hence applied to the Argentine region where early explorers thought silver abounded.

poncho—a wool blanket or shawl worn by Chilean cowboys.

porteño—an Argentine who lived in Buenos Aires city, as opposed to people who lived on the pampas.

portolani—a medieval sailing chart.

posada—an inn or hostel.

prensa—literally the "press," hence a famous newspaper in Buenos Aires.

preparatorio—an academic secondary school, either public or private. In Brazil the term is written *preparatário*.

presidencia—a regional government in the more remote Spanish colonies, an *audiencia* which is located at a place not having a viceroy or captain-general; hence president of an *audiencia*.

presidio—a spanish garrison, fort, or soldiers' barracks.

PRI—the *Partido Revolucionario Institucional*, the name for Mexico's major political party after 1946.

pronunciamiento—a "pronouncement," or declaration of policy made by a revolutionary leader.

protomédico—a medical inspector, first sent to the colonies in 1571.

Provincias Internas—Interior Provinces, a term applied in 1776 to the northern frontier in New Spain.

pueblo—the Spanish word for a town, sometimes also used for the people of a town; also refers to a tribe of Indians in New Mexico.

pulpería—an Argentine country saloon.

pulque—a mildly intoxicating beverage made by Mexican Indians from the juice of the *maguey* or century plant; *pulquería*, a place where *pulque* is sold.

puna—bleak, arid Andean tableland.

Q

quetzal—a tropical bird, native to Central America; Aztec word for feathers.

quilombo—a village of runaway slaves in the Brazilian backlands.

quinto—the "royal fifth," tax on precious metals mined in the colonies and paid to the Spanish royal treasury during the colonial regime.

quipu—Inca Indian knotted cord used for keeping accounts; a memory aid used in communications.

R

rancho—a farm or cattle ranch.

rancheros—middle-class ranch owners in northern Mexico, not as powerful as *hacendados*.

real hacienda—royal treasury, exchequer.

real de minas—a Spanish colonial mining community.

reales—small Spanish coins, valued at eight to the Spanish colonial *peso*, or "pieces of eight."

reconcentrados—concentration camps in Cuba in 1898.

Reconquista—the Christian reconquest of lands in Spain held by the Moors.

reducción—settlement of converted Indians by Jesuits in Paraguay.

regidores—elected members of the Spanish colonial town councils or *cabildos*.

repartimiento—a temporary allotment of Indian laborers and land to an individual Spanish settler in the early years of the conquest.

residencia—a judicial review of an official's conduct at the end of his term of office.

rotos—Chilean miners and industrial workers.

rumba—a Cuban dance.

rurales—mounted police squads in Mexico created by Porfírio Díaz to maintain order.

S

sabiá—a tropical bird in Brazil whose song symbolized Brazilian national feelings.

Santa Hermandad—the "royal brotherhood," or centralized police force in fifteenth-century Spain.

sarape—a Mexican Indian hand-woven blanket.

savanna—grassland.

selva—forested area; *selvas* (in Bolivia), the tropical plains spreading northeast toward the Amazon.

Sertão—the drought-stricken lands inland from the coast on the "bulge" of Brazil, behind Fortaleza. *Sertanejo* is an inhabitant of the *Sertão*.

Servicio Especial de Sauda Pública—The Brazilian Public Health Service after 1940.

Servicios—service branches of the Organization of American States to encourage technical cooperation in the 1960s.

sierra—Spanish word for mountain range.

siesta—a midday rest period.

simpático—pleasant, cordial, warm-hearted.

sones—sad poems on Cuban life written by Nicolas Guillén.

"Spanish Main"—The mainland of northern South America—i.e., the coasts of Colombia and Venezuela, as opposed to the Caribbean Islands.

SUDENE—the North Eastern Social and Economic Development agency, a Brazilian government program of the 1960s.

T

"Tacho"—nickname for the Christian name Anastasio, hence applied to Anastasio Somoza, dictator of Nicaragua in the 1940s—1950s.

Tahuantinsuyo—the Inca system of re-colonizing Quechua-speaking people into conquered territory, hence the whole Inca concept of a unified empire.

tango—Argentine-type ballroom dance.

"Tata"—affectionate word for "grandfather," applied by the conservatives to the Mexican dictator, Porfírio Díaz, and others.

teozintle—a wild grass from Central America similar to cultivated corn or maize.

tequila—a strong distilled liquor made from *pulque* or "cactus-plant beer."

tertulias—afternoon tea parties in Mexican society circles.

tierra—the Spanish word for earth or land; agricultural land belonging to peasants in Mexico.

tierra Caliante—the warm coastal regions of Mexico.

Tierra Firme—the northern Caribbean shore of South America, the "Spanish Mainland."

tierra Fría—the area of Mexico of highest altitude near the snow-covered volcanoes.

tierra Templada—the area of Mexico of temperate climate, the plateaus of central Mexico.

"Tierra y Libertad"—"Land and Liberty," the slogan of Emiliano Zapata and his peasant followers in the Mexican Revolution of 1910.

Tlachantín—the elected commander-in-chief of the Aztec army.

tortilla—a flat corn cake, a staple food in Mexico since Aztec times.

Tonton Macoute—the personal bodyguard of Haitian dictator Duvalier in the 1960s.

tribunal—court of justice, tribunal.

Trigarante—pertaining to the "Three Guarantees" of Iturbide under the Mexican *Plan de Iguala*.

U

Ultra-istas—young Latin American authors of ultra-modern poetry.

Unión Cívica Radical—a moderate reform party in Argentine politics at the turn of the twentieth century.

Index

England and the English *(cont.)*
  and economy of new nations, 322–23
  and First Pan American Congress, 314
  investments, 754–55
  and Mexican debts, 340–41
  Protestants in Chile, 388
  and recognition of new nations, 312–13, 354
  and Venezuelan Revolution, 289ff.
  War of 33 Immortals and, 397
  and William Walker's invasion, 452, 453
  17th-century rivalries, 219–21, 223–25, 227, 228
    privates, privateers, smugglers, 219, 220–21, 223–24
  20th-century, 725, 728–29
    Argentina and, 556, 557, 561, 562, 568, 569, 571ff.
    bases in Caribbean maintained by U.S., 734
    Brazil and, 510, 528, 533
    Chile and, 593
    Guatemala and, 683
    and Latin American Common Market, 728
    Panama and, 650, 676
    Uruguay and, 612, 659
    and World War II, 612
English language, 539, 808
  bibliography, 805–8
  Cultural Institutes and, 774
Enlightenment, Age of, 208, 233ff., 241, 246–49, 260
Enríquez, Carlos, 704
Enríquez y Carvajal, Francisco, 712
Entre Ríos, 371, 372, 375, 570
Equator, Federal Republic of the, 354
Ercilla y Zúñiga, Alonzo de, 211
Erosion Control Commission (Mexico), 488
Errázuriz, Federico, 389, 392
Escalante (explorer), 237
Esmeraldas, 629
España, José María, 277
Esquivel, Juan de, 98
Estancieros. See Hacendados
Estates. *See also* Land
  present-day, 574, 575–76, 596–98
Estevánico (slave), 113
Estigarribia, José Félix, 623
Estimé, Dumarsais, 709
Estrada, Genaro, 732
Estrada, Hector, 658
Estrada, Juan, 687, 688
Estrada Cabrera, Manuel, 450, 671, 680
Estrada Doctrine, 732
Estrada Palma, Tomás, 439, 440, 442, 696
Estremadura, 27
Eu, Comte d', 365, 366, 405
Europe, 3ff.

See also specific countries, wars
  events leading directly to revolution in Latin America, 285–87
  and recognition of new nations, 311ff.
  20th-century relations, 725–29
European Common Market, 728, 763
Experiment in International Living, 775
Export-Import Bank, 488, 490, 532, 585, 637, 698, 757, 758, 768, 769

Falcón, Juan Cristomo, 432–33
Falcón Dam, 487
Falkland Islands, 562, 728, 729
Falla, Manuel de, 579
Falls of Iguassú. *See* Iguassú Falls
Families, 177–78, 190, 198, 264, 347, 358
  Aztec, 66
  Mayan, 60
  nepotism, 156
  present-day, 460, 485, 535, 618
Family Compact, 235
FAO. *See* Food and Agricultural Organization
Far East, 4ff., 29–30
  See also Asia; Orient; specific countries
Farrell, Edelmiro, 557, 558
Fascism. *See also* Nazis; specific dictators
  Argentine, 555, 556, 557–58ff.
  Brazil and, 516, 519
  Mexico and, 477–78, 479, 481
Faucett, Captain, 535
Faustín I. *See* Soulouque, Faustín
Favelas, 536
Fazendas, fazendeiros, 262, 264, 265
Feathered serpent, 58, 62
Federalist War, 432
Federal Republic of the Equator, 354
Federal Savings and Loan Assns., 770
Federmann, Nikolaus, 130, 131
Fegari, Pedro, 617
Feijó, Diogo Antonio, 355
Felipillo (Indian), 122, 123
Ferdinand III (San Fernando), 20–21
Ferdinand V, 17, 23–24, 88, 92, 95, 99, 143, 145, 175–76
Ferdinand VI, 241
Ferdinand VII (Son of Charles IV), 285, 286–87, 289, 290, 294ff., 303, 306, 311, 312
Fernández, Félix. *See* Victoria, Guadalupe
Fernando, San. *See* Ferdinand III
Ferrelo (explorer), 113
Fertilizers. *See* Guano; Nitrates
Fiallo, Fabio, 712
"Fidelismo," 703
"Fidelistas," 700, 715, 773
"Fierro, Martín," 377–78
Fiesta de Hispanidad, 771
Fiestas. *See* Dances and dancing; specific celebrations, locations

Montemayor (lieutenant governor), 116
Montenegro, Carlos, 704
Monterey (California), 237
Monterey Bay, 118, 238
Monterrey (Mexico), 116, 336, 479, 486, 489
Monterrey Technical Inst., 496
Montesinos, Friar, 207
Montesquieu, Baron de, 246, 277
Monteverde, Domingo de, 291
Montevideo, 41, 201, 240, 282, 297, 298,
    372, 396–97ff., 401, 559, 728, 733
  film festival, 772
  Graf Spee incident, 612
  OAS meeting (1961), 759
  Pan American Conference (1933), 741,
    757
Montezuma, Count of, 228
Montezuma II, 63, 64, 65, 105, 106–7, 111
Montt, Jorge, 392
Montt, Manuel, 388–89
Moors, 19–20, 21, 22–23, 25
  See also Moslems
  in Portugal, 28
Mora, José A., 747, 749, 752, 765, 766
Mora, José Maria Luís, 337, 347
Mora, Juan Rafael, 450–51, 452
Moraes Barros, Prudente José de, 509
Morales, Ramón Villeda, 686–87
Morazán, Francisco, 448–49
Morelos, José María, 305
Morelos (Mexico), 464, 468, 486, 498
Moreno, Mariano, 297, 317
Morgan, Sir Henry, 200, 223–24
Morillo, Pablo, 294, 295
Moríñigo, Higínio, 623, 624
Morones, Luis, 470, 471, 473, 475, 476, 490,
    773
Morro Velho (Old Hill), 532
Morrow, Dwight W., 473
Mortgage Bank (Uruguay), 614
Mosaics, 215, 495
  See also Tiles
Moscoso, Teodoro, 760, 761
Moscow, 728, 773
  radio, 682
Moslems (Mohammedans), 3, 8, 17, 19, 29,
    185, 263
  See also Moors
Mosquera, Tomás Cipriano de, 426, 427
Mosquitoes, 537, 541
Motolonía (historian), 179
Mount Aconcagua; etc. *See* Aconcagua,
    Mt.; etc.
Movement of Nat'l Revolution (MNR),
    639, 640, 642, 818
Movies, 500, 544, 579, 580, 600, 772
Mules, 162
Mulattoes, 193, 278–79
  See also Negroes
  in 20th century:

  Dominican Republic, 711
  Haitian, 706, 707, 709ff.
Municipal government. *See* Politics; spe-
    cific periods, places
Mural painting. *See* Art
Murillo, Bartolomé, 26
Museums. *See* Science and research; specific
    places
Music, 216, 267–68
  19th-century, 347–48, 361, 362, 378
  20th-century:
    Andean Indians, 633
    Argentina, 578–79
    Brazil, 529, 543–44
    Chile, 603
    Colombia, 665
    Cuba, 703, 704
    Haiti, 710
    inter-American culture, 772–73, 775,
      776
    Mexico, 461–62, 464, 467, 497, 499–500
    Uruguay, 617
Mussolini, Benito, 516, 517, 558, 727
Mutis, José Celestino, 209, 247, 429
Mutton exports, Argentine, 570

Nabuco, Joaquim, 365
Nación, La (newspaper), 374, 550, 580
Nacional Financiera, 457, 460, 462, 819
Nâgo language, 263, 266
Nahuatl language, 68, 205
Nance, Gusta B., 232n
Napo River, 43, 646
Napoleon I (and Napoleonic Wars), 236,
    272, 273, 275, 282, 285–86, 289, 290,
    294, 296, 303, 305, 352
  and Haiti, 280, 281
  U.S. and, 311
Napoleon III, 341, 342, 726, 728, 730
Napoleon Wars. *See* Napoleon I
Nardone, Benito, 613, 614
Nariño, Antonio, 277, 293, 317
Narváez, Panfilo de, 107, 108, 112
Natal, 518, 735
Natchitoches, 237
National . . . *See under* specific countries
Nationalism, 457, 460, 462
  See also specific countries
Nationalization of industries.
  See also specific industries
  Bolivia, 629, 630, 638–43
  Colombia, 651
  Guatemala, 681–82
  Mexico, 4, 477, 481, 489, 491
  Uruguay, 614–15
Navajos, 237
Navarre, 20, 21
Navies. *See* Ships and shipping; specific
    countries
Navigation, 6, 90, 208